MW00812142

THE CAMBRIDGE DICTIONARY OF

Christian Theology

With over 550 entries ranging from 'Abba' to 'Zwingli' composed by leading contemporary theologians from around the world, *The Cambridge Dictionary of Christian Theology* represents a fresh, ecumenical approach to theological reference. Written with an emphasis on clarity and concision, all entries are designed to help the reader understand and assess the specifically theological significance of the most important concepts. Clearly structured, the volume is organized around a small number of 'core entries' which focus on key topics to provide a general overview of major subject areas, while making use of related shorter entries to impart a more detailed knowledge of technical terms. The work as a whole provides an introduction to the defining topics in Christian thought and is an essential reference point for students and scholars.

IAN A. McFARLAND is Associate Professor of Systematic Theology at Emory University. His publications include *Difference and Identity: A Theological Anthropology* (2001) and *The Divine Image: Envisioning the Invisible God* (2005).

DAVID A. S. FERGUSSON is Professor of Divinity and Principal of New College at the University of Edinburgh. His recent publications include *Church, State and Civil Society* (Cambridge, 2004) and *Faith and Its Critics* (2009).

KAREN KILBY is Head of the Department of Theology and Religious Studies at the University of Nottingham and President of the Catholic Theological Association of Great Britain. She is the author of *A Brief Introduction to Karl Rahner* (2007) and *Karl Rahner: Theology and Philosophy* (2004).

IAIN R. TORRANCE is President and Professor of Patristics at Princeton Theological Seminary. He is the author of *Christology after Chalcedon* (1988) and co-editor of *To Glorify God: Essays in Modern Reformed Liturgy* (1999) and *The Oxford Handbook of Systematic Theology* (2007).

THE CAMBRIDGE DICTIONARY OF

Christian Theology

Edited by

IAN A. McFARLAND, DAVID A. S. FERGUSSON,

KAREN KILBY, IAIN R. TORRANCE

CAMBRIDGE
UNIVERSITY PRESS

32 Avenue of the Americas, New York NY 10013-2473, USA

Cambridge University Press is part of the University of Cambridge.

It furthers the University's mission by disseminating knowledge in the pursuit of education, learning and research at the highest international levels of excellence.

www.cambridge.org
Information on this title: www.cambridge.org/9781107414969

First published 2011
First paperback edition 2014

A catalogue record for this publication is available from the British Library

Library of Congress Cataloguing in Publication data

The Cambridge dictionary of Christian theology / edited by Ian A. McFarland ... [et al.].
p. cm.
ISBN 978-0-521-88092-3 (Hardback)
1. Theology–Dictionaries. I. McFarland, Ian A. (Ian Alexander), 1963– II. Title.
BV2.5.C36 2011
230.03–dc22

2010022749

ISBN 978-0-521-88092-3 Hardback
ISBN 978-1-107-41496-9 Paperback

Contents

Contributors

William J. **Abraham** is Albert Cook Outler Professor of Wesley Studies and Altshuler Distinguished Teaching Professor at the Perkins School of Theology, Southern Methodist University. *Revelation*

Nicholas **Adams** is Senior Lecturer in Systematic Theology and Theological Ethics at the University of Edinburgh. *Frankfurt School, German Idealism*

Allan Heaton **Anderson** is Professor of Global Pentecostal Studies and Director of the Graduate Institute for Theology & Religion at the University of Birmingham. *Pentecostal Theology*

Andreas **Andreopoulos** is Lecturer in Christian Theology and Director of the Centre for Orthodox Studies at the University of Wales, Lampeter. *Transfiguration*

Edward P. **Antonio** is Harvey H. Potthoff Associate Professor of Christian Theology and Social Theory at the Iliff School of Theology. *Black Theology*

Kenneth **Appold** is the James Hastings Nichols Associate Professor of Reformation History at Princeton Theological Seminary. *Justification*

Willem J. van **Asselt** is Senior Lecturer of Church History in the Department of Theology at Utrecht University and Professor of Historical Theology at the Evangelical Theological Faculty in Louvain. *Synod of Dort*

Paul **Avis** is the General Secretary of the Council for Christian Unity. *Episcopacy*

Christine **Axt-Piscalar** is Professor of Systematic Theology and Director of the Institutum Lutheranum in the Theological Faculty of the Georg-August-Universität, Göttingen. *Liberal Theology*

Lewis **Ayres** is Bede Professor of Catholic Theology at the University of Durham. *Arian Controversy, Augustine of Hippo, Creeds, Council of Nicaea*

Vincent **Bacote** is Associate Professor of Theology and Director of the Center for Applied Christian Ethics at Wheaton College. *Abraham Kuyper*

Gary D. **Badcock** is Associate Professor of Divinity at Huron University College. *Vocation*

John F. **Baldovin,** S. J., is Professor of Historical and Liturgical Theology in the School of Theology and Ministry at Boston College. *Priesthood*

Hans M. **Barstad** is Professor of Hebrew and Old Testament Studies in the School of Divinity at the University of Edinburgh. *Biblical Theology*

The Revd Dr Michael **Battle** is Provost and Canon Theologian at the Cathedral Center of the Anglican Diocese of Los Angeles. *Nonviolence*

The Revd Mgr Dr F. J. **Baur** is Regent of the Priesterseminars St. Johannes der Täufer in Munich. *Occasionalism*

Tina **Beattie** is Professor of Catholic Studies at Roehampton University. *Abortion, Assumption, Human Rights, Immaculate Conception, Mariology, Nuptial Theology*

Dana **Benesh** is a PhD student in theology at Baylor University, with an interest in the history of exegesis. *Excommunication, Secularization, Tolerance*

Michael **Bergmann** is Professor of Philosophy at Purdue University. *Reformed Epistemology*

Nigel **Biggar** is Regius Professor of Moral and Pastoral Theology at the University of Oxford. *Moral Theology*

André **Birmelé** is Professor of Dogmatics at the Faculté de Théologie Protestante in Strasbourg. *Ecumenism, World Council of Churches*

C. Clifton **Black** is Otto A. Piper Professor of Biblical Theology at Princeton Theological Seminary. *Kingdom of God*

Paul M. **Blowers** is Dean E. Walker Professor of Church History at the Emmanuel School of Religion. *Maximus the Confessor, Monothelitism*

H. Russel **Botman** is Rector and Vice-Chancellor at Stellenbosch University. *African Theology*

John **Bowlin** is the Rimmer and Ruth de Vries Associate Professor of Reformed Theology and Public Life at Princeton Theological Seminary. *Aristotelianism*

Ian **Bradley** is Reader in Practical Theology in the School of Divinity at the University of St Andrews. *Pilgrimage*

Lucy **Bregman** is Professor of Religion in the Religion Department of Temple University. *Death and Dying*

Luke **Bretherton** is Senior Lecturer in Theology and Politics and Convener of the Faith and Public Policy Forum at King's College London. *Constantinianism, Divine Command Ethics*

James T. **Bretzke,** S. J., is Professor of Moral Theology in the Boston College School of Theology and Ministry. *Casuistry*

Lynn **Bridgers** is Director of Intercultural Religious Research at the College of Santa Fe. *William James*

John P. **Burgess** is the James Henry Snowden Professor of Systematic Theology at Pittsburgh Theological Seminary. *Baptism*

Stanley M. **Burgess** is Distinguished Professor of Christian History at the Regent University School of Divinity. *Perfectionism*

David B. **Burrell**, C. S. C., is Hesburgh Professor Emeritus in Philosophy and Theology at the University of Notre Dame and the Uganda Martyrs University. *Islam and Christianity*

Jason **Byassee** is the Director of the Center for Theology, Writing and Media at Duke Divinity School. *Allegory, Typology*

Euan **Cameron** is Henry Luce III Professor of Reformation Church History at Union Theological Seminary, New York. *Reformation*

Amy **Carr** is Associate Professor of Religious Studies at Western Illinois University. *Temptation*

Mark J. **Cartledge** is Senior Lecturer in Pentecostal and Charismatic Theology at the University of Birmingham. *Glossolalia*

Augustine **Casiday** is Lecturer in Historical Theology and Director of the MA in Monastic Studies at the University of Wales, Lampeter. *Hesychasm, Gregory Palamas, Platonism*

Christophe **Chalamet** is Assistant Professor in the Department of Theology at Fordham University. *Dialectical Theology*

The Revd Dr Mark D. **Chapman** is Vice-Principal of Ripon College Cuddesdon, Oxford, and member of the Faculty of Theology at the University of Oxford. *Ernst Troeltsch*

Sathianathan **Clarke** is Bishop Sundo Kim Professor of World Christianity at the Wesley Theological Seminary. *Dalit Theology*

Philip **Clayton** is Professor of Religion and Philosophy at Claremont Graduate University and Ingraham Professor at Claremont School of Theology. *Panentheism*

Francis X. **Clooney,** S. J., is Parkman Professor of Divinity and Professor of Comparative Theology at Harvard Divinity School. *Hinduism and Christianity*

Basil **Cole,** O. P., teaches Moral, Spiritual, and Dogmatic Theology at the Dominican House of Studies, Washington, DC. *Seven Deadly Sins*

Tim **Cooper** is Lecturer in Church History in the Department of Theology and Religious Studies at the University of Otago. *Antinomianism*

Paul **Copan** is Pledger Family Chair of Philosophy and Ethics at Palm Beach Atlantic University. *Moral Argument*

M. Shawn **Copeland** is Associate Professor of Theology at Boston College. *Womanist Theology*

John **Cottingham** is Professor Emeritus of Philosophy at the University of Reading and an Honorary Fellow of St John's College, Oxford. *Cartesianism*

S. Peter **Cowe** is the Narekatsi Professor of Armenian Studies in the Department of Near Eastern Languages and Cultures at the University of California, Los Angeles. *Armenian Theology*

James L. **Cox** is Professor of Religious Studies in the School of Divinity at the University of Edinburgh. *Traditional Religions and Christianity*

William Lane **Craig** is Research Professor of Philosophy at the Talbot School of Theology. *Cosmological Argument, Middle Knowledge*

Shannon **Craigo-Snell** is Associate Professor of Religious Studies at Yale University. *Patriarchy, Supernatural existential*

Andrew **Crislip** holds the Blake Chair in the History of Christianity at Virginia Commonwealth University. *Asceticism*

Garry J. **Crites** is Director of Evening and Weekend Courses at Duke University. *Fasting*

The Revd Dr Anthony R. **Cross** is Fellow of the Centre for Baptist History and Heritage at Regent's Park College, University of Oxford. *Joachim of Fiore*

Richard **Crouter** is John M. and Elizabeth W. Musser Professor of Religious Studies, Emeritus at Carleton College. *Enlightenment*

Lawrence **Cunningham** is the Revd John A. O'Brien Professor of Theology in the Department of Theology of the University of Notre Dame. *Catholic Theology*

Mary B. **Cunningham** is Lecturer in Theology at the University of Nottingham. *Divine Energies, Iconoclasm*

Ivor J. **Davidson** is Professor of Systematic Theology at the University of Otago. *Catechesis, Catechumen, Council of Chalcedon, Jerome*

Douglas J. **Davies** is Professor in the Study of Religion at Durham University. *The Church of Jesus Christ of Latter-Day Saints*

Andrew **Dawson** is Lecturer in Religious Studies at Lancaster University. *Base Communities*

Juliette **Day** is Senior Research Fellow in Christian Liturgy at Blackfriars Hall, Oxford. *Canon of Mass*

Gavin **D'Costa** is Professor of Catholic Theology in the Department of Theology and Religious Studies at the University of Bristol. *Anonymous Christianity, Inculturation, Religious Pluralism, Karl Rahner*

Celia **Deane-Drummond** is Professor of Theology and the Biological Sciences and Director of the Centre for Religion and the Biosciences at the University of Chester. *Ecotheology*

Paul J. **DeHart** is Associate Professor of Theology at Vanderbilt University Divinity School. *Postliberal Theology*

Ralph **Del Colle** is Associate Professor of Theology at Marquette University. *Mortal Sin, Penance, Venial Sin*

Gary **Dorrien** is the Reinhold Niebuhr Professor of Social Ethics at Union Theological Seminary and Professor of Religion at Columbia University. *Social Gospel*

Geoffrey D. **Dunn** is an Australian Research Fellow at the Centre for Early Christian Studies, Australian Catholic University. *Tertullian*

Mark W. **Elliott** is Lecturer in Church History in the School of Divinity at the University of St Andrews. *Nominalism, Pelagianism*

Noel Leo **Erskine** is Professor of Theology and Ethics at the Candler School of Theology, Emory University. *Caribbean Theology, Martin Luther King*

Wendy **Farley** is Professor in the Department of Religion at Emory University. *Phenomenology*

Douglas **Farrow** is Professor of Christian Thought in the Faculty of Religious Studies, McGill University. *Ascension and Session*

Richard **Fenn** is Maxwell M. Upson Professor of Christianity and Society at Princeton Theological Seminary. *Purgatory*

Paul S. **Fiddes** is Professor of Systematic Theology at the University of Oxford and Director of Research at Regent's Park College, Oxford. *Baptist Theology*

Stephen **Fields,** S. J., is Associate Professor of Theology at Georgetown University. *Symbol*

Duncan B. **Forrester** is Honorary Fellow and Professor Emeritus in the School of Divinity at the University of Edinburgh. *Political Theology*

Paul **Foster** is Senior Lecturer in New Testament in the School of Divinity at the University of Edinburgh. Logos

Nancy **Frankenberry** is the John Phillips Professor of Religion at Dartmouth College. *Natural Theology*

Mary McClintock **Fulkerson** is Professor of Theology at Duke Divinity School. *Feminist Theology*

Simon **Gathercole** is Lecturer in New Testament Studies in the Faculty of Divinity at the University of Cambridge. *Paul, Quest of the Historical Jesus*

Michelle A. **Gonzalez** is Assistant Professor of Religious Studies at the University of Miami. *Latino/a Theology,* Mujerista *Theology*

Todd **Gooch** is Associate Professor in the Department of Philosophy and Religion at Eastern Kentucky University. *Rudolf Otto*

Bruce **Gordon** is Professor of Reformation History at Yale Divinity School. *Heinrich Bullinger, Conciliarism*

Elaine **Graham** is Grosvenor Research Professor in the Department of Theology and Religious Studies at the University of Chester. *Practical Theology*

Gordon **Graham** is Henry Luce III Professor of Philosophy and the Arts at Princeton Theological Seminary. *Commonsense Philosophy*

Janette **Gray,** R. S. M., is Lecturer in Theology at the Jesuit Theological College, the United Faculty of Theology, Melbourne. *Celibacy*

Joel B. **Green** is Professor of New Testament Interpretation and Associate Dean for the Center for Advanced Theological Studies at Fuller Theological Seminary. *Soul*

Niels **Henrik Gregersen** is Professor of Systematic Theology in the Faculty of Theology at the University of Copenhagen. *Nordic Theology*

Mike **Grimshaw** is Senior Lecturer in Religious Studies in the School of Philosophy and Religious

Studies at the University of Canterbury. *Post-Christian Theology*

David **Grumett** is Research Fellow in Theology at the University of Exeter. Nouvelle théologie, *Pierre Teilhard de Chardin*

Ruben L. F. **Habito** is Professor of World Religions and Spirituality at the Perkins School of Theology, Southern Methodist University. *Buddhism and Christianity*

Roger **Haight,** S. J., is Scholar in Residence at Union Theological Seminary in New York City. *Juan Luis Segundo*

Douglas John **Hall** is Emeritus Professor of Christian Theology at McGill University. *Neo-Orthodoxy*

The Revd Stuart George **Hall** is Professor Emeritus of Ecclesiastical History in the University of London at King's College. *Historical Theology*

The Revd Dr Harriet A. **Harris** is Chaplain of Wadham College at the University of Oxford. *Orders*

John F. **Haught** is Senior Fellow in Science and Religion at the Woodstock Theological Center, Georgetown University. *Natural Science*

Nicholas M. **Healy** is Professor of Theology and Religious Studies and Associate Dean of the College of Liberal Arts and Sciences at St John's University. *Apostolic Succession, Thomas Aquinas, Ecclesiology, Infallibility, Marks of the Church, Vatican Council I*

The Revd Dr Brian L. **Hebblethwaite** is Life Fellow of Queens' College, and formerly Lecturer in the Philosophy of Religion in the Faculty of Divinity, University of Cambridge. *The Transcendentals*

Charles **Hefling** is Associate Professor of Theology at Boston College. *Liturgical Movement*

György **Heidl** is Associate Professor at the Center for Patristic Studies at the University of Pécs. *Origenism*

S. Mark **Heim** is the Samuel Abbot Professor of Christian Theology at Andover Newton Theological School. *Religion*

Scott H. **Hendrix** is Professor Emeritus of Reformation History and Doctrine at Princeton Theological Seminary. *Lutheran Theology,* Sola Scriptura, *Two Kingdoms*

Alasdair **Heron** is Professor of Reformed Theology at the University of Erlangen. *Reformed Theology*

Michael **Higgins** is President and Vice-Chancellor of St Thomas University, New Brunswick. *Canonization*

Mike **Higton** is Senior Lecturer in Theology in the Department of Theology at the University of Exeter. *Adoptionism, Anhypostasis, Christology,* Communicatio Idiomatum, *Hans Frei,* Homoousios, *Hypostasis, Hypostatic Union, Incarnation, Neo-Chalcedonianism*

Mary Catherine **Hilkert** is Professor in the Department of Theology at the University of Notre Dame. *Edward Schillebeeckx*

Harvey **Hill** is Associate Professor of Religion at Berry College. *Modernism*

Kenneth Einar **Himma** is Associate Professor of Philosophy at Seattle Pacific University. *Ontological Argument*

Bradford **Hinze** is Professor of Theology at Fordham University. *Tübingen School (Catholic)*

Andrew **Hoffecker** is Professor of Church History at Reformed Theological Seminary. *Charles Hodge, Princeton Theology*

Christopher R. J. **Holmes** is Associate Professor of Theology and Ethics at Providence Theological Seminary. *Ludwig Feuerbach*

Edward **Howells** is Lecturer in Christian Spirituality at Heythrop College, University of London. *Teresa of Avila*

Richard T. **Hughes** is Senior Fellow of the Ernest L. Boyer Center and Distinguished Professor of Religion at Messiah College. *Restorationism*

The Revd Mgr Kevin W. **Irwin** is Dean of the School of Theology and Religious Studies at the Catholic University of America. *Eucharist*

Lisa **Isherwood** is Professor of Feminist Liberation Theologies and Director of the Centre for Theological Partnerships at the University of Winchester. *Queer Theology*

Timothy P. **Jackson** is Professor of Christian Ethics at the Candler School of Theology, Emory University. *Adoption*

Paul D. **Janz** is Senior Lecturer in Systematic Theology at King's College London. *Metaphysics*

Werner G. **Jeanrond** is Professor of Divinity at the University of Glasgow. *Hermeneutics*

Willis **Jenkins** is Margaret A. Farley Assistant Professor of Social Ethics at Yale Divinity School. *Dietrich Bonhoeffer*

Robin M. **Jensen** is the Luce Chancellor's Professor of the History of Christian Art and Worship at Vanderbilt University Divinity School. *Icons and Iconography*

Darrell **Jodock** is the Drell and Adeline Bernhardson Distinguished Professor of Religion at Gustavus Adolphus College. *Adolf von Harnack, Alfred Loisy*

Mark D. **Jordan** is Richard Reinhold Niebuhr Professor of Divinity at Harvard Divinity School. *Body, Sexuality*

David G. **Kamitsuka** is Associate Professor of Religion at Oberlin College. *G. W. F. Hegel*

James F. **Kay** is Joe R. Engle Professor of Homiletics and Liturgics and Director of the Joe R. Engle Institute of Preaching at Princeton Theological Seminary. *Rudolf Bultmann, Demythologization*

Henry Ansgar **Kelly** is Professor Emeritus in the Department of English at the University of California, Los Angeles. *Devil*

Daren **Kemp** is a Director of Kempress Ltd and Co-Editor of the *Journal of Alternative Spiritualities and New Age Studies. Christian Science*

Fergus **Kerr**, O. P., FRSE, is Honorary Fellow in the School of Divinity at the University of Edinburgh and Editor of *New Blackfriars. Thomism*

Thomas S. **Kidd** is Associate Professor of History at Baylor University. *Revivalism*

Fr George **Kilcourse** is Professor of Theology at Bellarmine University. *Thomas Merton*

Sebastian C. H. **Kim** is Professor of Theology and Public Life in the Faculty of Education and Theology at York St John University. *Korean Theology*

Masami **Kojiro** is Professor of Systematic Theology at the Tokyo Union Theological Seminary. *Japanese Theology*

Steven **Kraftchick** is Director of General and Advanced Studies and Associate Professor in the Practice of New Testament Interpretation at the Candler School of Theology, Emory University. *Myth*

Alan **Kreider** is Professor of Church History and Mission at the Associated Mennonite Biblical Seminary. *Conversion*

Peter A. **Kwasniewski** is Professor of Theology and Philosophy and Instructor in Music at Wyoming Catholic College. *Teresa of Lisieux*

Lai Pan-chiu is Professor and Associate Dean of the Faculty of Arts at the Divinity School of Chung Chi College, Chinese University of Hong Kong. *Chinese Theology*

Dirk G. **Lange** is Associate Professor of Worship at Luther Seminary. *Divine Office, Inclusive Language,* Lex orandi lex credendi, *Community of Taizé*

Jacqueline **Lapsley** is Associate Professor of Old Testament at Princeton Theological Seminary. *Ten Commandments*

Emmanuel Y. **Lartey** is Professor of Pastoral Theology, Care and Counseling at the Candler School of Theology, Emory University. *Pastoral Theology*

Gordon W. **Lathrop** is Charles A. Schieren Professor of Liturgy Emeritus at the Lutheran Theological Seminary at Philadelphia. *Liturgy, Prayer*

David R. **Law** is Reader in Christian Thought at the School of Arts, Histories and Cultures, University of Manchester. *Kenotic Theology*

Frederick **Lawrence** is Professor of Theology at Boston College. *Bernard Lonergan*

Bo Karen **Lee** is Assistant Professor of Spirituality and Historical Theology at Princeton Theological Seminary. *Hildegard of Bingen*

Sang Hyun **Lee** is the Kyung-Chik Han Professor of Systematic Theology at Princeton Theological Seminary. *Asian-American Theology, Jonathan Edwards*

Mark R. **Lindsay** is Director of Research at the Melbourne College of Divinity. *Israel*

Thomas G. **Long** is the Bandy Professor of Preaching at the Candler School of Theology, Emory University. *Homiletics*

Janice **Love** is Dean and Professor of Christianity and World Politics at the Candler School of Theology, Emory University. *Kairos Document*

Robin W. **Lovin** is Cary Maguire University Professor of Ethics at Southern Methodist University. *Reinhold Niebuhr*

Walter **Lowe** is Professor of Systematic Theology Emeritus at the Candler School of Theology, Emory University. *Immanuel Kant*

Morwenna **Ludlow** is Lecturer in the Department of Theology of the University of Exeter. *Apostolic Fathers, Patristics*

F. Thomas **Luongo** is the Eva-Lou Joffrion Edwards Newcomb Professor at Tulane University. *Catherine of Siena*

Randy L. **Maddox** is Professor of Theology and Wesley Studies at Duke Divinity School. *Methodist Theology*

Lois **Malcolm** is Associate Professor of Systematic Theology at Luther Seminary. *Theodicy*

Mark H. **Mann** is Associate Professor of Theology and Director for the Wesleyan Center for 21st Century Studies at Point Loma Nazarene University. *Rationalism*

William E. **Mann** is Professor in the Department of Philosophy at the University of Vermont. *Anselm of Canterbury*

Neil A. **Manson** is Assistant Professor of Philosophy at the University of Mississippi. *Teleological Argument*

George M. **Marsden** is Francis A. McAnaney Professor of History at the University of Notre Dame. *Fundamentalism*

Bruce D. **Marshall** is Professor of Historical Theology at the Perkins School of Theology, Southern Methodist University. *Judaism and Christianity*

Hjamil A. **Martinez-Vazquez** is Assistant Professor of Religion at Texas Christian University. *Bartolomé de Las Casas*

Rex D. **Matthews** is Assistant Professor in the Practice of Historical Theology at the Candler School of Theology, Emory University. *John Wesley, Wesleyan Quadrilateral*

William C. **Mattison III** is Assistant Professor of Systematic Theology at the Catholic University of America. *Divorce, Marriage*

Bruce Lindley **McCormack** is the Charles Hodge Professor of Systematic Theology at Princeton Theological Seminary. *Atonement*

Joy Ann **McDougall** is Associate Professor of Theology at the Candler School of Theology, Emory University. *Androcentrism, Sin*

Bernard **McGinn** is Naomi Shenstone Donnelley Professor Emeritus of Historical Theology and of the History of Christianity in the Divinity School and the Committees on Medieval Studies and on General Studies at the University of Chicago. *Mystical Theology*

Alister **McGrath** is Professor of Theology, Ministry, and Education at King's College London. *Protestantism*

John A. **McGuckin** is Ane Marie and Bent Emil Nielsen Professor in Late Antique and Byzantine Christian History at Union Theological Seminary (New York) and Professor of Byzantine Christian Studies at Columbia University. *Ecumenical Councils, Origen of Alexandria*

Esther **McIntosh** is Assistant Editor at the *International Journal of Public Theology* and Research Associate in the Faculty of Education and Theology at York St John University. *Personalism*

Mark A. **McIntosh** is Van Mildert Canon Professor of Divinity in the Department of Theology and Religion at the University of Durham. *Hans Urs von Balthasar, Beatific Vision, Contemplation, Faith, John Henry Newman, Spirituality*

Steven A. **McKinion** is Associate Professor of Theology and Patristics at Southeastern Baptist Theological Seminary. *Cyril of Alexandria, Council of Ephesus*

The Revd Mgr. Paul **McPartlan** is Carl J. Peter Professor of Systematic Theology and Ecumenism in the School of Theology and Religious Studies at the Catholic University of America. *Henri de Lubac, Vatican Council II*

Néstor **Medina** teaches Theology at Queen's Theological College, Queen's University. Mestizaje

M. Douglas **Meeks** is the Cal Turner Chancellor's Chair in Wesleyan Studies and Theology at Vanderbilt University Divinity School. *Hope*

Linda **Mercadante** is Professor of Theology in the B. Robert Straker Chair of Historical Theology at the Methodist Theological School in Ohio. *Theology of Trauma*

Paul **Middleton** is Lecturer in New Testament Studies in the Department of Theology and Religious Studies at the University of Wales, Lampeter. *Martyrdom*

Daniel L. **Migliore** is Charles Hodge Professor of Systematic Theology Emeritus at Princeton Theological Seminary. *Lord's Prayer*

Bruce **Milem** is Associate Professor of Philosophy and Coordinator of the Religious Studies Program at the State University of New York, New Paltz. *Meister Eckhart*

R. W. L. **Moberly** is Professor of Theology and Biblical Interpretation at Durham University. *Prophecy*

Paul D. **Molnar** is Professor of Theology at St John's University. *Karl Barth*

The Revd Dr Andrew **Moore** is Fellow of the Centre for Christianity and Culture at Regent's Park College, University of Oxford. *Realism and Anti-Realism*

Susan Hardman **Moore** is Senior Lecturer in Divinity in the School of Divinity at the University of Edinburgh. *Deism*

Christopher **Morse** is the Dietrich Bonhoeffer Professor of Theology and Ethics at Union Theological Seminary, New York. *Soteriology*

Christian **Moser** is a staff member of the Institut für Schweizerische Reformationsgeschichte at the University of Zurich. *Huldrych Zwingli*

Rachel **Muers** is Lecturer in Christian Studies in the Department of Theology and Religious Studies at the University of Leeds. *Quaker Theology*

Francesca A. **Murphy** is Reader in Systematic Theology at King's College in the University of Aberdeen. *Aesthetics, Étienne Gilson*

David **Nash** is Reader in History at Oxford Brookes University. *Blasphemy*

Mark Thiessen **Nation** is Professor of Theology at Eastern Mennonite University. *Mennonite Theology*

Olga V. **Nesmiyanova** is Professor at the St Petersburg School of Religion and Philosophy. *Russian Theology*

Craig L. **Nessan** is Academic Dean and Professor of Contextual Theology at Wartburg Theological Seminary. *Orthopraxis*

Peter **Neuner** is Professor Emeritus at the Katholisch-Theologische Fakultät at the Ludwig-Maximilians-Universität in Munich. *Joseph Maréchal*

Damayanthi **Niles** is Associate Professor of Constructive Theology at Eden Theological Seminary. *D. T. Niles*

Paul T. **Nimmo** is the Meldrum Lecturer in Theology in the School of Divinity at the University of Edinburgh. *Scottish Theology*

The Hon. John T. **Noonan, Jr**, is a judge on the United States Court of Appeals for the Ninth Circuit, with chambers in San Francisco, California. *Usury*

Simon **Oliver** is Associate Professor in the Department of Theology and Religious Studies at the University of Nottingham. *Radical Orthodoxy*

Thomas **O'Loughlin** is Professor of Historical Theology in the Department of Theology and Religious Studies at the University of Nottingham. *Celtic Christianity*

Roger E. **Olson** is Professor of Theology at the George W. Truett Theological Seminary, Baylor University. *Arminianism*

Kenan B. **Osborne**, O. F. M., is Professor Emeritus of Systematic Theology at the Franciscan School of Theology, Graduate Theological Union, Berkeley, California. *Confirmation*

Gene **Outka** is Dwight Professor of Philosophy and Christian Ethics at Yale Divinity School. *Love*

Aristotle **Papanikolaou** is Associate Professor of Systematic Theology and Co-Director of the Orthodox Christian Studies Program at Fordham University. *Orthodox Theology*

David **Parker** is Edward Cadbury Professor of Theology and Director of the Centre for the Editing of Texts in Religion at the University of Birmingham. *Biblical Criticism*

George L. **Parsenios** is Assistant Professor of New Testament at Princeton Theological Seminary. *Mount Athos*

Paul **Parvis** is an Honorary Fellow in the School of Divinity at the University of Edinburgh. *Irenaeus of Lyons, Recapitulation*

Bonnie **Pattison** is Adjunct Professor of Theology at Wheaton College. *Poverty*

George **Pattison** is Lady Margaret Professor of Divinity at the University of Oxford and a canon of Christ Church Cathedral, Oxford. *Søren Kierkegaard*

Amy Plantinga **Pauw** is Henry P. Mobley, Jr, Professor of Doctrinal Theology at the Louisville Presbyterian Theological Seminary. *Election*

Lori **Pearson** is Associate Professor of Religion at Carleton College. *History of Religion School*

Michael Davey **Pearson** has served as Assistant Professor of Theology at Solusi University in Zimbabwe and is currently writing two books on the Holy Spirit for Andrews University Press. *Adventism*

Clark **Pinnock** is Professor Emeritus of Systematic Theology at McMaster Divinity College. *Open Theism*

Sarah **Pinnock** is Associate Professor of Contemporary Religious Thought at Trinity University, San Antonio, Texas. *Holocaust*

Alyssa Lyra **Pitstick** is Assistant Professor of Religion at Hope College. *Glory*

Paul-Hubert **Poirier** is Professor in the Faculté de Théologie et de Sciences Religieuses at the Université Laval. *Gnosticism*

Jean **Porter** is the Revd John A. O'Brien Professor of Theology at the University of Notre Dame. *Natural Law*

Robert W. **Prichard** is Arthur Lee Kinsolving Professor of Christianity in America and

Instructor in Liturgy at Virginia Theological Seminary. *Book of Common Prayer*

Inese **Radzins** is Assistant Professor of Theology and Dorothea Harvey Professor of Swedenborgian Studies at the Pacific School of Religion. *Simone Weil*

J. Paul **Rajashekar** is Luther D. Reed Professor of Systematic Theology and Dean of the Lutheran Theological Seminary at Philadelphia. *M. M. Thomas*

Shelly **Rambo** is Assistant Professor of Theology at Boston University School of Theology. *Anchoritism, Julian of Norwich*

Arne **Rasmusson** is Associate Professor in Theology and Ethics at Umeå University. *Christendom*

Paul **Rasor** is Director of the Center for the Study of Religious Freedom at Virginia Wesleyan College. *Unitarianism*

Stephen G. **Ray, Jr**, is Neal F. and Ila A. Fisher Professor of Systematic Theology at Garrett-Evangelical Theological Seminary. *Race*

Esther D. **Reed** is Associate Professor of Theological Ethics at the University of Exeter. *Forgiveness*

Fr Alexander **Rentel** is Assistant Professor of Canon Law and Byzantine Studies at St Vladimir's Orthodox Theological Seminary. *Ecumenical Patriarchate*

Joerg **Rieger** is Wendland-Cook Endowed Professor of Constructive Theology at the Perkins School of Theology, Southern Methodist University. *Materialism, Sanctification*

Cynthia L. **Rigby** is the W. C. Brown Professor of Theology at Austin Presbyterian Theological Seminary. *Barmen Declaration, Barthianism*

Michelle Voss **Roberts** is Assistant Professor in the Department of Religious Studies at Rhodes College. *Mechthild of Magdeburg*

Richard H. **Roberts** is Professor Emeritus of Religious Studies at Lancaster University and Emeritus Visiting Professor in the Department of Religious Studies at the University of Stirling. *Tübingen School (Protestant)*

Joan L. **Roccasalvo**, C. S. J., is Scholar-in-Residence at Fordham University. *Eastern Catholic Churches*

Eugene F. **Rogers, Jr**, is Professor of Religion at the University of North Carolina at Greensboro. *Holy Spirit*

Philip A. **Rolnick** is Professor of Theology at the University of St Thomas. *Analogy*

Paul **Rorem** is Benjamin B. Warfield Professor of Medieval Church History at Princeton Theological Seminary. *Dionysius the Areopagite*

Christopher **Rowland** is the Dean Ireland Professor of the Exegesis of Holy Scripture at the University of Oxford. *Apocalyptic*

Fr Neil J. **Roy** is a priest of the diocese of Peterborough, Canada, and teaches liturgy and sacramental theology at the University of Notre Dame. *Saints*

Tinu **Ruparell** is Assistant Professor and Graduate Coordinator in the Department of Religious Studies at the University of Calgary. *Pantheism*

Norman **Russell** is an independent scholar and translator. He is the author of several works on the Greek fathers and the translator of texts by several contemporary Greek theologians. *Deification*

Robert John **Russell** is Director of the Center for Theology and the Natural Sciences (CTNS) and the Ian G. Barbour Professor of Theology and Science in Residence at the Graduate Theological Union. *Divine Action*

Don E. **Saliers** is the William R. Cannon Distinguished Professor of Theology and Worship Emeritus at Emory University. *Theology and Music*

Marcel **Sarot** is UUF Chair for the History and Philosophy of Theology and Head of the Department of Theology at Utrecht University. *Diaconate, Patripassianism, Philosophical Theology, Theopaschite Controversy*

Hans **Schwarz** is Professor of Systematic Theology and Director of the Institute of Protestant Theology at the University of Regensburg. *Descent into Hell, Eschatology, Heaven, Hell, Universalism*

Fr Johannes M. **Schwarz** is Visiting Professor at the International Theological Institute, Gaming, Austria. *Limbo*

Fernando F. **Segovia** is Oberlin Graduate Professor of New Testament and Early Christianity at Vanderbilt University Divinity School. *Latin American Theology*

Frank C. **Senn** is Pastor of Immanuel Lutheran Church, Evanston, Illinois and has taught at Seabury-Western and Garrett-Evangelical Theological Seminaries. *Liturgical Calendar*

James W. **Skillen** is President of the Center for Public Justice in Washington, DC. *Covenant*

Natalia **Smelova** is Researcher in Syriac Studies at the Institute of Oriental Manuscripts, Russian Academy of Sciences, St Petersburg. *Syriac Christian Theology*

J. Warren **Smith** is Associate Professor of Historical Theology at Duke Divinity School. *Cappadocian Fathers*

James K. A. **Smith** is Associate Professor in the Department of Philosophy at Calvin College. *Deconstruction, Postmodernism*

Luther E. **Smith,** Jr, is Professor of Church and Community at the Candler School of Theology, Emory University. *Howard Thurman*

John **Snarey** is Professor of Human Development and Ethics at the Candler School of Theology, Emory University. *William James*

W. Becket **Soule,** O. P., is the former Dean of the Pontifical Faculty and Associate Professor of Canon Law at the Dominican House of Studies in Washington, DC. *Canon Law*

R. Kendall **Soulen** is Professor of Systematic Theology at Wesley Theological Seminary. *Scriptural Reasoning*

Bryan D. **Spinks** is Professor of Liturgical Studies at Yale Divinity School. *Sacramentology*

Max L. **Stackhouse** is Professor of Reformed Theology and Public Life Emeritus at Princeton Theological Seminary. *Civil Society*

Brian **Stanley** is Professor of World Christianity and Director of the Centre for the Study of World Christianity in the Faculty of Divinity at the University of Edinburgh. *Missiology*

Stephen J. **Stein** is Chancellor's Professor, Emeritus, in the Department of Religious Studies at Indiana University. *Jehovah's Witnesses*

James **Steven** is Lecturer in Theology and Ministry at King's College London. *Charismatic Movement*

The Right Revd Dr Kenneth W. **Stevenson** is the former Bishop of Portsmouth, England. *Blessing, Sacrifice*

Dan R. **Stiver** is Professor of Theology at Logsdon Seminary, Hardin-Simmons University. *Religious Language*

Jonathan **Strom** is Associate Professor of Church History at the Candler School of Theology, Emory University. *Pietism*

George W. **Stroup** is J. B. Green Professor of Theology at Columbia Theological Seminary. *Narrative Theology*

Elizabeth **Stuart** is Professor of Christian Theology at the University of Winchester. *Anointing of the Sick*

Phillip H. **Stump** is Professor of History at Lynchburg College. *Council of Constance*

Marjorie Hewitt **Suchocki** is Professor Emerita at the Claremont School of Theology. *Process Theology*

R. S. **Sugirtharajah** is Professor of Biblical Hermeneutics at the University of Birmingham. *Colonialism and Postcolonialism*

Steven **Sutcliffe** is Lecturer in Religion and Society in the School of Divinity at the University of Edinburgh. *New Age*

John **Swinton** is Professor in Practical Theology and Pastoral Care at the University of Aberdeen. *Disability Theology*

Mark Lewis **Taylor** is the Maxwell M. Upson Professor of Theology and Culture at Princeton Theological Seminary. *Paul Tillich*

M. Thomas **Thangaraj** is the D. W. and Ruth Brooks Associate Professor of World Christianity, Emeritus, at the Candler School of Theology, Emory University. *South Asian Theology*

John E. **Thiel** is Professor of Religious Studies at Fairfield University. *Tradition*

Deanna **Thompson** is Associate Professor of Religion and Chair of the Department of Religion at Hamline University. *Cross and Crucifixion*

N. J. **Thompson** is Lecturer in Church History at the University of Aberdeen. *Martin Bucer*

Susannah **Ticciati** is Lecturer in Systematic Theology at King's College London. *Job*

Terrence N. **Tice** is Emeritus Professor of Philosophy at the University of Michigan. *Friedrich Schleiermacher*

David **Tombs** is Lecturer and Programme Co-ordinator in Reconciliation Studies at the Irish School of Ecumenics. *Liberation Theology*

Joseph **Torchia**, O. P., is Professor of Philosophy at Providence College. *Manichaeism*

Jonathan **Tran** is Assistant Professor of Christian Ethics at Baylor University. *Excommunication, Secularization, Tolerance, Virtue Ethics*

Daniel J. **Treier** is Associate Professor of Theology at Wheaton College. *Doctrine, Evangelical Theology, Wisdom*

Carl R. **Trueman** is at Westminster Theological Seminary. *Assurance, Federal Theology,* Ordo salutis, *Puritanism*

Christopher **Tuckett** is Professor of New Testament at Pembroke College, University of Oxford. *John the Evangelist*

Lucian **Turcescu** is Associate Professor of Historical Theology at Concordia University, Montreal, Canada. *Sobornicity, Dumitru Stăniloae*

Max **Turner** is Professor of New Testament Studies at the London School of Theology. *Pentecost*

Cornelis P. **Venema** is President and Professor of Doctrinal Studies at Mid-American Reformed Seminary. *Predestination*

Medi **Volpe** is an Honorary Lecturer at Durham University. *Dorothee Soelle*

Andrew **Walker** is Professor of Theology, Culture, and Education at King's College, London. *Charismatic Movement*

Lee Palmer **Wandel** is Professor in the Department of History at the University of Wisconsin, Madison. *Humanism*

Bernd **Wannenwetsch** is University Lecturer in Ethics at the University of Oxford. *Just War, Virtue*

Kevin **Ward** is Senior Lecturer in African Religious Studies at the University of Leeds. *Anglican Theology, Thomas Cranmer, Richard Hooker*

Patricia A. **Ward** is Professor of French and Comparative Literature at Vanderbilt University. *Quietism*

Brent **Waters** is Stead Professor of Christian Social Ethics and the Director of the Stead Center for Ethics and Values at Garrett-Evangelical Theological Seminary. *Bioethics, Procreation*

Francis **Watson** is Chair of Biblical Interpretation at Durham University. *Scripture*

Darlene Fozard **Weaver** is Associate Professor of Theology and Religious Studies and Director of the Theology Institute at Villanova University. *Conscience*

Stephen H. **Webb** is Professor of Religion and Philosophy at Wabash College. *Animals*

Timothy P. **Weber** is Visiting Professor of Church History at Fuller Theological Seminary, Colorado Springs, Colorado. *Premillennialism*

John **Webster** is Professor and Chair of Systematic Theology at the University of Aberdeen. *Divine Attributes*

Timothy J. **Wengert** is Ministerium of Pennsylvania Professor of the History of Christianity at the Lutheran Theological Seminary at Philadelphia. *Martin Luther*

Merold **Westphal** is Distinguished Professor of Philosophy at Fordham University. *Atheism*

David **Wetsel** is Professor in the School of International Letters and Cultures at Arizona State University. *Blaise Pascal*

The Very Revd Stephen R. **White** is the Dean of Killaloe in County Clare, Ireland. *Agnosticism*

Jane **Williams** is Tutor in Theology at St Mellitus College, London. *Angels*

Stephen N. **Williams** is Professor of Systematic Theology at Union Theological College, Belfast. *Friedrich Nietzsche*

Thomas **Williams** is Associate Professor in the Department of Religious Studies at the University of South Florida. *John Duns Scotus, Voluntarism*

Ben **Witherington III** is Professor of New Testament Interpretation at Asbury Theological Seminary. *Dispensationalism*

John **Witte, Jr**, is Jonas Robitscher Professor of Law and Director of the Center for the Study of Law and Religion at Emory University. *Law*

Susan K. **Wood** is Professor of Theology at Marquette University. *Laity*

Thomas **Worcester,** S. J., is Associate Professor of History at the College of the Holy Cross. *Papacy*

A. D. **Wright** is Reader in Ecclesiastical History at the University of Leeds. *Council of Trent*

N. T. **Wright** is the Bishop of Durham. *Resurrection*

Randall C. **Zachman** is Professor of Reformation Studies in the Department of Theology of the University of Notre Dame. *John Calvin*

Editors

Ian A. **McFarland** is Associate Professor of Systematic Theology at Emory University's Candler School of Theology and a Lutheran lay theologian. He is a member of the American Academy of Religion and of the Nashville-based Workgroup for Constructive Theology. His most recent book is *The Divine Image: Envisioning the Invisible God* (2005).

David A. S. **Fergusson** is Professor of Divinity and Principal of New College at the University of Edinburgh. He has served as President of the Society for the Study of Theology (2000–2) and President of the UK Association of University Departments of Theology and Religious Studies (2005–8). He is a Fellow of the Royal Society of Edinburgh. His most recent book is *Faith and Its Critics: A Conversation* (2009).

Karen **Kilby** is Associate Professor of Systematic Theology and Head of the Department of Theology and Religious Studies at the University of Nottingham. She is President of the Catholic Theological Association of Great Britain. Her most recent book is *Karl Rahner: Theology and Philosophy* (2004).

Iain R. **Torrance** is President of Princeton Theological Seminary and Professor of Patristics. Formerly he held a Personal Chair in Patristics and Christian Ethics at the University of Aberdeen and served a term as Dean of the Faculty of Arts and Divinity. He was Moderator of the General Assembly of the Church of Scotland (2003–4). He has been co-editor of Scottish Journal of Theology since 1982 and edits the Cambridge monograph series on Contemporary Issues in Theology. His interests are in early Christianity, and he is the author of *Christology after Chalcedon* (1988).

Acknowledgements

The Cambridge Dictionary of Christian Theology has been over five years in the making, and many people have contributed towards seeing it through to completion. First in the list of those to whom thanks are due comes Kate Brett at Cambridge University Press, who was instrumental both in helping to conceive this project and for shepherding it through the early stages of development, not least through countless helpful suggestions of possible contributors for individual entries. We are also immensely grateful for the dedicated service of Rosanna Christian, Petra Michalkova, and Joanne Tunnicliffe, who handled with cheerful aplomb the mostly thankless task of organizing contracts for over two hundred contributors, as well as for Laura Morris, who managed a seamless transition in supervising the project when Kate moved to a new post at CUP.

Many thanks, too, are owed to the research assistants who helped along the way. Kristine Suna-Koro translated the article on Russian theology for us. Vance West collated entries from dozens of theological reference works as we struggled to come up with a final list of entries for the *Dictionary*. Over the final two years of the project, Diane Kenaston proofread virtually every article, rendering especially invaluable service (*inter alia*) in tracking down dates for some of the less well-known figures mentioned in various entries. And Maegan Gilliland and Bradley East provided sterling service in correcting the final proofs.

It goes without saying, however, that all this work behind the scenes would have been to no purpose without the co-operation of our many contributors. Given the many other demands on a scholar's time, composing articles for a reference volume is truly a work of supererogation, and we are correspondingly grateful for the participation of so many colleagues, who willingly condensed their expertise on complex topics into agonizingly restrictive word limits for the benefit of our readers. We have especially appreciated their grace and patience in dealing with the quibbles of four editors, and we hope that they find in the final product a tool that justifies their trust in us along the way.

Preface

There is no shortage of Christian theological reference works in print. Moreover, the proliferation of web-based resources (most notably the increasingly comprehensive Wikipedia) means that basic information about even the most obscure theological terms is rarely more than a few mouse clicks away. Under these circumstances the production of yet another theological dictionary may seem unnecessary at best and reactionary at worst. Consequently, before embarking upon this project, we discussed at some length what possible justification there could be for *The Cambridge Dictionary of Christian Theology.*

In part we were encouraged by our sister publication, Robert Audi's *Cambridge Dictionary of Philosophy,* which is widely recognized as having achieved remarkable compactness and accessibility without sacrificing accuracy or comprehensiveness. At the same time, we recognized that the extraordinarily pluriform character of contemporary Christian theology, including but also cutting across traditional confessional and juridical boundaries, raised particular challenges. Nevertheless, it seemed to us that there was a place – and, indeed, a need – for a single-volume reference work that was at once comprehensive in its coverage of topics, inclusive in the many perspectives of its contributors, and, most importantly, committed to a specifically *theological* examination of each topic considered. In short, we wanted a text that would exhibit what Hans Frei once referred to as a 'generous orthodoxy': coherent and capacious, but neither partisan nor blinkered.

In order to achieve these aims, we sought to enlist the services of a broad range of prominent theologians writing in English. Given the many commitments scholars face we have been able to reach this goal only very imperfectly, but we are all the more grateful for the generosity of the many colleagues who agreed to contribute to this volume. In enlisting their services, we judged it important to give the *Dictionary* a structure that would allow their individual contributions to be combined most effectively for the reader. Thus, while the *Dictionary*'s specifically theological (as opposed to historical or sociological) focus includes a comprehensive coverage of relevant topics, no less important than the range of material included is its level of integration. While the *Dictionary* is formatted conventionally, we have tried to ensure that the length and focus of individual articles make it as easy as possible for the reader to move between multiple entries in order to gain a well-rounded, appropriately contextual understanding of related theological concepts.

Entries range from a minimum of 250 to a maximum of 2,000 words in length. We settled on the minimum length of 250 words on the grounds that an important feature of a *theological* dictionary should be that it devotes enough space to terms and concepts to allow the reader to see how they are actually used in theological conversation. We have therefore not included any purely lexical entries. At the same time, we have opted for an upper limit of 2,000 words as an appropriate means of preserving the concision expected in a dictionary, which, we felt, would be eroded if individual entries were to encroach upon the length of a book chapter. Nevertheless, these longer entries contribute to the distinctive character of the *Dictionary,* since they provide a framework through which the various shorter entries are integrated both with one another and with larger conceptual fields.

CORE ENTRIES

We have conceived the 2,000-word articles as 'core entries'. Although they comprise only about 10 per cent of the total number of listings, they take up around a quarter of the total volume of text. As such, they are designed to provide the conceptual ballast for the volume as a whole, serving as the superstructure around and in terms of which many of the other entries are conceived and composed. The core entries fall into five basic categories that together map the territory of systematic theology from distinct, though complementary, conceptual perspectives:

- traditional doctrinal topics or *loci* (e.g., creation, ecclesiology, revelation);
- confessional orientations (e.g., Catholic, Lutheran, Orthodox);
- theological styles (e.g., evangelical, feminist, liberal);
- Christianity's relation to other faith traditions (e.g., Buddhism, Hinduism, Islam);
- academic disciplines (e.g., biblical theology, historical theology, systematic theology).

The inclusion of core entries on Christianity's relation to other faith traditions (as well as a range of articles of varying lengths on theologies emerging from non-western regions) is a feature driven by the recognition that the startling growth of Christian Churches in Asia, Africa, and Latin America, together with patterns of migration, make it likely that theology in the twenty-first century will cease to be dominated by western academic elites and that it will be increasingly conducted in close proximity with other religions.

The core entries include basic lexical orientation to the subject matter, historical and cultural contextualization, summary of key developments in the history of the topic, identification of continuing points of tension or debate, and evaluation of future prospects. Furthermore, core-entry authors were encouraged to use the comparatively large amount of space allotted to provide their own perspective on the topic as well as coverage of the basic conceptual terrain. The core entries were commissioned prior to the other articles, so that their content could be used by the editors to guide the composition of shorter articles on related topics. In this way, shorter entries are used to provide definition of and orientation to technical terms, freeing authors of core entries to sketch the main contours of their assigned topic without the need to make frequent explanatory digressions.

Needless to say, while the range of material covered by the core entries is large, it is not exhaustive. Some selection has inevitably been required in order to control the overall size of the volume, in line with our judgement of the relative significance of topics for the field as a whole. Thus, while all the major doctrinal *loci* feature in core entries, some significant theological styles (e.g., narrative and Queer theologies) have been assigned fewer than 2,000 words. Similarly, slightly shorter entries (generally between 1,500 and 1,750 words) have been allotted to other important topics that do not fall under any of the broader core-entry categories (e.g., baptism, monasticism, and philosophical traditions that have been important influences in the shaping of Christian thought). Finally, entries on the theologies associated with particular geographical regions vary widely in length and are, inevitably, somewhat arbitrary, though we have endeavoured to identify coherent centres of theological production both within (e.g., Scottish theology) and outside (e.g., South Asian theology) more established North Atlantic academic contexts. All these classes of articles function analogously to core entries, in that they have been used to help focus discussion on related topics.

BIOGRAPHICAL ENTRIES

Biographical entries fall into a separate category. Though in many cases individual theologians are directly relevant to the material covered in core entries and/or shorter articles relating to particular theological concepts or movements, we judged it important to treat significant thinkers in a more focused and deliberate manner. At the same time, because the number of figures who might qualify for entry is almost limitless, it was necessary to impose fairly severe limits on the number of figures granted individual entries. We have followed the practice of the *New Dictionary of National Biography* and the *Religion in Geschichte und Gegenwart* in not assigning separate entries to living persons (though living theologians are in many cases mentioned in other articles). Even with this means of exclusion, however, the list of those who might have been included remains vast, and we acknowledge a degree of unavoidable arbitrariness in the selection of those to be included.

In order to provide as balanced a list of figures as possible, we have tried to prioritize those theologians whose influence on the shape of central doctrines (e.g., Athanasius, Irenaeus), the subsequent history of the tradition (e.g., Aquinas, Luther, Palamas), or contemporary theology (e.g., Barth, Rahner) is widely recognized. Since the sociological complexion of Christian culture up to the twentieth century virtually guarantees that these criteria will produce a list that is overwhelmingly male and European, we have also endeavoured to include a significant number of women and persons of colour whose voices, though not as prominent in traditional academic theology, indicate something of the genuine, if often unacknowledged, diversity of Christian thought over the centuries.

In order to allow the maximum amount of space to subject entries, the vast majority of biographical entries have been set at either 250 or 500 words, though a few major figures have been assigned 1,000 words or more. Although the article's assigned length will constrain what is possible in each individual case, all entries include a summary of the figure's life, reference to the debates or controversies in which he or she was involved and the major ideas with which he or she is associated, identification of his or her most important works, and an evaluation of his or her influence.

USING THE *DICTIONARY*

As already noted, articles are arranged alphabetically, with each entry clearly identified in bold type and small capitals (e.g., **APOLOGETICS**). Core entries are further set apart by being printed in all capital letters (e.g., **CREATION**). Small capitals without boldface are employed within articles as a means of cross-referencing: when the reader comes across a term in small capitals in the body of an article (e.g., SCRIPTURE), this indicates that the term has an article of its own elsewhere in the *Dictionary.* Occasionally, cross-referencing is indicated by the addition of the conventional designations, 'see' or 'see also'. Because the core entries provide the conceptual centre of gravity for the text, readers are encouraged to refer to them in order to acquire a fuller sense of how concepts covered in related shorter entries mesh with the larger themes of Christian theological discourse.

Most entries include a brief bibliography of between one and six works. Obviously, given the enormous amount of writing available on almost every one of the entry topics, these bibliographies could be extended almost indefinitely, but stringency was necessary in order to meet the requirements of a one-volume reference work. The items listed at the end of the articles are, correspondingly, proposed in the vein of 'suggestions for further reading' for those wishing to pursue the topic in greater depth. In addition to these more formal bibliographic entries, however, two further sorts of references to other works are found in the *Dictionary.* First, biographical entries in particular generally include in the body of the article the titles and dates of the most important texts authored by the figure examined. Second, within all articles works cited are referenced by an abbreviated title and (where a portion of text is quoted) page, paragraph, or section numbers in parentheses. The full titles, original composition/publication dates, and (where relevant) the English translations (ET) from which the citations were taken are listed alphabetically by author (or, where no author is indicated, by title) in the 'References' pages at the end of the volume. Where material is cited from a modern or more contemporary edition of an older work, the date of the more recent edition is given in square brackets after the original publication date.

There are also a number of other, miscellaneous editorial conventions we have adopted in the *Dictionary* that the reader should note. First to note are the conventions we have adopted for biblical quotations. All such quotations are taken from the New Revised Standard Version, unless otherwise indicated, using the abbreviations for biblical and apocryphal books followed by the *Journal of Biblical Studies*; to save space we have also abbreviated the Old and New Testaments as OT and NT respectively. Second, throughout the volume we have chosen to use only Arabic numerals when referencing premodern texts (e.g., *Against Heresies* 3.20.3 means Book 3, Chapter 20, Section 3; *The City of God* 5.6–9 means Book 5, Chapters 6–9; *Summa theologiae* 1.93.2–4 means Part I, Question 93, Articles 2–4, and so forth). Third, we have uniformly referred to the Church of Rome as 'Catholic' rather than 'Roman Catholic'. Although we realize that this decision begs some significant ecclesiological questions, it was the easiest way to ensure consistency and economy of expression across a volume including contributors from a range of confessional traditions. (For similar reasons, we refer to the Chalcedonian Churches of the East as 'Orthodox' rather than as 'Eastern Orthodox'.) Finally, we have sought to provide dates for all figures mentioned within articles who do not have an article of their own elsewhere in the *Dictionary.* In most cases we have used dates of birth (if known) and death (where applicable), or, where both are unknown, *fl.* (Latin *floruit*, 'flourished'). For popes and monarchs, we have opted to use the dates of their reigns (indicated by the letter 'r.'). There are, however, two exceptions to this last convention. First, because the onset of the Roman emperor Constantine I's reign can be marked in several different ways, we have used his birth and death rather than reign dates. Second, in referring to the competing claimants to the papal throne during the Great Western Schism of 1378–1415, we have used birth and death dates to avoid confusion with respect to overlapping reigns, as well as disputed judgements regarding particular claimants' canonical status.

A

Abba The biblical record indicates that *abba*, the Aramaic word for 'father', was the form of address used by Jesus for God (see, e.g., Matt. 11:25–6; 26:39, 42; Luke 23:34, 46; John 11:41; 12:27–8; 17:5, 11, 21, 24–5). This usage appears to have been regarded as significant enough that it is one of the few pieces of Aramaic that is preserved untranslated in the Gospels (Mark 14:36). Jesus commended the same form of address to his disciples (Matt. 6:9; Luke 11:2; cf. John 20:17), and, again, its significance was such that it appears to have been preserved even among Greek-speaking communities in its Aramaic form (Rom. 8:15; Gal. 4:6).

While scholars disagree over whether or not Jews customarily addressed God as 'Father' before Jesus' time (cf. Isa. 63:16; Jer. 3:19), there seems little question that Jesus' use of the term was regarded by his followers as distinctive. The canonical evangelists understand Jesus' use of 'Father' as correlative of his own status as 'Son' (Matt. 11:27; John 17:1; cf. Matt. 3:17; 17:5 and pars.). From this perspective, later developed explicitly in the doctrine of the TRINITY, God's identity as 'Father' does not refer to a generic relationship between Creator and creature, but rather to a unique relationship with God's own co-eternal Word (John 1:1; see LOGOS), who, as 'Son', enjoys an intimacy with God that has no creaturely parallel (John 1:18). Thus, while Jesus is intrinsically God's Son, other human beings are children of God only by ADOPTION through Jesus' Spirit (Rom. 8:23; Gal. 4:5; see HOLY SPIRIT).

IAN A. MCFARLAND

Abortion Abortion is one of today's most contested moral issues, with many anti-abortionists taking an absolutist stand on the basis of the sanctity of innocent human life and the personhood of the unborn child, and many feminists taking an opposing stand on the basis of a woman's right to choose and her right to personal bodily autonomy. Between these polarized positions, there is a wide range of more nuanced historical and contemporary debates.

Christian attitudes to abortion are informed by SCRIPTURE and, in Catholic tradition, by NATURAL LAW. Yet it is difficult to derive an unambiguous conclusion from the diverse biblical passages which refer to life in the womb (e.g., Ps. 139:13–16), and to God's breathing of life into the human form (e.g., Gen. 2:7). Similarly, natural law lends itself to different interpretations as far as early human development is concerned, and there is ongoing debate regarding the personal identity and moral status of the embryo. Christianity has always regarded abortion as a serious SIN, and the early Church vigorously opposed practices of infanticide and abortion in surrounding cultures. Until the nineteenth century, however, there was a distinction in the Catholic theological tradition between early and late abortion in terms of the moral gravity of the act, relating to debates about when the soul enters the body ('ensoulment').

Although early abortion was not criminalized under English common law, during the nineteenth century legislative changes in Britain and the USA resulted in the criminalization of all abortion in response to pressure from the medical profession. In the late nineteenth century the Catholic Church stopped distinguishing between early and late abortion, and it is now the most absolutist of all religions on this issue. With the liberalization of abortion law in some countries since the 1960s (most famously, the 1973 decision of the US Supreme Court in *Roe* v. *Wade*), and with the more recent emergence of campaigns for women's reproductive rights, the Catholic hierarchy has sought to use its political influence wherever possible to block or abolish the legalization of abortion.

Modern Catholic teaching leaves open the question as to when the embryo acquires personhood, but it insists that the embryo must be accorded full human dignity from conception. Abortion might be permissible to save the mother's life, but only if the death of the fetus is an indirect rather than a direct consequence of the procedure (an ethical position known as the doctrine of double effect). Other Churches and religions such as Judaism and Islam adopt a more casuistic approach: although abortion is generally regarded as wrong, particular cases must be evaluated before a judgement can be made.

Abortion is a unique moral dilemma. There is widespread concern about high abortion rates and disputes about time limits for legal abortion are common in countries such as the UK and the USA. Significant ethical questions arise with regard to abortion on grounds of fetal disability, and scientific developments in embryology and biotechnology bring with them the risk of the commodification of human embryos and maternal bodies. Feminist pro-choice arguments sometimes show insufficient concern for questions regarding the dignity and vulnerability of the unborn child and the psychological wellbeing of women who are traumatized by abortion. On the other hand, the World Health Organization estimates that some 70,000 women die every year as a result of illegal abortions, and anti-abortion campaigners sometimes appear to be indifferent or even hostile towards the often profound suffering caused to women by unwanted pregnancies.

In view of the intractability of these issues, the traditional distinction between early and late abortion might serve society and the law well. For those who insist that there is no such distinction, the debate might more justly and effectively be conducted on moral grounds than through the law and politics. However, the ultimate credibility of any position might depend upon the extent to which it respects the moral authority of women and allows them to speak for themselves, recognizing that this will inevitably have a significant impact on an ethical debate from which women have historically been excluded, and yet which has such profound implications for women's lives.

R. M. Baird and S. E. Rosenbaum, eds., *The Ethics of Abortion: Pro-Life Vs. Pro-Choice* (Prometheus, 2001).

G. F. Johnston, *Abortion from the Religious and Moral Perspective: An Annotated Bibliography* (Praeger, 2003).

Tina Beattie

Abraham The biblical figure of Abraham, whose story is found in Gen. 11:27–25:10, is foundational for Judaism, Christianity, and Islam, to the extent that together they are sometimes named the three 'Abrahamic' religions. As the recipient of the covenant of circumcision, Abraham is regarded by Jews as the first Jew; his repudiation of idolatry for the worship of the one God means that he is sometimes described as the first Muslim in Islam (though formally most Muslims would accord this honour to Adam). While Abraham has never been popularly designated as the first Christian, his significance for the theology of Paul has given him a central role in the doctrine of justification, especially as developed in Protestantism.

In Galatians 3 and Romans 4, Paul cites Gen. 15:6 ('And [Abraham] believed the Lord; and the Lord reckoned it to him as righteousness') to argue that Abraham is the prototype of those who are justified by faith apart from works of the law. In this way, Paul argues, Abraham is ancestor not only of the Jews by virtue of his reception of the covenant of circumcision, but also of Gentile Christians, who, like Abraham, are reckoned righteous by virtue of their faith, apart from either circumcision (which was commanded only afterwards; Rom. 4:10–11) or the works of the Mosaic law (which was given hundreds of years later; Gal. 3:17). In this way, Abraham, as 'the ancestor of all who believe without being circumcised . . . and likewise the ancestor of the circumcised' (Rom. 4:11–12), points to the overcoming of the division between Jew and Gentile in the Church.

Ian A. McFarland

Absolution: see Penance.

Accommodation The concept of accommodation is a corollary of the doctrine of revelation and refers broadly to the processes by which God, though utterly transcendent of and thus intrinsically inaccessible to human investigation or knowledge, works within creation to make the divine self knowable to humankind. Accommodation thus refers to divine condescension to creaturely capacities and includes the use of any finite reality as a vehicle for divine self-disclosure. Most frequently, however, accommodation is associated specifically with God's use of Scripture as a vehicle of revelation scaled to the capacities of an unsophisticated audience. Thus, J. Calvin, following a tradition going back to Origen (*Cels.* 4.71) and Augustine (*Gen. lit.* 1.18.36), characterized the Bible's use of anthropomorphic language for God as analogous to a nurse's use of baby talk to communicate with an infant (*Inst.* 1.13.1).

Within this hermeneutical context, accommodation frequently serves as a tool of Christian apologetics. Calvin, for example, invoked divine condescension to account for discrepancies between biblical and scientific cosmologies (*CGen.* 6:14), as did G. Galilei (1564–1642) in his defence of heliocentrism (*Opere* 1.198–236). Divergence between Christian practice and the cultic and legal provisions of the OT is also explained in terms of accommodation, in line with Jesus' teaching that divorce was permitted by Moses only as a concession to hard-heartedness (Matt. 19:8). In Catholic thought accommodation is also used for the application of biblical texts to persons or circumstances other than those implied by their immediate context (e.g., the extension to all believers of God's promise to Moses, 'I will be with you', in Exod. 3:12).

See also Inerrancy.

Ian A. McFarland

Acculturation: see Inculturation.

Acedia: see Seven Deadly Sins.

Adiaphora Derived from the Greek for 'indifferent things', 'adiaphora' (singular: 'adiaphoron') was used in ancient Stoic philosophy for things (e.g., wealth) that were neither commanded as virtues nor proscribed as vices. In Christian theology it refers analogously to aspects of Church practice regarded as permissible but not obligatory. The category is implicit in Paul's pleas for toleration of diverse behaviours in the congregations to which he writes (e.g., eating or abstaining from meat; Rom. 14:1–4). In the second century Irenaeus likewise opposed papal demands for liturgical uniformity on the grounds that differences in practices of fasting did not preclude unity in faith (Eusebius, *EH* 5.24). The German Lutheran P. Meiderlin (1582–1651) appears to be responsible for perhaps the most well-known statement of this need to distinguish between what is and is not necessary in the Church: 'In essentials, unity; in inessentials, liberty; in all things, charity' (*Paraenesis* 128).

Although Meiderlin's formula has been taken up by a wide range of Christians from Moravians to Catholics (see Pope John XXIII, *Ad Petri*, §72), the topic of adiaphora achieved its greatest theological prominence during the Reformation, when Lutheran theologians debated the permissibility of submitting to certain Catholic practices judged to be adiaphora (e.g., the episcopal ordination of ministers) in the furtherance of Church unity. In adjudicating this controversy, the Book of Concord affirmed that adiaphora played the important role of maintaining good order and discipline in the Church; but while its authors conceded that in questions of adiaphora every effort should be made to avoid giving offence, they also insisted that, when the threat of persecution is present, compromise on adiaphora is forbidden, lest it appear that the practices in question are required and not a matter of Christian freedom (*FC, Ep.* 10).

Although the intra-Lutheran debates of the sixteenth century were not marked by disagreement over what counted as adiaphora, the criteria for distinguishing between essential and inessential matters remain a point of contestation among Christians, depending largely on the role they grant tradition as a guarantor of orthodoxy. The Protestant tendency to regard Scripture as the sole source of essential teaching reflects a view of tradition as fallible and, thus, subject to correction and change. The authors of the Westminster Confession of Faith (1647), following the Book of Concord's equation of adiaphora with ecclesial rites and ceremonies, distinguish between those things necessary for salvation, which are 'either expressly set down in Scripture, or by good and necessary consequence may be deduced from Scripture', and 'circumstances concerning the worship of God, and government of the Church . . . which are to be ordered by the light of nature, and Christian prudence' (1.6). By contrast, Orthodox, Catholic, and some Anglican Christians would include the content of the classical creeds, the decrees of ecumenical councils, and the apostolic succession of bishops in the list of essentials, reflecting a greater willingness to treat practices sanctioned by tradition as permanently binding on the Church.

Ian A. McFarland

Adoption Adoption as an ongoing, socially sanctioned *practice* does not exist in OT law. Three *acts* of adoption – of Moses (Exod. 2:10), Genubath (1 Kgs 11:20), and Esther (Esth. 2:7, 15) – are referred to, but these all take place outside Palestine and thus in contexts foreign to Jewish rule and custom. Torah tradition as such simply does not admit that someone who is not one's biological child can be rendered one's son or daughter by legal fiction. It was Paul who first introduced the notion of adoption into Christian theology.

The NT Greek word translated by the NRSV as 'adoption' is *huiothesia*, from *huios* ('son') and *tithēmi* ('to put or place'). The term appears five times in Paul's epistles (Rom. 8:15, 23; 9:4; Gal. 4:5; Eph. 1:5), but not once in the Gospels. Construed literally, *huiothesia* is gendered and connotes a legal placing or taking in as a male heir (i.e., one who may inherit) someone who is not one's biological son. One can readily see why Paul – that liminal figure at the dividing line between the historical Jesus and the Holy Spirit, Jew and Gentile, Roman and barbarian – would have been attracted to adoption metaphors. Paul knew himself to have been an outsider graciously allowed in (1 Cor. 15:8–10; cf. 1 Tim. 1:12–14), and he saw in his personal experiences a model of a fatherly God's salvific way with the wider world: 'When the fullness of time had come, God sent His Son, born of a woman, born under the law, in order to redeem those who were under the law, so that we might receive adoption as children' (Gal. 4:4–5).

See also Oblation.

Timothy P. Jackson

Adoptionism Adoptionism is the idea that the human being Jesus of Nazareth has some existence prior to union with the divine Logos, such that the union is something that *happens to* a particular human being. Some Ebionites, for instance, seem to have seen Jesus as a 'mere man' who fulfilled the law and was therefore anointed by the Holy Spirit (see Ebionitism). Something similar appears to have been taught in second-century Rome by Theodotus of Byzantium (*fl.* 180) and others, and later Paul of Samosata (d. *ca* 275) also seems to have emphasized the distinct existence of the man who was united to God's Word. The fourth-century theologian Marcellus of Ancyra (d. *ca* 375) is sometimes wrongly accused of adoptionism (though he could speculatively imagine the Word withdrawing from the human Jesus and the latter nevertheless continuing to exist); but one of his followers, Photinus of Sirmium (*fl.* 350), who stressed the unity of the *Logos* and the Father and downplayed the unity between the *Logos* and Jesus' humanity, argued that the *Logos* descended upon and eventually departed from Jesus. Considerably later, at the end of the eighth century, Elipandus of Toledo (*ca* 715–*ca* 800) and Felix of Urgel (*fl.* 800) drew upon distinctive Spanish liturgical traditions to authorize talk of the 'adoptive man' in Christ ('Spanish adoptionism'). They were opposed by Beatus of Liebana (*ca* 730–*ca* 800) and Alcuin of York (*ca* 735–804) who argued that 'adoption' language must be reserved for the Church's identity as child of God, in order not to obscure the difference between that relationship and the hypostatic union between Jesus' humanity and God.

Mike Higton

Advent: see Calendar, Liturgical.

Adventism Adventism grew out of the Millerite movement, whose members expected the return of Christ in judgement in 1844. When this did not occur as predicted (the 'Great Disappointment'), numerous clergy and LAITY combined their shared FAITH into a new movement. Its adherents adopted the name 'Seventh-Day Adventist' in 1860 and established its highest administrative body, the General Conference, in 1863. Seventh-Day Adventists have a representative four-tier administrative structure: congregations; conferences; union-conferences; and General Conference, which includes thirteen world divisions.

Since J. N. Andrews (1829–83) became the first missionary in 1874, Adventists have grown into one of the world's ten largest Christian denominations. Facilitators in Adventism's growth include its commitment to education (operating the largest educational system within PROTESTANTISM); preventive and curative health systems, hospitals, orphanages, and retirement homes (Adventist health practices contribute to an added life expectancy of six to ten years over the general American population); worldwide television, radio broadcasting, and publishing; and practical involvement in local communities through Adventist Community Services and the Adventist Disaster and Relief Agency, which facilitates humanitarian aid worldwide; and programs to counter AIDS in many developing countries.

Adventists come from the REFORMATION traditions of *SOLA SCRIPTURA*, *solus Christus*, *sola fide*, and *sola gratia*, and hold the DOCTRINES of an eternal TRINITY, literal six-day CREATION and young earth, stewardship of the earth, tithing, God's moral LAW as binding on all humanity, traditional Christian marriage, respect for life, Holy Communion (see EUCHARIST), and spiritual gifts (see CHARISM). Adventists are also part of the Arminian/Wesleyan tradition (see ARMINIANISM), believing in FREE WILL; restoration of the complete individual in the image of God through Christ (JUSTIFICATION); and the ministry of the HOLY SPIRIT (SANCTIFICATION and personal holiness).

Other Adventist doctrines include: adult BAPTISM by immersion; holding both OT and NT as of equal relevance; historicist interpretation of biblical PROPHECY; premillennial ESCHATOLOGY (see PREMILLENNIALISM); a temporary and literal great controversy between Christ and the DEVIL (viz., good and evil), concluding with the creation of a new earth; a literal HEAVEN; mortality of the soul, with immortality given as God's gift at Christ's PAROUSIA (Ezek. 20:12, 20; 1 Cor. 15:52–4); the imminent, literal second coming of Christ; a future, temporary HELL; the seventh-day sabbath of both testaments as relevant today; and strict separation of Church and State derived from Revelation 14.

Adventism also holds that the prophetic gift (1 Cor. 12:10) is one of God's gifts to the Church, and was evidenced through E. G. White (1827–1915). This conviction is understood in the context of a belief that non-canonical prophetic gifts throughout history have been lesser lights pointing humanity to God's greater light (i.e., Christ as revealed in SCRIPTURE). A product of early Methodism, White held that her writings were to exalt Scripture, never to replace it, and to encourage adherence to it as God's perfect standard of truth (see METHODIST THEOLOGY). Her view, and that of Adventism more generally, is that salvation is effected by one's submission to God's will as revealed in Scripture.

See also SABBATARIANISM.

G. R. Knight, *Reading Ellen White* (Review and Herald, 1997).

N. J. Vyhmeister, 'Who Are Seventh-Day Adventists?' in *Handbook of Seventh-Day Adventist Theology*, ed. R. Dederen Commentary Reference Series 12 (Review and Herald, 2000), 1–21.

MICHAEL DAVEY PEARSON

AESTHETICS, THEOLOGICAL Theological aesthetics addresses the place of beauty in Christian life. In classical metaphysics, beauty is taken to be an element of all reality, and therefore often numbered among the TRANSCENDENTALS. Because it cuts across (or 'transcends') categorization, and is thus, like truth and goodness, a property of being, beauty is an attribute of God. The beauty of God is the foundation of theological aesthetics. While goodness and truth are universal properties of being, the goodness of reality is best observed in individual moral acts, and truth is most easily analyzed in particular true judgements. Likewise, the finite, particular beautiful object, or 'aesthetic beauty', is our central means of access to transcendental beauty. Works of art capture aesthetic beauty in a lasting and socially transmissible form. Hence, works of art, and the aesthetic sensibility requisite to their appreciation, play a significant role in theological aesthetics. The high-intensity beauty of works of art represents the presence and appeal of divine beauty in all created reality.

The most influential modern proponent of theological aesthetics is the Swiss H. U. von BALTHASAR. Balthasar composed a trilogy which began with theological aesthetics (*The Glory of the Lord: A Theological Aesthetics*), moved thence to theological ethics (*Theo-Drama*), and ended with a theological consideration of truth (*Theo-Logic*). By presenting his theology in this sequence, he affirmed the need to anchor the theological senses and imagination in beauty before moralizing theologically or knowing theological truth. The ordering of Balthasar's trilogy reverses that of I. KANT's philosophical *Critiques*, which begin with judgement, move to ethics, and are completed by aesthetics. It likewise reverses the tendency of modern SYSTEMATIC THEOLOGY to work largely on a conceptual and moral plane, including aesthetics only as superficial, rhetorical decoration. For theological aestheticians, human imagination naturally desires the supernatural beauty of God because God calls it through beauty, which is gratuitously rooted in reality and graciously permeates it.

The aesthetic is what is sensorily perceived. One side of the western Christian attitude to aesthetic imagination is summed up in Augustine's adage, *ex umbris et imaginibus in veritas* ('out of shadows and images into truth', *Ep.* 75). This marked an attitude to aesthetic beauty which lasted from the patristic era to the nineteenth century, when the adage was carved over the doorway of J. H. Newman's oratory in Birmingham. While formally adhering to this deprecation of the imagination and sensory images as obstacles to transcendental Truth, medieval Thomism in its own way began with the 'aesthetic', by making sensation the first step in cognition, and by appealing to 'congruence' (*convenientia*) as a sign of theological plausibility. The Franciscan Bonaventure (1221–74) likewise subordinates the senses to the 'spiritual' but gives beauty a foothold by transforming Francis of Assisi's (1181/2–1226) Christocentric spirituality into a theology in which all reality is systematically envisaged as the expression of Christ. Many modern Christians have been motivated to make this starting point and foothold explicit in reaction to the way in which post-Kantian philosophy has heightened the early Christian depreciation of the aesthetic sensibility by removing its theological basis: for much modern thought the purer the philosophical reason of the aesthetic and sensory, the more attenuated its grip on reality and revelation.

In response to this depreciation of the sensory imagination, Balthasar countered that one reason for beginning with beauty was 'apologetic': unless one is first touched by its beauty, one will not grasp or be grasped by the Christian revelation at its most elemental level, and thus fail fully to recognize and desire the reality of the goodness and truth of the Trinity. Rather than eliminating the senses and imagination, one must baptize them. In line with this perspective, it is important to note that the most successful works of apologetics of modern times have been, in a broad sense, exercises in theological aesthetics. Works which have used beauty and imagination in service to revealed truth include those of G. MacDonald (1824–1905), C. S. Lewis (1898–1963), and J. R. R. Tolkien (1892–1973). Ever since J. Butler's (1692–1752) *Analogy of Religion* (1736), British theology has appealed to the reader's sense of harmony and congruity. In the nineteenth century, Romantic writers like S. T. Coleridge (1772–1834), MacDonald, and G. M. Hopkins (1844–89) explicitly turned to imagination as a witness to the supernatural, and used mythology, fairy tales, and poetry as a way of expressing Christian truths in symbolic, imaginatively attractive forms. Newman's idea of 'real assent' (which he originally called 'imaginative assent'), meaning assent to truth in the particular and concrete, is in the tradition of British empiricism. In this way, Romantic Christians of the nineteenth and early twentieth century (including Newman) effectively proposed a new, more positive interpretation of Augustine's 'out of shadows and images into truth'. Balthasar saw Hopkins and Lewis as exponents of an originally Anglican tradition which aimed to achieve supernatural realism through imagination.

Theological aesthetics is not a purely theoretical discipline. It has the practical and pastoral mission of educating the religious sensibility and physical senses to appreciate revealed beauty. Hence, art remains its most significant secular medium, and the ecclesial task of enabling worship to engender love for divine beauty belongs to the vocation of theological aesthetics. An important development in practical theological aesthetics has been the increased interest in Christian literature, from F. O'Connor (1925–64) to R. Hansen (b. 1947), religious film (e.g., the Orthodox movie, *The Island*, 2005), and Christian popular music (e.g., S. Stevens, b. 1975). Journals which link Christianity and contemporary aesthetics include *Image: A Journal of Art and Religion*; B. Nicolosi (b. 1964) trains Christian filmmakers at 'Act One', in Hollywood; and a dozen major universities offer MA programmes in 'Theology and the Arts'. To the extent that these enterprises are theological in spirit and do not merely serve niche markets, they cut across secular/Christian categories through the appeal to beauty; and they enable Christians to educate their aesthetic sensibility.

In so far as theological aesthetics appeals to common ground with non-Christians, it looks to a religious sense thought to be stimulated by contact with beauty. It was by admixture with a religious feeling for congruity and form that pre-Christian humanity developed the aesthetic sensibility which gave rise to the classical recognition that beauty is a property of everything that is real. Where nineteenth-century Romantic Christianity hoped mythology would revive this religious sense, contemporary theological aesthetics directs post-Christian humanity beyond the universal religious sense to its root in God's love for all humanity. The claim that aesthetics belongs to revealed theology comes down to the belief that the agapic love of the Trinity creates a counterpart to itself in the human desire or eros for God.

D. B. Hart, *The Beauty of the Infinite: The Aesthetics of Christian Truth* (Eerdmans, 2003).

A. Nichols, *Redeeming Beauty: Soundings in Sacral Aesthetics* (Ashgate, 2007).

P. Sherry, *Spirit and Beauty: An Introduction to Theological Aesthetics* (Clarendon Press, 1992).

R. Williams, *Grace and Necessity: Reflections on Art and Love* (Continuum, 2006).

Francesca A. Murphy

African Theology African theology is an academic endeavour developed at the nexus of theological (including, e.g., biblical, systematic, confessional, missiological, and practical) and contextual (e.g., geographical, anthropological, sociological, and geopolitical) specifics. It has emerged and progressed as a result of shifts at the nexus of these two sets of issues. On such shifting ground it has grown from a focus on colonial and cultural concerns mostly defined in missiological terms (from the 1960s), to political concerns closely associated with South African confessional forms (from the 1980s), and, most recently, to an African PUBLIC THEOLOGY interacting with geopolitical contexts that include public morality, local policy formation, Church–State relationships, and the developmental agenda (from the 1990s). African public theology is a contemporary thrust in African theology that feeds on the earlier trajectories and, as such, may rightly be called the defining progress leading to the emergence of a 'modern' African theology.

In its response to the impact of European COLONIALISM, the focus of African theology in the 1960s was largely on the meaning of African cultures or traditions. Reaction to the European colonial influence on African theology stressed the elements of cultural and spiritual enslavement that accompanied the slave trade and later commercialization. Across the continent cultural or traditional African theologies took on the form of pan-African, continental themes, or even local, tribal metaphors, which came to be known collectively as indigenous African theologies. Many of the earlier expressions of these theologies were theologically conservative and shaped primarily by concerns surrounding the themes of INCULTURATION.

The confrontational and reconstructive nature of these theologies was defined by historical conditions, both colonial and cultural. This early quest in African theology sought to understand the continuities and discontinuities between African traditional religions and identity, on the one hand, and Christian faith, on the other. Its leading representatives included J. Mbiti (b. 1931), K. Bediako (1945–2008), G. Setiloane (b. 1925), and K. Dickson (1929–2005), whose work helped to shatter negative theological stereotypes of indigenous African thought and provide a space for African theology to develop with greater independence from European models. Because a significant part of this theological engagement was brought about by the postcolonial African Christian experience of misrepresentation or marginalization within western theology, postcolonial African theology was partly driven by a HERMENEUTIC of suspicion as exemplified in the work of I. Mosala (b. 1950), T. Mofokeng (b. 1942), and M. Dube (b. 1964), and partly by the hermeneutic of reconstruction characteristic of J. Ukpong (b. 1940), D. Tutu (b. 1931), and A. Boesak (b. 1946).

Modern African theologies emerged from a framework of questions embedded in differentiated patterns of social exclusion expressed in oppositional thought structures. Such thought structures were used to distinguish the particular forms of African victimhood from a diversity of adversarial social constructs, most often missiological in nature, that were a legacy of the colonial opposition between the European (equated with Christian) and the African (equated with pagan). The ruptures in traditional African thought patterns resulting from the confluence of historical forces on the African continent were expressed as 'alienation', which could, in turn, be associated with some institutional context, aspect of continental geography, or political structure. Correspondingly, Africans' alienating experience with colonialism, suppressive African regimes, western Christianity, European culture, and European definitions of RACE, as well as with Marxist definitions of class, dominated this earlier discourse in African theology.

With the advent of the 1980s the increasing international prominence of the struggle against apartheid in South Africa added a new dimension to African theology. Influenced by strands of LIBERATION THEOLOGY developed in Latin America and among North American Black theologians, it included a strong focus on questions of HUMAN RIGHTS, as well as more specific social and theological analyses of racism. The specifically theological condemnation of apartheid as a HERESY and the call for prophetic denunciation of injustice that defined this period included the production of several internationally prominent theological texts, including the KAIROS DOCUMENT and the BELHAR CONFESSION.

Throughout the post-apartheid period in the 1990s African theologians wrestled with the continuities and the discontinuities of the former oppositional, anti-colonial model of theological reflection on its way to new forms of distinctively African theological reflection. This quest for a new or modern form of African theology, combining insights from earlier emphases on indigenization and liberation, has led to a number of serious experiments in constructive theology, including C. Villa-Vicencio's (b. 1942) 'theology of reconstruction', R. Botman's (b. 1953) 'theology of transformation', and a 'theology of reconciliation' promoted pre-eminently by Tutu, along with Botman, J. de Gruchy (b. 1939), and others.

In this transitional phase of theological reflection, many African theologians realized that a fundamental weakness of African theology resided in its inability to bring about a renewal of African ECCLESIOLOGY. African theology could not overcome the ecclesiological weakness embedded in its missiology. This inability was brought about by the strong oppositional nature of African anti-colonialist theology, with its tendency to formulate itself over against European models that had shaped churches established in the colonial period. However, in recognition of this problem new strains of African theologies are emerging as positive expressions that no longer posture in a deficit model. They seek their defining character in a critical, futurist form. This emergent critical form is being expressed as a 'modern' theology from Africa.

Most recently, African theologians such as Botman, D. Smit (b. 1951), J. Cochrane (b. 1946), and N. Koopman (b. 1961) have introduced 'PUBLIC THEOLOGY' as an example of this sort of definitive, positive, and ecumenical theological form that could also engage other theologies beyond an oppositional (i.e., north–south) or exclusively continental framework. In spite of its intended international reach, moreover, African public theology remains rooted in the context of Africa. This successful transformation to a 'modern' African theology can be ascribed to three historical stimuli: questions of gender, the persistent presence of ecumenical reasoning in African theology's political engagements, and the inherent methodological and hermeneutical restlessness of African theology. One can therefore speak of the theological 'bridges' of gender, ECUMENISM, and contextualization that have sustained and propelled the emergence of 'modern' African theology. Each of these needs to be explored in greater depth.

At each phase of its development, African theology encountered women's voices impacting its own theological meaning, such that the transformation to a modern African theology cannot be grasped without reference to the challenges raised by women theologians. Their work spans the breadth of the developments in African theology. The Circle of Concerned African Woman Theologians was born in Ghana in 1989. As such, it was formed on the not yet concluded foundations of the 1960s, with its focus on colonialism and culture. At the same time, some of its interlocutors related well to the 'confessional period' of the 1980s and beyond, and significant numbers of these theologians have become renewing public theologians.

African women played an important role in redefining ecclesiological identities in Africa. A significant part of this quest was a reaction to colonialism. However, it was sustained through the period of confessional engagement and has continued into the present. The Circle of Concerned African Woman Theologians guided the gender discourse in the African contexts in a formative fashion. Many of the women of the Circle have played a formidable role in establishing the public theological discourse of 'modern' African theology, sustaining the gender bridge throughout the transformations in African theology. The mothers of theology in Africa, including M. A. Oduyoye (b. 1934) of Ghana and D. Ackermann (b. 1935) of South Africa on the one hand, and younger scholars such as E. Mouton (b. 1952) and M. Dube on the other, fought the theological battle of women in African theological contexts. Their engagement with contexts, identity, and SPIRITUALITY has been presented through experience and storytelling, most programmatically in the volume *Claiming our Footprints* (2000). The scholarship of the Circle of Concerned African Woman Theologians will continually inform the future modalities of African theology, the significance of which as a legitimate endeavour is tied to the presence of gender-based critique in its midst.

Ecumenism has also played a significant role in sustaining African theology in the modern period. African theology has a persistent knack of exposing itself to ecumenical scrutiny and engagement, as seen in the work of figures such as Boesak, M. Buthelezi (b. 1935), J. Durand (b. 1934), and B. Naudé (1915–2004). In the early developments of the postcolonial period the major role-players (e.g., Bediako, Mbiti) deliberately sought exposure to ecumenical and international platforms where they tested and presented their contributions to African theology. Some of them studied in Europe and the USA, resulting in a certain ecumenical and international confidence about their skill and scholarship. In the time of 'confessing theology', the theologians of the Kairos Document (A. Nolan (b. 1934), F. Chikane (b. 1951), Villa-Vicencio, and others) and those of the Confession of Belhar (e.g., Boesak, Smit, Durand, and Daan Cloete (b. 1938)), immediately presented their work to the international and ecumenical world. Although both confessing documents arose within the apartheid context in South Africa, they have sustained their relevance also in a post-apartheid context. The Kairos Document was a radical rejection of theologies that support the status quo of apartheid while embracing a prophetic theology of the people. Even more significantly, the Confession of Belhar, as the first Reformed confession born on African soil to be received as having the same status as established confessions composed and adopted in Europe, leads this theological trajectory. Its central significance lies in the fact that, based on its identification and critique of the theological centre of the South African policy of apartheid, it treats racism as a confessional question. A significant number of Churches – European and American as well as African – have adopted Belhar as a confession of their own Churches. The major breakthrough in this theological initiative is vested in the strength of the argument that certain ethical questions should be regarded as equally important confessional issues. This discourse is also meaningful for questions related to gender justice and economic justice.

Contemporary African public theology builds on this ecumenical instinct. Therefore, it extends into the debates of the Christian, and sometimes inter-religious, ecumenical community (as in the work of John Pobee (b. 1937)). In this way modern African theology will continue its quest for being truly African but with an ecumenical and international reach, as exemplified in the work produced by African theologians at the Beyers Naude Centre for Public Theology at Stellenbosch University in South Africa.

Finally, the methodological transition from a liberation theological stance in the 1980s to a more explicit reconciling theology in the 1990s and beyond forms an important bridge in the transformation of African theology. African theologians of liberation were always at issue with each other with regard to their methodology and hermeneutics. The bridging role of LIBERATION THEOLOGY in the transformation of African theology resulted from a political engagement with the context that manifested itself – most notably in South Africa – in a legacy of methodological and hermeneutical 'restlessness' (T. Maluleke). However, this 'restlessness' can be seen in developments throughout the continent in Black theology, contextual theology, the theology of African religions, ecumenical and REFORMED THEOLOGIES, and theologies of reconciliation.

With the theme of reconciliation as its blazing flag, the drive to a secular, post-apartheid mode of theological knowledge on African soil connected well with the postcolonial mindset that guided the new thinking of African theologians. In this way, contemporary African theology incorporates the focus on issues of colonialism and cultural identity prominent in the 1960s and the confessional positions associated with the struggle against apartheid and racism in the 1980s to generate an African public theology for the twenty-first century. Although the agency of the victim, the poor, and the marginalized remain the *raison d'être* of African public theology, the methodological and hermeneutical restlessness about questions of identity, justice, race, class, power, forgiveness, confession, globalization, and gender will still have us see further transformation in future.

K. Bediako, *Christianity in Africa: The Renewal of a Non-Western Religion* (Orbis, 1995).

E. M. Conradie, ed., *African Christian Theologies in Transformation* (EFSA, 2004).

L. Hansen, ed., *Christian in Public: Aims, Methodologies and Issues in Public Theology* (SUN Press, 2007).

B. Knighton, 'Issues of African Theology at the Turn of the Millennium', *Transformation* 21:3 (July 2004), 147–61.

M. G. Motlhabi, 'Black or African Theology? Toward an Integral African Theology', *Journal of Black Theology in South Africa* 8:2 (1994), 113–41.

M. A. Oduyoye, *Introducing African Women's Theology* (Sheffield Academic Press, 2001).

H. RUSSEL BOTMAN

AGAPE: see LOVE.

AGGIORNAMENTO An Italian word that means 'updating', *aggiornamento* was, along with *ressourcement*, one of the two principal watchwords associated with the work of VATICAN COUNCIL II. Both terms denote movements that emerged from widespread dissatisfaction with the state of CATHOLIC THEOLOGY in the mid-twentieth century. Specifically, they reflected a desire to address the concern that rigid adherence to neo-Scholastic categories and methods developed in the nineteenth century had caused a certain ossification of Catholic thought. Yet, while advocates of *ressourcement* sought to rejuvenate the life of the Church by recovering the riches of patristic and medieval theology, the language of *aggiornamento* suggested that the best way for the Church to address the modern world was to appropriate the best insights of modern thought.

At the opening of Vatican II, Pope John XXIII (r. 1958–63) explicitly noted the need to ensure that DOCTRINE be 'explored and expounded in the way our times demand' ('Address', §6.5), but the implications of this summons have been sharply debated among Catholics. Liberals have seen in John's language at the Council and elsewhere a call for reform of Catholic practice comparatively free from captivity to established modes of thought. By contrast, more conservative voices argue that John's emphasis on the enduring substance (as opposed to the changeable form) of TRADITION suggests more caution, in order to ensure that engagement *with* modernity does not result in assimilation *to* it.

See also *NOUVELLE THÉOLOGIE*.

IAN A. MCFARLAND

AGNOSTICISM Since the term 'agnostic' was coined in 1869 by T. H. Huxley (1825–95) as a more epistemically responsible alternative to 'atheist', it and its cognate term 'agnosticism' have frequently come to be heavily value-laden, and thus need to be approached with some caution. Huxley's intention was value-neutral, but the concept has often been understood either as putting the whole God-question to one side as unresolvable or unimportant, or simply as reflecting a certain spiritual laziness.

There is a strong case that agnosticism, rightly understood, is a living part of faith – perhaps even its prerequisite: a notion which H. Mansel (1820–71) explored in his 1858 Bampton Lectures, *The Limits of Religious Thought*, although he did not use the actual term 'agnosticism'.

Agnosticism in the strict sense is an acknowledgement of the limitations and provisionality of all human knowledge, especially when finite minds attempt to explore the infinite and the divine. In the OT it surfaces especially in the Prophetic and Wisdom traditions, notably in the books of Jonah, Job, and Ecclesiastes, and profoundly in the book of Daniel also. In the NT it is present in Jesus' elliptical parabolic teaching, and in the frequent misunderstandings and blindness of the disciples, and highlighted particularly in their uneasy faltering towards some kind of post-resurrection understanding and faith.

Similarly, just as it is present in SCRIPTURE, though often as an undertone to the ongoing rush of story and event, so too agnosticism is witnessed to, *sotto voce* at least, throughout the history of Christianity. It even finds a voice in AUGUSTINE OF HIPPO (e.g., *Conf.* 1.4). Its flowering is richest in the mystical tradition through such concepts as *The Cloud of Unknowing* (late fourteenth century) and John of the Cross' *Dark Night of the Soul* (1619) in which all knowledge and even sense of God is stripped away.

Since the mid-nineteenth century, agnosticism has become an oft-neglected poor relation in the household of faith, and faith and theology have found themselves impoverished by its absence. A contemporary rediscovery of agnosticism is necessary, especially in a religious world which, in the face of challenges both internal and external, inclines more and more to the comforting illusions of certainty and even of fundamentalism.

A properly agnostic faith is one which prevents itself from being a closed circle of fixed and unchanging knowledge, and which, by acknowledging its own provisionality opens itself up to the insights of other disciplines, and places more stress on the relationality of faith and the category of 'personal knowledge' than it does on purely propositional knowledge – which it accepts is, in the case of God, unavailable to us in any definitive form. This in turn facilitates dialogue, both between the Christian traditions, and between Christianity and other world faiths.

Agnosticism, then, in spite of the relatively recent appearance of the word, is a concept as old as Christianity itself, and one which remains enduringly relevant. Its appositeness as a foundational strand in faith has never been better expressed than by the sixteenth-century Anglican divine, R. HOOKER: 'Dangerous it were for the feeble braine of man to wade farre into the doings of the Most High, whome although to know be life, and joy to make mention of his name: yet our soundest knowledge is to know that we know him not as in deed he is, neither can know him: and our safest eloquence concerning him is our silence, when we confesse without confession that his glory is inexplicable, his greatness above our capacitie and reach' (*Lawes 1.2.2.*).

S. R. White, *A Space for Unknowing: The Place of Agnosis in Faith* (Columba Press, 2006).

M. Wiles, 'Belief, Openness and Religious Commitment', *Theology* 101:801 (May/June 1995), 163–71.

STEPHEN R. WHITE

ALLEGORY Allegory can refer either to the reading of a text in some other sense than what would seem to be its literal meaning, or to a kind of text designed to be read in a non-literal way. For example, King David thinks Nathan's story of the rich man who steals the poor man's only lamb is a clear but abstract case of injustice that has nothing to do with himself. In reality it was about David's own treachery, designed to bring about his repentance: 'I have sinned against the Lord' (2 Sam. 12:13). An allegory is thus a reading meant (when applied to SCRIPTURE) to draw the reader and her community into the divine exchange between God and humanity that Scripture not only subscribes to but instantiates.

Many communities make use of allegorical modes of interpretation to read texts in counter-intuitive ways, especially when the community's core commitments change. Greeks read Homer (*fl.* 850 BC) and other ancient epics differently once the deeds depicted were deemed immoral. Christians could adopt similar strategies when reading the OT: the story of Sarah and Hagar no longer simply casts Abraham in an embarrassing light; it is an *allēgoroumena* (Gal. 4:24 – the only place the NT uses the term directly) about Gentile Christians and the LAW. But allegory is not only a defensive hermeneutic to apologize for awkward stories. It can also be employed because an ancient story (e.g., the Exodus) and a contemporary liturgical practice (e.g., BAPTISM) resonate in the community's experience (see 1 Cor. 10:1–11). Or it can be a way of reading greater significance into details than may seem warranted at first glance, as when the new COVENANT is seen in details of Israel's worship (Heb. 8–10), or when Gregory of Nyssa (see CAPPADOCIAN FATHERS) sees descriptions of the adornment of the soul with virtue in the story of the priestly vestments in Exodus in his *Life of Moses*. Allegory is an attention to the depth of things, their nature as 'mystery', where Christ meets the Church in judgement and grace. This new meeting can change things so dramatically that the old seems passé (2 Cor. 3:6). Once these NT readings are canonized, the practice of allegory itself (arguably) is as well.

Exactly how far can allegory go? When those who came to be called Gnostics seemed to other Christians to be allegorizing without limit, the nascent 'Orthodox' Church reacted by drawing some boundaries (see GNOSTICISM). For Clement of Alexandria (*ca* 150–*ca* 215), the Bible has to be read as a whole – one cannot find a teaching allegorically in one place that is not also present literally in another. IRENAEUS insisted that readings of Scripture had to conform to a single image – that of Christ. He mostly used texts that Christians had traditionally seen in Christological terms, such as those in Isaiah and Zechariah. ORIGEN took allegory and applied it more liberally throughout the Bible. To be sure, Origen thought that most of Scripture should be read literally and historically. Allegory was also an art for the advanced, since to discern Christ in counter-intuitive places could obviously be dangerous. But later Christians found him insufficiently circumspect in his application of these strictures. Antiochene theologians reacting against Origen attempted to recover the literal, plain meaning of the words on the page. Yet later Christians continued to imitate Origen in practice while vilifying his name.

This vacillation between eagerness to allegorize and worry over its randomness continued through the Middle Ages until today. Medieval Christians included allegory as the final level of reading in their fourfold *quadriga*. For example, if the literal 'meaning' of the word 'Jerusalem' is a city in Palestine, the tropological (moral) is the soul, and the anagogical (eschatological) is heaven, then the allegorical is the Church. These readings were reinforced in Church art in stained glass, iconography, and statuary. The Reformers reacted against allegory, worried that with its licence their Catholic opponents could defend non-biblical teaching with a veneer of Scripture without its depth. M. LUTHER continued to allegorize fairly regularly; J. CALVIN was more adamant in his efforts to root the practice out, even if he was never entirely successful.

Modern historical criticism has often seen itself as an ally of the Antiochenes and the Reformers in efforts to attend 'soberly' and not 'arbitrarily' to the words on the page. In the latter half of the twentieth century, the argument was made (citing the way in which Christians often coupled allegory with anti-Jewish polemic) that allegory erases not only the words on the page, but the Jewish bodies of those who hold to the literal sense. In the last generation or two Catholic scholars (including H. DE LUBAC, H. von BALTHASAR, and others) led the way in rehabilitating allegory as a hermeneutical move appropriate to those who are in Christ, looking to their Lord throughout all creation, including in the pages of the Bible.

J. O'Keefe and R. Reno, *Sanctified Vision: An Introduction to Early Christian Interpretation of the Bible* (Johns Hopkins University Press, 2005).

G. Anderson, *The Genesis of Perfection: Adam and Eve in Jewish and Christian Imagination* (John Knox Press, 2001).

JASON BYASSEE

AMILLENNIALISM 'Amillennialism' designates the belief that the 1,000-year reign of Christ and the SAINTS (viz., the MILLENNIUM) described in Revelation 20:4–6 does not refer to a future period of earthly history, but is rather a symbolic designation for the present period of the Church established at PENTECOST and ending with Christ's return and the Last Judgement. The term is problematic, both because it is easily misunderstood to mean a denial of the Millennium (leading some to prefer the phrase 'realized millennialism'), and because it is a neologism rarely used by the majority of those whose position it purports to describe. However named, the amillennial position is clearly distinct from PREMILLENNIALISM; its relationship to POSTMILLENNIALISM, whose proponents also identify Christ's return with the end of terrestrial history, is more ambiguous.

The denial of an earthly kingdom of Christ has been dominant in both eastern and western Christianity since the fourth century. The view of both the Catholic MAGISTERIUM and the Anglican, Lutheran, and Reformed traditions is indebted to AUGUSTINE's interpretation of the Millennium as referring to the indirect and contested way in which Christ reigns with the saints in the present (viz., in the Church), as contrasted with the immediate and uncontested way in which Christ will reign after the PAROUSIA (*City* 20.9). While defenders of this position stress its coherence with Christ's dissociation of God's kingdom from worldly politics (John 18:36), critics charge it with an undue spiritualization of the Christian hope that fails to take seriously God's commitment to realize God's purposes within rather than beyond history.

See also ESCHATOLOGY.

IAN A. MCFARLAND

ANABAPTISTS: see MENNONITE THEOLOGY.

ANALOGY While analogy is commonly used as a form of reasoning, as in an 'argument from analogy', or explanation, as in a PARABLE, the focus here is its use as a category of predication, one that is a mean between the settled meaning of univocation and the shifting meaning of equivocation. As a theory of how certain words are used when referring to God, analogy involves basic anthropological and theological understandings. In analogical predication, affirmative statements about God can be made that are based on REVELATION, and, more controversially, from the creaturely experience of perfections such as the good and the true (see TRANSCENDENTALS).

While the origins of analogy are unclear, early Greek mathematicians developed proportions, where a:b::c:d, e.g., 2:4::3:6. Plato (*ca* 430–*ca* 345 BC) subsequently moves to a non-mathematical application, as he sees something analogical in the proportional structure of things: 'the body of the world was created, and it was harmonized by proportion (*analogias*), and therefore has the spirit of friendship . . . having been reconciled to itself' (*Tim.* 32c). He is also the first to develop the framework of what will later be called participation metaphysics (see PLATONISM).

Aristotle lays out three kinds of predication: a term can be used with a single meaning; with multiple meanings (e.g., the meaning of 'sharp' changes when applied to musical pitch or knives); or, anticipating the category of analogy, with meanings that are partly the same and partly different (*Top.* 106a–108b). Aristotle's *pros hen* equivocation relates several terms to one that is primary, e.g., 'healthy' primarily said of a man, but also of what preserves health (food) and of what is its symptom (urine; *Meta.* Γ2, 1003a33). In the medieval period Aristotle's *pros hen* model becomes the basis of the analogy of attribution (see ARISTOTELIANISM).

T. AQUINAS is the benchmark in the history of analogy, as his synthesis and creative developments of Platonic, Aristotelian, and Christian uses generate a tradition that persists even today. Some important Protestant theologians, although increasingly interested in analogy, have remained critical of Thomistic accounts of how it works.

Univocity indicates a clear, one-to-one correspondence between a word and its referent, including certain words that apply to both creatures and God. It has an on-or-off, right-or-wrong, yes-or-no quality. J. DUNS SCOTUS and more recent thinkers (e.g., W. Alston, b. 1921; and W. Pannenberg, b. 1928) take the apparently commonsense view that *being* must be understood univocally of both God and creatures. Aquinas, however, holds that because the being of God, *ipsum esse subsistens* (subsistent being itself), is simple, infinite, eternal, lacking no perfection, and contained in no genus (*ST* 1.3–11), the divine being is fundamentally different from all else that is not God. Unlike the divine being, all creatures undergo the most fundamental change in the movement from non-being into being; creaturely being is limited; and its being is caused and sustained by another, viz., God (*ST* 1.8.1). Hence, no term can be applied univocally to God and creatures.

In contrast to univocity, equivocation, particularly metaphorical usage, forces a term outside its primary context in order to apply it to God (extrinsic predication). In the hymn which declares, 'a mighty fortress is our God', God is compared to a building of mortar and stone. The equivocation comes about because the literal, proper, or intrinsic sense must be denied (God is *not* a well-put-together arrangement of mortar and stone) in order to achieve the heightened poetic effect (God is strong and protects us). Biblically, liturgically, and rhetorically, metaphor is valuable, but it significantly differs from the theological use of analogy.

When comparing humans with God, metaphor always implies a denial of the literal, proper, intrinsic meaning of the term applied to God, but properly analogical terms, which are context transcendent, never do. For example, there is traditionally no context in which Christians would deny that God is good. Analogical terms must be flexible enough to be applied to humans in a finite context and to God in an infinite one, and they must do so without equivocation in either application. Although numerous metaphors can creatively describe the divine/human relation, only a short list of terms can qualify as properly analogical predicates for God and humans, such as 'being', 'unity', 'goodness', 'truth', and 'beauty'.

Even though an analogical term which refers intrinsically to both God and humans is first known in a creaturely application, its primary and most real reference is to God (*ST* 1.13.3). God's goodness, for example, is ontologically prior to, the ultimate cause of, and more eminent than (*via eminentiae*) creaturely goodness. In fact, God's goodness is infinite in extent and identical with the divine being (*ST* 1.13.2–3, 6). By contrast, all creaturely perfections like goodness and being are received and limited; hence, such shared predicates are analogical, not univocal. Analogical predication holds together *differences* between infinite Creator and finite creation, and *similarities* between them given by the causal bond of creation. It recognizes both the uniqueness of God and the necessary relation of creation to Creator.

The Thomistic use of analogy presupposes a doctrine of creation, in which God's 'ontological communication' (J. Richard, 'Analyse', 392) necessarily precedes analogical discourse or indeed any meaningful language about God, ourselves, and our world. Aquinas' commitment to creation distinguishes his use of participation from the Neoplatonic scheme, in that creation is not an emanation, a necessity born of the divine nature, but rather an act of divine intellect and will (*ST* 1.28.1.3). The non-necessity of creation renders it the first grace and creates the possibility of human response through movement toward the divine being.

While there are important controversies about the analogies of proportionality and attribution which go beyond the scope of this article, studies of chronological patterns in Aquinas' corpus indicate that participation metaphysics is Aquinas' most consistently used basis for the development and use of analogy. Numerous recent commentators have centred on participation metaphysics. Where God is said to be good essentially, in a way that is coterminous with the infinite divine being, human beings are said to participate in the good, i.e., to have a share of it but not the whole thing (*ScG* 1.32.7; *ST* 1.4.3.3). Hence, human life is given as a kind of incompleteness, a tension between what we are and what our relationship to God as our finality calls us to become: 'the closer anything comes to God, the more fully it exists' (*ST* 1.3.5.2). Participation metaphysics thus implies ongoing movement towards God as the path towards human fulfilment.

Participation does not mean that God's own being is participated, as though each human and the entire creation were chunks of the divine being. Participation is in *created* being, being in general (*esse commune*), being which is not divine (*Ver.* 21.4.7). Because divine and creaturely being are differentiated, there is an analogy of being (*analogia entis*), not a univocal sharing of being.

K. BARTH considered '*analogia entis* [the 'analogy of being'] as the invention of Antichrist' and the only good reason for not becoming Catholic (*CD* I/1, xiii). Through the efforts of E. Jüngel (b. 1933) and others, Barth came to see the importance of analogy for theology; however, neither Barth nor Jüngel accept the *analogia entis* – although they have very different reasons for rejecting it. Barth's (misplaced) concern is that *analogia entis* specifies God and human together through commonality of being. By contrast, Jüngel's concern is that *analogia entis* keeps God and human separated, that *analogia entis*, when warranted by the analogies of proportionality and attribution, is thoroughly apophatic and hides an AGNOSTICISM about the divine being (see APOPHATIC THEOLOGY).

Nonetheless, Jüngel asserts: 'there can be no responsible talk about God without analogy. Every spoken announcement which corresponds to God is made within the context of what analogy makes possible' (*God* 281). The crucial difference from the Thomistic account is that Barth and Jüngel variously propose the so-called *analogia fidei*, i.e., analogy understood as a correspondence (*Entsprechung*) of human words to God that is made possible through the coming of the God-human, Jesus Christ. From this perspective, if theology enters into the correspondence that God has already established in the coming of Christ and speaks from this place of light, the Christ event is recreated in human speech. Because the being of the human Jesus corresponds to the being of the divine Jesus, and thus to the being of God, 'the being of the human Jesus is the ontological and epistemological ground of all analogy' (*Mög.* 538). Analogy may thus only be understood Christologically. Given the corruption of SIN, Barth and Jüngel deny that humans can realistically know perfections apart from a starting point of FAITH. Therefore, they advocate *analogia fidei* and deny *analogia entis.*

The question about analogy, however it is resolved, invites further study of the relation between nature and GRACE. If there is an explicit or implicit faith at work in participation metaphysics, then the concern that promotes *analogia fidei* and excludes *analogia entis* might be averted. In this more harmonious understanding, since the grace of created reality cannot be antagonistic to faith in Christ, neither should *analogia entis* and *analogia fidei* be construed as mutually exclusive. The understanding of perfections discoverable in creation and faith in the Person who made the perfections possible should not be set in opposition. Analogy based on *being* is a moderate kind of predication, a mean between epistemological excess and ruinous deficiency. As such, *analogia fidei* should be seen as the fulfilment of *analogia entis*, not as its denial.

D. Burrell, C. S. C., *Aquinas: God and Action* (University of Notre Dame Press, 1979).

W. N. Clarke, S. J., *Explorations in Metaphysics: Being – God – Person* (University of Notre Dame Press, 1994).

E. Jüngel, *God As the Mystery of the World: On the Foundation of the Theology of the Crucified One in the Dispute between Theism and Atheism* (T&T Clark, 1999 [1977]).

Natural Theology: Comprising 'Nature and Grace' by Professor Dr. Emil Brunner and the Reply 'No!' by Dr. Karl Barth (Wipf and Stock, 2002).

P. A. Rolnick, *Analogical Possibilities: How Words Refer to God* (Oxford University Press, 1993).

PHILIP A. ROLNICK

ANAPHORA: see MASS, CANON OF.

ANATHEMA As the transliteration of the NT Greek word for something accursed (see, e.g., Rom. 9:1; 1 Cor. 12:3), the term 'anathema' is used in theology to identify teachings that a Church publicly rejects as inconsistent with or contrary to the Christian GOSPEL (see Gal. 1:8–9). Church COUNCILS have regularly included a list of anathemas (typically of the form, 'If anyone says . . ., let him be anathema'; cf. 1 Cor. 16:22) in their official acts as a means of specifying the theological positions that its positive definitions are meant to exclude. CATHOLIC THEOLOGY distinguishes between the anathematization of a particular proposition (*damnatio specialis*) and of a series of propositions, such as a book in its entirety (*damnatio in globo*). The practice of identifying rejected positions has also been characteristic of Protestant confessional documents, although the term 'anathema' is generally not used.

While the anathema has been associated with the violent repression of dissent within the Churches, its proponents defend its use as a necessary corollary to the positive declaration of Christian belief in times of crisis. K. BARTH, principal author of the BARMEN DECLARATION, argued, 'Without the No [of the anathema] the Yes would obviously not be a Yes', since it is 'by the No that the clarification of an obscure situation is accomplished in a confession' (*CD* I/2, 630). More provocatively, C. Morse (b. 1935) has proposed that the positive significance of the gospel is best revealed through the anathema, by identifying what Christians refuse to believe.

C. Morse, *Not Every Spirit: A Dogmatics of Christian Disbelief* (Trinity Press International, 1994).

IAN A. MCFARLAND

ANCHORITISM A religious order emerging in northern Europe in the eleventh century, anchoritism is distinct from other monastic orders in its call for men (anchorites) and women (anchoresses) to remove themselves from society to live solitary lives of devotion to God. The Greek term, *anachorētēs*, literally means 'one who has withdrawn'. The anchoress enters an anchorhold (a cell attached to the parish church) and lives out the duration of her life there, in prayer and contemplation. More popular among women, the anchoritic life is largely known from a set of thirteenth-century writings, foremost of which is the *Ancrene Wisse*, a guidebook written to girls considering this path of religious devotion. The *Wisse* outlines the motivations for becoming an anchoress and the anticipated temptations of this way of life.

Ancrene spirituality focuses on the inner life and is rooted in contemplation of the sufferings of Christ. The anchorhold's architecture reveals a great deal about daily life and spirituality. One window opened to a parlour, in which persons came to seek spiritual counsel. The other opened to the main sanctuary of the church, in which the anchoress viewed and received the EUCHARIST. There was also a door, in and out of which the domestic servant tends to the anchoress' basic needs. Despite their withdrawal from the world, the architecture suggests the social impact that anchoresses may have had in medieval society. JULIAN OF NORWICH is the most recognized anchoress in Christian history. The theme of enclosure permeates her text, *Showings*, and reflects a theological vision directly shaped by the form of life that she inhabited.

L. Georgianna, *The Solitary Self: Individuality in the Ancrene Wisse* (Harvard University Press, 1981).

SHELLY RAMBO

ANDROCENTRISM Derived from the Greek word for a male human being, the term 'androcentrism' refers to 'male centredness'. It describes a pattern of thinking that assumes the characteristics of ruling men to be the norm for all humankind. It emerges in patriarchal societies in which pyramidal structures place certain ruling males in the dominant position and subordinates women, children, and certain groups of non-elite men who depart from the norm (see PATRIARCHY). In androcentric thinking, women are considered to be human only in a derivative and deficient manner.

Feminist theory pioneered the use of the category as a tool of critical analysis by using it to expose the unconscious (or conscious) prejudice and partiality in what are presented as universal truths about the human condition, arguing that traditional understandings of such supposed universals as reason, power, and the good are one-sided expressions of the life-experiences, values, and goals of men. Feminists challenge that such false universals render women's life experience alien, marginal, and of lesser value. In S. de Beauvoir's (1908–86) pithy phrase, 'he is the subject, she is the other' (*Second* 16). In place of androcentrism, feminists propose gynocentrism, a pattern of thinking that does not simply exchange female-centredness for that of the male, but rather reflects consciously on its 'standpoint' and relinquishes any claim to objectivity and universality.

Since the 1970s, feminist theologians have challenged the androcentrism of the traditional Christian symbol-system, most notably, its notions of God, SIN, redemption, and its ECCLESIOLOGY. Particular attention has been paid to how androcentric patterns of thinking have distorted the Christian concept of God as Father and Lord, by accentuating God's absolute sovereignty and impassibility, and marginalizing female imagery and experiences of God. In their efforts to reconstruct Christian God talk, feminist theologians have sought to legitimize women's power of naming God's mystery from their own life-experiences and to develop alternative models of God's being based on compassion, friendship, and divine immanence in CREATION.

JOY ANN MCDOUGALL

ANGELS The OT takes the presence of angels for granted. They do not enter into the kind of speculation that marks later angel-literature (e.g., where angels came from, how they relate to human beings and to God, etc.). Angels simply turn up in stories with great regularity. Although angelology became a highly developed field of theological and spiritual writing in Christian theology in the patristic and medieval period, exegesis of SCRIPTURE is the starting point for these theologians. Christian theology speaks about angels, not just out of metaphysical or mystical interest, but because angels are in the Bible.

The word 'angel' (*aggelos* in Greek, *mal'ak* in Hebrew) means 'messenger', and it is not always clear in the Bible whether a given 'messenger' is a human carrier of God's news or an 'angel'. Most biblical texts assume that only the eyes of faith can tell the difference. Genesis 18 and Hebrews 13 are the classic texts that suggest that angels look like human beings or, at the very least, can choose to do so. Thus, in Genesis 18 the writer says that the Lord appeared to Abraham, but that when he looked up, he saw three men. Hebrews 13, which may well be commenting on the text from Genesis, recommends hospitality to strangers, because you never know when they may turn out to be angels.

Patristic authors, noting that angels appear much more frequently before the giving of the law in Exodus than afterwards, surmised that angelic messengers were more necessary as intermediaries between God and humans before the law gave God's people direct insight into the character and will of God. Much subsequent debate about angels among Christians has centred around their role in CREATION and the FALL. The first chapters of Genesis do not mention the creation of the angels. Non-Christian and heretical Christian sects used this as evidence against the doctrine of 'creation out of nothing'. They argued that God is not the sole power in the universe, and that other heavenly beings existed before the creation of the physical universe. Some co-operated with God, and some worked against him. In refutation of that, AUGUSTINE OF HIPPO and others argued that the angels are created with the 'heavens', even before the first 'day' of creation, and that the separation of light and darkness is a possible reference to the angelic fall (*City* 11.9).

This avenue of thought has proved suggestive in modern times in engaging with some of the questions of theodicy thrown up by scientific theories of evolution. If the angelic fall took place before the creation of the world, it might help to explain the evidence of 'sin' and 'evil' in the world before the evolution of human beings. It would also explain the presence of the serpent in the Garden of Eden – a creature whose will is opposed to that of God before Adam and Eve have sinned. At the same time, such speculations do not seem consistent with Christian theologies of humanity's responsibility for the fallenness of creation. Nor does it explain the more basic problem of how evil is possible in a universe created by a good God.

Most patristic writers concurred with Augustine's belief that the angels fell through pride, an assumption that inspired J. Milton (1608–74) in his great poem, *Paradise Lost.* Medieval theologians understood angels as incorporeal creatures of pure intellect and argued about whether or not fallen angels could be redeemed. Most argued that they could not, on the grounds that angels, unlike human beings, have a knowledge of God and a closeness to God that allow them to make a genuine and binding choice from the moment of their creation. According to Bonaventure (1221–74), developing a line of thought that can also be found in the work of ANSELM OF CANTERBURY and T. AQUINAS, human beings reject God out of ignorance of God's real nature, but angels do not have that excuse, so the angels who chose God before creation will never sin, and the angels that rejected God will never be redeemed. This perspective led to a belief that some human beings could, after death, become 'angels', to fill up the spaces left in the heavenly ranks by the defection of the fallen angels. Thus, when Bonaventure wrote his biography of Francis of Assisi (1181/2–1226), this is the prize he describes for Francis at the end of his saintly life.

The angelology of patristic and medieval theologians assumes a clear hierarchy in the angelic ranks. DIONYSIUS THE AREOPAGITE, in his *Celestial Hierarchy*, set a trend in this respect that was widely followed. It was assumed that there were different levels and types of angels, with different kinds of responsibilities with regard to human beings. Although the classification varies slightly from one author to another, the ranks most commonly referred to are: angels, archangels, principalities, dominions, authorities, powers, thrones, cherubim, and seraphim. These types are all mentioned in the biblical witness (see, e.g., Gen. 3:24; Isa. 6:2; Col. 1:16; 1 Pet. 3:22; Jude 9), though without the systematization that was introduced by later exegetes.

The interest in angelic hierarchies was not just theoretical. Bonaventure, in *The Soul's Journey into God*, saw a correlation between the orders of angels and the human spiritual ascent towards God. The ordered hierarchy of heaven is mirrored by, and helps to create, proper order on earth. In this, too, angels are messengers of God. Bonaventure is a testimony to the primary location of angelology in Christian theology, which is in devotional, mystical, and experiential writings.

Christian theologians from Justin Martyr (d. *ca* 165) onwards wished to make it clear that, although angels are heavenly beings, and carry out divine work, they are not to be worshipped as Jesus Christ is. Augustine contrasts the work of the Mediator, Jesus, with that of the angels (*City* 9–10). The angels may bring messages from God, but they do not bring human and divine life together as Jesus does. Like us, the angels praise and worship their Creator, rather than requiring worship from other creatures. Indeed, praising God is seen, both in the Bible and by Christian theologians, as the primary function of the angels. When Isaiah and Ezekiel receive their prophetic commission, they are given a glimpse of the heavenly courts, where the angels praise God continually (Isa. 6; Ezek. 1), and the author of Revelation sees as the final destiny of the world an intimacy with God which will enable all his creatures to worship as they were created to do. So it is appropriate that the most common setting in modern times for consideration of angels is in the LITURGY. On the Feast of Michael and all Angels, or the Feast of the Annunciation to Mary, the role of the angelic messengers is celebrated among those who witness to God's great work of creation and redemption.

J. Daniélou, *The Angels and Their Mission* (Christian Classics Inc., 1982 [1957]).

D. Keck, *Angels and Angelology in the Middle Ages* (Oxford University Press, 1998).

E. Peterson, *The Angels and the Liturgy*, 2nd edn(Herder and Herder, 1964).

JANE WILLIAMS

ANGLICAN THEOLOGY Anglicans have been reluctant to pin down too closely what is distinctive about their theology. Some would say that, in the area of SYSTEMATIC THEOLOGY at least, they are modest and have much to be modest about. There are a number of reasons for this unease. Most Anglicans do not regard themselves as belonging to a 'confessional' Church according to the pattern of the continental Churches of the magisterial REFORMATION. The Church of England's Thirty-Nine Articles of Religion do indeed borrow from Lutheran sources at certain points, and in many ways fit into a Reformed theological tradition. But Anglicans are reluctant, by and large, to see the Articles as constitutive either of their theology or indeed of their 'being church'. Rather, Anglicans place great importance on belonging to a Catholic Church which predates the Reformation and which can trace its origins back to the early Church.

R. HOOKER, writing at the end of the sixteenth century, at a time when the Elizabethan religious settlement had begun to take root, gave expression to what became a characteristic Anglican way of doing theology. He identified three sources from which the Church draws its sustenance, not least its theological method and content: SCRIPTURE, TRADITION, and reason. This 'three-legged stool' became the basis for what has been seen as a distinctively Anglican approach to theology. While at times Anglicanism has seemed to be a rather uneasy coalition of evangelical, Catholic, and liberal elements – and at times these elements have hardened into distinct and mutually suspicious parties – a distinctively Anglican theology can be characterized by its careful attention to each of the three sources and to their interconnections.

On this basis, Archbishop M. Ramsey (1904–88) can be described as an Anglican theologian par excellence: both because he encapsulates a particular method of doing theology which is characteristically Anglican in its moderation and scope, and because he addresses ecclesiological questions about the nature and form of the Church, a strong Anglican preoccupation. In his classic *The Gospel and the Catholic Church* (1936), Ramsey identifies a number of themes which he regards as central to Anglican theological thinking. First is a 'Platonic strain', which Ramsey understands as a 'classical HUMANISM' stemming from Hooker's emphasis on the accessibility of knowledge of God through the light of reason (see PLATONISM). Hooker distrusted theological systems which are overly biblicist in their emphasis and was concerned to allow flexibility for those matters which did not constitute the core of the faith (the ADIAPHORA, or non-essentials), and about which a local Church is at liberty to make decisions. Second, according to Ramsey, is a sensitivity to the importance of the worshipping community, its spiritual traditions, and the corporate life of prayer and worship, expressed pre-eminently in Archbishop T. CRANMER'S BOOK OF COMMON PRAYER.

For Anglicans, theological work should never proceed only, or primarily, from the academy. Anglicans are particularly indebted to those 'scholar' bishops and pastors whose theological work springs from their concern for the life of the Church as the people of God. Such scholarship is steeped in SCRIPTURE and the fathers of the early Church, both East and West. It is, therefore, conservative, but also mindful of the need to address contemporary concerns. Ramsey invokes the *via media* ('middle way'): the Anglican compromise, which (arguably) positioned the Church of England between Rome and continental PROTESTANTISM. Applied to theological method, this has produced a reluctance to press theology into a self-contained system, an ability to see both sides of an argument, and a desire to encapsulate important insights of both Catholic and Protestant theology.

Theology is thus most distinctively Anglican when it is questioning and fragmented, rather than systematizing and complete. *Essays and Reviews* (1860), *Lux mundi* (1889), and *Soundings* (1963) were each a series of essays by a variety of Anglican ecclesiastics and academics. Each collection aimed to probe the borderlines between theology and culture, theology and science, theology and ethics. Each encouraged an enquiring attitude rather than one of certainty and definition. Each came to express an Anglican theological way for that particular time. One of the most distinguished Anglican theologians of the twentieth century, D. MacKinnon (1913–94), raised the essay form to a very high level. His pieces probed and teased out issues, posing stimulating and pertinent questions, rather than providing definitive answers. In contrast, perhaps the most successful attempt to write a systematic theology from an Anglican perspective, has been the work of J. Macquarrie (1919–2007), a convert to Anglicanism from the Reformed tradition. Addressing the concerns of twentieth-century Protestant theology, Macquarrie brought an Anglican sensibility to the task, both in his attention to philosophical concerns (in this case mid-century existentialism) and in his sacramental and ecclesiological concerns.

Modern Anglican theology is often characterized as taking its starting point from the INCARNATION, rather than the crucifixion, which was so central to the spirit of the Reformation (see *THEOLOGIA CRUCIS*). Incarnational theology, rooted in the patristic legacy of the universal Church, tends to engage positively with philosophical and cultural themes, and upholds a sacramental view of the world. These emphases have wide implications for theological reflection on social ethics and political engagement. Archbishop W. Temple (1881–1944) was a pioneer in his concern to establish a mode of social engagement responsive to modern conditions while being grounded in a distinctively Anglican intellectual and theological tradition, though he, in turn, built on nineteenth-century antecedents such as F. D. Maurice (1805–72). His work was picked up and developed in thinking on the mission of the Church in an industrial society by the academic writing of R. Preston (1913–2001) and by such official documents as the archbishop of Canterbury's *Faith in the City* report (1985), which explored Christian believing in a post-industrial and multicultural Britain, and which gave a trenchant critique of the consequences of the government's neo-liberal economic philosophy. Incarnational themes can also be traced in the pioneer mission theologies of M. Warren (1904–77) and J. V. Taylor (1914–2001), with their reverence for other faith traditions and emphasis on a 'theology of attention', which takes seriously both the integrity and uniqueness of Christian FAITH and the presence of 'the other', who equally invokes respect.

Anglican theology has consistently been distinguished by a sense of responsibility among its theologians for sustaining what might be called the 'inner life' of the Church, in contrast with what was seen as an increasing academic tendency within Protestant theology. This has produced a number of important works of pastoral and sacramental theology, with a 'doxological' emphasis in, for example, the writings of W. H. Vanstone (1923–99), *Love's Endeavour, Love's Expense* (1977) and *The Stature of Waiting* (1982). There has been a recognition, too, of the importance of the mystical tradition, going back at least to the writings of JULIAN OF NORWICH and continuing after the Reformation in the works of the seventeenth-century Anglican divines and metaphysical poets like J. Donne (1572–1631) and G. Herbert (1593–1633). The modern embodiment of this concern is exemplified in the poetry of T. S. Eliot (1888–1965) and the Welsh poet and Anglican priest R. S. Thomas (1913–2000).

Not all Anglican theology fits into the general criteria outlined above. There is, for example, a strong evangelical tradition of theological writing, from Bishop J. C. Ryle (1816–1900) in the nineteenth century to J. Stott (b. 1921) and J. Packer (b. 1926) in the twentieth, and including writers such as T. Smail (b. 1928) and D. Watson (1933–84), influenced by the CHARISMATIC MOVEMENT. This writing by Anglicans has been important for the development of British evangelical thinking generally. It emphasizes distinctively evangelical rather than specifically Anglican traits, though its style of moderate reasonableness might be regarded as typically Anglican. The theological tradition of the diocese of Sydney in Australia, vigorously articulated in the writings of D. B. Knox (1916–94), understands itself to be both evangelical and an articulation of central themes of the English Reformation. Like evangelical theology generally, it is distrustful of Anglo-Catholic theology and its influence on the Anglican communion generally.

This antipathy has at times been reciprocated in much Anglican High-Church theology since the OXFORD MOVEMENT, with its emphasis on theology as based on the living tradition of the Catholic Church since ancient times. Anglo-Catholics such as Bishop C. Gore (1853–1932), Ramsey, and E. Mascall (1905–93), however, endeavoured to transcend these party animosities in order to represent Anglicanism as a whole. In the 1930s the theologian Sir E. Hoskyns (1884–1937) introduced K. BARTH and the concerns of continental Protestant 'neo-orthodoxy' into the Anglican theological world, and in particular to its Anglo-Catholic constituency. More recently, a theological movement known as 'RADICAL ORTHODOXY' expresses an Anglican sensibility in its critique of liberal modernity and its articulation of an alternative, Augustinian vision of society permeated by Christian values, an emphasis in accord with Hooker's vision of the Church.

For Hooker, the Anglican way embodied the ideal of a total Christian society in which Church and 'Commonwealth' (a term which incorporates both the State and more modern understandings of 'CIVIL SOCIETY') were mutually dependent. With the emergence of a non-established Episcopal Church in America at the end of the eighteenth century, American theologians utilized Hooker in a different way. Their Church was a small minority Church within American society as a whole, but they stressed the importance of the Episcopal Church as the sign of a Christian society with a different ethos from the State. The new American democracy had competing influences, including the secular, Enlightenment ideals of the founding fathers, and the democratic populism of evangelicalism. Episcopalianism positioned itself as a mediating influence. W. R. Huntington (1838–1909) articulated this in *The Church-Idea* (1870), aspiring towards a 'national church' around which American Christians could coalesce. As a practical experiment in American ecumenism, Huntington's theology was aspirational rather than practical, and remains unrealized. But his ideals were crucial for the self-understanding of the Anglican communion as a whole. They provided a way of transcending the origins of the communion in the established Church of England. The Chicago–Lambeth Quadrilateral (1888), which outlined the distinctive marks of the Church in relation to wider ecumenical relations, owed much to Huntington.

A renewed attention to providing a theological rationale for Anglicanism assumed importance again in the late twentieth century, as a response to the globalization of Anglicanism, and its need to escape the 'Anglo-Saxon captivity' of the Church, to utilize a concept of the Ghanaian Anglican theologian, J. Pobee (b. 1937). The American J. Booty (b. 1925) and the English bishop S. Sykes (b. 1939) have explored at length questions about the identity of Anglicanism as a distinctive ecclesial community, as has the Australian B. Kaye (b. 1939). But even these endeavours often appear too centred on the 'English' traditions of Anglicanism to serve adequately as the vehicle for a world communion. African Anglican theologians such as Pobee, J. Mbiti (b. 1931), and H. Sawyerr (1909–86), while rarely expressing their theological ideas in an exclusively Anglican framework, can be seen as embodying many typically Anglican themes, not least the search for a theology which is both warmly appreciative of the insights of African culture and engaged with the social, political, and economic issues facing Africa today. The theological critique of apartheid has always had a strong Anglican content. Archbishop D. Tutu's (b. 1931) commitment to justice and reconciliation is rooted in his Anglo-Catholic spirituality and in an incarnational theology with deep Anglican roots, while D. Ackerman's (b. 1935) theological writings reflect the importance of gender as well as race issues in the struggle for human integrity. The male bias of much classical Anglican thinking has been commented on and addressed by a growing number of Anglican women theologians throughout the communion.

In the post-Anglican and post-denominational world of India and China it would be invidious to write about a specifically Anglican theology. But in the theological writings of Bishop K. H. Ting (b. 1915), and T. C. Chao (1888–1979) in Mao's China, or S. Clarke (b. 1956) in modern South India, it is possible to see an inclusive, politically engaged, sacramentally enthused, theological perspective that gains its resonance, at least in part, from the Anglican tradition.

If all these recent developments can be seen as an extension and elaboration of a venerable Anglican way of doing theology, the conflict over the inclusion of gay and lesbian people in the life of the Church has endangered this self-understanding. Is Anglican comprehensiveness capable of comprehending radically different understandings of Christian truth, and indeed should it aim to do so? 'Traditionalists' accuse 'revisionists' of rejecting the balance between Scripture, tradition, and reason; 'progressive' Anglicans accuse the traditionalists of falling into a biblical FUNDAMENTALISM and theological dogmatism which is alien to Anglican ways of thinking. Whatever the outcome of these disputes, much of the trust and generosity of spirit which Anglicans have often conceived as the *modus operandi* of the theological endeavour have been called into question. Both sides see the dispute as a struggle for 'the soul of Anglicanism'. In this difficult situation, Archbishop R. Williams (b. 1950) has endeavoured to express the classic Anglican virtues of faithfulness to tradition and openness to theological change, in an age of dogmatic and combative formulations of belief.

M. D. Chapman, *Anglicanism: A Very Short Introduction* (Oxford University Press, 2006).
B. Kaye, *An Introduction to World Anglicanism* (Cambridge University Press, 2008).
S. Sykes, *The Integrity of Anglicanism* (Mowbray, 1978).
K. Ward, *A History of Global Anglicanism* (Cambridge University Press, 2006).
R. Williams, *Anglican Identities* (Darton, Longman and Todd, 2004).
A. Wingate, K. Ward, C. Pemberton, and W. Sitshebo, *Anglicanism: A Global Communion* (Mowbray, 1998).

KEVIN WARD

ANHYPOSTASIA Much CHRISTOLOGY after CHALCEDON insists that the humanity of Jesus has no independent existence of its own (no existence as a HYPOSTASIS – a really existing and fully identifiable reality) in abstraction from the HYPOSTATIC UNION. Rather, the human nature of Jesus acquires hypostatic (viz., particular, concrete) existence only in so far as it is held in being *as* the humanity of the *Logos*. It is brought into being for that union, and only exists within it; it is always and only the humanity of the *Logos*. No achievement or characteristic of this particular human life, therefore, is prior to the union, and so no achievement or characteristic can serve as the ground or reason for the union: all Christ's human achievements and characteristics flow *from* the union.

The most common way of putting this claim in recent theology has been to say that the human nature of Christ is, when considered on its own, anhypostatic, but that when considered as one nature of Christ's hypostasis, it is enhypostatic. The *enhypostasia/anhypostasia* distinction in this sense is often wrongly attributed to Leontius of Byzantium (*ca* 485–*ca* 540). Nevertheless, the idea behind the modern *enhypostasia/anhypostasia* distinction can be traced back at least to Leontius of Jerusalem (*fl.* 535), who denied that Christ's human nature was *idiohypostatic* (having its own hypostatic existence) or *heterohypostatic* (of a different hypostasis); rather, it subsists together (*synypostanai*) with the divine nature in a single hypostasis. It is also implicit in the Christology of JOHN OF DAMASCUS.

MIKE HIGTON

ANIMALS In the last twenty years or so, the animal-rights movement has put animals on the agenda of Christian theology. Before that, modern theology neglected the topic of animals, which is striking given how present animals are throughout the Bible. Since animal-rights advocates sometimes blame animal abuse on the Christian tradition, much theological work has been devoted to rebutting these charges. Contemporary theological scholarship, however, extends well beyond the limits of advocacy and practical ethics. Indeed, studies abound about the various roles of animals in the Bible and the changing attitudes towards animals in Church history. The topic of animals has arrived in theology in a fully nuanced and complex manner.

The Bible certainly values human life over the lives of non-human animals, but animals are not treated as morally dispensable. The OT assigns humanity the role of responsible stewardship, from Adam's task of naming the animals (Gen. 2:19–20) to legislation in the Mosaic covenant regulating the killing and consumption of animal flesh (e.g., Lev. 11). The book of JOB (chs. 39–41) has some of the most precise and poetic descriptions of animals to occur in all of ancient literature. The prophets regularly speak to the place of animals in God's plans. The depiction of human–animal peacefulness is a major motif in descriptions of the world restored to God's original purposes (e.g., Isa. 11:6–9).

In the NT Jesus spends time with the wild animals (Mark 1:12–13), a passage that inspired the Desert Fathers to enter into the wild themselves. Early disciples handled and tamed snakes as a sign of their holiness (Mark 16:18 and Luke 10:19; see Ps. 91:13). It thus should not be surprising that many stories about Christian SAINTS involve compassion towards animals. Some saints even tried to tame or otherwise domesticate wild animals as a sign of the coming peaceful KINGDOM OF GOD.

The OT tightly regulated the consumption of animals, but the NT, even allowing for a distinction between the GOSPEL and the LAW, was not immune to debates about whether Christians should eat animal flesh. PAUL had to balance the moral rigour of Christians who rejected meat-eating with those of more flexible dietary habits (Rom. 14–15). FASTING in the early Church ordinarily meant not eating meat, and early theologians like TERTULLIAN and Clement of Alexandria (*ca* 150–*ca* 215) drew on the Genesis portrait of a peaceful paradise, Greek medical philosophy, and the Noachic prohibition on consuming blood (Gen. 9:4) to defend moderate versions of vegetarianism. The meatless diet in Christianity was eventually inscribed into monastic practices with the dissemination of the *Rule* (ch. 39) of Benedict of Nursia (*ca* 480–*ca* 545).

Medieval Christians looked to the animal world to confirm and illustrate their moral convictions. Debates about whether animals have SOULS and, if so, what kind of souls, continue up to the present day. Indeed, the question of whether at least some animals will be in heaven is one of the most pressing among non-professional theologians. Even among academic theologians, however, interest in the moral status of animals has grown to the point where there is a specific subset of theological work, 'animal theology', that is devoted to exploring these issues.

Animal theology is growing, but it is not a homogeneous field. Some theologians provide biblical justifications for the idea that animals have rights, while other theologians identify more with the idea that animals deserve our compassion, even if they do not have any inherent claim to legal standing. Some animal theologians have been influenced by the way feminist philosophy has called for a re-evaluation of the role of the emotions in moral action, while others have argued that responsibility for animals can be sustained only by affirming the uniqueness of human nature and the biblical vision of human stewardship over the natural world. The animal-theology community has also been divided on the issue of companion animals, with some disparaging the natural resources that pets consume while others argue that human concern for non-human animals must begin in concrete and individual cases of personal engagement and bonding. There is also a growing interest in the use of pet-facilitated therapy in religious contexts and in the use of rituals like animal blessings in worship.

Although animal theologians have branched out into a variety of theoretical and practical issues, diet remains the topic that generates the most interest as well as the most controversy in this field. Theologians debate whether vegetarianism is a prerequisite for entering into discussions about the moral value of animals, since a carnivorous diet, some argue, is evidence of a prejudice that will prevent an objective examination of the issues. Other theologians worry that self-righteousness and exclusivity can undermine vegetarianism's goals. Most importantly, theological scholars are now looking at diet more broadly as a religious phenomenon that demands theological exploration. Although Christianity rejected the kosher rules that came to define Jewish religious practice, Christians in all eras have continued to surround eating with various proscriptions, rituals, and moral recommendations. The topic of diet has thus moved out beyond the specific field of animal theology and into the theological mainstream (see FASTING).

A. Linzey, *Animal Gospel* (John Knox Press, 1998).

S. H. Webb, *On God and Dogs: A Christian Theology of Compassion for Animals* (Oxford University Press, 1998).

STEPHEN H. WEBB

ANNIHILATIONISM The doctrine of annihilationism is a twentieth-century development in Christian ESCHATOLOGY that has emerged as a minority position within EVANGELICAL THEOLOGY. Traditionally, Christians have taught (on the basis of passages like Matt. 25:31–46 and Luke 16:19–31) that the ultimate destiny of all human beings is either eternal bliss in HEAVEN or eternal torment in HELL. Largely on the basis of the belief that a DOCTRINE of eternal torment is incompatible with Christian belief that God is love (1 John 4:8, 16), proponents of annihilationism like J. Stott (b. 1921) and C. Pinnock (b. 1937) teach that at the Last Judgement the lives of those who reject God are simply extinguished.

Though annihilationism is consistent with Gospel passages that refer to eschatological destruction (e.g., Matt. 10:28; John 10:28), its strongest biblical support arguably comes from PAUL, who never mentions hell (*gehenna*) and describes the destiny of the wicked in terms of destruction rather than torment (e.g., 2 Cor. 2:15; 4:3; 2 Thess. 1:9; 2:10). In contrast to UNIVERSALISM, which teaches that all persons are ultimately saved, annihilationists maintain that human rejection of God has eternal consequences: because eternal life is defined by a loving relationship with God, rejection of God entails death. Evangelical critics of annihilationism charge that it represents a capitulation to liberal sensibilities regarding the character of divine justice that fails to account either for the fullness of the biblical witness or for God's transcendence of human moral categories.

E. Fudge, *The Fire That Consumes: A Biblical and Historical Study of Final Punishment* (Verdict, 1982).

IAN A. MCFARLAND

ANNUNCIATION The term 'annunciation' refers to the story narrated in Luke 1:26–38: how the angel Gabriel was sent by God to announce to Mary of Nazareth that, by the power of the HOLY SPIRIT, she would bear a son named Jesus, 'who would be called holy, the Son of God' (v. 35). Christians typically commemorate this event exactly nine months before Christmas, on March 25, but, although the annunciation's place in the liturgical CALENDAR is in this way tied to the physiology of human reproduction, a central point of the narrative is that Mary's conception of Jesus was effected miraculously, without the involvement of a biological father. In other words – and against all male claims to be exclusive mediators of the divine to women (see ANDROCENTRISM) – in taking human flesh God completely bypassed male agency (see VIRGIN BIRTH).

Yet this eclipse of *male* agency did not extend to all human agency. On the contrary, a cardinal feature of Christian interpretation of the INCARNATION is that Jesus' conception occurs by way of Mary's FAITH in, and freely given consent to, Gabriel's announcement: 'Let it be with me according to your word' (v. 38; cf. Luke 1:45). To be sure, TRADITION insists that it was only by divine GRACE that Mary was able to give this 'yes' to God (see IMMACULATE CONCEPTION), but it remains the case here as elsewhere in the divine ECONOMY that God acts to save human beings by empowering and renewing rather than undermining human agency.

See also MARIOLOGY.

IAN A. MCFARLAND

Anointing of the Sick According to the Gospel of Mark it was during the last week of Jesus' life, at the house of Simon the leper, that a woman came and anointed Jesus with oil (Mark 14:3–9). It is common for scholars to root the sacrament of anointing the sick (or unction) in Jesus' healing ministry or in the practice of the early Church (attested to in Jas. 5:14–16), whereby the sick called for the elders of the Church to pray for them and anoint them with oil in the name of the Lord. But in fact, just as the sacrament of BAPTISM is rooted in Christ as the one who was baptized, so the sacrament of unction is rooted in the experience of Christ as the anointed one. This connection is made in the Orthodox tradition, where it is customary for the faithful to be anointed on the Wednesday before Easter. The Gospel reading for that service is the story of the woman anointing Jesus.

The sacrament of unction is for those who need to be reconnected with the mystery of the divine life and the Church because of suffering. This is made very explicit in one of the prayers included in the pre-VATICAN COUNCIL II rites of the Catholic Church which asks that the recipient will be raised up, strengthened, and given back 'to your holy Church'. This language clearly presupposes that there has been some sort of alienation from the group mind or body.

Much of the rite of unction recalls that of baptism. In most Catholic rites the rite of unction begins with the sprinkling of the recipient with holy water. Other elements which reprise baptism are confession and absolution, the anointing with oil, the laying on of hands and, in some rites, the EXORCISM.

Analyzed according to the formal elements of SACRAMENTOLOGY, the remote matter (the external sign) of the sacrament of unction is the olive oil, usually blessed at the Chrism Mass by the bishop. The proximate matter is the anointing of the person with that oil. Traditionally, eyes, ears, nostrils, mouth, hands, and feet were anointed. These were understood to be the apertures of the senses and therefore open channels into which both GRACE and evil could seep. Many of these channels were also anointed at baptism. In extremity the forehead only is signed. The laying on of hands is not essential to the rite but is present in some contemporary versions. The normal minister of the sacrament is a priest. In the Orthodox tradition it is considered desirable for the sacrament to be administered by seven priests, the mystical number of completeness.

It was in the Middle Ages that the sacrament of anointing became associated with the 'last rites' and thus became known as extreme unction. Just as baptism, CONFIRMATION, and the EUCHARIST initiated the recipient into the Church on earth, so PENANCE, unction, and the Eucharist came to be understood as initiating the recipient into the Church in HEAVEN.

P. Haffner, *The Sacramental Mystery* (Gracewing, 1999).
J. Macquarrie, *A Guide to the Sacraments* (SCM, 1997).
E. Stuart, 'The Sacrament of Unction' in *The Wounds that Heal: Theology, Imagination and Health*, ed. J. Baxter (SPCK, 2007), 197–214.

ELIZABETH STUART

Anonymous Christianity K. RAHNER's theory of the 'anonymous Christian' is based on two arguments. The first stems from Rahner's philosophy of the 'SUPERNATURAL EXISTENTIAL', in which he argues that all people have an implicit REVELATION of God which is adequate for salvation, even though it is only fulfilled in the historically particular revelation of Jesus Christ, and only partially thematized and expressed in other religious texts and practices. This means that, while Christianity is the absolute truth and Christ the source of all salvation, other religions can act as provisional mediators of saving grace. Working from this basis, Rahner could argue for both the notion of the 'anonymous Christian' (Christ's grace working implicitly in the individual) and 'anonymous Christianity' (the provisional saving structures called 'RELIGION', which have a telos towards Catholic Christianity).

The second type of argument takes the following form: since (1) God desires the salvation of all people, and (2) all people do not know the GOSPEL, and (3) God is loving and good, there must be (4) a means of salvation offered to all people. Rahner suggests that other religions may be deemed valid as provisionally 'lawful religions' until confronted by the truth of Christ, an ANALOGY with JUDAISM before the coming of Christ. It is through acts of FAITH, HOPE, and unconditional LOVE that those in other religions say 'yes' to God. However argued, the theory has been criticized as promoting Christian triumphalism, though Rahner himself was careful to specify that he intended it as a proposal internal to Christian dogmatics and not as a template for inter-religious dialogue.

See also SOTERIOLOGY.

GAVIN D'COSTA

Anselm of Canterbury Anselm was born in 1033 in Aosta, in the Italian Alps but at that time part of Burgundy. In

1059 he entered the monastery at Bec, in Normandy, to study with its prior, Lanfranc (*ca* 1005–89). Anselm became prior when Lanfranc left in 1063. In 1070 Lanfranc was summoned to England by William I (r. 1066–87) to become archbishop of Canterbury. Lanfranc died in 1089, and William II (r. 1087–1100) left the Canterbury see vacant for four years before appointing Anselm as archbishop in 1093. During the reigns of William II and Henry I (r. 1100–35), Anselm went to Rome in exile twice. His disputes with the kings centred on the relations between temporal and spiritual authorities in a highly feudal society: how much fealty in the form of military support Canterbury owed to the king in virtue of lands it possessed by the king's permission, and whether the king or the pope had the right the invest bishops with the insignia of their office. Anselm returned to England in 1106 from his second exile; he died at Canterbury in 1109.

Except for Scripture the main influences on Anselm's thought were various writings of Augustine and Boethius (480–524/5). He was inspired by Augustine's suggestive remarks in articulation of the doctrine of the Trinity that we see a vestige of the Trinity in the structure of the human mind, with the Father as memory, the Son as understanding, and the Holy Spirit as will (see *Vestigia Trinitatis*). He followed Augustine in espousing a doctrine of God's metaphysical simplicity, and he followed Boethius in defending a vision of God's eternality. Even while following the lead of his predecessors, however, Anselm exercises a kind of analytical rigour not found in their writings. Hand in hand with that rigour is a confidence in the powers of human reason to demonstrate the rationality of the tenets of the Christian faith. But, for Anselm, reason takes its inspiration and direction from faith itself; as he insists, if he did not believe, he would not understand.

Anselm's most distinctively original contributions to philosophical theology lie in his development of what later came to be called an ontological argument for the existence of God and in his position on the rational appropriateness of the incarnation.

In *Proslogion* (1078) Anselm suggests that we can conceive of God as that than which nothing greater can be conceived. Suppose that God did not exist in reality. If that were so, then we could conceive of something greater, namely, God existing in reality. Thus if that than which nothing greater can be conceived were not to exist in reality, then that than which nothing greater can be conceived would not be that than which nothing greater can be conceived. Therefore, God exists and cannot even be conceived not to exist. If this argument is sound, it shows not merely that atheists are mistaken; it shows that atheism is an impossible position to defend. During Anselm's lifetime the argument was criticized by Gaunilo of Marmoutiers (*fl.* 1080). Gaunilo's criticism and Anselm's reply have survived and are usually appended to *Proslogion*. In the subsequent history of philosophy, versions of the argument were endorsed by R. Descartes (1596–1650), B. Spinoza (1632–77), and G. Leibniz (1646–1716), while T. Aquinas, D. Hume (1711–76), and I. Kant rejected it. The argument still attracts considerable attention among contemporary philosophers.

Anselm's *Cur Deus Homo* addresses the question of why God became human – more precisely, why the second Person of the Trinity assumed a human nature. Anselm's answer connects the incarnation to the fall of humankind and to the subsequent need for atonement. Our earliest ancestors' disobedience dishonoured God so severely that it damaged not only them but also all their descendants. The damage is both cognitive and volitional: we lack the noetic certainty our earliest ancestors had, and our wills are disordered. The fall was thus so calamitous that no purely human acts, individually or collectively, can satisfy the debt of reparation owed to God. The quandary is that humans ought to pay the debt but cannot, while God can pay the debt but is under no obligation to do so. Nor can humans simply be forgiven by God, since that would amount to treating sinners in the same way as non-sinners and thus make sin subject to no regulation. Anselm's solution is that the incarnate Christ, both divine and human, can achieve by his non-obligatory, freely chosen sacrifice what humans ought to achieve but cannot.

B. Davies and B. Leftow, eds., *The Cambridge Companion to Anselm* (Cambridge University Press, 2004).

J. Hopkins, *A Companion to the Study of St. Anselm* (University of Minnesota Press, 1972).

William E. Mann

Anthropic Principle Coined by the physicist B. Carter (b. 1942) in 1973, the concept of the anthropic principle has played a significant role in contemporary discussions of the relationship between theology and natural science and, more particularly, in current versions of the teleological argument for the existence of God. Carter distinguished between 'weak' and 'strong' versions of the principle (WAP and SAP respectively), invoking both to explain why the material conditions in the universe are such as to allow for the emergence of intelligent life. According to the WAP this is simply a matter of logic: since intelligent life can exist only under particular physical conditions, it follows that any universe observed by such life will be compatible with their existence as observers. The SAP concretizes this principle in light of the fact that intelligent life exists: since humanity has evolved, the universe is necessarily such as to have allowed for its evolution.

More controversial interpretations of the anthropic principle were introduced by J. Barrow (b. 1952) and F. Tipler (b. 1947) in *The Anthropic Cosmological Principle* (1986). Their version of the SAP goes far beyond Carter's in arguing that the resolution of quantum indeterminacies renders the very existence of the universe contingent on the evolution of intelligent observers. Though Barrow and Tipler's physics remains highly controversial, theologians like J. Polkinghorne (b. 1930) have seen the fundamental – and seemingly unlikely – compatibility of physical constants with the emergence of intelligent life as evidence of a divine designer. Critics point out that this cosmological 'fine tuning' may eventually be explained by further scientific discoveries (e.g., the existence of an infinite number of parallel universes would arguably reduce even the strongest version of SAP to WAP), and that, in any case, arguments from design remain vulnerable to the logical objections raised by sceptics like D. Hume (1711–76).

Ian A. McFarland

Anthropocentrism In contemporary theology the concept of anthropocentrism (or humanocentrism) is as much an evaluative as a descriptive category. As a description, it points to the fact that human beings occupy a much more prominent place in Scripture than do other creatures, and that this prominence is reflected in the bulk of subsequent Christian theological reflection on creation. As a means of evaluation, the characterization of Christianity as anthropocentric marks this focus on the nature and destiny of humankind as problematic: for some it marks a failure to attend to the goodness and significance of all creatures implicit in the Christian doctrine of creation; for others it reflects a more deep-seated disregard for the non-human creation. While from the former perspective anthropocentrism is a corrigible shortcoming in the tradition, from the latter it is a defining feature of Christian faith that counts against its credibility at a time when the sciences of cosmology, ecology, and evolution have made clear both the vastness of the universe (see Extra-Terrestrial Life) and the radical interdependence of human and non-human life.

That Scripture and the various streams of Christian tradition that develop from it are at some level anthropocentric seems difficult to deny. In both of the Bible's opening creation stories, human beings take centre stage: in the first they are the climax of creation, given 'dominion . . . over every living thing that moves upon the earth' (Gen. 1:28); in the second they are creation's focus, with plants and animals described as though made for humanity's benefit (Gen. 2:8–9, 18–19). Yet, although the special status of human beings is affirmed at various points in Scripture (Ps. 8:3–8; cf. Sir. 17:1–7), there are also countervailing voices: even in Eden one tree is pointedly not for human use (Gen. 2:17), and elsewhere other creatures can be described as having a glory and purpose that has nothing to do with their utility for human beings (see, e.g., Ps. 104:18, 25–26; Job 38:1–39:30; 40:15–41:34). Thus, while Paul sees the redemption of humanity as the linchpin of the divine economy, he is also clear that the whole of creation is the object of God's saving work (Rom. 8:19–21; but cf. 1 Cor. 9:9).

Paul's language suggests that the crucial theological question is perhaps less whether Christianity is anthropocentric than how humanity's place at creation's 'centre' – and thus the scope of God's covenant with human beings – is to be understood. Is the rest of creation merely a stage (ultimately destined, according to 2 Pet. 3:10, to be 'dissolved with fire') on which a narrowly human drama takes place? Or does the hope for a 'new heaven and a new earth' (Rev. 21:1) implicate the whole of creation (Isa. 65:17–25; cf. 11:6–9)? The Christian tradition gives no unambiguous answer to this question. In classical Lutheran theology, for example, after the Last Judgement '[n]ot a transformation of the world . . . but an absolute annihilation of its substance is to be expected' (Schmid, *Doctrinal*, §66). By contrast, Orthodox theology stresses humanity's priestly and representative role as the creature commissioned to bridge the various divisions within creation (e.g., between heaven and earth, matter and spirit), so that everything might ultimately be offered to and united with God.

W. van Huyssteen, *Alone in the World? Human Uniqueness in Science and Theology* (Eerdmans, 2006).

P. Santmire, *The Travail of Nature: The Ambiguous Ecological Promise of Christianity* (Fortress, 1985).

Ian A. McFarland

Anthropology: see Theological Anthropology.

Antichrist The figure of the antichrist is a component of Christian eschatology that reflects the conviction that the ultimate triumph of the kingdom of God will be resisted by one who falsely claims Christ's lordship as his own (NB: the Greek prefix *anti-* connotes both opposition and substitution). In Scripture the term occurs only in the Johannine epistles, where the Church's encounter with 'many antichrists' is interpreted as a sign of the imminence of the end (1 John 2:18). Here the antichrist is identified by the teaching of false doctrine: a failure to confess the Son alongside the Father (1 John 2:22–3) and, more specifically, a denial of Jesus' fleshly humanity (1 John 4:2–3; 2 John 7). The 'lawless one' mentioned by Paul (2 Thess. 2:3–9) and the apocalyptic figure of the beast (Rev. 13:1–5 and *passim*) are also typically understood as referring to the antichrist.

Throughout the history of the Church, Christians have used the title of antichrist for their enemies both inside and outside the Church. Thus, the beast of Revelation is generally understood to refer to a Roman emperor, while Protestants from the time of the Reformation have frequently identified the papacy with the antichrist (see, e.g., M. Luther, *Smalc.* 4; WC 25.6).

Yet the references in the Johannine and Pauline epistles are less focused on identifying particular historical figures than on emphasizing the threat that HERESY and IDOLATRY, respectively, pose to the integrity of the Christian KERYGMA and the corresponding importance of testing all claims to inspired teaching (1 John 4:1).

IAN A. MCFARLAND

ANTIJUDAISM: see ISRAEL; JUDAISM AND CHRISTIANITY; SUPERSESSIONISM.

ANTINOMIANISM The label 'Antinomian' was first devised by M. LUTHER. It literally means 'against the LAW' (*nomos* is Greek for law), and Luther used it to describe those who said that the moral law should not be preached to believers. It was from the beginning a construction designed for polemical effect. It helped Luther to target those who thought (with good reason) that they were simply repeating what he had already said. In 1535 Luther had asserted that 'the law has been abolished' (*Gal.* 349). But in 1539 he asked, 'Why, then, should one wish to abolish the law, which cannot be abolished?' (*Anti.* 113). From its inception, then, the label was subject to polemic and freighted with irony, which should evoke a certain caution in how it is used and interpreted.

Antinomianism is best understood as a cluster of soteriological convictions that emphasized the passivity of the believer, the free GRACE of God and the imputation of Christ's righteousness in the process of salvation. All of these were convictions that the early Luther himself had advanced, until he began to see the kinds of ways in which they might be misused. The audience had changed, he said: where once the people needed to hear only grace, now they needed to be reminded of the law, not told that it had been abolished. His main target was J. Agricola (1494–1566), who took over Luther's teaching duties at Wittenberg during a brief absence in 1537. Agricola taught that too much emphasis on the place of the law in justification would give ground to Catholic understandings of human merit. An angry Luther turned on his friend. In 1539 he wrote a short work, *Against the Antinomians*, which was supposed to have served as Agricola's retraction. In it Luther gratuitously accused Agricola of saying that believers could sin as much as they pleased, thus linking a belief about the place of the moral law with a practical licentiousness. The aggrieved Agricola left for Berlin, the two men were never reconciled, and the debate between them largely faded from view.

The label was revived in early seventeenth-century England to slur one side in an intra-Puritan debate. All Puritans agreed that the law should be preached to sinners and that it played no part in JUSTIFICATION, but some argued that it also had no role in SANCTIFICATION. The imputation of Christ's righteousness to the believer meant that he or she was already holy in God's sight. God was a loving father who saw no SIN in his children, and who viewed them only with kindly goodwill. T. D. Bozeman (b. 1942) interprets this position as a 'backlash' against the harsh grind of Puritan piety that involved a lifelong watch of the heart in an endless war against sin and a constant search for assurance of salvation. Puritan preachers presented God as an angry judge who observed every sin, and who would bring punishment if each sin was not identified and confessed. One response to this devotional hegemony was to repudiate its underlying foundations, to replace an angry God with a loving one, and to say that all sin was covered by the imputation of Christ's righteousness to the believer. Historically, then, this version of Antinomianism was a revolt among the English Puritan community. In order to put it down, the Antinomian label was a handy weapon. It was conflated with that of the Libertines, an entirely different sixteenth-century group, to make the same connection forged by Luther between Antinomian doctrine and practical licentiousness.

Antinomian controversy also took place in the Puritan settlement of New England during the mid-1630s. The essential question was one of ASSURANCE: did the believer gain assurance of salvation from her sanctification, or from a direct communication from God to her SOUL? The label of Antinomian was again employed to beat down the losers in that debate, who were, for the most part, banished. When England experienced its own upheaval during the 1640s, Antinomian ideas came out into the open and seemed to flourish – to the horror of many. Antinomians like T. Crisp (1600–43) argued that no preparations were required in order for a person to be saved, in contradistinction to the lengthy Puritan process of cleansing the heart in preparation for Christ's entry. They went beyond Luther when they interpreted faith as the opening of one's eyes to a prior salvation already complete at the cross or even from eternity. But the civil war and the regicide were not a conducive context for urging even the smallest degree of freedom from the law. England emerged from the Interregnum with a lingering fear of Antinomian doctrine, which had, in a general sense, been discredited by the devastating experience of the war. English doctrine thereafter inclined towards moderation and moralism. Antinomian notions barely survived the century, and then only in very small pockets of the English-speaking Church.

Antinomianism is easily misjudged. It should not be linked with a practical immorality. Antinomian authors encouraged a life of godliness, though we cannot know how their ideas were applied by all of their readers. Despite its similarities with Calvinist doctrine, it should be seen as deriving from the early Luther. While Antinomian ideas could mix rather fluidly with Familism – yet another sixteenth-century sect that argued for perfection on mystical grounds – that, too, was a largely separate stream. The label is often read back into previous periods of Church history, but this is anachronistic and risks linking the Antinomians unfairly with heretical groups. Antinomianism was not a heresy, unless we are to interpret the imputation of heresy as merely an exercise in the projection of power. The Antinomians would contend that their beliefs were an attempt to recapture the core conviction of the Protestant Reformation – salvation by faith alone through grace alone – and the clear proclamations of the early Luther. Their claims should not be too quickly dismissed.

T. D. Bozeman, *The Precisianist Strain: Disciplinary Religion and Antinomian Backlash in Puritanism to 1638* (University of North Carolina Press, 2004).

D. R. Como, *Blown by the Spirit: Puritanism and the Emergence of an Antinomian Underground in Pre-Civil-War England* (Stanford University Press, 2004).

Tim Cooper

Antisemitism: see Judaism and Christianity.

Aphthartodocetism Associated principally with the figure of Julian of Halicarnassus (*fl.* 515), aphthartodocetism represents a radical form of miaphysitism. It was a common move in patristic Christology to suggest that in the incarnation the divine and human natures are united in much the same way as fire and iron in a red-hot poker. Julian took this analogy to the extreme, arguing that in Christ the divinity completely glorified the humanity in the same way that fire completely suffuses a red-hot coal. As a result, Christ's flesh was incorruptible (*aphthartos* in Greek) from the moment of his conception and not (as the majority of theologians taught) only from the time of his resurrection. This meant, in turn, that the incarnate Christ was not naturally susceptible to hunger, thirst, weariness, suffering, or death, though he voluntarily subjected himself to all these afflictions for the sake of the economy of redemption.

Because this teaching seemed to weaken Christ's consubstantiality with humanity, it was understood (and named) as a form of docetism. Unlike the docetists of earlier centuries, however, Julian did not deny that Christ had a genuinely human body, but only that his body shared the infirmities of fallen humanity. Nevertheless, his position was rejected not only by proponents of the dyophysite Christologies associated with the Council of Chalcedon, but also by other miaphysites like Severus of Antioch (*ca* 465–*ca* 540), who argued that denying the corruptibility of Christ's earthly flesh undermined the soteriological principle that he healed our nature by assuming it along with all its natural needs and vulnerabilities. At the same time, a modified doctrine of the incorruptibility of Christ's flesh became characteristic of later Armenian theology.

Ian A. McFarland

Apocalyptic The word 'apocalyptic' is an adjective which has come to be used as a noun to describe a discrete body of theological and eschatological themes which are to be found in many religions. The word itself, though derived from the Greek word *apocalypsis* (meaning 'unveiling' or 'revelation'), is a modern coinage, and it was only in nineteenth-century Germany that *Apokalyptik* came to be used as a noun.

There are two major ways of understanding apocalyptic, both of which are illustrated by Revelation 1:1 ('the revelation [*apocalypsis*] of Jesus Christ, which God gave him to show to his servants what must soon take place'). First, the word 'apocalypse' describes a literary *form* which, by means of visions, auditions, dreams, or some other unprompted divine stimulus, prompts the understanding of matters human or divine. Second, the eschatological reference at the end of the quotation to 'what must soon take place' suggests an interpretation of apocalyptic more in terms of the *content*, namely the terrible events which must precede the coming of the New Jerusalem on earth. In the light of this second approach, a widespread feature of the discussion of apocalyptic is its use as a way of describing a special expression of Jewish eschatology in which the following are characteristic features: a contrast between the present age and a new age, which is still to come; a belief that the new age is of a transcendent kind, which breaks in from beyond through divine intervention and without human activity; a universal concern; the belief that God has foreordained everything, and that the history of the world has been divided into epochs; and an imminent expectation that the present state of affairs is short-lived.

While it is true that the canonical books usually regarded as 'apocalyptic', namely, Daniel and Revelation, include eschatological matters, not all visionary texts do (the Slavonic Apocalypse of Enoch and the Ascension of Isaiah are two obvious examples from antiquity). Even Daniel and Revelation, which have so much in common (in large part because of Revelation's dependence on themes from Daniel, especially Dan. 10 in Rev. 1:13–17 and Dan. 7 in Rev. 13), differ in key respects, as M. Luther recognized in his later and more measured preface to Revelation. In this he usefully contrasted different kinds of prophecy and expressed the concerns of many religious leaders down the centuries about the difficulty in interpreting Revelation. He suggested that prophecy is of three types: (1) in words, without images and figures; (2) in images, but with the interpretation in words; and (3) exclusively in images, without either words or interpretations. Revelation is a challenge to exegetes, according to Luther, because it exemplifies the third type.

Christianity is an 'apocalyptic' religion in the sense that at the heart of its foundation documents is the assertion that the revelation of a new, distinctive, moment in the divine economy has come about. Its eschatological message is endorsed by apocalyptic means, by visions and other forms of revelation (e.g., the baptismal experience of Jesus in Mark 1:10, the 'conversion' of Saul in Acts 9:22–6). Even if the primary NT apocalyptic text, Revelation, seems to have a pessimistic view of future history, closer inspection reveals that it was (as it has continued to be) the motor of the hope of radical change in this world. The tribulation may have to precede the coming of the New Jerusalem but its coming will be on earth, not in heaven (cf. Matt. 6:10).

J. J. Collins, B. McGinn, and S. Stein, *The Encyclopedia of Apocalypticism*, 3 vols. (Continuum, 2000).
C. Rowland, *The Open Heaven: A Study of Apocalyptic in Judaism and Early Christianity* (SPCK, 1982).

CHRISTOPHER ROWLAND

APOCATASTASIS: see UNIVERSALISM.

APOCRYPHA JEROME gave the name apocrypha (meaning 'hidden' in Greek) to those books that were included in the SEPTUAGINT (LXX) but were not part of the Hebrew canon acknowledged by the rabbis. Though treated as SCRIPTURE by many early Christian writers and received as canonical by Orthodox Christians to the present day, for Jerome the fact that the apocryphal books existed only in Greek meant that they lacked the authority of what he called the 'Hebrew truth'. While Catholics continued to acknowledge the majority of these books as part of the canon, since the REFORMATION they have customarily classified them as 'deuterocanonical' in distinction from the 'protocanonical' books of the Hebrew Bible and the NT. Protestants exclude the apocrypha from the canon, though often including them in printed Bibles as an appendix.

Disagreement regarding the authority of the apocrypha has played some role in doctrinal disputes (e.g., Catholics traditionally adduce 2 Macc. 12:44–5/6 as biblical support for the doctrine of PURGATORY). It also has significant implications for the relationship between JUDAISM AND CHRISTIANITY. At the time of Christianity's origin, the shape of the Jewish canon was very much in flux, with many Jews regarding the LXX as Scripture. The Hebrew canon was fixed by the rabbis only from the second century – partly in reaction to Christian use of the LXX in disputes with Jews over biblical interpretation. Where Christians accept as authoritative a Jewish determination of the OT canon made in the Christian era, it would seem to follow that even after Christ the identity of the Church is not separable from the witness of the synagogue.

IAN A. MCFARLAND

APOLLINARIANISM Named after Apollinaris of Laodicea (*ca* 310–*ca* 390), Apollinarianism is the teaching that Jesus Christ, as the Word of God incarnate, lacks a human mind. Instead, Apollinaris taught that in Jesus the place of the mind was taken by the Word (see *LOGOS*). As a fervent supporter of ATHANASIUS and the Council of NICAEA, Apollinaris sought in this way to affirm that Christ was fully divine. Although this required that the INCARNATION be interpreted as the animation of a created human body by the uncreated divine Word – so that Christ could not be confessed as fully and completely human – Apollinaris defended his position by arguing that two complete natures could not co-exist in a single being. Yet, while Apollinaris apparently saw in the Word's displacement of Christ's human mind a plausible means of accounting for the sinless perfection of his earthly life, critics like Gregory of Nazianzus (see CAPPADOCIAN FATHERS) charged that if Christ did not possess a human mind, he could not redeem the mind from its sinful inclinations.

Apollinaris' qualification of Christ's humanity was formally condemned at the First Council of CONSTANTINOPLE in 381. Because his CHRISTOLOGY implies that Jesus is genuinely human in appearance only, it can be classified as a type of DOCETISM. In so far as Apollinaris' chief theological interest seems to have been the affirmation of the unity of Christ's person rather than the denial of his materiality, however, he is perhaps more fairly seen as a precursor of strict MIAPHYSITISM.

IAN A. MCFARLAND

APOLOGETICS Apologetics (from the Greek *apologia*, the speech for the defence in a law court) refers to that branch of theology that seeks to offer a persuasive account of Christian faith without direct appeal to the authority of biblical REVELATION, in accordance with the biblical injunction that believers should '[a]lways be prepared to make a defence [*apologian*] to anyone who calls you to account for the hope that is in you' (1 Pet. 3:15). More concretely, PAUL's claim that 'since the creation of the world [God's] . . . eternal power and deity ha[ve] been clearly perceived in the things that have been made' (Rom. 1:19–20) has been taken as implying that at least some of Christianity's claims can be sustained by apologetic arguments that appeal to general human experience outside the boundaries of the Church (cf. Acts 17:24–9).

In the first centuries of the Church, the attempt to defend Christianity against its detractors and commend it to the educated public as both religiously legitimate and intellectually serious was a major preoccupation of Christian writers. Most well known among these theologians (often referred to collectively as the apologists) are Justin Martyr (d. *ca* 165), Athenagoras (*ca* 130–*ca* 190), and TERTULLIAN, all of whom addressed their apologies of Christian faith and practice to the rulers of the Roman Empire. Later in the third century ORIGEN wrote his *Against Celsus*, a sweeping attempt to defend the credibility of Christianity against pagan attacks.

Beyond defending Christians against charges of sedition, these early apologetic works typically attempted to show the essential compatibility between Christian teaching and the best pagan philosophy, which was frequently identified with some form of Platonism. Often, Christianity was seen as the fulfilment of philosophers' teaching, though it also seemed reasonable to some to conclude that Plato (*ca* 430–*ca* 345 BC) had plagiarized many of his ideas from the OT (see Justin Martyr, *1Apol.* 59). Such arguments formed part of a broader programme to demonstrate both the antiquity (and thus, in the context of Greco-Roman intellectual culture, the authority) of the OT prophetical books and their fulfilment in the life of Jesus. In this way, the apologists typically argued their case on two inter-related tracks: defending Christianity's intellectual credibility as a comprehensive moral and cosmological framework on the one hand, and its religious credentials as the legitimate heir of an ancient faith on the other.

While a primary impetus for apologetic writing disappeared when Christianity became the religion of the Roman Empire in the fourth century, the genre did not die out. Augustine was spurred to write his monumental *City of God against the Pagans* by the charge that the fall of the Empire in the West had been caused by its abandonment of pagan worship. In the Middle Ages T. Aquinas' *Summa contra Gentiles* took the form of a defence of Christian claims over against Jews, Muslims, and other non-Christians. In later writings, however, Thomas argues that where one's interlocutor does not acknowledge the authority of revelation, then 'there is no longer any means of proving the articles of faith by reasoning, but only of answering his objections – if he has any – against faith' (*ST* 1.1.8).

Apologetics emerged as a distinct discipline among Protestant theologians in the seventeenth century, as the intellectual challenges of the Scientific Revolution and the Enlightenment put the Church on the defensive. Among Catholics apologetics was eventually subsumed under (though never simply identified with) the discipline of fundamental theology. Operating from diverse confessional orientations, theologians deployed a range of strategies in response to the charge that Christian claims were based on unsubstantiated appeals to authority. Pre-eminent among these was natural theology, or the attempt to establish at least some Christian beliefs (especially the existence of a creator God) on the basis of general experience of the world. Also important was the appeal to biblical miracles (and, as a corollary, the trustworthiness of the Bible as a historical record of those miracles) as evidence of the truth of Christian claims.

In the nineteenth and twentieth centuries the influence of liberal theology caused apologetic strategies among some Protestant theologians to shift from the attempt to demonstrate the truth of Christian claims to a focus on their meaningfulness as a particular form of human religious experience. According to this perspective, the proper goal of apologetics is to show that its teachings do address fundamental questions that arise out of the structure of a human self-consciousness, which, it is argued, presupposes some overarching framework within which to interpret and integrate the whole of reality. At the same time, more traditional approaches to apologetics continued to be pursued by more conservative theologians, especially in the Princeton theology and Dutch Reformed circles associated with A. Kuyper. Among contemporary evangelical theologians influenced by Kuyper, however, the goal of apologetics tends to be conceived less as a positive demonstration of the truth of Christianity than as the process of answering objections to the faith raised by sceptics (cf. Aquinas, *ST* 1.1.8).

Certain strands of twentieth-century theology (especially those influenced by K. Barth) reject the enterprise of apologetics as inconsistent with the absolute priority of Christ as the sole source and norm of Christian belief, as well as with God's absolute transcendence of the world. Such critics argue that to locate the truths of the Christian faith within the purview of general human experience of the world both marginalizes Christ and reduces God to purely worldly dimensions. Apologists respond that such a perspective is inconsistent with the essential unity of all truth, understood as corollary to belief in one God as the sole source of all that is. Furthermore, while acknowledging Christ as the sole *norm* of doctrine, they reject as excessive the claim that Christ is likewise the sole *source* of theological truth – and with it the implication that apologetics in any sense compromises the centrality of Christ for Christian belief.

See also Cosmological Argument; Eristics; Ontological Argument; Reformed Epistemology; Teleological Argument.

Ian A. McFarland

Apophatic Theology Apophatic or 'negative' theology refers to the practice of describing God by negating particular attributes of God (Latin *via remotionis* or *negationis*). As such, it is grounded in a widely accepted principle of Christian theology, namely, that God, as the unique, transcendent, and unoriginate Creator of all that is, is by definition prior to all creaturely categories and therefore can be neither conceived nor described in creaturely terms. In short, *Deus non est in genere* (Aquinas, *ST* 1.3.5). In line with this principle, many of the attributes traditionally associated with God in Christian theology are apophatic in form. Thus, immensity is the denial that God is contained by space, eternity that God is bound by time, simplicity that God is composed of parts, and immutability that God is subject to change.

Other traditional divine attributes, however, take cataphatic or 'positive' form, including designations of God as omnipotent, omniscient, wise, just, and merciful. Advocates of apophatic theology note that such positive forms of predication necessarily limit God and are therefore ultimately inadequate to the theological task, since God is by nature infinite (i.e., unlimited). Clement of Alexandria (*ca* 150–*ca* 215) made this point with great force as early as the turn of the third century (*Strom.* 5.12), drawing both on Scripture and on insights current in contemporary Platonism. At the same time, perhaps the greatest proponent of apophatic theology, the pseudonymous writer Dionysius the Areopagite, argued that cataphatic theology constitutes an important first step in Christian God talk, although it is one that must ultimately be left behind by the dedicated theologian, who, in contemplating the ineffable Godhead, must move from the presumption of knowing (cataphatic theology) to the mystery of unknowing (apophatic theology).

In his treatise *The Divine Names* Dionysius argues that the very plurality of names used for God in Scripture points to language's incapacity to name God, thereby drawing the theologian upwards towards the nameless, super-essential unity of God (*Divine Names* 1.5–7). The task of cataphatic theology is therefore preparatory. It allows language to exhaust itself in attempting to name God, and thereby opens the way towards an appreciation of God's surpassing of every name. Though God is the cause of the multiplicity of created goods, God (precisely *as* cause) is incapable of being categorized with those effects, in the same way that the fire that heats cannot itself be said to be heated (*Divine Names* 2.8). God is, rather, a goodness that transcends all creaturely good.

Dionysius' first great interpreter, Maximus the Confessor, used the transfiguration as a metaphor for the way in which God's being transcends all creaturely categories while at the same time bringing them into being, arguing that the blinding light of the transfigured Christ indicates God's essential unknowability (i.e., apophatic theology), which, however, illuminates the surrounding reality in such a way as to make affirmation (i.e., cataphatic theology) possible (*PG* 1165B–1168B). Also deeply influenced by Dionysius, T. Aquinas employed a classic mode of combining cataphatic and apophatic dimensions of theology in what is generally called the 'way of eminence' (*via eminentiae*). According to this approach, the presence of perfections in creatures implies that they are also present in the Creator as their cause (the cataphatic dimension), but God's absolute transcendence of the created world makes it impossible to predicate the same qualities of creature and Creator univocally (the apophatic dimension); it follows that it is only legitimate to predicate such qualities of God while affirming that they exist in God in a super-eminent way (see, e.g., *ST* 1.12.12). Thus, while we can be confident *that* such perfections exist in God, we remain ignorant of *how* they exist in God (*ST* 1.13.3).

For all these theologians, the negative way of apophasis is less a method to be used to derive theological propositions than a discipline to help guide the believer's apprehension of God as a supremely personal (and not simply cognitive) mystery. Nevertheless, the apophatic emphasis on divine transcendence provides the basis for affirming the radical divine freedom with respect to all that is not God that undergirds Christian beliefs regarding both God's incarnation and human deification. God's personal transcendence of the world as its Creator rules out cosmologies in which creatures are related to God by way of a hierarchically ordered sequence, with intellectual beings nearest to God at the top and inert matter languishing far from God at the bottom. Instead, God's radical difference from all that is not God means that this kind of emanationist ontology is ruled out from the start: as Creator, God is equally transcendent over every creature, but this does not translate into any sort of 'distance'; on the contrary, it allows God to be intimately present to creation (e.g., by assuming human flesh) without being any less God, even as it allows God to bring human beings to glory (viz., in deification) without their ceasing to be human. For this reason Nicholas of Cusa (1401–64) proposed a novel apophatic characterization of God as 'not-other' (*non aliud*). His aim was not to suggest that God could in any sense be identified with the material world (as in pantheism), but rather that God's 'difference' from all that is not God transcends the categories of opposition and distinction that determine the creaturely experience of otherness, so that God is 'not other' than (and, therefore, ineffably intimate to) all that is not God.

The principal criticisms of apophatic theology are threefold. First, many charge that apophatic theology of the sort practised by Dionysius is far more deeply shaped by Neoplatonic philosophy than by the Bible. A second, more substantive worry is that apophaticism's stress on what God is not results in a pattern of theological language that is overly abstract and insufficiently attentive to the qualities of love and mercy that Scripture depicts as central to divine identity. The third criticism reflects a similar concern, though it is based in the charge that apophatic theology does not in fact follow through on its promise to avoid a positive depiction of God, since any given theologian will invariably only focus on particular negations, which will invariably suggest a positive depiction of God. Thus, proponents of process theology in particular have argued that the traditional apophatic description of God as eternal and impassible have led to an all too cataphatic understanding of God as distant from and indifferent to creation. Defenders of negative theology, however, counter that such problems emerge only when apophasis is treated as a cognitive technique rather than as a summons to transcend cognition in its negative no less than its affirmative modes.

See also Meister Eckhart.

V. Lossky, *The Mystical Theology of the Eastern Church* (St Vladimir's Seminary Press, 1997).

A. Papanikolaou, *Being with God: Trinity, Apophaticism, and Divine–Human Communion* (University of Notre Dame Press, 2006).

D. Turner, *The Darkness of God: Negativity in Christian Mysticism* (Cambridge University Press, 1995).

R. Williams, 'Lossky, the *Via negativa* and the Foundations of Theology', in *Wrestling with Angels: Conversations in Modern Theology*, ed. M. Higton (Eerdmans, 2007), 1–24.

Ian A. McFarland

Apostasy The term 'apostasy' (from the Greek for 'defection' or 'rebellion') refers to the explicit rejection of the Christian faith as such, and is thus distinct from heresy, which refers only to the rejection of one or more particular doctrines. Though the Greek term is not used in this technical sense in the NT (see Acts 21:21; 2 Thess. 2:3), the problem of defection from the faith is raised in a number of biblical texts. In some cases (e.g., 1 Tim. 4:1; 2 Pet. 2:21; 1 John 2:18–19) it is unclear whether the offence the authors have in mind is apostasy or heresy, but the reference in Hebrews 6:4–6 to 'those who have once been enlightened . . . and tasted the goodness of the word of God . . . and then have fallen away' does seem to refer to those who have formally renounced their faith in Christ, presumably as the result of persecution.

The writer of Hebrews' claim that 'it is impossible to restore to repentance' those who had transgressed in this way (Heb. 6:4) led early Christians to class apostasy among the most severe sins: it was punished by excommunication without possibility of readmission to full communion prior to death. In the face of large numbers of apostasies brought on by the Decian persecution in the mid-third century, however, a more lenient policy eventually prevailed with respect to those who had apostatized under duress and later sought to be reconciled to the Church.

Ian A. McFarland

Apostle Derived from a Greek word meaning 'sent', apostle is used in the NT to refer to a class of Christian missionaries with prominent leadership roles in the primitive Church. The extent of this class is not depicted consistently across the NT. Luke, for example, generally limits his use of the title 'apostle' to twelve people separated out of the broader category of Jesus' disciples to serve as an eschatological symbol of the twelve tribes of Israel (Luke 6:13; 22:30; cf. Matt. 19:28). In Lukan perspective this group is definitive, except for the replacement of the apostate Judas by Matthias (Acts 1:15–26). By contrast, Paul, though normally distinguished from the apostles in Acts (9:27; 15:2, 22; but cf. 14:14), consistently identifies himself as one in his letters (e.g., Rom. 1:1; 1 Cor. 1:1; 1 Thess. 2:6) and applies the term to a broader class of Christian leaders (1 Cor. 12:28; cf. Rom. 16:7) – though even he may have conceived the title as applicable only to those whose ministry was rooted in personal witness to Jesus' resurrection (1 Cor. 9:1; cf. Acts 1:22).

Whatever the origins of the term, the later books of the NT clearly associate the class of apostles with the founding of, rather than an ongoing role in, the Christian community (Eph. 2:20; 2 Pet. 3:2; Jude 17). Likewise, in subsequent Christian theology the term is used to refer to those who were eyewitnesses to Jesus' earthly ministry and/or risen life. Because the content of the Christian Gospel is the historical person Jesus of Nazareth, the apostles' historical location gives them unique and irreplaceable authority, with the originating witness of the apostles serving as the touchstone for all subsequent claims of faithful witness to Jesus.

See also Apostolicity.

Ian A. McFarland

Apostles' Creed So named because of a legend attributing its composition to the twelve apostles, the text now known as the Apostles' Creed originated in what is now south-western France in the late sixth or early seventh century. It is a modified version of the so-called Old Roman Creed, which dates from the early third century and provided the template for virtually all early western (i.e., Latin) creeds. In its current form, the Apostles' Creed initially spread among Frankish Churches as part of Charlemagne's (r. 800–14) efforts to establish liturgical uniformity in his dominions. It was probably introduced to Rome in the tenth century as part of a programme of reform spearheaded by the Holy Roman emperors, where it soon became established as the official baptismal creed of the whole western Church – a position it retained among Lutheran and Reformed Churches even after the Reformation.

The Old Roman Creed (with which the legend of apostolic composition was first associated) most likely developed from the interrogatory creeds recited by converts at the time of their baptism. The unequal length of its three articles suggests that it is the conflation of a simple Trinitarian creed (itself based on the baptismal formula of Matt. 28:19) with an originally independent Christological confession of the sort found in many early Christian texts (e.g., Justin Martyr, *1Apol.* 1.21). The incorporation of this Christological material, with its emphasis on Jesus' birth, crucifixion, and death, may reflect a desire to affirm Jesus' materiality over against docetism.

L. T. Johnson, *The Creed: What Christians Believe and Why It Matters* (Image, 2004).

Ian A. McFarland

Apostolic Fathers The 'Apostolic Fathers' are the authors of various very early Christian writings which are generally regarded as orthodox, but which were not included in the final NT canon. There is no formal list, but the term normally includes the authors of *1* and *2 Clement*; the letters of Polycarp (*ca* 70–*ca* 155), Ignatius of Antioch (d. *ca* 110), and 'Barnabas'; the *Didache*; and *The Shepherd of Hermas*. Dates for individual works are uncertain, but most probably range from *ca* 90 to *ca* 150.

The term 'Apostolic Fathers' has been most popular in the Catholic tradition. It dates from the seventeenth century, but the *idea* it conveys is much earlier: already by the second century they were considered to have special significance because they had apparently received Christianity from Jesus' first followers. This assumption is reflected, for example, in the full title of the *Didache* ('The Teaching of the Twelve Apostles') and the common assumption that the *Letter of Barnabas* was by that apostle.

Several of these texts were letters which were addressed to a specific recipient or community, but were perhaps intended for a wider readership. Like Paul's letters they deal with some doctrinal concepts, such as the nature of Jesus Christ and the promise of resurrection, but these ideas are expressed very figuratively (perhaps reflecting liturgical language) and not through systematic or philosophical argument. *1 Clement* and the letters of Ignatius and Polycarp urge on their addressees the importance of Christian unity, the writers possibly fearing that schisms will make Churches more vulnerable to persecution. Ignatius' writing vividly presents his expectation of martyrdom, which he interprets as sharing in the death and resurrection of Christ. The motif of participation in the sufferings of Christ is a very common theme in the Apostolic Fathers.

Other writings take the form of a homily (*2 Clement*) or a collection of basic Christian ethical and spiritual principles (the *Didache*). Even the *Shepherd of Hermas*, which is written as a series of apocalyptic visions with accompanying interpretations, contains significant passages relating to personal behaviour and Church order. The *Didache* may well have been used for the teaching of new converts (that is, for catechesis): it contains examples of early Christian baptismal instructions and Eucharistic prayers closely related to Jewish mealtime blessings. Indeed, the Apostolic Fathers in general give tantalizing hints about the relation of second- and third-generation Christians to their Jewish contemporaries, although this evidence is notoriously difficult to interpret.

One striking aspect of the Apostolic Fathers is that (like several NT epistles) they seem to share a supposition that the basic message (kerygma) of the Christian faith has already been transmitted to their audience by word of mouth: they thus focus on exhorting Christ-like behaviour, encouraging fortitude in the face of persecution and giving guidance on issues that are dividing Christians. They show some awareness of the Hebrew Bible and parts of what became the NT canon, but usually quote very freely. Sometimes this may indicate quotation from memory; sometimes it suggests reliance on pre-Gospel collections of Jesus' sayings.

Morwenna Ludlow

Apostolic Succession The Nicene Creed states that the Church is 'apostolic', meaning that by the grace of the Holy Spirit its faith is fundamentally the same as that of the apostles. Apostolicity is an essential requirement or 'mark' of the Church. How, then, is contemporary faith derived from the apostles? For Protestant Churches the answer is largely through the authoritative teaching of canonical Scripture; for the Orthodox Churches, it is through their authoritative tradition and in communion with their bishops. Following developments initiated by Cyprian (d. 258) and Tertullian, the Anglican and Catholic traditions have believed apostolic faith is handed on through the bishops by apostolic succession, such that each episcopal generation consecrates the next in a line stretching from Peter and the apostles to the present. Consecration within this series gives bishops a unique charism enabling them to teach and govern the Church with an apostolic authority derived from Jesus' charge to the apostles and, through the apostles and succeeding bishops, to them.

In the nineteenth century, apostolic succession was used by Anglicans to argue for the legitimacy of their communion and its orders. It was denied (on seemingly flimsy grounds) by Pope Leo XIII (r. 1878–1903) in *Apostolicae Curae* (1896), from which he concluded Anglican orders must be invalid. For Episcopal Churches apostolic succession grounds the *iure divino* status of the episcopacy (see, e.g., Vatican Council II, *LG*,§3.20). In recent years, it has been criticized as unable adequately to acknowledge how no Church is ever fully apostolic, and as unwarrantably limiting apostolicity within the Catholic Church to celibate male clerics.

Nicholas M. Healy

Apostolicity Whether applied broadly as a criterion of Christian doctrine or more narrowly (following the Apostles' and Nicene Creeds) as an identifying mark of the Church, apostolicity refers to conformity with the faith and practice of the apostles. Already in the NT the apostles, as the eyewitnesses to Christ's ministry and resurrection, are viewed as the foundation of Christian teaching (e.g., Acts 2:42; Eph. 2:20; Rev. 21:14). The logic behind this position is developed by writers of the second century, who regard the apostles as the intermediaries through whom the Gospel was transmitted from Christ to the world (*1Clem.* 42:1;

Did.), and thus view agreement with them as a fundamental criterion of ORTHODOXY (Ignatius, *Eph.* 11:2). For many early writers a decisive mark of apostolicity was submission to the Church's duly appointed leaders, as the apostles' legitimate successors (Ignatius, *Trall.* 2:2; Irenaeus, *AH* 3.2–4).

There is broad ecumenical agreement that, because the Church is a community grounded in the commitments of Jesus' immediate followers, continuity with the faith of the apostles is a constitutive feature of Christian identity. At the same time, there is significant disagreement over the proper criteria of apostolicity. Catholic, Orthodox, and some Anglican theologians view institutional continuity, as established by an unbroken succession of bishops, to be a decisive test of apostolicity (see APOSTOLIC SUCCESSION). Protestant opinion, on the other hand, tends to regard apostolicity as a matter of teaching and practice that can be measured against the bar of SCRIPTURE without any reference to matters of ecclesiastical polity.

See also ECCLESIOLOGY.

IAN A. MCFARLAND

APPELLANCY In 1713 Pope Clement XI (r. 1700–21) issued the bull *Unigenitus,* which was intended to give definitive condemnation of JANSENISM. Though the PAPACY had condemned various DOCTRINES associated with Jansenism at several points in the seventeeth century, the comprehensive character of *Unigenitus* led four French bishops in 1717 to appeal against its judgements to a future ecumenical COUNCIL. Those who subscribed to the bishops' appeal came to be known as 'Appellants'. Thus, 'Appellancy' refers to a specifically eighteenth-century form of Jansenism.

The Appellants' opponents within Catholicism charged that their Jansenist doctrines of GRACE and SIN were indistinguishable from PROTESTANTISM, but Appellant ECCLESIOLOGY differed radically from Protestant doctrines of the Church. To be sure, both Appellancy and Protestantism were occasioned by the conviction that the Catholic hierarchy had given official approval to false doctrine; correspondingly, both saw the Catholic Church as deeply implicated in SIN. Yet while Protestants concluded that these facts justified – and even demanded – breaking with Rome, Appellants did not. On the contrary, though Appellants were suspicious of attempts to identify the Church's authority with a particular ecclesiastical office (e.g., the EPISCOPACY in general or the papacy in particular), they nevertheless insisted on the Catholic Church's indefectibility and thus differed from those Jansenists in the Low Countries who followed a path of SCHISM to form what became the Old Catholic Church in the Netherlands.

The Appellants' unique ecclesiological perspective is closely connected with the theology of grace they inherited from seventeenth-century JANSENISM. With a strong emphasis on God's immediate and sovereign guidance of the whole of human history, Appellant theologians trusted in God's ability to maintain the integrity of the Church even when it was most deeply implicated in the contradictions and ambiguities of history. Appellancy's opponents within Catholicism argued that the Church's integrity could be assured only when its members acknowledged the magisterium's authority to deliver a binding and definitive judgement on what was and was not orthodox doctrine. By contrast, Appellants believed that truth had to struggle against falsehood in the Church in the same way that Christ had to struggle with – without himself breaking from – the synagogue. Thus, while both Protestants and other Catholics saw the Church as a place of doctrinal unanimity (so that those espousing false doctrine by definition stood outside the Church), Appellants argued that the Church, as Christ's BODY, had to experience within itself the oppression and rejection of ORTHODOXY as well as its occasional triumph. Working from this perspective, Appellants argued that the church's integrity was ensured not by doctrinal consensus, but by the juridical structures, the sacraments, and the devotional practices that constituted it as the body of Christ.

J. M. Gres-Gayer, 'The *Unigenitus* of Clement XI: A Fresh Look at the Issues', *Theological Studies* 49 (1988), 259–82.

E. Radner, *Spirit and Nature: The Saint-Médard Miracles in 18th-Century Jansenism* (Crossroad, 2002).

IAN A. MCFARLAND

APPROPRIATION The DOCTRINE of appropriation is a feature of Trinitarian theology that emerged from the need to reconcile narrative conventions (characteristic of both SCRIPTURE and LITURGY) associated with the three divine Persons with dogmatic convictions regarding the essential unity of the triune God. According to classical Trinitarian doctrine, the Persons of the TRINITY, although *internally* differentiated by the relations that establish the Father as begetting, the Son as begotten, and the HOLY SPIRIT as proceeding from the Father (as well as, for western Churches, from the Son; see *FILIOQUE*) always act *externally* in unison, so that in their relation to creatures the actions of the Trinity are undivided (*opera Trinitatis ad extra sunt indivisa*). This claim seems flatly inconsistent with the way in which, for example, the APOSTLES' CREED specifies the Father as 'creator of heaven and earth'.

The doctrine of appropriation attempts to justify the practice of linking certain divine actions to particular Persons of the Trinity, notwithstanding the common participation of all three in every divine work. It is based on the principle that, while all three Persons are equally active in all God's works, each participates in a distinctive mode or manner that reflects the relationships between the Persons within the eternal life of the Godhead. Thus, the work of creation (i.e., the origination of all things other than God) is naturally 'appropriated' to the Father, since the Father is the source of the life of the Son and the Spirit within God. Similarly, the perfection of creatures (through sanctification and deification) is appropriated to the Spirit, as the one who completes and consummates the internal life of the Godhead.

Ian A. McFarland

Aquinas, Thomas Thomas Aquinas was born in 1224/5 near Naples to minor nobility. At an early age he was sent to the Benedictines for his education, but in 1244 joined the Order of Preachers, recently founded (in 1217) by Dominic (1170–1221). This was a significant decision, for the Dominican friars led a new and controversial form of the Christian life. Unlike the monks, they lived within the world, seeking perfect obedience to Christ through poverty and (often itinerant) preaching. In 1245 Thomas moved to the University of Paris where Albert the Great (*ca* 1200–80) encouraged his study of the works of Aristotle (384–322 BC), many of which were just then becoming available in the West. After a few years at Cologne, he began (probably in 1252) to teach at Paris and wrote his commentary on the *Sentences* of Peter Lombard (*ca* 1100–60). In 1256 he became *magister in sacra pagina*. As such, his responsibility was to preach upon Scripture (the 'sacred page'), analyze it, and engage in disputation over its interpretation.

Thomas wrote two further large-scale theological works, the *Summa contra Gentiles* (*ScG*), completed by 1265, and the *Summa theologiae* (*ST*) – his most important and massively influential work – which remained uncompleted at his death. Besides many shorter theological works, he wrote substantial commentaries on both Scripture and philosophy (predominantly the works of Aristotle). He died after a brief illness in 1274. Around the time of his death, propositions drawn from his theology were condemned by the archbishop of Paris. Soon, however, his work was generally acknowledged to be an outstanding constructive reconciliation of new learning with the tradition. Canonized in 1323, Thomas was named a doctor of the Church by Pope Pius V (r. 1566–72) in 1567.

Thomas is still sometimes interpreted from the perspective of one or other form of Thomism, and thus not as a theologian so much as a Christian–Aristotelian philosopher whose system provides the theoretical basis for the Catholic Church's self-presentation as the superior alternative to modernity. Since the 1980s, however, scholars have brought to light the thoroughly theological nature of his work and its consonance with the friars' preaching charism and their focus on Jesus Christ. For Thomas, Aristotelian and other philosophical thinking is useful, but only in a limited way. Theology, the enquiry into what we can know of God and of all things as they are related to God (*sub ratione Dei*), must always be governed by the knowledge of God (*scientia Dei*) that is revealed in and by Christ and the Holy Spirit, and made known to us only in Scripture.

To be sure, the considerable differences between Thomas' context, assumptions, and agenda and those typical of the modern period make misunderstanding relatively easy. Thus, for example, the first three books of the *ScG* treat for the most part what can be known about theological matters through natural reasoning, independently of revelation, before moving to focus on revealed truths only in the fourth and final book. Moderns have read this (whether disapprovingly or more positively) as a kind of apologetics, an attempt to show the truthfulness of Christianity by its congruence with natural theology. Scholars have argued recently, however, that given Thomas' context and interests, it is better understood as an appreciative yet critical engagement of pagan philosophical wisdom by Christian wisdom, showing their commonalities and differences, and demonstrating the inadequacy of non-revealed sources of knowledge and our need for revelation if we are to have true knowledge of God.

Thomas' Scholastic method can also be an obstacle for the contemporary reader of theology used to more historical and concrete approaches. In the *ST* he uses an approach derived from the disputation – the *disputatio* being the then common practice of having a *magister* engage in public debate on a given issue. Each larger theological topic is broken down into 'questions' that treat a particular sub-topic; these in turn are divided into short 'articles' that treat a single question (anything from, e.g., 'Whether God Understands Himself' to 'Whether Imprudence is a Special Sin'). Each article is made up of concisely stated arguments, usually three or four initially supporting a negative response, followed by a *sed contra* that briefly summarizes a positive argument (often by citing Scripture), then further arguments for the positive, and, finally, rebuttals of the initial negative case. Once the reader gets used to the Scholastic method, the insight and nuance of Thomas' arguments become increasingly apparent.

Its structure and method may give the initial impression that the *ST* is an intricate, massively logical, systematic theology that is perhaps too confident in its claims, too abstract, and too remote from Scripture and the concrete life of Christians. However, since Thomas wrote the *ST* as a textbook for his Dominican brethren, he could assume a good knowledge of Scripture and the economy of salvation in his readers. What they needed was a deeper theological understanding of what they already knew, so that they could preach with wisdom and insight. Hence (as he explains in the prologue), he chose not to follow the 'order of the subject matter' – i.e., not to begin with Scripture and its witness to Jesus Christ – but to proceed according to a more pedagogically oriented approach.

This approach is reflected in the overall structure of the work. The first part, for example, moves outwards from God as such through God as Creator to CREATION as such. The rest of the treatise charts creation's movement back to God, beginning in the second part with an exploration of how it is possible for people to act in accordance with the good (including a full-scale treatment of the virtues suitable for the confessional), and concluding in the third part with an extended discussion of Jesus Christ (who is 'our way' to God), followed by an account of the special gifts given through Christ: the Church, the sacraments, and life in HEAVEN. The *ST* as a whole thus describes a process of emanation and return (*exitus et reditus*) that Thomas abstracts from Scripture in order to allow his readers to return to Scripture with greater insight.

Thomas trains his readers, too, by turning to conceptual clarification before addressing more concrete issues. Thus he begins the first part of the *ST* with God as such in order to sort out ways to talk about God properly for use in the subsequent discussion of God's work in creation and redemption. So, too, in the second part he discusses human action in general before going on to consider moral action and the virtues; and in the third part he works out technical Christological concepts before proceeding to an extended discussion of Jesus' life and mission. Throughout Thomas is careful to note the limits of what we can know and say about the infinite God. His arguments are not deductive proofs, but aim only to show what can be said 'fittingly' (*convenienter*) in light of biblical revelation. As such, they are only 'probable' (like all theological argument) and so always challengeable.

In short, the ultimate goal of the *ST* and of Thomas' work in general is for his readers to acquire Christian wisdom through contemplation and practice. By acquiring intellectual and moral virtues within the theological virtues of FAITH, HOPE, and LOVE (*caritas*), we can become more like Christ and thus, in a human way, like God. The movement towards God raises us beyond our natural capacities so that we achieve our supernatural fulfilment. Becoming thus transformed is, however, only the penultimate goal for Thomas; it is not, in and of itself, the point of being a Christian. Rather, it prepares us for the ultimate gift of grace: the absolute happiness of the BEATIFIC VISION.

D. Burrell, *Aquinas: God and Action* (University of Notre Dame Press, 1979).

G. Emery, O. P., *The Trinitarian Theology of Thomas Aquinas* (Oxford University Press, 2007 [2004]).

N. M. Healy, *Thomas Aquinas: Theologian of the Christian Life* (Ashgate, 2003).

V. Preller, *Divine Science and the Science of God: A Reformulation of Thomas Aquinas* (Princeton University Press, 1967).

NICHOLAS M. HEALY

ARIAN CONTROVERSY In 318 or 320 Arius (*ca* 250–336), a priest in Alexandria, came into conflict with his bishop, Alexander (d. 326). The latter taught that the Son, although 'between created and uncreated', was always with the Father and eternally generated from the Father. If God is always Father, then the Son must always be with the Father: one cannot be a father without a child. Arius, preferring to see the language of Father and Son as secondary to other terminologies, objected that there is only one God, and that the Word or Son existed by the will of God from 'before the ages' but not eternally and without sharing God's being. Arius also, like a number of others associated with him, spoke of God's two Words or Wisdoms: that which is inherently God's, and that derivative Word or Wisdom present in the secondary reality – and which human beings name Word or Wisdom.

After some initial local meetings, a council of bishops met at the behest of the Emperor Constantine I (*ca* 275–337) at NICAEA in 325. The council issued a creed that said that the Son was generated 'from the substance of the Father' and was HOMOOUSIOS ('of the same substance') with the Father. Arius was exiled. This dispute reflected and stimulated tension between different theological trajectories present at the time it erupted: Nicaea did nothing to diffuse this tension. The technical terminology used in the creed seems to have been chosen as an ad hoc tool to censure Arius and was not clearly defined even by its supporters.

The events surrounding Arius were a catalyst for a continuing controversy. ATHANASIUS, bishop of Alexandria from 328, soon emerged at the centre of the ensuing debates and was eventually exiled in 336 on charges of malfeasance. A number of other supporters of Nicaea were exiled in these years, most notably Eustathius of Antioch (*fl.* 325) and Marcellus of Ancyra (d. 374). In his *Orations against the Arians* Athanasius ignored all angles of his case other than the theological and, following some hints in earlier authors, presented his enemies as followers of Arius, rather than representatives of an alternate theological tradition of long standing. This terminology of 'Arianism' was accepted by many western theologians, and increasingly by some easterners.

Many eastern bishops from 325 to 350 may be termed 'Eusebian', being broadly in a tradition that encompassed both Eusebius of Caesarea (*ca* 260–*ca* 340) and Eusebius of Nicomedia (d. 341). Such theologians hold that there is a basic ontological distinction between Father and Son, but also insist that there is an ineffable closeness between Father and Son such that the Son's being can be said to be 'from the Father' in some indescribable sense. For some the Son is 'the exact image of the Father's substance' (cf. Wis. 7:25; Heb. 1:3); for others the Son is a unique product of the Father's will. For all 'Eusebians' Athanasius' preferred language (viz., the Son as the Father's 'own' Word or

Wisdom) and Nicaea's talk of the Son coming from the Father's substance ignore a basic distinction between the one true God and the Word or Son who is created for the purpose of creating. The theology of these 'Eusebian' theologians is seen particularly clearly in the 'Dedication' creed of Antioch in 341.

The controversy shifted considerably during the 350s, as Emperor Constantius (r. 337–61) supported an increasingly subordinationist theology, according to which the Son is only 'like' (*homoios*) the Father: clearly distinct and ontologically inferior. These 'Homoians' rejected any use of *ousia* terminology. The most radical wing of this movement, represented by Aetius (*fl.* 350) and his disciple Eunomius (d. *ca* 395), insisted that Father and Son were unlike in *ousia*. Their teaching affected the perception of the Homoian movement generally and produced a strong reaction. During the 370s and 380s Eunomians or 'Heterousians' (from *heteros*, or 'other') increasingly became a distinct ecclesial group.

In 359 and 360 Constantius called two councils which, under pressure from him, promulgated a Homoian CREED intended to function as a universal marker of orthodox FAITH. In reaction, several groups – from supporters of Athanasius to some who owed far more to the 'Eusebian' tradition – coalesced around the creed of Nicaea as the only alternative to the Homoian creed. In the West also the events of 359–60 provided a stimulus for many theologians to agree on Nicaea as a standard. The different traditions among eastern and western theologians slowly came to recognize each others' theologies as mutually compatible, though this process took many years. As they slowly came together these groups agreed on the principles by which the creed of Nicaea should be understood: that God's immaterial and incomprehensible being is not divided and that the Persons are truly distinct from each other. Between 360 and 380 there was also an evolution of terminologies that distinguish what is one from what is three in God: God is one in nature, power, glory, or essence while there are three Persons or *hypostases*. The Father gives rise to a Son and a Spirit who possess the fullness of what it is to be God. This last development also occurred through polemic against those who doubted the full divinity of the HOLY SPIRIT.

These theologies represent a real development over those of Nicaea's original architects and have been called neo- or pro-Nicene by many modern scholars. In the East the CAPPADOCIAN FATHERS (Basil of Caesarea, Gregory of Nazianzus, and Gregory of Nyssa) were of particular significance in developing pro-Nicene theology; in the West Hilary of Poitiers (*ca* 300–68) and Ambrose of Milan (*ca* 340–97) were similarly significant. After the accession of the pro-Nicene emperor Theodosius I (r. 379–95), the Council of CONSTANTINOPLE promulgated a revised version of Nicaea's creed, adding clauses on the Spirit to insist that 'with the Father and the Son He is worshipped and glorified'. A parallel council held at Aquileia in the West under Emperor Gratian (r. 375–83) was much smaller, but it marked the triumph of the pro-Nicenes there also. Groups of non-Nicene Christians continued to be a real force within the Christian world through the next century (especially among the Germanic tribes who gradually took over the western empire), but increasingly they became distinct ecclesial groups.

L. Ayres, *Nicaea and Its Legacy: An Approach to Fourth Century Trinitarian Theology* (Oxford University Press, 2004).

R. P. C. Hanson, *The Search for the Christian Doctrine of God* (T&T Clark, 1988).

R. Williams, *Arius: Heresy and Tradition* (Darton, Longman and Todd, 1988).

LEWIS AYRES

ARISTOTELIANISM Understood as a collection of philosophical doctrines and a certain attitude towards philosophical enquiry derived from the Greek philosopher Aristotle (384–322 BC), Aristotelianism is usually contrasted with PLATONISM. Platonists assert the substantial reality of certain abstract ideas. Immaterial and changeless, these ideas are the only things with definite existence, the only things that can be truly known. Philosophy begins with the contingent and the material, but ascends to the necessary and the ideal, to the objects of certain knowledge. Its enquiries are thus more idealist than empirical, more speculative than practical. Aristotelians, by contrast, deny the independent existence of ideal form. Forms are always united with matter; a substance is nothing but this union. Matter accounts for change and individuation among substances; form guarantees their specific constancy and their rational intelligibility. Substances are known as their forms are grasped in thought. Philosophy begins with wonder about the things of this world, but also about human action and community, and then proceeds to reflection on causes that explain. Aristotelian enquiry thus tends to be this-worldly and practical. Speculation about transcendent things, while not shunned altogether, is reserved for the few at the close of the day.

In the modern period, 'Aristotelianism' is more a term of academic art than a name for the tradition inspired by Aristotle. This use of the term became prominent in ENLIGHTENMENT histories of philosophy where the traditions of the ancient schools were reduced to discrete philosophical positions – 'isms' of the now familiar sort. Polemical motives accounted for both the typology that emerged and for the tales that followed in turn. In the standard story, Aristotelianism broke in important ways with Platonism, was abandoned by Stoicism, corrupted by SCHOLASTICISM, and opposed by medieval Augustinianism. It was eventually revived by Renaissance HUMANISM, only to be denounced by PROTESTANTISM and eventually abandoned by CARTESIANISM and the new science. But this tale and these terms have never been very useful. One can not reduce philosophy to ideology and real philosophers to stock characters without distorting the relations of authority and influence that have actually obtained between concrete figures and texts. Far better, then, to ignore what the textbooks and the histories say and ask instead about the reception of Aristotle's texts, concepts, and distinctions in subsequent times and places. How were his efforts used by this theologian or that philosopher? Were they given independent standing or were they situated among other authorities and adapted to new purposes? Were his assumptions and conclusions inherited or only his vocabulary and distinctions? Was he used to address questions that he also shared (or at least might have) or was he asked to weigh in on matters that he could not imagine? Ask questions like these and the list of those we count among the Aristotelians becomes suddenly unfamiliar, as does their supposed 'Aristotelianism'.

One example should suffice. Mention Aristotelianism in Christian theology and many think of the thirteenth-century debate on a variety of topics between radicals (such as Siger of Brabant, *ca* 1240–*ca* 1285) and moderates (principally T. AQUINAS), with both sides pitted against the Augustinians (Bonaventure (1221–74) among others). But attend to the philosophical vocabularies employed in these debates and assess the authority given to Aristotle's actual views, and the historical tale can no longer be told in quite the same way. Consider, for example, the question of the will's relation to the intellect. In the standard story, the Augustinians opposed Aquinas' Aristotelianism precisely because it gave the intellect determinate authority over the will's acts. If the will desires only what the intellect has judged good, and if the intellect compels our willing when it judges some good best, then how can the will's acts be genuinely free? More, how can VIRTUE, which assumes freedom, reside in a power whose acts are determined by another, by the intellect's judgement about the good? And if the will's acts are always subsequent to that judgement, then how can we avoid reducing SIN to ignorance, to mere cognitive confusion about the good? Whither then the perverse will in the Christian drama of salvation?

This position was indeed assigned to Aquinas, and these anxieties were certainly expressed by his critics, and yet it is difficult to capture this debate in a tidy typology of Aristotelian intellectualists versus Augustinian voluntarists. In fact, with the exception of P. Olivi (1248–98), Aquinas' 'Augustinian' critics were all committed 'Aristotelians'. Walter of Bruges (d. 1307), W. de La Mare (*fl.* 1275), and R. Middleton (1249–1302) all employed terms and distinctions borrowed from Aristotle's ethics. All hoped to reconcile that vocabulary with their Augustinian commitments and all assumed they would succeed, that they could use that vocabulary to spell out those commitments. None doubted that Aristotle opposed the independence of the will or its primacy among the sources of human action. Rather, their complaint was with Aquinas, whom they accused of distorting Aristotle's ethics and defending a moral psychology at odds with their shared biblical and patristic inheritance.

Aquinas also used an Aristotelian vocabulary to explicate the GOSPEL, but he doubted its ability to account for an independent will and he doubted the necessity of an independent will to account for most of the things that human beings do. Most human actions can be explained by assuming that judgement precedes desire, and most of our moral failings can be assigned to judgement gone bad. In this, Aquinas followed Aristotle, or so he assumed. What remained was to account for Adam's FALL and our occasional perversity, and for this Aquinas changed vocabularies. He set aside Aristotle and borrowed from AUGUSTINE. So goes the opposition between 'Aristotelianism' and 'Augustinianism' in thirteenth-century ethics. Aquinas' Augustinian opponents defended Aristotle, and Aquinas, the Aristotelian, was an occasional Augustinian. Today we face a revival of Aristotelianism in the ethics of A. MacIntyre (b. 1929) and others, and one suspects that a similar complexity accompanies its return.

J. Bowlin, 'Psychology and Theodicy in Aquinas', *Medieval Philosophy and Theology* 7 (1998), 129–56.

M. Jordan, *The Alleged Aristotelianism of Thomas Aquinas* (Pontifical Institute of Medieval Studies, 1992).

B. Kent, *Virtues of the Will* (Catholic University of America Press, 1995).

A. MacIntyre, *After Virtue* (University of Notre Dame Press, 1981).

JOHN BOWLIN

ARMENIAN THEOLOGY Armenian Christianity gradually developed a highly distinctive form of theology out of its patristic matrix, significantly impacted by its geopolitical setting between the powers of Rome and Persia and their contrasting orthodoxies. Moreover, the Armenian people's tempestuous history was marked by an ongoing state of religious PLURALISM, resulting in the prominence of the genre of APOLOGETICS in defence of its characteristic tenets and liturgical practices. The centrifugal nature of Armenian society facilitated religious pluriformity; but a large number of texts, particularly for the later period, remain unpublished or lack critical editions, while relatively few sources overall are available in translation. Furthermore, texts promoting heterodox positions (e.g., those of the dualist Paulicians and Tondrakites) are usually preserved in only fragmentary condition. Traditionally, Armenian theology has been analyzed in terms of its continuing opposition to CHALCEDON, but arguably much more significant is its DOCTRINE of the incorruptibility of Christ's flesh.

Armenian theological writing emerged in the early fifth century, during which a rich library of Greek and Syriac patristic authorities and Greek philosophers was translated into Armenian. Greater Armenia had been represented at NICAEA, the canons of which remained for Armenians a primary standard of ORTHODOXY. After overcoming the Arian threat (see ARIAN CONTROVERSY), Armenian theology maintained a close affinity with the schools of Edessa and Antioch, and the suspicion of ALLEGORY associated with Antioch informed the early Armenian version of SCRIPTURE. However, under the influence of the Tome of Proclus (437) and other correspondence, it witnessed a gradual realignment towards the miaphysite theology associated with Alexandria (see MIAPHYSITISM), as manifest in the acceptance of the Henotikon at a synod in *ca* 500. The discussion of Chalcedonian Christology in Armenia from then until the 690s was framed by the anti-dualist context of relations with Zoroastrianism and the Nestorian Church in Persia (see NESTORIANISM), and by increasing contacts with the West Syrian (Jacobite) miaphysite Churches, by which the works of Timothy Aelurus (d. 477) and Philoxenus of Mabbug (d. 523) were transmitted to the Armenians.

The period between the sixth and the eighth century witnessed the anthropological debate between Severus of Antioch (*ca* 465–*ca* 540) and Julian of Halicarnassus (*fl.* 515) over the incorruptibility of Christ's flesh, in which their competing understanding of the effects of the FALL played a decisive role. Both sides found Armenian support, the Julianist Y. Mayragomec'i (*ca* 575–*ca* 640), whose circle produced the florilegium known as the *Root of Faith*, being especially extreme. He affirmed that in the INCARNATION Christ's nature remains purely divine, while the flesh he adopts through the VIRGIN BIRTH, escaping the corruption of human nature transmitted through carnal union, is only in the likeness of Adam. Hence, Christ's passions are voluntary, not 'natural'. These views then undergo systematic refutation by the theologians T. K'rt'enawor (*ca* 600–*ca* 675), Y. Ōjnec'i (*ca* 650–728), and X. T'argmanič' (*ca* 670–*ca* 730). Impugning Mayragomec'i's followers as proponents of APHTHARTODOCETISM, these latter theologians maintain that postlapsarian human nature is not per se corrupt, and that the passions are seminal to moral growth, thereby upholding Christ's consubstantiality with humankind and identifying the locus of SIN as the will. T'argmanič' in particular argued cogently against a narrow focus on Christ's flesh in isolation. Instead, he insisted that incorruptibility should be posed of Christ's synthetic nature within the union. Thus, he could assent to the passibility and mortality of Christ's flesh in itself and yet propose that through *COMMUNICATIO IDIOMATUM* the divine prevented the human from falling into sin, and hence preserved it from suffering corruption and death. He thus underscored the probity of affirming the incorruptibility of Christ's flesh from conception (and not merely after the RESURRECTION, as Severus had taught), while avoiding the charge of EUTYCHIANISM that had been applied to Julian. Subsequent theologians like P. Tarōnac'i (*ca* 1050–1123), Y. Sarkawag (*ca* 1050–1129), V. Aygekc'i (*ca* 1170–1235), and S. Ōrpēlian (*ca* 1260–1304) integrate this teaching symbolically with the unique Armenian practice of celebrating the EUCHARIST with the unmixed cup and unleavened bread, averring that adding water to wine results in vinegar and leaven leads to mold, both images of fleshly corruption.

M. Aramian, 'Yovhannēs Sarkawag's "Concerning the Symbol of Faith of the Three Hundred and Eighteen at the Council of Nicaea"', *St. Nersess Theological Review* 4 (1999), 1–32.

N. G. Garsoïan, *L'eglise arménienne et le grand schisme d'Orient* (Peeters, 1999).

S. PETER COWE

ARMINIANISM 'Arminianism' is the term used to identify a strain of Protestant thought that, contrary to Reformed ORTHODOXY defined at the Synod of DORT, emphasizes the grace-enabled free will of human beings for co-operation with saving GRACE for salvation. Some scholars consider Arminianism a branch of REFORMED THEOLOGY while others regard it as a full-blown alternative to Reformed theology.

The term derives from the Latinized name of Dutch minister and theologian Jacob Harmenszoon: Jacob Arminius (1559–1609). Arminius was not the first to teach the DOCTRINES associated with his name. One can find similar ideas in the early Lutheran theologian P. Melanchthon (1497–1560) and in the theologies of most Anabaptists such as B. Hubmaier (1480–1528) and M. Simons (1496–1561).

Debate surrounds the question of the 'essence' of Arminianism. Is it a humanistic belief in free will injected into an otherwise Protestant framework? Or is it a revival of the ancient heresies of PELAGIANISM and semi-Pelagianism, with their emphasis on good works? Or is it a concern for the character of God as perfectly good to the exclusion of any shadow of evil, as Arminians themselves insist?

Arminius was born into a respected family in the United Provinces (the present-day Netherlands). His family was slaughtered by the Spanish occupiers while he was away studying in another country. He completed his theological curriculum under J. CALVIN's successor in Geneva, T. Beza (1519–1605). Much controversy surrounds whether Arminius was a faithful follower of Beza until later, or whether he never fully subscribed to Beza's supralapsarian beliefs about the decrees of God (see INFRALAPSARIANISM AND SUPRALAPSARIANISM).

After completing his education in 1583, Arminius became in 1588 minister of a Reformed congregation in Amsterdam, where he distinguished himself for his piety, preaching, and pastoral care. In 1603 he was appointed professor of theology at the Reformed University of Leiden, where he fell into conflict with the other leading theologian, F. Gomarus (1563–1641). Gomarus was a supralapsarian and passionate advocate of the doctrine of unconditional predestination.

From 1603 until his untimely death of tuberculosis in 1609, Arminius was engaged in a heated dispute involving an inter-related set of doctrines: total depravity, unconditional election, limited atonement, irresistible grace, and perseverance of the saints. Arminius did not dispute total depravity and never entirely settled his mind about the perseverance of the saints. He was especially concerned to refute unconditional election of individuals to salvation or reprobation, limited or particular atonement, and irresistible grace.

Arminius was a prolific author whose published works fill three large volumes in English translation (*The Works of Arminius*, published in various editions over the centuries). Many of his sermons, essays, and treatises were never translated into English but remain in Latin and/or Dutch. He was a Scholastic thinker who relied heavily on logic to resolve theological conundrums. Because of his Scholasticism he was sometimes accused by his enemies of secret Catholic sympathies. He believed that the disputed doctrines were not necessary aspects of Reformed orthodoxy and worked tirelessly to demonstrate that one can be fully Reformed and believe in the freedom of the will enabled by God's prevenient grace.

There is very little doubt that Arminius was thoroughly orthodox on matters of classical Christian dogma such as the Trinity and the person and work of Jesus Christ (see Christology). He held to the satisfaction theory of the atonement, whereas some of his followers developed the so-called governmental theory. Arminius himself adhered to the Nicene Creed, the Chalcedonian Definition (see Chalcedon, Council of) and the Heidelberg Catechism (which was in his day the official confessional standard of Dutch orthodoxy).

Arminius' main works that spell out his theological views contrary to high Calvinism are: 'Declaration of Sentiments' (1608), 'A Letter Addressed to Hippolytus a Collibus' (1608), and 'An Examination of the Treatise of William Perkins Concerning the Order and Mode of Predestination'. In these and dozens of other essays, Arminius explicated and defended his belief that God limits divine sovereignty so as to be in no way responsible for evil or sin, and that predestination is based on God's foreknowledge of persons' faith and not vice versa.

The burden of Arminius' theological project was to protect and defend the character of God as love. Thus, he rejected limited atonement as well as unconditional election and irresistible grace. His key distinctive doctrine was prevenient grace as enabling the will, which voids the accusation that he was a semi-Pelagian who believed that the human will could initiate movement towards God by its own efforts. For him and all Arminians since, a free decision to accept the grace of God to salvation is possible for the fallen sinner only because of God's assisting grace empowering (but not bypassing) the will.

After Arminius died in 1609 his followers became known as the Remonstrants because of a document they promulgated known as the 'Remonstrance'. It affirmed the theology of Arminius and protested against the hegemony of high Calvinism within the Reformed Churches of the United Provinces. The leading Remonstrant was S. Episcopius (1583–1643), who wrote a lengthy and definitive account of Remonstrant theology in 1521 and became the principal of the Remonstrant Seminary in Holland.

The Remonstrants were tried as heretics at the Synod of Dort. Arminians generally consider this to have been a kangaroo court, because the accused were not allowed to defend themselves publicly during the trial. The Synod produced the canons which sought to refute Arminianism as heresy. The leading Remonstrants were banished from the United Provinces by the anti-Arminian ruler Prince Maurice of Nassau (r. 1618–25), but they returned as soon as he died. The contemporary Remonstrant Brotherhood is the descendant denomination of the Remonstrants and is a full charter member of the World Alliance of Reformed Churches. Arminianism subsequently spread from Holland to England and then to America and found acceptance in some quarters of the Church of England, in Methodism (J. Wesley was a passionate Arminian), among the General Baptists, and, later, among Pentecostals.

Beyond basic Protestant teaching, the hallmarks of Arminianism include belief in the grace-enabled free will of humans, the affirmation of the universal atonement of Christ, and confession of predestination as God's foreknowledge (rather than predetermination) of faith.

See also Baptist Theology; Methodist Theology; Pentecostal Theology.

C. Bangs, *Arminius: A Study in the Dutch Reformation* (Abingdon Press, 1971).

R. E. Olson, *Arminian Theology: Myths and Realities* (InterVarsity Press, 2006).

Roger E. Olson

Ascension and Session The Nicene Creed asserts that Jesus 'ascended into heaven and is seated at the right hand of the Father' (*ascendit in coelum, sedet ad dexteram Patris*). This reflects the narrative of Luke 24:50 and Acts 1:9–11, but also the theology of John 20:17, Acts 2:22–36, Philippians 2:9–11, Ephesians 1:15–23,

Hebrews 1:3, 1 Peter 3:22, Revelation 1:12–16, and numerous other NT passages that portray Jesus as having been exalted to the highest heaven.

The feast of the ascension entered the Christian calendar in the fourth century, though the ascension is said to have been celebrated on the Mount of Olives from early times. Ancient sermons, hymns, and liturgical prayers interpret the feast along the following lines: 'Thou, O God, didst on this day raise up, together with thyself, above all Principalities and Powers, the nature of Adam, which had fallen into the deep abyss, but which was restored by thee. Because thou lovedst it, thou placedst it on thine own throne; because thou hadst pity on it, thou unitedst it to thyself; because thou hadst thus united it, thou didst suffer with it; because thou, the impassible, didst thus suffer, thou gave it to share in thy glory' (*In Assumptione Domini, ad Vesperas*). This is in keeping with the rule of faith articulated by Irenaeus, who speaks of 'the ascension into heaven in the flesh of the beloved Christ Jesus our Lord', deploying this doctrine in anti-Gnostic fashion to emphasize the completion in Christ of the Creator's original plan and purpose for humanity, which is destined to ascend with him, 'passing beyond the angels and being made after the image and likeness of God' (*AH* 1.10.1, 5.36.3).

In the NT the ascension is already tied to the OT narrative of descent and ascent, exile and restoration, in which humanity, represented by the covenant people, retreat or advance in proximity to the promise of true fellowship with the living God. Jesus is depicted in his descent to the dead as retracing that journey, and in his ascent into heaven as attaining to the promise once and for all; hence as receiving both the priestly and the kingly power to effect the arrival of his people at the same goal (cf. Ps. 110, Dan. 7). Acts, Ephesians, Hebrews, and Revelation all undertake to expound that power, deploying Melchizedekian, Mosaic, Aaronic, and Davidic motifs to interpret the ascension and session for the life and ministry of the Church. Still more fundamentally, the NT connects the presence of Jesus in heaven with the bestowal of the Holy Spirit and so with the creation of the Church as the new covenant people. Jesus' ascension into heaven is the precondition of Pentecost and so of the Church.

But what does it mean to ascend into heaven? Just as in the Apostles' Creed *descendit ad inferna* indicates an alteration (through death) of condition and association, so also does *ascendit ad coelos*. To ascend into heaven is to begin to live in the immediate presence of the Father and as a full participant in the Spirit of glory. Where the body is concerned, we should think neither of a movement within time and space, nor yet (since resurrection precedes ascension) of an abandonment of time and space. We should think instead (though for us it cannot be entirely thinkable) of a transformation that generates the new creation; which means also the reorganization of heaven to exclude from it all opposition to God's purposes. This is the time and place and mode of existence to which the Eucharist gives provisional access, and to which the righteous dead are also made privy, until it is revealed openly at the parousia and unfolded in the renewal of all things (cf. Irenaeus, *AH* 5.2.3).

On the ascension and heavenly session rest the saeculum, the sacraments, the spiritual life, and salvation. The saeculum (or present age) receives its character as an age of grace in virtue of the fact that Christ has presented himself before the Father on humankind's behalf, with a view to the formation, growth, witness, and fullness of his ecclesial body. It also becomes a time of testing and choosing, for the mystery of lawlessness takes shape in the saeculum as a shadow cast by the reign of Christ, in so far as that reign is rejected on earth under the influence of the Devil, who is cast down from heaven in the purification effected by the ascension (Rev. 12; cf. 2 Thess. 2). The saeculum is thus bracketed by the ascension and the parousia as an age both of grace and of the refusal of grace.

The sacraments, in turn, are the means of grace determined for the Church in the saeculum in order to unite it to its head and to give it its catholic character; that is, its ability to reach into every human sphere with every kind of healing for mind, soul, body, and society (Cyril of Jerusalem, *CO* 18.23). The Eucharist in particular enables participation in the heavenly offering of Christ to the Father, on account of which judgement is suspended and the eschaton is both delayed and brought near.

The spiritual life is sustained by the ascension because it depends, as for Mary, on the grace that 'made us alive together with Christ . . . and made us sit with him in the heavenly places' (Eph. 2:5–6; cf. Pius IX, *Ineffabilis*). The liturgy itself follows the pattern of the ascension, the Spirit leading human beings to the Son, and the Son presenting them to the Father, who causes them to possess immortality (Irenaeus, *Dem.* 6–7). Moreover, the spiritual life is nourished by the resources of the *communio sanctorum*, in which the martyrs are pre-eminent in as much as the sprinkling of their blood upon the earth testifies to the offering being presented in heaven (cf. Heb. 9–12).

Salvation derives from the ascension since Christ's 'very showing of himself in the human nature which he took with him to heaven is a pleading for us' (Aquinas, *ST* 3.57.6); and because the 'one-ing' of God and humankind that is the goal of the incarnation is grounded in that way. For 'in him and by him we are mightily taken out of hell and out of the misery on earth, and honorably brought up into heaven and full blessedly one-ed to our essence, increased in riches and nobility, by all the virtue of Christ and by the grace and action of the Holy Spirit' (Julian, *Show.*, §58).

Because ascension, in other words, is ATONEMENT, both as saving grace and as perfecting grace. It is the foundation of that DEIFICATION of human beings for which the whole creation has been waiting. For the Son who goes to the Father prepares a place with the Father for those from whom he has gone (John 14:1–14; cf. 2:1–12).

Theologically, the most decisive issue in the treatment of the ascension and session of Christ is that of the controlling narrative. Where the biblical narrative controls, the doctrine moves along the lines indicated above: man, the whole man – the same indeed who walked the *via crucis* – hears the upward call into the presence of God. By contrast, when theological reflection begins with cosmological and soteriological preconceptions that deny to the whole human being the upward call, ascension in the flesh is forsaken for ascension of the mind only. If this does not lead to the GNOSTICISM with which Irenaeus battled, it leads nevertheless to an immanentism in which ascension and session begin to be viewed as functions of private spirituality on the one hand, and of universal history on the other; that is, as movements of the individual or collective mind in a process of self-deification. The traditional DOCTRINE forbids this mythological turn, and rejects the censorship of the human at which such alternative narratives sooner or later arrive.

J. G. Davies, *He Ascended into Heaven: A Study in the History of Doctrine* (Lutterworth Press, 1958).
D. Farrow, *Ascension and Ecclesia* (T&T Clark, 1999).
Ascension Theology (T&T Clark, 2011).
P. Guéranger, *The Liturgical Year: Pascal Time*, vol. III (French edn, 1871; St Austin Press, 2000), 167–265.

DOUGLAS FARROW

ASCETICISM Asceticism, from the Greek *askēsis*, denotes religious practices of self-discipline and self-mortification, such as FASTING, chastity, vigils, POVERTY, PRAYER, and manual labour. It has formed a central component of Christian religious practice and theology since the first century.

Literary theorists, philosophers, and historians of religion have conceptualized asceticism in a variety of influential ways. M. Foucault (1926–84) has characterized asceticism far more broadly than traditional students of Christian thought had, as the 'training of the self by the self' (*Care* 235). Literary theorist G. G. Harpham (b. 1946) has described asceticism even more broadly as the very core of culture, the underlying master code, 'the "cultural" element in culture' in fact, that allows the sub-routines of culture to function, and allows cultures to be compared (*Ascetic* xi). R. Valantasis (b. 1946) has presented asceticism as 'performances designed to inaugurate an alternative culture, to enable different social relations, and to create a new identity' ('Theory', 548). Each of these influential theorists has presented asceticism in a more self-conscious and reflective vocabulary that in important ways elucidates the social and psychological processes and forces that lie at the heart of asceticism. At the same time, these expansive definitions run the risk of construing asceticism so broadly as to render it almost coterminous with basic socialization. Within the context of recent theorization of asceticism, more phenomenological approaches still have use for historians and theologians.

Christian asceticism drew on Greek and Roman antecedents in developing a distinctive theory and practice of religious asceticism, as the pre-Christian Greek etymology of the term 'asceticism' entails. The earliest usages convey a semantics of athletic training and self-discipline rather than religious transcendence, but by the early Christian era the Mediterranean world (at least the literate class) was unified in commonplace medical-philosophical assumptions about the centrality of ascetic self-control for bodily health and philosophical advancement. While frequently differing in details and emphases, educated Greeks and Romans tended to agree that a regimen of self-training through sexual self-control (and sometimes enduring CELIBACY) and regulated diet formed a necessary component of civilized existence and a prerequisite for philosophical attainment.

The diversity of early Christian attitudes towards asceticism is especially evident in attitudes towards sex and diet. Some Christians displayed clear inclinations to integrate Christian communities with the moderate model of household asceticism (e.g., the Pastoral Epistles), while others advocated a strict asceticism, rejecting societal imperatives to marriage and childbirth, as well as such dietary commonplaces as wine and meat. While sometimes such Christian asceticism was rooted in a theological dualism that was rejected by the wider Church (e.g., followers of MARCION), the influential ascetic theology and lifestyle of ORIGEN, for example, demonstrates the debt that proto-orthodox Christianity owed to this strict, distinctively Christian asceticism.

In the course of the fourth century, ascetics would organize themselves in a variety of more formal institutions, including urban ascetics living itinerantly or as cloistered virgins, ascetically married couples, hermits living at the edges of villages, and – later – desert anchorites, who were as much a theological ideal as a social reality. A form of eremitical (i.e., reclusive) MONASTICISM emerged in organized form on the western outskirts of the Nile delta, characterized by a federation of small cells, each of which could house a master and one or more disciples. Cenobitic life, which may be traced to the foundations of Pachomius (*ca* 290–346) in upper Egypt, was characterized by walled separation from non-monastic society and a uniform regimen of communal work, prayer, and eating. Yet it is important to recognize that such distinctions are ideal types.

Organized ascetic behaviour fell on a continuum, and some communities included ascetics of different lifestyles. Regardless of social structure, early Christian monasticism was generally unified in its insistence on simplicity of life, ascetic regimen, and obedience to a spiritual director, ideals that would have an enduring influence on Christian theological traditions in the East and the West through such foundational works as the *Rule* of Benedict of Nursia (480–547).

At the core of early monastic theological reflection on asceticism is the understanding that Christian asceticism rectifies or heals the effects of the FALL, thus returning the body and mind to a prelapsarian state of unity. Early Christian ascetic literature is replete with such protological theology, reflected, for example, in the *Letters* of Antony (251–356), the *Asketikon* of Isaiah of Scetis (d. 489), and the burgeoning hagiographical literature in the wake of ATHANASIUS' *Life of Antony.*

Recent scholarship has recognized the theological diversity of the ascetic tradition in early Christian monasticism, complicating the traditional characterization of monasticism as the refuge of simple-hearted, unlettered saints. Emblematic of this shift is the recognition of the important enduring legacy of Origenist theology in Christian asceticism (see ORIGENISM), especially mediated by the theological works of Evagrius of Pontus (344–99). While anathematized with Origen posthumously, Evagrius' ascetic theology would influence Christian theology far and wide, not only in the Church of the East (where he was not condemned), but through ascetic theologians in the Greek and Latin Churches as well. Through his disciple J. Cassian (*ca* 360–*ca* 435), for example, Evagrius' foundational template for spiritual direction, the eight evil thoughts, was transmitted into the Latin theological and disciplinary tradition, to become the western tradition of the SEVEN DEADLY SINS under the influence of Pope Gregory I ('the Great', r. 590–604). Along with other, less theologically suspect traditions like Benedict's *Rule*, the theological traditions of early Christian monasticism left an enduring – though at times hotly disputed – legacy on the history of Christian thought and practice.

O. Freiberger, ed., *Asceticism and Its Critics: Historical Accounts and Comparative Perspectives* (AAR, 2006).

J. E. Goehring, *Ascetics, Society, and the Desert* (Trinity Press International, 2002).

G. G. Harpham, *The Ascetic Imperative in Culture and Criticism* (University of Chicago Press, 1987).

R. Valantasis and V. L. Wimbush, eds., *Asceticism* (Oxford University Press, 1995).

ANDREW CRISLIP

ASIAN-AMERICAN THEOLOGY 'Asian American' is a shorthand term that covers Pacific Islanders as well as East- and South-Asian Americans. Asian-American theology is theological reflection in the socio-cultural and political context of Asian Americans in the USA. In the 1970s the United Methodist minister, professor, and later bishop R. Sano (b. 1931) and others, working out of the Berkeley California area, compiled and made available to the public theological reflections of Asian-American pastors, theologians, and lay leaders. These compilations were among the very first examples of Asian-American theology to take published form.

Sano called for the liberation of Asian ethnicity from becoming suppressed in the process of Asian Americans' adjustment to American society, culture, and Church life. Sano's and others' main theme was liberation, and they were probably both influenced and encouraged by the liberation movement in Latin America and the Black civil rights movement in the USA (see BLACK THEOLOGY; LATIN AMERICAN THEOLOGY).

About the same time, S. H. Lee (b. 1938), a Korean American theologian, maintained that recently arrived Korean immigrants needed to face up to their newly adopted country in America instead of clinging to their Korean past, especially in their family and Church life. Citing Hebrews 11, Lee challenged Korean immigrants to appropriate the de facto situation of their having left their homeland as a divine calling for them to embark upon a pilgrimage or journey towards the goal of helping to make 'a better country'. Through Lee's writings and speeches Korean immigrant Christians were encouraged through understanding that their very human migration to America can have a theological meaning through a connection with Abraham's pilgrimage in response to God's promise.

In the 1980s and 1990s more Asian-American scholars began to think about exploring theology in an Asian-American context. Most theologians agreed that the Asian-American predicament in the USA was a situation of being 'in-between' Asia and America, as well as one of oppression. Asian-American theologians have embraced the in-between space as a potentially creative place and have called upon Asian-American Christians to use that in-between space as a place of resistance against the racist status quo and also as a place in which a new Christian experience and identity can be forged.

This in-between space is thought of in various ways: 'interstices' (R. N. Brock (b. 1950)), 'holy insecurity' (F. Matsuoka (b. 1943)), 'liminality' (S. H. Lee), and 'abjection' and the 'third space' (W. A. Joh (b. 1966)). For Brock, the divine power enables Asian Americans to maintain an 'integrity' of their interstitiality. For Matsuoka, faith enables Asian Americans to face up to their 'holy insecurity' instead of evading it. For Joh, the power of *jeung* (love) on the CROSS enables one to face one's abjection and to be healed. For Lee, God uses liminal spaces to bring about redeeming communion between God and believers as well as between persons previously alienated from one another.

Drawing on categories associated with LIBERATION THEOLOGY, A. S. Park (b. 1951) has written extensively about how the meaning of the GOSPEL and of salvation as experienced by oppressed people is different from the ways in which they are defined from the oppressors' perspectives. According to Park, forgiveness is for the oppressors, while liberation and healing constitute salvation for the oppressed, thereby pointing to the inadequacy of any one model of redemption to cover every human situation.

S. H. Lee, *The Liminal Christian: An Asian American Theology* (Augsburg Fortress, 2010).

F. Matsuoka, *Out of Silence: Emerging Themes in Asian American Churches* (United Church, 1995).

SANG HYUN LEE

ASSUMPTION In 1950 Pope Pius XII (r. 1939–58) promulgated the papal bull *Munificentissimus Deus*, in which he proclaimed as Catholic dogma the ancient Christian belief that Mary was taken up bodily into heaven at the end of her earthly life: 'the Immaculate Mother of God, the ever Virgin Mary, having completed the course of her earthly life, was assumed body and soul into heavenly glory.' The promulgation of the DOCTRINE makes it incumbent upon Catholics to accept it as divinely revealed truth, though its form leaves open the debated question of whether Mary died or merely fell asleep before being assumed into heaven. Other Churches point to the lack of scriptural support for Pius' claim, although many share the belief as an expression of devotion rather than doctrine. In the joint Anglican and Catholic statement, *Mary: Grace and Hope in Christ* (2005), Anglican contributors express reservations about the dogmatic status of the doctrine, but accept that it is consonant with SCRIPTURE and ancient TRADITION.

The most commonly cited textual evidence of the early devotional tradition is the apocryphal literature known as the *Transitus Mariae*, which may date from the fourth or fifth century, and which survives in numerous translations. More reliable historical evidence of widespread belief in the assumption can be found in sermons by JOHN OF DAMASCUS in the East and by Gregory of Tours (d. 594) in the West. By the late seventh century the assumption had become an established feast day celebrated across the eastern, western and Coptic Churches. It is celebrated on 15 August, and in the Orthodox Church it is known as the Dormition (or the falling asleep) of the Virgin.

Scriptural texts used during the liturgy of the assumption include the reference to the woman clothed with the sun in Revelation 12, references to the RESURRECTION of the dead in 1 Corinthians 15, the story of the visitation in Luke 1, and the reference in Psalm 45 to 'the queen in gold of Ophir' standing at the right hand of the king. The latter reference indicates the close association between the doctrine of the assumption and Mary's title as Queen of Heaven. Many biblical scholars question whether any of these texts can be used to support the assumption, although they have shaped western art as well as devotion in lavish representations of the assumption and the coronation of the Virgin.

There is considerable consistency to the theology of the assumption, in terms of both its historical and its doctrinal significance. Belief in the resurrection of the body is common to all Christians. Mary's bodily assumption is an eschatological sign which is inclusive rather than exclusive – it is not a unique privilege accorded to Mary but a promise given to all who have faith in Christ. Her assumption also symbolizes the efficacy of Christ's saving power: he is indeed the redeemer because at least one is fully redeemed. Moreover, the Catholic doctrine that Mary was conceived without SIN (see IMMACULATE CONCEPTION) is seen by some as entailing her freedom from the power of death, while others argue that the body which bore Christ could not be subject to decay. In proclaiming the dogma soon after World War II, Pius XII made clear that the assumption serves as an affirmation of the eternal destiny of the human BODY and SOUL in an era of catastrophic violence and moral corruption.

In some of the loveliest iconic images of the Dormition, Christ is shown beside Mary's bed, holding her infant soul in his arms, mirroring images of the infant Christ in Mary's arms. It is an image which suggests a maternal encompassing to the incarnation, and a delicate interweaving of themes of earthly birth and heavenly rebirth.

See also MARIOLOGY.

S. Shoemaker, *Ancient Traditions of the Virgin Mary's Dormition and Assumption* (Oxford University Press, 2006).

TINA BEATTIE

ASSURANCE One of the central DOCTRINES of PROTESTANTISM, assurance was the idea that every individual Christian could be certain that God was mercifully disposed towards them and that their salvation was secure. While medieval (and post-medieval) Catholicism regarded the notion as leading to rampant individualism and generative of a presumption that was lethal to the maintenance of the moral imperatives of the Christian life, Protestants from M. LUTHER onwards placed assurance at the centre of Christian life. Indeed, for Luther, the question of certainty was central to his REFORMATION project, as evidenced both in the struggles of his monastic life and, later, in works such as *The Freedom of the Christian* (1520) and *On the Bondage of the Will* (1525). The continuing importance of the notion in Protestantism is epitomized by the first question and answer of the HEIDELBERG CATECHISM. Rooted in the conviction that the promise of salvation was grounded entirely in the trustworthiness of God's promise rather than in human achievement, assurance was closely connected to the idea of JUSTIFICATION by

FAITH and, as such, entailed a fundamental revision of the role of the sacraments, the ministry, and the Church in Christian faith and practice.

In the earlier generations of Reformers, there was a tendency to regard assurance as of the essence of faith. For example, this appears to be the position of J. CALVIN in his *Institutes* (1559). When sermonic and pastoral material is taken into account, however, more nuance appears in their theology, including frequently a practical separation between possession of faith and possession of assurance. By the mid-seventeenth century, such a separation was routine. Arminian strands of Reformed Protestantism (see ARMINIANISM), as well as the more works-oriented modification of justification promoted by figures like R. Baxter (1615–91), led to the development of more legalistic and introspective understandings of assurance, including positions not too dissimilar to those of medieval Catholicism. Even within more mainstream confessional trajectories, the separability of faith and assurance was now acknowledged, as is evidenced by the teaching of the Westminster Confession of Faith (see WESTMINSTER STANDARDS), the autobiographical reflections of J. Bunyan (1628–88), and numerous texts on how to solve the problem of lack of assurance. Some have argued that this separation was the result of a doctrinal hardening, with later (particularly Reformed) Protestants emphasizing PREDESTINATION and LIMITED ATONEMENT in a way that led to introspection and a constant quest for so-called signs of ELECTION, which were necessary prior to an assured conscience. According to this perspective, this understanding of predestination and atonement helped facilitate in the mid-seventeenth century the theological reaction of Amyraldianism, which sought to ease believers' anxiety regarding God's disposition towards them by an emphasis upon universal atonement. Likewise, the thesis that the Reformed doctrine of election produced an anxious, introspective tendency had a profound influence on M. Weber (1864–1920), who saw in the tension between belief in predestination and the quest for assurance a primary dynamic in the rise of capitalism.

One area where later Protestant theology deviated significantly from earlier forms was in the role of the sacraments as means or aids to strengthen assurance. When Luther was tempted by the DEVIL, he would cry that he had been baptized, thus rooting his status before God in the sacrament as grasped by faith. The theology of the Reformed confessions (including the Anglican Thirty-Nine Articles) also reflected in various ways an emphasis upon BAPTISM and the EUCHARIST as part of the assured Christian life, though this emphasis declined dramatically in the later seventeenth century and still further with the advent of evangelicalism in the eighteenth.

In accounting for such changes, the best approach may be to recognize that the *problem* of assurance was only possible once the question had been raised – and that the question only emerged in problematic form (viz., 'How do I know that I am saved?') among later generations of Protestants. Thus, the novelty of the question, combined with the dramatic social and economic changes in western Europe from the late sixteenth to the seventeenth century (involving the rise of cities, the breakdown of rural life, and the transformation of the political map), inevitably generated new pastoral issues, which, in turn, could only be addressed by way of significant revision of earlier emphases. Such an interpretation, according to which attempts to distinguish between assurance and faith are seen as a product of serious efforts to interpret doctrine faithfully in light of changing circumstances rather than as a sign of dogmatic rigidity, may provide a more holistic, contextual understanding of the question of assurance in Protestant thought than the more purely doctrinal readings developed by an earlier generation of scholarship and appropriated by Weber.

See also PRACTICAL SYLLOGISM.

J. R. Beeke, *Assurance of Faith: Calvin, English Puritanism, and the Dutch Second Reformation* (Peter Lang, 1991).

R. C. Zachman, *The Assurance of Faith: Conscience in the Theology of Martin Luther and John Calvin* (John Knox Press, 2005).

CARL R. TRUEMAN

ATHANASIAN CREED Also known as the *Quicunque vult* after the first two words of the Latin original, the Athanasian Creed is commonly counted as one of the three great ecumenical CREEDS, though it has never secured the liturgical prominence of the APOSTLES' or the NICENE CREEDS, and its inclusion of the *FILIOQUE* has complicated its reception in the Orthodox Churches. The ascription of the Creed to ATHANASIUS is universally rejected, both because it was originally written in Latin and because its theology reflects much later (and distinctively western) forms of expression. Still, it retains a place in the Catholic daily OFFICE, is included in the Lutheran BOOK OF CONCORD and the Anglican BOOK OF COMMON PRAYER, and was approved by the Reformed Synod of DORT.

The influence of AUGUSTINE is especially clear in the Creed's Trinitarian theology, and parallels with other writers – particularly Vincent of Lérins (*ca* 400–*ca* 450) – suggest that the text originated in what is now southern France in the late fifth or early sixth century. Notwithstanding the severity of the Creed's opening and closing clauses (which declare that salvation is conditional on belief in its contents), the overall tone is catechetical rather than polemical. Though the tenets of MODALISM, ARIANISM, APOLLINARIANISM, and NESTORIANISM are clearly rejected, none is mentioned by name, and the carefully balanced phrasing of the Creed's forty-two clauses suggests that its primary purpose was summary exposition of the doctrines of the TRINITY and the INCARNATION, probably for the benefit of clergy in particular.

J. N. D. Kelly, *The Athanasian Creed* (Harper & Row, 1964).

IAN A. MCFARLAND

ATHANASIUS OF ALEXANDRIA Known as the principal opponent of subordinationist theology in the decades following the Council of NICAEA, Athanasius (*ca* 290–373) had a tumultuous career from the time he assumed the office of bishop of Alexandria in 328 until his death. Exiled from his see no fewer than five times (from 335 to 337, 339 to 346, 356 to 361, 362 to 363, and 365 to 366) as the result of the varied theological sympathies of successive emperors, Athanasius remained popular in Alexandria and, in spite of numerous setbacks, had by the time of his death made significant progress in forging a broad coalition of bishops across the empire willing to accept the Nicene confession of the Son as HOMOOUSIOS ('of the same substance') with the Father, thereby laying the political and theological groundwork for later Trinitarian DOCTRINE.

Athanasius appears to have been present at Nicaea as a deacon of the Church of Alexandria, accompanying Bishop Alexander, whose conflict with the presbyter Arius over the divinity of the Son or Word of God (see *LOGOS*) had occasioned the crisis that led to the summoning of the council (see ARIAN CONTROVERSY). Though Athanasius' contributions would prove decisive for later Trinitarian metaphysics, his early theology largely echoes Alexander's position (viz., that the Son shares the Father's eternity and immutability) and as yet lacks the technical theological vocabulary needed to clarify the relationship between Father and Son. Only at the end of the 330s (in his *Orations against the Arians*) does he begin to define his own position in opposition to a putatively well-defined group of 'Arian' theologians and, correspondingly, to make adherence to Nicaea the touchstone of ORTHODOXY.

Athanasius' 'Arians' were a rhetorical construct, representing a range of longstanding theological views that owed little if anything to Arius, but whose proponents were all worried that Athanasius' theology so elided the distinction between Father and Son as to result in a kind of modalism. For his part, Athanasius was eager to tar his opponents indiscriminately with the name of Arius for their failure to acknowledge the Son as eternal corollary to the Father. Even so, the term *homoousios* played little role in his polemics prior to his treatise *On the Decrees of Nicaea* in the early to mid-350s. At this point it acquires prominence as part of a theological strategy to secure the uniqueness of the Son's relationship to the Father: whereas all creatures were made by the Father, the Son was begotten (and therefore not a creature). Particularly in the face of theologies that argued that the Son was *unlike* the Father in substance, many found sympathy for this position, though it left unaddressed the chief difficulty many bishops had with Athanasius' position: his lack of a clear terminology for specifying the Son's distinction from the Father. Athanasius himself never fully resolved this problem, but by the early 360s he was willing to allow that fidelity to Nicaea was not inconsistent with the designation of Father and Son as distinct HYPOSTASES – a compromise that would later shape the orthodox doctrine of the TRINITY.

Though most widely known for his defence of the full divinity of the Son, his letters (*ca* 360) to Serapion, bishop of Thmuis (*fl.* 350), also helped lay the groundwork for the later Trinitarian theology of the HOLY SPIRIT. Against claims that the Spirit is a creature, Athanasius deployed many of the same sorts of arguments honed in his defence of the Son's divinity. For example, he averred that the Spirit's work is inseparable from that of the Son in the same way that the Son's is inseparable from the Father's, thereby emphasizing the equal divinity of the three by reference to the inseparability of their operations.

K. Anatolios, *Athanasius: The Coherence of His Thought* (Routledge, 1998).

IAN A. MCFARLAND

ATHEISM Within a specifically theological context, atheism may be understood as the absence of belief in the God of the Abrahamic monotheisms, i.e., a personal Creator, Lawgiver, Righteous Judge, and Merciful Saviour. To call God personal is to say that God is an agent and not just a cause, that God performs speech acts such as promises and commands, and that God is, among other things, capable of justice, mercy, and love.

Five types of atheism can be distinguished, two of them pre-theoretical and three theoretical or philosophical. The first occurs in lives from whom God, as described above, is simply missing but without much if any notice of that fact being taken. This atheist has no occasion to say, 'I am an atheist.' The second kind of atheism differs from the first only in being more reflective. Without theorizing in any formal or disciplined way, the atheist does find occasions to say, 'I am an atheist' or 'I don't believe in God.'

Like the second kind of atheism, the third is consciously affirmed, but for overtly theoretical reasons. It can be called 'evidential atheism' because those reasons consist either in saying, 'There is sufficient evidence, such as the nature and amount of evil and suffering in the world, to warrant denying the reality of God', or 'There is insufficient evidence to make it rational to believe in God.' The former concerns the truth of theistic belief, the latter its rationality. A witticism of Bertrand Russell expresses the evidentialist attitude clearly. When asked what he would say if some day he encountered God, who asked, 'Why did not you believe in me?' Russell said he would reply, 'Not enough evidence, God. Not enough evidence.'

Evidential atheism is linked to the inter-related rise of metaphysical scepticism and scientism in the modern period. When D. Hume (1711–76) and I. KANT published their powerful critiques of the traditional proofs for the existence of God, some concluded either that it was no longer rational to believe in God, absent this evidence, or even that such belief could now be seen to be simply false.

Evidential atheism is also linked to scientism, or the belief that only the natural sciences can tell us about the ultimate nature of reality. The emergence of this movement was spurred by the impressive results of modern (astro)physics from G. Galilei (1564–1642) to A. Einstein (1879–1955), as well as of evolutionary biology from C. Darwin (1809–82) to R. Dawkins (b. 1941). Metaphysical scepticism provided a hospitable environment for the growth of scientism: metaphysics (in some forms) pointed to God, but was not genuine knowledge; science was genuine knowledge but, far from providing compelling evidence of God's reality, suggested instead alternative (viz., purely materialist) explanations of the world. At the same time, scientism must address questions of self-reference, since the claim that only science can tell us the ultimate nature of reality is not itself a scientific claim.

In the fourth place there is the atheism of Sartre. Like Spinoza before him, Sartre does not discuss the evidence for or against the reality of a personal God. One could say that he simply postulates atheism, but that would not quite be fair. What he does is present an analysis of human life from which God is absent by definition; in other words, God is conceptually impossible, except for the fact that in each of us humans is the tragic and futile desire to be God ourselves. This suggests that the question of God's reality may be less like the question, 'Is there a kangaroo in the warehouse somewhere?' than like the question, 'Which overall story about the world and our life in it makes the most sense?'

Finally there is the atheism of suspicion. It is associated with K. Marx (1818–83), F. NIETZSCHE, and S. Freud (1856–1939). Since the middle of the nineteenth century it may well have been the most popular and influential form of theoretical atheism. The attack on theistic belief is not directed towards the evidence supporting the truth or rationality of such belief, but rather to the integrity of the believers in terms of the motivations and functions that such belief plays in the lives of individuals and societies.

What suspicion suspects is that believers believe in order to satisfy needs and desires that have little or nothing to do with truth or rationality. They believe because in some sense it would be nice if there were the kind of God monotheism affirms. Such believing needs to hide its true nature from itself, all the more so when the desires that are to be satisfied are themselves disreputable from the standpoint of the religion involved. Thus, according to the atheism of suspicion, theistic belief inevitably involves self-deception or bad faith in which the believer makes every effort not to notice what is really going on.

For Marx, who sees history as the history of class struggle, the ruling ideas of any epoch are those of the ruling class. Thus the primary function of religious belief is to legitimize the prevailing structures of economic exploitation. If religion simultaneously provides some consolation to the oppressed (opium for the masses), it is at the cost of accepting social domination as divinely ordained, at least for this life.

Nietzsche focuses on the resentments of the slaves whose political and economic impotence is compensated by moral revolt. The masters are evil (and the slaves, by default, are good). But God is good and will eventually punish the masters even more dramatically than the slaves could ever hope to do themselves.

Freud, too, sees theistic belief as wishful thinking. Would it not be nice if there were a God who could rescue us from the harshness of nature, death in particular? And would it not be nice if this God were a strict moral enforcer when it comes to our enemies but more like a doting grandfather when it comes to ourselves?

What the atheism of suspicion describes is surely not the whole story of religious belief. But history shows that it is all too true, all too much of the time. These atheistic analyses can thus be turned around and used for Lenten self-examination by believing individuals and communities. After all, the origin of this kind of critique is in the prophetic stand of the Bible.

J. Haught, *God and the New Atheism: A Critical Response to Dawkins, Harris, and Hitchens* (John Knox Press, 2008).

M. Westphal, *Suspicion and Faith: The Religious Uses of Modern Atheism* (Fordham University Press, 1998).

MEROLD WESTPHAL

ATHOS, MOUNT Mt Athos is at the centre of the Orthodox monastic world. Often called 'The Holy Mountain', it is actually a peninsula, the northernmost of three peninsulas extending into the Aegean Sea from the eastern coast of Chalcidice, Greece. The peninsula culminates in a 6350-foot peak, Mt Athos, which shares its name with the whole peninsula. Although protected by the Greek government, Mt Athos is politically autonomous and falls under the ecclesiastical authority, not of the Church of Greece, but of the ecumenical patriarchate of Constantinople. An abbot (*hēgoumenos*) oversees each monastery, and a representative body called the Holy Community addresses issues affecting the entire peninsula.

Mt Athos preserves a rich array of Byzantine and post-Byzantine art, architecture, and manuscripts. Its less tangible treasure is the living tradition of hesychastic spirituality, transmitted personally through the centuries from elder to disciple. Hesychasm is the cultivation of inner silence (Greek *hēsychia*) through various ascetical practices and the focused recitation of the Jesus Prayer. Hesychasm provides the foundation for the theological writings of Gregory Palamas, who was an Athonite monk before becoming archbishop of Thessalonica.

The monastic life is lived in various ways on Mt Athos: in monasteries, in sketes, and in hermitages. There are twenty monasteries. All are cenobitic, where monks live a 'common life'. They pray, eat, and work together, sharing all possessions under the direction of an abbot. Although only the twenty monasteries own land and send representatives to the Holy Community, Athos also contains several sketes, or 'ascetic settlements' (Greek *askētērion*). Sketes operate somewhat independently, but each is overseen by a ruling monastery. While some sketes reflect a modified cenobitic life, many are idiorhythmic, where monks tailor work and prayer schedules individually, and may own private property. Alongside the monks in monasteries and sketes, hermits pursue extreme asceticism in almost total isolation. Hermits occupy remote areas like the 'desert' of Athos at the furthest edge of the peninsula.

Ethnic diversity accompanies this variety in monastic routines. Although Athos is predominantly Greek in both language and ethos, and most monks are Greek, more and more monks are coming from abroad. Three monasteries are also traditionally reserved for Russians, Serbs, and Bulgarians respectively; and one skete is Romanian.

Athos' oldest surviving monastery, the Great Lavra, dates from 936. All other surviving monasteries were founded between the tenth and fourteenth centuries, except Stavronikita, founded in 1541. The current total population is approximately 2,000 monks. After decline in the mid-twentieth century, the monastic population is currently growing, for several reasons. The monasteries of Xenophontos and Simonopetra, for example, were rejuvenated in the 1970s when new abbots arrived with their monks from monasteries at Meteora, Greece. This renewal also has roots in Athos itself. Figures like Elder Joseph the Hesychast (1898–1959) and St Silouan the Athonite (1866–1938) inspired disciples who have not only revitalized several Athonite monasteries, attracting many new monks, but have also founded monasteries overseas on the Athonite model, especially in England and North America.

See also Monasticism, Orthodox Theology.

P. Sherrard, *Athos: The Mountain of Silence* (Oxford University Press, 1960).

Archimandrite Sophrony (Sakharov), *St. Silouan the Athonite* (St Vladimir's Seminary Press, 1999).

George L. Parsenios

Atonement Since the publication of G. Aulén's (1879–1977) classic typology, classifications of atonement theories have generally followed his lead: employing a more or less chronological order which moves from early Church theories, through western ideas from the Middle Ages through the post-Reformation period, to modern theories. Aulén's own rubrics for describing these theories were, respectively, the 'classic' or 'dramatic' view (which he also called the '*Christus Victor*' model), the 'Latin' view, and 'subjective' theories. The central question shaping this division of the material was not, however, historical, but dogmatic: who is the subject who performs the saving work accomplished in Jesus of Nazareth? Is the work a *continuous* divine work, in which God is the subject throughout? Is the work a *discontinuous* divine work, in which God is the architect of the plan of redemption but the human Jesus is the effective agent in its accomplishment? Or is the work a continuous *human* work as the more 'subjective' theories would suggest? A closely related issue for Aulén was that of locating the centre of gravity in the relation between the objective accomplishment of redemption in Christ and its subjective appropriation by the believer. Is the primary centre of gravity found in Christ's work? If so, the theory in question is an 'objective' one. Or is it found in the act of appropriation? If so, the theory is 'subjective'.

Aulén's book has been much criticized, but the basic questions with which he worked have to be taken into consideration by any historian of doctrine. However wooden the 'continuous/distincontinuous' distinction might have been, it did have the virtue of calling attention to the importance (1) of the understanding of the *Person* of Christ presupposed in any account of his work and (2) of the problem of how those separated from Christ by time participate in the salvation he either accomplished or bore witness to.

The problems facing Aulén's typology are fairly obvious today. In the first place, '*Christus Victor*' does not adequately describe patristic reflection on the work of Christ because it makes primary what for the fathers was a theme of secondary importance – enslavement to the Devil. For most of the fathers, the central problem needing to be addressed by the saving work of Christ was 'death' – understood as humanity's suffering a gradual deprivation of being as a consequence of having been cut off from the divine source of life in the fall. This would have culminated in a complete lapse into non-being had God not maintained the human race in existence until the One came in whom participation in the divine life was restored. The mechanism by means of which life was restored is usually described in terms of deification (*theopoeisis*, *theosis*), and Christ's triumph occurred chiefly by means of His obedience unto death (which restored human nature to its original integrity) and His resurrection (by which mortality was conquered by immortality and the connection to divine life was restored). Such reflection on Christ's work may be described as 'ontological' in nature.

Aulén's treatment of the 'Latin' type fared no better. Aulén was certainly right to find in Anselm a shift to juridical thinking. The problem was that he made Anselm's 'satisfaction' theory basic to his definition of the 'Latin' type. But Anselm made 'satisfaction' and 'punishment' alternatives: *either* God would receive an adequate satisfaction *or* God would have to punish. That 'satisfaction' might occur *through* punishment did not occur to Anselm, though it was basic to the thinking of a host of medieval and REFORMATION thinkers and represented a development whose importance Aulén underestimated. For if God was actively punishing sin in the death of Jesus, then God was no longer simply the passive recipient of Christ's voluntary self-oblation. Seen in this light, the 'double-sidedness' of divine activity and passivity, which Aulén associated with the 'classic' model alone, is also characteristic of penal substitution theories and does not provide an adequate basis for distinguishing between them. Aulén would have done better to locate all penal theories more loosely under the heading of 'judicial' thinking – a term which not only captures the distinctiveness of western atonement theology in the post-patristic period, but also allows for significant differences between Anselm and later thinkers.

Finally, while the use of the term 'subjective' as a description of moral influence theories has much to be said for it, it is woefully inadequate as a comprehensive term for the whole of nineteenth-century reflection on atonement. Of all the mistakes committed by Aulén, his interpretation of F. SCHLEIERMACHER is arguably the most egregious. However true it may be that the religious self-consciousness of the Christian constituted the starting point for at least one strand in Schleiermacher's approach to Christ's Person and work, Schleiermacher insisted that it was the influence of divine causality upon the God-consciousness of Jesus which grounded the accomplishment of redemption in Him, making his theory clearly 'ontological' in nature and 'objective' in its centre of gravity. Moreover, G. W. F. HEGEL does not even come in for consideration in Aulén's book, though it was Hegel's idea of a 'speculative Good Friday' which provided the historical root of much recent reflection on the theme of Jesus' death in God-abandonment. To treat either of these figures under the same heading as the moral-influence theories (see below) of A. Ritschl (1822–89) and his followers is seriously misleading.

These problems surrounding the rubrics employed in Aulén's typology can easily be addressed by a different nomenclature, with no loss of the valid insights in his work. If the generic headings of 'ontological', 'judicial', and 'moral influence' theories are used, all the major dogmatic theories can be located under one of these – though a separate category (a 'cultic' model, perhaps) would have to be devised for speaking of recent treatments of the 'sacrifice' of Jesus in NT studies.

A bigger challenge to atonement theology is that the ontological presuppositions that shape theological reflection in the modern period are dramatically different from those which pertained in the ancient world. By the same token, modern judicial theories, while not eliminating the element of retributive justice thought to be proper to God's righteousness, have not made that element central. What has changed, above all, is the concept of God presupposed by virtually all atonement theories elaborated prior to the ENLIGHTENMENT. Every atonement theory stands in an intimate relationship with particular understandings of God, CHRISTOLOGY, and THEOLOGICAL ANTHROPOLOGY. At the dawn of the modern era in Protestant theology, the virtual eclipse of classical METAPHYSICS required all three to be subjected to various strategies of reconstruction.

The reasons for the demise of classical metaphysics may be found in the rise of BIBLICAL CRITICISM and a loss of confidence that laws, order, and rationality are somehow embedded in the world and need only to be discovered. That epistemology fell out of favour due to the philosophical revolution associated with I. KANT and its aftermath in German IDEALISM, which eliminated the cosmological basis for classical metaphysics. The two-natures Christology of CHALCEDON was now suspect for its dependence on the old metaphysics; and the belief in divine simplicity and impassibility that hovered in the immediate background of all theorizing about Christ's work up to the post-Reformation period was felt increasingly to belong to an earlier era. Confronted by this shift in sensibilities, theologians went in one of two directions. Either they accepted the demise of classical metaphysics and sought to construct a new theological ontology more in line with the history of Jesus; or they tried to continue with business as usual, protesting that they had no principled commitment to the old metaphysics, and that their ad hoc use of it had no negative effects on their theology. The great danger which surrounded the latter option (favoured by a fair number of both Protestants and Catholics) was that the ontologies presupposed in their atonement theories became vague, even for those who made the healing of human nature central to their thinking about Christ's work.

The impact of this cultural shift upon atonement theology was also registered in the collapse of the traditional Protestant distinction between the Person and work of Christ. Schleiermacher collapsed the work of Christ into His Person. His was a Person-forming theory of redemption in which the completion of CREATION was understood to have taken place in the emergence of Christ as the 'Second Adam', the One in whose perfectly potent God-consciousness ideal humanity was instantiated. The treatment of the work of Christ which followed was designed primarily to show that Jesus' God-consciousness remained undisturbed by the tragic events which befell Him on the last weekend of His life. Hegel can be understood as having subsumed either the work of Christ into His Person or the Person of Christ into His work, depending upon whether one understands the being of God in his thinking to include a transcendent element which grounds history (as much traditional Hegelianism and PROCESS THEOLOGY insists) or whether one understands him to have completely identified the history of God with the history of human self-consciousness (as some recent American pragmatists have argued). Either way, he had set aside the classically Protestant distinction of Person and work. The same has to be said of T. F. Torrance's (1913–2007) understanding of the 'vicarious humanity' of Christ and the 'ontological healing' which occurred in it. Although Torrance was more traditional than either Schleiermacher or Hegel, his adoption of the idea that the *LOGOS* assumed fallen humanity constituted a modern element in his thinking. J. Zizioulas (b. 1931), with his critical retrieval of the CAPPADOCIAN FATHERS' understanding of the TRINITY and reconstruction of the idea of 'communion' along the lines of a relational ontology, also belongs here as a modern exemplification of the Orthodox theory of redemption.

The greatest representative of the 'judicial' frame of reference for understanding the work of Christ is K. BARTH. By grounding the outpouring of God's wrath upon the sinner in the cross of Christ in God's gracious ELECTION, however, Barth succeeded in de-centring the concept of retributive justice, making it the instrument of God's mercy. To the extent that he also grounded the being of both God and humanity in the eternal act of electing, Barth also made the eternal decision basic to his theological ontology. In addition, by making the category of 'correspondence' central to his explanation of how those separated from Christ in time and place 'participate' actively in His saving work, he also granted a significant role to the ethical. The result was a teleologically ordered judicial theory, with ontological implications – a model of models which took up all that was valid in the other two frames of reference and integrated them into the judicial. He was followed in this by H. von BALTHASAR and E. Jüngel (b. 1934).

Where moral-influence theories are concerned, Christ has typically been understood not so much as the instrument by means of which God achieves human salvation as the revelation of the way other humans must take if they are to be reconciled to God and to other persons. The emphasis here falls upon VOCATION, discipleship, and living the reconciled life in this world. The greatest representative of this outlook in the nineteenth century was Ritschl and, in the first half of the twentieth century, D. Baillie (1887–1954). Moral-influence theorists never had to concern themselves much with issues of ontology; for most, the divinity of Jesus was construed in terms of the quality of His humanity – which meant that the two-natures doctrine was moot.

The most important development impacting reflection on the work of Christ since the early nineteenth century has been the move away from the older attempts to construct a new metaphysical basis for ontology to more nearly post-metaphysical accounts. This move has been manifested in several ways: (1) through the later Barth's 'historicizing' of the two 'natures' of Christ; (2) through a focus on the *historical* reasons for the crucifixion of Jesus in the work of W. Pannenberg (b. 1928) and J. Moltmann (b. 1926); and (3) through a variety of 'non-violent' theories of the atonement, many of which (e.g., that of J. Weaver, b. 1941) go so far as to suggest that God did not will the death of the Son. In response to these developments, many have sought a revival of classical metaphysics and the *theosis* doctrine which was its primary legacy. But this has less to do with the stringency of arguments brought against 'modernity' than it does with the growing number of those dissatisfied not only with modern PROTESTANTISM, but with the Reformation as well.

See also LIMITED ATONEMENT.

G. Aulén, *Christus Victor: A Historical Study of the Three Main Types of the Idea of the Atonement* (Collier/Macmillan, 1969).

D. M. Baillie, *God Was In Christ: An Essay on Incarnation and Atonement* (Scribners, 1948).

K. Barth, *Church Dogmatics* (T&T Clark, 1956), IV/1, 157–357.

J. McIntyre, *The Shape of Soteriology: Studies in the Doctrine of the Death of Christ* (T&T Clark, 1992).

T. F. Torrance, *The Trinitarian Faith* (T&T Clark, 1995).

BRUCE LINDLEY MCCORMACK

ATTRIBUTES, DIVINE Characterizing God by enumerating properties of his being and activities is ubiquitous in the Christian TRADITION. From its beginnings, Christian FAITH defined itself in part by acknowledging that God is and acts in particular ways. In the primitive Christian tradition, such characterizations were given liturgical, homiletic, or catechetical expression, drawing on scriptural language, which constituted the comprehensive norm for Christian teaching. As the tradition developed, formal reflection upon God's attributes was shaped by the need to take stock of the effect of the saving presence of the Son and the HOLY SPIRIT upon concepts of God's being. This process involved complex negotiations between the kerygmatic, doxological, and scriptural resources of the faith and the conceptual inheritance of ancient PHILOSOPHICAL THEOLOGY. If the fullness of deity comes to dwell bodily in Christ, what is to be made of God's incorporeality or changelessness? The history is easy to oversimplify; severe critics of later 'theism', for example, commonly regard the fifth-century theologian Dionysius the Areopagite as emblematic of a wider and disastrous compromise with Greek metaphysics that was repeated in the thirteenth century by T. Aquinas. This reading seriously underestimates the corrective function played by the doctrines of the Trinity and the incarnation in determining the character of the Christian God in, for example, Augustine or John of Damascus.

Comprehensive formal presentation of the divine attributes was first achieved in the medieval *summas*; these, in turn, shaped the systematic accounts in post-Reformation Protestant dogmatics. When in the later seventeenth century Christian dogma ceased to be a commanding force in western intellectual culture, discussion of the nature of deity became preoccupied with two sets of issues. First, increasing authority was accorded to 'natural' religion and theology, that is, to a basic theism considered prior to 'positive' or 'revealed' religion. A classic example of this approach is the *Demonstration of the Being and Attributes of God* (1704) by S. Clarke (1675–1729). The principal concern of such theism was cosmological, that is, framing language about God in order to explain the existence and continuation of contingent reality. Accordingly, the divine attributes which received the greatest attention were those properties of deity deemed necessary for causal explanation of the world (e.g., self-existence or omnipotence). Neither Christian specifics such as Trinitarian or incarnational teaching, nor the temporal unfolding of God's saving dealings with creatures, played much role in describing the divine nature, which could be reduced to that of an infinitely powerful, independent, and eternal being. Similar moves continue to be made by some contemporary philosophers of religion who establish the divine attributes as the necessary properties of a perfect being (i.e., a being than which nothing is greater); once again, God's nature is conceived largely in isolation from his triune identity or his self-communication to creatures.

Second, from the late eighteenth century mainstream Protestant theology lost confidence in a dogmatic realism rooted in divine revelation. Correspondingly, the inadequacies of human talk about God's nature came to be explained not in terms of fallen reason's return to God, but by appeal to conceptions of rationality derived from German idealism. This entailed a shift in the object of theology away from the self-bestowing and reconciling presence of God to the historical reality of human religious–moral experience and action in the world. On this account, talk of God's attributes does not so much denote properties in God as characterize human experience of or response to God as the media in which God is schematized and through which alone God may be glimpsed. For some modern theologians, this approach enables recovery of a theology of the divine nature directed by God's 'economic' presence and activity rather than by speculative questions. In others, it engenders various kinds of nominalism, in which language about divine attributes is only remotely connected to God's being.

With the exception of some modern constructivist theologies, the majority position in the Christian tradition has been that knowledge of God's attributes derives from God, and so is 'revealed' knowledge. God alone knows himself and communicates this knowledge to creatures in suitably accommodated forms. The media of this communication are variously conceived. More directly, the divine nature is displayed in God's works in the world which enact (for example) God's faithfulness, goodness, or righteous wrath; these works are normatively rehearsed in the biblical writings. Less directly, God's nature may be known through rational contemplation of created reality, which participates in or reflects the creator's nature (e.g., created beauty echoes the beauty of God), but does so only inadequately, so that both eminent affirmation and negation of creaturely properties are required to speak of God. Both direct and indirect predication assume the dependence of knowledge of God's attributes on the revealing work of God, for even contemplation of created reality is anticipated and enabled by revelation, and so is not a work of purely natural reason.

If this is the case, then talk of God's nature is not a simple process of assigning properties to God as to some infinitely great entity. Rather, in the wake of God's self-presentation properties are 'confessed of' rather than 'attributed to' God. For this reason, 'attributes' may not be the happiest term for the kind of 'receptive' predication which is involved in talk of God. A number of consequences follow.

First, a Christian theology of the divine attributes goes beyond simply generating a conception of a perfect being, since its aim is to indicate the identity (in biblical terms, the 'name') of the divine subject. It is certainly the case that treatments of the divine attributes in both ancient and modern Christian theology have devoted attention to the question: 'What are the properties of deity?' However, much Christian theology has accorded only provisional significance to answers to that question. Although from the seventeenth century onwards such answers increasingly provided the ground for more specific Christian theological language, they properly serve only as that through which theology moves in order to attain the divine subject. The primary question for a theology of the divine attributes is thus: 'Who is this one (that is, YHWH, the God and Father of our Lord Jesus Christ)?'

Second, the one to whom the properties are ascribed is infinite personal subject and agent. God is *personal* in the sense that God is the free subject of relations, both within the divine being and externally. God is *agent* in the sense that the divine life is unrestrictedly self-moved and moving. This infinite divine subject precedes and exceeds all predication. Attribution of properties to God is thus not an exercise in conceptual comprehension of an inert object, but acknowledgement of a mobile, self-bestowing personal presence. In this context, it is important to note that in SCRIPTURE the primary idiom in which the divine attributes come to expression is doxological, through the recital of the acts in which God's being is declared. Ascription follows the divine self-enactment.

Third, there is a critical relation between a Christian theological account of the divine attributes and other conceptions of the nature of divinity. Strong claims about the distinctiveness of Christian teaching about God's nature are found in those theologians who insist that God's action in time in the incarnate Son is wholly determinative of God's attributes. Such claims may lead to heavy qualification of some traditional attributes (so that, for example, omnipotence is defined by God's 'weakness' at the cross), or to outright rejection of others (e.g., impassibility is sometimes judged an irredeemably sub-Christian property). Others argue that even though God's self-enactment is manifest in God's temporal works, it is not exhausted by those works, and therefore that – suitably corrected – properties such as immutability or incorporeality may legitimately be ascribed to God's infinite life.

Because of this, fourth, treatments of the divine attributes are closely related to conceptions of God as triune. When God's attributes are determined on the basis of a minimal theistic construal of how the world came to be (as they were by Clarke), God's triunity has little significance, because the properties ascribed to the deity are simply those of the world's efficient and formal cause. One effect of the widespread renewal of Trinitarian doctrine in the later twentieth century was much more expansive treatment of God's relation to and action in the world. When the Trinity is conceived as analogous to a community of persons, God is no longer thought of as a supreme mind or causal agent but as one who is internally differentiated and who engages in a diverse set of relations with created reality through the Son and the Spirit. This, in turn, shapes conceptions of God's attributes. Pushed hard, it may lead to appropriation of specific attributes to particular divine persons, though it is notoriously difficult to pursue this without calling into question the unity of God's essence. The most common effect of a Trinitarian conception of God is to emphasize that the divine attributes name God as God encounters us in God's works. This 'economic' conception is often set against abstract notions of deity apart from any relation to creatures, purportedly found in the tradition of negative theology which names God in terms of his sheer difference from creatures (see APOPHATIC THEOLOGY). By contrast, a theology of God's attributes, it is argued, should be derived from God's revelatory or saving encounter with creatures (a point sometimes reinforced by criticism of the 'substance metaphysics' thought to control classical doctrines of God in the western tradition, and by an emphasis upon God's being as God's act).

This shift to an economic register may resist abstract accounts of divine transcendence, but it is not unproblematic. Pressed hard, it may prove as narrowing as the theism which it tries to displace. This may happen when the economic activity of God is insufficiently grounded in God's immanent being, with the result that the inner depth of God's triune being ceases to play much role in theological descriptions of God's nature. In terms of the divine attributes, the corollary problem is that God's 'relative' attributes (the properties of God in his external operations, including, e.g., justice and mercy) are accorded much more weight than his 'absolute' attributes (the properties of his life in himself, including, e.g., omniscience and aseity). The distinction between 'relative' and 'absolute' is certainly unstable, and can be schematized in such a way that God's immanent being and his economic acts are sundered. Yet if it is a principle of Christian theology that God's relation to the world is such that the world adds nothing to God's essence, then God is not exhaustively defined by the properties of God's relation to the world, even though that relation enacts or repeats God's inner character. Thus, God's ('relative') omnipresence to all created reality is the economic expression of God's ('absolute') immensity as the one who is without limitation; likewise, God's extrinsic righteousness in judging and justifying creatures is grounded in God's intrinsic righteousness as the Holy One.

A final question, much discussed in the history of theology, concerns the multiplicity of God's attributes. We attribute many different properties to God – goodness, wisdom, love, omnipotence, holiness, and so on – but how does this range cohere with God's simplicity? It is important to be clear that divine simplicity is not mere absence of composition but singular, infinite fullness, perfect integrity, and abundance of life. God's simplicity does not lie behind the variety of God's attributes but *is* them (in this, it is not unlike God's unity, which is identical with God's triunity). Because of this, God's essence and God's attributes coincide. The divine attributes are not accidental properties of God, for God's being God is his being *this* subject in *this* way (i.e., with this identity and nature). Accordingly, the divine attributes do not name parts of God (God is not goodness plus wisdom plus love, and so forth), since they are identical with the divine substance and with each other. To ascribe goodness, wisdom, and love to God is, again, simply to indicate God's perfectly simple identity. Nevertheless, this ought not to lead to agnosticism about the fittingness of speaking of God by setting out a range of attributes, or to the suggestion that the divine attributes are simply creaturely projections. The distinctions between the attributes result from the creature's incapacity to comprehend infinite being in a non-discursive way. God knows God's self eternally and immediately; creatures must conceive of God serially and cumulatively, by enumeration and division of what is in itself one. And so to say 'God is good, wise and loving' is not to add anything to the statement 'God is', but simply to speak of God in the only way available to temporal, finite creatures.

K. Barth, *Church Dogmatics* (T&T Clark, 1957), II/1.
E. Farley, *Divine Empathy: A Theology of God* (Fortress, 1996).
C. Gunton, *Act and Being: Towards a Theology of the Divine Attributes* (SCM, 2002).
J. Hoffman and G. S. Rosenkrantz, *The Divine Attributes* (Blackwell, 2002).
W. Pannenberg, *Systematic Theology*, vol. I (T&T Clark, 1991).
C. Schwöbel, 'Exploring the Logic of Divine Perfection: Divine Attributes and Divine Agency' in *God: Action and Revelation* (Kok Pharos, 1992), 46–62.

JOHN WEBSTER

ATTRITION: see CONTRITION.

AUGSBURG CONFESSION The Augsburg Confession is arguably the defining document of LUTHERAN THEOLOGY, even though it is formally just one of the confessional standards included in the Lutheran BOOK OF CONCORD. Though derived from the theological ideas of M. LUTHER, it was drafted by P. Melanchthon (1497–1560) as a statement of the Lutheran confessional position for presentation to Emperor Charles V (r. 1519–56) at the imperial Diet of Augsburg in 1530. The Confession is composed of a total of twenty-eight articles, divided into two parts: the first (arts. 1–21) gives the Lutheran interpretation of the basic doctrines of the Christian faith, while the second (arts. 22–8) defends particular changes in Church practice (e.g., communion in both kinds, the marriage of clergy) introduced in Lutheran churches.

The Augsburg Confession was intended to be an irenic document. As such, the first three articles affirm the Lutherans' acceptance of traditional Catholic teaching regarding the TRINITY, original SIN, and CHRISTOLOGY. Likewise, at various points in the Confession care is taken to distinguish the Lutheran position from that of more radical opponents of Rome, like the Anabaptists. Nevertheless, the Confession clearly marks the Lutheran position off from that of the Catholic Church by ascribing JUSTIFICATION to FAITH and denying that human works are in any sense meritorious before God (arts. 4–6). The ECCLESIOLOGY of the Confession, according to which the Church is to be identified solely by proclamation of the GOSPEL and the right administration of the sacraments, without any reference to particular juridical or hierarchical arrangements (art. 7), also represented a clear break with CATHOLIC THEOLOGY.

IAN A. MCFARLAND

AUGUSTINE OF HIPPO Augustine was born in the North African town of Thagaste in 354 of a Christian mother (Monica) and a non-Christian father (Patricius). His immediate family had some means, but was not of great wealth. Through the help of a family patron Augustine was educated in rhetoric. He eventually left North Africa for Rome and then was called to Milan as an official teacher of rhetoric and speechmaker for the emperor.

Following an encounter with Cicero's (106–43 BC) now lost *Hortensius*, Augustine's public progress was mirrored by an inner search for the true philosophy. For some years he was associated with the dualistic Manichaeans (see MANICHAEISM). Finding their mythical explanations of scientific phenomena unpersuasive, he fell into scepticism. Gradually, under the influence of Ambrose of Milan's (*ca* 340–97) allegorical reading of the OT and some non-Christian Neoplatonic texts (see PLATONISM), Augustine returned to his mother's Christianity. He abandoned his secular career in 386 in favour of an ascetic and communal life.

In 388/9 Augustine returned to North Africa and founded a monastic community in Thagaste. After having been caught on a trip to Hippo and made to promise to accept ordination, the old bishop of this busy port – and the largest diocese in North Africa – ordained him priest and appointed him successor. From 395 until his death in 430 Augustine was the bishop of Hippo.

His initial writings in Italy attempt to copy earlier traditions of philosophical dialogue and also show a strong anti-Manichaean bent. Central to this polemic are his attempts to show that the created order is intelligible, and that it reflects the goodness of its one triune creator. His works after ordination show a new desire to present ideas within a language and genres that would fit with his position as an official spokesman for the Church. The text *On Faith and the Creed* of 393 shows him expounding the creed before a gathering of bishops, combining his own deep readings in Latin tradition with a deeply personal constructive bent. During 395 and 396 Augustine underwent a profound change in (or at least a deepening of) his views on GRACE. An exegesis of Romans 9 sent to Simplicianus (d. 400), Ambrose's successor as bishop of Milan, reveals the new Augustine. Here Augustine insists that all we have we receive and that we should be thankful for it, even as we confess the mysteriousness and incomprehensibility (to us) of God's providential ordering. Thus, God's choice of Jacob before he was born was based neither on knowledge of the works that Jacob would perform, nor even on the basis of knowing that Jacob would have faith, for faith itself is a gift (cf. Rom. 9:10–13).

Anthropologically Augustine now sets out with new clarity his fundamental principles. Human beings are created rational, good, and loving, naturally desiring the God who is the source of all existence. Through Adam's sin all are now marked by *ignorantia* (ignorance) and *infirmitas* (weakness), not knowing the good clearly and lacking the power to follow it. Through the incarnation of the Word and the sending of the Holy Spirit into the Church, God offers a vision of the blessed life that both draws human beings and provides them with the power of will to follow that vision. Augustine sees this process as the liberation of a will held in bondage by sin as the gift of a truly free will.

Between 397 and 400 Augustine wrote the *Confessions*. The first nine of its thirteen books read very easily to modern eyes as an autobiography, but Augustine's aim is to highlight aspects of the process through which God has drawn him to Christian faith. The book uses his own life to play out the theology of grace he has developed and covers events only up to the immediate aftermath of his conversion in 386. The final four books reflect on the nature of human existence in God's presence and the character of humanity's search for God, culminating in a powerful exegesis of Genesis 1, which offers important reflections on the character of Christian hermeneutics and the function of the Church.

As a bishop Augustine spent much time trying to bring about unity in the North African Church which was split between a Catholic section, in communion with the Church throughout the empire, and a section known to the Catholics as 'Donatist', who had emerged in the early fourth century (see Donatism). Augustine's writing against Donatists helped to define much of his ecclesiology. He taught that the Church's sacramental power is always Christ's power, and is not given as a result of the purity of the Church's members or leaders. The Church is the body of Christ animated and unified by Christ's Spirit, the Holy Spirit. It may well be (as Catholics had long claimed) that Donatist sacraments are valid, but these sacraments do them no good if they refuse the movement of love into unity that the Spirit imparts and is. Augustine distinguished strongly between Donatist leaders (who should have known better) and ordinary believers who had never known any alternative. Initially favouring a path of persuasion, Augustine eventually supported imperial legislation against Donatists, especially in the wake of the decisions of a conference held in Carthage in 411, at which almost the entire Catholic and Donatist hierarchies were present.

The decade between 410 and 420 was the high point of Augustine's career, a period of extraordinary intellectual creativity and sheer volume of writing. During this period Augustine composed much of his great works, *On the Trinity* (probably begun between 399 and 405), *The Literal Commentary on Genesis*, and *The City of God*. Augustine also wrote a significant proportion of his *Tractates on John's Gospel* and his *Interpretations of the Psalms*.

Augustine's Trinitarian theology begins in his own adaptation of previous Latin Nicene theology, particularly that of Ambrose and Hilary of Poitiers (300–68). Augustine distinguishes between what we should believe – at which level Trinitarian faith is a summary of biblical teaching – and our search for understanding. The latter he conceives as an exegetical and philosophical exercise in which we search to see how Scripture uses spatial and temporal language to speak of a God who transcends those categories. The legacy of his engagement with Neoplatonism is to be found in his understanding of God's omnipresence and yet transcendence of all, and in God's absolute mysterious simplicity.

Augustine's mature account of Father, Son, and Spirit rejects the usefulness of the philosophical terminologies of genus, species, and individual. Instead he finds multiple ways to speak of the three Persons as constituted by their acts towards each other, grounded in the Father's eternal generation of the Son and spiration of the Spirit. Post-nineteenth-century critiques of Augustine's supposed unitarian tendencies have been the subject of much critique in recent decades.

The decade between 410 and 420 also saw the emergence of Augustine's ongoing battle with what he saw as the erroneous views of Pelagius (*ca* 350–*ca* 420) and his associates on the nature of grace, free will, and the state of humanity following the fall (see Pelagianism). These debates saw the deepening of his views on grace, but little fundamental change.

The massive *City of God* finds its roots in Augustine's response to the capture of Rome by the Goths in 410 and ongoing attempts to explain Christianity to pagan circles in Carthage. Augustine presents Roman culture as a community which serves to inculcate violence and exposes Roman models of 'virtue' as exemplars of sin. He traces the emergence and beliefs of the two 'cities' – one based in love of this world, the other in love of God – through the course of history (where they lie intermingled) to their respective ends in hell and heaven. True justice is Christ and is known only through allowing one's growing appreciation of and participation in Christ's mystery and grace to pervade one's judgements.

In the final decade of his life Augustine completed *On the Trinity* and *The City of God*, and wrote extensively against Julian of Eclanum (*ca* 385–*ca* 455), one of the most cutting critics of Augustine's understanding of grace. This final period also saw a new series of works against certain anti-Nicene theologians he called 'Arians', and who were at this time associated with the Vandal kingdoms emerging in Spain and North Africa. Augustine died in 430, as Hippo was besieged by the Vandals.

L. Ayres, *Augustine and the Trinity* (Cambridge University Press, 2010).
P. Brown, *Augustine: A Biography* (University of California Press, 2000).
R. Dodaro, ed., *Augustine and his Critics* (Routledge, 2000).
C. Harrison, *Augustine: Christian Truth and Fractured Humanity* (Oxford University Press, 2000).
S. Lancel, *St. Augustine* (SCM, 2002).

Lewis Ayres

B

Balthasar, Hans Urs von Among the most influential Catholic theologians of the twentieth century, Hans Urs von Balthasar (1905–88) gave himself to the work of spiritual direction, translation, and publishing, founding and leading a religious community, and he produced a massive theological literature that, in many ways, is only explicable as the fruit of his spiritual life. His writings range from important studies of Origen, Gregory of Nyssa (see Cappadocian Fathers), and Maximus the Confessor, to analyses of the spiritual life as it unfolds in many different contexts (especially as it is revealed in the lives of the saints and mystical writers), to his great fifteen-volume trilogy in which theology unfolds according to three transcendentals of the beautiful (*The Glory of the Lord*), the good (*Theo-Drama*), and the true (*Theo-Logic*).

In each of these categories (in which he consciously inverts the order of Kant's critiques), Balthasar shows how the patterns of worldly being might become translucent to the consummate truth of their existence. A literary scholar by training, Balthasar often employed genealogies of cultural structures in order to portray their evolution and their transformation within the Gospel. Thus a central motif of his theology is the impression that the divine makes within the world, calling forth from the creatures a variety of finite expressions and echoes in which they are most themselves when they are also epiphanic of divine glory.

With this fundamental outlook, Balthasar's theology offers a distinct complement to other strands of modern academic theology, in which epistemological concerns and the anthropological starting point of all thought are understood to be determinative and, sometimes, final boundaries for theology. Balthasar proposes, alternatively, that human experience of reality, human freedom and action, and human apprehension of truth are all given their fullest and most comprehensive interpretations when they are seen to be elicited by God and discovered as finding the fullness of their truth in God. Thus the very perfection of worldly being points beyond itself, yet the mysterious *telos* of worldly existence cannot simply be extrapolated from finite to infinite; not even the analogy of being (*analogia entis*) in Balthasar's view can do this *in advance*. Rather, it is only in the light of God's own self-disclosure in revelation that theology can, as it were, read the analogy between Creator and creature *back downwards* – from the divine Being to its creaturely sign. But already Balthasar here shows the intrinsic role of Trinitarian thought throughout his theology: for the heart of the mystery of Being, the unfathomable and gracious surprise of this radical self-giving – from which flow all the creaturely forms of self-showing, self-bestowal, and self-expressiveness – turns out to be the infinite self-sharing of the three Persons of the Trinity. Thus Trinity defines Being in Balthasar, not the other way around. Trinity also grounds the finite traces of this infinite generosity, finite traces of self-giving that are the basis of all worldly beauty, goodness, and intelligibility. These traces are not, however, directly deducible from experience of the world, but 'reveal themselves as everlasting mysteries only when God's sovereignty permits him and occasions him out of free love ... to create the being of the world' (*Epilogue* 86). Only then can worldly being be seen to contain traces of the Trinity (see *Vestigia Trinitatis*). Balthasar thus sought to take the peculiarly modern concern with methodology and starting points and to propose a Trinitarian ontology at its very core.

From the 1940s, Balthasar developed a theological friendship and discussion with his fellow Swiss, K. Barth, and his monograph on Barth's theology was a landmark in the twentieth-century Catholic opening to other Christians. Also in 1940, while a university chaplain in Basel, Balthasar provided spiritual direction for one of Switzerland's first woman physicians, A. von Speyr (1902–67). Her conversion and baptism initiated a decades-long spiritual partnership with Balthasar, who perceived in Speyr's developing spiritual insights a profound grace. Her mystical participations in the paschal mystery of Christ seem to have deepened Balthasar's own sense of the profound ways in which the saints and mystical writers live into the reality of Christ, and, as it were, translate this mystery into their lives and teaching for the good of Christian theology.

Critical assessments of Balthasar's theology have tended to focus on three features of his work. First and most globally, his up-ending of the modern subjective turn in theology has sometimes met with misgivings, particularly among those who see no alternative to fundamentally Kantian presuppositions for any public theology. Second, Balthasar notably emphasizes the inner-divine kenosis of the three Persons of the Trinity. While this is an attempt to contemplate the eternal conditions of possibility for the historical missions of Christ and the Spirit, some critics have viewed his emphasis as unwarranted and inappropriate speculation regarding the inner-Trinitarian relations and as perhaps verging uncomfortably upon a kind of tritheism. Finally, Balthasar's striking portrayals of Christ's descent among the dead, coupled with his conviction that the reconciling power of God extends even to so radical a form of solidarity between Christ and the experience of human sinfulness has led some scholars to judge that here Balthasar has again made unwarranted claims extending beyond either the clear sense of SCRIPTURE or the limits of the TRADITION.

These concerns may perhaps be somewhat allayed by understanding that the goal of Balthasar's work was never a systematic or metaphysical account of reality per se. Rather, the reintegration of SPIRITUALITY and theology lay at the heart of Balthasar's many projects and writings. In everything, he sought to illuminate Christ's self-giving as the radical presence of the Trinitarian self-giving from which all creatures receive existence and the call towards the deep truth of themselves in God.

See also AESTHETICS, THEOLOGICAL; KENOTIC THEOLOGY.

M. A. McIntosh, *Christology from Within: Spirituality and the Incarnation in Hans Urs von Balthasar* (University of Notre Dame Press, 1996).

K. Mongrain, *The Systematic Thought of Hans Urs von Balthasar: An Irenaean Retrieval* (Crossroad, 2002).

E. T. Oakes, S. J., and D. Moss, eds., *The Cambridge Companion to Hans Urs von Balthasar* (Cambridge University Press, 2004).

A. Scola, *Hans Urs von Balthasar: A Theological Style* (T&T Clark, 1991).

MARK A. MCINTOSH

BAN: see EXCOMMUNICATION.

BAPTISM Most Christian Churches practise baptism, believing that Christ himself instituted it (Matt. 28:19). In baptism representatives of the Church apply water to an individual to mark the beginning of his or her life in Christ and the Church. Churches have differed, however, in their understanding of God's presence and activity in baptism (e.g., its status as a sacrament, its necessity for salvation), the preconditions for admitting a person to baptism (e.g., maturity, catechetical preparation), and modes of administering baptism (e.g., the amount of water used, those permitted to perform the rite). In recent years, Catholic, Orthodox, and major REFORMATION Churches have achieved greater theological consensus about these questions, generally recognizing baptisms performed by each other's Churches. At the same time, traditional understandings of baptism have been challenged in western societies, where baptism has often become little more than a social ritual.

In baptism God initiates a COVENANT, claiming people as God's own and promising to provide for them as his children. The baptized (or parents or community, on their behalf) promise, in response, to be loyal to God and to live in the way of Jesus Christ. Both covenantal trajectories are fundamentally communal: as God lays claim to an individual, God directs him or her into the life of the Church and asks the Church to recommit itself to the covenant; and as individuals declare faith in God, they agree to commit themselves to the community of faith, while the community pledges to care for them. This covenantal structure has five key dimensions:

First, *baptism sets forth the promises of God.* In baptism God promises to wash away a person's sins (Acts 22:16); to unite a person with Christ in his death and resurrection (Rom. 6:1–11; Col. 2:12); to grant a person the HOLY SPIRIT and new life in Christ (Acts 2:38; Titus 3:5); and to adopt a person into the family of God, represented by the community of faith (1 Cor. 12:13).

Baptism represents a fundamental reorientation of a person. One is no longer his or her own, but Christ's (1 Cor. 6:19). Traditional baptismal liturgies used imagery of a person's passage from the realm of darkness to the realm of light, and sometimes included EXORCISMS and acts in which the priest and the candidate (or his or her representatives) turned to the west (the realm of evil) and spat at the Devil. Contemporary liturgies often include declarations whereby the candidates renounce evil and pledge themselves to the way of Christ.

To be baptized is to be marked with a *new identity.* In the Church's first centuries, candidates stripped off their clothes, stepped naked into the baptismal waters, and received a white garment when they emerged. They understood themselves to be clothed with Christ (Gal. 3:27), in accordance with PAUL's declaration that, 'If anyone is in Christ, there is a new creation: everything old has passed away; see, everything has become new!' (2 Cor. 5:17).

Ancient baptismal pools and fonts were frequently eight-sided, representing the seven days of creation that culminate in an eighth day on which Jesus rises from the dead and recreates the world. In traditional baptismal liturgies, the priest or minister calls the candidate by his or her given name and declares, 'I baptize you in the name of the Father, and the Son, and the Holy Spirit.' A candidate's surname no longer identifies him or her; rather, he or she is now a child of the one God whom we know in Christ through the Spirit.

Second, *in baptism material things and communal actions help to set forth God's promises.* The Church accompanies its declaration of God's promises with application of water to the candidate. The Greek root for the word 'baptism', *baptizo,* implies being covered completely by water, though actual Christian practice varied widely. As early as the second century, the *Didache* recognized the need for flexibility: 'baptize' in running water . . . If you do not have running water, baptize in some other. If you cannot in cold, then in warm. If you have neither, then pour water on the head' (7.1–3).

Because symbolic actions appeal to the senses and emotions, they involve much more than the participants' mere intellectual assent to what is happening.

Baptism, like the EUCHARIST, employs matter and ritual to confirm and ratify God's promises in a way more deeply than words alone can. Thus, the use of water evokes the covenantal history of ISRAEL: the watery chaos that God separated from heaven and earth; the rivers flowing from Eden; the flood that destroyed and renewed the earth; the Red Sea, which parted for the people of Israel but drowned the Egyptians; water gushing from a rock in the wilderness in response to the Israelites' sinful rebellion (Num. 20:7–13); and the Jordan River, through which Israel passed into the Promised Land and in which JOHN THE BAPTIST would later declare forgiveness for the repentance of sins and baptize Jesus himself.

Different baptismal practices dramatize this salvation history. Immersion aptly represents drowning the old self of sin and birthing a new self, just as a child comes to life from the waters of the mother's womb. Sprinkling or pouring water over a candidate suggests the cleansing power of water and how precious every drop of water is to those who are thirsty and need reviving. Baptism in a lake or stream evokes the waters that flow through all creation; baptism in a pool or font, the waters that spring forth from the earth to refresh and sustain life. In each case, the water means nothing unless people clearly grasp the promises of God attached to it; yet, without these dramatic actions, the promises threaten to become mere words.

Third, *baptism sustains faith.* As representing *birth*, baptism is appropriately administered only one time. But as reminding Christians of who they really are, baptism, as M. LUTHER noted, is a sacrament for a lifetime that genuinely effects the acts of cleansing from sin and adoption as a child of God that it symbolizes.

Human faith is always weak and tottering. Trials and temptations, as well as identities of nation, class, race, and ideology, easily divert Christians from Christ's way. Experience of unjust suffering causes them to question who God is and therefore who they are. Whenever followers of Jesus remember that they have passed through the waters of baptism, they reaffirm their true identity as brothers and sisters of Christ. Baptism reassures Christians that God is faithful and will ultimately fulfil God's purposes, despite all evidence to the contrary.

Baptism sustains the faith not only of the individual candidate, but also of the church as a whole. Whenever Christians witness a baptism, they are invited to reclaim their foundational identity. Every baptism is a covenant-renewal ceremony between God and his people.

Fourth, *baptism is a public declaration of loyalty.* God's initiating activity calls forth humans' response: a candidate, normally before the assembled community, publicly pledges loyalty to Christ and the Church. Following ancient practice, the priest or minister may ask the candidate to recite a CREED and to promise to participate actively in the Church's worship and life.

In early centuries, baptisms often took place apart from the congregation in a special side room (the baptistery), but even then the community was represented by the ordained priest, and the newly baptized sometimes moved directly into the nave to receive their first Eucharist with the rest of the community. The Reformers believed that medieval Catholic practice obscured baptism's communal dimension, but today Catholic and Protestant Churches alike usually locate the baptismal pool or font in the nave itself and celebrate baptism as part of Sunday worship.

Fifth, *baptism is a spur to discipleship.* Those marked with a new identity in Jesus Christ commit themselves to his way of life. They promise to make common cause with the Church, and the community promises to instruct them and to encourage and hold them accountable in their discipleship. In the ancient Church, this instruction began as early as three years prior to candidates' baptism. In any event, baptism calls a person to begin a journey of witness and service that will end only in death. Some Churches cover the casket of the deceased with a white pall to signify this fulfilment of baptismal identity.

Baptism's covenantal structure clearly illuminates the baptism of persons who are old enough to grasp and respond to the promises of God. NT references to baptism presuppose that candidates come to baptism with a demonstrable FAITH. Baptism does not create this faith but rather marks and sustains it.

Nevertheless, the Christian Church early on came to see that baptism's covenantal resonances implicate children, and even tiny infants. Baptism does not guarantee their salvation, but it does mark the new life in Christ that God has promised the community as a whole, including its children. Because baptism of infants dramatically represents God's utter graciousness in claiming humans before they (can) respond to God, parents and the community can trust that their children's identity is secure in Christ, and the children themselves can be assured as they grow older that they have always belonged to God.

The practice of baptizing infants ('pedobaptism') has nevertheless been subject to sustained criticism since the Reformation and remains problematic in the Christian West. Baptists of both continental (see MENNONITE THEOLOGY) and English (see BAPTIST THEOLOGY) background have argued on biblical and dogmatic grounds that only those able to make confession of their faith should be admitted to baptism ('believers' baptism'). Even within the Reformed tradition, no less a figure than K. BARTH noted the tendency for baptism to be little more than a social rite of passage that guaranteed personal heavenly salvation but did not call a person into a new way of life in Christ and the Church. For Barth, baptism should be a means by which *adult* believers first make public witness of their faith and discipleship.

The problem, however, is not baptism of *infants*. All baptism – whether of adults or children – is tenable only if the Church lives as a covenant community that calls its members into patterns of mutual encouragement and accountability. In a culture shaped by excessive individualism and consumerism, Christians are challenged to clarify again what it means to be a member of the Church, and what it means for the Church to be the body of the living, resurrected Christ. Reform of baptismal practice will depend on a renewed vision of Christians' distinctive life together under the cross for the sake of the world.

See also Sacramentology.

Baptism, Eucharist and Ministry (World Council of Churches, 1982).

J. Calvin, *Institutes of the Christian Religion* (Westminster Press, 1960), 4.15–16.

'The *Didache*' in *Early Christian Fathers* (Westminster Press, 1953), 171–79.

J. A. Jungmann, *The Early Liturgy* (University of Notre Dame Press, 1959).

D. Wright, *Infant Baptism in Historical Perspective* (Paternoster Press, 2007).

John P. Burgess

BAPTIST THEOLOGY Baptists are a world Christian communion with Churches in every continent. Universally confessing faith in God as Trinity, they nevertheless show some diversity in their theology, owing partly to their congregational polity and partly to their origins. Baptist Churches tend to trace their heritage to work by English, North American, or German missionaries, the first being the oldest group. The earliest Baptist Church is reckoned to be a congregation of religious separatists from England who gathered under their minister John Smyth in Amsterdam in 1609 and restricted baptism to those who could profess their own belief in Christ. Members of this Church returned to set up the first Baptist church on English soil in London in 1612. Arminian in theology (see Arminianism), they came to be known as 'General Baptists'. The second main group of Baptists in England were 'Particular Baptists'. Calvinist in theology, they originated in a number of separatist congregations in London who adopted the practice of baptizing believing disciples in 1633 (see Reformed Theology). These two groups differed over the scope of the atonement, with Particular Baptists limiting its benefits to God's elect. The two streams were united in 1891 within what is now the Baptist Union of Great Britain, and today Baptists generally affirm in equal measure both the sovereignty of God and the need for a free human response to the offer of God's grace.

Baptist Churches in North America began in the British colonies in the mid-seventeenth century, showing at first the same distinction between Arminian and Calvinist congregations. Calvinist Baptists ('Regular Baptists') united in the late eighteenth century with new, evangelizing congregations formed out of the Great Awakening ('Separatist Baptists'), but then split in the mid-nineteenth century into Baptists in the northern states (the largest group now being the American Baptist Churches in the USA) and those in the southern states (the largest group being the Southern Baptist Convention) over the issue of slavery. Today the northern Churches are more moderate and ecumenical in theology than the southern. The mid-nineteenth century also saw the rise of African-American Baptist Churches, strongly committed to Christian social action. Today their three main conventions are together the second largest group of Baptists in the world, after the Southern Baptist Convention. Unlike southern Baptists, they are members of the Baptist World Alliance and (together with twenty-one other Baptist unions or conventions) the World Council of Churches.

The third main source of Baptist life has been German Baptists, whose first church was founded in Hamburg in 1834. Building on European pietistic movements of the nineteenth century, Baptists spread from Germany into western and eastern Europe, especially among Slavic-speaking peoples.

Although most national Baptist unions or conventions are members of the Baptist World Alliance, there is no single formulation of faith among Baptists throughout the world. Even some national bodies lack a central confession of faith, though most have adopted one in recent years. Despite their diversity, however, Baptist theologians generally stand within the tradition of the magisterial Reformation with its key principles of justification by faith and *sola Scriptura*, while drawing from the Reformation's more radical wing on matters of ecclesiology and baptism. Although the direct origins of the Baptist movement lie within separatism at the time of the English Reformation, there was some influence from the continental Anabaptist movement, especially with regard to the meaning and practice of baptism.

Baptists do not normally use creeds in their worship, preferring to appeal directly to the witness of Scripture, but several Baptist confessions of past and present have included reference to the ecumenical creeds and councils as reliable guides in matters of faith, and they have certainly never been rejected. Baptist theologians generally display a similar range of approaches to critical scholarship and to doctrines of God, creation, theological anthropology, Christology, soteriology, and eschatology as can be found in other branches of the church. Baptists have also contributed to critical biblical study in the twentieth century, especially in the area of the OT through the work of scholars like H. W. Robinson (1872–1945) and H. H. Rowley (1890–1969). Today there is an increasing interest among Baptist theologians in locating the Baptist movement within the whole 'Catholic' Church. While continuing the historic Baptist stress that Tradition must always be subject to the judgement of Scripture, there is a growing recognition that tradition will play a part in shaping the life of the Church as it interprets Scripture corporately.

The Baptist doctrine of the Church is based on two theological ideas: the rule of Christ in the congregation and the nature of the Church as a Covenant community. Baptists understand the local congregation to be 'gathered' by Christ in covenant relationship, sometimes expressed in a written covenant to which all assent, typically including an agreement to 'walk together and watch over' each other before God. Baptists affirm the freedom of this local church to order its own life and ministry, seeking the purpose of Christ within a 'church meeting' in which all the members have a voice and a vote. Freedom does not mean strict autonomy, however, as local congregations covenant together in regional associations and national unions or conventions for the purposes of fellowship, mutual counsel and mission. On the one hand, because the local church is the body of Christ, and its meeting stands under the direct rule of Christ who is present among his people (Matt. 18:20), it cannot be imposed upon by any external ecclesial authority. On the other hand, because churches when gathered together also stand under Christ's rule and are also a manifestation of his Body, the local church meeting must listen to the counsel of the wider Church as it seeks to find the mind of Christ for itself. It is the distinctive Baptist ethos not to define this sharing of oversight in a regulation, but to live in bonds of trust. Affirming the liberty of the local church under the rule of Christ also accounts for the emphasis of Baptists from their very beginning on the winning and preserving of religious liberty, not only for Christians but for all world religions. Baptists are opposed to any establishment of religion where the State either favours or interferes in the life of the religious community.

All Baptists understand the local congregation to be the most clearly visible unit of the 'invisible' universal Church, or the whole company of the redeemed, which exists through all space and time and will be completed in the new creation. Baptists, however, disagree about the extent to which the assembling of Churches together here and now *also* makes the Church visible, and about what corporate structures are necessary between the local and the universal levels of the Church. Most Baptists keep the term 'church' for the local congregation, although many recognize that associations and conventions have an ecclesial nature.

Baptist theology of baptism derives from the doctrine of the Church as a fellowship of believers. Only those who can profess their own faith are to be baptized, and Baptist biblical scholars have argued that this is a return to the practice of the NT Church. Baptists think that the growth of the tradition of infant baptism in the patristic period obscured the full meaning of baptism, in which there is an encounter between the transforming presence of God and the person who comes with his or her own faith. They think that the full range of metaphors attached to baptism in the NT (such as new birth, forgiveness of/cleansing from sin, death and resurrection with Christ, adoption as children of God, and membership in the body of Christ) cannot be applied to the baptism of a very young child, in which the only faith involved is that of the parents and the Church. Baptists think that the proper time for baptism is when a Christian believer can be commissioned for the ministry of the people of God, and endowed with gifts by the Holy Spirit for sharing in God's mission in the world. They practise immersion of candidates in the triune name of God as the normative mode of baptism, symbolizing death and resurrection; and many follow baptism with laying on of hands for a commissioning to Christian service. Young children are generally received into the covenant life of the Church through a service involving a prayer of blessing for the child, and dedication of the parents and Church to the task of Christian nurture. Since those who come to baptism already have faith and are already regenerated by the Spirit, it follows that Christian initiation is not a single point but a process, involving nurture, conversion, baptism, gifting with the Spirit for service, and sharing in the Lord's Supper (see Eucharist). In recent years Baptists have thus suggested to pedobaptist Churches that there is more ecumenical potential in affirming a 'common initiation' than a 'common baptism'.

The majority of Baptist Churches throughout the world believe that baptism as a believing disciple is essential for membership (so-called 'closed membership'). Like nearly all Baptists, these Churches affirm the unrepeatable nature of baptism; they do not regard the baptism of those already baptized as infants as rebaptism, since they decline to recognize the infant rite *as* baptism. Most 'closed membership' Churches now, however, offer hospitality at the Lord's Supper – 'open communion' – to all who confess Christ, regardless of baptism. A sizeable minority of Baptist Churches in the world (a majority in the UK) practise not only 'open communion' but 'open membership', where baptism as a believer is not required for Church membership, though this position may be taken for various theological reasons. Some follow one early Baptist view, notably expressed by J. Bunyan (1628–88), in which entry to the Church is based simply on the profession of faith of the believer, regardless of baptism. Others follow another early Baptist view that baptism is certainly essential for membership in the body of Christ, but that the conscience of those who regard themselves truly baptized as infants should be respected, and that they are to be accepted as fellow-members since 'God has accepted them' (Rom. 14:3). Some Baptist theologians have recently suggested that infant baptism might be given some recognition within an understanding of 'common initiation' as a process or journey, which is not completed until a personal profession of faith has been made and a disciple has been commissioned to share in the mission of God.

Baptists differ about whether baptism and the Lord's Supper are occasions for receiving the grace of God. Some follow the tradition of H. Zwingli and stress the nature of the Supper as a memorial of the sacrifice of Christ; in this they resemble the earlier General Baptists, though it should be added that the latter also followed Zwingli in stressing the presence of Christ in the congregation as his body. Others follow the tradition of the earlier Particular Baptists and affirm Calvin's understanding of a real communion with Christ through the elements in a 'spiritual eating and drinking'. The 'non-sacramentalists' among Baptists regard baptism as only a profession of faith and a declaration of the salvation that God has already brought to the life of the person baptized, while others affirm that God acts in baptism, coming graciously to meet and transform the believer as part of a process of salvation which has already begun. The first group insists on the language of 'ordinance' (i.e., what Christ has ordained) rather than sacrament, although the two terms were interchangeable in the early centuries of Baptist life.

Baptists generally hold to a twofold ministry in the local church. First there is the 'minister' or 'pastor' (often called either a 'bishop' or 'elder' by early Baptists), who has pastoral oversight of the congregation. While the local church is free to call its own minister, his or her call by Christ to ordained ministry is recognized by as wide a range of Churches as possible, since he or she represents the whole Church on the local scene and through a ministry of the Word helps to keep the local congregation faithful to the Gospel. The 'deacon', or pastoral assistant, though ordained up to the nineteenth century, is today usually a lay office and is filled by the local congregation acting alone. Some churches in addition appoint lay 'elders' who share in the ministry of oversight. Most Baptist unions or conventions also have a trans-local or inter-church ministry, called by a variety of names such as 'regional minister', 'executive minister', or sometimes even 'bishop'. These officers have no executive power in the local church but exercise a significant pastoral and missionary function among the churches. They are regarded as an extension of the local office of minister rather than constituting a third order of ministry. Theology of ministry and ecclesiology thus correspond in the Baptist ethos, in a relation between the local and the wider Church which is characterized more by trust than by regulation.

G. R. Beasley-Murray, *Baptism in the New Testament* (Macmillan, 1963).

P. S. Fiddes, *Tracks and Traces: Baptist Identity in Church and Theology* (Paternoster Press, 2003).

B. Leonard, *Baptist Ways: A History* (Judson, 2003).

W. Lumpkin, *Baptist Confessions of Faith* (Judson, 1959).

N. Wright, *Free Church, Free State: The Positive Baptist Vision* (Paternoster Press, 2006).

Paul S. Fiddes

Barmen Declaration The Barmen Declaration is a formal statement articulating the German Evangelical Church's theological argument for condemning the false doctrine (see Heresy) and political allegiances of the German Christians and calling for the Church's unity, spiritual renewal, and faithfulness to the classic confessions of the Reformation. It was adopted at the first Confessional Synod of the German Evangelical Church – commonly known as 'the Confessing Church' – held in Wuppertal-Barmen between 29 and 31 May 1934. Authored primarily by Swiss Reformed theologian K. Barth, it was signed by Reformed, Lutheran, and United Church pastors who rejected the German Christian Church's teaching that 'Christ, as God the helper and saviour, has, through Hitler, become mighty among us ... Hitler ... is now the way of the Spirit and Will of God for the Church of Christ among the German nation.' Against this position, the Declaration underscores the conviction that God alone is sovereign and that Jesus Christ alone is Lord. The text further insists on a Christocentric approach to discerning divine revelation, rejecting methods founded in natural theology. It was precisely because the German Christians approached the theological task 'in human arrogance', the signatories of the Declaration believed, that they falsely identified the ideology of National Socialism with the will of God.

The Declaration is divided into two parts. The first describes the context and motivation for its writing, challenging readers not to submit to the State's use of 'false doctrine' as a means to rally German Evangelicals, but instead to unite around shared biblical and confessional standards. The second rehearses the history of the union of confessional Churches comprising the German Evangelical Church, as well as the German government's initial recognition of this union in 1933. Six 'evangelical truths' are then 'confessed', each leading with a passage of Scripture and then making a theological statement to counter a 'false doctrine' espoused by the German Christians: (1) there is no Word of God other than that made known in Jesus Christ and attested to in Holy Scripture; (2) Christians belong to no lords other than Jesus Christ; (3) the Church is the property of Christ alone, and never of the State or of any ideology; (4) the presence of various offices in the Church does 'not establish a dominion of some over the others'; (5) while officers of the

State should be honoured by Christian believers, the State does not 'fulfil ... the Church's vocation', nor is the Church 'an organ of the State'; and (6) sermon and sacraments, as the 'Word and work of the Lord', may not be placed 'in the service of any arbitrarily chosen desires, purposes, and plans'.

The Barmen Declaration is considered, by many Protestant Christian believers, to have confessional status. It is included, for example, in the historical confessions of the Reformed Church in Germany, in the constitutions of many Lutheran and United Churches in Germany, and in the *Book of Confessions* of the Presbyterian Church (USA). It is commonly referenced as an example of how the Word of God heard in a specific, historical context can have, at the same time, broader – even universal – significance.

M. Ernst-Habib, 'A Conversation with Twentieth-Century Confessions' in *Conversations with the Confessions: Dialogue in the Reformed Tradition*, ed. J. D. Small (Geneva Press, 2005).

E. Jüngel, *Christ, Justice and Peace: Toward a Theology of the State in Dialogue with the Barmen Declaration* (T&T Clark, 1992).

CYNTHIA L. RIGBY

BARTH, KARL Karl Barth (1886–1968) was born and died in Basel, Switzerland. His father and both grandfathers were pastors. Barth studied in Berlin with A. von HARNACK, was influenced by F. SCHLEIERMACHER, and became seriously interested in theology after reading W. Herrmann's (1846–1922) *Ethics* (1901). Barth took the Christocentric impulse that was to define his theology from Herrmann, insisting that 'If the freedom of divine immanence is sought and supposedly found apart from Jesus Christ, it can signify in practice only our enslavement to a false god' (*CD* II/1, 319); thus a true understanding of humanity could only start 'from Jesus Christ as the object and foundation of faith' (*CD* II/1, 156).

Barth was ordained in 1908, and his thinking was influenced by his ten years as pastor at Safenwil (1911–21), World War I, his involvement in the Christian Socialist movement, and his years as professor of theology. His first appointments were at Göttingen, Münster, and Bonn. During the rise of the Third Reich, Barth took an active role in Church politics and was the primary author of the BARMEN DECLARATION, which rejected any assimilation of the GOSPEL to the politics of racial supremacy or nationalism. In 1935 the Nazis expelled him from his teaching post at Bonn for not taking a loyalty oath to A. Hitler (1889–1945), and he moved to Basel, where he remained until retirement in 1962 – at which point he travelled to the United States, speaking at Princeton, Chicago, and New York. These lectures later became *Evangelical Theology: An Introduction* (1963).

Barth broke with the LIBERAL THEOLOGY of his teachers in 1914, when he was disillusioned by the fact that most of his teachers signed a manifesto supporting war. In his search for a more viable biblical exegesis, he wrote two editions of his famous commentary on Romans (1919 and 1921). Influenced by S. KIERKEGAARD, Barth stressed God's otherness and ESCHATOLOGY in ways that he would later admit were one-sided but not absolutely wrong (*CD* II/1, 634–5). He consistently avoided any idea that God could be used by us 'to put the crowning touch to what men began of their own accord' (Busch, *Barth* 99) and promoted a 'DIALECTICAL THEOLOGY', so called because in it Barth sought to present the good news of the Gospel through conflicting ideas that could not be overcome through some theological synthesis. The only 'solution' to the problem of God talk was God's 'yes' to humanity in Jesus Christ; but this 'yes' included a 'no' in the sense that humanity could speak of God only by actually relying on God's GRACE in a way that brings all human speaking of God under judgement. In short, for Barth it is impossible for us to speak of God; but it becomes possible as God actually enables it.

Against all attempts to try to found human knowledge of God either in some already-existing prior knowledge of God that undermines the need for special revelation or in some general anthropology that reverses the roles of Creator and creature, Barth insisted, 'There is a way from CHRISTOLOGY to anthropology, but there is no way from anthropology to Christology' (*CD* I/1, 131). This same emphasis on God's priority in Christ was stressed in his DOCTRINE of reconciliation, wherein Barth maintained that FAITH'S possibility cannot be 'demonstrated and explained in the light of general anthropology' (*CD* IV/1, 740) and when he argued that the creation of world views was an attempt to circumvent revelation and reconciliation as actualized in Jesus Christ (*CD* IV/3, 257).

Barth came into conflict with E. Brunner (1889–1966), R. BULTMANN, and F. Gogarten (1887–1968), his fellow 'dialectical theologians', because he sensed that they attempted to ground theology elsewhere (e.g., in existentialist philosophy) and so compromised theology's nature as faith seeking understanding. Against those who imagined that his thinking, too, was grounded in some philosophical system, Barth abandoned his first effort at comprehensive theological statement (the 1927 *Christian Dogmatics*) and began his *magnum opus*, the *Church Dogmatics* (13 vols., 1932–67). In particular, he opposed NATURAL THEOLOGY on the grounds that it suggests that there is some generally available 'court of appeal' by which God can be known other than by grace. Natural theology for Barth amounts to a form of self-justification which was overcome once and for all in Jesus Christ for our benefit.

Barth's theology is Trinitarian in nature, beginning with his formal presentation of the doctrine in *CD* I/1, reaching a high point in his doctrine of God in *CD* II, and radiating out to pervade his view of CREATION (*CD* III) and reconciliation (*CD* IV) as well. God is both objective within the immanent Trinity and one who loves in freedom (primary objectivity), and objective to humanity as revealed in objects different from God (secondary objectivity). Barth insisted that a sharp distinction but not a separation between the immanent and economic TRINITY was important, and his entire theology is marked by the fact that in each doctrine our inclusion in relationship with God is based solely upon God's grace and cannot be said to be necessary for God.

Barth's revolutionary doctrine of ELECTION differed from the more traditional Calvinist double PREDESTINATION, in which some were saved and others damned according to an absolute fixed (static) decree preceding creation; against this Barth insisted that election had to be seen only in Christ, who, as electing God and elected human being, was both elected and rejected for us, and that it needed to be understood as a continuing action of the living God rather than as a fixed decree. Hence the rest of us stand in relation to God only in and through Christ himself, who experienced God's wrath in our place and so reconciled us with the Father. Rejecting both UNIVERSALISM and any idea that God could not in the end be gracious to all, Barth intended to affirm the power of God's gracious 'yes' over God's 'no' to sin which Christ himself endured for the human race in his death for us (*CD* II/2, 417, 477). Election then is the sum of the Gospel, an election of grace (*CD* II/2, 3 *et al.*): not a dark mystery concerning some arbitrary decree on the part of a distant God, but rather the establishment by an action of the living God of true human freedom and thus the very basis of Christian ethics, through which humanity is thus included within the doctrine of God itself (cf. *CD* II/2, 509ff.). In *CD* II/2 Barth's vision of the relation between ISRAEL and the Church, his thorough treatment of evil, and his fearless opposition to antisemitism all were marked by a hope engendered by the resurrection of Jesus himself from the dead.

Barth's later view of the sacrament (*CD* IV/4, fragment) has been vigorously criticized for: separating divine and human being and action too sharply (e.g., HOLY SPIRIT from water BAPTISM); rejecting infant baptism; insisting that Christ is the only sacrament (thus denying Barth's own earlier view that sacraments are means of grace in the more traditional Reformed sense); rejecting even his earlier sacramental views espoused in *CD* I/2 and II/1; and subtly redefining the sacraments as human ethical responses to God's actions within history instead of noticing that they represent our human inclusion in the life of the Trinity through Christ's own continuing high priestly mediation as the ascended and coming Lord. In his 'radically new view' of the sacrament, Barth's positive intention was to assert that Christ alone through his Spirit is our means of JUSTIFICATION and SANCTIFICATION and he wanted to avoid all forms of either sacramentalism, which would ascribe sacramental validity to the Church's action, or moralism, which would ascribe such validity to a person's own disposition or behaviour. Barth's positive aim was to stress that the visible Church is the historical form of Christ's presence on earth that could be experienced and understood only in faith and not directly discerned or validated in its visible actions as such.

E. Busch, *The Great Passion: An Introduction to Karl Barth's Theology* (Eerdmans, 2004).
G. Hunsinger, *How to Read Karl Barth: The Shape of His Theology* (Oxford University Press, 1991).
B. McCormack, *Karl Barth's Critically Realistic Dialectical Theology: Its Genesis and Development 1909–1936* (Oxford University Press, 1997).
T. F. Torrance, *Karl Barth: Biblical and Evangelical Theologian* (T&T Clark, 1990).

PAUL D. MOLNAR

BARTHIANISM 'Barthianism' refers to the school of thought following in the tradition of K. BARTH. It is a term which often bears a negative connotation, both in the view of those who count themselves students of Barth and by those critical of Barth's theology and its influence. For this reason, the argument is sometimes made that the truest Barthians are those who follow Barth's approach to theology while at the same time eschewing the label – even as Barth himself proudly declared he was not a Barthian!

A list of theologians influenced by Barth who arguably fall into this category of 'not Barthian' Barthians might include H. Gollwitzer (1908–93), T. F. Torrance (1913–2007), and E. Jüngel (b. 1933). They recognize, with Barth, that the focus of the Church's theology is not any particular theologian or theological school. Rather, just as JOHN THE BAPTIST pointed to the One greater than himself, theology should ever redirect us to Christ. In addition, these and other 'not-Barthian' Barthians seek to take seriously Barth's charge that they become theologians in their own right, rather than seeking to be little versions of him. They understand the work of theology to be ongoing and open ended, believing that the calling of every Christian is to discern the new shape of God's living Word. At the same time, they generally (1) uphold the sovereignty of God and the centrality of Christ; (2) reject any anthropological starting points for formulating claims about who God is or what God is up to in the world; (3) insist that we know God because God has acted freely in human history, revealing to us who God actually is; and (4) believe that the GOSPEL is good news for the whole world, and must therefore be proclaimed as well as considered.

Barthianism is roundly critiqued by liberal theological scholars who take issue with Barth's utter rejection of the ANALOGY of being (*analogia entis*). These theologians reject the Barthian assertion that God can be known, through the working of the Holy Spirit, solely on the basis of God's self-revelation in history. They further register the concern that Barthians reference the actions of God in ways that distance them from taking responsibility for historical occurrences or – even worse – in ways dangerously closed to conversation and correction. H. R. Niebuhr (1894–1962), for example, argued that Barthianism disallows the possibility of a public ethics, since it refuses to seek common ground upon which social issues can be discussed and negotiated.

Barthianism is also rejected as unorthodox by many evangelical scholars. C. van Til (1895–1987), for example, argued that Barthian reference to the Bible as the 'Word of God' is misleading, since Barthians understand the relationship between the Bible and REVELATION to be only indirect. Interestingly, some evangelicals take issue, along with liberal theologians, with the Barthian rejection of the analogy of being, understanding a point of contact to be a premise essential for effective evangelism and apologetics. In contrast to these thinkers, T. F. Torrance understood Barth's legacy to be consistent with evangelicalism in so far as it is centred on Christ, whose life, death, and RESURRECTION is proclaimed as good news for all the world.

See also Dialectical Theology; Evangelical theology; Liberal Theology.

T. Gorringe, *Karl Barth: Against Hegemony* (Oxford University Press, 1999).

C. van Til, *Christianity and Barthianism* (Presbyterian and Reformed Publishing, 1962).

Cynthia L. Rigby

Base Communities Emerging in the 1960s, the term 'base community' is common to both Catholic and Protestant traditions. Although theological interpretations and physical expressions differ between and within both traditions, the ethos of the base community is held, almost universally, to lie in its relatively small size. According to official Catholic interpretations, the *raison d'être* of the 'base ecclesial community' lies in its integration of the LAITY within the broader auspices of the Catholic Church. Here, emphasis rests upon its ecclesial status as a smaller component of the larger ecclesiastical whole, existing within (rather than in competition with) the parish or diocese.

Within conservative Protestant and, increasingly, Catholic charismatic circles, the significance of the base community rests on its ability to complement traditional ecclesiastical activity by enabling participants to access more readily the 'basics' of the Christian faith. Whether through mid-week Bible study or prayerful meditation, for example, the less formal environment encouraged by the base-community model is held to encourage a deepening of spiritual commitment and maturity.

For Christians of a more progressive persuasion, the significance of the base community resides in one or a number of key characteristics. For some (especially advocates of LIBERATION THEOLOGIES), the base community is valued as an instrument of socio-political empowerment of those at the economic base of society. To others, the meaningful interpersonal encounter facilitated by its relatively small scale allows for true Christian *communitas*. For those with an extra-institutional religious identity, the base community is championed as a viable alternative to large-scale, organizational Christianity.

A. Dawson, 'The Origins and Character of the Base Ecclesial Community: A Brazilian Perspective' in *The Cambridge Companion to Liberation Theology*, ed. C. Rowland, 2nd edn (Cambridge University Press, 2007), 139–58.

M. Hebblethwaite, *Basic is Beautiful: Basic Ecclesial Communities from Third World to First World* (HarperCollins, 1993).

Andrew Dawson

Basil of Caesarea: see Cappadocian Fathers.

Beatific Vision The DOCTRINE of the beatific vision holds that the redeemed come to see and know God in GLORY, and that this overwhelming gift of participating in the divine life makes them happy or blessed (i.e., it beatifies them) in the fullest sense possible for a human being. It means that they share in the beatitude or joy of the TRINITY forever.

The biblical witness offers a range of important texts, frequently taken up in the tradition. Jacob, referring to his night of wrestling with a stranger, declares, 'I have seen God face to face, and yet my life is preserved' (Gen. 32:30). Moses is told that he may not behold the face of God, for such a vision would bring his mortal human existence to its end, yet he is granted a vision of the divine glory while under God's protection (Exod. 33:20–3). In the NT the vision of God is more often spoken of in a heavenly or eschatological context. 1 John 3:2 ('when he is revealed, we will be like him, for we will see him as he is') holds together a final manifestation of Christ in glory with a transformation of believers that permits them to 'see him as he is'. 1 Corinthians 13:12 ('now we see in a mirror, dimly, but then we will see face to face') also emphasizes a transformed state in which seeing God 'face to face' will take the place of the partial vision available now. This future state will entail a personal relation grounded in God's prior knowing and loving of the believer: 'Now I know only in part; then I will know fully, even as I have been fully known' (1 Cor. 13:12).

As early as IRENAEUS, Christians had begun to understand this vision of God as the fulfilment of, or truest form of, human existence. Yet this divine self-disclosure to the creature is always understood as a free act of divine mercy and GRACE, a gift of a new form of sharing by the creature in God's own life: 'It is not possible to live apart from life, and the means of life is fellowship with God; but fellowship with God is to know God, and to enjoy his goodness. Humans therefore shall see God, that they may live, being made immortal by that sight' (*AH* 4.20.5–6). Various forms of the *visio Dei* ('vision of God') are alluded to and discussed throughout the tradition by major figures including the CAPPADOCIAN FATHERS, AUGUSTINE, ANSELM, BONAVENTURE, and T. AQUINAS. In 1311 the Council of Vienne affirmed that, while the beatific vision fulfils the deepest desire of the human person, it is granted only as a divine gift, not as an ultimate natural achievement.

Several theological *loci* intersect within the doctrine of the beatific vision. As a feature of the doctrine of God, the doctrine highlights a difference between Orthodox theologians such as G. PALAMAS, who emphasize that only the divine energies or glory can be seen in the vision of God, and western theologians such as Aquinas, who generally argue that it is precisely the vision of the divine essence itself that beatifies the redeemed – even though the infinity of God's essence means that the vision can never be comprehensive for either the ANGELS or the blessed. Within THEOLOGICAL ANTHROPOLOGY, the doctrine underlines the constitutive paradox of human existence: by nature, humanity's ultimate happiness is the vision of God, and yet that vision can only come as the gift of God in a way that entirely transcends natural human capacities: 'Man's happiness is twofold. One is the happiness found in this life ... [which] is imperfect. The other is the perfect happiness of heaven, where we will see God himself through his essence ... Even though by his nature man is inclined to his ultimate end, man cannot reach it by nature but only by grace, and this is owing to the loftiness of that end' (Aquinas, *CTrin.* 6.4.3–4). This paradox, importantly discussed by H. DE LUBAC in the twentieth century, raises the difficult question of how the desire for beatitude, if considered a natural and constitutive aspect of human existence, can nevertheless be addressed by an entirely free and unexacted gift of grace. As the ultimate term of all human knowing and loving, the doctrine of the beatific vision also plays important roles in theological epistemology, CHRISTOLOGY, and ESCHATOLOGY.

H. de Lubac, *The Mystery of the Supernatural* (Herder and Herder, 1998 [1965]).

MARK A. MCINTOSH

BEATIFICATION: see CANONIZATION.

BEATITUDES: see SERMON ON THE MOUNT.

BEAUTY, THEOLOGY OF: see AESTHETICS, THEOLOGICAL.

BELHAR CONFESSION The text of the Belhar Confession was commissioned by the South African Dutch Reformed Mission Church (DRMC) in 1982 and was officially adopted by that Church at its 1986 synod in the Cape Town suburb of Belhar. It was subsequently accepted as one of its confessional standards by the Uniting Reformed Church in South Africa, officially constituted in 1994 from the union of the two largest non-White South African Reformed Churches: the DRMC and the Dutch Reformed Church in Africa. Its composition was stimulated by the condemnation of the apartheid policy of the White South African Dutch Reformed Church (DRC) as a heresy at the 1982 General Assembly of the World Alliance of Reformed Churches in Ottawa, Canada.

As explained in the concurrently published 'Accompanying Letter', the Belhar Confession was occasioned by the conviction that 'the heart of the GOSPEL is so threatened as to be at stake' by the DRC's policy of apartheid (i.e., the enforced separation of racial groups within the Church). The Confession's five articles base this rejection of apartheid on the requirements of Christian unity, which (1) is grounded in the work of the TRINITY; (2) is 'a gift and an obligation' that 'must become visible' in the Church's daily life; (3) is belied by the enforced separation of believers according to RACE; (4) entails a mandate for the Church to work to alleviate suffering and injustice; and (5) demands obedience when resisted by any human authority.

IAN A. MCFARLAND

BIBLE: see SCRIPTURE.

BIBLICAL CRITICISM The term 'biblical criticism' is generally associated with a way of studying the Bible which emerged during the ENLIGHTENMENT, namely what is known as the historical–critical approach. During the modern period, biblical study generally seemed to require a choice between two extremes, historico-criticism on the one hand, or a theological (i.e., faith-based) interpretation on the other. In the postmodern age, the situation is more complicated, since there have emerged a number of 'readings' of the Bible, which take seriously the situation of the interpreter in a way that the historical–critical approach sometimes failed to do, while at the same time acknowledging the cultural relativity of the biblical writings in a way that theological approaches have often ignored.

But to begin with the historical–critical method and its aftermath is to tell the last part of the story first. Biblical criticism is better understood within the framework of the history of Christian thought and the emergence of a Christian canon of SCRIPTURE, in particular of the NT. It may then be recognized as the inevitable result of the direction taken by early Christianity. Most obviously, the adoption of a four-Gospel tradition set up a process of comparison and analysis. The significance of this may be seen in two second-century attempts to replace the fourfold Gospel with a single version. MARCION, taking seriously PAUL's statement that there is only one Gospel (see Gal. 1:6–7), made his own Gospel, which was a revision of Luke as it was known to him, with passages and wordings which he considered to be distortions of the Christian message removed or revised. A different approach was followed by Tatian (d. *ca* 185), who combined the Gospels by intricately interweaving their phrases, in order to produce a single version, known as the *Diatessaron* – a work so popular that in some regions it replaced the separate accounts. But, successful though these works were in their day and for some centuries after, their eventual failure is shown by the fact that neither of them survived antiquity. By contrast, the fourfold Gospel survives in thousands of copies and has been accepted as normative throughout the Church. In spite of various difficulties, most notably the ammunition that differences between the written texts gave to pagan writers such as Celsus (*fl. ca* 180), Christianity preferred this complex situation and developed ways of reading the written Gospels which found in them a richer meta-narrative. The same is true of the Epistles. The numbers – seven 'Catholic' letters, and fourteen in the Pauline collection (*NB*: doubling a number intensified its significance in ancient numerology) – imply that the sum of these sometimes contradictory letters contains a greater and universal wisdom.

Thus, the NT as a collection of writings can only be read within a process of critical comparison. From quite an early period, we find editions which provide paratext in order to facilitate this. The most influential system for the Epistles is the Euthalian Apparatus, which among other features contains a series of prologues setting each letter in its context.

Equally momentous was the claiming of the Jewish Scriptures as a part of the Christian heritage. To Marcion (and he was not alone in this), these Scriptures were not a part of Christianity. But the majority position was that they testified to Jesus as the Christ, and were inspired by the Spirit who also breathed life into the Church. The version which Christians adopted was the SEPTUAGINT, the Greek translations having their origin in the third-century-BC Jewish Diaspora in Alexandria. The textual complexity of the Septuagint, and the need for Christians to find interpretative methods which would justify their claims about its meaning, led to sophisticated readings relying heavily on allegorical techniques (see ALLEGORY). Here again, debate about the meaning of the text was essential to its use, since the 'plain' meaning was less important than what the reader found hidden.

The growth of the Christian canon therefore made biblical criticism an essential part of Christian self-understanding. This fact is easily overlooked, because of the well-known tendency of pre-modern scholars to explain or ignore discrepancies and historical difficulties. The meta-narrative always provided a framework in which such problems could be happily subsumed. It is of course all too easy to make broad statements about 1,500 and more years of biblical criticism. There was never a single meta-narrative. But the differences between a historical critic of the past 200 years and anyone before that are more pronounced than those between any two biblical scholars of the previous centuries. And yet it is hard enough to find a precise point at which the historical–critical method emerged. Does one locate it in the publication of B. Spinoza's (1632–77) *Tractatus Theologico-Politicus* (1670), in H. S. Reimarus' (1694–1768) *Fragments of a Life of Jesus* (1774), which proposed a radical historical account to replace the passion narratives in the Gospels, in D. F. Strauss' (1808–74) affirmation of the Gospels as MYTH, in J. Mill's (*ca* 1645–1707) *Novum Testamentum Graece* (1707), containing about 30,000 variant readings, in F. C. Baur's (1792–1860) article 'The Christ Party in Corinth' (1831), or in Bishop J. W. Colenso's (1814–83) remarks in the 1860s and 1870s on the historical impossibility of the Exodus account? In common to these approaches are analyses of the texts which, rather than accepting the theological issues at face value, draw on historical data and methodologies to question the claims which are made.

Of equal significance is the growth of the natural sciences, and in this process the conclusions reached by C. Darwin (1809–82), most notably in *On the Origin of Species* (1859). The emergence of an incontrovertible account based on observation, following previous upheavals such as the Copernican Revolution, could not fail to have a dramatic impact on biblical criticism. What followed was the emergence of the two extremes of historical–critical and theological approaches already described.

On the one hand, the destruction for ever of the biblical account as a historically inerrant framework led to research which challenged almost everything which had been believed hitherto. The traditional date and authorship of most of the writings were questioned, while many were convincingly shown to have emerged out of complicated composition histories. The effect of archaeology has been ever increasing, so that today the entire biblical history of Israel down to and beyond the Solomonic Empire has been shown to be tendentious. Biblical texts among the Dead Sea Scrolls have provided evidence that the Hebrew Scriptures existed in several different forms in the Second Temple Period, casting doubt on the theory that any single form of texts can be prioritized as the most reliable. The evidence of these scrolls, along with research on other texts from the ancient Near Eastern and Graeco-Roman worlds, has led to new reconstructions of the history of thought and the interpretation of all the biblical writings.

At the same time, the loss of historical credibility encouraged readers to find new theological interpretations in the Bible. Thus the first chapters of Genesis, robbed of any claim to literal truth, came to be treated as profound witnesses to the purpose and nature of life, as poetic accounts encouraging the hearers to make sense of the world. And periodically, attempts were made to marry historical analysis with theological interpretation. In English-speaking circles, the biblical-theology movement of the mid-twentieth century stands as one of the most significant examples. Making use of K. Barth's concept of Scripture as a witness to God's revelation in Christ, biblical theology sought to use the evidence from historical criticism to understand the text, that is, to find the theological content of the text within its historical setting rather than from outside. The popularity of the approach is shown by the success of G. Kittel's (1888–1948) *Theological Dictionary of the New Testament* (1933) in its English version (1964). Describing the history of each word in turn, the *TDNT* seeks to provide historical content which describes the theological concepts of early Christian writers. A famous example is J. Jeremias' (1900–79) research on the Aramaic word *abba* (see Mark 14:36; Rom. 8:15; Gal. 4:6), which, he argued, provided an insight on Jesus' relationship with God.

Postmodern readings of Scripture are possible because the historical–critical approach provided such cogent reasons why the biblical writings have to be read within a particular context. However, they argue that the historical–critical method claims an impartiality which no approach can ever achieve. Instead, they make a virtue out of the reader's necessary bias, suggesting readings of the text on a particular basis, such as postcolonial, gay, feminist, and womanist. The issue in the emergence of historical criticism was the conflict between a reading of texts which interpreted them within a reconstructed historical framework and one which treated them as components within a theological meta-narrative. The challenge of postmodern approaches is to both of these: they suggest that any historical reconstruction will owe a great deal to the situation of the historian; and they reject the universal validity of any single meta-narrative. Where they are most successful is in drawing on the characteristics of the Christian Bible as it was described above, namely the many-voiced character of the tradition. The debates will change. The debate is always with us, because the Bible is constructed out of biblical criticism.

J. Barton, *The Cambridge Companion to Biblical Interpretation* (Cambridge University Press, 1998).

B. D. Ehrman, *Misquoting Jesus: The Story Behind Who Changed the Bible and Why (HarperCollins, 2005);* UK edn: *Whose Word Is It? The Story Behind Who Changed the New Testament and Why* (Continuum, 2008).

D. C. Parker, *The Living Text of the Gospels* (Cambridge, 1997).

J. Pelikan, *Whose Bible Is It? A History of the Scriptures Through the Ages* (Penguin, 2005).

David Parker

BIBLICAL THEOLOGY Scholarly production on the subject of biblical theology is extensive, the terms 'biblical theology', 'biblical', and 'theology' all being used in a multitude of different ways. Consequently, a variety of definitions have been suggested, only the most important of which will be discussed here.

One immediately recognizable trait of the debates is a lack of clear distinction between the various uses of 'theology' in biblical studies. For example, when biblical scholars study the theology of the OT or the theology of the NT, the theology of Jeremiah or the theology of Luke (or certain theological ideas in the OT, the NT, Jeremiah, or Luke), they tend merely to build on their exegetical observations of the texts. From a methodological point of view, 'theological' is often interchangeable with 'exegetical' or 'literary'. In other words, the reason why the study is 'theological' is simply that the texts under investigation are themselves theological in character. Studies of this type seem intent on erecting a barrier against anything homiletic or confessional, the results appearing unrelated to the writer's own personal beliefs. For these and other reasons, 'biblical theology' is probably not the most appropriate term for these approaches. 'Theology of Hebrew Bible/OT' and 'Theology of NT' may be better expressions for this flourishing and worthy enterprise within biblical studies.

In assessing the various contributions to the debates over biblical theology, one can see how rooted they are in the historical–critical approaches of academic scholarship. Echoes of the distinction drawn by J. Gabler (1753–1826) between biblical and dogmatic theology as a means of insulating biblical exegesis from confessional prejudice can still be heard. In practice, however, what is intended is less a distinction between two different kinds of theology than one between biblical studies (understood as the more traditional and historical exegetical work described above) and a category of 'theology' that is used in a variety of different ways.

Many of the contributions to the debate appear to be kindled by a desire to come to terms with the enormous impact of historical research on the Bible, the results of which were occasionally regarded as problematic for belief. In this respect, biblical theologies represent a reaction against more dispassionate historical–critical approaches to the text. Several contributors to the debate, including K. Barth, J. Barr (1924–2006), R. Brown (1928–98), W. Brueggemann (b. 1933), B. Childs (1923–2007), and J. Levenson (b. 1949), have expressed the need to bridge the gap between uses of the Bible in the academy and in the life of the believer. This constitutes a core concern of biblical theology.

A principal feature of twentieth-century biblical-theology debates is their overwhelmingly Protestant and German setting. This has a historical explanation. Critical biblical studies started life in German universities, and the problems posed by critical scholarship were felt strongly from the end of the nineteenth century and throughout the twentieth century, as seen in the work of scholars like L. Köhler (1880–1956), W. Eichrodt (1890–1978), and G. von Rad (1901–71). Especially after 1945, scholars outside Germany, who took an interest in the debates there, increasingly contributed to the discussion. Nevertheless, the debate remained closely defined by Protestant and (especially in Switzerland, the Netherlands, Scotland, and the USA) Reformed theologians. A specifically Anglo-American development was the so-called 'biblical-theology movement'. This was exemplified by G. E. Wright (1909–74), who argued that the description of God's 'mighty acts' (Ps. 145:4) served as the Bible's overarching theological framework. However, this perspective has been subject to severe criticism by scholars such as J. Barr, who judged it exegetically unsound.

Since the biblical-theology debate was so closely bound up with traditions of Protestant interpretation, there was much less interest in the topic among Catholics. The reasons for this are not limited to differences between the Protestant and Catholic biblical canon. The Catholic stress on the importance of the tradition as against the *SOLA SCRIPTURA* of PROTESTANTISM meant that the impact of historical critical studies was much more dominant in Protestant circles. In addition, many Catholic seminaries and universities did not take an equal interest in the academic study of the Bible. Nevertheless, the voices of some very important Roman Catholic scholars have since been heard, including R. Brown, L. Goppelt (1911–73), M. Meinertz (1880–1965), R. Murphy (b. 1917), and R. Schnackenburg (b. 1914). And towards the end of the twentieth century, many important Jewish scholars have also engaged in the biblical-theology debate. Among them, we find names like M. Fishbane (b. 1943), S. Japhet (b. 1934), M. Goshen-Gottstein (b. 1925), J. Levenson, and M. A. Sweeney (b. 1953).

One important feature of twentieth-century biblical theology is that OT/Hebrew Bible scholars dominated the debate. For various reasons, NT perspectives did not enter the discussion to the same extent. One of the most important is that a driving feature behind the enterprise of biblical theology was to render the OT more theologically acceptable to Christians. Some Christian theologians viewed the Hebrew Bible as a fundamentally Jewish document that had been essentially superseded by the NT and, as such, was no longer necessary for the Church. This position goes back to MARCION and includes among its more recent proponents F. SCHLEIERMACHER, A. von HARNACK, and R. BULTMANN. But the OT is not so easily dispensable, since it has informed and shaped Christian belief from its very inception. It is because the OT is of great importance to Christian believers still today that the relationship between the testaments has proven a crucial and recurring question within biblical theology.

The fact that the texts of the OT and NT are literary creations of the past, written in Hebrew, Aramaic, and Greek, raises further textual and historical problems for biblical theology. Originating in ancient Near Eastern and Hellenistic/Roman cultural environments, they must be read and understood in the same way as other literary products of antiquity. If the Bible is not read in its historical context, it will be misunderstood and possibly misused. For this reason the Church itself has a stake in affirming the place of biblical studies in the academy. Exponents of biblical theology have attempted to come to terms with the historical–critical method without being unduly constrained by it: although its results cannot be ignored, its methodology is not exhaustive.

In any case, the historical–critical approach that dominated much of twentieth-century discussion is clearly not adequate by itself to meet the challenges of twenty-first-century scholarship. In fact, a complete change in the intellectual climate has taken place. Key concepts that shape current discussion of biblical theology include HERMENEUTICS and POSTMODERNISM. In addition, a challenge to history has come from sociology, especially via the work of figures like P. Bourdieu (1930–2002). As a result of developments in all these fields during recent decades, our understanding of what it means to refer to 'language', 'text', and 'history', as well as to the relationship between 'text' and 'history', has changed radically. To what extent and in what form do we have access to past reality at all?

Very little of this new knowledge is compatible with the mid-twentieth-century biblical-theology debates, steeped as they are in historicist positivism. It was formerly believed that it was the role of the exegete to reconstruct the past. Only after such a procedure could one discuss a text's relevance for the present (e.g., its use for HOMILETICS, SYSTEMATIC THEOLOGY, etc.). Among others, K. Stendahl (1921–2008) and H. Räisänen (b. 1941) are good examples of this false equation of 'what it meant' with 'what it means'. Similarly, the claim that the traditional historical–critical method belongs to science, and the implication that it is uniquely equipped to find the 'one truth' in the texts, have since the 1960s come under attack from postmodernist and hermeneutical theorists, for whom it is naive to claim that one can understand texts only in one, objective way, regardless of who the reader is. Clearly, Catholics read in a different way from Protestants. Jewish interpretations differ again, as do Muslim ones. Women read differently from men. An aggressive atheist reads a different text from that of a zealous fundamentalist. Different biblical scholars also read differently – to the extent that one might occasionally wonder whether they have read the same texts at all! Some critics have accused these more recent debates over hermeneutics as leading to relativism, and even nihilism. However, the relativism represented by various reader-based approaches to the text (e.g., reader-response criticism) is a necessary – and healthy – corrective to historical–critical claims to objective reading. However, there is a limit to the relativism. Texts cannot mean 'anything'.

Specifically, the story of how the OT came into being illustrates how earlier versions of beliefs, ideologies, theologies, and laws were reused and reinterpreted for later generations. One of the better-known examples of this process is the reinterpretation of the Deuteronomistic History of the Books of Kings in the Books of Chronicles, with its radically new King David ideology. In light of such examples, it is not only unhistorical but also unbiblical to claim that the biblical canon represents timeless truths; instead, canonization is a thoroughly historical process. Moreover, since we are dealing with texts, meanings are not fixed and invariable. New generations must read and understand the Bible in a manner proper and adequate to their own contexts. Recent biblical theologies have sought to take account of this awareness of the issues of historical accessibility, context, and difference across the various scriptural texts.

While the canonical approach represented by R. Rendtorff (b. 1925) has been important for Christian–Jewish relations, recent developments have above all been influenced by B. Childs' work on canon. Childs took a special interest in the relationship between the testaments, arguing for a 'canonical criticism' that takes the final form of the biblical books (including their ordering within the Christian canon) as hermeneutically decisive for Christian interpretation. By contrast, W. Brueggemann has stressed the pluralism of the Hebrew Bible, proposing 'a contextual shift from hegemonic interpretation . . . toward a pluralistic interpretive context (reflected in the texts themselves, in biblical interpreters, and in the culture at large)' (*Theology* 710). He correspondingly objects to canonical interpretations (such as that advocated by Childs) on the grounds that they are too authoritarian.

From a historical point of view, the texts of the OT are neither Jewish nor Christian. Rather, they represent a selection of what we might call the 'national literature' of ancient Israel. We should never stop reminding ourselves that the OT texts are in this sense both pre-Jewish and pre-Christian. It is, consequently, a misunderstanding to claim that the early Church inherited the Jewish Bible as its canon. In reality, Christianity started life as a movement within early Judaism. Later, both Christianity and Judaism grew, more or less simultaneously, out of the unique cultural inheritance of ancient Israel.

Among NT scholars, different approaches to biblical theology have been mapped out in the latter part of the twentieth century, particularly in Germany. P. Stuhlmacher (b. 1932) is a leading representative of a Tübingen School that also includes the OT scholar H. Gese (b. 1929). Here the importance of reading biblical texts in the context of Scripture as a whole is stressed. Particular reference is made here to the development of post-exilic Judaism, especially the inter-testamental period and its trajectories of interpretation that can be traced into the NT. And in the face of the separation of dogmatic and biblical theology that has dominated the academy since Gabler's day, F. Watson (b. 1957) has endeavoured to argue that later Church traditions of dogmatic theology are consistent with the best scholarly biblical interpretation.

The process of interpretation that had started already during the formation of the Bible has continued ever since. Readers of the present generation (non-believers no less than believers) represent the latest version of an interpreting community that has lasted for 2,500 years. That the Bible is not a dead corpus of meaningless texts that should be obeyed mechanically and for their own sake was shown also by Jesus. Jesus undertook one of the more radical reinterpretations of the Jewish Bible, leading ultimately to the creation of a completely new religion. The principles that he used, however, formed a part of contemporary (Tannaitic) Judaism, and were not simply invented by him. Just as recognition of the effects of context on interpretation means that it is not possible to reconstruct an 'original' meaning of the text, there is also no such thing as the 'final form' of the text. New readers and new historical settings will always create new understandings of the 'same' texts. Thus, a coherent biblical theology must operate with the understanding that literature can never be non-historical – and neither can exegetical or theological methods.

J. Barr, *The Concept of Biblical Theology: An Old Testament Perspective* (Fortress, 1999).

B. S. Childs, *Biblical Theology of the Old and New Testaments: Theological Reflection on the Christian Bible* (Fortress, 1993).

S. J. Hafemann, ed., *Biblical Theology: Retrospect and Prospect* (Apollos, 2002).

R. Rendtorff, *The Canonical Hebrew Bible: A Theology of the Old Testament* (Deo, 2005).

P. Stuhlmacher, *Biblische Theologie des Neuen Testaments*, 3 vols. (Vandenhoeck & Ruprecht, 1992–2005).

F. Watson, *Text and Truth: Redefining Biblical Theology* (T&T Clark, 1997).

HANS M. BARSTAD

BIOETHICS Bioethics is the disciplined study of a wide range of moral issues accompanying recent developments in biology, medicine, and biotechnology. Most bioethicists have received some formal training in philosophy, but the field is interdisciplinary, drawing upon the life sciences, social sciences, politics, law, and theology. A rough consensus has emerged among leading scholars in the field that medical practice and research should be guided by the principles of avoiding harm, beneficence, preserving patient autonomy, and protecting the free and informed consent of patients and research subjects.

The significance of bioethics for Christian thought is most apparent in questions pertaining to THEOLOGICAL ANTHROPOLOGY. Since humans bear the *imago Dei*, is there an inherent or divinely given human nature or essence that should be respected and protected? If so, what are the limits of medical interventions that need to be set in honouring this essence? If not, to what extent should humans use medicine to enhance their physical and mental capabilities? More concretely, how should healthcare be provided as an expression of the LOVE of neighbour? Ideally medicine strengthens the bonds of human association by providing care for and keeping company with those who are ill or injured. In this respect, medicine does not merely treat weakened or deteriorating bodies, but is a way of maintaining fellowship between the sick and the healthy.

These questions are addressed implicitly in traditional theological and creedal formulations of the INCARNATION. Since the Word was made flesh and dwelt among God's embodied creatures, the BODY is not to be despised but should be regarded as a divine loan and gift entrusted to the care of its recipients. Christ did not come into the world to save people from their bodies, but to redeem embodied sinners. Individuals should care for their bodies in ways that affirm this good gift, and medicine assists them in pursuing this care. It should be noted, however, that health and healthcare are penultimate rather than ultimate goods. Christian HOPE is not placed in preserving embodied life for as long as possible, but in the RESURRECTION of the body and eternal fellowship with the TRINITY. Consequently, Christians affirm good health and healthcare as relative goods that also serve as means for fulfilling the command to love God and neighbour.

The practical implications of these theological and creedal formulations are especially pronounced at the beginning and end of life when the bonds of human fellowship are most fragile. Early Christian teaching, for instance, prohibited ABORTION, infanticide, suicide, and euthanasia. Subsequent theologians, such as Ambrose (*ca* 340–97), AUGUSTINE, and T. AQUINAS wrote influential treatises reaffirming and clarifying these prohibitions, as well as stressing the good of PROCREATION and the care which should be given to the dying. Christians were also instrumental in establishing hospices to offer such care, and later hospitals to provide more general healthcare.

Recent and anticipated advances in contemporary medicine have helped to generate a number of highly controversial ethical issues associated with the beginning and end of life. The secular principle of autonomy noted above, for example, implies that competent adults should be free to either avoid or pursue reproduction. Medicine plays a growing role in assisting individuals to achieve both of these goals. Contraception and abortion are employed to prevent reproduction. For many individuals the use of contraceptive devices and techniques is not controversial, but public policies governing funding and distribution remain contentious. In addition, Christian ethicists, especially Catholics, may object that contraception is illicit because it disrupts the natural orientation of sexual intercourse towards procreation. The morality and legality of abortion continue to spark acrimonious public debate. Much of the controversy focuses upon the moral and legal status of the fetus, with no consensus over the point between conception and birth at which a fetus should be extended a moral and legal right to life.

A variety of techniques such as artificial insemination, *in vitro* fertilization, gamete donation, embryo transfer, and surrogacy are employed to assist infertile couples or individuals without suitable partners to pursue reproduction. The use of these techniques has again prompted divisive moral and political debates. Should gamete donation and surrogacy, for example, be subjected to governmental regulation, or treated as components of the free market? Moreover, objections have been raised against technological intervention into the natural reproductive process, purchasing gametes from 'donors' with 'desirable' characteristics (such as IQ or athleticism), and destroying unneeded embryos.

In addition, reproductive technologies are used to assert greater 'quality control' over the health of offspring. Fetuses can be tested and screened for a variety of chromosomal or genetic abnormalities and aborted if affected. Preimplantation genetic diagnosis, in conjunction with *in vitro* fertilization, may also be used to test and screen embryos prior to being implanted in a womb. A number of ethicists and handicapped advocacy groups are troubled by the prospect that the use of these techniques may prompt increased discrimination and prejudice against disabled persons and their parents.

A number of perplexing dilemmas are also associated with the end of life. To what extent, for instance, should physicians assist competent patients to die if they wish to do so? Ironically these questions have taken on greater urgency because of medical advances in prolonging life. These medical advances are adept at maintaining bodily functions indefinitely, even when patients become unconscious, thereby raising the issue of whether life-prolonging technologies should ever be withheld or withdrawn.

Since there is no fine line separating prolonging life from delaying death, some bioethicists, physicians, and patient advocacy groups support a 'right to die'. This right is exercised primarily through assisted suicide and euthanasia. Proponents assert that these options are needed to preserve the dignity of the dying patient. They argue that if a competent person (or the custodian of an incompetent patient) has determined that the quality of life has declined to such an extent that living is no longer desirable, then it is cruel and inhumane to refrain from helping such a person achieve a dignified death. Opponents counter that assisted suicide and euthanasia are unnecessary given recent improvements in palliative care. Moreover, frequent recourse to these options sends a less-than-subtle message to dying patients that they should not become a burden upon an already financially strapped healthcare system by lingering too long.

It should also be noted that medicine is drawing increasingly upon recent advances in human genetic testing in developing more efficacious diagnostic and therapeutic treatments. Although these developments provide better healthcare, they raise concerns regarding privacy. For example, to what extent, if any, should insurance carriers, potential employers, and public-health agencies have access to the genetic information of particular individuals? In addition, some fear that individuals suffering 'preventable' genetically related illnesses and disabilities, as well as their parents, will become victims of discriminatory attitudes and policies.

In participating in these contemporary debates, Christian theologians need to affirm health and healthcare as penultimate rather than ultimate goods. In the absence of this qualified affirmation contemporary medicine runs the risk of becoming an idolatrous and hubristic pursuit. In this respect, the incarnation serves as a powerful reminder that it is only God, not medicine or technology, that can redeem the finite and mortal human condition.

H. T. Engelhardt, Jr, *The Foundations of Bioethics* (Oxford University Press, 1996).

G. Meilaender, *Bioethics: A Primer for Christians* (Eerdmans, 1996).

BRENT WATERS

BIRTH CONTROL: see PROCREATION.

BISHOP: see EPISCOPACY.

BLACK THEOLOGY Black theology is characterized by a thoroughgoing diversity in its history, context, content, and expression. Although it originated in the USA, it now exists in many countries, including South Africa, the UK, Brazil, and the countries of the Caribbean. Thus no single definition of Black theology will do. This essay will focus on three constitutive dimensions of Black theology, shared by its various expressions in different countries: the political, the anthropological, and the theological.

The political dimension derives from Black theology's roots in both the civil rights and black power movements of the 1960s. Black theology is also political through being a PUBLIC THEOLOGY concerned with public political issues of RACE, equality, power, justice, and freedom. Of course, the political form of Black theology extends beyond its North American expression. In South Africa, where it established itself in the mid-1970s, it was defined by opposition to apartheid, a system of White rule premised on the separation of the races in which Blacks were deprived of power and regarded as inferior to Whites. In Britain Black theology was shaped by the presence of descendants of both Black ex-slaves and former colonial subjects from the Caribbean, Africa, and other parts of the British Empire.

Black theology is also anthropological. It represents a reworking of THEOLOGICAL ANTHROPOLOGY through race – a key category in modern definitions of the human self. Black theology takes seriously the centrality of race in modernity by reminding us of three historical dynamics. First, that it was through race that the being of Blacks was doubted and called into question. Blacks were often thought of as less than human; they were characterized as primitive, barbaric, and inferior to Whites. Second, the doubts contained in these definitions of Blackness received the backing of some prominent ENLIGHTENMENT thinkers, including Voltaire (1694–1778), D. Hume (1711–76), I. KANT, and G. W. F. HEGEL. This is important because in the philosophical anthropologies of these thinkers, in which some of the most influential modern ideas of the 'human' and the 'self' are presented, race functions as a powerful organizing presupposition. Although both philosophy and theology have been slow to acknowledge it, the human self in these modern philosophical anthropologies emerges as a totally racialized subject. Third, as a theological anthropology Black theology interrogates the commodification, exploitation, and consumption of Black bodies and Black labour in modernity beginning with the brutalities of slavery and eventually materializing in South African apartheid; colonial racism in the rest of Africa, Brazil, and the Caribbean; and racial segregation in the southern United States through much of the twentieth century. Far from being marginal to Black theology's self-understanding, these dynamics are at the centre of its historical identity.

Of course, the story of race and racism constitutive of that historical identity can be inflected and nuanced in different ways, depending on which version of Black theology one is dealing with. Thus, slavery in the

Caribbean and in Brazil was quite different from that in the USA, and Black theology in both places has developed differently as a result. Similarly, as indicated earlier, the trajectory of Black theology in South Africa was shaped by the systematic and comprehensive legalization of racial barriers under conditions of European COLONIALISM. Several points emerge from all of this. First, the existence of Black theology in these different geographical places attests to its global and pluralistic nature. This is one aspect which needs further comparative investigation, for it is no longer the case that Black theology can be reduced to the American version, even if it is true that historically the American version came first or inspired the rise of other theological articulations of Blackness around the world. Second, whatever the differences among these global articulations of Black theology, they are all more or less united by the effects of racism in modernity on Black human beings. Third, it is against the background of these dynamics that we must understand this theology as a redefinition of Black humanity, a quest for a 'new humanity' or a desire by Blacks to live as 'full human beings'. In Black theology these common phrases represent a critical rewriting of the history of anthropology in its philosophical, social, physical, cultural, and theological expressions.

This emphasis on race can obscure just how Black theology is specifically 'theological'. What has all of this to do with Christian theology? The answer is found in one of the inaugural texts of the discipline, J. Cone's (b. 1938) book *Black Theology and Black Power* (1969). In this text Black theology is understood as 'God Talk' which also seeks to be 'black talk' and its task *is* 'to analyze the black man's condition in the light of God's revelation in Jesus Christ with the purpose of creating a new understanding of black dignity among black people. . .' (117). The theological themes mentioned here – God, dignity, revelation, and Christ – are crucial, for they define the theological character of Black theology. Moreover, throughout its history Black theology has consistently construed itself as a systematic, critical, and constructive reflection on the relevance of the Christian GOSPEL for the victims of historic and contemporary racism. This theological grounding has been elaborated on three distinct but related planes: methodological, ecclesiological, and (in the context of the struggle for liberation) soteriological. The methodological aspect is evident in the logic of Black theology's articulation and organization of basic Christian themes such as God, humanity, CHRISTOLOGY, ECCLESIOLOGY, etc. These themes have continued to receive serious attention in the work of both first- and second-generation Black theologians, including M. Jones (b. 1919), J. D. Roberts (b. 1927), D. Hopkins (b. 1953), and K. B. Douglas (b. 1957). However, even when these theologians organize their claims through an infrastructure of authoritative Black sources, their presentation tends to follow the formal Euro-American models on which systematic and constructive theologies have traditionally been patterned. This criticism of Black theologians' approach to doctrine is not new; it was already being made within Black theology itself in the early 1970s.

This criticism notwithstanding, there are areas where Black theology clearly represents a distinct approach to theology. For example, its proponents claim that Christ is black. By this they mean not that Christ was biologically Black but that like Blacks throughout modernity he experienced discrimination, marginalization, and oppression because of his Jewish identity. The blackness of Christ typically functions as a symbol by way of which Black theology claims and asserts the identification of Christ with suffering Blacks. This is based on Black theology's re-reading of the traditional theological affirmation that Christ is 'God with us'. For Black theology, however, 'God with us' has a very specific theological content which resists reduction to an abstract generalization. 'God with us' means God has taken the side of the poor and the oppressed, and since Blacks are among the most oppressed of the earth, in taking their side God has specifically identified God's self as black.

The second plane on which the theological identity of Black theology is constituted is the Church. The Black Church is the historical foundation of Black theology, both because the latter has its beginnings in it and because it has inherited its spirit of resistance from – and thus stands in continuity with – it. Initiated, organized, maintained, and led by African-Americans, the North American Black Church represents the most powerful body in the history of Black Christianity. The Black Church was the only religious (and social) space of freedom in which African-Americans were not controlled by Whites, both during slavery and today. It was there that theological protest against racism was first actualized. Thus, it is the institutional criterion for the authenticity of Black theology's critique of white racism and of its other theological pronouncements. Most Black theologians today make the Black Church the most decisive and formative aspect of their thinking. Theologically, it is the body of Christ made up of believers living their lives in and through it; but sociologically it includes individuals, religious organizations, movements, and communities that sustain it structurally and that are sustained by it. Its ecclesial meaning consists in the belief that it is the gift of the HOLY SPIRIT bestowed upon the Black community in order to orient it towards the struggle for liberation and freedom.

This brings us to the third plane on which Black theology is 'theologically' constituted: as a theology of liberation (see LIBERATION THEOLOGY). Liberation means resisting racism and participating in the struggle to overcome all forms of oppression. Its goal is freedom.

Black theology sees the Exodus in the OT and Jesus' statements in the Gospels as models of such a theology of liberation. One frustrating aspect of Black theology's talk about freedom and liberation is, however, that these terms are usually not theologically developed or theoretically fleshed out. The fact that both terms come out of a complex history of an oppressive and racist modernity is hardly ever acknowledged, and there tends to be little sensitivity to the tensions that bedevil the relationship between 'theological' and 'secular' understandings of these terms.

In any event, within Black theology liberation has both a political and a theological dimension. The political dimension refers to the demand for equal rights, freedom from legal and economic harassment, and a demand for a better social life for Blacks. The theological dimension consists in the avowal that Black liberation is the work of God. It is what God is doing among Blacks in order to set them free from the structures of oppression. Black theology has always insisted on the unity of these two dimensions. This insistence is important for understanding its SOTERIOLOGY, according to which salvation is dialectically *both* about the redemption of individuals and communities from SIN and evil *and* about achieving freedom from racial oppression. Most Black theologians refuse to privilege the one or the other: properly speaking, there can be no salvation without liberation and no liberation without salvation. What gives salvation and liberation their Black content is the way in which the meaning of these terms is derived from, implicated in, and articulated through the structures of Black experience.

One of the greatest developments and challenges in the history of Black theology has been the emergence of WOMANIST THEOLOGY. Womanism arose as a critique of the early pretensions of Black theology to be an ungendered and unqualified voice for all Blacks, male and female. It represents the voices of Black women whose experience of racism and oppression has historically differed from that of Black men. Black women have found themselves subjected to a triple oppression involving White racism and white PATRIARCHY, racism by White women, and the patriarchy rampant in the Black community itself. Womanist theology challenges Black theology in all three dimensions of its identity discussed above.

On the international scene, there have been many developments in Black theology which call for further investigation. The existence of an international dimension to Black theology draws attention to pluralism within Black theology and says something about racism as a global reality. South Africa and Britain are two areas of particular importance in assessing these developments. The challenges facing Black theology in South Africa derive from the end of apartheid, which raised the question of the continued need for Black theology in that country. The answer depends on whether the collapse of legalized racism also entails the end of racism as such, and it is bound up with Black theology's failure to transform itself into a theology of liberation focused on social and economic problems in the post-apartheid period. There is also the further challenge posed by the fact that Black theologians in South Africa have largely entered into a new social class of the powerful and well-to-do. These developments partly explain why, in spite of the legacy of theologians like A. Boesak (b. 1945), S. Maimela (b. 1944), T. Mofokeng (b. 1942), and I. Mosala (b. 1950), there has not been any significant work in Black theology in South Africa in the last decade or so (see AFRICAN THEOLOGY).

In Britain Black theology faces the challenges of immigration and multiculturalism and the demands for an ethics of hospitality this involves. It also confronts the challenge of extensive religious PLURALISM. Muslims, Hindus, Buddhists, Rastafarians, Sikhs, Jews, Christians, and practitioners of indigenous religions are all a vibrant part of the context of Black theology in Britain today, including theologians like R. Beckford (b. 1965), K. Coleman (b. 1964), M. Jagessar (b. 1955), and A. Reddie (b. 1964). Given that British society is made up of many racial 'others', Black theology needs to reflect on how it can speak about racism and Christianity in non-exclusive ways.

J. H. Cone, *A Black Theology of Liberation* (Orbis, 1990 [1970]).

J. H. Cone and G. Wilmore, eds., *Black Theology: A Documentary History*, 2 vols. (Orbis, 1993).

D. N. Hopkins, *Shoes That Fit Our Feet: Sources for a Constructive Black Theology* (Orbis, 1993).

D. S. Williams, *Sisters in the Wilderness: The Challenge of Womanist God Talk* (Orbis, 1995).

M. N. Jagessar and A. G. Reddie, eds., *Black Theology in Britain: A Reader* (Equinox, 2007).

I. J. Mosala and B. Tlhagale, eds., *The Unquestionable Right to be Free: Essays in Black Theology* (Skotaville Pubishers, 1986).

EDWARD P. ANTONIO

BLASPHEMY Theologians and legislators have found this concept difficult to pin down, but the most helpful working definition is that blasphemy is a deliberate affront to God, a mocking of God's status and power, or an assumption on the part of an individual of divine attributes. Blasphemy (against the gods) was known in classical societies (e.g., in ancient Athens, which punished Socrates for this crime), and it is clearly presented as an offence in the Bible (see, e.g., Lev. 24:16). In both contexts blasphemy was seen as imperilling the safety of the community, resulting in attempts to isolate the offender.

Within the Christian Church blasphemy has often been understood as a matter of making light of Christian beliefs, in distinction from HERESY, which asserted different versions of those beliefs. It was categorized as a SIN in the work of P. LOMBARD (*ca* 1100–60) and T. AQUINAS, who emphasized the Church's right to discipline its adherents in response to blasphemy emanating from drunkards, gamblers, and others forgetting the reverence owed to God. Medieval society reacted to blasphemy with shame punishments involving public recantation or forms of mutilation. During the REFORMATION the polemical importance of blasphemy increased, since M. LUTHER used it as an accusation against Catholics. Later Reformed PROTESTANTISM deployed accusations of blasphemy to banish the veneration of images from Christian practice, while their Catholic opponents used the charge to revitalize their quite different vision of ORTHODOXY.

While in these earlier contexts accusations of blasphemy were based on the TEN COMMANDMENTS (which proscribed making images of God and misspeaking God's name), in the modern period blasphemy accusations have frequently centred on disputes over the divinity of Christ. This issue led to proceedings against Socinians in Western Europe (see SOCINIANISM), caused UNITARIANISM to be technically illegal in the UK until the early nineteenth century, and has re-emerged in close scrutiny of plays, poems, and films depicting Christ in the twentieth century. The last significant case prosecuted under the English common law of blasphemous libel (the *Gay News* case of 1977–78) made Christ the subject of homosexual fantasy and postulated a promiscuous lifestyle for him. More recent controversy over the film *The Last Temptation of Christ* (1988) involved ascribing to Christ heterosexual desires.

In both Protestantism and Catholicism, blasphemy accusations have seen something of a resurgence in recent years. In the Protestant world, this has been a marked feature of FUNDAMENTALISM, whose adherents see mainline denominations' lack of concern over the topic as indicative of wider surrender to the secular world. Public controversy over charges of blasphemy frequently shade into debates over freedom of speech. In the USA state action against blasphemy would breach the First Amendment of the Constitution, but this has not stopped lesser jurisdictions from excluding blasphemous material from the public sphere on the grounds of obscenity. In the UK the government has frequently been embarrassed by the attempts of individuals to use the law and has generally preferred to treat blasphemy as a public-order issue.

L. Levy, *Blasphemy: Verbal Offense against the Sacred from Moses to Salman Rushdie* (Knopf, 1993).

D. Nash, *Blasphemy in the Christian World* (Oxford University Press, 2007).

DAVID NASH

BLESSED VIRGIN MARY: see MARIOLOGY.

BLESSING In the pages of the Bible there lies a twofold use of the term 'blessing' that also runs through Christian liturgical practice and piety. On the one hand, to bless someone or something is to declare it special, set apart, a vehicle of God's GRACE. On the other hand, to bless God is to declare the wonders of God's grace and mercy. For example, in the EUCHARIST, PRAYER is offered for the blessing of the bread and wine, and for those who receive communion; but at the same time God is blessed in prayers and hymns, some of which (e.g., *Gloria in excelsis*) go back to the Church's first centuries.

This duality can also be seen in the OT. God blesses Adam and Eve, that they may increase and multiply (Gen. 1:28); but later on the same Hebrew word is used to bless God – a recurring theme in the Psalms (e.g., Ps. 16:7). And it is not just people who are declared blessed, but things as well, such as the sacrifice Samuel offers for Saul (1 Sam. 9:13). Perhaps the best-known blessing, taken into Christian liturgical use during the REFORMATION because of its scriptural origin, is the phrase Moses directs Aaron to use over the people of Israel: 'The Lord bless you and keep you' (Num. 6:24–6). Similarly, Jesus both blesses God before the feeding miracles (e.g., Matt. 14:19) and blesses the bread and cup at the Last Supper (e.g., Matt. 26:26). The Gospels also have many references to Jesus blessing the disciples, notably at the ascension (Luke 24:50). It is the blessing of people and things that gives rise to many of the prayers in Christian worship (e.g., blessing the husband and wife at marriage, as well as the rings they exchange).

The proliferation of the blessing of inanimate objects through the Middle Ages led to a reaction at the Reformation, where the emphasis was placed on the use of the objects in question (e.g., faithful reception of the elements of the Eucharist). Behind this debate lie sometimes quite different understandings of what the blessing is supposed to do, with (for example) Catholics stressing the objective nature of the act and Protestants emphasizing the inward life of the believer. Recently, common affirmation of the NT principle that things are to be blessed because they have been sanctified by God through prayer (1 Tim. 4:4–5) has pointed a way beyond these historic differences.

Many modern prayers link the blessing of objects closely with their use (e.g., the water at BAPTISM), and the revival of interest in Jewish worship (e.g., the food blessings in domestic sabbath rituals) has led to an increase among Christians in the number of prayers which bless God directly. At root, the notion of blessing is about the mutual relationship between God and God's people, where God is blessed for God's bounty, and God blesses both God's people in their life of faith and the tools given to them for that journey.

P. Bradshaw, *The Search for the Origins of Christian Worship: Sources and Methods for the Study of Early Liturgy*, 2nd edn (Oxford University Press, 2002).

Kenneth W. Stevenson

Body As the gospel of an incarnate God, Christianity might seem to exalt the human body. In fact, Christian theologies have valued bodies quite differently in response to diverging doctrines. Most theologians taught that all bodies, animate or inanimate, human or not, were created by an omnipotent and benevolent God who judged them good in their beginnings. They further claimed that, while God is completely bodiless, transcending even bodily images, God took on human flesh to accomplish redemption. Yet many of the same theologians regarded all human bodies in the present as deformed by sin and in need of punishing disciplines. Thus theological valuations ranged, even in a single author, from exalting the body as the summit of physical creation to denigrating it as the relentless enemy of the soul's salvation.

Theological meanings of 'body' are further complicated by the many biblical passages that undo ordinary assumptions about the basic bodily properties. The brief biblical narrative of the fall from innocence into sin suggested to many theologians that human bodies were created with quite different capacities from those they now have. Reading backwards from the details of the divine condemnations (Gen. 3:16–29) or the immediate consequences of original sin (3:7), they argued variously that bodies were originally free from death, disorderly passions, many cognitive or sensory failures, and at least some bodily pains. At the other end of biblical history, theologians inferred from stories of the risen Jesus what human bodies would be after the general resurrection. The canonical Gospels also record Jesus' startling teachings about his own body – for example, that it is identified with the bread and wine of a memorial meal (Matt. 26:26 and pars.) or with the bodies of the destitute and despised (Matt. 25:40, 45). Paul also understands the Christian community as Christ's new body (see, e.g., 1 Cor. 12:27).

When theorizing the human bodies actually present to them, however, theologians sometimes neglected these radical scriptural suggestions in favour of prevailing philosophical or cultural views. Many premodern theologians regarded embodiment as a limitation or degradation for any mind. They stressed the soul's yearning for liberation from the body, and their descriptions of the afterlife promise spiritual fulfilment rather than the completion of the resurrected body. Other theologians, wanting to emphasize God's generosity in becoming incarnate, dwell on the lowliness of the human body assumed by the Son. So too, and more vividly, do many theological or devotional retellings of Jesus' passion and death. The figure on the cross, drawing to itself all the world's sin, symbolizes the body's vulnerability, mortality, and ugliness.

Christian suspicion of the flesh became most vivid in Christian ethics and pastoral practice. Some theologians interpreted the cause of human sinfulness in Eden as fleshly pleasure in general and sexual desire in particular. From this, they concluded that the body was the great occasion for sin – the portal through which sin and death gained entrance to human history. If Christian theologians have disagreed about how far the ravages of original sin extended, they have often agreed that embodiment at present was a devastating effect and continuing manifestation of sinfulness. Following the usage in some Pauline passages, 'flesh' became a name for the source, condition, and stubborn resistance of sin (Rom. 8:3–13; Gal. 5:16–21).

Not a few contemporary theologians respond to the perceived denigration of the body in Christian Scriptures or traditions by offering more positive accounts, often in dialogue with sociological, anthropological, or philosophical rediscoveries of the body's importance in constituting human meaning. Some theologians have tried to resolve traditional contradictions by arguing that metaphysical or moral pessimism about the body belongs rather to Hellenistic overlays than to the core of Christian belief. Other theologians argue that denigration of the body causes large-scale damage by underwriting violence against particular bodies stigmatized for their race or gender or some other difference, even as it authorizes contempt for the rest of physical creation. On this sort of argument, rehabilitation of the body in Christian theology is important not only to undo past condemnations of bodily pleasure, but to reverse fundamental errors about the human role in the created cosmos.

In recent years, constructive theology has also turned back to the body as a source of forgotten knowledge about oneself and others. Embodiment is no longer an obstacle to some pure knowing, but the proper gift of human learning. This recognition leads in turn to reflection on the importance of bodily practice (including ritual) as a means of moral instruction and formation of the self.

S. Coakley, ed., *Religion and the Body* (Cambridge University Press, 1997).

J. B. Nelson, *Body Theology* (John Knox Press, 1992).

Mark D. Jordan

Bondage of the Will: see Free Will.

Bonhoeffer, Dietrich Dietrich Bonhoeffer (1906–45) was a German Lutheran pastor and theologian who began his career as a promising academic, but is chiefly remembered for his leadership in the Confessing Church movement and his involvement in a political conspiracy to assassinate A. Hitler (1889–1945), for which he was executed.

Bonhoeffer showed an early desire to reclaim the Church at the centre of Protestant theology. Written at the age of twenty-one, his first book, *Sanctorum Communio*, develops the social dimensions of God's self-revelation, in sympathetic correction to tendencies in the DIALECTICAL THEOLOGY of K. BARTH. Bonhoeffer's thesis – 'the church is Christ existing as community' – proposes to describe the shape of community from God's act of REVELATION. His second dissertation, *Act and Being*, secures the thesis by arguing that God's act for the world is nothing other than the community of persons created by and shaped in the Person of Christ.

As he became involved in the interwar ecumenical movement, Bonhoeffer found himself personally confronted by the SERMON ON THE MOUNT, especially its teaching of peace. Bonhoeffer pressed Churches and Christian organizations to more robustly and concretely proclaim Christ's command to peace.

After Hitler came to power Bonhoeffer helped organize a 'Confessing Church' in opposition to Nazi attempts to restrict ordained leadership to those of 'Aryan' descent. While most resisters objected to violation of a Lutheran 'TWO KINGDOMS' distinction between political and ecclesial spheres, Bonhoeffer also wanted the Confessing Church to address the worsening plight of Jews in Germany. His own break from antisemitism, however, remains a question of debate. His essay, 'The Jewish Question', pursues the dangerous strategy of subordinating the theological treatment of Judaism to a more formal analysis of the obligations of the Church to the State; at the same time, in that essay Bonhoeffer also suggests that a time may come for the Church 'to put a spoke in the wheel' of State oppression.

Bonhoeffer wrote the lectures that became *Discipleship* and *Life Together* for Finkenwalde, the secret seminary that he directed. *Discipleship* presents Christ's call to obedience, railing against the 'cheap GRACE' of religion without cost and Christ without discipleship. *Life Together* meditates on community as context for discipleship. Both underscored the concrete commitment of the life of FAITH.

After the seminary was disbanded, Bonhoeffer briefly accepted a lectureship in the USA, but felt compelled to return to share Germany's fate. Family connections obtained him a clandestine appointment to a military intelligence agency, where from 1938 to 1943 Bonhoeffer secretly worked in support of a coup plot. During this time Bonhoeffer wrote his *Ethics*, which articulates a discerning Christian responsibility for the world. The pattern of responsibility is christomorphic: 'vicarious representative action' that bears the burdens of others, without regard for one's own goodness or justification, but only the reality of the world's reconciliation in God.

Bonhoeffer was imprisoned in 1943, and his prison letters offer provocative theological fragments, including meditations on a 'religionless Christianity' (see DEATH OF GOD THEOLOGY). Here, thinking the INCARNATION anew, Bonhoeffer envisions a Church that can address a 'world come of age' by finding God in its midst, participate in God's sufferings at the edges of the world, and revive the ancient tradition of 'secret discipline' (*disciplina arcani*) through which the mysteries of the Christian faith are protected from commodification.

J. W. de Gruchy, ed. *The Cambridge Companion to Dietrich Bonhoeffer* (Cambridge University Press, 1999).

S. R. Haynes, *The Bonhoeffer Phenomenon: Portraits of a Protestant Saint* (SCM, 2004).

WILLIS JENKINS

BOOK OF COMMON PRAYER The Book of Common Prayer (BCP) is the liturgy of the Church of England and, in its several editions, of the various provinces of the Anglican Communion. T. CRANMER was the primary compiler of the first edition (1549), which contained significant innovations, including use of the vernacular, reduction of the eight daily hours to two, and the explicit rejection of sacrificial language for the EUCHARIST. Together with the King James Bible, it has shaped theological language and provided a reference point for liturgical development in Anglophone contexts ever since.

This first edition's retention of some traditional ceremonies was criticized by such Reformed theologians as M. BUCER. The combination of this critique and emphasis on Catholic elements by Catholic loyalists (e.g., S. Gardiner (*ca* 1497–1555)), led to a second, more Reformed edition (1552) under Edward VI (r. 1547–53). An ordinal (1550) was added to this and subsequent editions. Mary I (r. 1553–8) retired the prayer book in 1553, but Elizabeth I (r. 1558–1603) restored it in a 1559 volume that incorporated elements of both earlier editions. Since that time there have been translations (including the French and Latin versions of 1549), additional English editions (of which that of 1662 is most important), Scottish editions (from 1633), and editions for use outside Europe (beginning with the American edition of 1789). The late twentieth century brought multiple new editions, *A New Zealand Prayer Book* being among the most innovative.

Continuing points of debate in the interpretation of the BCP include Cranmer's intended Eucharistic theology, the validity of an ordinal that does not mention sacrificial priesthood (an issue for Anglican–Catholic dialogue), and the appropriateness of a marriage service that implies male headship (amended in most revisions since 1920).

See also ANGLICAN THEOLOGY; OXFORD MOVEMENT.

ROBERT W. PRICHARD

BOOK OF CONCORD Published on 25 June 1580 to coincide with the fiftieth anniversary of the initial reading of the AUGSBURG CONFESSION before the Emperor Charles V

(r. 1519–56), the Book of Concord was intended to serve as the definitive collection of confessional standards for the Lutheran Churches in the Holy Roman Empire. In its original form, the collection was prefaced with the three ecumenical CREEDS, followed by seven specifically Lutheran documents. Of these, three (the Augsburg Confession, the *Apology of the Augsburg Confession*, and the *Treatise on the Power and the Primacy of the Pope*) had been composed by P. Melanchthon (1497–1560), and three (the *Smalcald Articles* and the *Large* and *Small Catechisms*) by M. LUTHER himself.

Though all six of these documents were highly regarded by Lutherans, in the years after Luther's death disputes on a range of issues emerged among theologians who claimed the legacy of the Augsburg Confession, and the seventh document, the *Formula of Concord*, was drafted to bring definitive resolution to them. The successor to a number of formulae drafted during the early to mid-1570s, the *Formula* was completed in 1577 under the leadership of J. Andreae (1528–90) and M. Chemnitz (1522–86), and over the next three years was subscribed to by over 8,000 theologians and ministers in the Lutheran territories of the empire. In addition to confirming Lutheran distinction both from Catholics and from the radicals of the REFORMATION's left wing, it also highlighted important disagreements with REFORMED THEOLOGY in the areas of CHRISTOLOGY, the EUCHARIST, and ELECTION.

See also LUTHERAN THEOLOGY.

IAN A. MCFARLAND

BUCER, MARTIN Martin Bucer (1491–1551) was born in Sélestat, Alsace, and attended the local humanist school before entering the Observant Dominican convent in 1507. After ordination in 1516, Bucer pursued further theological study in the Dominican *studium generale* at Heidelberg. It was there in April 1518 that he heard M. LUTHER's public defence of his theological views. By 1523 Bucer had identified himself as a supporter of the REFORMATION. EXCOMMUNICATION followed swiftly, and he sought refuge in Strasbourg, where a programme of evangelical reform had already been initiated.

It was from Strasbourg that Bucer gradually emerged to prominence as a reformer, with an influence in the European evangelical movement surpassed only by that of Luther and P. Melanchthon (1497–1560). During the early 1540s Bucer assumed leadership of the church in Strasbourg. His correspondence testifies to a wide network of contacts as far afield as Hungary, Italy, and England. It was through these contacts that Bucer found asylum in England following the Protestant defeat in the Schmalkaldic war of 1546–7. At the invitation of T. CRANMER, Bucer assumed the Regius Professorship in Divinity at Cambridge in 1549. He died there in 1551.

Bucer endorsed the principal emphases of Luther's doctrine of JUSTIFICATION, and consistently described it as the chief article of the Christian FAITH. However, he laid particular stress on the effects and practical implications of saving faith: regeneration by the Spirit expressed in LOVE of God and neighbour; the outward fellowship of the Church; and the reordering of the Christian commonwealth. Bucer's understanding of faith drew a close connection between knowledge of God, persuasion by the HOLY SPIRIT, and the fruits of faith. Since those chosen and called by God might be more or less receptive to illumination by the Spirit, faith might be 'weaker' or 'stronger', and Bucer stressed the role of preaching, the sacraments, and godly discipline as the normal instruments by which the Spirit built faith up and rendered it more effective.

These considerations underlay Bucer's indefatigable work for unity within the evangelical movement, and, later, with Catholics. His collaboration with Melanchthon led to the 1536 Wittenberg Concord, which secured agreement on the EUCHARIST between the Churches of the AUGSBURG CONFESSION and those of the German imperial cities. Bucer also played a leading role in the short-lived agreement on justification that was reached between German Catholics and Protestants at the 1541 Colloquy of Regensburg. These efforts won him a reputation for doctrinal inconstancy that has endured in some later scholarship. In fact, Bucer made no secret of the fact that he had revised his views on sacramental efficacy. In matters of Church discipline his versatility was based on the principle of *epieikeia* or equity, whereby the demands of 'edification' in faith might determine how the Church's practice was adapted to particular circumstances. Yet Bucer maintained consistently that such moderation must never obscure the doctrine of justification by faith.

Despite his influence on J. CALVIN, the English Reformation and the Dutch Remonstrants (see ARMINIANISM), Bucer's memory survived more as a name and reputation than in an active intellectual legacy. But while Bucer's flexibility had only limited appeal in an era of increasing doctrinal polarization, the nineteenth century saw a revival of interest in his ideas among liberal Protestants in particular. This spurred a reappraisal of his thought and the gradual republication of his works in the twentieth and twenty-first centuries.

M. Greschat, *Martin Bucer: A Reformer and His Times* (John Knox Press, 2004).

C. Krieger and M. Lienhard, eds., *Martin Bucer and Sixteenth Century Europe: Actes du Colloque de Strasbourg (28–31 août 1991)*, 2 vols. (Brill, 1993).

N. J. THOMPSON

BUDDHISM AND CHRISTIANITY An early record of contact between Buddhism and Christianity is found in Clement of Alexandria (*ca* 150–*ca* 215), who refers to 'those among the Indians who follow the Buddha, revered as divine because of his extraordinary holiness' (*Strom.* 1.71.6). In seventh-century China, Nestorian Christians who had migrated from eastern Syria composed books in the style and format of Buddhist scriptural texts. The tale of Barlaam and Josaphat, popular in medieval Christian Europe from the eleventh century, has been traced to Buddhist origins. In the sixteenth and seventeenth centuries, Jesuit missionaries sent from Europe to China and Japan, while engaging Buddhists in public debates to convince listeners of the superiority of Christian doctrine and win them over as converts, also made use of adapted Buddhist (as well as Confucian, Taoist, and Shinto) terminology to convey Christian ideas. In nineteenth- and early twentieth-century Japan, Christians entered into alliances with Buddhists of various schools to manifest to the populace that religious commitment was not incompatible with their nationalistic sentiments.

Aside from these few documented cases, however, contact between Christianity and Buddhism throughout the centuries has been negligible and until recent times has made no significant impact on the organic development of either tradition. It is only from the latter part of the twentieth century on, as the result of the confluence of various factors, that a new situation has emerged, bringing forth new horizons in the ongoing historical unfolding of these two major religions.

One key factor in this new scene is the positive attitude towards other religions as expressed in official proclamations of Vatican Council II of the Catholic Church (1962–5). This stance towards other religions that came to be characteristic of the post-Vatican II era was prepared for by the theological work of Jesuits H. de Lubac, J. Daniélou (1905–74), K. Rahner, and others. Among Protestants, the influence of the theology of K. Barth, who viewed religion as an expression of human unbelief (in contrast to revelation, understood as God's self-manifestation to humankind), led to a stance largely indifferent to other religious traditions, or at best to one that regarded them as preparatory stages for receiving the Christian gospel. The work of P. Tillich provided a Protestant theological framework with a more positive stance towards other religions. Tillich's well-documented visit to Japan in 1960, where he was able to meet and engage in substantive conversations with prominent Buddhist intellectuals, made a profound impact on his subsequent work. Since the 1980s there have appeared many new and groundbreaking works by Christian theologians from Asia and the western hemisphere, mapping out more nuanced constructive approaches towards other religions, taking these latter seriously and engaging them in theological conversation. Some of these works not only lay the ground for further inter-religious encounters, but are also premised on and draw from the fruits of these encounters (see Pluralism, Religious).

Dialogical encounters between Christians and Buddhists grew in momentum from the 1970s on, notably in India, Sri Lanka, China, Japan, Europe, and North America. These encounters have been conducted under three general categories: first, the area of spiritual practice; second, the area of socio-political and ecological engagement; and third, matters of doctrine.

With respect to the first of these areas, increasing numbers of Christians have engaged in forms of Buddhist meditative practice over the last few decades. The life and work of the Cistercian monk and prolific writer T. Merton is noteworthy for blazing the trail in this direction. Another pioneer, who went a step further than Merton, is Fr H. E. Lassalle (1898–1990), a German Jesuit missionary who came to Japan before World War II and trained in Zen under Japanese Buddhist masters. He was granted authorization to teach Zen by Y. Koun (1907–89), then head of the Sanbo Kyodan Zen lineage based in Kamakura, Japan. From the 1970s until his death, Fr Lassalle led retreats at a Zen centre he established in the outskirts of Tokyo and also travelled to Europe on a regular basis for the same purpose. Now a new generation of Yamada Koun's authorized Zen heirs, a number of whom are committed Christians, continue leading Zen groups in Europe, North America, the Philippines, and Australia.

Various other forms of Buddhist spiritual practice, notably Vipassana or Insight meditation, along with Tibetan Buddhist practice, have also continued to attract spiritual seekers in the western hemisphere, and more and more Christians engage in these forms of practice while continuing to uphold their own faith. As more individuals engage in spiritual practice across traditions, a question that inevitably comes to be raised is that of the possibility of multiple religious belonging: can one be Buddhist and Christian at the same time? There are sociological as well as ecclesiological implications to this question that touch on (for example) whether it is possible to be a Buddhist Christian in ways analogous to the possibility of being a Jewish (or, for that matter, Yoruba or Aymara) Christian. These remain ongoing tasks for further theological reflection.

In the second category, encounters between Buddhists and Christians in the area of socio-ecological engagement have taken place in different regions of the world, as adherents of both traditions join hands in grass-roots movements towards peace, justice, and racial, ethnic, and ecological healing in their respective local contexts. Sri Lankan Jesuit theologian A. Pieris (b. 1934) describes the fruit of these kinds of encounters as an 'idiomatic exchange' between '*agapeic gnosis*' of one and '*gnostic agape*' of the other (Pieris, *Love* 110–35). As those motivated by Christian love towards socio-ecological action also drink from the wells of Buddhist wisdom, they are able to reclaim the contemplative dimension of their own heritage. As Buddhists, on the other hand, steeped in contemplative practice that opens to a realization of humanity's interconnectedness with all beings, work hand in hand with Christians in their shared tasks of promoting justice and peace and healing in this world, they are enabled to activate the compassion that is central to their own heritage, and carry it out into concrete action in history. For Christians, the Buddhist emphasis on NONVIOLENCE towards all living beings poses both a challenge and an invitation towards recovering a core message of the Gospel, and living it in the midst of a world caught up in violence on many levels. Also, the Buddhist view of the inherent Buddha-nature of all sentient beings and the interconnectedness of all constituents of the universe, which can ground a powerful and cogent ecological vision of earth community, challenges as well as invites Christians to go beyond anthropocentric ways of thinking, and acknowledge and embrace the entirety of CREATION as the *locus* of God's loving, salvific action. The cultivation of creation-centred Christian theologies and spiritualities is especially crucial in a world such as ours, threatened by impending global ecological destruction, towards empowering Christians for wholehearted engagement in ecological healing.

In the doctrinal sphere, many-levelled and fruitful dialogical encounters between Buddhists and Christians have been conducted since the latter part of the twentieth century, spurred by the establishment of institutes, dialogue centres, and scholarly associations dedicated to this purpose in various locations in Asia, North America, and Europe. A detached, comparativist scholar may, of course, find a wealth of data for academic research in these endeavours, and much writing can be found taking this approach. However, dialogical encounters between committed adherents of differing faiths presuppose a stance of also taking the claims of the other seriously and truly engaging the partner in dialogue on the level of truth claims. As a Christian committed to one's faith engages in dialogue with Buddhists, the theological framework that one brings into the dialogue can be brought into question in the process, and is cast in new light vis-à-vis Buddhist truth claims.

A key theme that has continued to draw attention in Buddhist–Christian dialogue through the years relates to the view of ultimate reality. Specifically, the Christian notion of God is examined vis-à-vis the Mahāyāna Buddhist notion of Emptiness or *śūnyatā*. The latter is brought out in clearer light as not at all nihilistic (as many westerners have taken it to be), but as a dynamic and open field of actuality. To offer a summary comment, these dialogical encounters addressing the question of the nature of ultimate reality can cast new light on elements in Christian tradition that have been underplayed in the historical development of doctrine. The apophatic and mystical dimensions of Christian FAITH are brought into fresh relief (see APOPHATIC THEOLOGY; MYSTICAL THEOLOGY). In conversation with Buddhists, we are led to a recovery of the *Deus nudus, incognitus, et absconditus* embedded right in the heart of Christian TRADITION. These dialogical encounters can thus bring back the focus in our God talk, towards a Middle Way that highlights the *Impersonal* as emphatically as the *Personal* dimension of the Divine, that acknowledges *transcendence* (God-as-Wholly-Other) as well as *immanence* (God-With-Us), all in the same breath.

An appreciation of the fecundity of the Buddhist notion of Emptiness can also open new approaches to the mystery of the TRINITY as a perichoretic and mutually kenotic Dynamic that is constitutive of our created being (see KENOTIC THEOLOGY; PERICHORESIS). It ushers us back as well to the mystery of the emptying Christ, as the revelation of this kenotic Dynamic who dwells among us (see CHRISTOLOGY).

The understanding of human nature and human existence is another important theme in the dialogue, with Christian views of human nature and the human subject set against the light of the Buddhist doctrine of non-self, or the self-less. This latter doctrine is a correlative of the notion of Emptiness and the interconnectedness of all constituents. Taking the Buddhist doctrine of non-self head on can correct certain individual-centred tendencies in Christian views of humanity, and can open the way for avenues in THEOLOGICAL ANTHROPOLOGY that highlight not only human creatureliness and no-thingness before God, but also human interconnectivity and interdependency with the whole of creation.

Another kind of endeavour that can be subsumed under encounter on the doctrinal level relates to the reading of sacred SCRIPTURE in both traditions. Buddhist readings of biblical texts can open new horizons of Christian understanding. Conversely, Christian readings of Buddhist Scriptures can also draw out dimensions in the latter that can be enriching to both traditions, as shown in the volumes in the series *Christian Commentaries on Non-Christian Sacred Texts* (2006–). Engaging in this kind of cross-reading, more than just offering new insights into these particular scriptural texts, raises the broader question of the relationship between REVELATION and texts. Answers to this question will necessarily touch on how Christians conceive the activity of the HOLY SPIRIT in light of new perspectives opened up as Christians take Buddhist (and other) truth claims to heart.

In sum, as Christians engage in dialogical encounters with Buddhists, we witness a process not unlike the breaking down of the old wineskins of our theological frameworks, calling for something fresh and new that will be able to contain the new wine pouring forth abundantly before us.

H. Kasimow, J. P. Keenan, and L. K. Keenan, *Beside Still Waters: Jews, Christians, and the Way of the Buddha* (Wisdom, 2003).

J. P. Keenan, *The Meaning of Christ: A Mahāyāna Theology* (Orbis, 1989).
S. King and P. Ingram, eds., *The Sound of Liberating Truth: Buddhist–Christian Dialogues in Honor of Frederick J. Streng* (Curzon, 1999).
W. Lai and M. von Brueck, *Christianity and Buddhism: A Multicultural History of their Dialogue* (Orbis, 2005).
J. S. O'Leary, *Religious Pluralism and Christian Truth* (Edinburgh, 1996).
P. Schmidt-Leukel, ed., *Buddhism, Christianity, and the Question of Creation* (Ashgate, 2006).

RUBEN L. F. HABITO

BULGAKOV, SERGEI Sergei Nikolaevich Bulgakov (1871–1944) is often considered the greatest Russian Orthodox theologian of the twentieth century, though the sophiology (or DOCTRINE of divine WISDOM) for which he is best known was condemned as a HERESY in his lifetime. The son of a priest, Bulgakov left seminary after a teenage crisis of FAITH and studied political economy at the University of Moscow. While engaged in doctoral research, he underwent a second spiritual crisis that turned him back to the Orthodox Church. Politically active as a Christian Socialist through the early years of the century, Bulgakov was ordained a priest in 1918. He taught for a short time in the Crimea before being exiled in 1922. After a brief sojourn in Prague, he moved to Paris, where he headed the St Sergius Orthodox Theological Institute from 1925 until his death.

Though Bulgakov introduced sophiology (or sophianism) in his early works *Philosophy of Economy* (1912) and *Unfading Light* (1917), his ideas achieved mature form in exile, culminating in the great trilogy *On Divine Humanity* (1933–45). Influenced by the work of V. Solovyov (1853–1900) and P. Florensky (1882–1937) as well as by German IDEALISM, Bulgakov argued that the divine Sophia is properly identified with the unity of the divine nature rather than with the second Person of the TRINITY. As such, it provides the basis for the unity of CREATION, which is inherently 'sophianic' (i.e., suffused with divine Wisdom). This correspondence between divine and creaturely Sophia is the ontological basis both for the HYPOSTATIC UNION of divine and human natures in the INCARNATION and for subsequent human DEIFICATION, as realized in the Virgin Mary, who, by virtue of the indwelling of the HOLY SPIRIT, is 'a creature and no longer a creature' (*Burning* 107).

That any human being – even Mary – should be described as 'no longer a creature' was central to the condemnation of Bulgakov's sophiology in the 1930s. As his simultaneous insistence that Mary always remains a creature implies, however, Bulgakov had no intention of simply obliterating the distinction between God and creation. That would be PANTHEISM, and Bulgakov characterizes his position rather as a kind of PANENTHEISM, in which everything is in God without being God. Although 'the being of the world is ... included in the very concept of God' (*Lamb* 130) by virtue of the fact that divine and created Sophia are one in their *essential content* (i.e., because the same Wisdom constitutes the ontological 'environment' in which both God and creatures have their being), they are absolutely distinct in their *modes of being* (i.e., eternal and temporal respectively). At the same time, Bulgakov's positing the divine essence rather than the Person of the incarnate *LOGOS* as the ontological basis for the relationship between God and humankind does run the risk of suggesting that humanity's eschatological realization of life with God is as much a matter of nature as of GRACE.

See also ORTHODOX THEOLOGY; RUSSIAN THEOLOGY.

B. Newman, 'Sergius Bulgakov and the Theology of Divine Wisdom', *St. Vladimir's Theological Quarterly* 22:1 (1978), 39–73.
R. Williams, *Sergii Bulgakov: Toward a Russian Political Theology* (T&T Clark, 2001).

IAN A. MCFARLAND

BULLINGER, HEINRICH Heinrich Bullinger (1504–75) was a Swiss Reformer, theologian, and leader of the Zurich church from 1531. His influence extended across Europe through his voluminous publications, correspondence, and networks of contacts. As H. ZWINGLI's successor, he defended, though not uncritically, the legacy of the fallen reformer and, together with J. CALVIN, was a luminary of the Swiss REFORMATION. His most well-known work was the *Decades*, but equally significant were his biblical commentaries, historical works, and pastoral tracts which focused on the principal theological questions of the sixteenth century: JUSTIFICATION, the sacraments, the Church, and the Christian life. Most of his writings arose from polemical battles with opponents such as the Anabaptists, Lutherans, and Catholics, as well as from pastoral engagement as head of a large church. His *Decades* were never intended as a treatise of SYSTEMATIC THEOLOGY, but in many ways they reflect his central ideas.

Bullinger's early theology was deeply influenced by Zwingli, M. LUTHER, and the 1521 *Loci communes* of P. Melanchthon (1497–1560). His attitudes were shaped by the dispute between Lutherans and Zwinglians over the EUCHARIST which broke out in 1525 and continued to his death. In his early work on the Eucharist, *De Testamento* (1534), Bullinger, following Zwingli, stressed the importance of the COVENANT. From the later 1530s, in response to a wide range of concerns, and following his extensive biblical commentaries, the centre of his thought shifted towards pneumatology (*De origine erroris*, 1539). This move found full expression in the *Decades* of 1549. In the *Decades* a range of key themes are in evidence, including the covenantal continuity of the OT and the NT, constituting a single, unified witness to God's REVELATION.

Bullinger was particularly interested in the ethical and communal nature of Christianity and continued Zwingli's emphasis on sanctification. To this end he wrote and preached extensively on the Christian life. Bullinger also followed Zwingli's conception of society as a *corpus Christianum*, in which magistrates exercised control over the Church, and the Church's authority resided in its prophetic witness to God's Word. On the sacraments, Bullinger refined Zwingli by stressing the spiritual presence of Christ in the Lord's Supper and baptism while rejecting, in discussions with Calvin, that the outward forms of the sacraments were instruments of God's grace. Bullinger stressed grace alone, but not passivity on the part of the believer; in regeneration a person is renewed to Christian living and strengthened to the imitation of Christ. In speaking of the Church, the sacraments, and the Christian life, Bullinger took particular interest in conversion, the restoration of the human person. In his mature theology the Spirit and its work of sanctification, vivification, and communion with Christ are central. He emphasized the commandment to love, and in his numerous vernacular, pastoral writings enjoined the faithful to good works in the service of the community. Bullinger saw himself as a pastoral bishop along the model of those in the early Church, and he devoted himself to the institutional life of the Church in the sixteenth century, passionately defending the historical orthodoxy of the Reformed faith and promulgating its doctrines.

Bruce Gordon

Bultmann, Rudolf Rudolf Bultmann (1884–1976) was the twentieth century's most influential NT scholar and theologian whose programme of demythologization dominated North Atlantic theological discussion throughout the 1950s and early 1960s. Born into the family of a Lutheran pastor near Oldenburg, Germany, Bultmann was educated in the heyday of Protestant liberalism at Tübingen; then at Berlin under H. Gunkel (1862–1932) and A. von Harnack; and finally at Marburg under A. Jülicher (1857–1938), W. Herrmann (1846–1922), and J. Weiss (1863–1914). At Marburg, Bultmann mastered the comparative methods of the History of Religion School typified by W. Bousset (1865–1920), even as he began to grapple theologically with the implications of Weiss' recovery of Jesus' proclamation of the kingdom of God as heralding the advent of the end of time. Taking the scientific character and limits of historical methodology seriously, Bultmann recognized the impossibility of demonstrating all the commonplaces of liberal theology: the superiority of Jesus over other foundational religious figures, the progressive unfolding of Christian values from historical data, identifying the kingdom of God proclaimed by Jesus with any political agenda, or reconciling the NT's apocalyptic world view with 'onward and upward' teleological assumptions.

After teaching briefly at Breslau and then Giessen, Bultmann returned to Marburg in 1921 with the publication of his form-critical study *The History of the Synoptic Tradition*. His retirement from Marburg in 1951 coincided with the appearance of his *Theology of the New Testament* (1948–53). While at Marburg, Bultmann also produced a book on Jesus (1926), his commentary on the Gospel of John (1941), and delivered his lecture on demythologization (1941), which set forth the controversial programme of an existentialist interpretation of the Christian message based on M. Heiddegger's (1889–1976) *Being and Time*. In retirement, Bultmann continued his lifelong practice of writing essays on philosophical and theological topics. These were collected and published (1933–65) in four volumes under the title *Glauben und Verstehen*.

Bultmann's lengthy tenure at Marburg overlapped with the rise and fall of the Third Reich. A Lutheran layman, Bultmann was active in the Confessing Church, organized in 1934 in opposition to the Nazi faction in the national Protestant Church of Germany (see Barmen Declaration). As early as May 1933, Bultmann called for the Church to serve the nation by exercising prophetic criticism. That same fateful year, he drafted a declaration by the Marburg theological faculty opposing any extension of the new Nazi laws that would have excluded 'non-Aryans' from Church office. Nevertheless, Bultmann was convinced that the NT does not prescribe a social ethic for political implementation. He thus consistently opposed throughout the 1950s any Church pronouncements on such issues as atomic energy or German rearmament.

Bultmann's students, such as G. Ebeling (1912–2001), E. Fuchs (1903–83), and E. Käsemann (1906–98), both extended and challenged his views. These 'post-Bultmannians' argued for hermeneutically grounding the Christian message in the life and teaching of the earthly Jesus, thereby giving rise to a 'new' quest of the historical Jesus. Bultmann also exerted a strong influence on many English-speaking theologians, including J. Macquarrie (1919–2007) and S. Ogden (b. 1928).

See also Dialectical Theology; Neo-Orthodoxy.

R. Bultmann, 'Autobiographical Reflections of Rudolf Bultmann' in *The Theology of Rudolf Bultmann*, ed. C. Kegley (Harper & Row, 1966), xix–xxv.

D. Fergusson, *Bultmann* (Liturgical, 1992).

James F. Kay

Byzantine Theology: see Orthodox Theology.

CAESAROPAPISM The term 'caesaropapism' was coined in the late nineteenth century by western scholars to refer to the supremacy of the civil authority (viz., 'Caesar') over the Church in the Byzantine Empire and throughout Orthodox (especially Russian) Christianity more broadly. Its aim was primarily contrastive: to distinguish the situation in the western Church, where the PAPACY was able to secure a high degree of autonomy in ecclesiastical matters, from that in the East, where the emperor effectively displaced the patriarch of Constantinople as the head of the Church. The sixth-century mosaic of the Byzantine imperial court in the Church of San Vitale in Ravenna is often cited as an illustration of this development, with the Emperor Justinian I (r. 527–65) in the centre, crowned with a halo, flanked by twelve attendants (including the local archbishop, standing well to the side), and performing the priestly function of carrying bread (or possibly the paten) for the EUCHARIST.

C

The roots of this imperial ascendancy in Byzantine ecclesiastical matters go back to the Emperor Constantine I (*ca* 275–337). Portrayed by Eusebius of Caesarea (*ca* 260–*ca* 340) in quasi-messianic terms for his support of the Church, Constantine set a precedent followed by successors like Justinian in convening and chairing the first ecumenical COUNCIL at NICAEA. At the same time, the fact that Byzantine theologians like THEODORE THE STUDITE felt it appropriate to criticize the imperial attempts to decide (rather than simply to enforce) orthodox teaching shows that imperial claims to full authority in Church affairs were not uncontested.

See also ERASTIANISM; PATRIARCHATE, ECUMENICAL.

IAN A. MCFARLAND

CALENDAR, LITURGICAL The Christian liturgical calendar developed as a way to celebrate the mystery of redemption in Christ by commemorating in discrete celebrations his life, death, RESURRECTION, and ASCENSION, as well as preparation for his coming and the outpouring of the HOLY SPIRIT. The liturgical observances sanctify time for Christians – the times of the day, the week, and the year. While special days based on natural cycles of the seasons also entered the liturgical calendar, its primary emphasis is the paschal mystery of Christ's death and resurrection. In this Christianity followed Judaism, in which the festivals of Passover, Weeks (Pentecost), and Tents (Tabernacles), though based in agricultural festivals, became historical commemorations.

The basic unit of the calendar is the day, subdivided into hours. The *Didache*, TERTULLIAN, ORIGEN, and the *Apostolic Tradition* testify that Christians, like Jews, had prescribed times of prayer in the evening (the beginning of the liturgical day), the morning, and at intervals during the day (third, sixth, and ninth hours). Sometimes a night vigil was kept. Cyprian of Carthage (d. 258) writes, 'We should pray in the early morning that by means of our morning prayer the resurrection of the Lord might be recalled; also at the setting of the sun and in the evening we should pray again. . .' (*Prayer* 35). These 'obligatory' morning and evening prayers became daily public services of Lauds and Vespers in the fourth century. Monastic communities developed these domestic prayers of Christians into the communal LITURGY of the hours (see MONASTICISM). Wednesdays and Fridays were fast days in commemoration of the Lord's passion (*Didache* 8).

Already in the NT (Acts 20:7; Rev. 1:10) there is evidence that Christians marked the first day of the week (Sunday) as the Lord's Day with a gathering (*synaxis*) in which they celebrated the presence of the crucified and risen Lord in the EUCHARIST. On this 'fixed day' of worship, Christians commemorated the resurrection of Christ (Justin Martyr, *1Apol.* 67). Clement of Alexandria (*ca* 150–*ca* 215) and Origen called Sunday the 'eighth day' in reference to the eschatological character of the resurrection as the beginning of the new creation. In 321 Constantine I (*ca* 275–337) proclaimed the Day of the Sun as a day of rest in the Roman Empire; thereafter sabbath ideas were imported into the Lord's Day (see SABBATARIANISM).

In the second century Christians in Asia Minor were commemorating the Pascha, or passover of Christ from death to life, annually in connection with the Jewish Passover (i.e., on 14 Nisan, which could fall on any day of the week). By contrast, the Roman Church always celebrated Easter – the day of Jesus' resurrection – on the first day of the week. This led to tensions that were ultimately resolved at the Council of NICAEA with the decision that Easter would be celebrated on the first Sunday after the first full moon of spring, thus keeping some connection with the Jewish Passover while also celebrating the resurrection on the Lord's Day. As the Jewish Passover was celebrated as a week of weeks ending with the Feast of Weeks (Pentecost), so Christians developed a fifty-day celebration of the resurrection ending with a commemoration of the outpouring of the promised Holy Spirit on PENTECOST. In the historicizing process that took place during the fourth century, with pilgrimages to sites of the life of Jesus in the Holy Land, Jesus' ASCENSION on the fortieth day after Easter became its own festival. In the same process the individual days of Holy Week (the week preceding Easter) were singled out for special devotion, especially Maundy Thursday (which commemorates Jesus' last meal with his disciples) and Good Friday (which commemorates the crucifixion). Perhaps motivated by a forty-day fast held after the beginning of the year in Egypt in imitation of Christ's fast in the wilderness, a forty-day fast developed throughout the Church, both as a preparation for Easter and as a time to prepare catechumens for baptism and to reconcile public penitents. This time of fasting – Lent – never included Sundays, and in the East it also excluded the sabbath. In the West the first day of Lent came to be called Ash Wednesday.

A second great cycle of commemorations developed around the INCARNATION. It used to be thought that Christmas was invented by bishops in the fourth century as a way of countering the pagan solstice festivals. The more likely explanation is that it arose as a matter of calendrical calculation. Both the creation of the world and its redemption were tied to the spring festival of Passover. Christians believed that the new creation also began in the spring with the ANNUNCIATION to Mary, which was observed on 25 March in the West and 6 April in the East; 25 December (Christmas) and 6 January (Epiphany) occur nine months later. There is evidence that Epiphany was already celebrated in Egypt in the third century as a commemoration of the baptism of Jesus, since the Gospel of Mark was read in the Egyptian Church starting at the beginning of the year. These eastern and western festivals were exchanged, with each observed in both places, providing a twelve-day celebration. In western Europe Advent emerged as a time of preparation for the nativity comparable to Lent, though not as rigorous.

New Year celebrations are associated with the incarnation. Rome continued to observe the old civil New Year on 1 January, but made it a celebration of Mary and the Holy Family. In some places the new civil year began on 2 February, the commemoration of the Presentation of Jesus in the Temple and the Purification of Mary (also known as Candlemas because of the blessing of candles). In England the annunciation on 25 March became the beginning of the new civil year. The liturgical new year in the western Church became the first Sunday of Advent.

In the Middle Ages great feast days were emphasized by having an octave (i.e., the observation of the eighth day or week after the feast). In Gaul, 1 January, the octave of Christmas, was celebrated as the circumcision and Name of Jesus. The octave of Easter, celebrated the eighth week after the resurrection, is Pentecost. Pentecost eventually acquired its own octave in the festival of the Holy Trinity. Corpus Christi became the octave of Maundy Thursday, observed after Trinity Sunday. By the high Middle Ages the western liturgical calendar was well established, with its seasons of Advent, Christmas, Sundays after Epiphany, Lent, Easter, and Sundays after Pentecost or after Trinity. This calendar was retained in Lutheran and Anglican reformations. Reformed practice rejected the Church-year calendar because of popular customs associated with certain days (e.g., dancing, fairs, blessing of wine, candles, ashes, palms, etc.) and in order to practise a continuous reading of biblical books. Recent ecumenical interest in a common three-year LECTIONARY has led to the restoration of the chief days and seasons in Reformed traditions. In revised calendars in western Churches the time after Epiphany is framed by the Baptism of our Lord and the TRANSFIGURATION of our Lord (except in the Catholic calendar) and the time after Pentecost is framed by Trinity Sunday and Christ the King/Reign of Christ Sunday.

The liturgical calendar also has a sanctoral cycle: the commemorations of SAINTS, usually on the day of their death (which is understood as the day of their birth into eternal life). Some of these dates are of great antiquity, especially martyrs' days such as Peter and PAUL on 29 June. Some are observed universally, including days of apostles and evangelists, the nativity of JOHN THE BAPTIST on 24 June, and the Dormition of Mary on 15 August; others are observed regionally, locally, or denominationally. A festival of All Saints is observed on 1 November and All Souls (commemorating all the faithful departed) on 2 November. Saints' days are related to the participation of the faithful in the mystery of Christ's death and resurrection – a theology implicit in the Orthodox celebration of a festival of all the saints on the Sunday following Pentecost as an application of the paschal mystery.

See also MARIOLOGY.

A. Adam, *The Liturgical Year* (Pueblo, 1981).

P. H. Pfatteicher, *New Book of Festivals and Commemorations: A Proposed Common Calendar of Saints* (Fortress, 2008).

A. Schmemann, *Introduction to Liturgical Theology* (St Vladimir's Seminary Press, 1986).

T. J. Talley, *The Origins of the Liturgical Year*, 2nd edn (Liturgical Press, 1991).

FRANK C. SENN

CALLING: see VOCATION.

CALVIN, JOHN John Calvin (1509–64) is best understood as a participant in two distinct but related movements of restoration in the sixteenth century: one focused on the restoration of arts and letters by the recovery of classical literature, and the other seeking the restoration of the Church by the recovery of the genuine meaning of SCRIPTURE. Calvin was first of all a highly learned person, skilled in the interpretation of Hebrew, Greek, and Latin texts, deeply committed to the recovery of letters brought about by the labours of G. Budé (1467–1540) and D. Erasmus (1466/9–1536). Calvin was also a teacher of the GOSPEL, whose teaching was strongly influenced by M. LUTHER. However, like H. ZWINGLI and J. Oecolampadius (1482–1531), Calvin was not only concerned with JUSTIFICATION by FAITH alone, but was also dismayed by what he took to be the superstitious Catholic worship of the signs of spiritual realities instead of those realities themselves, confining our minds and hearts to earth rather than lifting them by degrees to heaven.

Calvin was called in Geneva to the public ministry of teacher and pastor by G. Farel (1489–1565) in 1536. After their expulsion from Geneva in 1538, Calvin was called back to the ministry in Strasbourg by M. Bucer, who advanced his training both as pastor and as interpreter of Scripture. Calvin was decisively shaped as a teacher by P. Melanchthon (1497–1560), whose method of teaching via 'commonplaces' (i.e., traditional theological topics) Calvin followed in every edition of the *Institute* from 1539 to 1559. Under the influence of Bucer and Melanchthon, Calvin was profoundly committed to the cause of ecumenical unity among the evangelicals, even though his hopes in this regard were in large part frustrated. After his return to Geneva in 1541, Calvin saw himself as both a teacher and a pastor, called to restore the preaching of the Gospel to the Church of Christ, by restoring the right way to read Scripture both to pastors (in the *Institutes* and biblical commentaries) and to unlearned laity (in the *Catechism* and sermons), in the company of other learned and godly teachers and pastors.

Calvin was convinced that Rome had led the Church into captivity and ruin by teaching and preaching doctrines not drawn from the genuine sense of Scripture, and by preventing the reading of Scripture for ordinary, unlearned Christians. He therefore dedicated his life to restoring the practice of drawing doctrine from Scripture, so that pastors might better guide ordinary Christians in their own reading of Scripture. Calvin envisioned the Church as a school in which all are students as well as teachers, being instructed by God through Christ by the doctrine of the Holy Spirit set forth in Scripture. The goal of reading Scripture under the guidance of godly, learned interpreters was for Calvin the restoration of the proper worship of God the Creator. The Catholic Church, following the dictum of Pope Gregory I ('the Great', r. 590–604), had taught that images, and not Scripture, are the books of the unlearned, in spite of the repeated warning made by God through the prophets that images are teachers of falsehood. Taught by such images, Christians under the Catholic Church were led to the worship of a carnally imagined deity, culminating in the worship of the bread of the Eucharist as if it were the eternal Son of God himself. In order to restore the true worship of God, Calvin sought first to distinguish the true God, the Creator of heaven and earth, from the false gods and idols taught by Rome. He did this not by rejecting images altogether, but by pointing the godly from the dead images of superstition to the living images created by God, in which the invisible God becomes somewhat visible.

Calvin taught that the universe itself was such a living image of God, setting before the eyes of all the self-representation of God as the author of every good thing. Given Adam's fall into sin, we can no longer come to the true knowledge of God by means of the universe without the 'spectacles' God has provided for us in Scripture to contemplate the works of God, and we must be inwardly illumined by the internal testimony of the Holy Spirit. However, the fall has also brought about a change in the self-manifestation of God in the universe itself. Because we are sinners, the universe manifests the curse of God due to our sin – and the wrath of God against us as sinners – as much as it does the blessing of God towards us as creatures. If we are to come to know God as the author and fountain of every good thing, we must be directed to a new living image of God, one which not only manifests the benefits God wishes to lavish upon us, but which also takes away our sin and the curse and wrath upon us. It is the preaching of the Gospel that directs us to this new image of God set forth in Christ crucified and risen, and we must turn to contemplate this living image of God if we hope to know and worship God aright. In order for us to have access to the benefits bestowed on Christ on our behalf, Christ manifests and offers himself to us to be received and enjoyed by us in the living images of the Gospel, baptism, and the Lord's Supper. In these images Christ descends to us so that we might rise to heaven, where he is. The Supper is at the very heart of Calvin's understanding of Christian life, for through it God offers for our spiritual consumption the very flesh of Christ, in which the Father has placed every good thing that we lack. The entire ministry of the Church is meant to facilitate the experience of the power of Christ's flesh in the lives of the godly, so that they may be transformed into his image, and united with God unto eternal life.

Calvin's greatest contribution to theology comes from his ability to hold together two distinct yet related realities. Calvin claimed that the revelation of God comes first in the living images of God in the universe and in Christ, and called on the godly to contemplate both throughout their lives, thereby holding together God the Creator and the Redeemer. One sees a similar move made by J. Edwards, who never ceased being astonished by the beauty of God both in creation and in redemption. Calvin claimed that the contemplation of the powers of God in these living images would give birth to piety in the inmost affection of the heart, and this piety would be manifested in the ceremonies and celebrations of worship, thereby enkindling the pious affections of others. F. Schleiermacher was later to make this communication of pious emotions the central dynamic of all religious traditions, and especially of Christianity.

Calvin claimed that Christ himself was manifested first to the fathers and mothers in the history of Israel in the types, shadows, and symbols of the LAW, and then in the Gospel, which sets forth Christ as the reality symbolized by the law. To know Christ one must go from the law to the Gospel, and also from the Gospel to the law. This insight is most powerfully reflected in the theology of K. BARTH, who holds Jesus Christ together with the covenant made with Israel. Calvin taught that faith in Christ receives a twofold grace, repentance and justification, thereby effectively arguing against Rome that those who are sanctified always need to be forgiven, while countering certain evangelical excesses by maintaining that those who are forgiven are also sanctified throughout this life (see SANCTIFICATION). This combination of attention to both forgiveness and renewal is a hallmark of subsequent REFORMED THEOLOGY.

See also REFORMATION.

B. A. Gerrish, *Grace and Gratitude: The Eucharistic Theology of John Calvin* (Fortress, 1993).
T. H. L. Parker, *John Calvin: A Biography* (Westminster Press, 1975).
F. Wendel, *Calvin: Origins and Development of His Religious Thought* (Labyrinth, 1987).

RANDALL C. ZACHMAN

CALVINISM: see REFORMED THEOLOGY.

CANON LAW Canon law is a set of norms proposed, articulated, or approved by a competent authority in an ecclesiastical community, for the purpose of providing for the good order of ecclesial society. Since the sixteenth century canon law has typically been contrasted with 'ecclesiastical law': the latter is usually established by secular authority to regulate an ecclesiastical community, while 'canon law' refers to the law by which an ecclesial community regulates itself. The word 'canon' derives from the Greek *kanon*, literally meaning the stem of a reed used as a ruler, but it came to mean 'rule', 'model', or 'standard'. The *kanones* were distinguished from *nomoi*, or civil laws.

The relationship between theology and canon law is hotly debated; there are four major theories that attempt to describe this relation:

(1) The Church, based on charity, and LAW are mutually exclusive. This position, as presented most memorably by R. Sohm (1841–1917), finds no place in the Christian community for any law, since charity is paramount.

(2) Canon law is a species of law, just as secular law is. Although this theory is associated with both the Italian and the Navarra schools of canonists, it is widely held by many scholars of different nationalities. In this tradition, the rules for the interpretation of canon and secular law are the same, since the nature of law is identical in each; what makes canon law distinct is that the Church holds the same power over canon law as the State holds over civil law.

(3) Canon law is a species of theology, an 'applied ECCLESIOLOGY', and thus canon law and theology are identical. This theory is articulated in the writings of K. Mörsdorf (1909–89) and the Munich School of canonists, contending that canon law is theology with a juridical method.

(4) Both canon law and theology are generated and received by the Church. This theory is associated with the Jesuit canonist L. Örsy (b. 1921), emphasizing that there is an organic and ordered sequence from 'doing theology' to 'making law'. For a system of laws to be authentic, it must represent and be intimately bound to a system of theological values; otherwise it becomes destructive.

No Christian Church has officially adopted any of these theories, but adherents of each continue to discuss the inter-relation of law and theology, particularly in those denominations that have an identifiable juridical structure and legal system.

Regulations for early Christian community life are found in the NT, e.g., qualifications for various ecclesiastical orders in the Pastoral Epistles. Numerous writings from the apostolic and immediately following periods contained disciplinary norms and carried significant weight, particularly as they were digested and circulated in later collections. Beginning in the fourth century, canons from ecclesiastical synods and COUNCILS, sayings and writings of fathers, and (particularly in the East) imperial legislation were compiled in chronological collections. In the West, responses from the pope known as decretals received significant attention and quickly became a predominant source; principal collections include the late fifth-century *Collectio Dionysiana* and the *Collectio Hispana* (also known as the *Isidoriana*).

By the eleventh century, the profusion of sources and their apparent lack of organization hampered the Gregorian reformers in pursuing their objectives. With the production of systematically organized canonical collections – particularly those of Anselm of Lucca (1036–86), Burchard of Worms (*ca* 950–1025), and Ivo of Chartres (*ca* 1040–1115) – and the development of SCHOLASTICISM, canon law emerged as a distinct branch of learning.

The most significant text of this period is undoubtedly the *Concordia Discordantium Canonum* (also known as the *Decretum*), the product of Gratian, a shadowy twelfth-century Bolognese master. Probably written in stages around 1140, this work clearly distinguished canon law from theology and presented a synthesis of universally applicable norms adopted by all subsequent collections. Although completely unofficial beyond whatever force the original sources may have had, the method of the resolution of conflicting sources by recourse to authorities established the *Decretum* as the standard text for the teaching of canon law throughout the Middle Ages; only the Bible was more widely copied.

The production of legal texts did not cease with the *Decretum*, and the enormous number of laws made it difficult to determine which were still in force. Pope Gregory IX (r. 1227–41) commissioned Raymond of Penafort (1175–1275) to produce a single, unified, and authoritative compilation of all laws in force since the *Decretum*; this collection was known as the *Decretales*, in five books (1234). Gregory's successors produced other collections to supplement the *Decretum* and the *Decretales*: the *Liber Sextus* (1298) of Boniface VIII (r. 1294–1303), the *Constitutiones Clementinae* (1314) of Clement V (r. 1305–14), the *Extravagantes* of John XXII (r. 1316–34), and the *Extravagantes communes*. These works were all combined in an official edition by Gregory XIII (r. 1572–85) in 1582, under the title of *Corpus Iuris Canonici*; this was the official law of the Catholic Church until 1917.

By the middle of the nineteenth century, it had become clear that the laws of the *Corpus Iuris Canonici*, combined with the canons of the Council of Trent and papal pronouncements of the intervening three centuries, were badly in need of revision and adaptation. Although proposals for revision were presented as part of the preparatory phase of Vatican Council I, a Code (*Codex Iuris Canonici*) was not promulgated until 1917 by Benedict XV (r. 1914–22). Consisting of 2,414 canons, the 1917 Code was divided into five books, based on the divisions of classical Roman law.

While Benedict XV provided a procedure for updating the 1917 Code, these provisions were never implemented, and the Code soon needed revision. This was, in part, the result of a certain inadequacy in the Code's original provisions, but was more generally required by a major change in the understanding of the Church, law, society, and the human condition. John XXIII (r. 1958–63) in 1959 called for a revision of the 1917 Code at the same time as he convoked Vatican Council II; work began on the revision in earnest in 1967. The new Code of Canon Law was promulgated by John Paul II (r. 1978–2005) on 25 January 1983, and entered into force on 27 November 1983.

The 1983 Code bears the distinct imprint of Vatican II, and must be interpreted in the light of its documents. Containing 1,752 canons, the 1983 Code is divided into seven books – organized not according to classical Roman law, but according to an ecclesiology enunciated by Vatican II. Book II is entitled 'The People of God', and deals with the rights and obligations of the Christian faithful, the hierarchical constitution of the Church, and institutes of consecrated life and societies of apostolic life. As Book II deals in general with the Church's governing function, Book III presents the teaching function (magisterium), and Book IV regulates the sanctifying function (chiefly the law regarding sacraments). Book V organizes the Church's law on property, Book VI on sanctions and ecclesiastical penalties, and Book VII on procedures. An introductory Book I gives general norms and definitions for the application and interpretation of law.

The Eastern Churches in communion with the see of Rome, after being governed by a partial codification promulgated between 1949 and 1957, were granted their own, separate Code (*Codex Canonum Ecclesiarum Orientalium* or *CCEO*) on 18 October 1990; this Code came into force on 1 October 1991. The Eastern Code is the law common to the twenty Eastern Catholic Churches; in addition, each Church has its own 'particular' law to regulate matters not covered by the 1,546 canons of the *CCEO*, or to specify matters the *CCEO* has left to the individual Churches. Sensitive to the legal tradition of the Christian East, the *CCEO* is divided not into books, but into thirty 'titles'.

The canon law of the Orthodox Churches is founded on Scripture, tradition (the teaching of Christ and the apostles as preserved in the writings of the fathers of the first three centuries), and custom. The canons of ecumenical and regional synods, canons derived from the writings of the fathers, and certain imperial laws concerning the Church form the core of most Orthodox collections of canon law; the Churches of the Greek tradition follow a collection of canons and commentaries known as the 'Rudder' (*Pedalion*). One of the most notable Orthodox canonical concepts is *oikonomia*, the departure from or suspension of a strict application of law or discipline. While similar to the Catholic concept of dispensation, *oikonomia* can also be used in sacramental theology.

Within the Anglican Communion, the Submission of the Clergy Act (1533) abrogated those ecclesiastical laws inconsistent with the royal supremacy and common law. Many basic legal principles of pre-Reformation canon law, however, remained in force in England through the functioning of both ecclesiastical and secular courts. The current law of the Church of England is found in Measures and Canons enacted by the General Synod, the rubrics of the *Book of Common Prayer*, case law, and Acts of Parliament regarding the Church and its religious affairs. Other Churches of the Anglican Communion have their own law, and unlike Catholic or Orthodox Churches, most have a fundamental written constitution. Because of doctrinal disputes arising at the end of the twentieth century, Anglican canonists have begun to search for a *ius commune*, or legal tradition common to all Anglican Churches, that may present a way of resolving issues of autonomy and communion.

Many Churches tracing their origins to the Reformation have 'books of order' or other regulations concerning Church discipline, but none have as comprehensive or systematic a body of law as exists in the Catholic, Orthodox, and Anglican traditions.

J. P. Beal, J. A. Coriden, and T. J. Green, eds., *New Commentary on the Code of Canon Law* (Paulist Press, 2000).

J. A. Brundage, *Medieval Canon Law* (Longman, 1995).
N. Doe, *The Legal Framework of the Church of England: A Critical Study in a Comparative Context* (Oxford University Press, 1996).
J. H. Erickson, *The Challenge of our Past: Studies in Orthodox Canon Law and Church History* (St Vladimir's Seminary Press, 1991).
R. H. Helmholz, *The Spirit of Classical Canon Law* (University of Georgia Press, 1996).

W. BECKET SOULE

CANON: see MASS, CANON OF; SCRIPTURE.

CANONIZATION All Catholics are called to be SAINTS, but only a handful are officially recognized as such. The process of 'sainting' involves several steps, but the ultimate one is known as canonization – adding to the canon, or the list of those officially declared as God's intimate companions. In some cases, canonization can follow fairly quickly after the penultimate stage, beatification, but in many instances the *beati* enjoy their interim status for an indeterminate period of time.

In the early centuries of the Church, there was no juridical tribunal, survey, judgement, or official enquiry. The declaration or conferral of sainthood was a spontaneous affair – canonization by acclamation. In 973 we have the first documented case of a papal canonization: St Ulric of Augsburg (*ca* 890–973). He is known as a zealous bishop and he appears to have taken an active role in secular affairs. Pope John XV (r. 985–96) elevated him to the distinction of being included in the canonical lists.

In 1170 Pope Alexander III (r. 1159–81) wrote to the king of Sweden reminding him of the pontifical privilege in the area of canonization; this was the PAPACY's first major claim for exclusive jurisdiction. By 1234 Pope Gregory IX (r. 1227–41) cast nuance to the wind when he 'expressly and exclusively' reserved to the Holy See the right of canonization; but it was not until 1588, when Pope Sixtus V (r. 1585–90) established the Sacred Congregation for Rites that there was an effort to firm up control of the hitherto localized process of sainting. Sixtus ushered in the rule of the specialists, but it would not be until Pope Urban VIII (r. 1623–44) codified the practices in 1642 that we begin to see tight management from the centre.

In 1735 Pope Benedict XIV (r. 1740–58) published what would become a classic of its kind: *On the Beatification of Servants of God and the Canonization of the Blessed.* This work remained normative for centuries and provided substantive material for the 1917 *Code of Canon Law.* There were rumblings at VATICAN COUNCIL II for decentralization of the process, but nothing happened.

The modest tinkerings that had defined papal initiatives on the legislation governing sainting since Benedict XIV changed on 25 January 1983, when Pope John Paul II (r. 1978–2005) promulgated the new *Code of Canon Law* and issued the apostolic constitution *Divinus perfectionis magister*, a work that generated major reforms in the centuries-long process of sainting. The changes wrought by the new legislation included downplaying the juridical or adversarial approach that had previously governed the evaluation of candidates for sainthood by substituting a more historical and pastoral approach. This approach reintroduced the importance of local initiatives and placed greater focus on the use of a wide range of experts drawn from all over the world.

'Sainting' is not a uniquely Catholic exercise or prerogative. Other Churches in the apostolic and sacramental tradition – the Anglicans and the Orthodox – do likewise, although the elaborate liturgical, devotional, and juridical features of the Catholic iteration remain the pre-eminent model in Christian history.

M. Higgins, *Stalking the Holy: The Pursuit of Saint Making* (House of Anansi Press, 2006).
W. Woestman, *Canonization: Theology, History, Process* (Saint Paul University, 2002).

MICHAEL HIGGINS

CAPPADOCIAN FATHERS 'Cappadocian Fathers' is the modern appellation for Basil of Caesarea ('the Great', 329–79), Gregory of Nyssa (330–95), and Gregory of Nazianzus ('the Theologian', 329–90), who were the architects of the neo-Nicene theology that prevailed at the Council of CONSTANTINOPLE settling the ARIAN CONTROVERSY. Basil and his younger brother, Gregory of Nyssa, were third-generation Christians, their grandmother having been converted by disciples of ORIGEN's disciple, Gregory Thaumaturgos (*ca* 210–*ca* 270). Gregory of Nazianzus, the son of the bishop of Nazianzus, studied rhetoric and Neoplatonism (see PLATONISM) in Athens, where he entered into lifelong friendship with Basil. Their attraction to the study of rhetoric and philosophy led them to seek a synthesis of the Greek intellectual tradition and Christianity reflected in an anthology they made of Origen's writings, the *PHILOKALIA.* Although Nyssa had no formal training in philosophy and rhetoric and speaks only of his older sister, Macrina (324–79), as 'my teacher', his writings were more philosophical and speculative than Basil's or Nazianzus'. After succeeding Eusebius (*ca* 265–*ca* 340) as bishop of Cappadocian Caesarea in 370, Basil became the leader of the pro-Nicenes. To strengthen the ranks of pro-Nicene bishops, Basil made his brother bishop of Nyssa (371) and Nazianzus bishop of Sasima (372). In 379 Nazianzus was appointed patriarch of Constantinople by Theodosius I (r. 379–95) and presided over the Council of Constantinople. His *Five Theological Orations* became the canonical interpretation of the Council's final position.

Their theological methodology emerged in the dispute with Aetius (fl. 350) and Eunomius (d. *ca* 395), the leaders of the Anomoian or Heterousian party, who denied the Son's essential likeness and unity with the Father. Against the Council of Nicaea's formula that the Father and Son are 'of the same substance' (*homoousios*), Aetius and Eunomius argued that God's substance (*ousia*) is 'unbegotten' (*agennētos*), while that of the Son is 'begotten'. Since the substance of God is 'unbegotten', the Only-Begotten Son is, by definition, not *homoousios* with the Father. The divine substance, they argued, is knowable, for terms reveal the substance of a thing. In *Contra Eunomium* (364), Basil counters that concepts (*epinoiai*) about God arise from the process of reflection whereby the mind analyzes impressions of God from Scripture. Theology, therefore, does not give immediate knowledge of the divine substance but is a reflection upon the manner in which God revealed himself through the divine activities (*energeiai*). Reflection on the nature of God (*theologia*) centres upon the divine economy (*oikonomia*) described in Scripture. Nazianzus argues that the divine substance is wholly beyond human understanding and speech: 'to speak of God is not possible but to know God is even less than possible' (*Or.* 28.4). Since theological inferences are drawn from the divine activities in the sensible realm, our concepts and language about God arise from impressions in the material world. However, because God is incorporeal, our corporeal speech cannot properly represent God's substance. Even negative theology does not give this knowledge of God. Saying what something *is not* does not give knowledge of the substance; it does not tell what God *is*. 'Unbegotten', 'immutable', 'eternal', 'holy' are only properties of God's nature and not the substance itself. Since God is infinite mystery, no single term sums up all that God is. Moreover, theological discourse is appropriate only for those who have been initiated in baptism after catechesis and who have prepared themselves through ascetic purification of mind and body. Only then may the Holy Spirit dwell within and illuminate the mind, revealing the Son through whom the Father is known.

Basil's leadership of the Nicene cause began with his reconciliation of Nicene theologians with Basil of Ancyra (d. 362) and George of Laodicea (*ca* 300–61), who, not comfortable with *homoousios*, instead spoke of the Son's likeness to the Father's essence (*homoiousios*). For the Cappadocians, the names Father and Son denote the eternal relationship of the Unbegotten to the Only-Begotten who bears the divine image because he shares the same *ousia*. Guarding against charges of modalism, they argued that Father and Son are *hypostases* differentiated by their discrete 'modes of being' ('unbegotten' and 'begotten' respectively). The Holy Spirit proceeds from the Father and eternally abides *with* the Father and the Son, as heat and light exist together with the flame. As proof of their essential unity, the Son and the Spirit possess common power and glory with the Father without which neither the Son nor the Spirit could fulfil their creative and redemptive work in the divine economy or be worshipped with the Father. The creative and salvific activities are not divided between the three hypostases. Rather, Nyssa argues, there is a unity of operation in which all activities begin in the Father, are accomplished by the Son, and find their perfection in the Spirit. By claiming that the divine substance is unknowable and treating 'unbegotten', 'only begotten', and 'procession' as the respective characteristics of the three Persons, they undercut the Anomoian critique of Nicaea and established the theological grammar for speaking of the unity of God while being faithful to the NT depiction of Father, Son, and Holy Spirit as discrete.

Nazianzus also played a critical role in the condemnation of Apollinarius of Laodicea. Arguing that the divine *Logos* was the rational soul and governing principle of Jesus, Apollinarius contended that Jesus did not have a human soul but was a single nature (*mia physis*), a human body divinized by the *Logos* (see Apollinarianism). Nazianzus objected that 'what Christ did not assume he did not heal' (*Ep.* 101). In order for the whole person to be sanctified, the *Logos* had to be united with the rational soul as well as the body. Thus Christ must be fully divine and fully human.

See also Nicene Creed; Trinity.

L. Ayres, *Nicaea and Its Legacy* (Oxford University Press, 2004).

C. Beeley, *Gregory of Nazianzus on the Trinity and the Knowledge of God* (Oxford University Press, 2008).

J. Behr, *The Nicene Faith* (St Vladimir's Seminary Press, 2004).

M. Laird, *Gregory of Nyssa and the Grasp of Faith: Union, Knowledge, and Divine Presence* (Oxford University Press, 2004).

J. Warren Smith

Caribbean Theology Caribbean theology arose in the crucible of Africa and Europe vying for the souls of Black people in the Caribbean. Theology in the region was confronted by two peoples who represented two histories and two approaches to religion. The history of the Afro-Caribbean was nurtured in the memory of slavery, while the history of the European goes back to the search for conquest and expansion of empire and a quest for religious freedom. The East African theologian J. Mbiti (b. 1931) notes that African people are never without their religion. They take it to the fields, to festivals, to markets and funerals, and it shapes their beliefs and rituals. This was the case with Africans brought to the Caribbean as enslaved persons. As they adapted their religion to the new context, new expressions emerged such as Voodoo in Haiti, Santeria in Cuba, Shouter Baptist in Trinidad, and Myalism and Obeah in Jamaica.

Taking the last-mentioned tradition as an example, Afro-Caribbean people in Jamaica believed that the person who had the power of obeah had the ability to leave his or her body, to fly at night, and to cause great harm to befall the enemy. L. Barrett (d. 2003) indicates that obeah flourished not only because the society had lost its equilibrium and was in a state of disorientation but because there was a void for a religious practitioner. The traditional African priest had lost his power in this alien society, and as he joined forces with the obeah practitioner they became a formidable force in the society. Because Afro-Caribbean people were powerless to enforce their religious ideas it was mainly practised after dark and out of sight of the master class. In all the islands the religious practices of enslaved and African peoples were rendered illegal.

On the other side of African expressions of religion, which included drumming, dancing, and chanting, was Christianity as represented by mainline churches. Most of the Christian churches were staffed by missionaries who were invited to the islands by the planter class and were expected to use religion in the service of the plantocracy. What emerged throughout the Caribbean was quite unexpected. African peoples (who were always in the majority, as the vast majority of plantation owners resided in Europe) crowded missionary churches and proceeded to blend African ways of worship, which relied heavily on understandings of African spirits and COSMOLOGY, with the missionaries' teachings about Jesus, the Holy Spirit, HEAVEN, and HELL. The blending of these two approaches resulted in the emergence of a uniquely Caribbean consciousness as the point of departure for talk about God, spirits, humanity, and cosmology. This new consciousness, in turn, became the basis for the articulation of a theology centred on a new understanding of Caribbean community. Isaiah 65:20–5 was often cited as biblical warrant for this new community, which is understood as God's promise to Caribbean people. The idea of the nearness of God that resulted from the blending of Afro-Caribbean thought with the Christian GOSPEL lay at the heart of this communal vision, leading to a focus on gifts of health, healing, and long life marked by the eradication of poverty, as God's presence in the community became the basis of hope for a new future.

N. L. Erskine, *Decolonizing Theology* (Africa World, 1998).

L. Williams, *Caribbean Theology* (Peter Lang, 1994).

NOEL LEO ERSKINE

CARTESIANISM Cartesianism is the philosophical system founded by R. Descartes (1596–1650); the term comes from 'Cartesius', the Latin version of his name. Descartes is rightly known as the 'father of modern philosophy', since his philosophical ideas inaugurated a decisive shift away from the SCHOLASTICISM that had dominated European philosophy since T. AQUINAS in the thirteenth century, and towards a radically new philosophical and scientific outlook, many aspects of which remain with us today.

The Scholasticism that Descartes rejected was a comprehensive adaptation of Aristotelian philosophy to the demands of the Christian world view. It took over Aristotle's notion of 'final causes' (explanations by reference to purposes, goals, or end-states), and subsumed these under the overall framework of a providential universe in which the good for each creature lay in its moving towards the end laid down by the creator (see ARISTOTELIANISM). Descartes, though a committed theist, argued that appeals to divine purposes, however suitable for discussing the human condition, were, as he put it, 'utterly useless in physics'. Since the ends which God might or might not have proposed to himself in creating the universe were all hidden in the 'inscrutable abyss' of his wisdom, the workings of the cosmos had to be understood in a more straightforward way. Descartes found this way in the methods and procedures of mathematics, and in the decades following his death 'Cartesianism' became synonymous with a new quantitative approach to explanation in physics. In place of the Scholastic apparatus of 'substantial forms' and 'real qualities', where substances behaved the way they did because of their essential natures, Descartes proposed a purely quantitative model that aimed to explain all the material events throughout the universe by a few simple laws, invoking only the size, shape, and motion of particles.

The Cartesian approach was unificatory, in so far as all observable phenomena, both celestial (stars, planets, comets) and terrestrial (minerals, plants, animals), were regarded as composed of essentially the same physical stuff – what Descartes called *res extensa* or 'extended substance'. To understand matter was simply to grasp that it was something extended in three dimensions; and the particles of matter were differentiated one from another merely by their geometrical configuration. Yet where does their motion come from? The Cartesian view of matter is that it is essentially inert (since matter is simply extension, physics in a certain way is reduced to mere geometry). Hence matter, having no power of itself to move, has to be set in motion, and its motion conserved, by divine agency. 'God', wrote Descartes in his *Principles of Philosophy* (1644), is the 'primary cause of motion, and he always preserves the same quantity of motion in the universe'.

The new Cartesian approach was regarded with great suspicion in ecclesiastical circles, partly no doubt because of its hostility to Scholasticism, which had become the Church's favoured philosophy, and partly because it appeared (as Descartes' contemporary B. PASCAL pointedly alleged) to reduce the role of God to that of a distant motive force, rather than a providential creator. Nevertheless, Cartesianism is in no sense a 'naturalistic' or a secular outlook. The Cartesian programme for the mathematical explanation of all phenomena makes an abrupt halt when it comes to the phenomenon of human thought. 'There is a great difference between mind and body', wrote Descartes in his *Meditations* (1641), 'in so far as body is by its very nature divisible, while the mind is utterly indivisible.' So alongside the 'extended substance' of which every part of the physical universe is composed, Descartes maintains that each individual mind or SOUL is an indivisible and immaterial 'thinking substance' (*res cogitans*). Cartesianism places the mind entirely outside the domain of physical or mathematical explanation.

'Cartesian dualism', as it has come to be called – the assertion of a radical divide between the realm of matter and the realm of mind – is one of Cartesianism's most controversial aspects. In the twentieth century, it was stigmatized by the British philosopher G. Ryle (1900–76) as the 'dogma of the ghost in the machine', and it remains profoundly uncongenial to current naturalistic approaches to mental phenomena. If the mind is a ghostly immaterial substance mysteriously lodged in the body, it seems in principle impossible to give a scientific account of any of its workings, or of how it is related to the body. Descartes himself devoted a great deal of attention to the relationship between mind and matter, and plausibly argued in his *Discourse on the Method* (1638) that the creative and innovative nature of rational thought and language meant that they could never be entirely explained in physical and mechanical terms.

Cartesianism, as popularly understood nowadays, is often thought of as implying a subjectivist or individualistic outlook, a view which gains colour from the fact that the starting point of Descartes' philosophy is *je pense donc je suis* (in Latin, *cogito ergo sum*) – 'I am thinking, therefore I exist.' Because Descartes stressed that the only thing the meditator cannot possibly doubt is the certainty of his own existence, it has been supposed that he gave absolute primacy to the individual thinking subject, or, in the words of the late Pope John Paul II (r. 1978–2005), that he 'brought all reality within the ambit of the Cogito.' But although the individual subject has first place in the order of discovery, the Cartesian meditator very quickly becomes aware that he is a *dependent* subject. Descartes argues (as had Bonaventure (1221–74) before him) that the very idea of oneself as a finite being already presupposes the idea of an infinite being on whom one depends. The Cartesian meditator, aware of his own weakness and imperfection, soon realizes that he could not even exist from moment to moment unless there was an infinite substance that sustained him. Hence, although the Cartesian outlook has often been suspected of paving the way for the modern secular conception of a wholly 'autonomous' self, its actual character is quite different. Much of Descartes' own reasoning in the *Meditations* follows in a long tradition stemming from AUGUSTINE, in which the mind descends into itself in order to find the creator on whom it depends.

Cartesianism is thus a complex and in some ways ambivalent philosophical movement, in many respects prefiguring the modern scientific age, but also rooted in the theocentric culture out of which it grew. In struggling with the relationship between a physico-mathematical account of the universe and the realm of human thought, language, and meaning, it continues to mark out the ground on which we must continue to grapple with our existence and how it relates to what we know of reality as a whole.

J. Cottingham, 'The Role of God in Descartes' Philosophy' in *A Companion to Descartes*, ed. J. Broughton and J. Carriero (Blackwell, 2008), 287–301.

R. Descartes, *The Philosophical Writings of Descartes*, vols. I–II (Cambridge, 1985).

JOHN COTTINGHAM

CASUISTRY From the Latin *casus* ('case'), casuistry is a form of applied ethics which developed largely in connection with the Catholic sacrament of PENANCE. The *casus*, or moral case-study analysis, sought to apply moral principles to concrete situations. If the morally relevant features of a case could be identified and separated apart from the non-morally relevant features, then the application of the appropriate moral principles could be transferred to cases in which the features might be similar. This pedagogical method, often identified with Jesuit moralists, was especially used in helping seminarians and priests in their preparation for hearing confessions. This sort of practical confession case, termed a *casus conscientiae* ('case of conscience'), was discussed in seminary and young priests' training, and examples were collected and published as a vade-mecum (e.g., a pocket-sized edition), usually organized according to the TEN COMMANDMENTS and the Precepts of the Church, that the confessor could bring with him to consult if he encountered a difficult situation in the course of hearing penitents' confessions.

The traditional practice of casuistry was grounded in an understanding of the objective moral order, expressed in the NATURAL LAW, from which moral guidance could be derived in helping an individual determine what she or he ought to do (prescriptions) as well as what ought not to be done (proscriptions). Overemphasis on the so-called 'objective' nature of moral actions, however, led to an impersonal and inflexible ossification of moral analysis that was later criticized and caricatured (most famously in B. PASCAL's scathing critique of the Jesuits in his 1656 *Provincial Letters*). While the harsher critiques of casuistry often veered into caricature, nevertheless there was a legitimate critique of a moral analysis that trusted too much in human ability to achieve a high degree of practical moral certitude in complex situations, as well as the belief that anyone could see relatively easily into the inner recesses of another's heart.

The contemporary turn to a more personalist model of ethics led for a time to a further decline of the acceptance of traditional casuistry, but also supported a more nuanced approach to moral reasoning that better accounts for the individual's concrete situation. A number of key points in the traditional approach to casuistry also support this turn towards the subject. The notion of *casus conscientiae* recognizes that in the final analysis the ultimate criterion for judging moral decisions is the individual acting within the sanctuary of his or her own CONSCIENCE. Though casuistry is grounded in the natural law, this objective moral order is not equivalent to the physical laws of nature, but rather is oriented towards the human search for trying to discover and promote moral goods in the concrete, which must always take into account both particular changeability of individual circumstances and the limitedness of individual and collective moral wisdom. In this search for trying to do one's best to act on and promote the good, while avoiding or minimizing evil, casuistry can continue to make a very important positive contribution.

JAMES T. BRETZKE, S. J.

CATAPHATIC THEOLOGY: see APOPHATIC THEOLOGY.

CATECHESIS Catechesis (from the Greek *katêcheisthai*, 'to echo back', hence 'to be informed') might describe any kind of religious instruction, but the term is used classically of the teaching given to new Christian converts, especially in the context of BAPTISM. In the first century, Gentile believers especially required counsel on the moral and spiritual entailments of following Jesus, and the guidance they received seems to have had broadly similar aims to the teaching given to contemporary Jewish proselytes. Christian discipleship, like conversion to JUDAISM, meant a new way of life. However, to judge from the NT, instruction prior to baptism was generally quite limited; it is also difficult to identify teaching that must belong to an immediately post-baptismal setting. There is no evidence of a formal process for educating converts. Initiatory catechesis emerged in the later first/early second century. The *Didache*, a composite document probably originating in Syria, opens (1–6) with typically Jewish advice on the 'two ways' of life and death: baptism follows once these have been 'reviewed' (7.1). In Justin Martyr (d. *ca* 165), again, the 'enlightenment' of initiation is for those who have been taught the GOSPEL and pledge to live accordingly (*1Apol.* 61).

By the late second century, a clear distinction had arisen between full members of the Church and CATECHUMENS. Those under instruction were being taught the rudiments of the FAITH, especially its moral obligations, before baptism. Specific teachers or 'catechists' emerged: IRENAEUS' *Demonstration of the Apostolic Preaching* was probably written for one such. The duration and rites of instruction varied, but there would typically be a sustained period as a 'hearer' before admission to the final stages; to be 'elected' for baptism required evidence of good conduct. In the third-century *Apostolic Tradition* a three-year preliminary programme is prescribed, though this may represent a later ideal; due conduct is said to matter more than duration. The catechumenate involved scrutiny of motives, lifestyle, and employment; progression to the final phase involved examination, exorcism, prayer, and fasting. The whole process marked a dramatic journey from worldly society to sacred communion. Patterns varied, but by the later third/early fourth century some general sequences obtained. Easter was favoured as the time for baptism, with Lent as the season of advanced preparation; the demands of Lenten instruction were often compared to the rigours of athletic or military training. Scriptural exposition was central to the discipline; EXORCISMS, FASTING, vigils, and scrutinies were taken very seriously. Teaching was to be so internalized that it demonstrably 'echoed' in the entire character of the baptizand.

Catechesis reached its zenith in the fourth and fifth centuries. Imperial Christianity brought new challenges, making baptismal instruction all the more necessary. Doctrinal precision assumed heightened significance as an identity-marker, and theological content increased. This was especially true in the East; western emphases remained slightly more on moral formation. Final-stage catechumens would have the creed formally 'handed over' to them, then solemnly 'hand back' the symbol (from memory) prior to baptism. Local creeds were diverse, but there was a trend towards standardization of orthodox forms such as the APOSTLES' and NICENE CREEDS. Once baptized, neophytes might receive a course of 'mystagogical' instruction during Easter week on the meaning of the sacraments; only then would they remove their baptismal robes and become full members. Pre-baptismal catechesis and post-baptismal mystagogy came to be increasingly distinguished. Remarkable examples of both are provided in the *Catecheses* and *Mystagogical Catecheses* attributed to Cyril of Jerusalem (*ca* 315–87). We also have notable specimens from Ambrose of Milan (*ca* 339–97), John Chrysostom (*ca* 347–407), and Theodore of Mopsuestia (*ca* 350–428). Gregory of Nyssa's (see CAPPADOCIAN FATHERS) *Catechetical Oration* (*ca* 385) and AUGUSTINE'S *On Catechizing the Uninstructed* (*ca* 400) offered guides for teachers, respectively doctrinal and salvation-historical in style.

As infant baptism gradually became the norm during the fifth century, baptismal instruction declined. Enrolment, exorcism, renunciation, and profession (via sponsors) were compressed into a series of rapid steps at the start of the baptismal service. The traditional catechumenate disappeared; 'catechism' came to refer to the education of baptized children.

The twentieth-century Liturgical Movement generated renewed interest in classical patterns. Baptismal catechesis experienced something of a renaissance, both in missionary environments and, with the demise of Christendom, in contexts where infant baptism had declined in frequency or meaning. The Catholic catechumenate was officially restored after Vatican Council II, with the *Rite of Christian Initiation of Adults* (1972) prescribed for adult candidates. Anglican, Lutheran, Methodist, and other Churches also developed systems of counselling for new believers, covering various stages from enquiry to commitment. Orthodoxy, which in areas of the modern West has attracted significant numbers of converts, re-emphasized the importance of catechetical grounding for retention and formation. Popular induction programmes may share some of the instincts of older approaches. Catechesis today tends to be conceived as a lifelong journey of learning the implications of baptismal belonging.

T. M. Finn, *Early Christian Baptism and the Catechumenate*, 2 vols. (Liturgical Press, 1992).

M. E. Johnson, *The Rites of Christian Initiation: Their Evolution and Interpretation*, 2nd edn (Liturgical Press, 2007).

E. Yarnold, *The Awe-Inspiring Rites of Initiation: The Origins of the RCIA*, 2nd edn (T&T Clark/Liturgical Press, 1994).

Ivor J. Davidson

Catechumen The designation for a person undergoing catechesis first appears in the later second century. In the early Church, catechumens were regarded as Christians, not just enquirers after the faith, though not yet full members of the body. The catechumenate was entered by enrolment, involving moral and spiritual scrutiny, though children were also enlisted by Christian parents. Ordinary catechumens or 'hearers' did not attend special classes, but went to the normal services of the Church for a period of months or years. They were formally dismissed from the assembly prior to the Eucharist. By the fourth century, the sacraments were held to be sacred mysteries, not to be witnessed by the uninitiated, or even spoken of in their presence. Regular catechumens were expected to evince good conduct, but moral lapses were not regarded so seriously in their case as they were for the baptized; one consequence was that it became common to delay baptism for years (even to one's deathbed), a practice much deplored by Church leaders. To proceed to the final stages of baptismal preparation meant attending regular, sometimes daily, Lenten classes from which basic catechumens were barred. Individuals undergoing this training were known in the Greek East as *photizomenoi* ('those being illuminated'), in the West generally as *competentes* ('petitioners'), and in Rome as *electi* ('chosen ones').

Ivor J. Davidson

Catherine of Siena Catherine of Siena was a religious reformer and spiritual author famous for her public life. She was born in Siena in or around 1347 to a prosperous family of cloth dyers. In her late teens or very early twenties she joined a community of Dominican female penitents and developed a following that included a number of young Sienese noblemen. Between 1374 and her death in 1380, Catherine was engaged – especially through her letters – in matters of pressing political concern in Italy, including the 'War of the Eight Saints' between Florence and the papacy. In her letters she was an insistent advocate for peace in Italy, ecclesiastical reform, the return of the papacy to Rome from Avignon, and the Roman observance after the schism of 1378.

Catherine's writings include more than 380 extant letters; a visionary book, usually known in English as *The Dialogue*; and a number of prayers. The significance of her writings lies in the way in which she synthesized and communicated traditional theological teachings in her own highly energetic vernacular. The recurring theme in all Catherine's writings – whether addressed to the spiritual needs of individuals or to political crises – is love: the joy and consolation of perfect love of God; the love of neighbour as an expression of love of God; and self-love, which is the source of all vices, clouding the intellect and causing people to mistake truth for lies, and lies for truth. Catherine's career and writings make her a central figure in late medieval religion, and particularly its currents of affective spirituality and female sanctity.

F. T. Luongo, *The Saintly Politics of Catherine of Siena* (Cornell University Press, 2006).

F. Thomas Luongo

CATHOLIC THEOLOGY If 'theology' means a discrete academic discipline, then the roots of Catholic theology must be sought in the Middle Ages. In the post-NT period, the Greek word *theologia* meant different things. For the Greek fathers, *theologia* was understood to mean the mysterious inner life of the Trinity as opposed to *economia*, which meant the work of the Trinity as it poured itself out in revelation (see Economy, Divine). Others understood *theologia* to mean authentic discourse about God in prayer. Origen of Alexandria used the term to describe the third stage of the soul's ascent to God as it penetrated the mysteries of the *Song of Solomon*. Evagrius Ponticus (345–99) famously said that those who pray are theologians, so that at least one strand of the ancient tradition equated theology with prayer.

It is true that many of the Christian writers in the first millennium did engage in speculation and produce writings that we would recognize as theological in the modern understanding of the term. They did so in works of different genres that refuted erroneous theories, articulated the orthodox faith against heresies, or expounded levels of interpretation of sacred SCRIPTURE. The earliest attempts at a large account of the Christian faith can be traced in the West to the late second-century treatise *Against Heresies* by IRENAEUS OF LYONS and in the East in the third century to Origen's *On First Principles*.

Ordinarily, however, theology as an academic exercise is popularly traced back to P. Abelard (1079–1142), who was the first in the West to treat Christian themes by the application of dialectic in his famous work *Sic et Non*. It is with Abelard and, perhaps, his early contemporary ANSELM OF CANTERBURY in works like the *Proslogion* (1078) and *Cur Deus Homo* (1099), that intellectual reflection first began to be systematically applied to Christian doctrine. Anselm, famously, defined theology as 'faith seeking understanding' (*fides quaerens intellectum*). Abelard's *Sic et Non* was an attempt to juxtapose contrary theological positions from the tradition and resolve them by the application of dialectics – a strategy that would soon become common in the nascent universities.

Catholic theology, properly understood, is best seen as having developed when the subject matter of faith slowly shifted from the monastic cloister or the cathedral close to the newly emerging universities at the end of the twelfth century. While those holding chairs in the university saw themselves basically as commentators on the Bible, they were also convinced that the articulation of the truths of faith could best be uncovered by the application of dialectical reasoning and grounding in philosophy, first in the PLATONISM inherited from the patristic tradition and increasingly in Aristotle as his works became available to the West (see ARISTOTELIANISM). While this shift has been too generally known as 'SCHOLASTICISM' it was, in fact, a complex phenomenon of various hues. It was commonly said that the 'masters' had three tasks: to read the sacred text, to resolve cruxes arising from the text, and, finally, to preach.

T. AQUINAS and BONAVENTURE may stand as exemplars of two major trends in the thirteenth century. Bonaventure, a Franciscan friar, stood firmly in the Augustinian tradition, while Aquinas, a Dominican, though no stranger to Augustinian themes, made more conspicuous moves to distinguish philosophical from theological approaches to God. His 'style' of theology, best exemplified in his *Summa theologiae* (with its divisions of topics into questions, objections, and responses), was widely adopted after his own time, although this 'Scholastic method' often ended up somewhat mechanically applied by his later imitators, who lacked Aquinas' flexibility and sophistication in its application. In the opening question of the *Summa*, Aquinas insisted that theology was an intellectual enterprise (a 'science') rooted in ultimate principles (thus, also, a wisdom) whose foundational subject was God as God was revealed in Scripture. Hence, as a theologian, he saw his task as being an expositor of sacred Scripture.

The rise of the Renaissance humanists led to a strong reaction against the late Scholastic mode of doing theology. The humanists advocated recourse to patristic sources to recover the thought of the Greek and Latin fathers while also employing philology as an instrument of reform. The rise of the so-called 'trilingual schools' (in which students were taught Hebrew, Greek, and Latin) was the remote source for the later critical approach to biblical studies, as well as a refreshed impetus for vernacular translations and editions of the early Church fathers. The best known of these humanists – Erasmus of Rotterdam (1466/9–1536), J. Colet (1467–1519), T. More (1478–1535) – were profoundly influenced by their interest in biblical studies and their retrieval of the patristic tradition.

In reaction to the Protestant REFORMATION, Catholic theology took two directions. One was to put an emphasis on aggressive apologetical statements of Catholic doctrine in direct confrontation with the Reformers in works like the *De Controversiis Christianae fidei* (1586–93) of the Jesuit R. Bellarmine (1542–1621), which was widely known and widely excoriated in Protestant lands. The other emphasis was on a renewed Scholasticism, using as its launching point and organizing principle commentaries on the work of Aquinas. This renewed approach to Aquinas, often called 'baroque Scholasticism', had formidable champions both within the Dominican Order and among the Jesuits, especially in Spain.

Medieval writers like Aquinas attempted to give a full account of Christian faith and practice (as the very word *summa* implies), but, under the pressures of the Reformation and in response to exigent needs triggered by the reforming Council of TRENT, theologians began to carve off areas of theology into discrete disciplines. Thus, in the late sixteenth and early seventeenth centuries, free-standing manuals of MORAL THEOLOGY, mainly for the use of confessors and oriented towards CASUISTRY, began to be published in answer to pragmatic needs of improving the pastoral life of priests. The most influential of these works was the *Theologia moralis* (1748) of Alphonsus of Liguori (1696–1787); it went through at least seven editions before the author's death. In the same period there appeared single treatises on the Church (ECCLESIOLOGY) and, partially in reaction to the Reformation, separate treatises on the role of Mary in the Church (the term 'MARIOLOGY' first began to be used in the late 1500s). Thus, what was once a coherent whole now became separate 'tracts' of theology, which, in turn, became distilled into pedagogical manuals. Manual theology soon became the ordinary basis for instruction in seminaries established for the training of priests. This 'manualist' approach persisted well into the twentieth century.

The shortcoming of this 'manual theology' was apparent to some independent thinkers in the nineteenth century, such as those who flourished among the Catholic faculty of theology at the University of Tübingen in their attempt to retrieve the wisdom of the early fathers of the Church (see Tübingen School, Catholic). Independently, and blessedly untouched by Scholastic formation, J. H. Newman exercised his formidable intelligence on seminal issues like the development of doctrine and epistemological questions about the nexus between faith and reason.

It was also in the nineteenth century that Pope Leo XIII (r. 1878–1903) promoted the study of Aquinas as the model for doing Catholic theology in his encyclical *Aeterni Patris* (1879). That papal encouragement provided the impetus for theological renewal lasting well over a century, as scholars and teachers went back to Aquinas himself to free his thought from the encrustations of late medieval and baroque commentary. This retrieval of the authentic meaning of Aquinas took various directions, with one stream more concerned with the philosophical underpinnings of his thought while another (especially among the French Dominicans) made great strides in situating Aquinas more historically with a more precise focus on his status as a theologian.

In the same period, some Catholic thinkers began to attempt a new approach to theological thinking in response both to the Enlightenment and to the rise of the modern sciences. By the turn of the twentieth century, some of these more adventuresome writers, especially in France, drew the unwelcome attention of the Vatican for their more radical approach to the veracity of sacred Scripture and their desire to root faith in experience. The upshot of this attention was the wholesale condemnation of modernism by Pope Pius X (r. 1903–14) in 1907, as well as the subsequent imposition of an anti-modernist oath required of all those who taught theology and as a prerequisite for priestly ordination. Rome had enormous suspicion of the modernist thrust, which placed a strongly immanentist emphasis on the subjective reception and expression of religious faith. The Roman authorities also cast a critical eye on the historical turn that had been regnant in Protestant circles for over a century, and which seemed to have influenced the Catholic modernists excessively. The anti-modernist resistance of the twentieth century had deep roots in the Catholic Church's reaction against certain philosophical movements (to say nothing of its suspicions about the Enlightenment project in general) already condemned at Vatican Council I.

The net result of the anti-modernist reaction of Rome was to retard Catholic theological scholarship for decades. The slow reaction against such repressive measures began in the late 1930s when (mainly) European scholars started to retrieve the texts of classical theological sources from the early fathers and sought to integrate this historical scholarship with systematic theological reflection. These thinkers – including some of the most famous Catholic thinkers of the twentieth century like Y. Congar, M.-D. Chenu (1895–1990), H. de Lubac, and J. Daniélou (1905–74) – represented what was called (not always kindly) *la nouvelle théologie*. By mid-century their works also came under suspicion in Rome, and some of them found themselves condemned (though not by name) in the encyclical *Humani generis* (1950) by Pope Pius XII (r. 1939–58).

A major turning point for Catholic theology came at the calling of Vatican Council II, when the work of those theologians, so long under a cloud, became a shaping force in the conciliar documents. The work of the Council is reflected in two movements that have gone under two titles: the French word *ressourcement* ('back to the sources') and the Italian word *aggiornamento* ('bringing up to date'). Both of these movements encouraged a more sensitive approach to the historical development of theological positions with a concomitant critique of an ahistorical understanding of doctrinal formulations.

In the period after the Council, Catholic systematic theology followed two broad trajectories: a renewed Thomism that sought positive engagement with contemporary thought (K. Rahner) and a more literary approach privileging the patristic past (H. von Balthasar). However, other approaches of theology, under the pressure of more lay participation and the concerns of those outside the European context, also began to be heard in more contextualized theologies: feminist theology, liberation theology, various postmodern theologies reacting to the 'eclipse of God' in the West; and, very significantly after Vatican II, theologies that engaged world religions. Moral theology reacted strongly against the old casuist models of the late Scholastic manuals to turn either to accounts based on Christian theories of virtue or to accounts more rooted in the biblical witness.

Perhaps the greatest shift in Catholic theology in the last half-century concerned the issue of who was doing theology and where. Until the latter half of the twentieth century, it was uncommon to find lay theologians (of either gender) studying with a view towards a life vocation in that field. Second, in a more ecumenical climate it became more common for Catholics to study theology within ecumenical university faculties, especially as theology itself has moved outside the seminaries to university settings. With the increasing number of lay people studying theology, it was also inevitable that different kinds of theological questions and different forms of theological expression emerged.

These shifts in who was studying and where became intensified when increasingly theologians came from the non-European world. That shift towards what Rahner called the coming 'World Church' (*Weltkirche*) brought with it a more historically nuanced way of theological reflection. What did theologians have to say about the teeming world of the poor in the developing nations? How was theology to respond to such horrendous historical facts as the HOLOCAUST? What was to be made of the claims of Christianity in places where Christians were a tiny minority in a context where the world view was Buddhist or Hindu or Muslim? These are the essential issues facing Catholic theology in the twenty-first century.

Y. Congar, *A History of Theology* (Doubleday, 1968).

F. Kerr, *Twentieth-Century Catholic Theologians* (Blackwell, 2007).

J. Mahoney, *The Making of Moral Theology* (Oxford University Press, 1989).

LAWRENCE CUNNINGHAM

CATHOLICITY Derived from the Greek word for 'universal', catholicity (like APOSTOLICITY) is used in theology to name both a criterion of doctrinal orthodoxy and (following the language of the APOSTLES' and NICENE CREEDS) one of the classical marks of the Church (see ECCLESIOLOGY). In either case, it refers to the principle that the Church's FAITH and practice must not be limited by the prejudices and predilections of any particular time or place. Ecclesiologically, this means that the Church should be flexible enough in its form to be able to inhabit any culture (see INCULTURATION). Vincent of Lérins (d. *ca* 450) gave classic expression to the doctrinal implications of this ecclesiological point by defining genuinely Catholic teaching as that 'which has been believed everywhere, always, and by all' (*Comm.* 4.3).

This so-called 'Vincentian Canon' is not to be understood as a sociological test, as though the orthodoxy of any DOCTRINE could be secured by establishing that it had been explicitly affirmed by all Christians at all times and in every place. Instead, it is a summons to examine the ecumenicity of any proposed doctrine, and this in two senses: (1) Is it *consistent* with what Christians have said and done in other times and places? (2) Is it *necessary* for all Christians, regardless of the time and place in which they live? In this way, catholicity probes what is essential or non-negotiable in Christian teaching, over against matters that, while appropriate for a given context, may be altered without affecting the integrity of the faith (see ADIAPHORA).

IAN A. MCFARLAND

CELIBACY Celibacy, or the discipline of sexual abstinence, stands outside the pair-bonding or polygamous categories of most socially ordered human relationships. That celibacy occurs across different cultures and religious traditions leads to the assertion that it is as natural, if not as typical, as MARRIAGE and other forms of pair-bonding. Celibates also occur in varying non-intentional, circumstantial, or temporary ways in contemporary society. Despite its apparent rejection of more normal sexual pairing, celibacy is an expression of human sexuality. Christian understanding of celibacy means a life totally dedicated to union with God through non-marriage and sexual abstinence. Such a theology of celibacy values sexuality and human relationships as integral to God's creation of humanity, but it is also an expression of the diversity of human relations, beyond the sexual.

Celibate lifestyles can instantiate contrasting values: maintaining either a social order or the bodily transcendence of such order; natural purity or flight from natural human bonding; personal fulfilment or the overcoming of the self. The Catholic and Orthodox Churches (as well as some Hindu and Buddhist traditions) promote institutional forms of celibacy in MONASTICISM and in the lives of recluses or mystics. Within Christianity celibacy vowed by religious sisters and brothers is a voluntary relinquishing of sexual activity in order to give priority to PRAYER and service of God. Along with the vows of obedience and poverty, celibacy frees the person from familial and spousal commitments to serve God and others in eschatological witness to the KINGDOM OF GOD (Mark 12:25; Matt. 22:30). Priests and bishops in the Catholic tradition (and bishops in Orthodox traditions) are also obliged to be celibate, although priestly celibacy has another theological history and purpose than the more integrated celibacy in vowed religious life. Also, while there have always been more women exponents of celibacy in western Christianity, their theological understanding of celibacy has received little examination. Recent studies suggest that women's experience of an embodied, celibate sexuality that is not based in abjection or body-denying can address the negative concept of woman as sensual temptress which has figured widely in past theologies.

Christian theological discussion of celibacy falls into five categories: the biblical imitation of Christ with an eschatological orientation of spousal union with Christ; desert monastic and patristic renunciation of BODY, SEXUALITY, and the world; the psychological pathologies of failed celibacy, often presented with little theological reflection; theologies of the BODY that relate celibacy to other sexual and gendered experience; and an eco-ethical consciousness of the contribution of celibacy to the interconnectedness of life.

While Jesus is widely understood not to have married, the biblical warrants for a theology of celibacy are few. Prominent in theological treatments are Matthew's 'eunuchs for the kingdom' (Matt. 19:10–12) and PAUL's personal choice for celibacy explained in terms of the imminence of the kingdom of God (1 Cor. 7:5–7, 8, 17, 20, 24–35). The celibacy of the prophet Jeremiah has not been widely referenced for the theology of celibacy.

The traditions shaped by the Protestant Reformation viewed clerical and monastic celibacy as distortions of the Gospel ethic and complicit in the simony and corruption of the Renaissance Church, so in Protestant areas its validity as a Christian lifestyle was dissolved along with the monasteries that housed it. Recent scholarship on NT teaching on sexuality and asceticism has redressed the previous neglect in Protestant and Anglican biblical exegesis of such texts.

Early Christian understanding of celibacy as a 'white' (i.e., bloodless) martyrdom was derived from the same eschatological orientation that fuelled readiness for martyrdom when Christians were persecuted. Celibacy domesticated that radical willingness to die for God, while replicating the bodily sacrifice of the Saviour through the soul's exclusive and ascetic union with God. This eschatological imperative obviated the social obligation to provide emotionally and economically for family, partners, and progeny. This devaluation of sexual relations also reflected the contemporary Greco-Roman ascetic ideals of concentrating human energies and the moral power of control, and the spiritual disembodiment of Manichaean and other Gnostic beliefs. Traditional theology of celibacy denigrates all that is physical, the senses, women's sexuality, and marriage as being of this world and thereby corruptible. This discerns Godlikeness only in the spiritual and otherworldly 'angelism' promoted by eastern and western monasticism.

More recent theology judges such denial of the body and sexuality as restricting the humanity of its exponents, provoking a dissociated view of reality, and confusing personal detachment with a selfish lack of responsible commitment to anyone. Such an understanding of celibacy has also been blamed for not containing or converting sexual needs positively in destructive personalities. A contemporary theology of celibacy calls for more critical biological and psychological understanding of humanity and for a positive Christian anthropology that attempts to explain how the celibate has different needs and different expressions of sexuality, rather than none at all. Theologies of the body that have addressed celibacy are concerned with how abstinence from sexual activity can be understood not to devalue sex, the body, or women's sexuality, but to represent wider human types of sexuality and relationships than sexual intercourse. Celibacy that rejects neither the sexual nor the relational in humanity is the search for union with God, mediated in the diversity of human relationships other than sexual partnership. Then celibacy can be understood in terms of its likeness to other lives as much as in terms of its difference.

A theological appreciation of the commonality of the human condition demonstrates how celibacy contributes to God's gift of life through creation and through the interconnectedness of divine and all life reconciled in the incarnation and further sustained through the life of the Spirit. Celibacy seeks to unite the bodily and the spiritual in loving service of God. A Christian theology of celibacy can show how God is love even in situations where love appears unrequited by manifesting a form of human love that does not depend on the reciprocity of a partner. In this way, celibacy illuminates the diversity that is human love in the many ways that it manifests God's love.

See also Theological Anthropology; Virginity.

P. Brown, *The Body and Society: Men and Women and Sexual Renunciation in Early Christianity* (Columbia University Press, 1988).

J. Gray, *Neither Exploiting nor Escaping Sex: Women's Experience of Celibacy* (Slough, 1995).

W. Loader, *Sexuality and the Jesus Tradition* (Eerdmans, 2005).

A. W. R. Sipe, *Celibacy: A Way of Loving, Living and Serving* (Gill & Macmillan, 1996).

Janette Gray

Celtic Christianity That a distinctive form of Christianity existed in those parts of north-western Europe whose inhabitants in the early medieval period spoke a vernacular belonging to the Celtic language family is a widely held popular belief. For this view's proponents, this Christianity was distinctive in theology and spirituality from the Christianity of the Latin/Roman world of the time, and separate from it in its structures. It is, they argue, also to be distinguished from the 'Catholicism' or 'Roman Catholicism' that succeeded it and which held sway until the Reformation. In content, it is claimed that it is more sensitive to nature, closer to the earth's rhythms, to the feminine, less hierarchical, less interested in sin and non-Augustinian, and can provide the basis for a renewed liturgy. For some contemporary proponents it is, moreover, a lost, but recoverable, Christian wisdom ideally suited to contemporary situations, and which can interact seamlessly with New Age spirituality. However, the existence of 'Celtic Christianity' is denied by many scholars on either conceptual or historical grounds, or both.

For historians there never was a people covering north-western Europe who referred to themselves as 'the Celts'. The term 'Celtic' is primarily philological, and is used by analogy by literary historians and archaeologists to refer to literature and art which does not fall within the mainstream of western culture when that is defined by relationship to the Greco-Roman past. However, it is inappropriate when referring to Christianity which arrived in north-western Europe through its westward spread within the Roman Empire, establishing itself there as part of western

Christendom; every theologian writing in those lands saw himself belonging to a single religious body, and hence could move with ease in continental schools and monasteries.

However, in every region of the Latin West we find distinctive local features in their understanding and practice (hence descriptions such as 'North African Christianity'). This regional distinctiveness was facilitated by several factors. First, while the medieval West certainly had an image of its religious unity (expressed in language and canon law), it had no experience of the actual uniformity in such matters as liturgy or the desire for uniformity in doctrinal expressions that characterize recent centuries. The earlier the period one looks at in the West, the more one finds that local connections produce distinctive patterns in spirituality relating to local patterns of settlement, legal background, and language use. So, for example, a saint's life from Ireland will draw on the hagiographical models of ATHANASIUS and Sulpicius Severus, but express sanctity in a non-urban context, with its own traditions of law and social interaction, and in Latin, which was learnt as a second, specific-use language. Second, every feature of theology or practice first emerged somewhere, then later either became part of the mainstream or disappeared with the gradual spread of greater uniformity in practice or teaching: thus early medieval Spain produced a theology of the Eucharist as the sacred object, while early medieval Ireland produced a new system of penance which stands behind the later development of auricular confession and indulgences. Lastly, we have to be careful with using evidence in such as way that it appears to point to regional 'distinctive' variations when, in fact, it may merely be an earlier widespread form of Christian belief. For instance, the interest in the universe as sacramental reflects a common theme of pre-university theology, but when it is found in an insular text is taken as being somehow distinctive of works written in that area. When these considerations are kept in mind, the historical task is not that of finding a 'Celtic Christianity', but of being sensitive to the variations found throughout the medieval world and comparing them with other local theologies from the period; this process then leaves open the theological task of seeing whether or not these various phenomena pose questions as to the nature of later uniformities or of contemporary assumptions.

Thus, while discussions of Celtic Christianity often cite the Synod of Whitby (664) as a watershed moment in the confrontation between 'Celtic' and 'Roman' Catholicism, such interpretations are unfounded. The 'synod' was actually a royal court at Straeneshalch, the decisions of which regarding the dating of Easter were typical of many such meetings across Europe to standardize the liturgical calendar. Similarly, the decision regarding the proper form of monastic tonsure reflected a disagreement between monastic groups and should not be read in terms of a national distinctiveness.

The current interest in 'the Celtic past', whether well founded historically or not, has produced some interesting effects in Christian communities. First, it has often highlighted the historical nature of belief, and how culture and spirituality interact. Second, under the 'Celtic' label many Churches have experimented with liturgical practices which would otherwise be seen as incompatible with a Reformation heritage. Third, it has been used in several ecumenical endeavours to construct a common 'remembered past' that bypasses divided memories through the intellectual device that that which is now proposed is 'older' than the period of division.

T. O'Loughlin, *Celtic Theology: Humanity, World and God in Early Irish Writings* (Continuum, 2000).

'"A Celtic Theology": Some Awkward Questions and Observations' in *Identifying the 'Celtic'*, ed. J. F. Nagy (Four Courts, 2002), 49–65.

THOMAS O'LOUGHLIN

CENOBITISM: see MONASTICISM.

CHALCEDON, COUNCIL OF The fourth ecumenical COUNCIL of the Church convened in 451 at Chalcedon, just across the Bosphorus from Constantinople. It was called by the recently installed Emperor Marcian (396–457) to secure religious unity in the empire. Attended by around 500 bishops, the overwhelming majority from the East (the West was represented only by the delegates of Rome and two bishops from Africa), its proceedings were controlled by a group of nineteen imperial administrators, chosen to ensure that the will of Marcian and his consecrated wife Pulcheria prevailed.

By far the most significant achievement of Chalcedon was its definition of FAITH, generated by the gathering's reluctant members at the insistence of the imperial authorities. After much negotiation, a text was promulgated and signed in the emperor's presence by 452 bishops at the sixth session on 25 October, 451. At its heart lay the following statement:

> Therefore, following the holy fathers, we all with one voice teach the confession of one and the same Son, our Lord Jesus Christ: the same perfect in divinity and perfect in humanity, the same truly God and truly man, of a rational soul and a body; consubstantial with the Father as regards his divinity, and the same consubstantial with us as regards his humanity; like us in all respects except for sin; begotten before the ages from the Father as regards his divinity, and in the last days the same for us and for our salvation from Mary, the Virgin God-bearer, as regards his humanity; one and the same Christ, Son, Lord, Only-begotten, acknowledged in two natures, without confusion, without change, without

> division, without separation; at no point was the difference between the natures taken away through the union, but rather the characteristic property of each nature is preserved and comes together into a single person and a single subsistence; he is not parted or divided into two persons, but is one and the same Only-begotten Son, God, Word, Lord Jesus Christ, just as the prophets taught from the beginning about him, and as the Lord Jesus Christ himself instructed us, and as the creed of the fathers has handed down to us.

In a lengthy preamble to this formula, the delegates had endorsed the teaching of the Councils of Nicaea and Constantinople, and affirmed the findings of the Council of Ephesus. The bishops were accordingly committed to the position that Christ was consubstantial (*homoousios*) in divinity with God the Father; that Apollinarianism was erroneous; that Nestorianism was utterly wrong; and that (against the claims of Nestorius and his supporters) Mary deserved to be called *Theotokos* ('God-bearer'). These convictions are explicitly represented in the confession.

But the primary issue of the moment was the fierce dispute that had opened up in the late 440s over the teaching of Eutyches (*ca* 378–454), who had argued that there were two natures prior to the union of the divine Word and human flesh, but only one thereafter; and that Christ's humanity, though Virgin-born, was not consubstantial with ours (see Eutychianism). Chalcedon had undone the results of the so-called 'robber-synod' of Ephesus in 449, which had cleared Eutyches of error and mistreated his opponents. Against Eutyches, the Chalcedonian definition insisted that Christ was consubstantial with us in respect of his humanity, and there was a genuine distinction of natures after the union. In idiom drawn from a variety of sources, Christ was to be 'acknowledged *in* two natures' (the proposal 'from (*ek*) two natures' was rejected), 'without confusion, without change, without division, without separation': the first pair of negatives safeguarded the duality post-union, the second made it clear that there were not two distinct persons. There was one *prosōpon* (person) and one *hypostasis*, made known in two *physeis* (natures).

The formula represents a balancing act between the danger of swallowing up humanity into divinity (the perennial risk for 'Alexandrian' Christology) and the peril of rendering humanity quasi-independent of divinity (the corresponding challenge for the 'Antiochene' tradition). In responding to the issues generated by Eutyches, Chalcedon's leanings seem clearly Antiochene, though the council also explicitly invoked the authority of Cyril of Alexandria. As a solution to disagreement, Chalcedon failed. To a large majority of Christians in Egypt, Palestine, and Syria, the rubric of two natures after the union was unacceptable, and a betrayal of Cyril's essential reasoning. For them, Eutyches was wrong to deny the consubstantiality of Christ's humanity with our own; but it was vital to affirm that divinity entered into genuine, transformative union with human nature rather than merely being joined to it, as they took the council to be saying. A great deal of the history of the Eastern Churches over the following centuries is the story of diverse intellectual and political attempts to secure rapprochement between the supporters of Chalcedon and such Miaphysite ('one-nature') – but in their own terms orthodox and non-Eutychian – critics (see Miaphysitism). In the end, these efforts failed, though some of the reflection yielded significant theological achievements, not least the demonstration in the sixth century that the definition could indeed be read in a thoroughly Alexandrian fashion.

Chalcedon has remained a fundamental authority for Orthodox, Catholic, and a majority of Protestant Churches, but is officially rejected by the principal Coptic, Syrian, Armenian, Ethiopian, and Eritrean Churches to this day (see Oriental Orthodox Churches). Its divisive legacy in the East is undeniable, though modern ecumenism has yielded significant acknowledgements of common ground. In modern western theology the confession has been heavily criticized for its abstract language; for its general lack of scriptural reference; for its supposition that divine and human 'natures' can be spoken of in the same breath; and for its reticence about what it really means for these natures both to be present in a single subject. Yet other construals may commend themselves: the register is not nearly so desiccated or detached from the story of salvation as might first be supposed; the formula's boldness about the need to think God and humanity together presents a salutary challenge to unwarranted epistemic dualism; the negativity and minimalism may convey important principles about the inevitable boundaries of revealed mystery. So long as its central focus is recognized to lie not in the two natures in isolation but in their coming together in the one person, the Chalcedonian picture may be seen as an a posteriori conceptual description of a history rather than an exercise in speculation. Viewed thus, the definition may be regarded as marking out territory within which faith's reflection needs to operate if it is to think carefully about the object of its confession.

S. Coakley, 'What Does Chalcedon Solve and What Does It Not? Some Reflections on the Status and Meaning of the Chalcedonian "Definition"' in *The Incarnation: An Interdisciplinary Symposium on the Incarnation of the Son of God*, ed. S. T. Davis, D. Kendall, S. J., and C. O'Collins, S. J. (Oxford University Press, 2002), 143–63.

A. Grillmeier, *Christ in Christian Tradition*, 2nd edn, vol. I (Mowbray, 1975), 520–57; vol. II/1 (Mowbray, 1987).

R. V. Sellers, *The Council of Chalcedon: A Historical and Doctrinal Survey* (SPCK, 1953).

N. P. Tanner, ed., *Decrees of the Ecumenical Councils*, vol. I (Sheed & Ward/Georgetown University Press, 1990), 75–103.

IVOR J. DAVIDSON

CHARISM Transliterated directly from NT Greek, 'charism' (pl. 'charismata') in its broadest sense refers to any spiritual gift bestowed on human beings by divine GRACE (*charis* in Greek). The term is prominent in the letters of PAUL, where it is used principally to designate particular abilities (e.g., PROPHECY, exhortation, compassion, leadership, teaching, healing, GLOSSOLALIA) given to individuals for the benefit of the whole Church (Rom. 12:6–8; 1 Cor. 12:4–10, 28–31; cf. 1 Pet. 4:10). It can also function more generally to designate gifts bestowed by God on the community as a whole (Rom. 6:23; 11:29; 1 Cor. 1:7). In CATHOLIC THEOLOGY charism can be used in a way that combines these collective and individual meanings, referring to the form of service to the Church characteristic of a particular religious order, as derived from the VOCATION and practice of its founder.

Though Paul seems to assume that no believer is without some individual charism (1 Cor. 7:7), already in the NT the term comes to be used in a narrower sense for the gifts given specifically to Church leaders through the formal ritual of the laying on of hands (1 Tim. 4:14; 2 Tim. 1:6). In either case, the reception of charismata is closely associated with the operation of the HOLY SPIRIT. While through much of the Church's history a strong emphasis on order has led to stress on the institutional validation of charismata through formal processes like ordination, the contemporary CHARISMATIC MOVEMENT has placed renewed emphasis on the freedom of the Holy Spirit to bestow extraordinary gifts independently of institutional mediation.

IAN A. MCFARLAND

CHARISMATIC MOVEMENT 'Charismatic movement' refers here to two religious expressions of Pentecostal SPIRITUALITY that have found their voices outside the denominational structures of the classical Pentecostal tradition. Adding the prefix 'neo' to 'Pentecostal' is a way of identifying these voices, because it highlights the indebtedness neo-Pentecostals owe to their classical counterparts; but it also points to the fact that to be 'neo' is to be part of a distinctive constituency responsible for its own discourse and sure of its own identity (see NEO-ORTHODOXY). The charismatic movement, therefore, can be said to be neo-Pentecostal in its stress on personal encounters with the 'life-changing Spirit' and its acknowledgement that such encounters encourage 'signs and wonders', including MIRACLES, speaking in tongues (see GLOSSOLALIA), divine healing, and spiritual discernment. Charismatics also closely follow Pentecostals in their predilection for spontaneous and extempore liturgies, where repetitious singing of hymns and choruses replaces the more formal traditions of hymns, chants, and litanies.

The rubric 'neo-Pentecostal', however, also calls to attention that the charismatic movement, while experientially Pentecostal, is theologically diverse. This diversity amounts to what is really a bifurcation in neo-Pentecostalism itself (certainly in the USA and the UK). On the one hand there is the branch associated with a gentrified or middle-class Pentecostal spirituality that has taken root in the historic Churches. This branch is usually called Charismatic Renewal (shortened by participants to 'Renewal'). On the other hand, there is the branch whose taproots come from (usually more than one) newer religious constellations. Primarily evangelical and with a built-in propensity for SCHISM, this branch is often hostile to ECUMENISM and shows isolationist tendencies with the concomitant features of cultic behaviour and HETERODOXY.

Renewal did not explode on to the religious scene with the same ferocity as the Azusa Street revival of 1906. But once it arrived it spread like wildfire. The adoption of the term 'Renewal' (rather than 'Revival') by participants of this movement is an indication that they consider the existing denominations capable of being revitalized from within and see no reason to abandon their existing confessions. Enthusiastically ecumenical in its heyday (mid-1960s to 1980), Renewal was triggered by a number of priests and congregations in North America, notably Episcopalians D. Bennett (1917–91) from Van Nuys, California, and G. Pulkingham (1927–93) from Houston, Texas, and Catholics K. Ranaghan (b. 1940) at Notre Dame and F. MacNutt (b. 1925) in St Louis.

Ironically, despite the fact that the Renewal has attracted support from eminent scholars such as J. Moltmann (b. 1926) and M. Volf (b. 1956), it is hard to identify a specific charismatic theology from within the movement itself. It is almost a misnomer to talk of a charismatic theology, though there have been genuine recent attempts to outline its central features. Those theologians who did emerge as the intellectual apologists of the movement, including D. Gelpi (b. 1934) and T. Smail (b. 1928), did not adopt PENTECOSTAL THEOLOGY, but tried to make sense of it in terms of their own traditions. Catholics, for instance (most notably L. Cardinal Suenens, 1904–96), looked to the lives of Mary and the SAINTS as evidence of a charismatic tradition. But all those in the Renewal, Catholics in concert with Anglicans, Baptists, Presbyterians, and Methodists, held three things in common: none of them were cessationists who denied the presence of extraordinary spiritual gifts in the Church in the post-apostolic period; all of them were ecumenical in spirit and were open to each others' traditions; and all of them rejected the Pentecostal two-stage version of Christian initiation (the HOLY SPIRIT is received at BAPTISM and then more fully in the 'second blessing' of the baptism in the Spirit) and broadened the work of the Spirit to include 'inner healings' and spiritual therapy.

By highlighting the pastoral and intuitive side of ecstatic charismatic piety in the 1960s and 1970s, the Renewal shared in the wider cultural trends of late modernity that have moved away from the rational and logical epistemology of the ENLIGHTENMENT to broader and (some would say) wilder shores. It did, however, appeal to those committed Christians who felt that the 'Laodicean' Church (Rev. 3:14–16) needed revivification. In recent years the Renewal has perhaps lost momentum both in the USA and in Europe, though perhaps a better way of putting it is to see its influence continuing in diverse Christian initiatives, including the Emerging Church in America and Alpha in the UK.

The other half of neo-Pentecostalism (the second branch of the bifurcation) is more splintered than the Renewal, for it has been an upsurge of evangelical independent Churches jostling among themselves for position. In the UK from the late 1970s to the 1990s the Renewal and classical Pentecostalism both thought of these independents as rivals if not poachers. New Churches have drawn heavily on maverick and independent Pentecostal outsiders, notably the Healing Movement of the United States in the late 1940s and the Latter Rain Movement in Canada during the same period of time. A major theme in the Latter Rain Movement, reformulated by new Church leaders since the 1960s, has been the necessity for the Church to complete its restoration of spiritual gifts with a restored apostolate. The gist of the argument, based on Ephesians 4:9–12, is that spiritual gifts need to be grounded in a truly charismatic order for the Church to be itself again as it was in the NT.

One of the most prominent leaders in this arena is P. Wagner (b. 1930), who has championed and led the so-called 'apostolic reformation' since his days at Fuller Seminary in California. But it was one of his junior colleagues at Fuller, J. Wimber (1934–97), who emerged as the one major figure who successfully straddled the split ends of neo-Pentecostalism. The leading figure in the Renewal in the UK during the 1980s and 1990s, Wimber was welcomed both in new Churches hostile to ecumenism (New Frontiers in the UK, for example) and in mainstream Renewal (as found, for example, at Holy Trinity Brompton and St Andrew's Chorleywood). Wimber founded a denomination of his own (the Vineyard), and his flamboyant ministry was the precursor of the most controversial development in neo-Pentecostalism: the 'Toronto Blessing', a version of 'being slain in the Spirit' where one fell to the floor accompanied by raucous laughter or animal noises.

It is probably more accurate to talk of neo-Pentecostalism as a variation of classical Pentecostalism that has mainly impacted western Europe, the Antipodes, and North America. If we take a global perspective, however, the distinctions of classical or bifurcated neo-Pentecostalism do not begin to capture the revolutionary possibilities of a restless spirituality that is as resistant to classification as it is capable of mutation. In parts of Africa, for example, Pentecostal spirituality is better described as an indigenous syncretism that has adopted and adapted the classical and splintered ends of neo-Pentecostalism and given them new diversified lives and fresh theological voices.

See also CHARISM.

W. Abraham, *The Logic of Renewal* (Eerdmans, 2003).
M. Cartledge, *Encountering the Spirit: The Charismatic Tradition* (Darton, Longman and Todd, 2006).
D. Gelpi, *Charism and Sacrament: A Theology of Christian Conversion* (SPCK, 1997).
T. Smail, *The Giving Gift: The Holy Spirit in Person* (Hodder and Stoughton, 1988).
A. Walker, *Restoring the Kingdom*, 4th edn (Eagle, 1998).

ANDREW WALKER AND JAMES STEVEN

CHARITY: see LOVE.

CHICAGO–LAMBETH QUADRILATERAL: see ECUMENISM.

CHILIASM: see PREMILLENNIALISM.

CHINESE THEOLOGY The history and shape of Chinese Christian theology have been significantly influenced by the fact that Christianity, which had developed for centuries in the matrix of western culture, was introduced into China as a 'foreign' religion. In different periods of history, different branches of Christianity faced the questions derived from the Chinese context, a context which includes not only cultural, linguistic, philosophical, and religious dimensions, but also a socio-political dimension. Chinese Christian theologians have considered their basic theological tasks at times in terms of indigenization and at times in terms of contextualization, though they may have different positions on whether and how indigenization or contextualization is to be achieved (see INCULTURATION).

During the seventh century, a monk named Alopen (or Aluoben) brought a religion known to the Chinese as *jing jiao* (literally, 'luminous teaching') into China. Based on the theology and spirituality embodied in the monument and the scrolls found in Xi'an, it seems that this *jing jiao* employed some Buddhist or Daoist terms to translate some of its theological concepts, but its doctrine of God, Christology, and spirituality are quite similar to the Syrian Christianity at that time and there is no conclusive evidence indicating religious syncretism.

After the arrival of Catholicism in China in the sixteenth century, missionaries argued among themselves concerning whether Christianity should accommodate to the Chinese cultural tradition. For the Chinese Christians, who inherited the traditional Chinese culture as part of their upbringing, the question is more about 'which' and 'how' than 'whether' the

Chinese cultural resource should be used in theology. Yang Ting-yun (1562–1627), one of the 'three pillars' of the Catholic Church in China, had been attracted to Buddhism before his conversion to Catholicism. He continued to identity himself as a 'Confucian' even after his conversion and his theology bore some Confucian characteristics. Though Yang accepted the Christian belief concerning a Creator God bringing the world into being, he continued to use Chinese philosophical concepts to formulate his cosmology without making reference to the biblical account of a seven-day creation, or to Adam and Eve as the first man and woman. Through identifying the triune God as our 'Great Father–Mother' (*da-fu-mu*), instead of the sexually biased 'our Heavenly Father', Yang took filial piety, a cardinal Confucian virtue, as the cornerstone to form a theology which linked up piety (to revere heaven as a filial child), ethics (to love other people as brothers and sisters), and spirituality (to overcome oneself in order to serve God and other people). Yang seldom mentioned the doctrine of original sin and tended to assume the goodness of human nature. For him, God loved the people so much that God endowed human nature with a good conscience (*liang zhi*), so that human beings could serve God and love people accordingly. This is what Yang called 'teaching by nature' (*xing-jiao*), which is to be supplemented by 'teaching by book' (*shu-jiao*, referring to the OT books of Moses), and fulfilled in the 'teaching by grace' (*en-jiao*) of Jesus Christ.

In modern times, especially during the Republican period (1911–49), the most serious challenges to Christian faith came from nationalism, scientism, and the rapid social and political changes, rather than from the revivals of Confucianism and Buddhism prompted by the challenge of western colonialism. In response to the criticisms made by the anti-Christian movement during the 1920s, many Chinese Christians argued that Christianity was compatible with science and could contribute positively to social progress. Some Church leaders also attempted to indigenize Christianity, including its organization, liturgy, and theology. Since the 1930s, the focus of discussion has shifted from 'indigenization' (how to indigenize Christianity into Chinese culture) to 'contextualization' (how to make Christianity relevant to the contemporary socio-political context), though sometimes these two motifs intertwine.

Zhao Zi-chen (also known as T. C. Chao, 1888–1979), probably the best known Chinese theologian of his lifetime, suggested that Christianity could contribute to the rebuilding of the nation through the Christian way of cultivation of personality, as demonstrated in the perfect human personality of Jesus. Zhao's position is not only similar to the Confucian approach of governing the nation and the world through self-cultivation, but also in line with the political and theological liberalism popular at that time. However, some years later, Zhao's theology, under the influence of K. Barth's theology and Zhao's experience in prison during the Japanese invasion, shifted from theological liberalism to a more theocentric position, emphasizing the distinctiveness of Christian ethics vis-à-vis other ethical systems and the divine Word of God transcending other cultures without confusion or compromise.

Like Zhao, Wu Lei-chuan (or Wu Zhenchun, 1870–1944) also deliberated extensively on the relationship between Christianity and Chinese culture, but probably due to his understanding of the urgency of the political situation, Wu found that the most important aspect of the Christian legacy is the socialist ideal embodied in Jesus' message of the kingdom of God, which he thought more comparable with the Chinese philosophy of Mohism than with Confucianism.

Wu Yaozong (or Y. T. Wu, 1893–1979) was first attracted to the Social Gospel and pacifism, but he then found that a socialist revolution was inevitable for China. He became convinced that there was much common ground between Christianity and Marxism and that violence sometimes did not contradict the principle of love. Wu further suggested that Chinese theology should break with its western and capitalist tutelage in order to co-operate with the Communists for the rebuilding of China. After 1949, Wu became the leading theological voice in Mainland China.

After 1949, the theological discourses in Mainland China became highly focused on how Christianity might adapt to the new atheistic Communist regime. As it is articulated in the theology of Ding Guangxu (Bishop K. H. Ting, b. 1915), the theological mainstream in Mainland China took the idea of the 'cosmic Christ' as its key concept and stressed the following: (1) *agape* is an attribute of God's essence being expressed in his creation, providence, redemption, and sanctification; (2) all good things originate from God and therefore Christians should learn to appreciate all the good things taking place outside the Church; (3) all things will be redeemed, renewed, and reconciled in Christ; (4) the activities of the Holy Spirit are universal and not to be restricted to the visible Church; (5) human beings are created in the image of God, which was corrupted in the fall but not totally lost; and (6) 'glorifying God and serving fellow human beings' is the supreme principle for Christian living.

The 1980s saw the rise of 'Sino-Christian theology' proposed by a group of 'Cultural Christians' represented by Liu Xiao-feng and He Guang-hu, who are intellectuals from Mainland China engaging in theological studies without claiming any denominational affiliation. 'Sino-Christian theology' is thus more an approach to theology than a theological system. In contrast to a seminary-based, churchly theology aimed at articulating the official ecclesiastical doctrinal position, it tends to identify itself as an academic and humanistic discipline, aimed at expressing an individual's personal faith. In comparison with He, Liu is more critical towards theological indigenization. Liu argued that the Christ event, as divine REVELATION, was a critique of religion bringing forth the crisis of religion and national ideology. The fatal error of theological indigenization, Liu suggests, lies in its compromising the divine Word with human words.

Many Chinese theologians in Hong Kong and Taiwan continued theological indigenization through dialogue with Confucianism even after 1949. But in the 1970s, theologians in Hong Kong and Taiwan began to pay more attention to their particular socio-political contexts. In Taiwan, Homeland Theology and Chu-tou-tian (or Chut-hau-thi) Theology, which have been inspired by the theology of C. S. Song (b. 1929), emphasize the Taiwanese identity, the self-determination of the people of Taiwan, and the use of local Taiwanese cultural resources in theology. In Hong Kong, facing its return to Chinese sovereignty in 1997, Yang Mugu (Arnold M. K. Yeung, 1945–2002) proposed that, in comparison with LIBERATION THEOLOGIES, a theology of reconciliation is not only more proper to the context of 1997, but also better founded in SCRIPTURE and the Christian theological TRADITION.

The Chinese culture or context and its dramatic differences from western culture represent not only challenges but also opportunities for Chinese Christian theology with regard to the task of translating and interpreting the Bible and the classical Christian DOCTRINES in a way meaningful to the Chinese. For example, due to the lack of comparable terms in the Chinese language, Chinese theology has difficulties in translating or interpreting the concepts of *hypostasis*, *ousia*, *substantia*, etc., which reflect the substantialist bias of Indo-European languages, in which the idea of 'being' plays a key role. However, due to the characteristics of the Chinese language, Chinese Christian theology may be able to offer an alternative approach to the issue of 'overcoming onto-theology' in western theology. Whether or not Chinese Christian theology can offer better solutions to some of the western theological questions, it can enrich the discussion through making use of its cultural resources. Other than the theological usage of Chinese cultural resources, Chinese Christian theology may also raise a fundamental question of concern to both Chinese and non-Chinese Christians, regarding how to identify and distinguish those parts of their Christian heritage which are essential to the Christian identity from those which are merely dispensable products of western culture.

Lam W., *Chinese Theology in Construction* (William Carey Library, 1983).

R. Malek, ed., *The Chinese Face of Jesus Christ*, 5 vols. (Steyler, 2002–).

Ting K. H., *A Chinese Contribution to Ecumenical Theology: Selected Writings of Bishop K. H. Ting* (WCC Publications, 2002).

P. L. Wickeri, *Seeking the Common Ground: Protestant Christianity, the Three-Self Movement and China's United Front* (Orbis, 1988).

Yang H. and D. H. N. Yeung, eds., *Sino-Christian Studies in China* (Cambridge Scholars Press, 2006).

LAI PAN-CHIU

CHOSEN PEOPLE: see ELECTION.

CHRISMATION: see CONFIRMATION.

CHRIST: see CHRISTOLOGY.

CHRISTENDOM Christendom refers to the idea of Christian civilization as a religious, cultural, and political unity. The paradigmatic example is the Christian medieval world, but the term also refers to later forms of politically and culturally established Christianity, as well as to the idea of western civilization as a basically Christian civilization.

The early Church had no idea of Christendom. Christianity emerged inside Judaism, originally as one form of Diaspora Judaism. At that time diaspora (i.e., dispersion across many cultures) had been the normal form of Jewish existence for centuries. The experience of being a dispersed people living among other peoples and of not being in charge created a set of social innovations (e.g., the synagogue, the Torah, and the rabbinate) that made possible a social life without cultural homogeneity, a military, or other conventional political structures. This situation could be correlated with Jewish monotheism, in which God is Creator and Lord of the entire world, and justice is, correspondingly, not equated with the word of any earthly king or the emperor but transcends political order and is known through the Torah.

The early Church, which for quite some time maintained permeable borders with Judaism, similarly saw itself as a separate people that lived as resident aliens among other peoples. It continued to live with the social practices of the Jewish Diaspora communities. One could see the civil governments as used by God (see Rom. 13:1–7), but there was no systematic conception of Church and civil government as two co-working entities of one people. The Church rather introduced a 'counter politics' distinguished from the politics and moral ideals of the Roman Empire. 'Worldly politics' was not seen as the primary arena for the good life, as was the case in Greek city-states or in the Roman Empire. Instead, the Church created its own politics, with different social practices and moral vocabularies.

However, the Church grew and became the established religion, first of the ageing Roman Empire and then of what was to become western Europe. Christendom was the result. In this sense Christendom can be described not as a theological ideal, but as the actual result of Christian mission. Moreover, the fact that the Church originally emerged as a separate people and as an institution separate from the civil government continued, in different ways, to shape the world of Christendom as well as western civilization as a whole. The Church continued to be an institution separate from civil political institutions, although it was often closely aligned with them (and more closely aligned in eastern Christianity than in the West; see CAESAROPAPISM).

Though Eusebius of Caesarea (*ca* 260–*ca* 340) had described the conversion of Constantine I (*ca* 275–337) in glowing terms, the first major piece of systematic theological reflection on this new situation was AUGUSTINE's *City of God*. Within his analytical framework, the 'city of the world' can still be understood as a contingent historical formation built on a pagan lifestyle, and thus as standing in sharp contrast to the 'city of God' shaped by the love of God. But Augustine is also quite explicit that this worldly city is used by God's PROVIDENCE for the welfare of humanity. Building on this idea, later medieval theorists understood Christendom as one world governed by two powers, or 'swords', instead of talking about two cities. Church and civil government represented two different functions within one hierarchical cosmic order created by God. The OT descriptions of the Israelite monarchy became a main text for understanding Christendom in its political aspects. On the whole, Christendom can be seen as an attempt to unite faith, life, culture, and politics into a comprehensive and distinctively Christian social order.

The Protestant REFORMATION, which coincided with a struggle for the independence of the civil government from the Church and the rise of the modern State, led to the disintegration of unified western Christendom. Nevertheless, several of the basic theological ideas behind Christendom were transferred to the Protestant realms. Although in practice the model of Christendom was now restricted to each individual nation, Church and civil government were still two functions within one God-given polity. However, in the Radical Reformation and in some later 'free Churches', the practices and thinking of early 'diaspora Christianity' began to emerge again.

The American Revolution led to the separation of Church and State in the USA, but Christendom ideas and practices survived in changed forms. By contrast, the French Revolution was in part a radical revolution against Christendom. Much post-revolutionary continental European history was marked by struggle for social power and political influence between established Churches who held to the older model of Christendom and secularizing forces that rejected it.

Although Europe increasingly became secularized, conceptions of Christendom have continued to be presupposed in most European and American theology. For example, in much neo-Protestant theology the Reformation is described as the beginning of a process that led to the realization of Christianity in the modern liberal welfare state. From this perspective, Christianity has left its ecclesial period behind and reached its political–historical period, realized in liberal democracy. More radical forms of POLITICAL THEOLOGY (e.g., some LIBERATION THEOLOGIES) often tend to assume something similar, but replace the liberal meta-history with, e.g., a socialist one. In these theologies secularization is simply the legitimate realization of Christianity.

Such theologies have in common with more traditional Church theology a tendency to see the world 'from above': as an ordered whole that is the result of a historical development and the ground of a hoped-for future. The dominant forms of modern theology have therefore tried to understand the Church or Christianity as a function of a potentially harmonious and natural secular order and theology as part of a putative universal reason. This is Christendom under modern presuppositions.

Yet the Church has increasingly lost the position that made such positions intelligible; modern societies are increasingly pluralistic or fractured, and the so-called Third World (in which the Church has usually not been established in the way it was in Europe) is gradually becoming the centre of Christianity. In addition, it has also become more difficult to defend ideas of a unified secular society, of the State as a centred subject behind social development, and of unified secular reason.

An increasing number of theologians have therefore criticized the whole Christendom concept, both in its traditional and in its modern forms. According to such views, the Church rightly understands itself as a people that will share space with others, use various cultural and social resources, and show a relative and critical loyalty to other local entitities (such as regions, nations, international unions) in which they are living. But it will understand these relations in an unsystematic and ad hoc way. The Christian's primary identity is formed by the people called 'Church', not by nations or other communities. This 'Catholic' Church is thus transnational, and a diaspora identity can be seen as a concrete way of living the Christian catholicity in a world of nations in the time before the eschaton.

O. O'Donovan, *The Desire of the Nations: Rediscovering the Roots of Political Theology* (Cambridge University Press, 1996).

L. O. Sanneh, *Whose Religion Is Christianity? The Gospel Beyond the West* (Eerdmans, 2003).

J. H. Yoder, *For the Nations: Essays Evangelical and Public* (Eerdmans, 1997).

ARNE RASMUSSON

CHRISTIAN SCIENCE Christian Science, or the First Church of Christ, Scientist, was first established in 1879 in

Boston, Massachusetts, by M. B. Eddy (1821–1910). The Mother Church now has around 2,000 branch churches and 1,500 reading rooms around the world. Official membership numbers are not published, but the figure of 100,000 is often cited, which would represent a decline of over 50 per cent from the peak reached in the 1930s.

Church teachings follow Eddy's *Science and Health with Key to the Scriptures* (1875), which remains a global bestseller and can be understood as a reaction to scientific materialism. God, or Divine Mind, is our true spiritual nature, and the 'mortal world' of matter is an error of thought. Understanding this error brings healing.

Christian Science treatment may appear to the observer as similar to the prayers for healing that became widespread in Christian Churches in the late twentieth century. Healing is dispensed by lay, self-employed Christian Science practitioners who work full time, and by nurses who also offer physical care. Teachers authorized to impart the healing method are also registered, with worldwide listings now totalling around 2,500. Inevitably, there have been controversies over the acceptance of conventional medical attention, and this is left to individual conscience.

New members are required to be free from other Christian denominations. Eddy was raised a Congregationalist in the Reformed traditon (see Reformed Theology) and considered Christian Science part of mainstream Christianity. There is some debate as to how much Eddy's theology owes to that of P. Quimby (1802–66), who gave Eddy 'hands-on' mesmerist (magnetist) healing in 1862. Eddy claimed her own 'mental' system derived from a spontaneous healing experience and independent Bible study that followed a fall on ice soon after Quimby's death.

Church services remain loyal to Eddy's nineteenth-century format, with readings from her book and a repertoire of Christian Science hymns. Members offer testimonies of healing for arthritis, cancer, malaria, and the like; but as there are no clergy, no sermons are given. The Mother Church is governed by a board of directors guided by regulations set out in Eddy's *Church Manual* (1895). Strict governance led to some departures in the 1990s, and the Mother Church remains tightly managed. For example, it exerts trademark control over its Cross and Crown symbol, and members are still required to subscribe to *The Christian Science Monitor* magazine and other publications.

As with many sectarian groups, similar questions of authority were raised when Eddy's own students branched out. E. Hopkins (1849–1925) left the Mother Church in 1885 to found a College of Metaphysical Science. It is from Hopkins that the less hierarchical New Thought movement derives, including the Unity School of Christianity, founded in 1903.

Although the Mother Church continues today as a large global institution, the key contribution of Christian Science to the development of Christianity may lie in its early encouragement of mentalist approaches to healing. Appeals to science and healing techniques similar to those pioneered by Eddy were adopted by those open to alternative traditions such as New Age, and are now common in both mainstream Christianity and outside the Churches in contemporary spiritualities.

S. Gottschalk, *Rolling Away the Stone: Mary Baker Eddy's Challenge to Materialism* (Indiana University Press, 2006).

D. Kemp, *The Christaquarians? A Sociology of Christians in the New Age* (Kempress, 2003).

Daren Kemp

Christmas: see Calendar, Liturgical.

Christology Christology is discussion of the doctrine of Jesus Christ's *person* – i.e., his identity and nature, especially his humanity and divinity. It is sometimes (perhaps misleadingly) distinguished from discussion of his *work*, which is taken to come under the doctrine of salvation (see Atonement; Soteriology).

The Jewish healer, exorcist, and preacher, Jesus of Nazareth, emerged in a context deeply shaped by patterns of devotion to, trust and hope in, and belief about, the God of Israel. His earliest followers understood him as playing a decisive role in the relationship between God and God's people, as God's climactic judgement and renewal of the world approached. From the very start, however, there was variety in the ways in which such claims were articulated. Jesus was seen as the proclaimer of God's coming judgement, as God's obedient Son, as God's agent enacting God's good purposes, as the fulfiller and renewer of God's covenant, as the embodiment of God's wisdom, as the interpreter of God's law, as the focus of believers' obedience to God, as the exemplar of human life pleasing to God, as a gift from or sacrifice to God, as the incarnation of God's pre-existent Word (see *Logos*), or in numerous other ways.

In most of these interpretations, Jesus' identity and significance were understood primarily against the background of the Hebrew Scriptures, and he was understood as a decisive commentary upon those Scriptures. It was by bequeathing to later generations the Hebrew Scriptures (as the Christian OT), together with diverse early interpretations of Jesus' role in the ways of Israel's God (the NT), that early Christians made Christology an unavoidable question for later theology.

Christological reflection was already present in the ways that Christians preserved, interpreted, and passed on their memories of Jesus. It was there in the very fact that stories about this particular human being became central to Christian life, as well as in the way those stories highlighted the signs of the coming Kingdom of God in Jesus' life and ministry, in the recounting of particular episodes that illustrated Jesus' relationship with the God of Israel (the virgin birth, baptism, transfiguration, resurrection, and ascension), and in the ways reference to Jesus reordered Christians' ways of referring to God. It was also present in the Jesus-focused ways that Christians found of retelling the story of God's ways with the world in texts as diverse as the letters of Paul, the prologue of the Gospel of John, and the Epistle to the Hebrews.

Much modern investigation of this very early Christological reflection has focused on the titles the biblical authors use for Jesus, some of which he may possibly have used of himself: Messiah (Christ in Greek), Son of Man, Son of God, Lord, and *Logos*. The attempt has often been made to discern exactly what beliefs about Jesus' identity and significance are implied in each of these titles, but in recent years the focus has increasingly shifted away from particular terms to broader patterns of Christ-focused devotion among early Christians. The earliest available evidence suggests that Christians worshipped the God of Israel *as* the 'Father of our Lord Jesus Christ', and they appear to have begun referring to God *and* Jesus, or even to Jesus alone, in devotional contexts where one might have expected reference simply to God.

Yet it was not just in their devotion and in their interpretation of the Hebrew Bible that Christians focused on Jesus, but in their interpretation of their own lives (which they saw as patterned after, or sharing in, his life), of their communities (which they saw, e.g., as Christ's body), and of the whole world. Christian missionary activity, by assuming the propriety and necessity of bringing the message of this specific human being to all people everywhere, itself embodies strong Christological convictions (see Missiology).

The central Christological question the earliest Christians left to subsequent generations was how to do justice to this great variety of devotional and theological material, while at the same time continuing to make some kind of sense of the witness to Jesus as a particular human individual, beset by limitations, afflicted by suffering, betrayed, abandoned, and executed. One characteristically modern form of this controversy has been debate about the relationship between the 'Christ of faith' (i.e., the figure who emerges in the universal claims made by Christians in Jesus' name) and the 'Jesus of history' (i.e., the figure who emerges from historical–critical study of the Gospels). Another, closely related, form of this controversy in modern theology has been debate about the appropriateness or possibility of ascribing universal significance to one particular human being. On the one hand, there have been doubts that matters of ultimate significance to all human beings could depend on acquaintance with a particular religious tradition not accessible to all. On the other, there have been questions about the implications of claiming the centrality for all human life of one human being who is male, born and bred in one particular culture, and in various other ways decidedly *un*representative of all humankind.

The kinds of answers that were given to the basic Christological question in the early centuries of Christianity were shaped by the fact that the question was initially posed in a world where Jewish patterns of thought and practice had already for some time been interbreeding with Greek ones, and where the Hebrew Bible was already beginning to be interpreted with the help of the tools and vocabulary of Hellenistic philosophy. That process may have helped to bring to the fore an interest in asking ontological questions (i.e., questions about what *kind of being* Jesus was) that inevitably lay behind the functional questions associated with Christian devotional practice (i.e., questions about *what role* he plays, *as* that kind of being).

The process of asking and answering these questions was intensely controversial, and its early course is often charted in terms of the rise and fall of various 'heresies': answers to Christological questions that were ultimately rejected by what became the dominant Christian tradition in Europe (e.g., Ebionitism, Adoptionism, Docetism, Patripassianism, Arianism, Apollinarianism, Nestorianism, Eutychianism, Miaphysitism, Monothelitism). This 'orthodox' or 'Catholic' position is sometimes defined more by opposition to portrayals of these heresies than by direct positive statement.

The Catholic alternatives that slowly emerged in the process of debate with these alternative possibilities received classic expression in the Nicene Creed, and in the doctrine of the hypostatic union formulated at the Council of Chalcedon. Christological themes were subsequently explored further as Byzantine emperors sought to overcome miaphysite opposition to the two-natures formula of Chalcedon. For example, in 553 the Second Council of Constantinople confirmed that the hypostasis of Jesus was none other than the divine *Logos* and on this basis defended the proposition that in Jesus God suffered in the flesh (see Theopaschite Controversy). And in response to Byzantine iconoclasm, the Second Council of Nicaea (787) affirmed that the unity of Christ's incarnate person justified making images of him for Christian devotion. Christological themes were further developed in medieval debates about the necessity of a God-man for atonement, in Reformation disputes over the presence of the risen and ascended Christ in the Eucharist (see Ubiquity), and in many other contexts.

Broadly speaking, the answer that 'Catholic' Christians gave to the Christological question has two complementary sides. On the one hand, they claimed that the human being Jesus of Nazareth is not simply *illustrative* of God's ways with the world, but *central* to those ways, indeed *constitutive* of them. Jesus is God's way of loving the world; this one human life is what God is doing to share God's eternal life with the world; God is at work in and through this one human life to draw *all* life to Godself. If a Christian asks *who* she relates to (or who is relating to her) when she relates to Christ, the answer is 'God'. And this is not simply seen in those moments of glory or exaltation in the story of Jesus, but in the *whole* of that life, including Jesus' abandonment, suffering, and death, where the deadly but victorious encounter between God's loving life and the violent life of the world is played out.

On the other hand, Catholic Christianity has said that this one human life is the first fruit of the journey of all creaturely life into the life of God (see DEIFICATION). Jesus is a fully human being participating without reserve in the life of God, so blazing the trail along which all human beings are called. The way that Jesus marks out is the way of the CROSS, but also the way of resurrection to new life: others follow this path when God's grace unites them to Christ, making them die and rise with him. If on the first account Jesus was seen as the life of God reaching down into creaturely life, on this account Jesus is the life of humanity being drawn up into God's own life.

In the light of these two accounts, which Catholic Christianity has held together, reflection on the stories of Jesus and on the Christological questions that they pose has become a way of reflecting on what is meant by 'God's life', and so on what 'divinity' means (see TRINITY). Such an approach has led to God's life being seen not in pure opposition to the life of creatures, but as *open* for creatures – as capable of being *shared* with creatures. Only on some such view can the human being Jesus of Nazareth be fully divine; if one instead begins with a definition of divinity developed in abstraction from the Christian Gospel, Christology can become little more than a mind-numbing conundrum.

Similarly, reflection on these stories and questions has become a way of considering what it means to be human (see THEOLOGICAL ANTHROPOLOGY). 'Humanity' is not to be seen in simple opposition to divinity – and, in particular, SIN, however endemic it might be, is not to be seen as *essential* to human life – because in Jesus Christians see that human life *belongs* in God's life, and is freed to be most fully itself when it is most fully united to God's life. There is no true aspect of human life that cannot be so united to God, and so no need to deny the unadulterated fullness of Jesus' humanity in order to claim that he was divine.

The order in which these two aspects of Christology should be approached has been a matter for controversy in Christian theology. Some modern theologians (such as F. SCHLEIERMACHER) have begun by focusing upon a potential inherent in human life and graspable by psychological or philosophical analysis: a potential for awareness of, and communion with, God. Such theologians understand Jesus' divinity as God's unimpeded activation of that potential, and 'God' is to some extent defined as the referent of this activated potential. Other modern theologians (such as K. BARTH) begin instead by developing an account of God's freedom to share God's life with creatures, and only on that basis seek to understand creaturely participation in God's life. Rather than consisting in the activation of some universal human religious potential, some of these theologians see participation in the life of God as consisting in the specifically Jesus-shaped patterning of every aspect of corporate and individual life: as much a matter of polity as one of individual awareness. Other modern theologians (such as K. RAHNER) combine aspects of both poles.

See also *HOMOOUSIOS*; NEO-CHALCEDONIANISM; QUEST OF THE HISTORICAL JESUS; SYRIAC CHRISTIAN THEOLOGY.

D. Bonhoeffer, *Christology* (Collins, 1971).
D. Ford and M. Higton, *Jesus* (Oxford University Press, 2002).
L. Hurtado, *Lord Jesus Christ: Devotion to Jesus in Earliest Christianity* (Eerdmans, 2003).
W. Kasper, *Jesus the Christ* (Burns & Oates/Paulist Press, 1976).
J. Pelikan, *Jesus Through the Centuries: His Place in the History of Culture* (Yale University Press, 1985).
R. Williams, *The Dwelling of the Light: Praying with Icons of Christ* (Canterbury Press, 2003).

MIKE HIGTON

CHURCH: see ECCLESIOLOGY.

CHURCH AND STATE: see CIVIL RELIGION; CIVIL SOCIETY; POLITICAL THEOLOGY.

CIVIL RELIGION The phrase 'civil religion' was used by J.-J. Rousseau (1712–78) for the set of commitments (specifically, belief in a powerful God who oversees history, a future life where virtue will be rewarded and wickedness punished, and devotion to the society's laws) that need to be promoted in a society to ensure a loyal citizenry (*Social* 4.8). In contemporary sociology of religion, it refers to the religious sensibility of a society as a whole, as opposed to the ways in which individuals may claim a particular religious identity distinct from – though not necessarily over against – their political citizenship. For example, in the contemporary USA, one may identify as a Catholic Christian and still participate in American civil religion. While the former identity is realized through confessionally specific acts (e.g., attending mass) that distinguish practitioners from citizens with a different confessional identity (e.g., Reformed Jews), the latter is exemplified by practices (e.g., invocation of God in public speech, saluting the flag, rituals honouring those who have served and/or died in war) shared more broadly by citizens regardless of their formal religious affiliations.

Though Rousseau contended that governments should tolerate any particular religion so long as its teachings included nothing contrary to the duties of the citizen, totalitarian regimes of the left and the right have tended to view adherence to a particular religion as inconsistent with their demand for the citizen's total dedication to the state. By contrast, Rousseau's perspective has prevailed in western democracies, where – especially in the USA – the majority of Christian Churches have been willing (and often eager) to participate in civil religion. Among those who stand against this near consensus are the Jehovah's Witnesses, whose right to refuse to salute the American flag was ultimately affirmed by the US Supreme Court in *West Virginia State Board of Education* v. *Barnette* (1943).

The Witnesses' refusal to engage in the rituals of civil religion is rooted in the conviction that it represents a conflation of faith in God with faith in a particular socio-political order that amounts to idolatry. Over against this position, Christian defenders of civil religion argue that the charge of idolatry does not apply so long as loyalty to the State is understood to be subordinate to loyalty to God (in line with the situation evidently presupposed in 1 Pet. 2:17). Furthermore, they note that Christians' responsibility to influence public policy in a way consistent with their vision of God's purposes for humanity demands adaptation to the conventions of a society's public discourse. But theologians influenced by the radical traditions of the Reformation (see Mennonite Theology) have argued that participation in civil religion makes Christians captive to the interests of the nation-state, thereby impeding their ability to stand over against the wider society as agents of challenge and critique. Such reservations have led some theologians to introduce the idea of public theology as a more adequate conceptual framework for Christian engagement with civil society.

R. N. Bellah, 'Civil Religion in America', *Dædalus* 96:1 (winter 1967), 1–21.

S. Hauerwas, *After Christendom: How the Church Is to Behave if Freedom, Justice, and a Christian Nation Are Bad Ideas* (Abingdon Press, 1991).

Ian A. McFarland

Civil Society Current academic and activist focus on civil society is anticipated by a long history of debate about its nature and character, including the role of religion (and of the Christian Churches in particular) in securing its stability and growth. The dominant contemporary view defines civil society in terms of non-governmental forms of organization (e.g., businesses, schools, churches, social clubs) through which a community's members relate to each other. This definition derives in part from such authors as J. Althusius (1557–1638) and J. Locke (1632–1704) and differs from the older view of *societas civilis* (also associated with the reconstructive views of A. Ferguson (1723–1816) and G. W. F. Hegel), which refers to the development of the *polis* of ancient Greece, the *civitas* of Rome, and the nation-state of the Enlightenment as the basis for understanding the concept. According to the older definition civil society is a political order that forms, comprehends, and controls all other institutions.

Parallel disputes over the idea of civil society have arisen whenever accelerating forces of change have given rise to a sense that civilization was not based on a fixed pattern, but was being and could be reordered. What causes such a change in basic social ecology? Is it, for instance, the conquest and colonization of parts of the world where new patterns of life have to be constructed, in technological changes that alter older societies, or in revolutionary world views? Such developments reflect conflicts between statism and freedom, innovative and traditional economies, religion and secularism (or between religions), as well as between competing views of civil society. Historically, they also shape the social and intellectual forces that have issued in today's globalization.

The older view contrasted civil society with both 'barbarian' primal cultures and modern bourgeois practices based in private interests, and lauded a politically comprehensive regime that ruled over all other groups and institutions in a given territory. The more contemporary view reflects the fact that political orders are not eternal; they have to be repeatedly reconstructed through the cluster of non-governmental institutions called civil society. This latter perspective presumes a social theory of politics rather than a political theory of society. It does not view society as identical with, or a creature of, a political regime. Rather, it sees a political regime as a creature of civil society shaped by common interests, practical necessity, and an ethical world view that is usually religious in character.

Government is necessary to the wellbeing of civil society and it is charged with the duty of protecting members and organizations by regulating developments that threaten persons and institutions, using coercive force when necessary. But it can only do so within ethical, cultural, social, and legal limits that give the regime legitimacy. Thus, the ability to use coercive force cannot by itself create a viable society; and government is not the comprehending realm of public life, but a limited realm constructed for public service. To put it another way, the 'public' of civil society is ethically and historically prior to the 're-public' of political order.

The 'cluster' of spheres of interaction which constitute civil society is an interactive set of voluntarily constructed systems of co-operative institutions, each with a distinct purpose and function. Persons enter or exit these by admission or choice; and they can abolish, reform, or reconstruct them by modifying the systems, or by introducing new ones that are more reasonable or more materially or spiritually compelling. Religious organizations, advocacy and service associations, schools, hospitals, unions, corporations, political parties, and clubs are not natural phenomena: they have to be intentionally formed, joined, and made central to civilized life.

To point out the voluntary character of the organizational entities of civil society is to indicate that they have a distinct ethical dimension. Every society does (and must) have not only a political order, but a family structure, and in many societies these coincide with or even define the boundaries of those economic and religio-cultural systems to which people feel most loyal. A different order of ethics applies to the other entities of civil society, in that they require a moral will that transcends natural loyalties and a degree of independence from familial and political authority. Thus, in civil society patriarchy and arranged marriage is reduced and love-marriage becomes the ideal; chauvinism and authoritarianism is also reduced and free political parties and elections reflect democratic ideals.

Historically, the formation of the Church nurtured the decisive kind of institution beyond family and nation that brought about such change. The Church fostered and institutionalized a new kind of responsible freedom. It was a body defined by a religious world view made historically concrete in Jesus Christ, one that demanded a freedom to form new associations based in redefined ethical responsibilities and spiritual conviction. This is the mother of civil society, seldom acknowledged by classical or contemporary theorists. This social *novum* invited a new identity, established a new sense of rights and duties, and created new social spaces to form and re-form human associations on the basis of a transcendent ethic. From these roots came the clusters of organizations and practices that are the indicators of a vibrant civil society. In cultures where the Church is absent or weak, civil society is too, and people continue to live under kinship-based or regime-based systems.

There are other disputes as to the limits of the interactive systems that constitute a civil society. One dispute has to do with the efficacy of voluntary organizations. Is it so that the extension of the influence of non-governmental organizations can establish world peace and end the history of war-making between nations? This is the view of a number of liberal humanist and pacifist religious groups who believe that rational goodwill can solve all or most of human conflicts and lead to perpetual peace. More realist theorists doubt that human interests and passions can be so completely contained that the use of coercive force within and between peoples and nations will be unnecessary, even if some conflicts can be reduced or channelled.

A second dispute is connected with nineteenth- and twentieth-century critiques of capitalism. Are the modern corporation, especially in its transnational or multinational forms, and the market part of civil society? Or are these, like coercion-based political regimes, to be seen as outside of and a potential threat to the cluster of institutions that constitute civil society and make it flourish? Some Marxist scholars see them as essentially the instruments of a ruling class that inevitably exploit the poor and lead the world to an inevitable worldwide class conflict. Others, such as the more moderate German social philosopher, J. Habermas (b. 1929), argue that today's forms of economic organizations have grown so large that they tend to colonize the life-world, distort the possibilities of genuinely egalitarian communication and truncate the possibilities of meaning formation, all key tasks of civil society. The term, thus, should be reserved to those organizations, associations, and movements that emerge out of the concerns of the common life and that make a direct impact on interpersonal and practical life-worlds. But increasingly, international religious and ethical non-governmental organizations are working with corporations and seeking to utilize market forces to aid the poor.

Both of these disputes point to a still larger issue of whether a global civil society is being constructed beyond the control of any existing political order by the many-sided dynamic called 'globalization'. Of course, many see globalization as primarily an economic reality. Deeper analyses see globalization as a quite incomplete and often flawed dynamic that is developing the infrastructure of a global civil society, one that not only has compromised the sovereignty of every nation-state without establishing a centralized political order, but also is forming worldwide communications linkages, expanded international legal agreements, scientific, educational, technological, and professional organizations that operate across all borders, and foster widely shared ethical principles about human rights, the ideals of democracy as marked by pluralistic political parties, and especially freedom of religion and association. Indeed, it may well be forming new civilizational possibilities that demand a new theory of civil society. If that is so, and if no great civilizational development has ever endured without a religious vision at its core, then it is the task of the great religions of the world, including and especially Christianity, to develop a theology capable of giving moral and spiritual guidance to the emerging global civil society.

D. Elazar, *The Covenant Tradition in Politics*, vol. IV: *Covenant and Civil Society: The Constitutional Matrix of Modern Democracy* (Transaction, 1998).

M. Kaldor, *Global Civil Society: An Answer to War* (Polity, 2003).

J. Keane, *Global Civil Society?* (Cambridge University Press, 2003).

A. Seligman, *The Idea of Civil Society* (Free Press, 1992).
M. L. Stackhouse, *et al.*, *God and Globalization*, vol. III: *Christ and the Dominions of Civilization* (Continuum International, 2000–7).

MAX L. STACKHOUSE

COLLEGIALITY In CATHOLIC THEOLOGY 'collegiality' refers to the role of the EPISCOPACY within the Church's MAGISTERIUM. Modern reflection on collegiality is affected by past debates over ULTRAMONTANISM and CONCILIARISM as competing visions of the relationship between the local (viz., diocesan) and universal Church. Current discussion of the collegial principle involves particular attention to the relationship between the college of bishops and the PAPACY, with debates centring on the degree to which Catholic understanding of the supreme authority of the pope as defined at VATICAN COUNCIL I undermines genuinely collegial exercise of authority in the Church.

Vatican I emphasized that the pope's authority 'by no means detracts from that ordinary and immediate power of episcopal jurisdiction, by which bishops ... tend and govern individually the particular flocks which have been assigned to them', but also that papal jurisdiction is 'pre-eminent ... over every other church', 'immediate', and not subject to 'appeal ... to an ecumenical COUNCIL' (session 4, ch. 3). VATICAN COUNCIL II argued that papal supremacy serves collegiality by ensuring 'that the episcopate itself might be one and undivided' (*LG*, §18; cf. 23). Thus, the college of bishops can exercise its authority 'only with the consent of the Roman Pontiff' (*LG*, §22; cf. 21). While official Catholic teaching thus sees the collegial authority of the bishops as inseparable from their unity as defined by their submission to the papacy, other Christians involved in ecumenical dialogue with Catholics worry that the asymmetry of the relationship between pope and bishops undermines the collegial principle.

See also INFALLIBILITY.

IAN A. MCFARLAND

COLONIALISM AND POSTCOLONIALISM Colonial conquests are not new. They have happened throughout history. The current focus, however, is on modern European colonialism, which started in the fifteenth century with the Spanish and Portuguese, and was followed by the Dutch, British, French, German, and Italian powers acquiring, controlling, and, in certain cases, settling in the Americas, Asia, Africa, and the Pacific. Not all colonial expansion was from the West. In the East, there was a Mughal Empire in India, only finally extinguished in 1857, and Japan was a colonial power, occupying Korea and China. What is apparent in each case is the resilient nature of colonialism and its unending capacity to come up with new motives and rationales.

The old colonialism of the fifteenth to twentieth centuries was about conquering land, but there is also a neo-colonialism that is about conquering markets and has its own scheme of values. The old colonialists preached Christianity as a way of saving souls, whereas the current neo-colonialists promote the virtues of democracy and HUMAN RIGHTS in order to prepare countries for an intensified global economy. The old colonizers saw themselves as masters and used brute force to achieve their goals, but the new colonizers, no less violent, project themselves as liberators, or, to use the words of R. NIEBUHR: 'tutors of mankind in its pilgrimage to perfection' (*Irony* 71). Nor are colonialists always from the political right. The Communist USSR often functioned in a colonial way, and more recently, during the Iraq War, there emerged a group of humanitarian interventionists who argued, despite all evidence of misbehaviour and arrogance, that the West is a benevolent and progressive force. Despite such claims, colonial history has shown that no foreign power ever intervenes in other peoples' lives and cultures from purely unselfish motives.

Western Christian theology, which has been so robust in addressing such different ideologies as fascism, ATHEISM, RATIONALISM, Communism, Nazism, sexism, and secularism, has shown relatively little interest in offering a theological critique of colonialism and its political, cultural, and social consequences. Western theologians who were very vocal in dealing with internal controversies on such questions as the INERRANCY of the Bible or the VIRGIN BIRTH, rarely commented on the West's imperial intentions and expansion. The role of Christian theology in western colonial enterprise had much to do with supporting and justifying the cultural and economic exploitation of the colonies in the name of bringing salvation and morality to 'savage and senile peoples', as US Senator A. Beveridge (1862–1927) once put it (*CRS*, 56th Congress, Session 1, 9 January 1900, 711). In fact, two of the most celebrated hermeneutical activities of the nineteenth century occurred at the height of modern colonialism. One was the search for a historical Jesus, which was distorted by ethnic and nationalistic considerations (see QUEST OF THE HISTORICAL JESUS). The other was source criticism, which provided tools used to distinguish between 'authentic' and 'inauthentic' aspects of subjugated peoples' texts and religions. By and large, western theologians reflect the liberal position referred to above: that in spite of atrocities committed, the West still offers a better, more compassionate and enlightened alternative to the 'unregenerated' state of the colonized.

Western theologians such as F. SCHLEIERMACHER, F. D. Maurice (1805–72), W. Temple (1881–1944), Niebhur, K. BARTH, and P. TILLICH, to name a few, have used various arguments to legitimize western dominance. They might in some cases have shown an openness to other religions and expressed appreciation of other cultures, but the underlying hermeneutical presupposition of their work was that the Christian story informed and improved upon other religions, and that western culture was the ideal, universal model in spite of its tarnished record. A rough précis of the arguments of western theologians is that the western empire has a place and purpose in the PROVIDENCE of God, and the colonizers are the trustees and the chosen instrument of God. Often this sentiment was replicated by the subjugated peoples themselves (e.g., in the work of the Bengali reformers R. M. Roy (1772–1833), K. C. Sen (1838–84), and P. C. Mozoomdar (1840–1905)). Colonialism was seen as an inevitable stage in the progress towards the improvement and advancement of less civilized nations, and therefore it was a vehicle for the greater good of the subject peoples. Strong nations exercised authority over weaker ones, and the resultant atrocities were blamed on various incidental factors (e.g., human frailty, lack of morality, or hubris). Barth attributed this failure to a 'double activity' – a human being is capable of piety and reason as well as having the potential to hunt and sell slaves. The basic theological assumption behind such thinking is that western Christian culture is supreme, and inhabitants of other cultures need western tuition to come up to the required level. These theologians may not have harboured any explicitly racist views, but their rationale of dominating other peoples in order to civilize them implied that these subjugated peoples were inferior.

There are several characteristics of colonial theology. The first is the projection of a male monotheistic God. The Christian vision of a single-God framework has provided the impetus for many empires, ancient and modern, including the twentieth- and twenty-first-century US imperium, which has been justified and reinforced by such monotheistic and messianic ambitions. Biblical monotheism introduced into theological discourse notions of true and false RELIGION, and of the elect and the reprobate (see ELECTION). The religious intolerance characteristic of the monotheistic vision had devastating effects on religions in those colonies where indigenous religious ideas were expressed within a polytheistic framework, in which numerous gods and goddesses were venerated. The logic of monotheism is one that demands a choice between the one and the many as equivalent to that between truth and falsehood, and such an enforced choice fails people whose polytheistic context renders them self-consciously pluralistic and open to juggling multiple identities.

Another characteristic of colonial theology is the exclusive claim made for Christian SCRIPTURE as the only true oracle of God containing salvation for all, thus dismissing the stories and texts of other people as irrelevant. No less problematic is the idea of the elect people. Every empire claims that it is the chosen instrument of God, but the biblical idea of a chosen people and communal distinctiveness is given a contemporary urgency in colonial theologies and is read from a nationalistic perspective and put to use for every imperial expansion.

Christological claims, such as the Cosmic Christ and Jesus as a Lord and King sitting on a throne, have also proved to be problematic in the colonial world. When the idea of the Cosmic Christ was first mooted in the first Christian centuries, it provided an alternative to and a weapon against Roman power; but under different circumstances, the concept suggests a figure who controls the whole of the created order in a totalizing and exclusivist fashion. Such ideas reinforce the projection of Christianity as the supreme religion because of its divinely revealed status, and the corresponding dismissal of other faith traditions as inferior owing to their inability even at their best to move beyond the truths of general REVELATION. Linked to this stratification of religious systems is the notion of Christianity as historical and linear and other religions as mythical and cyclical. In such a linear perception of history, the subjugated peoples will always lag behind in the march towards progress by virtue of their defective understanding of time.

Labelling people of other faiths as 'anonymous', 'implicit', or 'hidden' Christians (see ANONYMOUS CHRISTIANITY) may not only appear condescending but also perpetuates the notions that adherents of other religions have a defective understanding, that they are in need of redemption as defined in Christian terms, and that everyone should embrace the Christian faith. It further instantiates a characteristic that runs throughout colonial theology: a conceptual binarism that divides humanity into contrasting pairs like Christian/non-Christian, believer/unbeliever, saved/damned, and chosen/rejected.

The term 'postcolonialism' refers to a way of thinking that developed in relation to colonial oppression and its aftermath. What postcolonial theology does is to place firmly at the centre of theological reflection colonialism and the economic, cultural, and political ramifications of both the old colonialism and the modern, neo-colonialism of globalization and market fundamentalism. It examines, categorizes, and explains a set of communal and cultural contingencies that result from colonialism, such as hyphenated identities, migration, diaspora, religious FUNDAMENTALISM, and the status of refugees.

There are two particularly significant contributions of postcolonialism to Christian theological discourse. One is contrapuntal reading. Its aim is to juxtapose the mainstream and the marginal, Christian and non-Christian, secular and sacred, and textual and oral traditions, and identify the linkages, contradictions, and discrepancies among them, not with a view to imposing artificial amicable alliances, but to achieve a counterpoint of various voices which maintain rather than iron out tensions. Such a method is an attempt to go beyond the earlier comparative hermeneutics used by both colonialists and nationalists. This older model was enlisted by colonizers to pass judgement on other peoples' stories and by colonized nationalists to dismiss western knowledge as tainted and to project the indigenous heritage as ideal and noble.

Another contribution is the theory of hybridity, where elements from both vernacular culture (which colonialists tried to undervalue) and metropolitan cultures are critically mixed in order to create what is now celebrated as a key element in postcolonial discourse: the 'third space' or in-between stage. Such a hybridized way of doing theology helps to readdress and re-enhance indigenous identity, infusing it with transformative insights. The idea of hybridity has challenged the missionary castigation of syncretism and the associated western insistence on either/or, and it has exposed the myth of cultural purity. Hybridity reminds us that there is no going back to or recovering a time when culture, tradition, or identity were an immaculate whole.

Postcolonialism stands within the liberative and progressive tradition of Liberation Theology, but it differs from it on a number of issues. First, there is a significant theological difference. Unlike liberation theology, which was devoted to overturning the God of the oppressor in favour of a God of the oppressed, postcolonialism does not see its role as replacing the God of the imperialists with the God of the subjugated, on the grounds that such an inversion simply replicates the classical colonial stratagem of divide and rule. Second, postcolonialism differs in the hermeneutical base it uses to interrogate sacred texts and traditions. In addition to economic and class interests, it invokes culture and draws attention to the cultural and intellectual control wielded by empires. Third, while liberation theology operates within and is defined by the metastories of Christianity, postcolonialism seeks to complicate these by underlining their enslaving as well as their emancipatory potential, and also by exposing Christianity's collusion with colonialism. Postcolonialism also differs radically from multiculturalism in that it critiques identity politics and is even more critical of nationalists and fundamentalists who resort to the cult of victimhood in order to espouse their claims and causes.

Postcolonialism, like any other modern theoretical category, has its own share of faults and weaknesses. Two in particular are pertinent to the theological discipline. One is that in its preoccupation with mainstream theology, it has neglected vernacular countertheological movements. The other is that in its excessive involvement with academic discourse, it has failed to reach and speak to the needs of ordinary people. The achievements of postcolonialism include a provincialization of European theologies, exposure of their collusion with empire, questioning their dominance and influence, and widening the resources for articulating theology. To Augustine, T. Aquinas, and M. Luther, postcolonialism has added O. Equiano (*ca* 1745–97), B. R. Ambedkar (1891–1956), T. C. Chao (1888–1979), and the experiences of Dalits, burakumins, indigenous peoples and women, and the religious texts of other religions, as worthy capital for doing theology. More pertinently, it has demonstrated that there exist other valid modes of thought apart from western forms of theorizing and representation.

K. Barth, *Protestant Theology in the Nineteenth Century* (Eerdmans, 2002 [1947]).

C. Keller, M. Nausner, and M. Rivera, eds., *Postcolonial Theologies: Divinity and Empire* (Chalice, 2004).

Kwok P., D. H. Compier, and J. Rieger, eds., *Empire and the Christian Tradition: New Readings of Classical Theologians* (Fortress, 2007).

R. Niebuhr, *The Irony of American History* (Chicago University Press, 2008 [1952]).

R. S. Sugirtharajah, *Postcolonial Reconfigurations: An Alternative Way of Reading the Bible and Doing Theology* (SCM, 2003).

R. S. Sugirtharajah

Commandments, Ten Sometimes called the Decalogue ('ten words' from the Septuagint, cf. Exod. 34:28; Deut. 10:4), the Ten Commandments are a series of injunctions said to be authored directly by God (Exod. 31:18; Deut. 4:13). They are the first and only commandments the whole people of Israel hear directly from God, as opposed to the rest of the Sinai legislation which is mediated by Moses (Deut. 5:4, 22). The commandments are numbered slightly differently in various traditions, e.g., Jewish traditions include as the first commandment (or 'word') what in Christian traditions is called the prologue ('I am the Lord your God, who brought you out of the land of Egypt, out of the house of slavery'); and the Jewish, Lutheran, and Catholic traditions combine into the first commandment (no other gods) what the Reformed tradition has taken to be two separate commands (no other gods, and no images).

The Decalogue appears twice in the OT: first as Israel is being formed as a people at Sinai (Exod. 20:1–17) and later when Moses is recalling that formative moment for the people just before they enter the land of Canaan (Deut. 5:6–21). While no claim is made that the entire will of God is revealed here, an ethical priority is given to the Ten Commandments by the foundational nature of their placement in the narrative. In both contexts, the Decalogue is set apart from the rest of the legislation that follows it. Indeed, the 'Book of the Covenant' in Exodus 20–23 and the material in Deuteronomy 12–26 have each long been viewed as an explication of the Ten Commandments, which precede them. These larger bodies of legislation show how the commandments are to work in the life of the community and, indeed, how they have worked in specific cases that the community has encountered.

Many prominent interpreters within Judaism and Christianity have understood the Ten Commandments as a summation of the moral LAW. As early as the first century, Philo of Alexandria (20 BC–AD 50) understood the Torah (that is, the whole of God's law) to be an elaboration of the Ten Commandments. In the Christian tradition, M. LUTHER organized his commentary on Deuteronomy around the commandments because he understood that book to be an elaboration of them, and J. CALVIN understood each commandment broadly, interpreting each of the 'negative' commandments (i.e., those in the form 'You shall not...') positively. Thus, he interprets the commandment against killing, for example, as an injunction to promote the neighbour's wellbeing. Recently, P. Miller (b. 1935) has proposed that a moral 'trajectory' emerges from each commandment, thus indicating the broad swathe of the moral life that the commandments encompass.

The so-called prologue (the first 'word' in the Jewish tradition) is crucial to understanding the Ten Commandments: 'I am the LORD your God, who brought you out of the land of Egypt, out of the house of slavery' (Exod. 20:2; Deut. 5:6). This divine self-presentation reveals the character of God as one who saves, who is gracious. Its position at the head of the commandments is vital to understanding the commandments not as coming from an abstract deity, but from this God with whom Israel is already in relationship, and whose character has already been revealed as one who acts for God's people. The prologue is then intimately connected to the first commandment ('You shall have no other gods before me'). Based on the truth of the prologue, of who this God is, the people are not to have any other gods. And the first commandment, together with the prologue, serves as the foundation upon which all the others stand. They affirm unequivocally that the vertical, divine–human relationship is prior to, and sustaining of, all horizontal relationships among human beings. Given the importance of the prologue to a correct understanding of the rest of the commandments, excising it (for purposes of 'posting' the Decalogue in public places, for example) violates the intent of the commandments.

The people are to obey the Ten Commandments not simply because God commands them to do so, but because obeying them is beneficial, making it possible for the community to flourish. The commandments thus are not designed to be a burden, but a gift. That the commandments are not arbitrary or purely for the sake of having people obey is illustrated by the presence of the motivation clauses (e.g., 'Honour your father and your mother, *so that your days may be long in the land that the LORD your God is giving you*'). These clauses suggest that from God's point of view the commandments are not self-evident. God seeks to persuade the people that this way of life is a *good* life, that obedience to the commandments is not only a recognition of the claim laid upon the people (i.e., an appropriate response to the gracious activity of the One who commands), but also inherently life-giving ('for our lasting good', in the words of Deut. 6:24).

So the commandments are designed to form a community whose members will thrive in their relationship with God and with one another. But to achieve this end, the commandments cannot simply be promulgated; they must be taught and interpreted for each new generation. Thus, when the young are taught the commandments, they are first reminded of the gracious character and identity of the God who commands (Deut. 6:21–3), and then instructed in the commandments themselves (Deut. 6:25). The centrality of the commandments for the life and faith of the community is indicated by the way in which SCRIPTURE equates the COVENANT itself with the commandments (Deut. 4:13; 9:11). Many interpreters understand them to function in a way akin to the US Constitution: as a founding document that must be reinterpreted by and for each new generation. In the NT, Jesus offers an authoritative interpretation of the commandments so that their true force and compass can be appreciated.

C. E. Braaten and C. R. Seitz, eds., *I Am the Lord Your God: Christian Reflections on the Ten Commandments* (Eerdmans, 2005).

W. P. Brown, ed., *The Ten Commandments: The Reciprocity of Faithfulness* (John Knox Press, 2004).

P. D. Miller, *The Ten Commandments* (John Knox Press, 2009).

JACQUELINE LAPSLEY

COMMONSENSE PHILOSOPHY The phrase 'Commonsense Philosophy' is chiefly associated with the eighteenth-century Scottish philosopher T. Reid (1710–96) who published an *Inquiry into the Human Mind on the Principles of Common Sense* in 1764, though there has always been some uncertainty as to how much Reid owed to the French philosopher C. Buffier (1661–1737). The purpose of Reid's *Inquiry* was to establish the scientific study of mental operations on a basis that would avoid the sceptical conclusions which had resulted from D. Hume's (1711–76) earlier attempt in his *Treatise of Human Nature* (1739). In order to do so, Reid gave certain 'principles of common sense' a rational authority that philosophical reasoning must respect.

According to Reid, Hume's philosophy was vitiated by its assumption of a Cartesian 'Ideal theory' which interpolated 'ideas' or mental representations between the world and the mind that apprehends it, thus opening up an unbridgeable gap that would forever admit scepticism (see CARTESIANISM). Reid attacked this assumption in two ways. One aimed to show that the Ideal theory was self-refuting, and the other that it conflicted with indispensable principles common to all forms of human reasoning. His sophisticated deployment of these arguments was widely regarded as providing a resounding refutation of Hume's scepticism not only in mental philosophy, but also in morals and religion where such scepticism struck contemporaries as dangerous. For some time, therefore, Reid gained an intellectual pre-eminence, especially in Scotland, resulting in a 'Scottish School of Common Sense', of which figures such as J. Beattie (1735–1803), J. Oswald (1703–93), and D. Stewart (1753–1828) are generally identified as members.

Reid's method involved striking a dialectical balance between philosophical theorizing and fundamental principles commonly exhibited in human thought and language. Arguably Beattie and Oswald adopted a 'vulgar' version of this method in which commonsensical opinion was simply preferred to philosophical theorizing, and Stewart was critical of Reid's adoption of the expression 'common sense' precisely because it so easily gave rise to this vulgar reinterpretation. The problem seems endemic, however. Any appeal to common sense in philosophy quickly lends itself to such vulgarization, and as time passed this tendency brought the School of Common Sense into disrepute in philosophical circles.

In some circles, however, it led to popularity. In North America Scottish educational ideals had been copied quite widely in the establishment of colleges, notably the College of New Jersey (subsequently Princeton University). The appointment of J. Witherspoon (1722–94) as president in 1768 led to curricular reforms in which Scottish commonsense philosophy played a large part, and its influence was renewed following establishment of Princeton Theological Seminary in 1812, when 'common sense' was hailed as the natural philosophical ally of REFORMED THEOLOGY.

Reid's *Collected Works* appeared in 1846, but his appeal to common sense was already falling out of favour. Only in the second half of the twentieth century, and divorced from the polemics of Beattie and Oswald, did it begin to receive sympathetic attention again.

S. A. Grave, *The Scottish Philosophy of Common Sense* (Clarendon Press, 1960).

L. Marcil-Lacoste, *Claude Buffier and Thomas Reid: Two Common-Sense Philosophers* (McGill-Queen's University Press, 1982).

N. Wolterstorff, *Thomas Reid and the Story of Epistemology* (Cambridge University Press, 2004).

GORDON GRAHAM

COMMUNICATIO IDIOMATUM The Latin phase *communicatio idiomatum* means 'communication/exchange of properties' and is used in Chalcedonian CHRISTOLOGY for the relationship between the divine and human natures in Christ. Most often it refers to a set of rules of proper predication – what one may properly say of Christ on the basis of the HYPOSTATIC UNION. Sometimes, however, the phrase refers to a description of the ways in which one nature acts upon or infuses the other in that union (see PERICHORESIS).

In the first perspective, the emphasis falls on the propriety of those apparently extravagant or paradoxical Christian patterns of speech such as TERTULLIAN's insistence that 'God was crucified' (*Carn.* 5) – patterns in which one says of the human Jesus of Nazareth things that are proper to the divine LOGOS, and vice versa. For instance, because in Chalcedonian Christology the human nature is always and entirely the human nature of the *Logos*, it is the *Logos*' humanity even when in Mary's womb and even when on the cross. One may therefore say that Mary's womb was the *Logos*' dwelling place, and that the cross was the site of the *Logos*' suffering – or, more strikingly, that Mary was the 'bearer of God' (*Theotokos*; see Council of EPHESUS) and that on the CROSS 'one of the TRINITY suffered' (see THEOPASCHITE CONTROVERSY).

While these patterns of speech first emerged in informal, non-technical contexts, they slowly became important bulwarks of Christology after the Council of CHALCEDON, and were taken to exclude certain alternatives (see NESTORIANISM), and to secure the claim that the human life of Jesus of Nazareth reveals God's life, enacts God's LOVE in the world, and draws the world to God precisely by being the fully human life that it is – and that what is active and making itself known in this human life is precisely God in the person of the eternal Son.

In the second perspective, the 'communication of attributes' refers not to a symmetrical interchange among the predicates that one may apply to Christ's two natures, but to the real divinization of Christ's humanity, blazing the trail for the divinization of those who share in his BODY. The divinization of the humanity consists in its receipt of all the communicable attributes of deity – all the attributes that are consistent with the flesh's continued creaturely existence. It is asymmetric in that, as JOHN OF DAMASCUS says, 'The nature of the flesh is deified, but the nature of the Logos does not become carnal' (*Jac.*, in *PG* 94:1461C).

In some post-Chalcedonian Christologies that trade on the understanding of the CAPPADOCIAN FATHERS that a HYPOSTASIS is simply some reality distinguished by a collection of individuating characteristics, the question arises as to why the human nature of Christ is not itself a hypostasis, if it is a particular human nature with specific differentiating characteristics. One response is to say that the central among the individuating characteristics of this human being are precisely those that derive directly from his unity with the Word: they are characteristics that are *communicated* to the humanity from the divinity. The narrative that fully identifies this particular human being is precisely a narrative of his coming from the Father and giving glory to the Father, revealing or enacting the nature of the Word in the world.

M. LUTHER and his followers developed a notable theory of the *communicatio idiomatum*, in the context of a theology deeply shaped by a related *communicatio*: the exchange of SIN and GRACE between Christ and sinners. As well as consistently defending the first sense of the Christological *communicatio* (insisting, for example, that the suffering of Christ's humanity is suffering that truly belongs to the person of the Son), Luther also insisted upon a real communication of properties from one nature to the other – arguing that however impossible it might be to say that divine nature considered in the abstract can suffer, that nature when hypostatically united to a human nature can (and must) truly share in the sufferings of the humanity if it is to be divinity *for us*. This *communicatio* from the humanity to the divinity is complemented by a real divinization of the flesh of Christ. Luther's theology of the EUCHARIST, for instance, depends upon an emphatic account of the receipt by the ascended humanity of Christ of a share in the attributes of the divine nature to which it is inseparably united, including the attribute of omnipresence. The ascended body of Christ is therefore ubiquitous, and its presence on the Eucharistic altar rests upon its presence everywhere (see UBIQUITY).

MIKE HIGTON

CONCILIARISM Conciliarism appeared as a coherent movement within the late-medieval church as a consequence of the crises of the Avignon PAPACY (1305–77) and the Great Schism (1378–1415). Its central principle, that the whole Church can be represented in a General Council, had long existed in medieval CANON LAW, though in the shadow of the papal monarchy that took shape with Innocent III (r. 1198–1216). Although as a movement it flowered and died quickly, conciliarism profoundly shaped the debate on Church authority in the fifteenth century, and its influence was felt in the REFORMATION. The immediate circumstances of its genesis were the desperate search for a means to restore unity to a Church divided by rival popes in the early fifteenth century. Two significant figures of this period were the Frenchmen P. D'Ailly (1350–1420) and J. Gerson (1363–1429), both of whom argued that a council was an exceptional instrument necessary when the hierarchical authority of the Church (the papacy) was incapacitated or had fallen into heresy. By the time of the Council of CONSTANCE, support for a General Council had grown exponentially, heightened by the threat posed to the Church by the Hussites in Bohemia. By this time there were three popes, all of whom were removed from office and replaced by Martin V (r. 1417–31).

Constance codified conciliar principles in two foundational canons, *Haec sancta* and *Frequens*. The former declared the superiority of councils to the papacy, while the second bound popes to summon regular councils. At this point, conciliarist thinkers did not view council and papacy in purely oppositional terms: the primary concern was to define the relationship between the two in order to preserve the unity of the Church. The Council of Basel (1431–49) proved the decisive battle. A magnet for the leading churchmen of the age, including G. Cesarini (1398–1444), Nicholas of Cusa, and E. Piccolomini (later Pope Pius II (r. 1458–64)), Basle embraced the epoch's spirit of institutional reform. Cusa wrote his *De concordantia catholica* (1433) in order to demonstrate the harmony of papal and conciliar views, but the Council's misguided deposition of Pope Eugenius IV (r. 1431–47) in 1439 sounded its death knell. Despite its decisive defeat, conciliarism's influence endured, particularly at the University of Paris and in the French Church through the writings of J. Almain (*ca* 1480–1515) and J. Major (1469–1550).

Although the idea that a council was superior to the papacy was dead, the conciliar period of the fifteenth century re-established the authority of councils within the Church. This was now taught in all the theological faculties. In the decades before the Reformation numerous calls rang out in German lands for reforming councils, and during the 1520s M. LUTHER predicated his message on the summoning of a General Council of the Church. The foundational principle of conciliarism, that Christ gave the keys of the KINGDOM OF GOD to the APOSTLES collectively and not to Peter alone, profoundly informed the ecclesiologies of sixteenth-century Protestant Churches, as the writings of H. ZWINGLI and J. CALVIN, among many others, bear witness. The role of councils has also continued to be a question in Catholic theology, shaping the definition of papal INFALLIBILITY at VATICAN COUNCIL I and the reflection on the nature of the Church in the documents of VATICAN COUNCIL II.

BRUCE GORDON

CONCUPISCENCE A transliteration of the Latin *concupiscentia* (which originally referred to any form of intense longing), concupiscence became a central concept in the western DOCTRINE of original SIN. Though used by TERTULLIAN for the 'lusts' of the old self in Ephesians 4:22 (*Resur.* 45), it is in the writings of AUGUSTINE that concupiscence comes to be used in a technical theological sense for disordered desire that turns the will away from God towards lesser goods. Augustine views it as a punishment for Adam's sin that is congenital in fallen human nature and remains an ongoing source of sinful acts even in the baptized, though it is not counted as sin after baptism (*Nupt.* 1.27–9; cf. 25).

During the REFORMATION the relationship between concupiscence and original sin became a point of contention between Catholic and Lutheran theologians.

Both sides agreed that original sin was defined by lack of FAITH, but the Lutherans insisted that it also included concupiscence. Catholics maintained that, while concupiscence is the occasion or 'tinder' (*fomes*) of sin, it is not in itself sin (see *Cat.*, §405, 2,515; cf. AQUINAS, *ST* 3.27.3 and 2/1.82.3). Thus, although both sides conceded that BAPTISM did not remove *concupiscence*, they disagreed over whether it removed all *sin* (as distinct from the penalty of damnation sin would otherwise incur). For the Lutherans, to waver on this point was to undermine the Christian's status as a sinner continually dependent on God for JUSTIFICATION (see *SIMUL JUSTUS ET PECCATOR*), while for Catholics the Lutheran position, by treating involuntary desires as sins, undermined human responsibility for sin.

IAN A. MCFARLAND

Concursus Along with *CONSERVATIO* and *GUBERNATIO*, *concursus* constitutes one of three components of classical Christian (especially Protestant) teaching on PROVIDENCE. The term means 'accompaniment' and refers to God's continual enabling of all creaturely activity. In other words, to speak of God's *concursus* is to confess that God's creative agency does not cease with the origination of creatures. Nor is God's ongoing involvement limited to the passive work of preserving creatures' existence in such a way as to allow them to act independently of God. Instead, *concursus* derives from the principle (enshrined in the DOCTRINE of CREATION from nothing) that God, as the sole source of every creature's being, must also be the source of the actions corresponding to and deriving from that being. Thus, the orbiting of the planets, the oak's growth, and the lion's hunting are, both as wholes and in each of their various parts, manifestations of divine *concursus*.

The logic of *concursus* seems to raise particular difficulties for creaturely freedom. If God is the cause of all creaturely activity, then it seems to make little sense to speak of creatures being responsible for their actions in a way that would allow for moral culpability or even genuine agency. While advocates of PROCESS THEOLOGY challenge the classical doctrine of *concursus* on these grounds, defenders of the tradition argue that there is no contradiction involved in seeing the free actions of creatures as the immediate product of divine agency: since creaturely freedom, too, is a gift of God, God's activity can never be in competition with it.

See also FREE WILL.

K. Tanner, *God and Creation in Christian Theology: Tyranny or Empowerment?* (Blackwell, 1988).

IAN A. MCFARLAND

Confession: see PENANCE.

Confirmation In today's Church the ritual of confirmation as an aspect of Christian initiation evidences a multiplicity of practices, a diversity of rituals, and a broad range of theological analyses. The Orthodox Churches' approach differs from that of the western Churches, where there are, in turn, divisions between Catholics on the one hand and the Churches of the REFORMATION on the other. Furthermore, contemporary Christian theologians across the ecumenical divide agree that in the NT there are no texts which offer a basis for a differentiation between baptism and confirmation. There is, consequently, no single meaning or theology for confirmation.

In the Orthodox Churches, the sacrament of initiation is a theologically and liturgically unified rite of BAPTISM, which includes a laying on of hands and anointing, and for which a presbyter (parish priest) is the ordinary celebrant. Some contemporary Catholic authors imply that the Orthodox Churches do have a separate sacrament of confirmation, which they call chrismation (*Cat.*, §1,289). This view Latinizes the Orthodox ritual.

In the West baptism–Eucharist was the original sacrament of initiation. In the course of time, this unity became a triunity that included the ritual of confirmation for four reasons. First, from around 400 onwards infant baptism gradually became dominant, due primarily to the rapid acceptance of a theology in which an infant needed to be baptized to remove original SIN and be assured of a place in heaven. Second, in this same period, presbyters became the pastors of outlying churches, with the bishop as pastor of the main (cathedral) church of a particular geographical region. Though presbyters' duties included baptism (owing to the consolidation of the doctrine of original sin described above), persons are not baptized into an outlying church, but into the larger Church. To provide a connection to the larger Church, it became the bishop's task to visit the outlying churches and anoint those who had been baptized. In time, the interval between baptism in the local church and the arrival of the bishop became longer, and the bishop's anointing of young children (rather than infants) took on new meaning. Third, no bishop simply came to a local church, anointed the baptized, and left. Liturgical prayers, readings, and hymns were added to his visit, thus making his 'confirmation visit' a sacred ritual distinct from the baptismal ritual. Lastly, western theologians reflected on this praxis, slowly providing a distinct theological meaning for confirmation. The theological descriptions ranged from a deepening of baptismal grace to a strengthening of the confirmed as a soldier of Christ.

During the Reformation, both M. LUTHER and J. CALVIN taught that a sacrament of confirmation could not be grounded in the NT and had been created by Church authority. For both the Lutherans and Reformed traditions, only baptism and the Eucharist were considered sacraments. Luther considered the ritual of confirmation *Affenspiel* (monkey business) and *Glaukelwerk* (mumbo jumbo). Calvin was even harsher in his denunciation. Correspondingly, in many Protestant Churches confirmation disappeared; and though in some Lutheran and Reformed communities a non-sacramental ritual of confirmation was retained, theologically it was considered a renewal of one's baptism, as was also the case in the Anglican Church.

The Catholic bishops at VATICAN COUNCIL II called for a renewal of confirmation. Part of this renewal appeared in the *Rite of Christian Initiation of Adults* (1972), in which initiation is a process involving baptism–confirmation–Eucharist. Baptism of infants, however, did not include confirmation and Eucharist. The *Catechism of the Catholic Church* (1994) seemingly attempts to theologize this discrepancy quantitatively: confirmation *completes* baptism; through confirmation the baptized are linked *more perfectly* to the Church; through confirmation Christians share *more completely* in the mission of Jesus (§§ 1303–5). This theology would seem to imply that those who are baptized only are less perfect than the confirmed, as though baptism were incomplete; yet confirmation does not make people 'super-Christians', and our language describing confirmation should not foster such a view.

The topic of confirmation is not a major theme in today's ecumenical discussion. It does not contribute to confessional division in a major way. In many ways, it is the question of age which dominates current discussion, as though age were the overarching and determining factor for a true understanding of confirmation. In the western Christian Churches, confirmation is a ritual which still needs a better theological analysis, especially as a framework for exploring how the sacrament of baptism (especially when given to infants) might productively be complemented by a later rite that testifies to its realization and public manifestation in the Christian life.

G. Austin, *The Rite of Confirmation: Anointing with the Spirit* (Liturgical Press, 1985).

M. E. Johnson, 'Confirmation' in *The New Westminster Dictionary of Liturgy and Worship*, ed. J. G. Davies (SCM, 2002).

A. Kavanaugh, *Confirmation: Origins and Reform* (Liturgical Press, 1988).

K. B. Osborne, *Sacramental Guidelines* (Paulist Press, 1995).

KENAN B. OSBORNE, O. F. M.

CONGREGATIONALISM: see POLITY.

CONSCIENCE Conscience typically designates the human capacity to know right and wrong; it encompasses our moral consciousness and practical moral decision-making. Conscience operates before and after moral action. The *antecedent* conscience refers to our capacity for apprehending good and evil (or discerning right and wrong), along with our appetite for the good. The antecedent conscience also includes the process of coming to a moral decision, determining how we ought to respond in a particular situation. The *consequent* conscience is our experience of peace or remorse after we act. Conscience may confirm that we acted according to our best moral judgement or it may bear witness against us, as in 1 Samuel 24:5: 'Afterwards David was stricken to the heart.'

The meaning of conscience has evolved within the Christian tradition. The OT does not contain a word for conscience but employs images such as the 'heart' to speak of the reality of conscience. The heart can be receptive to or hardened against God's voice; it can delight in or snub God's LAW. In the NT PAUL uses the word *syneidēsis* for conscience (the VULGATE translation is *conscientia*, or 'knowing with'). *Syneidēsis* is the capacity to know right from wrong; this capacity is grounded in reason. Thus, Paul says of certain Gentiles that 'the demands of the law are written in the hearts' (Rom. 2:14); conscience thus attests to a moral law which humans do not invent but which resonates within. The NATURAL LAW tradition that subsequently developed from Paul and other ancient sources affirms the existence of an objective moral order that is consonant with human flourishing, such that obedience to the moral law promotes the human good.

Medieval Christian theologians distinguished *syneidēsis* from *synderesis*. The distinction is attributed to JEROME and was actually a scribal mistake, but in the hands of subsequent theologians it became standard. For example, T. AQUINAS defined *synderesis* as our capacity to know first principles of morality, such as 'seek good and avoid evil.' By contrast, *syneidēsis* is the application of those principles to concrete situations in order to determine what we ought to do. Both dimensions of conscience belong to human reason. Aquinas argued that through their exercise of reason human beings participate in the objective moral order God establishes.

From the REFORMATION onwards, accounts of conscience vary with respect to emphases on either the consequent conscience or antecedent conscience, what a 'good' conscience primarily means, and how the objective moral reality to which conscience testifies is described and understood. Protestant approaches tended to emphasize the consequent conscience, feeling convicted of SIN, while Catholic approaches emphasized the antecedent conscience. For the reformers M. LUTHER and J. CALVIN a good conscience meant one assured of salvation by faith in Jesus Christ, and therefore free from anxiety over one's sinfulness. The objective moral reality to which conscience testifies is God. In Catholic accounts prior to VATICAN COUNCIL II a good conscience meant one that was true (i.e., in accord with objective morality, which was primarily described in terms of an extrinsic law). Vatican II, however, offered a more balanced description of conscience: on the one hand, conscience is the person's inner 'sanctuary', where he encounters God, and on the other hand conscience testifies to a law the person does not invent but discovers as obligatory (*GS*, §16).

Contemporary accounts of conscience often recognize its subjective and objective dimensions. Subjectively, conscience designates the interior 'space' in which we experience ourselves standing before or in dialogue with God. Objectively, conscience designates our awareness of particular moral values and principles as obliging us to act or refrain from acting. Particular accounts of conscience vary with regard to which dimension they emphasize. Taken together, these dimensions rule out both a moral subjectivism that would reduce morality to individual opinion and deny the reality of an objective moral order, and a blind obedience to moral authority that would lack the person's free, reasoned, and responsible appropriation of moral teaching.

The subjective dimension of conscience points to its dignity, even sanctity. It is wrong to force someone to violate their conscience, and wrong to act against one's own conscience. Yet conscience may err. Because of ignorance, prejudice, self-interest, or other factors, conscience may commend a course of action which is objectively wrong, or conscience may remain 'silent' when a person ought to be troubled by some occurrence or state of affairs. Christian ethicists sometimes distinguish between an invincibly and a vincibly erroneous conscience; the distinction concerns whether a person is morally culpable for her conscience's error. For example, one who sells food tainted with salmonella does something objectively wrong, but if she is ignorant through no fault of her own she does not incur subjective guilt. If her ignorance is cultivated, if we reasonably judge she ought to know otherwise, her conscience may be vincibly erroneous.

It is the teaching of the Catholic MAGISTERIUM that the settled judgements of conscience ought to be obeyed even though conscience may err. To act against conscience is to betray one's integrity. Given the risk of error, Christians have a duty to form their consciences well. Conscience formation is a lifelong and multifaceted task. It includes acquainting oneself with SCRIPTURE and TRADITION, though, of course, both are subject to varying interpretations. Moreover, the Church, as a community of conscience formation, is not immune from sin. Sometimes conscience formation leads to dissent. Regular prayer and consultation with trusted believers and relevant experts are important for forming conscience. We must also avoid influences that desensitize and distort moral perceptions, that dampen our appetite for the good.

The risk of error is nevertheless ineradicable, and conscience formation may reveal past sins to us, leading to a troubled conscience long after some wrongdoing or omission. Thus, the question of a peaceful conscience persists. P. TILLICH described the 'transmoral conscience' as our acceptance of our inevitably bad conscience in the faith that God accepts us though we are unacceptable. As grace draws us into the divine life we do not suspend the moral law but transcend it, experiencing the freedom that only faith in Christ gives.

P. Tillich, *Morality and Beyond* (John Knox Press, 1995).

DARLENE FOZARD WEAVER

CONSECRATION: see EUCHARIST.

CONSERVATIO The concept of *conservatio* (or *preservatio*), the divine preservation of the created order, constitutes one of three components of classical Christian (especially Protestant) teaching on PROVIDENCE, alongside *CONCURSUS* and *GUBERNATIO*. All three concepts follow from the DOCTRINE of CREATION from nothing, according to which God is the sole antecedent condition of the existence of all creatures, and therefore the ongoing source of all creaturely being and action. While various forms of DEISM limit God's role to that of a first cause that establishes creation in the beginning but thereafter lets it run according to its own laws, to affirm God's ongoing work of *conservatio* is to insist that, apart from God's continual willing of creation's existence, it would immediately cease to exist.

This classical form of *conservatio* also differs from the tenets of PROCESS THEOLOGY. While process theologians affirm God's ongoing interaction with every facet of creation in a way that deists do not, and while they also attribute to God a constitutive role in giving each entity the concrete form it assumes at any given moment, they nevertheless insist that a condition of God's being in genuine relationship with creatures is their ontological independence from God. The classical position (as developed most fully in Protestant SCHOLASTICISM of the seventeenth century) rejects this limitation, on the grounds that any compromise of the creature's dependence on God effectively establishes a second eternal reality alongside God and thus limits God's ability to perfect creation according to God's own purposes.

IAN A. MCFARLAND

CONSTANCE, COUNCIL OF The Council of Constance, the largest medieval general council, effectively ended the Great Western Schism, during which rival papal claimants reigned in Rome and Avignon. In 1409 the Council of Pisa deposed the rival popes and elected a new pope; the unintended effect of its actions was to create a triple SCHISM. The Council of Constance was convoked by John XXII (*ca* 1370–1419), successor to the pope elected at Pisa, and by the emperor-elect, Sigismund (r. 1433–7).

John XXII presided over the council; but in March 1415, fearing he would be forced to abdicate, he fled

Constance, threatening the council's existence. Then, on 6 April, the council enacted the decree *Haec sancta*, declaring that the council represented the universal Church and held its power directly from Christ and that all persons of every status, including the papal status, were bound to obey the council, and any other general council, in three principal matters, or *causae*: ending the schism, FAITH, and reforming the Church 'in head and members'.

The council addressed these *causae* with varying success. It succeeded in ending the schism by deposing two of the papal contenders, John XXII (Pisan line) and Benedict XIII (1328–1423, Avignon line), and accepting the resignation of Gregory XII (*ca* 1330–1417, Roman line) after this last had been allowed the privilege of issuing a *pro forma* re-convocation of the council. These actions made possible the election of a virtually undisputed pope, Martin V (r. 1417–31).

The *causa fidei* involved condemning the teachings of J. Wycliffe (*ca* 1325–84) and trying, condemning, and burning the Bohemian reformers, J. Hus (*ca* 1370–1415) and Jerome of Prague (1379–1416). Debate has focused on the motives and legality of Hus' trial, and on whether Hus in fact taught the DOCTRINES for which he was condemned. Though the trial probably did not violate norms of fifteenth-century CANON LAW, Hus' condemnation was in many ways unfair and ushered in a prolonged period of conflict.

The *causa reformationis* was hampered by conflicting interests and conceptions among reformers, but important monastic reforms and 'reforms of the head', which limited papal taxation and appointments to Church offices, were enacted. The decree *Frequens* required regular meetings of general councils (at a minimum once each decade) to make possible continuing reform.

Earlier scholars argued that the CONCILIARISM practised at Constance was radical and democratic. More recent scholars have traced its foundations in hierarchical views of theologians like J. Gerson (1363–1429) and in long-standing theories of canon law. *Haec sancta* and *Frequens* became fundamental documents for later conciliarists, who used them to support their assertion of conciliar superiority over the pope. Their papalist opponents argued against *Haec sancta*'s validity. Recent scholars have debated whether *Haec sancta* is still binding, whether it was primarily a dogmatic statement of faith or a legal decree, and whether it was intended to be of permanent validity or to address only the emergency situation of the schism, in which none of the papal claimants enjoyed undisputed legitimacy. The lasting significance of *Haec sancta* and *Frequens* lies in their reassertion of venerable traditions of collegial Church governance, traditions partially revived by VATICAN COUNCIL II.

See also PAPACY.

W. Brandmüller, *Das Konzil von Konstanz*, 2 vols. (Ferdinand Schöningh, 1991–7).

T. Izbicki, 'Papalist Reaction to the Council of Constance: Juan de Torquemada to the Present', *Church History* 55 (1986), 7–20.

PHILLIP H. STUMP

CONSTANTINIANISM A pejorative term meaning 'the alignment of the Church with political power for solely temporal purposes', the term 'Constantinianism' has its specific historical point of reference in the Edict of Toleration issued by Constantine I (*ca* 275–337) in 313, and the subsequent instalment of Christianity as the official religion of the Roman Empire under Theodosius I (r. 379–95) in 380. For many this is viewed as a watershed moment when the Church of the martyrs gave way to the Church of CHRISTENDOM and thereby lost its purity and integrity through colluding with the means and ends of the Roman Empire.

The origins of the term lie in an Anabaptist reading of Church history that views the 'Constantinian settlement' as a second fall. The key text is the *Martyrs Mirror of the Defenceless Christians* (1660) by the Mennonite T. J. van Braght (1625–64). The book documents the stories and testimonies of Christian martyrs from the time of Christ onwards. Its vision of Church history is that the true Church went underground at the time of Constantine only to become visible again with the non-resisting, non-violent ('defenceless') Anabaptist Churches. This Anabaptist vision of Church history is also the root of the distinctive elaboration of the term 'Constantinian' by J. H. Yoder (1927–97) and S. Hauerwas (b. 1940), who are the progenitors of its widespread use in contemporary theology.

Constantinianism is Yoder's term for that which the Church must 'disavow', namely, its claim not only to political, legal, and social establishment, but also all attempts to secure the Gospel through foundational epistemological strategies. Yoder contrasts a 'Constantinian' approach to Christian belief and practice to a non-violent, local, and ad hoc one. For Yoder the basic problem with Constantinianism is theological: from Constantine onwards, Christians begin to lose their eschatological conviction that the end and fulfilment of history is already given in the RESURRECTION of Jesus Christ. This leads them to collude with human attempts to define and achieve mastery over time. There is for Yoder an iterative series of 'Constantinianisms' through history as the relationship between Christianity and society develops.

Hauerwas focuses on and illustrates one such iteration: the PROTESTANT culture of North American Christianity, both liberal and conservative. For Hauerwas, Constantinianism denotes any attempt to adapt and domesticate the GOSPEL to fit with American values in order that the Church can be culturally and politically significant. For Hauerwas, if the Church conceives its *primary* task as forming a culture, or creating the virtues by which a liberal democratic (or any other) society can be sustained, it has betrayed its VOCATION: to form people to die well by explicitly forming an ecclesial community. Yoder and Hauerwas seek to recover the basis and witness of a critical, confessing Church within a context where the 'Constantinian synthesis' has broken down and the identification of a particular social–political order with Christianity can no longer be taken for granted.

Yoder and Hauerwas use 'Constantinianism' primarily in a normative, theological sense. However, its use in any historically descriptive sense is misleading: it fails to account for the multifaceted nature of the often dialectical relationship between ecclesial and political authority from Constantine onwards in the West; and ignores the almost continual persecution and minority status of Christianity in the Persian Empire and its Islamic successors. A striking contrast to the negative, historical use of the term is given in the Orthodox traditions, where Constantine is a SAINT and considered equal to the APOSTLES.

J. H. Yoder, *The Royal Priesthood: Essays Ecclesiastical and Ecumenical* (Eerdmans, 1994).
The Original Revolution: Essays on Christian Pacifism (Mennonite, 1971).

LUKE BRETHERTON

CONSTANTINOPLE, FIRST COUNCIL OF Reckoned as the second ecumenical COUNCIL, the First Council of Constantinople (Constantinople I) is responsible for the definition of the DOCTRINE of the TRINITY. Held in the imperial capital in 381, it constituted the dogmatic resolution of the debates over the status of the Son or *Logos* (as well as of the HOLY SPIRIT) that had remained unresolved after the Council of NICAEA in 325. The close conceptual linkage between the two councils is suggested by the fact that the confession of FAITH known as the NICENE CREED was in fact composed at Constantinople I. While the debates over the Person of Christ that occupied the next several ecumenical councils would result in ecclesial divisions lasting to the present day, the Trinitarian theology defined at Constantinople I achieved a degree of consensus that continues to serve as a basis for theological discussion across confessional lines.

The Council of Nicaea had secured the condemnation of Arius (see ARIAN CONTROVERSY), but its teaching that the Son who became incarnate in Jesus was *HOMOOUSIOS* with (i.e., of the same substance as) the God Jesus called Father proved highly contentious. Though vigorously defended by ATHANASIUS OF ALEXANDRIA, the claim that the Son shared the Father's divine nature was viewed with suspicion by many others. Some worried that it effectively collapsed the distinction between the Father and the Son in a way that amounted to MODALISM; they preferred to speak of the Son being *homoiousios* with (i.e., of like substance to) the Father. Others charged that any comparison of substances risked undermining the transcendent uniqueness of the Father and thought it best to speak more vaguely of the Son being 'like' the Father. And as the decades wore on, the same sorts of questions were applied to the Holy Spirit: was the Spirit, too, to be considered of the same essence as the Father?

By the time of Constantinople I (not least through the efforts of the CAPPADOCIAN FATHERS, who refined the terminological distinction according to which equality in substance or nature in the Godhead did not preclude difference in HYPOSTASIS or 'person'), theological reflection had progressed to the point where a broadly acceptable solution was possible. The Council confirmed the Nicaea confession of the Son as *homoousios* with the Father and also condemned those who denied the Holy Spirit's divinity (though, to minimize contention, the conciliar creed did not apply the term *homoousios* to the Spirit). In this way, it established the Trinitarian principle that the same worship was to be given to the Father, Son, and Spirit, confessed as three distinct but equally divine hypostases of the one God.

While best known for its resolution of the Christian doctrine of God, Constantinople I also condemned the Christological HERESY of APOLLINARIANISM (thereby anticipating the central preoccupation of subsequent ecumenical councils) and – much more controversially – affirmed the bishop of Constantinople as second only to that of Rome, thereby displacing the traditional pre-eminence accorded to the sees of Alexandria and Antioch in the East.

IAN A. MCFARLAND

CONSTRUCTIVE THEOLOGY: see SYSTEMATIC THEOLOGY.

CONTEMPLATION In the theology of the Christian spiritual life, the term 'contemplation' has generally been used for a state of PRAYER in which God draws one beyond visible things to 'contemplate something of divine and heavenly things and gaze at them with the mind alone' (ORIGEN, *CSong*, prologue); and, historically, the term's meaning intersects with the highest form of theology as a participation in divine truth. Contemplation is thus both an advanced form of prayer and, simultaneously, the highest state of theological reflection. *Contemplatio* translates into Latin the Greek term *theoria* (loosely, 'seeing'), which in Plato (*ca* 430–*ca* 345 BC) is used of the knowledge only available in the realm of unchanging reality, the world of the forms (see PLATONISM). In Aristotle, the moral or practical life is always a preparation for the *bios theoretikos*, the life of contemplation, in which, by pursuing understanding and wisdom, one arrives at true happiness (see ARISTOTELIANISM).

By the Christian era, it was common in the Mediterranean world to distinguish three pedagogical disciplines or phases: the moral, in which one developed freedom from the passions; natural contemplation, in which one entered into the truths of the natural world; and contemplation proper, in which one advanced, perhaps only fleetingly, towards wisdom. Important Christian spiritual teachers such as Origen, Gregory of Nyssa (see CAPPADOCIAN FATHERS), Evagrius Ponticus (345–99), and MAXIMUS THE CONFESSOR all translate this threefold pedagogical scheme into Christian terms. Origen famously associates the moral or practical discipline with the book of Proverbs, natural contemplation with Ecclesiastes (which teaches us not to value the world too highly), and contemplation itself with the Song of Songs (in which the bridegroom enraptures the bride with a passionate love of the divine reality). This progression via interior freedom to the stages of contemplation is conceived in profoundly Christological terms by Maximus. Christ the Word or *LOGOS* bestows the principles of intelligibility or *logoi* uniquely present in each creature, and these are what the mind seeks to understand in natural contemplation; by this practice, Christ prepares and perfects those who pray so that they may begin to sense him, the *Logos* himself, in the whole creation – and so be conducted towards the contemplation of the Word in God. In ORTHODOX THEOLOGY, contemplation is inherently transformative, leading those who pray towards a habitual recollection of God, holiness of life, and a capacity for WISDOM and discerning judgement.

In general, western theologies of contemplation develop less Christologically, though there is some analogy in AUGUSTINE's suggestion that in the INCARNATION the one 'by whom all things were made ... stretched forth his clemency to our misery' and gave himself in ways by which fallen humanity could be nourished: 'the rational creature feeds upon the Word as its own best food ... The food of the rational creature became visible ... in order that he might recall those who follow visible things to embrace him who is invisible' (*Lib.* 3.10.30; *Trin.* 1.27). Not only does Augustine emphasize the transformative nature of this encounter with the Word, but he clearly understands contemplation as an inherently theological act leading the mind to its truest fulfilment in gazing upon the divine Wisdom. So contemplation for Augustine is the partial presence to the mind even now of that fullness of vision which is the aim of all theology: 'There we shall see the truth without any difficulty, and enjoy it in all its clarity and certitude. There, there will be nothing for us to seek with the reasonings of the mind, but we will perceive by direct contemplation' (*Trin.* 15.45). Later Catholic spiritual theology will focus on these features already present in Augustine, namely the mind's passing over from discursive thought to passive vision, and from yearning to enjoyment, in order to trace a spiritual path from meditation to contemplation, and from acquired contemplation to a purely infused gift of inspired contemplation that carries the one who prays into 'a loving, simple, and fixed attention of the mind on divine things' (Francis de Sales, *Love*, 6.3). T. AQUINAS affirms this interpretation of contemplation as a drawing of the mind, inspired by love, into a joyful communion with the truth: 'Through loving God we are aflame to gaze on his beauty. And since everyone delights when he obtains what he loves, it follows that the contemplative life terminates in delight' (*ST* 2/2.180.1).

O. Clément and J. C. Barreau, *The Roots of Christian Mysticism* (New City, 1995 [1982]).
Jean-Pierre Torrell, *Saint Thomas Aquinas: Spiritual Master* (Catholic University of America Press, 2003).
A. N. Williams, *The Divine Sense: The Intellect in Patristic Thought* (Cambridge University Press, 2007).

MARK A. MCINTOSH

CONTRACEPTION: see PROCREATION.

CONTRITION A crucial term in western reflection on REPENTANCE, contrition refers to a person's full and genuine remorse for her own SIN. Defined by the Council of TRENT as 'sorrow of the SOUL and detestation for the sin committed, together with the resolution not to sin again' (*Poen.* 4; cf. *Cat.*, §1,451), contrition is understood in CATHOLIC THEOLOGY as necessary for the FORGIVENESS of sins committed after BAPTISM. It is thus central to the sacrament of PENANCE, which requires the penitent's contrition, along with subsequent acts of confession and satisfaction. In this context, contrition, as perfect sorrow for sin that is rooted in love of God, is distinguished from 'attrition', defined as regret for sin that is caused either by recognition of its ugliness or by fear of punishment. Trent stipulates that, although attrition is not sufficient to reconcile a person to God, it is nevertheless a divine impulse that disposes the sinner to obtain forgiveness through penance.

During the REFORMATION, Protestants rejected the claim that contrition was necessary for absolution on the grounds that this implied forgiveness was earned by human effort (viz., feeling sorry) in a way that led either to presumption ('Since I'm sorry, God has to forgive me') or to uncertainty over whether the conditions for forgiveness had been met ('Am I sufficiently sorry for God to forgive me?'). Catholics countered that the Reformers' understanding of faith as the sole condition of forgiveness was itself presumptuous and failed to reckon with God's commitment to work through rather than against human nature in granting GRACE.

IAN A. MCFARLAND

CONVERSION 'Conversion' means 'turning'. In Christianity's first centuries the Greek words *epistrepho* and *metanoia*, and the Latin *conversio*, denoted turning of two kinds. One kind involved a transfer of loyalties, in which people moved from one religion to another; the second involved an intensification of piety and praxis within their own tradition. Both kinds of turning led to new patterns of behaviour and social solidarity; both also commonly culminated in a ritual: BAPTISM.

In the Church's first three centuries, many people were converted as the Church, despite its illegality, grew rapidly. Joining it was risky; conversion involved a 'resocialization into an alternative community' (Meeks, *Origins*, 26). Its witness was rooted in its members' attractive behaviour, so the Church's leaders sought to ensure that those joining it absorbed the teachings of Jesus and had been freed of classic compulsions – sex, the occult, increasing wealth, and violence/xenophobia (see Justin, *1Apol.* 14–17). Candidates participated in an extensive CATECHESIS, often lasting several years, that formed them as Christians. Their journey to conversion culminated in baptism, whose ritual power expressed a death to old options and a rebirth to a transformed life within a new family.

The fourth century saw great changes. The emperor Constantine I (*ca* 275–337) transferred his loyalty to Christianity, which he made legal and attractive; at the century's end Theodosius I (r. 379–95) made orthodox Christianity the only legal religion; and in 529 Justinian I (r. 527–65) required all the empire's inhabitants to be baptized. The aim of these changes was to bring about a society comprehensively under Christ's Lordship. As this civilization – Christendom – took shape, the character of conversion changed.

Conversion no longer was career-endangering. It became advantageous to become a Christian; indeed, 'Many peoples were ... conquered by Roman weapons and so converted' (Cyril of Alexandria, *CIsa.* 2.4). Catechesis changed, taking less time and concentrating more on doctrine than on lifestyle. As infant baptism became general practice, catechesis largely disappeared. Baptism, which had been ritually imposing, became quick, private, and ritually shrunken. When Christendom expanded into northern Europe, missionary efforts led to the conversion of clans, whose decisions to transfer their loyalties to the new faith were made corporately. Even within societies in which everyone was a baptized Christian, conversion continued as individuals intensified their piety and practice. Some, sensing the call to *conversio*, took monastic vows (see MONASTICISM); others experienced 'continuing conversion' as lay people, devoting themselves to ascetic disciplines rooted in Jesus' teachings and way.

In the sixteenth century western Christendom fractured into competing groups. Catholics converted to Protestantism, and vice versa, often amidst intense conversion experiences. Both traditions gave new attention to catechesis, but in both baptism remained ritually unimpressive, except among Anabaptist and Baptist minorities, for whom the cost of conversion could be high. Calvinists gave intense analysis to the content and affective nature of personal religious change, as did Pietists in the Lutheran tradition (see PIETISM) and Wesleyans (see METHODIST THEOLOGY). Amidst evidence of the alienation of many people from the Churches, evangelistic preaching emerged, in England and America, which in camp meetings and revivals sought to convert the 'backslidden' believers. The emotional temperature of conversion was high; and the convert often prayed a simple prayer of surrender and gave mental assent to certain truths. The ethical content of conversion was typically the 'norms that society at large upholds' (Meeks, *Origins* 21).

In late Christendom, Catholic religious orders and Protestant mission societies sent missionaries to Latin America, Africa, and Asia, where people converted to Christianity. The character of these conversions was infinitely varied: at times voluntary, at times in response to inducement and compulsion; at times a matter of individual decision, at others of tribal decisions involving 'multi-individual conversions' (Costas, *Church* 128). Often the conversions were costly and led to persecution. Some missionaries experienced continuing conversion as they, 'through the eyes of others', saw God at work in cultures whose issues and world views were different from those of the West (Hiebert, *Transforming* 321). In the late twentieth century, as Churches in the West experienced 'one of the largest and fastest movements away from the Christian faith ever to have taken place' (Walls, *Cross* 63), the number of conversions to Christianity was burgeoning in the global South.

In the twenty-first century Christianity is worldwide. Some parts of Africa are virtually entirely baptized and elsewhere, as in China, conversions to Christianity are increasing rapidly. In many countries, nominal conversion is a problem and catechesis is urgently necessary. In the post-Christendom West, evangelistic traditions continue but in many places have lost effectiveness. Some new initiatives involve a reappropriation of the understandings and practices of the pre-Constantinian Christians. Conversion is emerging as a turning to Christ from western secularism and MATERIALISM. In many traditions conversion is increasingly preceded by CATECHESIS, which prepares Christians for life in hostile surroundings; in the *Rite of Christian Initiation of Adults* (1972), the Catholics have pointed the way. Baptism is re-emerging as a serious component of conversion, whose centrality is indicated by the ritual expressiveness with which Churches practise it. Christians in the West are also experiencing continuing conversion as an intensification of piety and practice in their commitment to the poor, environmental asceticism, and practical peacemaking.

A. Kreider, *The Change of Conversion and the Origin of Christendom* (Trinity, 1999).

L. R. Rambo, *Understanding Religious Conversion* (Yale, 1993).

R. D. Witherup, *Conversion in the New Testament* (Liturgical, 1994).

ALAN KREIDER

Cosmological Argument The cosmological argument is a piece of natural theology which seeks to demonstrate the existence of a Sufficient Reason or First Cause of the existence of the cosmos. Among its proponents stand many of the most prominent figures in the history of western philosophy: Plato (*ca* 430–*ca* 345 BC; see Platonism), Aristotle (see Aristotelianism), al-Ghazali (1058–1111), M. Maimonides (1135–1204), Anselm, T. Aquinas, J. Duns Scotus, R. Descartes (1596–1650), B. Spinoza (1632–77), G. Leibniz (1646–1716), and J. Locke (1632–1704), among others.

Three basic types of cosmological argument can be distinguished:

(1) The *kalam cosmological argument* originated in the efforts of Christian philosophers like J. Philoponus (*ca* 490–*ca* 570) to rebut the Aristotelian doctrine of the eternity of the universe. The *kalam* (Arabic for 'speech', used more broadly for natural theology) cosmological argument aims to show that the universe had a beginning at some moment in the finite past and, since something cannot come into being from nothing, must therefore have a transcendent cause. Although traditional proponents of the argument disputed the infinitude of the past on philosophical grounds, what has breathed new life into the *kalam* cosmological argument has been remarkable discoveries in astrophysics over the last century which suggest that the universe is not eternal in the past but had an absolute beginning about 13 billion years ago (see Cosmology).

(2) The *Thomist cosmological argument* seeks a cause which is first, not in the temporal sense, but in the sense of rank. In Aquinas' metaphysics every finite thing is composed of essence and existence and is therefore radically contingent. If an essence is to be instantiated, there must be conjoined with that essence an act of being. Essence is in potentiality to the act of being, and for that reason no substance can actualize itself but requires some external cause. Since an infinite regress of hierarchically ordered causes is impossible, we must arrive at a being which is not composed of essence and existence and, hence, requires no sustaining cause. This being's essence just *is* existence. Thomas identifies this being with the God whose name was revealed to Moses as 'I am' (Exod. 3:15).

(3) The *Leibnizian cosmological argument* frees the contingency argument from the Aristotelian metaphysical underpinnings of the Thomist version. Leibniz's driving question was, 'Why is there something rather than nothing?' On the basis of his Principle of Sufficient Reason that 'no fact can be real or existent, no statement true, unless there be a sufficient reason why it is so and not otherwise', Leibniz held that this question must have an answer. He argued that the Sufficient Reason cannot be found in any individual thing in the universe, nor in the collection of such things which is the universe, nor in earlier states of the universe, even if these regress infinitely. Therefore, there must exist an ultra-mundane being which is metaphysically necessary, that is, its non-existence is impossible. It is the Sufficient Reason for its own existence as well as for the existence of every contingent thing.

Contemporary defenders of the cosmological argument include W. L. Craig (b. 1949), R. Koons (b. 1957), D. Oderberg (b. 1963), A. Plantinga (b. 1932), R. Swinburne (b. 1934), and R. Taylor (1919–2003).

William Lane Craig

Cosmology Any account of the structure of the universe is a cosmology. Many cosmologies also include a cosmogony, or account of the universe's origin, though for others the universe is eternal and thus without a beginning. Similarly, the relationship between the phenomenal world and the divine is a central feature of many cosmologies, though not (for example) of materialist ones (see Materialism).

The majority of Christian theologians have sought to derive their cosmology from the Bible. The cosmologies which have resulted have for the most part agreed on the following points: the universe is not divine; it has been created from nothing by one God (see Creation); its history is directed by God (see Providence); and it is both spatially and temporally finite (i.e., it has a definite beginning and end). By contrast, in deist cosmologies the universe runs largely independently of divine direction (see Deism), while proponents of process theology question the doctrine of creation from nothing, the idea of an absolute beginning, and the positing of an absolute ontological distinction between God and the world.

Convinced that the witness of Scripture must be consistent with the structure of the universe as revealed to the senses, Christians have usually thought it important to assess the relationship between the biblical picture of the world and cosmologies developed outside the Church. In contemporary western theology, this assessment generally takes the form of exploring the compatibility between biblically derived cosmologies and those of natural science, but in the past it has entailed confrontation with Platonic (see Platonism), Aristotelian (see Aristotelianism), and Confucian (see Chinese Theology) cosmologies, to name just a few.

See also Panentheism; Pantheism.

Ian A. McFarland

Councils, Ecumenical Tertullian is one of the first to inform us that, by the mid- to late second century, Christian bishops in Asia Minor had instituted the practice of meeting together to resolve problems and agree on common religious policies (*Jejun.* 13). He thought it a good model for the West to emulate. These meetings, he says, were called 'synods'. Although the later Church has often looked to the first 'council' of the Apostles in Acts 15 as its paradigm in conciliarism, patristic writers do not refer to it in this light until after the fifth century. Instead, the idea of councils probably derived from the Hellenistic city-governance processes, where leaders would meet others of same rank under the aegis of the provincial governor's administration when matters of common policy were called for.

In any case, it was the Montanist crisis (see Montanism) that gave international prominence to the practice of the Churches in Asia Minor (Eusebius, *EH* 5.16.10), which may have emerged in part as a reaction to Rome's tendency to use the ancient system of letters to advance its right to adjudicate in other sees. Pope Victor I's (r. 189–99) treatment of the Montanists had been seen by many as too severe, and an alternative system of Church order using many voices to adjudicate, not simply one, was a natural reaction.

What this early system grew to look like can perhaps be seen from the life of Origen, who in the mid-third century was called in by a collective of Palestinian bishops to help them resolve problems of theology among them. His records of the meeting depict the gathering as a genuine dialogue seeking consensus through study. At the end, the dissident bishop was reconciled to the majority by admitting he had been convinced by the evidence. Only later did the synods assume the character of 'trials'. By the third century the principle of annual meetings of the bishops of a province became common. Cyprian (d. 258) shows that the North African bishops met regularly to decide disciplinary matters in their Churches (*Ep.* 55; 67.1). This practice established councils (at least in the Eastern Church) as the supreme source of canon law. The disciplinary decisions they published became known simply as 'the canons'.

Pope Leo I (r. 440–61) issued a set of guidelines in several letters explaining how the authority of councils was vested in the inspiration of the Holy Spirit, in the foundation of Scripture, and in harmony with universal tradition. He also taught that the council to be authentic had to agree with its predecessors, be popularly received (the consensus of the faithful), and be approved by the Holy See (*Ep.* 13–14, 106, 119, 129, 145–7, 162, 164, 166). The East concurred entirely with all these points except for the last, teaching instead that the council always had precedence in authority over any single bishop or patriarch and that the synod was expected to manifest a 'common mind'. Thus, when a crisis arose over doctrine or discipline, the collective mind of the bishops should be able to recognize immediately and acclaim authoritatively the true line of the tradition. The conciliar outcome was not to be decided by majority vote, and so there was always great pressure to ensure that the final vote should be unanimous. If this could not be achieved, the dissidents who refused to sign the conciliar Acts were denounced by the synod and anathematized as heretics (see Anathema; Heresy).

All the large synods remained governed by Roman (specifically, senatorial) conventions regarding debates, and by Hellenistic ideas about how philosophical ideas could be exchanged (more propositional than informative). After Constantine I (*ca* 275–337) achieved supreme power in the empire in 324, he determined that the Christians should be a force for cohesion. To promote this, he encouraged a much wider assembly of bishops, based on the model of the senatorial gatherings of the emperor's advisers. The first example of this 'ecumenical' kind of meeting (from the Greek *oikoumenē*, or 'worldwide') was the Council of Arles in 314 called to resolve the Donatist crisis (see Donatism). Though it failed in this aim, Constantine tried again in the East, calling an 'ecumenical synod' in Nicaea in 325 to settle the Arian controversy.

The Council of Nicaea determined that a provincial council of bishops should be held in every local area at least twice a year (Canon 5), and it also established the rule that the emperor was the one who should convoke an Ecumenical Council. Though its theological decisions would later become the standard of Orthodox Christology, in its aftermath a whole series of councils held throughout the fourth century conflicted with one another as the Arian crisis continued to play out. The fact that these numerous synods exposed conflicting views within the international episcopate caused the principle of synodical inspiration to take something of a battering in terms of popular faith. In reaction, synods from the fifth century on tended to mutate into a promulgation of patristic evidences, after the hearing of which the bishops passed a sentence of agreement with the standard authorities of the past. By this stage the idea of the synod as an open sharing of ideas had largely passed, and councils took on a forensic character – although at no stage was the idea abandoned that their decisions were governed by the Holy Spirit.

At the Council of Chalcedon the assembled bishops looked back and retrospectively declared that of all the numerous preceding synods, only three had hitherto been truly 'ecumenical': Nicaea, Constantinople, and Ephesus. After that point only momentously significant councils have earned the designation 'ecumenical'. Though the Catholic Church includes all twenty-one councils so designated by the papacy in this number, only seven are recognized as such by both the eastern and western Churches. All these are from the Greek Christian world and include (in addition to the first three mentioned above): Chalcedon, Constantinople II (553), Constantinople III (681), and Nicaea II (787). These have been commonly regarded in the Orthodox

Church in particular as the supreme authority, under God, for settling matters in the Christian Oecumene.

See also CONCILIARISM.

L. D. Davis, *The First Seven Ecumenical Councils (325–787): Their History and Theology* (Liturgical Press, 1990).

G. Florovsky, 'The Authority of the Ancient Councils and the Tradition of the Fathers' in *Glaube, Geist, Geschichte*, ed. G. Müller and W. Zeller (Brill, 1967).

J. A. McGuckin, *St. Cyril of Alexandria and the Christological Controversy* (Brill, 1994).

'Eschaton and Kerygma: The Future of the Past in the Present Kairos: The Concept of Living Tradition in Orthodox Theology', *St. Vladimir's Theological Quarterly*, 42:3–4 (winter 1998), 225–71.

JOHN A. MCGUCKIN

COUNTER-REFORMATION: see REFORMATION.

COVENANT 'Covenant' (Hebrew *b'rith*, meaning 'bond' or 'fetter that carries a sense of obligation') is arguably the most important biblical term characterizing God's relationship with ISRAEL and God's relationship, through Jesus Christ, with Jews and Gentiles alike. Some scholars argue that 'KINGDOM OF GOD' is more fundamental in the Bible than 'covenant'. Others contend that the two terms are interdependent, two sides of the same coin. Christians have chosen the word 'covenant' to characterize their Bible's fundamental division between the Old and New 'Testaments' (i.e., covenants).

For most of the Church's history, in both its eastern and western branches, the Bible's covenant framework faded from view until the time of the REFORMATION. Roman imperial influences, including the hierarchical ordering of authorities under a pre-eminent human figure, became predominant in Church governance and in biblical interpretation. With the Reformation, particularly in the work of J. CALVIN and his followers, renewed interest in the older testament and mastery of Hebrew came to the fore, leading to increased attention to the importance of covenant as a central theological and (more specifically) ecclesiological concept. It became the central concept for the interpretation of SCRIPTURE in seventeenth-century FEDERAL THEOLOGY, a role it also held in the emergence of modern DISPENSATIONALISM in the nineteenth century.

The confluence of the Reformation with the creation of modern states led, for better and for worse – and particularly in Reformed circles – to the adoption of covenant language in the shaping of Protestant states. Most influential in this regard were English and American Puritans, Scottish Presbyterians, and the Dutch Reformed. The Puritan settlers of New England, for example, saw themselves as a new covenant people entering a new promised land. The language of a 'new Israel' was then taken over by the American founders at the time of the Revolution as part of their self-identification as a political federation. The civil–religious consequences of those developments reverberate to this day, causing confusion and dissension about the relation of Israel (and modern Judaism) to Christianity and about the meaning of biblical law and moral obligation for law and government in regions of the world shaped by Judaism, Christianity, and Islam.

In the middle of the twentieth century, archaeological research led to the discovery of significant parallels between ancient Near Eastern kingship treaties and Israel's covenants. This threw new light on the complex meaning and importance of the biblical covenants. G. E. Mendenhall (b. 1916), interpreting the ancient suzerainty treaties from as far back as the third millennium BC, found a legal form with parallels to biblical covenants. Thus, God establishing a covenant with Israel at Sinai is parallel to a victorious Hittite king establishing suzerainty authority over a subject nation. Typically such a treaty or covenant began with (1) a preamble that was followed by (2) a historical prologue, (3) stipulations of the terms (i.e., obligations) of the relationship, (4) promised curses and blessings for those who break or keep the agreement, (5) succession or continuity arrangements, and (6) a ratification procedure that included the swearing of an oath.

Since the 1950s, much new research has been done on different types of ancient biblical and extra-biblical covenants. For example, suzerain–vassal treaties are distinguished from royal-grant treaties through which a king rewards a loyal people or person and pledges future blessings. God's covenant with Abraham or Noah, for example, can be interpreted in the latter way. And one of the most interesting avenues of biblical–theological exploration in recent years has taken scholars to the covenant structure of creation itself (and Gen. 1). W. J. Dumbrell (b. 1926) and others have led the way along this path. Here, attention is drawn to the Noachian covenant (Gen. 6 and 9), which is read as a perpetuation or renewal covenant, particularly a creation–renewal covenant. That in turn leads to the view that Genesis 1 has the structure of a founding covenant. Following from that, from a Christian point of view, all the biblical covenants, reaching their climax in the new covenant in Christ, are creation–renewal, creation–fulfilment covenants, loaded with eschatological promise.

While study of biblical and ancient Near Eastern covenants continues, there is little if any conversation between biblical scholars and the students of politics who are now debating the relative crisis of political liberalism in the West, with its 'contract' theory of the origin of society and government. To a significant degree, 'contract' is a reduced, weakened derivation from 'covenant', the latter having a richer, more communal and normative meaning than the former. D. Elazar (1934–99) is one of the few who has brought together study of biblical covenants and modern political thought. He has called attention to the great influence that Israel's way of life had on the formation of modern constitutionalism and political 'federation', particularly in countries influenced by Calvinism. A very lively and contemporary question, then, is whether a biblically informed understanding of covenant can make as important a contribution to the shaping of domestic and international politics as it can to the shaping of ecclesiastical and synagogal life as well as to the responsibilities humans bear in all other spheres of life.

If the biblical meaning of covenant obligation to God is rooted in the very meaning of creation and pertains to the recovery and fulfilment of creation through the covenant of redemption, then the potential for covenant thinking in all spheres of life in today's rapidly shrinking world is great indeed.

W. J. Dumbrell, *Covenant and Creation: A Theology of the Old Testament Covenants* (Paternoster Press, 1984).

D. J. Elazar, *The Covenant Tradition in Politics*, 4 vols. (Transaction, 1995–8).

E. W. Nicholson, *God and His People: Covenant and Theology in the Old Testament* (Clarendon Press, 1986).

JAMES W. SKILLEN

CRANMER, THOMAS Thomas Cranmer (1489–1556) is generally regarded as the chief architect of the Church of England as it came to be reformed in the sixteenth century, a Church which included both Catholic and Protestant elements. Cranmer himself has always been a controversial figure. He was appointed archbishop of Canterbury by Henry VIII (r. 1509–47), largely because of his diplomatic skills and ability in advancing theological arguments on behalf of the king's divorce from Catherine of Aragon (1485–1536). But he was never simply a bureaucrat. He was a realist, who understood that the monarch was the key to a reformation of the Church in England. From the early 1530s, however, he had become convinced of the truth of the Lutheran teaching on JUSTIFICATION, and he utilized his position as archbishop gradually to further the cause of reform, not merely as a SCHISM from Rome but as a positive appropriation of REFORMATION teaching.

During the reign of Edward VI (r. 1547–53), it became possible to implement this vision of reform in a thoroughgoing way. The Thirty-Nine Articles of Religion set forth the essentials of the Reformed faith (e.g., the supreme authority of SCRIPTURE, justification by faith), but also grounded the Church of England securely in a Catholic structure of the CREEDS and the threefold MINISTRY. The BOOK OF COMMON PRAYER was Cranmer's permanent legacy to the Church, both in its majestic English prose and in the ordering of its worship in a regular liturgical pattern. During Mary I's (r. 1553–8) attempt to restore Catholicism, Cranmer was tried and executed as a heretic, particularly for his Eucharistic DOCTRINE: that Christ's presence is real, but spiritual rather than corporeal. Whether his personal views were more influenced by Luther or by the Swiss theologians of the Reformed tradition continues to be debated. What is certain is that his 1552 service for Holy Communion beautifully expressed a central tenet of the Reformation – that the mass is not something which we offer to God. The free LOVE of Christ, crucified for us, can never be merited, but only received through FAITH. Our response is one of self-offering in love and service.

See also ANGLICAN THEOLOGY.

KEVIN WARD

CREATION Proclaimed in the first article of the NICENE CREED, the divine creation of the world is an axiom of all Christian FAITH. Although it derives from Judaism and is shared in part with Islam, the Church's doctrine of creation also reflects distinctively Christological themes. In recent times, the doctrine has attracted much attention, despite suffering neglect in mid-twentieth-century theological debates. Factors contributing to this renewed interest include concerns about the natural environment (see ECOTHEOLOGY), debates generated by modern scientific COSMOLOGY, the exegetical awareness that creation is not merely a preliminary but a pervasive theme throughout SCRIPTURE, and the comparative study of creation in the three Abrahamic faiths.

Despite the ambivalence of the opening verses of Genesis, where the formless void appears to pre-exist the divine act of creation, Christian theology was unanimously committed to a doctrine of *creatio ex nihilo* (creation out of nothing) from the latter part of the second century. This was articulated in conscious opposition to Greek philosophical notions of the eternity of matter and also to Gnostic (and later Neoplatonist) theories of emanation from the divine essence (see GNOSTICISM; PLATONISM). Although Justin Martyr (*ca* 100–*ca* 165) believed that Plato (*ca* 430–*ca* 345 BC) and Moses both taught creation out of pre-existent matter (*1Apol.* 59), theologians from Tatian and Theophilus of Antioch (both d. *ca* 185) onwards believed that matter itself was created by God out of nothing. The power, transcendence and goodness of God as expressed in Scripture all rendered *creatio ex nihilo* a more fitting account of the origin of the world and its relationship of dependence to its Creator. This view was accepted with surprising swiftness and unanimity, particularly by IRENAEUS and TERTULLIAN, the doctrine of creation never becoming the focus of significant doctrinal controversy in the early Church.

It has also been pointed out by historians of dogma that the development of the doctrine of the TRINITY further reinforced the *ex nihilo* doctrine. The relationship between God and the world was fundamentally different from that of the eternal relations of origin within the Trinity. What emerges, therefore, is an account of creation as a free and contingent act that is the expression of divine Grace rather than any necessity internal to God's being. This was widely accepted and repeated throughout the Middle Ages, for example in T. Aquinas' distinction between the unique act of creating and all subsequent creaturely actions of making (*ST* 1.45.5), and also in the Reformers, who further stressed creation as an act of divine grace. The classical doctrine thus structures the God–world relationship as asymmetric, with a stress on divine transcendence and creaturely dependence. At the same time, the ontological distance of God from creation also makes possible an account of divine interaction with creation. As J. Calvin insisted, the transcendence and condescendence of God must be held together in order to make sense of the forms of divine action in nature and history (e.g., *Inst.* 1.6.1). Recent Trinitarian theology has sought to rearticulate this account of creation as an event consistent with the divine being yet without necessity. In holding together the unconstrained action of God with the triune relations of love, theologians such as K. Barth and W. Pannenberg (b. 1928) present creation as a decision that is free, yet without randomness or caprice.

Creation was traditionally regarded not only as *ex nihilo* but also *per verbum* (through the Word). Following the Wisdom theology of the OT and the prologue to John, theology was able to connect the creation of the world, through the Incarnation, to its redemption in Christ. The world is created for a purpose that is inherently Christological. It has a social order, as well as a natural one, that reflects the wisdom of the divine *Logos*. The advent of Jesus is therefore not an epiphenomenon or accidental turn in the course of creation but, as the incarnation of the creative Word, its central event. In the Middle Ages, Franciscan theologians, especially J. Duns Scotus, speculated that Christ would have become incarnate, even had Adam not sinned, in order to raise the cosmos to its appointed destiny.

The assertion that the world is God's good creation out of nothing is further supported by related notions of sustaining. Especially in Orthodox theology, this has been extended to include the notion of a continuous creation (*creatio continua*) that remains the *locus* of God's ongoing activity. This concept has proved attractive against Deist patterns of thought with their tendency to reduce divine action to an initial and single providential ordering of the world (see Deism). As being continuously created, the world is not merely set in motion and held in being by God, but becomes the arena of an ongoing divine–creaturely drama.

The classical doctrine, however, with its twin stress on divine sovereignty and goodness, tends to heighten the problem of evil (see Theodicy). In face of this, theologians have responded with various strategies, particularly the notion of the original creation as damaged by a subsequent Fall and in need of redemption. More recently, a different strategy interprets the notion of creation's original goodness (see Gen. 1:31) as a matter of conforming to God's intentions for it rather than as referring to a primordial perfection from which it suddenly secedes. This appears more consonant with current scientific understanding of the evolutionary emergence of biological complexity in general and of hominids in particular.

Despite its largely uncontested position in the tradition, the standard account of creation out of nothing has been subject to recent criticism by process and feminist thinkers (see Feminist Theology; Process Theology). Its construction of the God–world relationship fails to reflect the immanence of the divine, it is argued, placing God in a hierarchical position over against the creation. For process thinkers, an account of creation out of chaos better reflects the mode of God's presence and action in the world as allurement rather than control. This has the advantage of softening the problem of evil, although its account of Divine Action is much more indirect than that of immediate causation, which has characterized most Christian thought (see *Concursus*). Feminist criticism of the *ex nihilo* tradition aims to achieve a more holistic, relational, and ecological approach to the God–human–world partnership. In this context, S. McFague (b. 1933) has sought to reintroduce the metaphor of the world as God's Body, though the loss of divine otherness and transcendence associated with this approach runs the risk of depersonalizing the interaction between God and creatures.

Since the publication of *On the Origin of Species* (1859) by C. Darwin (1809–82), significant tensions have developed between Christian understandings of creation and the modern scientific world view. Recent cultural conflict has been generated, particularly in the USA, by attempts to present Genesis 1–2 as offering an alternative cosmology to that of the Big Bang account. Instead of galaxies, planets, and life forms emerging from a violent explosion from a point of infinite density around 13 billion years ago, creation science has attempted to maintain a 'young universe' only thousands of years old (see Creationism). While allowing for some changes that are attributed to the effects of the flood described in Genesis 6–9, the world is perceived as created in much the same condition as we observe it today. The intellectual impossibility of this movement is evident from its attempt to challenge not merely biological Evolution but the confirmed theories of other scientific disciplines including cosmology, astronomy, physics, geology, and palaeontology. Intelligent-design theory, with its propensity to identify a God-of-the-gaps at points where current scientific explanation is inadequate, seems likely also to fail, since history suggests that the continual progress of science will tend to fill the gaps, thus further weakening the position of the theologian. A different approach, pursued by a diverse range of theologians from the mid-nineteenth century onwards, has been the attempt to develop an account of theistic evolution. This recognizes that the creative purposes of God may be served by an evolving cosmos at least as effectively as by one that is largely uniform across time.

The doctrine of creation needs to view theological and scientific explanation as functioning at different and complementary levels, thus avoiding a conflation of methodologies. This was already recognized by the early Church fathers, especially AUGUSTINE, in his tendency to interpret the six days of creation symbolically rather than literally (in, e.g., *Conf.* 12). If theology is concerned with first and final causes (roughly, the 'why' questions), science can then be viewed as dealing with intermediate physical processes (roughly, the 'how' questions). While there may be points of contact and tension arising in the pursuit of these different forms of explanation and the need to show their fit, they are radically different in the questions they seek to address and the methods of enquiry that are employed. In this respect, theology and science represent 'non-overlapping magisteria'.

Despite the historic tensions between religion and science, there has been a growth of interest in the relationship between these disciplines in recent years. In relation to the doctrine of creation, the argument for design has been revived by reference to those 'cosmic coincidences' detected by physicists (see TELEOLOGICAL ARGUMENT). The initial structure of the universe in the fractional moments after the Big Bang seems to suggest a series of finely tuned parameters that make possible the emergence of galaxies, planets, and carbon-based life forms. Much contemporary discussion is preoccupied with ways of explaining this highly particular structure by reference to the hypothesis of a multiverse either as an alternative or as a complement to divine design. At the same time, theologians need to avoid giving the impression that the doctrine of creation is restricted to the origin of the world.

Contemporary theology has noted the pervasiveness of ANIMALS in Scripture and suggested that many historical attitudes were seriously disordered. As fellow creatures, animals surround us and accompany us. Their presence may often be unobtrusive, but they are never far away in the teaching and life of Jesus. Our kinship with animals has been further stressed by recent evolutionary science that reveals common ancestral origins, genetic similarities, and behavioural traits. The bonding of humans with animals has always been a recurrent feature of human life, and not only in rural communities. The growing sense of the divine purpose as intending a community of creation has heightened ethical awareness of animals whether in terms of the conditions under which they are housed and slaughtered, or in terms of the threat of extinction that faces many species.

Similar issues arise with respect to the natural environment. The command to exercise dominion over the world (Gen. 1:26) has sometimes been taken as licence to utilize and exploit natural resources. A standard charge against Christian attitudes to nature is that these are hierarchical, domineering, and rapacious. The use of the Hebrew verb *rada* in Genesis 1 does indeed seem to connote the notion of mastery. However, some commentators have argued that in this initial pastoral setting it must be read in terms of a benign stewardship, the exercise of a divinely mandated duty of care for the earth and its inhabitants. Instead of undermining it, the textual tradition can thus be seen as promoting environmental responsibility. In the context of Genesis 1, the gift of 'dominion' must be viewed in terms of responsible representation. Theologies of stewardship have sought to develop this, often drawing on the priestly sense of representing the creation before God, another recurrent theme in Orthodox theology with its sense of the material universe as redeemed by Christ and suffused by the HOLY SPIRIT.

However, while this must ease some ecological concerns about a narrow ANTHROPOCENTRISM, other scholars have claimed that the role of human beings should not be seen as managing the entire creation on God's behalf. The world is not for us alone; it possesses a beauty and value under God's providence that are not dependent upon their instrumental function for human activity. More recent scientific recognitions of the age and size of the cosmos tend to reinforce this claim – animals inhabited the earth for hundreds of millions of years prior to the emergence of hominids. Attention in this context is likely to be given in future discussion to issues raised by the possible discovery of extraterrestrial life forms. There is already a rich tradition of theological reflection on the supramundane creation of ANGELS – God is the Creator of heaven as well as earth. Again this provides a reminder that the doctrine of creation is not only about cosmic origins but also directs us to the ongoing action and purposes of the Creator.

See also PROVIDENCE.

Z. Hayes, *The Gift of Being: A Theology of Creation* (Liturgical Press, 2001).
J. P. Mackey, *Christianity and Creation* (Continuum, 2006).
G. May, *Creatio ex Nihilo* (T&T Clark, 1994).
J. Polkinghorne, *Science and Creation* (SPCK, 1988).
H. Schwarz, *Creation* (Eerdmans, 2002).
M. Welker, *Creation and Reality* (Fortress Press, 1999).

DAVID A. S. FERGUSSON

CREATIONISM Understood as a particular interpretation of the doctrine of CREATION, creationism refers to the belief that all species were created immediately by God rather than arising through evolution from pre-existing species, as taught by the scientific theory of natural selection. Young-Earth Creationists like H. Morris (1918–2006) defend a literal interpretation of Genesis as providing an accurate account of life's origins, arguing that all species were created simultaneously no more than 10,000 years ago. Old-Earth Creationists like P. Johnson (b. 1940) do not take a definite position on the age of the earth and do not object to the idea that the creation of species was sequential rather than completed at one time. Creationist objections to the idea of evolution by natural selection centre on the charge that the theory is incompatible with the Christian doctrine of providence, since it views the emergence of species as a matter of chance rather than the product of deliberate divine action. Young-Earth Creationists supplement this objection with a commitment to the doctrine of biblical inerrancy.

In response to US court decisions ruling that the teaching of creationism in public schools violated the separation of Church and State, creationists began in the late 1960s to characterize their position as 'scientific creationism' or (later) 'creation science', arguing that their claims could be defended on scientific grounds. Most practising scientists have rejected the claim that creation science qualifies as natural science, primarily because it is not regarded by its proponents as falsifiable.

Within the field of theological anthropology, creationism is the belief that every human soul is created immediately by God, either at or soon after physical conception. As such, it is opposed both to the theory that souls pre-existed their bodies (held by Origen and, in modern times, by the Latter-Day Saints) and to the theory of traducianism, according to which the soul is transmitted biologically from parents to children and thus is not separately created by God. Creationism has been the dominant position in the Catholic Church since the time of Peter Lombard (*ca* 1100–60), though never subject to formal definition by the magisterium; it is also the majority position within Reformed theology.

While both traducianism and creationism support the position that human beings are composed of body and soul together over against theories of pre-existence, creationism is not as useful as traducianism in accounting for the transmission of original sin. At the same time, it is much more effective in affirming the essentially spiritual (i.e., non-material) character of the soul. The Reformed theologian F. Turretin (1623–87) defended creationism on the grounds that the unity of the human race required that all human beings must share the ontology of Adam. Thus, God created Adam by directly infusing a soul into pre-existing matter (Gen. 2:7), and God must form Adam's descendants in like manner (*IET* 5.13.3). Certain biblical texts (e.g., Eccl. 12:7; Isa. 57:16; Zech. 12:1) are also cited by proponents as supportive of creationism.

Ian A. McFarland

Creeds In a number of documents from the late fourth century we find a story that the apostles gathered together as they were about to take leave of each other and set out to convert the world. In order to protect them from teaching different doctrines in different places, the Holy Spirit fills them and they draw up a short definition of Christian belief, a creed (named after the first word in Latin, *credo* – 'I believe'). Often this original creed is taken to be that which we still know as the 'Apostles' Creed'. In one version each of the apostles speaks a different phrase of the creed, thus providing the basis for the idea that the creed contains twelve 'articles' of faith (from the Latin *articulus* or joint). The story is a legend: in a more primitive form the Apostles' Creed is first cited in 390, and Greek medieval theologians were indignant when Latin theologians claimed its apostolic authorship, as they had never heard of it.

The origins of creeds lie in the NT. From its inception Christians were concerned with the passing on of a formed tradition of belief. Jude 3 speaks of 'the faith once for all entrusted to the saints' and many other texts speak of a 'deposit' of faith or a 'confession' (1 Tim. 6:20; 2 Tim. 1:14; Heb. 3:1; 4:14; 10:23). Hebrews 6 also seems to speak of a stage of instruction in Christian belief. Similarly, Paul already speaks of traditions of belief passed down to new Christians (2 Thess. 2:15; Rom. 6:17; 1 Cor. 11:23; 15:3). We are uncertain about the precise content of this early teaching, although fairly convincing suppositions have been offered. We also possess fragmentary evidence of early formulae that could be committed to memory. The most well known is 'Jesus is Lord' (e.g., 1 Cor. 12:3; Rom. 10:9; Phil. 2:11), which may well be an allusion to a phrase used in or said at baptism (cf. Acts 8:16; 19:5; 1 Cor. 6:11). We also find evidence elsewhere in the NT that early Christians treated 'Jesus is the Christ' and 'Jesus is the Son of God' as confessional statements (Mark 3:11; 5:7; 1 John 2:22; Acts 8:37, the latter being especially good evidence for the link between these expressions and baptism).

Alongside these very brief expressions, we find some longer summaries of faith, especially at 1 Corinthians 15:3 (cf. Rom. 1:3–5; 2 Tim. 2:8; 1 Pet. 3:18–22). These formulae focus on narrating the achievements of Christ, others speak also of the Father and Christ (especially 1 Cor. 8:6 and 1 Tim. 2:5). There are in fact many passages which offer a parallel joining of Father and Son, some of which may be actual formulae, while others merely show the common practice of summarizing Christian belief in this way (e.g., 1 Tim. 6:13; 2 Tim. 4:1; Rom. 8:11; 2 Cor 4:14; 1 Pet. 1:21). These statements are mostly binitarian in structure, focused on God/Father and Christ/Son and the relationship between these two. There are also a number of Trinitarian creedal statements: both 2 Corinthians 13:14 and Matthew 28:19 offer formulae that link Father, Son, and

Spirit. With these should be joined a number of Pauline texts which link the three (e.g., 1 Cor. 12:4; 2 Cor. 1:21). The same style of formulae can be found outside the Pauline corpus (e.g., 1 Pet. 1:2). None of these formulae demonstrate that there was one common form of words in the earliest generations of Christianity: they all demonstrate the existence of a few common styles of summarizing belief and of handing on belief through preaching or catechesis.

The fragmentary evidence we possess from the second and third centuries includes creedal-type summaries that are Trinitarian in formulation, some that are binitarian, and others that seem to focus only on summarizing the story of Christ. There does not seem to be clear evidence that we can speak of a gradual evolution from the simple to the more complex forms: the diversity seen in the NT continues to be reflected. At the same time, the assumption that creeds simply grew or became fixed in response to battles over 'ORTHODOXY' and 'HERESY' should be avoided. Often formulae that received emphasis because of a particular doctrinal debate were already locally present. Nevertheless, and for a variety of reasons, during the period between 200 and 400 phrasing and formulae come gradually to be fixed.

It seems most appropriate to speak of three different types of creedal summary from the late second into the third century. First, there are sets of baptismal questions asked of candidates for baptism during the baptism ceremony itself. These were Trinitarian in form, asking first about belief in the Father, then about belief in the Son, and finally about belief in the Spirit. The very word *symbolum*, used later in Latin to designate the creed, seems first to have been used to refer to these questions.

Second, we have some evidence for confessions (most frequently binitarian or focusing solely upon Christ) that seem to have formed the basis for catechetical teaching. It is these that probably formed the basis for the later, formal creeds that emerged during the fourth century. In the third century, and possibly in Rome, we can first speak of declaratory creeds, designed to be learnt by candidates for baptism and then repeated back. It has been suggested that the growth of the Church, especially in the context of continuing tensions between the 'great' Church and other sects, prompted the need for a clear short form of words by which catechumens could indicate that they had learnt the basic core of Christian faith. These creeds also thus have a liturgical function, but one that arose subsequently to the baptismal questions. A similar process by which declaratory creeds gradually emerged from catechetical structures seems to have occurred in the eastern provinces, although we do not know much about it: claims that eastern creeds are dependent on an early version of the old Roman creed or upon a lost archetype have received little modern support. J. N. D. Kelly (1909–97) argued for the simple solution to the broad similarities in structure between eastern and western creeds that all declaratory creeds take their form from the threefold baptismal act (and the dominical command of Matt. 28:19) even if they are not simply unified versions of those questions. In this case similarity and local variety would be expected. Both my first and second types, then, have a clear liturgical origin and function.

Third, we find the 'RULE OF FAITH' or 'rule of truth'. A number of writers in the second and third centuries, such as IRENAEUS, TERTULLIAN, and ORIGEN, speak of this and offer short accounts of its contents. The texts they offer follow a standard threefold form but are never identical. The 'rule' seems to indicate the basic content of faith which is taken to be the content, or, for Irenaeus, the *hypothesis* (plot), of SCRIPTURE and Christian teaching. Given that a number of writers speak of this rule as being received at baptism, it seems likely that it is also a basic summary of the faith taught in CATECHESIS. The 'rule' thus precedes declaratory creeds proper. During the fourth century writers still occasionally speak of the 'rule of faith' and often mean by it the creed or the basic structure of Christian teaching.

During the second and third centuries there does not appear to have been a fixed form of words in any of these three cases. It may even be that we should not imagine local churches each possessing one local creed until the third century; since a variety of formulae may have been in use in any one location. As with the NT evidence, this does not mean that we can speak of immense plurality in belief, but we should not assume that clarity about the central core of belief means adherence to only one mode of expressing that faith. It is perhaps in the case of the baptismal interrogations that the actual phrasing became most quickly settled.

In the fourth century significant developments occurred. The early stages of the fourth-century Trinitarian controversies saw opponents quoting creeds or quasi-creedal summaries at each other. At the Council of NICAEA a short creed was drawn up for the purposes of anathematizing Arius. This move had some precedent: in 268 a group of bishops had written a long statement of faith and asked Paul of Samosata (*ca* 200–*ca* 275), who was under suspicion of heresy, to sign. A similar procedure was followed in the spring of 325 by a council preparatory to Nicaea. Nevertheless, Nicaea's creed is shorter and clearly a baptismal creed in form. Its precise origins have been the subject of much debate: it seems most likely to be a local creed from a Syrian or Palestinian context into which the famous Nicene phrases have been added. It was not clear to anyone present that this was a universal form of words or that it would have liturgical usage. Indeed, we find no mention of Nicaea's creed for more than fifteen years after the council: while there are some mention of Nicaea's judgements and one or two references to the key term *homoousios*, it was only in the 350s that the overt defence of the creed itself grew. This happened partly in response to attempts to impose an alternative creed. In this context Nicaea's creed appeared to be an obvious rallying point.

The form of the Nicene Creed known to most modern Christians is that drawn up by the Council of Constantinople in 381. The Council's members no doubt thought that they were not changing and could not change the faith itself, but they did feel able to make some minor changes and one significant addition to the creed. The clauses about the Spirit that we know today were added, possibly under the guidance of Gregory of Nyssa (see Cappadocian Fathers). Unfortunately we know little about the council itself, and its creed is not quoted in full until the Council of Chalcedon in 451. Already during the fifth century the principle that the content of the faith was unchangeable was combined with a growing perception that the creed was now fixed and irreformable (along with the decisions of major councils).

The creed of Nicaea (325) was not used liturgically even by its strong defenders in the second half of the fourth century. Local creeds continued in use, sometimes being supplemented with Nicene phrases, or by being interpreted as meaning what Nicaea said. The creed was, however, regularly affirmed by provincial councils and was a clear marker of ecclesial allegiance for bishops. By the end of the fourth century there thus emerges a new form of creed that had no immediate liturgical usage but which served as a marker of orthodoxy for bishops.

The creed of Constantinople (381) does seem to have been used in the baptismal liturgy fairly quickly in the region of Constantinople and its use spread widely through the East in the subsequent century. The same creed seems also to have been used in the Eucharistic liturgy from the end of the fifth century in the East and over following centuries in the West. In the West the final form of the Apostles' Creed emerged from earlier versions of the old Roman creed and by the Middle Ages had supplanted the creed of Constantinople in the baptismal liturgy following its (re)adoption in the liturgy at Rome itself. This new rise to prominence accounts for its importance not only in medieval Catholicism but also for the Lutheran and Reformed confessions in the sixteenth century. To be sure, some more radical Reformers rejected all formal creeds as inconsistent with the principle of *Sola Scriptura* and thus an unnecessary and illegitimate burden upon the conscience of the believer. This line of criticism has found echoes throughout the modern period (e.g., among advocates of Unitarianism and Restorationism). Nevertheless, that both the Apostles' and the Nicene Creeds (as well as the so-called Athanasian Creed) were upheld by so many on both sides in the upheavals of the sixteenth century has meant that they continue to constitute a central part of the Church's ecumenical heritage.

J. N. D. Kelly, *Early Christian Creeds*, 3rd edn (Longman, 1972).

J. Pelikan, *Credo: Historical and Theological Guide to Creeds* (Yale University Press, 2005).

F. M. Young, *The Making of the Creeds* (SCM, 1991).

Lewis Ayres

Cross and Crucifixion When Paul preached Christ crucified, he recognized it as utter 'foolishness' and 'a stumbling block' (1 Cor. 1:18, 23) for those who heard his message. The Hellenistic world viewed gods as eternal and unchanging, unaffected by the mortal world. To claim that a crucified man was also divine was offensive. Crucifixions were reserved for rebellious slaves, criminals, and enemies of the State. Known as the cruellest method of execution, it deliberately delayed death until maximum torture could be inflicted. For the divine to suffer such indignity was madness. For the Jews of Jesus' day, a crucified Messiah contradicted Deuteronomy 21:23, where a curse is laid on anyone hanged from a tree. Both Paul and the Gospel writers, however, emphasized that Jesus' life, crucifixion, and resurrection represented a fulfilment of Jewish Scriptures (cf. Mark 10:32–4; Matt. 20:17–19; Luke 24:44–7).

Yet the question of the offence associated with the cross emerges in other forms, as the Gospels' testimony to Jesus' arrest, trial, and condemnation by Jewish religious authorities led to centuries of Christian supersessionism. Even though Roman authorities crucify him, scriptural presentations of Jewish opposition to Jesus prompted Christians to claim that the Jews killed Christ. According to Christian Scripture, three days later Jesus rises from the dead, and commissions his followers to spread the gospel message. In the first two centuries after Jesus' death, Christians avoided public use of the cross out of concern for persecution. By the era of Constantine I (*ca* 275–337), the cross gained acceptance as the primary symbol of Christian faith, both because Christians ritually signed the cross with one another, and because Constantine himself had claimed it a symbol of victory. In a stunning example of symbolic reversal, the crucifixion of Jesus ceased to represent the deadly politics of Rome, standing instead for the empire's military victory over its enemies.

Though the cross has occupied a central place in Christian thought from that time, the explanation of how the crucifixion relates to Christ as saviour of the world has proven a persistent problem. Patristic theologians set forth what G. Aulén (1879–1978) called the *Christus Victor* theory, understanding the world as locked in a cosmic battle of good versus evil. The Devil defeats Christ in the crucifixion, but God triumphs over evil by raising Christ from the dead. The crucifixion of Jesus itself is not what saves; victory over sin and death comes in the movement from crucifixion to resurrection. The Middle Ages put the cross more at the centre of God's saving work. Using Latin forensic categories, Anselm of Canterbury portrayed God as a feudal lord dishonoured by human sin. The sinfulness is so great that no human can restore God's honour; only God becoming human will accomplish that feat. Jesus' obedience to God's will leads him to the cross, and God rewards his obedience. Because Jesus has no need for a reward, it is passed along to the rest of humanity. Anselm's view of Christ's death drew criticism from his contemporary, P. Abelard (1079–1142), who insisted that only a vindictive God demands the death of his own Son. He instead proposed that Christ's sacrificial love for others leads to the crucifixion, and this gift of love generates the response of love in his followers, working salvation through a subjective change in the human heart.

Even though the Church has not officially endorsed one atonement theory, it is nevertheless Anselm's focus on the cross that dominates Christian thinking about salvation. The Middle Ages also usher in the Crusades (from the eleventh to the fifteenth century), where Christians took up arms under the sign of the cross to convert by force (or kill) Muslims and Jews, and to liberate Jerusalem from Muslim rule. 'God wills it!' cried Pope Urban II (r. 1088–99), and thousands signed up to fight. Additionally, medieval Passion plays focused on the crucifixion and the Jews who called for Jesus' death. Thus an offence remained, but it was an offence that meant harm to Jewish lives. The Reformation theology of M. Luther centred on the crucifixion (see *Theologia crucis*), emphasizing the existential dimension of individual Christian responsibility – due to sin – for Christ's suffering while paradoxically also raging against Jews for killing Christ. The Europeans who colonized the Americas and Africa often used religious justification for their actions, claiming the indigenous people were redeemed by the blood of Jesus' death but did not know it yet. Slavery, too, was justified by arguing that the suffering of Jesus was greater than the suffering of slaves; therefore slaves should accept their lot.

Though the cross in this way remained prominent in situations of Christian domination over others, much theology during the modern period downplayed the soteriological significance of the cross. Theologians like A. Ritschl (1822–89) focused on Jesus as a moral exemplar for modern Christians, rather than as a crucified saviour. Arguably the most scornful rejection of the cross came from nineteenth-century thinker F. Nietzsche, who insisted that Christianity's embrace of the crucifixion as theologically meaningful valorizes weakness and contradicts the laws of evolution and humanity's will to power. A will to power unlike any the world had seen came in the twentieth century through the Holocaust, an extermination attempt not possible without the history of Christian anti-Judaism and its links to the cross.

Late in the twentieth century, feminist theologians joined in critiquing major theories of atonement. Feminists speak not only of scandal but also of the danger associated with claiming the crucifixion of Jesus is somehow salvific, since it often raises innocent suffering as a model to emulate (see Feminist Theology). Latin American liberation theologians refer to the Third World poor as 'the crucified people' who help bring about salvation through protest against oppressive structures (see Liberation Theology). Other contemporary theologians argue that the crucifixion exposes the world of violence for what it is, including the offensive acts perpetuated by Christians in the name of Christ. Contemporary attempts to seek meaning in the crucifixion must proclaim that the offence of the crucifixion is not a weapon to be used against others. Rather it is the proclamation that in the crucifixion Christ stands with all the violated and crucified of the world. When the whole story is told, Christ's brutal death opens to his followers, through the resurrection, a new future of reconciliation for a new humanity and a new creation.

See also Atonement.

G. Aulén, *Christus Victor* (Macmillan, 1951 [1931]).

J. Carroll, *Constantine's Sword: The Church and the Jews* (Houghton Mifflin, 2001).

M. Hengel, *Crucifixion in the Ancient World and the Folly of the Message of the Cross* (Fortress Press, 1977).

Deanna Thompson

Cyril of Alexandria Bishop and leading figure in the development of classical Christology, Cyril of Alexandria (*ca* 375–444) was a theologian in the tradition of Athanasius and the chief opponent of Nestorius of Constantinople (*ca* 385–*ca* 450) in the fifth-century Christological controversy that occasioned the Council of Ephesus. He is honoured as a saint both by those Churches that adhere to the Christology of the Council of Chalcedon and by the non-Chalcedonian Oriental Orthodox Churches.

In 412 Cyril succeeded his powerful uncle Theophilus as bishop of Alexandria. The early years of his episcopacy were marred by violent clashes between Christians and other groups, especially pagans and Jews. The murder of the pagan philosopher Hypatia (*ca* 360–415) is the most infamous of the clashes.

Cyril's corpus contains theological treatises, personal correspondence, circulars, and commentaries. Prominent among Cyril's earlier texts are commentaries on a large portion of Scripture, including the Pentateuch, Isaiah, the twelve minor prophets, and the Gospel of John, among many others. He also wrote several treatises articulating a Trinitarian theology against Arianism (see Arian Controversy), including his *Thesaurus* and *On the Trinity*.

The emergence of the Christological controversy altered the direction of Cyril's writing, consuming his attention until his death. In 428 Nestorius rejected *Theotokos*, the 'Bearer of God', as a proper appellation for the Virgin Mary. Upon hearing of this denial, Cyril wrote to Nestorius challenging his rejection of a well-established tradition. For Cyril, the term was a way to protect the FAITH from Arian corruption, since to call Mary 'Bearer of God' would enshrine the Christian confession that Jesus was nothing less than God incarnate. Eventually Cyril wrote to Nestorius with a collection of twelve ANATHEMAS that the latter deemed Apollinarian (see APOLLINARIANISM). The controversy led to the Council of Ephesus, at which Nestorius was condemned.

Following Ephesus, Cyril and John of Antioch (d. 441) agreed on a common expression of Christology in the *Formulary of Reunion*, which was a departure from much of the language Cyril had used initially. Early in the Christological controversy Cyril had preferred the phrase 'one nature of God the Word incarnate' to articulate Christ's reality. But in the *Formulary* Cyril adopted the formula 'one person from two natures'. Some of Cyril's followers considered this an abandonment of his earlier Christology, but Cyril defended the change in language, particularly in his two *Letters to Succensus*.

Cyril understood 'nature' (Greek *physis*) to be the set of defining characteristics or properties that distinguish one type of being from another. By contrast, the term 'person' (Greek *HYPOSTASIS*) was an individual representative of that type of being possessing a particular nature. For Cyril, then, the eternal Son of God possessed a divine nature, or the set of properties that make the Son God; and in the INCARNATION the Son added to himself a second set of properties, which defines a human being. The same Son who from eternity was God (and therefore possessor of a divine nature) had now in addition become a human being (as the possessor of a human nature). This formula allowed Cyril to maintain his single-subject Christology, in which the Son of God is the only subject of the experiences of Jesus Christ, including his birth and death.

See also MIAPHYSITISM; NESTORIANISM.

H. van Loon, *The Dyophysite Christology of Cyril of Alexandria* (Brill, 2009).

S. A. McKinion, *Words, Imagery and the Mystery of Christ* (Brill, 2000).

STEVEN A. MCKINION

DALIT THEOLOGY Dalits (literally meaning 'broken' or 'crushed ones') refer to the 180 to 200 million outcaste people in India. Cast out of human society and yet appropriated as slaves of the dominant Hindu caste communities, they were traditionally treated as untouchable and unapproachable because of their polluted status in the eyes of the Hindu caste communities. Even though the practice of untouchability was outlawed and a provision of reservation (affirmative action) was introduced through the Indian Constitution in 1950, Dalits continue to suffer under the cumulative effects of colossal economic marginalization and multi-layered social oppression brought on by the three millennia-old hierarchical, discriminatory, and comprehensive caste system.

D

In this historical context Dalit theology emerged in the 1980s as a liberation strand of Indian contextual thinking, reflecting upon the ongoing Christian mission of resisting oppression and advancing freedom, with special reference to the 'broken people'. Dalit theology developed in dialogue with LIBERATION THEOLOGY in Latin America and BLACK THEOLOGY in the USA. It also reflects a long history of Indian Christian attempts to inculturate the message of Christianity into the social, cultural, and historical contexts of South Asia (INCULTURATION). These theological currents aided in its oppositional stance towards forms of missionary and western theology that tended to be highly individualistic and calculatingly ahistorical.

Dalit theology correlates the 'pain-pathos' of those marginalized by the scars of untouchability with the HOPE of the Christian GOSPEL that encompasses and empowers them on a path towards overcoming the spirit of brokenness and celebrating the promise of new life in Jesus Christ. It arises out of the historical consciousness of Dalit communities, but is sustained by the experience that the God who sought all human beings in Jesus Christ is close at hand to free and liberate such 'crushed ones' into life in all its fullness. As with other theologies of liberation, Dalit theology is integrally related to the praxis of everyday living. Thus, Dalit theology consciously entwines the promise of abundant life with the power of Jesus Christ in an ongoing struggle against a world of death and destruction. It offers needed rationale and energy for sustaining liberation praxis as envisioned and legitimated by Dalit-framed worlds and God-injected words and actions of broken peoples on their journey towards wholeness.

The conceptual conundrum between articulating a need for methodological exclusiveness and conceding an obligation for theological inclusiveness provides an opportunity for Dalit theology to be both authentic to its own historical consciousness and resourceful to Christian theology as a whole. Three features of Dalit theology may be highlighted:

(1) *A theology of rejection and refutation.* Dalit theology seeks to guard itself against becoming co-opted by the homogenizing propensities of dominant theology. A certain kind of exclusivism safeguards the distinctively prophetic potentialities of Dalit theology. As a strategic posture, this exclusivism protects an oppressed community from expressing itself before God and other human beings in a mode and material that mimics dominant power groupings. Instead, Dalits endeavour to become outsiders, non-Hindus, outcaste, heterodox, and Christian defectors from traditional truth configurations.

(2) *A theology of aspiration and self-narration.* Even though Dalit theology is a counter-theology, it also nourishes the self-expressive character of the Dalit community. Dalits imaginatively utilize drums, dances, oral narratives, paintings, and sculptures to register and recall their sustaining and healing experience with the Divine, seeking continuity between Christianity and features of their own culture that antedate their encounter with the Church. These features make it possible to characterize Dalit theology as collective and comprehensive in scope, integrally humanizing, profusely (even if naively) dependent on God for help and succour, deeply rooted in the liberative teaching and practice of Jesus (understood either as a Dalit himself or as wholly Dalit-identified), organically connected with the natural world, and audaciously hopeful that life before death is both a gift from God and a right for all peoples.

(3) *A theology of negotiation for liberation of all creation.* Because of the inter-relatedness of human living and the inclusive character of the Christian gospel, Dalit theologians recognize that they need to be open and flexible in order to engage their context in a theologically responsible way. The diligent recovery and conscious integration of the distinctive identity of Dalit communities, along with a commitment to work with all other religious visions for the wellbeing of the entire human community, is a new-found challenge for Dalit theology. Reconciliation from below for the sake of all represents a twenty-first-century turn in Dalit theology and liberation praxis.

S. Clarke, *Dalits and Christianity: Subaltern Religion and Liberation Theology in India* (Oxford University Press, 1998).

V. Devasahayam, ed., *Frontiers of Dalit Theology* (ISPCK/GURUKUL, 1997).
A. P. Nirmal, ed., *A Reader in Dalit Theology* (GURUKUL, 1991).
M. E. Prabhakar, ed., *Towards a Dalit Theology* (ISPCK, 1988).

SATHIANATHAN CLARKE

DAMNATION Damnation is the state of eternal exclusion from God's presence, meted out by God to rational creatures in punishment for SIN. In traditional Christian theology (following biblical passages like Matt. 25:41–3), it is understood to be the irrevocable fate of the DEVIL and all his ANGELS (viz., demons), and of all human beings who die with their sins unforgiven. Christians have generally conceived damnation as a state of continuous and extreme torment (see HELL), in line with biblical language that describes the fate of the damned in terms of burning (Mark 9:48; Luke 16:23–4; Rev. 20:10, 14–15; 21:8). This agony is experienced by demons from the moment of their rebellion and FALL, and by reprobate human beings from the time of their death. Even as it is usually assumed that the blessedness of human beings who are saved will be augmented after the RESURRECTION of their bodies at the Last Judgement, so the same process will increase the sufferings of the damned.

This traditional picture of damnation has been challenged on the grounds that basic Christian convictions regarding God's identity as loving Creator are incompatible with the idea of God subjecting any creature to unending torment. Drawing on certain passages in the writings of PAUL in particular, proponents of ANNIHILATIONISM argue that, while the damned are eternally excluded from God's presence, this punishment takes the form of their final destruction rather than endless torture. Arguing that even this perspective is inconsistent with God's character, defenders of UNIVERSALISM insist that God will eventually restore all rational creatures to communion with God. Both these alternatives, however, remain minority views among Christians.

See also ESCHATOLOGY.

IAN A. MCFARLAND

DARWINISM: see EVOLUTION.

DE LUBAC, HENRI French Jesuit Henri de Lubac (1896–1991) was a leading pioneer of the 'return to the sources' (*ressourcement*) that underpinned VATICAN COUNCIL II's theological renewal. He entered the Society of Jesus in 1913, was ordained priest in 1927, and from 1929 taught fundamental theology at the Catholic University of Lyons. Influenced by M. Blondel (1861–1949) and P. Rousselot (1879–1915), he studied the relationship between nature and the supernatural, concerned that the Scholastic theory of 'pure nature' had severed the fundamental link between the two and consequently separated the Church from the world. He was convinced that the theory was a distortion of the authentic teaching of IRENAEUS, AUGUSTINE, and T. AQUINAS, arguing that 'the vision of God is a free gift, and yet the desire for it is at the very root of every soul' (*Cath.* 327). His fuller study, *Surnaturel* (1946) was thought (incorrectly) to have been criticized by Pope Pius XII (r. 1939–58) in *Humani generis* (1950), and de Lubac endured ten years of internal exile before being appointed to advise in the preparations for Vatican II, where his ideas became fundamental for the constitution *Gaudium et Spes* (1965), on the Church in the modern world.

De Lubac and J. Daniélou (1905–74) were founding editors of *Sources chrétiennes*, a series now numbering over 500 volumes. From study of the fathers, de Lubac formulated the principle, 'the EUCHARIST makes the Church' (*Corp.* 88), and strongly influenced modern Eucharistic/communion ECCLESIOLOGY. He also wrote on exegesis, most extensively in *Exégèse médiévale* (3 vols., 1959–64). Pope John Paul II (r. 1978–2005) named him a cardinal in 1983.

See also *NOUVELLE THÉOLOGIE*.

PAUL MCPARTLAN

DEATH AND DYING The phrase 'death and dying' is the title of the book by E. Kübler-Ross (1926–2004) that began the modern 'death-awareness movement' in the late 1960s. This movement makes *dying* as human experience its focus, while for most of Christian history, *death* is the eternal and ultimate event, and dying merely preparation for it. This contrast between traditional Christian thought and the modern 'death-and-dying' literature is important.

To speak of death as eternal and ultimate means that for Christians, death is a central theological category and – like SIN and judgement – one with a primarily negative aspect. In contrast to the contemporary movement, death is not conceived as a neutral, natural event. 'Death' in the NT is a cosmic, eschatological concept, pointing towards the final destruction of the old era. It is given a plentitude of meanings. Some of these evoke the death of Jesus, such as PAUL's baptismal theology in Romans 6. The pattern of death-to-life, with the new life promised in Christ, anticipates the general resurrection of the dead. So the claim that 'you have died, and your life is hidden with Christ in God' (Col. 3:3) makes the *now* of Christians a kind of death as well as a heavenly but hidden life. This multivalent use of 'death' relativizes biological death and clearly assumes that 'death' in all its dimensions is a transition into new, 'resurrected' existence. Jesus' own death, as well as those of Stephen and other martyrs, shaped Christian perspectives on death as painful and awful, yet also as the transition to a glorious future state. This understanding of death as followed by RESURRECTION and/or new life here and now is what Christians have traditionally pondered; in contrast, for Kübler-Ross what follows death as a 'natural event' is mourning.

There was no one ancient Christian theology of death. Within the above limits, ancient theologians could work the topic into a variety of perspectives, with more or less dependence upon the prevailing philosophy of their times. For some, the soul's eternal nature meant that death was a transition from a cave to the sunshine, while for others death was God's 'enemy' (cf. 1 Cor. 15:26). The latter view was revived in the twentieth century by G. Aulén (1879–1978) and was claimed to be *the* Christian position by O. Cullmann (1902–99), but it definitely was not the only one. This view personifies 'death' in a way that became a convention: up through the early twentieth century a Christian pastor could title a book of funeral sermons *When Death Speaks*. Today, however, such personification is rarely found in Christian thought.

For ancient theologians the issue of how salvation from sin and death is effected, and how creation and the cosmos itself participates in this, is the central matter. 'Death' was never merely a biological reality. It was thoroughly linked to sin, so that eventually a clear theological motif developed that 'death is punishment for sin', an idea found in Paul (e.g., Rom. 6:23) but elaborated in Latin theology especially by AUGUSTINE. To imagine Adam and Eve as immortal in their pre-sin condition makes death an 'unnatural' and intrusive reality, an idea utterly rejected by the modern death-awareness movement.

In ancient and Orthodox Christianity, Christ's status as cosmic, incarnate Word was emphasized over the human Jesus dying on the cross. Only in the Latin Christian Middle Ages did this latter focus gain ground. Increasingly gruesome verbal and artistic depictions of the crucifixion testify to this trend. When this happened, the dying Jesus became a model for our own death, as seen in the emergence of *Ars Moriendi* handbooks of preparation for death. Because Jesus' death was painful, there is no tendency in these texts to romanticize or minimize the physical, emotional, and spiritual pain of dying. Yet because for us, unlike for Jesus, death is also the time of judgement, preparation for death involved anticipation of God's judgement. So not only are death and the pain of dying a deserved penalty, but at the hour of one's own death (as well as at the universal Last Judgement) one would face God and Christ directly – a prospect replete with terrifying possibilities. The liturgical poem *Dies Irae* by Thomas of Celano (*ca* 1200–*ca* 1260) exemplifies this. Even the devout Christian will face the threat of wrath and universal destruction; 'death and nature' will be overwhelmed by the visible and awesome power of God. Contemporary death-and-dying writers interested in preparation for death include 'life review' as a possibility, but never focus on anticipation of immediate or eschatological judgement by God. On the other hand, some contemporary Christians see the awful possibilities of Judgement Day are reserved only for others, while believers are kept safe and saved and even 'raptured' away from the effects of divine wrath (see RAPTURE). Even for those (like K. RAHNER) who want to preserve some of the intentions behind the traditional idea of death as punishment for sin and occasion for judgement, more 'juridical' imagery is discarded in return for an existential focus on 'death's darkness'.

Yet death as positive transition into eternal life never vanished as a Christian hope. Use of PILGRIMAGE as a metaphor for life-into-death expresses this. Life is a journey, for the pious person a journey towards the goal of the Celestial City, as seen in John Bunyan's (1628–88) classic allegory *The Pilgrim's Progress* (1678). Here, this world is slated for destruction, and Christian life should be about leaving it behind in progress towards the sacred city. Biological death is only one of an enormous series of dangers and challenges in this process, and Bunyan's pilgrims cross the river of death in various spiritual states (fearful, brave, ignorantly conceited) that do not necessarily correspond to their ultimate fates. Here, Bunyan as pastor was aware that the experience of dying was not an absolute barometer for anyone's total spiritual condition. The 'life as pilgrimage' theme is absent from contemporary death-and-dying literature, since it assumes an 'otherworldly' goal that seems inevitably to devalue this life.

Bunyan had the restraint to be sparse in his description of the Celestial City, and typically traditional writers kept within the symbolic descriptions of the biblical book of Revelation. In the early nineteenth century, however, approaches to HEAVEN shifted so that human ties were not cut off or relativized by death, but continued in some fashion after it. This was the age of spectacular mourning for Western Europeans, and it became part of Christian thinking about death to consider partings as temporary, pending a family reunion in heaven. In order for this to happen, the focus on judgement had to be minimized or excluded, and death as a transition became a time for bereavement here on earth. Within this world view, death is not an Enemy, but a gentle transition, permitting family ties to continue.

When twentieth-century theologians wrote against this kind of domestic piety, they did not write primarily out of concern for developing a theology of death. They wanted to turn Christian attention towards social and political change, and to respond to critics of religious otherworldliness like K. Marx (1818–83). Personal death seemed too small-scale a topic, and even when major theologians such as E. Brunner (1889–1966) wrote about it, the focus was on the huge scope of eschatology, salvation, and history. This led to thoughtful Christian engagement with major historical events and secular ideologies, but it also led to Christian thought losing its moorings in pastoral care for the sick and dying, or preaching at funerals. This resulted in a vacancy, which the death-awareness movement quietly filled.

Today, if one wants to learn what Christians are saying about death and dying, the bulk of pastoral-care writings are shaped much less by traditional theological concerns than by the work of Kübler-Ross and her followers. Dealing with one's own impending death is modelled on 'loss', with major attention given to mourners. A book by a Christian pastoral-care expert entitled *Surviving Death* focuses on these two situations exclusively: no mention of any afterlife, positive or negative, can be found in its pages. Funeral sermons have now become 'preaching to mourners', another title that indicates this shift away from traditional topics. Moreover, the medicalization of death means that much Christian reflection on dying focuses on bioethics, hospice and end-of-life care: all very important, but not directly connected to traditional theological themes surrounding death.

Obviously, it is easy to bemoan this split between current pastoral and theological concerns on the one hand, and more traditional resources (including even mid-twentieth-century theologians like Brunner). The problem seems to be that the earlier eras produced and repeated ideas that simply do not serve well as 'resources' unless massively reinterpreted. The major obstacles to such appropriation are the 'otherworldly' focus of traditional Christian thought, and the heavy use of 'juridical' (legal/judgement) language. Even with continued high levels of belief in some form of afterlife, a model such as *Pilgrim's Progress* seems inimical to the basic goodness of creation, a central Christian rediscovery of our era. Moreover, most systematic theologians have already replaced juridical by existential and/or sacramental visions of ultimate, divine reality when dealing with other issues. The focus on Jesus' dying by torture may still be important and powerful enough to help Christians rethink our own dying and death, especially when his very human confusion and pain are stressed over against theologies of cosmic triumph. For many Christians in western cultures, however, this 'unnatural' death is not helpful to sort through their own quest for how a 'good death' should be pursued in the midst of a high-tech medical setting.

Meanwhile, some themes from the past do continue at a popular level that it is easy to scorn or ignore. Family reunions in the afterlife make no appearance in Brunner or Rahner, yet they are the subject of many greeting-card messages, and of newspaper obituary letters to the dead from family members (e.g., 'Happy Fiftieth Wedding Anniversary to Mom and Pop in Heaven'). This, along with popular fascination with near-death experiences, suggests that Christian repudiation of 'otherworldliness' is only part of the story, even if one finds such imagery unconvincing. Ironically, the death-awareness movement is now more receptive to such possibilities than are many Christian pastors and preachers, who do not want to encourage or collude in denial. How to restore or revision such imagery without repeating the mistaken emphases of the past is an important challenge.

See also ESCHATOLOGY; HEAVEN.

E. Brunner, *Eternal Hope* (Westminster Press, 1954).
E. Kübler-Ross, *On Death and Dying* (Simon & Schuster, 1969).
A. Lewis, *Between Cross and Resurrection* (Eerdmans, 2001).
J. Pelikan, *The Shape of Death: Life, Death and Immortality in the Early Fathers* (Macmillan, 1961).
K. Rahner, *On the Theology of Death* (Herder, 1961).

LUCY BREGMAN

DEATH OF GOD THEOLOGY In the late nineteenth century, F. NIETZSCHE proclaimed that 'God is dead' as a means of affirming that the concept of God no longer had a meaningful role to play in human self-understanding. Writing half a century later, D. BONHOEFFER, reacting against religious appeals to God's sovereignty as an excuse for avoiding responsibility in and for the world, suggested the possibility of a 'non-religious' interpretation of Christianity, in which the experience of God's absence becomes the basis for responsible engagement with the world. In the 1960s a number of theologians, including T. Altizer (b. 1927), P. van Buren (1924–98), and W. Hamilton (b. 1924), reflected more systematically on the possibility of maintaining Christian identity apart from belief in the existence of a transcendent God. The results were popularly termed 'death of God theology'.

The specific proposals of the figures associated with the 'death of God' movement were quite varied. Altizer accepted the traditional claim that the transcendent God took flesh in Jesus (see INCARNATION), but argued that this God's death on the CROSS meant that thereafter the sacred is found only in the world. By contrast, Hamilton and van Buren did not identify Jesus' crucifixion as the *locus* of God's death: their claim that 'God is dead' simply referred to the implausibility of traditional ideas of God in a modern context.

The 'death of God' movement drew attention to how frequently God is reduced to a projection: a distant, dominating figure rooted in human self-alienation and thus inimical to the GOSPEL message of 'God with us' (Matt. 1:23; cf. 28:20). Critics, however, charged that the rejection of any distinction between God and the world, though rooted in a desire to avoid a false understanding of God, was incapable of avoiding an equally idolatrous identification of the sacred with human self-consciousness. Others noted that Jesus' own practice of prayer to God, as well as the relationship between God and the world posited in traditional Christian accounts of CREATION and PROVIDENCE, suggested that incarnation and transcendence were not the mutually exclusive alternatives that the 'death of God' theologians supposed.

See also POST-CHRISTIAN THEOLOGY.

T. Altizer and W. Hamilton, *Radical Theology and the Death of God* (Bobbs-Merrill, 1966).

J. B. Cobb, Jr, ed., *The Theology of Altizer: Critique and Response* (Westminster Press, 1970).

IAN A. MCFARLAND

DECALOGUE: see COMMANDMENTS, TEN.

DECONSTRUCTION 'Deconstruction' refers to a strategy of philosophical critique often linked with 'postmodernism' and primarily associated with French philosopher J. Derrida (1935–2004). The term was introduced by Derrida in 1967 to describe his approach to the history of philosophy; unfortunately, the term is often employed as a synonym for critique or 'dismantling'. But for Derrida the term has a fundamentally *positive* meaning.

Deconstruction attends to the competing trajectories within a text or corpus of writings, showing the way in which a text often 'undoes' itself because of this internal tension. It is for this reason that Derrida asserts that deconstruction is not a 'method' or something that we 'do' to texts; rather, texts deconstruct themselves. According to Derrida, this is because texts attempt to exclude what they assume; they feed off of that which they claim to exclude. For instance, in his reading of Plato's understanding of writing in the *Phaedrus* ('Plato's Pharmacy', 1972), Derrida observes that Plato (*ca* 430–*ca* 345 BC) values speech over writing by construing speech as a realm of immediate presence, whereas writing is characterized by absence, since the author does not usually attend the text. But Derrida then goes on to show that the same 'absence' also characterizes speech. So the binary oppositions that Plato wants to make (presence/absence, speech/writing) cannot be so distinguished and dispatched.

Derrida's philosophical framework is derived from PHENOMENOLOGY, and at root his work is a claim about language. Famously, Derrida claims that 'there is nothing outside of the text' (*Gram.* 178). However, this has often been misunderstood. Derrida does not mean to deny that texts have referents; thus deconstruction should not be understood as a kind of linguistic IDEALISM. Derrida later clarified this, saying, 'there is nothing outside of context' (*Lim.* 136). Our access to the world beyond texts is always mediated by 'textuality'. 'Textuality', for Derrida, refers broadly to the system of signs and interpretation by which we navigate our existence in the world. Because these 'signs' are subject to a diverse array of interpretations, deconstruction suggests that there is a certain 'play' to texts and their meaning which cannot be pinned down by a simplistic appeal to authorial intent (though Derrida does not deny a limited role for authorial intent). While deconstruction is often understood as an 'anything-goes' approach to interpretation, Derrida himself explicitly rejects such a notion; however, some of his American heirs tend to foster this notion by their practice.

Deconstruction has had a significant impact on theology: a first wave can be found in the 'a/theology' of M. C. Taylor (b. 1945) who construed Derrida's work in the primarily Nietzschean terms of 'the death of God' (see NIETZSCHE). A second, more positive, appropriation of deconstruction for religion is found in the work of J. Caputo (b. 1940). However, this deconstructive 'religion' is evacuated of any determinate content and thus does not, properly speaking, have a 'theology'. A third approach is beginning to emerge which sees deconstruction as helpfully describing the conditions of finitude, and thus able to be incorporated into a theology of CREATION and INCARNATION.

J. D. Caputo, *The Prayers and Tears of Jacques Derrida* (Indiana University Press, 1997).

K. Hart, *The Trespass of the Sign: Deconstruction, Theology, and Philosophy*, 2nd edn (Fordham University Press, 2000).

JAMES K. A. SMITH

DECREES, DIVINE: see INFRALAPSARIANISM AND SUPRALAPSARIANISM.

DEIFICATION Deification, also termed 'divinization' or 'theosis', has become the subject of intensive study. Until the mid-twentieth century it was regarded as an esoteric topic peculiar to ORTHODOX THEOLOGY. A change of perspective began with the publication of *The Divinization of the Christian According to the Greek Fathers* (1938), a comprehensive survey by J. Gross (1913–?) of the Greek patristic material on divinization which established its mainstream character. This was followed by V. Lossky's (1903–58) classic *The Mystical Theology of the Eastern Church* (1944) and later by J. Meyendorff's (1926–92) *A Study of Gregory Palamas* (1959). These books, combined with the reissuing of the Greek *PHILOKALIA* in five volumes from 1957 to 1963, stimulated a renewal of interest in deification in the Orthodox world. One consequence of this was that western theologians too began to see in deification a possible enrichment of their own theology.

Theosis is not a straightforward concept. It refers first to a broad theological theme concerning the divine ECONOMY, a theme encapsulated in the so-called 'exchange formula': the Word 'was made human that we might be made divine' (Athanasius, *Inc.* 54). It refers also to a cluster of spiritual teachings: the incorporation of the believer through BAPTISM and the EUCHARIST into the new humanity hypostasized by Christ (see INCARNATION), the ascent of the SOUL through the ascetic life from the image to the likeness of God (see ASCETICISM), and the participation of the hesychast in the divine energies through the practice of noetic prayer (see HESYCHASM). These different ideas have all grown out of a single patristic insight, namely, that the 'gods [and] children of the Most High' of Psalm 82:6 are to be identified with those who, according to Paul, are by adoption siblings of and fellow heirs with Christ (Rom. 8:15–17).

Deification, as we find it expressed by the great fourth-century fathers, may have been elaborated in a Greek environment, but it has firm biblical roots and within the first few generations was already part of the Christian KERYGMA. The earliest Christian text to refer to Psalm 82:6 is JOHN. The 'gods', Jesus says, are those 'to whom the word of God came' (John 10:34). Jesus quotes this not to prove his divinity, but to underline the potential sonship which his hearers reject, the gods being sons of the Most High who nevertheless (as the following verse of the psalm declares) die like mortals. In early rabbinic tradition these verses were held to have been first addressed to Adam and Eve or to the Israelites in the Sinai desert who had worshipped the golden calf. The first Church father to quote Psalm 82:6–7, Justin Martyr (d. *ca* 165), took up this Jewish exegesis, setting it within the hermeneutic context of PAUL's teaching on the second Adam: Eve and the first Adam were to have become gods (i.e., were to have shared in immortality) but were judged and condemned because of their disobedience; the second Adam reversed their defeat, enabling Christians to share in his victory through their obedience (*Trypho* 123). The first explicit connection between this verse and baptism was made by IRENAEUS, who associates the 'gods' of Psalm 82:6 with Paul's teaching on adoption (*AH* 3.6.1, 3.19.1). He then goes on to connect the same verse with moral development: the 'gods' are not only the baptized but those who have conquered the passions and attained the likeness of God (*AH* 4.38.3). And finally he sets the 'gods' within the broader structure of the divine economy implemented by Christ, who 'because of his infinite love became what we are in order to make us what he is himself' (*AH* 5 Pref.). Thus before the end of the second century, the concept (if not the expression) of deification became established as a summary of the economy of salvation with reference both to baptismal incorporation into Christ and to moral growth into the likeness of God.

By the time Irenaeus died, his notion of our becoming gods by adoption had already arrived in Alexandria. It was there that a rapid development took place in the hands of Christian intellectuals influenced by PLATONISM, especially Clement (*ca* 150–*ca* 215) and ORIGEN. Clement devised a technical terminology, speaking for the first time of the 'deified' (*theopoioumenoi*) – the noun 'deification' (*theopoiēsis*) does not occur until the fourth century – as well as the 'gods'. His appropriation of this vocabulary was facilitated by his Euhemerism (the theory that all the pagan gods had been human beings who had achieved immortality). Following Philo of Alexandria (20 BC–AD 50), he also associated the creation of humanity in the image and likeness of God with the Middle Platonic conviction (drawing on Plato, *Theaetetus* 176b) that the purpose of doing philosophy was to become morally as like God as possible. Clement ties this in tentatively with the Irenaean version of deification, suggesting that the attainment of the divine likeness is fundamentally 'restoration to perfect adoption through the Son' (*Strom.* 2.134.2).

Clement's lead was followed closely by Origen, who is also the first to make the concept of participation an integral part of Christian thinking. Originally a Platonic term to express how the specific is related to the universal, or the contingent to the self-existent, 'participation' in Origen becomes a dynamic activity arising out of humanity's free response to God. This new strong version of participation is triadic in structure. Beginning as filiation through participation in the Son and spiritualization through participation in the Spirit, it finds its fulfilment in deification, which is participation in the Father, who alone is God in an absolute sense. Origen is, accordingly, the first Christian writer to cite 2 Peter 1:4: 'partakers of the divine nature'. In its original setting this verse refers to a sharing in God's attributes of glory and goodness. Origen gives it a more dynamic thrust, interpreting it as a sharing through the Son and the HOLY SPIRIT in the personal life of the TRINITY.

In the fourth century the CAPPADOCIAN FATHERS developed the notion of attaining likeness to God against the background of the gulf which was now perceived to exist between the created and uncreated orders of reality. Their emphasis is on the moral dimension of deification, the ascent of the soul to God. Only the body assumed by the *LOGOS* is deified in a literal sense. Gregory of Nazianzus coined the term 'theosis' (from the verb *theoō*, 'to deify') to express the sense of humanity's spiritual growth towards God. Basil of Caesarea reserves the term 'gods' exclusively for our eschatological state. Gregory of Nyssa does not use deification language of human beings at all, preferring to speak of 'participation' as the way in which we deepen our relationship with God.

In Alexandria Origen's heritage was treated differently. Deification came to be associated with the divine economy rather than with the idea of moral development. The Son's ability to deify proved his uncreated status. But in view of the ineffable nature of God, it was participation in the Word's deified flesh, not in the eternal Word as such, that produced deification in the believer. ATHANASIUS' focus on the deifying power of participation in the body of Christ was followed by CYRIL OF ALEXANDRIA, who abandoned the technical vocabulary of deification in favour of 'partakers of the divine nature' (2 Pet. 1:4), integrating more fully than Athanasius the recovery of the divine image or likeness with the reception of the sacraments. Cyril develops further the Origenian themes of the ADOPTION and SANCTIFICATION that lead to the attainment of incorruptibility, setting them firmly within the life of the Church.

The Byzantine approach to deification begins with DIONYSIUS THE AREOPAGITE, who gives us our first definition of deification: 'the attaining of likeness to God and union with him so far as possible' (*Hier.* 1.3.376A). Dionysius combines Gregory of Nazianzus' ascent of the soul with a reversion to unity adapted from the Neoplatonist Proclus (*ca* 410–85). He locates deification in the sacramental life, but in terms of the intellectual reception of symbols rather than corporeal participation in the body and blood of Christ. Symbols raise the mind to unity and simplicity, enabling it to participate in the divine attributes of goodness, oneness, and deity.

MAXIMUS THE CONFESSOR brings to the concept of theosis the structures of his Chalcedonian Christology. The interpenetration of the human and the divine in Christ is reflected in the divine–human communion to be attained in the believer. Deification is a transformation by grace attainable only in the life to come. But it can be initiated in this life. This transformative deification, of which the TRANSFIGURATION of Christ was a foretaste, is the purpose and goal of creation. The only real disaster that can befall us is failure to attain it.

Later, SYMEON THE NEW THEOLOGIAN (949–1022) and GREGORY PALAMAS (1296–1359) emphasized the experiential side of deification. For Symeon, theosis is a foretaste of paradise, a recovery of the original likeness lost in the FALL. The supreme image of theosis becomes that of participation in divine light. Symeon gives us autobiographical glimpses in his writings of the experience of such participation, when even the body becomes suffused with light. Participation in the divine light is also a central theme in Gregory Palamas. The Hesychast Controversy was centred on his explanation of how such participation takes place. Vision is participation. In his essence God is imparticipable, but in his operations, or ENERGIES, the believer may participate in something that is not other than God. The essence–energies distinction preserves the APOPHATIC transcendence of God while at the same time allowing communion with him. Those who are deified by grace through participation in the energies become *homotheoi* (wholly one with God), *anarchoi* (without beginning), and *ateleutētoi* (without end). They have not become what God is in God's essence, but through the divine ENERGIES they have come to share in God's attributes.

In his sermons to the people of Thessalonica Palamas presents an altogether more traditional version of theosis. But in his polemical works he develops a religious epistemology which attempts to preserve a fundamental antinomy: apophaticism and divine–human communion. Western assessments of his work have ranged from dismissive hostility to the judgement that his position is substantially the same as that of T. AQUINAS. In any case, Orthodox writers have generally been deeply committed to the essence–energies distinction. Thus, Lossky argues that God must exist in two different modes, totally unknowable and imparticipable in his essence but knowable and participable in his energies, if the human spirit is really to experience God. C. Yannaras (b. 1935) follows Lossky. The distinction between essence and energies is for him the starting point of all knowledge about God. We can know God only through the mode of being by which he makes himself accessible to us experientially, which is the energies. Knowledge implies participation. If God is only essence, theosis is impossible. For theosis is participation in the divine energies through communion with Christ in his body which is the Church.

J. Zizioulas (b. 1931), following a different strand of patristic tradition, dissents from this view. He does not define theosis in terms of participating in the divine energies but prefers to speak of divine–human communion. For him it is personhood that bridges the gulf between God and the world, not the energies. Theosis is therefore realized on the level of HYPOSTASIS, for the model and means of our realizing true personhood is the incarnate hypostasis of the *Logos* as defined by CHALCEDON, a theanthropic unity-in-diversity of love and freedom which is the model for the fulfilment of our own personhood. We have access to this in the Eucharistic assembly: 'There is no *theosis* outside the Eucharist, for it is only there that communion and otherness coincide and reach their fullness' (*Communion* 85).

In recent years Lutherans have been dissatisfied with their traditional emphasis on forensic JUSTIFICATION. Theosis has seemed to some of them, under the influence of T. Mannermaa (b. 1937), to offer a way of deepening the meaning of justification by giving it an experiential dimension. Others have been wary of what could be taken to be an assertion that faith automatically unites the believer to Christ, producing some kind of magical transformation. The work of Orthodox writers such as Lossky, Yannaras, and Zizioulas can be helpful to western Christians as well as to the Orthodox in the way that they set deification within the broader theological structures of ecclesial life.

E. Bartos, *Deification in Eastern Orthodox Theology: An Evaluation and Critique of the Theology of Dumitru Staniloae* (Paternoster Press, 1999).

M. Christensen and J. Wittung, eds., *Partakers of the Divine Nature: The History and Development of Deification in the Christian Traditions* (Fairleigh Dickinson University Press, 2007).

V.-M. Kärkkäinen, *One With God: Salvation as Deification and Justification* (Liturgical Press, 2004).

D. Keating, *Deification and Grace* (Sapientia Press, 2007).
A. Papanikolaou, *Being With God: Trinity, Apophaticism, and Divine–Human Communion* (University of Notre Dame Press, 2006).
N. Russell, *The Doctrine of Deification in the Greek Patristic Tradition* (Oxford University Press, 2004).

NORMAN RUSSELL

DEISM Deism, which flourished from the late seventeenth to the eighteenth century, is slippery to define. Its adherents ranged from questioning Christians to theists who sailed close to ATHEISM. In essence, deists shared a quest to find true RELIGION. They argued that the claims of Christianity must be measured against what can be known by reason, ethics, and humanity's innate sense of the divine. Religion should be rational, moral, and tolerant of diversity. Radical deists refused to accept supernatural 'mysteries' like PROPHECY and MIRACLES, and queried Christian belief in the TRINITY and the divinity of Christ.

The origins of Deism can be traced to the aftermath of the REFORMATION, which – in debates about Scripture and tradition, faith and reason – raised sharp questions about the nature of religious authority and knowledge. The political upheavals stirred up by the Reformation also played a part: the wars of religion turned freethinkers against rigid confessionalism. Although eighteenth-century admirers hailed Lord Herbert of Cherbury (1582–1648) as the 'father of Deism', this is not entirely true. Although Herbert set out 'common notions' of religion in all times and places – that a supreme being exists and is to be worshipped, that an understanding of moral truth is at the heart of religion – he still valued special REVELATION. J. Locke (1632–1704) opened the way to radical Deism with his arguments for 'reasonable Christianity', which placed special revelation under the judgement of reason. In *Christianity Not Mysterious* (1696), J. Toland (1670–1722) contended that 'by Christianity was intended a Rational and Intelligible Religion', adding that the claims of Christianity must be entirely understandable and possible when investigated by human reason (which was, after all, a trait of God's image). Other deists followed Toland's salvo with reinterpretations of biblical prophecy and miracles. Their determination to exclude the supernatural foreshadowed the thought of D. Hume (1711–76), and secular approaches to history. The 'Bible of Deism', M. Tindal's (1657–1733) *Christianity as Old as the Creation; or, the Gospel a Republication of the Religion of Nature* (1730), argued that a 'religion of nature' lay at the heart of all revealed religions, and that the time-bound traditions of Judaism, Christianity, and Islam threatened this. J. Butler's (1692–1752) riposte, *The Analogy of Religion, Natural and Revealed, to the Constitution and Course of Nature* (1736), delivered an antidote to Deism, as, later, did Hume's scepticism about NATURAL THEOLOGY.

Deism faded in Britain, but prospered in France (where its advocates included Voltaire (1694–1778) and J.-J. Rousseau (1712–1778)) and in revolutionary America, where T. Paine (1737–1809) promoted it in *The Age of Reason* (1794). Time has moved on, but questions the deists asked – whether belief is rational, how far an innate sense of the divine underlies all revealed religions, what the limits of religious TOLERANCE should be – still haunt twenty-first-century religion and politics.

P. Byrne, *Natural Religion and the Nature of Religion: The Legacy of Deism* (Routledge, 1989).
P. Gay, ed., *Deism: An Anthology* (Princeton University Press, 1968).

SUSAN HARDMAN MOORE

DEMYTHOLOGIZATION The term 'demythologization' (*Entmythologisierung*), with which R. BULTMANN is identified, first appeared in a 1930 Marburg dissertation by his student H. Jonas (1903–93), although whether Jonas or Bultmann originally coined the term is debated. Since Bultmann's programmatic essay of 1941 on 'New Testament and Mythology', demythologization has become virtually synonymous with his existentialist hermeneutics, informed by M. Heidegger's (1889–1976) analysis of human existence as radically temporal.

Demythologization refers to the exegetical procedure of divesting mythological concepts of their literal meaning in order to uncover the existential self-understanding latent within them. Thus, demythologization makes both a critical and a constructive move. Its critical task is to recognize and remove the mythical world view intertwined with the NT message or KERYGMA and rendered anachronistic by a modern world view shaped by scientific canons. Literal construals of the VIRGIN BIRTH and the bodily RESURRECTION of Jesus are problematic for modernity. The constructive task of demythologization is to render these problematic elements emblematic, that is, to interpret these forms symbolically in terms of their underlying existential self-understanding so that the NT can speak truthfully to modern human beings.

For example, by means of demythologizing, the resurrection of Jesus becomes transposed into a symbol for how the 'word of the CROSS', putting to death all that resists loving the neighbour, comes 'alive' in its hearers and affects in them the judgement and grace it proclaims. Jesus' resurrection is thus a mythological way of affirming the performative power of the Christian message as it becomes compellingly 'alive' in awakening the hearers' decision of FAITH. On these grounds, the resurrection is not a literal claim about the resuscitation of Jesus' corpse, but rather a symbolic affirmation that 'Jesus has risen into the kerygma' or that the Christian proclamation is the power of God that frees those who accept it into a new life determined by love and no longer by death. This is what it means to confess today 'the word of the cross' (1 Cor. 1:18) as 'the word of life' (Phil. 2:16). As this example shows, Bultmann's existentialist interpretation can be seen in continuity with older symbolic or 'spiritual' interpretations of SCRIPTURE, including allegorical readings, prompted whenever literal readings of the text proved unacceptable on any number of grounds.

Inherent in any programme of demythologization is some concept of MYTH, and, in Bultmann's case, there are multiple definitions at work. At the formal and literal level, myth is a comparative literary genre, stories of the gods, employed by researchers in the HISTORY OF RELIGIONS. Where such stories are accepted literally as part of a culture's given frame of reference, myth can also characterize an entire world view. The NT world view reflects for Bultmann the Gnostic Redeemer myth and Jewish APOCALYPTIC myths about the end of the world. On a deeper, symbolic level such myths employ earthly figures or events to represent transcendent powers, which is myth's way of acknowledging human finitude in the face of contingency and DEATH. Moreover, mythic representations employ 'objectivized' speech, that is, they speak of transcendence in a distancing way, outside the existential apprehension of faith, and thereby turn God into an empirical phenomenon or a controllable object of human thought or action. Demythologization as 'de-objectification' thus seeks to speak kerygmatically in such a way as to honour the mystery and freedom of the God of the Gospel and the mystery and freedom of human existence as related to this God.

R. Bultmann, *Jesus Christ and Mythology* (Scribner, 1958).
'New Testament and Mythology: The Problem of Demythologizing the New Testament Proclamation' in *New Testament and Mythology and Other Basic Writings*, ed. S. M. Ogden (Fortress Press, 1984), 155–64.

JAMES F. KAY

DESCENT INTO HELL Christ's descent into HELL (or Hades) is usually connected with 1 Peter 3:19–20 and 4:6. Both passages are quite obscure as to their actual meaning and might be influenced by Jewish apocalyptic literature (e.g., Enoch). Some exegetes suggest that the 'imprisoned spirits' in 1 Peter 3:19–20 are rebellious angels rather than human dead, and Christ's announcement declares their condemnation rather than their salvation. Approaching the right hand of power, the risen Christ announces to these demonic powers his victory and thereby their defeat. 1 Peter 4:6 involves an actual preaching to the dead; but the audience is those Christians who have died prior to Christ's return, and they receive assurance that their faith has not been in vain.

There is therefore no explicit mention of Christ's descent in the NT. Its antecedents lie in the ancient mythologies of Babylonia, Egypt, and classical antiquity, where heroes such as Heracles descended into the netherworld. Christian conviction, however, declared that Jesus is more than these deities and demi-gods. Christ says in Revelation 1:18: 'I was dead, and see, I am alive forever and ever; and I have the keys of Death and of Hades.' This shows that he has won victory over the forces of death's dominion. While the concept of a neutral sojourn in the realm of the dead proved stagnant for theological development, Christ's victorious entry was quite stimulating. M. LUTHER connected it with the liberation of the OT patriarchs from limbo, a theme shared by Orthodox ICONOGRAPHY. The *Catechism of the Roman Catholic Church* states: 'Jesus did not descend into hell to deliver the damned, nor to destroy the hell of damnation, but to free the just who had gone before him' (§633). Melito of Sardis (d. *ca* 190), Ephraem the Syrian (*ca* 306–73), and MARCION broadened this liberation to include all people, save perhaps some especially evil ones, and the Alexandrian theologians Clement (*ca* 150–*ca* 215) and ORIGEN extended the deliverance to those who had died before the great flood. Yet the Church never determined a specific doctrine concerning the beneficiaries of Christ's descent. Rufinus of Aquileia (*ca* 345–410) mentions a local creed referring to the descent, a phrase subsequently adopted by the APOSTLES' CREED. Its first official confessional appearance was in 359 in the Fourth Formula of Sirmium.

Early Christians had an existential interest in how far Christ's salvific power extended, since some of their forebears were historically and geographically disadvantaged in accepting Christ during their lifetime. From what they knew about 'God so loving the world', early Christians concluded that Christ's descent would offer their forebears the chance of salvation. While not expressly attested in the New Testament, this hope is certainly a legitimate inference from the Christ event, and it carries strong contemporary significance as well. Such salvific possibility would neither circumvent the Christ event nor cheapen grace; yet it would still involve a personal decision of acceptance, albeit one beyond this life.

See also CHRISTOLOGY; UNIVERSALISM.

W. J. Dalton, *Christ's Proclamation to the Spirits: A Study of 1 Peter 3:18–4:6* (Pontifical Biblical Institute, 1989).
H. Schwarz, *Eschatology* (Eerdmans, 2000).

HANS SCHWARZ

DEUS ABSCONDITUS The VULGATE uses the Latin *Deus absconditus* (literally, 'hidden God') to translate the predicate of Isaiah 45:15a ('Truly you are a God who hides himself'). Though used by Nicholas of Cusa as a means of stressing God's transcendence (*Vis.* 5), the phrase is most frequently associated with M. LUTHER. In his early work Luther cites Isaiah's reference to God's hiddenness to summarize the paradoxical nature of

REVELATION: God is most clearly seen as God hides the divine glory under the ignominy of the CROSS (*Heid.* 20). The concept plays a different role in Luther's later treatise *On the Bondage of the Will* (1525), where *Deus absconditus* refers to the secret will of God, in contrast with the will of God made known in SCRIPTURE (the *Deus revelatus*). Luther invokes this distinction to explain how it is possible for God (as *Deus absconditus*) to condemn the wicked even though the Bible says that God (as *Deus revelatus*) does not desire their death (Ezek. 33:11).

Though Luther stresses that Christians are 'to pay attention to the word and leave that inscrutable will alone' (*Bond.* 140), the distinction he draws between the *Deus absconditus* and *Deus revelatus* seems inconsistent with his own stress on the inherent trustworthiness of God's word. It also appears to conflict with the DOCTRINE of the TRINITY, according to which the Word incarnate in Jesus is fully God, thereby ruling out the possibility of a divine will other than that revealed in Christ.

IAN A. MCFARLAND

DEUTEROCANONICAL BOOKS: see APOCRYPHA.

DEVIL The English word 'devil' derives from *diabolos*, the Greek translation of the Hebrew *satan*, meaning 'adversary'. In the OT 'satans' can be human or angelic: God raises up human satans against Solomon (1 Kgs 11:14, 23), but against Balaam it is the Angel of God who comes as a satan (Num. 22:22, 32). Another supernatural satan appears among the sons of God to test Job, and yet another such satan accuses the High Priest Joshua in Zechariah (3:1–2). The SEPTUAGINT treats both these latter figures as a single angel with the proper name of the Devil (i.e., *Diabolos*), whose function it is to test and prosecute humans (cf. *Book of Jubilees* 10:8).

In the NT the Devil still performs his traditional adversarial functions with regard to humans (now including Jesus as the Son of Man), and, though he is intensely feared and disliked, there is no reason to believe that he is thought of as opposing God, or as having been discharged from the divinely assigned duties described in the OT. PAUL mentions Satan as an obstructer (1 Thess. 2:18; Rom. 16:20) and tester (1 Thess. 3:5; 1 Cor. 7:5; 2 Cor. 2:10–11; 11:14). He also considers him to be in charge of punishing and rehabilitating sinners (1 Cor. 5:5; cf. 1 Tim. 1:20). Satan operates against Paul himself, with God's explicit approval, to keep him from the sin of pride (2 Cor. 12:7).

In the Gospels the HOLY SPIRIT drives Jesus into the wilderness to be tested by Satan (Mark 1:13), who has been given the rule of the kingdoms of the world (Luke 4:6; cf. Satan's association with the angelic governors of nations in Eph. 6:11–16). Jesus predicts that he will be ousted from this position (Luke 10:18; John 12:31), but for the time being he remains in power. As in Job, Satan is depicted as urging the need to test the apostles, a negotiation witnessed by Jesus, who intervenes to mitigate the tests (Luke 22:32). And as in Zechariah, Satan retains his role as accuser, a position from which he will be dismissed only after he is defeated by the testimony of Christian martyrs (Rev. 12:10–11). He has also taken over the functions of the Angel of Death, but that office too will come to an end when Jesus 'destroys' him (Heb. 2:14).

At times, the sins that Satan urges upon humans when testing them are attributed to him as well: he is a murderer from the beginning (John 8:44), and Jesus' mission is to put an end to the Devil's works (1 John 3:8). After Satan's future ousting from HEAVEN, he will be active for a time on earth, and then locked in the Abyss for 1,000 years, to be finally released again, and then, at the end of time, thrown into the Lake of Fire, along with Hades, Death, and sinful humans (Rev. 12–20); but in the meantime he deserves respect, according to Jude, who commends the archangel Michael for not 'blaspheming' the Devil when disputing over the body of Moses (Jude 8–9). Matthew teaches that uncharitable people will be sent to 'the eternal fire', which is prepared for the Devil and his angels (25:41), whether as punishers, or punished, or both.

Theologians of the patristic period systematized the variegated and often contradictory glimpses of Satan in the Bible and thereby infused him with a different character and history from what he had had before. So far, he had not been tied to the sin of Adam and Eve; the envious *diabolos* who introduced Death into the world was not Satan but Cain (Wis. 2:24; 10:1–4), and 'that ancient serpent who deceives the whole world' (Rev. 12:9) refers to the dragon of Isaiah (27:1). It is Justin Martyr (d. *ca* 165) who seems to have first identified the Devil with the serpent of Eden, thus setting him in opposition to God (*Trypho* 45, 79, 124). Cyprian of Carthage (d. 258) locates the Devil's decisive offence earlier: he refused to worship God's image in Adam, and so was expelled from heaven, whereupon he mounted his attack on humankind (*Jealousy* 4–5).

ORIGEN OF ALEXANDRIA came up with an even earlier first sin for Satan, namely, pride and rebellion against God, by interpreting Isaiah 14, where the king of Babylon is compared to an arrogant Morning Star (*Lucifer* in Latin), as referring to Satan (*Prin.* 1.5.5). Origen's scenario of Satan as God's enemy from the beginning received general acceptance as biblical, and this theology of the Devil has remained in place to the present day. Once Satan came to be regarded in this way as a principle of evil, Christianity took on a more dualistic aspect.

One new idea that developed after Origen, especially at the hands of AUGUSTINE (*Trin.* 13.15), was that Satan actually received title to all of humankind after deceiving Adam and Eve, so that Jesus had to 'redeem' them, that is, buy them back from Satan with the payment of his death. This notion was modified by ANSELM OF CANTERBURY, who denied that any payment was due to or received by Satan; but it was still widely held that fallen humanity was deservedly put under the Devil's control. T. AQUINAS considered Satan and his fellow fallen angels to be pure spirits of immense intelligence. These angels were identified not only with the principalities and powers, but also (somewhat incongruously) with the parasitic possessing demons of the Gospels.

Another medieval development was the notion that Satan had been consigned to HELL, and that he was placed in charge of tormenting damned souls as they arrived in hell. But, whether bound or not, he was generally believed to have access to the world above. Satan's supposed involvement with sorcery, which came to a head in the witch hunts of the early modern period, did not constitute any new theology of the Devil. The idea that Satan might be an object of worship is rather an extension of the patristic identification of the pagan gods as diabolical. Satan's portrayal in J. Milton's (1608–74) *Paradise Lost* (1667) is a good embodiment of the usual beliefs.

Christian beliefs about the Devil have proved remarkably consistent and uncontroversial across the theological spectrum up until the modern period: Satan sinned irretrievably in the first instant of his creation; he was punished at once, but allowed, under God's strict control, to work for the damnation of human souls. Reactions by Christians to the constant threat of the Devil's machinations have ranged from great fear (especially evident in the witchcraft persecutions) to great confidence. The Devil, our Accuser, goes about like a roaring lion, looking for victims (1 Pet. 5:8–9); but if we stand up to him, he will flee (Jas. 4:8).

Doubts about the existence of the Devil can be dated to the liberal Protestant theology of F. SCHLEIERMACHER (*CF*, §§44–5). Similar doubts did not surface in Roman Catholic circles until the 1960s. The question as to whether there is a real supernatural entity named Satan is usually conditioned by the prehistory imposed on Satan in the patristic period. In other words, the Devil whose existence is affirmed or denied is invariably Lucifer, Origen's ousted rebel, rather than the satans or Satan of the Bible.

G. B. Caird, *Principalities and Powers: A Study in Pauline Theology* (Oxford University Press, 1954).
H. A. Kelly, *Satan: A Biography* (Cambridge University Press, 2006).
J. B. Russell, *Satan: The Early Christian Tradition* (Cornell University Press, 1981).

HENRY ANSGAR KELLY

DIACONATE The diaconate is one of the three ordained offices of ministry in the Catholic, Anglican, and Orthodox Churches, besides priests and bishops. It is a lay office in Protestant Churches.

The Greek *diakonos* (servant, intermediary, courier) is used to designate a specific office already in the NT. In Acts 6, seven men, traditionally understood as the first deacons, were by the imposition of hands appointed to look after widows. Preaching, or the proclamation of the GOSPEL, is in Acts 6:4 characterized as the *diakonia* of the Word. The NT (unlike *Didache* 15:1–2) does not explicitly mention this as one of the tasks of the deacon, but Acts 6:4–8:40 shows that the seven participated in such proclamation. Acts also mentions the seven exorcizing and baptizing (8:38), and in the early second century deacons performed liturgical tasks at the EUCHARIST. 1 Timothy 3: 8–13 discusses the qualifications of a deacon, who must be in all respects irreproachable; Romans 16:1 makes clear that women could also serve as deacons.

In Ignatius of Antioch (d. *ca* 110) there is found for the first time a clear distinction between deacons, priests, and bishops, with the clear implication that deacons are of lower hierarchical rank than priests and bishops. Nevertheless, in the early Church the diaconate could become a position of power and influence, because deacons were in charge of alms and other Church funds. Besides looking after the poor and managing the ecclesiastical property, liturgical tasks and the proclamation of the Gospel continued to be part of the office of a deacon until well into the Middle Ages, though the task of looking after the poor was gradually taken over by monks. Little by little, the diaconate lost its character as a permanent position and became a stage on the way to the priesthood. In the nineteenth century, however, there were still cardinal-deacons who had not been ordained priests. VATICAN COUNCIL II restored the permanent diaconate in the Catholic Church; married persons may be candidates for the office, but deacons can only remarry in exceptional cases.

Current discussions within Catholicism concentrate on two issues: the diaconate of women and the distinguishing characteristic of the diaconate. With respect to the first, in the NT, the early Church, and the Middle Ages, there were female deacons. To what extent was their position the same as that of male deacons? Should a female diaconate be reintroduced? With respect to the second, if all three traditional tasks of the deacon (liturgy, proclamation, poor relief) are tasks of the priest as well, and if every priest should first be ordained deacon, what is the distinguishing characteristic of the diaconate? Should diaconate and priesthood not be separated, and should deacons not have their own specific tasks, which cannot ordinarily be carried out by priests?

In Orthodox Churches and in the Anglican Church, the position of deacons is similar to that in the Catholic Church (though Anglican deacons may marry also after ordination and may be female). Presbyterian

Churches, following J. CALVIN, have sometimes identified a fourfold ministry: pastors, elders, doctors, and deacons, these last charged with looking after the poor and needy. In Lutheran Churches the function of deacons varies widely.

MARCEL SAROT

DIALECTICAL THEOLOGY 'Dialectical theology' commonly refers to the school which emerged around K. BARTH and F. Gogarten (1887–1968) in the years immediately following World War I. The use of dialectical tensions and paradoxes, however, runs throughout the Christian tradition and can be traced back to PAUL's epistles in the NT (e.g., 1 Cor. 1:18–25). Though AUGUSTINE prays to God 'most hidden from us and yet most present amongst us' (*Conf.* 1.4), it is arguably M. LUTHER who, at least until the twentieth century, made the most use of paradoxes and polarities in Christian theology: writing about the freedom and bondage of Christians, about their status as justified sinners (*SIMUL JUSTUS ET PECCATOR*), about God hidden in REVELATION (see *DEUS ABSCONDITUS*), about God's Word as LAW and GOSPEL. In the nineteenth century, dialectical thinking was prized by S. KIERKEGAARD, who emphasized the unresolvable duality of God and world, and G. W. F. HEGEL, who, dissatisfied with mere dualities, had a deep interest in the syntheses which surmount them.

The expression 'dialectical theology' seems to have been first used in 1922 to describe the theology of Barth and Gogarten, as well as that of E. Brunner (1889–1966), E. Thurneysen (1888–1977) and – shortly thereafter – R. BULTMANN. In retrospect, 'theology of the Word' would have been a better characterization of the school, but 1922 saw the publication of the second edition of Barth's commentary on Romans and of his lecture on 'The Word of God as the Task of Theology', two texts in which he unambiguously advocated a dialectical way of thinking. With his article '*Zwischen den Zeiten*' ('Between the Times'), published in 1920, Gogarten became the other key thinker of the school. Both pastors were fighting the theology of the preceding generation, which they thought had lost sight of the God who, in judgement and GRACE, remains hidden even in revelation and thus cannot be used to legitimize (all-too) human purposes. In 1922 they founded a journal which took the title of Gogarten's article as its name.

With his sympathetic review of Barth's Romans commentary, Bultmann became closer to the school. Like Barth, he had been sensitized to the importance of paradoxes and dialectical tensions in theology as an enthusiastic student of W. Herrmann (1846–1922). As for Brunner, he had been in regular contact with Barth since 1916. But even as the school was beginning to take shape, differences in orientation were becoming apparent: Gogarten wanted to begin by clarifying notions like 'modern historical consciousness' using philosophical resources, Bultmann rejected the possibility of speaking of God without speaking of oneself, and Brunner wished to complement the theology of the Word with a NATURAL THEOLOGY for apologetic and missionary purposes. Barth saw all this as a return to the sort of LIBERAL THEOLOGY he wanted to overcome.

By the end of the 1920s, it was obvious that the 'dialectical school' was in disarray, yet it was only in October 1933 (after Gogarten briefly joined the German Christians) that Barth and Thurneysen separated themselves from *Zwischen den Zeiten*. The journal was dissolved. Even after the demise of the school, most members maintained, each in his own way, a dialectical orientation: Bultmann's programme of DEMYTHOLOGIZATION, for instance, rests on the idea that God is hidden in his revelation and thus never 'objectively' available at our disposal. Ironically, Barth's doctrine of analogy, with its dialectic of similitude and dissimilitude, and his opposition to the various forms of natural theology advocated by former members of the school, rest on that same idea. For Barth, dialectics says something about revelation itself, in its veiling and unveiling, and not just about our finite ways of thinking. It is never identical with a dualism in which the polarities are equivalent, for it has an irreversible direction, a purpose: God's 'yes' – the RESURRECTION – is victorious beyond any tensions or antinomies. Yet Barth could only point to it and understand this 'yes' in light of the CROSS, of God's 'no' to our human rejection of God.

In order to avoid misunderstandings of his theology as dualistic, already in the 1920s Barth made progressively less use of terms like 'paradox' and 'dialectic'. But he remained a theologian who thought dialectically. Decades after the death of Barth and his erstwhile dialectical colleagues, even as theologians are required to think not only *with* but also *after* them, the use of dialectical tensions remains an inevitable and indeed fruitful way of thinking theologically. This will be the case as long as theology is a theology of wayfarers who live 'between the times' and who do not yet see 'face to face' but only 'in a mirror, dimly' (1 Cor. 13:12).

See also NEO-ORTHODOXY.

C. Chalamet, *Dialectical Theologians: Wilhelm Herrmann, Karl Barth and Rudolf Bultmann* (TVZ, 2005).

J. M. Robinson, ed., *The Beginnings of Dialectic Theology* (John Knox Press, 1968).

CHRISTOPHE CHALAMET

DIONYSIUS THE AREOPAGITE After the Council of CHALCEDON in 451, the ongoing arguments over Christ's natures and Person included various appeals to earlier authorities, including the newly 'discovered' works of an apostolic author, Dionysius the Areopagite (Acts 17), first cited during the colloquy at Constantinople in 532. They were quickly introduced, edited, and commented upon by John, bishop of Scythopolis in Palestine, around 540.

Despite some initial questions over its authenticity, the Dionysian corpus was for many centuries considered apostolic and thus highly authoritative. Only in 1895 was there proof that these writings used works by the Neoplatonist philosopher Proclus (410–85) and therefore date from the late fifth or early sixth century. Perhaps nothing more about the author's identity can ever be proven. In any event, he knew late Athenian Neoplatonism (not only Proclus but also Damascius (*ca* 460–*ca* 540)), and used earlier patristic literature, especially the Cappadocian Fathers. Thus, a corpus that was once noted for its original features ironically now seems increasingly dependent on prior works.

The first treatise in most early manuscripts is the Dionysian presentation of the angelic ranks, *The Celestial Hierarchy.* It begins with the general method for interpreting symbols, whether biblical or liturgical. Chapters 4–10 present the angels in three triads, a distinctively Dionysian pattern: seraphim, cherubim, and thrones; dominions, powers, and authorities; principalities, archangels, and angels. Chapter 15, in conclusion, interprets many details of the biblical descriptions, such as the angels' physical features and equipment.

The Ecclesiastical Hierarchy presents the rituals and orders of a Christian community in seven chapters. Chapter 1 introduces the vocabulary and general idea of a hierarch and a hierarchy. The next three chapters present and interpret the three sacraments: baptism (called illumination), the Eucharist (or synaxis), and the consecration of the myron ointment that is used in other rites. Chapters 5–6 present the clergy and laity, including monks (see Monasticism). Chapter 7 concludes the work by describing and interpreting the funeral rite. The longest work in the Dionysian corpus is *The Divine Names.* Chapter 1 presents the basic point that Scripture can praise God by many names, some more appropriate than others, and yet also by a 'wise silence' confess that God is actually beyond every name and thus unknowable. With Chapter 4, *The Divine Names* exegetes its first specific name for God, namely, the 'good', as well as 'light', 'love', and 'beauty'. Chapter 13 culminates the work with the names 'perfect' and 'one', leading to the subject of union with God.

Only a few pages long, but dense and difficult, *The Mystical Theology* begins with a prayer and advice to 'Timothy' that he should ascend above sense perception and conceptual achievement towards union with the One who is beyond perception and conception. The programmatic use of affirmation and negation is illustrated by Moses entering into the cloud or the 'darkness of unknowing' on Mt Sinai. Chapter 3 characterizes three previous Dionysian treatises (the lost or fictitious *Theological Representations, The Divine Names,* and the lost or fictitious *Symbolical Theology*) as a descending sequence of affirmations, to be followed by an ascending series of terse negations in this approach to the ineffable God beyond affirmation and negation. Chapter 4 then negates every category of sense perception, while Chapter 5 goes 'higher' to negate every type of concept regarding God, even the very titles of *The Divine Names.* Finally, no affirmations or assertions suffice, and the Godhead even transcends all denials.

Last in the corpus are ten *Letters,* ostensibly to apostolic figures and arranged in a specific pattern. The fourth letter, on Christ, has been carefully examined from the beginning for clues to the author's Christology: is it orthodox (i.e., Neo-Chalcedonian), or does it tend towards a Miaphysite emphasis on the divine nature (see Miaphysitism, Neo-Chalcedonianism)?

Translated into Latin by J. Scotus Eriugena (*ca* 800–*ca* 875) in the ninth century, Dionysius profoundly influenced medieval theology and spirituality. After Hugh of St Victor's (1096–1141) appropriation in the twelfth century came the Scholastic interest by Albert the Great (ca. 1200–80) and especially T. Aquinas, as well as spiritual interpretations by Richard of St Victor (d. 1173), T. Gallus (*ca* 1200–46), Bonaventure (1221–74), the author of the late fourteenth-century *The Cloud of Unknowing,* and many others. Further, the Dionysian corpus provided the medievals with some angelology, liturgical allegory, key terms such as 'hierarchy', 'supernatural', and 'anagogy', and perhaps an influence on 'Gothic' architecture. Current interest in negative theology frequently invokes the Dionysian legacy, albeit loosely.

See also Apophatic Theology; Platonism.

A. Louth, *Denys the Areopagite* (Continuum, 2002).

P. Rorem, *Pseudo-Dionysius: A Commentary on the Texts and an Introduction to Their Influence* (Oxford University Press, 1993).

Paul Rorem

Disability Theology Disability theology is the attempt by disabled and non-disabled Christians to understand and interpret the gospel of Jesus Christ, God, and humanity against the backdrop of the historical and contemporary experiences of people with disabilities. It has come to refer to a variety of perspectives and methods designed to give voice to the rich and diverse theological meanings of the human experience of disability. This theological movement emerges from theoretical roots within the sociological critique of cultural perceptions of disability provided by disability studies.

Disability studies highlight the implicit and explicit social oppression of people with disabilities and the underlying cadences of 'ableism' (an equivalent to racism, sexism, etc.) that are prevalent within culture. Disability studies in the UK have focused on the 'social model of disability', which assumes (in contrast to medical models) that it is the ways in which society is structured (including the values and assumptions that underpin this structure) rather than particular impairments or pathologies that cause disablement. For example, a person in a wheelchair is not disabled if they have adequate access to buildings, transport, etc.; likewise, a person with an intellectual disability is disabled by the fact that western culture prioritizes reason and intelligence over friendship and dependence. In the USA the social model has been developed in line with the civil rights movement, such that people with disabilities are considered to be an oppressed minority group pushing towards civil rights and liberties.

Disability theology picks up on and develops theoretical perspectives such as these and presents a constructive critique of Christian theology and the practices that emerge from it in relation to the experiences of people with disabilities in Church and world. Disability theology recognizes that the meaning of the term 'disability' is diverse and complex, constructed and reconstructed according to particular times, cultures, contexts, and intentions. As a socially constructed way of naming difference, the term 'disability' can serve to advantage some people and disadvantage others. Disability theologians have recognized that theology has mostly been constructed without consideration of the experience of people with disabilities. Consequently, the ways in which particular theological understandings and Christian practices have been developed have disadvantaged and at times served to exclude and oppress people with disabilities through, e.g., the equation of disability with sin or the exclusion of people with intellectual disabilities from the sacraments based on sacramental theologies that emphasize intellect and knowledge. Even when it has not so explicitly disadvantaged or excluded people with disabilities, Christian theology and practice have often ignored their perspectives in a way that leads to tacit exclusion.

Disability theology is *informative* in so far as it seeks to raise people's consciousness to the experience of disability and its significance for the development and practice of Church, theology, politics, and culture. It is also *transformative* in so far as, in seeking to challenge the primacy of disabling theological and cultural interpretations, attitudes, assumptions, and values, and in presenting creative theological alternatives to the status quo, it offers a different basis on which to understand God and value human beings.

Recent analyses have begun to question the all-encompassing explanatory power claimed by social models of disability. Appeal to civil rights presupposes autonomy and self-representation, something that is unavailable for people with (for example) profound intellectual disabilities or dementia. This line of critique suggests a need for new models of disability theology that embrace more effectively the broad range of the human experience described as 'disability'. This may be the next phase of development within this field.

N. Eiesland, *The Disabled God: Toward a Liberatory Theology of Disability* (Abingdon Press, 1985).

H. Reinders, *Receiving the Gift of Friendship: Profound Disability, Theological Anthropology and Ethics* (Eerdmans, 2008).

John Swinton

Dispensationalism Dispensationalism is a term given to a reading of the Bible based on a particular and distinctive hermeneutic, namely, the principle that biblical history is made up of a series of 'dispensations', or specific temporal periods within the divine ECONOMY. The idea of separate dispensations is arguably implicit in classical Christian distinctions between the periods of LAW, of GRACE, and of eschatological GLORY, as well as in the idea of distinct COVENANTS characteristic of seventeenth-century FEDERAL THEOLOGY. But the majority of those who describe themselves as dispensationalists follow the list of seven dispensations given in the *Scofield Reference Bible*. These comprise the dispensations of innocence, prior to Adam's fall (Gen. 1:1–3:7); of conscience, from Adam to Noah (Gen. 3:8–8:22); of government, from Noah to Abraham (Gen. 9:1–11:32); of patriarchal rule, from Abraham to Moses (Gen. 12:1–Exod. 19:25); of the Mosaic LAW, from Moses to Christ (Exod. 20:1–Acts 2:4); of grace, from Pentecost to the rapture (Acts 2:4–Rev. 20:3); and of an earthly, millennial kingdom yet to come (Rev. 20:4–6). This schema is modified by those who identify themselves as progressive dispensationalists.

The distinction between the various dispensations is not simply temporal. Each dispensation represents a different way in which God relates to human beings over the course of earthly history. Individual dispensations are defined by the transmission of a divine revelation to a particular group of people (e.g., all humanity in the case of the dispensation of conscience, Israel only in the case of the dispensation of the law). Each revelation discloses an aspect of God's will for human beings that demands the obedience of those to whom it is revealed. In every period the ground of salvation remains Christ's ATONEMENT on the cross, so that under all the dispensations one is saved by FAITH rather than works; but only under the dispensation of grace is Christ the explicit object of that faith. Prior to that time, the object of saving faith for an individual is the revelation corresponding to the dispensation then in force.

Modern dispensationalism emerged only in the nineteenth century, largely due to the influence of British evangelical preacher J. Darby (1800–82). Darby, who was to become the founder of the Plymouth Brethren denomination, developed a doctrine of the PAROUSIA according to which Christ would return twice: first in secret to RAPTURE the Church out of the world and up to heaven, and then again after seven years of worldwide tribulation to establish the MILLENNIUM. Darby made numerous evangelistic trips to America between 1859 and 1877 and won many American converts to his premillennial theology (see PREMILLENNIALISM). His theology was further popularized by evangelist D. Moody (1837–99), though by far the single most enduring tool for spreading this theology was the publication in 1909 of the enormously popular *Scofield Reference Bible*, which annotated the text of the King James Version with extensive notes, maps, and charts, all coordinated with Darby's dispensational scheme.

Dispensationalism arose in part due to a concern about apparently unfulfilled biblical prophecies. Dispensationalists recognized that the NT has a profoundly eschatological orientation, and that its writers based many of their claims on the conviction that the ministry of Jesus fulfilled prophetic predictions in the OT. If the truth of the GOSPEL was in this way linked with the fulfilment of prophetic texts, in cases where OT prophecies seemed not to be fulfilled, the overall credibility of Christianity was at risk: biblical prophecy might be seen as false prophecy, or, worse, God might appear to be unfaithful and correspondingly untrustworthy. Dispensationalists attempt to respond to this problem by fitting the OT prophecies into a coherent series of episodes that together constitute the full context of God's saving work.

To its credit dispensationalism has forced a re-evaluation of much of the Bible's prophetic, eschatological, and apocalyptic language. Perhaps still more significantly, with its emphasis on the enduring significance of God's covenant with Israel, dispensationalists have also stood firm against supersessionist readings of SCRIPTURE, according to which God's promises to Abraham had been somehow annulled by Christ's resurrection (see SUPERSESSIONISM). Furthermore, dispensationalism has reaffirmed the hermeneutical wisdom of beginning with the plain or apparent meaning of a text. It has also rightly recognized that God has related to God's people in different ways at different times, and that the earliest Christians did anticipate a reign of God upon the earth in space and time, not merely in heaven.

Nevertheless, Christians operating outside a dispensationalist framework have criticized the dispensationalist system on several fronts. From a purely literary perspective, they charge that dispensationalist interpretation of all prophecy as the literal foretelling of the *future* ignores prophecy's primary function in Israel: to shape the life of the community by revealing God's perspective on the *present*. Thus, even the large amount of prophetic material that is predictive in character usually focuses on the near term, for the simple reason that it is addressed to the prophets' contemporaries and not to an audience in the remote future. Similar criticisms are levelled against dispensationalist tendencies to interpret apocalyptic literature like Daniel or Revelation without regard for the metaphorical character of its language.

On a more distinctly theological level, dispensationalism is criticized for a failure to reckon with the finality of Christ as the one in whom all OT prophecy finds its fulfilment (2 Cor. 1:19–20), reducing his ministry to one mode of God's dealing with humankind rather than the ground and goal of the divine economy in every age. In opposition to the dispensationalist understanding of the time of the Church as a sort of parenthesis between the time of OT prophecy and the time when those prophecies are fulfilled for Israel literally on the earth, the majority of Christian tradition sees the Church as encompassing all the faithful from Abel till the end of time.

See also ULTRADISPENSATIONALISM.

C. A. Blaising and D. L. Bock, *Progressive Dispensationalism* (Bridgepoint, 1993).

C. Hill, *In God's Time* (Eerdmans, 2002).

B. Rossing, *The Rapture Exposed* (Westview, 2004).

B. Witherington, *Jesus, Paul, and the End of the World* (InterVarsity Press, 1992).

The Problem with Evangelical Theology (Baylor University Press, 2005).

BEN WITHERINGTON

DIVINE ACTION At the heart of Christian faith and praxis lies the LORD'S PRAYER, which includes the petitions: 'your kingdom come, your will be done, on earth as it is in heaven' (Matt. 6:10). The reality of powerful – and seemingly sufficient – scientific explanations of nature raises important questions for Christians about whether it still makes sense to speak of God acting in the world; scholars over the last two decades have achieved new and promising breakthroughs in the problem of divine action. The breakthroughs have come through arguing that various key discoveries in the NATURAL SCIENCES can be interpreted through a philosophy of nature in which emergence replaces the reduction of all events to purely physical processes, and indeterminism replaces causal closure. These insights make it possible to envision God acting in the world without intervening in (i.e., breaking or suspending) the regularities of nature.

There are theologically powerful reasons for wanting to affirm that God acts in the world in such a non-interventionist fashion. According to the traditional Christian DOCTRINE of CREATION, God creates the world out of nothing and holds it in being at all times. Furthermore, the doctrine of PROVIDENCE holds that God is also the continuous Creator, who shapes some or all events in nature (see *CONCURSUS*; *GUBERNATIO*). At the same time, because God's ultimate intent is to bring the created world and all its processes to perfection, Christians also affirm that divine action should be consistent with (and thus not override or violate) natural processes. Given the enormous capacity of modern science to account for worldly processes in natural terms, Christian theology has since the Enlightenment been dominated by the assumption that it is necessary to choose between two mutually exclusive options: either God's action includes *objective interventions* into the world that suspend or violate the ordinary processes of nature; or 'divine action' is merely our *subjective response* to God's ordinary, uniform action of holding the world in existence through natural processes.

Because of developments in the natural sciences that call into question the model of a causally closed, deterministic universe, these mutually exclusive alternatives are no longer the only options. There is now a third possibility: divine action can be viewed as at once *objective* and *non-interventionist*. I call this theory of divine action '*non-interventionist objective divine action*' (NIODA). For this theory to be scientifically defensible, the events that result from God's action must occur within a domain of nature in which the corresponding scientific theory can be interpreted in terms of *ontological indeterminism* – since where there is no determinism, there is no scientific 'law' for God to violate.

There are at least four distinct approaches to NIODA based on claims that a particular scientific theory implies an indeterministic view of nature. There are two additional approaches to divine action which have figured prominently in the theology–science dialogue, but which are based primarily on an overarching metaphysical framework rather than on specific scientific theories. The following is a brief summary and assessment of each of these six approaches.

Top-down approaches to divine action explore how processes at a higher level of complexity might have a degree of causal efficacy on processes at a lower level of complexity. Scholars exploring this approach include P. Clayton (b. 1956) and N. Murphy (b. 1951). A promising example is the 'mind/brain' problem, which explores whether (higher-level) mental states, though the result of the brain's activity, can nevertheless effect changes in the (lower-level) neurophysiology of the brain. If successful, this top-down account of causality offers a robust defence against a reductionism that interprets mental states as nothing more than brain states. In order to be plausible, however, such accounts need to be able to show that at least some processes at the neurophysiological level are indeterministic.

The *whole–part* approach to divine action focuses on the way the boundary conditions of a complex system influence the evolution of that system. An everyday example is the formation of vortices in a pot of boiling water. Working from such a model, A. Peacocke (1924–2006) asked whether God might be viewed as acting on the boundary of the universe, or on what Peacocke called 'the universe-as-a-whole'. If so, this would avoid God's intervening in particular processes within the universe; but this approach raises the question of what it means to speak of the universe having a 'boundary'. If taken in a physical sense, the concept runs up against the problem that according to the theory of general relativity the universe does not have a physical boundary. Of course, if the 'boundary' of the universe is taken in a purely metaphysical sense (i.e., as referring to God's radical transcendence of the universe), the challenge from physics is overcome – but then Peacocke's approach also ceases to be a properly scientific account of divine action.

The *lateral-amplification* approach to divine action works from the fact that small differences in the initial state of a system produce large differences in the final state of a system (as in, e.g., the 'butterfly effect' in chaos theory). Though such systems are generally viewed as deterministic (indeed it is the determinism of chaotic processes which produces their unpredictability), J. Polkinghorne (b. 1930) argues that they might actually be ontologically indeterministic, in line with a theory he calls 'holistic chaos'. If such indeterminism were vindicated, God could change initial states of complex systems without violating natural laws. The challenge is that Polkinghorne's proposal involves a wager that his theory can be defended empirically.

Bottom-up approaches to divine action look for evidence for ontological indeterminism at lower levels in nature, where the effects of divine action could play out at higher levels of complexity. The most likely domain for such divine action is the subatomic level of quantum physics, which physicists since W. Heisenberg (1901–76) have interpreted as pointing to ontological indeterminism in nature. Defended in the writings of T. Tracy (b. 1948) and R. Russell (b. 1946), this approach works from the view that quantum events (e.g., spontaneous radioactive decay) lack a sufficient efficient natural cause. Because such processes are ontologically indeterminate, God's acting in, with, and through them is by definition non-interventionist. The challenge to such approaches is that other interpretations of quantum physics may eventually win out over indeterministic ones.

Two other approaches to divine action depend specifically on a metaphysical philosophy of nature rather than on a specific theory in science. The first of these is based in contemporary Catholic philosophy. E. McMullin (b. 1924), D. Edwards (b. 1943), and W. Stoeger (b. 1943) draw on T. Aquinas' distinction between primary and secondary causality to argue that God's action as primary cause is entirely identified with the creation of the world *ex nihilo*. God holds the world in being and bequeaths to nature a large degree of autonomy, letting nature 'make itself' through the unbroken chain of natural, secondary causes. From this perspective, speculation about divine action in relation to special events in nature (with the exception of miracles like the INCARNATION and RESURRECTION of Jesus) would risk making God into a secondary cause. The challenge here is whether the restriction of divine action to primary causality is adequate to the biblical account of God's relation to creation.

Finally, advocates of process theology writing on science, including I. Barbour (b. 1923) and C. Birch (b. 1918), have argued that God's action in nature is necessarily non-interventionist, given the metaphysical framework found in A. N. Whitehead (1861–1947) and C. Hartshorne (1897–2000). Here God provides the subjective 'lure' for each actual occasion as it comes into existence. The contribution to the world made by each actual entity is thus partly the result of the influence of the past, partly the result of divine influence, and partly the result of the novelty expressed through the occasion itself. An advantage of process theology is that non-interventionist divine action is 'written into' the METAPHYSICS of the world at every level. The challenge is to show that the sciences at all levels are consistent with this metaphysics' claim of indeterminism. If they are not, it seems hard to avoid the conclusion that the novelty guaranteed in principle by the metaphysics is actually expressed in nature.

See also MIRACLES.

R. J. Russell, *Cosmology from Alpha to Omega: The Creative Mutual Interaction of Theology and Science* (Fortress Press, 2008).

R. J. Russell, N. Murphy, and W. R. Stoeger, S. J., eds., *Scientific Perspectives on Divine Action: Twenty Years of Challenge and Progress* (Center for Theology and the Natural Sciences, 2008).

O. Thomas, ed., *God's Activity in the World: The Contemporary Problem* (Scholars Press, 1983).

ROBERT JOHN RUSSELL

DIVINE COMMAND ETHICS Divine command ethics (DCE) refers to the position that the good life is one lived in obedient response to God's command as mediated primarily through SCRIPTURE (e.g., the TEN COMMANDMENTS) but also through the order, mandates, or spheres of responsibility given in CREATION (e.g., family). The commands establish obligations or duties to be fulfilled.

Critique of DCE stems from the 'Euthyphro dilemma', first articulated in Plato's dialogue of that name: 'Does God command the good because it is good, or is it good because it is commanded by God?' The problem is that if something is good because willed by God (as DCE appears to suggest), then God can will atrocities, and they are still good. The emphasis on the freedom of God's will in theologians like J. DUNS SCOTUS and M. LUTHER leaves open such a possibility. S. KIERKEGAARD addresses this dilemma by emphasizing how ethics (understood in terms of regnant social norms) may be suspended by God's command, which demands the seemingly immoral in order that ethics itself may be held to account. Kierkegaard's paradigm example of this is God's command to ABRAHAM to sacrifice Isaac.

Conversely, the dilemma implies that if something is good in itself (i.e., if its goodness is independent of God's will), then not only is God's sovereignty limited but also morality is not founded on the command of God so that both God and humans are bound by a moral framework autonomous of both. In this case God's commands are simply a source of information about morality, not the basis of morality itself. Some understandings of NATURAL LAW take this view, as does I. KANT, so that, for example, the Ten Commandments are a republication of either the natural law or a rationally derived moral standard. DCE seeks to counter this implication.

In the twentieth century K. BARTH provided the most sustained theological development of DCE. Barth represents a refutation of the dilemma. He argues that God elects to act in certain, self-limiting ways, and that humans can only be good through obedient response to this God who is encountered in Christ. Thus, for Barth, DCE understands humans as God's creatures, as sinners pardoned by God, and as the heirs-expectant of the coming KINGDOM OF GOD (*CD* IV/4, 7). Obeying God's command requires that we respond appropriately as those who are creatures, sinners, and heirs-expectant. For Barth, the Decalogue represents neither an arbitrary assertion of divine power, nor the republication of an autonomous ethics, but the delimitation of the sphere in which human life, in relationship with God, may be free and fulfilled (*CD* II/2, 699).

For Barth, while God's commands enable us to make generic statements about what constitutes good action, the commands are always addressed to a particular person in a particular context. As personal address, God's command is simultaneously a boundary, an invitation and empowerment. In being confronted by God's command one is forced to turn away from self and respond to one's neighbour. The commands demand recognition that one cannot live alone, that one is not the source of one's own being and that one's freedom means being free for relationship with others. VOCATION is the context and 'the place of responsibility' where God's command is heard in continual interaction with the neighbour.

Barth has been criticized for overemphasizing Christology in his ethics. In response, more Trinitarian accounts of DCE have been developed by theologians like R. Mouw (b. 1940). Contemporary philosophical developments of DCE are represented in the work of P. Quinn (b. 1940) and R. Adams (b. 1937).

P. Helm, *Divine Commands and Morality* (Oxford University Press, 1991).

R. Mouw, *The God Who Commands: A Study in Divine Command Ethics* (University of Notre Dame Press, 1991).

LUKE BRETHERTON

Divine Office 'Divine office' refers to the daily rhythm of prayer in a Christian community or daily (primarily) public prayer. It is distinguished by its primary focus on the meditation of God's Word in Scripture rather than on the celebration of the Eucharist. Vatican Council II replaced the designation 'divine office' with 'liturgy of the hours', a shift that highlights daily prayer as a means of timekeeping grounded in Scripture. Among the Churches stemming from the Reformation, the Anglican Communion has either kept the designation 'divine office' or used 'daily office'. The Lutheran tradition tended to keep the classic Latin designations for particular services (e.g., Matins for morning prayer, Vespers for evening prayer). Today, it is common simply to speak of 'daily prayer'.

The history of the divine office is much broader than simply the history of a book such as the breviary, and its origins in the early Church are difficult to trace. Jewish prayer is often cited as a source, but very little is known about the practice of Jewish prayer at the time of Jesus or shortly afterwards. One thing that is clear is that morning and evening were the principal times for daily prayer. In the second and third centuries, daily prayer took on various manifestations. A great diversity of practice is witnessed in the surviving sources, though one insight common to almost all sources is that the various practices in place are conceived as a response to Paul's admonition to 'pray without ceasing' (1 Thess. 5:17).

In the fourth century in both the East and the West, various forms of the liturgy of hours emerge. Modern scholars, developing the ideas of A. Baumstark (1800–76), have categorized these as 'cathedral office', 'urban monastic', and 'desert monastic'. The cathedral office brought together the people of a local community for daily prayer in the bishop's church. All ranks of clergy and laity participated and the prayer or liturgy was constituted of a diversity of ritual forms and expressions (e.g., psalms, hymns, readings, intercessions, as well as more symbolic ritual such as the use of incense and light). The desert-monastic office (associated primarily with Egypt) followed the pattern of prayer in the morning and evening. It was, however, focused more on a meditation of God's word, both psalms and other Scripture readings. The urban-monastic office, though quite varied in practice, was an amalgamation of both the cathedral and the desert-monastic office. A particular noteworthy ritual – the lighting of the lamps or *Lucernarium* at Vespers – has remained one of the most popular expressions of daily public prayer: in the deepening darkness, the community of believers proclaims the one true light Jesus Christ.

In the East the urban-monastic office established the regular hours of the divine office, drawing on both public (morning and evening) and private (third, sixth, and ninth hours of the day) prayer practice. In the West various monastic traditions came together in the *Rule* of Benedict of Nursia (*ca* 480–*ca* 545). Benedict sought a pastoral reform of daily public prayer. He redistributed the Psalter over one week, rather than having it repeated (in some cases) every day. He eliminated the repetition of the same psalms at the same offices, except for some of the classic introductory psalms, such as Psalm 95 at Nocturnes (after Vatican II sung at Matins). He also introduced hymnody, Gospel canticles, and a reading to interrupt the long recitation of psalms. The classic pattern of the liturgy of the hours in the West arose out of Benedict's reform: Nocturnes (preparatory prayer to the morning prayer, often at 2 or 3 a.m.), Matins (or Lauds), Prime (at the first hour of the day, or 6 a.m.), Terce (at the third hour, or 9 a.m.), Sext (at noon), None (at the ninth hour, or 3 p.m.), Vespers (evening prayer), and Compline (prayer before retiring).

With the Reformation came a considerable simplification of the practice of the divine office. M. Luther attacked 'the babbling of the seven canonical hours' (*LC*), though he continued to insist on the need for daily public prayer, either in community or (especially) in the home. It was, however, the Church of England and T. Cranmer in particular who had the most success in translating the form of the divine office into prayers for the local church community through the Book of Common Prayer. The Anglican Communion has kept the tradition of morning and evening prayer alive in the local parish for the whole Church.

Today, liturgical renewal has again sought to lift up this ancient practice of prayer. Vatican II's terminological choice of 'Liturgy of the Hours' has helped focus the attention back to the office as meditation on God's Word throughout the day and the week, from Sunday to Sunday. This renewal has found expression in many worship resources among Churches of the Reformation as well, notably in the *Book of Common Worship* of the Presbyterian Church USA (1993) and *Evangelical Lutheran Worship* (2006). Another significant factor in the reawakening of daily public prayer has been the Community of Taizé. Taizé simplified the liturgy of the hours, though always keeping the ancient pattern of psalm–Word–prayers, and through its use of repetitive chants and silence has introduced several generations of young people to this spiritual discipline that is at the heart of the Christian Church.

P. F. Bradshaw, *Daily Prayer in the Early Church: A Study of the Origin and Early Development of the Divine Office* (Wipf and Stock, 2008).

Liturgy of the Hours, 4 vols. (Catholic Book Publishing, 1975).

Juan Mateos, 'The Origins of the Divine Office', *Worship* 41 (1967), 477–85.

R. Taft, S. J., *The Liturgy of the Hours in East and West: The Origins of the Divine Office and Its Meaning for Today*, 2nd revised edn (Liturgical Press, 1993).

Dirk G. Lange

DIVINIZATION: see DEIFICATION.

DIVORCE Divorce, most simply understood as the termination of a marriage, poses a great challenge to Christian ethics, given Jesus' stark words on the subject in the NT. Biblical scholars contextualize the question posed to Jesus in Matthew 19:3–12 within a first-century rabbinic debate over the valid conditions for divorce. The question at the time was less about the permissibility of divorce than about its conditions: can a man divorce his wife 'for any cause' (v. 3)? Jesus startles his audience with a broad prohibition of divorce, claiming that from 'the beginning' God made them male and female, and the two become one body such that 'what God has joined together, let no one separate' (vv. 4–6; cf. Gen. 1:1, 27; 2:24). When the Pharisees note this is contrary to the LAW of Moses, which permits divorce, Jesus replies that this was a concession by Moses due to the people's hardness of heart (v. 8). He then adds, 'I say to you, whoever divorces his wife, except for unchastity, and marries another commits adultery' (v. 9).

We see here a clear prohibition of divorce, a position which biblical scholars concur is Jesus' own. Yet we also see an immediate exception ('except for unchastity'), which is one of the two Matthean 'exception clauses' (see also Matt. 5:32). These exceptions are noticeably absent in the Markan (Mark 10:11–12) and Lucan (Luke 16:18) parallels, and scholars believe they are additions by Matthew. They are canonical SCRIPTURE nonetheless, and they are not unique. PAUL also indicates Jesus' strict teaching on divorce, but offers his own instruction, according to which a marriage can be considered terminated and the person remarry when an unbelieving spouse initiates a separation (1 Cor. 7:10–15). This is the origin of the so-called 'Pauline privilege'.

Different Christian traditions attempt to embody the above scriptural texts in varying ways. The Catholic Church prohibits divorce, though it does recognize the Pauline privilege (as well as a Petrine privilege) in dissolving marriages. There is also a practice of annulment, though this recognition that the bond of a marriage (God's 'joining together') was never in place is importantly distinct from divorce, which is the termination of the bond. There are Orthodox Churches which allow divorce, but only once. Protestant traditions generally permit divorce, though even these practices usually recognize divorce as a tragic human failure rather a merely private, contractual choice to leave a spouse.

The tensions in the scriptural texts on divorce and the varying ways different traditions honour those texts engender a host of complicated ethical issues. Can the Church even recognize divorce if no one is to separate what God has joined together? When has a binding marriage been entered into, and when has it not? What is the relationship between civil marriage and Christian marriage? How is the Church to regard people who have divorced and remarried, especially in the Catholic Church concerning reception of the EUCHARIST? Despite these difficult and painful questions among Christians regarding divorce, C. S. Lewis was surely right to state that 'It is a great pity that Christians should disagree with each other about such a question; but ... they all disagree with ... the modern view that it is a simple readjustment of partners' (*MC*, 105).

R. Collins, *Divorce in the New Testament* (Michael Glazier Books, 1992).

T. Mackin, *Divorce and Remarriage* (Paulist Press, 1982).

WILLIAM C. MATTISON III

DOCETISM The term 'docetism' is applied to all forms of CHRISTOLOGY that deny or diminish confession of Christ's full humanity. In its most extreme form, it refers to the position, associated with certain forms of GNOSTICISM, that Jesus only seemed (*dokein* in Greek) to have a human body and thus did not genuinely suffer or die on the cross (some Gnostics allegedly went so far as to deny that Jesus left footprints). By extension, the term is also applied to positions like APOLLINARIANISM, which affirms that Jesus had a human body, but denies that he had a genuinely human mind.

Docetic Christologies work from two related presuppositions. The first is that Christ is fully divine. The second is that divinity and humanity are so utterly irreconcilable that Christ can only be genuinely God if his divinity displaces some or all of his humanity. While various NT texts (e.g., 1 John 4:2–3; 2 John 7; cf. Gal. 4:4) give witness to rejection of docetic Christologies from a very early date, the classic theological objection to docetism was formulated by Gregory of Nazianzus (see CAPPADOCIAN FATHERS): 'That which he has not assumed he has not redeemed, but what he has taken up is healed' (*Ep.* 101). In other words, because Christ's work involves the renewal of the whole of human nature, it is necessary for his life to have been human 'in every respect' (Heb. 2:17). Correspondingly, the idea that Jesus' divinity is ontologically incompatible with his full humanity is denied (see CHALCEDON, COUNCIL OF).

IAN A. MCFARLAND

DOCTRINE Doctrine denotes teaching, whether understood objectively as a communicable proposition or subjectively as a churchly activity. This duality also pertains to doctrine's conceptual cousins, such as theology, TRADITION, and WISDOM. Doctrine binding within a particular Church is 'dogma' (a Greek word for a public decree). Many define ORTHODOXY as doctrine shared by major streams of Christianity, including, e.g., the Trinitarian RULE OF FAITH embodied in the classical CREEDS, and perhaps other deliverances of ecumenical COUNCILS.

Doctrine judged to be false and contrary to the gospel is defined as heresy.

Difficulties for classic Christian doctrine and practice stemmed from Renaissance and Enlightenment historical criticism. J. H. Newman famously sought to address these difficulties in *An Essay on the Development of Christian Doctrine* (1845). His argument contrasts development – legitimate and even necessary doctrinal change – with corruption. Newman then specifies seven distinctive tests by which to recognize faithful development: (1) preservation of type or idea, (2) continuity of principles, (3) power of assimilation, (4) early anticipation, (5) logical sequence, (6) preservative additions, and (7) chronic continuance.

Newman acknowledges that some orthodox Christian doctrines might appear to have greater differences over time – in language, for instance – than alternative formulations. Yet he appeals to the analogy of physical growth, in which developments are consistent with and even necessary for continuity of identity. And he argues that certain doctrinal flowers that Protestants accept as having developed from earlier biblical seeds (e.g., the Trinity) are not substantially different in kind from those they do not accept (e.g., Marian dogmas). Newman's analogies have not proven convincing to everyone; in the twentieth century many historians involved in doctrinal criticism became increasingly suspicious of Trinitarian orthodoxy and fostered a revival of something like Arianism (see Arian Controversy). Moreover, the German historian of dogma, A. von Harnack, influenced many to see in patristic theology the unhealthy dominance of Greek philosophy; this 'Hellenization thesis' has only recently faced significant criticism and controversy.

One of the more noted contemporary typologies of doctrine stems from G. Lindbeck (b. 1923). He characterizes the classical approach, which dominated until the early modern period and continues among most 'conservatives' today, as 'cognitive–propositional': doctrines are descriptive propositions – truth claims with realist cognitive content. By contrast, modern 'liberals' hold an 'experiential–expressivist' approach, in which doctrines communicate truth indirectly. Doctrines express religious experiences using symbols, whose significance for knowledge of God must be discerned with the help of philosophy and other disciplines. Lindbeck characterizes his own approach as 'cultural–linguistic', in which doctrines are second-order rules (like grammar) shaping first-order religious discourse (e.g., prayer). According to Lindbeck, doctrines are not directly descriptive of reality; rather, since their meaning is inseparable from their use, their reference to reality involves the Christian form of life of which they are part. Thus, for example, 'Christ is Lord' might be a central Christian doctrinal claim, but on the lips of a Crusader splitting an infidel's skull, the claim is false because it expresses something alien to the Gospel.

Lindbeck's impulse was ecumenical: to explain how different doctrinal formulations might be reconciled by reference to commonalities in Christian practice. At the same time, his typology has drawn criticism from all sides for oversimplifying or caricaturing alternatives. Liberals worry that his anti-apologetic focus on Christian identity and Church practice undermines theology's public accountability. Conservatives worry that his approach reduces doctrine to talk about talk rather than talk about God. Nevertheless, Lindbeck's recognition of the inseparability of doctrinal language and communal practices has dominated subsequent discussion of the topic.

Several theologians have taken up the performative turn implicit in Lindbeck's cultural–linguistic model. K. Vanhoozer (b. 1957) offers a 'canonical–linguistic' approach, modifying Lindbeck's focus on Church practice by viewing the biblical canon as containing the Church's initial and regulative linguistic practices. The canon provides the 'script' for knowing what God has done in Christ and thereby what role God intends for the Church. Accordingly (and following K. Barth), doctrine is not repetition of what the apostles and prophets said, but is rather what the Church must say on that basis. In short, doctrine is direction for how to participate fittingly in the drama of redemption, in a way that rules out 'modern' forms of separation between doctrine and ethics. A. Thiselton (b. 1937) likewise relates doctrine to the questions of 'life', via hermeneutics. He uses 'dispositional' accounts of belief to understand how doctrines embody personal and communal stances in public contexts of action, rather than simply containing propositions momentarily and mentally held. Such approaches are salutary reminders that doctrine is about teaching and learning, not simply knowing or believing.

See also Systematic Theology.

E. Charry, *By the Renewing of Your Minds: The Pastoral Function of Christian Doctrine* (Oxford University Press, 1997).

G. Lindbeck, *The Nature of Doctrine: Religion and Theology in a Postliberal Age* (Westminster Press, 1984).

K. Vanhoozer, *The Drama of Doctrine: A Canonical-Linguistic Approach to Christian Theology* (John Knox Press, 2005).

Daniel J. Treier

Dogma: see Doctrine.

Dogmatics: see Systematic Theology.

Dominion Theology Sometimes known as dominionism, dominion theology refers broadly to a range of movements within North American Protestantism that seek to make the legal precepts of the Bible the basis for the reform and governance of civil society. In line with this perspective, advocates of dominion theology tend to deny the virtue of religious tolerance and promote instead a vision of the United States as a Christian nation. The most radical form of dominion theology is Christian Reconstructionism, founded by R. J. Rushdoony (1916–2001), a Presbyterian minister whose most influential work, *The Institutes of Biblical Law* (1973), invoked the concept of theonomy (from the Greek for 'God's law') to outline a programme for making biblical LAW (e.g., OT prescriptions against adultery and blasphemy) the template for civil law.

Dominion theology is a form of POSTMILLENNIALISM grounded in the command to exercise worldwide dominion given to humanity by God in Genesis 1:28. Rushdoony argued that this 'creation mandate' was renewed and fulfilled in Jesus' claim to have been given 'all authority on heaven and on earth' (Matt. 28:18). Most interpreters read Genesis 1:28 as referring to stewardship of the natural world and not to political supremacy, rendering the idea of a 'creation mandate' problematic. Also, it has been a matter of virtual consensus among Christians since the second century (on the basis of passages like Mark 7:19; Acts 15:19; Gal. 3:24–5) that the legal precepts of the OT do not apply either outside ISRAEL or after the coming of Christ.

IAN A. MCFARLAND

DONATISM The chief theological significance of the Donatist SCHISM, which divided North African Christianity from the fourth century until the rise of Islam, was its role in clarifying the way in which the holiness of the Church was to be understood. In the aftermath of the Decian persecution (250–1), Cyprian of Carthage (d. 258) had taught that bishops who had committed apostasy disqualified themselves from office. This principle was invoked in the wake of the 'Great Persecution' (303–11) by a significant group of African Christians to reject Caecilian as bishop of Carthage, on the grounds that one of the bishops who had ordained him had apostatized, rendering the ordination invalid. Though Caecilian continued to be recognized as legitimate by the other bishops in the empire, his opponents organized a separate Church, known to its enemies as Donatist, after one of its most effective early leaders, Donatus the Great (*ca* 310–*ca* 355).

Though formally condemned at the Council of Arles (314), Donatism flourished owing to many factors, including tensions between Roman and native Berber populations (Donatism was particularly strong among the latter) and the movement's ability to claim the mantle of the tradition of moral rigorism long characteristic of African Christianity. The chief theological point of dispute with the wider Church was, however, very narrow. The Donatists argued that sacramental acts performed by sinful clergy were invalid and, correspondingly, that a Church led by such clergy was no Church. The 'catholic' party, whose most articulate spokesman was AUGUSTINE, countered that the foundation of the Church was Christ and not the clergy. Thus, even if a bishop were a sinner, the sacraments he performed were effective, because the object of the believer's FAITH in receiving it was not the celebrant (however personally virtuous he might be) but Christ's promise. In short, the validity of a sacrament was guaranteed *EX OPERE OPERATO* (i.e., by virtue of its having been performed in accordance with the canons of the Church) and not *ex opere operantis* (i.e., by virtue of the celebrant's personal moral worth).

Augustine cited the parable of the weeds (Matt. 13:24–30, 36–43) to support his contention that the Church is properly conceived as a 'mixed body' (*corpus permixtum*) of SAINTS and sinners rather than a spotless society of perfected saints (see, e.g., *Pet.* 2.26.6, 3.2.3). Though in the parable the field where the weeds grow is the world, not the Church, Augustine's central point remains: prior to the Last Judgement the saved are not separated in any clearly identifiable way from unbelievers. Correspondingly, to confess the Church's holiness is to trust in the GRACE of Christ rather than in the personal sanctity of its members. Augustine certainly did not think that the holiness of individual Christians was unimportant, but he was insistent that it be understood as a consequence – not a prior condition – of the grace communicated through word and sacrament.

J. Alexander, 'Donatism' in *The Early Christian World*, ed. P. F. Esler (Routledge, 2000), 2.952–74.

IAN A. MCFARLAND

DORDRECHT, SYNOD OF: see DORT, SYNOD OF.

DORMITION: see ASSUMPTION.

DORT, SYNOD OF During the Twelve Year Truce (1609–21) interrupting the war with Spain, Church and society in the Dutch Republic were torn apart by theological controversies which started at Leiden University with an academic dispute on the doctrine of PREDESTINATION that soon turned into a public debate. The discussions touched not only upon theological matters, but also upon political issues (e.g., Church–State relations) and existential questions (e.g., the fate of children dying in infancy). Eliciting violent conflicts among the population in the Dutch Republic, the contrasts arising from these theological disputes grew into a struggle for power, in which ecclesiastical and political interests became intricately woven together.

In 1604 the Leiden professor J. Arminius (1560–1609) started the discussion. Driven by both pastoral and exegetical motives, he distanced himself from the established Reformed doctrine of predestination. Unlike F. Gomarus (1563–1641), his academic opponent at Leiden, Arminius denied that faith was a result of divine ELECTION, describing it instead as a necessary condition, foreseen by God, on the ground of which God decides to choose or to reject an individual. The basic structure of Arminius' predestination doctrine therefore was determined by the concept of God's foreknowledge of future contingents that occur independent from the divine will, including especially human beings' free choice to believe or not. The main question Arminius posed to REFORMED THEOLOGY was: 'How can God's grace be effective, without undermining human freedom?' Arminius maintained that God does not grant FAITH except where the offer of GRACE is met by the free assent of the individual human being. His opponents, led by Gomarus, posed the question of whether it is possible to accept the idea of future contingents which lie outside of, or are prior to, the general divine will that actualizes all things. In their view God alone is self-existent and necessary; the entire contingent order depends on the divine will. Moreover, they objected that Arminius' position implied that there are two separate wills in God and thus two different acts of predestination: first, a predestination of qualities (people with the quality 'faith') and, secondly, a predestination of concrete believing individuals based on their foreseen faith. They also accused Arminius of PELAGIANISM, since it was assumed that he abolished the sovereignty of God's grace by making its effectiveness dependent on human factors.

The most important document left by Arminius concerning his teaching is his *Declaration of Sentiments*, or *Verclaringhe* (1608). In this text Arminius rejected various views on predestination held by his Reformed contemporaries by arguing for an order of priorities in the mind of God corresponding with four divine decrees. The first of these was the general decree to appoint Christ as a mediator of salvation without reference to individual people. The second decree was the determination of the means of salvation (preaching, sacraments). In the last two decrees God establishes the conditions for the future contingent acts of individual human beings, and then acts on the basis of his foreknowledge of the result. Within this framework it is not the case that the elect believe, but that believers are the elect.

Arminius was an advocate of government interference in matters of the Church and argued at the States General for the convocation of a national synod for an official settlement of the dispute. Three months after Arminius' death his followers drew up a 'Remonstrance' (*Remonstrantie*), which for the most part concurred with the central tenets of Arminius' *Verclaringhe*. This Remonstrance was presented to the States of Holland and West Friesland in June 1610. A majority of the States General, supported by the famous Dutch jurist H. Grotius (1583–1645), reacted favourably and wished for 'Arminians' and 'Gomarists' (or Counter-Remonstrants) to tolerate one another. A minority wanted to exclude the Remonstrants.

In response to this crisis, the States General called a national synod in Dort (or Dordrecht). It lasted 180 sessions, from 13 November 1618 to 29 May 1619, and included twenty-six Reformed theologians from Great Britain, Switzerland, and German territories alongside a Dutch delegation that included fifty-eight ministers and elders, five theologians from different Dutch universities, and eighteen political commissioners.

Presented in five chapters, the Canons of Dort closely followed the five points of the Remonstrance. Each chapter opens with a positive declaration of the orthodox point of view, followed by a refutation of the Remonstrant position, as follows: (1) God elects and reprobates, not on the basis of his foreknowledge, but by his sovereign and free will (see UNCONDITIONAL ELECTION); (2) Christ died sufficiently for all, but effectively only for the elect (see LIMITED ATONEMENT); (3) through the fall, humanity was totally corrupted, though it remained human (see TOTAL DEPRAVITY); (4) God's grace works effectively in conversion, though not by coercion (see IRRESISTIBLE GRACE); (5) God preserves the elect so they cannot totally and finally fall from grace (see PERSEVERANCE).

Promulgated on 6 May 1619, the Canons functioned as a confessional document that became authoritative for the further development of the Reformed Church and its theology. It should be noted, however, that the Canons were a document of consensus, and the 'solutions' presented were in fact less radical than the positions of M. LUTHER and J. CALVIN. They were based on statements (*judicia*) of members of all nineteen sections into which the synod had been subdivided, and these *judicia*, in turn, show enough diversity in their formulation of the doctrine of predestination in particular to preclude a monolithic interpretation. Thus, though the Canons affirm the importance of that doctrine in Reformed thinking, they do not make it a 'central dogma' or a *principium theologiae*, as is often suggested in secondary literature.

See also ARMINIANISM; FREE WILL.

C. Bangs, *Arminius: A Study in the Dutch Reformation* (Eerdmans, 1971).
G. P. van Itterzon, *Franciscus Gomarus* (M. Nijhoff, 1930).
H. Kajaan, *De groote synode van Dordrecht in 1618–1619* (De Standaard, 1918).
R. A. Muller, *God, Creation and Providence in the Thought of Jacob Arminius* (Eerdmans, 1991).
K. D. Stanglin, *Arminius on the Assurance of Faith: The Context, Roots, and Shape of the Leiden Debate, 1603–1609* (Brill, 2007).

WILLEM J. VAN ASSELT

DULIA Derived from the Greek word for 'service', 'dulia' is the technical term in CATHOLIC THEOLOGY for the veneration of ANGELS and SAINTS as opposed to the worship (or latria) rightly offered to God alone. The distinction is first made by AUGUSTINE, who uses the Greek terms to contrast 'the service that consists in the worship of God' with 'the service owed to human beings, as when the Apostle commands slaves to be subject to their masters' (*City* 10.1). A similar distinction was later invoked during the eighth-century iconoclastic controversy by John of Damascus, who (in *Three* 1.8) defended the liturgical use of icons against the charge of idolatry on the grounds that they were the object of veneration (*proskynēsis*) rather than worship (*latreia*). In later Catholic theology the veneration of saints is specified as dulia in an absolute sense, while dulia in the relative sense refers to the veneration of objects associated with them (i.e., relics and images). Also, public veneration is limited to figures whose sanctity has been validated through the ecclesiastical process of canonization.

T. Aquinas offers a detailed exposition of the theology of dulia. He defines it quite generally (and in line with Augustine's usage) as the virtue whereby honour is shown to other human beings by virtue of some excellence they possess. As such, he argues that it is properly offered in some respect to all people (*ST* 2/2.103.2.3). Because people display different forms of excellence, however, he also allows that it is possible to speak of different types of dulia, corresponding to the particular characteristics of those to whom it is given. Most specifically, he allows that the unique and unsurpassable excellence of the Virgin Mary justifies her being offered a superlative degree of veneration, with the technical designation of hyperdulia (*ST* 2/2.103.4.2).

For Catholics the dulia of the saints includes both veneration (honouring them for their virtues) and invocation (appealing to them to intercede with God on someone's behalf). Biblical passages cited in support of such practices include the prostration before an angel described in Joshua 5:13–14 (cf. Rev. 22:8–9, where similar behaviour is presumably forbidden because it constitutes latria rather than dulia) and the request for the prayers of other Christians found in passages like Romans 15:30 (on the grounds that if it is permissible to ask saints on earth for prayers, it cannot be wrong to request them from saints in heaven). Protestants, while not necessarily objecting to the commemoration of the saints (through, e.g., prayers of thanksgiving), have generally rejected the distinction between dulia and latria as untenable in practice and contrary in spirit to the biblical stress on God as the only proper object of devotion (e.g., Deut. 10:20; Matt. 4:10) and on Christ as the sole mediator between God and humankind (1 Tim. 2:5).

Ian A. McFarland

Duns Scotus, John John Duns Scotus was born in Duns, Scotland, probably between 23 December 1265 and 17 March 1266. He was ordained to the priesthood in 1291 and lectured on the *Sentences* of P. Lombard (*ca* 1100–60) at Oxford in the late 1290s and at Paris in 1302 and 1303. In early 1305 he was incepted as Franciscan regent master at the University of Paris. In October 1307 he took up duties as *lector* in the Franciscan *studium* at Cologne, where he died on 8 November 1308.

Scotus accepted a basically Aristotelian epistemology according to which all our knowledge is ultimately derived from sensory experience (see Aristotelianism). Like T. Aquinas, however, he was confident that even from such humble beginnings, we can come to a rational understanding of God. Accordingly, Scotus developed a highly complex argument for the existence of a being that is the origin of all agency (first in efficient causality), the ultimate goal of all activity (first in final causality), and maximally excellent (first in preeminence). He argued that any being that is first in one of these three ways will also be first in the other two ways, and further that any being enjoying the triple primacy is endowed with intellect and will. Finally, he argued that any such being is infinite, and that there can be only one such being.

Scotus argued for the doctrine of univocity: the thesis that some words that are said of both God and creatures are univocal – have exactly the same meaning – in those disparate uses. Specifically, any word that names a 'pure perfection' (i.e., a perfection that does not imply any limitation or deficiency) can be predicated univocally of God and creatures. Scotus takes the doctrine of univocity to be a consequence of the Aristotelian view of knowledge. For since concepts derived from our experience of creatures are the only concepts we can have, it follows that if we cannot apply to God the concepts we derive from creatures, we cannot apply any concepts to God at all; and that in turn means, absurdly, that we cannot know or think about God at all (see Analogy).

On the question of universals, Scotus was a realist, and indeed more of a realist than Aquinas. Scotus calls the extra-mental universal the 'common nature' (*natura communis*) and the principle of individuation the 'haecceity' (*haecceitas*). The common nature is common in that it is 'indifferent' to existing in any number of individuals. But it has extra-mental existence only in the particular things in which it exists, and in them it is always 'contracted' by the haecceity. So the common-nature humanity exists in both Socrates and Plato, although in Socrates it is made individual by Socrates' *haecceitas* and in Plato by Plato's *haecceitas*. The humanity-of-Socrates is individual and non-repeatable, as is the humanity-of-Plato; yet humanity itself is common and repeatable, and it is ontologically prior to any particular exemplification of it.

Scotus rejected the theory of illumination he found in Henry of Ghent (*ca* 1220–93), arguing that it led to scepticism, which he attacked vigorously. In ethics Scotus was a voluntarist concerning both human action and the moral law, although he recognized a core of the moral law – the natural law 'in the strict sense' – that was unchangeable even by divine decree (see Voluntarism).

Scotus became known as the 'Subtle Doctor' because of the difficulty and penetrating insight of his thought, and as the 'Marian Doctor' because of his defence of the Immaculate Conception. He was highly influential in later medieval philosophy, though the excesses of some over-subtle followers, stigmatized as 'Dunsmen', gave us the English word 'dunce'. He was beatified in 1993. In recent years Scotus has been the target of sustained criticism from theologians identified with the movement known as Radical Orthodoxy, particularly over the doctrine of univocity.

R. Cross, *Duns Scotus* (Oxford University Press, 1999).
T. Williams, *The Cambridge Companion to Duns Scotus* (Cambridge University Press, 2003).

Thomas Williams

Dyothelitism: see Monothelitism.

Easter: see Calendar, Liturgical.

Eastern Catholic Churches The Eastern Christian Churches are divided into two groups: the Orthodox Churches and the Eastern Catholic (sometimes referred to as Uniate) Churches. Until the eleventh century, all Eastern Churches were visibly in communion with Rome, though as early as the fifth century Church unity had been weakened due to Christological, political, and cultural difficulties. In 1054, the eastern and western branches separated from one another. To this day, the former have been known as the Eastern Orthodox Churches, and the latter, the Catholic (or Latin) Church. The separation was visibly expressed by the Orthodox Churches' rejection of the western way of understanding the primacy of the Pope (see Papacy).

The Orthodox Churches include autocephalous (i.e., self-governing) groups, such as the Greeks, Russians, Ukrainians, Bulgarians, and others. Between the sixteenth and eighteenth centuries, various Orthodox communities within these autocephalous groups re-established communion with Rome. In this way, each of the Eastern Catholic Churches (except for the Maronite Church) has an Orthodox counterpart. Though they hold their eastern heritage in common with the Orthodox Churches (and, like the latter, continue to have their own patriarchs), they are in communion with the Holy See. These developments can be seen as part of papal attempts to secure unity with the Orthodox that date from the thirteenth century and continue today, most recently with the publishing of John Paul II's (r. 1978–2005) encyclical, *Ut unum sint* (1995).

Eastern Catholic Churches have undergone Latinization, a term that refers to the modification of eastern liturgies and customs under the influences of western Catholic practices. The most significant of all Latinizations in the USA is the discipline of clerical celibacy, which, while long established in the western Catholic Church, had not been characteristic of Eastern Catholic Churches prior to a 1929 proscription of married clergy outside traditional patriarchal territories.

The major liturgical rites of the Christian East developed in five locations. They may be classified according to (1) Syriac influence, located in Edessa, and (2) the Greek influence, whose Churches originated in Antioch, Alexandria, Armenia, and Constantinople. The Eastern Churches also share with the Orthodox Churches four main emphases of spiritual theology: love of patristics (i.e., the writings of the fathers of early Christianity), deification, hesychasm, and the importance of Lent and Pascha (i.e., the feast of Christ's resurrection). Each of these calls for some comment.

The Eastern Church fathers of the fourth and fifth centuries built a solid foundation in dogmatic theology and a vibrant liturgical life for the universal Church. Remarkable for their timeless beauty of expression, their writings have remained a living part of the Eastern Churches, and without them the early Church could not have developed. Their concept of deification (Greek *theosis*) takes seriously the all-encompassing view that men and women, made in the image and likeness of God (Gen. 1:26) and a little lower than God (Ps. 8:5), are called to be new creations, transformed into Christ.

Hesychasm (from the Greek *hēsychia*, 'quiet') refers to an inner quiet expressed in the psalm verse, 'Be still, and know that I am God' (Ps. 46:10). Hesychasm embraces an apophatic posture that refuses to form concepts of God (see Apophatic Theology) and is best expressed in the Jesus Prayer, 'Jesus, Son of David, have mercy on me a sinner.' Repeated and synchronized with a person's breathing, the prayer was popularized in *Franny and Zooey* (1961) by J. D. Salinger (1919–2010).

The asceticism of Lent calls for fasting from certain foods and intensifying one's prayer. The austere Lenten season is superseded by the great joy of Pascha, when special foods are relished. 'Christ is risen! Indeed he is risen': this is the greeting of the Paschal season.

The beauty of eastern Christian worship can overwhelm a first-time visitor because the rich liturgical life of these Churches embraces both sensory and spiritual faculties. It engages the whole person – mind, heart, and body in praise of God. An essential part of worship in the Eastern Churches is the iconostasis: a screen of icons measuring several feet high. The screen may be viewed either as a link between the sanctuary and the nave or as a point of separation. In Oriental liturgies, leavened bread has been traditionally used. The deacon serves as a liturgical master of ceremonies, a fact that influenced the establishment of the Office of the Permanent Diaconate in the Catholic Church at Vatican Council II. The cultural history of the Eastern Catholic Churches has contributed to world culture, as have their indigenous art forms, such as chant, hymnography, iconography, art, and architecture.

M. A. Fahey, *Orthodox and Catholic Sister Churches: East is West and West is East* (Marquette University Press, 1996).

R. Payne, *The Holy Fire: The Story of the Early Centuries of the Christian Church in the Near East* (St Vladimir's Seminary Press, 1997).

J. L. Roccasalvo, *The Eastern Catholic Churches: An Introduction to their Worship and Spirituality* (Liturgical Press, 1992).

Joan L. Roccasalvo

Eastern Orthodox Theology: see Orthodox Theology.

Ebionitism Derived from the Hebrew word for 'poor', Ebionitism refers in the first instance to the beliefs of an early sect of Jewish Christians. According to Irenaeus, who is the first to describe them, the Ebionites were close followers of the Mosaic law whose only Gospel was a version of Matthew (*AH* 1.26). This latter claim was echoed by Epiphanius of Salamis (*ca* 310–403), though the few passages he cites from what is now known as the *Gospel of the Ebionites* suggest that the text was in fact a harmony of all three synoptic Gospels. After the destruction of the Jerusalem temple in AD 70, the Ebionites appear to have lived primarily in rural areas in and around Palestine, surviving until around the sixth century. Despite their marginal status, many modern scholars think it likely that the Ebionites were the direct descendants of the earliest Christian communities, formed before the transformation of the Christian movement by the Gentile-oriented ministry of Paul.

Apart from their devotion to the law, the chief theological characteristic of the Ebionites was a low Christology, according to which Jesus was the natural son of Joseph and Mary, though specially anointed by God to be Israel's Messiah and given the power to perform miracles. From this specifically Christological perspective, Ebionitism can be seen as a form of adoptionism, and in the later history of the Church the term was applied loosely to any teaching that was perceived to compromise confession of Jesus' divinity.

Ian A. McFarland

ECCLESIOLOGY Ecclesiology can be defined as constructive theological enquiry into the Church's nature, function, organization, and/or practices. Full-blown theoretical treatments of the Church are uncommon prior to the nineteenth century, though ecclesiological concepts of varying complexity and depth have been operative throughout the Church's history. Many historical, cultural, political, sociological, economic, and other non-theological factors – often unrecognized or unacknowledged – have contributed to the Church's self-understanding, though they cannot be discussed here.

The ecclesiology of the NT is somewhat diverse, countering the traditional and still common belief that Jesus directly founded the Church, its sacraments, and some, at least, of its structures. Nonetheless, the NT clearly links the Church to Jesus' earthly ministry and the apostolic leadership (see, e.g., Matt. 16:13–20; John 20:15–19; 1 Cor. 11:23–6). The Church is seen as the fruit of the resurrection and gift of the Holy Spirit. Its members have been called to anticipate and prepare for the kingdom of God by preaching the gospel and practising the obedience of faith. The Church is the body of Christ in which the Holy Spirit brings about *koinonia* (communion) with God and among its members (see, e.g., Rom. 12:4–8; 1 Cor. 12:12–13).

These and other NT themes inform Augustine's theology of the Church, a complex synthesis of previous developments and the basis for ecclesiology in the West for more than a millennium. Augustine rejected both Eusebius of Caesarea's (*ca* 260–*ca* 339) subsumption of the Church under a Christianized Roman Empire and Donatism's restriction of the Church to the pure, separated few. The Church is the one mystical body of the whole Christ, made up of everyone since creation moved by saving grace. It thus extends beyond the pilgrim Church on earth to the saints and angels in heaven. The earthly Church and its sacraments, particularly baptism and the Eucharist, are the means by which Christ imparts his grace. Led by its bishops (see Episcopacy), it is a 'mixed body' comprising not only those who desire God above all else, but also of those whose chief desire lies elsewhere. The Church is thus found in pure form only in heaven.

While Augustine acknowledged the primacy of the pope, it was for him balanced by the unity of the Church enabled by the Spirit and displayed in the decisions of Church councils. By the end of the Middle Ages, the Church in the West had become a hierarchical institution governed by canon law. The pope claimed sovereign authority not only over the Church – the spiritual realm – but over kings and other laity – the temporal realm – as well. Failure to submit to him ruled out the possibility of salvation (see Papacy).

The Reformation brought greater ecclesiological pluralism and experimentation. The reformers' acknowledgement of the critical function of Scripture and the role of the Holy Spirit in its interpretation and application undercut an over-reliance upon tradition and past doctrinal decisions. The juridical and hierarchical ecclesiology of the Roman Church, the sacramental system, and the restriction of mediation of the Word of God to the clergy were rejected or considerably modified by the Protestant reformers. Various alternative forms of worship and Church life were instituted in which the laity were often accorded a far greater leadership role. While these efforts were rejected by the Catholic Council of Trent, henceforth ecclesiology had more examples of concrete Church life to draw upon than had been the case during the Middle Ages.

Critical philosophy and the Romantic reaction to the Enlightenment had a major effect on ecclesiology, which to this point had been a secondary theological *locus*. With F. Schleiermacher's great work, *Christian Faith*, ecclesiology moved to a more dominant position. Schleiermacher argued that religious experience or 'feeling' (*Gefühl*) is a more basic aspect of our humanity than either knowledge or ethical action and that it is diverse and particular, since human consciousness of God is formed within a particular Church or religion. The function of Christian Churches is to mediate Christ's particular experience of God through their patterns of life. Thus the lived experience of a Church is prior to – and to some degree normative over – its interpretation of Scripture and doctrine. Ecclesiology – in the form of a theological description of this distinctive communal experience – therefore provides the overarching context and criteria for the Church's theological enquiry.

At about the same time, a Catholic ecclesiology inspired by Romanticism and the Church fathers was developed by J. Moehler (1796–1838), according to whom the Church's vital internal essence finds organic expression in the external elements of the visible Church (see Tübingen School, Catholic). The Church's essence is 'unity in love', the communion with God and one another brought about by the Holy Spirit. This deep ecclesial core remains self-identical despite external differences and changes over time. In his later career, Moehler shifted to a Christocentric ecclesiology more concerned with unity in truth and its external expressions. In this he supported the work of the Roman school of ecclesiology that, in various forms, became the dominant ecclesiology of the Catholic Church through the first half of the twentieth century. Central to this ecclesiology was the claim that the Church was established by Christ and is governed by his Vicar, the pope, who is the infallible interpreter of revelation. Without the pope, there could be no true Church, since his office guarantees the truth of the Church's doctrinal and moral teachings.

By the end of the nineteenth century, A. Ritschl (1822–89) had shifted some Protestant ecclesiologies away from communal consciousness towards moral action. Popular among his students – most significantly A. von Harnack – was Ritschl's idea of the Church as a community of brotherly love that seeks progressively to build the kingdom Jesus founded, thus promoting this-worldly redemption. Another student of Ritschl, E. Troeltsch, brought social–historical study of the Church to the fore and developed an influential typology of religious forms found in the Church's history.

Just before World War II, D. Bonhoeffer argued that theology must begin with the Church, since all Christian doctrine is social in intention. For K. Barth, theology is a practice of the Church, though it is not (contra Schleiermacher) governed by the Church's religious experience, but by the centre and norm of all doctrine, Jesus Christ. On the analogy of the incarnation, the Church can be described in two ways, according to two distinct agencies: the human community and the Spirit of Christ. God is always at work in the Church (as in the world more generally), and some of that activity can be discerned; but the Church's life can also be described in thoroughly human terms. Sometimes Barth seemed reluctant to link these two agencies securely together, especially in his late sacramental theology. However, his main concern was to acknowledge the Church's humanity, and thus its sinfulness and frailty, while also affirming God's free, gracious activity within the Church that enables it to be effective in its witness.

Within Catholic ecclesiology Vatican Council II was the main event of the twentieth century. It had been prepared for by a remarkable group of courageous theologians and to some degree reflects their work. Of particular significance were H. de Lubac's efforts to redescribe the Catholic Church as truly catholic, in the sense of inclusive and affirming of all that is good everywhere. Y. Congar's historical studies brought to the fore the work of the Spirit within the Church's traditions and supported a greater role for the laity. K. Rahner developed an influential theology of the Church as sacrament. As the community that makes Jesus Christ – the primary sacrament – effectively present, the sacramental Church is itself the ground of its sacramental actions (see Sacramentology).

The most pressing issues for contemporary ecclesiology are inter-related: the widespread challenges to traditional forms of Church authority; the implications of ecclesiological, religious, and moral diversity; the status and application of traditional doctrines and moral norms; and the growing awareness of the many non-theological factors at work in the construction of past ecclesiologies. Most laity are now well aware of alternative ecclesial forms and the diversity of religions, and many are too well educated to accept uncritically official *dicta* regarding moral or doctrinal questions, or claims to authority that strike them as illogical, self-serving, or unnecessarily divisive. Some have characterized calls for more open discussion and tolerance of difference as the voices of relativism and individualism. The difficulty is exacerbated by the tendency among both clergy and laity, guided by conservative, liberal, or other ideologies, to insist that the Church must take a stand on a particular – often moral – issue.

Of the various contemporary ecclesiologies, perhaps the most popular are those based upon the idea of 'communion' for which some Catholics have drawn upon Moehler or Orthodox ecclesiology, while some Protestants have been influenced by J. Moltmann's (b. 1926) 'social Trinitarianism' (see Trinity). For Moltmann, the mutual indwelling of the divine Persons is regarded as the form of perfect, non-hierarchical community and therefore the template for the Church to emulate in itself and promote in the world. Communion ecclesiology (often drawing on the correlation of 'Church' with the 'communion of saints' in the Apostles' and Nicene Creeds) has penetrated a number of official documents, where it is used to promote the idea of unity-in-diversity: we can be in communion and work together even though we differ in some relatively inessential aspects. While the idea is commonly used to support inclusivist or pluralist ecclesiologies, it can also be exclusivist, as when the Orthodox theologian J. Zizioulas (b. 1931) seems to suggest that, unless one is part of the Church, one is not fully a person. It has been suggested that a focus on communion can too easily become confused with the self-celebration of bourgeois communities. Others have pointed out that true communion is too unrealizable an ideal this side of the eschaton for it to be especially useful in addressing the issues noted above.

An alternative approach, found most influentially in the work of S. Hauerwas (b. 1940), is to focus on the Church's practices (sometimes the Eucharist in particular) as primary. Hauerwas draws on Aristotle and T. AQUINAS to describe the Church as schooling its members in Christian VIRTUES to create a community with an ethos that counters modernity's individualism and, correlatively, many Christians' assumption that Christianity is primarily about belief in a set of doctrines. This approach, too, has been criticized as inadequate or misleading in its treatment of the realities of ecclesial existence. The Churches are more complex, diverse and conflicted in their practices and cultural forms than it acknowledges. Further, the focus on practices sometimes comes with a relative neglect of doctrine, suggesting a tendency to a less than fully theological approach to the Church.

More recently, some have proposed introducing more realistic descriptions of the Church's life into ecclesiological enquiry by drawing upon social scientific methodologies. One significant example is R. Haight's (b. 1936) broad, comparative ecclesiology 'from below'. Other versions have adopted a more ethnographic approach, whether largely descriptive or, drawing upon doctrine and Scripture, more normative. One of the difficulties with these realist approaches may be that they are less able to address issues of authority and the normativity of doctrine; indeed, they may accentuate the problematic nature of these concepts.

We seem to be in a period of transition for the Churches and ecclesiology, in which it is difficult to see the way ahead. Achieving open, honest, nonpolitical, and reprisal-free discussion with all parties is obviously a vital first step, as is engagement with all knowledges that bear upon the Church. It may be that ecclesiology should become somewhat less central than it has been for some time. Ecclesiological enquiry, after all, is not concerned to promote the Church as such, let alone to bolster support for some group within it. Perhaps by re-centring theological enquiry upon Jesus Christ and the gospel, the Church will gain some insight as to how it should reform itself so as to serve its Lord more truly.

See also MARKS OF THE CHURCH.

Y. Congar, *L'église: de Saint Augustin à l'époque moderne* (Cerf, 1970).
R. Haight, S. J., *Christian Community in History*, 3 vols. (Continuum, 2004–8).
G. Mannion and L. S. Mudge, eds., *The Routledge Companion to the Christian Church* (Routledge, 2008).

NICHOLAS M. HEALY

ECKHART, MEISTER Meister Eckhart (*ca* 1260–1327/8) was a German Dominican theologian and preacher. His work, written in both Latin and Middle High German, includes scriptural commentaries, disputed questions, sermons, and treatises on spiritual matters. A gifted writer, he was equally adept at poetic images, startling hyperbole, and rigorous dialectic. He was tried for heresy near the end of his life but died before the trial concluded. Afterwards, Pope John XXII (r. 1316–34) condemned several of Eckhart's views as heretical. Today, many Catholics and other Christians regard this condemnation as mistaken, and Pope John Paul II (r. 1978–2005) mentioned Eckhart favourably.

Eckhart's thought is not systematic, but certain themes and images recur, such as the ethic of detachment, the birth of the Son in the SOUL, and the Godhead beyond the TRINITY. One important theme is the relationship between God and creatures. For Eckhart, the fact that God created everything means that every creature is dependent on God for all that it is. As Eckhart says in German Sermon 4, 'All creatures are a pure nothing ... Creatures have no being because their being depends on God's presence. If God were to turn away from creatures for an instant, they would turn to nothing.'

Consequently, the being that God gives to creatures is God's own being. For anything to exist, it must take part in God's being and in some sense be one with God. Eckhart develops this idea in a brilliant passage in his Latin *Commentary on Wisdom*. Since creatures exist only through being one with God, God then is indistinct from creatures. Still, creatures differ and are distinct from each other. This flower is different from that cup. So God, in being indistinct from all creatures, is for that reason different and distinct from creatures. Thus, Eckhart concludes, God is distinct from creatures by virtue of God's indistinction, and indistinct from creatures by virtue of God's distinction.

This conclusion expresses a familiar thought in Eckhart: that God is both immanent in creation and utterly transcendent, both identical to and wholly different from creatures. Moreover, the fact that God is described in paradoxical, if not contradictory, ways reflects Eckhart's oft-stated view that nothing we say about God really captures what God is. For some scholars, this claim, familiar from 'negative theology', provides the inner logic of Eckhart's distinctive use of language (see APOPHATIC THEOLOGY). Careful not to let his sermons and texts end with positive and therefore misleading claims about God, Eckhart frequently undermines his own assertions by the use of paradox, contradiction, and image. In doing so, he compels his readers and listeners to confront their own inadequate beliefs about God. In this sense, Eckhart may be considered a mystic, not because he puts stock in extraordinary experiences of a temporary union with God, but because his work aims towards an awareness of God as present and identical to oneself and everything else while remaining transcendent and wholly other.

See also MYSTICAL THEOLOGY.

McGinn, Bernard, *The Mystical Thought of Meister Eckhart* (Crossroad, 2001).

BRUCE MILEM

ECONOMY, DIVINE Beginning in the patristic period, the category of the 'economy' (*oikonomia*, a word referring originally to the management of a household) has been used for God's actions externally towards and in CREATION, in distinction from the internal relationships of the TRINITY that were the subject of 'theology' (*theologia*, or 'talk about God' in the most literal and exclusive sense). This idea of a divine economy is rooted in NT usage, where reference is made to God's 'plan [*oikonomian*] for the fullness of time, to gather up all things in [Christ]' (Eph. 1:10), and to 'the plan [*oikonomia*] of the mystery hidden for ages in God' (Eph. 3:9). Following the immediate context of both these passages, patristic talk about the divine economy tends to refer quite specifically to the INCARNATION as the focus and climax of God's dealings with the world.

The relationship between economy and theology is at the crux of many of the controversies that have shaped theology from the early centuries to the present day. For, while Christians have wanted to maintain (in opposition, for example, to MODALISM) that it is precisely through God's 'economy' that God's eternal identity (viz., the proper content of 'theology') is revealed, they have also wanted to avoid any confusion of the two spheres. Thus, during the Trinitarian and Christological debates of the fourth to the seventh centuries, much turned on whether particular aspects of Jesus' earthly life (e.g., his apparent subordination to the Father in passages like Luke 22:42) were seen as matters of 'economy' or as disclosing the eternal relationships of 'theology'. Similarly, an important feature of the ongoing debate between eastern and western Christians over the FILIOQUE has to do with the relationship between the Son's 'economic' sending of the HOLY SPIRIT on the Church and the eternal mode of the Spirit's procession within the Godhead.

IAN A. MCFARLAND

ECOTHEOLOGY Ecology, like EVOLUTION, is more than simply an aspect of NATURAL SCIENCE, in that it has political, social, and cultural ramifications. Ecology is about human and non-human creatures and their interrelationship and interdependencies on the planet Earth, and for this reason it incorporates global as well as local considerations. Although at one time ecology was perceived as being simply connected with nature conservation, it is now conceived in much broader terms that also impact on issues of global justice. The market economy, for example, tends to encourage patterns of consumption that are unsustainable in terms of global resources and energy availability, and this has a negative ecological impact on the poorest communities of the world. Although ecologists have warned of the dangers of human impacts on the planet ever since R. Carson's (1907–64) *Silent Spring* (1962), the seriousness of the problem has only come into public view since a consensus started to be reached on the human impact of climate change – especially the realization that the greenhouse gases that are a by-product of energy use in industrialized societies are affecting the global climate. Ecotheologians argue that theology should take ecology, thus broadly conceived, as a key context for theological reflection. Such reflection will take different shapes according to the particular Christian tradition under review, leading to a rich mosaic from different cultural contexts. All ecotheologians take the disproportionate impact of climate change on the poorest communities of the world seriously, though their voices have also been joined more recently by liberation theologians such as L. Boff (b. 1938).

The early accusation made by historian L. White (1907–87) that Christianity, with its blatant ANTHROPOCENTRISM and affirmation of human dominion in Genesis 1:28, was responsible for the ecological crisis, spawned a series of replies that sought to discredit such notions. Much of the response was directed at White's interpretation of Genesis, which was rejected in favour of more benign readings of dominion. More recently, scholars have acknowledged that Genesis has often been invoked in the way White argued, but have also defended the possibility of alternative readings of Scripture orientated around ecojustice principles.

More constructive approaches to ecotheology have become less defensive and have taken up a wide range of more systematic issues for discussion. Within this broad remit of the task of theology, different ecotheologians will have different foci of interest. The breadth of theologies represented range from more traditional Orthodox teaching, through those that are more liberal or radical, including ecofeminist positions. Those attracted to more classical interpretations of theology argue that the traditions themselves contain sufficient insights to inform a Christian theology that gives due weight to ecological concerns, including, for example, a greater focus on the DOCTRINE OF CREATION, a widening of the scope of CHRISTOLOGY that takes up classic notions of Christ as Pantocrator (literally, 'ruler of all'), a review of pneumatology that is inclusive of creation as such rather than confined to ECCLESIOLOGY, a re-evaluation of THEOLOGICAL ANTHROPOLOGY that takes seriously humanity's interdependence with the whole created order, a broadening of THEODICY so that it takes account of the suffering of non-humans in evolutionary history, and so on. Specific biblical themes, like those exemplified in the WISDOM tradition, or key figures in the tradition such as Benedict of Nursia (*ca* 480–*ca* 545) or Francis of Assisi (1181/2–1226) may also be invoked as a way of affirming the natural world. While Francis encourages a theology that is linked with a contemplative approach to the natural world, Benedict allows for more active intervention on the part of humanity.

On the other hand, more liberal scholars argue for a greater reformulation of classical doctrines so that ecological themes become more explicitly embedded in theology, veering towards more pantheistic interpretations of Christianity that seek to affirm creation by seeing it as divine (see PANTHEISM). There are also those who set out in a deliberate way to address the political and social aspects of the debate, and incorporate such discussion into theological reflection. The social-justice agenda is also not lost on those who are seeking to develop ecotheologies that make sense in a contemporary context, and in as much as this includes voices from the global South as well as the North, ecotheology represents a very broad movement that encompasses virtually every distinctive class of theology.

See also ANIMALS.

E. Conradie, *Christianity and Ecological Theology: Resources for Further Research* (SUN Press, 2006).

C. Deane-Drummond, *Ecotheology* (Darton, Longman and Todd, 2008).

N. Habel and S. Wurst, eds., *The Earth Bible,* vol. II: *The Earth Story in Genesis* (Sheffield Academic Press, 2000).

CELIA DEANE-DRUMMOND

ECUMENISM *Oikoumenē*, the past-participial form of the Greek verb *oikein*, was used in the ancient world to refer to the inhabited world, as reflected in the SEPTUAGINT translations of the Psalms (e.g., Pss. 9:9; 18:5; 23:1, LXX). In the NT the term has several meanings: the universe as a whole (Rev. 12:9; 16:14), the inhabited world (Luke 4:5; Acts 17:6; 19:27; Rom. 10:18), the Roman Empire (Matt. 24:14; Luke 2:1), and the eschatological unity of God and humankind (Heb. 2:5). In the ancient Church 'ecumenical' could be used to refer to all Christians, but also more specifically to those of the Roman Empire. Thus, synods or COUNCILS were called 'ecumenical' to the extent that their decisions were understood to be binding on all Christians throughout the empire.

After the fall of the Roman Empire, 'ecumenical' was used to designate the Church universal. From the sixth century the patriarch of Constantinople claimed the title 'ecumenical' in order to signify his primacy over the various Eastern Churches. The Churches of the REFORMATION generally described the universal Church as 'ecumenical' rather than 'Catholic' in order to avoid any confusion with the Catholic Church of Rome. In this same vein the Lutheran BOOK OF CONCORD described the creeds of the ancient Church as 'ecumenical'. Today 'ecumenical' is synonymous with the fullness and unity of the Church universal, comprising Christians of all nations as gathered and guided by the Holy Spirit. This meaning of the term emerged in revival movements in the post-Reformation period and was also a crucial term at the founding meeting of the Evangelical Alliance in 1846.

In the twentieth century 'ecumenical' has emerged as the adjective used to describe all efforts designed to further rapprochement and reconciliation among Christian Churches. The Swedish bishop N. Söderblom (1866–1930) preferred it to 'universal Christianity'. The goal of ecumenism – and the heart of that which is called the ecumenical movement – is the unity of the Church: a unity given in and by God and manifest in the service that the Churches are called to give jointly to the world. In contemporary discourse 'ecumenical' is also used in less specifically ecclesial contexts to describe any effort towards greater unity among persons or groups (secular ecumenism), including dialogue between different religions (inter-religious ecumenism).

During the nineteenth century the profound social changes resulting from industrialization and western colonial expansion brought forth the first ecumenical initiatives at both local and national levels. These initiatives reflect a renewed spiritual awareness. The divisions between Churches were viewed as unacceptable because inconsistent with the confession of the Church as one, holy, Catholic, and apostolic. Conscious of the need for a general renewal and conversion of the established Churches, Christians of a variety of confessional backgrounds met in groups for prayer and fellowship. This spiritual ecumenism found three basic expressions: a stress on unity in missionary activities, common witness in the face of social problems, and the pursuit of a common confession of faith that transcended established doctrinal divisions.

The first institutional manifestations of ecumenism followed rapidly on these developments. Organizations like the Evangelical Alliance (1846) and the YMCA (1855), which were both non-denominational and transnational, were followed by the establishment of international bodies of Churches with shared confessional backgrounds (e.g., the Presbyterian Alliance in 1875, the World Methodist Council in 1881, the International Congregational Council in 1891, and the Baptist World Alliance in 1905). In 1888 the third international Anglican Lambeth Conferences (the first of which had been held in 1867) proposed what became known as the 'Chicago–Lambeth Quadrilateral', which outlined four points (SCRIPTURE, the NICENE CREED, the sacraments of BAPTISM and EUCHARIST, and the historic episcopate) as the proper basis for the restoration of Christian unity in the face of existing ecclesiastical divisions.

Important as these developments were, the origin of the modern ecumenical movement is generally traced to the World Missionary Conference held in Edinburgh in 1910. Though participation was limited to Churches that traced their origins to the sixteenth-century Reformation, the Edinburgh Conference established four major trajectories for further work: (1) a missionary trajectory pursued via various international conferences (Jerusalem in 1928; Tambaram, India, in 1938; and Whitby, Canada, in 1947); (2) a peace movement taking shape in the World Alliance for Promoting International Friendships (founded in 1915, with a conference held in Prague in 1928); (3) Life and Work, concerned with the Churches' joint engagement in social justice, ethics, and political activism (with international conferences held in Stockholm in 1935 and Oxford in 1937); (4) Faith and Order, occupied with doctrinal questions (officially founded in Lausanne in 1927 and consolidated in Edinburgh in 1937). These four lines of development provided the groundwork for the foundation of the WORLD COUNCIL OF CHURCHES (WCC) in 1948.

At the outset the ecumenical movement involved comparatively informal movements linked to the Churches that originated with the Reformation, with the participation of institutional Churches emerging only gradually. Nevertheless, the ecclesiology characteristic of the Churches of the Reformation facilitated this development. While they understood themselves as full and true expressions of the one Church of Christ, these Churches also acknowledged that this one Church existed under other forms and with other traditions than their own. They viewed the division and mutual non-recognition of Churches as correspondingly unacceptable. The shared concern of Anglicans, Lutherans, Reformed, Methodists, Baptists, etc., was twofold: on the one hand, they wanted to overcome the doctrinal controversies that had occasioned the divisions among them; on the other, they wished to find common ways of participating in mission and of engaging with secular society.

Though somewhat cautious, the Orthodox Churches quickly grasped the urgency of the ecumenical movement. In a 1920 ENCYCLICAL the patriarchate of Constantinople expressed a desire for worldwide communion of Churches, which soon led to involvement in Life and Work and Faith and Order. Drawing on a conciliar understanding of the Church universal derived from the first seven ecumenical COUNCILS, the autocephalous Orthodox Churches have always sought dialogue and co-operation with other Christian communities without committing themselves to a definitive judgement regarding their ecclesial character. The Churches of the Orthodox tradition joined the WCC in 1961, all the while noting their many reservations and naming differences as they arose.

The Catholic Church remains more hesitant, having rejected the very idea of ecumenism in the encyclicals *Satis cognitum* (1896) and *Mortalium animos* (1928), which forbade all contact with the nascent ecumenical movement. In the wake of the decree on ecumenism (*Unitas redintegratio*, 1964) adopted at VATICAN COUNCIL II, however, Catholicism has undergone a conversion to ecumenism. While continuing to insist on the singularity of the Catholic Church as the one *locus* of the Church in its fullness, Vatican II nevertheless proposed common prayer, dialogue on matters of doctrine, and collaboration in service to the world (*UR*, §4.12). While membership in the WCC was not envisioned, the Catholic Church did commit itself to participation in Faith and Order and to the establishment of a secretariat for ecumenical affairs (ultimately realized as the Pontifical Council for Promoting Christian Unity).

After 1945 the ecumenical movement underwent rapid expansion. With so many Churches emphasizing the importance of common prayer and shared worship, ecumenical meetings became increasingly popular and frequent on the local level. Such work was sustained by the conviction that the unity of the Church is primarily the work of the Holy Spirit, and thus a spiritual reality given by God. At the regional, national, and even continental levels, councils of Churches were instituted in many places. Biblical translations were produced for use by speakers of a single language across denominational lines, and in many areas theological education and research have been characterized by close co-operation between different Churches. Within the WCC, Faith and Order has been particularly important in working towards doctrinal consensus among the Churches, including the publication of the Lima document, *Baptism, Eucharist and Ministry*, in 1982.

Especially following the entry of the Catholic Church into the ecumenical movement, bilateral ecumenical processes have emerged alongside the multilateral work of the WCC. Christian confessions representing very different traditions have organized themselves into Christian world communions (e.g., the Anglican Communion, the Baptist World Alliance, the Lutheran World Federation, the World Alliance of Reformed Churches, the World Methodist Council) that both pursue development projects (generally in close co-operation with the WCC) and engage in bilateral talks that have resulted in formulae of agreement that go far beyond the levels of convergence envisioned by Faith and Order. Among the Anglican, Lutheran, Methodist, and Reformed families, these processes have in many countries led to declarations of mutual recognition and communion that put an end to historical divisions. Even the Catholic Church has participated in this movement, having signed doctrinal agreements with non-Chalcedonian and Lutheran Churches.

Multilateral work has often been opposed to bilateral negotiations. Even if there is today general recognition of the complementarity of the two approaches, the model of unity to be pursued remains an open question. Within the WCC, some wish to promote a model of 'conciliar community' that replaces historical confessional traditions, leading to a certain degree of ambivalence with the contemporary ecumenical movement. With the onset of the twenty-first century, the numerous, undeniable advances that have been made also point to challenges ahead. For example, while the growing participation of two thirds of world Churches is a major success of the ecumenical movement, it also entails 'paradigm change' in light of the recognition that social justice, education, racism, and the marginalization of minority groups are significant obstacles to the unity not only of the Churches but of humankind as a whole. In trying to make itself more representative of these constituencies and modifying its priorities accordingly, the ecumenical movement has taken up this challenge, but this shift has often failed to elicit interest among those for whom the ecumenical vision is primarily about achieving doctrinal consensus in order to achieve greater communion among Churches.

A further development over the last decades is the emergence of numerous more informal, locally based Church groups with a strongly charismatic orientation (without, however, it necessarily being possible to identify them with classical Pentecostalism). In many places these groups count more members than the traditional Churches, yet their participation in the ecumenical movement is made difficult because of their comparative lack of interest in any dimension of Church life beyond the local or regional level.

In the light of such challenges, the ecumenical movement needs to take stock of its future course. The movement has helped overcome historical oppositions among the traditional Churches, but now is the time to proceed less tentatively. Some are content with peaceful co-operation while maintaining separate identities; others hope for a true universal communion of Churches. Where the latter goal is not kept in sight, the ecumenical movement risks degenerating into a simple forum for dialogue without a well-defined objective.

At the level of doctrine theological dialogues have been undertaken, and they have permitted the stakes to be raised. It is now necessary to move from consensus to communion. The Catholic and Orthodox Churches are confronted with the question of whether they will recognize the legitimacy of ecclesial forms different from their own. By the same token, the Churches of the Reformation must accept the challenge posed to them regarding their catholicity, their capacity to be the Church beyond the boundaries of their traditional spheres. This involves dealing with the question of ecclesiastical authority above the local or national level. The Churches are struggling to address these challenges.

Finally, it is necessary to say something about the general evolution of the world, which at the start of the twenty-first century is marked by a reassertion of local identities – a turning inwards that promotes a growing opposition between cultures and civilizations. In this context, the ecumenical movement needs to be ready to reaffirm its vision of unity and pursue it with vigour.

S. W. Ariarajah, *Gospel and Culture: An Ongoing Discussion within the Ecumenical Movement* (WCC, 1994).

A. Birmelé, *Crisis and Challenge of the Ecumenical Movement: Integrity and Indivisibility* (WCC, 1994).

G. R. Evans, *Method in Ecumenical Theology: The Lessons So Far* (Cambridge University Press, 1996).

M. Kinnamon, *Why It Matters: A Popular Introduction to the Baptism, Eucharist and Ministry Text* (WCC, 1985).

N. Lossky, J. M. Bonino *et al.*, *Dictionary of the Ecumenical Movement*, 2nd edn (WCC, 2002).

H. Meyer, L. Vischer *et al.*, *Growth in Agreement: Report and Agreed Statements of Ecumenical Conversations on a World Level*, 3 vols. (WCC, 1984–2007).

André Birmelé

Edwards, Jonathan Jonathan Edwards (1703–58), arguably the most creative American philosophical theologian, was born in East Windsor, Connecticut, as the only son in a family of eleven children. He entered the College of New Haven (now Yale) before he was thirteen, and during his student years came under the influence of the British empiricism of J. Locke (1632–1704), the new science of I. Newton (1643–1727), and the moral philosophy of the Cambridge Platonists. After serving as a pastor for almost thirty years in Northampton and Stockbridge, Massachusetts, Edwards became the president of the College of New Jersey (now Princeton) in January 1758, but died in March from an illness caused by smallpox vaccination. The twenty-six-volume critical edition of Edwards' works was completed by Yale University Press in 2009, and all his writings are electronically available from the Edwards Center at Yale University.

The most innovative element in Edwards' thought – and one with obvious affinities to the emerging empirical science by which he was so deeply influenced – is his conception of reality as a system of law-like habits or dispositions. Dispositions are defined by Edwards realistically rather than nominalistically, and thus are ontologically present in creatures even when they are not being exercised. Dispositional laws constitute the relative but real permanence and structure of the created world, and God's direct action according to those laws constitutes the actual existence of entities.

This ontology of dispositions is not limited to the creation. For Edwards, God is essentially the eternal disposition to love and beautify. God's being, therefore, is inherently dynamic. The divine disposition is fully and completely exercised, according to Edwards, through the immanent TRINITY. God in God's internal being (i.e., God as God) is therefore completely and fully actual (i.e., in God, actuality and disposition coincide). In addition, however, God seeks to exercise the divine disposition *ad extra*, in time and space. Thus, though God is fully God in God's own being and needs no further actualization *ad intra*, by exercising this disposition *ad extra* God seeks to 'repeat' God's internal being and beauty in time and space. For that purpose, God creates the world and human beings who, through their perception and love of God's beauty as realized through the world, effect this repetition. Moreover, in order to redeem fallen human beings who by their sin fail to promote the end for which God created the world, God becomes incarnate and thereby provides the world with a true and concrete image of God's beauty.

Edwards' emphases in his *Treatise on Religious Affections* on FAITH as an experience of God's beauty and upon Christian practice are both to be understood in the context of God's project of 'repeating' God's internal being in time and space. The converted person's experience is conceived as 'a sense of the heart', an apprehension of beauty in which the sense ideas one receives from the outside and the imaginative activity inspired by the HOLY SPIRIT within the mind coalesce together as a sensation that involves the whole person and repeats in concrete temporal and spatial context God's internal knowledge of beauty. This apprehension of the divine beauty by the whole person, according to Edwards, then leads to its expression in concrete, virtuous actions on the part of Christians, through which converted men and women participate in God's own temporal repetition of God's self.

R. W. Jenson, *America's Theologian: A Recommendation of Jonathan Edwards* (Oxford University Press, 1988).

S. H. Lee, *The Philosophical Theology of Jonathan Edwards* (Princeton University Press, 1988).

SANG HYUN LEE

ELECTION Election is the demonstration of unshakeable divine faithfulness through God's gracious relationship to an identifiable group of people. God's promise to ISRAEL is that 'the Lord your God has chosen you out of all the peoples on earth to be his people, his treasured possession' (Deut. 7:6). The election of Israel is grounded not in their merit but in God's LOVE and faithfulness alone (Deut. 7:7–8). The same themes of divine GRACE and faithfulness are carried into the NT, where Christ is God's elect, and those whom God chooses in Christ 'before the foundation of the world' become participants in this election 'according to the good pleasure of his will, to the praise of his glorious grace' (Eph. 1:4, 6). The promises of election are unconditional because they are rooted in God's self-consistency; they are not invalidated by the manifold failings of the elect (see UNCONDITIONAL ELECTION). The faithlessness of God's people incurs divine judgement but does not nullify their election: 'if we are faithless, he remains faithful – for he cannot deny himself' (2 Tim. 2:13). Yet for both Israel and the Church, divine election brings with it an ethical corollary: no one in the COVENANT community, including the strangers in its midst, is to be neglected or mistreated. God's faithfulness is to be mirrored by human faithfulness, particularly towards those who are vulnerable.

The temptation to construe election as an exclusive privilege afflicts both Israel and the Christian community throughout their histories. The outworkings of this misconstrual, reflected already in the biblical writings, include vengeful fantasies of divine retribution and even outright violence towards those outside the community. But the heart of the DOCTRINE of election is grace, not privilege or exclusion: God works through the particular for the sake of the universal. Election is a penultimate strategy in the overall ECONOMY of divine blessing. The election of a particular group is a blessing from God that enables them to become a sign of God's faithfulness and a source of blessing to others. In God's blessing to the family of Abram, 'all the families of the earth shall be blessed' (Gen. 12:2–3). God's bent is towards the wellbeing of the entire creation, and the bestowal of God's particular gifts to Israel and through Jesus Christ must be seen within this larger frame of reference.

In APOCALYPTIC portions of the NT, paralleling Jewish apocalyptic writings (cf. 2 Esdr. 8:1–3; 2 Bar. 44:15), election becomes primarily concerned with the eternal salvation of individuals, rather than with the witness and service of a visible community. 'Many are called but few are chosen' for membership in the Messiah's kingdom (Matt. 22:14), and the number of God's elect is fixed, its exact composition to be revealed at the end of time (Rev. 7:4–8; 14:1). This shift from a visible communal election to the eternal election of a finite number of individuals introduces large conceptual changes in the doctrine. From being a penultimate strategy in the manifestation of divine faithfulness towards 'every living creature of all flesh' (Gen. 9:15), election becomes the ultimate divine response to the irredeemable wickedness of the world: the eternal rescue of a small group of SAINTS. This doctrinal shift also has significant ethical ramifications, as it creates an enormous group of people for whom the elect community's obligations of respect and care no longer apply: the wicked, who 'will be tormented with fire and sulphur in the presence of the holy angels and in the presence of the Lamb. And the smoke of their torment goes up for ever and ever' (Rev. 14:10–11).

This dualism between the elect and those destined to eternal torment becomes articulated in post-biblical reflection in a doctrine of double PREDESTINATION: those not in the finite number elected to eternal salvation are reprobate, predestined by God to eternal damnation. In this transmogrification, suspicions of divine caprice and of a scarcity of grace cloud election's original witness to God's unshakeable faithfulness. These suspicions in turn create theological pressure on the doctrine to migrate from an economy of divine grace to an economy of human desert: the saints deserve their election on account of their faithfulness. This theological migration can be observed as the Church becomes almost wholly Gentile. The Pauline conviction that Gentiles share in God's irrevocable election of Israel (Rom. 11:29) gives way to a SUPERSESSIONISM in which Christians claim to take Israel's place as God's chosen people. Their status as the 'new Israel' is predicated on their faithfulness, in contrast to the alleged disobedience and unbelief of the Jews. The Church thereby loses its sense of identity with the story of the triumphs and failings of God's chosen people of Israel. Thus the doctrine of election that enters into the mainstream theological reflection of the Church is shorn of its connection to Israel and focused on the eternal salvation of a predetermined number of Christian individuals.

In ORTHODOX THEOLOGY the emphasis on election is muted by co-operative understandings of the effect of divine grace in the lives of believers. In the western Churches (both Catholic and Protestant), stress on the bondage of human SIN complements the doctrine's portrayal of the sovereignty of God in human salvation. AUGUSTINE, as usual, provides the landmark western statement. Against his theological opponent Pelagius, Augustine insists that sinners must place all their reliance for salvation on God's grace (see PELAGIANISM). Election thus counters both the pride of saints and the despair of sinners. Since the identity of the elect is unknown, believers are to refrain from judging others and hope for the salvation of all. But in the end, their benevolent hopes will be dashed, for God has from eternity chosen only a small number from the mass of damned humanity for salvation.

For T. AQUINAS, the cause of the election of particular persons to salvation is divine love, and predestination, as the plan of the divine intellect ordering persons towards an end, presupposes election (*ST* 1.23.4). However, most of the western tradition continues to use the terms 'election' and 'predestination' interchangeably. Election takes on special importance in emerging Protestant (especially Reformed) movements as part of their resistance to ecclesial claims to mediate salvation. Salvation is rooted in God's eternal election alone, and participation in the visible Church is no guarantee of membership in the invisible Church of God's elect. God's grace is victorious in whomever God chooses (IRRESISTIBLE GRACE) and the elect will assuredly persevere in their godliness (PERSEVERANCE of the saints).

Though J. CALVIN did not make election the doctrinal centrepiece of his theology, Calvinism becomes particularly associated with a double predestination grounded in God's secret and 'terrible' eternal decree. Calvin's pastoral intent in expositing the doctrine is clear: 'But I do not merely send men off to the secret election of God to await with gaping mouth salvation there. I bid them make their way directly to Christ in whom salvation is offered us, which otherwise would have lain hid in God. For whoever does not walk in the plain path of faith can make nothing of the election of God but a labyrinth of destruction . . . Christ there is for us the bright mirror of the eternal and hidden election of God, and also the earnest and pledge' (*Predest.* 113, 127). Trust in the righteousness and mercy of Christ is here put forward as a remedy to those who doubt whether they are included in God's 'secret' election. But within Calvinist traditions this pastoral assurance falters, as those who experience wavering faith conclude that they were never truly 'in Christ', and thus not among God's elect. Pastoral concerns that rooting election in 'the secret counsel and good pleasure of God's will' alone (WC 3.5) encourages either despair or spiritual complacency led some to abandon the notion of a predetermined number of elect. Theological followers of J. Arminius (1560–1609) hold that God elects those whom God foreknows will make use of the grace bestowed (see ARMINIANISM). As this develops in Wesleyan traditions, it is possible for believers to have assurance of present salvation, but the teachings of irresistibility and perseverance are denied (see METHODIST THEOLOGY). F. SCHLEIERMACHER untethers election from double predestination by linking election to the fellowship of Christ and seeing a 'vanishing' distinction between those inside and outside the Church as Christ's redemptive work unfolds. While Schleiermacher succeeds in restoring a communal, public understanding of divine election, he leaves no role for the Jews as people of God's choosing. The rise of dispensationalist theology in the nineteenth century posits two peoples of God elected to two distinct destinies: Israel to an earthly destiny, and the Church to a heavenly destiny (see DISPENSATIONALISM).

Two major developments in twentieth-century Christian views of election after World War II deserve notice. The first is the deliberate effort to abandon Christian 'teaching of contempt' towards Jews, as encouraged by the work of the French Jewish scholar J. Isaac (1877–1963). This is reflected in VATICAN COUNCIL II's insistence that 'the Jews should not be presented as rejected or accursed by God' (*NA*, §4). Reaffirming God's permanent and irrevocable election of the Jews has increasingly become a non-negotiable element in Christian theological understanding, though the issue of whether Jews and Christians are elect through one covenant or parallel covenants remains unresolved. A second major development is the Christological reformulation of election doctrine by the Reformed theologian K. BARTH. Barth rejects the double decree of election for some and reprobation for others, seeing this teaching as the unfortunate result of the theological separation of the God of election from Jesus Christ. Instead, he affirms Christ as the basis of divine election, functioning as both elect human and electing God. As electing God, Christ reveals God's eternal act of unconditional self-determination to be gracious to humanity. As elect human, Christ takes our rejection upon himself, and is the guarantor of the election of all humanity. Barth thus shifts the focus of the doctrine from individual salvation back to communal service and witness. Israel and the Church are the pre-eminent witnesses to both the grace and the judgement of God's election, though in Barth's scheme Israel is more associated with divine judgement and the Church with divine grace.

The 'scandal of particularity' inherent in the doctrine of election invites some new theological objections in the contemporary period. One charge is that election is hopelessly anthropocentric, eclipsing biblical witness to God's gracious purposes for all of creation, with deleterious ecological consequences. An adequate theological response must insist that the faithfulness of God to the entire creation remains the larger horizon within which the faithfulness of God in human redemption is displayed (see ANTHROPOCENTRISM; ECOTHEOLOGY). The natural world has become 'the new poor', to whom the elect community's obligation of faithfulness should be directed. Another charge is that election is an inherently hierarchical, exclusive doctrine that legitimates injustice towards those deemed outside God's special choosing. By contrast, liberation theologians have shown how God's liberation of the chosen people from bondage in Egypt provides hope for oppressed people everywhere (see LIBERATION THEOLOGY). But their interpretations sometimes reject the permanent chosenness of Israel and posit the oppressed as morally superior and hence deserving of their special elect status. An adequate theological response must affirm the 'friendliness of God' towards all human sinners, and a corresponding human ethical obligation to the wellbeing of all.

Prospects for the doctrine of election depend on recovering its focus on the visible community of faith (both Jewish and Christian) and its location in an economy of divine grace, not human desert. The main visible outworkings of a doctrine of election must be a community of worship and service in which God's grace is celebrated and displayed to the world. Election must again be affirmed as a penultimate good, what God is doing in this time between the times, towards the ultimate divine aim of universal blessing. While it is impossible at this stage of theological development to disentangle the doctrine of election from questions of ultimate human salvation, the doctrine must be freed from associations with divine partisanship or caprice, with an eternally predetermined abandonment of some. As K. Tanner (b. 1957) notes, 'the unconditionality of God's giving implies the absolute inclusiveness of God's giving: God gives without restrictions to everyone and everything, for the benefit of all' (*Economy* 72).

K. Barth, *Church Dogmatics*, II/2 (T&T Clark, 1957).
J. Calvin, *Concerning the Eternal Predestination of God* (John Knox Press, 1997).
K. Stendahl, 'The Called and the Chosen: An Essay on Election' in *The Root of the Vine: Essays in Biblical Theology*, ed. A. Fridrichsen *et al.* (Dacre Press, 1953), 63–80.
K. Tanner, *Economy of Grace* (Fortress Press, 2005).
M. Wyschogrod, *The Body of Faith: Judaism as Corporeal Election* (Jason Aronson, 1996).

AMY PLANTINGA PAUW

ENCYCLICAL As the term itself (which derives from the Greek word for 'in a circle') suggests, an encyclical is a general or circular letter sent to multiple addressees. Originally (and to this day in the Anglican and Orthodox communions) an encyclical could be issued by any bishop or group of bishops. In contemporary Catholic (and popular) usage, however, it refers specifically to letters addressed by the pope to all bishops in communion with Rome, though sometimes the address is limited to the EPISCOPACY in a particular country. Encyclicals are generally identified by the first two or three words of the Latin text following the salutation.

Encyclicals are the second highest level of papal pronouncement (after apostolic constitutions) and have been the customary form given to papal decisions on matters of DOCTRINE and morals since the time of Pope Pius IX (r. 1846–78). As such, they serve multiple purposes: outlining the general principles of Church teaching on a given topic (e.g., the great social encyclicals from *Rerum novarum* (1891) to *Centesimus annus* (1991)), clarifying particular issues (e.g., the place of historical-critical study of SCRIPTURE in *Divino afflante spiritu* (1943), the Church's approach to ECUMENISM in *Ut unum sint* (1995)), and condemning error (e.g., MODERNISM in *Pascendi dominici gregis* (1907), ABORTION and all forms of artificial contraception in *Humanae vitae* (1968)). Judgements rendered in encyclicals are not an expression of the supreme MAGISTERIUM of the Church, and their dogmatic status is correspondingly debated. While some regard them as sufficiently binding to preclude further discussion among theologians (following Pius XII, *Humani*, §20), others view such discussion as appropriate to the ongoing process of clarifying Church teaching.

See also PAPACY.

IAN A. MCFARLAND

ENDO, SHUSAKU Shusaku Endo (1923–96) was a distinguished Japanese Catholic novelist of rare theological perception. Endo was baptized in 1935 at the age of twelve. He studied French literature at the University of Lyons from 1950 to 1953 and became personally aware of the historic cultural rootedness of Christianity in Europe. In contrast, he spoke of his own Christianity as 'a kind of ready-made suit' which could be easily removed. This interested him in cross-cultural communication, which, together with Japanese identity, he explored in a series of books, including *The Sea and Poison* (1958), *Wonderful Fool* (1959), *Silence* (his most famous work, 1966), *A Life of Jesus* (1973), *The Samurai* (1980), and *Deep River* (1993).

Developing a distinctively Japanese understanding of the awareness of God, he wrote, 'The religious mentality of the Japanese is ... responsive to one who "suffers with us" and who "allows for our weakness" but their mentality has little tolerance for any kind of transcendent being who judges humans harshly ... In brief, the Japanese tend to seek in their gods and buddhas a warm-hearted mother rather than a stern father' (*Jesus* 1). Following this, and avoiding any triumphalism, Endo developed a narrative CHRISTOLOGY of Christ as perpetual companion. Jesus was one from whom those who had failed – and Endo saw failure as the pervasive cross-cultural human condition – could find compassion. Acutely aware of the apparent silence of God, Endo understood silence not as God's withdrawal, but as the silence of pitying solidarity or accompaniment.

IAIN R. TORRANCE

ENERGIES, DIVINE The 'divine energies' are defined in ORTHODOX THEOLOGY as the activity of God both in the CREATION of the universe and in God's continuing involvement, or immanence, therein. The concept has its roots in Aristotle's thought, but was further refined by later philosophers including Philo of Alexandria (20 BC–AD 50), Plotinus (204–70), and Porphyry (*ca* 230–*ca* 310), as well as by various Greek patristic thinkers. Philo was the first to describe God's mode of existence in the form of a triad consisting in the divine essence (*ousia*), powers (*dynameis*), and energies (*energeiai*). The divine energies, while not participating in God's essential nature, are signs or impressions in the created world through which he may be glimpsed.

In Christian theology, the antinomy between an uncreated and eternal God and the created universe has, from as early as the second century (when the doctrine of *creatio ex nihilo* was first made explicit), posed the question of how any relationship between the two is possible. With respect to the divine essence, God can only be described by apophatic terminology as inaccessible and unknowable (see APOPHATIC THEOLOGY). According to Greek patristic thinkers, who were influenced by Philo, the divine energies are the aspects of divine existence that can be named. The CAPPADOCIAN FATHERS, for example, believed that they are the active powers of God that can be discerned by meditating on God's works. Thus, words such as 'Lord', 'Master', 'Light', and 'Truth' designate not God's unknowable essence, but rather God's energies which, like rays of the sun, are perceptible to human beings in the created world. The sixth-century Syrian theologian DIONYSIUS THE AREOPAGITE adapted this concept to a Neoplatonic structure, seeing the divine energies as the force that flows both down and up between God and creation. In the seventh century MAXIMUS THE CONFESSOR developed this idea in terms of the concept of *logoi*, that is, the God-given qualities that define creatures in their particularity and allow them to originate, grow, and attain their appropriate goals. About a century later, JOHN OF DAMASCUS also stressed the distinction between the divine essence and energies, insisting that, whereas the former is unknowable, the divine energies illumine creation, reflecting the eternal glory of God.

Further development of the Orthodox understanding of God's presence in creation, and the distinction between his essence and energies, occurred in the fourteenth century during the debate between GREGORY PALAMAS, an Athonite monk and archbishop of Thessalonica (see ATHOS, MOUNT), and the Calabrian monk Barlaam (*ca* 1290–1348). This controversy was inspired by an increasing focus on the manner in which human beings may achieve union with God through hesychastic PRAYER (see HESYCHASM). If God's essence, which is shared by Father, Son, and Holy Spirit, is unknowable, how can mystics experience a sense of participation in divine being? How, to state this biblically, can they become 'participants of the divine nature' (2 Pet. 1:4)? Palamas, building on a theological tradition that was by now well established, described this dynamic force as the 'energies' of God. These energies are not the essence, or unchanging being, of the Trinitarian Godhead; rather, they emanate from God like rays from the sun. Palamas uses various terms to describe the divine energies, including 'divinities', 'uncreated light', and 'grace'. As V. Lossky (1903–58) puts it, 'The energies might be described as that mode of existence of the TRINITY which is outside of its inaccessible essence. God thus exists both in his essence and outside of his essence' (*Mys.* 73). This is the glory of God, which revealed itself quintessentially in the TRANSFIGURATION (Matt. 17:1–13; Mark 9: 2–13; Luke 9:28–36), when Christ manifested his divinity to three APOSTLES, appearing to be 'shining' or infused with light. Palamas' opponents, including especially Barlaam, objected to the concept of divine energies because they believed that it detracted from God's essential simplicity and could lead to ditheism or, worse, polytheism. The upholding of Palamas' distinction between essence and energies at several councils held in Constantinople in the mid-fourteenth century resulted in the formal adoption of this doctrine in the Orthodox Church.

The concept of divine energies has important implications for monastic theology and, in particular, for the concept of *theosis* or DEIFICATION. It allows the antinomy according to which God, in his essence, remains unknowable, but in his energies may be present in creation and especially in particularly holy people who have purified themselves to the extent that they may be transfigured by this divine power. The union to which they are called is, however, not hypostatic: in other words, they do not participate in God's essential being. What they experience is, according to Palamas, a form of union which God grants by GRACE, even though they remain creatures in nature. This is in fact the original state of grace which God intended not only for human beings but for the whole of creation, and which was disfigured, though not entirely lost, through the FALL. Orthodox tradition regards the divine energies as manifestations of the eternal effulgence of God, and recognition and participation in these energies may be recovered – in fact *should* be recovered – within the limits of the created world and of temporal existence.

The western Christian tradition remained largely unaware and unreceptive of Greek interpretations of the divine energies, mainly because of the pervasive influence of AUGUSTINE's emphasis on the simplicity of God's essential being. Although it has often been assumed that later western theologians therefore ruled out participation, or synergy, between God and his creation, a revisionist view suggests that, at least according to T. AQUINAS, God is present in all things precisely because all things depend on God. In a sense, this formulation goes further than the eastern concept of essence and energies since it applies not only to a sanctified, or transfigured, form of existence but to *all* created beings that owe their existence to God. The divergence, or similarities, between the eastern and western views of the 'divine energies' represent a current topic in ecumenical debate.

D. Bradshaw, *Aristotle East and West: Metaphysics and the Division of Christendom* (Cambridge University Press, 2004).

V. Lossky, *The Mystical Theology of the Eastern Church* (St Vladimir's Seminary Press, 1998).

J. Meyendorff, *A Study of Gregory Palamas* (St Vladimir's Seminary Press, 1998).

D. Stăniloae, *The Experience of God: Orthodox Dogmatic Theology*, 2 vols. (Holy Cross Orthodox Press, 1994–2000).

MARY B. CUNNINGHAM

ENLIGHTENMENT As an intellectual catchword 'the Enlightenment' (*Aufklärung*, Age of Reason, *le siècle des Lumières*) names a historical epoch (broadly eighteenth-century Europe) as well as a set of philosophical tenets and moral sensibilities articulated within this era. First construed in the nineteenth century as a distinct period, the Enlightenment encompasses diverse thinkers with varied appeals to critical reasoning and to promoting human betterment. With antecedents in the seventeenth century among popular English deists, J. Locke's (1632–1704) advocacy of natural religion, and R. Descartes' (1596–1650) quest for a principle of human certitude, Enlightenment thought flourished in England, Scotland, Germany, and among the *philosophes* in pre-revolutionary France.

By the 1790s the movement had reached a turning point. I. KANT's critical philosophy brought the impasse between intellectual–moral autonomy and received religious teachings to a head, while the French Revolution led to rethinking the meaning of liberty, fraternity, and equality and called forth new paths of theological and moral reflection. Today the intellectual challenge of the Enlightenment extends to all aspects of life, including debates about multiculturalism (in contrast with a universal humanity), the cogency and place of religion (alongside NATURAL SCIENCE), the rise of secularism, and the origins of modernity and (if it indeed exists) of postmodernity.

C. Becker's (1873–1945) thesis in *The Heavenly City of the Eighteenth-Century Philosophers* (1932) has generally been sustained. For Becker the Enlightenment 'climate of opinion' aims at the good life on earth for its own sake, with posterity replacing the classical 'heavenly city' of AUGUSTINE. With some exceptions (e.g., Baron d'Holbach (1723–89) in France, K. Bahrdt (1741–92) and J. Basedow (1724–90) in Germany, and D. Hume (1711–76) in Scotland), the movement did not foster MATERIALISM or naturalism. Thus, belief in God, virtue, and immortality, hallmarks of the DEISM of Lord Herbert of Cherbury (1583–1648), informed the American founders' concept of God-given natural rights. The Pietists' emphasis on introspection also fed the self-discovering impulses of Enlightenment thinkers: it is no accident that Halle, the German university most closely associated with PIETISM, also hosted the rationalist C. Wolff (1679–1754). The political liberalism of J.-J. Rousseau's (1712–78) *Social Contract* (1762) called for a public CIVIL RELIGION to supplant extant faiths, thus challenging traditional belief in God, SCRIPTURE, and religious DOCTRINE. G. Lessing's (1729–81) *The Education of the Human Race* (1778) cast revelation as a progressive, rational unfolding of history, and J. Herder's (1744–1803) *The Spirit of Hebrew Poetry* (1782–3) enquired into the aesthetics that inform OT teaching. The early philological–historical criticism of J. Ernesti (1707–81), J. Michaelis (1717–91), and H. Reimarus (1694–1768) challenged received views of the Bible.

Ever since its rise, the Enlightenment has been defined as much by its opponents as by its advocates. In the 1790s, to be an *Aufklärer* was to risk being viewed as anti-religious, whether that was justified or not. Amid this ferment, Kant's essay *What is Enlightenment?* (1784) remains emblematic. For him, freedom of expression is a prerogative of scholars, though our duties in CIVIL SOCIETY require subservience to authority. Kant's injunction to knowledge ('Dare to know') was thus incomplete, and his tract, correspondingly, distinguishes between a present 'age of Enlightenment' and 'an enlightened age' yet to unfold. Anticipating the stance of S. KIERKEGAARD, writers like J. Hamann (1730–88) and F. Jacobi (1743–1819) criticized Kant's moral–religious philosophy in the name of faith and inner religious experience. While in an attempt to fulfil the legacy of the Enlightenment, G. W. F. HEGEL and other figures of German IDEALISM set forth a philosophical rationalism that marks the apogee of western philosophy's attempt to reconcile reason with nature, the human self with history, society, and deity.

Recent critics of Enlightenment rationality like A. MacIntyre (b. 1929) and R. Rorty (1931–2007) call attention to the limits of universal reason, while emphasizing the relative, deeply anchored, historical-truth perspectives within diverse communities. By probing the ambiguity of what J. Habermas (b. 1929) calls 'the modern project', critical theorists, feminists, and liberation theologians use the tools of social and political theory to plumb the un-emancipatory rationality of the Enlightenment (see FEMINIST THEOLOGY; LIBERATION THEOLOGY). Such critics implicitly build upon the revolt against RATIONALISM of early nineteenth-century Romantics, who demanded that its teachings embrace the fullness of life, including human subjectivity. For the German Romantic theologian F. SCHLEIERMACHER rationality was radicalized, not diminished, by criticism; common moral assumptions were deepened, not eradicated, by individual subjectivity; and institutions were challenged, not overthrown, by the imperative to preserve human freedom.

Though a 'typical' Enlightenment thinker probably does not exist, eighteenth-century models of relating rationality to the claims of religious faith stubbornly persist amid the debates of contemporary philosophers, theologians, and historical–critical theorists. In its general anti-authoritarianism the Enlightenment still shapes the contours of our intellectual landscape.

F. C. Beiser, *Enlightenment, Revolution, and Romanticism: The Genesis of Modern German Political Thought, 1790–1800* (Harvard University Press, 1992).

M. A. Gillespie, *The Theological Origins of Modernity* (University of Chicago Press, 2008).

P. Hyland *et al.*, eds., *The Enlightenment: A Sourcebook and Reader* (Routledge, 2003).

RICHARD CROUTER

ENTHUSIASM Derived from the Greek for 'being possessed by a god', 'enthusiasm' is a pejorative term, the sense of which was captured by the third earl of Shaftesbury (1671–1713): 'Inspiration is *a real* feeling of the Divine Presence, and Enthusiasm *a false one*' (*Charac.* I, §7). While Christians have debated the criteria of genuine INSPIRATION (i.e., speech by the power of the HOLY SPIRIT) from the beginning (see, e.g., 1 Cor. 12:3; 1 John 4:2–3), the charge of enthusiasm pertains as much to ECCLESIOLOGY as to REVELATION, since it is generally made against persons or groups who invoke the Spirit against established forms of piety and ministry in the Church.

Although the Spirit has been invoked to such ends at least since the rise of MONTANISM in the second century, the category of enthusiasm dates only from the REFORMATION period. M. LUTHER condemned radicals like T. Müntzer (*ca* 1490–1525) as *Schwärmer* or fanatics (the term was meant to suggest swarming insects) for their disregard of civil and ecclesiastical authority in favour of personal revelation. In Britain from the mid-seventeenth to the early nineteenth century, 'enthusiasm' was used for any movement that opposed the religious establishment as in some measure tepid, decadent, or corrupt and advocated a more immediate relationship between the individual believer and God. It was applied equally to Quakers, who rejected the whole apparatus of ordained ministry and sacraments, and early Methodists, whose stress on the importance of individual conversion entailed no such opposition to the structures of the established Church.

Though polemical overuse led to the gradual disappearance of 'enthusiasm' as a category of academic theology, the concerns that had prompted its use have continued to mark the reaction of established Churches to charismatic movements, including especially the emergence, explosive growth, and widespread influence of Pentecostalism from the early twentieth century. In their rejection of established forms, 'enthusiasts' are accused of subverting the Church's CATHOLICITY, and their criticism of the faith and practice of other Christians is interpreted as an offence against LOVE that, even where it does not lead to open SCHISM, threatens the Church's unity. By contrast, those so accused argue that they are merely recalling the Church to the demands of APOSTOLICITY and HOLINESS characteristic of the primitive Church in the face of routinized forms of piety.

Historically, movements charged with enthusiasm have often proved highly fissiparous. At the same time, many have also served as catalysts for renewal and reform across the wider Church (e.g., in challenging slavery and acknowledging women in positions of leadership). Theologically, the problem of 'enthusiasm' reflects tensions inherent in pneumatology: since the Spirit 'blows where it chooses' (John 3:8), it cannot be controlled by the Church, which must therefore guard against whatever threatens to 'quench the Spirit' (1 Thess. 5:19). At the same time, the fact that 'God is a God not of disorder but of peace' (1 Cor. 14:33) means that the relationship between charismatic leaders and established practice cannot be disregarded when assessing such leaders' claims to be moved by the Spirit.

See also Charismatic Movement; Marks of the Church; Methodist Theology; Pentecostal Theology; Quaker Theology.

Ian A. McFarland

Ephesus, Council of The Council of Ephesus is reckoned as the third ecumenical council both by those Churches that adhere to the Christology of the Council of Chalcedon and by the Oriental Orthodox Churches. It was called to settle the Christological controversy that had arisen between Cyril of Alexandria and Nestorius of Constantinople (*ca* 385–*ca* 450) over Nestorius' rejection of *Theotokos* ('Bearer of God') as an appellation for the Virgin Mary.

The Councils of Nicaea and Constantinople had condemned Arianism (see Arian Controversy), and formulated the doctrine of the Trinity. A crucial aspect of this Trinitarian confession was the insistence that Christ was fully God, and the designation of Mary, Christ's mother, as 'Bearer of God' served to highlight this point. In 428 Nestorius rejected the term, leading Cyril to question his commitment to the Nicene faith. Cyril argued that withholding the title of *Theotokos* from Mary reduced Christ's status to that of a mere man and thereby made the Church's worship of him equivalent to idolatry. He correspondingly stressed human nature's unity with God in the incarnation, in what became the defining slogan of later miaphysite ('one-nature') Christologies: 'one nature of God the Word incarnate' (see Miaphysitism). Cyril presented Nestorius with a list of twelve anathemas, to which Nestorius was expected to agree. Nestorius responded by claiming the anathemas were Apollinarian (see Apollinarianism) and charging Cyril with heresy.

The controversy led Emperor Theodosius II (r. 408–50) to summon an ecumenical council to meet at Ephesus in June 431. Two groups of bishops were initially delayed in arriving, including most notably the group led by John of Antioch (d. 441). After waiting two weeks, Cyril proceeded to assemble the bishops who were present, who condemned Nestorius. As a concession to western theological concerns, they also condemned Coelestius (*fl.* 415), Pelagius' (*ca* 355–*ca* 420) most well-known disciple (see Pelagianism). When John eventually arrived, he condemned Cyril; when word reached Theodosius (who was a supporter of Nestorius), he initially concurred in revoking the decisions of Cyril's council. Subsequently, however, he was persuaded to accept them.

Cyril was the obvious victor following Ephesus, with Nestorianism condemned and his twelve anathemas vindicated. But reconciliation with the eastern bishops, particularly John of Antioch, was important, both politically and ecclesiastically, so Cyril agreed in 433 to a *Formulary of Reunion*. In this document Cyril set the stage for both the theology of Chalcedon (as well as for later miaphysite Christologies) by conceding that the language of 'one person from two natures' represented an orthodox account of the incarnation. Terminological conservatives never accepted the concessions Cyril made to John, and their objections heralded the deeper and permanent split between the miaphysites and the imperial Church which took place after Chalcedon.

See also Mariology; Syriac Christian Theology.

P. B. Clayton, *The Christology of Theodoret of Cyrus* (Oxford University Press, 2007).

J. A. McGuckin, *St. Cyril of Alexandria and the Christological Controversy* (St Vladimir's Seminary Press, 2004).

Steven A. McKinion

Episcopacy Ostensibly a ministry of unity centred on the office of bishop (a word ultimately derived from the Greek *episkopos*), episcopacy has proved divisive in Church history. Catholics, Orthodox, and Anglicans are wedded to episcopacy and, in spite of frustrations with actual bishops, believe it to be apostolic and therefore ecumenically non-negotiable.

In the NT *episkopē* means 'pastoral responsibility' or 'oversight', sometimes 'visitation'. Jesus Christ is the great shepherd and *episkopos* of the Church (1 Pet. 2:25). The earliest reference to the plural *episkopoi* is Philippians 1:1, where the term is functional and the 'bishops' are linked with the equally functional *diakonoi* ('deacons'). *Episkopoi* are sometimes synonymous with *presbyteroi* ('elders'), as in Acts 20:17, 28. In the Pastoral Epistles the figures of Timothy and Titus represent a stage between apostle and bishop: they remain in local churches, have delegated apostolic authority, receive some kind of 'ordination' and themselves ordain elders (though in Tit. 1:5–9 *presbyteroi* and *episkopoi* are equated). The moral and spiritual qualities of 'bishops' are set out, but not their duties.

In the later NT books the apostles have a collective identity and are the foundation of the Church (Eph. 2:20; Rev. 21:14). The turn of the first century saw a gradual and patchy development towards a 'monarchical' episcopate: one bishop for one church in one place. In *1 Clement* (*ca* 100) the episcopate is collegiate and transmitted authority is important. In the letters of Ignatius of Antioch (d. *ca* 110) the bishop is the representative of Jesus Christ and the image of God the Father. He gathers his presbyters and deacons and his authority legitimates celebrations of the Eucharist. In the late second century Irenaeus sees the bishop as the guarantor of apostolic truth against Gnostic aberrations (see Gnosticism), through continuity in the bishop's seat or see. In Cyprian of Carthage (d. 258) the bishop is the successor of the apostles and the bond of unity, presiding in the councils of the Church. The episcopate is a unified entity and the Church and the episcopate are indivisible. This idea was taken up in later Catholic ecclesiology, for which the apostles collectively constitute the 'apostolic college', and bishops are successors of the apostles. Jerome, however, argued that bishops evolved out of the presbyterate in Alexandria, rather than being delegated in succession from the apostles.

After the Constantinian establishment of the Church bishops became imperial administrators as well as pastors and theologians. The majority view among medieval theologians was that bishops were priests with enhanced jurisdiction, not a third holy order alongside priests and deacons. By the later Middle Ages, bishops had become politicized and were often engaged in power struggles with the pope and with civil rulers. The conciliar movement mobilized bishops and rulers against a dysfunctional papacy, largely unsuccessfully (see Conciliarism).

The majority of bishops resisted the Reformation, though M. Luther was willing to accept the episcopacy, provided that bishops preached the gospel. J. Calvin, too, did not reject episcopacy on principle (as he did the papacy), though he preferred an alternative form of Church order. The English Reformation continued the medieval fabric of bishops and dioceses, but without much theological rationale. R. Hooker defended the apostolic and divine origin of episcopacy, but held that the episcopate could be abolished if it became unreformable and could be reconstituted from the presbyterate. Lutheran Churches in Scandinavia generally retained episcopacy, without making it essential. These Churches and the Lutheran Churches of North America now have bishops in 'the historic episcopate' (defined in ecumenical theology as 'in intended visible continuity with the mission of the apostles'). The Chicago–Lambeth Quadrilateral of 1888, designed to provide a template for rapprochement among the divided Churches, included 'the historic episcopate, locally adapted in the method of its administration to the varying needs of the nations and peoples called of God into the unity of his church' as an essential element of Christian unity, but does not require it in order to recognize a Church or to reach agreements that fall short of full ecclesial communion with an interchangeable ordained ministry.

Episcopacy by divine right (*de iure divino*) was asserted by the Council of Trent and Vatican Council I and has been embraced by High-Church Anglicans. The spiritual character of episcopacy was rediscovered in the Catholic Church by J. A. Möhler (1796–1838) in the early nineteenth century (see Tübingen School, Catholic) and articulated by Vatican Council II. According to this theology (articulated in, e.g., the conciliar decree *Christus Dominus* of 1965) the episcopate is a third order of ministry and receives the fullness of holy orders. The bishop's authority comes directly from God, and collectively the bishops comprise a college with the pope at its head. However, the authority of the episcopate and of local organs of consultation tends to be repressed in contemporary Catholic practice.

In ecumenical discussion the World Council of Churches document *Baptism, Eucharist and Ministry* (1982) encouraged non-episcopal Churches to embrace episcopacy, though recognizing the reality of personal *episkope* in non-episcopal Churches as a stepping-stone to unity. Some Anglican and some Lutheran Churches have ordained women to the episcopate, though this is condemned by the Catholic Church. Similarly, the fact that the bishops (male and female) of the United Methodist Church and of some Lutheran Churches are not at present within the historic episcopate makes their status a subject of current ecumenical dialogue. Despite such disagreements, however, the framework provided by the *BEM* was successfully implemented in *Called to Common Mission* (2001), involving the majority of Lutheran and Anglican Churches in the USA. In Europe the Porvoo Agreement (1996) between the Nordic and Baltic Lutheran Churches and the British and Irish Anglican Churches showed how the loss of the historic episcopate could be repaired when Churches come together within a shared theological framework and a common intention.

J. Halliburton, *The Authority of a Bishop* (SPCK, 1987).
W. Kasper, *Leadership in the Church* (Crossroad, 2003).
Women Bishops in the Church of England: A Report of the House of Bishops' Working Party on Women in the Episcopate (CHP, 2004).
J. Zizioulas, *Eucharist, Bishop, Church: The Unity of the Church in the Divine Eucharist and the Bishop During the First Three Centuries* (Holy Cross Orthodox Press, 2001).

Paul Avis

Epistemology, Theological: see Revelation.

Erastianism Named after the Swiss theologian T. Erastus (1524–83), the term 'Erastianism' functions in most theological literature for a Protestant doctrine affirming the supremacy of the civil authority over the Church in ecclesiastical matters. It is perhaps most often associated with the position within Anglican theology that defends the English monarch as (in the words of the Act of Supremacy of 1534) 'the only supreme head on earth of the Church in England', with the right to appoint bishops and supervise the work of ecclesiastical courts. In the early seventeenth-century Netherlands, Erastianism was advocated by the Remonstrants (see Arminianism) over against the majority of the Dutch Reformed, who advocated a Presbyterian polity operating independently of the civil magistrate.

Erastus himself did suggest that the 'ecclesiastical' role of the monarch in ancient Israel provided an appropriate model for Church–State relations in a Christian context, but he did not offer a comprehensive theory of Church–State relations. Instead, his primary focus was the narrower question of the validity of excommunication. Against the insistence on the importance of this distinctly ecclesiastical form of discipline characteristic of Reformed theologians like J. CALVIN and T. Beza (1519–1605), Erastus argued that the sins of Christians should be punished by the civil authority only and not by the clergy withholding the sacraments. His defence of this position rested both on a strong correlation between ancient Jewish and Christian sacramental practice (e.g., he argued that the fact that the OT excludes no one from the Passover sacrifice for their sins implies that the Church should not exclude any member from the EUCHARIST) and on the parallelism between word and sacrament as divinely appointed means of GRACE (so that it makes no more sense to exclude a person from the sacraments than from the word). Though defended by some English Puritans, Erastus' position was rejected in the Westminster Confession (see WESTMINSTER STANDARDS), which specifies that 'Jesus, as king and head of His Church, has therein appointed a government, in the hand of Church officers, distinct from the civil magistrate', and that this government has powers including 'suspension from the sacrament of the Lord's Supper for a season; and . . . excommunication from the Church; according to the nature of the crime' (WC 30.1, 4).

While Erastianism in its broader sense runs afoul of modern western political sensibilities regarding the separation of Church and State, its chief theological significance has to do with the question of whether a ministry of exclusion from the sacraments is properly part of Christian practice. Generally, Christians have affirmed that it is, with some (e.g., Mennonites and related groups, as well as some Reformed Churches) going so far as to claim such discipline as an identifying MARK OF THE CHURCH. Yet the fact (stressed by Erastus himself) that Judas was not excluded from the Last Supper, as well as the scandalously inclusive character of Jesus' general practice of table fellowship (see, e.g., Matt. 9:10–11), has been used in contemporary theology to argue for a position similar to Erastus'.

IAN A. MCFARLAND

ERISTICS Derived from the Greek word for 'dispute' (*erizein*), the term 'eristics' was coined by the Swiss Reformed theologian E. Brunner (1889–1966) for his own distinctive understanding of Christian APOLOGETICS as a matter of attacking – rather than merely defending against – challenges to the FAITH launched from outside the Church. He was careful to distinguish eristics from theological prolegomena, arguing that the eristic task was merely to clear a space for the formulation of DOCTRINE and not in any sense to provide a foundation for it (which can only be God's Word). Citing PAUL's charge to 'destroy arguments and every proud obstacle to the knowledge of God' (2 Cor. 10:5) as a summary description of eristics, Brunner regarded B. PASCAL and S. KIERKEGAARD as past masters of eristic theology for their reasoned engagement with unbelievers and their attacks on non-Christian philosophies.

The propriety of eristic theology became a notorious point of contention between Brunner and K. BARTH. The latter charged that eristics amounted to an abandonment of theology's proper focus on God's Word in favour of a preoccupation with the capacities of human reason, as though the reception of God's revelation depended on right thinking rather than the other way round. Brunner countered that Barth's denial of any 'point of contact' between divine revelation and human reason falsely construed all natural human reason as equally far from the truth in a way that failed to recognize unquestionable areas of overlap between Christian and non-Christian knowledge (e.g., in the realms of mathematics and NATURAL SCIENCE).

IAN A. MCFARLAND

EROS: see LOVE.

ESCHATOLOGY The concept of eschatology comprises all views and tenets of faith associated with the so-called 'last things' (*ta eschata* in Greek). The destiny of this world, as well as that of the individual person and everything it encompasses, has been thematized in eschatology: HEAVEN and HELL, paradise and immortality, RESURRECTION and transmigration of souls, rebirth and reincarnation, final judgement and doomsday, the return of the Lord, etc. Since the way in which these different topics are answered affects the life and destiny of persons and communities, eschatology shapes both our current life together and our outlook on the future. For instance, Buddhists striving for Nirvana will not cling to this life; they adhere to the notion of rebirth and therefore treat other life forms with reverence. Likewise, Christians, who believe in the resurrection of the BODY, have only in recent years retracted their long-standing view of cremation as a denial of resurrection.

At the time of Jesus, the Sadducees, one of the main parties in first-century Palestinian Judaism, rejected the notion of resurrection. Indeed, the main outlook in the Israelite community was focused on this life and not the hereafter. God's blessing consisted in a long life and a continued existence through one's descendants. Upon death the individual continued to exist in a shadowy form in Sheol, but this was not actual life and therefore undesirable. One expected Yahweh to punish wrongdoings and reward people of good conduct. But as the Psalms and the book of JOB attest, this simple reward/punishment system did not always coincide with reality. The Israelite covenant community expected preferential treatment on the Day of Judgement, which they regarded as God's wrath imposed primarily on other nations. But the prophets like Amos and Jeremiah forcibly included Israel in their announcement of divine judgement. The Day of the

Lord was not light, but darkness (Amos 5:18). Yet simultaneously with this word of calamity there emerged the hope of rejuvenation for the Davidic kingdom, albeit in nationalistic and political terms. And in post-exilic Judaism (e.g., Deutero-Isaiah and Daniel) there surfaced an otherworldly hope, including the affirmation of a resurrection of the dead. Though actual monotheism emerged relatively late in Israel, the understanding that Yahweh was creator, sustainer, and redeemer provided a clear demarcation from the cyclical-fertility religions of Israel's neighbours.

In Jewish apocalyptic, history was perceived as a unity comprising all nations and the whole universe. The final battle between Yahweh's heavenly legions and the forces of evil would inaugurate the future eon of God's ultimate victory and the establishment of a new heaven and earth where justice would rule. The present age remained one of turmoil, anguish, and sorrow. This universal scope of the future transcended all ethnic and national boundaries. A heavenly saviour would usher in God's eternal rule.

While John the Baptist still pointed to the proximity of judgement and the kingdom of God in his call for repentance, Jesus of Nazareth emphasized the present as the time of salvation, connecting it to his person, proclamation, and mission. In and with him salvation became a present possibility. Though his claims could be interpreted in eschatological and messianic terms, his identification of himself with the suffering servant in Isaiah 42, 52–3 made the contemporary religious establishment reject his claims and demand his death.

Following the hermeneutic of the resurrection event, the NT writers identified the complete fulfilment of the OT promises in the life and destiny of Jesus. They accorded to him the title 'Christ', the anointed messianic saviour. Accepting the belief in Christ's resurrection, many of his followers concluded that the final events (universal judgement and Christ's inauguration to power) would occur immediately. The Gospel writers attempted in various ways to address the possible disappointment of eschatological delay; for instance, the Church was seen as the interim institution between Christ's resurrection and his parousia, or second coming. Also, spreading the good news of Christ's salvific action was seen as a precondition for his return. Paul proclaimed a baptismal dialectic: through baptism into Christ's death, Christians are already a new creation, foreshadowing some of the destiny in which they hope. Though living in the old eon, they fervently await the final public disclosure of God's kingdom.

Under the influence of I. Kant and F. Schleiermacher, the nineteenth century emphasized the ethical import of the Christian message. At the close of the century, J. Weiss (1863–1914) and A. Schweitzer (1875–1965) rediscovered eschatology as the main tenor of Jesus' proclamation and the NT witness. Schweitzer claimed that Jesus' message was entirely eschatological and should either be interpreted literally or discarded as literary fabrication: there is no middle ground. Schweitzer himself opted for a literal understanding and admitted that Jesus was mistaken. Most scholars after him were unwilling to follow that route. R. Bultmann opened the way for a more positive approach and evaded the vexing question concerning eschatological delay. The NT imagery, he claimed, should be understood neither cosmologically nor historically, but existentially. Just as Jesus himself confronted his audience, the NT kerygma confronts us with a fundamental question: do we want to understand ourselves as being tied to the past and to this world or to be radically open for God and his future? Bultmann draws heavily on the Pauline letters and the Gospel of John. In the here and now, we encounter the liberating Gospel and live out our Christian existence.

A variation of this approach is the 'realized eschatology' of C. H. Dodd (1884–1973) and J. Robinson (1919–83). They claimed that the decisive event of Christ's coming has already occurred. What the Christian still anticipates is Christ's coming beyond history, the incorporation of all history into God's eternal purpose. Alongside these existentialist and transcendentalist approaches are those emphasizing the future-directedness of eschatology. For instance, O. Cullmann (1902–99) asserted that Jesus proclaimed the kingdom of God as a future event and anticipated it proleptically in his person. This caused a tension between the already fulfilled resurrection and the not-yet-completed eschatological event. According to W. Kümmel (1905–95), Jesus conjectured an interval between his resurrection and the parousia, a notion which gradually gained more importance. Conservative scholars such as G. Maier (b. 1937) argue that the NT contradicts the idea that the Christian community (or Jesus himself) mistakenly expected the imminent end of the world. They assert that Jesus did not err concerning the kingdom's fulfilment, nor did he talk about a delay. Similar to Paul's solution, these theologians emphasize a bipolar tension between present and future in the kingdom proclamation. The kingdom has already begun but presses on for its universal, visible fulfilment. W. Pannenberg (b. 1928) made significant headway in this model with his notion of prolepsis. In Christ's resurrection, the end of all history has already occurred in proleptic anticipation. What is still to come cannot be anything fundamentally new, only the universal disclosure of that new life which the Resurrected One already inaugurated. J. Moltmann (b. 1926) adopted a similar approach, expressing that Christian hope embraces both the object hoped for and the hope inspired by it. Eschatology both talks about the last things that have yet to occur and informs us about how to regard our present life on earth.

Moltmann's approach has been very important for liberation theologies, because socio-political liberation lies at the core of advancing the kingdom here and now. Eschatology cannot be spiritualized but must enunciate hope in the present. Theologians influenced by process thought, such as J. B. Cobb, Jr (b. 1925) and R. Ruether (b. 1936), assert that subjective immortality, meaning the survival of the self or the person, should never be paramount. There is a universal hope which transcends divisive individuality and ushers us into a more complete community with fellow human beings and all things, so that Christ will finally be all in all. The early Christian emphasis on the resurrection of the individual and of the body is abandoned here in favour of a communal future existence in and with God.

While the destiny of the individual and of the community still remains important, some recent NT scholars such as M. Borg (b. 1942) suggest that Jesus' eschatology is not to be understood in temporal terms referring to an end of actual time. Rather, 'the kingdom of God' points to God's power and sovereignty, compassion and justice. Instead of teaching about the breaking in of the kingdom, Jesus was a teacher of subversive wisdom. Thus, at the end of the twentieth century, scholars returned full circle to the same non-eschatological, ethical, precept-centred Jesus embraced throughout most of the nineteenth century.

'If you confess with your lips that Jesus is Lord, and believe in your heart that God raised him from the dead, you will be saved' (Rom. 10:9). This is one of the earliest Christian creeds, underscoring that there is no hope beyond this life if there has been no resurrection. The lordship of Christ connected with his resurrection determines both future and present. 'Therefore we have been buried with him by baptism into death, so that, just as Christ was raised from the dead by the glory of the Father, so we too might walk in newness of life' (Rom. 6:4). In baptism Christians participate in the salvific effect of Christ's death and resurrection and are made new creatures, so that – as Paul expects – they will lead a different life. Eschatology and ethics are intimately related in a cause-and-effect sequence. Since the expectation of a resurrection like Christ's is contingent upon Christ's own resurrection, the cause-and-effect sequence cannot be reversed into our resurrection being a reward for good conduct.

Though the NT distinguishes between body, soul, and mind, it always sees the person as a unity. Both body and soul are marred by estrangement from God. Any existence beyond death, therefore, is contingent upon God and not on the constitution of an immortal soul. The God who has upheld us in this life will, through undeserved GRACE, also uphold us in the beyond. There will be neither an annihilation of the person nor the ascent of an immortal soul immediately to God. Since God is not subject to time, there is no 'waiting room' until the final judgement (see PSYCHOPANNYCHISM). We are immediately received into the presence of God, as Jesus told the criminal on the cross (Luke 23:43). Though death is both a relief (this earthly journey is over) and a risk (the fear of the not-yet-seen), Christians are confident that the one who is their saviour will be their judge.

While baptism is the initiation into the new existence, the EUCHARIST is continuing participation. 'Until he comes' (1 Cor. 11.26), we participate in this meal which foreshadows the celestial banquet, where all are called together regardless of rank and class. The assertion in the words of institution, 'Do this in remembrance of me' (1 Cor. 11:24) is twofold: Christians should certainly remember Christ's SACRIFICE, but the words are also an appeal to God to remember the sacrifice of the Son and accelerate the completion of the kingdom. Petitions for the coming of the kingdom, deliverance from evil, and the manifestation of God's power signify the LORD'S PRAYER as thoroughly eschatological.

The interim between Christ's resurrection and his return in glory has often tempted Christians to speculate about a date for his return or the inauguration of a millennial rule. Yet Jesus admonished his followers: 'But about that day and hour no one knows, neither the angels of heaven, nor the Son, but only the Father' (Matt. 24:36). Whether Franciscan spiritualism in the Middle Ages, T. Müntzer's (*ca* 1490–1525) prediction in the REFORMATION period, or A. Hitler's (1889–1945) secularized vision of the Thousand-Year Reich: every millennial aspiration, no matter how forcefully proclaimed, has proven untenable. Christian existence is characterized not by second-guessing God but by a faithful existence proleptically anticipating in this life what is expected and promised in the life to come.

See also DISPENSATIONALISM; MILLENNIUM.

A. Kelly, *Eschatology and Hope* (Orbis, 2006).

H. Küng, *Eternal Life? Life After Death as a Medical, Philosophical, and Theological Problem* (Crossroad, 1991 [1984]).

W. J. La Due, *The Trinity Guide to Eschatology* (Continuum, 2004).

J. Moltmann, *The Coming of God: Christian Eschatology* (Fortress Press, 1996).

G. Sauter, *What Dare We Hope? Reconsidering Eschatology* (Trinity Press, 1999).

H. Schwarz, *Eschatology* (Eerdmans, 2000).

HANS SCHWARZ

ETHICS: see MORAL THEOLOGY.

EUCHARIST Derived from the Greek word for 'thanksgiving', 'Eucharist' is a term Christian Churches use to describe their central act of worship. Other terms include: action of thanksgiving, breaking of bread, Eucharistic assembly, synaxis, memorial, holy SACRIFICE, divine LITURGY, sacred mysteries, most Blessed Sacrament, Holy Communion, Lord's Supper, Holy MASS (see *Cat.*, §1,322–1,419).

The OT background to Jesus' command to 'do this in remembrance of me' (Luke 22:19; 1 Cor. 11:24–5) is the

Passover feast, in which God's act of saving intervention on behalf of the chosen people in the Exodus is actualized and experienced anew through a meal (Exod. 12:1–28; 16:1–36; 24:1–11). The foundations of Jewish liturgical piety in the gathered assembly for worship (synagogue) and meal fellowship (sabbath) with sacrificial overtones (Temple) undergird the accounts of Jesus' table fellowship in the NT. In particular, the proclamation of the *berakoth* ('blessings') in Jewish ritual recounted what God did in history, through which proclamation contemporary congregations experienced the selfsame salvation. Eucharist as an act of remembrance derives from the Hebrew term *zikkaron* (Greek *anamnēsis*) whereby contemporary believers are drawn into and become partakers in the paschal mystery of Christ (including his obedient life, betrayal, suffering, death, resurrection, and ASCENSION looking to his PAROUSIA). The NT accounts of Jesus' last supper are a rich source of theological and liturgical insight (Matt. 26:26–9; Mark 14:22–5; Luke 22:15–20; 1 Cor. 11:23–6). More recently exegetes have gained additional insight from Jesus' meal fellowship during his public ministry (e.g., John 2:1–11; Matt. 9:10–13; Luke 10:38–42; 15:1–32), his discourse on the 'bread of life' (John 6:1–71), and his post-resurrection meals (Luke 24:13–35).

The earliest descriptions for the Eucharistic rite are the early Church documents dealing with the Christian way of life, the *Didache* (late first century), and the *First Apology* (*ca* 150) of Justin the Martyr (d. *ca* 165). The *Didache*'s description of thanksgiving prayers (chs. 9–10) is best appreciated against the biblical background for memorial, the value placed on human productivity in making the bread and wine, Church unity imaged as the individual grains of wheat becoming the (broken) bread, and the requirement that partakers be baptized and believe in Jesus. The *First Apology* (chs. 65, 67) adds important information about the proclamation of the word, the PRAYER of the faithful (derived from the Jewish synagogue service), the kiss of peace, and the collection of gifts for the poor. Justin delineates various liturgical roles (reader, deacon, presider), and emphasizes the assembly's affirmation – 'Amen' – at the end of the Eucharistic prayer.

The *Apostolic Tradition* (generally dated to the third century) describes two Eucharists: one after an ordination and the other after a baptism. In both cases the structure replicates that given by Justin. The term *anaphora* is given to the prayer of thanksgiving by which the bread and wine become the body and blood of Christ. Particularly important is the structure of this Eucharistic prayer, which gives thanks for creation, the incarnation, redemption (especially the Last Supper), the memorial prayer (*anamnēsis*, part of which explicates the community's act of offering the blessed bread and wine back to God the Father), the invocation of the HOLY SPIRIT (*epiclēsis*) over the bread and wine and for the unity of the Church, and the final doxology, concluding with 'Amen'.

After the time of Constantine I (*ca* 275–337) the liturgy underwent a period of expansion with respect to the structure and ritual of the Eucharistic rites (across a number of cultures), and the beginnings of technical theological descriptions of the Eucharist emerged. For example, from the Syrian city of Edessa came the Liturgy of Saints Addai and Mari, closely modelled on the structure from Justin and reflecting the contents of the anaphora of the *Apostolic Tradition* – except that it contains no account of the institution of the Eucharist at the Last Supper. The Liturgy of St Basil, possibly brought to Egypt by Basil of Caesarea himself (see CAPPADOCIAN FATHERS), is often used in the Coptic Church today (see ORIENTAL ORTHODOX CHURCHES) and serves as the basis for the third Eucharistic prayer in the contemporary Roman rite and in the American BOOK OF COMMON PRAYER. Notable, when compared with the *Apostolic Tradition*, is the addition of the *Sanctus* acclamation ('Holy, Holy, Holy') and intercessions within the Eucharistic prayer itself for the wider Church community, its leaders and ministers, for the earth's fruitfulness, and for the deceased.

The *Apostolic Constitutions* from fourth-century Antioch is similar to the *Didache* and the *Apostolic Tradition* in that it lays out the liturgy as part of a broader account of Christian beliefs and practices. The structure reflects that of Justin with the inclusion of a dismissal after the homily for catechumens and penitents. The anaphora is the most elaborate in content and structure. The Liturgy of St John Chrysostom originated in the same period and is the principal rite for the Orthodox Church today. Its particularities include descriptions of the 'little entrance' at the start of the liturgy and the 'great entrance' with the gifts of bread and wine after the dismissal of the catechumens. Of particular note is the way that the epiclesis in this prayer explicitly asks that the bread and wine be transformed by the power of the Holy Spirit.

Among the descriptions of what the Eucharist is and does, the *Mystagogical Catecheses* of Cyril of Jerusalem (*ca* 315–86) stand out. These five lectures were given to the newly initiated in mid-fourth-century Jerusalem during the octave of Easter. In the fourth lecture he cites the dominical words 'this is my body/blood' as the basis for Christian belief that in fact the bread and wine are the body and blood of Christ. He uses the important patristic term *figure* to distinguish the consecrated host from the flesh of Jesus that walked this earth. In the fifth lecture he describes the Eucharistic rite, which includes the *Sanctus*, anamnesis and epiclesis, intercessions, and the Amen. He describes how to receive communion, standing with palm outstretched and saying 'Amen' to the gift of Christ's body.

For the cup one bows as a gesture of adoration and reverence and says 'Amen'.

In the West as early as the mid-fourth century are indications of what became the Roman canon of MASS, likely composed of a number of independent prayers. One of the clearest descriptions of the Roman rite for the Eucharist comes from the *Ordo Romanus Primus* (*ca* 700). Today's Catholic mass resembles this structure, including particularities like musical chants at the beginning, two readings from SCRIPTURE, and a rather elaborate procession of gifts at the 'offertory'. The text of the canon had been in continual use as the sole anaphora in the Roman rite up until VATICAN COUNCIL II. In 1969 the Catholic Church made slight adjustments to this text and approved three additional prayers to be prayed in its stead, at the discretion of the celebrant. A particular feature of the Roman rite is the number and variety of prefaces making up the first part of the Eucharistic prayer. Today there are over ninety.

Beginning in the ninth century theologians began to focus on what the consecrated bread and wine were in themselves. Two French monks, Radbertus (*ca* 790–865) and Ratramnus (d. *ca* 870) wrote treatises 'On the Body and Blood of Christ' with the former holding a 'symbolic' view and the latter a 'realistic' view of Christ's presence in the elements. In the eleventh century Berengar of Tours (*ca* 1000–88) tried to describe the Eucharistic change in symbolic terms, but his views were judged heretical. These theologians, along with Alan of Lille (*ca* 1130–1202) and Lanfranc (*ca* 1005–89) struggled to chart a path between crass realism and empty symbolism in describing the Eucharist. T. AQUINAS won the day by speaking of TRANSUBSTANTIATION, according to which the accidents (appearance, smell, touch, etc.) of the elements remain while the substance is transformed into Christ's body and blood.

Also during the Middle Ages the communal celebration of the Eucharist was altered, with the withholding of the wine from the laity becoming established practice. It was also supplemented by masses said by individual priests or small groups often with no one other than the priest receiving communion ('private masses'), as well as by devotions to the Eucharist (e.g., outdoor processions, benediction from the consecrated host, etc.). In the sixteenth century M. LUTHER, J. CALVIN, and others protested against these practices, arguing for good preaching, restoration of communion under both species, and the abolition of private masses. Luther never favoured the term 'transubstantiation' since it was in his opinion too philosophical. Nor did he like 'consubstantiation', though others in the period used it to describe the fact that the body and blood of Christ were contained within the bread and wine after consecration. A foe of indulgences, Luther decried the stipend system whereby priests would receive income from celebrating the mass and sought to purge the mass of any sacrificial references. As a result, in Luther's *Formula Missae* (1523) and *Deutsche Messe* (1526) the Eucharistic prayer was reduced to the words of Jesus at the Last Supper. The Reformed tradition followed Luther's liturgical focus on the words of institution, but rejected both Catholic and Lutheran doctrines of Christ's presence in the consecrated elements in favour of a doctrine of spiritual communion between the believer and Christ.

In response to this and other challenges, the Council of TRENT issued the decree on the Eucharist as sacrament in 1551, affirming the use of transubstantiation to describe the change from bread and wine to the body and blood of Christ. In 1562 they issued their decree on the Eucharist as SACRIFICE and reaffirmed that in the Eucharist 'a sacrifice is offered'. In 1570 Pope Pius V (r. 1566–72) approved the publication of the normative Roman missal for the whole Church, with exceptions made for some religious communities (e.g., Dominicans) and locales (e.g., Milan).

One result of the REFORMATION was a separation between Catholics and various Protestant Churches in the celebration of mass and a consequent inability to share communion at each other's services. This separation continues, with some traditions insisting on fuller doctrinal agreement between the Churches before communion can be shared (Orthodox, Catholic) and others allowing communion across confessional boundaries (e.g., some Lutheran and Anglican Churches). At the same time, the biblical and patristic revival of the late nineteenth and early early centuries, coupled with papal encouragement for participation and frequent communion, led to a growing consensus in Eucharistic practice associated with the flowering of the LITURGICAL MOVEMENT. Among Catholics, the promulgation of the Constitution on the Liturgy (*Sacrosanctum concilium*, 1963) at Vatican II ushered in an unprecedented set of reforms and changes in the mass, including the use of the vernacular, the restoration of a variety of roles in the liturgy, and the singing of various genres of music.

See also UBIQUITY.

A. J. Chupungco, ed., *Handbook for Liturgical Studies*, vol. 3: *The Eucharist* (Liturgical Press, 1999).

K. W. Irwin, *Models of the Eucharist* (Paulist Press, 2005).

R. Jasper and G. Cuming, eds., *Prayers of the Eucharist: Early and Reformed*, 2nd edn (Liturgical Press, 1990).

X. Leon-Dufour, *Sharing the Eucharistic Bread: The Witness of the New Testament* (Paulist Press, 1987).

N. Mitchell, *Cult and Controversy: The Worship of the Eucharist Outside Mass* (Pueblo, 1982).

KEVIN W. IRWIN

EUTYCHIANISM Eutychianism refers to a form of MIAPHYSITISM that was condemned at the Council of CHALCEDON. An archimandrite in Constantinople, Eutyches (*ca* 380–*ca* 455) was a vehement opponent of all forms of dyophysite (or two-nature) CHRISTOLOGY, which he associated with the NESTORIANISM condemned at the Council of EPHESUS. Though Eutyches drew his inspiration from CYRIL OF ALEXANDRIA's teaching of the "one nature" of the incarnate Word, he seems to have concluded that, because Christ was (following the decrees of the Councils of NICAEA and CONSTANTINOPLE) 'of the same substance' (HOMOOUSIOS) with the Father, he could not also be *homoousios* with human beings. Over against this position – and in line with the soteriological principle that Christ could only heal a nature that he had truly assumed – Chalcedon affirmed Christ's full humanity as well as his full divinity by way of a modified dyophysitism, according to which Christ, though one person and HYPOSTASIS, was to be acknowledged in two natures.

The two-nature language of Chalcedon was rejected by the miaphysite Churches of Syria, Egypt, and Ethiopia, but these communities also repudiated the Eutychian denial of Christ's consubstantiality with humanity; and Eutyches was likewise condemned in the formula of union promulgated in 482 by Emperor Zeno (r. 474–91) in an unsuccessful bid to reconcile these miaphysite Churches. Essentially, Eutychianism transformed the miaphysitism of Cyril into monophysitism by insisting that confessing Christ in one nature (*mia physis*) implies that he has *only* one nature (*monē physis*) in a way that precludes his being confessed as fully and truly human.

IAN A. MCFARLAND

EVANGELICAL THEOLOGY The adjective 'evangelical' attaches to theology in various ways, including a commitment to norm theology by the Christian GOSPEL (*euangelion* in Greek); the nomenclature of European PROTESTANTISM, particularly in Germany, where Lutheran Churches are called *evangelische*; and a global network of Christians, parachurch organizations, and Protestant Churches. This article addresses evangelical theology in the third, most common, sense.

This evangelical movement possesses four basic characteristics according to the influential definition of D. Bebbington (b. 1949). First, *conversionism* identifies an expectation that people must experience a turning from SIN to God via the Christian message. Second, *activism* follows as these Christians – laypersons and clergy alike – spread the gospel via evangelism and good works. Third, *biblicism* points to a high view of SCRIPTURE as the central authority over these believers' lives. Fourth, *crucicentrism* highlights the central message around which the Bible orients the activity of the converted: the CROSS of Jesus Christ as God's 'good news' (gospel). Building on these identifiers, this sketch of evangelical theology will provide (1) further historical nuance, (2) doctrinal depth regarding treatments of Scripture and the message of the cross, (3) deliberation over its complicated relation to the life of the Church, and (4) a brief examination of its contemporary situation and future prospects.

With respect to the first of these points, because Bebbington's characteristics could seemingly apply (for example) to Francis of Assisi (1181/2–1226), who clearly was no 'evangelical' in Bebbington's sense, additional factors are needed to specify further the scope of the term. Bebbington's work assumed and addressed a certain time period and place. Thus, many would add to Bebbington's four characteristics that an evangelical stands in historical continuity with the eighteenth-century revival movements associated with figures like J. WESLEY and G. Whitefield (1714–70). A minority or revisionist view tries to trace the origins back still farther, closer to the Protestant REFORMATION itself. In any case, from these Anglo-American revival movements of the 1730s, along with some of their partners in Continental PIETISM, worldwide communities have since formed and proliferated. As with any social network, especially one lacking strong institutional definition, the boundaries are fuzzy and dynamic, but this approach to defining evangelicalism allows for the appropriate overlap, hybridity, and distinctiveness between the various Anglo-American contexts and their non-Western parallels and partners.

One key point of contention among contemporary evangelicals is whether the movement's theological parameters have been defined too tightly in 'Reformed' terms, connected to early, magisterial Protestants like J. CALVIN and his heirs. Some, like D. Dayton (b. 1942), have claimed that the energy and blurrier doctrinal frameworks of later holiness movements stemming from Wesley need greater attention as evangelically normative. An additional complication is the degree of theological similarity, along with a combination of relational overlap and tension, between evangelicalism and PENTECOSTAL or CHARISMATIC movements. T. Larsen (b. 1967) addresses this issue by locating conversionism and activism more clearly under a particular evangelical emphasis on the work of the Holy Spirit, thus drawing more Pentecostal and charismatic Christians into the definition. Not all conservative Protestants are thereby comfortable in such an evangelical network, and the same would be true of some 'Pentecostal' Christians worldwide (in the increasingly generic sense of this term), among whom there are historical connections to both the evangelical movement and to other independent, indigenous catalysts.

Second, this historical complexity problematizes any detailed doctrinal sketch of evangelical belief. Evangelicals tend to follow the content of the classical Christian CREEDS in the content of what they affirm, although many of them are non-creedal in their formal confessional and ecclesiastical structures. Thus, evangelicals almost without exception – perhaps by definition, depending on one's view – embrace forms of theism consistent with the Church's Trinitarian RULE OF FAITH embodied in the NICENE CREED. Similarly, the content of classic CHRISTOLOGY appears in evangelical textbooks, although it does not tend to elicit dogmatic contemplation but instead gets entwined in apologetics. Evangelical theological anthropology is broadly Augustinian (see Augustine of Hippo), although a more traditional notion of humans being 'in the image of God' has come under recent critique as too individualistic and rationalistic.

Evangelical soteriology, too, is broadly Augustinian yet ever more pluralistic, and in this context it is possible to give further definition to the characteristic of crucicentrism. For evangelicals, following the Protestant Reformers, the core question concerns how particular persons may be 'right with God' based on the work of Jesus Christ. M. Luther, tormented in conscience over whether he could co-operate sufficiently with sacramental grace, longed for assurance of divine favour. Based on his reading of Paul's letter to the Romans he came to view justification not as being made righteous but as being declared righteous; not as the infusion of Christ's righteousness into his being but as the imputation of that righteousness brought about by his relation to Christ in faith. Hence justification is 'by faith alone', because faith looks to Christ for assurance rather than to a moral change in oneself based on internal reception of Jesus' merit.

In line with this account of justification, atonement is somehow objectively rooted in the crucifixion as a sacrifice 'for' us. Evangelicals generally hold some version of a substitutionary atonement theory, though some non-Reformed evangelical scholars increasingly criticize 'penal' substitutionary theories as historically alien to their traditions, ethically underdeveloped (especially in their relation to violence), and legally rather than relationally focused. Some of these scholars likewise criticize the specific Lutheran–Reformed architecture of justification by faith alone, finding the imputation of Christ's righteousness to be a dogmatic imposition upon Scripture that minimizes the need for sanctification of Christian lives. At the same time, evangelicals across the board have always insisted that, while justification is by faith alone, the faith that justifies is never alone; good works do not merit divine favour but follow as its gift, a consequence of the covenant relationship with God in which people obey out of gratitude.

Evangelical biblicism likewise generates doctrinal elaboration and dispute. Evangelicals maintain the classic Protestant commitment to the principle of 'Scripture alone' (*sola Scriptura*), which means not that Scripture is the sole theological source but rather that it is the final authority over all others. Evangelicals interpret the inspiration of Scripture (as described in 2 Tim. 3:16–17) to mean that, although composed via human activity, it counts as divine speech. Most evangelicals affirm that inspiration is 'verbal' (i.e., including the particular words used and not just the message communicated) and 'plenary' (i.e., involving the entirety of what the words convey).

For many American evangelicals, facing controversies with 'modernists' from the late nineteenth to the twentieth century, inspiration entailed the Bible's inerrancy (see Modernism). If Scripture says what God says, and God tells the truth, then Scripture must tell the truth. This basic position is subject to careful qualification (as seen in, e.g., the 1978 Chicago Statement on Biblical Inerrancy), having to do with identifying what Scripture actually says in light of literary genre, ancient versus modern standards of precision, and so forth. Nevertheless, other evangelicals have rejected full inerrancy in favour of a limited version in which the Bible's infallibility pertains to Christian faith and practice without including history, science, and the like. Evangelicals outside North America have not always weighed in on these debates, generally affirming a high view of biblical inspiration and authority with less specification.

Third, evangelicalism's relation to Church life is also complex. Several recent works have highlighted and sharply criticized evangelical neglect of ecclesiology – or at minimum its 'Low-Church' instincts – and associated individualism. Evangelicalism is neither a denomination nor a congregation, and some would say that it is not even a tradition. Its nature as a movement is usually parasitic and reformist: evangelical people and congregations seek to bear witness within and transform orthodox but 'dead' structures towards a more lively piety, or sometimes 'liberal' pieties in the direction of more orthodox belief.

Evangelicals frequently ignore or seem unaware of Luther's sacramentalism, Calvin's affirmation of the Church as our mother, and their heritage of ecclesiastically ordered devotion more generally. Evangelical denominations usually stem from earlier divisions, and can often be traced to departures from established or mainline Churches. Where evangelical presence remains within established and mainline Churches (e.g., the Church of England, the Presbyterian Church USA), congregational life tends to be more voluntarist, autonomous, entrepreneurial, and institutionally marginal. It can be difficult to discern whether these tendencies to individualism and ecclesiastical inattentiveness are a function of the traditions (often theologically and culturally North American) feeding into evangelicalism, or rather of evangelical habits influencing these contexts in the first place.

Evangelicalism needs such ecclesiological confrontation, particularly in moments of triumphalism about its North American vitality relative to the established Churches of Europe or its vibrancy in the rapidly growing, broadly Pentecostal Christianity of the 'global South'. Yet the ecclesiological situation is not entirely bleak. Evangelical literature and subcultures have begun to criticize the individualism and dualism lying behind the earlier evangelical cultural retreat. Theologians have sketched ecclesiological emphases that evangelicals might offer in conversation with others, and some have begun drawing upon the distinctive roots of their particular ecclesiological traditions and emphasizing that 'evangelical' is an adjective rather than a noun. Meanwhile, evangelicalism may allow for unique forms of ecumenical effort, since it already networks people and congregations across many institutional lines, and since its forms of networking are rooted in shared mission rather than mutual toleration or conversation. As ecumenical theology turns towards considering various forms of Church communion alongside institutional reunion, evangelical life at best may embody realistic possibilities for principled ECUMENISM.

Of course, evangelicals are not often characterized by such long-term, persevering co-operation. Hence, fourth, any sketch of their contemporary situation risks becoming quickly outdated in the face of perennial, internal debates over boundaries. In recent decades we have seen disputes such as those over whether OPEN THEISM, with its denial of God's exhaustive foreknowledge, can be orthodox; whether ecumenical discussion with Catholics and interest in 'new perspectives' on Paul violate commitment to justification by faith alone; whether 'seeker-sensitive' Churches and contemporary praise music pander too much to consumer culture; and whether the 'emergent Church' conversation can coherently look backwards to ancient tradition and forwards to 'postmodern', more relaxed forms of mission (see POSTMODERNISM).

Aside from material issues, however, the challenge for evangelical theology may be the more formal one of scholarly engagement. Between the time of J. EDWARDS and the twentieth century, some evangelical theologians were briefly important, at least within pockets of American or British life. But few would surface indisputably on everyone's list of lasting influences. The PRINCETON theologians such as C. HODGE and B. B. Warfield (1851–1921) are, deservedly or not, largely associated with propagating the inerrantist doctrine of Scripture, while P. T. Forsyth (1842–1921) probably remains underappreciated for his evangelical anticipation of themes later elaborated by K. BARTH. After the American renewal of evangelical identity in the mid-twentieth century, theologians such as C. Henry (1913–2003) and J. Packer (b. 1926) undertook serious intellectual work; yet, while aware of and engaged with university-based theology, their work remained marginal to it. Evangelicals in the UK produced important biblical scholars (e.g., F. F. Bruce (1910–90) and I. H. Marshall (b. 1934)) who, through doctoral supervision and the establishment of Tyndale House at the University of Cambridge, eventually fostered a similar renaissance among Americans. But most evangelical theologians lacked such resources, and the theological direction of evangelicalism is set at a more popular level by pastors or other charismatic leaders, including, ironically, the writings of non-evangelical C. S. Lewis (1898–1963). While at best this mantle of leadership rests on scholarly churchfolk such as J. Stott (b. 1921), at worst it entails fundamental suspicion and neglect of academic theology.

At the start of the twenty-first century, beyond senior statesmen like D. Bloesch (b. 1928) and T. Oden (b. 1931), the most academically renowned, explicitly evangelical theologians are probably A. McGrath (b. 1953), K. Vanhoozer (b. 1957), the late S. Grenz (1950–2005), and the biblical scholar and churchman N. T. Wright (b. 1948). Much evangelical discourse continues to reflect a measure of influence from the Reformed tradition and is increasingly (and somewhat controversially) engaged with the thought of Barth. Evangelical theology globally takes institutional form in a variety of parachurch organizations (e.g., the International Fellowship of Evangelical Students, stemming from the InterVarsity movement), in particular the World Evangelical Alliance.

Resurgence in academic forms of evangelical theology will inevitably heighten evangelicalism's identity issues. To what extent will Churches support such an enterprise? Will further self-discovery in non-Reformed traditions make definition of a coherent evangelical heritage even more contested? Will resulting encounters with various others – mainline Protestants, Catholics, Orthodox, non-Christians, and so on – water down or deepen evangelical theological commitment(s)? How will the need to pursue racial reconciliation and acknowledge cultural plurality alter such new-found scholarly enterprise along with evangelical self-definition?

Evangelical theology must ultimately concern itself neither with such societal challenges nor with the perennial temptation of excessive self-definition. Its Anglo-American crucicentric Christological preoccupation needs careful supplementation from its charismatic effervescence in contemporary world Christianity, highlighting the perfecting work of the HOLY SPIRIT who raised Jesus from the dead. As God's empowering presence creating, unifying, and sending the Church to participate in the divine mission, the Lifegiver fosters evangelical devotion in a way that upholds both Christian and cultural integrity – part of making all things new.

D. Bebbington, *Evangelicalism in Modern Britain: A History from the 1730s to the 1980s* (Unwin Hyman, 1989).

D. Dayton and R. Johnston, eds., *The Variety of American Evangelicalism* (InterVarsity Press, 1991).

W. Elwell, ed., *Evangelical Dictionary of Theology*, 2nd edn. (Baker Books, 2001).

T. Larsen and D. Treier, eds., *Cambridge Companion to Evangelical Theology* (Cambridge University Press, 2007).

M. Noll, *The Scandal of the Evangelical Mind* (Eerdmans, 1994).
R. Olson, *Westminster Handbook to Evangelical Theology* (John Knox Press, 2004).

Daniel J. Treier

Evolution 'Evolution' is a shorthand term for the dominant theory in the biological sciences describing the emergence of new species from existing species. As such, it refers to what is otherwise known as neo-Darwinism or (more accurately) the 'modern synthesis', as developed in the second quarter of the twentieth century through the work of scientists like T. Dobzhansky (1900–75) and E. Mayr (1904–2005). The synthesis in question combines the theory of evolution by natural selection (as developed independently by C. Darwin (1809–82) and A. R. Wallace (1823–1913)) with modern genetic theory (especially the statistical application of G. Mendel's (1822–84) work on the inheritance to entire populations by R. A. Fisher (1890–1962), S. Wright (1889–1988), and J. B. S. Haldane (1892–1964)).

In his *On the Origin of Species* (1859) Darwin had argued that the ground of speciation was the fact of natural variation within a species. Within any given set of environmental conditions, certain of these natural variations will give greater reproductive success to organisms that possess them (e.g., plants with slightly thicker leaves that minimize loss of moisture will do better in a dry climate; molluscs with slightly harder shells will be better able to survive attacks by predators). Drawing an ANALOGY with the way human beings deliberately select for particular traits in breeding new strains of plants or animals, Darwin argued that new species emerge gradually from a common ancestral type, as such adaptive traits accumulate over many generations through this process of 'natural' selection. Yet, while Darwin was able to appeal to a wide range of evidence in support of his theory (e.g., descent from a common ancestor was suggested by the phenomena of anatomical homology and similarity in embryological development across species, as well as by the geographical proximity of phenotypically similar species), he did not have a theory of inheritance that allowed him to explain how particular traits would maintain their integrity over the generations, rather than being gradually diluted through hybridization. Modern genetic theory, by establishing the gene (ultimately correlated in the mid-twentieth century with particular sequences of base pairs in the DNA molecule) as a fixed unit of heredity, provided a solution to this problem; and the field of population genetics furnished mathematical models showing how adaptive traits could accumulate in a particular population of organisms in exactly the way that Darwin's theory demanded.

Particularly within the English-speaking world, considerable attention is given to the incompatibility of evolutionary theory with a literal interpretation of Genesis 1, according to which all species were created instantaneously by God over a short period of time in the relatively recent past. Proponents of CREATIONISM, strongly committed to a doctrine of biblical INERRANCY, argue that the modern synthesis is incompatible with Christian FAITH in so far as it diverges from this biblical account of the origin of species. While the creationist position has considerable support in some conservative Protestant circles, however, it cannot claim to represent any consensus in the wider Christian tradition, given that classical thinkers from AUGUSTINE (*Gen. lit.* 2.9) to J. CALVIN (*CGen.* 6.14) have explicitly denied that the Genesis creation stories need to be interpreted as literal accounts of natural history.

Nor was the theological response to Darwin's theory as uniformly negative as popular characterizations often suggest. After 1859 many theologians in both Europe and the USA welcomed evolution and argued for its compatibility with Christian belief. To be sure, Darwin's explanation of the match of species to environment cut the ground from under that popular version of the TELEOLOGICAL ARGUMENT propounded earlier in the nineteenth century by W. Paley (1743–1805), but the emergence of increasingly complex species, especially human beings, could still be viewed as a manifestation of divine wisdom in the created world. Instead of a remote and occasionally active deity, theology could now envisage a divine accompanying of and constant involvement in biological evolution, the laws of which were here viewed as providentially ordered. Among Anglican writers in particular, this resonated with a commitment to KENOTIC THEOLOGY and divine passibility, with A. Moore (1848–90) famously claiming that Darwinism, appearing in the guise of a foe, had done the work of a friend. Subsequently, different theistic theories of evolution have emerged in both Catholic and Protestant theology, the most ambitious being perhaps that of P. TEILHARD DE CHARDIN in the twentieth century.

The most serious theological questions raised by modern evolutionary theory relate to the doctrine of PROVIDENCE. If, as the modern synthesis teaches, the mechanism of evolution is random variation based in unpredictable mutations in organisms' genetic code, then God's capacity to guarantee particular outcomes to the evolutionary process seems limited. In this context, different interpretations of evolutionary theory have significantly different theological implications. If, as argued by scientists like R. Dawkins (b. 1941) and S. C. Morris (b. 1951), the evolutionary process naturally inclines towards the emergence of more complex forms of life over time, then it is possible to understand God as having initially established a set of conditions under which the emergence of complex (i.e., intelligent) life would have eventually emerged. But if the evolutionary process is inherently directionless (i.e., has no natural tendency to promote greater complexity over greater simplicity), as argued by palaeontologist S. J. Gould (1941–2002), it would seem to be impossible for God to ensure the emergence of intelligent life without the violation of natural law – though this objection holds only for a zero-sum model of DIVINE ACTION, according to which the integral operation of creaturely causes precludes direct divine involvement.

A further area in which evolutionary theory impacts theological reflection is ethics (see MORAL THEOLOGY). Evolutionary science is inclined to interpret all forms of human behaviour, whether traditionally judged good or bad, as products of the evolutionary process. From a theological perspective, this tendency can be viewed as either helpful in illuminating traditional Christian teaching or as deeply problematic. Thus, for example, it is possible to interpret original SIN as reflecting the persistent influence of primitive survival impulses that are 'hard-wired' into the brain (though such strategies require that 'sin' be seen as the original condition of human creation rather than the product of a declension from a state of original righteousness). Also, the apparently conflicting experiences of freedom and determinism can be seen as complementary features of existence, in which the latter provides the stable context for the possibility of calculated engagement with the environment characteristic of the former. On the other hand, evolutionary biologists' success in explaining apparent instances of altruism among animal species (e.g., individual ants sacrificing themselves for the colony) as adaptive strategies that maximize the survival potential of a particular genome raises questions regarding the degree to which acceptance of evolutionary theory is compatible with traditional Christian understandings of VIRTUE.

See also NATURAL SCIENCE; NATURAL THEOLOGY.

P. Hefner, *The Human Factor: Evolution, Culture, and Religion* (Fortress Press, 1993).

S. C. Morris, *Life's Solution: Inevitable Humans in a Lonely Universe* (Cambridge University Press, 2003).

M. Northcott and R. J. Berry, eds., *Theology After Darwin* (Paternoster Press, 2009).

M. Ruse, *Can a Darwinian Be a Christian?* (Cambridge University Press, 2001).

IAN A. MCFARLAND

EX OPERE OPERATO The Latin phrase *ex opere operato* (literally, 'by the work having been worked') is a key phrase in the history of SACRAMENTOLOGY, associated both with the Donatist controversy in fourth- and fifth-century North Africa (see DONATISM) and with the REFORMATION.

The Donatists maintained that the validity of the sacraments depended on the character of the celebrant, a position summarized by the phrase *ex opere operantis* (literally, 'by the work of the worker'). For the Donatists a sacrament performed by a sinful priest was no sacrament at all: his BAPTISM did not effect the forgiveness of sin, and EUCHARIST received from his hands did not bring communion with Christ's body and blood. Over against this position, the view received as orthodox by both western (Catholic) and eastern (Orthodox) Churches was that, because the sacraments were fundamentally God's work, rooted in God's promise to the Church to be present and active in them, their reality was guaranteed by the faithfulness of God rather than the faithfulness of the minister. It followed that they were valid *ex opere operato*, or by the mere fact of their being celebrated according to the established canons of the Church, regardless of the moral qualities of the celebrant. Otherwise, it was argued, the faithful would be in constant doubt about the efficacy of the sacraments, since it was impossible for one receiving a sacrament to be certain of the state of the minister's SOUL.

At the time of the Reformation, both Lutheran and Reformed theologians accepted the principle of *ex opere operato* in its anti-Donatist sense. By this point, however, the phrase had acquired a further meaning that was the source of dispute between Catholics and Protestants. It was the Catholic position that the sacraments (the Eucharist in particular) conferred GRACE by the mere fact of being validly celebrated (i.e., *ex opere operato*), so long as the recipient did not introduce some obstacle (Trent, *Sacr.*, Canons 6, 8). Over against this position, both Lutheran and Reformed theologians insisted that FAITH was necessary as the means of appropriating the grace of the sacrament. They argued that the sacraments were simply a visible means of communicating the GOSPEL promise of FORGIVENESS, and that reception of the benefits of any promise requires faith or trust on the part of the one to whom it is addressed. In short, while the Catholic position can be seen as concerned to stress the objectivity of God's grace in the sacrament independent of human merit, the position of the reformers reflects a desire to stress the relational character of the sacrament as a communicative act between God and the individual, including the active participation of the recipient.

IAN A. MCFARLAND

EXCOMMUNICATION Excommunication refers to the exclusion of a member from the associational involvement and sacramental life of a particular religious community. Excommunication, in Christian understanding, is viewed as having a scriptural basis in passages like 1 Corinthians 5:1–13 and 2 Corinthians 2:5–11 (with reference to the exclusion of an unrepentant sinner), 2 Timothy 1:20 (regarding blasphemers handed over to Satan), and Matthew 18:15–18 (with reference to the sinning brother and the power to bind and loose). In the western tradition both the Churches of the Reformation and the Catholic magisterium have traditionally held that, while excommunication does affect one's status within a religious community, it does not necessarily affect one's salvation. While it is the most severe form of discipline in the Church, it has as its goal repentance, restoration, and peace.

Excommunication, comprised of both religious and social exclusion, was the primary sanction of the early Church. Four forms of excommunication were practised in the early and medieval Church. Excommunication could include temporary refusal of the Eucharist; censure with denial of the Eucharist and communal activities; absolute exclusion from the Church; or the exclusion of a group within the Church. The early Church practised excommunication in association with repentance. An offender presented to the bishop as one desiring to repent of a serious sin would, in a liturgical excommunication, be designated a 'penitent' who was assigned penitential works. Upon completion of the period of penitence, the bishop, with the community's consent, would receive the penitent back into communion through the laying on of hands. After the sixth century, excommunication was separated from the sacrament of penance, and the practice of avoiding all excommunicated persons arose. In the thirteenth century Pope Innocent III (r. 1198–1216) identified excommunication as a disciplinary but also medicinal penalty, having the purpose of healing and restoring the offender. By the fifteenth century, a distinction emerged between those excommunicated who were to be avoided entirely due to the grave nature of their sins (the *vitandi*), and those others who were only denied the sacraments (the *tolerati*).

Both the Reformation and the Council of Trent addressed the issue of excommunication. For the Reformers the practice of excommunication was an appropriate means of ensuring Church discipline and purity, motivating the sinner to repent, and preserving God's reputation. J. Calvin promoted the involvement of the Church body in the excommunication process, and he considered it essential that the excommunicated continue to hear the preaching of the Word, so that they might be moved to repentance. The Council of Trent dealt with excommunication by reminding bishops of its use as a spiritual discipline, not a political instrument; by encouraging restraint in the practice of excommunication; and by reaffirming its medicinal purpose.

The contemporary practice of excommunication in the Catholic Church involves the refusal of the sacraments, Christian burial, and ecclesiastical office and revenue. Excommunication is generally imposed only if there is serious sin or refusal to repent of a practice or position, and only after warnings and time for repentance have been given. But it also may directly follow certain acts, such as abortion, as well as being instituted as the consequence of an ecclesiastical investigation. In either case, however, repentance continues to be the desired outcome.

Excommunication today is not commonly practised among Protestant bodies, although 'shunning' or withdrawal of Church membership may occur, and the Church of England still has canons dealing with excommunication (see Canon Law). The Anabaptist tradition has spoken of excommunication in terms of 'the ban' and understands it not as the act of excluding a member from the community but rather as one of formally acknowledging an exclusion that the excommunicated member has already chosen for him or herself. Accordingly, the excommunicated can seek reinstatement through a process of rehabilitation outlined in counsel with the Church; in a manner that is the converse of the way in which the excommunicated chose to exclude themselves, so they can now, with the community, commence a process by which they can re-enter communal life. In this way, here, too, the goal of excommunication is not punishment but reconciliation (see Mennonite Theology).

Recent examples of excommunication include the Catholic excommunication of two Chinese bishops who had been appointed by the Chinese government rather than the Vatican; of an archbishop who installed four married men as bishops; of a theologian for his views on papal infallibility and other doctrines; and of Church members who join organizations viewed as opposed to Church teachings (e.g., Masonic groups, and groups supportive of birth control, abortion, euthanasia, assisted suicide, and the ordination of women). In *Torture and Eucharist* W. Cavanaugh (b. 1962) offers an example of the productive possibilities of excommunication, citing the Catholic Church's excommunication of Chilean political leaders who utilized kidnapping, torture, and murder for the purpose of State control. Cavanaugh argues that the doctrine of the catholicity of the Church provides the framework within which this practice of excommunication occurs: in the same way that the Church eucharistically gathers a body of individuals around the one body of Christ, so political use of violence individuates and eviscerates ecclesial communities that might otherwise resist the State's totalizing apparatus. In such contexts, excommunication bespeaks a prior violation against the Church. Chile's political leaders were excommunicated because, in a sense, they excommunicated themselves by disregarding the communal authority of the gathered Church. Thus, although particular instances of excommunication differ, they articulate the same warrants: community, corporate discipleship, witness, and repentance.

See also Apostasy; Heresy.

W. T. Cavanaugh, *Torture and Eucharist: Theology, Politics, and the Body of Christ* (Blackwell, 1998).

E. Vodola, *Excommunication in the Middle Ages* (University of California Press, 1986).
J. H. Yoder, *Body Politics: Five Practices of the Christian Community Before the Watching World* (Herald Press, 1994).

Dana Benesh and Jonathan Tran

Exorcism The term 'exorcism' (derived from the Greek word for 'charging under oath') refers to the act of driving an evil spirit out of a person or object. In the NT exorcism is portrayed as a defining feature of Jesus' ministry (see, e.g., Matt. 9:32–3; Mark 1:21–7, 34, 39; Luke 13:32), as well as that of his disciples (see, e.g., Matt. 10:8; Acts 5:16; 8:6–7), whose power over evil spirits is connected with the invocation of Jesus' name (see Mark 16:17; Luke 10:17; Acts 19:11–17). In subsequent Christian tradition exorcism is conceived broadly in terms of release from the power of the Devil, so that, e.g., Catholic and Orthodox Christians include prayers of exorcism in the rite of baptism, on the grounds that catechumens are subject to demonic influence, even though not possessed.

Though the exorcism of evil spirits from persons judged to be possessed has been part of Christian experience from the earliest periods, in contemporary practice great care is taken to distinguish demonic possession from physical or mental illness more appropriately treated medically or psychologically. In Catholicism, for example, exorcism may not be performed until after medical examination has ruled out alternative diagnoses, and then only by a priest who has obtained the consent of the local bishop (*Cat.*, §1,673). These strictures dictate that exorcisms are performed only rarely in Catholic and most Protestant (e.g., Anglican, Methodist) contexts. In many Pentecostal Churches, however, exorcism is performed more routinely, often featuring as a regular part of public worship.

Ian A. McFarland

Extra Calvinisticum The idea of the *extra Calvinisticum* (a Latin phrase that may be translated as 'the Calvinist remainder') derives from a fundamental disagreement between the Lutheran and Reformed branches of the Reformation over the proper interpretation of the doctrine of the incarnation. Proponents of Reformed theology (including J. Calvin) argued that the orthodox Christology of Chalcedon, according to which the divine and human natures are united in Christ without confusion or change, implied that Christ's finite human nature is incapable of containing the infinite divine nature of the Son (*finitum non capax infiniti*). Consequently, the infinite Son is completely within the flesh of Jesus, but also completely outside (*extra*) Jesus' finite – because truly human – flesh.

Lutherans coined the phrase *extra Calvinisticum* as a pejorative characterization of this Reformed position. They charged that, by claiming that the divine Son was not exhaustively present in the incarnate Christ, the Reformed undermined the integrity of the gospel, since Jesus could only be trusted as Saviour if his life was truly God's – and therefore revealed the fullness of God's will towards humanity – without remainder. The Lutherans defended their position by arguing that, while the divine and human natures remained ontologically distinct in Christ, their union in Christ's person was so profound that, in accordance with the doctrine of the communication of attributes (*communicatio idiomatum*), the *properties* of the divine nature (including especially omnipresence) were communicated to the human, thereby justifying an exhaustive identification of the Son with Jesus after the incarnation. The Reformed held that the Lutheran distinction between a nature and its properties violated the Chalcedonian principle that Christ's two natures remained unconfused: since a nature is defined by its properties, they argued, any sharing of properties necessarily implies a confusion of natures.

See also Hypostatic Union; Ubiquity.

Ian A. McFarland

Extra-Terrestrial Life As the phrase itself suggests, any living organisms originating outside the earth's biosphere would constitute extra-terrestrial life; but in theology the question of extra-terrestrial life generally focuses on the possibility of intelligent life elsewhere in the universe. No definitive evidence of such life has yet been found, but many cosmologists judge that the sheer size of the known universe makes it extremely likely that intelligent life would have evolved elsewhere. Most famously, F. Drake (b. 1930) developed an equation to quantify the various factors constraining the evolution of intelligent life and concluded that it was reasonable to suppose that there might now be ten advanced civilizations in the Milky Way galaxy alone. On the other hand, scientists like S. J. Gould (1941–2002) have argued that, while the appearance of life on other planets may be extremely common, the random character of evolutionary processes makes the emergence of intelligent life an extraordinarily rare and possibly unique event.

The chief theological question raised by intelligent extra-terrestrial beings is their place in the economy of salvation and, more specifically, their relationship to Jesus Christ. Would it make sense (following, perhaps, a broad interpretation of Mark 16:15 and Rom. 8:19–21) to speak of the Word who took human flesh in the incarnation as saviour of a non-human species? Or is it more theologically appropriate to imagine the divine Word becoming incarnate in other species on other worlds? In this way, extra-terrestrials serve much the same theological function as angels did in medieval theology: as a basis for thought-experiments designed to explore issues related to the general characteristics of creatures' relationship to God.

Ian A. McFarland

FAITH Along with HOPE and LOVE, faith has been understood in the Christian tradition (following 1 Cor. 13:13) as a theological virtue: a settled disposition enabling one to move towards God by GRACE. As the young AUGUSTINE observes, without faith one would not believe there was anything to hope for; without hope one would despair of attaining the realities of which faith speaks; and without love one would not even desire to come to that goodness in which one had come to believe (*Sol.* 6.12). It is in this sense that the TRADITION has generally interpreted the most famous biblical statement about faith – as making present even now something of the reality to which one is journeying: 'Now faith is the assurance of things hoped for, the conviction of things not seen' (Heb. 11:1).

F

Faith in the theological sense is thus only possible as a gift of God, for one cannot by oneself have natural certain knowledge or even right opinion of the divine realities which the teachings of faith seek to express. Classically, therefore, faith is considered according to two fundamental dimensions: it refers both to the *beliefs* or DOCTRINES to which one assents (*fides quae creditur*), and also to the *act* of trust or adherence by means of which these beliefs are accepted as true (*fides qua creditor*, or, especially in the work of M. LUTHER, *fiducia*). But, because the divine realities adhered to by faith inspire one with the hope of attaining them, and also arouse love of the divine goodness which never ends, living faith is always seen to be at work in one's manner of life and one's moral imagination. Because of the foretaste of the divine granted to faith, it intrinsically searches and longs for an ever fuller understanding and participation in the divine realities which the truths of faith announce: 'faith is a habit of mind, by which eternal life begins in us, making the understanding assent to what does not appear' (T. AQUINAS, *ST* 2/2.4.1). Thus faith makes present to human consciousness something of the communion with God which is the consummation of the human person, but which is nonetheless so superabundant that in this present life it can only be sensed by the human mind as a kind of darkness. In the life to come, faith reaches its end, for it is succeeded by the vision of God: hope is relinquished in favour of beatitude; while love journeys without end ever deeper into the life of the TRINITY (see BEATIFIC VISION).

In SCRIPTURE faith is not only an interior or cognitive state but a determining characteristic of one's whole manner of life – adherence, fidelity, obedience – as contrasted with mistrust or disobedience: paradigmatically, Adam and Eve are led by the serpent into mistrusting the divine command, and so into disobedience; by contrast, ABRAHAM's obedience to God's calling and trust in God's promise reflect God's prior truthfulness and trustworthiness. In the book of JOB, the accuser (or *Satan*) argues that Job's faith is merely mercenary, only as deep as the divine largesse showered upon Job. Yet under Satan's testing, Job persists in testifying to the greatness and trustworthiness of God. This indomitable belief turns out to be the most authentic faith: 'I know that my Redeemer lives, and that at the last he will stand upon the earth, and after my skin has been thus destroyed, then in my flesh I shall see God, whom I shall see on my side' (Job 19:25–7).

This conviction that God's goodness and truth shall unfailingly overrule all, despite the most appalling and apparent facts to the contrary, finds its profound culmination in the NT accounts of Jesus' own fidelity and trust in the One he calls Father – and in the Father's own trustworthiness in raising Jesus from death (see *ABBA*). In correspondence to this, Jesus calls forth an echoing faith in his followers. The Gospel of JOHN portrays the growing awareness within the community that Jesus is truly God's Christ, 'the way, and the truth, and the life' (14:6) in whom, by the adherence of faith, one comes to the Father. In an analogous fashion, the letters of PAUL unfold faith in Christ and trust in him as involving a sharing in his death so as to share in his resurrection. Paul regards this living adherence to the truth of Jesus' death on the cross and his resurrection from the dead as the crucial opening of believers to God's Spirit: 'It is no longer I who live, but it is Christ who lives in me. And the life I now live in the flesh I live by faith in the Son of God, who loved me and gave himself for me' (Gal. 2:20).

A perennial question for Christian theology has been the role of faith in relation to reason. In the ancient and medieval periods, faith and reason were generally conceived as complementary. For Augustine or Aquinas, faith is a rational activity. It does not mark the end point of the mind's reach but the beginning – just as a student advances in a discipline by starting from teachings that, to begin with, need to be accepted as true even though one does not yet know how they are so. In religious faith, the truths proposed for belief enable a continual search for deeper comprehension. One believes *in order to* understand; the truths that faith presupposes become the basis for deeper participation in the truth which is the mind's fulfilment. As Aquinas puts it: 'Since the goal of human life is perfect happiness [*beatitudo*], which consists in full knowledge of the divine realities, the direction of human life toward perfect happiness from the very beginning requires faith in the divine, the complete knowledge of which we look forward to in our final state of perfection' (*CTrin.* 3.1). Early modern thinkers, by contrast, tended to emphasize faith and reason as entirely distinct activities, holding reason solely responsible for what it could know by its own unaided activity, and reserving faith for the apprehension of those few extraordinary beliefs that are apparently unavailable to reason. Not infrequently (as for instance in J. Locke (1632–1704) and many later advocates of DEISM) this isolation of reason from faith led to the view that faith can only be preserved from fanaticism or superstition either if it is subject to reason (i.e., may only propose as worthy of belief what is always already credible at the bar of reason), or if it is regarded as a merely private personal opinion without public significance.

Also central has been the question of the full term or goal of *statements* of faith – and the role of the will in the *act* of faith as, by means of these statements or teachings, it extends towards this goal. Augustine had observed that 'what we hope for is that faith in true things will eventually be transformed into the things themselves' (*Trin.* 13.3). Aquinas also affirms that the true reach of faith is not confined to doctrinal formularies themselves: 'The act of the believer does not reach its end in a statement, but in the thing: we do not form statements except so that we may have apprehension of things through them' (*ST* 2/2.1.2). So the doctrinal language is an absolutely *necessary* dimension of faith, yet it is not *sufficient* in the sense that both the mind and the will reach out by means of the doctrines of faith to the reality of God which the doctrines name. The role of the will in this is vital, for, in the classical view, the love of God poured into a believer's heart by the HOLY SPIRIT (Rom. 5:5) animates the believer's own love to sustain the mind in reaching out towards the divine truth and goodness that a believer genuinely seeks but cannot fully grasp. Thus classical discussions of faith have emphasized the integrated role in genuine faith of mind *and* heart, doctrinal statements *and* affective believing.

The ultimate object of faith is always God himself, present as illumining the mind and animating the heart in order, by grace, to bestow faith on a believer: 'the light of faith, which is, as it were, a faint stamp of the First Truth in our mind, cannot fail, any more than God can be deceived or lie' (Aquinas, *CTrin.* 3.1.4). Classically, this has been seen as the ground of faith's certainty, not that the truth of God is grasped by the mind, but that the One who is believed foundationally in every genuine act of faith is always God himself. This emphasizes the personal or relational dimension of faith, as a bond that God establishes with a believer – who believes not only *that* God exists, or *what* God teaches, but also believes *in* God himself as faithful and true.

T. Aquinas, *Summa theologiae* 2/2.1–16.

Augustine, *The Enchiridion on Faith, Hope, and Charity* (New City, 2008 [421–3]).

K. Barth, *Church Dogmatics* (T&T Clark, 1958), IV/2, 312–77.

R. Cessario, *Christian Faith and the Theological Life* (Catholic University of America Press, 1996).

A. Dulles, *The Assurance of Things Hoped For: A Theology of Christian Faith* (Oxford University Press, 1997).

MARK A. MCINTOSH

FAITH AND ORDER: see ECUMENISM.

FALL In Christian theology 'fall' is the term used to name the first act of creaturely disobedience to God and its consequences. In certain contexts, it refers to a primordial rebellion and punishment of angelic beings (see DEVIL) alluded to in some NT texts (2 Pet. 2:4; Jude 6; cf. Luke 10:18). Usually, however, it refers to the first human beings' transgression of God's command as described in Genesis 3. Although Genesis clearly states that this transgression was punished by a series of permanent changes in human beings' relation to one another and to the natural world (Gen. 3:14–19), the story does not play a central role in subsequent reflection on the human condition in the OT. In the writings of PAUL, however, the figure of Adam acquires new prominence as the one who introduced a fundamental change in the human situation made good by Christ (Rom. 5:12–14; 1 Cor. 15:21–2; cf. 1 Tim. 2:13–14).

While these Pauline texts served as a stimulus for the subsequent development of a doctrine of the fall, Christian writers of the first few centuries did not move much beyond Paul's brief references to Adam's disobedience as the occasion for the entrance of sin and death into the world, the effects of which are overcome through the redemptive work of Christ. Only with AUGUSTINE does the fall become a central theological category. While pre-Augustinian theologians viewed Adam's disobedience as occasioning a weakening of human capacities (a stance that continues to be characteristic of ORTHODOX THEOLOGY to the present day), Augustine (largely in response to PELAGIANISM) argued that the effects of the fall were more extreme: it did not merely increase human susceptibility to sin, but resulted in a turning of the will from God that rendered all human acts inherently sinful. In subsequent Augustinian tradition (both Catholic and Protestant) this interpretation of the fall led to an expansion of the meaning of original SIN as naming not only a past event (viz., the first sin of Adam), but also a congenital state of estrangement from God characteristic of all post-Adamic humanity.

The idea of the fall as a historical event producing catastrophic consequences for the human race serves several theological purposes. First, it helps to absolve God from responsibility for evil by ascribing suffering and mortality to contingent human actions rather than to eternal divine intentions. Second, it provides a framework for affirming the universal significance of

Christ's work, since Christ can only be confessed as the Saviour of all people if it is the case that all people stand in need of salvation. Third, the fall demands of Christians a recognition of universal solidarity – and equality – in sin, since if all persons, by virtue of the fall, stand equally in need of salvation by Christ, there is no basis for any one person claiming any merit over another.

At the same time, the doctrine of the fall has come in for severe criticism. The modern period in particular has forced Christians to confront the fact that the most credible scientific accounts of human origins (see EVOLUTION) are not consistent either with the idea that all human beings descended from a single pair (see MONOGENESIS), or with the belief that suffering and death in the natural world arose only as the result of human disobedience. While some theologians (e.g., P. TILLICH, R. NIEBUHR) have attempted to address this concern by reinterpreting the fall as an inevitable feature of every individual human life rather than as a primordial historical event, such proposals run the risk of impugning Christian belief in the inherent goodness of creation (and thus of the Creator) by tracing the fall to human ontology.

A further charge levelled against the Augustinian doctrine of the fall in particular is that the idea of a congenital sinfulness implies a moral determinism that is inconsistent with basic Christian convictions regarding individual freedom and moral accountability. In other words, the claim that human beings are inherently and necessarily sinful seems to make it meaningless to regard their sin as blameworthy. Consequently, theologians who seek to defend an Augustinian understanding of the fall have to show (e.g., by careful examination of the ontology of the will) how the defence of universal human solidarity in sin can be affirmed without undermining the integrity of human beings as responsible creatures before God.

See also *CONCURSUS*; FREE WILL.

M. Suchocki, *The Fall to Violence: Original Sin in Relational Theology* (Continuum, 1994).

N. P. Williams, *The Ideas of the Fall and Original Sin: A Historical and Critical Study* (Longmans, Green and Co., 1927).

IAN A. MCFARLAND

FASTING Fasting is the practice of going without food and drink, usually for a spiritual benefit. In the OT fasting was practised as a supplement to prayer for God's intervention in a time of crisis (as for healing or aid in battle; see, e.g., 2 Chron. 20:3). The prophetic books also stressed the role of fasting as a rite of mourning, whether for the dead or for one's own sin (e.g., Jer. 36:9). By the post-exilic period, fasting had become increasingly ritualized into a Jewish practice to be exercised on specific days of spiritual discipline.

By comparison to the frequent allusions to fasting in the OT, the NT references to the practice are far less common, reflecting a growing sense of uncertainty as to the place of fasting within the developing religion. While the synoptic Jesus advocated fasting as a necessary complement to effective PRAYER (e.g., Matt. 6:16–18), and the Church of Acts practised fasting during times when God's direction was being sought (Acts 13:2–3; 14:23), some NT writers express clear ambivalence towards the public displays of fasting which marked its routinization (e.g., Col. 2:16; 1 Tim. 4:3).

Within the patristic period, many Christian writings reflected Greco-Roman thought on food and fasting as much as the biblical tradition. Following the pagan physician Galen (129–200), Ambrose (*ca* 340–97) and JEROME argued that the amount and types of food that one eats stimulate sexual urges, and thus that fasting should be a prime weapon in combating lust. In particular, Christians should avoid red meat, wine, and other foods which were thought to trigger sexual desire. Some fathers also deemed fasting a demonstration of one's mastery over physicality: just as eating was the source of sin's entry into the world (Genesis 3), rigorous fasting was the sign of its defeat.

In the medieval Church, fasting was increasingly situated as the central prescription of Christian PENANCE, especially in the monastic movements of both East and West. Because the life of a monk was considered a perpetual penance, the life of the religious was to be marked with regular fasting. In medieval handbooks of penance, most notably the Irish Penitentials, very specific lengths of fasting were indicated as remedy for various sins, with the longest fasts often prescribed for those sins which affected the stability of the monastic community (see MONASTICISM).

Fasting could involve the renunciation of all food and drink or only certain foods. It could be performed for one day (or part of a day) as routine devotional practice, over a set number of days for extended penance, or during liturgical seasons such as Lent. There were also so-called special fasts that were added to the end of liturgical fast days for penance. In some Protestant contexts (e.g., colonial New England) 'Fast Days' were proclaimed as expressions of collective, public penitence.

For all its perceived spiritual benefit, fasting had undeniable social implications in Christianity. Not only were ascetics given positions of honour within the early and medieval Church, but fasting also provided a penitent means of re-entry into, and upwards movement within, the community. In recent years, fasting has been reclaimed as a spiritual discipline by some Christian traditions, most notably by evangelicals, although its practice is not as widespread as in earlier centuries. While some have attempted to delineate a theology of fasting, it is most often advocated as a return to the biblical model of focused prayer through ascetic discipline.

See also Asceticism.

C. W. Bynum, *Holy Feast and Holy Fast: The Religious Significance of Food to Medieval Women* (University of California Press, 1987).

T. Shaw, *The Burden of the Flesh: Fasting and Sexuality in Early Christianity* (Fortress Press, 1998).

Garry J. Crites

Federal Theology Federal theology is a term applied to a trend in Reformed theology, particularly in the late sixteenth and seventeenth centuries, which tended to structure itself around the notion of covenant (Latin *foedus*). While not monolithic in terms of detail, it did enjoy significant confessional and ecclesiastical status, being important to both the Three Forms of Unity and the Westminster Standards, the confessional documents, respectively, of the continental Reformed Churches, and British-American Presbyterianism respectively.

The Bible itself contains explicit references to numerous covenants between God and human beings (with Abraham, Noah, etc.), and also to the supplanting of the covenant with Israel with a more glorious covenant at the end of time. Thus, federal theology rests upon a notion which is central to the Bible's own account of the development of salvation history, and which was picked up and developed by the Reformed in the sixteenth century to fulfil a number of theological purposes.

The first major articulation of federal theology was by H. Zwingli in the 1520s, who used the notion of covenant to defend the practice of infant baptism in the face of Anabaptist criticism. This allowed him to draw a clear connection between circumcision and baptism, thus defending his sacramental position and, at the same time, offering an account of how the OT and NT were connected to each other. Other early Reformers, such as H. Bullinger, W. Tyndale (*ca* 1495–1536), and J. Hooper (*ca* 1495–1555), used covenant as a means of articulating the relationship between divine sovereignty and human responsibility, possibly influenced by the earlier work of D. Erasmus (1466/9–1536).

J. Calvin brought an emphasis upon a single covenant of grace to Reformed theology. This covenant, while one in substance, can be distinguished into various historical dispensations, which, in turn, involved both unilateral and bilateral elements. As such, this covenant provided a basic unity to the Bible and became the context for understanding the role of the moral law in the life of the believer. For most Reformed, for example, the Sinaitic covenant was seen as gracious, with the Mosaic law providing the framework for living life in the context of prior redemption. This single covenant notion can be found in the Heidelberg Catechism and so came to enjoy significant confessional status within the Reformed Churches in the Low Countries.

In the late sixteenth century some Reformed theologians started to argue for a second covenant, a covenant of creation, nature, or works, which referred to an arrangement between God and Adam in the Garden of Eden prior to the fall. While the language of covenant is absent from Genesis 1 and 2, the stipulations imposed upon Adam in his state of creation were considered to indicate the existence of a covenantal relation between two parties, the divine and the human. Linked to the idea of a probationary period for Adam, the successful fulfilment of which would be rewarded with an exalted state of being, this covenant effectively fulfilled for Reformed theology what the doctrine of the *donum superadditum* had done for medieval Catholic theology and clearly built upon earlier, pre-Reformation discussions of the nature of merit: it allowed for finite works to merit a reward of which they are not strictly and intrinsically worthy. Scholars are divided as to how far this development of a covenant of works is consistent with Calvin and other early Reformed theologians, but the basic concepts which it embodies (divine condescension in creation; Adam's representative headship of humanity; and divine stipulations for obedience and promises of reward) are present in the earlier Reformed literature.

Structurally, the covenant of work set the basic framework for understanding the person and work of Christ as the last Adam, with the Reformed understanding of his work as a recapitulation of the first covenant, with Christ as the representative of the elect. Thus, there is a close connection between the covenant of works and the covenant of grace in the developed federal theology of the seventeenth century.

In the mid-1640s, a further soteriological covenant was introduced, the covenant of redemption (in English) or *pactum salutis* (in Latin). The Reformed argued that the relationship between God the Father and God the Son, whereby the Father appointed the Son as Mediator, and the Son willingly submitted himself to the Father to take the role, was a covenantal one. This was driven in part by linguistic work on the definition of covenant then applied to the soteriological relations within the Godhead; but also by the need to clarify, in the face of Catholic criticism, how Christ could be Mediator according to both natures, not simply the human. The term 'covenant of redemption' does not enjoy confessional status, as it developed too late for incorporation in the Westminster Standards in the 1640s, but it is arguably built upon discussions of Christ's mediation as far back as the work of Calvin.

By the early eighteenth century, federal theology was in decline, in part because of significant philosophical shifts in the broader intellectual culture but also because, in England at least, the Reformed had effectively lost the intellectual and political battle. Only the Baptist J. Gill (1697–1771) mounted a particularly notable defence of federalism, as one born out of time;

and in the American colonies, Reformed Orthodoxy's most able defender, J. EDWARDS, while clearly knowledgeable about the work of previous generations, found other idioms for articulating and defending the Reformed system.

R. S. Clark, *Caspar Olevian and the Substance of the Covenant* (Rutherford House, 2005).

R. W. A. Letham, 'The *Foedus Operum*: *Some Factors Accounting for Its Development*', *Sixteenth Century Journal* 14 (1983), 457–67.

P. A. Lillback, *The Binding of God: Calvin's Role in the Development of Covenant Theology* (Baker Books, 2001).

CARL R. TRUEMAN

FEMINIST THEOLOGY Feminist theology emerged in the USA in the 1970s, in part as an outgrowth of the activism of Second Wave Feminism. This 1960s secular movement addressed sexism in contemporary society by working to expand women's rights, draw public attention to sexual exploitation and other long-invisible forms of gender discrimination, and promote recognition and enhancement of women's agency beyond the bounds of the domestic sphere. These Second Wave concerns have also shaped feminist theology, but its drive to combat sexism (i.e., the view that women are inferior to men), has been defined by R. Ruether (b. 1937) as the promotion of the full humanity of women, a principle generated in relation to the Christian tradition as well as other social-change discourses. Feminist theologies draw constructively from FAITH traditions to envision change, but many also employ a HERMENEUTICS of suspicion, which critiques the failures of these traditions to recognize and support women's full humanity. Feminist theological projects are as varied as the many forms of sexism.

A long-standing issue for feminist theology has been women's access to leadership and full participation in the life of Christian communities. A number of nineteenth-century women from, e.g., Pentecostal, Holiness, and African Methodist Episcopal traditions, are known for their preaching. However, access to preaching did not typically include full clergy rights. Thus twentieth-century feminist theology saw the rise of advocacy movements for women's ordination, which included protest activities as well as theological arguments. The irregular ordination of eleven Episcopal women in 1974 and the Catholic Women's Ordination Conference (WOC) in 1975, for example, are historic displays of feminist theology's convictions gone public. In part a result of such pressures and the influence of secular progress achieving women's equality, the ordination barrier has been lifted in many denominations: denominations which ordain women went from 7 per cent in 1890 to about 50 per cent by the late twentieth century (Chaves, *Ordaining* 18). The feminist battle for ordination for the remaining 50 per cent still goes on, as illustrated by the continued activism of one of feminism's oldest organizations, the WOC.

Theological activism around issues of female leadership addresses sexism by arguing that women be given access to the same rights, power, and privileges granted to men, i.e., an approach defined by *inclusion*. An inclusive theological approach is also found in evangelical feminism, with its primary focus on biblical authorization for women's equal participation in the life of the Church. Biblical scholarship aimed at finding permission for women to speak and act as leaders has made much of Pauline 'prohibition' passages (e.g., 1 Cor. 14:34–6; 1 Tim. 2:12) and Jesus' relationship to women in attempts to reinterpret the negative passages in women's favour. Feminist focus on the authoritative function of SCRIPTURE in light of women's issues has also yielded a great deal of literature recovering previously ignored stories of women agents in both the OT and the NT, along with female images of the divine. With the attention to female images and metaphors, the inclusivity approach is also employed in the focus on liturgy with demands for INCLUSIVE LANGUAGE for God and human beings.

A theology generated by human brokenness as complicated as sexism is not limited to one strategy of change. As feminist exploration of the causes of women's exclusion expands, proposals for theological remedies also move beyond the idea that women simply want to be included in existing structures. Classic claims by feminist theologian V. Saiving (1921–92) in the 1960s that mainline definitions of SIN and LOVE are shaped by male experience are an early example of the case that normative religious texts and traditions are inflected with male perspectives, a social constructionist view that feminist theologians have continued to develop. Saiving's point was that a male-defined notion of sin as pride (as exemplified in the work of R. NIEBUHR) and its redress by self-sacrifice (associated with the thought of A. Nygren (1890–1978)) invite self-destructive responses for women, who generally lack an adequate sense of self.

While the particulars of Saiving's analysis are outdated, her basic point that symbols, images, doctrinal narratives, and discourses are shaped by gendered experience is not. Sexism is not simply a problem of prohibitive practices and the texts that authorize them. To be sure, classic theologians' views on women matter, e.g., the impact of Aristotle's view that a woman is a 'misbegotten male' (T. AQUINAS), that she is fully *imago dei* only when joined with a man (AUGUSTINE and K. BARTH), that woman's subordination to man is punishment for Eve's sin (M. LUTHER). However, the sexism of the tradition is more complex. DOCTRINE with no apparent reference to women can function to render them as lesser beings. The traditional periodization of Church history is problematic, for it is defined as if the only agents who count are male. Recognition that discourses not directly about women can be constitutive of world views that oppress them has become a key assumption of feminist theology and continues to generate new readings of religious history, tradition, and classic doctrine.

Feminist theologies that investigate the oppressive functions of religious and secular discourse are akin to Latin American LIBERATION THEOLOGY, as well as to BLACK THEOLOGY, postcolonial theologies (see COLONIALISM AND POSTCOLONIALISM), and other POLITICAL THEOLOGIES. Such theologies are generated by the struggles of marginalized groups with oppressive social structures and the Christian tradition that renders them invisible or less than human. Distinctive in the thinking of feminist theologies of liberation is the concept of gender, i.e., the social construction of the difference between male and female. A shift to gender analysis means that feminists cannot limit their concern to women, but must attend to the social definitions of maleness as well as femaleness and ask how these constructed identities have been used to socially locate and constrain populations. Gender criticism explores the use of difference in ways that sometimes exaggerate, but, most importantly, exploit difference in a way that denies the full humanity of all involved. Consequently, for liberation feminists Scripture's exclusionary discourse cannot be interpreted as 'really' inclusive of women if properly interpreted, but must be acknowledged to be deeply shaped by ancient patriarchal societies and the gendered ideological interests that drove its authors. Redress of such oppressive traditions requires not only a hermeneutics of suspicion towards Scripture, but analyses of the power structures that produce and maintain authoritative texts and the emergence of liberatory movements to counter their effects.

The focus on gender in feminist theology has been accompanied by criticism and productivity alike. Early on, African-American feminists, self-described womanists, and Black feminists argued that feminist theology's focus on gender as the defining identity marker did not represent the experience of all women (see WOMANIST THEOLOGY). For these women social constructions of RACE had as much or more impact than gender as a marginalizing factor. Recognition that the 'women's experience' of feminist theology constitutes a false universal (sometimes called 'essentialism') is also evidenced in the constructive work on identity markers such as ethnicity and class. Latina and *MUJERISTA* THEOLOGIES and ASIAN-AMERICAN THEOLOGIES (along with those which complexify 'Asian') are a few examples of the generative work in second- and third-generation feminist thinking that attends to the effects of the very different social realities that construct 'women'. While debates over the attractiveness of feminism for non-Caucasian, non-Western women are common, a recent Native American feminist claim is that Native American women were the real 'first wave' of feminism on the continent now known as North America. Another critical/constructive development in feminist theology is the challenge to its binary accounts of gender, i.e., the heteronormative assumption that there are only two kinds of people, males and females. QUEER THEOLOGIES not only expand concepts of sexual desire and difference, but 'out' the ignored sexuality of the tradition in provocative ways.

As second- and third-generation feminist thinking demands attention to markers besides gender (race, ethnicity, SEXUALITY, class), there is no agreement on how best to understand the intersection of these markers of both privilege and marginalization. One of the important implications for feminist theological work is the need to recognize the additional marker of 'Whiteness' on theologies in which that 'invisible privilege' is also shaping gender. For example, how might the limitations of liberal 'add-on' strategies be addressed? To simply begin with gender and add the harm of racism does not recognize the fundamentally altered nature of gender for women 'of colour'. Alternative ways to understand complex identity markers and avoid essentializing the notion of woman include such concepts as intersectionality, geographies, subject positions, poststructuralist destabilizations of the subject, and strategic essentialism. Some worry about the limitations of what has been called 'identity politics', noting that, while identity markers have enabled feminist theology to identify formerly invisible forms of injustice, there are questions about the granting of an almost religious authority to marginalized identities. Feminist theologians like S. Parsons (b. 1945) who worry that the Christian tradition and orthodoxy have been given short shrift by previous thinkers see identity politics as unwilling to engage communal norms. Some argue that identity politics invites overly simple accounts of power, allowing a kind of dualistic categorizing of the oppressors and the oppressed.

Classic Christian doctrine has received considerable feminist theological attention. Two early feminist constructions of SYSTEMATIC THEOLOGY include a kind of parody of the patriarchal force of the traditional *loci* in *Beyond God the Father* (1973) by M. Daly (1928–2010), and a trenchant critique of the oppressive work and inter-relation of official beliefs in R. Ruether's *Sexism and God-Talk* (1984). Since the publication of these feminist classics, others have focused on particular doctrines. A first of three doctrines receiving significant attention for their real and potential harm is the doctrine of God. As it is dominated by male images for the divine, the classic TRINITY of Father, Son, and HOLY SPIRIT has been contested for its symbolic valorization of maleness as most akin to the divine. Closely related is CHRISTOLOGY, which, in the form defined at CHALCEDON, identifies the man Jesus of Nazareth with the full presence of God. Again the feminist critique focuses on the doctrine's problematic valorization of maleness, as Jesus' divinity has historically functioned to privilege males as the only legitimate representatives of God. Even when such ordination restrictions are not in place, feminists argue that images shape the social imagination, communicating the superior value of maleness. While womanists have maintained that maleness is not Jesus' most important feature for the African–American community, and Queer feminist critiques move beyond the denigration of women to the homosocial resonances of classic imagery, all seek to offer more liberative readings of this central doctrine.

A third area of concern develops around doctrines of sin and salvation. Saiving's critique that identifying sin with pride continues to reinforce women's inordinate lack of a self has been expanded and connected to doctrines of ATONEMENT that valorize suffering. Feminist theologies explore ways that such doctrines reinscribe self-destructive cultural images of femininity and, in the work of R. N. Brock (b. 1950), compare sacrificial atonement to 'divine child abuse'. The call to take up the cross and suffer for Jesus is a particularly harmful imperative for African–American women, as many womanists argue. Moral imperatives to self-sacrifice have been connected to much harmful pastoral advice given victims of domestic abuse (see TRAUMA, THEOLOGY OF). Feminist theologies, Queer feminists, and womanists basically concur that the alternatives of self-sacrifice or egoism are inadequate to the full-bodied, gendered, and complex character of human beings, and strive to offer alternatives honouring this complex diversity.

Challenges to definitions of gender and the role of Christian and other religious traditions will continue for feminist theology. The effects of globalization, for example, must be factored in for all locations, from capitalism's effects on two thirds of the world to the religious and cultural hybridity constituting the USA. Globalization also requires that feminist theology acknowledge its western character and widen its vision of human suffering, oppression, and flourishing. Recognizing the 'false universal' of the western Christian world and its role in historic colonialism raises even more questions about feminist theology's relation to the classic Christian tradition beyond the way in which it properly connects to so-called ORTHODOXY. 'TRADITION' will mean quite different things for different international locations, as it does even now in the globalized USA.

M. P. Aquino, D. L. Machado, and J. Rodriguez, eds., *A Reader in Latina Feminist Theology: Religion and Justice* (University of Texas Press, 2002).

P. Cochran, *Evangelical Feminism: A History* (New York University Press, 2005).

D. Juschka, *Feminism in the Study of Religion: A Reader* (Continuum, 2001).

M. Kamitsuka, *Feminist Theology and the Challenge of Difference* (Oxford University Press, 2007).

R. S. Keller and R. R. Ruether, eds., *Encyclopedia of Women and Religion in North America* (Indiana University Press, 2006).

P. Kwok, *Postcolonial Imagination and Feminist Theology* (John Knox Press, 2005).

MARY MCCLINTOCK FULKERSON

FEUERBACH, LUDWIG Ludwig Feuerbach (1804–72) was a philosopher who practised, in K. BARTH's words, 'anti-theology'. In Feuerbach's greatest work, *The Essence of Christianity* (1841), he set out to describe RELIGION as a human activity along realist and materialist terms (see MATERIALISM; REALISM AND ANTI-REALISM). Contra G. W. F. HEGEL's theoretical IDEALISM, Feuerbach maintained that at the heart of religion is a God who is not abstract and distant but rather present in human beings as their true nature: God is nothing else than human nature purified of limitations. Accordingly, for Feuerbach religion attributes to God human qualities that should be returned to their proper subject – the human being – in order to secure a more authentic form of human existence: 'The human being – that is the secret of religion; God is the human, and the human is God.'

Feuerbach calls his readers to cease to project perfections onto the divine being, arguing that such projection only incurs religious misery – the acute recognition of that which one lacks as an individual (but which humanity possesses as a species). The essential insights that Feuerbach promotes, then, are that religion is concerned above all else with humanity, and that God is but the quintessence of the qualities of the human species. Accordingly, to be related to God is to be related to ourselves: humanity's essential being is the measure of all things, most especially of God. Human reason, will, and affection are, correspondingly, self-referring, self-reflecting, and self-grounding.

Unlike D. F. Strauss (1808–74), Feuerbach is not concerned with articulating a critique of BIBLICAL THEOLOGY or of Christianity as such; but like F. SCHLEIERMACHER and Hegel, he is deeply concerned with questioning the objectivity of God as an immediate object of human knowledge. This enables him to distil the essence of religion into a system of belief that trades upon maintaining the antithesis between the divine and human, the I and the Thou. Religion, for Feuerbach, needs to progress, and to overcome such an antithesis, in order that the object of religion might be understood as identical with the self-consciousness of the human person.

ATHEISM, for Feuerbach, is but the culmination of religion, precisely because atheism recognizes religion for what it is: human divine-object-making. That Feuerbach understands there to be this kind of natural progression in religion's development is testimony to the optimism underlying his project and that of much nineteenth-century thought. But what Feuerbach never fully realized is that because the humanity of the man or woman he describes is (as a species) immortal, it is too abstract to reflect the concrete reality of mortal human lives. Indeed, because Feuerbach vested his hopes in the human being as the one with whom God is identified – the human in whom there is no lack – neither death nor the sinfulness of human beings are themes present in his writings.

In this way, Feuerbach demonstrates what happens when theology ceases to be interested in God per se, and becomes only interested in what God is for human beings. Feuerbach's philosophical theology is but the culmination of a long tradition in European Protestant divinity in which, according to Barth's famous words, 'theology has long since become anthropology'.

H. Van Austin, *Feuerbach and the Interpretation of Religion* (Cambridge University Press, 1997).

CHRISTOPHER R. J. HOLMES

FIDEISM Derived from the Latin word *fides* (FAITH), fideism is a term used – often pejoratively – to refer to the conviction that certain claims (e.g., that God exists) cannot be justified by appeal to reason but must be accepted or rejected by faith. A fideist position may be maintained on the grounds that religious beliefs are *contrary* to reason (irrational), that they are *logically distinct* from the kinds of propositions that can be supported by rational argument (arational), or that they articulate truths that are *beyond the scope* of rational demonstration (suprarational). Also, certain forms of Christian APOLOGETICS sometimes characterized as fideist aver that all rational arguments work from beliefs that are not themselves subject to rational defence and must therefore be presupposed (prerational).

The idea that Christian beliefs are both true and irrational is often attributed to TERTULLIAN, based on a misquotation from one of his treatises (*Carn.* 5); but such a position is in fact very hard to ascribe to any major Christian theologian, even though some (e.g., M. LUTHER) speak very disparagingly of the power of reason in order to emphasize God's transcendence of human capacities (cf. Isa. 55:9). Likewise, though CATHOLIC THEOLOGY teaches that certain DOCTRINES (e.g., the TRINITY) can be known only through REVELATION and are thus suprarational, the MAGISTERIUM has explicitly rejected fideism as contrary to the fundamental unity of all truth (John Paul II, *Fid.*, §§52–3, 55).

The most common form of explicit fideism treats religious language as arational: logically distinct from forms of discourse for which reason is an appropriate criterion. Though with antecedents in the thought of B. PASCAL and S. KIERKEGAARD, this position is most often associated with the philosophy of L. Wittgenstein (1889–1951), who argued that different uses of language constituted distinct 'forms of life', with their own criteria of deployment and assessment (*PI*, §§23, 241). The philosopher D. Z. Phillips (1934–2006) applied Wittgenstein's analysis specifically to religious belief, arguing that the meaning of concepts like 'God' and practices like 'prayer' can only be assessed from within the specifically religious contexts where they are used. To try to evaluate them in the same way that one would concepts like 'proton' or 'experiment' in physics is a category error, equivalent to critiquing a tennis match by appealing to the rules of badminton.

The most common criticism of fideism in theology is that it implies an epistemological relativism in which all religious claims are equally justified, so that it becomes impossible to defend a given religion as either uniquely true or superior to any other. Similarly, strict fideism would appear to disallow any arguments within a religious community over any disputed matter of faith or practice. Both these positions appear inconsistent with the behaviour of many (if not most) religious people, who view their faith as more than a matter of personal preference and, correspondingly, offer arguments for and against particular beliefs. In this way, fideism, while rightly noting the differences between religious and other forms of speech, fails to recognize that the facts of religious practice render any claim of absolute incommensurability between religious and non-religious language untenable.

See also REFORMED EPISTEMOLOGY.

D. Z. Phillips, *Faith and Philosophical Enquiry* (Schocken Books, 1979).

A. Plantinga, 'Reason and Belief in God' in *Faith and Rationality: Reason and Belief in God* ed. A. Plantinga and N. Wotterstorff (University of Notre Dame Press, 1983), 16–93.

IAN A. MCFARLAND

FIDES QUA/QUAE CREDITUR: see FAITH.

FIGURAL READING: see TYPOLOGY.

FILIOQUE The Latin word *filioque* is theological shorthand for the chief doctrinal issue separating the eastern (Orthodox) and western (Catholic and Protestant) Churches. As originally drafted, the NICENE CREED states that the HOLY SPIRIT 'proceeds from the Father' (cf. John 15:26). Beginning in the sixth century, western Church councils, drawing on the thought of AUGUSTINE (*Trin.* 15.26), revised the text to read 'proceeds from the Father *and the Son*' (*filioque*), stressing the full equality of the first two Persons of the TRINITY in order to counter the continuing influence of Arianism (see ARIAN CONTROVERSY). The *filioque* was formally adopted by Rome in 1014 and was retained after the REFORMATION by the Anglican, Lutheran, and Reformed Churches.

The Orthodox object to the *filioque* on a number of grounds. Juridically, they argue that it constitutes the kind of alteration of the Creed explicitly forbidden by the Council of EPHESUS (Canon VII). Dogmatically, they charge that it confuses the divine economy (where the Son does send the Spirit on the Church) with the Spirit's eternal, intra-Trinitarian procession as described in John 15. Moreover, they contend that it undermines Christian monotheism by replacing confession of the Father as the sole source (*aitia*) of divinity with the positing of two such sources within the Godhead. In response to this charge, western theologians counter that the Orthodox position fails to do justice to the Holy Spirit's specific identity as the Spirit of Jesus Christ (cf. Acts 16:7; Phil. 1:19; 1 Pet. 1:11). In an effort to respect both the Father's logical priority within the Trinity and the intrinsically Christological shape of the Spirit's being and action, theologians from both eastern and western traditions have proposed compromise language, according to which the Spirit proceeds from the Father *through* the Son, or proceeds from the Father and *rests on* the Son.

Ian A. McFarland

Film, Theology and The question, 'What is cinema?' is hardly straightforward. The popular nature of the film industry and its alliances with pornography, violence, and entertainment, may make the relation of cinema to theology seem even harder to construct persuasively than others of the arts. Yet both cinema and the other arts have multiple forms of expression and provide powerful ways to express what may not easily be put into words.

Cinema is a relatively new art form. A. Bazin (1918–58), arguably one of the greatest film critics, writing on the ontology of the image, contrasted the arts of painting and photography. Painting, he argued, is tugged in two directions at once. One is to create an image of such vitality, perceptiveness, depth, and interest to the viewer that it even surpasses that to which it referred. It can stand on its own. The other tug is to reproduce faithfully, to copy, to duplicate. Bazin argued that photography freed painting from its anxiety about resemblance, but photography, in turn, could not aspire to the creativity and even eternity which may belong to painting. Photography, Bazin argued, freezes time and embalms objects like insects in amber. The contribution of cinema, then, is to reconnect time and image, much as the discovery of perspective added a dimension to form.

Cinema early on developed its own language which was subsequently taken still further with the addition of sound. Its early art lay in two directions: the creativity of the director in *mise en scène* (lighting, composition, framing, set) and skill in montage. Skill in montage of various kinds could suggest simultaneity, speed, or a completely different idea by association. For example, an item or two of clothing tossed to the floor might suggest physical intimacy without that ever actually being displayed. It was montage, Bazin argued, which set film apart from animated photography, which gave it language and made it an art form. Great directors like S. Eisenstein (1898–1948) did not need to show an event as they merely alluded to it with enormous skill (in, e.g., *The Battleship Potemkin* (1925) and *Ivan the Terrible* (1944)).

This point can be illustrated further. The Italian neorealist film *Bicycle Thieves* (*Ladri di biciclette*, 1948), directed by V. De Sica (1901/2–74), is about as far removed from Hollywood as one can get. It was low budget, shot in the street, without professional actors. This shielded it from artificiality. Located in a time of disillusion, it carries a strong message: at a certain stage of poverty, the poor will steal from each other. Yet the genius of De Sica is such that the film is not a documentary (which would only describe and record), not propaganda (in which its meaning would be subordinated to an ideology), and not a sermon (which might be didactic or hortatory). In the heat of the desperate search for the lost bicycle (the means of employment), the camera pauses to watch a group of Austrian seminarians. With neither engagement nor polemic, a sensation of anticlericalism is introduced. De Sica displays such artistry that one is caught into the flow of connection to such an extent that one oneself provides the necessity, and draws the conclusion, without the need of special effects or blood and guts to induce sympathy. Direction of such felicity can enable the contrivance of actor and set to disappear, and cinema itself, Bazin ventures, becomes more of a hybrid between the novel and the theatre than either the one or the other.

It is evident that there are several well-known films which, though made for a mass audience, could well be called 'religious'. Examples might include C. B. DeMille's (1881–1959) *The Ten Commandments* (1956) or W. Wyler's (1902–81) *Ben Hur* (1959). There were others which were less successful. In exploring the relation of theology and film, the issue is not, 'Is there a genre?' but, 'Does cinema have a particular capacity to explore and deepen unresolved issues in religion or believing?' Similarly, in the work of some critics, the Catholic assumptions (for example) of A. Hitchcock (1899–1980) are laid bare, or the Lutheran childhood of I. Bergman (1918–2007), but these in themselves do not make their films theological. The stance of films most constructively interesting to theology may (as suggested) not be the overtly sermonic or pious but one which stands aside and like some forms of painting permits both an outsider and an insider perspective. Such a stance in which tentative proposals are advanced, explored, and revised may be illustrated especially in the work of Bergman with respect to intergenerational and inter-sibling forgiveness; K. Kieślowski (1941–96) on bereavement and creativity, providence, superstition, presentiment; and A. Tarkovsky (1932–86) on loss, bewilderment, identity, and sacrifice. There are many others (e.g., C. Dreyer (1889–1968), J.-L. Godard (b. 1930), R. Andersson (b. 1943)), all characterized by a probing and observant openness to the human condition. And though documentary is not a genre treated here, it may be argued that, at its most sensitive (e.g., J. Yu's (b. 1966) Academy Award-winning *Breathing Lessons: The Life and Work of Mark O'Brien* (1996), which addresses severe disability), it transcends documentation and becomes an avenue for heightened awareness and self-reflection.

It should not be thought that all film interesting to theology must be representational. S. Brakhage (1933–2003) strove to create visionary experiences which could not be analyzed or described in words. He wrote: 'there is a pursuit of knowledge foreign to language and founded upon visual communication, demanding a development of the optical mind, and dependent upon perception in the original and deepest sense of the word' (*Essential* 12). In its full range of forms, film is increasingly used as a teaching resource in theology for the purpose of drawing attention to the spiritual, emotional, and ethical dimensions of faith.

A. Bazin, *What Is Cinema?*, 2 vols. (University of California Press, 1971 [1967]).

P. Coates, *Cinema, Realism and the Romantic Legacy* (Ashgate, 2003).

P. A. Sitney, *Eyes Upside Down: Visionary Filmmakers and the Heritage of Emerson* (Oxford University Press, 2008).

Iain R. Torrance

Five-Point Calvinism: see Reformed Theology.

Forgiveness The forgiveness of sins through the grace of God in Christ is at the heart of the Christian gospel (Acts 13:38–9; Eph. 1:7; Col. 1:14). Yet a tragic paradox of Church history is that issues concerning forgiveness have been the cause of conflict and separation. The possibility of forgiveness for sins committed after baptism was one of the earliest controversies in the Church. The nature of the authority bestowed in 'the keys' (Matt. 16:18–19; 18:15–19; John 20:22–3) has been contested in the politics of papal primacy. Feminists have exposed how forgiveness has featured in the exercise of power in the Church (see Feminist Theology). Doctrinal debate has veered – in the West especially – between divine forgiveness as a conditional, quasi-legal victory pronounced over sin that entails some kind of exchange, and an unconditional act of grace that disregards wrongdoing without qualification.

Why these tensions? Philological investigation yields initial answers. The Hebrew *salach* ('pardon') is used of God pardoning the iniquity of the people, albeit not lightly or readily, when they return to their covenant obligations (Exod. 34:9; 1 Kgs 8:39; Num. 14:19) – though there are instances where God's pardon does not wait for Israel's repentance (Isa. 40:1–2; Jer. 31:31–4; 33:6–8). *Nasa* ('to lift or take away') is used frequently of God's forgiving iniquity and transgression (Exod. 34:7; Job 7:21; Ps. 25:18) and implies a sense of lightness and relief. *Kaphar* ('to cover over, propitiate, or atone for sin') is used in Genesis 6:14 for covering the ark with pitch but has cultic associations with sacrifice and appeasement (Exod. 29:36; Lev. 5:13; Neh. 10:33). Rendered by the Greek verb *aphienai* (or noun *aphesis*) in the Septuagint, its sense of release from imprisonment or remission of penalty is linked by NT writers with the Person of Christ Jesus and subsumed by Paul into his fuller doctrine of justification. *Kalyptein* is also used for the covering over of sins (1 Pet. 4:8; Jas. 5:20) such that they are not regarded. *Charizesthai* ('to give graciously or restore one to another') is used in contexts where something is given to another.

Issues lie deeper than simply a matter of definition, however. Questions arose in the third century, for instance, about forgiveness for post-baptismal sin. Some Christians had sacrificed to Roman gods. Others had not actually offered sacrifices but obtained certificates declaring that they had. Did the Church have the means to admit them back into fellowship? The Novatianists held that a Church containing lapsed members was not truly a Church. Cyprian of Carthage (d. 258) replied that the unity of the Church was found in the episcopate, not in the moral purity of its members. Eventually, the Council of Carthage (251) recognized forgiveness for lapsed Christians through the practice of public confession and absolution from the hands of the bishop. Subsequent councils, notably Ancyra (314) and Nicaea, regulated the practice of penance more closely.

The meaning and practice of forgiveness in Christian tradition has rarely been unaffected by socio-political pressures. Church historians probe, for instance, how the weakness of the papacy at the fall of the Roman Empire contributed to Pope Leo I's (r. 440–61) allowing of private confession, whereas its strength permitted Lateran Council IV (1215) to make confession to a priest compulsory at stated intervals, and the Council of Trent to confirm the reality of the effect of the priest's utterance of the formula 'I absolve you.' The political convictions of the English reformer J. Wycliffe (1325–84) coincided with his challenge to the necessity of confession to a priest and penance.

The politics of forgiveness should not, however, predominate in our historico-theological investigation. Consider further the tension between God's forgiveness as a legal or forensic victory pronounced over sin and as an unconditional offer of love. Anselm of Canterbury argued that it was not proper for God to forgive sins by compassion alone without any punishment or payment for the honour taken from him; only Christ, who was at the same time human and divine, could reconcile sinners to God by making good the satisfaction that every sinner owes. T. AQUINAS used the concept of satisfaction to explain the authority by which Christ, the mediator of God and humanity, took away the punishment due to sin. The Reformers taught that JUSTIFICATION by FAITH consists solely in the forgiveness of sins and emphasized PAUL's teaching that God's reconciling work in Christ covered over human sin (Rom. 4:7–8) thereby imputing to humanity an 'alien' righteousness.

By contrast, Protestant theologians of the ENLIGHTENMENT de-emphasized forgiveness obtained through Christ's communication of his righteousness to humanity and rejected images of forgiveness resulting from anything like a 'divine court'. For F. SCHLEIERMACHER, the problem besetting human nature was not captivity to the DEVIL or God's wrath but the underdevelopment of God-consciousness. He was less concerned with the forgiveness of sin on the cross than with the ideality of Christ's God-consciousness and subjective experience. In the twentieth century A. Nygren (1890–1978) argued that God is not held to any requirements of justice other than those of his own nature as *agape*-LOVE; forgiveness means disregarding the manifold faults and failings of our outward lives and the recognition of inward value not destroyed by sin.

What are we to make of this history? Christian teaching tends, in the West especially, to fall into either/or ways of thinking that affirm one pole at the expense of another (e.g., relational or quasi-legal, objective or subjective, conditional or unconditional). Yet the experience of forgiveness remains irreducibly heterogeneous and resistant to antinomies, including reconciliation among human beings as well as between human beings and God (Matt. 6:14–15; 18:21–35; Luke 6:37; 17:3–4). Correspondingly, an adequate theological analysis of the concept must recognize that the role of the HOLY SPIRIT in bringing about forgiveness is both sacramentally located and more diffuse. Yet all the Spirit's modes of acting are entailed in the NICENE CREED's confession of 'one baptism for the forgiveness of sins' and the claim that the cup shared in the EUCHARIST is 'for the forgiveness of sins' (Matt. 26:28). Here, especially, believers may learn that forgiveness is not primarily a moral concept but an integral part of the transformation of sin into repentance and new life.

See also ATONEMENT; CROSS AND CRUCIFIXION.

A. Bash, *Forgiveness and Christian Ethics* (Cambridge University Press, 2007).
L. G. Jones, *Embodying Forgiveness: A Theological Analysis* (Eerdmans, 1995).
H. B. Swete, *The Forgiveness of Sins* (Macmillan, 1916).

ESTHER D. REED

FRANKFURT SCHOOL The Frankfurt School is the informal name given to a group of German intellectuals employed by the Institute for Social Research, directed from 1931 by M. Horkheimer (1895–1973). The Institute was based initially in Frankfurt. Its most well-known first-generation contributors were Horkheimer, T. Adorno (1903–69), W. Benjamin (1892–1940), and H. Marcuse (1898–1979), together with E. Fromm (1900–80), F. Pollock (1894–1970), and others. Its emblematic writings are *Dialectic of Enlightenment* (1944), *Traditional and Critical Theory* (1937), *Eclipse of Reason* (1946), *Negative Dialectics* (1966), *Minima Moralia* (1951), *Eros and Civilization* (1955), and *One-Dimensional Man* (1964). Its principal members were Jewish, and in the face of severe threat from National Socialism in Germany the Institute moved to New York in 1934, where its work influenced a generation of American scholars, before moving back to Frankfurt in 1951.

The purpose of the Institute for Social Research was to investigate problems in social life, utilizing categories and methods of enquiry drawn from philosophy, sociology, and psychoanalysis. It pioneered the relation of these disciplines to each other. The problems it investigated included questions of economic and social injustice, false consciousness, authoritarianism, and alienation. It addressed the contradictions and anxieties of modern life in European and North American urban settings whose size, technological complexity and social anonymity had ballooned during the later nineteenth century.

The Frankfurt School's importance derives from the scope of its enquiries and the tools developed in its analyses. Its focus on critique was an adaptation of I. KANT's late eighteenth-century project for 'reason' to understand its own conditions and limit itself. Its focus on alienation drew on G. W. F. HEGEL, via K. Marx (1818–83), identifying contradictions between aspirations and institutional reality or – using Aristotelian terms – between possibility and actuality (see ARISTOTELIANISM). It had a particularly strong focus on forms of widespread social self-deception and the ways mass-marketed culture tends to simultaneously increase social alienation and conceal its effects. Its attention to the unconscious drew on F. Schelling (1775–1854), via S. Freud (1856–1939), attempting to explain societal repression of certain ideas and the spread of authoritarianism using Freud's model of individual repression of trauma. Finally, the School's understanding of rationality drew on A. Schopenhauer (1788–1860) and F. NIETZSCHE, via M. Weber (1864–1920), in its identification of the irrational habits of action that accompany even the most technologically rationalized forms of social action. In all this work the category of 'contradiction' is central: the central thrust of investigation is to identify clearly where contradictions in thinking lie, what material contradictions they express, and what material changes would resolve them.

The School's significance for theology lies in five broad areas. First, its critique of established categories of social analysis; second, its focus on suffering; third, its heritage of Jewish philosophy; fourth, its concern with justice; fifth, its explicit interest in theology. Horkheimer and Adorno insisted that theological discourses continue to express forms of HOPE and social life repressed by technological society and mass culture. Before 1968 these intersections led to generative interaction between Marxists and left-wing Christian theologians, especially in Germany, which shaped the theologies of J.-B. Metz (b. 1928) and J. Moltmann (b. 1926) and those they influenced.

NICHOLAS ADAMS

FREE WILL Human freedom is the subject of some of SCRIPTURE's most well-known passages. Jesus promises to make his followers free (John 8:36), and PAUL echoes this point: 'For freedom Christ has set us free. Stand firm, therefore, and do not submit again to a yoke of slavery' (Gal. 5:1). As both these passages suggest, the characteristic understanding of freedom in the Bible is that of liberation *from* external forms of oppression (e.g., captivity to the powers of SIN and death), though it also includes freedom *for* renewed life empowered and guided by the HOLY SPIRIT (see 2 Cor. 3:17). This way of talking about freedom, however, raises questions that have fuelled debates in the Church over the character of human freedom. If freedom is viewed as a gift of Christ, does that mean that non-Christians lack freedom? And what does it mean to define genuine freedom as a 'slavery' to Christ (Rom. 6:17–19) so complete that Paul can say, 'it is no longer I who live, but Christ who lives in me' (Gal. 2:20)?

In later theological discourse answers to these questions have generally turned on individual theologians' beliefs about free will, or the conditions of responsible agency: the experience that *I* am the author of my actions, and thus responsible for them. Often theologians have equated free will with an individual's autonomy over against possible causes of her action that can be distinguished from herself, such as genetic or environmental influences. It is possible to deny such freedom of the will by arguing that all human actions can be accounted for by some combination of external causes apart from any reference to an autonomous 'I'. At the other extreme, it is possible to affirm that the willing of the 'I' is the one necessary and sufficient explanation for every human action. While it would be difficult to find any theological defenders of either of these positions, they are approximated in radical forms of MATERIALISM and IDEALISM respectively.

In the Church's first centuries, reaction against what was seen as the fatalism of pagan culture in both its elite philosophical and popular religious forms led Christians to stress free will as an inalienable feature of human nature as created by God – and to exhibit a corresponding hostility towards theologies (e.g., various forms of GNOSTICISM and MANICHAEISM) that were believed to threaten it. Thus Theophilus of Antioch (d. *ca* 185) put God's creation of humankind as 'free and self-directing' (*eleutheron kai … autexousion*) at the heart of his THEOLOGICAL ANTHROPOLOGY (*Aut.* 2.27). For Theophilus human freedom was closely correlated with individual autonomy. In direct contrast to any sort of ontological determinism, to be free was to have a nature that was in certain crucial respects *in*determinate or open-ended: as free creatures, human beings were naturally neither mortal nor immortal, but endowed with the capacity to achieve either state. This basic perspective was shared by IRENAEUS (*AH* 4.37), ORIGEN (*Prin.* 2.8.3), and the CAPPADOCIAN FATHERS (see, e.g., Gregory of Nyssa, *Or.* 5), who agreed on humanity's God-given powers of self-determination for all their differences on other matters of theological anthropology.

The situation was complicated in the fifth century by AUGUSTINE's response to PELAGIANISM. Worried that Pelagius' high estimation of human beings' capacity to keep God's LAW rendered the GRACE of Christ unnecessary, Augustine argued that the effects of the FALL did not simply hamper human beings' ability to obey God but actually rendered them incapable of doing so. He insisted that humans did not thereby cease to be accountable for their sins, however, for they ineluctably remained the responsible authors of their sinful acts. Augustine defended this seemingly paradoxical claim that human beings sin necessarily and yet freely by proposing a particular ontology of the will. According to Augustine, human willing naturally follows desire (i.e., we will what we want), and one of the effects of the fall was to pervert human desire so that human wants are turned away from God. In short, although fallen human beings will what they want, their wants are congenitally perverse and their wills correspondingly bound to sin. Deeply influenced by Paul's notion of fallen humanity's slavery to sin, Augustine equated free will with the pursuit of the good that was possible only after God had healed human desire through the gift of grace.

Though Pelagianism was officially rejected by the Church, Augustine's insistence on the bondage of the fallen will to sin was viewed with unease by many and has continued to be a point of contention even in traditions otherwise strongly influenced by his thought. Thus, when at the time of the REFORMATION M. LUTHER and, even more consistently, the tradition of REFORMED THEOLOGY defended a strongly Augustinian DOCTRINE of the bondage of the will to sin, many worried that free will was in danger of being displaced completely by the powers of original sin and divine grace. Among Catholics, theologians like L. Molina (1535–1600) sought to square human freedom with God's sovereign guidance of history by developing a theory of divine 'MIDDLE KNOWLEDGE' of what rational creatures would freely will in any given set of circumstances. Among Protestants,

ARMINIANISM represented a similar attempt to carve out a space for free will to operate independently of divine determination.

With the rise of empiricism and RATIONALISM in the seventeenth and eighteenth centuries, the idea of free will was subjected to new forms of assessment. The success of mechanistic explanations of phenomena by the emerging NATURAL SCIENCES led some to wonder whether seemingly free human actions were also subject to explanation in terms of physical causes. According to the theory of compatibilism, given classic form by philosophers like T. Hobbes (1588–1679) and D. Hume (1711–76), the physical determinism of the sciences is 'compatible' with free will, so long as the latter is understood as the absence of compulsion rather than ontologically as an action of the 'I' with no antecedent external cause. 'Incompatibilists' refuse to define free will in such purely psychological terms and therefore conclude that either freedom is an illusion (in the case of strict materialism) or that physical determinism is false (in the case of 'libertarian' interpretations of free will). While the emergence of quantum mechanics in twentieth-century physics has called strictly deterministic interpretations of physical phenomena into question, it does not necessarily lend support to belief in libertarian free will, since the probabilistic calculus associated with quantum events arguably rules out assigning events *any* determinate cause – including free will.

In light of the continuing problems associated with scientific accounts of causation, Augustine remains an important touchstone for a contemporary theological assessment of free will because of his refusal to equate the will's freedom with its capacity for self-causation. In certain respects, his position is similar to compatibilism, since he believed that human action was never externally compelled, even when (as for fallen human beings apart from grace) it was necessarily sinful. Yet, unlike compatibilists, Augustine did not identify this psychological 'freedom of choice' (which he usually termed *liberum arbitrium*) with freedom of the 'will' (*voluntas*). For Augustine the latter referred exclusively to willing that is shaped by grace and therefore corresponds to God's will. Apart from grace, the human will, though unconstrained, is bound to sin and therefore emphatically unfree.

The equation of true freedom with action determined by grace seems oxymoronic to those who equate freedom with the capacity to pursue more than one possible course of action. Thus, while proponents of PROCESS THEOLOGY hold that God always seeks to persuade human beings to will particular ends, they judge that an Augustinian picture of God directly turning desire towards such ends destroys rather than establishes human freedom. By contrast, an Augustinian perspective treats the will's freedom not as a matter of its neutrality between possible courses of action, but rather as its correspondence with the good. In this way, the will's freedom is not constituted by the *autonomy* of its operation (i.e., the sense that I could will otherwise than I do), but rather by the agent's recognition of its correspondence to the proper end of human life (i.e., the sense that I will as I ought to). In short, to be a free and responsible agent is not to be able to will independently of God, but precisely to will under God and thereby to fulfil God's purposes willingly rather than (as is the case with irrational creatures) unconsciously.

This perspective provides a way of approaching the two questions raised at the beginning of the article regarding the rhetoric of human freedom in Scripture. In answer to the first, it follows that, apart from the grace of Christ, who is for Christians the measure of God's will towards and for humanity, no person is free (though, importantly, it is a separate question whether Christ's grace is present either only or always among those who identify themselves as Christians). In answer to the second, in the same way that God is supremely free although incapable of choosing evil, so, in line with Paul's affirmation in Galatians 2, human beings are most free when they will in accord with God, the transcendent Good who is their source and end as creatures.

A. Farrer, *The Freedom of the Will* (Charles Scribner's Sons, 1958).

G. O. Forde, *The Captivation of the Will: Luther vs. Erasmus on Freedom and Bondage* (Eerdmans, 2005).

P. van Inwagen, *An Essay on Free Will* (Oxford University Press, 1983).

K. Tanner, *God and Creation in Christian Theology: Tyranny or Empowerment?* (Blackwell, 1988).

J. Wetzel, *Augustine and the Limits of Virtue* (Cambridge University Press, 1992).

IAN A. MCFARLAND

FREI, HANS Hans W. Frei (1922–88) was a German-born American theologian and influential teacher best known for his work on biblical HERMENEUTICS and his contributions to NARRATIVE THEOLOGY. Following doctoral work on K.BARTH, Frei's early writings explored a shift in eighteenth- and nineteenth-century hermeneutics that he called the 'eclipse of biblical narrative'. He charted the demise of a pre-critical consensus in which realistic ('history-like') narrative texts in SCRIPTURE were taken to make available to the reader the history of God's ways with the world, such that a literary exploration of the narratives would at the same time be an exploration of history and of the providential patterns of God's activity that shape it. However, with the rise of critical questioning of the connection between biblical narratives and their historical referents, these texts were increasingly taken (by both conservative and liberal interpreters) as more or less reliable evidence for the reconstruction of the history behind the text – or, where that reliability was in question, as mythic triggers for the development of a religious way of seeing the world. The reading of biblical texts *as* realistic narrative, and the exploration of the patterns that link different narratives, slipped into the background.

Frei argued that a post-critical reading of these narratives could see them as providing a narrative identification of their central character, Jesus Christ, such that their narrative meaning would simply be the story about Jesus that they tell. According to Frei, such literary exploration could proceed before any questions of factuality or of significance for the reader are raised. While those questions can and must be raised eventually, their posing should be governed by the meaning that narrative reading uncovers. Frei argued, for instance, that in the Gospels it is the way that Jesus is identified in the RESURRECTION narratives that most urgently presses historical claims – albeit of a rather odd kind; he also argued that the narratives stake a claim on the reader's personal, ecclesial, and political life by demanding some kind of typological or figural interpretation, looking for patterns of resemblance between differing biblical narratives, and between those narratives and the events of the present (see TYPOLOGY).

Frei later distanced himself from the idea that narrative reading was justified simply by the literary qualities of the texts, arguing instead that it is rooted in a long-standing practice of Christian reading, the *sensus literalis*, which takes the Gospels primarily as realistic depictions of their central character, Jesus. He further distinguished theologians who understand theology as the internal discourse of a particular community from those who understand it as the reinterpretation of Christian claims according to a general philosophical scheme and he argued that his hermeneutical claims would flourish best at the point on that spectrum where theologians let their philosophical claims about realism, reference, and meaning be governed by the particular shape of the Gospel narratives as they are read within the Church.

See also POSTLIBERAL THEOLOGY.

M. Higton, *Christ, Providence and History: Hans W. Frei's Public Theology* (T&T Clark, 2004).

MIKE HIGTON

FRIENDS, SOCIETY OF: see QUAKER THEOLOGY.

FUNDAMENTAL THEOLOGY Although the phrase first appeared at the turn of the eighteenth century, it was not until the first half of the nineteenth century that 'fundamental theology' emerged as a clearly defined discipline within CATHOLIC THEOLOGY in particular. Fundamental theology deals with the foundations of theological knowledge, focusing on the conditions of its possibility and its credibility. This attention to foundations renders fundamental theology distinct both from the analysis and interpretation of particular Christian DOCTRINES (SYSTEMATIC THEOLOGY) and from Christian reflection on the way in which those doctrines shape the life of believers in their encounter with the world (PRACTICAL THEOLOGY). Thus, whereas other forms of theology engage more directly with the substance of Christian claims about God and the world (e.g., the TRINITY, CREATION, CHRISTOLOGY, SACRAMENTOLOGY), fundamental theology focuses more on formal questions of how such claims are derived and disseminated and tends, correspondingly, to be marked by a greater degree of methodological abstraction from particular dogmatic content.

Though fundamental theology's concern with the plausibility of Christian beliefs gives it a definite apologetic cast, it is often distinguished from APOLOGETICS, on the grounds that the latter discipline attempts to argue for the truth of Christian claims based entirely on non-theological grounds (e.g., by appeal to natural reason and experience only), while fundamental theology operates explicitly from within the context of Christian FAITH. As such, it is a part of the broader enterprise whereby Christians seek to move towards greater self-understanding of their faith and not simply a contingent response to external challenges to Christian beliefs. Thus, while the form and content of a purely apologetic theology will be subject to enormous variation depending on the particular criticism(s) the apologist is trying to answer, fundamental theology has greater formal stability, owing to its location within the community of faith. At the same time, by virtue of its particular focus on the metaphysical and epistemological grounds of the Christian faith, fundamental theology shares with apologetics a natural orientation towards those outside that community.

Whether or not conducted with the explicit aim of engaging non-believers, the character of fundamental theology is preparatory: to provide a basis for the faithful reception of Christian claims by establishing the reasonableness of the metaphysical and epistemological framework within which those claims are made. In so doing, fundamental theology may deploy arguments and appeal to criteria that are not specific to the Church, but which engage the reason of all persons of good will, whatever their explicit religious convictions. In any case, these arguments have often been conceived as having a twofold structure: to establish, first, that in the GOSPEL God has communicated saving truth to humankind (the *demonstratio Christiana*) and, second, that God has established the Catholic Church as the authoritative interpreter of that divine communication (the *demonstratio Catholica*). So conceived, fundamental theology seeks to defend the plausibility of supernatural REVELATION as the source of specifically Christian beliefs and the Church as the means by which those beliefs are communicated to the world.

While older versions of fundamental theology (e.g., those typical of nineteenth-century Catholic SCHOLASTICISM) could include extensive use of formal philosophical proofs, more contemporary approaches often rely on appeals to human experience that are less directly tied to more traditional forms of philosophical demonstration, as well as on historical analyses of Christian texts and traditions. These methodological developments render fundamental theology better able to attend to the ways in which personal, social, and historical contexts affect the reception of Christian claims. Reflecting this attention to the human context within which Christian beliefs are received, contemporary fundamental theology tends to begin neither with revelation nor with the Church, but with FAITH, in order to identify those basic ontological features of human existence that render people open to the possibility of receiving divine revelation in the first place. This identification of the principles that structure human encounter with the world provides a framework within which it is possible for Christians to discuss their beliefs meaningfully with persons from the widest possible range of religious commitments. Adding this attention to anthropological concerns to more traditional discussion of revelation and the Church, fundamental theology can be understood as addressing three foundational questions: *why* faith is humanly significant, *what* its proper object is, and *how* knowledge of that object is communicated.

An important dimension of contemporary treatments of the first of these questions is a refusal to limit faith to the cognitive assent to propositions (the faith which one believes, or *fides quae creditur*) and a corresponding emphasis on faith as a mode of engagement with the world (the faith by which one believes, or *fides qua creditur*). The thought of K. RAHNER has been particularly influential in proposing that the basic conditions of human knowing include an ultimate horizon of meaning that at once conditions all experience (i.e., provides the context within which it is appropriated by the subject as a concrete experience) and itself is not reducible to any particular item of experience (i.e., as the horizon of experience it remains unthematized). For Christians it is natural to identify this horizon with God, since God's status as the ground and source of all that is implies that God is necessarily present in every experience. In contrast to more traditional arguments that treat God's existence as a fact to be deduced from particular bits of sense data (see COSMOLOGICAL ARGUMENT; TELEOLOGICAL ARGUMENT), this approach views the human encounter with God – and thus the possibility of faithful assent to God's presence – as characteristic of every experience.

This sort of transcendental, a priori experience of God within every experience is the basis for the concrete, a posteriori experience of God in supernatural revelation: those explicit acts of divine communication that call for the equally explicit human response of faith as personal assent to and trust in God. Fundamental theology moves towards these events that define Christian faith's explicit object by noting that the temporal form of human life means that any explicit (i.e., thematized) knowledge of God comes in history. Because God, as the ultimate horizon of experience, is irreducible to any particular item of experience, such revelation is not simply given with the order of things and will for that reason be supernatural. At the same time, because human experience is spatio-temporal, such revelation, if it takes place, will take the form of particular divine communicative acts in space and time. As such, it will undoubtedly include particular propositions about God, humanity, and the world as a whole; but, in so far as the object of revelation is God, it will also be experienced as personal: a process of *self*-communication in which God, acting in loving freedom, presents God's own self to be the object of human love. For Christians Jesus Christ is the supreme and unsurpassable instance of divine self-presentation to which every human being is summoned to respond. And, while Christians cannot prove that Jesus is this definitive event of divine self-disclosure (indeed, to presume to do so would be to undermine the individual's relationship with God in Christ as one of personal trust), they can and should endeavour to show why faith in Christ is reasonable. Such efforts may take a variety of forms, including the arguments for the credibility of Christian claims (including, e.g., considerations of the reliability of SCRIPTURE as a historical record and the evidentiary role of MIRACLES), the distinctive illumination they give to the human condition, their coherence, their correspondence with the general range of human experience, and their capacity to give stable yet flexible contours to believers' lives.

With respect to the question of *how* the revelation of God in Christ is received and disseminated, anthropological criteria come once again to the fore. In addition to being historical, human beings are social, and what knowledge they possess is held in the social medium of language: transmitted from others within one's linguistic community, which functions as the touchstone for reflection on, interpretation of, and debate over the meaning of particular statements. Again, while such considerations cannot in themselves definitively establish the authority of any social group to decide what counts as authentic revelation, they do point to the impossibility of avoiding the question of the external, mediating grounds of the internal experience of faith.

The claim of Catholic fundamental theology is that the Church (and, more specifically, the Catholic Church) provides the God-given means by which human beings are related in faith to Jesus Christ. Faith is for Christians fundamentally directed towards Jesus

Christ. Because Jesus (who is, of course, known only as certain facts about him are known) is a particular historical person, he cannot be known by introspection: one can only believe in Jesus if one is told about him. And because Jesus' earthly life is irrevocably past, all present knowledge of him derives from (and depends on) those who had immediate experience of him as the risen Lord. Thus, since the concrete way in which their experience of Jesus is handed down is by a summons to join them as members of the community that confesses Jesus as Lord, the Church is as much the condition of the possibility of belief as is revelation itself.

In addition to giving attention to these general features of faith, revelation, and the Church as foundations of Christian belief, fundamental theology also looks at the specific forms in which these realities have developed within Catholic (as well as the broader Christian) TRADITION. This feature of fundamental theology further highlights its difference from a narrowly conceived programme of apologetics. Once again, fundamental theology's task is not simply to defend the truth or relevance of particular faith claims in general terms, but to explicate their form and meaning within a specifically Christian context. Thus, part of what it means for fundamental theology to give a foundational account of Jesus Christ as the definitive instance of God's self-communication is to explicate the form that self-communication takes in Jesus' birth, ministry, death, and RESURRECTION, as well as to locate it within the broader context of God's earlier acts of self-communication to ISRAEL. Similarly, the treatment of the Church in fundamental theology includes reflection on the relationship between Scripture and tradition, as well as discussion of the role of COUNCILS, CREEDS, and the MAGISTERIUM in defining, articulating, and interpreting doctrine. This process of justification by way of explication reflects T. AQUINAS' view that, where the particular claims of revelation are disputed, attempts to prove doctrine must give way to the more modest task of answering objections and resolving potential misunderstandings (*ST* 1.1.8). It thereby provides fundamental theology some defence against the charge that 'apologetic' attempts to establish the credibility of Christian claims for a general audience invariably dilute their force by allowing the terms of argument to be determined by non-Christians.

H. Fries, *Fundamental Theology* (Catholic University of America Press, 1996 [1985]).

J. B. Metz, *Faith in History and Society: Toward a Practical Fundamental Theology* (Crossroad, 2007).

J. H. Newman, *An Essay in Aid of a Grammar of Assent* (Oxford University Press, 1985 [1870]).

G. O'Collins, S. J., *Fundamental Theology* (Paulist Press, 1981).

D. Tracy, *The Analogical Imagination: Christian Theology and the Culture of Pluralism* (Crossroad, 1981).

IAN A. MCFARLAND

FUNDAMENTALISM As a designation concerning Christians, fundamentalism refers to the outlooks of various militantly conservative evangelical Protestants since the 1920s. The great majority of fundamentalists have been in the revivalist tradition (see REVIVALISM), although some influential militants have been shaped more by confessional traditions. The term 'fundamentalist' was coined in 1920 as a self-designation for conservatives fighting against theological modernism in the Northern Baptist Convention. Soon it became a generalized term for any militant conservative Protestant in the USA, where the movement has always been the most influential. Fundamentalism has had some counterparts in Canada, the UK, and the rest of the English-speaking world, but nowhere else has it been nearly so much a popular movement. It also has many outposts around the world growing out of missionary efforts from the USA.

In its paradigmatic form fundamentalist militancy has typically involved reactions to two dimensions of modernity. First, it was a reaction to the modernist or LIBERAL THEOLOGY that had made inroads into many major Protestant denominations by the early twentieth century. Second, it was fuelled by alarm over a much broader set of issues in mainstream American culture, including changes in sexual mores, fears of Bolshevism, growth of secular thought in education (often symbolized by the teaching of EVOLUTION), and concerns over the resulting cultural relativism. Fundamentalists are usually distinguished from earlier militant conservatives by being shaped specifically by their reactions to aspects of modernity. They are, however, not entirely anti-modern since they have often excelled at using modern communication technology and have typically been defenders of twentieth-century capitalism and an American-style political system.

At the heart of fundamentalist theological concerns are classic evangelical emphases (see EVANGELICAL THEOLOGY). God sent his Son into the world to die on the CROSS for the salvation of sinners. There is no other hope of salvation or of avoiding an eternity in HELL. Therefore by far the kindest thing one can do for other people is to share this message of salvation with them. That is the central task of both the Church and individuals in it. The authority for this message is God's Word in SCRIPTURE, which is perspicuous to any competent reader and which, along with personal heartfelt PRAYER, should be at the centre of one's devotional life. In reaction to higher criticism of Scripture, fundamentalists have emphasized the Bible's INERRANCY. They have also retained strict behavioural mores regarding sexuality, alcohol, tobacco, card-playing, theatre, films, and the like.

Most self-styled fundamentalists have taken pains to distinguish their teachings from those of Pentecostals (see PENTECOSTAL THEOLOGY). Nonetheless, they have many similarities in attitudes, behavioural expectations, and basic evangelical doctrines drawn from their common revivalist heritage. Pentecostals were often influenced by fundamentalist militancy and many became at least cobelligerents with self-styled fundamentalists.

Those who did the most towards building the fundamentalist coalition into a distinct and lasting movement were dispensational premillennialists (see PREMILLENNIALISM). Much of what became the standard fundamentalist version of this DISPENSATIONALISM was developed by J. Darby (1800–82) of the Plymouth Brethren movement. In late nineteenth-century America these teachings spread among the interdenominational revivalists associated with D. Moody (1837–99). In the early twentieth century they were codified in the notes of the *Scofield Reference Bible* (1909), which became a standard authority in many fundamentalist Bible institutes, of which Moody Bible Institute in Chicago was the prototype.

Dispensationalism teaches that history is divided into seven dispensations. Each of these historical eras involves a test that humans fail and ends with judgement. The current 'Church age' is a dispensation of GRACE, and is nearing its end. False Churches and a civilization that forsakes God signal imminent judgement. Prophecies in Daniel and Revelation predict an exact end-time scenario. First will be the 'secret RAPTURE' in which the saints will 'meet the Lord in the air' (1 Thess. 4:17). Then will be seven years marked by the alliance of the 'ANTICHRIST', a religious leader, and the 'beast', the political leader of a revived Roman Empire, the return of Jews to Palestine, and a final three and a half years of the 'great tribulation'. Then Christ will return with the SAINTS, defeat the evil powers, and set up his millennial kingdom for a literal 1,000 years (see MILLENNIUM). The prediction of the return of Jews to ISRAEL in this scenario has made fundamentalists strong supporters of the State of Israel.

Since fundamentalists have always proclaimed that these events will commence within a generation, social reform might seem a futile task. Nonetheless, while rejecting the liberal SOCIAL GOSPEL, many dispensationalist fundamentalists have also spoken as though reclaiming their nation through revival and reform was among their major goals. Opposition to the teaching of evolution in public schools has long been a political manifestation of this reform impulse. More broadly, popular rhetoric about restoring a lost Christian America made many fundamentalists prone to embrace American CIVIL RELIGION. 'Fundamentalism' in other parts of the Anglophone world, while also alarmed by modern secularism, tended to be defined more by strong doctrinal conservatism and less by local patriotism.

W. ('Billy') Graham (b. 1918) started out as a classic fundamentalist, but his evangelistic success precipitated a division and change in the definition of the movement. When Graham co-operated with mainline Protestant Churches in his New York campaign of 1957, the most militant fundamentalists condemned him, thus culminating a campaign to make ecclesiastical separatism a new test for being a true fundamentalist. Graham and his more open associates began calling themselves simply 'evangelicals'. They repudiated fundamentalist separatism and dispensationalism and typically drew on a broadly Reformed theological heritage (see REFORMED THEOLOGY). British Protestant conservatives like J. Packer (b. 1926), who had been using 'fundamentalist' as a broader equivalent of 'conservative evangelical' soon also adopted the new terminology and distinction between 'evangelicals' and the more extreme 'fundamentalists'.

Since then self-styled fundamentalists have been ecclesiastical separatists, typically independent or sectarian Baptists, dispensationalists, and strong proponents of the inerrancy of Scripture. In the late 1970s fundamentalists re-emerged to prominence in American cultural life as among the leading participants in the 'religious right' political coalition. More than ever they manifested the tension between their prophetic theology that the near return of Christ is the only hope for civilization and their hope to restore Christian civilization through political action. More broadly, fundamentalists constitute the most militant wing of non-Pentecostal conservative evangelicals throughout the world.

J. A. Carpenter, *Revive Us Again: The Reawakening of American Fundamentalism* (Oxford University Press, 1997).

G. M. Marsden, *Fundamentalism and American Culture*, 2nd edn (Oxford University Press, 2006 [1980]).

E. R. Sandeen, *The Roots of Fundamentalism: British and American Millenarianism*, 1800–1930 (University of Chicago Press, 1970).

GEORGE M. MARSDEN

Gay and Lesbian Theology: see Queer Theology.

Gender: see Feminist Theology; Sexuality.

Gilson, Étienne Étienne Gilson (1884–1978) was a Parisian Thomist (see Thomism). Like C. Péguy (1873–1914) and J. Maritain (1882–1973), he listened spellbound to the lectures of philosopher H. Bergson (1859–1941) at the Collège de France. He simultaneously heard L. Lévy-Bruhl (1857–1939) lecture on D. Hume (1711–76). While Bergson attuned Gilson to metaphysical realism, Lévy-Bruhl inspired and trained him to be a historian of ideas. Gilson wrote his PhD under Lévy-Bruhl on R. Descartes (1596–1650). His first major works were on T. Aquinas (1919) and Bonaventure (1924). After founding the Institute for Mediaeval Studies in Toronto in 1929, Gilson taught half the year in Paris, as professor of medieval philosophy at the Collège de France, and half in Toronto.

G

Gilson made three principal contributions to twentieth-century theology. Neo-Scholastic ideology and the exigencies of Catholic apologetics had made Aquinas the theoretical standard by which to judge, and the historical model to which to assimilate, the other medieval thinkers (see Scholasticism). Gilson's first service to modern theology was as a historian. With his highly readable, text-based studies of Augustine, Bonaventure (1221–74), Bernard of Clairvaux (1090–1153), P. Abelard (1079–1142), Dante (*ca* 1265–1321), J. Duns Scotus, and lesser lights, Gilson demonstrated the diversity of medieval Christian thinkers. Such historical research by a respected historian and Thomist laid the groundwork for the *ressourcement* movement of the 1950s. A friend to the *ressourcement* leader H. de Lubac, Gilson endorsed de Lubac's contention that Augustine, Bonaventure, and Aquinas taught that human beings have a natural desire for the supernatural vision.

Along with helping to alter the image of the Middle Ages, Gilson changed the perception of Aquinas from a philosopher to a theologian. As a text-oriented historian, Gilson was well placed to show that Aquinas' *Summa theologiae* was a work of theology. From his groundbreaking 1919 study of Thomas, to the greatly enlarged 1945 benchmark edition, to its final 1966 revision, the major thesis of *Introduction au système de S. Thomas d'Aquin*, Gilson's 'work of a lifetime', was that Aquinas used philosophical demonstrations within a theological plan and with a theological design and purpose. Gilson was thus the first to propound what is now the most widely received conception of Aquinas. Contemporary historiography has not reversed his findings, and all twenty-first-century Thomist philosophy and theology is indebted to Gilson.

Third, believing that it was because 'Saint Thomas was essentially a theologian' that 'he constituted a new and original system of philosophy' (*Intro.* 23), Gilson defended and practised what he called 'Christian philosophy', the discipline of using revealed truths to show philosophy how to ask realistic questions. A rigorous Thomist and Aristotelian (see Aristotelianism), Gilson said on occasion that Christian theology could inspire many different kinds of philosophy. Commended by John Paul II (r. 1978–2005) in the encyclical *Fides et ratio* (2001) as a model of the relation of faith and reason, Gilson's conception of 'Christian philosophy' has also influenced Benedict XVI (r. 2005–).

J. F. X. Knasas, 'Does Gilson Theologize Thomistic Metaphysics?' in *Thomistic Papers V*, ed. T. A. Russman (University of St Thomas, 1990), 3–19.

F. A. Murphy, *Art and Intellect in the Philosophy of Etienne Gilson* (University of Missouri Press, 2004).

Francesca A. Murphy

Glory 'Glory' refers to God and the splendour of God's perfection, directly (the glory of God), by participation (the glory of creatures and, in a particular way, of Christians), or by contrast (when referring to human vainglory). In the OT the primary term for 'glory' in a positive sense is *kābôd.* From its root meaning of 'mass' or 'weight' derive connotations of importance and worth, the splendour manifested by things of such nature, and the honour due them. 'The glory of the Lord' is a technical expression used of God's sovereign and self-revelatory actions in creation (Isa. 6:3), history (Exod. 24:16–17), and liturgy (Lev. 9:6–24; 1 Kgs 8:11), all of which are to be perfected in God's eschatological dominion (Dan. 7:13; Ezek. 43:5). Since actions manifest the presence of the one who acts, 'the glory of the Lord' implies God's presence and the divine attributes revealed thereby (e.g., mercy in Bar. 4:21–4; cf. Eph. 4:19).

Significantly, God's transcendence is not jeopardized by this kind of self-revelation, for one may see God's glory but not God's face (Exod. 33:18–23). This combination of revelation and 'hiddenness' (as certain modern theologians call it) is a particular characteristic of the suffering servant in whom God's glory will shine to the nations (Isa. 49:3, 6; 53).

In response to God's self-manifestation, creatures should give glory to God, that is, acknowledge God's glory, praise God in word and deed, and rejoice in doing so. All creation glorifies God by its existence, but rational creatures are to do so knowingly and freely (see Ps. 86:9, 12), including by CONVERSION (Jer. 13:16). God's supreme merit and eternal claim on glorification contrast starkly with ephemeral human success and the often improper praise humans give each other (Ps. 49:17–18).

Kābôd is dramatically translated in the SEPTUAGINT with *doxa*, which means 'opinion' in non-biblical Greek. The NT continues to use *doxa* to mean *kābôd* (occasionally also in the sense of 'repute' or 'honour', though never as 'opinion'). *Doxa* appears in hymns (Eph. 3:21), connects brilliance with God's presence (e.g., ANGELS as God's messengers, light as characteristic of heaven), and, as in the OT, characterizes God's salvation of the faithful and punishment of the wicked (Exod. 15:1–2; Matt. 25:31–46).

What is new in the NT is the identification of the glory of God with the glory of Christ. Christ's entire life is an event of divine glory: His birth (Luke 2:14), His miracles or 'signs' (John 2:11), His TRANSFIGURATION (Luke 9:32), the 'hour' of His passion and RESURRECTION (Luke 24:26; John 17:1), His PAROUSIA (Matt. 25:31). By applying to Christ a term specific to God inherited from the OT, the NT writers profess Christ's divinity (Heb. 1:3; 2 Cor. 4:6). On the one hand, Jesus reveals God's glory (i.e., what it is); on the other, it reveals Him (as God). Thus in Himself Christ possesses glory from eternity (John 17:5), while in the flesh He receives it permanently after His passion (Heb. 2:9).

Those who respond properly to the glory of God in Christ by glorifying Him in deed (Matt. 5:16), word, and worship comprise the Church. Already in the OT God not only revealed His glory but also communicated it (e.g., in creation, in the glory shining on Moses' face in Exod. 34:29–30). Christians are adopted into God's glory by the gift of the HOLY SPIRIT (Gal. 4:5–7; 2 Cor. 3:18). In this way, the GRACE given human beings on earth is the seed of heavenly glory (2 Cor. 4:17; Rev. 21:11).

In order to summarize the different ways in which glory was predicated of God and God's works, the Scholastics distinguished among intrinsic fundamental glory (God's essence), extrinsic fundamental glory (God's works in creation), intrinsic formal glory (God's self-knowledge), and extrinsic formal glory (rational creatures' praises).

Glory has figured as a central topic within SYSTEMATIC THEOLOGY at a number of points in the history of the Church. The fathers of the Council of NICAEA considered that Christ's proper possession of glory indicates His divinity. From the patristic era to VATICAN COUNCIL I (DS 3,025), theologians reflected on what it means to say the purpose of creation is the glory of God: does this glorification consist in creatures' mere existence, the praise of rational creatures, or the latter's rejoicing in God? Ultimately the three are, as it were, inseparable: the creature who praises God simultaneously exists, is perfected, and rejoices in praising. God, however, does not create narcissistically *in order* to receive praise, nor does God *acquire* glory through creatures, for they merely participate in God and God's own knowledge of God's goodness. If then God in no way depends on creaturely glorification, it is clear God creates out of goodness and benevolence towards creatures, not out of need.

The medieval Scholastics reflected on the nature of the elect's participation in heavenly glory: whether it is by an act of the mind, the will, or both; and whether the body's RESURRECTION or the salvation of loved ones increases one's glory. The idea that the elect enjoy different degrees of glory was defended by T. AQUINAS and given classic literary illustration by Dante Alighieri. According to M. LUTHER, by contrast, the elect do not merit glory, so all in heaven have the same degree of glory (a teaching which, defended by Jovinian for different reasons, was condemned by synods at Rome and Milan in the fourth century).

Luther also called for a return to what he termed a 'theology of the cross' (see THEOLOGIA CRUCIS) from the 'theology of glory', of which he accused the Catholic Church. He characterized the former as stressing the hiddenness and self-abasement of God in Christ crucified, the other as focusing on human self-glorification. Catholic theologians of the period did not notably engage this polemical mischaracterization of the Catholic position.

God's glory was also prominent in Reformed and Jesuit SPIRITUALITY, with different emphases: Reformed piety stressed that history, its good and evil, inevitably glorifies God. By his motto, 'For the greater glory of God', Ignatius of Loyola (1491–1556) encouraged his followers always to choose the action that best serves God. In contemporary theology H. U. von BALTHASAR made the theme of God's glory central to his systematic theology through an analysis of the true, the good, and the beautiful.

See also BEATIFIC VISION; DEIFICATION; ESCHATOLOGY.

H. Bavinck, *Reformed Dogmatics,* vol. II: *God and Creation*, 2nd edn (Baker Academic, 2004 [1908]).

Benedict XVI, *Jesus of Nazareth* (Doubleday, 2007).

ALYSSA LYRA PITSTICK

GLOSSOLALIA The term 'glossolalia' is derived from the Greek phrase *glossais lalein*, which literally means 'in tongues to speak'. The concept is found in the longer ending to Mark, Acts, and 1 Corinthians. In Mark 16:17 it is associated with the commission to proclaim the GOSPEL. In Acts it is associated with the coming of the HOLY SPIRIT on PENTECOST upon the disciples as they 'declared the wonders of God' in different languages and dialects (2:1–13). Luke records further glossolalic utterances in Acts 10:46, when the Spirit comes upon the Gentile household of Cornelius, and again in 19:6, when the Ephesian disciples of JOHN THE BAPTIST receive the Spirit. PAUL mentions the phenomenon in the list of *charismata* in 1 Corinthians 12:10 (see Charism) and in 14:2 states that the gift is a matter of speaking 'mysteries in the Spirit' whose public understanding requires the presence of an interpreter. Paul considers this speech to be praying with the Spirit (14:15), which bypasses the mind, and he instructs the Corinthians to limit the use of this gift within the assembly so that order may prevail.

The linguistic nature of glossolalia within the NT has been a subject of considerable debate. It can be argued that Luke regarded the speech as real human languages, or foreign speech (*xenolalia*). The evidence of 1 Corinthians 13:1 suggests that Paul probably also regarded it as real human speech ('tongues of mortals'), although he also uses a secondary mysterious category 'and of angels'. Contemporary examples of tongues speech have tended to defy full normal linguistic criteria.

Glossolalia made a significant return to theological attention with the explosion of global Pentecostal Christianity at the beginning of the twentieth century (see Pentecostal Theology). In this tradition it was understood as a sign that the Holy Spirit had descended upon believers as on the day of Pentecost itself. It was regarded as a sign not only of a post-conversion outpouring of the Spirit on individuals, but also of the 'latter rain' associated with Christ's second coming (see Parousia). Many early Pentecostals regarded glossolalia as an unlearnt human language given for the preaching of the gospel in foreign lands. Unfortunately, the gift they received proved inadequate for the task and most were required to learn the local language by traditional means. Over time, Pentecostals regarded it as a prayer language, to be used for intercession and, when interpreted in the assembly, as equivalent to prophecy. With the rise of the charismatic movement in the 1960s, its role as a signifier of baptism in the Spirit subsided and its role as a mysterious prayer language became the dominant understanding. Today many Pentecostal and charismatic scholars have focused on new ways of understanding glossolalia using language game, speech-act, and transpositional theories, as well as sacramental and apophatic theology.

M. J. Cartledge, *The Gift of Speaking in Tongues: The Holy Spirit, the Human Spirit and the Gift of Holy Speech* (Grove Books, 2005).

ed., *Speaking in Tongues: Multi-Disciplinary Perspectives* (Paternoster Press, 2006).

Mark J. Cartledge

Gnosticism The development of the earliest forms of Christian theology can only be properly understood when considered against the backdrop of contemporary movements associated with the claim to be in possession of a special salvific knowledge (Greek *gnosis*). The Gnostic movement never reached the level of homogeneity known in other movements which emerged among second- and third-century Christians, like those of Marcion or Montanus (see Montanism). The knowledge the Gnostics claimed consisted in a rather loose set of doctrines that exhibited a number of common features, which we have come to know through texts written between the second and fifth centuries. Though most of these doctrines were shared by Christians and non-Christians alike during that period, research from the eighteenth century on has attempted to define 'Gnosticism' as an exclusive and exaggerated quest for *gnosis* at the expense of faith and characterized by a dualism which promoted hatred of the world, the body, and matter.

This approach to Gnosticism has met with justified criticism, since it fails to explain many features of the complex religious and spiritual movement to which it is supposed to refer. When original 'Gnostic' sources are examined, for example, they often lack characteristics generally thought to be central to this standard definition of 'Gnosticism'. Many 'Gnostic' texts of the first centuries show no more exaggerated a pursuit of knowledge than did other contemporary Christian literature, much of which was also clearly concerned with an overriding desire to attain the 'knowledge of salvation' (Luke 1:17; cf. Rom. 15:14; John 8:32). How, then, did the Gnostic quest for knowledge differ from that of other Christians? To answer this question, one has to consider all the information available on groups characterized as Gnostic from both direct and indirect sources.

In his work *Against Heresies*, Irenaeus of Lyons fought against the followers of Valentinus, a Christian thinker active in the eastern part of the empire and in Rome between 140 and 160. After describing the system of Valentinus' disciples, Irenaeus reconstructs the prehistory of the Valentinian movement and lists its ancestors. According to Irenaeus the list of the immediate predecessors of the Valentinians stretched from Simon Magus (*fl.* 50) to the 'Gnostics' of his day. The Coptic papyri discovered at Nag Hammadi in 1945 contained texts which convey ideas and doctrines similar to those attributed to these Gnostics by Irenaeus.

According to Irenaeus and other heresiologists, there were groups which adhered to common doctrines and who either referred to themselves as 'Gnostics', or had been so named by their contemporaries. But this designation was hardly exclusive to such groups. Even 'orthodox' Christian authors like Clement of Alexandria (*ca* 150–*ca* 215) and Evagrius Ponticus (346–99) used the term 'Gnostic' to refer to Christians who had reached the highest degree of spiritual achievement. Moreover, many of the groups characterized as 'Gnostic' do not actually refer to themselves in this way in their own texts. They seem to have preferred circumlocutions to describe the way they saw themselves: 'the unmovable or kingless generation', 'the perfects', 'the sons of light', and 'the spirituals'. Despite this fact,

Christian writers tended to follow the example of Irenaeus and used the label for authors who never applied it to themselves and whose doctrines were very far from those that tend to be associated with Gnosticism.

Beyond the issue of who is to be called a Gnostic, however, lies the question of how 'Gnosticism' itself is to be defined – a problem rendered all the more difficult since it seems nearly impossible to draw any clear line of demarcation that reliably separates what might and might not be categorized as Gnostic. Contrary to MANICHAEISM, for example, Gnosticism never constituted a distinct social reality or a religion in the strict sense of the word. Rather, Gnosticism appears to be a polymorphous religious current that historically has been attested to exclusively in Christian contexts. In other words, 'Gnosticism' is essentially one more expression of the diversity within early Christianity: during the Church's first few centuries, being 'Gnostic' was essentially just one more way of being Christian.

Why, then, was 'Gnosticism' eventually rejected by the Church? The factors that explain the rejection of the Gnostics by their fellow Christians appear to be many, especially the notion that the lower world, radically cut off from the world above, could not possibly have been intentionally created by a benevolent and omnipotent God. In addition to these beliefs, the Gnostics' fascination with the origin of evil also caused problems. Refusing both the Christian doctrine of CREATION and the Platonic procession, those generally characterized as Gnostics opted for an explanation of evil based on deficiency and fall. Thus, they distanced themselves from Judaism and PLATONISM, as well as from the theological conceptions that were becoming normative in most Christian Churches. Furthermore, whereas a theologian like Irenaeus championed the harmony of the OT and the NT, and the unicity of God as Creator, Revealer, and Saviour, the Gnostics came to the conclusion that the Creator known through the Jewish Scriptures cannot be the true God – a claim which helps to distinguish Gnostics from other early Christians.

From a historical point of view, labels such as 'Gnostic' and 'Gnosticism' cannot help but prove inadequate. Some scholars have therefore proposed not to rethink the category of Gnosticism but simply to get rid of it. Nevertheless, for want of better labels, it appears more reasonable to retain the terms 'Gnostic' and 'Gnosticism' to refer to certain streams of belief within early Christianity. These labels, when used in ways similar to terms like 'pagan' and 'paganism', are useful conventions, on the condition that one remain alert to their limitations and avoid applying them to movements (e.g., Manichaeism or Marcionitism) that in doctrine and organization diverge significantly from the 'Gnostic' sensibilities described in the previous paragraph.

K. L. King, *What Is Gnosticism?* (Belknap Press, 2003).
C. Markschies, *Gnosis: An Introduction* (T&T Clark, 2003)
M. Meyer, ed., *The Nag Hammadi Scriptures: The International Edition* (HarperCollins, 2007).
M. A. Williams, *Rethinking 'Gnosticism': An Argument for Dismantling a Dubious Category* (Princeton University Press, 1996).

PAUL-HUBERT POIRIER

GOD: see TRINITY.

GOOD FRIDAY: see CALENDAR, LITURGICAL.

GOSPEL The word 'gospel' translates the Greek *euaggelion*, or 'good news'. By the time the NT was written, it had become the standard term used by Christians to characterize their message and was often described more specifically as the 'gospel of God' (e.g., Rom. 1:1; 15:16; 2 Cor. 11:7; 1 Thess. 2:2, 8–9) or the 'gospel of [Jesus] Christ' (e.g., Rom. 15:19; 1 Cor. 9:12; 2 Cor. 9:13; Gal. 1:7; 1 Thess. 3:2). A further development of this convention is reflected in the custom of calling written accounts of Jesus' ministry – especially the four texts eventually adopted as the core texts of the NT canon – Gospels (see Mark 1:1).

Among first-century Jews the concept of 'good news' may already have had some theological resonance connected with God's expected eschatological vindication of ISRAEL (Isa. 52:7; cf. Rom. 10:15). In any event, Matthew and Luke see the proclamation of 'good news' to the poor as integral to Jesus' identity as Israel's promised Messiah (Matt. 11:5; Luke 4:18) and interpret the content of that news to be precisely the advent of God's reign (Matt. 4:23; 9:35; 24:14; Luke 4:43; 8:1; 16:16). A particular feature of this reign as proclaimed by Jesus was evidently the forgiving of SIN (Mark 2:5–12; Luke 5:21–5; 7:47–9), and soon after Easter Jesus was interpreted as the one in whose name FORGIVENESS had been secured for all who believed in him (Luke 24:47; Acts 2:38; 5:31; 10:43; 13:38; Eph. 1:7; Col. 1:14). In line with this development, the gospel itself came to be identified with Jesus. So PAUL, speaking of his own service to God as centred on 'the gospel of his Son' (Rom. 1:9), clearly regards Jesus as the content of the good news and not just its messenger.

This identification of the good news with Jesus evidently underlies Paul's subsequent description of the gospel as 'the power of God for salvation to everyone who has faith' (Rom. 1:16), since elsewhere he equates this 'power' with the 'word of the cross' (1 Cor. 1:18), or the proclamation of 'Christ crucified' (1 Cor. 1:23; 2:2; cf. Gal. 3:1). In short, for Paul Jesus is the eschatological vindication of God's promises to Israel (Rom. 3:21–6; 2 Cor. 1:20; Gal. 3:15–16). Yet, if to believe in the gospel is in this way to be subsumed under the power of Jesus' crucified and risen life (Rom. 6:3–8; Gal. 2:19–20), it is also to subscribe to a message with a definite content (1 Cor. 15:1–11; cf. 2 Tim. 2:8) that can be ignored or rejected (Rom. 10:16; cf. 1 Pet. 4:17). Moreover, this message contains very specific implications for behaviour, such that persons can be condemned for 'not acting consistently with the truth of the gospel' (Gal. 2:14; cf. Phil. 1:27), the goal of which remains participation in the reign of God (Gal. 5:21; cf. 1 Cor. 15:50).

This dual characterization of the gospel as commitment to the person of Jesus on the one hand, and to a corresponding way of life with concrete behavioural demands on the other, has led to disagreement among theologians over the relationship between the gospel and God's LAW. In certain respects this disagreement can be related to differing understandings of Paul's claim that Christ is 'the end of the law' (Rom. 10:4). Some have interpreted this passage as highlighting Christ's role as the one who fulfils the law (see Matt. 5:17–18) and have correspondingly argued for a fundamental continuity between law and gospel. Thus, T. AQUINAS described the gospel as a 'new law', which, like the 'old law' of Moses, is given to make human beings righteous, even though the gospel is more perfect in so far as it explains the law's true sense, provides instruction on how to meet its demands, and grants the GRACE that makes it possible for human beings to meet those demands (*ST* 1/2.106.2, 107.1–2).

By contrast, M. LUTHER saw the relationship between law and gospel in sharply dialectical terms, arguing that the gospel, as God's freely given *promise* of forgiveness in Jesus Christ, is essentially discontinuous with the law, which speaks of God's *demands*. Though both law and gospel are integral to the economy of salvation for Luther, they operate in radically different ways: the law convicts the individual of her inability to fulfil God's commands, thereby driving her to abandon all attempts at self-justification in order to rely exclusively on God's free gift of grace in Jesus Christ (*Bond.* 766–7). In short, while the law demands action, the gospel is to be received in FAITH – a division alien to Thomas' view that the gospel combines grace with its own set of behavioural demands on the believer (*ST* 1/2.106.4).

In subsequent LUTHERAN THEOLOGY the distinction between law and gospel became the basic framework of biblical interpretation, according to which any commands (even those spoken by Jesus) are 'law' and any words of promise or comfort (whether in the OT or the NT) are 'gospel' (see, e.g., *FC, Ep.* 5). This perspective has been criticized by both Catholic and Reformed theologians as overly formalistic and as failing to take seriously the fundamental unity of God's word in Christ as that which both graciously claims and forms the believer. While all sides agree in defining the gospel as the good news of God's having reconciled humanity in Christ (2 Cor. 5:19), there remains sharp disagreement over whether the shape of this reconciled human life is rightly viewed as part and parcel of the message or, on the contrary, whether such inclusion undermines the good news by making grace conditional on human performance.

See also JUSTIFICATION.

K. Barth, *Evangelium und Gesetz* (Kaiser, 1935).
W. Elert, *Law and Gospel* (Fortress Press, 1967).

IAN A. MCFARLAND

GRACE 'Grace' is the English word normally used to translate the Greek *charis* in the NT and the SEPTUAGINT. The verbal cognates of *charis* point to its connotations of (divine) favour (Luke 1:28; cf. v. 30) and, still more specifically, gift (e.g., Rom. 8:32; 1 Cor. 2:12). In SCRIPTURE grace is associated pre-eminently with the figure of Jesus: not only did divine favour rest upon him personally (Luke 2:40, 52; John 1:14), but he is understood as the means by which that favour is transferred to others (John 1:16; Acts 15:11; Rom. 3:24; Eph. 1:7). Thus, while grace is not God's only gift to humankind, its association with Christ establishes it as that gift which completes and perfects humanity's relationship with God: 'The LAW was indeed given through Moses; grace and truth came through Jesus Christ' (John 1:17).

The contrast between grace and the law suggested by John becomes a prominent theme in the letters of PAUL. For example, he argues that those who affirm that the JUSTIFICATION of sinners comes through the law nullify God's grace (Gal. 2:21). Paul thereby seeks to highlight the status of grace as an unmerited gift rather than a reward that is earned (Rom. 4:4, 16). Because it originates with and is secured by God prior to any human merit or demerit, grace is the sole basis for human beings' ability to stand before God (Rom. 5:2), so that (in words that would be a focal point of debate in later theological controversies) 'by grace you have been saved through faith, and this is not your own doing; it is the gift of God – not the result of works, so that no one may boast' (Eph. 2:8–9; cf. Rom. 11:5–6). At the same time, grace is not only viewed in forensic terms as an antidote to SIN. It also has the character of a sphere of power that both defines and animates the Church: Christians are 'under grace' (Rom. 6:14), which in its abundance overflows on the community (2 Cor. 4:15; 9:14), to the extent that Paul can go so far as to ascribe his own achievements not to himself, but to 'the grace of God that is with me' (1 Cor. 15:10).

Particularly in the western Churches, later theological reflection on grace was decisively shaped by AUGUSTINE OF HIPPO's response to PELAGIANISM in the early decades of the fifth century. Though the exact shape of Pelagius' (*ca* 355–*ca* 420) own views remains difficult to assess, Augustine attacked those associated with him (especially Caelestius (*fl.* 415) and, later, Julian of Eclanum (*ca* 385–*ca* 455)) on the grounds that they effectively denied the Pauline principles that human beings are saved by God's grace by their stress on the role of human obedience in securing salvation. As Augustine himself recognized, his opponents did not deny the role of grace in salvation, but they interpreted it quite broadly, as encompassing all those means by which God enabled human beings to live righteously, including those capacities with which humanity had been naturally endowed in CREATION (especially FREE WILL) and the gift of the law, as well as the effects of Christ's work. By contrast, Augustine believed that the FALL had rendered human beings incapable of any good work: their natural freedom had been destroyed, and the gift of the law (which communicated only the knowledge of the good and not the power to effect it) was therefore of no help. Grace was God's response to this situation, and was, correspondingly, to be interpreted narrowly as the power, given through the HOLY SPIRIT, by which God healed fallen humanity so as to enable them both to will and to do the good.

Although the debate over the role of grace in salvation continued for a century after Augustine's death, his insistence that all good – including even the desire for faith – comes only through grace prior to every human effort was given synodical approval at the Second Council of Orange in 529 (see DS 373–8). Over the next several centuries, however, the implications of Augustine's views continued to be matters of extended reflection in medieval CATHOLIC THEOLOGY. For example, in light of Christian belief in the unity and consistency of God, it was important to clarify that an Augustinian emphasis on grace's role in healing fallen human nature did not imply any essential opposition between the nature God created 'in the beginning' and the grace bestowed by God in time. It thus became a commonplace of medieval theology that the gift of grace never cancels or overrides creatures' natural capacities, but rather brings them to perfection (*gratia non tollit naturam sed perficit*).

A further element of medieval theology that would later become a matter of contention was the gradual emergence of ways of speaking about grace that implied it might be conceived along the lines of a physical quality present 'in' the SOUL (see, e.g., Aquinas, *ST* 1/2.110.1). This perspective was closely connected with developments in SACRAMENTOLOGY, according to which the consecrated elements of the EUCHARIST in particular were seen as 'containing' grace, which was then conferred on the communicant in the act of receiving them (see *EX OPERE OPERATO*). Yet it is probably best seen as a corollary of the Augustinian principle that grace is God's gift: as an objective good, it renders the soul to which it is given objectively good and thus can be said to continue to inhere in the soul *as* a good in addition to turning the soul to the good (*ST* 1/2.110.2; see *HABITUS*). Nevertheless, at the time of the REFORMATION both Lutheran and Reformed theologians objected to this idea of 'infused' grace, arguing that such language undermines the correlation between the concept of grace and fallen humanity's absolute dependence on God by implying that grace changes the soul in such a way as to render it objectively good independently of God's activity. They argued that it was more appropriate to speak of grace as 'imputed': exclusively a matter of active regard on God's part *towards* creaturely reality and never any sort of substantial reality *in* the creature.

These debates over the proper language to use when speaking of God's grace reflect a larger dispute between Catholics and Protestants over the process of human salvation. Specifically, both sides followed Paul (and Augustine) in maintaining that human beings were justified by grace, but they differed sharply over its anthropological implications. The Reformers insisted that the principle of justification by grace was preserved only if interpreted as 'by FAITH alone' (*sola fide*): trust in God's forgiving grace towards sinners as revealed in Christ without any consideration of the capacities or merits of the believer. By contrast, Catholic theologians insisted that the Reformers' insistence on the extrinsic character of justifying grace lacked the resources for correlating God's forgiveness of sin in grace with sin's objective destruction. The Catholic Council of TRENT thus held that faith, though undoubtedly a gift of grace, is merely the beginning of justification, which is brought to fulfilment only as God's grace continues to work in and through the believer to turn her will more and more to God. Here again, while Protestant theologians have interpreted justifying grace as a *relation* (and thus not subject to quantitative variation) in order to stress its grounding in divine LOVE, Catholics have interpreted it as a transformative *power* (and thus capable of being present in greater or lesser degree) in order to attend to its effects in perfecting human nature.

Despite their insistence on the principle of justification by faith alone, Protestants have been no less concerned than Catholics to affirm the transformative effects of grace. In this context, it is important to note that, in the centuries following the Reformation, Catholic and Protestant theologians alike were happy to appropriate (albeit with a considerable range of variation in interpretation) earlier medieval distinctions between prevenient, operating, and co-operating grace. Speaking very generally, prevenient grace was used to refer to the activity of grace *prior to* CONVERSION. Initiated entirely by God, it comes before (Latin *praevenire*) any human activity towards, thought of, or desire for God. Operating grace referred to the process by which God unilaterally works (Latin *operari*) to turn a person's will towards faith *in* conversion, while co-operating grace referred to God's enabling and strengthening of the believer (whose will is thus brought to 'co-operate' with God) in her progress towards SANCTIFICATION *after* conversion. At the same time, fierce debates took place within both Catholic and Protestant circles over whether or not belief in divine prevenience implied that human beings were incapable of rejecting God's grace (see IRRESISTIBLE GRACE).

Whether grace is understood as imputed or infused, its status as gift demands an account of its transmission from God to humankind or, in traditional theological language, the means of grace. Since human beings exist in time and space, God's communication of grace to them must make use of spatio-temporal reality. There is considerable weight behind the identification of these means as word preached and sacraments celebrated in the community of faith. In Christian preaching, human beings are confronted with God's promises as words of grace. After all, if the proper response to the news of God's grace is faith, Paul himself insists that 'faith comes from what is heard' (Rom. 10:17). Indeed, in line with this perspective Protestant theologians have generally understood the sacraments as 'visible words' – the promise communicated with the aid of material aids for the aid of material creatures. By contrast, Catholic (as well as Orthodox) theologians, while not discounting the kerygmatic dimension of the sacraments as signs of God's grace, also emphasize their power to sanctify those who receive them.

In spite of the often contentious and complex debates among Christians over the character of grace, it is possible to identify several common themes that continue to shape Christian theologies of grace across confessional divisions. First, grace originates exclusively in the life of the TRINITY: rooted in the eternal love of the Father, manifest in the life, death, and RESURRECTION of the Son, and poured forth on creatures through the power of the Holy Spirit. Second, grace is absolutely free: having its origin solely in divine love for creatures, its bestowal is never necessary for God's wellbeing. Importantly, however, the fact that God gives grace freely and without any possibility of diminishment does not mean that grace is cheap. The fact that grace is shown forth pre-eminently in the giving forth of God's own life in Jesus indicates that the divine life that constitutes its inexhaustible ground is also the measure of its infinite cost.

Turning from consideration of the ground of grace within God to its external effects, it may be stated, third, that grace is given to all creatures (so that, in the language of REFORMED THEOLOGY, it may be termed 'common grace') and is absolutely necessary for their wellbeing. Since (according to the majority of the Christian tradition) God brings all creatures into existence from nothing, so that creatures have no basis for existence in themselves apart from God, creatures' continued subsistence, activity, and flourishing is absolutely dependent on God's gracious favour (see *CONCURSUS*; *CONSERVATIO*; *GUBERNATIO*). Fourth, grace is the only bulwark against creaturely defeat by the power of sin. Since all creatures are utterly dependent on God by virtue of their very status as creatures, the fact that human beings have inexplicably yet radically turned away from God means that they actively undermine the only possible basis for their existence. Rather than resting in God's creative and sustaining grace, human beings have opened up a breach between themselves and God, choosing death over life. Grace is the means by which God overcomes this breach, defeating sin and death by reaffirming God's faithful commitment to creaturely flourishing in spite of the creature's faithlessness (2 Tim. 2:13), both effecting and perfecting creatures' communion with God.

See also ARMINIANISM; DORT, SYNOD OF; FEDERAL THEOLOGY.

Augustine, *Nature and Grace*, in *Answer to the Pelagians I*, ed. J. E. Rotelle (New City Press, 1997 [*ca* 415]).

K. Barth, *Epistle to the Romans* (Oxford University Press, 1968 [1921]).

D. Bonhoeffer, *Dietrich Bonhoeffer Works,* vol. IV: *Discipleship*, ed. G. B. Kelly and J. D. Godsey (Fortress Press, 2003 [1937]).

H. de Lubac, *A Brief Catechesis on Nature and Grace* (Ignatius Press, 1984).

S. Jones, *Feminist Theory and Christian Theology: Cartographies of Grace* (Fortress Press, 2000).

J. Sittler, *Essays on Nature and Grace* (Fortress Press, 1972).

IAN A. MCFARLAND

GREGORY OF NAZIANZUS: see CAPPADOCIAN FATHERS.

GREGORY OF NYSSA: see CAPPADOCIAN FATHERS.

GUBERNATIO The divine *gubernatio* (or *succursus*) refers to God's guiding of CREATION towards a particular end. It is one of three dimensions of classical Christian (especially Protestant) teaching on PROVIDENCE and, arguably, the one that corresponds most closely to the popular understanding of the term. The idea of *gubernatio* follows from the DOCTRINE of creation in two respects. First, the very act of God's bringing the world into being suggests the intention to achieve some end. Second, the related beliefs that God sustains the world in its being (CONSERVATIO) and activity (CONCURSUS) at every moment of its existence imply God's continually working to bring the world to that end.

Theological reflection on *gubernatio* centres on how God works and the degree to which God is able to achieve God's intended purposes for creation. According to classical REFORMED THEOLOGY, God's sovereignty is absolute: because God is at every point the sole condition of the world's existence, all that God intends for the world infallibly happens. Critics argue that this position vitiates the freedom of creatures and thereby compromises one of the chief aims of God's creative activity. Thus, in PROCESS THEOLOGY divine omnipotence is expressly denied: while God has purposes that God is always seeking to realize, God does so in such a way (viz., by persuasion) that God's aims may be thwarted by creatures choosing not to follow the divine lead. In other words, while the classical Reformed position maintains that the kind of absolute FAITH in God demanded by the GOSPEL only makes sense on the presupposition that God's purposes must ultimately triumph, process theology worries that such inevitable triumph renders the acts of creatures irrelevant in a way that is inconsistent with God's purposes.

IAN A. MCFARLAND

HABITUS Although it is the etymological root of (and sometimes translated as) 'habit', the Latin term *habitus* is used in theology to refer to a more particular quality than the more or less idiosyncratic patterns of behaviour designated by its English cognate. On the most general level, *habitus* is a creature's disposition to act in a particular way, as considered in relation to its nature (so that a *habitus* is good when it accords with nature and bad when it does not). Such dispositions are subject to modification and manifest themselves in regular patterns of behaviour that in their familiarity are experienced by the agent as 'natural'. Because the possession of proper *habitus* is crucial to facility in any complex action (e.g., listening, writing, riding a bicycle), their acquisition can be considered an aspect of creaturely perfection. From a specifically moral perspective the totality of a person's *habitus* constitutes her character.

Within the specifically theological context of medieval SCHOLASTICISM (see T. AQUINAS, *ST* 1/2.51.1–2, 4), a distinction is drawn between *habitus* that are innate to an agent (e.g., knowledge of first principles), *habitus* that are acquired by the action of the agent that comes to possess it (e.g., reasoning from first principles), and *habitus* that are infused into an agent by God (e.g., wisdom). The category of infused *habitus* is particularly significant as a means of explaining how human beings acquire perfections (ultimately, the BEATIFIC VISION) that are supernatural and therefore by definition beyond their natural capacities. Because it is important for Aquinas to affirm that the GRACE by which God perfects human nature always works with rather than against that nature (see *ST* 1.1.8.2), he argues that God effectively gives human nature powers it would not otherwise have by infusing certain *habitus* into human beings, so that the human perfection is achieved by enhancing rather than bypassing or overriding human agency (see *ST* 1/2.110.2).

During the REFORMATION Protestant theologians objected to the idea of infused *habitus* on the grounds that it made of grace something that inhered in – and thus became a property of – the SOUL (as *gratia habitualis* or 'habitual grace') in a way that undermined humanity's absolute and continuous dependence on God for salvation. In order to guard against the implication that grace ever becomes a property of the soul in such a way as to diminish human dependence on God, CATHOLIC THEOLOGY in fact denies that habitual grace includes an actual disposition to act righteously; instead, the concept of habitual grace serves only to name the renewal of the soul whereby it is enabled to grow in the VIRTUES of FAITH, HOPE, and LOVE (which, in turn, only manifest themselves in particular acts when enabled by the further gift of 'actual grace'). Nevertheless, in LUTHERAN and REFORMED THEOLOGY any language that suggests that grace inheres in the soul as a *habitus* continues to be viewed as problematic in so far as it suggests that a person's status before God is subject to quantitative variation that is in some way a function of human effort or ability.

IAN A. MCFARLAND

H

HAMARTIOLOGY: see SIN.

HARNACK, ADOLF VON Adolf von Harnack (1851–1930), a German Protestant historian of theology, began his teaching career in 1874 at Leipzig, with subsequent positions at Giessen (1879), Marburg (1886), and finally Berlin (1888). By 1888 his views were controversial enough for approval of his appointment to take nine months. He enjoyed the confidence of the faculty and the Kaiser but not of the ecclesiastical authorities, who regarded the conclusions in the first volume of his *History of Dogma* to be incompatible with orthodox teaching.

Harnack learnt the art of historical criticism and investigating sources from M. von Engelhardt (1828–81), at Dorpat. A second influence was A. Ritschl (1822–89), apart from whom, Harnack said, his own *History of Dogma* (3 vols., 1885–90; ET 7 vols., 1896–99) would probably never have been written; moreover, 'the future of Protestantism as a religion and a spiritual power lies in the direction which Ritschl has indicated' (Zahn-Harnack, *Harnack* 135, 64). Ritschl had emphasized the sociological context of the Church's development and objected to the influence of classical philosophy on Christian teaching. For him, change occurs because each embodiment of the Christian ideal is inadequate.

Harnack incorporated many of Ritschl's themes into his portrait of the early Church. The essence of Christianity, he said, was not so much a set of ideas as a way of life inspired by Jesus. DOCTRINE came about because of the Hellenization of the gospel. Harnack's goal was to free evangelical Christianity from its false entanglements; historical study gave the Church freedom to reassess doctrinal developments.

Harnack was deeply involved in the society and culture of his time. For example, in 1890 he was elected to the Prussian Academy of Sciences, directed the Royal Library from 1905 to 1921, and was the president of the Evangelical Social-Congress. In 1911 he was named the first president of the Kaiser-Wilhelm Society for the Advancement of Science. In 1902 the royal court awarded him the Order of Merit, and in 1914 he was granted nobility.

During the winter semester of 1899–1900, Harnack gave public lectures on 'The Essence of Christianity', the English title of which became *What Is Christianity?* (1900). Here he recommended a *historical*-theological analysis. In an effort to avoid confessionalism or dogmatism, he urged his hearers to look for the spiritual stance that gives rise to the various forms Christianity has taken and to be captivated by that spirit.

Harnack was involved in several controversies, including one about the APOSTLES' CREED and another about the SOCIAL GOSPEL. During the later years of his life, he tangled with K. BARTH regarding the relation between historical study and theology. He found Barth's evaluation of the historical to be frightening and its motivations quite incomprehensible.

A highly productive scholar, Harnack's many other writings include *Christianity and History* (1896), *The Mission and Expansion of Christianity in the First Three Centuries* (1902), *The Acts of the Apostles* (1908), *The Constitution and Law of the Church in the First Two Centuries* (1910), *Geschichte des altchristlichen Litteratur bis Eusebius* (4 vols., 1893–1904), and *Marcion, Das Evangelium vom fremden Gott* (1920).

W. Glick, *The Reality of Christianity: A Study of Adolf von Harnack as Historian and Theologian* (Harper & Row, 1967).
C. Welch, *Protestant Thought in the Nineteenth Century*, vol. II: 1870–1914 (Yale University Press, 1985).

DARRELL JODOCK

HEAVEN The distinction between heaven and sky is not usually present in antiquity. Heaven can denote the space above the earth; the dwelling place of angelic beings, the gods, or the highest God; and the dwelling place of those who will reside in eternity with the divine. This remains true for the biblical understanding of heaven, albeit with some modifications.

The Israelites did not assign God a definite locale. Heaven was simply a part of CREATION, distinguished from the earth by being stretched out above it. Some passages identify heaven as the domain from which God descends and to which he subsequently returns (Deut. 26:15), and others describe God as transcending both heaven and earth: 'Will God indeed dwell on the earth? Even heaven and the highest heaven cannot contain you, much less this house that I have built!' (1 Kgs 8:27). In late Judaism, heaven becomes synonymous with God in order to avoid pronouncing God's name (1 Macc. 4:10). While Elijah is taken up to heaven (2 Kgs 2:1), Enoch 'was no more, because God took him' (Gen. 5:24). This identification continues in the NT with the 'kingdom of heaven': Jesus teaches his disciples to pray to 'our Father in heaven' (Matt. 6:9); the Resurrected One is lifted up towards heaven (Acts 1:10); Christ 'is at the right hand of God' (Rom. 8:34); Paul assures that we have 'a house not made with hands, eternal in the heavens' (2 Cor. 5:1); and there will be 'a new heaven and a new earth' (Rev. 21:1).

Early Christians commonly held that Jesus reopened the earthly paradise that had been shut since the FALL. Christ's promise to the criminal on the cross seems to imply such a restoration: 'Truly I tell you, today you will be with me in Paradise' (Luke 23:43). John Chrysostom (*ca* 345–407) and JOHN OF DAMASCUS supported this conception. Yet Theophylact (*ca* 1050–1108), archbishop of Ochrid and Bulgaria, was wary of such conflation: 'Let no one say to me that paradise and the kingdom are one and the same. For eye hath not seen, nor ear heard, neither have ascended into the heart of man, the good things of the kingdom' (*Luc.* 23.43). Rather than a return to the beginning, a cyclical view of time, the kingdom of heaven is fulfilment and completion. What existence in this new creation will be like, even PAUL can only express by negating present experience (1 Cor. 15:42–4). There will be unrestrained, continuous existence in the presence of God. To discard this image as a utopian dream is to forget that Jesus Christ attained this fulfilment through his death and RESURRECTION. Our immanent and perpetual yearning for self-transcendence, deification, perfection, and the elimination of death will be complete in life everlasting. The *Catechism of the Catholic Church* declares: 'Heaven is the ultimate end and fulfilment of the deepest human longings, the state of supreme, definitive happiness' (§1,024). As to God's habitation: it is the non-localized dimension that encloses all others and defies all efforts of human conceptuality.

C. McDannell and B. Lang, *Heaven – A History* (Yale University Press, 1988).
H. Schwarz, *Eschatology* (Eerdmans, 2000).

HANS SCHWARZ

HEGEL, GEORG WILHELM FRIEDRICH G. W. F. Hegel (1770–1831) grew up in a world of upheaval. As a young man he grappled with the collapse of the Holy Roman Empire and with the subsequent seizure of German territory by French Republican armies under Napoleon (1769–1821). He was also immersed in the fertile philosophical and religious ideas of the eighteenth and early nineteenth centuries. These factors shaped his development of an influential meta-narrative that is deservedly considered a pre-eminent achievement of modern philosophy. His meta-narrative recounted the movement of 'spirit' (German *Geist*), Hegel's richly multifaceted concept encompassing individual and communal self-consciousness culminating in the fullness of freedom. The enormity of Hegel's influence on modern thought is difficult to overestimate and can be measured by the fact that subsequent influential and original thinkers – Christian (e.g., S. KIERKEGAARD and K. BARTH) and secular (e.g., L. FEUERBACH and K. Marx (1818–83)) – positioned themselves in terms of Hegel's intellectual project.

Shortly after Hegel enrolled at the seminary of the University of Tübingen in 1788, the French Revolution became a catalyst for his intense intellectual focus on the dynamics and development of freedom. Later, as a lecturer at the University of Jena, Hegel followed closely the events in France and worked to develop what would become his mature philosophical framework. Politics and philosophy converged (literally and metaphorically) when he completed his most famous work, *Phenomenology of Spirit* (1807), as Jena was taken by Napoleon's army. Hegel associated the spirit of freedom of the French Revolution with the Protestant REFORMATION (with its emphasis on subjective inner freedom) and saw both as crucial moments of spiritual renewal and social betterment. However, Hegel was also critical of the excesses of the French Revolution such as the brutal and repressive 'Reign of Terror' when, in the name of freedom, frenzied revolutionary agents tore down the religious and social structures, some of which made civic freedom possible. This revolutionary reign, Hegel argues in a haunting passage from the *Phenomenology*, left an undeveloped form of freedom whose 'sole work and deed' was 'the coldest and meanest of all deaths, with no more significance than cutting off a head of cabbage', suggesting the horrific yet indifferent image of the guillotine.

The aftermath of the French Revolution proved for Hegel that a holistic inner spiritual and rational principle of life must be the basis of modern cultural development. Not lacking in ambition, he set out to conceptualize spirit as the key to the interpretation of civil society, the State, and religion. Most striking about Hegel's system of thought is that God is everywhere related to it: God is the beginning (premise) of all things and the end (telos) of all things as spirit. The essence of God as eternal idea (abstract spirit), manifested concretely in human subjectivity (finite subjective spirit) and society (finite objective spirit), moves towards fullness and reconciliation in the sublation (German *Aufhebung*) of difference to produce absolute spirit. Historically, Hegel envisioned this movement as a dialectical process in which cultures and subjects become more explicitly self-reflexive and self-determining. Hegel's overarching philosophical project is squarely theological and, in its emphasis on the realization of the divine in history, incarnational. He interpreted finite spirit's rise to the Absolute and reinterprets the traditional doctrine of the TRINITY by correlating Christian Trinitarian imagery with moments of the dialectic: Father (identity), Son (difference), and HOLY SPIRIT (identity-in-difference). The essential truth of the Christian Trinity discloses in representational form (*Vorstellung*) the truth of life itself – a truth that philosophy grasps fully in terms of its essential idea (*Begriff*). Christianity is the 'consummate' or 'absolute' representational fulfilment of RELIGION, just as 'absolute knowing' is the conceptual fulfilment of reason. As such, consummate religion and philosophy articulated the inner spiritual and rational principle at work in the world. Armed with this meta-narrative of absolute spirit, Hegel set out to evaluate religions, and cultures more generally, in terms of their contribution to the development of spirit.

As chair of philosophy at the University of Berlin, Hegel produced *Elements of the Philosophy of Right* (1821), along with what would become his posthumously published *Lectures on the Philosophy of Religion* (1832) and *Lectures on the Philosophy of History* (1837). In these works, among others, Hegel endeavoured to articulate the development of the consciousness of freedom on the part of spirit, and the consequent realization of that freedom. Moreover, as he observed in his *Philosophy of History*, this 'development implies a gradation – a series of increasingly adequate expressions or manifestations of Freedom, which results from its Idea'. Given the close association of the history of religion and the history of cultures, it is not surprising that the concrete evolution and gradations of the consciousness of freedom on the part of spirit present themselves similarly in both historical accounts. In his *Lectures on the Philosophy of Religion,* Hegel used this evolutionary and hierarchical development to interpret non-Christian religions as inadequate prefigurations of true religion, which Hegel defined as the full 'self-knowing of divine spirit through the mediation of finite spirit'. In other words, religion is not simply finite consciousness of the infinite but also the self-consciousness of absolute spirit mediated through finite consciousness – a self-consciousness that is only fully represented religiously in Christian Trinitarian and incarnational language. Non-Christian religions 'are not indeed *our* religion', Hegel suggests to his Christian audience, 'yet they are included in ours as essential though subordinate moments … and the recognition that this is so is the reconciliation of true religion with false'.

Hegel made more of an effort to learn about religions of the world than most other European thinkers of his day. Nonetheless, the perspective he credited as universal more nearly reflects a western and Christian ethnocentrism; hence, many contemporary critics have noted how deeply problematic Hegel's totalizing project is on both philosophical and ethical grounds. However, for all his totalizing ambitions, driven by his deep sense of the need for making overarching sense of his chaotic historical moment, and for all his ethnocentric conviction that German Protestant culture's prized export to the rest of the world was the fullness of spirit, Hegel remained convinced of the philosopher's need for self-critique.

As recognized by secular left-wing Hegelians in his own day, as well as by contemporary students of Hegel, his philosophical, cultural, political, and economic vision must also give way to his dialectical method.

Every thesis generates its antithesis; every synthesis is yet another thesis. In Hegel's thought there is an ongoing 'restlessness of the negative', to quote the title of J.-L. Nancy's (b. 1940) essay on Hegel. In his more self-reflective moments, Hegel was keenly aware of this too. The job of the philosopher is 'to comprehend what is', Hegel wrote in the preface to the *Philosophy of Right*; yet, he observed, 'every individual is a child of his time; so philosophy too is its own time apprehended in thoughts'. What we get with Hegel, one might say, is totality but not finality.

P. C. Hodgson, ed., *G. W. F. Hegel: Theologian of the Spirit* (Fortress Press, 1997).

T. Pinkard, *Hegel: A Biography* (Cambridge University Press, 2000).

C. Taylor, *Hegel* (Cambridge University Press, 1975).

DAVID G. KAMITSUKA

HEIDELBERG CATECHISM Drafted at the behest of Frederick III (r. 1559–76), elector of the Holy Roman Empire's Palatinate region (of which Heidelberg was the capital), the Heidelberg Catechism was initially adopted by a local synod in 1563. Although written in a mostly irenic style and commissioned in the hope of providing a basis for rapprochement between Lutheran and Reformed theologians, the Catechism was rejected by Lutherans because its DOCTRINE of the EUCHARIST was judged too close to that of J. CALVIN. Subsequently approved by the Synod of DORT, it remains perhaps the most widely received confessional standard among Reformed Churches.

Though the catechism is traditionally ascribed to the joint efforts of Z. Ursinus (1534–83) and C. Olevianus (1536–87), the former is generally recognized as the text's principal author. Its sequence of co-ordinated questions and answers is divided into three unequal parts: 'Of Human Misery' (qu. 3–11), which focuses on human inability to keep God's LAW; 'Of Human Redemption' (qu. 12–85), which reviews the ATONEMENT, the TRINITY (through an exposition of the APOSTLES' CREED), JUSTIFICATION, and SACRAMENTOLOGY as a means of describing how God has overcome the effects of humanity's failure; and 'Thankfulness' (qu. 86–129), which describes the proper response to God's redeeming work through a survey of good works, REPENTANCE, the TEN COMMANDMENTS, and PRAYER. The catechism is noted for its Christological focus and for the pastoral functionality seen both in its consistent use of the second person and in the way its subdivision into fifty-two groups of questions facilitates systematic review of the whole text over the course of a year.

IAN A. MCFARLAND

HELL The word 'hell' stems from the Old Icelandic *Hel*, the Nordic mythological netherworld and its ruler. Not specifically Jewish or Christian, the concept of hell appears in virtually all religions as a place of punishment and is usually thought to be located somewhere beneath the earth.

The early OT writings portray Sheol as the shadowy existence of alienation in death (see Ps. 89:48). Perhaps through the post-exilic influence of Parsism, Sheol came to be understood as temporary, to be superseded by a twofold outcome of history: 'Many of you who sleep in the dust of the earth shall awake, some to everlasting life, and some to shame and everlasting contempt' (Dan. 12:2). In late Judaism and in the NT, Gehenna is a fiery realm where the wicked receive justice. The name stems from the Hinnon valley at the foot of Mount Zion, a locale which served as the city dump. The perpetual burning of refuse gradually made the valley synonymous with eternal anguish in fire. Gehenna presupposes resurrection and final judgement: the whole person will be tortured, resulting in 'weeping and gnashing of teeth' (Matt. 13:50). Unlike apocalyptic literature, the NT rarely provides a graphic description of hell; when it does, the intention is to awaken the conscience of the listeners (e.g., Matt. 10:28).

The early Church conveyed optimistic certainty concerning salvation and focused its attention on the coming kingdom. When Christianity became the official State religion under Constantine (*ca* 275–337), theology gave greater emphasis to final judgement and eternal punishment. ORIGEN's understanding of hell as a fiery purification that was temporary, even for the devil, received neither ecclesial nor imperial approval. AUGUSTINE (*City* 21), and Gregory I ('the Great', r. 590–604) discussed hell extensively, and the doctrine intensified in the Middle Ages through the influence of the fourth-century *Apocalypse of Paul*. The twelfth century marked the distinction between VENIAL and MORTAL SINS: the latter led to eternal punishment in hell, the former to temporary punishment in PURGATORY. Various levels were designated for unbaptized children, Old Testament patriarchs, etc. The fear of hell drove many to monastic life (see M. LUTHER). The REFORMATION rediscovery of divine GRACE did not lead to the dismissal of hell, only its unbiblical exaggerations. The ENLIGHTENMENT, however, regarded hell as inconsistent with a gracious God. Recent emphasis on grace by theologians like K. BARTH and J. Moltmann (b. 1926) has devalued the notion of hell. Yet the *Catechism of the Catholic Church* still teaches: 'To die in mortal sin without repenting and accepting God's merciful love, means remaining separated from him forever by our own free choice. This state of definite self-exclusion from communion with God and the blessed is called "hell"' (§1,033). Evangelical and Orthodox Christians share this view.

Rather than an eternal torture chamber, hell is the state of utter despair, of knowing the holy destiny that one has missed without the possibility of ever reaching it. It is the task of the faithful to hope, pray, and witness to the GOSPEL that such despair is never realized.

H. von Balthasar, *Dare We Hope 'That All Men Be Saved'? With a Short Discourse on Hell* (Ignatius Press, 1988).
D. Powys, *'Hell': A Hard Look at a Hard Question: The Fate of the Unrighteous in New Testament Thought* (Paternoster Press, 1997).

Hans Schwarz

Heresy The Greek term *hairesis*, from which the word 'heresy' derives, originally referred simply to a school or sect, and it retains this neutral sense in parts of the NT (see, e.g., Acts 5:17; 15:5; 24:5). Already in the letters of Paul, however, it is used in a negative sense to describe division or factionalism in the Church (1 Cor. 11:19; Gal. 5:20), and it is this pejorative sense of the term that dominates its later use. By the end of the second century, Ignatius of Antioch (d. *ca* 110) uses the word to describe alien or confused teaching about Jesus (*Trall.* 6.1), though he also preserves the more general sense of sectarianism (*Eph.* 6.2). In the fourth century heresy was formally defined by Augustine (*Fid.* 10), Basil of Caesarea (*Ep.* 188.1; see Cappadocian Fathers), and Jerome (*Tit.* 3.10) as false teaching (i.e., error in doctrine).

As false teaching, heresy is that which is judged contrary to the gospel of Jesus Christ. In Catholic teaching it refers specifically to any teaching directly opposed to a doctrine that has been explicitly defined as dogma by the magisterium. It is a theologically necessary category in so far as explicit commitment to a particular set of doctrines implies the no less explicit rejection of others. At the same time, false teaching must not be equated with false belief. The condemnation of heresy is not about trying to guarantee that every member of the Church has exactly the same understanding of God, but rather about ensuring the consistency of the Church's public witness. Given that God invariably transcends every conceivable theological category, it is a reasonable assumption that no Christian can escape the charge of false belief; a heretic is not a person who happens to have erroneous ideas, but someone who actively promotes opinions contrary to the public teaching of the Church.

See also Schism.

Ian A. McFarland

Hermeneutics Hermeneutics is the art or theory of interpretation. Christian theology has always been involved in hermeneutical activity. The continuous interpretation of biblical, doctrinal, liturgical, canonical, literary, and other texts in the Church requires general reflection on the conditions of human understanding and a sensibility to the particular character and demands of communication through texts.

As a result of the Enlightenment and related philosophical, theological, and historical developments, in recent centuries western hermeneutical consciousness has been particularly sharpened. However, all people everywhere attempting to understand written or oral forms of communication have been implicitly or explicitly concerned with hermeneutical issues. Moreover, text interpretation has always been linked in some way to the interpretation of human selves and their communicative existence in this universe. Hence, like any other academic discipline concerned with questions of understanding (e.g., law, philosophy, literary studies, psychology, sociology, etc.), theology must rise to its hermeneutical challenges.

Inspired by the Jewish hermeneutical tradition and by the ancient Greek hermeneutical schools of Alexandria and Antioch and their respective philosophical traditions, theologians in the early Church approached biblical texts with the help of allegorical and/or philological interpretation. Origen, for instance, stressed the need for both a grammatical–philological and a spiritual–allegorical interpretation of the biblical texts. Augustine further explored the connection between the function of linguistic signs (semiotics) and theological interpretation. Medieval theologians approached biblical texts through the theory of the fourfold sense of Scripture (or the *Quadriga*), thus exploring the text's literal, tropological (moral), anagogical (eschatological), and allegorical meanings. However, the natural tension between attention to the literal sense, on the one hand, and to the three 'spiritual' senses, on the other hand, was further increased by the shifting weight attributed to the one or the other according to different theological and ecclesiastical interests.

The problem can be stated in terms of two questions. Should biblical interpretation respond more to theological expectations and the Church's codified criteria of understanding (i.e., rule of faith, creeds, doctrinal presuppositions, tradition, theological programmes, ecclesial authorities) – that is, to the concerns of the community of interpreters? Or should appropriate attention to the literal sense of the biblical texts guide and challenge the Church's extant practices of interpretation? The question of whether biblical interpretation finds its authority in the biblical text itself or in the community of its interpreters has been at stake in Christian theology from the very beginning in so far as Christians have been reading the OT through their experiences of God's revelation in Christ, i.e., typologically (see Typology). The dialectics between text and interpretation requires renewed attention in every generation of Christian interpreters.

The Reformation was partly the consequence of hermeneutical adjustments. Protesting against the deplorable state of the Church and finding spiritual orientation in a renewed interpretation of the biblical texts (partly because the invention of printing made books more widely available in a wide range of European vernaculars as well as Latin), Protestant theologians criticized allegorical interpretation and attended afresh to the literal sense of Scripture. The Bible, understood as the ultimate norm for Church and theology, was expected to provide its own criteria of interpretation, in contrast to the Catholic doctrine of the Church's teaching authority as the ultimate judge in matters of biblical interpretation.

Both the DOCTRINE of the verbal INSPIRATION of the biblical texts and the authority of the teaching office were challenged in the Enlightenment with reference to the authority of human reason. This conflict promoted the emergence of an explicit hermeneutical consciousness in theology. Bridging the distance between textual communication (biblical and doctrinal) and text reception demanded critical attention to the general rules of linguistic communication, to the deepening awareness of historical consciousness, and to claims of any authority to control the dynamics of human communication.

In response to this challenge, F. SCHLEIERMACHER proposed a genuinely critical approach to text interpretation in theology. He rejected external authorities imposed on the text and thus freed the interpreter to concentrate on the semantic potential of the text itself. Theological interpretation must not claim any special privileges but follow the general rules of interpretation. Every interpretation ought to attend to the tasks of 'grammatical' and of 'psychological' understanding. Grammatical understanding explores the objective linguistic conventions through which the individual meaning is communicated to the interpreting subject. Psychological understanding refers to the subjective dimension of all textual understanding. Hermeneutics is thus always dipolar, combining objective and subjective dimensions in one single act of reconstructing the meaning of a text. As a result of this dipolarity, interpretation at best is an approximation to the text's semantic potential, and hermeneutics is to be understood as an art.

Schleiermacher paid critical attention to the demands of both reason and subjectivity in the process of understanding. His hermeneutics challenged theologians to consider whether or not they wish to accept the priority of general hermeneutics over against the particularities of biblical text interpretation. Responses to this challenge varied and were motivated not only by hermeneutical considerations but also by specific doctrinal and ecclesiological convictions and concerns. K. BARTH, for instance, rejected any attempt to subordinate theological hermeneutics to general hermeneutical rules. Against Schleiermacher's hermeneutics of signification (i.e., the claim that divine revelation through the Bible requires from interpreters a complex combination of linguistic and subjective approaches to the biblical text), Barth defended a hermeneutics of REVELATION: the biblical text will reveal its own message to any properly attentive and obedient reader. Followers of Barth (e.g., H. FREI, G. Lindbeck (b. 1923), K. Vanhoozer (b. 1957)) have urged biblical readers to allow the biblical text fully to absorb their reality and imagination, whereas followers of Schleiermacher (e.g., R. BULTMANN, H. Küng (b. 1928), D. Tracy (b. 1939)) have supported the development of a public, general and fully interdisciplinary hermeneutics that allows theological text interpretation to become as critical and self-critical as possible. While theologians in Barthian (see BARTHIANISM), EVANGELICAL, and POSTLIBERAL traditions have rejected the co-operation between philosophical and theological hermeneutics, and theologians associated with the 'New Hermeneutic' movement (e.g., G. Ebeling (1912–2001), E. Fuchs (1903–1983), R. Funk (1926–2005)) have called for a limited co-operation between theology and philosophical hermeneutics, theologians in LIBERAL, correlational, FEMINIST, LIBERATION, contextual, pluralist, and POSTMODERN traditions have welcomed all critical insights into the hermeneutical process.

Philosophers like M. Heidegger (1889–1976), H.-G. Gadamer (1900–2002), E. Levinas (1906–95), P. Ricœur (1913–2005), J. Habermas (b. 1929), G. Vattimo (b. 1936), and others have continued to explore the hermeneutical condition of humankind and to examine the particular challenges facing the understanding of otherness and radical otherness in our time. More recently, a number of theologians have responded positively to Gadamer's hermeneutics. He approached understanding in terms of a 'fusion of horizons': the horizon of the text is fused with the horizon of the interpreter without any need for additional methodological moves. Other theologians, following Habermas' and Ricœur's critique of Gadamer's anti-methodological attitude, are exploring a combination of central dimensions in the interpretative process (understanding, explanation, and assessment) in order to tackle ideological distortions present in both texts and interpreters. Further influenced by recent studies in linguistics and literary criticism, these theologians study the communicative process itself in order better to appreciate the textuality of texts (viz., over against any reduction of textual meaning to propositional communication in isolated sentences) and the ensuing demands on the interpreter. Any reading process aiming to be responsible to the challenges of the text as text must explore the genre, style, conventions, strategies, and functions of textual communications in order to decide which means of text-reception are most appropriate. Moreover, all theologians are faced with multiple ambiguities (both in the text and in text interpretation) and with the necessary plurality of readings.

At the same time, theologians also need to consider explicit and implicit power structures operative in the hermeneutical process. Feminist hermeneutics has exposed androcentric distortions in biblical and theological hermeneutics and demanded a hermeneutics of suspicion equipped to detect, highlight and overcome patriarchal, hierarchical, and kyriarchal dimensions in texts and their interpretation (see ANDROCENTRISM; PATRIARCHY). The awareness of a global humanity has further highlighted the need to reflect on the overall global, ecological, social, and political conditions of human text interpretation and self-interpretation. Since no act of human communication in general and of theological interpretation in particular can ever be free of interests and expectations, it is the perennial task of theological hermeneutics to make these 'pre-understandings' thematic, to show how they are necessary for initiating and energizing the process of interpretation, and to lend their voice to the texts themselves so that they may challenge any pre-understanding and prejudice in the interpretative process itself.

The conversation in theology on adequate hermeneutics will continue as long as theology exists. Whether Christian theologians are willing to participate in the interdisciplinary and inter-religious conversation on the possibilities and limitations of human communication and interpretation will depend on their particular approach to human otherness, to the radical otherness of God, and to the nature and scope of God's self-revelation in this universe.

W. G. Jeanrond, *Theological Hermeneutics: Development and Significance* (SCM, 1994).
A. C. Thiselton, *New Horizons in Hermeneutics* (HarperCollins, 1992).
D. Tracy, *Plurality and Ambiguity: Hermeneutics, Religion, Hope* (Harper & Row, 1987).
K. J. Vanhoozer, *First Theology: God, Scripture and Hermeneutics* (InterVarsity Press, 2002).

WERNER G. JEANROND

HESYCHASM From the Greek *hēsychia* (meaning 'silence', 'tranquillity', and 'stillness'), 'hesychasm' denotes a major current in Greek Christian spirituality that fosters an intimate, contemplative relationship with God, typically through an ascetic regimen of FASTING, vigilance, and PRAYER. Hesychastic spirituality emerges as a distinct movement in the monasteries of Mt ATHOS during the fourteenth century, though it draws on a literature and a heritage of monastic practice that stretches back 1,000 years to the golden age of Egyptian MONASTICISM. For purposes of convenience, four major periods can be identified: that of the Egyptian Desert Fathers (*ca* 250–400); that of the monastery of Sinai (seventh and eighth centuries); that of Athonite hesychasm (fourteenth century); and that of the 'Philokalic' revival (late eighteenth century to the present).

In early Egyptian Christian literature, the term *hēsychia* can be synonymous with 'solitude', and the hesychast is basically a hermit (cf. *AP*, Poemen 90). It may be a constituent part of the monastic VOCATION to sinlessness (e.g., *AP*, Arsenios 2; Athanasius, *Ant.* 30.2), but it is unclear that the terms have a well-defined meaning. However, the references in the early literature of Egyptian monasticism provided sufficient resources for subsequent generations to consolidate into a coherent teaching. John Climacus (*ca* 579–649), abbot of the monastery of Sinai, developed these teachings in his *Ladder of Divine Ascent*, especially at Step 27. The monastery at Sinai appears to have been a major centre for the furtherance of ascetical theology, such as can be found in *On Watchfulness and Holiness*, written probably in the eighth century by a priest of Sinai known (fittingly enough) as Hesychios. In that writing there appears a robust presentation of the *method* of hesychastic prayer that will be increasingly common.

The ongoing articulation of this method and its underlying theology reaches its apogee in the monasteries of Mt Athos some centuries later. Gregory of Sinai (*ca* 1265–1346) was one major proponent of 'inner prayer'. He lived through huge debates about hesychastic theology, which centred on the question of whether the Athonite experience of divine light was or was not a direct encounter with God, but did not contribute to them. His namesake, G. PALAMAS, embroiled himself in these debates, championing the cause of the hesychasts, who were ultimately vindicated. Eventually the theological tides ebbed and the observation of the practices fell away, but the literature was preserved.

In the late eighteenth century, a movement of revival on Athos witnessed the publication of a corpus of ascetical literature reaching back a millennium: the PHILOKALIA, edited by Makarios of Corinth (1731–1805) and Nikodimos of the Holy Mountain (1749–1809). Shortly thereafter, P. Velichkovsky (1722–94) edited a similar collection in Church Slavonic: the *Dobrotolyubie* (1793). These collections and their subsequent vernacular translations have fostered a renewal of hesychastic practice that is at home in the monasteries but also finds a following among secular Christians, as memorably recounted in the anonymous Russian spiritual travelogues *The Way of the Pilgrim* and *The Pilgrim Continues His Way*.

See also ASCETICISM.

T. Špidlík, *The Spirituality of the Christian East*, vol. II: *Prayer* (Cistercian Publications, 2005).

AUGUSTINE CASIDAY

HETERODOXY Originally coined as an antonym for 'ORTHODOXY', 'heterodoxy' (from the Greek for 'different opinion') refers to any DOCTRINE or set of doctrines at variance with the official teaching of a particular Church. In contemporary use by many Catholic, Orthodox, and Protestant writers, the term is used for teachings which, while not officially approved, nevertheless do not entail the kind of logical inconsistency with official teaching that would constitute HERESY. In this way, the holding of heterodox doctrines would not constitute grounds for EXCOMMUNICATION in the way that the profession of heretical doctrines would.

The theological ground for heterodoxy as a distinct category over against orthodoxy and heresy was given classic expression by F. SCHLEIERMACHER (*CF*, §25). Defining orthodoxy as that which is unquestionably in conformity with a Church's confession and heterodoxy as that which is not, Schleiermacher noted that there is nothing to impede (and, based on historical precedent, good reason to allow) that heterodox views might one day be vindicated as orthodox. Correspondingly, he argued that, in so far as proponents of a heterodox (in distinction from a heretical) opinion remain committed to defending their claims in terms of orthodox teaching, Christians should anticipate a future resolution of the disagreement that precludes regarding heterodoxy as grounds for division.

IAN A. MCFARLAND

HILDEGARD OF BINGEN Hildegard of Bingen (1098–1179), 'Sibyl of the Rhine', was one of the most extraordinary figures of the twelfth century. Known as a visionary and prophet in her own day, she preached publicly and powerful clerics supported her theological works. She wrote the first known morality play (*Ordo virtutum*), has more musical works securely attributed to her than any other composer of the period, and was the author of several scientific texts (e.g., *Physica*, *Liber simplicis medicinis*, and *Causae et curae*). Hildegard is best known for her theological trilogy (*Scivias*, the *Book of Life's Merits*, the *Book of Divine Works*), and for her letters to Church leaders calling for reform. Most famous is the copy of *Scivias* that was illuminated in her own monastery.

Born to a noble German family, Hildegard was offered by her parents as a 'tithe' to the Church, and at the age of eight she joined the anchoress Jutta of Sponheim (1092–1136), to learn the ways of PRAYER (see ANCHORITISM). From her earliest childhood, Hildegard experienced intense visions, 'a light so dazzling that [her] soul trembled'. However, it was not until she was forty-three that Hildegard recognized in this 'fiery light' her prophetic call. At the encouragement of her trusted teacher and scribe, Volmar (d. 1173), Hildegard explored God's command to 'cry out and write' what she saw. She began composing *Scivias* (from *Scito vias Domini*, 'Know the ways of the Lord') in 1141. Until recently, it was widely held that in 1148 Bernard of Clairvaux (1090–1153) and Pope Eugene III (r. 1145–53) officially approved her as an authentic mouthpiece of God, with the pope commanding Hildegard to continue recording her visions. This is now questioned by the American historian John van Engen.

Hildegard completed *Scivias* in 1151. A masterful *summa* of Christian DOCTRINE, it comprises twenty-six visions in three sections on CREATION, redemption, and SANCTIFICATION, covering such topics as divine majesty, the TRINITY, the FALL, the INCARNATION, the Church and its sacraments, and ESCHATOLOGY. The second book of her trilogy, *Book of Life's Merits* (1158–63), expounds on six visions and juxtaposes VIRTUES with vices. Finally, the *Book of Divine Works* (1163–73) presents a complex cosmology concerning life's origins, the nature of HEAVEN, and the history of salvation. Here, she emphasizes God the Word as 'fiery life' and as verdure, vitality, and fruitfulness. She concludes this treatise with a critique of the contemporary Church and a call to reform.

Hildegard was also an abbess and founder of two houses (one at Rupertsberg and one at Eibingen, the latter still thriving today). A bold preacher, she embarked upon four preaching tours from the age of sixty to her late seventies. Both in her sermons and in her extensive correspondence with popes, emperors, priests, abbots, and LAITY, she denounced 'lukewarm and sluggish' clergy as well as ecclesiastical abuses like simony and moral laxity. Her APOCALYPTIC prophecies made a keen impression, and even the prelates whom she attacked invited her to preach and send them transcripts of her sermons.

Despite her successes, Hildegard most frequently described herself as a 'frail human being' (*Sciv.* 1.1). She was sure, however, that God delighted to use her weakness to shame the wise, calling herself 'a small sound of the trumpet from the living Light' through which 'the mysteries of God' (*Ep.* 201) were 'poured out' in a 'fountain of abundance' (*Sciv.* 1.1). Defying categorization, Hildegard is much studied among various academic disciplines today, engaging scholars from musicologists and art historians, to medical historians, medievalists, and scholars of spiritual theology.

C. Burnett and P. Dronke, eds., *Hildegard of Bingen: The Context of Her Thought and Art* (Warburg Institute, 1998).

B. Newman, *Voice of the Living Light* (University of California Press, 1998).

BO KAREN LEE

HINDUISM AND CHRISTIANITY Christianity and Hinduism are two of the world's largest and most varied religions; indeed, each in its own way is endlessly productive of rich theological insights offering fruitful possibilities for inter-religious reflection. Common creed and practices notwithstanding, 'Christianity' may be taken to designate a family of communities and theologies, while 'Hinduism' indicates very many distinct but interwoven traditions with widely varied faith and theological perspectives. Even if they are notably different in important ways, Christianity and Hinduism share remarkable and important affinities and are complementary regarding theological doctrine and practice. This essay reviews their historical relationship, the nature of their theological encounter, and examples of theologically fruitful similarities and differences.

In the early Christian era there are Roman and Greek accounts of encounters with Indian ascetics and sages in the East, as well as detailed references to Brahminical and Buddhist teachings in both pagan and Christian literature. Tradition holds that St Thomas the Apostle preached the GOSPEL in South India. Christian communities in the East Syrian tradition (see NESTORIANISM) were certainly established in India in the first millennium. The modern encounter began with the opening of the European colonial period, and the arrival of the Catholic Portuguese on the west coast of India in 1498. From then on, the religious interactions of Hindus and these newly arrived Christians have been intense and complex, inextricably intertwined with economic and political calculations; in controversy and debate, specifically religious factors have sometimes seemed secondary to various communal, political, and social issues at work on both sides.

Early missionaries such as F. Xavier (1506–52) knew little about Hinduism, and had little opportunity to learn of its traditions in detail. Later missionaries, such as R. de Nobili (1579–1656), J. Bouchet (1655–1732), and G. Cœurdoux (1691–1777), developed more sophisticated notions of culture and religion, and argued that the Catholic engagement of Hinduism is best grounded in detailed knowledge of Hindu tradition. As for the Protestant missionary tradition in India, likewise rich and varied, one could begin with the pioneer Lutheran missionary B. Ziegenbalg (1682–1719) and figures such as N. Goreh (1825–85). It is also important to acknowledge the variety of Hindu responses to this encounter with Christianity and its theological possibilities. Traditional Hindu scholars argued with missionary scholars, defending Hindu beliefs against unanticipated new challenges. In the nineteenth century figures such as R. M. Roy (1772–1833), K. Chandra Sen (1838–84), and Swami Vivekananda (1863–1902) engaged Christian thought in theologically interesting ways, while the early twentieth century witnessed impressive comparative studies by the Vaisnava scholar A. Govindacharya (*fl.* 1910) and the Saiva scholar J. M. Nallaswami Pillai (1864–1920). In recent decades Hindu intellectuals have been more vigorously critical of (foreign) Christian presence in India, and of social and political dimensions of Christian mission. Mostly reactive to Christian initiatives, Hindus seem in general to have been only minimally interested in Christian theology; even the potentially useful word 'theology' has not been widely used. Given the growing Hindu population in the West, and the engagement of young Hindu scholars in the study of religion, it may be that the Christian–Hindu theological exchange will now flourish more vigorously outside India.

History has not fixed the Hindu–Christian encounter in any definite mould and there is no single dominant set of issues on the agenda. Precisely because there is no single, fixed connection between Hinduism and Christianity, there is no urgency to clarify, heal, or resolve the relationship (tensions and misunderstandings notwithstanding); the myriad possibilities for exchange can liberate and enliven the Christian theological imagination, and innumerable starting points in text, ritual, and practice present themselves. So too on an institutional level Hindu communities come in many different configurations and with differing modes of authority. None is without structure, but none is neatly comparable to any specific Christian analogue. While this fluidity may frustrate those seeking a single route to the resolution of religious and theological differences, Hinduism's variety precludes the possibility of any single path of dialogue, and so again puts a premium on inventiveness and multiple strategies of engagement rather than on a quest for definitive conclusions about the meaning of the two religions for one another. All this adds up to a difficult but creative site for theological exchange, in which both Christians and Hindus can participate, with no one in a position to determine when the theological exchange is complete.

With this fluid context, Christianity and Hinduism invite comparison on a wide range of specific theological themes. Both include subtle theory and developed Scholastic systems (see SCHOLASTICISM), liturgy performed and theorized, APOLOGETICS, and devotional and erotic mysticism (see MYSTICAL THEOLOGY), along with local and popular devotions that elude easy comprehension. Analogies and differences in theological perspective and with respect to particular doctrines are numerous and striking, and here I can give only a few examples.

One of the oldest comparisons is that of the TRINITY and a popular Hindu conception of the divine as 'tri-formed' (*trimurti*). Christian missionary theologians were struck by the apparent similarity of Trinity and *trimurti*, and by way of often negative contrast compared the Christian God with Brahma, Visnu, and Siva. While the comparison was never resolved – differences are actually greater than similarities – the exchanges illumined issues essential to each tradition. The nineteenth century brought more subtle analogies between the Trinity and the triple reality of Being, Consciousness, and Bliss (*saccidananda*), a much more promising site for insightful reflection. Similarly, a long tradition compares Christ and Krsna, particularly with respect to the nature of *avatara* and INCARNATION, and the meaning of divine embodiment. And while it is important to avoid facile comparisons of the HOLY SPIRIT with Hindu concepts of divine breath (*prana*) or divine energy (*sakti*), the parallels cannot be discounted; as the theology of the Spirit becomes more developed, these new parallels may provoke still further interesting exchanges. Although Hindu polytheism seems rather distant from Christian piety and theology, the core insight that the Divine is in fact imagined diversely in accord with the capacities and inclinations of individuals and communities is a dynamic worthy of deeper consideration. Devotion to the Virgin Mary can also be compared with the worship of the goddesses so prominent in Hindu piety and theology. Hindus and Christians have a strong sacramental sense, cherish sacrament and affirm the possibility of an embodied presence of the divine, and ritualize material images in places of worship (see SACRAMENTOLOGY); both appreciate the importance of ritual participation, the sharing of food (though within different social constructions), and the variable roles of priest and people in communal worship. Art and music too offer highly promising starting points for Hindu–Christian conversations on matters of faith. Specific and technical theological parallels appear as more refined theological topics are examined. There is striking common ground in explanations of grace and salvation, and even regarding the mysterious balance of grace and free will. Within quite different cosmologies, both traditions have explored the meaning of death and life thereafter. Christian theologians can profitably learn from Hindu theorizations of devotion, GRACE, and liberation, even if the philosophical and cultural expressions of beliefs and doctrines differ greatly. REVELATION is a topic of shared concern, along with related questions about experience and reason in human knowledge of God; given shared linguistic sensitivities, theological language itself is a topic for discussion.

Even more stubborn differences open possibilities. Christian theologians have long pondered radical nondualist (Advaita) Vedanta, which sees personalizations of the divine as only provisionally necessary for the sake of people not ready for higher understanding; the Christian theologian is thus invited to consider a divine fullness that is neither personal nor less than personal, and yet able to fulfil human being beyond itself. Yoga, a spiritual practice rich in implications for THEOLOGICAL ANTHROPOLOGY, is not necessarily contrary to Christian spirituality and anthropology, even if the structures involved differ greatly. With diligent intellectual labour, connections can be made, and yoga shown to put in a new light the goals and methods of a Christian spiritual theology.

At the same time, however, some differences are not easily turned to advantage. For many Hindus, it is simply undesirable and theologically dubious to claim that God has only one name; as a result, the cult of multiple deities is preferable, for the sake of more adequate relations to the divine. Or one may take up the matter of IDOLATRY: while missionary apologetics seem to have been fuelled as much by misunderstanding as by substance, at a very deep level common Christian discomfort with images of the divine may reveal a very different underlying view of divine corporeality and visibility, differences not softened simply by notice of the Catholic and Orthodox veneration of images (see ICONS AND ICONOGRAPHY). And, even as Christian theologians do well to appreciate analogies between Mary and Hindu goddesses, difficulties arise if further thought is given to the presence and importance of goddesses as divine persons equal to or greater than male deities. The very idea of goddesses is largely alien to the biblical tradition, as so too the Hindu belief that divine persons can be gendered male or female. Finally, the real parallels in Christian and Hindu claims about revelation and SCRIPTURE may also accentuate the inevitable difficult question: which texts, which message, form *the* revelation? While Hindus might well find it possible to respect the NT as revelatory, Christian theologies still struggle in characterizing the authority of the Vedas, Upanisads, and other Hindu texts.

Ethical issues too may provoke theological reflection. Hindus and Christians share a wide range of values, regarding religious freedom, democracy, the importance of family, and (in differing ways) the centrality of social responsibility. Christian and Hindu views on NONVIOLENCE, respect for ANIMALS and the environment are complementary, each tradition filling gaps in the other. But here too robust disagreement is possible, as when Christians criticize the persistence of caste distinctions in Hindu society and the seeming tolerance of POVERTY, or when Hindus point to the intricately interwoven histories of colonialism and Christian mission, or the perceived disruption of social order by Christian evangelical and liberation movements. Controversies over practice imply underlying notions of world, social order, human progress, and the relationship of culture and religion, and theologians and ethicists can profitably go deeper into such problems and underlying theological foundations.

Does an increasing Christian knowledge of Hinduism and its theological possibilities for Christians affect faith in the uniqueness of Jesus as saviour of all, or change how Christians estimate the relationship of Christianity to world religions? On the one hand, such questions are largely internal to the Christian tradition, and there is no data in the Hindu traditions that would resolve such questions in any particular conservative or progressive way. On the other, a consideration of the distinctive manifold possibilities presented by Hindu traditions with respect to every level of Christian faith and understanding should affect profoundly every avenue of Christian theology, in both content and method. Even if the great Christological questions remain central, the theologians who consider such questions will change due to their encounter with Hinduism, and on that basis assess from a new perspective any of the available Christian views of other religions. Even as Christians confess the universal salvific centrality of Christ and the Church, they will necessarily become more careful in how they bring their faith positions into encounter with complex living traditions such as the Hindu. Erudition, imagination, affective engagement, and nonviolent learning are all virtues prerequisite to any productive Hindu–Christian theological encounter. How Hindu theologians might proceed with respect to the possibilities latent in the Christian tradition lies beyond this essay, in the constructive Hindu theologies that will develop during the twenty-first century.

A. Amaladasas, S. J., ed., *Indian Christian Thinkers/ Christian Thinkers in India*, 3 vols. (Satya Nilayam, 2005–7).

J. B. Carman, *Majesty and Meekness: A Comparative Study of Contrast and Harmony in the Concept of God* (Eerdmans, 1994).

F. X. Clooney, *Hindu God, Christian God: How Reason Helps Break Down the Boundaries between Religions* (Oxford University Press, 2001).

'Restoring "Hindu Theology" as a Category in Indian Intellectual Discourse' in *Blackwell Companion to Hinduism*, ed. G. Flood (Blackwell, 2003), 447–77.

'Hinduism and Christianity' in *SCM Press Dictionary of Spirituality*, ed. P. Sheldrake (John Knox Press, 2005), 336–8.

K. Satchidananda Murty, *Reason and Revelation in Advaita Vedanta* (Columbia University Press, 1959).

FRANCIS X. CLOONEY, S. J.

HISTORICAL THEOLOGY Christian faith is inextricably-bound up with events. It is not a timeless philosophy or a code of ethics. It is rooted in the events surrounding Jesus Christ, themselves seen and interpreted in the light of earlier scriptural texts, the OT. When believers summarize their FAITH, as in the APOSTLES' CREED and NICENE CREED, much of the summary is about these events, past, present, and future. So what they say about God (i.e., theology) is based on things that happen. But the relevant events do not stop at the end of the NT. This is because faith in God the Father and in Jesus Christ is received in the life of the community of believers, that is, by inspiration of the HOLY SPIRIT in the Church. So a comprehensive theology takes account of what continues to happen, because God makes himself known in events. This works in various ways.

First there is Church (or ecclesiastical) history. Ever since Eusebius of Caesarea (*ca* 260–*ca* 340) pioneered this discipline, Church historians have tried to put together coherent accounts of how the Church originated, spread, organized itself, and established itself, first in the Roman Empire and neighbouring regions, and then in other parts of the world. It recounts the disputes and reconciliations, including the history of theology itself: how ideas developed, what norms were established, and what teachings were ruled out as false. It included the way the books that form the canon of SCRIPTURE were identified. This is a decisive question for theology, for while the limits of the canon were largely settled in the fourth century, they have never been completely agreed between all branches of the Church.

Usually Church history was itself partly governed by criteria of ORTHODOXY. Because Churches and governments condemned, or neglected to copy, alternative views of how things were, little attempt was made to assess conventional history objectively. In the ancient world, for instance, people often wrote works pseudonymously, under the name of some accepted authority. Most of the books of the Bible are like that, but so are many of the other books and records that have come down to us, sometimes out of pious and humble respect, sometimes from deliberate deception. Only with the Renaissance of the fifteenth and sixteenth centuries did the determination to sort the wheat from the chaff emerge. Finding and sorting good ancient copies, exposing frauds, and going, in D. Erasmus' (1466/9–1536) famous slogan, 'to the sources' transformed people's views of the past. By challenging traditional justifications for the powers of the pope, investigation of ancient texts shook western CHRISTENDOM to its foundations. The philological work of establishing the true text, nature, and value of ancient handwritten sources remains an important adjunct of Church history and therefore of historical theology.

These processes were greatly advanced after the ENLIGHTENMENT in the eighteenth century. New techniques of critical study have produced sounder copies of ancient documents, methods of comparative history have been applied to the Church, and revisions have constantly been made in estimates of past personalities. A notable feature has been the reassessment of many who (especially in the ancient Church) were condemned as heretics, and whose writings are largely lost. Here from time to time archaeology helps, not only with material evidence from excavations about how people lived and worshipped, but with new finds like the Nag Hammadi codices, which give evidence about sects in the past dismissed as 'Gnostic' (see GNOSTICISM).

Historical theology proper is a discipline in which the theology of the past is described and expounded in its own historical context. It is a form of intellectual history, since the ideas are generated in a context of thought, itself affected by social and political events. Much early theology is unintelligible without the context of ancient Greek philosophy, but Latin and Semitic (Syriac) influences were also strong. Furthermore, the documents of past ages always need verification. Modern scholars have sometimes written histories of doctrine or of theology, elaborated and presented as an objective account of the past, but inevitably reflecting their own intellectual and religious preconceptions. A famous example is the *History of Dogma* (1885–90) by A. von HARNACK, written from a liberal Protestant standpoint; but there are many others. Those involved in other kinds of theology, systematic, moral, philosophical, will often use past authorities as a source of truth. Among Catholics, for instance, J. H. NEWMAN wrote his justification for his conversion to Catholicism in his *Essay on the Development of Christian Doctrine* (1845), and the influential Jesuit K. RAHNER has in various writings based a modern Christology on the decree of the Council of Chalcedon.

The principle was early established that the true faith had never changed: Jesus had given all truth to his apostles, and they had delivered it whole and perfect to the world. Modern critical history now sees that variety rather than uniformity marked the earliest stages. But even on the old assumption, the growth of the Churches, and the spread of the faith among different languages and cultures, brought different aspects to the fore, and different ways of living, worshipping and believing appeared. In the face of this, emperors and bishops tried to discriminate between true and false traditions, and to establish principles for such discernment.

One way is to expound creeds and other statements already judged authoritative. Coinciding with the adoption of Christianity by the Roman Empire in the early fourth century, theological disputes arose. Though it had earlier roots, the most famous of these divisions were associated with a thinker in Alexandria called Arius (*ca* 250–336), and the many disputes which followed are often called the 'Arian Controversy'. They involved debates over the way the Son of God relates to the Father. All held that Jesus was the earthly manifestation of one who existed with and in God the Father before the world was created, and who was responsible for the creation as well as the salvation of the world, and so in some sense was God. But whether he was a second God beside his Father and junior to him, or pre-existed only within the Father – not to mention what should be said about the Holy Spirit, who was confessed and worshipped in a variety of ways alongside Father and Son – caused great controversy. The attempt to resolve the issue at the Council of Nicaea had limited success. A consensus arose, represented by some very famous names, including Athanasius of Alexandria, Basil of Caesarea (see Cappadocian Fathers), and Augustine of Hippo. This consensus, in which the equal deity of Father, Son, and Holy Spirit was confessed in one God, who exists as Trinity, is nowadays called 'Nicene'. This position became dominant in the 380s, and is represented by the creed adopted by the Council of Constantinople, which in almost all respects is the 'Nicene Creed' used in Churches today. Once it was confessed, however, that the Son of God was no less divine than his Father, questions arose as to how such a being could become fully human in Jesus Christ, and there were attempts to come to a general conclusion backed by the Roman Empire. The Councils of Ephesus and Chalcedon were only partly successful in resolving this issue. One creedal confession, the 'Chalcedonian Definition' of the faith, became normative for most of the Churches, declaring Christ as one person with two natures. It left substantial numbers of eastern Christians outside the imperial Church; their descendants remain to this day in the various eastern Churches, Armenians, Syrians, Assyrians, Copts, and others (see Oriental Orthodox Churches; Syriac Christian Theology). These Churches still often bear the abusive labels 'Nestorian' and 'monophysite', given them by their critics in the main bodies of Orthodox, Catholic, and Protestant Churches (see Miaphysitism; Nestorianism). The point, however, is that theologians still use the creeds of Nicaea, Constantinople, and Chalcedon as points of reference.

In addition to creeds, the Churches came out of these disputes with a large corpus of other authoritative writings. During the fifth century it was already customary to support an argument with a chain (*catena*) of testimonies from 'the fathers', that is from past thinkers of recognized orthodoxy. Soon this became the norm and, for many, quoting chapter and verse replaced free argument. Different groups would, of course, allow different authorities, and gradually the Greek, Latin, and Syriac parts of the Church drifted apart. For example, among the Latins, Augustine prevailed; among the Greeks, Gregory of Nazianzus (see Cappadocian Fathers) and John Chrysostom (*ca* 347–407); for many Syrians Theodore of Mopsuestia (*ca* 350–428); and for the Miaphysites Cyril of Alexandria. But all adopted the principle inherent in the discipline of patristics: identifying and following the 'fathers' in the faith. One of the consequences is the hardening of attitudes towards those of a differing tradition, from which we have all suffered.

In the medieval West intellectual life flourished and usually assumed the truth of past heroes of the faith, whose views were presented and expounded in the light of contemporary issues. The form and government of the Church had of course greatly changed. The collapse of the old Roman Empire under the northern barbarians was met with a learned and powerful papacy (a good example is Gregory I, 'the Great' (r. 590–604)) representing civilization and learning, and soon claiming universal dominion. At the same time monastic communities everywhere sprang up, and kings and emperors promoted pious learning to help govern and civilize their subjects: Charlemagne (r. 800–14) and Alfred of England ('the Great', r. 871–99) are good examples. As time went by communities of scholars (called 'universities') flourished in centres like Paris and Oxford. In these schools it was common practice to lecture on an authoritative text, a process which came to fix itself on the *Sentences* of P. Lombard (*ca* 1100–60), a masterly assembly of authoritative extracts from Scripture and the fathers; it was the custom for new teachers to write a commentary on the *Sentences*, and some of these became famous. Such minute exposition of traditional authorities is often called 'Scholastic', from the university 'Schoolmen' who practised it (see Scholasticism). Despite many changes in philosophical and theological thinking, and occasional protests by such as P. Abelard (1079–1142/3), these practices prevailed until displaced by a new comprehensive authority, the great synthesis of T. Aquinas.

Though for a time controversial, Aquinas received papal commendation in 1567 and was made required reading for ordinands by a papal bull of 1879. His thought, however, was not merely a textbook, but has been repeatedly revived and renewed (see Thomism). Similarly, with the rise of Protestantism, even among those for whom 'the Bible only' was the authority, new masters were found whose thought could be developed and reworked. To this day M. Luther and J. Calvin are constant sources of ideas and new debate among theologians. Sometimes such figures are so highly regarded that a new orthodoxy grows up, and we hear of 'Lutheran orthodoxy' or 'Calvinist Scholasticisim'. With such great thinkers, however, as with Aquinas, the creative impulse can break out again.

After the Enlightenment new attitudes appeared. The philosophies of idealism, following I. Kant and G. W. F. Hegel, were allowed to interpret, and often to denigrate, theological traditions. At the same time history was liberated from the past orthodoxy, and Bible and Church were reconceived in contemporary guise by figures like D. F. Strauss (1808–74) and A. Ritschl (1822–89). It was a guise generally optimistic about the future of science and of western culture. Harnack, already mentioned above, belongs here.

In the twentieth century new factors altered perspectives on the past. Worldwide mission led members of diverse Church traditions to see how much they had in common, in contrast to those they aimed to convert; that led towards an 'ecumenical' theology, and a relativizing of confessional traditions formerly held sacrosanct. A new openness among westerners to the largely unknown and varied religions of the East also came into this. Globalization of cultures leads to engagement with non-Christian religion, whose nature and insights must be set alongside the historical perspective of the Church. The carnage of European wars recalled theology from its progressive idealism. K. Barth in particular insisted on a transcendent God and the authority of his Word as a basis of all true theology; his ideas, elaborated with great detail and stunning power, transformed Reformed theology, stimulated other theologians (including the Catholic H. von Balthasar), and continue to attract research and exposition on a large scale. But historical continuities should be noted. On the one hand, Barth himself constantly works to his conclusions from previous thinkers, such as F. Schleiermacher, the first great creative theologian of the Enlightenment. On the other hand, a kind of Barthian orthodoxy sometimes creates a new Scholasticism, from which historical theology must again rescue him.

Barth is not all of twentieth-century theology. All kinds of creative developments have occurred, not least in the Catholic Church. Vatican Council II released historical study from limitations formerly enforced, encouraged the reinterpretation of the past, and thereby fulfilled some of the ideas already adumbrated in the work of figures like Newman and Rahner. At the end of the twentieth century, a massive attempt was made by German Protestants to compile a synthetic account of contemporary theology on a basis at once ecumenical and open to the insights of modern philosophy, ethics and non-Christian religions, in the thirty-six-volume *Theologische Realenzyklopädie* (1977–2004). While in this collection other disciplines required only one editor each, six or seven were engaged in *Kirchengeschichte*, the theological history of the Church. This shows how theology is bound to become more and more historical, the longer the Church lives, grows, and thinks.

A. von Harnack, *History of Dogma*, 7 vols. (Williams & Norgate, 1896–9).

H. Jedin and J. Dolan, eds., *History of the Church*, 10 vols. (Herder and Herder, 1987).

J. H. Newman, *An Essay on the Development of Christian Doctrine* (J. Toovey, 1845).

J. Quasten, *Patrology*, 4 vols. (Christian Classics, 1983–6).

K. Rahner, *Theological Investigations*, vol. IV (Helicon, 1966).

E. Stöve, 'Kirchengeschichtsschreibung' in *Theologische Realenzyklopädie*, ed. G. Krause and G. Müller, vol. XVIII (W. de Gruyter, 1989), 535–60.

Stuart G. Hall

History of Religion School The History of Religion School refers to a group of late nineteenth-century German Protestant scholars who shared a set of convictions about historical research and its importance for a proper scientific understanding of Christianity as a historical phenomenon. The term has come to symbolize a comparative and non-theological approach to the study of Christian origins and indeed to the study of religious traditions generally. Yet the scholars who were associated with this method had their own set of theological concerns and their own vision of the nature of religion and its possible contributions to modern culture. Both a proper translation of the term *Religionsgeschichtliche Schule* and an understanding of these scholars' shared interest in religion (and not in religion*s*) demand that this term be rendered 'History of *Religion* School'. Members included such figures as: W. Bousset (1865–1920), Albert Eichhorn (1856–1926), H. Greßmann (1877–1927), H. Gunkel (1862–1932), H. Hackmann (1864–1935), W. Heitmüller (1869–1926), E. Troeltsch, J. Weiss (1863–1914), and W. Wrede (1859–1906).

Scholars have long pointed out that 'school' is a misleading way to refer to the circle of mostly young biblical scholars who found themselves at Göttingen beginning in the 1880s. These individuals did not share one clearly defined ideology or programme of research. Most of them were drawn to Göttingen by the work of

A. Ritschl (1822–89), who became their teacher but against whom they all would rebel to greater or lesser extents. Originally, Ritschl represented for these scholars a viable approach to LIBERAL THEOLOGY that was grounded in a modern historical method and relevant for societal concerns of the time. Ritschl rooted his conception of Christianity in the historical reality of Jesus and the early Christian community's reception of his teachings concerning the KINGDOM OF GOD. Thus, for Ritschl, Christianity was a practical religion whose ethical message could be articulated through a careful consideration of the gospel norm as historically given in the person of Jesus Christ. While theology entailed a judgement of FAITH, it was also deeply rooted in history.

For many of his students who would embrace a history-of-religion approach, Ritschl's work was nevertheless insufficiently historical and too closely shaped by dogmatic interests. Ritschl's portrait of Jesus, for example, was predicated on the claim that Jesus preached about a this-worldly kingdom rooted in ethical concerns of community. Yet the research undertaken by many of these scholars, including Ritschl's son-in-law J. Weiss, revealed instead a Jesus who was deeply shaped by Jewish APOCALYPTIC, and who therefore anticipated an imminent end of the world. While Ritschl's work on early Christianity served a modern liberal theological agenda, it did not represent the thoroughgoing historicist portrait that these scholars sought.

Many of these erstwhile students of Ritschl found a mentor in P. de Lagarde (1827–91), professor of oriental languages, whom Troeltsch called the true father of the school. Lagarde sought to 'free' the historical science of religion from the partiality of theology. Inspired by him and by B. Duhm (1847–1928), the young scholars at Göttingen began to pursue research that resisted any tendency to exempt Christianity from the rigorous historical analysis applied to all other religious phenomena. Instead of turning primarily to canonical texts of the OT and NT, they placed earliest Christianity in its pluralistic first-century Greco-Roman and Jewish contexts. They sought to understand the religious life and world view reflected in both canonical and non-canonical sources. They therefore developed a style of research that was quite distinct from traditional biblical theology; instead of producing a history of dogma, they sought to craft a history of the Christian religion.

Contemporary scholars have argued that the History of Religion School was unified by a common conception of the nature of religion as an irrational life force having to do with 'the spiritual', and not primarily with dogma or morals. Thus, its proponents portrayed the apostle PAUL as a 'man of the spirit' who founded a religion based not on DOCTRINE but on individual religious experience. Similarly, where they took interest in M. LUTHER, it was for his 'mysticism', and they argued that the study of religion should focus on exemplars of religious experience and the piety of the masses, and not just on the writings of elite Scholastic theologians or the history of dogmatic formulations.

In many ways this conception of religion as rooted in spiritual experience was one they thought could be investigated by 'objective' historical research. Yet, it is important to see what members (e.g., Gunkel and Troeltsch) themselves saw: that a 'purely historical' method entails a particular world view, one that partakes (at least in part) of an idealist view of history and that sees 'the religious' as essential to human life (see IDEALISM, GERMAN). Theirs was not, then, a plea for 'neutrality' or 'value-free' scholarship. On the contrary, many of these scholars aimed to show the superiority of Christianity through a historical method that appealed not to supernatural or absolute truth, but to the depth of religiosity displayed within its history. Further, their work can be seen in the context of the political culture of the German Empire, wherein theologians engaged in methodological debates that were tied up with questions about political order and that had to do with the place of the Church and religion in a rapidly modernizing culture. The members of the School belonged to what can be called the liberal Protestant 'theological left'. While they were opposed to an authoritarian Church and resisted (what they saw as) simplistic appeals to a German Lutheran tradition that could be harmonized with bourgeois values, they nevertheless saw an important role for religion in modern culture.

It was Ernst Troeltsch who articulated the twofold theoretical vision of the school: first, an interest in research that rejects a dogmatic supernatural perspective and that embraces a cultural–historical one; and second, the development of a philosophy of religion that seeks to ground the validity of Christianity within the historical development of religions generally. Thus, the school did not reject theological tasks, but sought a new relation between the historical and the systematic. This relation continues to vex theologians and scholars of religion today. As Troeltsch himself saw, there is 'no escape from history' and its relativizing effects. At the same time, normative questions and concerns (even when unacknowledged) remain central to the study of religion. The work of this school points both to the distorting effects of overly dogmatic readings of history and to the fiction of an objective science of religion.

M. D. Chapman, *Ernst Troeltsch and Liberal Theology* (Oxford University Press, 2001).

F. W. Graf, 'Der "Systematiker" der kleinen Göttinger Fakultät: Ernst Troeltschs Promotionsthesen in ihr Göttinger Kontext' in *Troeltsch-Studien*, vol. 1: *Untersuchungen zur Biographie und Werkgeschichte*, ed. F. W. Graf and H. Renz (Gütersloh, 1982), 235–90.

E. Troeltsch, 'The Dogmatics of the History-of-Religions School' in *Religion in History* (Fortress Press, 1991), 87–108.

Lori Pearson

HODGE, CHARLES Prominent American Presbyterian theologian, churchman, and educator of the nineteenth century, Charles Hodge (1797–1878) was schooled at Princeton College and Seminary. Convinced of the necessity of a highly educated clergy, he studied in Europe from 1826 to 1828 to bolster his knowledge of ancient languages and acquaint himself with modern scholarship. He served as professor of biblical literature at Princeton Seminary until 1840, when he became professor of didactic theology. He advocated Old School confessional allegiance to the WESTMINSTER STANDARDS and traditional forms of piety, over against New School efforts to alter Reformed DOCTRINE and polity and to advocate the crisis conversions of the Second Great Awakening.

A prolific writer, his works spanned literary genres: biblical commentaries (on Romans, Corinthians, and Ephesians), theologies (the popular *The Way of Life*, 1841, and his magnum opus, the three-volume *Systematic Theology*, 1872–73), history (*Constitutional History of the Presbyterian Church*, 1839) and NATURAL SCIENCE (*What is Darwinism?*, 1874). The most accessible source for his expansive grasp of biblical, theological, ecclesiastical, and cultural topics are his 142 articles for the *Biblical Repertory and Princeton Review*, which he founded and edited until 1871. Through this prestigious journal Hodge rapidly emerged as a leader of 'PRINCETON THEOLOGY', which became synonymous with Old School Presbyterianism. In articles occasionally exceeding a hundred pages he analyzed proceedings of the annual General Assembly, championed an authoritative SCRIPTURE and Reformed ORTHODOXY, opposed interdenominational voluntary societies, and lamented the tragic events of America's Civil War. By his death Hodge had trained over 2,000 students, and his scholarship established the theological basis for American evangelicalism.

J. W. Stewart, *Mediating the Center: Charles Hodge on American Science, Language, Literature and Politics* (Princeton Theological Seminary, 1995).

ANDREW HOFFECKER

HOLINESS MOVEMENT: see PENTECOSTAL THEOLOGY.

HOLOCAUST The Holocaust refers to the annihilation of Jews under Nazi German leader A. Hitler (1889–1945) during World War II, as well as the associated mass murder of other groups such as gypsies, homosexuals, the disabled, and non-Jewish Poles. Some scholars prefer the Hebrew term *Shoah* (destruction) because the biblical Greek term *holocaustos* (burnt offering) is theologically offensive in connoting that the deaths of two thirds of European Jewry were a ritual sacrifice to God. Also, the use of the term 'holocaust' in its broad meaning – large-scale destruction – is problematic in obscuring the unique features of the Nazi atrocities, including the bureaucracy, technology, ideology, and intention to exterminate all Jews in total genocide.

Holocaust theology emerged in the 1970s among Jewish and Christian thinkers, parallel to the growth of popular interest in the Holocaust generated by the increasing availability of survivors' memoirs and media depictions. For these writers, the Holocaust is a crisis and turning point. THEODICY looms large. Is the Holocaust part of God's plan? If not, does it signify God's absence or rather God's vulnerability? Theologically more conservative thinkers uphold God's omnipotence and goodness, and argue either that the Holocaust served a purpose for God's plan in history, or that we cannot fathom God's inscrutable designs. Other authors maintain that God's participation in human suffering is the only theodicy that effectively defends God from accusations of sadism or neglect. For Christians this idea is often developed in terms of Christological and Trinitarian accounts of divine suffering, while Jewish thinkers may deploy Kabbalistic ideas of divine withdrawal and the exile of God's *Shekhinah* (presence) to explain earthly evils.

More radically, there are scholars who believe variously that the Holocaust shakes the credibility of REVELATION, requires protest against God, makes theodicy impossible, or necessitates new religious outlooks, including secularism. Ethical and religious responses by Jewish authors who lived through the Holocaust, such as survivor E. Wiesel (b. 1928) and philosopher Emmanuel Levinas (1906–95), are viewed by many as authoritative for guiding authentic interpretations of the Holocaust.

Certain concerns remain specific to Jews or Christians. Jewish theologians ponder the meaning of the COVENANT and Jewish identity after the Holocaust, as well as the significance of the State of ISRAEL and genocide prevention. The post-Holocaust commandment that Jews must not grant Hitler posthumous victory, formulated by E. Fackenheim (1916–2003), is widely accepted as religious, cultural, and political in import. The primary preoccupation for Christian theologians is addressing and providing correctives to the legacy of anti-Judaism in the NT and Church history. Doctrinal triumphalism and SUPERSESSIONISM are repudiated, while the Jewish roots of Christianity and the relevance of Jewish thinkers for Christian theology are embraced. There is asymmetrical interest on the part of Christians in learning from Jewish writings and seeking reconciliation for past wrongs, whereas Jewish priorities are establishing survival as a people and rethinking the covenant without necessarily engaging with Christian texts or groups.

Although the Holocaust occurred on European soil, much theological and dialogical activity in response to it has occurred in North America, due to its sizeable Jewish population and popular interest in the Holocaust. In Europe post-Holocaust reflection has been most prominent in Germany, England, and the Vatican. Catholic and Lutheran Churches in particular face accusations of complicity with National Socialism that compel a response. More broadly, various ecumenical statements have sought to revise Church theology and repair relations with Judaism. The WORLD COUNCIL OF CHURCHES made a statement against Christian antisemitism as early as 1948, while the Vatican documents *Nostra aetate* (1965) and *We Remember: A Reflection on the Shoah* (1998) affirm the validity of the Jewish covenant with God and acknowledge past wrongs.

Since the 1990s, controversies have arisen about certain assumptions in Holocaust thought. Some authors have questioned the selective use of Holocaust testimony to support theological conclusions, the appropriation of Jewish voices by Christians, and the exoneration of Christianity by emphasis on its Jewishness. Other recent thinkers correlate Holocaust representation in popular culture with trends in religious responses and analyze the rhetorical deployment of the Holocaust in biblical studies and theology. Appealing to the moral lessons of the Holocaust, a few Jewish and Christian writers have spoken against Israel's policies towards Palestinians, although most Holocaust thinkers enthusiastically support Israel, and some evangelical theologians view the Holocaust and Israel as preparation for the Messiah. Finally, there are new initiatives among Jewish and Christian thinkers to look at the implications of more recent genocides, and to incorporate Muslims and representatives of other religions into Holocaust dialogue.

See also JUDAISM AND CHRISTIANITY.

D. Cohn-Sherbok, ed., *Holocaust Theology: A Reader* (New York University Press, 2002).

C. Rittner, S. D. Smith, and I. Steinfeldt, eds., *The Holocaust and the Christian World: Reflections on the Past, Challenges for the Future* (Continuum, 2000).

SARAH PINNOCK

HOLY SPIRIT Traditional Christian theology understands the Holy Spirit as the 'third' Person (see HYPOSTASIS) of the TRINITY, equal in divinity with the Father (see *ABBA*) and the Son (see CHRISTOLOGY). The DOCTRINE of the Holy Spirit, or pneumatology, has become a hot topic in twentieth and twenty-first-century Christian theology because of repeated Trinitarian revivals. And yet, the more theologians proclaim a revival of Trinitarian thinking, the more they tend to focus on Christ. This fact prompts the question: is there anything the Spirit can do that Jesus cannot do better? And if Jesus can do everything better than the Spirit, what is the Spirit for? The western solution of AUGUSTINE – making the Spirit the 'bond of love' (*vinculum caritatis*) between the Father and the Son – labours under dual disadvantages: Orthodox Churches suspect that it subordinates the Spirit to Father and Son, while a 'bond' or 'chain' sounds more like a thing than a 'person'.

Any attempt to answer these questions must reckon with two models of the Trinity as the matrix for the Spirit's work: (1) the Trinity as crossing a distance, and (2) the Trinity as a community to join. If the Trinity crosses a distance – from God in HEAVEN to the human being on earth – then the picture of the divine ECONOMY seems clear, but the Spirit fares badly. In the distance-crossing model, God the Father remains in heaven, and Christ crosses the infinite distance from heaven to earth. On this model, the Spirit then crosses the much smaller distance between the exterior history of Jesus in the world to the interior of the human heart. In other words, the distance-crossing model measures the work of the Spirit in inches – and it is not clear that Jesus cannot do that work even better than the Spirit (as in the slogan 'Let Jesus into your heart'). The Spirit seems superfluous, even dispensable.

In versions of Christianity focused on REVELATION, the problem gets worse. In many of these versions, it is packets of information – 'revelation' – that cross the distance between God and humanity. Jesus conveys it; FAITH receives it, understood as the believer's act without reference to the Spirit's gift. This leaves both God and the believer Spirit-free. The same problem plagues the CHARISMATIC MOVEMENT, too, if what the Spirit conveys is an 'experience' that works like information. In traditions that reduce the Trinity to revelation and faith, it is the human being who is exhorted, 'Have faith! Believe the Good News!' – as if the human being were the agent of faith, and the Spirit became our creature. If Christ conveys information, and the human being believes it, then, once again, the Spirit looks superfluous. The Spirit is at best the believer's assistant, and even here, Christ may seem a safer bet, such that a person who has trouble believing should call on Christ, in preference to the Spirit, to 'help my unbelief' (Mark 9:24). Even K. BARTH, credited with the most powerful of the twentieth century's Trinitarian revivals, has been charged in this way. It is a symptom of this Spirit-forgetfulness that Barth can announce the Spirit, but then go on to speak of Christ for hundreds of pages.

Perhaps the disappearance of the Spirit is only an apparent problem. Perhaps it marks the Spirit to become small, to whisper, to retire. P. Florensky (1882–1937), independent of western Christianity's Trinitarian revivals, notes the same pattern, points out that it is not confined to modernity, and treats it with bemusement rather than alarm. If Barth fumbles, Florensky shrugs. Theologians 'hardly [give] a clear and precise explanation of anything', but 'turn out to be almost mute, or clearly confused'. This applies not to modern theologians, but to 'all the holy fathers and mystical philosophers'. They paint merely a 'false window' for symmetry's sake. Even the ascetics, Florensky notes, speak of the Spirit as '"grace," ... something completely impersonal', because they recognize 'not the Holy Spirit but His grace-giving energies, His powers, His acts and activities' on human beings, so that they blur the Holy Spirit and the human spirit. 'If, by their indecisiveness or silence, the dogmatist fathers show their inner uncertainty concerning ... the Holy Spirit ... the ascetic fathers by their copious words reveal the same state of consciousness even more clearly' (*Pillar* 81, 83, 90).

The final shock comes from the LITURGY. Eastern and western theologians tend to agree in crediting the East with more prominent invocations of the Spirit, especially in the liturgy. Florensky turns to the Slavonic liturgy of PENTECOST, where three prayers appear. The first addresses the Father; the second addresses the Son; the third begins with epithets of the Spirit (emphasis added): 'Eternally *flowing, living, and illuminating Spring*, consubstantial with the Father, *enabling Power*, You who wonderfully *perfected* the economy of human salvation...' Florensky notes that according to the meaning of the day, to the place of the third PRAYER, and to the opening epithets, one expects the prayer to continue, '"O Holy Spirit" or "O Comforter" or "King of Truth" or some other name of the Third Hypostasis of the Holy Trinity... This expectation is so natural', Florensky continues, 'that, in listening to the prayer, one inevitably hears something like this and remains convinced that it is addressed to the Holy Spirit. But that is not in fact the case. Here is the immediate continuation of the prayer ... : *"O Christ our God."*' And yet Florensky finds it 'ridiculous to see in this incompleteness ... a defect' because the Spirit promises 'only a betrothal', 'a kiss of the Bride', before the prayers 'Come Holy Spirit' and 'Thy Kingdom come' shall be fulfilled (*Pillar* 87–8, 91, 81, 101–4).

If Florensky is only bemused and not alarmed that the Spirit retires behind the Son, that is because he has left the distance-crossing model behind. The Spirit, however anonymous, is anonymous not as crossing a distance, but as *relating to the Son.* The Son and Spirit do not trade off a baton in a relay: they *interact.* They inter-relate, even they do so in a process such that as one steps forwards the other steps back. They appear on stage together; they dance. And that makes all the difference. If they appear together, neither is dispensable. If they inter-relate, neither is superfluous. This is the second pattern: not crossing a distance, but joining a community, a dance; not linear, but interactive. And that pattern shows up in many and various ways, in versions where the Spirit is depicted not only as retiring, but also as coming to the fore.

In the twentieth century theologians as diverse as R. Norris (1930–2005), R. Jenson (b. 1930), R. Williams (b. 1950), and S. Coakley (b. 1951) direct us to Romans as the place where the second, joining model of the Trinity is at home. 'When we cry "Abba! Father!" it is that very Spirit bearing witness with our spirit that we are children of God, and if children, then heirs, heirs of God and joint heirs with Christ – if, in fact, we suffer with him so that we may also be glorified with him' (Rom. 8:16–17). In this passage, the Trinity is not something that Christians 'stand off from and gawk reverently [at] from a safe distance. On the contrary, their worship is a kind of participation in the relations among the members of the Trinity' (Norris, 'Trinity' 20–1). In this passage, the Spirit relates Christians to the Father, identifies them with the Son, and incorporates them into its own, Trinitarian community. The Spirit, in short, makes the Trinity a community to join. Florensky puts it like this:

> 'But more than three? Yes, there can be more than three – through the acceptance of new hypostases into the interior of the life of the Three. But these new hypostases are not members which support the Subject of the Truth, and therefore they are not inwardly necessary for this subject's absoluteness. They are conditional hypostases, which can be but do not have to be in the Subject of the Truth. Therefore, they cannot be called hypostases in the strict sense, and it is better to call them deified persons (*Pillar* 380).

Human beings become therefore not the hosts but the guests at the Trinitarian feast that Christians see prefigured in the hospitality of Abraham (Gen. 18:1–8), the Last Supper (Matt. 26:20–9 and pars.), the Eucharistic celebration, and the wedding of the Lamb (Rev. 19:9): 'you prepare a table before me ... my cup overflows ... I shall dwell in the house of the LORD my whole life long' (Ps. 23:5–6).

This can sound otherworldly and disembodied, but to interpret it in that way would be a mistake. PAUL associates the Spirit's catching Gentiles up into the Trinitarian life with the RESURRECTION of the BODY: in a dense phrase he identifies all three members of the Trinity – the Spirit, Jesus, and the one who raised Jesus, the Father – by the body of Jesus dead and raised. Significantly, they appear again in a clause about the work of the Spirit in joining other mortal bodies for Jesus' sake into that Trinitarian raising: 'If the Spirit of him who raised Jesus from the dead dwells in you, he who raised Christ from the dead will give life to your mortal bodies also through his Spirit that dwells in you' (Rom. 8:11). This applies not only in bodily death and resurrection, but also in bodily suffering ('if ... we suffer with him', Rom. 8:17) and weakness ('the Spirit helps us in our weakness; for we do not know how to pray as we ought, but that very Spirit intercedes with sighs too deep for words', Rom. 8:26). This picture is strikingly different from that of the Spirit merely conveying information to us. Here it is rather us whom the Spirit conveys into the Trinitarian life. And this life is not all otherworldly, but with and through our bodies.

JOHN OF DAMASCUS suggests a summary of how this works. The Spirit *rests upon* and *radiates from* the body of the Son. The 'resting' is no stillness or lack of activity, but the place in which the Spirit is to be found. The 'radiation' is a constant going out, in illumination, expansion, dilation, witness, and celebration. And 'the body of the Son' rings in all its analogical registers: the Spirit rests on the body of the Son in the BAPTISM of the historical Jesus; the Spirit rests on the body of the Son in expanding the Church; the Spirit rests on the body of the Son in the consecration of the bread and wine in the EUCHARIST; the Spirit rests on the body of the Son in the resurrection of the dead. In all these cases the Spirit both relates to the Son and gives a gift to the Son – and is so neither dispensable nor superfluous. And in all these cases the Spirit does not float free of bodies, but sticks close to matter for the Son's sake, because the Son re-befriended the body in the INCARNATION.

Although the relationship between the Son and the Spirit remains a point of contention between eastern and western Christianity (see *FILIOQUE*), this language of the Spirit resting on and radiating from the body of the Son provides a possible basis for rapprochement. It also has consequences for the reading of NT narratives and for looking at Christian art. It means first that you can see the Spirit at work in Trinitarian epiphanies or appearances in iconic stories of Jesus. The Spirit hovers over the womb of Mary at the ANNUNCIATION. The Spirit appears over the waters of Christ's baptism in the Jordan. The Spirit drives Jesus into the wilderness thereafter. The Spirit figures in the clouds that accompany the TRANSFIGURATION that comes upon Jesus at prayer. The Spirit also rests upon the dead body of Jesus in the resurrection. And the Spirit rests on and radiates from the body of Christ in the Church, in descending upon the disciples at Pentecost.

The question of the personal pronoun to be used for the Spirit is a problem derived from the fact that the word for Spirit is famously neuter in Greek, masculine in Latin and German, and feminine in Hebrew and Syriac. Romans 8:22–3, 26 associates the Spirit with labour pains, which the Spirit seems at once to cause (as if gendering the Spirit male) and to express (as if gendering the Spirit female). Rupert of Deutz (*ca* 1075–1129) portrays the Spirit as a mother bird incubating future Christians to be (re)hatched from the font (*DO* 7). Thomas AQUINAS portrays the Spirit as 'the semen of the Father' bearing him new sons (Rom. 8:17). In either case, this pattern remains: the Spirit expands the identity of Christ in the most bodily of metaphors. The Spirit becomes, you might say, paraphysical, befriending and accompanying the physical for Christ's sake, making holiness in people, places, and things.

S. Brock, *The Holy Spirit in the Syrian Baptismal Tradition*, 3rd edn (Gorgias Press, 2008).
S. Coakley, *On Desiring God: An Essay 'On the Trinity'* (Cambridge University Press, in press).
R. W. Jenson, *The Triune Identity* (Fortress Press, 1982).
E. F. Rogers, Jr, *After the Spirit: A Constructive Pneumatology from Resources Outside the Modern West* (Eerdmans, 2005).
ed., *The Holy Spirit: Classic and Contemporary Readings* (Wiley-Blackwell, 2009).

Eugene F. Rogers, Jr

Holy Week: see Calendar, Liturgical.

HOMILETICS Today the word 'homiletics' primarily describes an academic field of theological enquiry involving the study of preaching – its history, theology, and practice – and the analysis of sermons – their composition, delivery, and reception. The term 'homiletics' is drawn from the Greek *homilia*, meaning 'conversation' or 'discussion', the Latin cognate of which is *sermo*, from which the term 'sermon' is derived. Originally, 'homiletics' and 'homiletical' were employed to refer not to the academic study of preaching but to the practice of preaching, to aspects of the actual event of crafting sermons and delivering them in worship or other settings. The continuing use of the word 'homily' to refer to a sermon is a legacy of this earlier use of 'homiletics'. While contemporary homiletics as a theological academic discipline is found in a variety of religious traditions – Judaism and Islam, for example – the vast majority of homiletical literature has been generated by the Christian tradition.

AUGUSTINE'S *On Christian Doctrine* (*De doctrina christiana*) is generally considered to be the first sustained and comprehensive work in homiletics. We can already discern in this very earliest treatment a tension that has continued to be felt through the history of homiletics, namely the question of whether preaching is mainly a form of public speaking like all others (with the exception that it involves religious themes), or whether it is a unique and theologically shaped form of address. Augustine provides some comfort to both sides of this debate. On the one hand, as a teacher of classical rhetoric before becoming a pastor and a theologian, Augustine discusses preaching by employing the larger and familiar rhetorical categories outlined by Cicero (106–43 BC), such as speaker, hearers, and style of speech. On the other hand, Augustine considers the NT to be the speech act par excellence, and he employs the rhetorical styles and strategies of the biblical writers as a way to correct and finally to transform the 'secular' and morally neutral Ciceronian rhetoric.

This tension between preaching as a form of public rhetoric and preaching as theologically governed speech can be seen partially as the result of underlying currents in the developing Christian Church. Because Christianity originated as a movement within Judaism, the earliest Christian preaching modelled itself on images of inspired prophetic address in the OT and on the methods of biblical interpretation and application found in synagogue preaching more than it relied on the canons of classical rhetoric. The idea of preaching as charismatic, biblically shaped speech can be seen in the account of Jesus' preaching in Luke 4 and in the reports of sermons in the book of Acts (e.g., Peter's PENTECOST sermon in Acts 2). While these are surely the literary creations of the author of Luke to Acts, they almost certainly reflect the basic patterns of early Christian preaching in terms of direct address, biblical citations, and call for faithful and ethical response. The letters of PAUL, however, already display some features of Greek rhetoric, and as the Church became Hellenized and then Latinized, the marks of classical rhetoric increased in its preaching. As preaching became more and more formal, took its place as an element of stable liturgy, developed as an instrument for the building up of congregations, and became a practice that needed to be taught to larger and larger numbers of clergy, the more rhetorical features and categories assumed prominence.

In the medieval period, the ingredients for the later academic discipline of homiletics began to take shape, as evidenced by the appearance of a burst of homiletical textbooks, collectively called *Artes predicandi*, providing practical counsel on sermon structure and content. One of the earliest of these, and in many ways the most influential, was Alan of Lille's (*ca* 1125–1202) *The Art of Preaching*, which appeared around 1200. By the middle of the thirteenth century, homiletics was established as an academic discipline in many European universities. With the reorganization of theological curricula that occurred in universities in the early nineteenth century, under the influence of F. SCHLEIERMACHER and others, homiletics became, along with liturgics, catechetics, poimenics (pastoral care), and archagics (mission), a branch of PRACTICAL THEOLOGY, that is, theology reflecting on the work of the Church and its ministry.

The continuing influence of rhetoric upon homiletics can be seen in the fact that many teachers of homiletics in the nineteenth century, especially in the English-speaking world, were known as professors of 'sacred rhetoric'. In the latter part of that century, however, homiletics experienced something of a crisis when classical rhetoric gradually disappeared from university curricula. Deprived of its traditional academic conversation partner, and relegated to the region of PRACTICAL THEOLOGY, which was increasingly viewed as 'applied' theology rather than a generative theological field, homiletics in the late nineteenth and early twentieth centuries became preoccupied with matters of technique and nuts-and-bolts practicality. Increasingly, the homiletical literature became dominated by books of practical advice written by practitioners, and original theological and theoretical research in the field declined.

At least five developments in the twentieth and twenty-first centuries, however, have reinvigorated the discipline of homiletics. First, there has been a move from classical rhetoric to HERMENEUTICS as an academic framework for reflection on homiletics. The theology of K. BARTH, with its strong emphasis on preaching as an event of the Word of God and with its rejection of rhetorical strategies in sermons, had an enormous impact on homiletics. Even among homileticians who did not embrace the full array of Barthian claims, the idea of preaching as an event of biblical hermeneutics took root. Sermons, instead of being viewed as religious content arranged in patterns derived from rhetoric, could be understood to be reverberations generated and shaped by encounters with the biblical texts themselves. Subsequent developments in biblical interpretation, such as the so-called 'new hermeneutic', with its emphasis upon the eventfulness of biblical language, and literary and rhetorical criticism, have furthered the connection between homiletics and biblical hermeneutics.

Second, homiletics began to incorporate literary theory and poetics. In the last third of the twentieth century, homiletics, especially in the USA, began actively to engage literary theory as a way of fashioning a new kind of effective preaching. Inspired by thinkers such as NT scholar A. Wilder (1895–1993), whose work emphasized literary imagination and the rhetorical inventiveness of early Christian preaching, homiletics initiated experiments integrating sermons with features of other literary genres, especially narrative, PARABLE, poetry, dialogue, and short stories. The result was that sermons broke out of traditional patterns ('three points and a poem') and assumed a wide variety of creative forms.

Third, homiletics has seen a new emphasis on the hearer. Recent homiletical theory has afforded a much larger place to the role of the hearer and to the process of listening to sermons. This began in the 1940s and 1950s essentially as an attempt to factor into the equation of preaching insights gained from psychology. It was realized that listeners to sermons were not clones of each other or blank tablets upon which the sermon could be inscribed, but highly individual, and in some ways idiosyncratic, processors of information. More recently, however, psychological motifs have been supplemented, and to some degree replaced, by sociological and cultural themes. Homiletics has increasingly recognized that most congregations, as homogenous as they may appear, are in fact composed of clusters of listening groups, marked off by age, gender, ethnicity, class, and other social constructs. The effect of this new framing of the preaching context has been twofold. First, many homileticians today encourage preachers to assume multiple approaches to sermons in terms of language, theme, and structure in order to address the multiplicity of the hearers. Second, some homileticians have fashioned the image of the 'roundtable pulpit', that is, preaching that involves not just one-way proclamation but occurs in the midst of congregational conversation and response.

Fourth, homiletics has been influenced by conversation with communication theory. In the middle of the twentieth century, some homiletical theories began to be developed around scientific 'source–channel–receiver' concepts of human communication. More recently, these approaches have advanced and expanded into explorations of the impact of electronic media upon how hearers participate in the event of preaching and also into experiments in the use of media in sermons. A recent challenge to homiletics has been the rise of the internet age and the alteration this has inevitably brought to the ways that hearers receive and process communication.

Fifth, homiletics has benefited from the fact that in the last half century practical theology has been able to break free from the label 'applied theology' and redefine itself as a generative field of theology, one that studies theologically laden and historically shaped religious practices. One result of this development is that preaching is no longer viewed as merely the practical product of wisdom developed elsewhere but rather as a living expression of theological activity performed 'on the ground'. Also, homiletics as a theoretical and academic discipline is now taught at the research level in a number of universities and theological schools.

O. C. Edwards, *A History of Preaching* (Abingdon Press, 2004).

J. F. Kay, *Preaching and Theology* (Chalice Press, 2007).

R. Lischer, ed., *The Company of Preachers: Wisdom on Preaching, Augustine to the Present* (Eerdmans, 2002).

THOMAS G. LONG

HOMOOUSIOS The Council of NICAEA established a key feature of the later DOCTRINE of the TRINITY in defining the Son of God as *homoousios* (Greek for 'of the same substance') with the Father (see *ABBA*). The term was adopted chiefly because it was known to be unacceptable to Arius (*ca* 250–336), despite nervousness on the part of some that it implied a material relationship between Son and Father (i.e., making the Son quite literally a 'chip off the old block'). Theologically, the word seems to have been understood to imply not so much that the Son and Father were of equal rank as that the Son was generated by the Father in a unique way (viz., not by an act of will, by which all other reality came to be), and that the Son therefore shared to some extent in the Father's way of being.

The term was reaffirmed at the First Council of CONSTANTINOPLE, by which time it was taken to mean that the Son is not a lesser God: everything that the Father is, the Son is also, except that the Father is the begetter of the Son and the Son the one begotten by the Father, so that these relationships are the individuating idioms that mark out the Son and Father as distinct HYPOSTASES sharing the same substance or *ousia*. The still later Christological definition of the Council of CHALCEDON further specifies that Christ is not only *homoousios* with the Father as regards his divinity, but also *homoousios* with all other human beings as regards his humanity: like us in all respects, except for sin (cf. Heb. 4:15).

See also ARIAN CONTROVERSY.

MIKE HIGTON

HOMOSEXUALITY: see SEXUALITY.

HOOKER, RICHARD Queen Elizabeth I (r. 1558–1603) brought stability to the Church of England, a Church clearly Reformed, but still in living continuity with the ancient Catholic tradition. Richard Hooker's (1554–1600) achievement was to set forth, systematically and with theological rigour, a defence of the Elizabethan settlement in the eight volumes of *The Lawes of Ecclesiastical Polity* (1593). His ideas were worked out while he was master of the Temple Church in London, in debate with his colleague, the Puritan W. Travers (*ca* 1550–1635). Travers wished for a further reformation of the Church of England along the lines developed in Geneva (see PURITANISM). He held that SCRIPTURE ordained a particular order and DOCTRINE for the Church, which the Church of England, with its Catholic survivals, hardly demonstrated. Hooker countered this by arguing that Church order is one of the ADIAPHORA of FAITH, which God allows each national community to regulate for itself. He agreed that SCRIPTURE is the ultimate authority, but the reading of Scripture must be guided by reason, by common sense (nature), and by context: 'Words must be taken according to the matter wherof they are uttered' (*Lawes* 1.14.3). Hooker was appreciative of the teachings of T. AQUINAS and also admired J. CALVIN, though he felt the need to oppose what he saw as the narrow and exclusive approaches to discipline and Church governance of Calvin's disciples in England.

Hooker's approach to biblical HERMENEUTICS and Christian dogmatics – moderate and inclusive, irenic and questioning – has been seen since the time of the OXFORD MOVEMENT as expressing the essentials of ANGLICAN THEOLOGY. His 'three legged stool' presents the image of a Church which acknowledges the authority of Scripture, TRADITION, and reason, and which consistently searches for ways of harmonizing these three principles for the more perfect understanding of God's REVELATION. Hooker's approach was seen as particularly valuable for the Episcopal Church in the USA, as its members reconstituted their life after the American Revolution. It supplied a vision of a Church of stability and order, reason and faith, over against what at times seemed the excesses of individualistic and undisciplined evangelicalism.

KEVIN WARD

Hope Certain strands of Greek thinking, as seen in the myth of Pandora's box, denigrate hope as preventing us from being resigned to our destiny. If freedom, as Aristotle asserts, is living according to the necessity of one's existence, then hope, the Christian tradition counters, is living according to God's promised future. Hope energizes life by contradicting the negations of the present through the power of suffering LOVE.

Dogmatic studies prior to the REFORMATION tended to treat hope, together with FAITH and love, as a theological VIRTUE. Like faith and love, hope is a 'theological' virtue because God is both its object and its source. Hope is a gift of God, though it entails human effort as well and, as PAUL suggests, is closely connected to patience and passion: 'For in hope we were saved. Now hope that is seen is not hope. For who hopes for what is seen? But if we hope for what we do not see, we wait for it with patience' (Rom. 8:24–5). Hope is the primary virtue of the human being's pilgrim journey through time. The debilitating disease of human existence is denial that we are 'on the way'. Hope, while directing us to what is beyond time, maintains our creaturely temporal existence. The proximate threats to hope are suffering and failure; the extreme trial of hope is DEATH. Hope, then, is fragile, but nonetheless an absolute condition of life. Where hope ceases, the powers of SIN, evil, and death enter.

According to AUGUSTINE 'hope deals only with good things, and only with those that lie in the future, and which pertain to the [person] who cherishes that hope' (*Ench.* 2.8). Augustine proffered the TRADITION's standard way of conceiving the inter-relation of faith, hope, and love. Hope stems from faith, from which it receives its object, and serves love, which achieves its object. It keeps faith alive and, partaking of love's desire, opens the way for perfect love. Facing the future, hope relies on God finally to realize what faith partially grasps and what love most desires. Thus, hope without faith would be blind. Without love it would be futile. But faith and love without hope wither in the present oppositions.

T. AQUINAS is the second magisterial theologian of hope as a theological virtue (*ST* 2/2.17–22). Four characteristics emerge in Aquinas' treatment. First, hope is directed towards a future good, difficult *but not impossible* to attain. This good is 'eternal life [or happiness], which consists in the enjoyment of God Himself'. We may hope for eternal happiness, because it belongs to God's infinite power 'to lead anyone to an infinite good'. Hope, therefore, differs from natural optimism or human planning because it moves towards a future that only God can give. Second, hope seeks a *future* good. Even though we already participate in God on the way, 'it has not yet appeared what we shall be' (1 John 3:2). What is hoped for is genuinely outstanding. And yet, in the third place, good hope seeks a *possible* good, in a future that may be confidently expected according to God's fidelity. Finally, hope's orientation towards its object is *arduous.* Hope pursues a difficult good, for hope entails the self-giving love involved in following Christ's way. Hope belongs to the *will* rather than the appetite; it is the elevation of the will made possible by GRACE so that the enduring character of hope depends on the love that 'bears all things, believes all things, hopes all things, endures all things' (1 Cor. 13:7).

Sin against hope takes two forms: despair, as the anticipation of what negates us, and presumption, as the unwarranted anticipation of fulfilment. In both cases we seek an illusory release from our pilgrim existence and expect the security of our lives other than from the hand of God. Servile (as opposed to filial) fear destroys the wayfarer's movement towards the promised good and finds its only antidote in hope.

In the modern period Christian theology increasingly focuses on hope for this world in line with the third petition of the LORD'S PRAYER, 'Your will be done on earth as in heaven.' From the period of the Reformation the character of hope has had much to do with the timing of the KINGDOM OF GOD. Hope takes on different shapes in the Lutheran 'TWO KINGDOMS' doctrine, the Reformed doctrine of the rule of Christ (*Herrschaft Christi*) in the world, and the evangelical option of the premillennial or postmillennial reign of Christ (see PREMILLENNIALISM; POSTMILLENNIALISM). In all cases hope takes its shape and power from the shape and power of God's rule. Where God does not rule or will not rule, there is no hope.

The ENLIGHTENMENT insistence that reason can take the place of hope as the human way of managing history, or that hope can be manufactured by the manipulation of nature and history, prompted theology to take history with utter seriousness and to treat the relation between the world's hope and Christian hope. Replacing God's PROVIDENCE, the secular DOCTRINE of progress lodged deep within the process of history and the human direction of history made hope seem redundant. Over against these trends, twentieth-century theology sought the relevance of hope to a world ravaged by two world wars, the HOLOCAUST, the threat of nuclear destruction, the degradation of nature, and the seemingly incorrigible conditions of POVERTY. Theology has had to confront three responses to this shattering of faith in progress: (1) the temptation to despair and nihilism, (2) the new Stoicism expressed in A. Camus' (1913–60) slogan 'Think clearly, don't hope', and (3) APOCALYPTIC and the politics of fear. In response to these strong anti-hope impulses, modern dogmatics judges it no longer sufficient simply to discuss the virtue of hope. The object of hope becomes not just the being of God as the ultimate good, but the promises and acts of God towards history and the CREATION.

Several movements in which the theological significance of hope has been developed are prominent, the rediscovery of biblical ESCHATOLOGY being the first. Theological reflection on hope becomes inextricably connected to the eschatological character of the kingdom of God and the eschatological dimension of salvation. Hope becomes key to Christian theology because, as K. BARTH claimed, theology is thoroughly eschatological, a theme that was revived by J. Moltmann (b. 1926): 'from first to last, and not merely in the epilogue, Christianity is eschatology, is hope' (*Hope* 16). But hope takes on different contours depending on whether eschatology, for example, is viewed with A. Schweitzer (1875–1965) and R. BULTMANN as realized, with Barth as grounded in God's eternity, with W. Pannenberg (b. 1928) as future proleptically revealed, or with Moltmann as grounded in the Messianic hopes of ISRAEL stemming from the promises of God.

The debate over the theological significance of the RESURRECTION opened a new perspective on hope. The eschatological act of God's raising Christ from the dead orients hope lived in history towards God's new creation of all things. This hope is the awareness of God's *novum* by which we are awakened to the contradictions of God's promises for the world and the power by which we can resist the principalities and powers that negate God's future. In some ways Ernst Bloch's (1885–1977) *The Principle of Hope* (1954–9) was a foil for Moltmann's reflection on hope. Bloch locates hope in historical progress as the animation of movements of freedom towards a new society. Moltmann, too, wants to remove the modern suspicion of hope as a utopian vague aspiration and to see it as an objective, realistic anticipation of just society. But Moltmann is radically different from Bloch in grounding hope not in history but rather in God's act of resurrection. Resurrection hope, nevertheless, is meant for history and creates the peculiar form of history between Christ's resurrection and the new creation of all things, namely, the history of mission (see MISSIOLOGY).

Contemporary theological views of hope have also been deeply affected by the rediscovery of the centrality of the doctrine of the TRINITY for theology. If the Christian community lives *in* the communion of God's own life, hope becomes the gift and power of the HOLY SPIRIT in ways little noticed by the tradition. Hope is empowered by God's very being for the world. This, in turn, has led to many new theological insights on the place of hope in relation to ecology and the BODY. God's hope for the creation and God's intention to indwell creation as God's home lead to energized hope for human rejoicing in embodied existence and peace with all of God's creatures.

Finally, recent theology sees hope trusting in God's promises as the energy of the life of PRAYER, meditation, and doxology. Furthermore, sacramental theology has viewed the sacraments as hope's anticipation of the eschatological reign of God in the midst of everyday suffering and joy: Christians are baptized into the community of hope and eat Christ's meal as the primary sign and realization of hope's yearning under the conditions of history (see BAPTISM; EUCHARIST).

K. Barth, *Church Dogmatics* (T&T Clark, 1961), IV/3, 1.
M. D. Meeks, *Origins of the Theology of Hope* (Fortress Press, 1974).
J. Moltmann, *Theology of Hope: On the Ground and Implication of Christian Eschatology* (SCM, 1967 [1964]).
The Coming of God: Christian Eschatology (Fortress Press, 1996 [1995]).
W. Pannenberg, *Basic Question in Theology: Collected Essays*, 2 vols. (Fortress Press, 1970–1 [1967]).

M. DOUGLAS MEEKS

HOURS, CANONICAL: see DIVINE OFFICE.

HUMAN RIGHTS There is ongoing debate about the origins and foundations of human rights. Some argue that human rights are rooted in the secular ENLIGHTENMENT concept of natural rights, others trace them back to Judeo-Christian influences, and others claim that the fundamental vision of human dignity is inherent in all major RELIGIONS. The 1948 Universal Declaration of Human Rights (UDHR) borrows its language from the American Declaration of Independence (1776) and the French Declaration of the Rights of Man and the Citizen (1789). However, while those declarations were primarily concerned with the rights and responsibilities of the citizen, the UDHR was a response to the catastrophe of World War II and the HOLOCAUST, and it takes the human per se, 'born free and equal in dignity and rights', as the bearer of fundamental rights that take precedence over all other interests. It is an educative and visionary document, which does not claim to describe human beings as they are but to shape a vision of what they might become (and, indeed, must become) in order to avoid the 'barbarous acts' of recent history and achieve 'the highest aspiration of the common people'. There are thirty articles in the Declaration, of which Articles 1 to 21 are concerned with civil and political rights, and the remainder with economic and social rights. Of the fifty-six member states of the United Nations (UN) in 1948, forty-eight voted for the Declaration, and no nation voted against it; there were eight abstentions.

In its privileging of democracy, equality, and political and personal freedom, the Declaration universalizes a set of values associated with the modern secular nation state. The world's religious traditions may agree with some of these principles, but they have their own tried and tested ways of ordering the world, usually in forms of gendered social and religious hierarchies and communal values which come into conflict with rights-based egalitarian individualism. To the extent that a concept analogous to human rights might be found in some religions, this is always understood in the context of the individual's primary responsibility to God and to the believing community. Thus there is an ongoing struggle between religious world views which command passionate allegiance among their followers and which are home to powerful vested interests, and secular, rights-based world views which command just as much passion and are home to just as many vested interests.

Among Christian thinkers, some argue that the lack of a theological perspective and the abstract universalism of the concept 'human rights', detached from any particular cultural, legal, or religious context, renders it incoherent and vulnerable to abuse and manipulation. Others argue that the Christian DOCTRINES of CREATION and INCARNATION lend strong theological support to the idea of universal human rights, vested in the belief that the human is made in the image of God and is therefore endowed with intrinsic dignity, and that in Christ God entered fully into the vulnerability and suffering of the human condition.

Throughout its history the mostly Protestant WORLD COUNCIL OF CHURCHES has strongly supported the concept of human rights and encouraged the UN and its member nations to be active in their defence. The Catholic Church expressed its support for the UN and the concept of human rights in Pope John XXIII's (r. 1958–63) ENCYCLICAL *Pacem in terris* (1963), and there is ongoing advocacy for economic and social rights in Catholic social teaching. However, the Catholic hierarchy remains firmly opposed to the extension of rights to the sexual and reproductive sphere (see ABORTION; PROCREATION). Recent debates about euthanasia and the right to die have also alienated mainstream Catholicism from some aspects of human rights, although there are many Catholics who distance themselves from the Church's official position and support the idea of sexual and reproductive rights, women's rights and, in certain carefully defined circumstances, the right to die.

See also BIOETHICS; THEOLOGICAL ANTHROPOLOGY.

M. R. Ishay, ed., *The Human Rights Reader: Major Political Essays, Speeches, and Documents from the Bible to the Present*, 2nd edn (Routledge, 2007).

R. Ruston, *Human Rights and the Image of God* (SCM, 2004).

TINA BEATTIE

HUMANISM The term 'humanism' was coined in the nineteenth century to characterize a movement associated in the first instance with a set of thinkers in fourteenth- to sixteenth-century Europe who called themselves 'humanists'. Figures usually viewed as representative of early modern humanism include F. Petrarch (1304–74) and L. Valla (*ca* 1405–57) in Italy, and D. Erasmus (1466/9–1536) and T. More (1478–1535) in northern Europe. Among historians, there is no consensus on a definition of 'humanism'. Nevertheless, some of the most influential attempts to characterize the humanism of the Middle Ages, Renaissance, and REFORMATION have suggested complex links between humanism and Christian theology. By contrast, in contemporary western culture, 'humanism' is generally associated with intellectual trends either indifferent or hostile to theology, especially in the forms of the 'secular humanism' championed by the philosopher P. Kurz (b. 1925) and the 'scientific humanism' of the biologist E. O. Wilson (b. 1929).

In the 1950s the émigré scholar P. Kristeller (1905–99) eschewed definitions then at play in American universities and public life, which were anchored to human potentiality or FREE WILL, and offered in a series of lectures a concrete and specific delineation, not of 'humanism', but of what distinguished a group of fourteenth- and fifteenth-century Italian and fifteenth- and sixteenth-century German, French, and English authors from their contemporaries – on what grounds they called themselves 'humanists'. These authors, Kristeller argued, shared an education, the *studia humanitatis*: grammar, rhetoric, history, poetry, and moral philosophy. That education, to which we shall return, endowed two significant sensitivies: to language – words and when they were used, syntax, style, rhetorical techniques – and to history, or, more precisely, to thinking of humankind as existing not simply within time, but along a line of chronology in which each human being could be precisely located.

In 1962, at least in part in reaction to claims on the part of Italian Renaissance scholars to have found the origins of 'humanism' in fourteenth-century Italy, the English medievalist R. Southern (1912–2001) published an article which argued for 'medieval humanism' which accorded dignity to human nature and held the universe to be both intelligible and accessible to human reason. In 1995, in the first volume of a two-volume study of 'Scholastic Humanism', Southern moved closer to Kristeller's definition, in attending to the programme of study of Scholastic theologians, and expanded his own earlier definition to encompass self-knowledge and the affective self. Southern was concerned with linking a group, Scholastic theologians, who have received more opprobrium than most, to the modern age and a cluster of attributes then considered positive.

Southern and Kristeller occupy two durably influential poles in discussions of 'humanism' in past societies. On the one hand is a definition which consciously seeks to link a past moment, a group of thinkers, to the present; on the other, a definition that equally consciously seeks to circumscribe a particular group and distinguish it from all others before and after. For neither, however, was Christianity integral, essential, to the humanism of the thinkers they studied.

In 1959 B. Moeller (b. 1931) published an article, 'Die deutschen Humanisten und die Anfänge der

Reformation', in which he stated, 'No humanism, no Reformation.' Moeller argued that, M. LUTHER aside, 'the Reformation was led by humanists', such as K. Peutinger (1465–1547) and P. Melanchthon (1497–1560). And yet, in the end, Moeller insisted that Luther himself was no humanist (the driving argument of his article), and that the humanists who at first followed the charismatic and electrifying Luther broke with him on the dignity of humankind. Humanism, Moeller argued, preceded the Reformation and ended with it.

In 1963 L. Spitz (1922–2000) argued the case for the deep interdependence of the Reformation and humanism, linking the two explicitly in the term, 'Christian humanism'. After a meticulous review of the literature, Spitz called for a more complex understanding of individual humanists, who were diverse in their engagements, but were all critical of Scholasticism, the increasing formalism of religious life, its concomitant loss of immediacy, its rote sacramentalism, as well as the value the Church placed on hierarchy and priests. The foundation for this criticism, Spitz wrote, was a return to classical Christian sources. Spitz differentiated among those who had been classified as 'German humanists', and located Luther firmly among them, in his education and in his particular approach to reform – even as he underlined Luther's anthropology and its divergence from the optimism attributed to humanism.

For most of these scholars, 'humanism' was inseparable in some way from 'human', and with it, a sense that human beings' potentialities were not limited by their nature. Among them, Spitz acknowledged most explicitly the artificiality of the construction of 'humanist' in medieval and early modern Christianity as somehow occupying a separate mental world from the teachings of the Church on fallen humanity. For these scholars, 'humanists' were more optimistic about humankind's ability to change and improve. 'Christian humanists', as Spitz suggested, studied the Christian past, using 'literary studies', as Moeller had called them, but represented an eddy, a dead end, in the face of Luther's and then J. CALVIN's radical anthropology. The overwhelming majority of scholars differentiated 'Christian humanism' from Italian or Renaissance or even medieval humanism: 'Christian humanists' were northern Europeans, who sought to foster a 'Christian Renaissance' that paralleled the 'Italian Renaissance', which was itself then constructed as 'secular'.

In 1970 C. Trinkaus (b. 1911), who had studied with Kristeller at Columbia, published *In Our Image and Likeness: Humanity and Divinity in Italian Humanist Thought*. Trinkaus proposed a very different approach to the question, what is the relationship of 'humanism' to Christianity? Rather than positing a priori a shared sense of human nature, Trinkaus proposed to study how Italian Renaissance thinkers, primarily the humanists, defined the nature, condition, and destiny of humankind within the framework of Christianity. Trinkaus argued that Renaissance thinkers could not be abstracted from the Christian world in which they lived. He revealed in the most influential humanists – from Petrarch to Valla – close biblical readings informed by deep reading in the Christian fathers.

In 1977, M. O. Boyle (b. 1943) connected the particular emphasis of the *studia humanitatis* on the historicity of language to Erasmus' work on the Greek NT. Boyle argued that Erasmus' approach to the texts of the NT was informed by a conceptualization of language itself that arose from the *studia humanitatis*: a sense, there in Valla's work on eloquence, of each word's existence within time, spoken in historically specific human societies.

Boyle pointed to an essential characteristic of the thinking of those whom many had identified as Italian humanists: an intellectual commitment to philology, a conviction that words are spoken and written in specific times and places. That sense of language as historical was taken up by evangelicals in the sixteenth century, in their own attentiveness to Jesus' speaking and preaching. It links Erasmus' *textus receptus* to the beginnings of modern biblical HERMENEUTICS. Thus, if we return to Kristeller's narrow definition of a shared education, that education provided ways of thinking about Christian sacred SCRIPTURE that would open new horizons of thinking about Christian theology in the sixteenth century.

Contemporary appropriations of the term 'humanism' centre on the affirmation of human dignity and worth, often in reaction to what is seen as the diminishment of the human in relation to the divine associated with traditional forms of Christianity in particular. The term began to be appropriated to designate an alternative to traditional Christian FAITH and practice in the early twentieth century, with the 1933 publication of *A Humanist Manifesto* (now generally referred to as *Humanist Manifesto I*) by the philosopher R. W. Sellars (1880–1973) and Unitarian minister R. Bragg (1902–79). Though the beliefs outlined in this document include the rejection of REVELATION as a source of truth in favour of a reliance on reason alone, its authors nevertheless define their project as that of 'religious humanism'. They stress, however, that it is a new religion, with a specifically secular orientation designed to supplant previous forms of organized religious life. Its purpose is 'the complete realization of human personality' (§8) through 'a heightened sense of personal life and in a cooperative effort to promote social well-being' (§9) rather than through practices of PRAYER or devotion to any transcendent deity.

The principles enshrined in this first *Manifesto* were given organizational form with the founding of the American Humanist Association in 1941. Subsequently, the AHA has overseen the release of the successor documents, *A Humanist Manifesto II* (1983) and

A Humanist Manifesto III (2003), neither of which designate humanism as a religion. The term has over this same period been used by others, including the International Humanist and Ethical Union (founded in 1952), an umbrella organization analogous to the World Council of Churches that unites a range of humanist groups, and the Council for Secular Humanism, which split off from the AHA in 1979.

As already noted, early modern humanists (especially in northern Europe) often had keen interest in theology. Many of the most influential theologians of the sixteenth century, both Protestant and Catholic, were products of humanist-inspired curricula and exemplified humanist commitments in their writing; and the humanist emphasis on the careful study of original sources (both biblical and non-biblical) in their original languages has played a central role in western Christian theological education and scholarship ever since. By contrast, contemporary humanism's characteristic rejection of revelation as the source and measure of ultimate truth places it in obvious tension with Christianity. At the same time, all major Christian Churches share the humanist emphasis on the importance of promoting human dignity, leading writers such as J. Maritain (1882–1973) to defend Christianity as the truest form of humanism. From a strictly Christian theological perspective, the problem with 'secular humanism' as it has emerged in twentieth-century polemics is threefold. First, its ontology does not acknowledge any divinity. Second, its epistemology places the measure of truth exclusively in human reason. Third, its anthropology does not acknowledge sin as Christian theologians have tended to understand it (viz., as a force that vitiates and distorts humanity's efforts at self-improvement).

A. J. Balfour, *Theism and Humanism* (Hodder and Stoughton, 1915).
M. O. Boyle, *Erasmus on Language and Method in Theology* (University of Toronto Press, 1977).
P. Kurtz, *In Defense of Secular Humanism* (Prometheus Books, 1983).
J. Maritain, *Integral Humanism: Temporal and Spiritual Problems of a New Christendom* (Scribner, 1968).
C. E. Trinkaus, *In Our Image and Likeness: Humanity and Divinity in Italian Humanist Thought* (Constable, 1970).

Lee Palmer Wandel and Ian A. McFarland

Humankind: see Theological Anthropology.

Humanocentrism: see Anthropocentrism.

Hyperdulia: see Dulia.

Hypostasis In theology after the Cappadocian Fathers, the Greek term *hypostasis* was used to refer to the threeness of the Trinity: God is one substance in three hypostases (traditionally named 'Father', 'Son', and 'Holy Spirit'). In Christological formulations derived from the Council of Chalcedon, the term was also used to refer to the oneness of Christ: he is two natures, divine and human, in one hypostasis. Because *persona* is the theological term used for these purposes in Latin, 'hypostasis' is often, perhaps misleadingly, translated as 'person'.

In early theological usage, something might be called a 'hypostasis' simply in order to emphasize its real existence (as opposed to existence simply in thought), though perhaps with an emphasis on the *distinct* existence of that reality. The first of these emphases still dominates in the anathemas of the Council of Nicaea, where 'hypostasis' is taken as a synonym of *ousia* (substance); the second emphasis, occasionally present in earlier authors, came to play an increasing role after Nicaea, until the Cappadocians established a clear distinction between *ousia* as the name for what is common to the Persons of the Trinity, and *hypostasis* as the name for their distinctness: each Person is a hypostasis precisely to the extent that it is characterized by specific individuating characteristics (or *idiomata*). The Son, for example, is everything that the Father is (i.e., with respect to *ousia*) except that the Son is begotten and the Father the one who begets (the particular characteristics of their respective hypostases). In the case of the Persons of the Trinity, these individuating characteristics are given only by the ways in which the Persons relate among themselves. In these contexts, 'hypostasis' plays a fairly bare grammatical or logical role (though a vital one). Later theologians have sometimes, however, found grounds for a richer account of 'relational personhood' which may be applied analogously to the Persons of the Trinity and to human persons.

Hypostasis was later appropriated in Christology to give a name to the unity of Christ: the God-man is one hypostasis, in which the divine Word has united humanity to itself (see Hypostatic Union). In this context, hypostasis can have two different shades of meaning. On the one hand, it can mean something like 'distinguishable reality', and the insistence that Christ is one hypostasis is tied to the joint claims that (1) one may no longer speak adequately about the divine Word without speaking of the human life that this Word has taken on, and (2) one cannot properly speak about this human life without identifying it as the human life of the divine Word. To refer either to Christ's humanity or to his divinity in abstraction is to identify each incompletely. To use a different theological idiom, one could say that to tell the story of the human being Jesus is to tell the story of the Word's way of being for the world, and to tell the story of the Word is to tell the story of the human life the Word has taken on for the world. For this shade of meaning of 'hypostasis' there is a certain symmetry to the ways in which consideration of the hypostasis relates to consideration of the two natures, human and divine, united in it, and 'hypostasis' refers first and foremost to the composite divine–human whole produced by the hypostatic union.

On the other hand, the emphasis in the definition of 'hypostasis' can fall on the idea of 'that which subsists by itself'. With this emphasis, the consideration of the two natures is much more asymmetrical, with the emphasis falling on the claim that the humanity of Christ has no independent existence, but exists only as the outworking in history of the Word's act of being: the hypostasis of the God-man *is* the hypostasis of the Word (see *Logos*). Here 'hypostasis' language points to the idea that the *Logos* is the one metaphysical subject of the Incarnation – though it does not refer to *psychological* subjectivity, as if the human nature of Jesus lacked a human mind, will, or subjective centre. The idea is that Jesus' humanity has no independent existence – it is not a *distinct* hypostasis because it does not subsist by itself; it exists, and is what it is, only in so far as it exists in union with the *Logos* (see Anhypostasia). It is this second shade of meaning that is in view when one says that 'hypostasis' language answers a 'Who?' question (as opposed to the 'What?' questions answered by 'nature' language). Whom does one meet when one meets Christ? One meets God the divine Word. It is fundamentally the Word who is at work, who is sharing the divine life in its Word-shaped form with the world, in this fully human life.

Mike Higton

Hypostatic Union In Christology after the Council of Chalcedon, the 'hypostatic union' is both (1) the act by which a divine nature and a human nature are united in one hypostasis, and (2) the state of unity that results from that act.

From the first perspective, the emphasis falls on the act of assumption by which the divine *Logos* actively unites to its existing divine nature a new human nature. In other words, the hypostasis in question is the hypostasis of the *Logos*, the subject or ground of the act of union.

From the second perspective, the emphasis falls on the accomplished fact of the union, and on the symmetrical holding together of the divine and the human natures in one hypostasis. Sometimes, where the meaning of 'hypostasis' is taken from the Trinitarian theology of the Cappadocian Fathers, this perspective leads to an emphasis on the collection of individuating characteristics (or *idiomata*) of the two natures united (i.e., both the *idiomata* that pertain to the humanity and those that pertain to the divinity), which together fully mark out or individuate this one divine–human reality.

Hypostatic union is sometimes distinguished from the 'union according to nature' associated with miaphysite Christologies, in which the unity of Christ is a matter of a new divine–human nature in which the defining properties of divinity and humanity have been united to become the defining properties of the one God-man. It is also distinguished from the 'union according to grace' held to be available to all Christians, who can by adoption become co-heirs with Christ – becoming by grace what he is by nature.

See also Eutychianism; Miaphysitism; Nestorianism; Syriac Christian Theology.

Mike Higton

Iconoclasm Iconoclasm (literally 'breaking of images') refers to Christian opposition to the production and use of religious images in private or public worship. The prohibition of images has traditionally been based on the Ten Commandments: 'You shall not make for yourself an idol, whether in the form of anything that is in heaven above, or that is on the earth beneath, or that is in the water under the earth. You shall not bow down to them or worship them' (Exod. 20:4–5; cf. Deut. 5:8–9). The idea that the production of representational art leads to its worship – in other words, to idolatry – has been used to justify the destruction of images at various times throughout the history of the Church.

The traditional scholarly explanation for the absence of religious art during the Church's first two centuries (the earliest examples are preserved in the house-church at Dura Europas, dated to *ca* 240) has been that early Christians adhered rigorously to the Mosaic commandment. Others, however, view the absence of artefacts as the result of historical accident, arguing that the literary sources do not yet associate the production of religious art with idolatrous practices in this period. Patristic references to images are scattered and have been interpreted in various ways by scholars; problems also exist with regard to the authenticity of certain texts. Nevertheless, early Christian writers, including Tertullian, Clement of Alexandria (*ca* 150–*ca* 215), Eusebius of Caesarea (*ca* 265–*ca* 340), and Epiphanius of Salamis (*ca* 315–403), did express hostility to religious images. Occasionally this attitude reflected a belief in the value of 'imageless' prayer over physical or visionary reminders of God's manifestations in the created universe. Some of these texts were employed for polemical purposes in later Church councils, but without consideration of their historical or theological backgrounds.

The defence of religious images against more organized opposition, which now began to be called 'iconoclasm', developed in the course of the seventh century, especially in the eastern Churches. Iconoclast polemic against the production of painted panel paintings, or 'icons', and growing popular belief in the link of icons with divine power may have emerged first in Jewish and Muslim circles and only later in some groups of Christians. This forms the backdrop for the first major outbreak of iconoclasm as an organized policy. From approximately 730 the Byzantine emperor Leo III ('the Isaurian', r. 717–41) began to enforce iconoclast policies within the Byzantine Church: according to later, and certainly biased, historical sources, he, and to an even greater extent his son Constantine V (r. 741–75), ordered the destruction of all religious art, including not only panel icons, but also wall paintings and mosaics in churches. These emperors received the backing of a significant number of bishops in their enforcement of iconoclasm. During this period of Byzantine history (in two phases, from 730 to 787 and 815 to 843), theological arguments both for and against religious images developed further. Most iconoclast writings were subsequently destroyed, but enough fragments survive (mainly in the writings of iconophile, or 'image-loving', opponents) for us to reconstruct at least some of their main arguments.

At the beginning of the controversy, iconoclasts appear to have focused primarily on the charge of idolatry. This appeal to the Decalogue was answered in various ways by iconophile thinkers such as John of Damascus: the most usual method was to list examples in the OT – indeed in Exodus itself – of God himself overturning the commandment as, for example, when he ordered Moses to construct cherubim above the ark of the tabernacle (Exod. 25:18–22). Philosophical and Christological arguments followed, focusing, respectively, on the relationship of an image to its prototype and on the significance of the incarnation for the possibility of religious art. It is not clear which side was the first to introduce these lines of thought, but credit is usually given to John of Damascus. Constantine V, who took a keen interest in theological debate and was rigorous in his enforcement of iconoclast policies, appears to have opposed all manner of popular practices, including veneration of saints, relics, and the Virgin Mary. Judging by the *Horos* (or 'Definition') of the iconoclast Council of Hiereia (754), however, it appears that the majority of iconoclast bishops focused exclusively on religious art as an innovation within Church tradition which had no basis in apostolic or early Christian practice. The triumph of the defenders of icons at the Second Council of Nicaea (787) and again, definitively, in 843 led to the acceptance of a coherent 'theology of images' in the Orthodox Church. This theological position was enriched in the course of about a century by the sophisticated, often philosophical, arguments of John of Damascus, Theodore the Studite, and the patriarch Nicephorus of Constantinople (*ca* 760–829).

Western responses to the Byzantine iconoclastic controversy varied. Whereas Pope Hadrian I (r. 772–95) sided with iconophiles and accepted the decisions of Nicaea II, Frankish theologians at the court of Charlemagne (747–814) maintained an iconoclast position. After studying a Latin translation of the acts of Nicaea II, they rejected its decisions at a synod in Frankfurt in 794, expressing a moderate form of iconoclasm which allowed religious art in churches for educational reasons, but banned the veneration of images as idolatrous.

Iconoclasm featured again in the period of the REFORMATION, especially in England, in the course of the sixteenth century. Here the opposition to religious art was connected with a more general suppression of all forms of Christian devotion that were not believed to be based on scriptural or apostolic authority. The reformers also identified 'abuses', verging on idolatrous practice, associated with monasteries, the Virgin Mary, saints and their relics, and religious images. This led to the destruction of sculpture, wall paintings, and other artistic representations throughout England.

See also DULIA; ICONS AND ICONOGRAPHY.

E. Duffy, *The Stripping of the Altars: Traditional Religion in England 1400–1580* (Yale University Press, 1992).

E. Kitzinger, 'The Cult of Images before Iconoclasm', *Dumbarton Oaks Papers* 7 (1954), 86–150.

K. Parry, *Depicting the Word: Byzantine Iconophile Thought of the Eighth and Ninth Centuries* (Brill, 1996).

J. Pelikan, *Imago Dei: The Byzantine Apologia for Icons* (Yale University Press, 1990).

MARY B. CUNNINGHAM

ICONOSTASIS A transliteration of the Greek word for 'icon stand', iconostasis can be used of any such stand, but it refers primarily to the screen of ICONS that separates the altar from the nave in Eastern Orthodox, as well as EASTERN CATHOLIC, churches. This screen evolved from the Byzantine templon: a low rail that marked off the chancel area from the rest of the church and which (like the iconostasis) could be entered by way of either a central door or one of two side doors. The practice of hanging icons from the templon rail led to its gradual augmentation, culminating in the fifteenth and sixteenth centuries in the complete visual barrier between altar and nave that is the modern iconostasis.

There are liturgical rubrics governing the arrangement of icons on the iconostasis, as well as which persons are allowed to pass through each of the three doors. Critics of the iconostasis worry that this highly formalized separation of the altar from the rest of the church effectively cuts off the LAITY from the celebration of the EUCHARIST. Its defenders counter that the iconostasis symbolizes the way in which heaven (the altar) is united with earth (the nave) by way of the intercession of Christ and the saints. In this way, at the same time that the opacity of the iconostasis accentuates the ontological difference between heaven and earth, its constituent icons highlight the incarnational connection between them in a way that furthers the inclusion of the whole people of God in the Church's Eucharistic worship.

IAN A. MCFARLAND

ICONS AND ICONOGRAPHY An icon is a visible image or representation of something existing or imagined – divine or created. According to Genesis 1:26–7 God made humanity in the divine image, while Colossians 1:15 refers to the Son as the visible image (*eikon*) of the invisible God. Thus, in its broadest definition, the term 'icon' can be applied to Christ, human persons, sacramental elements, painted portraits, photographs, and even buildings. With reference to pictorial art, however, an icon is any artistic image especially created for devotional purpose, including images in paint or mosaic on walls; woven or embroidered on textiles; enamelled on silver; or carved on gems, precious metals, or ivory. In its most limited sense an icon is a two-dimensional painting of Christ, a SAINT, or a narrative scene, painted according to traditional techniques and materials (egg tempera or wax encaustic often with gold leaf added) and closely following a prototype. Such images are the focus of prayer and liturgical celebrations, particularly in the Orthodox Churches, which have a highly developed account of their role in Christian DOCTRINE and worship. This theology asserts that the image offers a means by which the worshipper may come into closer contact with its model (Christ or the saint). The veneration and PRAYERS that appear to be offered to an image are, in fact, offered to the prototype that is made mystically present through the icon.

An icon is therefore a kind of SYMBOL – a thing that points to a reality that far surpasses or transcends itself, but in which it participates. It is not the reality itself, but relates to it in such a way as to make it genuinely known or understood. The veneration offered to icons is therefore intended to be extended to the prototype or model, and is not the worship of a material, or human-made object (see DULIA). In this sense, an icon functions like the elements of the sacrament (e.g., bread, wine, water) in that earthly, visible material mediates a transcendent and invisible reality. Thus, Christians in some traditions show the same reverence for an icon that others might for the consecrated host of the EUCHARIST. Many icons have also been credited with working MIRACLES, through the agency of the saint whose image they portray.

Frontally composed portraits of Christ and the saints did not appear in any quantity until the fifth century. The earliest Christian images, discovered mostly in funereal contexts from the late second to the mid-fourth centuries, were initially comprised of simple, symbolic motifs that were commonplace in Roman art (e.g., the peacock, dove, anchor, or fish). Certain more complicated images were transferred from a pagan to a Christian context such as representations of small children (*putti*) harvesting grapes or wheat, the caretaking shepherd with his flock, a praying figure (usually a veiled female with her hands outstretched), and diners reclining at a meal. Early narrative images included scenes from the OT or the Gospels, including Adam and Eve; Noah; ABRAHAM and Isaac; Daniel; Jonah; the BAPTISM of Christ; and Jesus shown healing, raising the dead, and working wonders. After the legalization and establishment of Christianity in the fourth century, more types appeared, including scenes of Christ enthroned, Christ giving the law to his APOSTLES, and the first passion images that often included an empty CROSS surmounted by a Christogram.

Although based on Scripture, the narrative images that appeared in the third and fourth centuries were not illustrations of stories as much as typological or symbolic allusions to those stories' deeper meanings. Thus the images functioned exegetically in ways that paralleled contemporary commentaries or homilies. For example, the image of Jonah omitted many aspects of the biblical narrative in order to point to Jonah as a sign of Christ's death and resurrection – itself a symbol of the Christian's hope, through baptism, for a blessed afterlife. Daniel, often presented as a heroic nude in the posture of prayer, was a symbol both of God's rescue from death and of the promise of resurrection. The three magi arriving to adore the Christ child probably signified several different things, including the overcoming of idolatry, the extension of the covenant to the nations, or a testimony to the Trinity.

This typological or allegorical function of iconography demonstrates the ability of images not only to interpret Scripture, but (as icons) to point beyond its literal meanings in order to disclose higher, more spiritual truths. The possibility of venerating saints' images may well have been established by this exegetical function of early Christian art. In addition, the ancient Roman practice of allowing a portrait image to signify the presence of an absent model (as in the emperor's image serving as a proxy for his person) eventually came to be applied to Christian holy images. As Christianity became the dominant religion in the empire, and the cult of the pagan gods was no longer a serious threat, the definition of idolatry became more focused on the worship of false gods than on the veneration of carved or painted images. For example, Athanasius of Alexandria's treatise *On the Incarnation* 14, written in the first half of the fourth century, compared the incarnate *Logos* with the restorer of a portrait, remaking the human soul in the image of God by revealing its original beauty (*Inc.* 14). Fifty years later, Basil of Caesarea (see Cappadocian Fathers) explained the identification of the Son and the Father in the Trinity by the generally understood identification of the emperor with his official portrait (*Spirit* 18.45).

In the West, from the time of Pope Gregory I (r. 590–604), images were more often perceived as pedagogical aids than as mediators of sacred realities. Gregory's famous dictum that what Scripture was to the educated, images were to the illiterate (*Ep.* 9.105; 11.13) was frequently echoed in the writings of western theologians from Bede (672/3–735) to Bonaventure (1221–74) to T. Aquinas. For this reason, western Christian iconography tended more towards didactically oriented art, including illuminated Bibles and office books, and illustrations of biblical narratives on church walls, in stained-glass windows, and sculpted in relief on the portals of Gothic cathedrals. By the high Middle Ages, however, iconography had become more oriented to fostering a devotional attitude in viewers, by appealing to the imagination and emotions in elaborated biblical images as well as images of the suffering Christ, his grieving mother, or the agonies of the saints. Like the meditations developed out of Franciscan spiritual practices, this iconography encouraged the viewer to enter the narrative in a deeply personal sense.

The Byzantine iconoclastic controversies of the eighth and ninth centuries denounced the Orthodox veneration of images by claiming that images made of wood and paint should not be granted the same status as the elements of the Eucharist. The iconoclasts argued that Christ's divine nature was invisible and therefore could not be portrayed in a pictorial image. The same objections were raised out of the Protestant Reformation in the West, beginning in the sixteenth century and most thoroughly exemplified in the writings of J. Calvin (*Inst.* 1.11). Holy images were declared to be idols and their veneration a form of idolatrous worship – and in both instances the images were taken down and destroyed by those zealous to purify worship from such practices. Although the images were reinstated in the Orthodox Churches through the decrees of the seventh ecumenical council in 787, the Protestant Churches of the West never completely resolved their differences on the validity of visual images for use in corporate worship, private devotion, and theological reflection.

The Council of Trent (Session 25) approved the value of religious iconography as a means of instructing and inspiring the faithful through portraying the stories of redemption, miracles, and the saints as salutary models. Using language very much like that contained in the dogmatic statements from the seventh ecumenical council, it affirmed that honour and reverence might be duly offered to images of Christ, the Blessed Virgin, and the saints, not because images were intrinsically holy, but because the honour paid to them was referred to the original they represented. This position led to a flowering of Catholic religious art in the late sixteenth and seventeenth centuries. Meanwhile, such Protestant artists as Rembrandt (1606–69) produced masterworks on biblical themes or portraits of the saints or apostles that were commissioned or purchased by private patrons for the adornment of their homes or for civic rather than ecclesial institutions. The ultimate legacy of this more private or secular function of religious art was a general diminishment of theological reflection on the role and value of pictorial art in Christian practice and worship until recent decades.

See also Allegory; Dulia; Iconoclasm; Orthodox Theology; Theodore the Studite; Typology.

H. Belting, *Likeness and Presence: A History of the Image before Art* (University of Chicago Press, 1994).

A. Besançon, *The Forbidden Image: An Intellectual History of Iconoclasm* (University of Chicago Press, 2000).

J. L. Koerner, *The Reformation of the Image* (University of Chicago Press, 2004).

J. Pelikan, *Imago Dei: The Byzantine Apologia for Icons* (Yale University Press, 1990).

ROBIN M. JENSEN

IDEALISM, GERMAN German Idealism refers to the writings of German philosophers responding to the work of I. KANT. Its principal figures were J. G. Fichte (1762–1814), G. W. F. HEGEL, and F. Schelling (1775–1854), who built on insights by J. G. Hamann (1730–88), J. G. Herder (1744–1803), F. Hölderlin (1770–1843), F. H. Jacobi (1743–1819), and K. Reinhold (1757–1823). Fichte's main writings were *Wissenschaftslehre* (1794) and *Foundations of Natural Right* (1796). Hegel's main writings were *Phenomenology of Spirit* (1807), *Philosophy of Right* (1821), *Science of Logic* (1812), and *Lectures on the Philosophy of Religion* (1827). Schelling's main writings were *System of Transcendental Idealism* (1800), *Philosophical Investigations into the Essence of Human Freedom* (1809), *Ages of the World* (1811–15), and several series of lectures which were unpublished in his lifetime, including *Philosophy of Mythology* and *Philosophy of Revelation*.

Kant's philosophy had three significant features. It was unsystematic (in the German Idealist sense that it did not attempt to develop all its dimensions from one single principle); it investigated questions of natural causality independently of questions of human freedom; and it treated questions of NATURAL SCIENCE, LAW and morality, and aesthetics as relatively independent areas of enquiry. German Idealism represents a concerted effort to complete Kant's project. It attempted to be systematic, reconciling and harmonizing 'theoretical' and 'practical' philosophy (including the split between subject and object) in an account where reality has the structure of a mind.

Fichte articulated two key idealist insights: (1) an object is only an object in so far as it is thought by us; but (2) it is only genuinely an object if it offers some resistance to our subjectivity. He fruitfully explored many of the difficulties arising from these two principles but did not resolve them.

Hegel attempted to reconcile subject and object historically and socially. He argued that concepts express historically specific relations between persons in relation to objects: our ideas are expressions of our history. Objects are objects 'for us' (we think them); but objects have their own integrity as products of history – a history which includes the subjects who think objects. Hegel overemphasized the objectivity of his own historical account and underestimated the extent to which objects exceed the concepts we use to describe them.

Schelling saw subjectivity as nature's agency, in which human action participates, rather than as the activity of discrete individuals. He acknowledged that objects exceed the concepts we use to describe them and suggested that artistic production offers a model for reconciling subject and object in a way that cannot be captured by thinking. He saw subjectivity as a product of a system, not the producer of the system. Thus, although the 'I' is free, it is a predicate of 'being'. This insight led the later Schelling away from German Idealism towards an interest in how being is 'revealed'.

The importance of German Idealism for theology is threefold. First, Fichte's suggestion that the subject produces its objects transferred a model of divine creativity to human agency, in a way that seemed to leave little space or need for talk of God. Second, Hegel's turn to history transformed theology in many ways, including spurring the QUEST OF THE HISTORICAL JESUS. Third, Schelling's turn to REVELATION challenged philosophy's claim to comprehend reality and offered ways to think about being that are taken up, in very different ways, by M. Heidegger (1889–1976) and K. BARTH.

NICHOLAS ADAMS

IDOLATRY The prohibition of idolatry, or the worship of manufactured images, is deeply rooted in the Jewish traditions out of which Christianity emerged and takes classic form in the TEN COMMANDMENTS (Exod. 20:4–6; Deut. 5:8–10). It probably originated in the practical concern to prevent the kind of identification of God with an image that would allow the image to be used to control or manipulate God. In the OT, however, the reason given for why images of God *may* not be constructed is that they *cannot* be: since the people of Israel saw 'no form' when God spoke to them from Sinai, they should not depict God 'in the form of any figure' (Deut. 4:15–16). In short, the prohibition of images is understood as a means of preventing any confusion between the phenomenal world and God. As the Creator of heaven and earth, God is utterly distinct from the world and so cannot be identified with or depicted by any part of it (see Ps. 115:3–4; Acts 17:29; Rom. 1:23).

While biblical and other early Christian prohibitions against idolatry focus on participation in pagan worship (see Acts 15:20; 1 Cor. 10:14; 1 John 5:21), later theologians have dissociated idolatry from explicitly cultic activity. For example, M. LUTHER argued that because 'to have a God properly means to have something in which the heart trusts completely' (*LC* 366.10), even a professing Christian commits idolatry if she puts her trust in wealth, learning, or some other finite good. Still more recently, theologians have identified the danger of 'Jesusolatry', in which the figure of Jesus becomes the sole focus of Christian piety in a way that is inconsistent both with the doctrine of the TRINITY and with the distinction of created human and uncreated divine natures characteristic of Chalcedonian CHRISTOLOGY (see CHALCEDON). In both cases, the perspective is the same as that of SCRIPTURE: to worship God means *not* to worship any particular fact or thing in the world (still less the world itself) and therefore to be always alert to ways of speaking and acting – whether inside or outside the Church – that threaten to confuse God with the world.

H. R. Niebuhr, *Radical Monotheism and Western Culture* (Harper & Row, 1943).

IAN A. MCFARLAND

IMAGO DEI: see THEOLOGICAL ANTHROPOLOGY.

IMMACULATE CONCEPTION The Immaculate Conception refers to the Catholic DOCTRINE that the Virgin Mary was conceived free from original SIN and not to Mary's virginal conception of Christ, with which it is often confused. Some devotional writers have attributed a virginal conception to Mary as well as to Christ, but Catholic doctrine has always taught that Mary was sexually conceived by her parents. A feast celebrating Mary's conception has been celebrated in the Eastern Churches since the seventh century and spread to the West during the eighth century. In 1476 Pope Sixtus IV (r. 1471–84) officially established the Immaculate Conception as a solemnity to be celebrated on 8 December.

Debates about Mary's sinlessness can be traced back to the early Church. Some patristic theologians such as IRENAEUS OF LYONS, TERTULLIAN, and John Chrysostom (*ca* 347–407) attributed actual sin to Mary, but most accepted her sinlessness while differing as to whether this related to the conditions of her conception or to her subsequent development in the womb. The debate continued until the late Middle Ages, drawing in religious orders and secular leaders alike, with Franciscans generally defending the doctrine and Dominicans opposing it. The nineteenth century saw a surge in Marian devotion – perhaps as a reaction against the spread of secular modernity across Europe – and this generated widespread popular support for the promulgation of a doctrine on the Immaculate Conception. In 1854 Pope Pius IX issued the constitution *Ineffabilis Deus*, which states that the Virgin Mary, 'in the first instance of her conception, by a singular privilege and grace granted by God, in view of the merits of Jesus Christ, the Saviour of the human race, was preserved exempt from all stain of original sin' (DS 2,803). The apparition to B. Soubirous (1844–79) at Lourdes in 1858 was said by the young visionary to have identified herself as the Immaculate Conception, which was interpreted by many Catholics as potent affirmation of the dogma.

Protestants reject the doctrine of the Immaculate Conception because they argue that it lacks scriptural justification and denies the unique sinlessness of Christ. The Orthodox Church rejects the western doctrine of original sin so that, although it believes Mary to be perfectly holy, it does not accept the categories that shape the Catholic dogma of the Immaculate Conception. The report of the Anglican–Roman Catholic International Commission (ARCIC), *Mary: Grace and Hope in Christ*, accepts that the Immaculate Conception, like the ASSUMPTION, is consistent with SCRIPTURE and the early shared TRADITION, but questions how far Anglicans can accept such doctrines as binding in FAITH.

The Immaculate Conception establishes an intimate relationship between the woman of the original creation – Eve – who disobeyed God's commandment and was responsible for introducing suffering and death into human experience, and the woman of the new creation in Christ – Mary (the New Eve) – who was obedient to God and brought life and salvation to humankind. In art and popular devotion, the tradition of the Immaculate Conception has also been shaped by the association of Mary with the woman of the Song of Songs, and with the second-century apocryphal text, the *Protevangelium of James*, which tells of Mary's conception and birth to her elderly parents, Anna and Joachim. Medieval iconography portrayed the Immaculate Conception as a warm marital embrace between Mary's parents at the golden gate of Jerusalem, symbolizing the moment of her conception. The Council of TRENT discouraged such imagery, and the seventeenth century saw the emergence of a new iconographic style which depicts Mary as the woman crowned with stars from Revelation 12:1.

In recent years there has been theological debate about the doctrine of original sin, with some arguing that it presents an excessively negative view of the human condition. Feminists argue that this is exacerbated by the dualistic representation of Mary and Eve, with Mary's sinless perfection constituting an unattainable ideal of virginal maternal femininity, and Eve's association with SEXUALITY and death contributing to a culture of misogyny. However, others have suggested that the Immaculate Conception resonates with a contemporary theological quest for a new appreciation of the grandeur and mystery of CREATION, with Mary symbolizing the cosmic transformation of matter through the redeeming grace of Christ. It may also be that the art and devotions of the medieval Church, with their emphasis on the maternal genealogy of Christ and their association of married sexual love with Mary's conception, offer a resource for the emergence of new theological possibilities relevant to the Christian understanding of the goodness of creation, sexuality, and female embodiment.

S. J. Boss, 'The Development of the Doctrine of Mary's Immaculate Conception' in *Mary: The Complete Resource*, ed. S. J. Boss (Continuum, 2007), 207–35.
S. L. Stratton, *The Immaculate Conception in Spanish Art* (Cambridge University Press, 1994).

TINA BEATTIE

INCARNATION Incarnation (from the Latin *incarnatio*, meaning literally infleshing or enfleshment) is, in CHRISTOLOGY, the process by which God is understood to have become human flesh (i.e., taken on a human life) in Jesus of Nazareth. This is one of the deepest patterns in Christian thinking about Jesus: he is understood to be

'Immanuel', 'God with us', God come into the world to save sinners (cf. Matt. 1:23 and 28:20).

This central idea has been refracted through a variety of metaphors and images. Perhaps the most familiar is that of 'descent', as in the words of the NICENE CREED which declare that the eternal Son of God 'came down from heaven' so as to be 'incarnate of the HOLY SPIRIT and the Virgin Mary'. That descent is sometimes understood as a matter of God's voluntary self-emptying or humbling, as God's decision to appear in the form of a weak, mortal creature, and so as a 'veiling' of God's glory (see KENOTIC THEOLOGY).

At the same time, incarnation has been understood as a matter of the making visible or making tangible of God's life – and so a proclamation or REVELATION of the nature of God. Jesus has therefore been understood as the true prophet who has not simply been given God's self-revelatory Word to speak, but has himself been given to the world as the embodiment of that Word, and as the true image or representation of God's being (see *LOGOS*).

From a somewhat different direction, the incarnation has been seen as the catching up of a human life into perfect union with God (see DEIFICATION), and so as a matter of the perfection or SANCTIFICATION of human life. Jesus' life has been understood as God's temple, as the perfect tabernacle in which the God of Israel meets with God's people; he has been seen as the sinless high priest who alone has been made worthy to stand in the presence of God and intercede for his people.

Jesus has also been seen as the embodiment of the KINGDOM OF GOD, and the incarnation as the establishment of that kingdom in history. All people are understood to be called into this kingdom, and the incarnate Jesus is seen both as the perfect model for their citizenship and as the embodiment of their king – or, in language drawn from the letters of PAUL, Christians are understood to become members of a BODY which *is* Jesus' body (Rom. 12:5; 1 Cor. 12:27) and of which he is the head (Eph. 5:23; Col. 1:18).

Various questions emerged as Christian theologians tried to give more precise conceptual form to these incarnational beliefs. Is it truly God, the one creator God of Israel, who has become flesh in Jesus of Nazareth? Has God become *fully* human? And in what sense has the one 'become' the other?

The classic Christian answer to the first of these questions, honed particularly during the fourth-century controversies leading to the Councils of NICAEA and CONSTANTINOPLE, is that it is indeed truly God (viz., the divine Word, the second Person of the TRINITY) who has become incarnate in Jesus of Nazareth (see ARIAN CONTROVERSY). As such, the Son or Word is not a creature, nor a being of a lesser rank or glory than the Father, but one who is everything that God the Father is ('God from God, Light from Light'), though with the specific individuating feature of eternally coming *from* the Father and giving glory back *to* the Father.

The classic Christian answer to the second question is that the Word has indeed become fully human: there was no hint of pretence or seeming about Jesus' human life (see DOCETISM), and Jesus lacked nothing that is essential to fully human life. He had a human body, a human mind (see APOLLINARIANISM), a human soul, a human will (see MONOTHELITISM); he was capable of real suffering; he was genuinely beset by those limitations of knowledge and strength that necessarily characterize finite, creaturely life. The one qualification that classic incarnational theology has made is that Jesus was without SIN. This, however, was not understood as a diminishment of his humanity, but rather as confirmation of the fact that sin is not an essential feature of fully human life (even if it is endemic in all human beings except Jesus after the FALL).

The classic Christian answer to the third question, about what it means for God to 'become' fully human, is that the incarnation is not a matter of the eternal Word 'turning into' a human being (i.e., of the Word losing or changing its characteristics in order to live as a human being, swapping omnipresence for finite locality and so on). Nor is it a matter of the eternal Word 'adopting' an already existing human being – a human life with its own independent existence logically or temporally prior to the incarnation (see ADOPTIONISM). Rather, the incarnation has been understood as involving the eternal Word 'assuming' a human life: bringing into being a fully human life which only exists, and is only fully individuated, because of this act of God (see ANHYPOSTASIA), and bringing this life into being in *union* with the Word (see HYPOSTATIC UNION). That is, the eternal Word takes on, in addition to its existing divine way of being, a human way of being, and this human life is the Word's way of being in the world, and for the world. Classic incarnational theology presents no theory of *how* this 'bringing into being' took place, but insists that this whole life exists only for this, and there is nothing in this human life that is not derived from this union and devoted to it.

In the formulations of incarnational theology which flow from the Council of CHALCEDON (and which have been regarded as central or definitive in many, though by no means all, Christian Churches – see SYRIAC CHRISTIAN THEOLOGY), the eternal Word is understood to be of the same substance (*HOMOOUSIOS*) as the Father, and the human life of Jesus of Nazareth is understood to be of the same substance as the rest of humanity; but the union between these two 'natures' is such that together they form one distinct reality (i.e., one HYPOSTASIS or 'Person').

Incarnational theology affects how God is understood, in that for this theology to make sense, the act of incarnation must be understood not simply as *possible* for God, but as *proper* to God: an act in which God's immanent nature is made known. Incarnational theology has therefore pushed Christians towards the understanding that

God's life is a life of self-giving LOVE, a love that pours itself out for another; incarnational theologies draw analogies between the eternal pouring out of the Father for the Son, the incarnation of the Son in Jesus of Nazarath, and Jesus' own passion (see CROSS AND CRUCIFIXION).

Incarnational theology also affects how humanity is understood. At the heart of incarnational theology is the claim that God's life has been lived out under the conditions of creatureliness, so revealing or ensuring that it is possible for creaturely life to be intimately united to God without ceasing to be creaturely. Creatureliness – finitude, bodiliness, enmeshment in webs of interdependence with other creatures, being one animal among others – is therefore not to be understood as a barrier to godliness, but is rather the medium in which godliness can be lived out. 'Incarnational theology' can also therefore refer to an understanding of the Christian calling precisely as a call to such godly humanity, to Christ-like self-giving engagement with the world, and therefore to life as the incarnation of God's self-giving love in situations of need.

Incarnational theology has been subjected to sustained and serious questioning, and has received equally sustained and serious defence. Some query the conceptual coherence of traditional formulations – does it make sense, for instance, to speak of the unchanging *Logos* 'becoming' composite, by taking on another, human, way of being? Others point out the dependence of classical incarnational theology upon what some deem an inappropriate or outmoded METAPHYSICS, with the suggestion being made that the whole machinery of 'substances', 'natures', 'persons' is either implausible or inadequate. Still others wonder whether the identification of this male human being as *the* embodiment of God's life suggests that maleness is closer to godliness than femaleness (see FEMINIST THEOLOGY). And questions have been raised about the scriptural grounding of incarnational theology: whether the claim that Jesus is the embodiment of God's life in the world is supported by the NT portrayals of Jesus; or whether there is really scriptural support for the idea that between the eternal Father and the human Jesus there is another subject, the eternal Son. On these and other fronts, incarnational theology remains controversial.

See also VIRGIN BIRTH.

S. T. Davis, D. Kendall, S. J. , and G. O'Collins, S. J., *The Incarnation: An Interdisciplinary Symposium on the Incarnation of the Son of God* (Oxford University Press, 2004).

H. McCabe, *God Matters* (Continuum, 2005).

W. C. Placher, *Jesus the Savior: The Meaning of Jesus Christ for Christian Faith* (John Knox Press, 2001).

B. Studer, *Trinity and Incarnation: The Faith of the Early Church* (T&T Clark, 1993).

MIKE HIGTON

INCLUSIVE LANGUAGE Praise, thanksgiving, lamentation, supplication, and the many other dimensions of public LITURGY all come to expression through language – language understood broadly as not only the use of words, but also that of space, architecture, art, music, and kinetics (bodily movement). However, throughout western history, the language of PRAYER has reflected and also shaped the predominantly patriarchal and hierarchical ethos and structure of the Church. The ritual embodiment of a particularly exclusive and male-dominated theology where God is known only as Father and referred to only through male pronouns, and where architecture places emphasis on a high-holy place (apse or high altar) reserved only for male celebrants was challenged by many women thinkers, theologians, and activists beginning in the mid-twentieth century.

Language, it was argued, is not neutral. Language does not simply reflect or communicate a given reality; through its utterance, language forms reality. Classic liturgical language has reinforced a hierarchy in which many are excluded or cannot identify with either the object or the subject of the prayers and the rituals. The proposal of inclusive language entails, first of all, a deepening awareness of the power of language (both verbal and non-verbal) in defining the believer's relationship to God and to other believers in the community; second, a liberation of language from structures that are oppressive, not only to women, but also to many who are marginalized; and third, a renewal of space and ritual practices that will be more attuned to silenced voices.

Inclusive language has been one response to the problem of limited metaphors for God and the human experience within worship. At its best, it does not simply replace male references for God with female references but consists in the hard work of finding a balance between male and female imagery, as well as drawing on the rich treasure of natural metaphors for God found within SCRIPTURE. It seeks to free language in all its forms (verbal and non-verbal) and thereby open a space for worship to be a dialogue with God that includes both sexes, all orientations, races, and experiences. It is not only for women but seeks to connect everyday experience with an experience of both the presence and the absence of God.

Inclusive language has called to attention the simple fact that God has no gender and thus cannot be contained in any one gendered metaphor or image. Inclusive language thereby shifts the focus of speech away from a simple identity issue, with its proponents arguing, for example, that when we refer to God's name, we do not refer to a proper name (like Sally or Bill) but to God's power to act in a particular way – though opponents argue that this is not true of the traditional Trinitarian names for God (viz., Father, Son, and HOLY SPIRIT). Proponents note that inclusive language not only renews language for God, but also speaks the truth about the wide spectrum of human experiences – and does so through an enhanced awareness of the beauty and poetry of Scripture rediscovered and reawakened in liturgical language.

See also ANDROCENTRISM; FEMINIST THEOLOGY; PATRIARCHY.

M. Procter-Smith, *In Her Own Rite: Constructing Feminist Liturgical Tradition* (Abingdon Press, 1990).

J. R. Walton, *Feminist Liturgy: A Matter of Justice* (Liturgical Press, 2000).

DIRK G. LANGE

INCULTURATION Inculturation (or acculturation) is a very new term for an extremely ancient question: the relation of FAITH to culture. The early Christians struggled over the issue whether non-Jewish followers were bound by Jewish cultic requirements (Acts 15). In choosing to allow certain Gentile practices that were not permissible within Judaism as part of Christian discipleship, the Church implicitly determined that at every new cultural step the task of discipleship had to be worked out anew, albeit in continuity with Christian REVELATION. PAUL's preaching at Athens (Acts 17) might also be viewed as inculturation. What Paul first saw as 'IDOLATRY' he seemingly came to understand as really pointing towards Christ. Paul's was a critical evaluation of culture, drawing on elements that might help proclaim the GOSPEL. This process of sifting through culture has continued throughout Christian history through its moves into Greco-Roman, Ethiopian, Syrian, and other local cultures.

The Council of NICAEA exemplifies inculturation in employing the term *HOMOOUSIOS* to define Christological ORTHODOXY. It is a non-biblical Greek philosophical term that gained special prestige in the Christian tradition, but, as in many cases of inculturation, it came to bear a meaning different from the one it originally had. A different form of inculturation happened when Latin was introduced as the liturgical language of the western Church as a medium for binding different linguistic groups together.

The use of 'inculturation' in modern discussion has often been related to the insertion of the Christian Church into non-European cultures associated with the discovery of the 'New World' in the sixteenth century (a usage which points to the Eurocentric bias of many discussions of the subject). A typical critical issue regarding inculturation in general, and inculturation in the 'New World' in particular, emerged during the sixteenth and seventeenth centuries and regarded the use of indigenous local customs by Christian converts, sometimes in the liturgy. In China, for instance, the Jesuit M. Ricci (1552–1610) was successful in establishing Catholic communities and was held in high esteem by the Chinese emperor. Ricci and his successors permitted the Chinese cultic practice of veneration to the ancestors, seeing in it no more than a healthy regard for the dead. However, Pope Clement XI (r. 1700–21) viewed this 'veneration' as an act of worship. He banned the practice on the grounds of its idolatrous nature. Clement's action had disastrous social repercussions that were redressed 200 years later in 1939 when Pope Pius XII (r. 1939–58) ordered the ban lifted, viewing 'veneration' now as an 'honourable' manner of giving 'esteem' to ancestors. But there were real issues that Clement faced. For example, he had also banned the liturgical use of the Chinese term *Shangti* (Heavenly Lord) for God and insisted on the Latin *Deus* because of reports that the Chinese emperor had accepted Christianity only because he believed that it paid homage to the 'Heavenly Lord' of Confucianism.

Because the Bible was actively translated into indigenous languages this sort of problem was inevitable and has been replicated in almost every mission context right into the present. For example, the Vatican recently required that some experimentation in the Indian liturgy come to an end because it was charged that it was almost impossible to discern the mass from Hindu *puja* (the rite of devotion to Hindu gods). This problem was heightened because of the many artistic and cultural changes implemented in such experimentation centres. For example, when the Holy TRINITY was depicted in iconographic terms drawn from representations of Brahma, Vishnu, and Shiva, as creator, preserver, and destroyer respectively, this raised fertile imaginative representational possibilities as well as controversy. The Indian Catholic artist J. Sahi (b. 1944) was taken to a civil court by small groups of Hindus and Catholics for just such an artistic representation: by Hindus, because they considered it a defilement of their religious heritage; and by Catholics, because they considered it a desecration of their holy site.

Because the question of inculturation is not an issue solely concerning non-European cultures, recent discussion has highlighted tensions between non-European and European Churches. Should non-European theological developments be subject to judgement from European theological frameworks? The Indian Christian liberation theologian F. Wilfred (b. 1948) is not alone in arguing that this judging process is cultural imperialism, the imposition of western modes of theology upon non-western indigenous Churches and non-western theological modalities. In response, it has been argued that, because the heritage of Church TRADITION is a constant explication of the gospel, it is not European culture per se that is being exalted, but rather the gospel within the tradition of the western Church. It is added that in the not-too-distant future the rich Indian tradition will also constitute part of the organic normative tradition by which future Christian communities will be judged. This position was advanced by Pope John Paul II (r. 1978–2005), who also defined inculturation as the constant movement between faith and culture (*Red.* 52; *Fid.* 72). This debate remains unresolved, especially in highly centralized Christian communities like the Catholic Church.

A question of inculturation facing European theology is theology's own relation to modernity. Catholicism again provides examples that are not limited to this denomination. Philosophical and political 'modernity' had been condemned by a number of popes ever since the French Revolution, and likewise the application of modern historical–critical scholarship to SCRIPTURE. However, in the 1960s many of these condemned 'values' were seen to be legitimated during VATICAN COUNCIL II. Thus many 'liberal' Catholics were deeply concerned with Pope John Paul II's and then Pope Benedict XVI's (r. 2005–) constant criticisms of modernity. They argued this was a betrayal of the spirit of the Council and signalled the Church's retreat from contemporary challenges. These unresolved debates highlight the complex relation between (modern secular) culture and faith – the ever-developing Christian tradition.

In Protestant circles S. Hauerwas (b. 1940) has argued that, despite the sophisticated examination of ways of relating Christ to culture found in H. R. Niebuhr's (1894–1962) *Christ and Culture* (1951), Niebuhr ultimately elevates (modern, western) culture as an independent norm that determines the significance of Christ. Hauerwas criticizes both modernity and forms of Christianity that have capitulated to it – an approach that echoes K. BARTH's criticism of his teachers' support of World War I.

Inculturation affects every aspect of Christian witness: the liturgical, ethical, doctrinal, philosophical, social, and so on. The critical questions revolve on whether particular new cultural elements, as part or as a whole, are compatible with the gospel, how they are transformed in their interaction with Christian practices and doctrines, and how they might serve in proclaiming the gospel afresh. One might see something of this debate as an aspect of the ecclesiological balance between the local and universal Church. Ecclesiologies that emphasize the former usually facilitate inculturation more naturally. Nevertheless, the history of the Church testifies that no pre-Christian culture was accepted as it stood, although many such cultures contained much that was good and true, but they required the fire of the gospel to bring about a purification and transformation. The rigour of discernment, prayer, loyalty to the gospel and Christian communities are all required in this extremely complex but absolutely necessary and never-ending task.

See also ECCLESIOLOGY.

M. P. Gallagher, *Clashing Symbols: An Introduction to Faith and Culture*, revised edn (Darton, Longman and Todd, 2003).

G. F. Snyder, *Inculturation of the Jesus Tradition: The Impact of Jesus on Jewish and Roman Cultures* (Trinity Press International, 1999).

P. Tovey, *Inculturation of Christian Worship: Exploring the Eucharist* (Ashgate, 2004).

GAVIN D'COSTA

INDIGENOUS RELIGIONS: see TRADITIONAL RELIGIONS AND CHRISTIANITY.

INERRANCY Within a specifically Christian context, inerrancy refers to the DOCTRINE that SCRIPTURE is completely without error in every respect, including matters of, e.g., history and cosmology. For example, an inerrantist would claim that the account of the sun standing still during the battle of Gibeon (Josh. 10:12–13) is a historically accurate report of a miraculous astronomical event. Inerrancy is a position generally associated with conservative PROTESTANTISM and has proponents across a range of confessional traditions (e.g., Baptists, Lutherans, and Reformed). Especially (though by no means universally) prominent among evangelicals, inerrancy has been a defining mark of Christian FUNDAMENTALISM since the latter's emergence as a distinct movement.

Probably the most influential and well-known account of the inerrantist position is 'The Chicago Statement on Biblical Inerrancy' (1978). The authors of the 'Statement' argue that the doctrine of inerrancy, though strictly applicable only to the original autographs of the biblical books (Article 10), is a necessary implication of Christian belief in biblical authority, which 'is inescapably impaired if this total divine inerrancy is in any way limited or disregarded' ('Short Statement', 5). In short, if the authority of the Bible is denied at any point, then its trustworthiness everywhere is open to question. Thus, the authors derive the Bible's inerrancy (Article 12) from its INFALLIBILITY (i.e., its essential reliability as a guide for faith and practice) arguing that it is impossible 'for the Bible to be at the same time infallible and errant in its assertions' (Article 11).

Opponents charge that the inerrantist position misconstrues Scripture as a collection of propositions demanding intellectual assent rather than a divine address calling for personal trust. They also note that inerrancy is a relatively recent development, and that earlier generations of Christians acknowledged inaccuracies in biblical accounts as instances of divine ACCOMMODATION or even of human carelessness.

IAN A. MCFARLAND

INFALLIBILITY Infallibility is applied in Christian theology both to SCRIPTURE (see INERRANCY) and to the PAPACY. The DOCTRINE of papal infallibility was defined at VATICAN COUNCIL I, called by Pius IX (r. 1846–78), at its final session on 18 July 1870, in the dogmatic constitution, *Pastor aeternus*. The definition is the culmination of the council's emphatic reassertion, against modern critical questioning, of the certainty of the Catholic Church's teaching, based on the pope's absolute authority as the vicar of Christ. When speaking *ex cathedra* – in the explicit exercise of his universal office as pastor and teacher of all Christians – the pope's teaching in FAITH and morals cannot err. The pope may define a doctrine in this way without calling a COUNCIL, and the broader

Church's consent is not necessary for a papal doctrine to be irreformable. There can be no appeal to a council.

The definition moved the Catholic Church considerably beyond the commonly held belief in the Church's indefectibility: the doctrine that the HOLY SPIRIT maintains the Church, taken as a whole, in the truth of the GOSPEL. After Vatican I, there was a tendency to assume that much of papal teaching is infallible. However, VATICAN COUNCIL II tacitly rejected significant earlier papal teachings, including those of Pius IX himself, and clarified some of the conditions for an infallible statement: the pope's teaching is not infallible when he speaks as a private person, as bishop of Rome, or as a theologian; there is a difference between the infallible doctrine and the form in which it is stated, which may need development; the Holy Spirit is the ultimate basis for infallibility.

See also APPELLANCY; CATHOLIC THEOLOGY; CONCILIARISM.

NICHOLAS M. HEALY

INFANT BAPTISM: see BAPTISM.

INFRALAPSARIANISM AND SUPRALAPSARIANISM The distinction between infralapsarianism and supralapsarianism derives from a debate within REFORMED THEOLOGY over the proper interpretation of the DOCTRINE of ELECTION. According to the Reformed ORTHODOXY defined at the Synod of DORT over against ARMINIANISM, all creaturely events are the product of divine PREDESTINATION; that is, they are ultimately determined by God's eternal and unchangeable decree. The debate between infra- and supralapsarians focused on the relative order of the decree by which God predestined a certain number of human beings for salvation on the one hand, and the decree by which God permitted that all humankind fall into a state of SIN (and thereby merit eternal DAMNATION) on the other. Broadly speaking, infralapsarians argue that the decree of election comes later (*infra*) than the decree whereby God permits the FALL (*lapsus*); supralapsarians argue that the decree of election comes earlier (*supra*).

The infralapsarian position, defended by F. Turretin (1623–87) and C. HODGE, has generally been more popular within the Reformed tradition. It describes a logical sequence according to which God determines: (1) to create human beings, (2) to permit the human beings so created to fall, (3) to elect some of those who have fallen for salvation and to allow the rest to be damned, and (4) to appoint Christ, the Word of God incarnate, as the means of salvation for the elect. Because the fall is logically prior to election on this scheme, the emphasis falls on God's love and mercy in choosing to rescue a portion of humankind from the damnation they deserve: God loves and elects fallen human beings in spite of their objective unworthiness. From the supralapsarian side, this is precisely the problem: the infralapsarian emphasis on God's mercy comes at the expense of God's sovereign freedom, since election now appears as a kind of divine reaction to the fall rather than as the foundation of God's dealings with humankind. Moreover, since the damnation of the reprobate is in the infralapsarian system a consequence of the fall rather than intrinsic to God's eternal purposes for human beings, it appears to detract from, rather than to serve, God's glory.

In placing election before the fall, the supralapsarian position, held by T. Beza (1519–1605), W. Perkins (1558–1602), and F. Gomarus (1563–1641), among others, changes the tenor of the divine ECONOMY. According to supralapsarians God determines: (1) to predestine a fixed number of human beings for salvation and the rest for damnation, (2) to create the human beings so predestined, (3) to permit all the human beings so created to fall, and (4) to appoint Christ, the Word of God incarnate, as the means for the salvation of the elect. In contrast with infralapsarianism, God elects fallible (*labiles*) – but not fallen (*lapsi*) – human beings. As a result, the emphasis falls upon God's freedom in electing some and damning others over God's love and mercy. But because the fall is now logically subsequent to the primordial decree, infralapsarians note, it no longer has the appearance of a violation or surd that disrupts God's plans for creation and risks appearing a means deliberately chosen by God to reveal the divine mercy and justice. Furthermore, infralapsarians charge that the whole idea of God electing and rejecting *possible* human beings runs against SCRIPTURE's emphasis on God's election of *particular* human beings. In short, while supralapsarianism presents a thoroughly consistent picture of divine sovereignty, this consistency comes at the expense of fidelity to the dramatic texture of the biblical narrative, with its emphasis on mercy and love as the motives shaping God's dealings with humankind.

Since all participants to the debate agreed that all God's decrees were eternal, the question of their relative priority was a logical rather than a temporal one. Even so, some Reformed theologians, including H. Bavinck (1854–1921), reject the whole debate on the grounds that the eternal character of all the divine decrees renders debates over their order moot. Bavinck argued that, because God's decree is comprehensive and all-inclusive in its ordering of the universe in all its interdependent parts, it cannot be exhaustively or exclusively described in terms of the kind of linear sequence characteristic of both infra- and supralapsarianism.

Still more trenchant is the critique of K. BARTH, who faults both the infra- and supralapsarian positions for their agreement on placing Christ's election last in the sequence of decrees. Barth charged that in either case the God who elects is, quite against the central thrust of the GOSPEL, considered in complete abstraction from Jesus Christ, as a 'hidden God' who stands behind (and, by implication, above) the incarnate God revealed in time and space (see *DEUS ABSCONDITUS*). Against this perspective, he countered that, in so far as Christ is the one in and through whom God's will for the world in all its dimensions is both effected and revealed, he is the immediate object of election, the one in whom the election of all other human beings is accomplished, and thus has absolute priority in any consideration of the order of divine decrees. By placing Christ, the one, simultaneous manifestation of God's freedom and love (indeed, of God's freedom *as* love) at the foundation of God's electing, Barth seeks to avoid the kind of relative prioritization of one attribute over the other characteristic of the infra- and supralapsarian positions.

K. Barth, *Church Dogmatics* (T&T Clark, 1957 [1942]), II/2, 33.

H. Bavinck, *Reformed Dogmatics*, vol. II (Baker Academic, 2004 [1918]), 361–74.

J. R. Beeke, 'The Order of the Divine Decrees at the Genevan Academy: From Bezan Supralapsarianism to Turretinian Infralapsarianism' in *The Identity of Geneva: The Christian Commonwealth, 1564–1864*, ed. J. B. Roney and M. I. Klauber (Greenwood Press, 1998), 57–76.

IAN A. MCFARLAND

INSPIRATION Whether used broadly to refer to any claim to speak by the power of the HOLY SPIRIT or more specifically to characterize the mode of divine self-communication in SCRIPTURE, the concept of inspiration is subsidiary to the DOCTRINE of REVELATION. As applied to Scripture, its primary purpose is to affirm that the biblical books are the product of divine rather than human willing, notwithstanding their having been written by human authors (see 2 Pet. 1:21). The term 'inspiration' itself is rooted in an analogy between divine and human communication: as human speech is physically a product of breathing, so, according to 2 Timothy 3:16, Scripture is 'God-breathed' (*inspirata* in the VULGATE).

While belief in the inspiration of the Bible is a matter of virtual consensus among Christians, the modern period has seen considerable disagreement over the kind of interaction between God and the Bible's human authors entailed by the concept and, correlatively, over the character of the text produced. Drawing on the work of B. B. Warfield (1851–1921), some conservative Protestants (especially those committed to FUNDAMENTALISM) promote a doctrine of 'plenary' or 'verbal' inspiration, according to which God is conceived as directing the biblical writers in such a way that the resulting texts (at least in their original form) are free from error of any sort (see INERRANCY).

Defenders of plenary inspiration worry that the propensity in LIBERAL THEOLOGY to refer inspiration to the disposition of the Bible's human authors rather than to the words of the text inevitably subverts Scripture's normative status in the Church: by abstracting what God says from what is written, they charge, liberals open the door to arbitrary interpretation. Yet, while proponents of plenary inspiration deny that they reduce the composition of Scripture to an impersonal process of dictation, their critics argue in turn that the model of biblical author as divine amanuensis invariably downplays the Bible's historical, human character in a way that risks collapsing the distinction between God's word and human witness to it.

Another option allows (with more conservative approaches) that inspiration extends to the very words of Scripture, but (against 'dictation' theories) conceives of inspiration as a particular case of God's providential use of creaturely realities to effect God's purposes rather than as a form of divine intervention bracketed off from the rest of human history. The latter perspective is viewed as problematic both because it is inconsistent with Scripture's own depiction of revelation as exceeding (even as it includes) the composition and reception of the Bible (see, e.g., 1 Cor. 14:26), and because it construes biblical authority as rooted in a purely *formal* property of the text (viz., its mode of production) rather than in its *content* (viz., divine self-communication). The alternative conceives of inspiration as a matter of God's use of the biblical texts in the ongoing process of revelation rather than as an intrinsic property of those texts that makes them revelatory independently of God's action.

See also ENTHUSIASM.

B. B. Warfield, *The Inspiration and Authority of the Bible* (Presbyterian and Reformed Publishing, 1948).

J. Webster, *Holy Scripture: A Dogmatic Sketch* (Cambridge University Press, 2003).

IAN A. MCFARLAND

INTELLIGENT DESIGN: see CREATIONISM.

IRENAEUS OF LYONS Perhaps the outstanding theologian of the second century, Irenaeus of Lyons was almost certainly from Smyrna in the Roman province of Asia, though he eventually became bishop of Lugdunum (modern Lyons) in southern Gaul. The year of his birth and that of his death are unknown, though his predecessor as bishop, Pothinus, perished in a savage local persecution in or very near the year 177.

Though his *Demonstration of the Apostolic Preaching* also survives, Irenaeus' great work, in five books, is the *Refutation and Overthrow of Knowledge Falsely So-Called*, usually known simply as *Against the Heresies*, which must have been written in the early 180s. In it he exposes and attacks the views of a motley group of sects holding views lumped together under the modern label GNOSTICISM. Against the Gnostics' denigration of the material world, Irenaeus affirms its goodness. Against their distinction between an inferior creator god and the transcendent God who lies beyond, he stresses the unity and coherence of God's dispensations.

According to Irenaeus Adam and Eve were created as children (*AH* 3.22.3), which is why they did not have sex in Eden, and the story of God's dealings with their progeny is the story of humankind growing up, a story which reaches its climax but not its end in Christ, who draws all things to himself (see RECAPITULATION). One of the meanings Irenaeus can give to the 'image' of God in which humankind was created is that it is the human body, in which God was to become visible in Christ (*AH* 5.6.1).

The definitive *revelation* given by and in Christ is entrusted to the APOSTLES and by them to the Church, passed on in the several Churches, from bishop to bishop. Irenaeus thinks that it is in principle possible to give for each of the apostolic Churches a list of bishops stretching back to the beginning. But in practice he undertakes to do so only for 'that greatest and most ancient church, known to all, founded and established at Rome by the two most glorious apostles Peter and PAUL' (*AH* 3.3.2) – though he adds that in his youth he himself had heard Polycarp (*ca* 70–*ca* 155), who was 'appointed by the apostles as a bishop in Asia in the church in Smyrna' (3.3.4).

In order to understand Irenaeus' view of APOSTOLIC SUCCESSION, it is important to realize that he is not saying that the bishops *are* what the apostles *were*, but that the bishops *teach* what the apostles *taught*. They are publicly accredited witnesses to a teaching TRADITION, and what they succeed to is understood in those terms, rather than in terms of authority or power. This tradition is, he passionately believes, uniform and unchanging, in contrast to the ever-shifting positions of fissiparous HERESY. SCRIPTURE is fully adequate for establishing the truth, but its meaning is continually twisted by the heretics and its pattern distorted – his analogy is with a fine mosaic of the emperor's son, the individual stones of which are prised loose and rearranged in the shape of a dog or a wolf (*AH* 1.8.1). The right pattern is given by the living tradition handed on in the Church and summarized in a proto-creedal set of propositions he calls the rule of truth or RULE OF FAITH, which functions rather like the picture on the lid of the box of a jigsaw puzzle – it shows you what the whole should look like.

D. Minns, *Irenaeus* (Geoffrey Chapman, 1994).

E. Osborn, *Irenaeus of Lyons* (Cambridge University Press, 2001).

PAUL PARVIS

IRRESISTIBLE GRACE The DOCTRINE that God's gift of GRACE cannot be resisted or rejected by human beings is a centrepiece of classical REFORMED THEOLOGY as defined at the Synod of DORT, which decreed that where God acts to convert a person to FAITH, it is not in the power of that individual to decide whether or not to be converted (3/4.12). At about the same time, similar views were associated with Catholic JANSENISM, and the claim that after the FALL human beings are unable to resist the interior operation of divine grace was among the propositions condemned by Pope Innocent X (r. 1644–55) in the anti-Jansenist bull *Cum occasione* (1653).

Both at Dort and among Jansenists, the idea of irresistible grace was closely connected with a belief that the effects of SIN are so pronounced that human beings would be incapable of benefiting from grace if its reception depended in any way on their own efforts. For Reformed theologians the doctrine of irresistible grace (like that of UNCONDITIONAL ELECTION) is also a corollary of the doctrine of JUSTIFICATION: if salvation is completely independent of human merit, then the gift of grace whereby a person is saved must be irresistible, since otherwise its efficacy *would* depend on a proper human response. Critics, however, worry that this exclusive focus on God's work implies a divine disregard of human agency inconsistent with God's commitment to human freedom.

See also APPELLANCY; ARMINIANISM; REFORMED THEOLOGY.

IAN A. MCFARLAND

ISLAM AND CHRISTIANITY To delineate the relations between Islam and Christianity, Judaism, too, has to be kept in mind, since it is necessary to invoke each of the three Abrahamic faiths to make fruitful comparisons. For a Christianity rooted in the REVELATION of God's promise to ABRAHAM and the LAW (or Torah) to Moses, into which Jesus had led his erstwhile followers by fulfilling both promise and Torah, the very thought of a yet further revelation of the sort claimed by Islam was unthinkable. However Christians have attempted to think of their relation to God's COVENANT with the Jews, that covenant remains the grounding fact for FAITH in Jesus, whose advent is quite unintelligible without the initiating promise and the subsequent gift of Torah (see JUDAISM AND CHRISTIANITY). But what was the Church to do when it encountered a further revelation to a man named Muhammad in the Arabian desert in the early seventh century?

It was a traumatic encounter, since Muhammad's followers had overrun the then civilized world (excepting China) within a century of their prophet's death. Not that their advent was always overtly threatening: a half-century after the Persian invasion of the Holy Land, which wreaked untold havoc and decimated monasteries, the bishop of Jerusalem, Sophronius (560–638) welcomed the forces of Islam, who showed a respect for Christian lives and sites which contrasts starkly with the later rampage by the Crusaders. Yet, because it was impossible for Christians to think of a 'new revelation', the only theological category available for Islam was that of a Christian HERESY.

Here the disanalogies among the three Abrahamic faiths are instructive: even those Christians who believed that the 'New' Testament had effectively replaced the

'Old' had to tolerate the presence of Jews in their societies, for they could not utterly deny their own spiritual ancestry (see Supersessionism). Yet Jews seldom posed a threat, as social arrangements reinforced the conviction that Judaism is for Jews only. But a competing revelation expressly destined for the entire human race had to be on a collision course with Jesus' command to 'proclaim the gospel to the whole creation' (Mark 16:15), even if Islam expressly provided privileged niches for Jews and for Christians as possessors of a divine revelation. So as the 'Muslim world' gained territory and power, it was destined to be a geographic as well as a spiritual 'other', for Christendom could hardly find room for so potent an adversary in its midst – not even the grudging space granted to Jews.

Yet a burgeoning medieval and early modern Europe could hardly resist the charms and allurements of the renowned Islamic civilization, especially as its elites sought elegant accessories from India and China which passed through the heart of the Muslim world on their way to Europe along the fabled 'silk road'. However, Europeans' desire to find a tax-free route to those very accessories would spell the end of such fated interaction between Christendom and the Islamic world, as the European discovery of America opened up far more than the Indies. After arresting the Ottoman forces at the gates of Vienna in 1683, western Europe could confidently turn its back on Islam to pursue the mercantile missionizing of North and South America, a development that ultimately led to western colonization of the Muslim Ottoman and Moghul Empires.

In breathlessly short compass, that is a summation of Christian history with Islam, though it is marked as well by fruitful philosophical and theological exchanges in medieval times among interlocutors like Avicenna (980–1037), al-Ghazali (1058–1111), and T. Aquinas, as well as by a continuing fascination for the 'marvels of the East'. Also, it should not be forgotten that the 'Islamicate' had provided room for Jews as well as Christians, who were always to be found among 'Arabs' (a shifting ethnic identity which includes but 20 per cent of present-day Muslims).

Globalization is eroding the geopolitical isolation of the Islamic from the traditionally Christian, or western, world: Europeans and Americans find Muslims in their midst. Specific historic and economic narratives account for the Muslims who are present in each distinct society, and the ways they are present: guest workers (largely from Turkey) in Germany, Algerians in France, British Commonwealth subjects in the UK and Canada, and immigrants from the Asian subcontinent in the USA, along with African-American Muslims. Yet, to undercut the palpable fear which the very presence of Muslims can so easily elicit in Europe, something else has to happen, including a seismic shift in mentality towards 'other believers'. It is worth noting how Vatican Council II's Dogmatic Constitution on the Church (*Lumen gentium*, 1964) already anticipated the groundbreaking initiatives of its Declaration on the Relation of the Church to Non-Christian Religions (*Nostra aetate*, 1964), and in some cases spoke even more forthrightly regarding the salvific faith of other-believers (and even of non-believers). Noting that 'those who have not yet received the gospel are related in various ways to the People of God', the document speaks first of the Jewish people, who remain 'most dear to God, for God does not repent of the gifts He makes nor of the calls He issues'. Then it mentions those who 'acknowledge the Creator', notably Muslims 'who, professing to hold the faith of Abraham, along with us adore the one and merciful God, who on the last day will judge mankind' (*LG*, §16). To feel the sea-change one need only contrast this with F. Xavier's (1506–52) letter to Ignatius of Loyola (1491–1556), imploring Ignatius to send more Jesuits to Asia, to 'save souls perishing'. As Vatican II avers, the principal issue is not salvation, which is a matter that belongs to God alone. The issue is rather how Christians can come to a more fruitful understanding of our own faith and its implications in our world through interaction with Muslims.

One such mutual illumination occurs when Christians discover just how central the book known as the Qur'an is to the lives of Muslims. There are a number of steps required here, for Christians can easily be misled by the Muslim categorization of them as 'people of the book' into comparing the Qur'an with the Bible. This often produces tendentious questions, like 'When will Muslims admit historical–critical methods to the study of their scriptures?' Or 'If the Qur'an is taken to be the very word of God, does that not mean that all Muslims must be "fundamentalist"?' In opposition to such an approach, attention to the way Muslims use the Qur'an actually helps to distinguish the Qur'an from the Bible. More fruitful is W. C. Smith's (1916–2000) suggestion that the better parallel is between the Qur'an and Jesus. Exploring this living comparison will clarify the way Christians relate Jesus to the Bible as well.

A first step is to realize how the Muslim phrase 'peoples of the book', meant to embrace Jews and Christians by including them in a Muslim commonwealth, is in fact false to traditional Christian self-understanding, as it presumes that God gave Jesus the NT in the same way that God gave Muhammad the Qur'an. We should not find it surprising that Muslims will view Christian revelation in parallel with theirs. But what is surprising is that this way of regarding God's revelation in Christ comes uncannily close to the view of many Christians, who in practice often privilege the Bible over the very person of Jesus, though for Christians the revelation of God in Christ is in a person, and not primarily in a book (even though we gain access to that person largely through the biblical books). This crucial difference is reflected in the parallel formulae inviting us to compare Jesus with the Qur'an: Christians believe that Jesus is the Word of God made human while Muslims believe that the Qur'an is the Word of God made Arabic. In this way Muslims of the Sufi tradition meditating on the 'names of God' gleaned from the Qur'an can be compared to Christians receiving the body and blood of Christ in the EUCHARIST. Far from embracing scriptural 'FUNDAMENTALISM', Muslims are rather directed to an interior appropriation of their scripture like that to which Ignatius calls Christians through his *Spiritual Exercises* (1548). Moreover, the rich commentary literature surrounding the Qur'an, recast in each epoch, vitiates any charge of Muslim 'fundamentalism'. As the Sufi example suggests, for Muslims the Qur'an is unlike any book in much the same way that, for Christians, Jesus is unlike any other human being.

A fruitful way into this crucial point of comparison is to note how Muslims use the Qur'an in ritual contexts: verses from the Qur'an might be said to flow over those engaged in the bodily movements which constitute the five daily prayers, much as the words of the Eucharistic prayer flow over believers who anticipate its delivering them the body and blood of Jesus. Outside ritual contexts, and in contact with daily demands, Muslims will be more inclined to have recourse to the hadith: stories telling how the Prophet Muhammad responded, in word or action, to situations. Passed on from parents to children to regulate playground behaviour, they can also animate statesmen. The NT contains similar sorts of stories, of course, which animate 'imitation of Christ' strategies among Christians. But the literary genre of the Qur'an is quite different and defies any easy characterization. The most that can be said is that, unlike hadith (which offer directives to action), Qur'an verses cumulate to create a world in which believers 'live, move, and have their being' (Acts 17:28). This is the way Christians will find faithful Muslims (many of whom know the Qur'an virtually by heart) employing its verses in the midst of their daily lives, as a way of continuing the ritual practices of prayer.

Here is where personal experience with Muslims can be so telling. One can marvel at the palpable, pervasive sense of the presence of God. In overwhelmingly Muslim Bangladesh, plans to meet for lunch are invariably suffixed with '*in sh'Allah!*' – which translates into the language of western Ireland as 'God willing!' but is too easily misconstrued by western hearers as 'Muslim fatalism'. Yet it need not be 'fatalism' to see one's life 'in God's hands', any more than believing the Qur'an to be God's word makes one 'fundamentalist'. Indeed, employing such labels can lead to ignoring the rich opportunities to which the contemporary world opens Christians: to let the practices of other-believers show them fresh ways to the God worshipped in both traditions (however differently), thereby letting difference enrich Christian faith and its distinctive revelation. There is no inherent danger of syncretism here; only respect for difference suggesting ways our transcendent God is revealed in the immanence of interpersonal exchange, especially in friendship.

As Christians ask how the confession of Islam may or may not inform the political strategies of Muslim countries, they may find it more salutary to follow the lead of the masses of the Muslim faithful, who give daily witness to their revelation, rather than of Islam's putative public spokespersons, whether religious or political. In any case, the sea-change that is now taking place in interfaith relations directs Christians to more 'ordinary' interchanges, where they can begin to intimate the 'extraordinary' in Islam, precisely as it is nourished by and gives voice to a particular faith commitment. Interfaith friendship can in this way lead both Christian and Muslim believers to a more humble posture, by reminding them how much they have to learn from the other about what must be of paramount interest to both of them: humanity's way to God.

A. H. al-Ghazali, *Ninety-Nine Beautiful Names of God* (Islamic Texts Society, 1992).
K. Armstrong, *Islam: A Short History* (Modern Library, 2000).
K. Cragg, *Readings in the Qu'ran* (HarperCollins, 1988).
M. L. Gude and L. Massignon, *Crucible of Compassion* (University of Notre Dame Press, 1996).
S. Murata and W. Chittick, *Vision of Islam* (Paragon House, 1994).
J. Sacks, *Dignity of Difference* (Continuum, 2002).

DAVID B. BURRELL

ISRAEL The Hebrew word 'Israel' literally connotes a struggle with God, but it is within Christian theology that 'Israel' has often had to struggle most. The place and function of Israel within Christian discourse has been a perennially controversial question. Indeed, the still-unresolved nature of the relationship between the Church and Israel stands at the very centre of what it means for the Church to be the Church. One of the first consequences of this controversy has been how 'Israel' is in fact to be defined, a question to which numerous answers have been proposed. Adding significantly to the confusion has been the particular continuation of Israel, even after the destruction of the Second Temple in 70, in the specific forms of Jews as a distinct people and Judaism as a religion. While much of traditional Christian theology has assumed the destruction of 'Israel', its continuing existence has proven to be a challenge to the Church's understanding of both Israel and itself.

In its most minimal, but paradoxically most profound, meaning, 'Israel' refers to the relationship between God and God's people. Throughout SCRIPTURE, the COVENANT community of God is always to some extent 'Israel'. Even in the NT, the identity of this people of God can never be entirely divorced from the OT applications of this word. Indeed, almost invariably, whenever the NT authors speak of the 'people of God', it is to 'Israel' that they are referring. This minimalist definition implies therefore an inclusivity that goes beyond a specific geography, ethnicity, or religious determination. However, the nature of the community described by the term 'Israel' remains hidden from view behind that designation. Of the numerous attempts that have been made to give fuller meaning to this name, there are three that have achieved most currency.

In the first instance, the name can refer simply to the historical tribal confederacy and (later) kingdom, and therefore by extension to the land over which a succession of judges and kings ruled from the Exodus to the fall of Jerusalem in 587 BC. In this case, a distinction is typically made between the northern kingdom, to which the name 'Israel' continues to adhere, and Judah in the south. By this definition, Israel's existence as such ceased when Jerusalem was destroyed by the Babylonian army, and was only properly restored as an independent political entity in 1948. During the intervening centuries, 'Israel' was little more than an outlying province of other empires, its ultimate embodiment being viewed, in both Jewish and Christian theologies, primarily in eschatological terms.

Alternatively, 'Israel' can refer more broadly to the entire OT community of God's people, descending from the patriarch Jacob, upon whom the name 'Israel' was divinely bestowed at Peniel (Gen. 32:28–30). According to this view, the trajectory of the community passes through several distinct stages: under the patriarchs, a loose family of tribal and religious affiliations; from the Exodus until Samuel, a theocratic nation under YHWH (see Tetragrammaton); from Saul to the exile, an institutional State; and from the exile until the restoration, a suffering and persecuted remnant. There is no distinction made here between the northern and southern kingdoms, as the definition is primarily a theological one that seeks to articulate the embodiment of the covenantal relationship until the time of Christ.

More contentiously, 'Israel' has been used as a synonym for the community of Jesus' followers – the Church – that is thereby believed to have superseded the Hebrew people as God's chosen covenant-partner (see Supersessionism). Although there is neither linguistic nor theological justification for the synonymity of 'Israel' and Church within the Gospels, some disputed Pauline phraseology in the epistles (e.g., Rom. 9:6; 1 Cor. 10:18; Gal. 6:16) has historically lent support to this idea. Indeed, the term 'new Israel' has been used widely in both academic and popular theological discourse as a designation for the Church since it was first proposed by Tertullian. This last usage has, however, declined sharply since the burgeoning of post-Holocaust theology in the 1960s. There has been a corresponding recognition among many Church leaders that this sort of marginalization of present-day Judaism in Christian theological discourse has all too often been a precursor to and justification for social and political ostracism that, after Auschwitz, must forever be rejected.

None of these three major definitions of 'Israel' is completely apposite, and a more faithfully theological definition encompasses aspects of each. The name must primarily be associated with both biblical and post-biblical Jewish communities, including their relationship to the land of promise *and* their separation from it, their relationships to *and* their estrangements from one another, their fidelity *and* their infidelity to YHWH, and their ancient and modern political structures. As YHWH's covenant partner, Israel is Israel in *all* its manifestations, glories and faults; it is not only Israel in its faithfulness, nor is it only Israel in its waywardness. In other words, Israel is Israel in the fullness of its social humanity.

However, the community of the Church cannot be entirely absent from the definition, even if it is not, as some would want to suggest, the primary referent. Notwithstanding that the Church is in no sense the 'new Israel', it has become part of Israel (Rom. 11:17–19), and so now shares also in the original covenant partnership.

In recent decades, the nature of 'Israel' and its place within Christian theology has arisen in two main *loci*; the meaning of the Israeli State, and the necessity of inter-faith dialogue. What place does, or should, the modern-day political State, founded in 1948, have in theological considerations? This question is especially pressing for Palestinian Christians, but it is not limited to them. For some Christians, the re-establishment of the Jewish people on their traditional homeland is an indication of 'end-times' prophetic fulfilment (see Dispensationalism). For others, the new political entity is an entirely secular affair, with no religious significance. Still others, conscious that the foundation of the State was in part a direct result of the Holocaust, conceive modern Israel as both a political and a theological reality, precisely because the Holocaust itself is viewed as a theologically determinative event. Similarly, the ubiquity of inter-religious violence in the twentieth century has forced religious leaders to concede that global peace requires greater dialogue between religious traditions, and so Christians have again had to consider the relationship between Christianity and Israel.

See also Judaism and Christianity.

K. Barth, *Church Dogmatics*, (T&T Clark, 1957, 1960) II/2, 34–5, and III/3, 49.3.

M. Barth, *The People of God* (JSOT, 1982).

R. Davidson, 'Theology of Land and Covenant' in *Reports to the General Assembly of the Church of Scotland 2003*.

R. K. Soulen, *The God of Israel and Christian Theology* (Fortress Press, 1996).

Mark R. Lindsay

James, William The psychologist and philosopher William James (1842–1910) is best known as a founder of the psychological–phenomenological study of individual religious experience and the philosophical tradition known as pragmatism. In theological studies, James is best known for his books *The Will to Believe* (1897) and *The Varieties of Religious Experience* (1902). Following the publication of the former, James speculated that he should have titled it 'the right to believe'. In it he rejected the widely accepted views of D. Hume (1711–76), I. Kant, and G. W. F. Hegel by choosing theism and the right or will to believe over absolutism, agnosticism, and determinism. James observed that for many persons religion is a 'live option' (defined as an unavoidable and significant choice, upon which a believer is willing to act) and defended the intellectual legitimacy of adopting a religious faith. In *Varieties*, he rejected objectivism and advocated a radically inclusive empiricism. He argued for the validity of sensory and religious experience and hypothesized that the human 'subconscious' functioned as a doorway between the 'conscious self' and 'The More' that, when open, allowed an individual to receive an experience of the 'reality of the unseen'. For James, in both volumes, strict adherence to logical reason resulted in deterministic monistic systems, while reality – as it is shaped by free will – remains empirically pluralistic.

Born into a theologically rich world, James made four significant contributions to contemporary American liberal theology: (1) he influenced both R. Niebuhr and his brother, H. R. Niebuhr (1919–62); (2) he contributed to the development of process theology; (3) he influenced Black theology; and (4) he made seminal contributions to the psychology of religion.

James' theological methodology, which combined elements of pragmatism and empiricism, deeply influenced R. Niebuhr, who also adopted James' ideas of religion as a motive for and agent of social change and social justice. In addition, Niebuhr incorporated James' eschatological view – the belief in the eventual triumph of one's ethical values – as central to religious philosophy. H. R. Niebuhr recognized James' understanding of the phenomenology of consciousness and the interactive and selective nature of human response. He saw attention and imagination, combined with deliberate action, as foundational for morality.

James' radical empiricism and empirical theology also influenced B. Meland (1899–1993) and A. N. Whitehead (1861–1947) at the University of Chicago, who were foundational figures in the development of process theology. Meland adopted James' idea of a 'stream of consciousness' (defined as the continuous, uninterrupted flow of consciousness in which every thought and feeling is immersed) and argued for human participation in a stream of experience that is not fully recognized at the cognitive level or easily expressed in conceptual terms.

James' pragmatism played an important role in Black theology. W. E. B. Du Bois (1868–1963), who studied under James at Harvard University, became a 'devoted follower' when James was developing pragmatism. Du Bois applied pragmatic philosophy to a historical interpretation of race relations. Numerous Black theologians have addressed the importance of James' pragmatism, particularly its focus on the validity of experience. C. West (b. 1953) has explored pragmatism in the legacies of James and Du Bois, while African-American humanist A. Pinn (b. 1964) continues to document the importance of experience in Black liberation theology as well as the pragmatic reconstruction of African-American theology. Theologian C. T. Smith (b. 1961) sees pragmatism as influential in womanist theology, particularly the continuity between theory and praxis.

From the work of his student E. D. Starbuck (1866–1947) on conversion, to A. T. Boisen (1876–1965), who revolutionized the training of chaplains through Clinical Pastoral Education, James' influence is writ largest in the area of psychology of religion. More broadly, *The Will to Believe* and *Varieties* continue to serve as foundational texts across many subfields of religious studies.

L. Bridgers, *Contemporary Varieties of Religious Experience* (Rowman & Littlefield, 2005).

C. West, *Race Matters* (Vintage Books, 2001).

John Snarey and Lynn Bridgers

Jansenism Named after Cornelius Jansen (1585–1638), bishop of Ypres and author of the posthumously published *Augustinus* (1640), Jansenism refers to a movement within Catholic theology that was influential in France and the Low Countries from the seventeenth to the early nineteenth century. Especially in its early period, the Jansenist spirituality practised by the nuns of the convent of Port-Royal-des-Champs and their sympathizers (including B. Pascal) took the form of a moral and sacramental rigorism that included wariness of frequent participation in the Eucharist. In this as well as in their teaching on grace and sin, Jansenists stood in stark and deliberate opposition to the theology and practice of the Jesuits, who coined the epithet 'Jansenist' as a derogatory term for their opponents.

As the title of Jansen's treatise suggests, Jansenists advocated a strongly Augustinian interpretation of Christian doctrine. Jansen's views had been formed in opposition to the Catholic theological position known as Molinism, according to which the choices of free creatures, though infallibly known by God, are nevertheless independent of God's will (see Middle Knowledge). Jansenists regarded this attempt to defend human free will against the threat of divine determinism as an attack on the sovereignty of God's grace that amounted to semi-Pelagianism. At the same time, the Jansenist emphasis on the degree to which original sin vitiated human freedom, their corresponding stress on the sufficiency of grace, and their teaching on predestination were viewed by opponents as indistinguishable from the tenets of Reformed theology as defined at the Synod of Dort.

Though *Augustinus* was condemned by the papacy as early as 1642 for violating a moratorium on publication of works on grace, the controversy came to a head in 1653, when Pope Innocent X (r. 1644–55) issued the bull *Cum occasione*, which condemned five propositions associated with Jansen's book, including irresistible grace, limited atonement, and the claim that even the just are unable to obey God's commands by their own efforts. The Jansenist theologian A. Arnauld (1612–94) responded by accepting the pope's condemnation of the five propositions, but denying that they were to be found in *Augustinus*. He went on to argue more generally that, while the magisterium had the power to decide matters of *doctrine* (e.g., whether the five propositions were orthodox), it had no authority to pronounce on matters of *fact* (e.g., whether those propositions were in *Augustinus*).

Though Arnauld's distinction between doctrine (*droit*) and fact (*fait*) was rejected both by the University of Paris and by Pope Alexander VII (r. 1655–67), his decision to defend himself by reference to questions of ecclesiology (rather than by explicitly opposing papal teaching on sin and grace) set the tone for much later Jansenist apologetics. Further papal condemnations of Jansenist positions over the following decades were associated with increased attention among Jansenists to the specifically ecclesiological implications of their theology of grace, leading eventually to the conclusion that the integrity of the Church was a function of its devotional and sacramental practice rather than of doctrinal unanimity as defined by the magisterium.

See also Appellancy.

N. Abercrombie, *The Origins of Jansenism* (Oxford University Press, 1936).

J. Delumeau, 'Jansenism' in *Catholicism between Luther and Voltaire: A New View of the Counter-Reformation* (Westminster Press, 1977 [1971]), 99–128.

Ian A. McFarland

Japanese Theology The phrase 'Japanese theology' is used here in its narrowest sense, i.e., systematic theology undertaken in Japan by the Japanese. Such Japanese theology has always been on the boundary between Christian faith and Japanese culture. As a result, Japanese theology has mainly developed in two directions.

On the one hand, there is a type of theology which tries to maintain the evangelical faith (especially in the atonement of Jesus Christ) as well as to play a prophetic role in society. This type of theology was first represented by M. Uemura (1857–1925), one of the preeminent leaders of Christianity in Japan in its early years. This type is interested not only in dogmatic theology but also in the significance of Protestant Christianity or Puritanism for reforming contemporary Japanese society. It is represented mainly by the works of Y. Kumano (1899–1982), T. Sato (1923–2007), Y. Furuya (b. 1926), H. Ohki (b. 1928), and K. Kondo (b. 1943). They all learnt much from K. Barth, while taking seriously the historical reality of Christianity as analyzed in the works of E. Troeltsch. Recently, T. Haga (b. 1952), influenced by postliberal theology, has developed a strong support for the uniqueness of the Christian community and the significance of its presence in the Japanese cultural situation.

Over against this evangelical–prophetic theological type, there is a Japanese form of liberal theology, which tries to mediate between Christianity and Japanese culture more positively. These two types have been in conflict with each other. The first representative of the liberal type was D. Ebina (1856–1937); he had a debate with Uemura on Christology in the early twentieth century. Ebina was close to an adoptionist understanding of the divinity of Jesus Christ (see Adoptionism), while Uemura clung to a traditional, Chalcedonian Christology. More recent and remarkable representatives of the second type are K. Takizawa (1906–84) and S. Yagi (b. 1932), who insist that the essence of Christianity and that of Zen Buddhism are ultimately the same. Though their works are provocative, they tend to go beyond the boundary of theology into the philosophy of religion.

In relation to such a liberal position, one might expect Japanese theology to be indigenous to Japan. There have been, however, few such successful theologies which have tried to be more harmonious with Japanese culture. Buddhism, which was introduced to Japan around 500 and is now quite indigenous to Japan, has experienced several transformations with regard to its essence, so that it now has teachings and moral codes far different from the original Buddhism. Japanese Christian theologians are cautious about such dangers of inculturation. It goes without saying, however, that Japanese theology – even the evangelical–prophetic type – has its background in Japanese churches and culture, which leave an undeniable trace in it.

To date, one theology in particular is noteworthy for its attempt to remain both distinctively Christian and distinctively Japanese. *Theology of the Pain of God*

(1946) by K. Kitamori (1916–98) is inspired by M. Luther's notion of the *Deus absconditus*, but at the same time, it utilizes a traditional Japanese word, *tsurasa*, which refers to the human inner conflict between personal love and social responsibility, in order to explicate the pain quintessential to God's being. More recently, N. Miyahira (b. 1966) has been developing a 'theology of the concord of God'. He makes use of another traditional Japanese notion – *wa* (concord) – as a tool to understand the Trinity. The project is attractive but problematic, for *wa* refers not only to concord but also to a kind of rigid social code, and thus constitutes a hindrance for freer and more spontaneous actions among the Japanese.

One may point out two general characteristics of Japanese theology. First, Japanese theologians are quite eager to learn theologies from abroad, especially theologies in Germany and the USA. Theological studies in Japan started just as westernization in Japan did, with the result that theological 'import' has been and is still more important than 'export' in Japan. A most striking example of this is the richness of the Japanese translations of the works of many modern western theologians such as Barth, P. Tillich, R. Bultmann, R. Niebuhr, J. Moltmann (b. 1926), W. Pannenberg (b. 1928), T. F. Torrance (1913–2007), and others. On the other hand, despite the fact that the many pre-eminent Japanese theologians received their degrees in European or American institutions (especially in the period since World War II), their works are not so popular outside Japan, and only a limited number of them are available in other languages.

Second, Japanese Protestant theology is more ecumenical and less 'denominational' in focus. This characteristic has a historical background. Japanese Protestantism started in the late nineteenth century, and its theological orientation was basically determined by that of the World Evangelical Alliance established in the same century. The theological attitude of the Alliance can be traced further back to 1795, the year the London Missionary Society was established. Participants of the Society insisted that they should proclaim Jesus Christ, rather than their own denominations. Japanese theology thus has been ecumenical and open from the outset. In this context, the 'No-Church Movement' associated with the early twentieth-century theologian K. Uchimura (1861–1930) may be regarded as a radical criticism of denominational Churches.

This same ecumenical tendency is also seen in the establishment of the United Church of Christ in Japan (UCCJ) in 1941. The UCCJ is currently the largest Protestant denomination in Japan and comprises Presbyterians, Congregationalists, Methodists, and others. Most of the active theologians in Japan belong to the UCCJ, and the fact that UCCJ is a united Church makes theology in Japan much broader than in many more traditional European and North American contexts. UCCJ theologians have had lively conversations with different denominational traditions, as well as with both conservative and liberal theologies. Both conservative and liberal theological currents – as well as the tensions between them – can be found in the UCCJ.

Finally, with regard to liberation theologies, T. Kuribayashi (b. 1948), in his *Theology of the Crown of Thorns* (1986), develops a theology which is deeply rooted in the life and reality of discriminated communities in Japan. Though there are some remarkable feminist theologians in Japan, their works tend to concentrate on biblical exegesis and no important work by them has appeared in the field of systematic theology so far (see Feminist Theology).

Yasuo Furuya, ed., *A History of Japanese Theology* (Eerdmans, 1997).

C. Michelson, *Japanese Contribution to Christian Theology* (Westminster Press, 1959).

Masami Kojiro

Jehovah's Witnesses The Watchtower Bible and Tract Society is a Christian sectarian body founded by C. T. Russell (1852–1916) in the USA during the closing decades of the nineteenth century. The group adopted the name 'Jehovah's Witnesses' in 1931. Russell's spiritual journey began with doubts about several Christian doctrines. In time, however, he came to accept the authority of the Bible and the imminence of Christ's second coming (see Parousia). Russell subsequently became a master at both organization and publication. He published, for example, a magazine, *Zion's Watchtower*, and seven volumes entitled *Studies in the Scriptures* (1886–1917) which articulated a theology that evolved over time.

The Witnesses regard the Bible as the final authority in matters of religion and make use of their own *New World Translation* (1961). For them the Bible is a dark book with hidden meanings and therefore requires assistance in interpretation. The community disseminates proper interpretations through the *Watchtower* magazine and a host of other publications.

God's proper name, the Witnesses state, is Jehovah, which they equate with the Hebrew YHWH (see Tetragrammaton). They reject belief in the Trinity as a form of polytheism and regard neither Jesus nor the Holy Spirit as divine. Jesus (or Christ) was the archangel Michael before his human birth. Born of Mary, he was a perfect human, but not God in the flesh, nor the second Person of the Trinity. He died on a torture stake, not a cross, and he was not resurrected. Instead, a new Jesus was created to live at the right hand of Jehovah. Christ's death was a ransom sacrifice to bring back what Adam lost when tempted by the Devil, namely, the opportunity for humans to live on a paradise-like earth for ever. Adam and his descendants lost the right to life and thus were subject to death. The Holy Spirit has no divine or personal nature; rather it is an impersonal, invisible, active force of Jehovah which motivates Witnesses to do Jehovah's will.

Human beings, beginning with Adam, lost perfection through the FALL and became depraved in both body and mind. Yet they have FREEDOM OF WILL and are responsible for their actions. They are not immortal; when dead, they have no consciousness. Salvation is obtained by following Jehovah's law and working for his cause. Everlasting life comes to those who follow God's will. Christ's life set an example for others to emulate. Jehovah's Witnesses spend time 'witnessing', whether by conversation, distributing literature, or conducting Bible-study sessions.

Jehovah's Witnesses who are faithful and fulfil their responsibilities may be either part of the 144,000 anointed ones who will reign with Jehovah God in HEAVEN for eternity (see Rev. 14:1–3) or part of the 'Great Crowd' or 'other Sheep' who will live for ever on a paradise-like earth, which will never be destroyed. The wicked, who will not participate in either of these glorious situations, following the battle of Armageddon will be destroyed by Jehovah God and cease to exist. The Witnesses reject as unscriptural and unjust the notion of the wicked suffering eternal torment in HELL. At the battle of Armageddon, Christ and the forces of good will destroy the wicked institutions of the world – Churches, governments, and businesses. Death will cease for ever.

The Witnesses practise BAPTISM by immersion. They have a 'memorial communion service' once a year, but only those of the 'elect class' or the 144,000 participate. Jehovah's Witnesses do not celebrate any holidays or religious festivals, including either Christmas or Easter. They use no images in their worship. They also obey only those human laws they find consistent with Jehovah's statutes. Therefore they do not accept blood transfusions, serve in the military, salute the flag, or participate in elections.

Jehovah's Witnesses have prospered not only in the USA, but also worldwide, often attracting converts from the social, cultural, and economic margins of society. They have frequently suffered hardship and persecution as a result of their beliefs and practices.

M. D. Curry, *Jehovah's Witnesses: The Millenarian World of the Watch Tower* (Garland Publishing, 1992).

A. Holden, *Jehovah's Witnesses: Portrait of a Contemporary Religious Movement* (Routledge, 2002).

M. J. Penton, *Apocalypse Delayed: The Story of Jehovah's Witnesses*, 2nd edn (University of Toronto Press, 1997).

STEPHEN J. STEIN

JEROME Jerome (*ca* 347–420) was a major exegete, translator, controversialist, and ascetic. Born in Stridon (Dalmatia) and educated in Rome, he travelled widely in his youth, spending time as a hermit in the Syrian desert. An assistant of Pope Damasus I (r. 366–84), he became a prominent advocate of ASCETICISM and critic of clerical morality. Forced to leave Rome, he travelled in the East, accompanied by a wealthy Roman widow, Paula, and her daughter Eustochium. In 386 they settled in Bethlehem, where Paula's wealth financed the establishment of a double monastery, with Jerome in charge of the male house. He devoted the rest of his life to learning and left a remarkable legacy of intellectual achievements.

Jerome is most famous for his revisions and translations of SCRIPTURE, which laid the foundations of the VULGATE. He was the first in the West to return to 'the Hebrew verity' rather than relying on Greek versions of the OT, and his work had no rival until the REFORMATION. He published major commentaries on OT and NT texts; though interested most in the literal sense, he also exploited spiritual interpretation and made use of Jewish exegetical traditions. He wrote history and biography, and translated theologians such as ORIGEN into Latin (though he later became a fierce critic of Origen's ideas). A sharp polemicist and literary satirist, he found many targets: Helvidius (*fl.* 380), who denied the perpetual VIRGINITY of Mary; Jovinian (d. *ca* 405), a monk who considered marriage equal to virginity; the early supporters of Pelagius (see PELAGIANISM) – and others. His construal of ascetic ideals reflects his own inner struggles and his doctrinal contributions were often none too acute, but he saw himself as champion of ORTHODOXY, expositor of scriptural wisdom, and teacher of serious devotion. His extensive correspondence offers a rich mine of information on the dynamics of the late antique theological world.

S. Rebenich, *Jerome* (Routledge, 2002).

IVOR J. DAVIDSON

JESUS OF NAZARETH: see CHRISTOLOGY.

JOACHIM OF FIORE Joachim of Fiore (*ca* 1135–1202) was born in Calabria and is chiefly known for his theory of history and for the development of Christian apocalypticism in general and millennialism in particular. No earlier than 1171 he entered the Benedictine monastery of Corazzo, becoming abbot in 1177. While visiting the house at Casamari in 1183 and 1184, he received two visions, one on the book of Revelation, the other on the TRINITY. In his own lifetime and the early thirteenth century, he was primarily known for his concordances between the OT and NT, and for his predictions of the coming of the ANTICHRIST; it was only later that his views of the future progress of the earth gained widespread influence.

By the time Corazzo was accepted into the Cistercian order, Joachim and some of his followers had become disillusioned by the order's lack of spiritual vitality and indiscipline, and between 1190 and 1192 he founded a new house at San Giovanni da Fiore. As such he was a reformer, not so much seeking a return to the idealized perfection of the primitive Church, as looking to the future Church in the third age of the Holy Spirit which was soon to dawn (in the year 1260, according to his followers). While the Florensians initially enjoyed popularity, they fell into sharp decline in the early thirteenth century. Joachim's theories were later developed by the Spiritual Franciscans and others, invariably in ways not to the liking of the Church. Although the fourth Lateran Council (1215) condemned his Trinitarian doctrine and its misinformed attack on Peter Lombard (*ca* 1100–60), Joachim himself was not condemned.

Joachim wrote three major works, beginning in the 1180s: *The Book of Concordance of the Old and New Testaments*, *Exposition of the Apocalypse*, and *Ten-Stringed Psaltery.* These works are lengthy, often repetitious, filled with difficult exegesis, elaborate symbolism, and patterns of numbers (especially twelves, sevens, sixes, fives, and twos – though threes eventually dominate, reflecting the centrality of the Trinity in his thought), which were later compiled in the *Liber Figurarum.* His visions led him to the conviction that through the gift of understanding (*intelligentia spiritualis*) the spiritual/intellectual person (*spiritualis intellectus*) could understand Scripture.

Joachim's focus was the Trinity's involvement in history. He divided history into three states (Latin *status*), each corresponding to one of the divine Persons. He avoided a dynamic modalism (in which each Person reveals a different aspect of the one God in historical succession) by teaching that all three Persons are active in each *status* and, more specifically, that the ages of the Son and the Spirit overlap, analogously to the way that both the Son and Spirit proceed from the Father. The first *status* of the Father began with creation. The second commenced with the rise of the messianic hope in the OT and extended through the incarnation down to Joachim's day. The third age of the Spirit would be the culmination of history, in which humanity would enjoy the peace of God.

Although the main pattern of history for Joachim was that of his three *status*, he also affirmed two dispensations, corresponding to the two biblical testaments. Moreover, from Augustine he adopted the idea of seven ages corresponding to the seven days of creation – five leading up to the incarnation, the sixth lasting to his own day, and the seventh to begin soon thereafter. After the final destruction of the antichrist, the eighth day of eternal bliss would come.

The chief stimuli of his work were Scripture (particularly Revelation) and the Latin fathers. He opposed Scholastic theology and developed biblical hermeneutics into a complex scheme that emphasized seven 'typical' senses by which each of the seven Augustinian ages of history had literal concordances in the other six. Joachim used these concordances to draw connections between the two testaments, but his real originality lay in his use of them as a method of understanding the future; for he believed that in the same way that the Spirit proceeds from the Father *and* the Son, so the spiritual understanding of Scripture that would cast light on the future age proceeds from both the OT *and* the NT.

See also Apocalyptic, Premillennialism.

B. McGinn, *The Calabrian Abbot: Joachim of Fiore in the History of Western Thought* (Macmillan, 1985).

M. Reeves, *Joachim of Fiore and the Prophetic Future: A Medieval Study in Historical Thinking*, revised edn (Sutton, 1999).

M. Reeves and B. Hirsch-Reich, *The Figurae of Joachim of Fiore* (Oxford University Press, 1972).

D. C. West, ed., *Joachim of Fiore in Christian Thought: Essays on the Influence of the Calabrian Abbot*, 2 vols. (Franklin, 1975).

Anthony R. Cross

Job In its prose frame (1:1–2:13 and 42:7–17) the book of Job narrates a wager between God and Satan (see Devil) over a pious and prosperous individual from the land of Uz. Job's piety is tested by the destruction of his livestock and children, and finally by bodily affliction. Urged by his wife to curse God and die, he continues to bless God and ultimately receives back God's blessing in double. The proverbial 'patience of Job' (Jas. 5:11) comes from this simple folktale. But in the book's centre erupts something quite different in poetic form (3:1–42:6). The arrival of Job's friends sets the scene for Job's outcry against his fate, as they attempt to explain his suffering, arguing above all that it is the consequence of his sin. Dissatisfied with their platitudes, Job seeks to bring his complaint before God, whose response alone will satisfy him. God does indeed respond to Job, bringing him to silence. But it is Job, not his friends, who is in the end commended by God (42:7–8).

In the light of a modern preoccupation with theodicy, the climax of the poem in God's speeches can only be unsatisfying, because it fails to provide an explanation for Job's suffering. But in the Christian tradition the problem of undeserved suffering has not been viewed as something to be reconciled abstractly with a just and loving God, but is explored in the context of much richer doctrinal resources, e.g., in typological relation to the redemptive suffering of Christ and the Church (Pope Gregory I, 'the Great' (r. 590–604)), within philosophical discussion of God's providential knowledge (T. Aquinas), and in investigation of the divine law and God's hiddenness (J. Calvin).

A common feature of these traditional interpretations is belief in personal immortality. When read through a modern lens this looks like an easy solution to the problem of unjust suffering: retributive justice might not hold in this life, but it will in the afterlife.

This complaint, however, presupposes that immortality is a continuation of time rather than something which brings about an alternative (eschatological) perspective on temporal life.

K. BARTH brings some of these traditional themes to culmination in his reading of Job as a witness to Christ. Within this doctrinal frame his main concern is with the question of whether Job is right or wrong to argue with God, concluding that he is both at once (echoing the *SIMUL JUSTUS ET PECCATOR* of M. LUTHER). This highlights a theme which was a persistent problem for earlier interpreters: how God could commend Job when his speech was so unchastened and even blasphemous.

If, in this vein, Job is read as a book about human SANCTIFICATION, God's speeches might be viewed as the culmination of Job's persistent struggle with God. The God who speaks is the One with whom Job has been wrestling all along, but seen now as the Creator, whose ways are irreducible to retributive justice. Thus, while the text may not offer theoretical solutions, it does address Job's practical dilemma: it narrates his tortured exploration of God's incomprehensible ways and its issue in a transformed relationship with God.

K. Barth, *Church Dogmatics* (T&T Clark, 1961), IV/3, 70.
S. Ticciati, *Job and the Disruption of Identity: Reading Beyond Barth* (T&T Clark, 2005).

SUSANNAH TICCIATI

JOHN OF DAMASCUS Often considered the last great theologian of the patristic era, John of Damascus (nicknamed Chrysorrhoas, or 'Golden-Stream' for his eloquence) was born into a family of Christian civil servants sometime in the latter half of the seventh century. He followed his father as an official in the Muslim government in Damascus until the caliph sought to islamicize his administration, at which point Mansur (John's Arabic name) became a monk, spending the rest of his life in a monastery (according to later tradition, that of Mar Saba) near Jerusalem. He is thought to have died around 750.

John's reputation as a theologian rests on two distinct achievements. First is his *Exposition of the Orthodox Faith* (actually the third part of a more comprehensive work, *The Fountain of Knowledge*), a classic compendium of ORTHODOX THEOLOGY that (thanks to a twelfth-century Latin translation) also proved tremendously influential in the West. In this volume John gave definitive statement to the Trinitarian and Christological dogmas that had been the focus of the first six ecumenical COUNCILS and was also the first to apply the term 'PERICHORESIS' to the relationship among the Persons of the TRINITY. No less significant are his *Three Treatises on the Divine Images*, in which he outlined a specifically Christological defence of the veneration of ICONS, arguing that because God had in Christ assumed a fully human nature, one could not object to images of Christ without denying the INCARNATION (see, e.g., *Three* 1.16, 3.8).

See also DULIA; ICONOCLASM.

IAN A. MCFARLAND

JOHN THE BAPTIST A Jewish eschatological prophet in first-century Palestine, John was known as the 'Baptist' (or 'Baptizer') for his practice of dipping his followers in the Jordan River as a sign of their repentance in the face of imminent divine judgement (cf. Mark 1:4–5 and Matt. 3:1–6). According to Luke, John was born to a priestly family (Luke 1:5–13), though his later career in the wilderness has led modern scholars to associate him with the Essenes, an eschatologically oriented Jewish sect who rejected the Jerusalem priesthood and the Temple cult. In any case, it is clear that John attracted a large group of disciples who continued to be associated with him after his death (see Acts 19:1–3). Josephus (*ca* 37–*ca* 100) suggests that John was arrested and killed by Herod Antipas (*r.* 4 BC–AD 39) because his followers were viewed as a political threat (*Ant.* 18.5.2); the NT ascribes his execution to John's criticism of Herod's marriage to his brother's wife (Matt. 14:1–12 and pars.; cf. *Ant.* 18.5.1).

The relationship between John and Jesus is complex. Luke states that they were of virtually the same age and related through their mothers (1:36–44). Be that as it may, the fact that Jesus was baptized by John (Mark 1:9) could easily give an appearance of dependence on him, and the Gospel writers employ various strategies to avoid any such implication: Matthew claims that John consented to baptize Jesus only after Jesus ordered him to do so (3:13–15), and Luke carefully omits any explicit mention of John as the agent of Jesus' baptism (3:21). Nevertheless, it seems clear that Jesus' early preaching was modelled on John's (cf. Matt. 3:2 and 4:17), and according to JOHN THE EVANGELIST Jesus' first disciples were drawn from the Baptist's followers (1:35–42).

In the synoptic Gospels John is identified with the prophet Elijah, whose return was expected immediately prior to the last days (Matt. 11:13–14; Mark 9:11–13; Luke 1:17; cf. Mal. 4:5–6), and Christians, following this lead, have generally interpreted John as the last of the OT prophets. As the one who 'prepares the way' for Jesus (Matt. 3:3 and pars.; cf. Isa. 40:3; Mal. 3:1), he is in the Orthodox Churches officially known as St John the Forerunner (*Prodromos* in Greek). For all Christians he embodies the link between the two testaments of Christian SCRIPTURE, symbolizing in his person the transition from the time of the LAW to that of the GOSPEL (see John 3:25–30; cf. Gal. 3:23–6).

C. M. Murphy, *John the Baptist: Prophet of Purity for a New Age* (Liturgical Press, 2003).

IAN A. MCFARLAND

JOHN THE EVANGELIST John the Evangelist is above all the author of the Gospel that bears his name, and hence the primary evidence about him is the Gospel itself. We can try to identify him with a figure known from elsewhere in early Christian tradition (e.g., John son of Zebedee, or 'John the Elder' mentioned by Papias in the early second century). But such attempts are probably fruitless and not in the end very helpful. The Gospel itself identifies its author as the 'beloved disciple' (21:24), mentioned (in the third person) at a number of points earlier in the Gospel (cf. 13:23; 19:26; 20:2). However, this person remains mysterious and anonymous. Debates have raged about his identity, but perhaps the Gospel's enigmatic silence on this should be respected: the identity of the beloved disciple is perhaps meant to be hidden and anonymous, to exhibit 'ideal' discipleship, pointing away from oneself to the person of Jesus.

John's Gospel presents us with a version of the story of Jesus which is radically different from that of the synoptics. The differences range from the relatively trivial (a longer ministry of Jesus, with longer periods in Jerusalem) to those which go to the heart of Jesus' ministry and teaching, e.g., there is no institution of a EUCHARIST at the Last Supper; Jesus' teaching focuses on 'eternal life' (rather than the KINGDOM OF GOD) and above all on himself as the revealer of God and as the object of 'believing'. As such, John's Gospel is widely thought to reflect less the historical Jesus and more the theology of its author.

The conceptual background of John's theology has been much debated. An earlier view regarded John as 'Gnostic', and/or heavily influenced by Greek philosophical thought. With regard to GNOSTICISM, there is no doubt that (later) Gnostics found John's Gospel very congenial, and verses such as John 17:3 (equating 'eternal life' with 'knowing God') can be interpreted in a Gnostic way. However, John has none of what are now regarded as the essential features of Gnosticism (e.g., a view of the CREATION as the work of an ignorant or malevolent Demiurge). In fact, many of the most characteristic features, often thought to make John very 'Greek' (or even 'Gnostic'), are now to be found in the radically Jewish Qumran scrolls (e.g., language about 'light' and 'darkness'). It seems most likely that John's background of thought is to be located in Judaism, possibly in a 'heterodox' form of Judaism at the end of the first century.

The relationship of John's Jesus to 'the Jews' of his story, and the Judaism of his day, is complex. In one way, there are very positive links. The story of Jesus fulfils Jewish Scripture (12:40; 19:36–7). Jewish traditions are alluded to elsewhere (1:51, alluding to the story of Jacob's ladder); the Johannine prologue (1:1–18) is full of echoes of talk about WISDOM in Jewish tradition; and much of Jesus' teaching takes up themes and motifs associated with Jewish feasts. 'Moses' witnesses to Jesus (5:46–7) and 'salvation is from the Jews' (4:22).

Yet, alongside this, there are powerful negative elements. 'The Jews' are regularly vilified in the story as Jesus' opponents, at one point being called children of the DEVIL (8:44). The discourse about the bread in 6:31ff. appears to leave no positive place for OT history (cf. v. 32: the manna is *not* the true bread from heaven); and 1:17 can be read as adversely contrasting 'Moses' (the medium of the LAW) with Jesus Christ (who brings GRACE and truth).

John thus appears to be indebted to Jewish traditions in a deep way, but is also implicitly claiming to break with many aspects of that tradition in light of his beliefs about, and commitment to, the person of Jesus.

One other factor should not be ignored. Many today would regard it as essential to recognize that John is not writing as an isolated individual but comes from a community situation. Moreover, that situation is one where the Christian group has been expelled from the synagogue (9:22; 12:41; 16:2), experiencing perhaps persecution, possibly even MARTYRDOM, from other Jews (see especially 16:2). John's bitter language about 'the Jews' thus has to be seen in the context of this situation of violent antagonism. Just how this has affected his theology is not so clear. Some (e.g., W. Meeks, b. 1932) have argued there is a close relationship between the social situation of John's community, as isolated in the world and alienated from its neighbours, and John's CHRISTOLOGY of Jesus as a 'stranger' on the earth whose true home is in HEAVEN.

John presents us with a Christology that is, on the surface, considerably 'higher' than much of the rest of the NT. The Jesus of John is the pre-existent Word (1:1), 'one' with the Father (10:30), the unique Son of God, and even called 'God' on occasions (1:1; 20:28). Equally though, the Johannine Jesus is strictly subordinate to the Father (14:28). Parts of John's Christology lead seamlessly to the later creedal formulations of Jesus as fully divine, 'true God from true God'. However, more 'subordinationist' verses such as 14:28 should make us wary of reading John as too 'Chalcedonian' before his time (see CHALCEDON, COUNCIL OF). Locating John within the broad spectrum of Jewish thought at the end of the first century may mean that John's language about Jesus could be better interpreted in other categories (e.g., that of a divine 'agent'). But, on any showing, John's presentation of Jesus has had a profound influence on subsequent Christian debate about who Jesus was/is.

J. Ashton, *Understanding the Fourth Gospel*, 2nd edn (Oxford University Press, 2007).

W. A. Meeks, 'The Man from Heaven in Johannine Sectarianism' in *In Search of the Early Christians*, ed. A. R. Hilton and H. G. Snyder (Yale University Press, 2002), 55–90.

D. Moody Smith, *Johannine Christianity: Essays on Its Setting, Sources and Theology* (University of South Carolina Press, 1984).

Christopher Tuckett

JUDAISM AND CHRISTIANITY Christianity began as a Jewish movement. It differed from other interpretations of Judaism in the first century by proclaiming and worshipping Jesus as 'both Lord and Christ' (Acts 2:36), the Messiah of ISRAEL, in whom all the promises of God to the elect people find their fulfilment. The first generation of Christians, however, had already come to the conclusion that they had a divine mandate to proclaim its message about Jesus to the Gentile world as well as to their fellow Jews (cf. Rom. 1:5–6, 16; Acts 10:34–48), without requiring that the Gentiles observe the Torah (see LAW). The resulting fellowship of Jews and Gentiles, united by BAPTISM and FAITH in Jesus apart from Torah observance, guaranteed that most Christians would eventually be Gentiles.

The proclamation of Jesus as the Messiah to whom the law and the prophets bear witness (Rom. 3:21) met considerable resistance within Judaism from the start. The crisis created for all Jews by the Roman destruction of the Second Temple in 70 greatly intensified the conflict between those Jews who believed Jesus to be the Messiah, and the majority who did not. By 100 Jesus-believing Jews had effectively been excluded from the life of the synagogue and the Jewish people.

But Christianity's relationship to Judaism was never simply adversarial. The rejection of the GOSPEL by the majority of Jews, coupled with its growing acceptance among the Gentiles, posed a theological problem with which Christians wrestled, well before the separation of the two communities became irrevocable. PAUL poses the problem with great clarity. On the one hand, the unwillingness of most Jews to believe in Jesus Christ is 'trespass' (Rom. 11:12), calling forth the 'severity' of God (11:22). On the other hand, this trespass in no way nullifies the election of Israel (11:1–2) or the salvation of the Jewish people, to whose ancestors God promised his love for ever (11:26–9). Although for most of the Church's history Israel's trespass has been more obvious to Christians than God's COVENANT fidelity to the Jews, Paul's insistence on both has meant that Christian theology has not been able to look upon Judaism as simply one religion among many.

This was not inevitable. Early in the second century, MARCION proposed a form of Christianity that would have rejected all things Jewish. The Church, however, repudiated Marcion and began to develop readings of the OT in which everything – not only the narrative of patriarchs, exodus, kingdom, exile, and return, but also the most obscure cultic prescriptions – was inherently pertinent to Christ, the Church, and the Christian life. If not precisely a literal promise to be fulfilled, then it was a figure or type of Christ to come (see TYPOLOGY). The primary model here was Paul, who spoke of the events of Israel's history 'as a figure ... written down for our instruction' (1 Cor. 10:11). By this radically Christocentric and ecclesiocentric reading of the OT, the Church from an early point yoked her understanding of God, Christ, and her own mission to the Jewish people.

With this traditional insistence on a permanent link between the Jewish people and the Church were bound up several basic theological commitments.

(1) It meant that Christians were irrevocably committed to worshipping the one God of Israel. The DOCTRINE of the TRINITY deepens and specifies this commitment, but cannot contradict it. Judaism has traditionally rejected this doctrine and regarded Christianity as *Avodah Zarah* (false worship), though in the Middle Ages a contrary view began to develop, which does not regard Christianity as IDOLATRY. In modern times Jewish thinkers have sometimes strongly embraced this more positive view of the Church's relation to the God of Israel.

(2) Christian theology could not consistently neglect the ELECTION of Israel. Earlier Christian writers sometimes held that, with the Jewish rejection of the promised Christ, God no longer has any special regard for Israel according to the flesh (e.g., Justin Martyr, *Trypho* 44, 135; Irenaeus, *AH* 4.36.2). But at least as common has been the view that God's love for and covenant with the fleshly descendants of ABRAHAM are everlasting. As T. AQUINAS, for example, reads Romans 9–11, Paul 'ascribes to the Jews a particular dignity on account of their origin ... namely that according to the flesh they are descended from the patriarchs, who were most beloved of God' (*CRom.* 9.1). Therefore even the 'enmity' (*inimicitia*) of the Jews towards the gospel can make void neither God's love for them nor their future salvation (*CRom.* 11.4).

(3) Israel and the Church are not two peoples, but one, from Abraham to the end of time. Within this one people, however, the Jews have a priority which is not merely temporal, but natural and enduring (Rom. 11:16–24). Even when Christians think of the Church as the 'true Israel', they cannot forget that the saviour of the world is a Jew, through union with whom the Gentiles have been grafted into the one Israel of God. Jesus Christ remains, as Augustine observes, 'the king of the Jews', not 'the king of the Greeks or Latins', and Christ reigns over all nations, precisely as the one in whom the Jewish root 'was so strong that it could change the engrafted wild branches into itself; but the wild olive could not take away the [Jewish] name which belongs to the cultivated olive root' (*Serm.* 218.7).

(4) Israel's biblically narrated history includes events yet to come as well as those which have been, so the Church is tied to the Jewish people prospectively as well as retrospectively. God's promises to the patriarchs guarantee the persistence of the Jewish people, even though they have for the most part turned away from the fulfilment of those promises in Christ. God's faithfulness also

guarantees the eschatological salvation of the Jewish people, their full reintegration into the one people of God, to which they naturally belong (Rom. 11:24). Their salvation is Christ's work, and will come about by a final conversion to him. In the meantime the Jewish people are dispersed across the world, a witness to the nations of promises and prophecies in whose accomplishment they do not yet believe (see Augustine, *City* 18.46). This means that Christians should not molest them, but leave them to their own worship and communal life – though from the First Crusade (1096) onwards, this traditional stricture was frequently violated.

This thoroughly Christological understanding of the Jewish people is now often labelled 'supersessionism'. If supersessionism is defined as the view that God has rejected *the Jewish people*, then the traditional teaching is not supersessionism. God's unfailing love for Israel according to the flesh is, on the contrary, one of its basic structural features. At the same time, this traditional outlook was bound to regard *Judaism* – a communal life lived according to the full requirements of the Torah – as superseded. Precisely because the law of Moses is a figure of Christ yet to come, to continue observing it after Christ is to reject his coming, to cling to the shadows when the reality which casts the shadow is immediately at hand (Heb. 10:1 was often cited in this connection).

Thus a remarkable juxtaposition characterizes Christian theological reflection on the Jews and Judaism from the early Church to the Enlightenment: the Jewish people can never be superseded, but Judaism must be. What unites the Church to the Jewish people – the figural significance of this people's biblical history – is also what opposes Christianity to Judaism. With that comes a problem, which this theological tradition has seen but never entirely resolved: how can the Jewish people abide as God's elect until the end of time without Judaism?

Since the Enlightenment two main alternatives have arisen to traditional Christian interpretation of Judaism and the Jewish people. Though diametrically opposed in some respects, both stem from a rejection of the traditional figural way of linking the Jewish people and their religion to Christianity.

First, in the late eighteenth century, liberal Protestantism began to argue that the biblical history of the Jewish people and their religion is not (as the tradition had insisted) necessary for the intelligibility of Christian faith. The context needed to understand the redemption wrought by Jesus Christ, as F. Schleiermacher and many others maintained, is not the law and the prophets, but a universal human consciousness of the need for redemption (see Schleiermacher, *CF*, §13.2). That Jesus and the first Christians were Jews is merely a historical accident. In its religious essence Christianity is no closer to Judaism than to any other religion, and the Jewish origins of Christianity must, in fact, be regarded as unfortunate, given the unattractive features of the Jewish religious consciousness – particularly the Jews' conviction of their own election by God (cf. Schleiermacher, *CF*, §8.4). On this basis some Protestant theologians (e.g., Schleiermacher, A. von Harnack) have argued, echoing Marcion, that the OT should be excluded from the canon of Scripture. More recent versions of this view do not share this low estimate of Judaism, but continue to insist that Judaism cannot be more than historical background for Christianity.

The second alternative acquired particular salience in the wake of the genocide of European Jews during the Holocaust. In light of these events, the traditional figurative approach has often been rejected precisely because it claims that Christianity provides ultimate religious truths (e.g., salvation through Christ alone) not recognized by post-biblical Jewish faith. This outlook is basically the mirror image of the first: the idea that Christianity fulfils Judaism is Judaism's misfortune, since it inevitably denies God's enduring covenant with the Jews. Some advocates of this view hold that God has made two covenants with humanity: one through the Torah for Jews, and the other through Jesus for Gentiles. Others hold that there is finally only one covenant, but two irreducibly different faiths, each an equally legitimate route to covenant fellowship with the one God. Either way, this approach clearly upholds both the permanence of Israel's election (as the tradition had also generally done) and the permanent divinely willed character of Judaism. At the same time, its advocates are hesitant to affirm any notion of the finality and universal saving mission of Jesus Christ. As a result this approach, while it regards Christianity as needing ever more profound shaping by Judaism, effectively treats it as a religion for Gentiles only.

Recently, another way of looking at the relationship between Judaism and Christianity has emerged within Christian theology, that of Messianic Judaism. Like the traditional figurative view, this approach holds that faith in Jesus as Israel's Messiah is the religious fulfilment of Judaism. At the same time, Jews who have faith in Jesus should remain Torah observant, and thus be clearly recognizable as Jews: they should, for example, worship on Saturday and keep kosher. In striving to uphold the continuing practice of Judaism for Abraham's descendants according to the flesh, Messianic Judaism has affinities with the 'two covenants' view. But in seeing this as compatible with full Christian faith it departs dramatically not only from this view, but also from the traditional Christian mainstream, which held that Jesus had broken down any wall that might separate Jews and Gentiles who believe in him (cf. Eph. 2:14–16).

The traditional figurative understanding of the Jewish people and their role in the history of salvation has also continued to find potent advocates, such as C. Journet (1891–1975), J. Maritain (1882–1973), and K. Barth. These modern versions of the traditional outlook not only underline the permanence of God's covenant with the Jews, but emphatically reject anti-semitism, any notion that the Jewish people are collectively responsible for the death of Jesus, and any political arrangement which fails to accord full equality to the Jews. Though anticipating the post-Holocaust positions of many Churches, particularly of Vatican Council II (*NA*, §4) and parallel Protestant statements, they continue to regard Judaism itself as largely a barrier, rather than a means, to the Jewish people's proper relationship with God.

Still more recently, various suggestions have been made for ameliorating the traditional idea that the practice of Judaism after the coming of Christ is opposed to Christian faith (see, e.g., the treatment of Judaism in *The Catechism of the Catholic Church*). But an understanding of Judaism which does full justice both to Jesus Christ's 'primacy in everything' (Col. 1:18) and to God's unfailing love for the Jewish people has so far, even after two millennia, eluded Christian theology.

S. Boguslawski, O. P., *Thomas Aquinas on the Jews: Insights into his Commentary on Romans 9–11* (Paulist Press, 2008).
M. C. Boys, ed., *Seeing Judaism Anew: Christianity's Sacred Obligation* (Rowman & Littlefield, 2005).
T. Frymer-Kensky, D. Novak, P. Ochs *et al.*, eds., *Christianity in Jewish Terms* (Westview, 2000).
M. S. Kinzer, *Postmissionary Messianic Judaism: Redefining Christian Engagement with the Jewish People* (Brazos Press, 2005).
R. K. Soulen, *The God of Israel and Christian Theology* (Fortress Press, 1996).

Bruce D. Marshall

Julian of Norwich Medieval mystic and theologian, Julian of Norwich (1342–*ca* 1416) is best known for her *Showings*, an account of her sixteen visions of Christ on the cross. Vowing a life of solitary devotion and prayer as an anchoress (see Anchoritism), she wrote within the anchorhold of the church of St Julian in the context of England's Black Death. A product of over three decades of interpreting the visions, the long text of *Showings* (the expanded version) contains rich theological reflections on the nature of God, the Trinity, and redemption. Her interpretation of atonement, conveyed in the parable of the lord and the servant (Chapter 51), is one of her most significant contributions to Christian theology. In this parable, she replaces the forensic language of humanity as guilty before God, with a depiction of humanity as weak and vulnerable, willing to do God's will, but lacking strength. In her visions, Julian receives a view of the world through the eyes of the suffering Christ. Her frequently quoted statement – 'all manner of thing shall be well' – provides a vision of wellness from the site of suffering. This vision is expressed in multiple Trinitarian iterations, in which sin is contained within a vision of God as creating, loving, and sustaining the world in its fragile goodness. Although she claims to be both 'unlettered' and fully aligned with the teachings of the Church, her writings display significant theological acumen and innovations on medieval theology. She exposes the inadequacy of divisions between 'spiritual' and 'theological' writings, and her references to God and Jesus as Mother provide insights for rethinking gendered language for God.

G. Jantzen, *Julian of Norwich: Mystic and Theologian* (Paulist Press, 2000).

Shelly Rambo

Just War The just-war tradition evolved as a form of Christian political witness to the need to curtail violent conflict in the form of a reflective and deliberative response to the understanding of God's eternal peace as the aim of history and human susceptibility to the temptation of violence. The overriding purpose of this train of thought has been to scrutinize and direct conduct towards armed conflict and during warfare. Guided by the overall aim of peace (*recta intentio*), warfare itself was understood as a moral act of judgement with the threefold objective of protecting, penalizing, and restoring justice.

It is possible to distinguish three main historical incarnations of the just-war tradition: (1) its emergence during the patristic era with cautious attempts at systematizing in the medieval period, but treated typically as a side aspect in the broader discussion of the duties of the Christian ruler; (2) the widening of its scope and shifting of its rationale in the classical early modern period when the tradition was employed in conjunction with and as a means of promulgating the concept of *ius gentium*, an international law of nations to counter national absolutism and regulate international conflict in the age of sovereign nation states; (3) its late modern revival brought about by the need to respond to the challenge of new types of weaponry of mass destruction following World War II and the development of international institutions (e.g., the World Court) and legislation such as the Hague conventions (1899, 1907).

The just-war *tradition* assumes an underlying continuity of three principal convictions: (1) the need to question war, as such and in each concrete instance, in the spirit of neighbourly love; (2) the concomitant need to understand war as an 'impossible possibility' (*ultima ratio*, or 'last resort'), that may justly be deliberated upon, but if entered into then; (3) conducted only under constant moral vigilance, in the hope of success but never triumph.

Modern sensitivities against war may need reminding that it was the revolutionary contribution of

Judeo-Christian political thought that turned war into something questionable and demanding justification. The philosophies that undergirded the Greco-Roman world might have questioned the usefulness or proportionality of particular wars, but not the legitimacy of war as such. Pre-Christian world views that idolized violent strife and competition, and saw the welfare of cities and empire dependent on the favour of gods and goddesses of war, were forever challenged by the beliefs and practices of a fast-growing sect that confessed their Lord as both 'prince of peace' (Isa. 9:6) and ruler of the universe (Col. 1:15–20). Belief in the ontological priority of violence and the inevitability of war gave way to belief in peace as the ultimate end of history. Reconciliation became the genuine mode of existence in conformity with the reality of the new CREATION that God has brought about in Christ who 'is our peace who has made us both one, and has broken down the dividing wall of hostility' (Eph. 2:14).

Theological pacifism and the theological just-war tradition are distinct but closely related ways of articulating neighbourly love in the face of violence – both an external threat of assault and an inner temptation to exercise such an assault. When the rulers of the earth in the vast territories of the Roman Empire attended to the call of Christ and asked, as Christians, for spiritual guidance in the discharge of their office, theological argument tended to interpret the right to carry the sword (Rom. 13) in the light of the overriding duty of Christians to love their neighbours. The authority of rulers to judge and penalize the wicked was now understood as their peculiar service of love: towards their protégés but also towards the offenders by giving them 'their due' – confronting them with the truth about their conduct and bringing them to justice as an opportunity to repent and better themselves. The transposition of the domestic paradigm of policing and of the 'sword' as a symbol of protective love to a people's external (international) relations stands at the cradle of the just-war tradition. The crucial point in this transposition was not a legitimizing one of making warfare a Christian possibility; rather it was a critical one of ensuring that the *same* criteria and principles applied in both domestic and international affairs, such as distinguishing retaliation from revenge and public from private action. These distinctions, which were implicit in the ruler's monopoly on the use of force in domestic affairs, came also to bear on the way in which the question of war was to be fought.

Hence the main purpose of the just-war tradition has been to *prevent* war from happening, not to justify its pursuit. The critical scrutiny it requires with regard to the exercise of lawful authority (*legitima potestas*), appropriate intention (*finis pax*), and legitimate cause (*iusta causa*) implied the prohibition of arbitrary imperial warfare and revenge. Ambrose's (*ca* 340–97) famous excommunication of the Christian emperor Theodosius I (r. 379–95) in the year 380 illustrates the principle. The emperor's decision to destroy the city of Thessalonica, whose inhabitants had mistreated his ambassadors, was judged by Ambrose as expressing the imperial lust for revenge rather than as a loving act of justice. According to the standard of the emerging just-war tradition, even waging war had now to be understood as an act of justice that needed to be tempered by mercy and love in order to be genuinely 'just'. What later came to be called the 'principle of proportionality of means' (*debitum modus*) can thus be understood as directly springing from the Christian's duty to love.

Having stressed the continuity in the Christian tradition of just-war thought, it is also necessary to point out internal fissures and moments of heterogeneity in the development of the tradition from its patristic origins to its classical and modern versions. Central to the rationality of the just-war tradition has been the attempt to reconcile the radical challenges of the SERMON ON THE MOUNT (especially, e.g., Matt. 5:38–9) with the ruler's prerogative to use the sword in Romans 13. AUGUSTINE famously emphasized the renunciation of violent responses as a matter of the Christian's inner disposition (*Faust.* 22.75). This reflected a sensitivity peculiar to this tradition, that the Christian, even when fighting legitimately and successfully in a war, is to be a sort of 'sad soldier' (*City* 19.7) – less prone to revel in triumph than to moan the death and harm done to the enemy whom the Christian is called to love even as a soldier.

The medieval solution of differentiating between counsel and command was more robust, but only at the expense of effectually dividing the Christian body into camps of 'ordinary' and 'perfect' members. T. AQUINAS (in *ST* 2/2.41) argued that the Christian might be praised for abstaining from self-defence (according to the dominical counsel of the Sermon on the Mount), but is not commanded to do so. The theological permission for self-defence Thomas found in human nature itself, with its created inclinations such as the one towards self-preservation (*ST* 2/2.94).

The Reformers objected to the distinction between commands binding on all Christians ('evangelical precepts') and supererogatory acts ('evangelical counsels') applicable only to the religious on the grounds that it introduced an improper division within the Christian BODY. Instead, they offered an alternative distinction between public and private duties. According to M. LUTHER the decisive difference is between the Christian as private individual in relation to him- or herself – a capacity in which he or she must abstain from retaliation, as long as only his or her own goods are concerned – and the Christian in public office or ministry. With respect to the latter, the Christian is not only permitted but obliged to do what is necessary to protect those who are entrusted to him. Hence both, non-retaliation and retaliation, can be asked of the same person according to his or her role or office, and either reaction must be understood as actualizing the one overriding command to love the neighbour.

What the Reformers rejected in the medieval synthesis of love and self-defence raised its head again in the modern version of the just-war tradition. Modern just-war thought, emerging in the work of F. di Vitoria (*ca* 1490–1546), H. Grotius (1583–1645), and I. KANT, tended to revolve around the idea of accommodating and balancing the rights of individual sovereign nation states to defend themselves from outward aggression. This new, rights-based paradigm caused the just-war tradition to shift in several interconnected ways. First, its scope was extended with and through the development of international law. Second, the list of criteria to be applied during deliberation about war was refined; in particular a number of criteria to be applied during conflict (*in bello*), such as 'probability of success' and 'discrimination of non-combatants', were added. The growth of this list of criteria suggests, however, also a more technical and legalist understanding of the tradition. Along with the shifting focus from love of neighbour to the right of self-defence came a shift from scrutinizing to legitimizing. Just-war thought was originally motivated and sustained by a set of particular Christian commitments and practices, including the willingness to suffer rather than wage unjust war, or to suffer defeat if success could only be had by, say, the use of unproportionate means. Modern thought has led to a universal 'just-war theory' whose criteria are meant to be applied by everyone in every situation. Ironically, it seems as though is it precisely this modern shift towards wider applicability which threatens the relevance of just-war thought today.

S. Hauerwas, *Dispatches from the Front: Theological Engagements with the Secular* (Duke University Press, 1994).

O. O'Donovan, *The Just War Revisited* (Cambridge University Press, 2003).

P. Ramsey, *The Just War: Force and Political Responsibility* (Scribner, 1968).

M. Walzer, *Just and Unjust Wars* (Basic Books, 1977).

BERND WANNENWETSCH

JUSTIFICATION Justification refers to how people become 'just' in God's eyes. According to Christian theology, justification is an act of God: it is God who justifies. Human beings are recipients of God's justification: it is they who are justified.

Reflection on how justification happens, how humans relate to it, whether they are merely passive or somehow contribute to the process, and how it affects its recipients are issues that have occupied theologians through the centuries and given shape to justification as a DOCTRINE. Historically, debates over these issues have been more prominent in the Christian West than in the East, and often went hand in hand with the process of Christianization in medieval Europe. Those debates reached a high point during the REFORMATION. For nearly five subsequent centuries, perceived differences in doctrines of justification divided Catholic and Protestant Churches. Thanks to ecumenical dialogue, Catholics and many Protestants today recognize a core consensus on justification.

The doctrine of justification finds its biblical point of departure in Pauline theology, particularly as it is articulated in Romans and Galatians. In both letters, PAUL addresses a pivotal situation in the history of Christianity: the nascent religion's expansion beyond its original Jewish–Christian origins. Paul's 'mission to the Gentiles', aimed at persons for whom obedience to the LAW, exemplified in this case by the rite of circumcision for men, could not be presupposed, brought about a reassessment of what it meant to be Christian. Should non-Jews be required to be circumcised when becoming Christian? Paul's answer, summarized in Galatians 2:16, is no: 'a person is justified not by the works of the law but through FAITH in Jesus Christ'.

A more extensive statement of the same point comes in Romans 3:22–5. In these and similar passages, Paul appears to establish an opposition between 'law' and 'faith', or 'law' and 'GRACE'. People are justified not by virtue of their obedience to the law but by God's grace. All – whether observant Jews or virtuous Gentiles – have fallen short according to the law; their redemption depends on the gift of grace. That in turn is made possible by Christ's sacrificial ATONEMENT and is effective for those who believe.

Over the centuries, two questions have remained central to the exegesis of these passages and have fuelled extensive theological debates. The first has to do with the relationship of 'faith in Christ' to 'the law'. Does faith in Christ obviate, or in some way even prohibit, doing works of the law? Put another way: can one be righteous in God's eyes without works? The Letter of James, exhorting early Christians to greater moral accountability, argues forcefully to the contrary: 'So faith by itself, if it has no works, is dead' (Jas. 2:17). Historically, the most compelling theological models have found ways to maintain both points: justification comes by faith/grace alone, and faith without works is dead. Paul's emphasis, though, is clearly on the former.

Second, exegetes have long differed in their assessment of how central justification is to Paul's SOTERIOLOGY. Paul's forensic language about God's righteousness and believers becoming righteous stands alongside notions of being 'in' Christ, of being united with Christ, filled by the HOLY SPIRIT, and of participating in the GLORY of God. The twentieth century, in particular, saw numerous voices, ranging from A. Schweitzer (1875–1965) to contemporary proponents of 'new perspectives on Paul', emphasize participatory aspects of Paul's soteriology.

The first significant post-biblical debate over justification took shape in AUGUSTINE'S rejection of PELAGIANISM. According to Pelagius (*ca* 355–*ca* 420), people either choose to SIN or they choose to obey God. On the one hand, their will is free to make those choices. On the other hand, choices are habit-forming, and, once habituated to sin, people require liberation through Christ. Christ 'justifies' those who have faith and frees them to redirect their lives by imitating his moral example. Pelagius understands justification as forgiveness of past sins only. Once forgiven, the believer's subsequent holiness is a consequence of his or her own volition. In Augustine's view, Pelagius overemphasized human capacities while underestimating human dependence on God. For Augustine, humans are not only burdened by sins actually committed; they are fundamentally compromised by inherited original sin, which has left them with no capacity at all to love and obey God. Their 'FREE WILL', while not extinguished, is nonetheless incapable of choosing holiness; it invariably chooses a path of self-interest. Any volitional movement persons make towards God comes as a result of God's grace working upon them.

Responding to Pelagius, Augustine fashions a radically God-centred doctrine of justification. Not only are humans entirely dependent upon God's grace for justification, they would also be incapable of accepting that offer if it were not for a preceding gift of preparatory grace. God prepares their will for acceptance, offers them justification, and enables them to accept that offer. All salvific acts are accomplished by God and correspond to God's eternal PREDESTINATION. These views carried the day, and Pelagius' positions were condemned at the Council of Carthage (418) and at the second Council of Orange (529).

The outcome of Augustine's debate with Pelagius over grace and free will established boundaries for the doctrinal development of justification in the Middle Ages. That narrative was driven by a second theme, as well. Having accepted that justification comes by grace alone, medieval theologians began reflecting on the *means* by which that grace is bestowed. Set in a time of ecclesial institutionalization, those means, defined as sacraments, were tied tightly to the ordained ministry of the Church.

Augustine himself had connected justification to BAPTISM by highlighting this sacrament's power to wash away original sin. During the eighth and ninth centuries, theologians such as Alcuin of York (*ca* 735–804) also began to link justification with confession, though Alcuin did not view the practice as a sacrament nor regard the involvement of a priest as necessary. Regular self-accusation and confession were part of Alcuin's monastic ethos, which he and his followers sought – successfully – to extend to the wider Church. By the twelfth century, theologians like Hugh of St Victor (1096–1141) had come to regard confession, now a component of PENANCE, as a sacrament. Peter Lombard (*ca* 1100–60), whose *Four Books of Sentences* was one of the most influential theological works of the Middle Ages, cements the link for posterity by discussing justification within the context of penance.

Linking justification with penance had important consequences for the doctrine's development. Conceptually, justification became tied more tightly to forensic language of guilt, remission of sins, and satisfaction, at the expense of Paul's participatory notions of a life 'in' Christ. Practically speaking, the fourth Lateran Council's (1215) decision to make annual penance mandatory for all Christians both universalized justification's application and embedded it in a host of pastoral and missional concerns. One could not simply discuss concepts of free will and grace in the abstract, one needed to consider their application to practice and preaching. Those pressures became particularly evident whenever the question of human involvement in justification arose.

Most medieval theologians followed Augustine in stressing the need for some sort of preparation that readies a person for the receipt of justifying grace. They differed in their judgement of the human role in that process. Many argued that God had endowed humans with enough natural sense of what is good that, by 'doing what is within them' (*facere quod in se est*), they could remove obstacles to the grace that God wants to give them. Its logic was taken a step further by G. Biel (*ca* 1420–95), who argued that God has made a commitment to bestowing grace on those who 'do what is within them'. That commitment, or covenant, is grounded in the sacrament of penance: while God is free to bestow grace any way God sees fit, God has identified specific means of grace (such as sacraments) upon which humans may rely unfailingly. According to Biel, if a person approaches the sacrament of penance with a proper attitude of repentance (CONTRITION), God will follow up with the grace that enables the journey towards justification to continue.

Though not all medieval theologians followed this line of argument, most agreed that justification effects a genuine change in the believer. Quoting Augustine, theologians identified justification with a moment of conversion, when love of self (*amor sui*) turns to love of God (*amor Dei*). Grace, once infused, gives rise to habits of righteous behaviour, transforming the believer into someone who, increasingly, *is* just.

Throughout the medieval period, many of the thinkers who stressed the importance of human efforts in justification and who took an optimistic view of natural human capacities for change were reformers exhorting the Church to greater discipline and rigorous imitation of Christ. By contrast, the most famous reform movement in Church history, the Reformation, took the opposite approach. M. LUTHER, drawing on his readings of Paul and Augustine, viewed human nature as utterly incapable of doing anything that could contribute to its justification. Much like Augustine,

Luther saw original sin as a human condition marked by radical self-love, so that even their apparently good deeds are motivated by hope of reward or fear of punishment rather than by love of God. Prior to receiving the grace of justification, their self-love is all-encompassing. Luther therefore rejects Biel's contention that preparatory acts might indirectly merit justification. With respect to justification, humans can 'do' nothing at all, according to Luther; they can only receive. Their role is passive. Their response is one of trusting faith (*fiducia*). Thus, Luther speaks of justification 'by grace alone' (*sola gratia*) and 'by faith alone' (*sola fide*).

Luther understands justification itself as 'imputative'. That is, justifying grace means that a person is *reckoned* just in the eyes of God; it does not *infuse* the person with righteousness of his or her own. Luther introduces the distinction in order to make the point that justification is based entirely upon the righteousness of Christ, which is attributed to the believer by grace, and not upon any qualities inhering in the believer. He does not, however, deny that justification transforms the believer; he merely insists that such a transformation is not the condition for, but a consequence of, justification. Through faith Christ 'takes up residence' in the justified believer, working in and through that person. Luther describes the process eloquently in *Freedom of a Christian* (1520), speaking of a spiritual union of the believer with Christ. The ensuing effects of SANCTIFICATION include charity. As Luther's early modern followers systematized his insights, they embedded a narrowly understood imputative notion of justification within a more comprehensive order of salvation (*ORDO SALUTIS*) that included mystical union, sanctification and other transformative elements. These aspects have been rediscovered by contemporary scholars such as T. Mannermaa (b. 1937).

Among theologians who remained loyal to Rome, reactions to Luther's new conceptual language, though generally critical, were mixed – largely because there was no 'official' doctrine of justification as of yet. Thomists, Franciscans, and Augustinians all espoused varying models of the doctrine, and there was disagreement over whether Luther's could be included among them. The Council of TRENT was called in part to address this problem. In its famous Session 6 (1547), Trent accomplished two things. It forged an agreement on justification among those present, and it anathematized what it took to be Luther's teachings on the subject. In doing so, it actually integrated some of Luther's criticisms of medieval theology into its consensus position, rejecting particularly optimistic assessments of natural human capacities or of human involvement in justification. On the other hand, it also targeted exclusively imputative understandings of the doctrine, defended the transformative effects of justifying grace, and upheld an ability of the free will to co-operate with that grace. While not resolving all disputes, Trent remains remarkable for its unprecedented formulation of a normative Catholic doctrine of justification.

Luther's understanding of justification became central to most Protestant traditions. J. CALVIN adopted its main features, while linking justification more closely to predestination and adding a more explicit emphasis on sanctification. That latter emphasis is shared, if in different systematic contexts, by both Anabaptists and Methodists. It is accentuated further in nineteenth-century Holiness movements and in subsequent Pentecostalism, all of whom retain Luther's doctrine of justification. The Anglican doctrine of justification, confessed in the Thirty-Nine Articles of Religion, is compatible with Luther's understanding as well.

Twentieth-century ECUMENISM provided opportunities for re-evaluating the historic condemnations of Trent and of Protestant confessional statements such as those of the Lutheran BOOK OF CONCORD. Capping several decades of dialogue, the Lutheran World Federation and the Catholic Church agreed in the *Joint Declaration on the Doctrine of Justification* (1999) that the sixteenth-century condemnations formulated by both sides did not apply to the actual teachings of each confession as understood today. Differences in conceptual language remain, but can be understood in part as resulting from the varying conceptual models (e.g., an 'infused' versus an 'imputed' understanding) prevalent in the two traditions. Both sides affirmed a core consensus on justification; they were joined by the World Methodist Council in 2006.

Now that the main protagonists of the Reformation-era debates over justification no longer condemn each other, attention can focus on other challenges. One of these comes as a consequence of Christianity's globalization, which has seen the emergence of non-western centres of theological discourse. Given justification's embeddedness in western European intellectual history, most obvious in its use of forensic categories specific to that tradition, it will be interesting to see how voices in areas that do not share those conceptual presuppositions come to appropriate and interpret Paul's theology.

K. Lehmann and W. Pannenberg, eds., *The Condemnations of the Reformation Era: Do They Still Divide?* (Fortress Press, 1990).

T. Mannermaa, *Christ Present In Faith: Luther's View On Justification* (Fortress Press, 2005).

B. L. McCormack, ed., *Justification in Perspective: Historical Developments and Contemporary Challenges* (Baker Academic, 2006).

A. E. McGrath. *Iustitia Dei: A History of the Christian Doctrine of Justification*, 3rd edn (Cambridge University Press, 2005).

H. A. Oberman, *The Harvest of Medieval Theology*, 3rd edn (Baker Academic, 2000).

O. H. Pesch, *Theologie der Rechtfertigung bei Martin Luther und Thomas von Aquin: Versuch eines systematisch-theologischen Dialogs* (Matthias-Grünewald-Verlag, 1967).

KENNETH APPOLD

Kairos Document The Kairos Document is a theological comment on the crisis in South Africa, originally published in 1985. Written by a group of theologians who were brought together by F. Chikane (b. 1951), later to become general secretary of the South African Council of Churches, the document arose from discussions among primarily Black Christians. They were eager to develop biblical and theological models that would inspire activism to end apartheid, the system of racial separation and subjugation that characterized South Africa until 1994, when the first democratic elections were held. The 1985 edition was signed by 151 Church leaders, theologians, and others, despite the country being under a partial state of emergency. It was revised slightly and reissued in 1986 at a time of a total state of emergency, but with thousands of Christians openly endorsing it.

K

The *kairos* is defined as 'the moment of grace and opportunity, the favorable time in which God issues a challenge to decisive action'. The text critiques 'state theology', which defends the status quo, and 'church theology,' which cautiously criticizes apartheid. The document promotes instead a 'prophetic theology', which calls for action to confront 'the evils of the time' and announces 'the salvation that we are hoping for'.

Many inside South Africa denounced the document. Some theologians in other parts of the world criticized the text as too millenarian and APOCALYPTIC (see PREMILLENNIALISM). Widely hailed as a turning point in theological debates within the country, however, the text inspired similar efforts across the world.

See also BELHAR CONFESSION.

The Kairos Document: Challenge to the Church, 2nd edn (Eerdmans, 1986).

JANICE LOVE

Kant, Immanuel Modern theology, like modernity at large, is constantly tugged to and fro by the sibling rivalry of the ENLIGHTENMENT and Romanticism. Immanuel Kant (1724–1804) is a decisive figure for understanding and assessing this rivalry. Professor at the University of Königsberg (the city in which he was born) from 1755, Kant emphasized individual intellectual and moral autonomy in a way that makes him the paradigmatic Enlightenment thinker, but he also contributed crucially to Romanticism's rise. The magisterial character of his three *Critiques* (the *Critique of Pure Reason* (1781), the *Critique of Practical Reason* (1788), and the *Critique of Judgement* (1790)) renders him indispensable to critical awareness of what human reason can and cannot do.

Plato (*ca* 430–*ca* 345 BC) taught that knowing involves 'seeing' a particular form with the mind's eye. However active the mind might be in this process, its purpose was to achieve a clear, unbiased correspondence; to communicate the form of the 'given' (see PLATONISM). In contrast, Kant in his first *Critique* assembled telling evidence that even in knowing human reason is more radically creative. It actually *gives form* to what it receives. The knowing subject thus exercises a sovereign – albeit limited – generativity vis-à-vis that which is apparently 'given' by sense experience. Ironically, Kant's critical shift towards the role of the knowing subject precipitated a somewhat uncritical 'turn to the subject' in modern thought, in which creative subjectivity assumed centre stage.

The idea that the subject contributes actively to the thing known is the basis for Kant's link with Romanticism, for which the creativity of the subject was a central concern. Romanticism resists any suggestion of insuperable limit. It tends to interpret each experience of transcendence as a communion with infinite transcendence (viz., God). Theologians steeped in PIETISM were drawn to the Romantic contention that the subject's creativity exhibits a kind of godhood. Kant regarded such claims as naive ('transcendental illusion'). His chosen realm was something more recognizably human – let us call it *finite transcendence.*

The Enlightenment was cosmopolitan, transcending national boundaries. Thus it staunchly defended reason as the indispensable safeguard of mutual understanding. Kant conceived of 'pure reason' as something which 'inhabits' the human mind, yet which simultaneously transcends the mind in so far as 'mind' suggests a sort of object existing *within* the world. Kant remained quasi-Platonic in his respect for reason's own internal operations. Truth is not whatever we want it to be; properly exercised, it represents an open, utterly shareable form of authority. If I should rashly declare that 'there is no truth', others are fully entitled to observe that I am implying that this one statement, at least, is true. Similarly if a dictator proclaims, 'It is I who will determine what is reasonable', all reflective persons will share in the empowering awareness that *ipso facto* the speaker, however powerful, has effectively forfeited any reasonable claim to authority. By contrast, Romanticism's emphasis on the transcendental value of the particular gave it much closer affinities with European nationalist movements of the late eighteenth and early nineteenth centuries. Since nationalism can easily be invoked to stifle dissent, with the result that cosmopolitan openness to other voices is thereby lost, the Enlightenment defence of reason is no less relevant today than it was in Kant's time.

At the same time, Kant was an admirer of one of the great early Romantics, J.-J. Rousseau (1712–78). He knew there was more to life than the pure reason epitomized by science. In his second *Critique* he turned his attention to 'practical reason', giving attention to the innumerable choices we make in living an embodied, interpersonal life. Kant developed these ideas further in *Religion within the Limits of Reason Alone* (1793) – a book whose thesis may sound less onerous when understood (as Kant intended) as referring to religion within the limits of *ethical* reason alone.

In exploring Kant's views on practical reason, the negative example of the dictator is once again apposite. By its very nature reason is something that is shared; it tacitly requires that people be treated on an even footing and that no one can unilaterally determine what counts as reasonable. In furtherance of this basic principle, Kant affirmed a 'categorical imperative', according to which persons are to be treated as ends in themselves and not simply as means. In this way he sought to use reason's unique transcendence to underwrite the cause of justice. This may be Kant's true revolution: that according to the basic principles of practical reason otherness (i.e., the moral claim of the other person to be treated *as* a person) is installed within reason itself. For Kant, in other words, the most authentic witness to humanity's transcendence is the individual's capacity to honour the otherness – the fact that there are other persons different from and irreducible to oneself – that testifies to human finitude.

A further dimension of Kant's reflections on practical reason relates to the motivation for ethical behaviour. Although Kant was insistent that ethical behaviour needed no further motive than one's inherent sense of duty, he also held that such behaviour could only be considered rational if there was some assurance that the goodness at which it aimed would ultimately be realized. At the same time, he recognized that consideration of any short-term reward will bias ethical judgement. To resolve this conundrum, he posited a reward so resolutely long-term as to be quasi-eschatological, yet worth the wait. He termed it 'the [unqualifiedly] Highest Good'. But anything that good sounds too good to be true. How can we trust that such a Good will in fact be available to us? The question gives voice to the anguish of ethical effort. It is in this context of utterly human, utterly reasonable anguish – and only in this context – that the ever-cautious Kant found justification for affirming the existence of God, on the grounds that nothing less than God can provide the rationally requisite Assurance of the realization of the Highest Good (see Moral Argument).

This proposal places theology within very strict limits indeed. But with it Kant demonstrates a profound awareness of the existential conflicts inherent to human existence, without falling prey to the debilitating dualisms of heart versus head and Faith versus reason that afflict so much of later religious existentialism. Moreover, in light of F. Nietzsche's denunciation of Christianity for professing selfless love while smugly anticipating a (highly selective) celestial reward, Christianity may need to cleave rigorously to the kind of dialectical character of faith that Kant's analysis of practical reason suggests. Christianity may need to set firmly between itself and any thought of reward a fierce allegiance to the ethical in its own right; something like Kant's occasionally off-putting adherence to the categorical imperative.

H. Caygill, *A Kant Dictionary* (Blackwell, 1995).

C. L. Firestone and S. R. Palmquis, eds. *Kant and the New Philosophy of Religion* (Indiana University Press, 2006).

R. Kroner, *Kant's Weltanschauung* (University of Chicago Press, 1956).

W. Lowe, *Theology and Difference: The Wound of Reason* (Indiana University Press, 1993).

Walter Lowe

Kenotic Theology The term 'kenosis' is derived from *ekenōsen* in Philippians. 2:7, which states that, although Christ was in the form of God, he did not exploit his divine equality for his own self-interest, 'but emptied himself [*heauton ekenōsen*], taking the form of a slave, being born in human likeness'. Although the term is derived from Philippians, 'kenosis' denotes an issue that is fundamental to the entire NT. On the one hand, the NT affirms Christ's divine status: he is the pre-existent divine Word who is one with the Father (see Abba). On the other hand, the NT affirms the reality of Christ's humanity: he weeps, he is tired, he suffers anguish, pain, God-forsakenness, and death. Kenotic theologies attempt to reconcile these two sides of the NT witness and to show how Christ, though divine, could live a real human life. What is distinctive about kenotic theologies is that they do this by reflecting upon the notion of *self-emptying*, arguing that Christ 'emptied himself' of his divine nature or prerogatives in order to live as a human being. Where kenotic theologians differ from each other is in their understanding of what it is that Christ emptied himself of, the extent of this emptying, and what impact this emptying had on Christ's divinity.

Although kenotic elements appear in the theology of the Church fathers, the fathers' emphasis on the immutability and impassibility of Christ's divine nature prevented them from developing the kenotic motif beyond the idea of a partial concealment of Christ's divine glory beneath his human form, a view advanced by Hilary of Poitiers (*ca* 300–68).

Unresolved Christological tensions arising from Eucharistic controversy led to kenosis becoming an important issue in the 'kenosis-krypsis' controversy between the Lutheran theologians of Tübingen and Giessen in the early seventeenth century. The Tübingen theologians argued for the concealment (Greek *krypsis*; Latin *occultatio*) but continued use of the divine powers by the incarnate *Logos*, while the Giessen theologians argued for a 'kenosis of use' (Greek *kenōsis chrēseōs*), whereby Christ abstained from using some of his divine powers for the duration of the incarnation (see UBIQUITY).

The classic age of kenotic theology was the nineteenth and early twentieth centuries. The influence of PIETISM's emphasis on Jesus' suffering, the insights of BIBLICAL CRITICISM, the impact of the Hegelian notion of God's self-development in history, and the rise of psychology raised questions concerning Christ's self-consciousness, personality, and human experience. The result of this was increasing awareness of the reality of Christ's humanity and the problems this raised for the affirmation that he was both truly divine and truly human. Kenosis offered a way of holding fast to the affirmation of Christ's divinity – albeit in a reduced form – while doing justice to the concrete reality of Christ's humanity. The problem is: what aspects of his divine nature can Christ lay aside without undermining his divinity?

Kenotic theology in nineteenth-century Germany was advanced primarily by Lutheran theologians, notably those of the 'Erlangen School': J. C. K. Hofmann (1810–77), F. H. R. Frank (1827–94), and above all G. Thomasius (1802–75). Thomasius argued that on becoming incarnate the *Logos* renounced the 'relative' attributes of omnipotence, omniscience, and omnipresence; but retained the 'immanent' or 'absolute' attributes of truth, holiness, love, and absolute power (which Thomasius identified with God's unconditioned FREE WILL rather than with the power over the universe characteristic of the relative attribute of omnipotence). Kenotic theologies were also advanced by some Reformed theologians such as J. H. A. Ebrard (1818–88) and W. F. Gess (1819–91), the latter of whom advanced the controversial theory that the *Logos* became the 'human' SOUL of Jesus, and that Jesus only gradually recovered a memory of his divine origin and status during his earthly ministry.

Although kenotic theology lost popularity in Germany in the 1880s, at about the same time it experienced a second flowering in Britain lasting through the 1920s, a delay that can be attributed to the late arrival of biblical criticism there. Influential in introducing kenotic theology to the English-speaking world was A. B. Bruce's (1831–99) *The Humiliation of Christ* (1876). The notion of kenosis was taken up and elaborated in different ways by A. M. Fairbairn (1838–1912), P. T. Forsyth (1848–1921), C. Gore (1853–1932), F. Weston (1871–1924), and H. R. Mackintosh (1870–1936).

The kenotic motif has been extended by some theologians beyond CHRISTOLOGY to the internal relations of the TRINITY and its relations to the world. Examples of this can be found in the nineteenth century in the theologies of Hofmann and K. T. A. Liebner (1806–71). In the twentieth century this approach became increasingly influential. The Russian Orthodox theologians M. Tareev (1866–1934) and S. BULGAKOV, and the Catholic scholar H. von BALTHASAR, describe the Father's generation of the Son as a kenotic relationship underpinning God's creation and sustaining of the universe. God 'empties' or limits the divine self in order to allow the universe to come into existence and human beings to live lives of freedom.

The intense debate on kenosis in Germany exposed problems in the Christologies of the kenotic theologians. It was argued against Thomasius that there can be nothing non-essential in God and that his distinction between absolute and relative attributes is artificial and misleading. Similarly, it was argued that Gessian-type kenotic Christologies, which reduce the incarnate *Logos* to an initially unconscious human soul, undermine the Trinity and make it doubtful that believers genuinely encounter God in a Christ who has given up so much of his divine nature. From the 1880s the theology of A. Ritschl (1822–89), with its emphasis on theological statements as value judgements, seemed to offer a way of addressing theological questions that avoided the conceptual problems thrown up by the highly complex metaphysical systems of the kenoticists.

Despite its problems, however, some version of kenosis is arguably necessary if Christianity is to hold fast to the doctrine of the INCARNATION, for only if Christ lays aside or scales down some aspect of his divine nature is it possible to conceive of him being divine and yet able to live a genuinely human life. Furthermore, kenosis is central not only to Christology, but to Christian life and discipleship as such. The notions of self-giving, self-sacrifice, service, and love of others which it denotes are essential for Christian existence.

See also ATTRIBUTES, DIVINE; CHALCEDON, COUNCIL OF; SACRIFICE.

D. G. Dawe, *The Form of a Servant: A Historical Analysis of the Kenotic Motif* (Westminster Press, 1963).

C. S. Evans, ed., *Exploring Kenotic Christology: The Self-Emptying of God* (Oxford University Press, 2006).

DAVID R. LAW

KERYGMA The term 'kerygma' is the Greek word for a proclamation or public notice cried by a herald (*kēryx*). The public character of kerygma led Basil of Caesarea (see CAPPADOCIAN FATHERS) to invoke it theologically in contrast to dogma: whereas *kērygmata* were clearly and openly taught, *dogmata* were passed on privately, in order to avoid their being profaned (*Spirit* 66). Current theological use of kerygma, however, is rooted in much more recent developments, especially M. Kähler's

(1835–1912) contrast between the putative 'historical Jesus' that had been the object of extensive theological investigation in the nineteenth century and the risen Christ proclaimed in the Church as the object of FAITH. In this way, the 'kerygma', understood as the heart of the Christian GOSPEL, refers specifically to the proclamation of Jesus Christ as the risen Lord.

Kähler's point, taken up and developed by R. BULTMANN and others, was that Christian faith could not and did not depend on the shifting and always uncertain results of scholarly historical investigation, since 'the real Christ is the Christ who is preached' (*Hist.* 66). In this respect the kerygma theology of the mid-twentieth century understood faith in Christ principally as a matter of personal decision in response to the kerygma rather than as a matter of historical judgement. As such, this emphasis on the centrality of proclamation for the Christian life found strong support in parallel developments, connected with both the emergence of DIALECTICAL THEOLOGY and the renaissance of scholarly interest in M. LUTHER, in which the category of the Word of God – understood precisely as God's claim on humanity made real in proclamation – emerged as a leading focus of theological interest.

Over against attempts to understand the gospel in terms of general patterns of human religious experience and assess it in terms of the canons of historical investigation, the gospel as kerygma was interpreted as witness to Christ, and faith as an event born of the individual's encounter with that witness. For advocates of kerygma theology like Bultmann, critical attention to the form of the NT texts themselves supported this approach, as the Gospels were not (as the practitioners of the nineteenth-century 'QUEST OF THE HISTORICAL JESUS' supposed) biographies of Jesus, but rather preaching documents: collections of disparate literary units (PARABLES, MIRACLE stories, wisdom sayings, etc.) that were themselves expressions of the earliest Christian communities' witnesses to the risen Christ. The task of theology is, correspondingly, not to persuade people of the divinity of Jesus or the moral worth of Christian teaching, but simply to clarify the content of the kerygma (e.g., using DEMYTHOLOGIZATION to rid the biblical message of anachronistic imagery) so that the preacher can confront people with its existential challenge.

While emphasis on the Word proclaimed has continued to be an important topic in theology, during the latter half of the twentieth century kerygma theology was subject to two important lines of critique. First, some (including a number of Bultmann's own pupils) argued that it was illegitimate to divorce the substance of Christian faith from the historical facts about Jesus as sharply as Bultmann himself seemed to do, noting that, in so far as the object of the kerygma's witness is a set of particular historical events (principally, the life, death, and resurrection of Jesus), its validity cannot be separated from the question of whether or not those events actually took place. In short, it was objected that kerygma theology's focus on the individual's decision for or against the kerygma threatened to loosen faith from dependence on the person of Jesus Christ its object and reduce it to a purely subjective matter of transformed self-understanding.

The second line of critique against the Bultmannian understanding of the kerygma also focused on its risks of subjectivism, but this time motivated by its tendency to focus on Christian faith as a reality purely internal to the believer, without reference to the broader social context of which she or he is part. Proponents of LIBERATION THEOLOGY in particular argue that the transformed self-understanding that Bultmann rightly sees as a crucial dimension of Christian encounter with the kerygma needs to be understood as extending beyond the individual to include the faith community as a whole, in relation to the wider society of which it is a part. In the absence of this attention to the communal dimension of faith, they argue, Bultmann's project ignores the political dimensions of Jesus' message, with its emphasis on concrete deeds of liberation for those afflicted by injustice and oppression (see especially Luke 4:18).

P. Althaus, *Fact and Faith in the Kerygma of Today* (Muhlenberg Press, 1959); UK edn, *The So-Called Kerygma and the Historical Jesus* (Oliver and Boyd, 1959).

R. Bultmann, H. W. Bartsch *et al.*, *Kerygma and Myth: A Theological Debat* (HarperCollins, 2000 [1953]).

W. Pannenberg, 'Kerygma and History', in *Basic Questions in Theology* (Fortress Press, 1970 [1961]), 1.81–95.

Ian A. McFarland

Kierkegaard, Søren Søren Aabye Kierkegaard was born in Copenhagen in 1813 and spent virtually his entire life within a mile's radius of Copenhagen's Church of Our Lady, which he attended as a child, in which he delivered some of his communion meditations, and where his funeral service was held in 1855. The most chronicled events of his life are a troubled relation to his father (who was nevertheless a major influence on his view of Christianity), his agonized renunciation of marriage (1841), being mocked in a satirical newspaper (1846), and a pamphleteering attack on the established Church (1854–5) that caused extensive debate throughout Scandinavia. After his death his work gradually became known outside Scandinavia, first in Germany, and by the 1930s he had become a major figure in modern philosophy and theology, being seen as an inspiration for both NEO-ORTHODOXY and existentialism.

After a protracted study of theology, Kierkegaard's Masters thesis *On the Concept of Irony* signalled a lifelong fascination with Socrates (469–399 BC) and Socrates' maieutic art. He applied this in his own strategy of 'indirect communication', seeking to reawaken a sense for authentic Christianity in the flaccid environment of bourgeois Christendom. A primary means to this end was the series of books he published under pseudonyms such as Victor Eremita and Johannes Climacus and which he called his 'aesthetic' writings. Several of these, portraying the seductive but also destructive power of aesthetic existence, have a strongly literary character (e.g., *Either/Or* (1842), *Repetition* (1843), *Stages on Life's Way* (1845)); others explore more explicitly philosophical and theological topics (e.g., *Fear and Trembling* (1843), *Concept of Anxiety* (1844), *Philosophical Fragments* [1844], *Concluding Unscientific Postscript* (1846)). Themes of these writings include the opposition between aesthetic and ethical views of life, the limitations of ethics in relation to faith ('the teleological suspension of the ethical'), the paradox of the INCARNATION, the moment of intersection of time and eternity, and what has been called a 'phenomenology of moods' that explores the psychological dimensions of human beings' spiritual situation. These 'moods' and 'movements' (as Kierkegaard also calls them), include melancholy, anxiety, absurdity, despair, and 'the leap' that brings about contemporaneity with Christ. Collectively these works attack both Romanticism and Hegelianism (see HEGEL), not sparing either theological ('Right Hegelian') or anti-theological ('Left Hegelian') versions of IDEALISM. At the same time Kierkegaard published under his own name a series of what he called 'upbuilding (or "edifying") discourses' that explored and applied the biblical sources of his understanding of Christian existence. However, as he said himself, most of the world ignored these works, preferring the more poetic or intellectually satisfying pseudonymous works.

In the second half of his authorship, he expressed an ever bleaker view of the present age and of the insincerity of the Christianity practised in 'CHRISTENDOM'. Again, he used pseudonyms, only this time because he was expressing a 'high' view of faith that he could not claim to live up to himself. This is found especially in works attributed to 'Anti-Climacus' (*Sickness unto Death* (1849), *Training in Christianity* (1850)). He also continued to publish discourses under his own name, notably *Upbuilding Discourses in Various Spirits* (1847), *Works of Love* (1847), and *Christian Discourses* (1848), as well as a number of smaller collections. In these two strands of writing he sought both to articulate the demands of following one who was despised and rejected by men, warning that all would-be disciples must expect hostility and persecution from the world, and to offer assurances as to the basic goodness of creation and the unconditionality of the forgiveness of sins (especially in the several discourses on Matt. 6:24–34 and Luke 7:36–50). The final 'attack on Christendom' was occasioned by a sermon preached by H. Martensen (1808–84) on the occasion of the death of Denmark's primate, J. Mynster (1775–1854). Mynster had been the leading figure of Danish Church life, and Kierkegaard had known and admired him for many years. However, he also regarded him as a quintessential compromiser unworthy of Martensen's epithet: 'a witness to the truth'. He also saw the sermon as serving Martensen's own (successful) jockeying to become Mynster's successor. The newspaper articles and pamphlets that Kierkegaard wrote were personal to the point of scandalous, but they also highlighted the paradoxes of preaching a kingdom that was not of this world from within the privileged position of a comfortable establishment. Kierkegaard's health gave way in the midst of the attack and he died after a short illness, refusing communion but affirming his faith in divine love.

J. Garff, *Søren Kierkegaard: A Biography* (Princeton University Press, 2005).

B. Kirmmse, *Kierkegaard in Golden Age Denmark* (Indiana University Press, 1990).

R. L. Perkins, *International Kierkegaard Commentary*, 24 vols. (Mercer University Press, 1985–).

GEORGE PATTISON

KING, MARTIN LUTHER When R. Parks (1913–2005) was jailed for refusing to relinquish her seat to a White man on a Montgomery city bus on 1 December 1955, she not only staked out her claim to become the mother of the American civil rights movement, but also catapulted Martin Luther King, Jr (1929–68), a twenty-six-year-old African-American clergyman, into the leadership of that movement. The following year King successfully led the Montgomery Bus Boycott and became the first president of the Southern Christian Leadership Conference, which served as an organizing centre for the American civil rights movement. His 'I Have a Dream' speech, delivered on 23 August, 1963 in Washington, DC, is regarded as one of the great oratorical feats of the twentieth century, while his 'Letter from Birmingham City Jail', written in April of that same year, is similarly viewed as a classic Christian confessional document, emphasizing the believer's duty to resist injustice wherever it is found.

King worked assiduously to alleviate and eradicate racism, which he saw as a blemish on the American soul. He regarded segregation and discrimination as expressions of the SIN of racism, which he described as 'the white man's burden and America's shame'. In 1964 he became the youngest person ever to receive the Nobel Peace Prize for his work in exposing racial oppression and segregation in the USA and for his commitment to NONVIOLENCE. His own theological vision, outlined in sermons, letters, and books centred on the idea of 'the beloved community', in which peace and justice would prevail.

King was assassinated on 4 April, 1968 in Memphis, Tennessee while pushing for better wages and working conditions for sanitation workers. Towards the end of his life he spoke out forcefully against the harm that poverty inflicts on the powerless and with equal passion opposed the Vietnam War. His lasting contribution is his work in civil rights, encouraging and informing people of all races, religions, and nationalities that they can realize their dreams and fulfil their potential.

D. J. Garrow, *Bearing the Cross: Martin Luther King, Jr., and the Southern Christian Leadership Conference* (William Morrow and Company, 1986).

NOEL LEO ERSKINE

KINGDOM OF GOD The English phrase 'kingdom of God' (*mlkwt yhwh* in Hebrew/Aramaic; *basileia tou theou* in Greek) refers to a transcendently righteous power, congruent with God's will. The phrase is central in Jesus' teaching and important in subsequent Christian theology. It never appears in the OT, though God is on various occasions identified as 'King' (e.g., 1 Sam. 8:7; Isa. 6:5; cf. 2 Macc. 13:4) or as exercising royal prerogatives (Exod. 15:18; 1 Chron. 28:5; 2 Chron. 13:8). Particular psalms (22, 24, 29, 47, 93, 96, 97, 99, 145) highlight God's theophany, holiness, governance, creative power, and future judgement. In Daniel (4:34; 6:26), *1 Enoch* (10:1–11:2), and the *Testament of Moses* (10:1–10), visions of God's dominion become increasingly apocalyptic, contrasting this world and the next.

In the first century BC *Psalms of Solomon* the phrase 'kingdom of our God' first appears in a hymn that awaits the coming of a Messiah who shall destroy lawless Gentiles and unite ISRAEL in righteousness (17:1–32). The metaphor becomes emphatic in Jesus' teaching, appearing in all the earliest Gospel traditions: Mark, Q, sources unique to Matthew and Luke, and (though to a much lesser degree) JOHN. PARABLES (Matt. 13:1–52) and aphorisms (Matt. 7:21; Luke 16:16), not theoretical disquisitions, are the preferred mode for describing it. The LORD'S PRAYER includes a petition that God's kingdom come (Luke 11:2; Matt. 6:9). The kingdom is also associated with Jesus' exorcisms and his disciples' acts of healing (Luke 10:9; 11:20).

In Jesus' proclamation the kingdom is not coterminous with Israel or any geopolitical entity; neither is it styled as inner spirituality or a utopian dream. The kingdom is a metaphor for God's dynamic sovereignty throughout eternity (Matt. 13:36–43), already yet secretly erupting in human history (Matt. 13:18–23; Mark 4:22; Luke 17:20–1). Its timing is ambiguous: the kingdom is variously described as on the verge (Mark 1:15; 9:1), already present (Luke 6:20), and yet to be consummated (Matt. 13:24–30; Luke 13:29). A gift from God, not a human achievement (Mark 10:23–7; Luke 12:32; John 3:3), the kingdom upends conventional expectations (Matt. 20:1–16; Luke 9:59–60). It requires radical acceptance (Matt. 18:23–35) and infant dependence (Mark 10:14–15). Those with faith anticipate its surprising future with joy and wonder (Luke 14:7–24); the faithless are hardened in their rejection (Mark 4:11–12, 25).

Outside the synoptic Gospels the theme of 'the kingdom of God' is muted; for though the rest of the NT is no less eschatological than the Gospels, that ESCHATOLOGY assumes a more clearly defined Christological shape. PAUL, for example, is not preoccupied by the idea of the kingdom, although he uses the term in association with God's vocation, peace, and righteousness (Rom. 14:17; 1 Cor. 6:9–10; Gal. 5:21; 1 Thess. 2:12). Accordingly, he forecasts Christ's delivery of the kingdom to God (1 Cor. 15:20–8). John (18:36), Ephesians (5:5), Colossians (1:13), and Revelation (11:15; 12:10; 22:1) effectively equate God's kingdom with Christ's. Believers who endure this world's torments are assured salvation in Christ's heavenly kingdom (2 Tim. 4:18; 2 Pet. 1:10–11; Rev. 3:21).

In earlier post-biblical Christian literature references to the kingdom follow two intersecting lines. Questions about temporality persist: whether its coming is uncertain (Ignatius, *Eph.* 11.1; 19.3), provisionally realized (*1Clem.* 5.4, 7; *Barn.* 8.5–6), or a future event (*1Clem.* 42:3; *Barn.* 21.1). For IRENAEUS and ORIGEN the kingdom is an ultimate stage of human maturation for communion with God. 'Our face shall see the Lord's face, and shall rejoice with joy unspeakable' (Irenaeus, *AH* 5.7); apprehension of God comes by honouring Christ as the *autobasileia*, or 'kingdom itself' (Origen, *CMatt.* 14.7). Later ORTHODOX THEOLOGY tends to pursue 'the kingdom of God hidden within [the believer's] soul' (Isaac the Syrian, *Asc.* 2) without disavowing the Church's position at the intersection of mortal life and God's eternity.

After the Council of NICAEA, AUGUSTINE explored socio-political aspects of God's kingdom in *The City of God* (*ca.* 413–*ca.* 427). Although he makes the Latin *civitas* rather than *regnum* the presiding metaphor, Augustine draws the connection: 'the church even now is the kingdom of Christ and the kingdom of heaven' (*City* 20.9), thereby following Cyprian of Carthage (d. 258) in transposing the kingdom of God into an ecclesiological key. Directly counter to God's city is that of the DEVIL (20.8–15). Caught in the middle is the *civitas terrena*: corporate humanity, created in God's image and wounded by the FALL.

Centuries later Peter's receipt of 'the kingdom's keys' (Matt. 16:18–19) occupies a critical place in Pope Gregory VII's (r. 1073–85) assertion of papal authority over Emperor Henry IV (r. 1084–1105). After the Concordat of Worms (1122) the way was paved for the promulgation of a universal pontifical power answerable to God alone. Resistance to this papal transmogrification of God's kingdom came from JOACHIM OF FIORE, whose spiritual interpretation of history minimized all civil authorities while inadvertently inspiring later radicals like T. Müntzer (*ca* 1488–1525) to attempt violent imposition of 'the kingdom of God' onto society.

Neither fanatical nor pontifically centred – though dependent on German nobles for his security – M. LUTHER contrasted a gracious *Reich Gottes* and a severe *Reich der Welt*. Christians have a foot in each world: God has ordained the powers that be (Rom. 13:1), and both God and Caesar are to be recompensed (Mark 12:17). Luther also preached that both kingdoms are collateral operations of one God: worldly government is the 'alien work' (*opus alienum*) by which Adam's children are governed; the 'proper work' (*opus proprium*) of God's kingdom is confession of God's unique lordship and succour for the poor (see TWO KINGDOMS).

After the REFORMATION's challenge to attempts to identify the kingdom of God with the Roman Church, the concept became increasingly anthropocentric during the ENLIGHTENMENT. I. KANT translated the kingdom into a philosophical principle that could be known through unassisted reason in his *Religion within the Limits of Reason Alone* (1793). Under Pietist influence (see PIETISM), F. SCHLEIERMACHER regarded God's kingdom as Jesus' mediation to humanity of his uniquely potent 'God-consciousness'. Following Kant, A. Ritschl (1822–89) argued that Christians *are* the kingdom of God in so far as they recognize their common humanity, act lovingly, and expand the community of moral conviction and moral goods. A. VON HARNACK defined the kingdom as 'the rule of the holy God in the hearts of individuals', establishing the human soul's infinite value (*Christ.* 56). Whereas Harnack reckoned Jesus no social reformer, W. Rauschenbusch (1861–1918) viewed God's kingdom precisely as 'the Christian transfiguration of the social order' (*Theol.* 145). Affirming the Church as God's kingdom already present 'in mystery', VATICAN COUNCIL II distinguished its growth from human ideologies of progress (*LG*, §3). In line with Vatican II, LIBERATION THEOLOGIES struggle with the temptation to political messianism associated with Rauschenbusch's SOCIAL GOSPEL, and thus tend to distinguish the growth of the kingdom through political liberation from its definitive advent.

Debate has erupted at every stage of Christian reflection on the kingdom of God. Though biblically supportable, Augustine's bifurcation of the Heavenly City's glory of God and the Terrestrial City's self-glorification (cf. Matt. 6:24 and *City* 14.28) stimulated both Eusebius of Caesarea's (*ca* 260–*ca* 339) praise of empire as 'the imitation of monarchical power in heaven' (*Con.* 5) and Pope Gregory the Great's (r. 590–604) allegorization of the Church as the kingdom of heaven (*HGos.* 2.38). Attempts to identify the kingdom with worldly political or ecclesiastical structures were repudiated by Menno Simons (1496–1561), and the Quaker G. Fox (1624–91) refused 'war against any man ... neither for the kingdom of Christ nor for the kingdoms of this world' (*Journal* 1,660). From the perspective of REFORMED THEOLOGY, K. BARTH asserted 'the radical and indissoluble antithesis of the kingdom of God to all human kingdoms' (*CD* IV/2, 177). While sympathetic to Ritschlian theology and ethics, both J. Weiss (1863–1914) and A. Schweitzer (1875–1965) argued that Jesus' teaching about the kingdom had to be interpreted in purely apocalyptic terms. In this way, almost every theological assertion made for the kingdom of God has provoked an equal and opposite reaction.

The significance of God's kingdom in Christian thought lies at the nexus of the Church's memory of Jesus, the paradox of his GOSPEL, and the Church's life amidst history's vagaries. Because Jesus' ministry was centred on the kingdom, its understanding bears on both CHRISTOLOGY and the QUEST OF THE HISTORICAL JESUS. Because God's redemptive invasion of this world lies at the heart of Jesus' preaching, the kingdom raises fundamental questions for the Church's DOCTRINE of God, SOTERIOLOGY, and POLITICAL THEOLOGY. ECCLESIOLOGY is implicated, because in every age the church has depicted the kingdom in accordance with its own aspirations and follies. The paradoxical form and substance of Jesus' gospel of the kingdom reflect its eschatological character and import. Accordingly, a pilgrim Church does well to follow its Lord by bearing truthful witness to the kingdom while abjuring identification with it.

B. E. Daley, *The Hope of the Early Church* (Cambridge University Press, 1991).

E. P. Sanders, *Jesus and Judaism* (Fortress Press, 1985).

E. Staehelin, *Die Verkündigung des Reiches Gottes in der Kirche Jesu Christi*, 7 vols. (Reinhardt, 1951–65).

C. Walther, *Typen des Reich-Gottes-Verständnisses* (Kaiser, 1961).

C. CLIFTON BLACK

KOREAN THEOLOGY Ham S.-H. (1901–89), a Korean philosopher and peace activist, described Korea as the 'Queen of Suffering', which is a fitting portrait of a nation which, surrounded by the superpowers of China, Russia, and Japan, has suffered great turmoil throughout her history. Christianity was introduced to the Korean peninsula in the late eighteenth century and experienced a turbulent history, including persecution of Catholics by the government, Japanese occupation, the Korean War, postwar poverty, military-backed governments, and the division between North and South. Korean theological discourse has been developed as a result of Christians struggling to respond to these challenges. It has incorporated Christian theologies brought from outside on the one hand and responded to traditional religions such as Buddhism, Confucianism, and shamanism on the other (see BUDDHISM AND CHRISTIANITY; TRADITIONAL RELIGIONS AND CHRISTIANITY).

In response to the poverty and injustice in postwar Korea, two theological responses emerged: a theology of holistic blessing and minjung theology. Both can be described as major contextual theologies intended to address these problems. The GOSPEL of holistic blessing became dominant in Korean Christianity in the Protestant revival meetings that started in the early twentieth century and became increasingly popular among Christians after World War II. The man who epitomizes this approach is D. Yonggi Cho (b. 1936) of the Full Gospel Church in Seoul. It was the harsh reality of extreme poverty in postwar Korea that brought Cho to seek the meaning of the gospel and adopt the theology of 'threefold blessing': 'spiritual wellbeing, general wellbeing, and bodily health'. The theology of holistic blessing is not limited to the Full Gospel Church. As revival is characteristic of the Korean Church regardless of denomination, so the message of the expected blessings for those who seek is common to most of the mainline Protestant Churches.

Minjung theology played a key role during the 1960s and 1970s in challenging the military-backed governments and the mistreatment of factory workers by *jaebul*, or family-run mega-companies. Suh N.-D. (1918–84) presented his thesis arguing that Jesus identified with the poor, sick, and oppressed (minjung), and that the gospel of Jesus is the gospel of salvation and liberation. For him, this is manifested in a struggle with those evil powers and so liberation is not individual or spiritual but rather communal and political. Suh systematized minjung theology in the following years, seeing the minjung as subjects of history and introducing 'han', or anguish and despair, as the key theme for theology in the Korean context. Ahn B.-M. (b. 1922), another well-known minjung theologian, asserted that Jesus identified with the oppressed in such a way that 'Jesus is minjung and minjung is Jesus', and that the event of the cross is the climax of the suffering of the minjung. He also insisted that the minjung is the owner of the Jesus community and that this is fundamentally a community which shares food. Minjung theology captured people's imagination and was a major instrument of the minjung or civil movement that challenged both the Church and society to deal with problems of socio-economic and political injustice in South Korea.

The integration of Christianity with Korean religiosity was much discussed in the 1960s. The two foremost theologians in this field were Ryu D.-S. (b. 1922) and Yoon S.-B. (1916–80). Ryu in his thesis on 'Tao and Logos' suggested that the use of eastern philosophy of the Way is necessary for conveying the message of the Christian gospel in Asia. He also described the dynamics of the development of Korean theology as the result of constant interaction between paternal and maternal movements of the HOLY SPIRIT. The former approach is rooted in the Confucian tradition and leads to the conservative and hierarchical aspects of Korean Church life; the latter embraces a shamanistic approach to the FAITH and is closely related to the revival movements and Pentecostal Churches in Korea. Yoon believed that Korean theology would blossom through creative exploration of the religious meaning of the Tankun myth – the story of the origin of the Korean people from the union of the son of heaven and a female bear – in the light of Christianity. He insists that Confucianism provides the background for Korean thinking, and so is an indispensable tool for Korean theology, arguing that the Confucian concept of 'sincerity' can integrate dichotomized concepts in traditional theology, such as LAW and gospel, sacred and secular.

Although the desire for reunification of North and South Korea has been the most important agenda item for political leaders, the ways to achieve the goal have differed widely, as the two Koreas were at the forefront of the Cold War ideological conflict. Developing a theology of peace and reconciliation is a recent attempt of Korean Christians to deal with this sharp division not only between the North and South but also between conservatives and liberals in South Korea. In 1988 the Korea National Council of the Churches issued the 'Declaration of the Korea National Council of the Churches toward the Unification and Peace of Korean People', which made a significant impact both within the Church and on the whole nation. The declaration affirmed that Christ came to the earth as the servant of peace and proclaimed the KINGDOM OF GOD, which represents peace, reconciliation, and liberation. It also acknowledged and confessed the SIN of mutual hatred, used to justify both the division of Korea and the citizens of the two Koreas' acceptance of their respective governments' ideology as absolute in a way contrary to God's absolute authority. The declaration proclaimed the year 1995 as a jubilee year for peace and unification when Koreans could celebrate together the fiftieth anniversary of the liberation from Japan. The declaration exhibits the Korean Christians' articulation of a theology of peace and reconciliation as they trust God's sovereign power over the problem of division, the slavery of hatred, and the bondage of ideological conflict.

The four theological movements above are distinctively Korean approaches to the Christian life, but the majority of Korean Protestants are deeply conservative and hold an attitude of ardent commitment to SCRIPTURE. This earnest adherence to the Bible has become an integral part of the daily lives of Christians, both individually and collectively, and they tend to take the text literally. Christian Churches are characterized as incorporating the dynamics of the occasional *sakyunghoe* (Bible-examining meetings), *buhoenghoe* (revival meetings), and weekly home group meetings, which include Bible study, sharing of testimony, and *tongsung kido* (the whole group praying aloud, separately but simultaneously). These are key aspects of faith for most Christians in Korea, and often result in the revival of their faith and deepening of their commitment.

Although the problems of poverty and injustice still remain, Korea's emergence as the world's thirteenth largest economy and the establishment of democracy mean that some of the distinctive theologies of the second half of the twentieth century arguably have less relevance in twenty-first-century South Korean society. There are emerging challenges to the integrity of the Church: a lack of authentic spirituality in Church leadership and a lack of social and personal ethics. The exploration of theology of peace and reconciliation in the Korean peninsula is still the most urgent agenda item for the Korean Churches, and articulating a relevant theological discourse which can be accepted by both liberal and conservative sections is an imperative for the Korean Churches.

CTC-CCA, eds., *Minjung Theology: People as the Subjects of History* (Orbis, 1983).

S. C. H. Kim, 'The Word and the Spirit: Overcoming Poverty, Injustice and Division in Korea' in *Christian Theology in Asia*, ed. S. C. H. Kim (Cambridge University Press, 2008), 129–53.

W. Ma, W. Menzies and H.-S. Bae, eds., *David Yonggi Cho: A Close Look at His Theology and Ministry* (APTS Press, 2004).

D. K.-S. *Suh, The Korean Minjung in Christ* (CCA, 1991).

Sebastian C. H. Kim

Kuyper, Abraham Abraham Kuyper (1837–1920) was born into the home of a minister in the Dutch Reformed Church (*Nederlands Hervormde Kerk*). His education in Leiden University was strongly influenced by J. H. Scholten (1811–85), who modelled for Kuyper an emphasis on the logical development of ideas from root principles and an orientation to the primary ideas of the Reformation. Kuyper embraced modern theology, and became a minister in the NHK, but experienced a conversion to a more traditional Reformed orthodoxy due to his reading of the Christian allegorical novel *The Heir of Redclyffe* (1853) and the influence of parishioners. Kuyper entered politics in 1874 but remained active in Church life. In 1879 he helped form the Reformed orthodox Anti-Revolutionary Party, and served as editor for the party's weekly paper (*De Heraut*) and daily (*De Standaard*).

In 1880 he helped to found the Free University of Amsterdam, which he believed had an important role to play both in furthering the mission of the Church and in shaping contemporary culture through its impact on the life of common people. 'Sphere Sovereignty' was the title of Kuyper's inaugural address for the Free University and the label for his idea that human life is rightly characterized by pluralism with respect to both social structures and world views. According to Kuyper, God is sovereign over the entire creation, but there is also a derivative sovereignty distributed across social spheres such as the family, schools, and the State. This pluralism of spheres allows for a diversity of world views, manifested concretely in a diversity of public institutions like the Free University.

In 1886 Kuyper led the Doleantie, a schism from the NHK prompted by concerns about the national Church's theological liberalism, and in 1892 Kuyper's group merged with the Christian Reformed Church in the Netherlands to form the Reformed Churches in the Netherlands. Kuyper served as Prime Minister of the Netherlands from 1901 to 1905, though his tenure was unremarkable. His continuing influence is a function both of the example of his own committed engagement with contemporary culture and of his ideas, which encourage a committed and public Christianity.

In 1898 Kuyper gave the Stone Lectures at Princeton Seminary, which presented his distinctive interpretation of Reformed theology. This perspective, later labelled 'neo-Calvinism' (initially a pejorative designation that eventually became an accepted label), saw Christianity as a world system which yielded a comprehensive view of life and reality. In addition to articulating his idea of sphere sovereignty, the lectures also highlighted two of Kuyper's distinctive theological emphases: common grace and the antithesis. Kuyper stressed the importance of common grace (i.e., that which God bestows on all humankind) as the divine restraint in creation that allows positive contributions to history from all human beings and thus justifies Christian engagement with the public realm. By contrast, Kuyper coined the idea of the antithesis, which distinguished Christians (beneficiaries of both special and common grace) from non-Christians (beneficiaries of common grace only) to emphasize the distinctiveness of Christian belief. Kuyper never resolved the tension between these two emphases, and his legacy includes those who emphasize one or the other as more central to Christian participation in the world.

J. Bratt, *Abraham Kuyper: A Centennial Reader* (Eerdmans, 1998).

C. van der Kooi and J. de Bruijn, eds., *Kuyper Reconsidered: Aspects of His Life and Thought* (VU Uitgeverij, 1999).

Vincent Bacote

L

Laity The Greek word *laikos*, from which the word 'lay' derives, does not occur in the Bible, although the noun *laos*, meaning 'people', is frequent, specifically designating the people of God as distinct from the Gentiles. Thus, the word *laos* properly refers to a sacred or consecrated people, distinct from a people who are not so consecrated. Several scholarly studies have shown that, although *laikos* is philologically related to *laos*, the use of the former term suggests that it refers to a further distinction within the people of God, according to which the *laikos* is opposed to the priest and Levite as one who is not consecrated for leadership in worship. In short, *laikos* designated a segment of the Christian population that were not leaders of the community and who exercised no cultic function. It referred to those who were not priests, deacons, or clerics.

Y. Congar (1904–95) argued that in 1 Peter the priestly themes and levitical ethic of the OT are carried over to the people of God as a whole (see, e.g., 1 Pet. 2:9). By contrast, Clement of Rome (*fl.* 95) is the first to contrast *laikos* to 'priest' (*1Clem.* 40:5), and uses the former term to refer to that part of the people which is neither priestly nor levitical; nevertheless, for him *laikos* refers to the non-priestly, non-levitical element among the *holy* people.

Gratian (*fl.* twelfth century), in a canon which he attributes to Jerome, declared, 'There are two types of Christians' (*Decr.* 100.12.1.7), effectively dividing humankind into two classes: those of religion and those of the world. In Gratian's text, lay people are allowed to possess temporal goods needed for use, to marry, to till the earth, to pronounce judgement on disputes and to plead in court, to lay their offerings on the altar, and to pay their tithes. They can be saved if they do good and avoid evil. Gratian's description presents the lay condition as a concession to human weakness and denies to the laity, concerned in temporal affairs, any active part in the sphere of sacred things. Gratian's division was echoed by other medieval writers, most notably Hugh of St Victor (1096–1141). Their perspective was shaped by an ambivalent attitude towards the world as essentially good because of its divine source, but also as a source of evil and a distraction from spiritual things. The latter emphasis led to an attitude of contempt towards the world that undercut the very structures and values inherent to the lay state and placed a correspondingly high value on the ideal of flight from the world in monasticism.

From the fifteenth century two competing ecclesiologies developed: a tendency by some writers to identify the Church with the clergy and a reaction (culminating in the Protestant Reformation) that identified the Church with a lay society, with no theological distinction between a priesthood of the baptized and a hierarchical priesthood.

A more positive view of the laity in Catholic theology developed in the nineteenth century, when growing secularization, a more positive attitude towards the world, and waning ecclesiastical temporal power required a new form of witness in an increasingly pluralistic and secular world. Pius XI (r. 1922–39) and Pius XII (r. 1939–58) officially accepted and promoted Catholic Action, a movement which enabled the laity to cooperate with or even participate in the hierarchy's own apostolate, but the apostolate was still essentially that of the hierarchy. In the encyclical *Mystici corporis* (1943), Pius XII acknowledged the laity's share in responsibility for the Church's total mission.

This brief overview of the history of the laity shows that the very concept excluded the laity from any active part in the sphere of sacred things. It does not account for the truth that the laity, like clergy and monks, are ordered to a heavenly inheritance (Col. 1:12), even though they are also involved in the activities of the world and, indeed, accomplish God's work in and through their work in the world. The laity cannot be identified simply by reference to the world, secular work, or merely temporal occupations. These provide the conditions, not merely the matter, of their Christian activity, which can be quite spiritual.

Vatican Council II and, later, the 1983 Code of Canon Law identify the Church as the people of God, treating all Christians in common before differentiating the various states of life and offices. They stress the oneness of the chosen people of God. Members of the Church share a common dignity from their rebirth in Christ, possess in common one salvation, one hope, and one undivided charity (*LG*, §32). All are called to holiness. The people of God as a whole is active, consecrated, and a witness and sacramental sign of God's grace active in the world. This people is constituted by baptism and shares properly in Christ's priestly, prophetic, and kingly offices, although these are carried out differently according to one's office and state in life. As part of the people of God, the laity is entrusted with a common sacred mission, which is also secular: the transformation of the present order into the kingdom of God. The laity has an active responsibility for the evangelizing mission of the Church. The apostolate of the laity is inherently their own, received in baptism and confirmation (*LG*, §11).

The secular quality properly attributed to the laity is not to be interpreted in an exclusive sense. As the development of lay ecclesial ministry has shown, lay people also legitimately engage in ministerial service within the Church. These new activities are raising new questions about the relationship between lay and ordained ministry. While some fear that laypeople are usurping what is properly ordained ministry, others fear a clericalization of the laity and a devaluation of the laity's traditional influence and mission in the secular sphere. At the same time, the older dualism between the spiritual and secular spheres is being questioned today.

Y. Congar, *Lay People in the Church* (Geoffrey Chapman, 1965).
L. Doohan, *The Laity: A Bibliography* (Michael Glazier Books, 1987).
John Paul II, apostolic exhortation, *Christifideles laici* (1988).

SUSAN K. WOOD

LAMBETH QUADRILATERAL: see ECUMENISM.

LAS CASAS, BARTOLOMÉ DE While his work as a historian seems to be one of his major contributions to the understanding of the conquest and colonization of the Americas, Fray Bartolomé de Las Casas (*ca* 1485–1566) is best known as the 'defender of the Indians' for his work in protection for the human rights of native population in the Americas. He challenged the myth of superiority that constructed the Amerindians as barbaric, deficient, irrational, naturally inferior, and created to serve. His hope was that this challenge would transform the treatment of Amerindians by the Spaniards *conquistadores.*

Las Casas arrived in the Americas in 1502 and observed the mistreatments of indigenous populations first hand, but it was not until 1511, after listening to a sermon in which the Dominican priest A. Montesino (1480–1540) denounced the behaviour of Spanish conquistadores towards indigenous people, that Las Casas began his quest for the elimination of the *encomienda* system. Las Casas saw the *encomienda* system as a mortal sin because it was a legal way of enslaving Amerindians in order to use them as forced labour. He was not against the missionary endeavour; indeed, he saw it as the only just motive for the colonization of the Americas. But he was against the violence that, in his eyes, had prevented the establishment of a real missionary enterprise.

Las Casas understood that while it was important to confront the actions of the Spaniards, it was more important to challenge the ideology behind those actions. This ideology, which defined Amerindians as less than human, was supported by a philosophy that talked about two different kinds of human beings: those born to be served, and those born to be servants or slaves. Against this perspective, Las Casas believed that all humans were created equal and that the idea of two different types of humans would imply that God somehow failed in the CREATION (see THEOLOGICAL ANTHROPOLOGY).

After twice presenting his defence of the Amerindians before Spain's King Charles I (r. 1516–56) and having been named bishop of Chiapas, Las Casas officially presented his arguments in favour of the humanity of the Amerindians during his famous debate against J. Ginés de Sepúlveda (1494–1573) in 1550. Two years later, he published his best-known work, *The Destruction of the Indies*, where he not only narrates the atrocities committed by the *conquistadores* but also engages in a more general condemnation of Spanish actions, including the killing of Amerindians. At the same time, it is important to acknowledge that Las Casas did not make the same defence of Africans: although he later regretted it, he suggested that Africans should be used as workforce in the sugar mills, as this would liberate the Amerindians from that hard labour.

The work of Bartolomé de Las Casas is still important in today's society in Latin America, as indigenous communities still struggle for HUMAN RIGHTS. The resurgence of Las Casas' message has become present in the theological discourse called *teología india.*

G. Gutiérrez, *Las Casas: In Search of the Poor of Jesus Christ* (Orbis, 1993 [1992]).

HJAMIL A. MARTINEZ-VAZQUEZ

LATIN AMERICAN THEOLOGY Latin America was the crucible for the development of LIBERATION THEOLOGY, a theological–religious movement that was closely tied to its social and cultural context. The contextual character of liberation theology was emphasized and theorized by Latin American liberation theologians themselves, intent as they were on reading and confronting 'the signs of the times'. In retrospect, such a judgement can be not only readily confirmed but also amply extended. From the beginning liberationists argued that all theological systems or visions had a context, that such contexts represented particular needs and challenges, and that all theologies should scrutinize and address such challenges and needs, if they hoped to be of relevance and service to their respective societies and cultures. No theology was beyond history, or outside society and culture; all theology was, and should be, contextual.

What liberationists posited of all theological visions or systems, past or present, they readily applied to themselves. As a theological–religious movement, Latin American liberation theology sought to be keenly cognizant of and directly responsive to the context of Latin America, from which it was emerging and in which it sought to intervene. This was the Latin America of the late 1960s and early 1970s – that period of sharp global turmoil that followed the consolidation of the Cold War through the 1950s and into the 1960s.

Socially, this context was marked by key material developments: (1) the process of decolonization at work in the Third World, involving wars of liberation and independence in the face of the western empires, yielding a host of new states (see Colonialism and Postcolonialism); (2) the emplacement of a geopolitical binomial between the democratic systems of the West and the socialist systems of the East, with a drive for a third way on the part of would-be non-aligned states; and (3) the underlying geo-economic struggle between western market capitalism, with its emphasis on human rights, and eastern centralized Communism, with its focus on social rights. In Latin America in particular, two crucial developments can be singled out as of particular significance for the emergence of liberation as a central theological theme: the triumph of the Cuban Revolution and the rise of other resistance movements to the established order. In 1959, within a long-standing historical context of US imperial and neo-imperial dominance over Latin America, Cuba veered away from the orbit of the USA towards that of the USSR. In its wake liberation movements spread across the continent in the 1960s, bringing about a chain reaction of military overthrows and repressive national security governments, largely in league with the USA.

Culturally, this context was also characterized by pivotal discursive developments, including: (1) worldwide proliferation of artistic productions critical of imperial regimes and policies; (2) sharp critiques of capitalism and socialism from opposite sides of the binomial; (3) the intensification of civil rights campaigns within the West; (4) the beginning of a breakdown of the modernist consensus across the spectrum of academic disciplines, leading to the discourses of postmodernism and poststructuralism; and (5) a corresponding turn to cultural studies, with its focus on the local, the popular, and the ideological. Again, within a specifically Latin American context, two striking developments can be noted: a sharp attack on received economic theory and a remarkable outbreak of cultural production. Thus, the model of developmentalism, which outlined the path the un- and underdeveloped nations needed to follow to achieve progress, was challenged as dependency, with liberation advanced instead as ideal model. Similarly, a boom in artistic production of all sorts took place, focusing on the societies and cultures of the continent.

Against this social–cultural background, the role of Christianity in general and the shape of the Catholic Church in particular underwent transformative developments as well, propelled by the teachings and directives of Vatican Council II. Theologically, a sense of *aggiornamento* was urged, involving attention to and relevance for the modern world. Religiously, an ethos of dialogue was launched that was both ecumenical and inter-religious in scope. Ecclesially, a sense of shared governance characterized by regional consultation, as well as of accountability and ministry to the local context, requiring close analysis and corresponding action, was promoted within the Church. The result was a change in relations with the world, with other Churches, with other religious traditions, and with the multiple variations of Catholicism itself.

In Latin America, this spirit of renewal unleashed by the Council found a ready home. Critical analysis of the continent's cultural and social context was undertaken by a group of young, progressive theologians with the aim of providing secure grounding and firm direction for the message of Christ in and to the modern situation of Latin America. Not long after the Council, a symbolic marker of such early endeavours emerged in the series of documents adopted by the Conference of Latin American Bishops (CELAM) at their epochal meeting in Medellín, Colombia, in 1968. In such circles the concept of liberation, conceived as including political and economic as well as human and spiritual dimensions, was broadly circulated. Similar stirrings were afoot in theological circles of the historical Protestant Churches, where younger theologians were also engaged in the development of a new theological vision for Latin America that would best suit the message of the gospel in times of change. The organization Iglesia y Sociedad en América Latina in 1961 emerged as gravitational centre for these theologians, while its journal, *Cristianismo y Sociedad*, launched in 1963, functioned as a means of propagating its ideas. In such circles the notion of revolution was widely entertained.

It was against the backdrop of this combination of social–cultural turmoil and theological–religious upheaval that liberation theology, bringing together the developing concepts of liberation in Catholic circles and revolution in Protestant circles, was forged and irrupted on the Latin America scene. A number of foundational publications, clustering around 1968 to 1972, constitute a multiple point of origin. On the Catholic side, several works become key referents, including a series of five volumes by J. L. Segundo entitled *Theology for the Artisans of a New Humanity* (1968–72) and G. Gutiérrez's (b. 1928) *A Theology of Liberation: History, Politics, and Salvation* (1971). On the Protestant side, the following two works were essential: R. Alves' (b. 1933) *A Theology of Human Hope* (1969) and H. Assmann's (1933–2008) *Teología de la liberación: una evaluación prospectiva* (1970; ET: *Theology for a Nomad Church*).

To be sure, a number of proposals and exchanges had taken place prior to this explosion. In fact, the period between 1961 and 1968 – from John XXIII's (r. 1958–63) call for the Council (1961) to the declarations adopted at Medellín – may be regarded as a phase of incubation. Within this period, the years 1967 and 1968 proved especially fertile and decisive. What followed afterwards was a torrent of projects and publications. Thus, the period between 1969 and 1975 – from the first flurry of groundbreaking works to the initial contact with other theologies of liberation at the 1975 Theology of the Americas Conference in Detroit – may be regarded as a phase of consolidation. During this period, an early sense of euphoria and unlimited possibilities yielded sombre reflections on captivity and exile. Within a very short period of time, therefore, liberation theology had quickly become not just a Latin American phenomenon but also a hemispheric as well as a global happening. In the process, the way of Christian thought and life in the twentieth century had been radically and irrevocably changed.

In general, liberationists developed their theological reflections within the framework of concrete engagement with the situation of the Church and people in Latin America. As such, their thought and writing was marked by critique of imperial regimes and policies (with respect to both the historical legacy of the European conquest of America and the contemporary power exercised by the USA over the region), alongside vocal espousal of the ideals of human dignity and social justice for all. Similarly, liberationists critiqued capitalism as the model for political economy and expressed support for socialism, foregrounding the problematic of economic class in theology and the Church alike. Most significantly, liberationists turned to the people, to local contexts and communities, and to the dynamics and mechanics of dominant ideologies as a context for producing theology, a practice most clearly visible in works like the multi-volume compendium *The Gospel in Solentiname* (1975) by E. Cardenal (b. 1925) and in the overall project of C. Mesters (b. 1931).

The chief stimulus of liberation theology in Latin America was the overwhelming presence of POVERTY in the continent, with the 'irruption of the poor', understood as the refusal of the poor to continue to suffer their condition in silence, being identified by many liberationists as the fact that, more than any other, has given form to liberation theology. As Catholic and Protestant theologians alike focused their attention on Latin America as both matrix for and target of their respective theological visions and ecclesial programmes, they brought to the fore the dire state of social destitution and cultural marginalization that gripped the vast majority of its peoples. Such reality was seen as demanding a new approach altogether on the part of Christian theology and practice. Indeed, poverty would serve as a framework and perspective (a first order of reflection) for theological construction and religious action (a second order of reflection). In this process of conscientization, the whole of Christian TRADITION and practice came to be reconceptualized and reformulated in what became known as the PREFERENTIAL OPTION FOR THE POOR. This revision would encompass all theological disciplines and all religious practices, and saw its fruit in more detailed studies of particular DOCTRINES, including CHRISTOLOGY (in, e.g., J. Sobrino's (b. 1938) *Christology at the Crossroads* (1978)) and ECCLESIOLOGY (in L. Boff's (b. 1938), *Church: Charism and Power* (1981)).

Central to this enterprise was biblical studies and the interpretation of SCRIPTURE, where liberationists adopted a mixed hermeneutical position: theoretically conservative, but socially radical (see HERMENEUTICS). On the one hand, the Bible was the Word of God, authoritative and normative for the people of God. Its meaning was objective and univocal. On the other hand, Scripture had been wrested away from the poor, to whom it had been addressed by God, and placed in captivity by bourgeois ecclesial and academic traditions. Faced with this situation, liberationists insisted that Scripture had to be rescued for its rightful heirs. This was carried out in two inter-related ways: the formation of base ecclesial communities, involving small-group readings paying explicit attention to local contexts; and the development of a materialist hermeneutics, foregrounding the role of political economy in texts and interpretations.

Through the 1980s and 1990s, Latin American liberation theology experienced a twofold development. On the one hand, its influence declined markedly in Latin America as the result of various factors, including internal pressure from unsympathetic Church authorities, external persecution from national as well as transnational governmental authorities, the depopulation of rural areas that were a strong centre of liberationist BASE COMMUNITIES, and a shift in world economy from industrial to global capitalism. On the other hand, its impulse was appropriated in new and multiple directions: by Third World theologians in Africa and Asia as well as by minority theologians in the First World. The question of its future in the twenty-first century is very much to the point. Here G. Gutiérrez's observation proves most insightful: liberation emerged as a response to massive poverty in Latin America; such poverty not only remains but has actually increased; therefore, liberation, properly reconfigured, remains a valid and urgent theological–religious response to the Latin American context ('Theol.').

L. Boff and C. Boff, *Introducing Liberation Theology* (Orbis, 1987).

O. E. González and J. L. González, *Christianity in Latin America: A History* (Cambridge University Press, 2007).

A. T. Hennelly, *Liberation Theology: A Documentary History* (Orbis, 1990).

I. Petrella, *The Future of Liberation Theology: An Argument and Manifesto* (Ashgate, 2004).

C. Rowland and M. Corner, *Liberating Exegesis: The Challenge of Liberation Theology to Biblical Studies* (John Knox Press, 1989).

D. Tombs, *Latin American Liberation Theology* (Brill, 2002).

FERNANDO F. SEGOVIA

Latino/a Theology Latino theology places the everyday faith and culture of Latino/as as the starting point of their theological reflection. Drawing from the religious practices, spirituality, and socio-cultural context of US Hispanics, a fundamental dimension of Latino/a theology's method is its commitment to the faith of the people as the centre of its writings. Latino/a theologians are a diverse group of scholars, yet what unites them is their shared dedication to giving voice to the millions of Latino/as in the USA; a community, they argue, that is often marginalized and ignored by the theological academy.

Several central themes appear repeatedly within the corpus of Latino/a theology, some of which have become fundamental concepts within the theological academy as a whole. Latino/a theologians' work on *mestizaje* and later *mulatez*, first explored by V. Elizondo (b. 1935), is groundbreaking. This emphasis on cultural and biological hybridity (indigenous and Spanish in *mestizaje*; African and Spanish in *mulatez*) predates later theological musings on this topic and challenges simplistic and dualistic understandings of race, culture, and identity. For Latino/a theologians *mestizaje* and *mulatez* are not only descriptive but also epistemological categories. They reveal the both/and, in/between, hybrid reality that Latino/as embody (though not exclusively) in their everyday lives. In addition, *mestizaje* and *mulatez* reveal the complex historical processes of identity and culture in the Americas.

Popular religion is a second fundamental concept within Latino/a theology. In this area the contribution of O. Espín (b. 1947) has been profound. From his work emerges a multitude of Latino/a voices that make the popular religious practices of Latino/as a fundamental source for theological reflection. These localized, contextualized practices, Latino/a theologians argue, are the most authentic avenue for tapping into any community's experience of the sacred. All religious rituals are ultimately contextual. Popular religion, however, is not seen in opposition to official or institutional religion. Latino/a scholars use the term to designate local, contextual, and everyday religious practices that are not in tension with institutionalized religion but can function outside the institution. Popular religion does not just refer to religious practices, but also to an accompanying world view. The emphasis on popular religion within Latino/a theology is linked to its commitment to elaborate the faith of Latino/a peoples.

The inter-relationship between the academic and pastoral realms is yet another significant theme within Latino/a theology. In their emphasis on the organic unity of the pastoral and the academic, Latino/a theologians view any strong distinction between them as foreign to their theological projects. This attempt to bridge the pastoral and the academic, the elite and the popular, is found in the sources privileged by Latino/a theologians. The unity of the pastoral and the academic is exemplified by the presence of Latino/a theologians as active participants in both areas, with the emphasis on the pastoral sometimes leading to the critique that Latino/a theology can be too ecclesiocentric.

Lo cotidiano (daily life) is yet another fundamental theme within Latino/a theologies. The primacy of *lo cotidiano* has been a key feature of Latina theologies. Since their earliest work, both M. Aquino (b. 1956) and A. M. Isasi-Díaz (b. 1943) have emphasized the daily life of Latinas as *the* starting point for their theologies. Daily life is not only material, but also cultural. It does not refer exclusively to the private or domestic sphere. Epistemologically, it is linked to 'common sense'. *Lo cotidiano* is thus the foundation of social systems. One cannot sharply distinguish one from the other, for everyday relationships serve as the model for systemic social structures.

A final central theme within Latino/a theology is the question of identity. Latino/a theologians struggle to articulate a theology that is representative of Latino/a communities broadly while not erasing the diversity that exists among the various Latino/a communities in the USA. This tension between a broader category of 'Latino/a' and the specificity of the different national groups in the USA is one that will continue to haunt Latino/a theology. While the significance of representing Latino/a culture and identity is fundamental to their theological task, Latino/a theologians must be careful not to reduce and limit their discourse to identity politics. Similarly, the ecclesiological focus of Latino/a theology can, at times, limit its scope. The future of Latino/a theological discourse would be greatly enriched by dialogue with scholars in the field of religious studies, who will add yet another dimension to the study of Latino/a religious experience.

V. Elizondo, *Guadalupe: Mother of the New Creation* (Orbis, 1997).

O. O. Espín, *The Faith of the People: Theological Reflections on Popular Catholicism* (Orbis, 1997).

R. S. Goizueta, *Caminemos Con Jesús: A Latino/a Theology of Accompaniment* (Orbis, 1995).

J. González, *Mañana: Christian Theology from a Hispanic Perspective* (Abingdon Press, 1990).

Michelle A. Gonzalez

Latria: see Dulia.

Latter-Day Saints, The Church of Jesus Christ of The Church of Jesus Christ of Latter-day Saints (LDS) is based in Utah's Salt Lake City. Its prophet-founder, J. Smith, Jr (1805–44), confused by denominational multiplicity within Christianity, reported divine encounters when still a teenager in New York State. According to LDS belief God, saving Smith from a sensed evil presence, later revealed to him previously hidden gold plates. These told of migrants from ancient ISRAEL populating ancient America. Disobedient to God despite both prophetic calls to repentance and a post-resurrection American appearance of Christ, they were annihilated through warfare. Smith produced these narratives as the Book of Mormon in 1830, the year of the LDS Church's foundation.

The small Reorganized LDS Church (RLDS, renamed The Community of Christ in 2000) long continued to be headed by Smith's direct descendants after Smith's murder in 1844. The majority of converts to the Church, however, migrated to the Salt Lake Valley in 1847 under the leadership of B. Young (1801–77). The westward-bound Saints (popularly known as Mormons) built chapel-like temples at Kirtland, Ohio (1836), and Nauvoo, Illinois (1845), and developed many distinctive rites, including BAPTISM for the dead. This practice is underpinned by extensive genealogical research, as well as by a theology of MARRIAGES binding for eternity and death-transcending 'endowments' (a technical term for rituals performed in LDS temples). Special clothing worn within temples and a distinctive undergarment worn at all other times symbolize these endowment COVENANTS with God. These developments were, in turn, closely interwoven with ideas of plural marriage practised by Smith from the 1830s, made known to his core associates in the 1840s, and formally publicized in 1852, only to be abolished in the 1890s under severe pressure from the federal government of the USA (though Fundamentalist LDS maintain this practice, which they hold to be divinely mandated).

Smith identified the Church as a Restoration of truth known by Adam but spoilt through APOSTASY. The juridical structure of the Church includes an 'Aaronic Priesthood' (divided into deacon, teacher, and priest) for boys older than twelve and a 'Melchizedek Priesthood' for men over nineteen, many of whom serve a two-year voluntary mission period. The Church is directed by a prophet-president who, together with two counsellors, provides the model for all offices. They, in turn, lead the Church's Twelve Apostles and Quorums of Seventies in managing world regions, which are divided locally into Stakes and Wards.

Encouraged to marry, men bring their wife and children within their priestly responsibility. Regional patriarchs also exist to give patriarchal blessings by direct inspiration of the Holy Spirit. Privately treasured, these blessings help inspire Saints in their lives. All, however, are also encouraged individually to seek direction from the HOLY SPIRIT.

While formally maintaining the terminology of Father, Son, and Holy Spirit, LDS theology is not traditionally Trinitarian, for it holds that there are an indefinite number of eternal intelligences, all of which are essentially like God in kind if not in degree (see TRINITY). These intelligences become spirit-children of God and are born as humans to gain experience and demonstrate obedience. All are potential 'gods in embryo'. Divine GRACE, effective through Christ's suffering ATONEMENT as achieved both in Gethsemane and on Calvary, ensures universal RESURRECTION into one of three Kingdoms, representing three degrees of glory: the Telestial, the Terrestrial, and the Celestial. The precise degree of glory gained by any individual matches his or her moral achievement on earth. The ideal family, with spouses who have been 'sealed' in celestial marriage in a temple, progressively expands for ever within the highest degree of the Celestial Kingdom.

C. L. Blomberg and S. E. Robinson, *How Wide the Divide? A Mormon and an Evangelical in Conversation* (IVP, 1997).

D. J. Davies, *The Mormon Culture of Salvation* (Ashgate, 2000).

DOUGLAS J. DAVIES

LAW Christianity was born into the intensely legal worlds of rabbinic Judaism and imperial Rome. The early Church largely rejected the Jewish law (or Torah) in favour of Christ's GOSPEL and his example of disregarding Jewish rules of purity, diet, DIVORCE, sabbath observance, and more. 'Christ is the end of the law' (Rom. 10:4), PAUL wrote, and 'the letter [*gramma*, i.e., written code] kills, but the Spirit gives life' (2 Cor. 3:6). Christ freed his followers to live by GRACE and follow the moral law written in the hearts and consciences of all people (Rom. 2:14), distilled in the commandment to 'love the Lord your God' and 'your neighbour as yourself' (Matt. 22:37–9; cf. Deut. 6:5; Lev. 19:18; Rom. 13:8–10). The NT furnishes ample illustrations of proper Christian living that continue to guide believers to this day and provide starting points for Christian ethics, CATECHESIS, and ecclesiastical discipline.

In comparison to its virtually wholesale rejection of Jewish law, early Christianity was more ambiguous in its treatment of Roman law and authority. Christ had, after all, enjoined his followers to 'give ... to the emperor the things that are the emperor's' (Matt. 22:21). Paul and Peter had both called Christians in good conscience to be subject to the governing authorities, paying them taxes, tributes, honour, and obedience (Rom. 13:1–7; 1 Pet. 2:13–17). But early Christians soon found they could not accept the Roman imperial cult nor readily partake of the pagan rituals attached to Roman commerce, litigation, festivals, or military service. The early Churches thus organized themselves into separate communities with, eventually, their own internal laws and ecclesiastical government. Early Church constitutions, such as the *Didache* (*ca* 100) and *Didascalia apostolorum* (*ca* 250), set forth internal rules for Church offices, clerical life, ecclesiastical discipline, charity, education, family, property, and other relations among the faithful. Early Christian leaders also urged their Roman rulers to reform their laws of slavery, education, concubinage, infanticide, and more. Such legal independence and reformist agitation eventually condemned Christians to intermittent waves of persecution.

The Christian conversion of Constantine I (*ca* 275–337) in 312 and the legal establishment of Christianity in 380 eventually allowed the Church to imbue the Roman law with a number of its basic teachings. Particularly the great synthetic texts of Roman law, the *Theodosian Code* (438) and the *Corpus iuris civilis* (529–34) of Justinian I (r. 527–65), were heavily sprinkled with Christian teachings on the TRINITY, the sacraments, LITURGY, holy days, sabbath observance, sexual ethics, charity, education, and much else. This legal establishment of Christianity contributed greatly to its expansion throughout the empire and to its canonical preservation for later centuries, but it also subordinated the Church to imperial rule. Roman emperors and other political rulers convoked many of the Church COUNCILS and major synods; appointed, disciplined, and removed the higher clergy; administered many of the Church's parishes, monasteries, and charities; and legally controlled the acquisition, maintenance, and disposition of Church property. This pattern of 'CAESAROPAPISM' persisted throughout much of the Germanic period in the Catholic West and throughout the Byzantine Empire of the Orthodox East.

Beginning in 1075, the Catholic clergy, led by Pope Gregory VII (r. 1073–85), threw off their civil rulers and established the Catholic Church as an autonomous legal and political corporation in the West. The Church now claimed personal jurisdiction over clerics, pilgrims, students, the poor, heretics, Jews, and Muslims. It claimed subject-matter jurisdiction over doctrine and liturgy; ecclesiastical property, polity, and patronage; sex, MARRIAGE and family life; education, charity, and inheritance; oral promises, oaths, and various contracts; and all manner of moral, ideological, and sexual crimes. The Church predicated these jurisdictional claims in part on its authority over the sacraments and in part on the papal 'power of the keys' bequeathed by Christ to Peter (Matt. 16:18–19); it developed an elaborate body of CANON LAW to support these jurisdictional claims. A hierarchy of Church courts and officials administered the canon law in accordance with sophisticated rules of procedure and evidence, and a vast network of ecclesiastical officials presided over the Church's executive and administrative functions.

Drawing parallels between medieval ecclesiastical legislation and the Jewish legal practices rejected by early Christians, the sixteenth-century Protestant REFORMATION rejected the Catholic canon law as an intrusion on Christian freedom as well as a usurpation of State authority. To most Protestant reformers, canon law obstructed the individual's relationship with God and obscured biblical norms for right living. The clergy's legal rule in a united Christendom further obstructed the Church's divine mission of preaching the Word, administering the sacraments, and caring for the poor and needy. While they insisted that the Church must have internal rules of order to govern itself and that its leaders must prophesy against injustice and tyranny, most Protestants regarded law to be the province more of the State than the Church. Theologically, Lutherans in particular stressed the distinction between gospel, understood as that which defines humanity's relationship with God, and law, which governs relationships among human beings only. This insistence led to conflicts among Protestants over the role of the biblical law in shaping the life of the Christian in Church and society (see THIRD USE OF THE LAW).

These new Protestant teachings permanently broke the international rule of the medieval Church and canon law, splintering western CHRISTENDOM into competing nations and regions, each with its own religious and political rulers. The Reformation also triggered a massive shift of power and property from the Church to the State. The early modern State now claimed jurisdiction over numerous subjects previously governed by the Church: marriage and family life, property and testamentary matters, charity and poor relief, contracts and oaths, moral and ideological crimes. Particularly in Lutheran and Anglican polities, the State also came to exercise considerable control over the clergy, polity, and property of the local established Churches, in emulation of the earlier laws of Christian Rome and in expression of the new theories of absolute monarchy (see ERASTIANISM).

These massive shifts in legal power and property from Church to State did not suddenly deprive western law of its dependence upon religion. Catholic canon law still governed the Catholic Church in France, Spain, Portugal, and Italy, and their many colonies, and the clergy's moral pronouncements continued to shape the State law of these Catholic lands until the French Revolution. Protestant teachings on marriage and divorce, public education and social welfare, democracy and rule of law, and constitutionalism and natural rights all came to direct and dramatic expression in state law, and provided some of the driving forces for early modern democratic revolutions in Europe and North America.

While many of these traditional Christian legal ideas and institutions were gradually eclipsed by the various secular political regimes born of the ENLIGHTENMENT, western law still today retains important connections with Christianity and other religions. Law and religion remain conceptually related. They both embrace closely analogous doctrines of sin and crime, covenant and contract, righteousness and justice that invariably bleed together in the mind of the legislator, judge, and juror. Law and religion are methodologically related, through overlapping hermeneutical methods of interpreting authoritative texts, casuistic methods of converting principles to precepts (see Casuistry), and systematic methods of organizing and teaching their subject matters. Law and religion are institutionally related, through the multiple relationships between political and religious officials and through their common commitment to protect the religious freedom of all.

Even today, the laws of the secular State retain strong moral and religious dimensions. These dimensions are reflected not only in the many substantive doctrines of public, private, procedural, and penal law that were developed in earlier Christian eras. They are also reflected in the characteristic forms of contemporary western legal systems. Every legitimate legal system has what L. Fuller (1902–78) called an 'inner morality': a set of attributes that bespeak its justice and fairness. Like divine laws, human laws are generally applicable, publicly proclaimed, uniform, stable, understandable, nonretroactive, and consistently enforced. Every legitimate legal system also has what H. Berman (1918–2007) calls an 'inner sanctity': a set of attributes that command the obedience, respect, and fear of both political authorities and their subjects. Like religion, law has authority – written or spoken sources, texts or oracles, which are considered to be decisive or obligatory in themselves. Like religion, law has tradition – a continuity of language, practice, and institutions, a theory of precedent and preservation. Like religion, law has liturgy and ritual – the ceremonial procedures, decorum, and words of the legislature, the courtroom, and the legal document aimed to reflect and dramatize deep social feelings about the value and validity of the law.

Even today, Christianity and other religions maintain a legal dimension, an inner structure of legality, which gives religious lives and religious communities their coherence, order, and social form. Legal 'habits of the heart' structure the inner spiritual life and discipline of religious believers, from the reclusive hermit to the aggressive zealot. Legal ideas of justice, order, dignity, atonement, restitution, responsibility, obligation pervade the theological doctrines of countless religious traditions, not least Christianity. Legal structures and processes, including Catholic and Orthodox canon law and Protestant forms of ecclesiastical discipline, continue to organize and govern religious communities and their distinctive beliefs and rituals, mores, and morals. The modern western State still protects, respects, and reflects these religious beliefs, values, and practices in its law.

H. J. Berman, *Law and Revolution: The Formation of the Western Legal Tradition* (Harvard University Press, 1983).

L. L. Fuller, *The Morality of Law*, revised edn (Yale University Press, 1969).

M. W. McConnell, R. F. Cochran, Jr, and A. C. Carmella, eds., *Christian Perspectives on Legal Thought* (Yale University Press, 2001).

J. Witte, *Law and Protestantism: The Legal Teachings of the Lutheran Reformation* (Cambridge University Press, 2002).

J. Witte and F. S. Alexander, eds., *Christianity and Law: An Introduction* (Cambridge University Press, 2008).

John Witte, Jr

Lectionary Derived from the Latin word for 'reading', a lectionary is any collection of biblical texts (called lections or lessons) for use in Christian public worship or private devotion. Generally, lectionaries are closely co-ordinated with the liturgical calendar, so that, for example, texts read during Lent reflect the themes of that season. The widespread adoption of an ecumenical lectionary by Catholic and many Protestant Churches over the last thirty years or so is testament to the influence of the liturgical movement, as well as of Catholic–Protestant rapprochement in the wake of Vatican Council II. This lectionary follows a three-year cycle, with primary focus in each year given to one of the synoptic Gospels, with readings from John interspersed across all three years. In addition to a Gospel text, a reading from the OT (usually somehow connected to the Gospel reading), one from the NT epistles or Revelation, and a psalm are also appointed for each week.

The aim of a lectionary is to provide for use of Scripture in worship that is at once comprehensive (covering both testaments and the widest possible range of books within them) and systematic (so that large sections of texts are read in sequence from week to week, following the old monastic practice known as *lectio continua*). Protestant free-Church traditions tend to resist the use of a lectionary as an artificial constraint that risks quenching the Holy Spirit (1 Thess. 5:19). Defenders of lectionary use counter that it helps to prevent arbitrariness or personal prejudice in the preacher's selection of texts.

Ian A. McFarland

Lent: see Calendar, Liturgical.

Lex orandi lex credendi The phrase *lex orandi lex credendi* ('the rule of prayer [is] the rule of belief') has played a critical role in the theological and historical debate concerning the place and importance of the liturgy in the life of the Church. The simplified form of the adage leaves open several interpretations, including the view that theology (belief) establishes practice (prayer), and its opposite: that practice is actually determinative of belief.

The original (and less equivocal) form of the phrase appears in a text by Prosper of Aquitaine (*ca* 390–*ca* 455): *legem credendi lex statuat supplicandi* ('the law of prayer grounds the law of belief', *Cap. 8*). Writing against the semi-Pelagians (see Pelagianism), Prosper was insisting that the necessity of grace was confirmed by the apostolic tradition of supplication, PRAYER, and intercession. Specifically, he argued that the practice of *unceasing prayer* for God's grace refuted the semi-Pelagian claim that people could initiate the life of FAITH apart from grace.

The adage itself reflects an ongoing tension within the discipline of theology over the role of practice. The pendulum has continually swung from one side to the other, sometimes privileging the argument from practice and then moving back to a heavier reliance on belief as the ultimate criterion of ORTHODOXY. The REFORMATION has often been seen as the triumph of *lex credendi*, though this does not apply to M. LUTHER, who developed his radical CHRISTOLOGY through reflection on sacramental practice (see UBIQUITY). Today, with emerging interest in the critical role of practices in theological scholarship, the adage is once again in the midst of an effort to rethink a methodology not only in liturgical theology but in the wider field of SYSTEMATIC THEOLOGY.

K. Irwin, '*Lex orandi, lex credendi* – Origins and Meaning: State of the Question', *Liturgical Ministry* 11 (spring 2002), 57–69.

DIRK G. LANGE

LGBT THEOLOGY: see QUEER THEOLOGY.

LIBERAL THEOLOGY Liberal theology is a form of theology based in reaction to the challenges of modern times and fundamentally determined by the will to mediate between the specific content of Christian religion and the entire cultural situation. This is the common feature of all forms of liberal theology, despite many specific differences in procedure. Aiming at a theology that is oriented towards the present, liberal theology criticizes and transforms the doctrine of the Church and the traditional self-understanding of Christianity in general. Interpreting liberal theology as a theological agenda for communication between theology and the entire (modern) cultural situation allows the concepts of liberal theology to be viewed against the backdrop of the problematic social and scientific situations to which they try to respond. This context varies between the nineteenth and the twenty-first centuries and shows different characteristics in the USA, Germany, Britain, and predominantly Catholic countries.

Within the discipline of HISTORICAL THEOLOGY, 'liberal theology' can be used in a more narrow sense for German theology of the last third of the nineteenth century. As such, it includes A. Ritschl (1822–89) and his school, A. von HARNACK, E. TROELTSCH, and the HISTORY OF RELIGION SCHOOL, as well as those thinkers and movements influenced by them that helped shape theology in the USA and the UK. Understood in a broader sense, 'liberal theology' denotes those theologies that productively refer to the ENLIGHTENMENT and try to implement its principles. In this case, the relevant period stretches from the eighteenth century to the present, and the movement includes theological rationalists like J. Semler (1725–91), as well as F. SCHLEIERMACHER and a 'speculative branch' (influenced by G. W. F. HEGEL) represented by D. F. Strauss (1808–74), F. Baur (1792–1860), and the (Protestant) TÜBINGEN SCHOOL. In the UK and later in the USA, J. Priestley (1733–1804) and T. Lindsay (1843–1914) were influential. In the USA H. Bushnell (1802–76) is one of the key figures of liberal theology, influential on both Church politics and academic theology; also noteworthy are W. Rauschenbusch (1861–1918) as the most important exponent of the SOCIAL GOSPEL and the theological MODERNISM represented by the Chicago School (e.g., S. Mathews (1863–1941)).

Liberal theology is primarily a phenomenon located within PROTESTANTISM. In England it became significant for the Church through the Anglican Broad Church Party. Liberal traditions were also formative influences behind UNITARIANISM in the UK and the USA. In Germany liberal theology is bound first and foremost to the academic context and shapes the lived religion of those feeling alienated from confessional Churches and their doctrine. In the context of European CATHOLIC THEOLOGY, liberal theology is far less influential due to the Vatican's condemnation of the liberal modernist movement in the early twentieth century. However, Catholic theology and the Catholic Church in North America are an exception to this rule.

Despite this broad spectrum of positions, it is possible to isolate from the history of liberal theology certain features regarding content and method that continue to be formative. Not all of these features may be found in every type of liberal theology, and they may appear with different weight in different versions. The following analysis will be restricted to liberal theology in Protestant Christianity.

In the age of Enlightenment, the necessity of reframing both the traditional DOCTRINE of the Church and the self-understanding of Christianity became crucial, owing to the perceived distance between NATURAL SCIENCE, CIVIL SOCIETY, and individual consciousness on the one hand, and the authoritative claims of Church and theology on the other. Reason was called upon as a critical authority against the established teachings of theology and Church. A conception of rational religion developed, which, freed from objectionable dogmatic content, could build a binding religious foundation for society and promote the individual's capacity for self-determination. In this framework the basic components of liberal theology are the critique of doctrine – especially in its denominational forms – and the claim for individual autonomy.

Another component of liberal theology is the high estimation it attributes to historical thinking. The literal understanding of SCRIPTURE as God's word and as a sacrosanct text with incontestable authority is superseded by an understanding of Scripture as subject to historical development. This not only makes way for a historical–critical approach to the Bible's text, but also raises the question of what really belongs to the 'essence' of Christianity, and what, contrarily, has to be perceived as a dispensable form of expression.

To answer the question of the 'essence of Christianity', liberal theology turns to the historical Jesus, critically distinguished from the 'dogmatic' Christ (see QUEST OF THE HISTORICAL JESUS). The two-natures CHRISTOLOGY of CHALCEDON is subject to criticism, as are traditional accounts of the ATONEMENT. Instead, Jesus of Nazareth's person and practice, as they are accessible by means of historical research, are made the criterion for identifying Christianity's essence; they also represent a point of reference for the individual's lived religion, as liberal theologians draw a picture of Christ's person designed to serve as an ethical example to be followed.

For more speculative branches of liberal theology (e.g., D. F. Strauss), Jesus' personality is less important than the idea he brought to the world. Nevertheless, several classical representatives of liberal theology emphasize 'Jesus' religion' as the unique feature of his personality, by means of which he has the divine power to take the believer with him into relation with God. References to Jesus' 'God-consciousness' (Schleiermacher), 'Son-consciousness' (Harnack), 'inner life' (W. Herrmann (1846–1922)), and the description of Jesus as 'the face of God turned towards us' (Troeltsch) denote more than mere 'Jesusology' or reduction of Jesus to the status of moral exemplar; rather, they emphasize the unique power in Jesus' personality that brings redemption – and which can be apprehended and appropriated personally only through FAITH.

Nor is this faith understood as a *solely* religious relation. Rather, it has *simultaneously* an ethical dimension: the individual and the religious community are encouraged to take active responsibility in creating a world more in accord with God's will. The possibility and necessity of the individual's and the community's religious–ethical contribution is stressed, leading to less emphasis on human depravity. The Reformed concept of double PREDESTINATION and the notion of the divine wrath are also all but abandoned. God is thought of as LOVE and WISDOM aimed at remodelling the individual and the whole world. Under the key phrase 'KINGDOM OF GOD', the ethical, world- and culture-forming power of Christianity is emphasized, appearing in different shapes (democracy, HUMAN RIGHTS, the Social Gospel, Christian Socialism) depending on the varying political context.

In turning towards the historical Jesus, liberal theologians focus on the transition from the 'Jesus of history' to the primitive Church's KERYGMA and on the development of the Church doctrine in its dogmatic form. This approach, with its emphasis on historical science and history of ideas, leads to the development of 'history of dogma' as an autonomous theological discipline. For example, Harnack's 'history of dogma' (*Dogmengeschichte*) is determined by his understanding of the 'simple gospel of Jesus' and the 'religion of Jesus' as Christianity's core. From this position he criticizes the formation of dogma in the early Church, which he believes is a Hellenistic alienation of Christian thought. For Harnack the idea has to be contested that right faith is dependent on assent to authoritative doctrine, a characteristic not only of Catholic and Orthodox thought but also of confessional Lutheranism.

Such critique of dogma on behalf of the individual's religious experience is a characteristic trait of liberal theology. Most of its representatives, however, do not reject all forms of Church doctrine but argue in favour of its being put into appropriate contemporary form. So long as it is cast in a form that is oriented towards religious experience and ethical practice, the importance of Church doctrine for the forms of religious community remains uncontested by most liberal theologians, just as is the importance of religious community as the context in which religion is communicated. It is thus incorrect to suggest that liberal theologians promote individualism and foster a strong disinclination for community. It is true, however, that liberals tend to stress the independence of the local congregation, particularly in the USA and the UK.

Responding constructively to the challenge of historicism is a decisive characteristic of liberal theology. For Troeltsch, however, this challenge is not sufficiently dealt with by means of a historical–critical approach to Scripture and a conception of Christian history through 'history of dogma'. His main concern lies in Christianity's power to shape the cultural whole. This leads him to include sociology in theology alongside the historical method and, finally, to call for a realization of theology via cultural studies. Especially since the 1980s, a Troeltsch renaissance has developed in Germany, whose representatives regard the approach of cultural studies as the most appropriate contemporary form of liberal theology, with parallel developments in the USA and Great Britain.

In all forms of liberal theology the concept of religious experience stands in the foreground. Through religious experience the individual experiences his or her religious autonomy. This stress on religious self-reliance is a critical component of liberal theology. Liberal theology aims at unfolding the religious experience and those statements regarding God and world that stem from it. Theology is thus better characterized as 'teaching of faith' (*Glaubenslehre*) than as 'dogmatics'. Correspondingly, Schleiermacher's demand that all propositions of the doctrine of faith have to be deduced from the pious self-consciousness (*CF*, §15) became programmatic for liberal theology. In American and

British theology, W. James' analysis of religious experience has achieved comparable importance.

A further characteristic of liberal theology is the importance it attaches to a foundation of theology in philosophy of religion, in order to prove that religion belongs to the essence of being human, with the result that the distinct features of Christian religion become apparent against the backdrop of a general concept of religion. The 'History of Religion School' calls for a comparative view on religions. This comparative focus of religion led Troeltsch to abandon Christianity's claim for absoluteness. Still, he viewed Christianity as valid for western culture, in so far as it places individualism and ethical personality in the centre of religion and cultural self-understanding. The emphasis on this central notion of Christianity connected with a concept of a personal God is the answer that the classical representatives of liberal theology in late nineteenth-century Germany gave in reaction to Darwinism and the great rise of natural science in general. In contrast, liberal theology in Britain and the USA tries to encourage the mediation between theology and natural science more strongly. In the course of this process, theologians are able to argue for a more pantheistic concept of God while interpreting incarnation as a process taking place in the context of the world.

Normally, fundamentalist, confessional, and Pietist theologies and Churches have tried to attack liberal theology. A special impulse for this critique came from dialectical theology, which denigrated basically the whole of neo-Protestantism as an apostasy from true Christianity. As R. Bultmann wrote, 'The object of theology is God, and the charge against liberal theology is not to have dealt with God, but with man.' Conservative and 'neo-orthodox' theologies consider liberal theology as a counter-programme, just as conservative theology is understood as a counter-programme from the liberal perspective. Nevertheless, liberal theology has to address the question of whether its intended mediation between theology and the modern world can preserve the autonomy of religion and the distinctive characteristics of Christianity, or whether, contrariwise, communication and mediation invariably end in fatal compromise with the cultural Zeitgeist.

L. J. Averill, *American Theology in the Liberal Tradition* (Westminster Press, 1967).

K. Cauthen, *The Impact of American Religious Liberalism* (Harper & Row, 1962).

D. Fergusson, ed., *Blackwell Companion to the 19th Century Theologians* (Blackwell, 2009).

W. R. Hutchison, ed., *American Protestant Thought in the Liberal Era* (University Press of America, 1981).

B. Reardon, *Liberal Protestantism* (Stanford University Press, 1968).

C. Welch, *Protestant Thought in the Nineteenth Century*, 2 vols. (Yale University Press, 1985 [1972]).

Christine Axt-Piscalar

Liberation Theology Liberation theology is a collective term for a group of related theologies, which rose to prominence in the last three decades of the twentieth century. Latin American liberation theology is probably the best known of these, and it originated, along with Black theology, in the USA in the late 1960s and early 1970s. In subsequent years contextual theologies in Africa and Asia, along with other contextual theologies in the USA (e.g., Latino/a theology), also sought to articulate liberationist themes. While the public prominence of some of these theologies peaked in the 1970s and 1980s, the impact of the movement is likely to be long-standing. Liberation theology's impact on theological method and Christian thinking on social-justice issues have been especially profound.

Liberation theologians adopt a prophetic approach to doing theology. The word 'liberation' reflects the concern for what early proponents called 'integral salvation'. That is, the theological world is engaged at the same time as, and through, an engagement with the social and political world. God is encountered in a special way within the struggles of everyday life. Liberation theology typically stresses the need for practical social commitments linked to the theological reflection in response to experiences of injustice and social exclusion. For example, Latin American liberation theology has focused especially on poverty, political oppression, and economic injustice. Black liberation theology has focused on racism and discrimination in the USA and apartheid in South Africa. African liberation theology has focused on colonial legacies, African identity, and cultural imperialism. Asian liberation theology has focused on poverty and religious pluralism in a continent where Christianity is very much a minority religion. Latino/a liberation theologies, in the USA, have focused on experiences of social and political marginalization, and the richness of hybrid cultural identity.

Although they raise different concerns, liberation theologians share the desire to address their social context as part of their reflection and their response to it. The variety of social contexts absorbed into this process makes liberation theology an inherently pluralist movement. It is therefore as appropriate to talk of 'liberation theologies' in the plural as it is to speak of 'liberation theology' in the singular. Even within each regional or thematic grouping, there is significant variety, and many participants prefer to speak of 'Latin American liberation theologies', 'Black liberation theologies', 'African liberation theologies', and so on. This tendency is especially notable in Asia, with clearly defined movements of Dalit theology (India), minjung theology (see Korean Theology), and Filipino theology. Likewise in the USA, along with Black and Latino/a theologies, there are also Native American theologies and Asian-American theologies.

Furthermore, each form of liberation theology has shown a history of internal growth and development; it would be mistaken to see any of them as fixed or static. Later expressions of both Latin American and Black liberation theology are significantly different from the pioneering works of the late 1960s and early 1970s, especially in their greater appreciation of FEMINIST THEOLOGY. However, this dialogue has sometimes been difficult. Liberation theologies have often been as male-dominated as other theologies, and were sometimes slow to recognize and incorporate gender analysis in their work. Early versions had a tendency to downplay gender equality, or dismiss it as a secondary issue. For their part, many liberation theologies were critical of early feminist theologies that seemed to take little account of class, race, cultural identity, and global justice. Over time, however, the encounters between liberation theologies and feminist theologies have been mutually positive, and distinctively new theologies such as WOMANIST and *MUJERISTA* THEOLOGIES have emerged. The challenges have been even greater, and the dialogue more difficult, in relation to issues of sexual orientation, with most liberation theologies showing little engagement with QUEER THEOLOGIES.

Liberation theologies are usually more attentive to *praxis* (practice and reflection) than simply to DOCTRINE. They speak of 'doing theology' to emphasize the practical orientation of theological work, and they speak of transformation to indicate ambitious aims for fundamental changes in societies. Latin American liberation theology was particularly noted for its promotion of grass-roots theological reflection in BASE COMMUNITIES. Theologians in these contexts have tried to incorporate marginalized voices and/or neglected traditions in their theological activity, and sought to question conventional theological approaches and established authorities. At times this has created severe tension between Catholic liberation theologians and Church authorities. During the 1980s there were a number of clashes between the Catholic MAGISTERIUM and high-profile Latin American theologians, such as G. Gutiérrez (b. 1928) and L. Boff (b. 1938), over the use of social analysis in theology. However, in recent years the primary tension has shifted from Latin America to Asia, with concerns over pluralism taking more attention in investigations of T. Balasuriya (b. 1924) and P. Phan (b. 1943).

Given the importance of distinctive identities and contexts for developing these theologies, there has been an unfortunate tendency for observers to identify all liberation theologies as forms of – and/or dependent upon – Latin American liberation theology. Some sensitivity is required when using the term 'liberation theology' in an inclusive sense to refer to the strands other than the Latin American variant. Some theologians deliberately seek to make public perception of 'liberation theology' more global and inclusive by claiming the term for their work, including 'Asian Liberation Theology', 'African Liberation Theology', or 'Palestinian Liberation Theology'. Others are wary that preconceived ideas about Latin American liberation theology will distort perceptions of their work, and prefer to speak of their work as African theologians or Asian theologians in more generic terms as just 'contextual theologies' or 'Third World theologies'.

The most significant forum for creative dialogue between the different branches of liberation theology has been the Ecumenical Association of Third World Theologians (EATWOT). Established in 1976 to promote dialogue between theologians drawn primarily from Africa, Asia, and Latin America, but also including Black theologians from the USA, EATWOT has allowed different liberation theologies to explore shared values and develop their distinctive identities in relation to each other. Missio, a Catholic mission institute headquartered in Aachen, Germany, has also made a significant contribution to the dissemination of Third World liberation theologies through its annual report on *Theology in Context: Information on Theological Contributions from Africa, Asia, Oceania and Latin America*. With a comprehensive bibliography of journals and books, summaries of selected articles, and fully indexed reports about theological conferences, this report remains an invaluable resource on liberation theology.

C. Rowland, ed., *The Cambridge Companion to Liberation Theology* (Cambridge University Press, 1999).

R. S. Sugirtharajah and V. Fabella, eds., *Dictionary of Third World Theologies* (Orbis, 2000).

DAVID TOMBS

LIFE AND WORK: see ECUMENISM.

LIMBO 'Limbo' (Latin for 'border', 'hem', 'fringe') is a term in Christian ESCHATOLOGY describing the state and place of souls that have neither been proportioned to the vision of God, nor merited eternal punishment through personal SIN. It is understood not as a third intermediary state between HEAVEN and HELL, but, owing to the lack of BEATIFIC VISION, as a realm on the border of hell. As such it is twofold:

(1) The 'Limbo of the Fathers' (*limbus partum*), which Christian theology has traditionally identified with the scriptural term 'bosom of ABRAHAM' (Luke 16:22), refers to the resting place of the just souls before Christ, who could not attain the vision of God prior to the advent of the Redeemer. With Christ's descent into hell and the completion of the paschal mystery the limbo of the fathers is considered dissolved.

(2) The 'Limbo of Children' (*limbus infantium*) on the other hand has a permanent character and was developed in response to the theological question of the fate of those dying with original sin only; thus generally limited to children dying before BAPTISM. The issue became the central argument in the Pelagian controversy, in which AUGUSTINE

argued the reality of original sin from the sacramental theology and practice of the Church, asserting the damnation of unbaptized children over and against the Pelagian idea of them attaining a third place different from heaven and hell (see PELAGIANISM). The non-salvation of these children was subsequently an articulated Catholic DOCTRINE, though the nature of the presumed punishment remained vague. Augustine himself had spoken only of the 'lightest punishments' (*poena levissima*).

Building on Augustine, but with Scholastic refinements in the understanding of original sin, a more specific description of the state of unbaptized children was attempted and limbo (i.e., *infantium*) emerged as both a theological concept and an eschatological term. Theological developments allowed a clearer differentiation between the punishments of hell and their causes, assigning only the exclusion from the beatific vision to the state of the children. In authors following T. AQUINAS, this state is compatible with a natural beatitude, while some later theologians even assert the possibility for relations with the supernatural order (e.g., F. Suarez (1548–1617)).

Over the next centuries limbo became the common teaching of Catholic theologians, despite the attacks of JANSENISM and rigorous post-Reformation Augustinianism denouncing limbo as identical to the 'third state' of the Pelagian HERESY. Outside the Catholic Church, Reformed theologians, due to their sacramental theology, affirmed the possibility of the salvation of unbaptized children by extraordinary means of GRACE.

Since the beginning of the twentieth century a number of theologians have argued the salvation of unbaptized children based on God's universal will of salvation (1 Tim. 2:4). Most attempts seek an explanation along the lines of the classic substitutes for baptism in CATHOLIC THEOLOGY. Some propose a variation of *baptism of blood*, with H. Schell (1850–1906) calling death itself a *Quasisakrament*. Others propose versions of *baptism of desire* along three distinct lines: illumination after death; vicarious desire on the part of the parents or the Church; unconscious desire along the lines of K. RAHNER's 'ANONYMOUS CHRISTIANITY'.

Apart from problems inherent in some of the proposed solutions, a point of contention with defenders of the limbo theory is the level of authority to be assigned to a number of Church documents teaching or presupposing the non-salvation of children.

JOHANNES MARIA SCHWARZ

LIMITED ATONEMENT One of the defining points of Reformed ORTHODOXY, the DOCTRINE of limited (also known as 'definite' or 'particular') ATONEMENT teaches that, although Christ's death is of infinite value (and thus more than sufficient to atone for the sins of the whole world), Christ did not die for all people, but only for those whom God had eternally elected to salvation. Given classic formulation at the Synod of DORT (Canon 2.8), limited atonement is logically dependent on three further theological assumptions: (1) that Christ effects salvation by paying a penalty human beings owe to God (i.e., a substitutionary model of atonement); (2) that this work of Christ's is the sole effective and meritorious cause of salvation; and (3) that some human beings will be damned (i.e., that UNIVERSALISM is false). For, if Christ paid the penalty for all people, and that payment is the sole condition of salvation, then it would follow that no human being is damned. Since for the divines at Dort it was axiomatic that some people are damned, Christ cannot have died for them. The atonement he makes on the cross is therefore 'limited' to that subset of human beings who are the object of God's eternal ELECTION.

The plausibility of limited atonement is tied to that of the soteriological and eschatological presuppositions with which it is connected. At the time of Dort, proponents of ARMINIANISM taught that Christ died for all people, but that all were not saved because FAITH was also necessary for his death to be effective. In more recent times limited atonement has been challenged by theologians who do not regard damnation as a theological given, as well as by those who reject substitutionary models of the atonement as one-sidedly stressing God's demands for justice in disregard of SCRIPTURE's emphasis on God's boundless LOVE and mercy.

IAN A. MCFARLAND

LITURGICAL MOVEMENT The name 'Liturgical Movement' is commonly used to refer to a series of related changes in the theology and practice of Christian worship that from its beginnings early in the twentieth century has been centred in the Catholic Church, but has affected many Churches of the Protestant REFORMATION. Like most important movements, it had its harbingers and antecedents. Among these were the reforms introduced by Dom P. Guéranger (1805–75) at the Abbey of Solesmes, which had been refounded in 1833, especially with respect to plainsong (or 'Gregorian chant'). More generally, the recovery of earlier and, it was argued, more authentic practices owed something to the 'historical mindedness' of the nineteenth century, and to Romanticism's protest against the disintegration of 'CHRISTENDOM'.

The Liturgical Movement drew much of its strength from a renewed appreciation of patristic theology, as contrasted with (neo-) SCHOLASTICISM, and from a corresponding admiration for pre-medieval rites and ceremonies. But, although the movement promoted and relied on historical scholarship, it was not primarily antiquarian. There was at the same time a strong pastoral and in some sense a populist emphasis.

Monastic communities, not surprisingly, provided much of the impetus, especially at first; but the watchword that came to be associated with the movement – 'full, conscious, active participation' – always referred to the whole people of God in virtue of their BAPTISM.

The complexity of the Liturgical Movement reflects the concreteness of what it sought to reform. In different ways, nearly all the elements of the Church's being converge in its worship. Where worship is corporate and therefore liturgical, it entails some way of understanding not only the Christian GOSPEL and its proclamation, the role of different 'orders' of MINISTRY, and the work and witness of those who gather, but also doctrinal matters that pertain to the INCARNATION, GRACE, the HOLY SPIRIT, and the TRINITY. All these, arguably, are co-variables: how any of them is construed affects the others.

In its theological aspect, the Liturgical Movement demonstrates the interdependence of ECCLESIOLOGY, CHRISTOLOGY, SACRAMENTOLOGY, and MISSIOLOGY. Conversely, innovations and restorations in liturgical practice, initially advocated on historical grounds, have raised important theoretical questions for SYSTEMATIC THEOLOGY. It seems likely that the influence of the movement both on the actual performance of LITURGY and on theological reflection will continue. Perhaps, as some would hold, it has only begun.

The beginning of this beginning is usually dated to 1909. It was then that Dom L. Beauduin (1873–1960) delivered to the Congress of Catholic Works at Malines a report on 'La vraie prière de l'Église'. Its central idea was that the whole Christian people should be allowed to live the liturgy. For Beauduin this participatory view of worship, which he expounded at greater length in his book *La Piété de l'Église* (1914), was inseparable from other concerns: the unity of the Church, reform of MONASTICISM, and social activism. All these, in various degrees, motivated the later movement as well. Developments in Belgium and France were complemented, somewhat independently at first, by a German and Austrian line of renewal centred on the Abbey of Maria Laach. Here a number of important publications, including what is now the *Archiv für Liturgiewißenschaft*, were inaugurated. Here, too, Dom O. Casel (1878–1948) wrote the papers that set out his 'theology of mysteries', which sees worship in general and the EUCHARIST in particular as not only a re-enactment but a making-present of the 'paschal mystery' (as it would later be termed) of Christ's life, death, and RESURRECTION.

Only after World War II, and in some respects because of it, did the impact of the Liturgical Movement begin to be felt outside specialist circles. Its incipiently ecumenical character also began to emerge. Official prohibitions from the Catholic side had prevented participation in the dialogues and conferences that led to the formation of the WORLD COUNCIL OF CHURCHES in 1948, but there had been co-operation with Protestant biblical and patristic scholars, and eventually among liturgiologists. Many of the same concerns that the movement sought to address had been recognized in the Church of England, notably by A. Hebert (1886–1963), a member of an Anglican religious community, whose *Liturgy and Society* (1935) remains a classic exposition of the Church as Christ's BODY, enacting in its liturgy a God-given mission to the world. But, while the Anglicans had the strongest liturgical tradition outside Catholicism, their BOOK OF COMMON PRAYER could be altered, in England, only by act of Parliament, and Parliament had twice rejected proposed revisions. Then in 1945 came *The Shape of the Liturgy*, probably the most influential book to which the Liturgical Movement gave rise. In it Dom G. Dix (1901–52), another Anglican monk, proposed that the meaning of Eucharistic liturgy is conveyed, not by any specific ritual text, 'primitive' or otherwise, but by the structure or 'shape' of what is *done* in the liturgy. His thesis, in its main lines, has come to be accepted all but universally, and its practical application can be seen in the formal congruence of the liturgies now authorized by nearly every western Christian Church that worships liturgically.

It was at VATICAN COUNCIL II, however, that early twentieth-century efforts on the part of individuals, organizations, and commissions came to fruition most effectively. The Council's Constitution on Liturgy, *Sacrosanctum concilium* (1963), sets out a theological rationale for Christian worship, which, like other conciliar texts, avoids for the most part the niceties of Scholastic definition and concentrates on biblical warrants and antecedents. Like those texts too, it has a strongly pastoral character and emphasizes the Church's missionary VOCATION. It does not deal directly with every aspect of liturgical life (that was left to a 'Commission for the Implementation of the Liturgy Constitution'); but with *Sacrosanctum concilium* the Liturgical Movement entered a new phase, genuinely ecumenical in scope, which has not yet come to a definitive close.

On the Protestant side, the Liturgical Movement was in part to thank for the remarkable contents of 'Baptism, Eucharist and Ministry', the so-called Lima Document approved by the World Council of Churches' Faith and Order Commission in 1982. Liturgical reforms have undoubtedly brought different Churches closer together with respect to the *manner* in which they worship, especially at the Eucharist. Still, there remain divisive questions concerning what those Churches teach and believe about what they are doing when they take part in liturgical action. Such doctrinal issues, as the Lima Document makes clear, have a bearing on every aspect of worship as practised in the traditions that flow from the Protestant Reformation, and while there is convergence on those issues, there is as yet no consensus.

The Liturgical Movement began with a recognition, not always explicitly articulated, that Christian worship has not been, and need not be, exactly the same regardless of place and time. While innovations such as the use of vernacular language could be justified – as they were at the time of the Reformation – by an appeal to ancient precedent, they were at the same time informed by present needs. *Sacrosanctum concilium* spoke of 'liturgical adaptation', by which it meant what has more recently been termed 'INCULTURATION'. With Christianity's demographic shift away from Europe, where the Liturgical Movement began and to which it addressed itself for the most part, the theological questions surrounding inculturation are becoming more urgent than ever.

J. F. Baldovin, S. J., 'The Liturgical Movement and Its Consequences' in *The Oxford Guide to the Book of Common Prayer*, ed. C. Hefling and C. Shattock (Oxford, 2006), 249–60.

J. Fenwick and B. Spinks, *Worship in Transition: The Liturgical Movement in the Twentieth Century* (Continuum, 1995).

J. Fenwick, B. Spinks, and André Haquin, 'The Liturgical Movement and Catholic Ritual Revision' in *The Oxford History of Christian Worship*, ed. C. Wainwright and K. B. Westerfield Tucker (Oxford University Press, 2006), 696–720.

G. Wainwright, 'Ecumenical Convergences' in *The Oxford History of Christian Worship*, ed. G. Wainwright and K. B. Westerfied Tucker (Oxford University Press, 2006), 721–54.

Charles Hefling

Liturgy The public and communal event in which Christian symbols and rituals are enacted by an assembly and its ministers sometimes bears the title 'liturgy'. That word has also been used to denote the ordered and printed texts that a ritualizing community might be using. But the more common application of the word in current scholarship is to indicate the whole event of a Christian assembly's symbolic practice – its words, songs, actions, and ritual repetitions – implying that this practice is, as in the ancient Greek use of the word *leitourgia*, a 'public work' with public meaning, whether or not printed texts or prescribed orders are used. In so far as a communal meeting with some symbolic content is important to every Church, every Church may be said to have a liturgy. The very idea that such an event is meaningful makes liturgy a matter of intense theological interest.

This liturgical event has also been known by a great variety of other names, some of them more at home in one Christian Church or another, each of them bringing some theological nuance to expression. For example, the word 'service' may be used. This English expression is like the Germanic *Gottesdienst* or *gudstjänst* in that it leaves interestingly ambiguous whether it is the assembly that is serving God or God the assembly. Similarly and with the same intentional ambiguity, the communal symbolic event may be called 'divine service' or 'divine liturgy'. Or it may be called 'worship' or a 'worship service', pointing to the fact that a large part of most Christian symbolic and ritual practice involves the public praise of God and a sense of standing in humility and adoration before God. It may be called 'common prayer', 'holy communion', or a 'sermon', other titles also taken from the diverse important contents of the event as a part for the whole, implying that one or the other of these is at the heart of what is happening there. If the event involves the full, classic Christian ritual of word and table, it may be named 'EUCHARIST', from the Greek for the 'thanksgiving at table' over bread and cup, or 'mass'. This title is most likely derived from the old Latin dismissal at the end of the event: *Ite, missa est* – 'Go, it is sent', the 'it' probably originally meaning the *fermentum* (i.e., the Eucharistic bread uniting the bishop's liturgy with that of other communities), but ultimately coming to mean the assembly itself. Both 'Eucharist' and 'mass', then, also involve naming the whole from the part, with interesting implications: the whole event is a standing before God in thanksgiving or the whole event is a sending in mission. Or this event may be called a 'meeting' or a 'meeting for worship', indicating that a gathering of people, an assembly, does this thing, but perhaps also suggesting that the meeting is with God, at God's initiative. Similarly and perhaps most evocatively, it may be called simply 'having Church', expressing the confidence that 'Church' subsists in and comes to expression through what happens in this meeting.

None of these titles is quite right. Each of them is theologically suggestive. But using 'liturgy' does invite us to see that Christians do everywhere share the practice of a meaningful communal event, even while this title may inadequately express the widespread Christian conviction that the primary actor here is not so much the *assembly* doing its public work as *God* going out in love towards the world. Still, even where that conviction is strong, the Christian assembly does act, coming together to participate in symbols and rituals. And there is meaning to be found in its action.

For the great majority of Christians, the pre-eminent occasion for this communal event is Sunday. Liturgical events also occur on other days, but they circle around the Sunday liturgy like planets around a sun. That timing begins to give a sense of the important theological meaning woven through the Christian meeting. The Christian tradition holds that Jesus Christ was raised from the dead on the first day of the week, that he was encountered in a gathering of the community on that day, and that a meeting on that day continues as a memorial of and a continued encounter with his RESURRECTION. Furthermore, the biblical tradition has taken the seven-day week as an image and symbol of the CREATION of the world. In Genesis 1 God creates light on the first day. For Christians, then, the first-day meeting also is a witness to and an encounter with the One who continually creates the world. Indeed, in so far as the meeting is on the Day of Light, it points to the light of the Risen One restoring human beings' capacity to see the creation and live before the Creator. Yet further, the meeting on the 'Lord's Day' is a meeting 'in the Spirit' (Rev. 1:10) poured out from God and from the resurrection of Jesus – a continued memorial of both the creation (Gen. 1:2) and PENTECOST (Acts 2:2). The Sunday meeting, then, is an expression of the Christian FAITH in God as TRINITY. Indeed, to use the metaphors employed by the Danish theologian R. Prenter (1907–90), this liturgy is the encounterable 'body' of the Christian dogma of the Trinity, and the classical doctrine of the Trinity is the 'soul' of the liturgy ('Liturgie'). Thus, holding the principal symbolic and ritual event of Christians on Sunday already suggests a set of basic, shared meanings.

The full range of such meanings is explored in the discipline called 'liturgical theology'. This discipline emerged out of the twentieth-century ecumenical LITURGICAL MOVEMENT, which has sought a renewed Christian identity in the world through a renewal of Christian symbolic practice. The hope for that renewed identity inevitably led to further reflection on what public worship actually says about God and the world, as well as what it means for the Church. A variety of methods are used by the diverse theologians who engage in this work. Some have sought out the ways in which the data of the Christian meeting can be seen to be in dialogue with the *loci* – the principal topics – of systematic theology. The work of G. Wainwright (b. 1939) may illustrate this method. Yet others have argued that liturgical practice is itself the Christian *theologia prima*, the primary thing that is being said about God among Christians. Writing secondary reflections on that primary experience, they have sought then to explore what actually comes to expression in the meeting. The works of A. Schmemann (1921–83) and A. Kavanagh (1929–2006) are at the heart of this method. More recently, figures like G. Hughes (b. 1937) and S. Garrigan (b. 1969) have enquired more fundamentally about how meaning occurs at all and applied these reflections to meaning in liturgy; or they have sought to find access to what the participants in a particular local liturgy actually understand is occurring there, with the hope of enabling a more ethically responsible mutual communication of Christian meaning. There remain yet further methods, but all of these theologians share in the conviction that the public liturgy of Christians should be seen as of central significance to the meaning of Christian faith and the identity of the Christian Church.

One classical way that liturgical theologians speak of this central significance is with the use of the dictum *LEX ORANDI, LEX CREDENDI* ('the rule of prayer [is] the rule of faith'). Practically every liturgical theologian gives some attention to commenting on this dictum, diversely reflecting on the mutual interactions of Christian doctrine and theology with the enacted symbols of Christian faith. Not uncommonly, liturgical theology hopes to invite people to see the ways that theology arises out of communally read and preached SCRIPTURE and shared PRAYER and sacraments. But the actual source of the dictum can be found in the more nuanced phrase of Prosper of Aquitaine (*ca* 390–*ca* 455): *legem credendi lex statuat supplicandi* ('the rule for interceding should establish the rule for believing', *Cap.* 8). Prosper meant to argue for an Augustinian conception of GRACE by pointing to the fact that Christian assemblies everywhere are urged to follow the advice of 1 Timothy 2:1: to pray for everybody. For Prosper, it followed that everybody needs grace and everybody can receive grace. The 'rule' of this interceding is a rule of universal human need and of all-embracing divine grace. Faith arises out of need and trusts that grace. But this symbolic practice of interceding and its implications for faith are also dependent on both the scriptural word and the great theological work of AUGUSTINE. Thus, liturgy is not independent of the Bible and theology, and yet Bible and theology come into their own and invite us into faith by means of liturgy.

This example of reflection on the theological significance of one of the Christian assembly's symbolic practices may provide a model for the ways that many parts of liturgy may function theologically. The public reading of Scripture (see LECTIONARY), the public use of prayer, the thanksgiving at the holy table (see MASS, CANON OF), the use of the LORD'S PRAYER, the practice of BAPTISM, the ANOINTING OF THE SICK, the singing of daily prayers (see DIVINE OFFICE), and the practice of a pattern of seasons and feasts (see CALENDAR, LITURGICAL) have all been at the centre of theological reflection and even of major theological controversy. Yet their very practice – like the practice of interceding for all people – renewed again and again in dialogue with biblical texts, also meets the assembly with God's grace and calls it to faith. The same could be said for communal singing, for preaching, for confessing the faith, for eating and drinking the holy gifts and carrying them to the absent, for taking a collection for the wretched and the hungry poor, and for many other symbolic practices of liturgy, small and great, from candle-lighting to public processions to speaking in tongues (see GLOSSOLALIA). One central source for theological meaning has been the way in which these things stand beside each other and work together. The great shape of the mass or the Eucharist has provided the most basic of these juxtapositions, as word and sacrament enacted together on Sunday have formed for many Christians a primary source for meaning and for faith, a basic way in which the Church has been gathered into the life of the triune God going out in mercy towards the world.

But as theologians and reflective Christians generally continue to think about the diverse ways that one might chart the relationships between liturgy, theology, and faith, a number of questions remain quite alive: what unites Christian liturgies? Is there a single basic structure, drawn from Scripture and Christian TRADITION, or is liturgy always locally determined and quite diverse? Or, then again, should Christian liturgy be both local and more-than-local at once? And what role does the history of liturgy play in making these decisions? Furthermore, what does renewal of liturgy – renewal of the central symbols of this event but also renewal of the assembly's participation in those symbols – actually look like? And how can one tell what the event means to its participants? Furthermore, besides the *Lex orandi* and the *Lex credendi*, must not the *Lex agenda* also be considered? That is, does the way we pray also flow into what we do, into ethics, especially into the communal response to the poor and the care for the earth? Finally, does Christian liturgy reinforce Christian division or can it contribute to Christian unity? Besides the continuing questions of meaning, these questions of shape, history, renewal, access, ethics, and unity form the fascinating frontier of liturgical theology today.

S. Garrigan, *Beyond Ritual: Sacramental Theology after Habermas* (Ashgate, 2004).
G. Hughes, *Worship as Meaning: A Liturgical Theology for Late Modernity* (Cambridge University Press, 2003).
G. Lathrop, *Holy Things: A Liturgical Theology* (Fortress Press, 1993).
J. Puglisi, ed., *Liturgical Renewal as a Way to Christian Unity* (Liturgical Press, 2005).
T. Schattauer, 'Liturgical Studies: Disciplines, Perspectives, Teaching', *International Journal of Practical Theology* 11 (2007), 106–37.
D. Vogel, ed., *Primary Sources of Liturgical Theology: A Reader* (Liturgical Press, 2000).

Gordon W. Lathrop

Logos The Greek word *logos* is a highly significant technical term in pre-Christian Greek philosophy. It is employed in the SEPTUAGINT to translate important Hebrew ideas; it occurs in the NT in various senses to refer to SCRIPTURE, divine utterance, or as a Christological title, and it is a key term in early Christological formulations. Furthermore, its significance in Hellenistic philosophy continued with the middle Platonic schools as exemplified in the writings of Plotinus (*ca* 205–70) and Porphyry (*ca* 235–*ca* 305), it functioned as part of the cosmological formulations of writers who represent trajectories in early Christianity usually grouped together under the heading of 'GNOSTICISM', and the term has retained widespread currency in Christian writings (both theological and popular) down to the modern period.

The semantic field of the term *logos* is related to the verb *legō*, 'I say, recount, utter.' In this primary semantic sense *logos* represents the product of the act of speech – 'a word' or 'an utterance'. It should be noted, however, that the term *logos* is not usually employed in a grammatical sense to refer to the unit of speech that linguists would classify as a lexeme (a 'word-type' unit). Rather, for that precise sense Greek writers would employ the term *lexis* (see Aristotle, *Rh.* 1406bl). Thus, the term *logos* encapsulates the more active or performative aspect of speaking, which is perhaps better understood from the perspective of speech-act theory, whereby the act of utterance is seen as having an illocutionary function – by saying something, something is done or instantiated.

The term, however, is not limited to this primary sense, but encompasses a rich range of related meanings. In Greek literature of the classical and Hellenistic periods it is widely used to denote 'computation' or 'reckoning', often of monetary value, but also more widely of dues and penalties in general. Related to this it can refer to the esteem or value of objects or people. Perhaps deriving from this notion of 'computation', or 'quantification', it becomes the term used to denote 'principles' or 'rules'. In a mathematical sense, in the writings of the Pythagorean School, it denotes 'ratios' or 'proportions'. Related to this designation of 'rules', it describes 'hypotheses', 'rules of conduct', and 'reasons' or 'grounds' of an argument. Derived from this, its utility in philosophical and theological reflection can be clearly seen, since the term has the versatility to incorporate simultaneously ideas of utterance, rationality and existential categories.

Within extant early Greek philosophical traditions, *logos* became a key term to describe the faculty of human reason and notions of rationality in general. Thus, for example, in Plato's (*ca* 430–*ca* 345 BC) *Theaetetus* the idea of *logos* refers to the whole rational enterprise. Within the writings of Aristotle (384–322 BC), *logos*, as argument from reason, is one of the three basic modes of persuasion. Such ideas were exploited by the first-century Jewish writer and thinker Philo of Alexandria (*ca* 20 BC-*ca* AD 50), who related the idea of *logos* to the creative principle and coupled this with his reflection on the purposes and work of the God of Judaism.

Within the context of the NT, *logos* is used in a variety of ways, some drawing on previous usages in Jewish and Hellenistic texts, while at other times it is used in more innovative ways. The term can refer to the Jewish scriptures in formulations such as John 10:35, where the Johannine Jesus refers to 'the word of God' and immediately explains this reference with the clarification that 'scripture cannot be broken', thereby making explicit the equation between 'word' and 'scripture'. More generally, the term *logos* may signify divine utterance in terms that resonate with the prophetic experience of transmitting divine oracles (e.g., 'the word of God came to John son of Zechariah' in Luke 3:2). For PAUL *logos* terminology is used to denote the central content of his proclamation. Thus, 'the word of God', although directed to Israel initially, has not failed (Rom. 9:6) and is understood as representing the GOSPEL message which Paul is commissioned to preach to Gentiles (1 Cor. 1:18; 1 Thess. 1:8; 2:13).

Undoubtedly the theological high point of the use of *logos* terminology in the NT occurs in the Johannine writings. The striking and creative affirmation of the pre-existence of the *logos* in the Johannine prologue is not without antecedents. This passage appropriates language that was readily recognizable in the wider Hellenistic philosophical traditions, but that had also been habilitated in pre-Christian Jewish thinking, especially in the so-called wisdom literature. Thus, in the Greek rendering of Hebrew Scriptures *logos* language was used in a manner that gave an active and independent role to the actions and existence of the word in a way that made it distinguishable (at least on the surface level) from its divine origin. It has been suggested that this reflects the first stages of the tendency to hypostasize the 'word of God' as an entity or being in its own right (cf. Ps. 107:20; Isa. 55:10–11; Wis. 18:14–16). However, it has been questioned whether classifying these verses as representing the hypostasization of the *logos* is an accurate portrayal of their sense, or if this does not in fact represent the retrojection of later Christological concerns onto the OT texts under discussion. Notwithstanding these background issues, in Johannine theology the word is seen both as pre-existent and as having become incarnate in the person of Jesus. As part of this perspective the Johannine epistles are unfortunately often overlooked. These writings strengthen the affirmation of the incarnate word (1 John 1:1) and offer the promise of participation within the existential sphere of that word (1 John 2:14).

Notions of the word as an autonomous, pre-existent and possibly hypostasized entity, which occur *in nuce* in the NT, become the centre of much theological reflection in subsequent periods. In the second century the prevailing view was to equate both the word and the wisdom of God (Justin, *Trypho* 129.3–4; Tertullian, *Prax.* 6–7). One of Justin Martyr's (d. *ca* 165) most innovative moves was to exploit *logos* terminology to claim that there was wisdom in the pagan philosophical traditions, but that it was partial in comparison to the fullest expression of wisdom that finds articulation in Christ. Thus Justin was able to claim that Plato, albeit dependent upon and not fully understanding the writings of Moses, recognized the *logos*-centric nature of the universe (*1Apol.* 50.7). Justin's open attitude to pre-Christian Hellenistic thought has been used as an important resource for exploring contemporary Christian attitudes to other faiths (see K. RAHNER and VATICAN COUNCIL II).

However, perhaps almost certainly in response to the later ARIAN CONTROVERSY, Christological creedal affirmations move more uniformly to confess the second Person of the TRINITY as the unbegotten Son. In part the unease with *logos* language arose from the way such terminology was used by those perceived to be Arians to advance their own viewpoints. Thus, Marcellus of Ancyra (*ca* 280–*ca* 375) argued that the term reflected the ontological unity that existed between the Father and his *Logos* to the extent that the existence of two *hypostases,* at least prior to the INCARNATION of the Son, was denied (see HYPOSTASIS). However, it should be clearly stated that ATHANASIUS had no problem in speaking of the second Person of the Trinity as the Word of God (see *Gent.* 47). Yet even after this period, partially under the continuing influence of Middle Platonic thought, *logos* language retained a prominence especially among the fathers of the eastern Church.

In the twentieth century there has been renewed interest in *Logos* Christology and this may in part be related to the prominence given to the *logos* in Jungian thought, where it represents the masculine principle of rationality and consciousness. *Logos* Christology has been viewed as a rich vein of theological reflection on the solidarity of the divine with universal humanity. In this regard the true essence and centre of earthly life is seen as being realized when human nature exists in union with the *Logos.* The concept of the *Logos* has been important in PROCESS THEOLOGY especially in its exploration of Christology. In line with the affirmation of pluralistic approaches, *logos* language is utilized to express openness to other religious traditions (as noted, this has a precursor in the writings of Justin Martyr), to raise awareness of ecological concerns, and to emphasize the need for humanity to live together harmoniously. For process theologians the *Logos*, especially through the incarnation, represents dynamic transformation of being and consequently the challenge to humanity is to live incarnational lives that constantly aim to find the full potentiality of each new situation and thus refuse to simply habituate or to repeat sterile modes of existence.

Regardless of the cause of this renewed interest, this direction of thought has once again brought the Christological perspectives of the fourth Gospel into sharper relief. The notion of Christ as the incarnate *Logos* is consequently being explored as an important theological resource for addressing inter-faith issues and questions of THEODICY. In part, this is due to seeing the incarnation of the *Logos* as expressing solidarity with all humanity and at the same time entering fully into the experience of human sufferings.

See also CHRISTOLOGY; JOHN THE EVANGELIST; PLATONISM.

J. M. Dillon, *The Middle Platonists* (Duckworth, 1996).

J. D. G. Dunn, *Christology in the Making: A New Testament Inquiry into the Origins of the Doctrine of Incarnation* (SCM, 1989).

T. E. Pollard, *Johannine Christology and the Early Church* (Cambridge University Press, 1970).

PAUL FOSTER

LOISY, ALFRED Alfred Firmin Loisy (1857–1940) was a French biblical scholar who advocated a constructive dialogue between Catholic theology and modern historical study. Ordained a priest in 1879, he studied and taught at the Institut Catholique in Paris. Dissatisfied with both highly traditional and more recent rationalist approaches to biblical interpretation, he sought an alternative that allowed an interpreter to be both an objective historian and a faithful Catholic. To accomplish this, he adopted a more dynamic sense of theological development. A living Church, he thought, needed to change.

French Catholicism had been relatively uninfluenced by modern historical criticism (see BIBLICAL CRITICISM), and its leaders were not hospitable to Loisy's proposals. In 1893 he was dismissed from his teaching position at the Institut. Six years as a chaplain at a Dominican convent renewed his desire for reform, and *The Gospel and the Church*, his best-known book, was published in 1902. It was simultaneously a critical response to A. von HARNACK's *What Is Christianity?* (1900) and a proposal for a more developmentalist understanding of SCRIPTURE and Church DOCTRINE. The book portrayed the Church as the natural and necessary outgrowth of Jesus' work. The historian's job was to trace its organic development, and the theologian's was to identify its contemporary religious significance. In 1903 the Vatican placed it and four other texts by Loisy on its Index of Prohibited Books.

Pius X's (r. 1903–14) ENCYCLICAL *Pascendi dominici gregis* (1907) condemned 'MODERNISM', calling it the 'synthesis of all heresies'. Included were statements lifted from Loisy's writings. Clearly the Vatican considered him a modernist, and he was excommunicated the following year. Appointed to a chair in the history of religions at the Collège de France which he held until his retirement in 1931, Loisy continued his scholarly work apart from CATHOLIC THEOLOGY.

H. Hill, *The Politics of Modernism: Alfred Loisy and the Scientific Study of Religion* (Catholic University of America Press, 2002).

DARRELL JODOCK

LONERGAN, BERNARD Canadian philosopher-theologian Bernard Joseph Francis Lonergan (1904–84) entered the Society of Jesus in 1922. While reading philosophy at Heythrop College, he earned an external degree in mathematics, Greek, Latin, and French from the University of London (1926–30); he also studied economic theory to grasp how moral precepts can be grounded in economic process; and he re-read the theoretical parts of J. H. NEWMAN's *Grammar of Assent* 'five or six times'. Newman, J. Stewart's (1846–1933) *Plato's Doctrine of Ideas* (1909), the dialogues of Plato (*ca.* 430–*ca* 345 BC), and AUGUSTINE's early dialogues influenced his ideas about knowledge. In his first period at the Gregorian University (1933), Lonergan began intensive study of T. AQUINAS; in papers on philosophy of history (published posthumously) he used Aquinas' notion of the intellect as infinite in potency and Christopher Dawson's (1889–1970) ideas about culture to respond to G. W. F. HEGEL and K. Marx (1818–83).

Lonergan's doctoral dissertation at the Gregorian, a genetic study of operative grace and freedom in Aquinas, resolved issues of philosophical and theological interpretation, overturning the dominant Bañezian and Molinist schools of baroque SCHOLASTICISM. Five articles (published in 1967 as *Verbum: Word and Idea in Aquinas*) written while Lonergan was teaching in Montreal (1940–6) and Toronto (1947–53) corrected prevalent misinterpretations of Thomist Trinitarian theory. His extrication of Aquinas' theory of knowledge from medieval metaphysical discourse revealed the primacy of the act of understanding (insight) over concepts, propositions, and deductions, enabling Lonergan to ground a modern cognitional theory (What are we *doing* when we are knowing?) and epistemology (Why is doing that *knowing*?), and to explain a methodically controlled metaphysics (*What* do we know when we understand and judge correctly?). Teaching dogmatic theology at the Gregorian (1954–65) immersed him in post-Kantian continental philosophy and theology; and in *Insight: A Study in Human Understanding* (1957) he re-contextualized the discoveries of *Verbum* in the thought-world of modern mathematics, science, common sense, and dialectical aspects of human living. *Method in Theology* (1972) transformed Catholic ORTHODOXY by integrating the modern notions of empirical science, scholarship, and history into theology while avoiding scientism, relativism, or historicism. *Method* envisions theology as an eightfold, functionally specialized, collaborative effort, moving from research, interpretation, history, and dialectics through foundations, DOCTRINES, and systematics to the massive project of communications.

Lonergan considered functional specialization important to any humane discipline that anticipates the future in light of the past. After *Method* and until his death, Lonergan revised drafts of an economic theory of monetary circulation written in the 1930s and early 1940s. He also wrote papers elaborating a HERMENEUTICS of LOVE grounded in the gift of God's love, which pivots on religious, moral, and intellectual CONVERSION to engage the hermeneutics of achievement's upward spiral through repeated acts of experience, understanding, judgements of fact and value, decisions, and actions.

See also CATHOLIC THEOLOGY, THOMISM.

I. Coelho, *Hermeneutics & Method: The 'Universal Viewpoint' in Bernard Lonergan* (University of Toronto Press, 2001).
W. A. Mathews, *Lonergan's Quest: A Study of Desire in the Authoring of Insight* (University of Toronto Press, 2005).

Frederick Lawrence

Lord's Prayer Taught by Jesus to his disciples, the Lord's Prayer is found in two versions in the NT (Matt. 6:9–13; Luke 11:2–4). Since the earliest years of the Church, it has deeply influenced Christian prayer, worship, instruction, and theology.

As many commentators note, the purpose of the Lord's Prayer is not to limit Christian prayer to certain words mechanically repeated but to provide a model or pattern of prayer. In both its Matthean and Lucan versions, the prayer includes an opening address, followed by petitions for the honouring of God's name and the coming of God's reign (see Kingdom of God), and then petitions for human needs. This order of priorities sets the proper pattern for the whole of Christian life.

Addressing God as 'Father' (Aramaic *Abba*) expresses both respect and intimacy. While not unique in Jewish prayers of the time, calling on God as father is distinctive of Jesus' prayers, teaching, parables, and ministerial practice. By encouraging his disciples to pray with confidence in the trustworthiness of God and with reliance solely on God's sovereign grace, Jesus calls them to take part in his own personal relationship with the one he calls Father.

The Lord's Prayer is strikingly corporate as well as personal in character. Its petitions reflect a communal rather than an individualistic spirit: '*Our* Father', 'Give *us*', 'Forgive *us*', 'Deliver *us*'. Guided by this prayer, Christians pray not only for themselves but also with and for other Christians, and, representatively, with and for all people.

Another feature of the Lord's Prayer is its profoundly eschatological orientation. This is evident in the first set of petitions that look to God to secure recognition of God's holy name, to bring in God's reign, and to establish the doing of the divine will throughout the creation. Yet while recognizing that God alone can accomplish these things, the prayer sets in motion a life of faithful witness and joyful service in response to the holy, trustworthy, and gracious God. One cannot pray from the heart for God to bring in God's reign and establish his rule without living in a way that corresponds to these petitions.

The second set of petitions, which concern human welfare, is similarly oriented to the future as well as to the present. The petition for daily bread asks for the satisfaction of basic human needs here and now but also implicitly looks to the messianic banquet of the end of time. Likewise, the prayer for forgiveness has in view not only our need of forgiveness and our responsibility to forgive others in the present but also the coming completion of God's righteous and merciful purposes throughout the creation. Finally, the petition for help in the time of temptation and for deliverance from the evils that daily threaten our destruction gives expression both to our awareness of our utter dependence on God and to our hope in the final triumph of God.

The concluding doxology, while a later addition to the earliest scriptural texts, gathers up the themes of the prayer as a whole and has been widely adopted by the Church as entirely fitting.

J. Jeremias, *The Lord's Prayer* (Fortress Press, 1964).
J. Lochman, *The Lord's Prayer* (Eerdmans, 1990).

Daniel L. Migliore

Lord's Supper: see Eucharist.

Love The testimony of Scripture renders language of love (*agapē* in the Greek of the NT – a term translated in the King James Bible as 'charity') central to Christians. Jesus brings together and makes central the commandments to love God and neighbour (Matt. 22:36–40 and pars.); Paul elevates love above both faith and hope as the chief virtue (1 Cor. 13:13); and John goes so far as to identify God with love (1 John 4:8) and to affirm that all love is of God (1 John 4:7). Later influential thinkers in the Church, moreover, both East and West, from Augustine and T. Aquinas to K. Barth and K. Rahner, reiterate and extend these scriptural testimonies. Liturgies incorporate them as well (e.g., in the confession that 'we have not loved God with our whole heart, and we have not loved our neighbours as ourselves').

References to love in Christian theology and ethics remain indispensable in two respects. First, the biblical witness affirms that love refers fittingly both to God's action and ours. It is not the only such term (e.g., justice is another one). Still, it is suggestive of two overlapping sets of questions. The first set has to do with *how much* our own loves can and should resemble and differ from the content of God's love. How far can and should we love whom and what God loves in our own actions and interactions? The second set derives from the fact that human beings are created to love both God and one another, in accordance with Jesus' two commandments. This feature of theological anthropology raises questions of its own, since the two commandments appear to be *mutually irreducible* to each other and yet to be *mutually bound together.* Furthermore, the second of the two commandments, with its specification that we are to love our neighbours as ourselves, also generates a widely canvassed question about how neighbour-love is to be related to self-love.

The first question of the relationship between God's actions and ours requires reference to Christian convictions regarding God's identity and God's relation to the world, as well as to convictions regarding human beings and the human situation. These convictions may be elaborated with reference to the biblical texts' comprehensive witness to the overall shape of God's self-disclosure and governance of the world. A traditional way of conceiving this shape is in terms of the narrative sequence of CREATION, FALL, the COVENANT with ISRAEL, the INCARNATION, the Church, salvation, and ESCHATOLOGY. The scope of this scheme is suggestive of the comprehensive range of convictions that must be assessed and inter-related in developing a specifically Christian account of divine and creaturely love. By adding substance and narrative density to depictions of love, the biblical story provides clues to the answers to the questions of *how much* and *how far* human love can and should resemble God's.

Each of the components of the Bible's broader narrative sequence describes a basic conviction regarding God and God's relationship to the world and illustrates how an account of love may be influenced by it. The Christian DOCTRINE of *creation* refers to God as the sole antecedent condition of the origin and preservation of the world, including whatever order and coherence is found there. In this way, it suggests that love be understood as radical and joyous freedom dedicated to promoting the flourishing of another. At one level this claim suggests a radical incommensurability between God's love and ours, since only God, as Creator, is able to promote the flourishing of what is other than God's self absolutely, by bringing it into being. At the same time, it is also suggestive that human beings may appropriately affirm God's preserving action (see *CONSERVATIO*) by caring for non-human ANIMALS and nature for their own sake and reject ANTHROPOCENTRISM.

The *fall* refers to the appearance of SIN and evil, and the distortions and derangements they bring into the world. In so far as sin and evil threaten the wellbeing of creatures, they are in no way the product of God's will, yet they remain a painful feature of created reality in which human beings find themselves complicit. The reality of the fall thus raises the question of how in practice human loving may at once affirm the fundamental goodness of others as good creatures of God (and thus reject any anthropology that portrays human beings as 'essentially' antisocial, aggressive, and competitive), while at the same time taking seriously the way in which sin has distorted human loving (thereby also belying the view that human beings are 'essentially' harmless).

The *covenant with Israel* refers to God's particular relation to a people God chooses, a people in whom the history of redemption is rooted and by whom all of the nations will bless themselves. It thereby raises the question of how human love shall honour the terms of God's ELECTION and governance, respecting the particularity of love without rendering love exclusive of certain individuals or groups. Further, it points to a model of covenant love as promoting a mutually engaging, dialogical model of human communion. Along the same lines, the Christian confesssion of Jesus of Nazareth as the *incarnation* of the divine Word in human flesh affirms his status as both Saviour and exemplar, thereby raising the question of how human love can hold together but not equate the claims that Jesus is a saviour *of* us *and* a model *for* us. Christian understandings of VOCATION have long included the idea that love of Christ promotes imitation of Christ (1 Cor. 11:1), yet not in such a way that in our love we ever confuse ourselves with Christ. In this sense, genuine love of Christ requires genuinely following Jesus, but at a distance.

The *Church* refers to the Christian community in its corporate life and in the lives of persons who identify with it, and in its relations to surrounding social worlds. In line with Jesus' second great commandment, Christian love suggests that the Church regard itself as a collective person and affirm that humanity at large is the neighbour given to the Church. Christian reflection on the character of *salvation*, with its twin reference to both JUSTIFICATION (God's utterly free love that rescues human beings from the power of sin) and SANCTIFICATION (God's action in and through the HOLY SPIRIT to regenerate and transform human beings), pushes the question of Christian practice further. Combined with Christian convictions regarding the enduring power of sin, it raises the question of how love may be practised in such a way as to affirm both that no one attains complete love for God and neighbour, and that the more one loves God and one's neighbour as oneself, the more virtue and less vice one has.

Eschatology refers to God's absolute future when God's purposes are fulfilled, the promise of which warrants a manner of life in the present dominated by the three 'theological virtues' of faith, hope, and love. The promise of the full realization of God's purposes raises the question of how human beings should shape their loves so as to bear witness that they live at present in the 'uncompleted interim'. Christian love should embody a recognition of the tension between that which God has already accomplished in Christ, and that which is not yet realized, and thereby reflect something of Christian convictions regarding the elements of continuity and discontinuity between present experience and future hope that is already realized in God.

The second set of questions regarding the relationship between *our love for God* on the one hand and *God's and our love for our neighbours and ourselves* on the other deals with how to understand our fitting attachments and actions as we stand before God in comparison with our fitting attachments and actions as we face other human beings. The mutual irreducibility of the two commandments means that each set of attachments has its own integrity and exigencies, even as Jesus' explicit ordering of theme teaches that relation to God has the higher status. Thus, love for God includes our unlimited obedience, but love of neighbour and love of self do not. Yet we join Jesus' two commandments together in opposing inordinate ambitions to dominate and control everything, including God and other people. These ambitions violate both commandments.

In addition to the question of the relationship between the two commandments, further complexities also arise *within* the second commandment regarding the relations between *our love of our neighbours* and God's and our love of ourselves on the one hand, and the relations between *our love of ourselves* and God's love, and our love of our neighbours on the other. Three considerations merit ongoing attention: the *similarities* between neighbour-love and self-love are a permanent part of what the second love commandment enjoins us to honour (as exemplified in the colloquialism 'what's sauce for the goose is sauce for the gander'); the *unlikenesses* or *asymmetries* between one's relation to one's neighbour and one's relation to oneself (where each of us retains a distinct 'pocket of agency'); and the importance we accord to *special relations* among persons (e.g., where our neighbours include co-religionists, family members, friends, and compatriots: all are neighbours, but special bonds vastly thicken how we perceive and engage particular neighbours).

K. Barth, *Church Dogmatics* (T&T Clark, 1958), IV/2.
R. Canning, *The Unity of Love for God and Neighbor in St. Augustine* (Augustinian Historical Institute, 1993).
A. Nygren, *Agape and Eros* (University of Chicago Press, 1982 [1930–6]).
G. Outka, *Agape: An Ethical Analysis* (Yale University Press, 1972).
K. Rahner, 'Reflections on the Unity of the Love of Neighbour and the Love of God' in *Theological Investigations*, vol. VI (Helicon, 1969), 231–49.

GENE OUTKA

LUCIFER: see DEVIL.

LUTHER, MARTIN Born in Eisleben in 1483, Martin Ludher (as he initially spelt his name) was the eldest son of Hans, a mine worker and (later) owner, and Margaret, whose brother was mayor of Eisenach. Sent to school in Mansfeld, Magdeburg, and Eisenach, Luther received his Masters degree at the University of Erfurt in 1505. Later that same year he was caught in a thunderstorm while journeying from his parents' home to Erfurt to begin his studies in law and vowed instead to become a monk, entering the 'Black Cloister' of observant Augustinians in Erfurt. In 1507 he was ordained a priest and began to study theology both there and in Wittenberg, where he was exposed not only to the regnant nominalist theology but also to HUMANISM and where he succeeded J. von Staupitz (1460–1524) in 1512 as professor of Bible. In addition to lecturing on the Psalms, Romans, Galatians, and Hebrews from 1513 to 1518, he also became an assistant to the ailing pastor at Wittenberg's city church and oversaw several Augustinian monasteries in Saxony. With the (presumed) posting on 31 October 1517 of the *Ninety-Five Theses* questioning the theological justification for the sale of indulgences, Luther became embroiled in controversy not only over his understanding of JUSTIFICATION but also over his view of papal authority.

Declared a heretic by papal decree (1520) and pronounced an outlaw of the Holy Roman Empire by the imperial diet meeting in Worms (April 1521), Luther was first put into protective custody in the Wartburg Castle by his prince, Elector Frederick the Wise of Saxony (r. 1486–1525), before returning in March 1522 to Wittenberg, where he remained for the rest of his life as a professor and assistant to the city pastor. In 1525 he married K. von Bora (1499–1552), an escaped nun. Under the leadership of Frederick's brother, Elector John of Saxony (r. 1525–32) and his son Elector John Frederick I (r. 1532–47), Luther oversaw the religious transformation of Wittenberg and the electoral Saxon lands, writing liturgies and hymns in German, translating the Bible (1522–33), helping to lead an official visitation of churches there (1527–29), co-authoring with P. Melanchthon (1497–1560) the *Instruction by the Visitors for the Parish Pastors of Saxony* (1528) and publishing his *Small* and *Large Catechisms* (1529). At the same time, he continued to oppose a variety of theological adversaries in print, including D. Erasmus (1466/9–1536) on the bondage of the will and H. ZWINGLI and others on the presence of Christ in the EUCHARIST. He also produced numerous works of devotion; tracts on social matters such as education, secular authority, and usury; and exegetical works (the most important being his second exposition of Galatians in 1535 and his lectures on Genesis, published between 1544 and 1554). He prepared the *Smalcald Articles* (1537) as his theological last will and testament for an anticipated Church council. In 1539, he published his masterpiece on ECCLESIOLOGY, *On the Councils and the Church(es)*. Intermittently plagued from 1527 on by various physical ailments, he finally succumbed in February 1546 while on a mission to Eisleben to craft a political agreement among the feuding counts of Mansfeld.

Scholars have debated for over a hundred years the exact moment of Luther's 'breakthrough' to an evangelical (Lutheran) view of salvation by God's mercy in Christ, dating it anywhere between 1509 and 1518. Already in his earliest lectures on the Psalms (1513–15), Luther challenged the traditional ways of interpreting SCRIPTURE, abandoning the regnant definition of 'letter and spirit' (cf. 2 Cor. 3:6) as escaping the literal meaning in favour of the spiritual and replacing it with the notion that God's Word kills and makes alive. He also clearly was moving away from defining the righteousness of God (*justitia Dei*) as God's righteous judgement against the sinner (*justitia activa*) to God's merciful promise to forgive sinners and thereby make them righteous (*justitia passiva*). By October 1518, when he was interviewed by Cardinal Cajetan (1468–1534) in Augsburg, Luther insisted that a person could be certain of God's forgiveness by trusting the priest's word of absolution. This contradicted the late medieval belief that humility required the penitent to remain uncertain whether God forgave them, so that they would continue to work to merit God's GRACE. Thus, for Luther, 'FAITH' meant not simply knowledge of correct DOCTRINE or the mind's assent to it, but rather trust and confidence in God's word of forgiveness. By 1521 Luther also began defining God's grace not as a force or power but simply as God's undeserved mercy.

These exegetical and linguistic shifts provided the underpinnings for Luther's theology throughout his career. First, Luther held that the sinners, curved in upon themselves (*incurvati in se*), are justified by GRACE alone (*sola gratia*). Only God's merciful promise of forgiveness and reconciliation and thus not human effort or merit makes a person right with God (i.e., declared righteous by virtue of Christ's righteousness alone). Second, God effects this justification by means of God's Word (*solo Verbo*), which functions first as LAW (revealing SIN and putting to death the old creature) and then as GOSPEL (revealing Christ as humanity's gracious saviour), and which is received by faith alone (*sola fide*). The sacraments (which Luther reduced to two, BAPTISM and the Lord's Supper) were, following AUGUSTINE, 'visible words' of God, also providing God's unconditional promise of grace to the sinner. Third, Luther also transformed certain aspects of medieval mystical theology into what he called the 'theology of the cross' (*THEOLOGIA CRUCIS*), defined as God's REVELATION under the appearance of its opposite. This included not only Christ's death on the cross, but also all other aspects of Christ's past coming in the flesh and present encounter with people in the Church. In the latter, God speaks, hidden in the weak words of a pastor, or God comes in sacramental elements, and in all cases must be received by faith, since this hiddenness works first as an alien work (*opus alienum*; cf. Isa. 28:21) to destroy human reason and its quest to control God before it performs God's proper work (*opus proprium*) of creating faith and declaring the sinner righteous. Thus, the believer, living by faith alone, is at the same time sinner and righteous (*SIMUL JUSTUS ET PECCATOR*).

These three aspects of Luther's theology imply a fourth: a distinction between human and divine righteousness (sometimes referred to as the doctrine of the TWO KINGDOMS). With the 'left hand', Luther argued, God rules this world through the so-called first or civil use of the law, restraining sin and the DEVIL and maintaining order; here reason and human laws rightly have a place. With the 'right hand', God declares a new world, coming fully at the end of time but received fully in this world by faith alone. God brings in this realm through the theological, or second use of the law (which convicts and slays the sinner) and the unconditional promise of the gospel. The Christian lives by faith in this promised world to come and, at the same time, works in this world to love the neighbour and tend creation through the God-given VOCATIONS and spheres of life (*Stände*): society, household, and Church.

These core beliefs affected every other aspect of Luther's theology. Thus, in *The Bondage of the Will* (1525), written against Erasmus, he argued that sinners could not freely choose God or earn salvation but were curved in upon themselves and could only be made believers when the HOLY SPIRIT used God's Word to terrify (law) and comfort (gospel). In fights with Zwingli and others over the Lord's Supper, Luther emphasized the power of God's promise to be present under the forms of bread and wine and thereby to forgive sinners. Against what he viewed as papal incursions into God's left hand, he championed the God-given duties of prince and citizen. The Church, which Luther defined already early in his career as the assembly of believers and SAINTS hidden among sinners, was made visible through tangible signs of the Word and the sacraments (see MARKS OF THE CHURCH) and is not fixed to a particular person or place (e.g., the pope or Rome). Because faith and God's promise are oriented towards God's future work, Luther's theology and view of history was always eschatological and even apocalyptic. Luther assumed that he was living near the end. At the same time, by tying the gospel to God's merciful comfort of the terrified sinner, Luther also placed his pastoral concerns at the centre of his theology. Thus, many of his most popular writings were intended for pastors and parishioners and the life of faith.

See also LUTHERAN THEOLOGY.

P. Althaus, *The Theology of Martin Luther* (Fortress Press, 1967).

C. P. Arand and R. Kolb, *The Genius of Luther's Theology: A Wittenberg Way of Thinking for the Contemporary Church* (Baker Academic, 2008).

B. Lohse, *Martin Luther's Theology: Its Historical and Systematic Development* (Fortress Press, 1999).

TIMOTHY J. WENGERT

LUTHERAN THEOLOGY Lutheran theology originated in the early Reformation with the writings of M. LUTHER and his colleagues at the University of Wittenberg. Luther was a professor of biblical interpretation and never compiled a medieval *summa* or system of doctrine. Although he believed the Wittenbergers had recovered the gospel centre of Christianity, he never claimed to have a theology of his own but preferred the term 'our theology' for those teachings that undergirded the evangelical or Lutheran movement. His Wittenberg colleague, P. Melanchthon (1497–1560) published in 1521 the first organized treatment of evangelical themes. Melanchthon's *Loci communes* was praised by Luther and became the first textbook of Lutheran theology.

The *loci* or topics treated by Melanchthon – sin, law, grace, justification – were taken from PAUL'S epistle to the Romans. The Wittenbergers had challenged Scholastic SOTERIOLOGY on these points and debated the same issues with their opponents after the indulgence controversy erupted in 1517. It quickly became a dispute about matters that belonged to the third article of Christian CREEDS: the transmission of grace through the Holy Spirit, the sacraments, and the nature and authority of the Church. Consequently, these third-article issues also dominated the confessional writings that were later collected in the BOOK OF CONCORD (1580): Luther's *Large* and *Small Catechisms* (1529), the AUGSBURG CONFESSION (1530), Melanchthon's *Apology of the Augsburg Confession* (1531), Luther's *Smalcald Articles* (1537), Melanchthon's *Treatise on the Power and Primacy of the Pope*, and the *Formula of Concord* (1577). Except for the catechisms, the confessional writings were generated by intra-Lutheran debates and by conflicts with Catholic and Calvinist theologians. Unlike the tradition of REFORMED THEOLOGY, Lutherans have not awarded Churchwide confessional status to any writings since 1580; hence, the *Book of Concord* remains an important source of Lutheran theology.

Specific doctrines distinguished Lutherans from their early opponents. Foremost is JUSTIFICATION by faith alone, which was the heart of Luther's teaching that faith in Christ, not human merit, was the only means of salvation. Without accepting TRANSUBSTANTIATION, Lutherans asserted that the body and blood of Christ were truly present 'in, with, and under' bread and wine in the EUCHARIST. This assertion positioned Lutherans between a Catholic view of the mass and a Reformed view of the sacrament, and it led to an emphasis on the union of natures in Christ, because that union allowed the human nature (body and blood) to be present *everywhere* the divine nature was (the doctrine of UBIQUITY) and hence also present in the sacrament. In contrast to the medieval designation of clerical and monastic callings as uniquely religious and superior to lay occupations, Luther argued that all Christians were priests and lived in TWO KINGDOMS – a spiritual realm under the GOSPEL and a temporal realm under the LAW – both of which were ruled by God and possessed equal integrity. When the validity of infant BAPTISM was challenged, Lutherans insisted that the HOLY SPIRIT imparted grace through baptism at any age and through other external means like the Lord's Supper, absolution, the word of God, and the mutual forgiveness and encouragement of believers. Some of these doctrines were accepted by other Protestants, but the emphases on real presence, the two kingdoms, and external means of GRACE are regarded as typically Lutheran emphases.

Finally, Lutheran theology incorporates the reflection, discussions, and publications that are supported by regional Churches and by the Lutheran World Federation (LWF), founded in 1947. The LWF made theology one of its early portfolios, and that work continues through its Department of Theology and Studies. In addition to symposia and theological analyses of current issues, the department sponsors ongoing dialogues between Lutherans and other Christians, as well as inter-religious conversations. Some Lutheran Churches have their own departments of theology, for example, the Commission on Theology and Church Relations in the Lutheran Church–Missouri Synod (LCMS), and dialogues involving Lutherans also occur within national and synodical settings. In 1956 the LWF initiated international Luther research congresses that meet and publish their proceedings every five years.

The *Book of Concord* was never accepted as authoritative in its entirety by all Lutherans, and, as a collection, it did not provide a systematic structure or an explicit *ORDO SALUTIS*. After 1580 academic theologians, mostly at German universities, made up for that deficit during a period called Lutheran ORTHODOXY, which lasted into the ENLIGHTENMENT. One of its chief representatives, J. Gerhard (1582–1637), professor at Jena, applied the *loci* method to a comprehensive and ordered list of topics in his *Loci theologici communes* (1610–22). Orthodox polemics clarified the lines between Lutheran and other confessional theologies by insisting that Luther's thought was the correct interpretation of God's word in SCRIPTURE. Although rich in study, worship, and music, orthodoxy in Lutheranism (as in other confessions) was challenged by the Pietist movement (see PIETISM). A Lutheran pastor-theologian in Frankfurt, P. J. Spener (1635–1705), published one of the earliest Pietist critiques, which advocated that 'the teaching of theology', called by him a practical discipline, 'be carried on not by the strife of disputations but rather by the practice of piety' (*Pia*, 50).

In eighteenth- and nineteenth-century Europe Lutheran theologians were influenced by the intellectual currents of rationalism, Romanticism, and idealism. A reaction against these currents led to a movement called neo-Lutheranism, which revived Lutheran confessional identity in the face of the Prussian union. Prominent neo-Lutheran theologians taught at Erlangen and elsewhere in Germany, but they were also found in Scandinavia and the USA, where in 1847 C. F. W. Walther (1811–87), who had emigrated from Saxony, became the first president and theological mentor of the LCMS.

A similar revival of Lutheran theology occurred in Germany in the early twentieth century concurrent with the rise of NEO-ORTHODOXY. The catalyst was the rediscovery of Luther's early lectures and their analysis by K. Holl (1866–1926), professor in Berlin. This Luther renaissance, which lasted long after Holl, exerted vital influence on twentieth-century theologians. Among those whose scholarly work was enriched by Luther's writings were R. Hermann (1867–1962), G. Aulén (1879–1978), P. Althaus (1888–1966), E. Hirsch (1888–1972), H. Iwand (1899–1960), R. Prenter (1907–90), G. Wingren (1910–2000), G. Ebeling (1912–2001), G. Forell (b. 1919), G. Forde (1927–2005), O. Pesch (b. 1931), T. Mannermaa (b. 1937), and O. Bayer (b. 1939). Ecumenical dialogues and intramural debates also devoted attention to the confessions; and while Lutheran theologians were influenced by neo-orthodoxy, PROCESS THEOLOGY, and other forms of modern thought, the writings of Luther remained the primary source of Lutheran theology.

As a consequence, Luther reception and interpretation have become a contentious issue in contemporary Lutheran theology. Scholars with strong ecumenical priorities stress the Catholic nature of Luther's sacramental views and draw mainly on his early writings, the Augsburg Confession, and Melanchthon's *Apology*. They assert that Lutherans are evangelical Catholics, not Protestants, and locate Lutherans on the Orthodox and Roman Catholic end of the theological spectrum. These scholars generally support the 1999 *Joint Declaration on the Doctrine of Justification* signed by the president of the Pontifical Council for Promoting Christian Unity and by eight officers of the Lutheran World Federation.

In contrast, scholars with strong confessional priorities insist that the *Book of Concord* restated the biblical and evangelical truth that Luther discovered, and that Lutheran theologians should uphold it for the sake of Christendom. They emphasize Luther's critique of the medieval Church, draw on his polemical writings and treatises like *Bondage of the Will* (1525), and are wary of agreements between Lutherans and other Churches. Some Evangelical Lutheran Church in America (ELCA) pastors and teachers have refused to accept commitments made by the ELCA to the Episcopal Church and to four Reformed Churches.

The authority of Scripture and its corollary, confessional subscription, are perennial points of debate. They come to the fore when social and ecumenical matters are at stake or when mergers between Lutheran Churches are contemplated. The *Formula of Concord* contains an explicit statement of biblical authority, and some Lutheran theologians have associated its position with a notion of INERRANCY that grew out of later Christian FUNDAMENTALISM. Even theologians who would not make that connection prefer a literal reading of verses that apply directly to social issues like homosexuality. Luther himself sometimes applied the Bible literally, but he also prioritized the gospel message about Christ over a literal reading that considered all biblical verses to be of equal authority. Lutheran Churches that agree with his hermeneutical priority have ranked the *Formula of Concord* below Luther's catechisms and the Augsburg Confession, but other Churches insist that unconditional subscription to the entire *Book of Concord* – not in so far as it agrees with Scripture but *because* it agrees – is necessary.

Ever since the sixteenth century Lutheran theologians have debated the effect of justification. Does the classic Lutheran description of the justified sinner as *SIMUL JUSTUS ET PECCATOR* mean that God both pronounces and makes the sinner righteous, or does it mean the believer is pronounced righteous in spite of remaining only or mainly a sinner? At times both Luther and Melanchthon expressed a forensic view of justification, but the modern Finnish school of Luther interpretation, citing evidence mainly from his lectures on Galatians (1531), argues that Luther also believed the justified sinner was both pronounced and truly made righteous.

Luther's concepts of two kingdoms and true Christian orders (Church, household, and government) were used by a few German theologians in the 1930s to disallow resistance to the Nazi dictatorship. Arguing that even unjust governments were divine orders of creation and therefore legitimate, they rejected the BARMEN DECLARATION (1934) and exposed Luther's concepts to blunt criticism by K. BARTH and D. BONHOEFFER. Luther's concepts were, however, misapplied by them, and contemporary theologians like R. Saarinen (b. 1959) would like to rehabilitate the three orders, because they epitomize not submissiveness in the face of misrule but commitment to ethical Christian participation in the public sphere. In this context, Luther himself wrote that there 'is the common order of Christian love, in which one serves not only the three orders, but also serves every needy person in general with all kinds of benevolent deeds' (*Supp.* 365).

In the twenty-first century ecumenical and global concerns will force Lutherans to articulate the ethical and political resources of their theological tradition. Luther's theology of the cross (see *THEOLOGIA CRUCIS*) is already being used to address human suffering, and a proper understanding of two kingdoms encourages action to relieve and prevent that suffering. Women theologians are finding resources in Luther's thought to support empowerment and equality. The relationship of Lutheran theology to other religions has only begun to receive attention; the global diversity of Lutheranism will accelerate and enrich that conversation. Lutheran Churches are growing faster outside Europe and North

America than within those traditional strongholds, and theologians in Latin America, Australia, Asia, and Africa, supported by the LWF, are seeking ways to adapt traditional Lutheran concepts to their cultures. Does justification by faith alone mean the same thing in Namibia as it does in Porto Alegre or Minneapolis or Leipzig? In addition to answering that question, Lutheran theologians can utilize Luther's notion of the universal Church to strengthen co-operation among Christians throughout the world.

C. E. Braaten, G. O. Forde, P. R. Hefner *et al.*, *Christian Dogmatics*, 2 vols. (Fortress Press, 1984).

G. Gassmann and S. H. Hendrix, *Fortress Introduction to the Lutheran Confessions* (Fortress Press, 1999).

N. H. Gregerson, T. Peters, B. Holm, and P. Widman, eds., *Gift of Grace: The Future of Lutheran Theology* (Fortress Press, 2004).

R. Kolb and T. J. Wengert, eds., *The Book of Concord: The Confessions of the Evangelical Lutheran Church* (Fortress Press, 2000).

H. T. Lehmann and J. Pelikan, eds., *Luther's Works*, 55 vols. (Fortress Press, 1955–86).

B. Lohse, *Martin Luther's Theology: Its Historical and Systematic Development* (Fortress Press, 1999).

SCOTT H. HENDRIX

Magisterium Derived from the Latin word for 'teacher', 'magisterium' is a term in Catholic theology for the teaching office of the Church, rooted in Christ and transmitted through apostolic succession to all bishops in communion with the papacy. According to the *Catechism of the Catholic Church*, because its task is to preserve the faithful from error (§85) through authoritative interpretation of Scripture and tradition, the magisterium possesses the charism of infallibility with respect to matters of faith and morals (§890). Yet, because this charism can be exercised in different ways, a distinction is drawn between the supreme and the ordinary magisterium. The former is exercised when the pope, either by himself or together with the college of bishops, proclaims a doctrine 'by a definitive act ... for belief as being divinely revealed' (*Cat.*, §891; cf. §88). By contrast, the ordinary magisterium refers to the process by which bishops (and especially the pope) propose 'a teaching that leads to better understanding of Revelation' through less formal means like preaching or catechesis (*Cat.*, §892).

It is Catholic teaching that the magisterium, while not itself a source of revelation, nevertheless forms a functional unity with Scripture and tradition, such that 'one of them cannot stand without the others' (*Cat.*, §95). This claim that proper interpretation of Scripture requires a teaching office is a central point of disagreement between Catholics and the Churches of the Reformation. Protestant theologians worry that the Catholic position effectively divinizes the Church. In order to affirm God's capacity to judge the whole Church (including its official leadership) through Scripture, they are therefore inclined to challenge the idea of an infallible magisterium. By contrast, Catholics counter that for Christians the true meaning of Scripture as God's word for the Church cannot be determined independently of the Church (including especially its leadership), since it is only by reference to the Christian community that it is possible to define what Scripture's genuinely 'Christian' sense is.

Ian A. McFarland

M

Magnificat The Gospel of Luke reports that after the annunciation, Mary visited her kinswoman, Elizabeth, who was herself pregnant with John the Baptist. The canticle sung by Mary in response to Elizabeth's greeting, recorded in Luke 1:46–55, is known as the Magnificat, from the first word in the Vulgate translation of the text. In setting, style, and theme it echoes the song of Hannah in the OT (1 Sam. 2:1–10), on which it appears to have been modelled. Both are hymns of praise to God sung by women in joyous response to unexpected pregnancy (cf. 1 Sam. 2:1 and Luke 1:47–9), and both take the form of a recital of reasons for such praise. The grounds given relate generally to God's power to vindicate God's cause (cf. 1 Sam. 2:2–3, 10 and Luke 1:51, 54–5) and more specifically to the fact that God manifests this sovereignty by reversing earthly relationships of power and prestige (cf. 1 Sam. 2:4–5, 8 and Luke 1:52–3).

Later incorporated into the vespers service of the divine office, the Magnificat is most naturally seen as a summary confession of God's way of working in the world. For M. Luther it pointed to the *theologia crucis* (as well as to the doctrine of creation from nothing) by confirming that 'God is the kind of Lord who does nothing but ... break what is whole and make whole what is broken' (*Magn.* 299). Along similar lines, the historical-critical judgement that the canticle may have originated among marginalized Jewish Christians known as the 'Poor Ones' (*Anāwim* in Hebrew) resonates with its contemporary appropriation by advocates of liberation theology, for whom it is evidence of God's preferential option for the poor and corresponding commitment to overturn entrenched relationships of social inequality.

Ian A. McFarland

Manichaeism Manichaeism was a highly eclectic, radically dualistic religion based upon the teachings of its Persian founder, Mani (216–76). Mani's father was Patik, a member of a community of Judaizing Christians that performed baptism. Mani professed two revelations convincing him that he was God's final prophet and an apostle of Christ, and prompting his veneration as the Paraclete. After travelling to India, he returned to his homeland, where he initially enjoyed imperial favour; after opposition by the official fire-worshipping religion, he was executed.

While Manichaeism drew heavily upon Zoroastrianism, Christianity, and Buddhism, twentieth-century scholarship has affirmed the special influence of Christian teachings. But the very fact that Manichaeism engaged in such successful proselytization (east to China and Manchuria, and west to North Africa and Rome) warrants its characterization as a world religion in its own right rather than as a mere offshoot or heresy of any one religion. H. Puech (1902–86) proposed several reasons for Manichaeism's worldwide appeal: its portrayal as a universal, ecumenical creed; its broad missiological reach; and its revelatory claims, supported by a voluminous Scriptural *corpus* (*Man.* 61–6). Manichaeism can also be considered a late expression of Gnosticism, in view of its pessimism towards matter, body, and world; its teaching of the soul's divinity; an emphasis upon salvific knowledge; and a conflictual dualism between substantial principles of good and evil (represented by Light and Darkness respectively).

Manichaean dualism supported an elaborate cosmogony that can be outlined on the basis of three 'Moments' or 'Times' (Decret, *Mani* 80). In the Former Time, Light and Darkness occupied separate regions, an uneasy co-existence shattered by the hostile invasion of Darkness. That onslaught precipitated the Present Time, when the commingling of Light and Darkness (through a series of evocations), eventually produced the visible universe and humans. Matter confines the luminous particles ingested by the agents of Darkness. The soul's very embodiment attests to the ongoing conflict characterizing reality as a whole.

Only an illuminating *gnosis* allows humans to free their souls (their true selves) from subjection to corporeal nature. The Manichaean Elect exemplify the proper response to this enlightenment, abetting the release of Light by adhering to a rigorous asceticism comprising the Three Seals (mouth, hands, and womb) and Five Commandments, and refraining from any activity (e.g., sexual intercourse) perpetuating Light's penal condition. Finally, the Future Time encompasses an eschatological age when the luminous particles will be fully liberated, and everything will be consummated in a state of peacefulness.

Manichaean cosmology represents an acosmic perspective strongly at odds with the Christian assumption that creation is fundamentally good – and it was attacked on these grounds by the former Manichaean, Augustine of Hippo. Manichaeism relegated the material universe and bodily existence to the status of mere expedients or necessary evils instrumental in freeing the luminous particles from matter, the hypostasization of Evil.

A. Bohlig, 'Manichaismus' in *Theologische Realenzyklopädie*, ed. G. Krause and G. Müller, vol. XXII (W. de Gruyter, 1991), 1.

S. Lieu, *Manichaeism in the Later Roman Empire and Medieval China: A Historical Survey* (Manchester University Press, 1985).

Joseph Torchia, O. P.

Marcion Though often treated by his opponents as representing many of the ideas characteristic of Gnosticism, Marcion proposed a Christian theology based on significantly different principles. He was born in Sinope in Asia Minor in about 110, the son of the local bishop, and came to Rome around the year 140 as a wealthy ship owner. Though he quickly joined (and made a substantial monetary donation to) the Church in Rome, his theological views caused him to be excommunicated (and his gift returned) in 144. Marcion went on to found his own, well-organized Church, which persisted in the western part of the empire into the fourth century and in eastern areas (especially Syria) considerably longer. He returned to Asia Minor soon after his split with the Roman Church and died there around 160.

Marcion's one book, the *Antitheses*, survives only in fragments, but the title highlights his central theological conviction: the gospel of Jesus Christ stands in irreconcilable contradiction to the teachings of the OT. While the tensions between Christian teaching and the Jewish Scriptures (e.g., regarding the status of the Jewish law) were an important topic of theological reflection in the early Church, Marcion's solution was radical: he argued that the God of Jesus Christ was a different being than the God of the Jews and, correspondingly, rejected the OT as Christian Scripture. In its place, Marcion was the first to define a specifically Christian canon of Scripture, which he limited to Paul's letters and the Gospel of Luke, restored to what Marcion believed was their original condition by the removal of all references to the OT.

Marcion's theology was strongly dualistic. While the God of Jesus was a loving and merciful Spirit, the God of the Jews, creator of the material world, was a lesser and hard-hearted being who demanded obedience. Jesus himself had nothing to do with the world of matter, the corruptibility of which was the source of all evil: as an emissary of the purely spiritual Father, he did not assume flesh, and therefore did not experience bodily resurrection. Similarly, Jesus' followers were to wean themselves from all things material in order to attain a purely spiritual life with God.

Though Marcion's dualism has commanded little sympathy in the Church, theologians continue to be challenged by his emphasis on the radical character of Paul's gospel. F. Overbeck's (1837–1905) famous quip – that Marcion was the only Christian who really understood Paul, and that even he misunderstood him – remains insightful. For, while Marcion's rejection of any continuity between the God of Abraham and the God of Jesus is clearly inconsistent with Paul's theology (see, e.g., Rom. 4 and 9–11), Marcion did appreciate the contrast between the righteousness of God as revealed in law and gospel in Paul's thought (see, e.g., Rom. 3:19–28; Gal. 3:23–8). This same insight (though not derived from Marcion) was crucial to Augustine's theology of grace, and, during the Reformation, to the doctrine of justification developed in Lutheran and Reformed theology.

E. Blackman, *Marcion and His Influence* (SPCK, 1948).

A. von Harnack, *Marcion: The Gospel of the Alien God* (Labyrinth Press, 1990 [1921]).

Ian A. McFarland

Maréchal, Joseph Joseph Maréchal (1878–1944) was born in Charleroi, Belgium, and pursued university studies in biology (in which he received a doctorate in 1905), philosophy, and theology at the University of

Louvain. He joined the Jesuit order in 1895, was ordained to the PRIESTHOOD in 1908, and served as professor of psychology and the history of philosophy in Louvain between 1910 and 1914, and again from 1919 to 1935. He sought to free neo-Scholasticism from its tendency to woodenness through a re-examination of the philosophy of T. AQUINAS. In his groundbreaking *Le Point de départ de la métaphysique* (5 vols., 1923–47), he applied a transcendental epistemology based in the work of I. KANT and J. G. Fichte (1762–1814) to Thomistic METAPHYSICS (see THOMISM). The result was an identification of the a priori conditions of knowledge in Kant's transcendental idealism with the formal objects of knowledge in Thomistic SCHOLASTICISM. Further, Maréchal argued (against Kant) that the intrinsic, dynamic orientation of reason to God allows Being itself to be grasped in such a way as to give a firm ground to metaphysics.

Alongside his work in metaphysics stands Maréchal's important analysis of the psychology of mysticism (*Studies in the Psychology of the Mystics*, 2 vols., English version: 1927/French version: 1937). Maréchal exerted a wide-ranging influence on the history of Catholic thought in the twentieth century through the so-called 'Maréchal School', which counted among its members K. RAHNER and B. LONERGAN, alongside a number of francophone philosophers and theologians.

A. M. Matteo, *Marechal: Quest for the Absolute* (Northern Illinois University Press, 1992).

PETER NEUNER

MARIOLOGY The Virgin Mary's significance for Christianity is one of the most disputed of all theological issues, for it goes to the heart of questions about the relationship between nature and GRACE, the Christian understanding of CREATION, and the role of humankind in Christ's saving work. Since the REFORMATION Mary has been a marker of division, and more recently of tentative dialogue, between Catholics and Protestants. In the Orthodox and Coptic Churches she remains a figure of iconic holiness intimately identified with the suffering and glorification of her Son, while the 2004 document produced by the Anglican–Roman Catholic International Commission (ARCIC), *Mary: Grace and Hope in Christ*, expresses fundamental agreement between Catholic and Anglican DOCTRINE on many previously disputed questions.

Mary's scriptural role is most often portrayed in terms of the ANNUNCIATION and nativity (Matt. 1:18–24; 2:1–12; Luke 1:26–38; 2:1–20), the visitation and the MAGNIFICAT (Luke 1:39–56), the presentation of the infant Jesus and the finding of the twelve-year-old Jesus in the temple in Jerusalem (Luke 2:22–51), the flight into Egypt (Matt. 2:13–17), the wedding at Cana (John 2:1–12), and the crucifixion (John 19:25–7). Mary is also referred to in the context of Christ's genealogy (Matt. 1:12–16), in references to his family background (Matt. 13:55; Mark 6:3; John 6:42), in disputes about the relationship between Jesus' family and his disciples (which some interpret as implicitly critical of her, particularly in Mark 3:31–5; cf. Matt. 12:46–50; Mark 3:31–5; Luke 8:19–21; 11:27–8), and in the account of the praying community after Christ's ascension (Acts 1:14). Less explicitly, there is a reference in Galatians to Christ's birth from a woman (4:4), while the reference in Revelation to a woman giving birth to the Messiah (12:1–18), though traditionally associated with Mary, is now thought to refer to the Church. Luke and JOHN seem to attach more significance to Mary than Matthew and Mark.

In addition to scriptural references, the second-century text known as the *Protevangelium of James* had a formative influence on the early cult of Mary. Inspired partly by the OT story of Hannah and Samuel (1 Sam. 1:2–11), it tells of Mary's early life, from her conception by her parents to the infancy of Christ. Although suppressed in the western Church for several centuries, the *Protevangelium* has had a continuous influence on eastern Christianity, and in medieval Catholicism it was a source for widely popular works such as the *Legenda Aurea* or *Golden Legend*, and the Gospel of Pseudo-Matthew. In its association of Mary with the temple and with the book of Samuel, it is an example of how the first Christians sought to interpret the story of Christ in terms of the characters, motifs, and prophecies of the OT. Most common among these typological readings is the interpretation of Mary as the New Eve in relation to Christ as the Second Adam (cf. Rom. 5:12–21; 1 Cor. 15:21–2, 45–9).

The earliest theological references to Mary as the New Eve are found in the second-century writings of Justin Martyr (d. *ca* 165), IRENAEUS OF LYONS, and TERTULLIAN. Irenaeus offers the most extended reflection in *Against Heresies*, portraying Mary as the virgin earth from whom the second Adam was made, and as the first woman of the new creation who, by her virginal obedience, undoes the effects of Eve's disobedience in the Garden of Eden. This intricate TYPOLOGY is an example of the poetic analogies by which patristic theologians laid the foundations for what would later become doctrinal ORTHODOXY.

Much early Marian theology was formulated as a response to challenges from movements which would later be deemed heretical. Central to these were disputes about the relationship between the divinity and humanity of Christ. To those who contested the full humanity of Christ, the early defenders of Christian orthodoxy responded by insisting upon his birth from a human mother. To those who questioned his full divinity, they pointed to the mystery of Mary's virginal conception as evidence of the power of God beyond nature and human intervention. Thus the virginal motherhood of Mary became the linchpin upon which the doctrine of the INCARNATION rested, and the seal was set on this position when the Council of EPHESUS declared Mary *Theotokos* or Mother of God, bringing an end to the Nestorian controversy and establishing a doctrine which has remained undisputed within both Chalcedonian and ORIENTAL ORTHODOX CHURCHES. Protestant theologians such as K. BARTH who would deny Mary any active role in salvation still affirm the title Mother of God because of its Christological significance. By the end of the fourth century, these theological roots had begun to flourish in forms of Marian piety and devotion which focused attention on her personal qualities of divine motherhood and virginal holiness as well as on her significance for Christ's identity and mission.

In order to consider how these trends subsequently developed, it may be helpful to view Marian theology in terms of the relationship between nature and grace, and between divine initiative and human co-operation. Although veneration of Mary has been compared with goddess worship, the Christian distinction between creation and God means that no creature becomes one with the Godhead in a way which would dissolve the difference between them. Mary belongs within the order of creation, and she therefore remains human even when this is expressed in terms of the closest possible union with her divine Son or, more generally, with the Persons of the TRINITY. Within this context, the central question dividing Protestant and Catholic theologies is the extent to which humankind contributes to its own redemption in the person of Mary, which opens into a larger question about the extent to which the original grace of creation retains its revelatory capacity, as a form of natural REVELATION alongside the revelation of SCRIPTURE.

The Augustinian doctrine of original SIN was never accepted by the Orthodox Church, which thus has a more positive understanding of the enduring goodness of creation than its western counterparts. Mary's divine motherhood is an iconic affirmation of the grace of a material creation in which the mystery of God is manifest. As one intimately associated with the incarnation, she is the sinless perfection of our humanity in an inclusive rather than an exclusive sense: we are all ultimately called to participate in deification (*theosis*) and union with God that she exemplifies.

Although Augustine's doctrine of original sin would have far-reaching consequences for the western Church and its attitudes towards nature, until the late Middle Ages western Catholicism also retained a fundamentally positive understanding of the relationship between creation and grace. From the tenth century, the growing identification of Mary with the motherhood of the Church created a vast maternal presence at the heart of medieval society, in which Marian devotion was closely intertwined both with the cycles of nature and with the domestic worlds of women. By the twelfth century the cult of Mary was giving rise to a proliferation of devotional literature and practices. These included Marian litanies and antiphons, the increasing popularity of the Hail Mary and the introduction of the Rosary, and the development of new forms of Marian spirituality.

The Reformation led to the eradication of Marian devotion across large sectors of European Christianity. Reformers such as M. LUTHER and J. CALVIN refocused the Christian faith exclusively on the biblical revelation rather than the cumulative TRADITION of the Church. This resulted in the rejection of the cult of the SAINTS and of many of the sacramental practices and devotions of medieval Catholicism. The theological perspectives of the reformers emphasized the sacrificial and redemptive power of the cross rather than the redeeming totality of the incarnation, and they posited a radically fallen creation and a human consciousness cut off from any awareness of revelation and grace except through salvation in Christ. From this perspective, no human being can play an active role in their own salvation, and the Catholic belief that Mary's *fiat* – her 'yes' to God in the annunciation – constitutes a responsive initiative which makes her both redeemed and redemptive, actively participating in Christ's saving mission, is, correspondingly, viewed as heretical.

In response to the crisis of the Reformation, the Council of TRENT sought to bring a greater sense of order and scriptural coherence to Catholicism. Marian theology, art, and devotion in the centuries following Trent reflect wider cultural changes in the understanding of nature, gender, and maternal femininity. The fertile virgin mother of medieval devotion was replaced by representations of idealized virginal femininity, suggestive of a world-transcending spirituality in which grace no longer constitutes the fulfilment and perfection of nature, but is instead locked in a struggle against nature (including human nature) as the western world surged into modernity through its embrace of scientific rationalism. Mary thus enters modernity under a cloud of Protestant suspicion on the one hand, and floating disembodied on a cloud of Catholic sentimentality on the other, in a cult far removed from the incarnational exuberance of the medieval Church. The promulgation of the doctrines of the IMMACULATE CONCEPTION and the ASSUMPTION intensified divisions between Protestants and Catholics.

VATICAN COUNCIL II transformed Catholicism and paved the way for ecumenical dialogue across all the contested frontiers of doctrine and theology, including the role of Mary. The Council was divided between a minority of bishops resistant to the proposed modernization of the Church, and a prevailing majority which introduced widespread and controversial changes. After prolonged and heated debate, conservatives who campaigned for a separate document on Mary were narrowly defeated by those who argued that Mary should be incorporated into the document on the

Church, *Lumen gentium*. Although *Lumen gentium* acknowledges the uniqueness and greatness of Mary as Mother of God, it also situates her within the Church as an exemplar and model of the life of faith for the pilgrim people of God. There was a dramatic decline in Marian devotion in the decade following the Council, to be followed by a revival during the PAPACY of John Paul II (r. 1978–2005), whose personal devotion to Mary is evident in many of his theological writings, especially his ENCYCLICAL *Redemptoris Mater* (1978).

The Council ushered in a more humanized, less transcendent sense of Mary, and this gained particular significance for LIBERATION THEOLOGIES of the 1970s and 1980s. Mary's Magnificat was seen as a rallying cry for the poor and the marginalized, and Mary became a symbol of divinely inspired resistance to the politics of domination. Feminist theologians were more concerned to expose ways in which the cult of virginal motherhood had had a repressive effect on Christian attitudes to female sexuality, promoting an impossible ideal over and against which Eve constituted the identification of the female body with sexuality, sin, and death. As debates over the role of women in the Church and the exclusion of women from the Catholic priesthood have intensified, Mary has been invoked in support of both sides of the argument. Among conservative Catholics she is held up as the perfect example of obedient and receptive femininity. Those supporting women's ordination have pointed to a long tradition of according a priestly role to Mary, as a potential role model and justification for a female sacramental priesthood.

If gender is a significant feature of these debates, the environmental crisis has also precipitated a reappraisal of Mary's potential to symbolize the goodness of creation, so that questions of nature and grace remain close to the surface of Marian theology. The combined influences of feminism and environmentalism have led some contemporary theologians to explore the contours of a Mariology suffused with a sense of cosmic wonder at the creative and generative power of God, so that, paradoxically, while feminist theologians of the late twentieth century were resistant to the 'high' Mariology of the preconciliar Church, a new generation of feminists has sought to rediscover the significance of Mary as Mother of God and Queen of Heaven, for a revitalized appreciation of the mystery, grace, and glory of creation.

Today, Christianity faces different challenges from those of its formative years, but the questions remain substantially unchanged. Who is Jesus Christ in relation to God, humankind, and creation? Already by the late fourth century, Christians had found that it was impossible to address these questions without turning to the shadowy biblical figure of Mary and bringing her into the limelight of Christian doctrine and devotion. Today, Mary remains a persistent challenge to Christians in their quest for theological agreement and ecclesial unity. She still haunts the edges of the western secular imagination, in art and music, in cinema and popular culture, while in many Catholic countries she remains a focus of popular devotion which often eludes the controlling influence of doctrinal orthodoxy. As the elusive m/other of the incarnate Christ, she both reveals and conceals what it means to profess belief in a God who was born of a woman and was woven into the fabric of creation, in order to redeem that same creation and restore it to a state of wholeness and grace.

H. U. von Balthasar, *Mary for Today* (St Paul, 1989).
T. Beattie, *God's Mother, Eve's Advocate: A Marian Narrative of Women's Salvation* (Continuum, 2002).
S. J. Boss, *Empress and Handmaid: On Nature and Gender in the Cult of the Virgin Mary* (Cassell, 2000).
H. Graef, *Mary: A History of Doctrine and Devotion* (Sheed & Ward, 1994).
E. A. Johnson, *Truly Our Sister: A Theology of Mary in the Communion of Saints* (Continuum, 2003).
K. Rahner, *Mary, Mother of the Lord: Theological Meditations* (Catholic Book Club, 1963).

TINA BEATTIE

MARKS OF THE CHURCH What are the signs that indicate the presence of the Church of Christ? The NICENE CREED states that it is by the working of the HOLY SPIRIT that the Church is one, holy, Catholic, and apostolic. For the Orthodox and Catholics, these are four 'marks' (*notae*) that constitute the Church's nature and way of life. Each mark has been variously interpreted, but it is generally agreed that the Church is: *one* in its faith, though not uniform; *holy* in the Spirit and set apart for Christ, though its members commit SIN; *Catholic* in being fully present locally and universally; and *apostolic* because in communion with the faith of the APOSTLES as it follows the guidance of SCRIPTURE and the teaching of its bishops.

Following the REFORMATION, the Catholic Church used these marks apologetically, arguing that it alone is truly the Church, since it alone displays all four marks. Although the Protestant Churches fully accepted the creedal statement, they drew up their own marks by which to discern the true Church (*notae verae ecclesiae*). The Lutherans traditionally have two: pure preaching and proper use of sacraments (see AC 7). To these some Reformed Churches add a third: the disciplined Christian life. M. LUTHER himself counts seven marks in his *On the Councils and the Church* (1539): the presence of the Word, BAPTISM, the EUCHARIST, the practice of confessing and forgiving sins, the pastoral office (*iure divino*), PRAYER, cross-bearing. With the advent of ECUMENISM, the marks have been used more constructively, particularly after VATICAN COUNCIL II's claim that the true Church 'subsists in the Catholic Church' (*LG*, §8) has suggested to some

Catholic theologians that it may 'subsist' in other communions as well.

NICHOLAS M. HEALY

MARRIAGE Marriage is one of the most familiar topics in Christian ethics. If anything is 'natural', in any of the varying uses of that term, it is marriage. Of course, just because something is 'natural' does not mean its meaning is uncontested. Thus Christian thinking on marriage has for two millennia addressed two important and related yet distinct questions. The first concerns the 'nature' of marriage as a part of God's CREATION in relation to other world views, which have interpreted the meaning of marriage in radically different ways, including as an artefact of human social construction, an institution subservient to State or political purposes, or a radically individualistic and/or Romanticist endeavour. The second question concerns the ongoing role and shape of marriage in the context of the KINGDOM OF GOD.

In answering the first question, Christianity has consistently maintained that marriage is part of God's creation. Thus it is good, and serves a role in God's plan for humanity. As to the second, from the eschatological perspective of the kingdom – be it the kingdom's inauguration in this life or its coming to fulfilment in the next – marriage has been variously suppressed, transformed, transcended, and even understood as an epitomization of God's relationship with God's people. Thus marriage serves as a perfect arena for reflection on and living out the complicated relationship between nature and GRACE.

Four crucial scriptural claims about marriage shape the Christian perspective. First, marriage is good and plays a role in God's creative purposes. The key texts here are Genesis 2:24 and Matthew 19:1–12 (cf. Mark 10:2–12), in the latter of which Jesus refers to the former: 'For this reason a man shall leave his father and mother and be joined to his wife, and the two shall become one flesh' (Matt. 19:5; cf. Gen. 2:24). The passage from Genesis has consistently been interpreted as a reference to marriage between a man and a woman, and as vindicating the view that marriage is part of God's creation. The two becoming one flesh is generally understood as a reference to sexual union. Marriage and its concomitant sexual union are not by-products of the FALL or original SIN, but rather part of God's plan for humanity. Also, when questioned by the Pharisees, Jesus bases his prohibition of DIVORCE on a direct reference to Genesis 2:24, claiming divorce was not how it was 'in the beginning', when the two became 'one flesh'. He therefore concludes by declaring, 'what God has joined together, let no one separate' (Matt. 19:6). The repeated reference to 'the beginning' (vv. 4, 8) and the claim that one must not undo what God has done firmly establish the role of marriage in God's creative purposes.

It is likely due to this theme of a definitive 'joining together' that marriage has served as a consistent metaphor for God's relationship to God's people. This metaphor is the second foundational scriptural claim about marriage. Marriage is frequently used in the OT to depict the COVENANT between God and ISRAEL, and in the NT PAUL, alluding to Genesis 2:24, claims that 'This is a great mystery [*sacramentum* in the VULGATE], and I am applying it to Christ and the church' (Eph. 5:32). This passage provides a springboard for many claims in the TRADITION regarding the distinctively Christian facets of marriage, including the status of marriage as one of the Church's seven sacraments in the Catholic and Orthodox traditions.

Yet coupled with these extraordinary affirmations of the goodness of marriage are equally stark subordinations, and even suppressions, of marriage in the Christian life. Thus, a third scriptural claim about marriage is that it is not part of humanity's ultimate destiny. In Mark 12:18–27 (cf. Matt. 22:23–33; Luke 20:27–40), Christ claims there is no marriage in heaven. Thus, despite the aforementioned aptness of marriage as a metaphor of the relationship between God and God's people, there are discontinuities enough between this life and resurrected life to prompt Jesus to claim marriage does not exist at the RESURRECTION.

Though this particular teaching could be explained by naming the differences between this life and the next, other NT passages state in no uncertain terms that it is better not to marry even in this life. This is the fourth foundational aspect of scriptural teaching about marriage. PAUL never disparages marriage, but he thinks it better not to marry (1 Cor. 7:8–9). And Jesus, in the very passage where he points to the binding of spouses by God as intended from the beginning, seemingly affirms his disciples' claim that it is better not to marry when he speaks of those who 'have made themselves eunuchs for the sake of the kingdom of heaven' (Matt. 19:11). These passages explain a consistent claim in the Christian tradition (e.g., AUGUSTINE, T. AQUINAS) that CELIBACY is a higher calling than marriage.

What can we take from this survey of biblical texts? Marriage is indeed part of God's creative plan, and its binding nature makes it an apt metaphor for understanding God's relationship with God's people. But it is also radically subordinated to discipleship and life in Christ. It is reminiscent of family relationships, which must be absolutely rejected to the extent they impede discipleship (Matt. 10:37; Luke 14:26) and yet which may be the very locale of salvation when transformed by grace (John 19:26–7). The Christian tradition has consistently tried to maintain this balance, against people who have problematic understandings either of the nature of marriage or of the role of marriage in a life of Christian discipleship.

In the Roman world of early Christianity, the Christian subordination of marriage to the KINGDOM OF GOD was a potent check on powerful forces in pagan culture. Christian praise of celibacy as an honourable way of life, its claim that widows need not remarry, and its insistence on communal care for widows, orphans, and other vulnerable members of the population, all served to weaken the role of marriage in perpetuating a social order that concentrated power on the (male) head of the family and, ultimately, in the Roman Empire. Bishops like John Chrysostom (*ca* 345–407) called on Christians to practise marriage, an institution shared with non-believers, in a manner reflective of specifically Christian belief.

At this time there were also forces, claiming to act in the name of FAITH, who understood marriage (and sexuality) to be a worldly phenomenon that was either irrelevant to Christian living (see 1 Cor. 6:12–20) or unworthy and hence incompatible with it. It is against the latter perspective – specifically associated with MANICHAEISM – that Augustine wrote his treatise *On the Good of Marriage*, which has in many ways set the agenda of theological thinking about marriage ever since. There Augustine identified three 'goods' of marriage: *proles* (PROCREATION), *fides* (fidelity), and *sacramentum* (sacramental bond). All marriages are good because they are characterized by an orientation towards procreation, and entail the exclusive fidelity of spouses. Augustine treats the permanence of marriage under the good of *sacramentum*, which is distinctive to Christian marriage. Though Augustine's belief that the permanence of marriage is distinctive to Christian marriage will not be shared by later thinkers, his articulation of these three goods is the basis of centuries of subsequent Christian thought on marriage.

A similar twofold defence of marriage can be seen in the Middle Ages. In part prompted by the subjugation of marriage to political purposes, medieval thinkers like Aquinas identified consent as the essence of marriage. Marriage is consensual union with a spouse for a purpose: family life and the raising of children. In a break from Augustine, Aquinas understands even natural marriage as inseparable, though he does affirm Augustine's claim that only Christian marriage is sacramental. Like his predecessor, Aquinas affirms the goodness of marriage against those who rejected such an embodied and procreative practice as unworthy of Christian life; yet he also follows Augustine in subordinating the practice of marriage in the context of discipleship, by continuing to praise celibacy as an exalted calling for the Christian. This latter stance would be challenged in the REFORMATION, when figures like M. LUTHER and J. CALVIN refused any such subordination of marriage to celibacy.

The nature of marriage remains a contested issue, with the Christian traditions witnessing to an inherent meaning of marriage as part of CREATION, over and against more modern understandings of marriage as a private endeavour whose parameters are set by the participants. More specific questions on the nature of marriage include: how essential is procreation to marriage and sex? How does the contemporary understanding of marriage as a loving partnership correlate with the Christian tradition on the goods of marriage? Need marriage be between a man and a woman? What is the good of vowed permanence such that intimate living arrangements outside marriage are lacking something important? These questions are contested not only between Christians and non-Christians but even among Christians. Though they concern the nature of marriage, from the Christian perspective of grace perfecting nature their answers are also crucial for understanding the shape of marriage in the graced life of Christian discipleship.

See also NUPTIAL THEOLOGY; SACRAMENTOLOGY; SEXUALITY.

P. Evdokimov, *The Sacrament of Love: The Nuptial Mystery in the Light of the Orthodox Tradition* (St Vladimir's Seminary Press, 1985).

T. Mackin, *What Is Marriage? Marriage in the Catholic Church* (Paulist Press, 1982).

E. Schillebeeckx, *Marriage: Human Reality, Saving Mystery* (Sheed & Ward, 1965).

K. Scott and M. Warren, eds., *Perspectives on Marriage: A Reader*, 2nd edn (Oxford University Press, 2000).

A. Thatcher, *Marriage after Modernity: Christian Marriage in Postmodern Times* (New York University Press, 1999).

WILLIAM C. MATTISON III

MARTYRDOM One of the features of the life of the early Church was its experience of persecution and suffering. Although in the first two centuries this persecution was local and sporadic, the reality of suffering and the possibility of undergoing death for Jesus left its imprint on the theology of the early Christians. The term *martys* (witness) was not in fact used unambiguously to refer to one who had been killed for the faith until *The Martyrdom of Polycarp* (*ca* 155). Nonetheless, the link between witnessing and dying was not itself an innovation and is found in the NT, in the cases of Stephen (Acts 22:20; cf. Acts 7) and Antipas (Rev. 2:13). Furthermore, sayings attributed to Jesus reveal the possible dangers early Christian communities faced in witnessing to or confessing his name, including the possibility of death (Mark 13:9–13; 8:34–5; Matt. 10:38–9; cf. John 12:25). Experiences of persecution and possible martyrdom are found throughout the NT, perhaps most graphically in Revelation, where the Whore of Babylon is said to be drunk with the blood of both the saints and witnesses/martyrs (*tōn martyrōn*) of Jesus (Rev. 17:6).

Much Christian reflection on martyrdom begins with the death of Jesus; Jesus is himself the faithful *martys* (Rev. 1:5; 3:14), and those who follow him on the road of suffering and martyrdom directly and most faithfully imitate his example. This meant that suffering and death could be interpreted positively, a move found as early as PAUL (e.g., 2 Cor. 6:10; Phil. 4:4–6); indeed, many early Christians eagerly anticipated death, most famously Ignatius of Antioch (*ca* 35–*ca* 110; see especially *Rom.* 4.1–5.3). Moreover, so positively regarded was suffering and death that many Christians actively sought martyrdom, willingly handing themselves over to arrest or engaging in provocative behaviour designed to attract the authorities' attention (e.g., *Acts of Euplus*; Tertullian, *Scap.* 5.1; *Perp.* 4.5). Such enthusiasm for death was by no means shared by all early Christians, and martyrdom itself was scorned by those of a 'Gnostic' leaning (e.g., *Testament of Truth* 31–2). Readiness for martyrdom, therefore, became one significant criterion for distinguishing between true and false Christians (Justin Martyr, *1Apol.* 26; Tertullian, *Scorp.* 1–7).

Early Christians created an alternative world view within which they understood their experiences of persecution, suffering, and death. In martyr acts, popular stories of martyrs, the climactic moment where the hero could confess or deny Christ became a point of cosmic conflict; the protagonist was an athlete trained in combat to fight against the DEVIL and his legions, who sought to steer her from her confession. Martyrdom took place under public and cosmic gaze, and often the reaction of the crowd (both hostile and positive) is noted. Those who recant under torture are said to be weak, untrained for combat, and the devil's prey (see especially *Martyrs of Lyons*). The central point of each martyr act is the confession, 'I am a Christian', where the martyrs explicitly identify themselves with the fate of their master. However, not only do they follow Christ's example in death, but they also participate in his victory over death and Satan; charging towards death becomes in reality rushing towards life (*Martyrdom of Pionius* 20.5; 21.4). Martyrdom is said to be a second baptism (Tertullian, *Pat.* 13.7), cleansing the martyr from SIN, according him an honoured place in HEAVEN. It was believed that those in prison awaiting martyrdom possessed power to heal and to forgive sins. This world view helps explain the enthusiasm for death found among early Christians.

However, readiness for martyrdom as a measure of ORTHODOXY broke down by the third century, when the proto-orthodox had to face the twin problem of 'heretics' – especially followers of MONTANISM – who enthusiastically gave confession and were martyred while the 'orthodox' lapsed in substantial numbers under the Decian persecutions. Clement of Alexandria (*ca* 150–*ca* 215) acknowledged the deaths of his theological opponents looked like true martyrdom, but their beliefs, together with their over-eagerness for martyrdom, rendered their sacrifice ineffective (*Strom.* 4.16–17). Augustine later confirmed Clement's view with his influential (though problematic) dictum that 'not the punishment but the cause' (*non poena sed causa*) makes the martyr.

The need to separate true and false martyrs was important not only for reasons of doctrinal purity, but for ecclesiastical order. Martyrs were celebrated and remembered by the early Church, and their graves were used as meeting places for worship. As a rudimentary cult of the martyrs developed, with calendar, intercessions, and importance attached to relics, spiritual and ecclesiastical authority were accorded to imprisoned confessors awaiting execution, creating an alternative power structure to that of presbyters and bishops. The efforts of rigorists in relation to those who had lapsed during periods of persecution were often thwarted by confessors who had not been executed issuing certificates of reconciliation to them.

After Christianity had become the State religion, opportunities to undergo martyrdom disappeared, though the rhetoric of martyrdom was retained in the developing monastic movement, so called 'white martyrdom'. With the exception of the Crusades and the few missionary expeditions at the edge of the Christian empire, there was little opportunity for martyrdom in the Middle Ages – T. Becket (*ca* 1120–70) and P. Martyr (1206–52) being significant exceptions, although their deaths were arguably more political than religious. Nonetheless, the cult of the martyrs, now transformed into the cult of the SAINTS, remained important as martyr-saints, who had won God's favour by their heroic deeds, were asked to intercede for the faithful.

The dawn of the REFORMATION ushered in a new period of martyrdom, beginning with the Hussite movement. In July 1412, three men, whose names are now unknown, were beheaded for protesting against papal indulgences. Supporters carried their bodies through the streets of Prague bearing placards reading: *Ita sunt martyres* (these men are martyrs). At Bethlehem chapel, J. Hus (*ca* 1370–1415) held a mass for martyrs for them. Hus was himself later arrested, imprisoned, and then executed. To the Church hierarchy, these men were heretics, but to others, they were added to the numbers of the martyrs. So seriously did the authorities view such unauthorized popular CANONIZATION, it became a capital offence to deny the execution of Hus was 'just and holy'. As the Reformation movement advanced, and Protestants, Anabaptists, and Catholics died at the hands of other Christians, reports and counter-reports circulated both proclaiming and denying the executed the title 'martyr'. These books and pamphlets proved popular, with the most famous, *Foxe's Book of Martyrs* (1563), undergoing three printings in the author's lifetime. The commitment of those who lost their lives in this period cannot be questioned, and even hostile witnesses comment on the manner in which they faced horrific deaths, which acted as evangelical rallying points more often than deterrent. It is less clear to what extent both execution and resistance were political rather than religious, especially in

England under Elizabeth I (r. 1558–1603) and to a lesser extent Mary I (r. 1553–8).

Similar ambiguity exists over two famous twentieth-century figures, D. BONHOEFFER (1906–45) and O. Romero (1917–80), both killed for essentially political reasons, yet remembered as Christian martyrs. The example of Bonhoeffer raises an important martyrological question: the place of violence in the rhetoric of martyrdom. Christianity has not been immune to the juxtaposition of violence and martyrdom. The popular acceptance of Bonhoeffer as a martyr suggests tacit approval of his involvement in the plot to assassinate A. Hitler (1889–1945) and brings to mind other occasions where Christianity has juxtaposed violence and martyrdom. For example, an inducement offered to boost recruitment for the Crusades was the guarantee that those who died in them would be considered martyrs and have their sins forgiven. More ambiguously, traditions regarding the remembrance of war dead, where the sacrifice of the soldiers is often linked with that of Jesus (by way of, e.g., the reading of John 15.13 at remembrance services), chime with rhetoric of martyrdom, as does the political language in the more recent 'War on Terror', where combatants are understood to die for the sake of democracy and freedom.

A distinction is often drawn between these cases and the example of the passivity of the early Christians; if their example is appropriated for any modern political cause, it is passive resistance movements. But again, the relationship between early Christian martyrs and violence is ambiguous. Many early Christians provoked their own deaths and took their own lives. Furthermore, eschatological violence is not far from early martyrologies; the demands of the martyred souls under the altar for bloody retribution (Rev. 6:9) are more than satisfied in Revelation. Persecutors are promised violent judgement for their actions, and the martyrs themselves are cast in the role of combatants in a cosmic battle; their bodies are the weapons by which the war will be won. Jewish Holy War tradition – which combined explicitly with martyrdom in the books of the Maccabees – is an important source for early Christian martyrological rhetoric.

Such tensions and ambiguities cannot be resolved by attempts to formulate ever tighter definitions of martyrdom; martyrs are acclaimed, not defined. Martyrs provide examples of bravery and loyalty to a cause for good or ill. The way in which these deaths are subsequently remembered and retold ultimately determines whether or not they gain a place in the ever-growing *Acts of the Martyrs*.

C. Bruno *et al.*, *The Book of Christian Martyrs* (SCM, 1990).

E. A. Castelli, *Martyrdom and Memory: Early Christian Culture Making* (Columbia University Press, 2004).

B. S. Gregory, *Salvation at Stake: Christian Martyrdom in Early Modern Europe* (Harvard Univeristy Press, 1999).

P. Middleton, *Radical Martyrdom and Cosmic Conflict in Early Christianity* (T&T Clark, 2006).

PAUL MIDDLETON

MARY MAGDALENE The figure of Mary Magdalene is mentioned twelve times in the NT. She is characterized in each of the four Gospels as a follower of Jesus. Her name presumably refers to her being from the town of Magdala Nunayya on the Sea of Galilee. Luke claims that she had at one time been possessed by seven demons, and that she was one of a number of women who provided material support to Jesus and the twelve APOSTLES during their ministry (8:2–3). All four evangelists place her among the women who witnessed Jesus' crucifixion and found his tomb empty on Easter morning. John describes her as the first person to see the risen Lord and, correspondingly, as the first to proclaim Jesus' resurrection to the other disciples (20:11–18; cf. Mark 16:9). On the basis of this account, she is sometimes called the 'apostle to the apostles' (*apostola apostolorum*).

In later Church TRADITION a variety of legends about Mary became popular. In the third century she began to be identified with the Mary of Bethany mentioned in John 11:1–2 and thereby with the sinner in Luke 7:36–50. Based on this conflation, Mary came to be regarded in western (but not Orthodox) Christianity as a repentant prostitute. This unflattering view of Mary's past may have emerged in part as a reaction against streams of early Christianity in which she was viewed as a figure of authority (e.g., the *Gospel of Philip* 59 describes her as one of Jesus' closest companions, and the *Gospel of Mary* 10 describes her as having received secret wisdom from Jesus).

IAN A. MCFARLAND

MARY OF NAZARETH: see MARIOLOGY.

MASS, CANON OF The canon is the historic PRAYER of the EUCHARIST in the Catholic Church used predominantly in the West until the REFORMATION. Following the Council of TRENT it became the sole Eucharistic prayer of the Church until the revised missal of 1970.

The canon's origins have been sought among Jewish meal prayers, the *Apostolic Tradition*, and early Latin euchology, with mixed success. Despite valiant attempts, it is impossible to show direct or indirect lineage between first-century Jewish table prayers, the biblical narratives of the Last Supper, and the Latin prayer that emerged in the late fourth century. Investigations in light of a model Eucharistic prayer in the *Apostolic Tradition* were based upon its (now refuted) attribution to Hippolytus (*ca* 170–*ca* 235). If Pope Damasus I (r. 366–84) initiated the adoption of Latin for the liturgy, then looking beyond him for the canon's origins will be unrewarding: parts are probably translations from existing Greek prayers, others are Latin renderings or compositions.

Leaving aside the unreliable *Liber Pontificalis*, which attributes elements of the canon to second-century popes, the first evidence of its structure and content is provided by Ambrose of Milan (*ca* 340–97). The developed form emerged between the time of Pope Leo I (r. 440–60), who composed numerous prefaces, and Pope Gregory I (r. 590–604), who revised existing material. Another attempt to provide an authoritative Roman missal was initiated by Charlemagne through Alcuin (*ca* 740–804), who revised the *Gregorian Sacramentary* using Gallican missals and is credited with introducing the prayers for the dead. Subsequent amendments included 'Amens', new prefaces, seasonal material, and local SAINTS. The Protestant Reformers objected to the sacrificial imagery and interpretation of the canon, and although some (e.g., M. LUTHER, T. CRANMER) initially only amended it, the canon was ultimately rejected by them. In the Catholic Church, however, the 1570 missal fixed the text of the canon for the next 400 years. The twentieth-century LITURGICAL MOVEMENT and new liturgical scholarship provoked some calls for revision before VATICAN COUNCIL II; however, the 1970 missal contained only minor changes. More radical were three new prayers modelled on early eastern Eucharistic prayers; and, with the further publication of Eucharistic prayers for use with children, the place of the canon has diminished.

The canon's presentation as separate paragraphs, known by their opening words in Latin, has provoked two distinct scholarly responses: a historical approach seeking the origin and development of each paragraph; and a literary approach promoting the canon's essential unity over its apparent inconsistency. The canon does contain literary devices to connect the paragraphs, for example in the use of 'therefore', but, as will be seen from the summary below, there is considerable repetition, for example, of petitions for the offering, such that the prayer gives the impression of being a collection of separate prayers.

The variable preface (*Vere dignum*) responds to the opening dialogue with a statement of thanksgiving related to the feast or LECTIONARY theme, and concludes by recalling the concelebration of the ANGELS as the congregation sings the *Sanctus* (Isa. 6.3) and *Benedictus* (Matt. 21.9). The first offering petition occurs in *Te igitur*, where the Father is asked to accept and bless what is offered and for whom (the Church, the pope, and bishops), continued by a petition for the salvation of those present (*Memento domine*). Medieval missals separated the variable prefaces and congregational parts so that medieval commentators, the Council of TRENT and some modern writers erroneously considered the canon to begin with the *Te igitur*, not the opening dialogue.

After remembering the dead in general there follows a list of saints (Mary, the apostles, and early Roman martyrs) whose fellowship and prayers are invoked (*Communicantes*). The following two paragraphs (*Hanc igitur* and *Quam oblationem*) both contain further requests that the offering be acceptable to God; the latter has been considered as an *epiclesis* (i.e., an invocation of the HOLY SPIRIT) over the bread and wine that they may become the body and blood of Christ, although nowhere in the canon is the Holy Spirit explicitly invoked. With few exceptions a recitation of the events of the Last Supper form a central feature of all Eucharistic prayers. Commonly known as the 'Institution Narrative', it paraphrases the biblical accounts. In the canon this section (*Qui pridie*) recounts Christ's actions and words at the Last Supper and expands them with some particular features, including the description of Christ's 'holy and venerable hands' before the words over the bread and cup.

It is customary in eucharistic prayers to situate the Last Supper in the context of Christ's ministry – especially his death and RESURRECTION. In the Canon the passion, resurrection, and ASCENSION are mentioned only in the paragraph *Unde et memores*, where they are followed by yet another petition for the acceptance of the offering. The biblical sacrifices of Abel, ABRAHAM, and Melchizedek are invoked as precedents for the acceptance of this 'holy sacrifice' (*Supra quae*). There follow the *Supplices te rogamus* petitions, which ask that the people receive the fruits of the EUCHARIST, ratified at the heavenly altar by the transfer and return of the gifts by an angel. Once again there are intercessions for the dead (*Memento etiam*), followed by a further list of saints in the *Nobis quoque*. The canon concludes with the Trinitarian doxology (*Per ipsum*) and a congregational 'Amen'.

The canon repeatedly petitions God concerning the offering: it is the divine acceptance which consecrates the elements, not an invocation of the Holy Spirit. Correspondingly, there is no formal epiclesis, or invocation of the Spirit, despite a tradition identifying *Quam oblationem* as a consecratory epiclesis and *Supplices te rogamus* as a communion epiclesis. TRADITION and ritual practice have identified the *Qui pridie* as consecratory, but its grammatical dependence upon the preceding and following petitions suggests that it serves rather to place the offering in narrative context. Contemporary interpretations emphasize the consecratory effect of the whole prayer.

B. Botte and C. Mohrmann, *L'Ordinaire de la messe: texte critique, traduction et études* (Cerf, 1953).

J. A. Jungmann, *The Mass of the Roman Rite: Its Origins and Development* (Benziger, 1951–5).

E. Mazza, *The Eucharistic Prayers of the Roman Rite* (Liturgical Press, 1986).

JULIETTE DAY

Materialism At first sight, the concerns of materialism seem to be diametrically opposed to the concerns of theology. If God is Spirit (John 4:24), and if the term 'spirit' is understood in a disembodied sense, matter appears to be foreign to theology. This impression of an irreconcilable conflict between materialism and theology is further confirmed if materialism is understood as an exclusive concern for matter without interest in concerns for spirit or mind.

There are indeed materialisms (e.g., scientific naturalism) that focus on matter to the exclusion of everything else. In this tradition human feelings and emotions, for instance, are understood as nothing more than biochemical processes in the brain, and they are to be treated as such. Another form of unilateral materialism holds that economic processes totally determine cultural and intellectual developments. Insights derived from these perspectives merit serious consideration in Christian theology, which has frequently been marked by an unwarranted idealism that lacks any concern for how theological ideas might be shaped by material realities. It is thus appropriate that the relationship between mind and brain has been an important feature of contemporary dialogue between theology and the natural sciences, and that economic processes have been an important focus for many liberation theologies.

There are other forms of materialism, however, that are of more fundamental interest to theology and that overcome the spectre of determinism, which is so often the result of unilateral materialisms. Dialectical materialism holds that material and spiritual phenomena influence each other in a mutual relationship. In the work of K. Marx (1818–83), the way material economic processes shape the world – including the world of the mind and spirit – is investigated with great seriousness, but the result is not determinism. Later thinkers in the tradition of dialectical materialism, like J. C. Mariátegui (1894–1930) and A. Gramsci (1891–1937), studied how the world of the mind and spirit, as expressed in culture and religion, shapes and reshapes material realities, just as it is shaped by them.

Christian theology itself is grounded in material realities. The incarnation of God in Jesus Christ is the primary example: 'The word became flesh and lived among us' (John 1:14). Furthermore, Christ became flesh in a particular body, in a particular place and time, in a particular social location, the son of a day labourer and an unwed mother at the margins of the Roman Empire, in solidarity with the 'least of these'. Christianity has often overlooked the importance of these facts, and the Apostles' Creed and the Nicene Creed make no reference to the earthly ministry of Christ. Yet this tendency of spiritualization and abstraction has never gone uncontested, and it can be argued that the Gospels were at least in part written to combat it (see, e.g., John 19:33–5).

These materialist strands in Christian theology have their roots in the Jewish traditions, where God creates heaven and earth and reaffirms this commitment to the material world and its rhythms once and for all after the Great Flood (Gen. 8:21–2). In the Hebrew Bible, the concern of theology is not the divine as it relates to non-material realities or the afterlife (an idea that appears only very late) but life in this world and its wellbeing. Spirituality, in this context, is inextricably bound up with the material at every turn.

Joerg Rieger

Maximus the Confessor A former secretary in the Byzantine imperial court in Constantinople, Maximus the Confessor (588–662) withdrew to monastic life in Asia Minor, moving later to Carthage with other refugee monks from the Arab invasions. As a theologian, Maximus' career can be divided into two broad phases. In the first he emerged as a prolific monastic pedagogue, authoring spiritual and exegetical works and theological commentary on earlier patristic tradition, most notably (in his *Book of Ambiguities*) on the work of Gregory of Nazianzus (see Cappadocian Fathers) and Dionysius the Areopagite. In the second phase Maximus was consumed by an extended battle against imperially sponsored monothelite Christology.

Maximus followed Irenaeus, Origen, Athanasius, and the Cappadocian Fathers in articulating a cosmic theology that envisioned the whole economy of creation, redemption, and deification (or recreation) through the lens of the incarnation. As the Creator-*Logos* through whom all things were made (Col. 1:16), Jesus Christ integrated within himself the *logoi*, the graced principles or patterns of all created existents, and projected the true end (*telos*) and consummation of the created universe. As the New Adam (Rom. 5:12–21; 1 Cor. 15:22, 45) he both restored humanity to its true origin (*genesis*) and, by his virginal conception under the conditions still of human birth (*gennêsis*), redeemed human passibility (*pathos*) as a whole. In the unfolding work of his passion, death, resurrection, and ascension Christ pioneered a whole new eschatological 'mode' (*tropos*) of human existence.

Though forcefully criticizing Origen's speculative cosmology, Maximus significantly rehabilitated Origen's ascetical gospel, especially as expanded by Evagrius Ponticus (345–99), whose insights Maximus appropriated despite the condemnation of Origenism and Evagrius in the Council of Constantinople of 553. Maximus' own spiritual doctrine focused substantially on the outworking of baptismal grace, the cultivation of *agapē* and the virtues, the reintegration of the human will, the transformation of the affections supporting the soul's desire for God, and the progressive contemplation of the Trinity – all within the context of participation in the deifying mystery of Jesus Christ.

Maximus' Christology was galvanized in the refiner's fire of the monothelite controversy, which he entered in earnest in Carthage in 645 in a public debate with Pyrrhus, the former patriarch of Constantinople (r. 638–41). Here and in some carefully argued theological and polemical *Opuscula* he defended the two wills of Christ as proper to his divine and human natures and as implicit in the Christological definition of Chalcedon. Having concurred with Leontius of Byzantium (*ca* 485–*ca* 545) that the person of Christ is not only 'from' two natures and 'in' two natures but 'is' the two natures compositely, Maximus developed a refined interpretation of the internal hypostatic mystery by which Jesus' human will submitted to the divine so as to effect salvation. Christ's agony in Gethsemane (Matt. 26:42 and pars.) became his definitive exegetical evidence.

Having joined with Pope Martin I (r. 649–53) in a council in Rome to condemn imperial monothelitism in 649, Maximus was deported, tried in Constantinople, exiled, and eventually died in Lazika (Georgia). His epithet 'Confessor' stems from his defence of dyothelitism, which was vindicated by the third Council of Constantinople of 680–1.

A. Louth, *Maximus the Confessor* (Routledge, 1996).

L. Thunberg, *Microcosm and Mediator: The Theological Anthropology of Maximus the Confessor*, 2nd edn (Open Court, 1995).

Paul M. Blowers

Mechthild of Magdeburg Mechthild of Magdeburg (*ca* 1208–*ca* 1282) was a German mystic and poet associated with the Beguines, a lay women's movement that flourished during the twelfth and thirteenth centuries but waned amid accusations of heresy. Mechthild received her first 'greeting' from the Holy Spirit at the age of twelve, left home to join a community of Beguines in Magdeburg in her twenties, and wrote her book, *The Flowing Light of the Godhead*, beginning in her forties. The courtly imagery of her poetry suggests that she was born and educated among minor nobility, yet her theology emerged largely from her personal visions and her life with the Beguines. Mechthild moved to the Cistercian convent at Helfta at the end of her life, probably driven there by poor health and criticism of her book.

Mechthild's work exemplifies a new trend towards vernacular writing that made room for women's voices alongside Scholastic and monastic idioms. Her visions and poetry express the mutual passion of God and the soul, in which fleeting experiences of mystical union alternate with the estranged longing of the earthbound, embodied human condition. The metaphor of fluidity running throughout *The Flowing Light* is one of Mechthild's most significant contributions to Christian thought. Imagery of flowing, dissolving, rising, and sinking conveys a matrix of relations – between God and world, soul and body, and self and other – that defies rigid binaries and hierarchies. Mechthild thus offers a subversive vision of love from the margins of mainstream theology: the 'Holy Spirit flows by nature downhill' (*Flowing* 2.26) to the most humble.

See also Mystical Theology.

F. J. Tobin, *Mechthild von Magdeburg: A Medieval Mystic in Modern Eyes* (Camden House, 1995).

Michelle Voss Roberts

Mennonite Theology Mennonites locate their origin in the radical wing of the Reformation. These radical reformers were scornfully labelled Anabaptists, referring to their practice of rebaptism. This practice reflected their theological understanding of the call to follow Christ in all of life, including offering primary allegiance to Christ and his community (i.e., the Church) rather than to the civil community. Many contemporary Mennonites reach back to their Anabaptist roots to define their core identity. For this reason the central beliefs of the early Anabaptists serve as an appropriate reference point for understanding Mennonite theology today.

'Fear of the Lord' is one of the most common expressions found in early Anabaptist testimonies and writings. This emphasis reflected Anabaptists' vivid awareness of the presence of God, coupled with a great consciousness of their need for repentance. The possibility of new birth through the power of God entailed a yielding to God, the only One they believed was worthy of worship and total allegiance. Thousands of Anabaptists were martyred for this allegiance. In the face of death many quoted Scripture in a way that spoke of their fear of the Lord – the only One with the prerogative to judge their faithfulness (see Martyrdom).

Contrary to accusations that early Anabaptists were Pelagian (see Pelagianism), historical writings evidence that they generally believed in both human sin and the need for redemption through Christ. Menno Simons (1496–1561), a leader among Dutch Anabaptists after whom Mennonites are named, testifies: 'Outwardly before men I was moral, chaste, and liberal, and none reproved my conduct. But inwardly I was full of dead men's bones, stench and worms' (*Writings* 77). Simons writes that he

> prayed to God with sighs and tears that He would give to me, a sorrowing sinner, the gift of His grace, create within me a clean heart, and graciously through the merits of the crimson blood of Christ forgive my unclean walk and frivolous easy life and bestow upon me wisdom, Spirit [and] courage . . . so that I might . . . make known . . . His glory (*Writings* 671).

He goes on to say that he did come to know the 'illumination of the Holy Ghost', 'the gracious favor and gift of God' (*Writings* 669). What sets Simons and other Anabaptists apart from many other reformers of the sixteenth century is their refusal to embrace justification by grace through faith *alone*. As Simons wrote, 'Show us one single word in the whole Bible saying that an unbelieving, refractory, carnal man without regeneration and true repentance was or can be saved simply because he boasts of faith and the death of Christ' (*Writings* 95).

Properly to understand why rebaptizing was viewed as a crime for which many Anabaptists were executed requires an acquaintance with the political arrangements in early sixteenth-century Europe. In the context of European Christendom mandatory infant baptism provided the means through which everyone was registered as a citizen as well as a Church member. As such, infant baptism served to affirm the alignment of Church and State. Upon reaching maturity, citizens reaffirmed their loyalty to this arrangement through the swearing of civil oaths, acts considered vital for the health of the civil community.

This is not to say that for Anabaptists themselves baptism was not primarily a theological act. It was. It followed new birth, what Austrian Anabaptist H. Schlaffer (d. 1528) referred to as 'the baptism of fire ... the ardor of the love of God and the neighbor in the heart' (Snyder, *Footsteps* 71). Baptism was a public response to what God had done, an act of being incorporated into the body of Christ. It thus served as Anabaptists' defining oath, their covenant with God and the people of God. This baptismal oath defined their spiritual relationship with God *and* their embodied personal and social existence. J. Yoder (1927–97) has argued that this is perhaps the most radical insight of the Anabaptists. Theologically, this returned them to the biblical idea that the Church comprises those who have believed and said yes to God's offer of salvation. This led to what sociologists have called *believers'* Churches. Put differently, it named both the visibility of the Church *and* the visibility of that which is not the Church – the world.

In light of their understanding of the community of believers, Anabaptists interpreted Scripture together. Brothers and sisters, educated and uneducated, sought to discern together – with leadership but fundamentally under the active guidance of the Holy Spirit – what Scripture was saying. They determined to respond in faithfulness to what they heard through Scripture. As H. Denck (*ca* 1495–1527), a South German Anabaptist, famously put it: 'No one can know Christ unless that person follows after him in life, and no one may follow him unless that person has first known him' (*Schriften* 2.45). The testimony of jailers or executioners often expressed astonishment that illiterate peasants had memorized considerable portions of Scripture, attesting to the seriousness with which they 'read' Scripture together.

The communal study of Scripture led Anabaptists to hear Jesus' call to love and serve their neighbours and their enemies. The practice of footwashing served to remind them that they were following Christ, the One who cleansed them and called them to serve. In response to hearing that the gospel of Jesus Christ was 'good news to the poor', many Anabaptists sympathized with 'peasants' revolts'. Expressing their protests in theological terms, peasants appealed for relief from excessive taxation and for access to forests and streams for hunting and fishing. J. Stayer (b. 1935) contends that Anabaptists, many of whom were themselves peasants, embodied the concerns of the peasants' revolts after the revolts themselves ended, through the creation of structures for sharing their possessions so as to ensure that no one among them was in need. Also, most Anabaptists refused to kill the Muslim Turks, who were perceived to be enemies of Christendom. They likewise refused to kill their persecutors, many of whom claimed to be brothers in Christ.

These core convictions and practices of early Anabaptists – love of neighbour and enemy, communal interpretation and discernment, conversion and faithfulness, believer's baptism and believers' baptism, and a vivid awareness of the living and active presence of God among believers – continue to resonate in contemporary Mennonite theology. Mennonite theologian J. Yoder, more than anyone else, has translated Anabaptist ideas into contemporary theology and ethics in a way that has garnered wide academic respect and in many cases has changed paradigms. In the 1950s Yoder studied theology with K. Barth and the Scriptures with O. Cullmann (1902–99) and W. Eichrodt (1890–1978) at the University of Basel. He also wrote his doctoral thesis there on the disputations between the magisterial Reformers and the developing Anabaptist movement in the 1520s and 1530s in Switzerland. During a career spanning more than forty years Yoder wrote more than a dozen books and hundreds of articles, but it is his *Politics of Jesus* (1972) that both conveyed many of his central passions and established his reputation as one of the most influential theological ethicists in the second half of the twentieth century. Here we see at work a careful Scripture scholar, a subtle theological mind and a brilliant polemicist. This book, along with Yoder's other writings, has convinced many outside the Mennonite tradition to take seriously the social and political dimensions of the gospel of Jesus Christ – and their claims upon the life of the body of Christ. Moreover, his powerful arguments have caused more than a few to at least give serious consideration to the varied implications of shaping their lives to reflect love for enemies as well as neighbours.

Yoder's witness is still very much alive today partly because his most famous 'convert', S. Hauerwas (b. 1940), is himself very influential. Though Hauerwas is much more than simply a convert of Yoder's, his writings frequently point the reader to Yoder. In addition to affirming Yoder's pacifism, he stresses the centrality of Jesus for moral as well as doctrinal theology, and he sees the vital connection of ethics to the life of the body of Christ, so that the most important ethical task of the Church is to *be* the Church. Hauerwas has enriched and broadened contemporary understanding of Yoder through an energetic retrieval of virtue ethics, as well as through creative engagement with a broad range of issues and an array of contemporary thinkers. Both he and Yoder have reconfigured the field of Christian ethics while also influencing other theological disciplines. Though both would point all Christians fundamentally to Jesus (and the biblical witness that finds its focal point in him), both have also known that some of the reading strategies for seeing Jesus were acquired from Anabaptist witnesses.

T. N. Finger, *A Contemporary Anabaptist Theology* (InterVarsity Press, 2004).

M. T. Nation, *John Howard Yoder: Mennonite Patience, Evangelical Witness, Catholic Convictions* (Eerdmans, 2006).

C. A. Snyder, *Following in the Footsteps of Christ: The Anabaptist Tradition* (Orbis, 2004).

J. C. Wenger, ed., *The Complete Writings of Menno Simons* (Herald Press, 1956).

Mark Thiessen Nation

Merton, Thomas A native of Prades in southern France, Thomas Merton (1915–68) was educated in French and English boarding schools before matriculating at Clare College, Cambridge, in 1933. In January 1935 he entered New York City's Columbia University where he earned BA and MA degrees in English literature. Merton was provisionally baptized a Catholic on 16 November 1938, following his conversion experience narrated in *The Seven Storey Mountain* (1948). Important early Catholic influences were neo-Scholastic philosophers J. Maritain (1882–1973) and É. Gilson. On 10 December 1941, he entered the Cistercian Abbey of Gethsemani in Kentucky where he was known as 'Louis' and spent twenty-seven years as a contemplative, spiritual writer, poet, essayist, social critic, and catalyst for inter-faith dialogue.

His early spiritual writings such as *Seeds of Contemplation* and *Thoughts in Solitude* reflect the wisdom of the Desert Fathers, monastic formation and its disciplines, and emphasis upon silence, solitude, and the liberation of the 'true self'. In the 1940s and early 1950s he wrote significant religious poetry. Merton cultivated the apophatic mystical tradition, influenced by John of the Cross (1542–91) and Meister Eckhart (see Apophatic Theology, Mystical Theology). His theology was Augustinian, emphasizing the action of grace on the unaided will and the primacy of love of God and neighbour. *Contemplative Prayer* (1969) gathers Merton's most mature spiritual reflections, integrating the way of unknowing and darkness (spiritual dread) with a growing sense of the activist contemplative's responsibility to the Church and world.

In the last decade of his life, Merton reclaimed a commitment to the world beyond the cloister with urgent social criticism in works such as *Conjectures of a Guilty Bystander* (1966) and *Faith and Violence* (1968). Social-ethics concerns included the Holocaust, racism, nonviolence, consumerism, 'mass-man', the 'post-Christian' world, technology, peacemaking, and dialogue. When Nicaraguan E. Cardenal (b. 1925) arrived in 1957 as a novice at Gethsemani, he awakened Merton to Latin American social, political, and economic realities that presaged liberation theologies. His poetics and spirituality were influenced through contacts with a circle of Latin American poets including P. Cuadra (1912–2002) and O. Paz (1914–98). During a decade of correspondence, Polish poet C. Milosz (1911–2004) challenged Merton to refocus his wrestling with the role of the contemplative in a world of action by grasping religion as a personal vision. The result was Merton's series of existentially informed literary-critical essays exploring the religious transcendental freedom that he discovered in the work of B. Pasternak (1890–1960), W. Faulkner (1897–1962), A. Camus (1913–60), and F. O'Connor (1925–64).

The frontier of inter-religious dialogue engaged Merton with Judaism, Islam, Buddhism, and other world religions. The desire for dialogue with Asian contemplatives led him to three months of travel in late 1968. He died from accidental electrocution at the Bangkok Red Cross, where he was speaking at a conference with western monastic leaders. Merton's writings endure as a matrix for twenty-first-century Christians seeking mature spiritual identity through contemplative and mystical practices. His reflections and personal witness are prescient catalysts for social justice initiatives and inter-faith dialogue.

G. Kilcourse, *Ace of Freedoms: Thomas Merton's Christ* (University of Notre Dame Press, 1993).

M. Mott, *The Seven Mountains of Thomas Merton* (Houghton Mifflin, 1984).

George Kilcourse

Mestizaje The label of *mestizaje* was first used in the Americas to identify the mixed progeny of Spanish and indigenous people. At different times, in different places, and over the years *mestizaje* became identified with independence, cultural assimilation, and the national ethnocultural interest and agendas of the ruling classes of the countries of today's Latin America. More recently, Latino/a theologians have appropriated *mestizaje* to identify the presence of indigenous, African, and Spanish culture in Latino/a culture and religion. Latino/a theologians in the USA have used the multivalent character of *mestizaje* in four key ways: (1) to reclaim their mixed cultural heritage; (2) to identify their present condition of social exclusion and ethnocultural discrimination, and attitude of resistance against the dominant Anglo culture of the country; (3) to describe the Latino/a experience of cultural 'in-betweenness' in the complex process of identity formation as a people; and (4) to name the characteristically mixed and complex religious world of Latino/as, expressed in their religious symbols by weaving together indigenous, African, and Spanish-European elements.

Despite the important role *mestizaje* played when Latino/a theology was first launched, subsequent generations of Latino/a theologians are beginning to challenge some of the limitations of the term in disallowing indigenous and African–Latino/a voices outside the paradigm of *mestizaje*, because of its potentially culturally homogenizing force. It is also being complexified by the various communities in Latin America and over the world that are reclaiming *mestizaje* as an appropriate category to describe their own historical reality and experiences.

N. Medina, *Mestizaje: (Re)Mapping 'Race,' Culture, and Faith in Latina/o Catholicism* (Orbis, 2009).

NÉSTOR MEDINA

METAPHYSICS The adjective 'metaphysical' is in both religious and non-religious contexts often used loosely and in a broadly undefined way to signal a concern with certain points of reference – e.g., the divine, the supernatural, the noumenal, the incorporeal, the religiously visional, etc. – that are taken to be real even though they are not physically or spatio-temporally sensible. Under its more rigorous academic definition, however, the philosophical discipline of 'metaphysics' has a more exact denotation that makes the term less readily amenable to religious or theological application.

Although there is continuing dispute about the intended meaning of 'metaphysics' as it was applied to a group of Aristotelian writings by a later editor, what the term has come most commonly to designate after Aristotle (384–322 BC) is that exercise of philosophy concerned with 'the first causes and principles of things' (*Meta.* 981b29). Metaphysics as such is concerned with investigating the most basic or general kinds of questions that human beings ask as they reflect critically upon themselves, the world, and their place in the world: questions of identity and composition, quality and quantity, space and time, causality, modality and reality, 'the meaning of life', and, most basic of all, the question of existence itself, or of 'being *qua* being' in Aristotelian terminology (see ARISTOTELIANISM). Thus, what we know today as the discipline of 'ontology', as the philosophical science of existence or being, has traditionally taken the primary place in metaphysical questioning.

Theology faces certain fundamental problems in speaking 'ontologically' about God and thus 'metaphysically' about God. For while theology must of course be able to affirm that God really exists (Heb. 11:6) and that God is the Creator of all that is, it does not suppose itself thereby to be affirming that God exists in the same way that created things exist, or that God 'is' in the same way that created things 'are'. In other words, it does not view God's eternal and immortal 'being' or 'existence' as merely another being or 'existent' among other existents. This means also that God's 'being' or reality cannot appear within the essentially comparative structures of any natural ontology within metaphysics. To assume that we could place God's infinite and eternal 'being' within an intellectual endeavour concerned with the existence of finite things would be to engage in the error of what is today spoken of, usually pejoratively, as 'onto-theology'. In fact this error is exactly what T. AQUINAS recognizes better than he is often given credit for by his critics. For, as Aquinas stipulates, even the very 'being' or existence of God (i.e., not only what theology also speaks of as God's attributes or perfections) must be spoken of '*ana*logically' and thus indirectly, and not (as we would say today) '*onto*logically', that is, not directly within a cognitive ordering of being.

It will be helpful, therefore, to distinguish very roughly between three different kinds of dispositions that have been assumed with regard to the nature of metaphysics as a legitimate philosophical exercise: (1) a 'classical' view of metaphysics which predominated in various forms from early Greek thought through to seventeenth-century rationalism; (2) metaphysics after the rise of modern science, especially in light of D. Hume's (1711–76) and I. KANT's critiques of the classical approaches; and (3) metaphysics as it is taught and pursued today in the so-called Anglo-American 'analytical' schools of thought.

In its 'classical' manifestations the discipline of metaphysics was engaged in as one form or another of what today is often referred to as 'metaphysical realism', meaning the postulation of a supposed objectively real 'suprasensible realm' surpassing or lying beyond the physical (hence '*meta*physical') or material world of space and time we live in. This was understood as a sphere 'out there', an objectively existing or 'subsisting' realm of unchanging and constant realities which are not susceptible to the transience and passingness of sensibly embodied existence, and which thus 'transcend' our own embodied life in space and time.

It is generally accurate to say that metaphysical questioning here was usually, at least early on, pursued roughly along either Platonic or Aristotelian lines of thought, even in theology. Those following Plato (*ca* 430–*ca* 345 BC) approached the question of suprasensible reality by appealing to what were postulated as the eternal and ultimately real Platonic 'Forms' or 'Ideas' like 'the good', 'the true', or 'the beautiful' (see PLATONISM). These meta-physical Forms were seen as having their being or essence in themselves, in suprasensible purity and perfection; and the particular empirical things constituting and encountered in sensibly embodied life were then deemed to have their subsidiary integrity of character and identity to the greater or lesser degrees that they 'participate' in (i.e., reflect or 'instantiate') these Forms.

Those following Aristotle approached metaphysics somewhat differently. The direction followed here did not proceed from the higher reality and perfection of the Forms down to their imperfect instantiations in empirical particulars, but rather began from empirical particulars and proceeded from there to underlying suprasensible 'substances' or 'essences'. In all cases, however, what was sought in the metaphysically real was something essentially unchanging, reliable, and constant; something not susceptible to the contingencies, vicissitudes, and transience of passing and corruptible spatio-temporal existence. Christian theologians during this time often deemed further that this suprasensible, 'metaphysical' reality also afforded a certain leverage to address questions about the reality of God, since divinity likewise transcends the corruption and decay of sensible or empirical reality in the extensive magnitudes of space and time.

In the seventeenth-century RATIONALISM of the early modern period, substantialist metaphysics or metaphysical realism reached a kind of zenith, through a new and speculatively sharpened reinforcement of the earlier 'pre-modern' metaphysics of substances and essences. G. Leibniz (1646–1716), for example, located the elementary and metaphysically real components of nature in 'simple substances' or windowless 'monads' which, having neither parts nor spatially extensive dynamism, are dynamically inert. R. Descartes (1596–1650) likewise located the elementary and foundational basis of human being not physically in sensible embodiment, but rather meta-physically in the '*thinking* substance'. Others, such as B. Spinoza (1632–77), can be added to this group. But what brings this otherwise disparate set of metaphysical thinkers together under the designation of 'seventeenth-century rationalism' is the shared supposition that 'pure reason' by itself, unaided by any sensible input or experience, which always introduces misapprehension, confusion, and error, is able to give us the clearest and most certain insight into the true underlying metaphysical 'nature of things'.

This seventeenth-century rationalism was at its heart precisely the quintessential 'project of pure reason' that Kant, in his *Critique of Pure Reason* (1781) would expressly bring under sustained attack as the 'old metaphysics', which he saw as systemically afflicted with the error of what he polemically called 'dogmatism' (i.e., an overreaching and thus illegitimate activity of the purely speculative use of reason by which it makes claims to objective metaphysical realities in ways that cannot themselves be rationally justified). In other words, Kant argued that rationalism's reification of its metaphysical 'substances', 'essences', 'substrates', 'monads', and so on, is itself an *ir*rational move. Kant's objective, however, was not to destroy metaphysics per se, but rather to return it to its proper place and full critically rational dignity. And he did so by introducing a more 'modest' metaphysics, which no longer inadmissibly reifies into objective realities what reason itself can only show to be its own purest ideas, but which concerns itself instead merely with the ways in which reason, as a 'faculty of unity', must comport itself as it searches into the conditions for the possibility of human experience of self and the world.

Whatever the subsequent disagreements with Kant and departures from him, continental philosophy changed fundamentally after him. Even though defenders of the Platonic metaphysics of emanation and effusion still remain today (not least in some theological circles), it is generally accurate to say that the effects of NATURAL SCIENCE and Kant's critique of traditional metaphysics proved so forceful that theology, just as much as subsequent philosophy, has found itself unable any longer to sustain its questioning about God and the world through straightforward substantialist appeals to a putative objectively real suprasensible metaphysical 'realm' underlying physical reality.

The theological reaction to this collapse of substantialist metaphysics has been mixed. Several important theological voices have taken it as an opportunity to refocus fundamental theological questioning back to a robustly incarnational centre in sensibly embodied life. But in both the nineteenth and twentieth centuries, by far the more prominent and influential reactions to the collapse of objectivist metaphysics have been to move in the opposite direction: in following post-Kantian idealistic and romantic thought, to turn to the 'non-objective' metaphysical domains of human 'subjectivity' or to mental domains of 'inwardness' in order to account for the intelligibility of its foundational claims about the relation of God to the world (see LIBERAL THEOLOGY). A further and currently even more predominating trend has been towards the theological restriction of fundamental questioning about God to the theoretically self-securing domains of grammar, language, hermeneutics, and doctrine (see POSTLIBERAL THEOLOGY). In pursuing this path theology follows in the footsteps of the decidedly anti-metaphysical 'linguistic turn' which emerged almost simultaneously on several intellectual fronts in early twentieth-century thought and therefore with massive impact.

The so-called 'analytical school' of philosophy in North America and Britain has in one way been similarly anti-metaphysical in orientation. However, its grounds for the rejection of classical metaphysics are different, in as much as it usually has the more radical Humean (rather than the more nuanced Kantian) critique of metaphysics as its implicit point of orientation. Yet in another way this school has also fostered a resurgence of metaphysical interest as it focuses around particular kinds of problems: the relation of mind and BODY, the constitution and identity of material objects (mereology), the problem of FREE WILL in relation to the findings of modern science, *de dicto* and *de re* modality, the REALISM/ANTI-REALISM debate and so on. Terms like 'ontology', 'substance', 'subsistence', etc., arise here in new ways in the relation of physical materiality and language.

M. Heidegger, *Introduction to Metaphysics* (Yale University Press, 2000 [1953]).

I. Kant, *Prolegomena to Any Future Metaphysics* (Cambridge University Press, 2001 [1783]).

D. MacKinnon, *The Problem of Metaphysics* (Cambridge University Press, 1974).

W. Pannenberg, *Metaphysics and the Idea of God* (Eerdmans, 2001).

P. van Inwagen and D.W. Zimmerman, eds., *Metaphysics: The Big Questions* (Blackwell, 2008).

Paul D. Janz

METHODIST THEOLOGY Methodism emerged in the mid-eighteenth century as a renewal movement within the Church of England. The branch of this movement led by J. WESLEY and his brother Charles (1701–88) has grown through the past two centuries into a global family of Methodist Churches, in addition to spawning several Wesleyan 'holiness Churches' and conveying through the latter some characteristic theological emphases to the Pentecostal and charismatic movements (see CHARISMATIC MOVEMENT; PENTECOSTAL THEOLOGY). J. Wesley established the major theological precedents for this family of Churches, which reflect his commitments as an Anglican priest at the outset of the ENLIGHTENMENT who embraced key emphases from continental PIETISM.

Wesley was trained in and embraced the 'Anglican' reframing of the Church of England in the late seventeenth century, with its vision of providing a 'middle way' between the Reformed and Catholic Churches (see ANGLICAN THEOLOGY). Thus, while he stressed SCRIPTURE as the norm for theological reflection – at times referring to himself as 'a man of one book' – he also valued the creedal affirmations and theological voices of the early Church as guides in interpreting Scripture. Wesley's training at Oxford cultivated interest in several Greek patristic theologians. These added voices served as a counterweight to the dominant influence of AUGUSTINE's thought in western Christian theology on such issues as TOTAL DEPRAVITY, UNCONDITIONAL ELECTION, and pessimism about the possibility of attaining Christlikeness in this life. This counterweight allowed Wesley, like most Anglicans, to adopt a moderate ARMINIANISM and to stress the importance of 'holy living'.

Another Anglican trait which Wesley shared was affirmation of the contribution of reason to theological reflection. But he was uncomfortable with the rationalist stream of the emerging Enlightenment. Shaped by the Aristotelian tradition at Oxford (see ARISTOTELIANISM), Wesley valued reason not as an independent source but as a processor of knowledge, organizing and drawing inferences from the input of Scripture, TRADITION, and experience. As this suggests, Wesley aligned more with the empiricist stream of early Enlightenment thought, although he did not share the scepticism of advocates like D. Hume (1711–76). Rather, Wesley embraced the 'common-sense' assumptions that human knowledge is at best probable, not infallible, and that our sense impressions are generally reliable indicators of reality.

Attention to experience was also central to the Pietist dimension of the Methodist revival. Wesley championed a personal experience of assurance of God's love as typical of 'real Christianity'. This emphasis was expressed a few times in the strong contrast 'that ORTHODOXY, or right opinions, is, at best, but a very slender part of religion' (*Works* 9:254–5). When questioned, Wesley denied that he was dismissing all concern for DOCTRINE in Christian life; he was stressing that Christian life involved more than *mere* affirmation of correct doctrine.

But Wesley went on to suggest a hierarchy of significance among theological claims. He affirmed that there are core doctrinal convictions, central to the early CREEDS (TRINITY, INCARNATION, human SIN, ATONEMENT, etc.), that are essential to Christian life and constitutive of Christian identity. Those who deny these convictions place themselves outside the Christian fold. But Wesley was quick to insist that there is room for legitimate variation of 'opinion' in philosophical articulation of these core doctrines. Moreover, there are a number of theological debates that are less clearly defined in Scripture and the creeds, and are, correspondingly, less pivotal to authentic Christian life. In his sermon 'Catholic Spirit', Wesley encouraged allowing for alternative 'opinions' on these debates while maintaining Christian fellowship with all who agree on the 'main branches of Christian doctrine'. As an example, while Wesley staunchly rejected unconditional PREDESTINATION, he usually classed this difference with G. Whitefield (1714–70) and the Calvinist wing of the Methodist revival as a matter of 'opinion', affirming their full standing in the Church.

At the same time, Wesley tired of Calvinist Methodist preachers using preaching houses that he had built to turn audiences against Arminian theology. So Wesley developed the 'Model Deed', which restricted the pulpit in his preaching houses to those who preached in accordance with his four published volumes of *Sermons* (1746–60) and his *Explanatory Notes upon the New Testament* (1755). This set a precedent for specifically *Wesleyan* Methodists that their theological teaching and reflection should emulate not just Wesley's embrace of the core doctrines of the whole Christian family but also his characteristic 'opinions' on other major theological issues (while showing irenic openness to those of other 'opinions').

This precedent was formalized when the remnants of the Methodist societies in North America were gathered after the Revolutionary War and organized as the Methodist Episcopal Church in 1784. Wesley sent over for the new Church an abridged set of the Articles of Religion of the Church of England, to serve as the articulation of core Christian doctrine, while continuing the expectation of preaching in accordance with characteristic emphases as found in his *Sermons* and *Notes*. Although the two sides of this expectation are not formally adopted in every current branch of the Methodist family of Churches, the general expectation remains in place. So does Wesley's precedent of bringing tradition, reason, and experience into engagement with Scripture in theological reflection (see WESLEYAN QUADRILATERAL).

Wesley's response when asked about the distinctive doctrines of Methodism was often to deny that there were any, emphasizing instead a distinctive concern for spiritual life (e.g., *Works* 9:33). At other times he allowed that Methodists placed special emphasis upon certain traditional doctrines, particularly in the area of SOTERIOLOGY. Wesley's concern in this area was to reclaim the holistic account of the human problem and God's salvific response that is evident in Scripture. On one front this meant defending the universal reality of human spiritual need, in the face of idealized accounts of human nature by some Enlightenment thinkers. Wesley's longest single treatise was devoted to *The Doctrine of Original Sin* (1757). The treatise focuses less on debates over inherited guilt, or the modes of transmitting depravity, than on demonstrating the shared human experience of spiritual infirmity and bondage.

Turning the focus around, Wesley was equally concerned to reject depictions of depravity as the *final* word about humanity (or of all but the 'elect'). Convinced that 'God's mercy is over all God's works' (Ps. 145:9), Wesley insisted that God reaches out in love to all persons in their fallen condition. Through that encounter, which Wesley termed 'prevenient GRACE', God awakens sufficient awareness and upholds sufficient volitional integrity that we can *either* responsively embrace God's deeper salvific work in our lives *or* culpably resist it.

This brings us to Wesley's dominant soteriological concern: countering the tendency to restrict present salvation largely to forensic JUSTIFICATION. As he put it: 'By salvation I mean, not barely (according to the vulgar notion) deliverance from hell, or going to heaven, but a present deliverance from sin, a restoration of the soul to its primitive health' (*Works* 11:106). Wesley placed SANCTIFICATION at the centre of soteriology, valuing justification as the 'doorway' into this larger focus. He called his people to 'holiness of heart and life' nurtured in the full range of the 'means of grace', affirming the possibility of attaining *entire* sanctification, or 'Christian Perfection', in this life. The possibilities, limits, and dynamics of sanctification have been central to Methodist proclamation and debate ever since.

Given the coherence of the Christian world view, Wesley's focal concerns in soteriology were reflected in characteristic emphases (or 'opinions') within the other *loci* of theology. For example, he identified God's reigning attribute as LOVE – in specific contrast with sovereignty. Accordingly, he privileged a 'parent' analogy for God over the analogy of a sovereign lord. He also placed strong emphasis on the responsive relationship between God and humanity, which opened the door for many later Wesleyans to critique atemporal models of God's existence.

Wesley's most characteristic emphasis in CHRISTOLOGY was on valuing Christ 'in all his offices' – not just as the priest who atones for guilt, but also as the prophet who teaches the ways in which we are to live, and as the king who oversees the restoration of wholeness in our lives (see THREEFOLD OFFICE).

A characteristic that stood out to Wesley's peers was his heightened attention to the work of the HOLY SPIRIT. It begins with Wesley's stress on the ASSURANCE of God's pardoning love, or the 'witness of the Spirit', which evokes and empowers our responsive love for God and neighbour. This 'new birth' makes possible the journey of sanctification, or growth in the 'fruit of the Spirit'. Then there is Wesley's concern to reclaim (within the western tradition) the 'gifts of the Spirit', like the gift of preaching, for lay men and women.

Finally, it is important to note that Wesley's optimism about the transformative impact of the Spirit in individual lives led him to embrace an early form of POSTMILLENNIALISM in his later years. This embrace was reflected in his encouragement of the Methodist people to get involved not just in works of mercy but also in the work of social transformation.

John Wesley's era in Methodist theology was dominated by his contributions – sermons, catechisms, hymn collections, etc. Developments following his death were shaped by Methodism's transition into an independent Church. In England Methodists tended to align with the dissenting traditions, playing down many of the Anglican threads in Wesley's thought. In the USA the stronger pressure was a primitivist mentality that 'all we need is the Bible'. Moreover, in a situation where most Christians who accepted a role for theological standards conceived of them along the lines of J. CALVIN's *Institutes*, Wesley's *Sermons* did not measure up. This pushed Methodists to develop Scholastic compendiums of theology. These compendiums were generally conservative in scope and more 'Protestant' in tone than Wesley's precedent. The most prominent example is R. Watson's (1781–1833) *Theological*

Institutes (1823–4), the standard Methodist theology text for over fifty years.

Towards the end of the nineteenth century, Methodist theologians in both England and the USA were interacting more with currents in their culture. They also turned attention to the new theological trends being championed in Germany. This resulted, by the turn of the century, in a stream of 'modernist' or 'liberal' Methodist theologies. Mixed within this stream were concerns for cultural apologetics, for undergirding the Social Gospel, and for addressing the challenge of the historical and natural sciences. Many of these agendas resonated with Wesleyan emphases, and there was the occasional attempt to claim him as a forerunner. The more common tendency was to ignore Wesley's writings as products of an outmoded age.

In the mid-twentieth century the optimism of liberal theology was subject to critique by the movement known as neo-orthodoxy. Methodists who resonated with this critique, but who were less comfortable with the one-sided alternatives being championed, began to reclaim Wesley's soteriological balance. This renewed interest spawned an ongoing project to provide a critical edition of Wesley's works, and a growing range of scholarly engagements with Wesley's theology.

Far from encouraging parochialism, engagement with Wesley has led to interaction with his wide range of sources and a broadened dialogue with ecumenical Christianity. Similarly, attention to Wesley's proposed parallel between God's synergistic transformation of our lives and God's synergistic transformation of social–political structures has provided a fruitful perspective for engaging the various liberation theologies that emerged in the last third of the twentieth century (see Liberation Theology). Wesley's emphasis on the responsive nature of God's interaction with humanity has placed Methodists in prominent roles within debates over the adequacy of Process Theology and Open Theism. Finally, Wesley's underlying assumptions about the nature and purpose of theology have proved helpful in addressing issues of contextualization as Methodism has spread across the globe.

T. Campbell, *Methodist Doctrine: The Essentials* (Abingdon Press, 1999).
T. Langford, *Methodist Theology* (Epworth, 1998).
R. Maddox, *Responsible Grace: John Wesley's Practical Theology* (Kingswood Books, 1994).
C. Marsh *et al.*, *Methodist Theology Today* (Continuum, 2006).
G. Wainwright, *Methodists in Dialog* (Kingswood Books, 1995).
J. Wesley, *The Works of John Wesley*, ed. F. Baker and R. Heitzenrater (Abingdon Press, 1984–).

Randy L. Maddox

Miaphysitism Miaphysitism (from the Greek for 'one nature') is the name given to a wide range of perspectives upon Christology. A number of miaphysite theologies were condemned as heresies (e.g., Apollinarianism, Eutychianism), but the perspective was not necessarily heretical, and some of the greatest theologians of the early Church were miaphysites, including Cyril of Alexandria and Severus of Antioch (*ca* 465–*ca* 540).

To explore and assess the miaphysite perspective – the belief that in Christ we encounter '*one nature* of God the Word incarnate' – it is helpful to distinguish a number of overlapping strands. To begin with, it is important to clarify that *mia*physitism (which stresses the unity of the incarnate Christ) is not the same as *mono*physitism (according to which the Word's taking flesh undermines the integrity of Christ's humanity).

This distinction is helpful in appreciating the ways in which questions of *terminology* (the limitation of vocabulary) relate to questions of theological *instinct* in the early Church. Among post-Nicene theologians there was a general acceptance that only God can save, and that for 'saving' to take place there must be real engagement with real humanity. This double conviction threw up two different strategies. One was to stress the real *unity* of the divine and the human in Christ and thus the real engagement with humanity. This tended in a miaphysite direction (viz., *one* nature of God the Word incarnate). The other strategy was to stress on the undiminished *integrity* of both natures in Christ: we encounter *real* God and *real* humanity. This tended in a *dyo*physite direction (*two* natures).

As theologians developed their positions, theological instinct was often out of step with available terminology. That is, some theologians could have a burning understanding that Christ is one being, but not have an adequate way of expressing the oneness. There were a number of false starts, including that of Apollinaris (*ca* 310–*ca* 390), who depicted the union of the human and divine in organic terms as a *living union*, like that of body and mind in a person. His instincts were laudable, but his model and terminology (which suggested that the divine *Logos* replaced Christ's human mind) were inadequate. A more promising start was made by Cyril of Alexandria, when he explained that not all things which are *single* (i.e., having one nature) are *simple*. This more complex vision opened the way for stretching the vocabulary of 'oneness', though it took years for more adequate models to emerge.

Alongside Apollinaris' living-union model of Christ's oneness (which exercised lasting influence on the early Christian imagination), another model was to look at the ways substances mix. Mixture had been discussed by Aristotle, who distinguished between 'juxtaposition' (as of beans and wheat), 'confusion' (or flowing together, as when a cup of wine is absorbed by the sea), and 'mixture' (when two or more ingredients do not overwhelm each other, but balance each other, producing a third entity different from all of them). Another model was to look at the way fire apparently interpenetrates iron when it is red hot: they do not disturb or destroy each other, and there is no confusion, but they are totally inter-involved. In these cases, contemporary physics had a considerable bearing on how union could be conceived and expressed.

These models (or variations on them) mesmerized certain early Christian thinkers. They dominated the ways in which the incarnation was understood. And part of the difficulty was that these models illustrated union *in static terms*, so that the union of God and humanity in Christ came to be seen by many as something performed upon two static, pre-existing entities. Such static understandings of union brought out the most problematic tendencies of miaphysitism. For example, Julian of Halicarnassus (*fl.* 515) came adrift partly because he extended the fire model too far, arguing that just as the red hot coal becomes all fire, so the body of Christ becomes suffused with the divine GLORY. This suggested a kind of interior divinization, which threatened the reality of the human nature (see APHTHARTODOCETISM).

The greatest of the miaphysites, Cyril of Alexandria and Severus of Antioch, resisted seeing the union in static terms, because they did not see it as being an end in itself. Because the Word became incarnate *for our sake*, the union was always to be understood as something which was purposive, probing, healing, and creative – and thus as *dynamic*, not static. The greatest miaphysites maintained this dynamism by using language about *kenosis* (self emptying; cf. Phil. 2:7) and the picture of a journey (the eternal Word came down from heaven and returned there, clothed with our humanity; cf. John 16:28).

However, this developing theology tended to put more and more pressure upon the ability of the one nature terminology to express it. By the middle of the fifth century, the miaphysite paradigm was beginning to look rather old-fashioned. A change of meanings had gradually been taking place. In older terminology the three words *ousia*, *physis*, and *HYPOSTASIS* all meant much the same thing and referred to being. However, in developing the doctrine of the TRINITY, Basil of Caesarea (see CAPPADOCIAN FATHERS) had distinguished between *ousia* and *hypostasis*, and this distinction fed into Christological discussion as well, so that Christ was said at the Council of CHALCEDON to be one *hypostasis* in two *physeis*. The miaphysites of the fifth and sixth centuries reacted bitterly to Chalceon's two-nature paradigm and refused to accept the Council. They accused it of NESTORIANISM and separated to form their own miaphysite Churches, which today are called the ORIENTAL ORTHODOX CHURCHES.

Were the Chalcedonians 'Nestorian'? That is still debated, but it can certainly be argued that Chalcedon tended in a dualist direction, affirming the *independence* of the two natures in Christ, rather than simply their *integrity*. This potential misunderstanding suggested that the dyophysite terminology also needed to evolve (as happened with the development of NEO-CHALCEDONIANISM during the sixth century). The classic non-heretical miaphysitism of Cyril of Alexandria and Severus of Antioch was also capable of dealing with such subtleties, and could speak movingly and illuminatingly about traditionally difficult Christological questions (e.g., the THEOPASCHITE CONTROVERSY), but ultimately the perspective came to be seen as having lost elasticity, and as being hampered by an unnecessarily restricted vocabulary.

P. T. R. Gray, *The Defense of Chalcedon in the East (451–553)* (Brill, 1979).

I. R. Torrance, *Christology after Chalcedon: Severus of Antioch and Sergius the Grammarian* (Canterbury Press, 1988).

IAIN R. TORRANCE

MIDDLE KNOWLEDGE Christian theologians have traditionally affirmed that by virtue of being omniscient God knows, for example, what would have happened if the Canaanites had been spared from destruction, what Napoleon would have done had he won the Battle of Waterloo, or how Jones would respond were he to hear the GOSPEL. What was disputed, however, was, so to speak, *when* God has such knowledge.

According to the Jesuit theologian L. Molina (1535–1600), logically prior to God's decree to create a world, God possesses not only knowledge of everything that creatures *could* do (natural knowledge) but also knowledge of everything that creatures *would* do in any appropriately specified set of circumstances (middle knowledge). Then logically posterior to the divine decree God has knowledge of everything that creatures *actually* do (free knowledge).

God's *natural knowledge* is God's knowledge of all necessary truths. By means of it God knows what is the full range of possible worlds. God knows, for example, that in some possible world Peter freely denies Christ three times and that in another world Peter freely affirms Christ under identical circumstances, for both are possible.

God's *middle knowledge* is God's knowledge of all contingently true subjunctive conditionals concerning creatures, including truths about creaturely free actions. It is 'middle' because it stands 'between' God's knowledge of all possible worlds and God's knowledge of the actual world. For example, logically prior to God's creative decree, God knew that *if Peter were in circumstances C, he would freely deny Christ three times.* Such conditionals, when *C* is fully specified, are called counterfactuals of creaturely freedom by contemporary Molinists.

Such conditionals serve to delimit the range of possible worlds to worlds that are feasible for God to actualize. For example, there is a possible world in which Peter freely affirms Christ in precisely the same circumstances in which he in fact denied him; but given the truth that if Peter were in precisely those circumstances he would freely deny Christ, then the possible world in which Peter freely affirms Christ in those circumstances is not feasible for God. God could *make* Peter affirm Christ in those circumstances, but then his confession would not be free.

By means of middle knowledge, God knows what is the proper subset of possible worlds which are feasible for God, given the counterfactuals of creaturely freedom that are true. God then decrees to create certain free creatures in certain circumstances and simultaneously decrees how God would act in any circumstances, thereby bringing about the truth of counterfactuals of divine freedom, which are not true logically prior to God's decree.

God's *free knowledge* is God's knowledge of the actual world, including foreknowledge of future contingents (i.e., events produced by creatures' free decisions). On the basis of God's middle knowledge of how creatures would freely act under any circumstances and God's knowledge of God's own decree to create certain creatures in certain circumstances, God knows how creatures will in fact freely behave. In this way, God knows, for example, that Peter will freely deny Christ three times.

J. Arminius (1560–1609) was the first Protestant advocate of middle knowledge. Contemporary proponents include W. L. Craig (b. 1949), T. Flint (b. 1954), A. Freddoso (b. 1946), J. Kvanvig (b. 1954), A. Plantinga (b. 1932), and E. Wierenga (b. 1947).

WILLIAM LANE CRAIG

MILLENARIANISM: see PREMILLENNIALISM.

MILLENNIUM The 'Millennium' (from the Latin for '1,000 years') is a term in Christian ESCHATOLOGY derived from Revelation 20. The seer here relates a vision of the end times: after the DEVIL has been bound for 1,000 years (v. 3), 'those who had been beheaded for their testimony to Jesus and for the word of God . . . came to life and reigned with Christ for a thousand years' (v. 4). After the conclusion of this 1,000-year period, the Devil is released, engages in a final battle against Christ and the SAINTS, and goes down to eternal defeat (vv. 7–10). There follows the Last Judgement and the end of history (vv. 11–15).

Christians have interpreted the meaning of this millennial reign of Christ in a number of different ways. The majority of the earliest Christians (including, e.g., IRENAEUS OF LYONS) understood it literally as referring to a future historical period (see PREMILLENNIALISM). Though it had become theologically marginal by the fourth century, this position has periodically attracted vigorous support and finds contemporary defenders among Christians ranging from liberation theologians on the left to dispensationalists on the right. The majority of Christian Churches have preferred to interpret the Millennium symbolically as referring either to the era of the Church as a whole (i.e., the entire period between PENTECOST and the PAROUSIA), or to a period of steady expansion of the KINGDOM OF GOD extending from some point in later Church history until Christ's return (see AMILLENNIALISM; POSTMILLENNIALISM).

See also DISPENSATIONALISM; RAPTURE.

IAN A. MCFARLAND

MINISTRY As the English word most often used to translate the NT Greek term *diakonia*, 'ministry' refers to the service Christians are obliged to render to one another and to the world by virtue of their having been called by God in Christ, whose own ministry is the foundation of that exercised in his name (Heb. 8:6). The precise form and character of Christian ministry is described in various ways in the NT. Sometimes the focus is on the ministry of the whole Church, whether directed outwardly to the world as 'the ministry of reconciliation' (2 Cor. 5:18) or inwardly to the community as 'building up the body of Christ' (Eph. 4:12). At other times it is used to refer to the specific ministry of an individual within the Church. For example, PAUL speaks of his own ministry (Rom. 11:13; 2 Cor. 6:3; cf. Acts 20:24; 21:19), and other figures are likewise instructed to fulfil their particular ministries (Col. 4:17). Paul interprets these various ministries of individual believers as a function of the diversity of gifts (see CHARISM) bestowed by the HOLY SPIRIT (1 Cor. 12:5).

The book of Acts bears witness to the belief that Jesus' closest followers (those for whom Luke generally reserves the title 'APOSTLE') exercised a special ministry within the Church that was associated specifically with proclamation and set them apart from the body of believers (Acts 6:2–4). Whereas Paul's correspondence suggests a highly diversified and relatively informal hierarchy of ministries that includes all the community's members (1 Cor. 12:28), the narrative of Acts points towards (though it does not explicitly define) a more fixed distinction between a small subset of members exercising a formal leadership role in the community (the clergy) and the majority of Christians (the LAITY), whose ministerial role is less well defined. Already in the NT there is reference to rites beyond BAPTISM used to set apart individuals for such leadership roles (see, e.g., Acts 6:6; 14:23; 1 Tim. 4:14).

While various forms of ministry (prayer, prophecy, distribution of food to the poor, etc.) continued to be practised by members of early Christian communities, by the third century the distinction between clergy and laity was well established, with the ministry of word (viz., public preaching) and sacrament (especially the EUCHARIST) limited to those authorized through formal rites of ordination. This distinction continues to define the shape of Christian ministry in the majority of Churches, with the more refined idea of a threefold form of ordained ministry, structured around the offices of the diaconate, the presbyterate or priesthood, and the episcopacy, assuming something of a formal status in both Orthodox and Catholic (and, later, Anglican and Methodist) communions. While this threefold division is based on biblical terminology (see, e.g., 1 Tim. 3:1–13; 5:17–18), however, few would claim that the current understandings of the roles of the three offices directly mirrors NT practice.

At the same time, it would be mistaken to suppose that the Church's ministry was ever understood as limited to the clergy. In the West monastic orders were often organized and authorized to pursue particular forms of ministry, including care of the sick, education, and missions (see Monasticism). During the Reformation the Augsburg Confession suggested a still more provocative position, affirming the importance of clergy for good order in the Church (14), but defining ministry as *God's* work of giving the Spirit to believers through word and sacrament rather than by reference to the clerical office (5). Correspondingly, it became characteristic in Protestantism to affirm that all the baptized could claim a specifically Christian vocation (see Priesthood of All Believers). More recently, Vatican Council II emphasized from a specifically Catholic perspective that Christian ministry includes the whole people of God: because 'all are called to sanctity and have received an equal privilege of faith', the layperson, too, is 'a witness and a living instrument of the mission of the Church' (*LG*, §32–3). Finally, perhaps the most influential document to emerge from the World Council of Churches, while honouring ordained ministry in general and its traditional threefold form in particular, stresses that ministry 'in its broadest sense denotes the service to which the whole people of God is called, whether as individuals, as a local community, or as the universal Church' (*BEM*, 'Ministry', §7b).

E. Schillebeeckx, *Ministry: Leadership in the Community of Jesus Christ* (Crossroad, 1981 [1980]).

S. Wood, ed., *Ordering the Baptismal Priesthood: Theologies of Lay and Ordained Ministry* (Liturgical Press, 2003).

Ian A. McFarland

Minjung Theology: see Korean Theology.

Miracles Derived from a Latin word for 'wonder' or 'marvel' (*miraculum*), miracle refers to an event that is unusual, comes from God, and is revelatory of God. A variety of Greek words are used for such events in the NT (e.g., *dynamis, teras, sēmeion*), all of which can also be applied to demonic acts (cf. Acts 2:22 and 2 Thess. 2:9). Much theological discussion of miracles, especially in the modern era, centres on how God is understood to be active in them. Specifically, are miracles to be understood *objectively*, as a particular kind of divine activity (e.g., the violation of a law of nature), or *subjectively*, in terms of their revelatory impact on those who witness them?

Though subjective interpretations of miracles are often viewed as a modern development, no less a figure than Augustine defined 'miracle' in terms of the response of the person confronted with it (*Cred.* 16). For Augustine, since everything that happens happens by God's will, miracles are distinguished from other events only by their rarity and the relative obscurity of their cause. In the modern period F. Schleiermacher emphasized the subjective character of miracles even more strongly, arguing that miracle is 'merely the religious name for event' (*Speeches*, 49).

Perhaps the most influential version of the objective approach comes from T. Aquinas, who defined a miracle as an event caused immediately by God without the intervention of any creaturely causes (*ST* 1.105.6). Nevertheless, since for Aquinas God is the One who at every moment enables creatures to have causal effects on each other, it is not true to say that God is quantitatively more active in miracles than in other events, but only that in miracles God is active in a qualitatively different way (*Pot.* 3.7). Thus, even for Aquinas the communicative aspect of miracles remains fundamental in distinguishing them from 'ordinary' events. Moreover, he argued that, since miracles are scientifically inexplicable (since they lack a created cause), they cannot count as evidence for faith (*ST* 1.105.7); rather, they serve to confirm faith in the believer (*ST* 2/2.178.1).

Notwithstanding Aquinas' views, during the Enlightenment miracles came increasingly to be viewed as evidence for Christian belief and, still more specifically, as proof of the revealed truth of Scripture. Their credibility as such was famously attacked by D. Hume (1711–76) in his *Enquiry concerning Human Understanding* (1748). Working from the premise that a miracle was by definition inconsistent with human experience, and that human experience was the only court of appeal that could be used to judge the veracity of testimony that a miracle had occurred, Hume concluded that no such testimony could possibly be so compelling as to outweigh doubt as to its trustworthiness. Hume's argument remains influential, though it has been criticized on a number of grounds, including his assumption that the weight of experience is the only legitimate basis for according belief to a proposition.

Contemporary evaluation of the credibility of miracles as supernatural occurrences is closely bound up with theological reflection on divine action. Given that Scripture also ascribes extraordinary events to demonic influence, specifically theological criteria must also be used to evaluate the claim that any 'miraculous' event is revelatory of God. Such criteria arguably include the ability to show that the alleged miracle is consistent with existing knowledge of God, that it contributes to the furthering of God's purposes in history, and that it builds up the unity of the Church.

IAN A. MCFARLAND

MISSIOLOGY Missiology, or the academic study of the theology and practice of Christian mission, has not secured universal recognition as a distinct branch of theology. The missionary expansion of both Protestant and Catholic Churches during the nineteenth century stimulated the development of what became known as 'missionary science' or *Missionswissenschaft*, which attempted to apply modern scientific method to the problems of the overseas mission field. Such approaches made greatest headway in Germany, the Netherlands, and Scandinavia. G. Warneck (1834–1910), professor of mission at the university of Halle from 1897 to 1908, and J. Schmidlin (1876–1944), professor of missiology at the university of Münster from 1914 to 1934, are generally recognized as the respective founding fathers of Protestant and Catholic missiology. In Britain, a chair in 'evangelistic theology' had been created in 1867 at New College, Edinburgh, for the celebrated India missionary, A. Duff (1806–78), but the chair had only one other holder after Duff, and ceased to exist as a permanent post in 1892.

Mission studies never secured a firm foothold in British university departments of theology, and the term 'missiology' was slow to gain acceptance in theological vocabulary in both Scotland and England in the course of the twentieth century. However, the World Missionary Conference held in Edinburgh in 1910 led to the publication from 1912 of the first international journal of mission studies, the *International Review of Missions*. The conference also stimulated the study of missions as an academic discipline outside Britain, especially in the USA. Yale University already had a chair in missions, from 1906, and its example was followed after 1910 by several other leading American institutions, such as Boston University (1910) and Princeton Theological Seminary (1914). However, missiology did not enter the mainstream of academic theology in North America to the extent that it did in continental Europe: the American professional body, the American Society of Missiology, was not founded till 1973.

In the postcolonial era (see COLONIALISM AND POSTCOLONIALISM), the place of missiology in the secular academy has become increasingly vulnerable, and many European university posts in missiology have either disappeared or been redenominated as posts in intercultural theology. Nevertheless, since the 1960s there has been a gathering swell of theological writing on the subject of mission. Three reasons for this trend may be identified.

The first is that the focus of missiology since 1945 has shifted from the older 'missionary science' (the empirical analysis of how obstacles to the agreed objective of making 'heathen' nations into Christian ones could be overcome) to a more fundamental debate on the very nature and goals of mission. This realignment has created more space for specifically theological reflection on the missionary purposes of God. Trends in BIBLICAL THEOLOGY also encouraged an emphasis on discerning the missionary tenor of Christian SCRIPTURE as a whole, in place of the preoccupation with obedience to the so-called 'Great Commission' of Christ (a phrase that had become almost exclusively affixed to Matt. 28:18–20), which had characterized evangelical thinking in the nineteenth and early twentieth centuries. The concept of the *missio Dei*, which broke surface at the Willingen meeting of the International Missionary Council in 1952, has conventionally been traced to a paper by Karl Barth in 1932 describing the Trinitarian God as the author of mission, though the trajectory from Barth has recently been disputed. In a statement drafted by Lesslie Newbigin (1909–98), Willingen affirmed that mission derives its essential character from the sending of the Son by the Father, and of the Spirit by the Father and the Son. During the 1960s the idea of the *missio Dei* spread to other sections of the world Church, including, after VATICAN COUNCIL II, the Catholic Church, and acquired new overtones that reflected the secular theologies of that decade. A book by the Dutch Protestant missiologist J. C. Hoekendijk (1912–75), *The Church Inside Out* (1966), was of particular importance for its insistence that the Church was of only secondary significance in the divine mission of establishing the KINGDOM OF GOD in the world. The change of title in 1969 from the *International Review of Missions* to the *International Review of Mission* symbolized the change of mood. After the Upssala assembly of the WORLD COUNCIL OF CHURCHES in 1968 Protestants became embroiled in hot debates about the relative priority on the mission agenda of evangelism and liberation or humanization. Post-Vatican II Catholics have engaged in similar arguments, though the employment of the different terminology of a single process of evangelization moderated the polarization to some extent. All alike faced the challenge posed to Christian truth claims by the plurality of religions – no new issue in itself, but one that now gained unprecedented prominence in the consciousness of Christians in the West (see PLURALISM, RELIGIOUS). Definitions of mission were fiercely contested and increasingly broad. From the 1980s onwards they began to include the renewal of CREATION, and the boundary between Christian ethics and missiology became less distinct.

The second reason for the resurgence of interest in missiology is the intensifying awareness of Churches in the western hemisphere that they now exist in a post-CHRISTENDOM context that demands critical missiological engagement with post-Enlightenment western cultures: the later writings of L. Newbigin have been a major influence in this respect. Much writing on Christian responses to postmodernity has had a broadly missiological intent (see Postmodernism).

Third, and perhaps most important, the de-centring of Christianity from its centuries-old concentration in Europe to new plural centres of gravity elsewhere has opened up new horizons for the theology of mission. The Churches of the 'global south' have challenged the Churches of the north by their active commitment to mission, both within their own countries and increasingly also on an international scale: countries such as Korea, Nigeria, and Brazil are now major exporters of missionaries. Much missiology emanating from the south has a quite different character from that which traditionally obtained in Europe or North America. Pneumatology has a new salience, as theologians debate the work of the Holy Spirit both within and beyond the Church. Even theologies of mission emanating from the Pentecostal and evangelical Churches that are now so numerous in the global South are increasingly including within their scope questions of structural injustice and poverty, neo-colonialism, and inter-religious encounter. Asian, African, and Latin American voices have broken the White monopoly of the discipline of missiology. No longer is it a discourse among western strategists alone; it is now a global conversation.

D. Bosch, *Transforming Mission: Paradigm Shifts in Theology of Mission* (Orbis, 1991).
J. C. Hoekendijk, *The Church Inside Out* (SCM, 1966).
K. Kim, *The Holy Spirit in the World: A Global Conversation* (SPCK, 2008).
O. G. Myklebust, *The Study of Missions in Theological Education*, 2 vols. (Egede Instituttet, 1955, 1957).

Brian Stanley

Modalism Also known as Sabellianism, modalism (or modal monarchianism) refers to any account of the Trinity in which the Father, Son, and Holy Spirit are regarded as features of God's relationship to creation (i.e., as matters of the divine economy only) rather than as intrinsic to God's eternal being. Sabellius (*fl. ca* 220) allegedly taught that the Father, Son, and Spirit were merely three modes or manifestations of one underlying divine reality in the same way that light, heat, and astrological effect are three forms of the sun's energy. A more nuanced version of modalism seems to have been taught by Paul of Samosata (*ca* 200–*ca* 275), who was condemned for denying any real distinction between the Father and the Son (see *homoousios*).

Early Christian doctrines of God were marked by the struggle to balance the demands of monotheism (see, e.g., Rom. 3:30) with the Trinitarian language of Scripture and worship (see, e.g., Matt. 28:19). Modalist insistence on a single divine reality safeguarded the oneness of God; moreover, modalism affirmed the equality of the Father, Son, and Spirit more effectively than adoptionism, which implied that the Son was less divine than the Father. Yet the idea that Father, Son, and Spirit are merely ways in which God appears rather than essential features of God's being makes it difficult to explain accounts of the interaction between them in the NT (e.g., Matt. 26:39; Luke 3:21–2; John 12:27–8). Furthermore, by refusing to identify Father, Son, or Spirit with God's eternal being, modalism implicitly undermines the conviction that their activity in history reveals God's eternal will.

See also Patripassianism.

Ian A. McFarland

Modernism A particular variant of liberal theology, modernism flourished from about 1880 to about 1930 in Western Europe and North America. The movement drew its name from the desire of its adherents to adapt Christian theology to modern culture. This desire stemmed from two fundamental beliefs. First, particular aspects of Christianity could no longer speak to the modern situation. Second, the Christian tradition, properly renovated, had much to teach modern people.

Although different modernists emphasized different features of modern culture and consequently arrived at different theological positions on many issues, certain ideas were broadly shared. Modernists typically found I. Kant's refutation of metaphysics persuasive, and therefore denied the absolute value of dogmatic claims. In place of metaphysics, Kant emphasized practical reason, and modernists tended to share his emphasis on morality, but modernists generally found F. Schleiermacher's emphasis on religious feeling even more valuable. Modernist religion was not so much a set of beliefs as it was a set of feelings or experiences of God. Christian doctrinal claims, modernists believed, simply articulated these experiences in theological language.

Not all modernists acknowledged Kant and Schleiermacher as sources for their own theological reflections, however. For many, German biblical criticism was the conduit for the ideas that Kant and Schleiermacher articulated more systematically, and some of the bitterest fights between modernists and their more conservative co-religionists stemmed from competing claims about Scripture. Modernists typically repudiated a literal reading of Scripture, instead interpreting the biblical writings as human responses to God that reflected the limitations of their historical and cultural contexts. These limitations did not lead modernists to reject the authority of the Bible, but they did encourage modernists to think carefully about how the Bible might function in a modern context quite different from that of the biblical authors.

The emerging theory of evolution reinforced the doubts that many modernists had about literal interpretations of the Bible, but evolution also offered a way forward. Central to virtually every modernist theology was a sense of ongoing human progress. Unlike conservatives, who looked to the past as the repository of human wisdom, modernists celebrated the great advances in human knowledge in the present, and they expected even more to come in the future. This belief in inevitable progress could be more or less naive, but it was the intellectual basis for the modernist conviction that Christian truth should take modern form.

At the turn of the twentieth century, modernists and their more conservative co-religionists battled for control of their denominations. Among Protestants, the fight revolved around the question of biblical inerrancy. For example, the Presbyterian C. Briggs (1841–1913) was charged with heresy in 1891 for raising critical questions about SCRIPTURE and found guilty after a bitter trial. Catholics also fought over biblical inerrancy, but Church authority loomed even larger. Modernists like A. LOISY in France insisted that historical scholarship on the Bible was not subject to Church oversight. Concerned at the theological implications of scholarship like Loisy's, the Vatican condemned modernism by name in 1907 and excommunicated Loisy himself the following year.

By the mid-twentieth century, modernism had faded as a theological movement on the cutting edge. Among Catholics, a vigorous anti-modernist campaign had already by the 1920s ensured that theologians did not openly advocate modernist ideas or describe themselves as modernist. For many Protestants, the two world wars, economic depression, and ideological conflict with Communism seemed to discredit the optimistic assessment of human nature and human progress common to modernists. However, modernist assumptions continue to shape much biblical criticism, and the central modernist question about how best to co-ordinate contemporary intellectual life and the Christian tradition remains alive and well.

W. R. Hutchison, *The Modernist Impulse in American Protestantism* (Duke University Press, 1992).

M. O'Connell, *Critics on Trial: An Introduction to the Catholic Modernist Crisis* (Catholic University of America Press, 1994).

HARVEY HILL

MOLINISM: see MIDDLE KNOWLEDGE.

MONASTICISM Though derived from a Greek word meaning 'solitary' (*monachos*), within Christianity 'monasticism' refers to a wide range of lifestyles, many explicitly communal in character, that defy easy categorization. Most broadly, Christian monasticism is characterized by a life of ASCETICISM that sets the monastic (whether a male monk or a female nun) apart – often physically as well as with respect to behaviour – from the wider society. In so far as Christian monasticism typically entails commitment to both CELIBACY and POVERTY in imitation of Christ and the APOSTLES, monastic distinctiveness has normally included abstinence from MARRIAGE and PROCREATION on the one hand, and from secular forms of economic production and exchange on the other. Such deliberate and formal renunciation of worldly attachments and pursuits has as its aim the cultivation and perfection of a life dedicated to the LOVE of God (cf. 1 Cor. 7:32–5).

The value accorded to VIRGINITY in the NT (Matt. 19:10–12; 1 Cor. 7:8, 25–6; Rev. 14:1–5), as well as the evidence for distinct groups of 'virgins' and 'widows' during Christianity's first centuries (Hippolytus of Rome, *Trad.* 10, 12; cf. 1 Tim. 5:3–16), suggests that some Christians were set apart from other believers for non-clerical ministries of PRAYER, FASTING, and service from the earliest period. Nevertheless, it is only from the fourth century, beginning in Egypt, that Christian ascetics began to order their lives as monastics. In contrast to earlier Christian ascetics, these early monastics followed a VOCATION characterized by withdrawal (Greek *anachōrēsis*, from which 'anchorite' is derived) to the desert (Greek *erēmos*, the root of the words 'eremite' and 'hermit'), and thus separate from the life of the local congregation under its bishop. Traditionally, the forms of Christian monasticism that emerged are divided into two basic types: eremitical and cenobitic.

Possibly the most famous of Christian monks, Anthony of Egypt ('the Great', *ca* 250–356) became the model for eremitical (i.e., solitary and reclusive) forms of monastic life. Taking literally Jesus' injunction in Matthew 19:21 to give all his possessions to the poor, Anthony first became the disciple of a local Christian hermit, before eventually retiring on his own to increasingly remote desert regions of the Nile delta. Anthony inspired and instructed others, including Macarius the Elder (*ca* 300–91), in his form of the monastic life, which spread throughout the desert regions of northern Egypt and Syria. While many followed the eremitical life strictly (by, e.g., deliberately living out of earshot of their nearest neighbours), in other cases Christian hermits congregated in groups, each living in his own cell yet in close proximity with one another and often with a de facto superior – an arrangement sometimes known as semi-eremitical monasticism.

Despite the predominantly eremitical character of the earliest forms of Christian monasticism, cenobitism (derived from the Greek for 'life in common') emerged relatively quickly as an alternative manifestation of the monastic impulse, with the Egyptian Pachomius (*ca* 290–346) generally recognized as the first to organize a formal community of monks. The distinguishing characteristics of cenobitism are the community's submission to an abbot or abbess and subscription to a rule ordering the monks' or nuns' common life, making obedience a defining feature of cenobitic monasticism alongside celibate chastity and poverty. In the Orthodox Churches the *Rule* of Basil of Caesarea (see CAPPADOCIAN FATHERS) is dominant, though it is less a communal constitution than a catechetical treatise stressing the basic principles and virtues of monastic life, drawing parallels especially with the common life of the early Jerusalem Church as described in Acts 2:44. By contrast, the later *Rule* of Benedict of Nursia (*ca* 480–*ca* 545), which quickly became the prevailing model in the West, provides much more detail with respect to the internal organization of the monastery.

Both Basil and Benedict agreed that the chief virtue of monastic community over more solitary forms of Christian asceticism was the strength that came from the mutual support and encouragement of the monks. Correspondingly, both sought to merge the basic monastic principles of poverty, celibate chastity, and obedience with a moderation that avoided extreme ascetic practices. Benedict's injunction, 'Work and pray' (*ora et labora*), summed up the basic framework for the monks' communal life, which combined physical labour, the study of SCRIPTURE (*lectio divina*), and common worship, with the last taking the particular form of the DIVINE OFFICE.

While cenobitism remained the dominant form of monastic life in the West throughout the medieval period, a distinctive form of eremitism developed in northern Europe beginning in the eleventh century (see ANCHORITISM). Moreover, the rise of large urban centres in medieval and early modern Europe led to the foundation of new religious orders distinct from both eremite and cenobite forms of monasticism, including the Mendicant Orders (e.g., the Dominicans and Franciscans) in the thirteenth century and the Jesuits in the sixteenth. Seeking to model engagement with rather than withdrawal from the world, these newer groups were dedicated especially to public preaching, missions, and the combating of HERESY, though the mendicants (named from the Latin word for 'begging') also laid particular stress on the strict observance of apostolic poverty. While these religious, like the members of the older cenobite orders, also adhered to an ecclesiastically approved rule to which they were bound by vows, their commitment to engagement with the secular world set them apart from established forms of monasticism, so that (for example) consideration of the flexibility required by missionary activity led the Jesuits to be exempted from the common recitation of the daily office – a practice that had to that time been one of the defining features of western religious orders.

In medieval Europe a particular theology of monasticism developed that became the basis for sharp criticism by Protestants during the REFORMATION. Whereas all Christians were under obligations to follow the so-called 'evangelical precepts' (viz., the TEN COMMANDMENTS) as necessary to salvation, monastics also undertook to follow the 'evangelical counsels' (also known as 'counsels of perfection'), including the classical commitments to poverty (following Matt. 19:21 and pars.) and celibacy (following Matt. 19:10–12). It was widely understood that the merits accrued by the monks through their more rigorous calling redounded not only to the benefit of their own SOULS, but also to the other members of society (as well as to the dead in PURGATORY). The Reformers, beginning with the former monk M. LUTHER, rejected the distinction between precepts and counsels as unfaithful to the principle that all Christians are bound to keep the whole law, even as they invariably fall short of doing so (Luke 17:7–10; cf. Matt. 5:20). They correspondingly denied that Christians' different VOCATIONS either reflect or enable differing levels of merit before God, leading to the rapid dissolution of monasteries in Protestant territories. At the same time, other groups from the radical wing of the REFORMATION (e.g., the Hutterites) could share Luther's disdain for the notion of different classes of Christians, yet insist against him that it was both possible and obligatory for Christians to follow evangelical principles of nonviolence and communalism that set them apart from the wider world.

In the present day, monasticism continues to be an important feature of both the Orthodox and the Catholic communions (indeed, Orthodox bishops are traditionally drawn from the ranks of monks), and has since the nineteenth century also become a feature of Anglican and (to a lesser extent) Lutheran Church life as well. The ecumenical Community of TAIZÉ provides yet a further model of an interdenominational, largely Protestant monastic community organized around the traditional monastic principles of common work and worship. Especially among Protestant monastics the idea of meritorious vows is rejected, in line with Luther's criticism, and the monastic vocation seen rather as a matter of witness to the promise of the KINGDOM OF GOD. With their focus on the life of prayer, contemplation, and the cultivation of distinctively Christian forms of SPIRITUALITY, contemporary monasteries often serve as places of PILGRIMAGE and retreat for Christians and non-Christians alike.

See also ATHOS, MOUNT.

W. Capps, *The Monastic Impulse* (Crossroad, 1983).

D. J. Chitty, *The Desert a City: An Introduction to the Study of Egyptian and Palestinian Monasticism Under the Christian Empire* (St Vladimir's Seminary Press, 1997 [1966]).

M. Dunn, *The Emergence of Monasticism: From the Desert Fathers to the Early Middle Ages* (Blackwell, 2000).

K. S. Frank, O. F. M., *With Greater Liberty: A Short History of Christian Monasticism and Religious Orders* (Cistercian Publications, 1993 [1975]).

T. Merton, *The Silent Life* (Farrar, Straus and Giroux, 1957).

IAN A. MCFARLAND

MONENERGISM: see MONOTHELITISM.

MONERGISM: see SYNERGISM.

MONOGENESIS Monogenesis (or monogenism) is the DOCTRINE that the whole human race is descended from a single male and female pair. Though this first couple is traditionally identified with the biblical figures of Adam and Eve, monogenesis is not necessarily linked to a literal interpretation of Genesis 1–3. It is historically the majority position among Christians across confessional traditions and is opposed to polygenism, which posits multiple sets of human ancestors for the present human population. Monogenesis is the official teaching of the Catholic Church, which rejects polygenism as incompatible with the doctrine of original SIN (Pius XII, *Humani*, §37).

Strict monogenesis is incompatible with modern scientific theories of EVOLUTION, according to which new species emerge from relatively self-contained breeding populations and not from a single mating pair. Yet it is not clear that monogenesis need be understood in a strictly biological sense, since its primary purpose is to make sense of original sin (viz., the doctrine that sin is a universal though not essential characteristic of human nature). If all humans are congenitally sinful, then this sinfulness is inherited from one's progenitors, all the way back to the first human being, who, on this account, is 'first' precisely by virtue of being the first sinner and not because of particular biological criteria. From this perspective, monogenesis can be correlated with a metaphysical rather than a biological understanding of the human species, in a way that does not clash with scientific accounts of human origins.

See also FALL.

IAN A. MCFARLAND

MONOPHYSITISM: see MIAPHYSITISM.

MONOTHELITISM The focus of the last major phase of Christological controversy in the early Church, monothelitism was the fruit of attempts by Byzantine emperors and patriarchs of Constantinople to resolve enduring cleavages stemming from the Council of CHALCEDON. Monophysite Churches had continued to repudiate the Chalcedonian Definition's language of two distinct natures, divine and human, in Christ, on the grounds that it compromised the integral unity of Christ as Saviour and smacked of NESTORIANISM.

In the sixth century, Emperor Justinian I's (r. 527–65) various tactics to reconcile the increasingly alienated monophysite Churches of Egypt and Syria failed miserably. In the seventh century, the politically stressed emperor Heraclius (r. 610–41), anxious to reunify the empire at all levels, allied himself with Patriarch Sergius I of Constantinople (r. 610–38) in a new strategy of appeasement. Innovating on a phrase from DIONYSIUS THE AREOPAGITE, they asserted the principle of a single 'theandric energy' in Christ, a formula favourably received by some Egyptian monophysites in 633. Despite protests from Patriarch Sophronius of Jerusalem (r. 634–8), whose insistence on dual operations proper to the two natures of Christ anticipated the position of his disciple MAXIMUS THE CONFESSOR, this 'monenergism' entered a controversial new phase when Heraclius officially endorsed Sergius' *Ecthesis* (638), which stated that Christ had 'one will' (*monon thelêma*).

Monothelite theologians like Theodore of Pharan (*fl. ca* 610) grounded their 'one will' CHRISTOLOGY in the idea that only a single volition, the divine will, could have effected salvation through the *LOGOS* incarnate. Sergius cited no less an authority than Gregory of Nazianzus (see CAPPADOCIAN FATHERS), whose interpretation of John 6:38 was construed as forfeiting a human will in Christ, since such a will would inherently imply *opposition* to the divine will.

In a public debate with Pyrrhus, the deposed patriarch of Constantinople (r. 638–41), in Carthage in 645, Maximus the Confessor clearly emerged as the leading critic of monothelitism. Here and in various theological *Opuscula* Maximus targeted the 'one will' doctrine as a betrayal of Chalcedon. Salvation was effected in the INCARNATION precisely through the glorious reciprocity of divine and human wills in Christ's two-natured person. Contra Sergius, the duality of wills indicated *difference* but not *opposition*, a fact dramatically demonstrated in Jesus' actively conforming his human will to the divine will in the agony of Gethsemane. In 649 Maximus joined Pope Martin I (r. 649–53) in a Lateran Council in Rome that condemned monothelitism and incurred the wrath of the Byzantine emperor Constans II (r. 641–68). Martin died in exile and Maximus underwent humiliating trials and exiles, dying in 662 the principal champion of dyothelite Christology.

In 680 the emperor Constantine IV (r. 668–85), concerned to heal the Christological rift between Rome and Constantinople, convened the third Council of Constantinople (the sixth ecumenical COUNCIL), which subsequently witnessed an emerging consensus to reclaim the ORTHODOXY of dyothelite Christology. Though not named in the council's decrees, Maximus' position was vindicated in the affirmation of 'two natural volitions or wills in [Christ] and two natural energies that know no division, change, partition, or confusion, in accordance with the teaching of the holy fathers'.

See also MIAPHYSITISM.

D. Bathrellos, *The Byzantine Christ: Person, Nature, and Will in the Christology of St. Maximus the Confessor* (Oxford University Press, 2004).

PAUL M. BLOWERS

MONTANISM Called by its proponents the 'New Prophecy', Montanism was a charismatic movement that arose in Phrygia in the latter half of the second century. Founded by Montanus and two associates, the prophets Priscilla and Maximilla, the movement was defined by belief that, in fulfilment of Jesus' promise to send the Paraclete (John 14:16), the Holy Spirit had been poured out anew to supply the Church with ongoing revelation. This emphasis on the extraordinary manifestations of the Spirit became one of the chief sources of controversy surrounding the movement, for Montanus and his associates apparently identified themselves with the Holy Spirit when prophesying (Montanus is supposed to have referred to himself as a lyre played by the Spirit), and some later adherents seem to have believed that Montanus was the Spirit's incarnation.

Montanists viewed the outpouring of the Spirit as a sign of the imminent end of the world (the Phrygian town of Pepuza was to be the site of the new Jerusalem), and this apocalyptic outlook influenced its general ethos, which was characterized by a puritan ethic born of the conviction that moral decline was the cause of the waning of the Spirit's activity in the wider Church. This implicit criticism of the ecclesiastical status quo led to Montanism's being rejected almost immediately by local Church leaders in Asia Minor. Though it was ultimately condemned by (probably) Pope Eleutherius (r. *ca* 175–*ca* 190), Montanism was viewed sympathetically by Irenaeus (see *AH* 3.11.9) and made a notable convert of Tertullian, who admired its moral rigour.

Ian A. McFarland

Moral Argument Moral arguments for God's existence rest on the postulate of a deep connection between a good God and objective moral values (human dignity, rights, virtues, duties). Most basically, proponents of moral arguments have sought to exploit this connection to argue from moral objectivity to God, as follows:

(1) If objective moral values exist, then a personal, good God (most likely) exists.
(2) Objective moral values do exist.
(3) Therefore, a personal, good God (most likely) exists.

According to the first premise, God's non-existence would entail the absence of objective moral values. Correspondingly, proponents of the moral argument have to defend the appropriateness of belief in objective moral values in the face of naturalistic accounts that deny that appeal to God is necessary to make sense of moral behaviour. At the same time, many naturalists concede that objective values (if they exist) would best be explained as proceeding from God. For example, J. L. Mackie (1917–81) acknowledged that, if objective moral values exist, this would be a strong argument for God's existence. As an atheist, Mackie therefore denied their existence.

A defence of moral objectivity might begin with human beings' persistent sense of the overriding character of ethical obligation, the universality of moral claims, and their essentially disinterested character. While the fact of such basic moral intuitions regarding, say, the wrongness of rape, child abuse, or torture for pleasure does not establish their truth, it arguably does suggest that they should be taken seriously as sources of data regarding the basic order of things. Moreover, defenders of the moral argument aver that such data imply a source of goodness that is both transcendent and personal. That this source is *transcendent* follows from the idea that basic moral values are invariant across time and space; that it is *personal* follows from the fact that their content centres on the valuing of individuals as persons (i.e., as ends in themselves rather than means).

In perhaps the most famous example of the moral argument, I. Kant argued that morality does not need God in one sense, because epistemologically human beings are immediately aware of the unconditional and binding character of their moral intuitions independently of belief in God. Nevertheless, he argued that the intelligibility of moral action only makes sense on the assumption that there is an ultimate consonance between moral behaviour and individual happiness, and that such consonance can only be guaranteed by postulating the existence of a God who is omnipotent and good. Many have sought to see in his account of the unconditional, binding, and objective demands of morality a transcendent dimension of experience that can be identified with the God of traditional theism.

A classic challenge to the link between moral objectivity and belief in God at the heart of moral arguments is Plato's (*ca* 430–*ca* 345 BC) 'Euthyphro dilemma': is the good good because God so decrees (i.e., on the basis of an arbitrary divine fiat that appears to undermine the objectivity of morality), or does God decree the good because it is good (i.e., on the basis of a standard independent of God that renders divine sanction superfluous)? This conundrum can be evaded by seeing God's nature as the ground of moral value, rather than as an independent variable that logically precedes or follows it. On this view, God neither acts out of obligation nor arbitrarily defines the good; rather, what God decrees is good because God is intrinsically good.

P. Copan, 'God, Naturalism, and the Foundations of Morality' in *The Future of Atheism: Alister McGrath and Daniel Dennett in Dialogue*, ed. R.B. Stewart (Fortress Press, 2008), 14–62.

J. E. Hare, *God and Morality: A Philosophical History* (Blackwell, 2007).

Paul Copan

Moral Evil As distinguished from natural evil, moral evil is a categorical designation for all causes of creaturely suffering that can be attributed directly to creaturely (viz., human) agency. Traditionally, discussion of moral evil has focused on discrete and deliberate acts by particular, readily identifiable agents: adultery, lying, murder, theft, usury, and the like. In the modern period attention to the social dimensions of sin among advocates of liberal theology (especially the Social Gospel movement) and, more recently, liberation theology has expanded the idea of moral evil to include acts of collective evil that are clearly the product of human agency, but are neither necessarily deliberate or easily reducible to the actions of particular individuals. Such sins include, for example, patterns of discrimination based on class, gender, and race, or degradation of the environment caused by pollution.

The contrast between these two dimensions of moral evil can be illustrated by contrasting bigotry with racism. The former is an individual act identifiable by reference to particular words and actions spoken or uttered with the aim of degrading a person identified as racially other. The latter refers to broader patterns of social marginalization (e.g., statistically higher levels of poverty or incarceration) associated with racial difference but not the product of explicitly discriminatory actions. In such cases the evil effects are the cumulative product of individual actions, but the sorts of changes required to alleviate the evil are often difficult to identify. For example, while it is relatively easy to specify the kinds of changes in behaviour that would allow one to cease being a murderer, it is more difficult to specify the actions that would end a person's complicity in racism or environmental degradation.

Ian A. McFarland

MORAL THEOLOGY While Catholics and Anglicans prefer 'moral theology', and many Protestants incline towards 'theological ethics' or 'Christian ethics', the various titles amount to the same thing: disciplined reflection on moral matters in the light of theological presuppositions. It is a traditional belief of Christian orthodoxy that the world is the creation of one, benevolent God. Accordingly, Christian moral theologians expect the world to contain a moral order, which can be known in principle through reflection on common human experience – that is, through 'reason'. This given moral order is usually known as natural law in Catholic circles and as 'orders of creation' in Protestant ones. At this point moral theology can find common ground with moral philosophy, which confines its study to what can be known apart from special manifestations of God in history.

Since Christian theology holds that human life and understanding have become sinful, moral theologians assume both that actual human grasp of created goods is deficient and in need of correction, and that a realistic description of human flourishing must take into account the problem of sin and its overcoming. Reason, then, is not enough. Attention must be paid to God's gracious initiatives in history to save humans from sin. Accordingly, Christian moral theology takes as its primary authority 'special revelation' as contained in Scripture – especially the life, death, and resurrection of Jesus Christ as reported and interpreted in the NT. Moral theologians who follow Augustine – M. Luther, for example – tend to view the ravages of sin as grave, reason as crippled, and the need for intellectual and moral grace through Scripture as acute. Those, on the other hand, who stand in the tradition of T. Aquinas are inclined to think that the deliverances of reason remain valid in spite of sin, and are more in need of supplementation than correction.

While Christians believe that something decisive about salvation was wrought in Jesus Christ, they recognize that its outworking still awaits completion at the eschaton, or end of history (see Eschatology). Some moral theologies emphasize the nearness of the transformative end and espouse social and political ethics that are accordingly radical. Others, emphasizing its remoteness, are more provisional and conservative. Christian pacifism would be an example of the former; just-war doctrine, an example of the latter.

Biblical thought was never purely Hebraic, and ethics in the NT already bear some marks of Greek influence. The imprint becomes larger in subsequent moral theology. The seminal ethic of Augustine draws from Aristotle the 'eudaemonistic' view that the desire for happiness or wellbeing (*eudaimonia*) motivates all human action, and from Neoplatonism an understanding of the virtuous life as one in which various desires or loves are properly ordered – all the while following the Bible in identifying the sum of human wellbeing as the fulfilment of love for God (see Aristotelianism; Platonism). Aquinas not only retained this fundamentally 'teleological' conception of moral life as defined by the pursuit of goods or 'ends', but also developed Augustine's 'deontological' conception, according to which certain types of action are necessary for achieving final fulfilment. This he did by adumbrating a doctrine of double effect, which observes that an action might have several consequences or effects, some good and some evil, and that what determines its moral rightness is whether the agent intends only the good effects and whether the evil effects that he accepts are proportionate (in some fashion) to the good ones. Thus Aquinas launched a tradition of moral analysis in which intention is primary, and which continues to vie with 'consequentialist' alternatives such as utilitarianism, where the results of action are all that matter.

With his deep sense of human sinfulness and his correlative conviction of humankind's utter dependence for salvation upon God's grace, Luther regarded this Augustinian–Thomistic heritage of moral theology as flawed in two respects. First was the presumptuous emphasis on the human work of ascent to God, rather than on God's gracious descent to helpless humanity. And second was the vitiation of neighbour-love through spiritual egocentricity: since the agent's driving concern is to secure his own good through reunion with God, all his apparently charitable dealings with other people are selfishly instrumental. Instead, Luther proposed that virtuous life should be reconceived as beginning where eudaimonism ends: with reunion with God, effected by the free gift of God's gracious JUSTIFICATION, and appropriated by FAITH. On this basis of grace and faith, the moral agent is freed from spiritual egocentricity to love his neighbour genuinely and per se. In the 1930s this Lutheran view led A. Nygren (1890–1978) to draw an absolute distinction between acquisitive pagan *eros* and altruistic Christian *agape*, and to declare, problematically, that self-love has no place at all in a Christian ethic.

One of the main objections that the Catholic Church levelled against the Lutheran doctrine of justification was that it issues in a moral freedom that amounts to laxity. The Council of TRENT therefore sought to tighten moral discipline by reasserting the sacrament of PENANCE as the means of restoring the state of justification after post-baptismal sin. Thus was created a need to educate priests in the making of moral judgements with a view to imposing appropriate penances. Such clerical preparation for the confessional dominated subsequent Catholic thinking about moral matters, and led to the development for the first time of a separate science of moral theology distanced from dogmatic and spiritual theology, and focused on the transgression of moral laws.

Alarm at the Lutheran perspective was sometimes shared by the followers of J. CALVIN, who were less allergic than Lutherans to the discipline of moral law. The Puritan W. Ames (1576–1633) inaugurated a Protestant tradition of analyzing cases in the light of moral rules in order to counsel the laity, and without the Catholic orientation to penitential practice. This Protestant CASUISTRY came to flourish in Anglican and even Lutheran quarters before it disappeared at the end of the seventeenth century, partly because of complacency, and partly because of a pietistic reaction against moral 'rationalism' and in favour of the cultivation of spiritual life (see PIETISM). The assertion of the primacy of the spiritual dimension of moral life was also the driving concern of S. KIERKEGAARD. Whereas the rationalist I. KANT had used the biblical story of Abraham and Isaac to argue that putative divine commands should be subject to the judgement of reason, Kierkegaard deployed it to illustrate how individuals may be called by God to transcend what passes for ethical rationality. Up until World War I, however, it was Kant's voice that dominated Protestant ethics. A. Ritschl (1822–89) propounded an ethical, rather than metaphysical, reading of the dogma of the INCARNATION. In calling Jesus 'divine', he argued, Christians make no claim about his metaphysical status; rather, they ascribe to him an absolute moral worth as initiator of the KINGDOM OF GOD – that is, the community where consciousness of God as Father issues in fraternal love for human beings. This conception of the kingdom of God became central to religious socialism in Europe and the SOCIAL GOSPEL movement in the USA at the turn of the twentieth century, as Protestants sought to provide a moral response to the challenges of modern industrial society.

Protestants, of course, were not alone in trying to address the 'social question' that industrialization had raised. In 1891 Pope Leo XIII issued his famous encyclical, *Rerum novarum*, appealing to natural rights against both capitalism and socialism and inaugurating a continuing tradition of papal statements on social justice, whose most recent expression was Pope John Paul II's *Centesimus annus* (1991).

In the early twentieth century liberal Protestant faith in social progress was shaken by the intractable realities of conflict. In the USA, R. NIEBUHR developed 'Christian realism', which recognizes the severe constraints that the selfish interests of groups place on the socially redeeming power of love. On the other side of the Atlantic, K. BARTH was chastened first by the willingness of his liberal theological mentors to line up behind the Kaiser's cause in World War I, and then by the readiness of the 'German Christians' to find a messiah in A. Hitler (1889–1945). In reaction he articulated a position (sometimes described as NEO-ORTHODOXY), which stressed the strangeness to human reason of the commands of the 'free' God, and which grounded ethics in a Trinitarian theology that issues from the doctrine of the incarnation understood as a statement about the character of God, and not merely about the moral authority of Jesus.

While Barth was asserting the primacy of faith in God in such a way as to confound moral 'reason', K. Kirk (1886–1954) was articulating the view that careful moral analysis and love for God need not be alternatives: on the one hand he sought to revive casuistry, while on the other he gave his most famous book the title of *The Vision of God* (1931). Kirk's typically Anglican insistence on thinking moral and spiritual life together finds a strong echo in the late twentieth-century Orthodox ethics of C. Yannaras (b. 1935) and S. Harakas (b. 1932).

The issue of the bearing of moral rules upon concrete cases resurfaced in Protestant moral theology in the 1960s, when another Anglican, J. Fletcher (1905–91), propounded 'situation ethics'. From this viewpoint, all rules of conduct are subordinate to the principle of love (deployed in consequentialist fashion) and may be suspended by it. Fletcher's most formidable critic was P. Ramsey (1913–88), who insisted on the need for more specific and reliable indications of right conduct, and contended for a casuistry that is capable of learning from morally novel situations.

At the same time, a form of theology was rising to prominence in Europe (see POLITICAL THEOLOGY) and Latin America (see LIBERATION THEOLOGY) that stressed the need to think in the context of 'praxis' – that is, active political commitment to the cause of the poor and oppressed. Of the criticisms that this ecumenical movement has attracted, one emanated from moral theology, namely, that its wont to bypass ethics and move directly from theological premises to political pronouncements robs its judgements of precision and credibility. A species of liberation theology in its method, FEMINIST THEOLOGY has also made its mark on Christian ethics since the 1970s, emphasizing the embodied nature of human existence, criticizing the concept of Christian love as impartial and disinterested, and drawing attention to the building of community at the ordinary level of personal relationships.

In the opening decade of the third millennium, the dominant influence on contemporary Anglo-Saxon moral theology – mainly Protestant, but also some Catholic – is S. Hauerwas (b. 1940). Influenced by MENNONITE THEOLOGY, Hauerwas insists that moral theology concentrate on articulating the distinctive practices of communities that live in the Christian 'narrative' – that is, the orthodox reading of salvation history running from creation to the eschaton, whose key lies in Jesus' 'NONVIOLENCE'. While this approach has the Barthian virtue of bolstering theological and ecclesial integrity, its counter-cultural posture hinders it from dealing carefully and charitably with non-ecclesial points of view, and from having much to offer those who bear responsibility for grappling with the complexities of public policy.

Meanwhile Catholic moral theology, liberated by VATICAN COUNCIL II from the legalistic orientation that followed the Council of TRENT, has restored to human flourishing its proper priority to moral law. Nevertheless, debate continues over how best to understand natural law, with 'physicalism' (e.g., *Humanae vitae*, 1968) contending for the human body as the locus of what is normative, and 'PERSONALISM' (e.g., B. Häring, 1912–98) contending for the good of human persons as a whole. Another important point of ongoing controversy attends the role of weighing up 'quantities' of good and evil in making moral judgements, pitting 'proportionalists' such as R. McCormick (1922–2000) against 'absolutists' such as G. Grisez (b. 1929).

These debates should set moral theology's agenda for the foreseeable future: to reconcile theological integrity, charitable openness, and analytical meticulousness; to develop a cogent account of what in 'nature' is normative; and to articulate a more convincing account of the deontic constraints necessary to discipline the crude 'calculation' of consequences.

See also PASTORAL THEOLOGY; PRACTICAL THEOLOGY; VIRTUE ETHICS; VIRTUES.

D. Atkinson and D. Field, *The New Dictionary of Christian Ethics and Pastoral Theology* (InterVarsity Press, 1995).
N. Biggar, 'Ethics' in *The Blackwell Encyclopedia of Modern Christian Thought*, ed. A. McGrath (Blackwell, 1993), 164–83.
R. Hays, *The Moral Vision of the New Testament* (T&T Clark, 1996).
J. Mahoney, S. J., *The Making of Moral Theology* (Oxford University Press, 1987).
G. Meilaender and W. Werpehowski, eds., *The Oxford Handbook of Theological Ethics* (Oxford University Press, 2005).
A. Nygren, *Agape and Eros* (University of Chicago Press, 1982 [1930–6]).

NIGEL BIGGAR

MORMONS: see LATTER-DAY SAINTS, THE CHURCH OF JESUS CHRIST OF.

MORTAL SIN SIN is a breach in one's relationship with God. It is an offence against God and against truth and reason in the created order. The human being sins by an act of will and in doing so turns away from God's LOVE. This distorts the image of God in humanity and results in alienation from neighbour and oneself. According to Catholic tradition there are different types of sin with regard to their gravity and their effects vis-à-vis the state of GRACE of the one who sins. They differ according to the matter of the sin, the knowledge of the sinner, and the nature of her consent. Traditionally, Catholic theology identifies two types of sin in this regard: mortal and venial.

Mortal sins concern more serious matters than VENIAL SINS, matters that are objectively grave. They destroy a person's state of GRACE, depriving them of charity and sanctifying grace. Without repentance they lead to a loss of salvation and eternal death. FAITH may persist but the loss of charity is spiritually fatal. Because of the seriousness of mortal sin, it requires full knowledge and complete and free consent on the part of the sinner. If either of these is lacking the sin is not mortal. In a state of mortal sin the reception of the sacrament of reconciliation (i.e., PENANCE) is required before one is able to receive the EUCHARIST. A perfect CONTRITION is acceptable if sacramental penance is unavailable. In either case, the spiritual harm is so severe that a new initiative of divine grace and human CONVERSION is necessary.

RALPH DEL COLLE

***MUJERISTA* THEOLOGY** *Mujerista* theology is a Latina feminist theological voice that centres on the faith and struggles of grass-roots Latina women. Central to the task and methodology of *mujerista* theology is making grass-roots Latinas the subject and authors of contemporary theology. *Mujerista* theology is one of several Latina feminist voices within the contemporary theological arena. In contrast to embracing the term 'Latina feminist' or *feminista hispana*, proponents claim that the term *mujerista* is more inclusive of Latinas, who often feel feminism is an Anglo construction. Nonetheless, a feminist hermeneutic is fundamental to the *mujerista* position, which is primarily articulated by A. M. Isasi-Díaz (b. 1943). Three dimensions of Isasi-Díaz's corpus best summarize the central concerns and features of *mujerista* theology: her emphasis on the fluidity and hybridity of identity, the significance of *lo cotidiano* (daily life), and her use of autobiography and narrative.

Isasi-Díaz's emphasis on hybridity appears in her analysis of *MESTIZAJE/mulatez*, her understanding of difference, her use of Latina philosopher M. Lugones' (b. 1944) notion of world-travelling, and in her interpretation of all these concepts as revelatory of identity. *Mestizaje/mulatez* refers to the Latino/a condition as racially and culturally mixed people attempting to negotiate their identity within the dominant culture of the USA. As the primary *locus theologicus* of LATINO/A THEOLOGY, this category functions ethically in Isasi-Díaz's corpus as a condemnation of racism and ethnic prejudice. A fundamental aspect of Isasi-Díaz's emphasis on difference is a conceptualization of this notion as relational. As she points out, difference is often understood as exclusionary and divisive. Instead, Isasi-Díaz constructs difference in terms of relationships, showing that differences are relative. Similarly, Isasi-Diáz uses the category of world-travelling to refer to the survival tactics appropriated by Latino/as as they co-exist and travel between the Latino/a world and the dominant Anglo culture. At the core of all these categories is the insight that the traditional, oppositional, and static categories of identity that have been imposed on Latino/as do not speak to their lived realities. For Isasi-Díaz, theoretical concepts must ring true to people's daily lives or they are of little value.

Isasi-Díaz's writings on *lo cotidiano* are the foundation of many of the concepts and terminology that saturate her theology. This interest in *lo cotidiano* began early in her corpus with her use of ethnography and the inclusion of the voices of everyday Latinas in her academic publications. *Lo cotidiano* has in turn developed into a sophisticated concept that is fundamental to understanding her research project. As Isasi-Díaz has repeatedly pointed out, *lo cotidiano* has been traditionally deemed irrelevant and insignificant for academic reflection; even within LIBERATION THEOLOGIES it has been subsumed under the structural. Isasi-Díaz counters that structural change must be grounded in *lo cotidiano*, if it is to be significant and lasting. *Lo cotidiano* also functions hermeneutically for her as the lens through which we capture reality. In other words, Isasi-Díaz understands *lo cotidiano* as the epistemological horizon from which *mujerista* theology is written and lived. These explorations of *lo cotidiano* are a fundamental and distinctive contribution of her corpus. While other Latino/a theologians acknowledge *lo cotidiano* as a source for theology, Isasi-Díaz also presents it as the basic framework for academic theological reflection.

The autobiographical voice Isasi-Díaz embraces within many of her writings is an example of the significance of *lo cotidiano* for her work. She is not afraid to show her readers that she is passionate about a topic and why. Linked to this is the importance of emotions within her epistemology as fundamental to knowing. As she points out, to know something one must be impacted by it. A theology that claims any sort of social commitment must be grounded in compassion and love. This autobiographical starting point is also reflected in the ethnographic methodology of *mujerista* theology, which interweaves the voices of everyday Latinas as equal contributors to the Christian theological corpus alongside the great thinkers of the Christian tradition.

Within Latino/a theology, the *mujerista* corpus pushes the question of feminism and sexism. The biggest challenge that *mujerista* theology faces is the relationship between the various voices within Latina theology. *Mujerista* theology needs to engage those voices in Latina theology that challenge its viability precisely to be true to its commitment to the broadest possible range of Latina experience.

A. M. Isasi-Díaz, *En la Lucha/In the Struggle: Elaborating a Mujerista Theology* (Fortress Press, 1993).
Mujerista Theology: A Theology for the Twenty-First Century (Orbis, 1996).
La Lucha Continues: Mujerista Theology (Orbis, 2004).

MICHELLE A. GONZALEZ

MUNUS TRIPLEX: see THREEFOLD OFFICE.

MUSIC, THEOLOGY AND Theology is typically regarded as reflective language about God, sometimes ordered into systems of thought. *Christian* theology may then be conceived as an ordered set of claims, based on the reality of God and the world as revealed in the incarnate Word, Jesus Christ. This fact would seem to make music and musical settings of sacred texts entirely secondary to what theologians do. Music as such is not propositional, nor is it a 'language' with concrete reference and semantic sense. Yet theology may also be conceived as address to God – as PRAYER in the modalities of doxology as well as lament. This viewpoint opens the possibility of music as a form of theology. Some music may be said to explore the mystery of God and the depths of our humanity before God. Any theology of music must take this into account.

Within the Christian tradition there has long been a close association between music and theology. Early on figures like TERTULLIAN and Epiphanius of Salamis (*ca* 315–403) offered theological criticisms of singing and instrumental practices, reflecting their suspicion of the highly sensual qualities of music and worries about its association with pagan theatre and cultic religious practices. Gradually there emerged theological interpretations and commentaries on the Psalms that often carried positive theological affirmations of musical practices, and which have continued to influence Catholic and Orthodox theologies of music. Of particular significance in this respect are AUGUSTINE'S *De musica* and the *De utilitate hymnorum* of Niceta of Remesiana (d. *ca* 415). At the heart of the REFORMATION, M. LUTHER claimed that music was a wondrous gift from God. In his prefaces to the *Wittenberg Hymnal* (1524) and to George Rhau's hymn collection, *Symphoniae iucundae* (1538), Luther praised music as theological expression, noting that 'next to the Word of God, music deserves the highest praise' ('Preface', 321). Luther's theology of music stands at the head of a subsequent tradition of theologies of music, particularly influenced by J. S. Bach (1685–1750) and his interpreters.

There are several distinct elements in the task of a theology of music. First, it tells the story of how music and theology have mutually influenced one another. Second, a theology of music takes seriously how musical settings and performance practices may deepen as well as interpret the theological meanings of biblical and liturgical texts. At the same time such theological enquiry seeks to uncover the theological significance and import of the great instrumental and vocal works from all traditions, many of which do not deal with explicitly theological material. Furthermore, a theology of music examines what theologians can learn from the intrinsic values in various forms of music. This will include questions about time, temporality, and human self-understanding. How does music encode and express deep human emotions that are required for understanding the world? This question itself stands on the threshold of theological reasoning. Finally, but not exhaustively, theological reflection investigates how creativity is displayed in various forms of music, and how this may reflect the divine creativity itself.

Music can project us into the affective knowledge of God and of human existence. In music we often receive in sonic form the very patterns of how we experience the world: its pitch, tempo, rhythms, dissonances, harmonies, and complex simultaneity of pain and pleasure, life and death, time and eternity. This in turn opens a dialogue between music and theological wonder in which Christian conceptions of the goodness of CREATION, the depth of SIN and alienation, the sanctifying power of God's GRACE, the prophetic call to witness, and the central conception of the mystery of 'God among us' is at stake.

Theology has an interest in tracing different relationships between music (both texted and wordless) and explicit and implicit features of Christian belief and experience. Much depends upon context and the living performance of 'sound'. Music does not consist in the notes in a score, or in the 'mind' of the composer, much less in the abstractions of music theory. Rather, it is the lived encounter with the power of ordered sound (in itself a mysterious concept) that opens up new worlds. Among the matters that are deepest are how God is acknowledged and becomes palpable in the hearing of ordered sound.

Few can deny the powers of ordered sound on both SOUL and BODY. Humanity, to put it simply, is vulnerable to music. Both emotional and intellectual import and somatic and communal effects provide a framework for further exploration of music's theological significance, whether in so-called 'classical music', 'indigenous folk music', or in the wide range of popular music that so dominates the listening practices in contemporary societies.

When music is fused with language *addressed* to God it manifests a *doxological* element in theology. This doxological element is found first in SCRIPTURE in the prophets' heightened speech, the psalms, the canticles, or in the great hymns of Revelation, later taken up in the music of Bach, G. F. Handel (1685–1759), and F. J. Haydn (1732–1809). The doxological element is ubiquitous in many of the writings of the early Church theologians. Treatises that speak conceptually and analytically about God may suddenly break into ecstatic poetry: addressing God in heightened speech that is 'song'. This practice suggests that limiting 'real theology' to rationally ordered speech free of the doxological element means that something crucial is lost – a theme echoed in K. BARTH'S and H. Küng's (b. 1928) writings on W. A. Mozart (1756–91).

Music, especially in the context of the worship of God, is not merely an ornamentation or emotional expression of conceptual thought. There is an *intrinsic* relationship between thinking about God and acknowledging God in praise as well as lament. Furthermore, in so far as theological discourse about God must contain the element of silence that acknowledges the limits of our language, it opens the door to music as an alternative medium of Christian faith and practice.

J. S. Begbie, *Theology, Music and Time* (Cambridge University Press, 2000).
I. H. Jones, *Music: A Joy For Ever* (Epworth, 1989).
D. E. Saliers, *Theology and Music* (Abingdon Press, 2007).
P. Westermeyer, *Te Deum: The Church and Music* (Fortress Press, 1998).
D. Zager, ed., *Music and Theology: Essays in Honor of Robin A. Leaver* (Scarecrow Press, 2007).

DON E. SALIERS

MYSTICAL THEOLOGY The term 'mystical theology' (*theologia mystikê*) did not appear until the sixth century in the short treatise of that name by an anonymous author writing under the pseudonym of DIONYSIUS THE AREOPAGITE. Nevertheless, V. Lossky (1903–58) was correct when he stated, 'In a certain sense all theology is mystical, in as much as it shows forth the divine mystery' (*Mys.* 7). If the eastern Christian tradition did not make a break between mysticism and theology, this has also been true of many chapters in western Christian history. Mystical theology, broadly conceived as correct thought and speech about God (*theologia*) leading to DEIFICATION (*theosis*), is rooted in the encounter between Christian faith and Hellenistic culture. Neither 'mystical' (signifying the hidden dimension of outward religious objects and practices) nor 'theology' occurs in the Bible, but early Christians soon adopted these terms to describe their belief that the inner appropriation of SCRIPTURE, PRAYER, and LITURGY was meant to lead to the heights of contemplation of God (*theôria theou*), even 'becoming like God' through deifying union.

Mystical theology in an implied sense is found as early as Clement of Alexandria (*ca* 150–*ca* 215), the first to import major themes of Greek philosophy into Christian discourse. Mystical theology becomes explicit, if not yet thematized, in the work of ORIGEN. Origen's account of the progress of the fallen soul back to God through a programme of ascesis, meditation on Scripture, prayer, and contemplation, embraces three stages, which later came to be called the purgative, illuminative, and unitive ways: 'Having completed those stages by which the soul is purified through actions and virtues, it is led into the knowledge of natural things, and comes in a fitting way to the truths of faith [*dogmatica*] and ascends to mystical matters [*mystica*] and to the contemplation of divinity in pure spiritual love' (*CSong*, prologue). With Origen, as with many of his successors, mystical theology, whether taken in an implicit or an explicit way, was not primarily a way of thinking, but rather a programme for living, involving ascetic practice and participation in the sacramental and liturgical life of the community, always guided by the goal of increasing LOVE of God and neighbour.

Origen's mystical theology was developed in the patristic period by Evagrius Ponticus (*ca.* 345–99) in the East and his student John Cassian (*ca* 360–*ca* 435) in the West. The CAPPADOCIAN FATHERS of the late fourth century were important for emphasizing the negative, or APOPHATIC, dimension of mystical theology. The ungraspable infinity of God makes all striving towards the divine an endless pursuit (see Phil. 3:13) characterized by the paradox of insatiable satisfaction. Dionysius was the heir of these traditions, as well as of the mystical thinking of pagan Neoplatonic thinkers, especially Proclus (*ca* 410–85). His mystical theology is the summit of a complex interaction of the ways of practising and contemplating biblical and liturgical faith (the symbolic, positive, and negative theologies) aiming towards a 'mystical union' with the God who is both named with all names and beyond all names. This theology is a spiritual discipline aimed at deconstructing human forms of knowing, perceiving, and loving by 'plunging into the truly mystical darkness of unknowing' (*Mys.* 1.3).

Mystics of the Middle Ages recognized this holistic meaning of mystical theology, or the art of contemplation. All three of the major modes of medieval theology – the monastic, the Scholastic, and the vernacular – involved mystical theology, though in differing ways. 'Mystical theology' was not a term used by western monks during the period of the dominance of monastic theology between the sixth and the twelfth centuries. The only thinker who employs *theologia* and *mystica* often was J. Scotus Eriugena (*ca* 810–*ca* 880), who translated the Dionysian corpus into Latin and initiated western Dionysianism. Nevertheless, the monks remained true to the thought of Gregory the Great (*ca* 540–604), the 'Doctor of Contemplation', in their insistence that the study of Scripture include both an understanding of faith (*intellectus fidei*) and a deeper grasp of divine love (*intelligentia amoris*) aimed at divinization. Monastic mystical theology reached its culmination in the twelfth century, especially among the Cistercian mystics like Bernard of Clairvaux (1090–1153) and William of Saint-Thierry (*ca* 1080–1148), but it was an integral aspect of all monastic theology in the early Middle Ages.

The rise of the new scientific, professionalized, and differentiated model of theology that we call Scholastic in the late eleventh and twelfth centuries had a dual effect on the mystical element of theology. On the one hand, the distinction of various theological operations (*lectio–quaestio–disputatio–praedicatio*), coupled with the desire to produce systematic presentations of Christian DOCTRINE, tended to uncouple theology from the goal of contemplation and deification. On the other hand, many Scholastic authors attempted to reap the fruits of the new methods for more systematic ways of presenting the riches of mystical teaching. Among these were the Augustinian canons of Saint Victor outside Paris, where Hugh (*ca* 1095–1141) and Richard (d. 1173) stand out as important contributors to the development of SCHOLASTICISM and as major mystical authors whose writings influenced late medieval and early modern mystics. The twelfth century also witnessed the beginning of a long line of mystical handbooks composed by monks, Victorine canons, and later by members of other religious orders. In the thirteenth century, Bonaventure (1221–74) was another witness to a seamless theological programme that contributed both to scholasticism and to mystical theology through such widely read works as *The Mind's Journey into God* and *The Threefold Way.*

Also important for evaluating the Scholastic contribution to mystical theology was the role the schoolmen took in the Dionysian revival of the late Middle Ages. Apart from Eriugena, few read Dionysius in the early Middle Ages. The Victorines initiated renewed study of Dionysius, and the last major Victorine mystical author, T. Gallus (*ca* 1200–46), wrote the first full commentary on the Dionysian corpus, interpreting the master of mystical theology as the supreme authority for the negative aspect of mysticism, just as the Song of Songs was the main authority for its positive side. Gallus' interpretation has been called affective Dionysianism in that he taught that the 'supreme point of love' (*apex affectus*) was the place where the soul meets God beyond all positive and negative modes. This programme, especially through its adoption by Bonaventure, various Carthusian authors, and the anonymous English *The Cloud of Unknowing* (fourteenth century), formed an important strand in late medieval mystical theology. Shortly after Gallus' affective Dionysianism began to spread, the Dominican Albert the Great (*ca* 1200–80) also commented on the Dionysian corpus. His interpretation can be described as intellective, or better 'super-intellective', in that he and his followers among the German Dominicans, especially Meister Eckhart, insisted on the role of intellect in the drive towards reaching a deep union with God that surpasses all categories of human loving and knowing. The conflict and interaction of these two modes of understanding Dionysian mystical theology continued for centuries, not least in the fourteenth-century debates over mystical theology that engaged theologians like J. Gerson (1363–1429) and Nicholas of Cusa (1401–64).

Not all mystical theology was exhausted by the monks and the Scholastics. From the thirteenth century on, a flood of literature, much of it mystical, began to be produced in the vernacular languages of Western Europe. This vernacular theology was a real theology, though it necessarily differed from the monastic and Scholastic modes in context, presentation, and audience. Like the monastic theologians, its adherents saw deification and union with God as the direct goal of their teaching and practice. This theology was pioneering, not only in many of its themes and forms of languages, but also in the fact that women played such a large role in it, as the names of Clare of Assisi (1194–1253), Hadewijch of Antwerp (early thirteenth century), Mechthild of Magdeburg, Angela of Foligno (*ca* 1250–1309), M. Porete (d. 1310), Catherine of Siena, Julian of Norwich, and Catherine of Genoa (1447–1510) demonstrate. Male theologians writing in the vernacular were also significant, such as H. Suso (*ca* 1300–66) and J. Tauler (*ca* 1300–61) in Germany, J. van Ruusbroec (1293–1381) in the Low Countries, and R. Rolle (*ca* 1300–49) and W. Hilton (d. 1396) in England. Some of the teachings advanced by late medieval mystics about the need for annihilation and the possibility of attaining indistinct union with God proved controversial, so the period from the thirteenth through to the seventeenth centuries saw a series of conflicts between some mystics and the guardians of orthodoxy: bishops, councils, and popes.

It is not easy to summarize the many forms of teaching found in the new vernacular mysticism of the late Middle Ages and of early modern times. While many authors did not use the term 'mystical theology', even the supposedly unlearned knew what it meant. Teresa of Avila, speaking of her direct contact with God, says: 'I used unexpectedly to experience a consciousness of the presence of God of such a kind that I could not possibly doubt that he was within me and that I was totally engulfed in him. This was in no sense a vision: I believe it is called mystical theology' (*Life* 1.10). The mystical theology of Teresa and her collaborator, John of the Cross (1542–91), represents the high point of sixteenth-century Catholic mysticism. The seventeenth century was the 'Golden Age' of French mysticism with figures like P. de Bérulle (1575–1629) and F. de Sales (1567–1622), but towards the end of the century the long-simmering tensions between mysticism and orthodoxy exploded in the Quietist controversy, in which some mystics were accused of teaching that the prayer of quiet and the attainment of a state of pure love freed one from the obligations of the Christian life and even the constraints of the moral law (see Quietism). The condemnations of the Spanish mystic M. de Molinos (1628–96) in 1686, and of Archbishop F. Fénelon (1651–1715) and Madame Guyon (1648–1717) in the 1690s reduced mystical teaching to a carefully circumscribed division of theology (often called 'Ascetical and Mystical Theology') under the watchful eyes of dogmatic theologians like the Jesuit G. Scaramelli (1687–1752). The marginalization of mystical theology was aided by the fact that it was in the seventeenth century that 'mysticism' as a special category of study, and not as a way of life, first appeared. For several centuries, down to the revival of serious interest in mysticism in the twentieth century, mysticism was severed from its theological roots, most often being seen as a species of psychological (especially paranormal) experience, rather than as a programme for living and appropriating correct thought and speech about God.

Mystical theology had an ambiguous place in the Churches of the Reformation. Luther was not a mystic and opposed Dionysian mystical theology. He was, nevertheless, indebted to aspects of late medieval vernacular mysticism, such as the writings of Tauler, and therefore there was a place for mystical theology in Protestantism, as can be seen with J. Arndt (1555–1621) and the Pietists (see Pietism). Similarly, the Anglican tradition contained a mystical tendency evident among seventeenth-century Puritans and in a number of later spiritual writers and theologians. The problems that mystical theology encountered after 1700 did not affect the Christian East, where the late eighteenth century saw the publication of the *Philokalia*, and nineteenth-century Russia played host to a series of mystical guides and teachers.

The extent to which the revival of theological interest in mysticism in the twentieth century will see fruit is difficult to discern. Mystical theology has become important today not only due to efforts of academic theologians, but also because of the emergence of original mystical teachers, such as P. TEILHARD DE CHARDIN, S. WEIL, and T. MERTON. The contours of a mysticism that is deeply theological, not just a branch of abnormal psychology, remain to be determined, but many will agree with the statement of K. RAHNER that the Christian of the future will either be a mystic or not be a Christian at all.

F. von Hügel, *The Mystical Element of Religion as Studied in Catherine of Siena and Her Friends*, 2nd edn, 2 vols. (James Clarke, 1923).
V. Lossky, *The Mystical Theology of the Eastern Church* (SPCK, 1957).
J. Maréchal, *Studies in the Psychology of the Mystics* (Burnes, Oates & Washbourne, 1927).
B. McGinn, *The Presence of God: A History of Western Christian Mysticism*, 4 vols. (Crossroad, 1991–).
M. A. McIntosh, *Mystical Theology* (Blackwell, 1998).
A. Stolz, *The Doctrine of Spiritual Perfection* (Crossroad, 2001).

BERNARD MCGINN

MYTH Fundamentally, Christian theology has adopted one of four positions in determining the relationship between myth and its sacred narratives: (1) rejection – because myth and the narratives are incompatible, (2) historical – the early religious narratives adapted contemporaneous myths as they were developed; (3) translation – myths are deficient or deceptive forms of expressing the sacred narrative that must be recast in non-mythical (usually philosophical) language in order to be understood; and (4) poetic – myth is the necessary and fullest form of expressing the sacred narratives' truth.

Initially, Christianity adopted the first position and insisted on a clear distinction between its foundational stories and the 'myths' of its competing religious neighbours. Thus, when the NT uses the Greek term *mythos*, it does so only in a derogatory manner (cf. 1 Tim. 1:4; 4:6–7; 2 Tim. 4:4; and Titus 1:14). These 'myths' are rejected as false, particular, and local stories that were historically unreliable and destructive depictions of reality. In contrast, the Christian narrative is considered as universally true, grounded by 'eyewitness' accounts that verify its truth, and revelatory of the meaning of existence (cf. 2 Pet. 1:16).

This position dominated Christian thinking until the eighteenth century, when the investigatory methods of the Renaissance and the philosophic sentiments of the ENLIGHTENMENT combined to render it problematic. As interpreters such as J. G. Eichorn (1753–1827) brought historical and non-polemic understandings of myth to bear on the biblical narratives, it became evident that SCRIPTURE itself contained myths (e.g., creation and flood myths) and mythic elements (e.g., depictions of healings, miracles, resuscitations, and divine interruption of nature's typical courses). Further, analyses of ancient non-biblical myths demonstrated that they were not occasional, local stories or fables, but rather pre-scientific constructions of world views with intrinsic logics of their own.

The publication of D. F. Strauss' (1808–74) *The Life of Jesus Critically Examined* (1835) signalled a further change. In opposition to interpreters who explained the origins of the Gospels as supernatural narratives or by recourse to rationalist reconstructions, Strauss argued that the Gospels did not simply contain mythic elements, but were composed entirely of mythic material from their most extraordinary and miraculous stories to their most mundane descriptions of everyday behaviour. More critically, these mythic constructs were inchoate and deficient forms of the truth, which needed to be replaced by a new philosophic treatment of the intersection of the divine and the human in history.

Strauss' initial analyses of the Gospels are amplified in the work of R. Bultmann, who argued that not only the Gospels, but the entire NT was mythic. Like Strauss, Bultmann sought to eliminate this myth, but not because he thought that its message was defective. According to Bultmann, the NT used a mythic three-story depiction of the universe to announce the fundamental relationships of God and human beings in a manner which was no longer comprehensible to modern thought. The ancient myth thus obscures the true Christian proclamation. Only when the myth had been translated into a modern vernacular would a contemporary hearer be encountered by the message embedded in the mythic form. Thus, Bultmann proposed 'demythologizing' or recasting the mythic depictions into the philosophical language of existentialism, which, he thought, best revealed its essential nature.

Finally, more recent study that considers the structural and literary functions of myth has argued that it is a necessary form for expressing sacred narrative. This conception of myth is most evident in the work of scholars such as L. Gilkey (1919–2004), P. Ricœur (1913–2005), and S. McFague (b. 1933), who argue that myth is not simply a vehicle for truth but is essential to the expression of truth. Myth therefore cannot be rejected or translated if the sacred narratives are to be communicated. Obvious questions arise with this position as they do with the others. For instance, given the range of genres found in Scripture, what is the relationship of the truths conveyed by narrative or figuration to those expressed with prosaic and literal language? Second, what methods of interpreting myth are appropriate to discern the truth that is being expressed? Finally, if mythic narration is essential to the truth-value of the myth, what myths will communicate in modern contexts? However these questions are answered, the relationship of myth to the sacred narrative will persist because the nature, origin, and means of discerning the truth-values of myths remain open questions.

STEVEN KRAFTCHICK

Narrative Theology Unlike other theological movements in the last third of the twentieth century – such as process, feminist, and various liberation theologies – narrative theology is not so much a coherent, identifiable school or movement as it is a theme. Narrative has become a prominent topic for discussion not just in theology, ethics, biblical studies, homiletics, pastoral care, and Christian education, but also in psychology and psychotherapy, philosophy, literary studies, anthropology, law, and medicine. And in addition to the attention it has garnered in the academy, narrative has also drawn the attention of practising religious communities both within and outside Christianity. Rarely has a single theme attracted such widespread interest.

There are many factors in the emergence of narrative as a theme in theology. During the last thirty years of the twentieth century questions about identity – personal, racial/ethnic, cultural, and ecclesial – surfaced in both Churches and society. In North America and western Europe some theologians struggled with the question of the meaning of Christian identity in a post-Christian and postmodern world. Many racial/ethnic groups, women, and Christians in non-western communities rejected White, male, North American and western European interpretations of Christian faith and began to explore new paradigms for doing theology.

Additionally, biblical scholars and theologians recognized the limitations of historical criticism and the importance of reading biblical texts in the ecclesial contexts in which they originated and have their primary function. Many turned to different forms of literary criticism in order to interpret texts within the larger biblical canon. OT scholars pointed to the central role of narrative in the Pentateuch, and NT scholars, using redaction and reader-response criticism, focused not just on individual pericopes but on parables as extended metaphors and on Gospels as a literary genre.

S. Crites (1931–2007) provided important impetus in the early discussion of narrative theology by arguing that 'the formal quality of experience through time is inherently narrative'. He found evidence in traditional folk cultures of 'sacred stories', stories that are ritually re-enacted but cannot be directly told 'because they live, so to speak, in the arms and legs and bellies of the celebrants' ('Narrative', 291, 295). Although these sacred stories cannot be directly told, they come to expression in what Crites described as 'mundane stories', stories that create a world and are the means by which people articulate and clarify their sense of identity. Individual and communal identity assumes the form of narrative because there is something about the nature of temporal experience that requires narrative expression.

Crites' essay raised a question that continues to be debated in narrative theology: is narrative a convenient but still arbitrary category for describing the nature of Christian identity or is there something about human identity in general and Christian identity in particular that requires the use of narrative and explains its centrality within the various genres of Scripture? In other words, is narrative a foundational or an ad hoc category for Christian theology?

During the 1970s and 1980s the debate concerning the foundational status of narrative became one aspect of a larger debate in theological hermeneutics, a debate between what was sometimes identified as a 'Yale School' of theology (sometimes described as postliberal theology) and a 'Chicago School' of theology. The best-known figures in the former were H. Frei (1922–98) and G. Lindbeck (b. 1923) and in the latter P. Ricœur (1913–2005) and D. Tracy (b. 1939). In *The Eclipse of Biblical Narrative* (1974) Frei traced the 'eclipse' of a realistic reading of Scripture, prominent before the Enlightenment, in which the Bible renders its own world and truthfulness and the emergence during and after the Enlightenment of a form of interpretation that stood realism on its head, separated the issues of meaning, truth, and reference, and argued the primacy of the reader's world over that of the text. The hermeneutical challenge became not the demands made by the plain sense of the biblical text on the reader, but the necessity to reinterpret the text in light of the primary reality of the reader's world, a world in which meaning and truth have been sundered and the text's truthfulness becomes a matter either of the text's historical accuracy or of its remythologization by those sitting in front of the text.

Narrative theology, as Ricœur understood it, is a specifically Christian task that must attend not only to the constitutive narratives of the Christian community but to the larger field of narratology, to the nature of temporality, to what passes away and what endures, and to the art of emplotment. In his three-volume work on *Time and Narrative* (1981–85) Ricœur explored the relation between historical and fictional narratives in relation to temporality and concluded that life stories, for both individuals and communities, interweave historiography and fiction in narrative identity. In *Oneself as Another* (1992) he argued that personal identity can be articulated only in the temporal dimension of human existence and as a dialectic of selfhood and sameness that attains its fullest development in narrative theory.

The critical difference between Frei and Ricœur is whether narrative theology should interpret Christian identity in light of those particular narratives – namely, Scripture – that give Christian readers their distinctive faith or by means of a general theory of narratology.

Since the early 1970s several attempts have been made to use narrative to reconstruct Christian doctrine, including reinterpretations of revelation, the reality of God and the Trinity, the identity of Jesus Christ, and the nature of the Church. In particular, Frei, R. Krieg (b. 1946), G. Loughlin (b. 1957), and M. Cook (b. 1936) have made intriguing proposals for a Christology that is more directly related to the NT than the classical Christology of Chalcedon.

M. L. Cook, *Christology as Narrative Quest* (Liturgical Press, 1997).

H. W. Frei, *The Identity of Jesus Christ* (Yale University Press, 1975).

G. Loughlin, *Telling God's Story: Bible, Church and Narrative Theology* (Cambridge University Press, 1996).

P. Ricœur, *Figuring the Sacred: Religion, Narrative, and Imagination* (Fortress Press, 1995).

George W. Stroup

Natural Evil As distinguished from moral evil, natural evil is a categorical designation for all causes of creaturely suffering that cannot be attributed directly to creaturely (viz., human) agency, including disease, famine, and natural disasters (e.g., earthquakes, floods, storms, volcanoes, and the like). Prior to the modern period, theologians attributed even these sorts of events indirectly to human agency, in so far as they understood creation's susceptibility to suffering and decay to be a by-product of the fall (see Gen. 3:17–19; cf. Rom. 8:20–1). Contemporary scientific understanding of natural history makes it clear that various forms of natural evil were features of the earthly environment long before the advent of the human species. Nevertheless, the line between natural and moral evil remains very hard to define, in so far as (for example) deaths resulting from earthquakes are inseparable from human decisions about constructing buildings, and 'natural' phenomena like global warming seem at least in part to be caused by human activity.

While these qualifications are important, natural evil is generally seen as posing a greater challenge to Christian theodicy than moral evil, both because the scale of destruction tends to be extraordinarily large and because it appears more difficult to absolve God of responsibility for the suffering that results. Process theology addresses this problem by ascribing some degree of agency to all creatures. A more common approach among Christians has been (following passages like Rom. 11:33) to stress divine incomprehensibility and trust that such events fall within the scope of divine providence. Critics of such attitudes worry that they promote a complacency towards suffering inconsistent with Jesus' teaching and practice.

Ian A. McFarland

Natural Law The natural law is commonly said to be a set of moral norms, or evaluative principles, grounded in some way in nature or reason, and therefore accessible to all. However, there is no consensus on what the natural law is, even granting that such a thing exists. Nonetheless, it is possible to trace a more or less continuous tradition of reflection on the natural law from the Stoics, through patristic and medieval jurists and theologians, continuing through the modern period to the present day. It would be a mistake to identify the object of this tradition with any one construal of nature or reason, or with a specific set of moral injunctions. Rather, the natural-law tradition is grounded in a distinctive form of normative analysis, in which the conventions of society are interpreted and evaluated in terms of their relation to pre-conventional principles.

Such analysis need not imply that what is non-natural, in the sense of conventional, is thereby wicked or bad, but it does presuppose that we do have access to a pre-conventional natural order of some kind, which provides a basis for the normative evaluation of social conventions. For the Stoics, this pre-conventional origin tended to be identified with the innate rational order of the cosmos, whereas the eclectic philosophers writing near the beginning of the Common Era often interpreted it in terms of a synthesis of Stoic and Platonic elements (e.g., Cicero (106–43 BC)) or through an identification with the decrees of a supreme deity (as in Philo of Alexandria (20 BC–AD 50)). In any case, nature is construed as an intelligible principle of operation or causality, and, in the intellectual ethos of Hellenistic philosophy, this implies that it is also a normative principle – understood in terms of Platonic exemplars, or in the Aristotelian terms of the innate teleologies informing living creatures, or (most often) some synthesis of both (see Aristotelianism; Platonism).

The versions of the natural law that would be most familiar among Christians today first began to take systematic shape in the early twelfth century through the work of Scholastic jurists and theologians. Patristic theologians had already appropriated the idea of natural law, which they construed in scriptural and theological terms. The natural law thus understood lies at the intersection of two distinct yet complementary points of access to God's creative wisdom and providential care: nature, understood as comprising the fundamental principles of order and causality structuring created existence; and Scripture, which attests to the existence of a natural law and draws out its practical implications. Following well-established patristic trajectories, the Scholastics identify the natural law with the 'inner law' referred to at Romans 2:14, where PAUL asserts that the Gentiles discern what the LAW requires through an inner law. Furthermore, they identify the two scriptural formulations of the Golden Rule and the TEN COMMANDMENTS as basic precepts of the natural law. At this level, natural-law precepts are thus taken to be both natural and revealed, and the revealed precepts of the natural law set the basic parameters for any account of the normative significance of nature.

However, the line of interpretation does not run in one direction only. While the Scholastics relied on Scripture to provide a basic outline of natural-law precepts, they also drew on their overall concept of natural law in order to distinguish those scriptural precepts which are permanently binding from those that are in some way conditional, and they further appealed to judgements about what is natural and proper in order to interpret and harmonize even those precepts which were regarded as unconditionally binding. The revealed precepts of the natural law, or at least those that had some specific content (such as the precepts of the Decalogue) were not generally regarded as constituting natural law most properly understood; rather, the Scholastics, in accordance with very long-standing traditions, identified the natural law with pre-conventional principles for action, which are further specified through divine decree or human deliberation. Thus, whatever can be construed as a pre-conventional principle for human action, including fundamental metaphysical principles of causality and the inclinations humans share with other living creatures, can be identified as a principle of natural law.

At the same time, the normative significance of these diverse principles cannot simply be read off from observations of (putatively) natural activities and processes. The Scholastics were well aware that the activities and processes of non-human creatures offer limited guidance at best for human action, and recognized that we can only determine the normative force of natural principles through rational reflection. Partially for that reason, they tended to identify natural law understood in its most proper sense with reason itself. What is more, Scripture itself strongly suggests just such an interpretation, most notably at Romans 2:14. Whatever their reasons, the Scholastics clearly identified the natural law in its primary sense either with rational capacities for practical judgement, or with the foundational principles through which practical judgement operates. It is easy to overlook the significance of this claim, since the Scholastics continued to express themselves in the traditional language of their classical forebears. Yet this represents the first time that the natural law is identified directly with an innate capacity for rational discernment, rather than with an objective normative order discerned through reason. This identification, in turn, allowed the jurists to identify the natural law, through which we stand in right relations to God and neighbour, with the rights through which we exercise our own claims to freedom and forbearance.

The Scholastics interpret the relation between human law and the natural principles from which it stems in terms that acknowledge the indeterminacy of natural principles and allow room for considerable variation at the level of specific expressions of those principles. Rather than regarding social conventions as more or less direct and unchangeable expressions of human nature, they emphasized the need for processes of rational, communally shared deliberation, in order to move from natural principles to their conventional formulations. The natural law, thus construed, comprises the dynamic originating principles underlying the mores, institutions, and laws of particular societies, but it leaves considerable scope for flexibility and variation at the level of specific formulations.

When we turn from the medieval to the early modern period, we come to another decisive moment in the formulation of the natural-law tradition. Most of those reflecting on the natural law in this period identify themselves as Christians attempting to draw out the implications of Christian thought for the changing social conditions of their time. Nonetheless, there is a fundamental difference between modern natural-law thinkers and their medieval forebears, grounded in a very different construal of reason and REVELATION. On the modern view, these are two mutually compatible, complementary, but ultimately distinct sources for moral knowledge. Reason does its work, and *then* revelation steps in to confirm, correct, and supplement the moral code which reason generates independently. The Scholastics also said that the precepts of the natural law are (at least) rationally defensible. Yet, at the same time, they interpreted reason itself in theological, and ultimately scriptural terms. That is why they did not hesitate to draw on Scripture as well as rational argument in order to determine the concrete content of the natural law, and it is also why they did not attempt to derive a system of natural-law thinking out of purely natural data or rationally self-evident intuitions.

In contrast, the modern natural lawyers attempt to do precisely that. Now for the first time we see the emergence of the ideal of a scientific knowledge of morality, grounded in perspicuous principles of rational judgement, and developed through demonstrative arguments and deductive reasoning. Note that, by now, the natural law has come to be seen as primarily a set of specific rules which can be derived with certainty from first principles. This further separates the modern appropriation of the natural-law tradition from its medieval version, since now the universality of the natural law is recast as a universality of rationally compelling norms, not the universality of a human capacity. Many contemporary theories of natural law similarly construe it as a set of norms grounded in practical reason, which can as such be derived to a high degree of rational certainty without reference to natural, metaphysical, or theological claims. At the same time, the Scholastic approach to the natural law is once again beginning to receive respectful attention, thanks to a renewed interest in the scriptural and theological presuppositions of medieval accounts of natural law, on the one hand, and a return to Aristotelian and broadly naturalistic approaches in moral philosophy, on the other.

M. Crowe, *The Changing Profile of the Natural Law* (M. Nijhoff, 1977).

A. P. d'Entrèves, *Natural Law: An Introduction to Legal Philosophy*, 2nd edn (Hutchinson, 1970).

J. Porter, *Nature as Reason: A Thomistic Theory of the Natural Law* (Eerdmans, 2005).

B. Tierney, *The Idea of Natural Rights* (Scholars Press, 1997).

JEAN PORTER

NATURAL SCIENCE Natural science is a modern method of understanding the physical universe based on observation, hypothesis formation, and experimental verification. It strives to express its understanding of natural phenomena as far as possible in terms of testable hypotheses. Natural science is thus distinct from what had traditionally been called natural philosophy not only by virtue of its emphasis on experimentation, but also because of a preference for expressing the intelligibility of observed data in quantitative terms. The book of nature, said G. Galilei (1564–1642), 'is written in mathematical language, and the letters are triangles, circles and other geometrical figures, without which means it is humanly impossible to comprehend a single word' (*Opere* 4.171). Although contemporary philosophy of science has shown that the practice of assessing the relative merits of different hypotheses is often less procedurally regular than classic models suggest, it remains the case that the combination of experimentation and mathematical formulation has dominated natural scientists' self-understanding of their work since the seventeenth century.

Natural science comprises the disciplines of astronomy, geology, chemistry, physics, and biology, as well as numerous cross-disciplines such as oceanography, environmental science, and computer science. Its method corresponds to patterns of human cognition consisting of experience, understanding, and judgement. Science begins with the observation of a deliberately restricted range of data in the natural world. Second, it formulates hypotheses (ideally in mathematical terms) in order to express the intelligible relationships of the various elements observed. These relationships may then be correlated with the data of additional scientific experiments and hypotheses so that a comprehensive 'theory' will emerge, such as the Copernican heliocentric theory, I. Newton's (1643–1727) and A. Einstein's (1879–1955) gravitational theories, and C. Darwin's (1809–82) theory of EVOLUTION. Third, the method of natural science requires an ongoing process of testing and critical reflection in order to arrive at an accurate judgement as to whether its hypothetical or theoretical understanding in fact corresponds to the observed data. As new data become available the hypotheses and theories may need to undergo revision.

Both the method and discoveries of the natural sciences have enormous implications for Christian theology. Because of the widespread influence of scientific method and its impressive applications to technology, the question has often arisen in the modern and contemporary world as to whether the natural sciences have rendered theological understanding of the world intellectually superfluous. Methodologically speaking, there are at least four distinct ways of responding to this question: conflict, contrast, contact, and confirmation.

Conflict thinks of scientific method and theology as mutually exclusive. Both theists and non-theists may claim that science and theology are cognitively incompatible. Some theists since the time of Galileo have considered science inferior, erroneous, or negligible in comparison with the blinding truth of REVELATION. Since the time of Darwin a considerable number of Christians, for example, have taken evolutionary biology to be incompatible with biblical faith.

However, the conflict approach is also endorsed by scientists and scientifically educated intellectuals who have come to believe that scientific method, as described above, is the only reliable way to arrive at truthful understanding of anything whatsoever. This belief is usually called 'scientism'. It is the epistemic foundation of the world view known as 'scientific naturalism'. Scientific naturalism, in turn, is the belief that only the world available to science can appropriately be called real. Accordingly, theological reference to God or anything 'spiritual' is considered obsolete and illusory.

Logically speaking, in order to take science and theology as conflicting methods of understanding, one first has to assume that they are both attempting to accomplish the same cognitional objective. Devotees of scientism and scientific naturalism, for example, almost invariably assume that theology is a primitive *scientific* attempt to understand phenomena that modern natural science can now explain much more accurately.

Advocates of the 'contrast' approach, on the other hand, argue that science and theology cannot really compete, contradict, or conflict with each other since they are addressing radically distinct kinds of questions. Proper theological method does not and should not claim to provide scientific information, nor should theologians ever embrace particular scientific hypotheses or theories for theological reasons. The methods and results of scientific and theological enquiry exist in sharp contrast, not contradiction, to each other.

The contrast approach, therefore, nullifies the common claim made by followers of scientism and scientific naturalism that 'Ockham's razor' demonstrates the superiority of scientific explanations over theological ones. Ockham's razor is a maxim that instructs enquirers not to multiply explanations unnecessarily. It maintains that, in explaining natural phenomena, a good rule of thumb is to choose the simplest hypothesis – the one that makes the fewest assumptions – *if there are competing hypotheses.* However, the whole point of the contrast approach is to make it clear that science and theology cannot be competing ways of understanding – in which case it makes no sense to compare them or choose between them.

There is, of course, a real conflict between theology and *scientism*, as well as between *scientific naturalism* and any particular theological world view. But there can be no real conflict between science and theology rightly understood from a contrast perspective. Hence, Ockham's razor has no meaningful application to real issues in science and theology. It only seems to be a useful device if one first assumes, as advocates of scientism often do, that theology is an alternative and competing set of attempts to provide scientific explanations.

A third approach agrees that it is important to distinguish carefully between scientific and theological methods. However, it maintains that contrast alone fails to bring a satisfying resolution to the question of theology's relationship to the natural sciences. The mind needs to make clear distinctions, of course, but not as an end in itself. Human beings naturally strive to unify knowledge, but to do so without oversimplification they need to relate different kinds of understanding to one another in comprehensive syntheses that preserve rather than blur necessary distinctions.

This 'contact' approach acknowledges that in the real world it is the same human mind that entertains both scientific and theological ideas. At the origins of both science and theology lies one and the same human desire to understand and know. So theology and science are not opposed. Nor are they so independent of each other that theological understanding remains unaffected by new scientific discoveries.

It is the task of a constructive theology of nature, therefore, to clarify some of the ways in which scientific discoveries and theories, without being confused with theology, can nonetheless have a bearing on theology's understanding of God, creation, sin, redemption, and eschatology. Such a task becomes imperative especially during and after periods of fresh discovery and theoretical innovation. Since it is not the task of religious FAITH or theology to make scientific discoveries or to provide scientific information, it is clearly inappropriate for scientific thinkers to reproach biblical authors for not having revealed the exact age of the universe, the evidence for biological evolution, or any other information that human reason can arrive at on its own. But, if it is inappropriate to fault theologians for not having anticipated Darwin's theories, it is worthy of comment, if not reproach, that even at the beginning of the twenty-first century Christian theologians have barely begun the project of developing a theology of evolution that would allow Christians everywhere to embrace enthusiastically the well-established scientific evidence for life's evolution.

A fourth approach highlights the significant ways in which theology in the West positively supports or 'confirms' the adventure of scientific discovery. No scientist, this approach proposes, can initiate or sustain a process of enquiry into nature apart from possessing from the start a tacit faith that the real world is intelligible. Science, like all kinds of human knowing, begins with what philosopher M. Polanyi (1891–1976) calls a deeply personal 'fiduciary' aspect (from the Latin *fides*, 'trust') consisting especially of the belief that deeper understanding will reward judicious enquiry.

However, is there any basis for such trust? The confirmation approach declares that there is, but only if God exists. The reality of an infinitely intelligent ground of rationality would justify the scientist's trust in the world's endless and inexhaustible intelligibility. Theology does not need to seek intellectual legitimacy by placing itself alongside science as a competing set of 'answers' to questions that science can deal with quite well on its own. Rather, theology's appropriate function in relationship to science is that of responding to ultimate questions such as why the scientist should bother to seek intelligibility and truth at all. Believing in the existence of an infinite horizon of intelligibility – God, in other words – should justify and confirm the scientific search for understanding and truth.

I. G. Barbour, *Religion and Science: Historical and Contemporary Issues* (HarperSanFrancisco, 1997).
J. F. Haught, *Science and Religion: From Conflict to Conversation* (Paulist Press, 1995).
B. Lonergan, *Insight: A Study of Human Understanding*, 3rd edn (Philosophical Library, 1970).
M. Polanyi, *Personal Knowledge* (Harper & Row, 1964).
A. N. Whitehead, *Science and the Modern World* (Free Press, 1925).

JOHN F. HAUGHT

NATURAL THEOLOGY Natural theology is, traditionally, the attempt to establish rational theistic claims through observation of nature and the use of human reason, without recourse to purported special REVELATION. A more contemporary view of natural theology suggests that, although proofs for the existence of God are out of the question, reason may still seek to integrate and provide coherence and consistency to religious convictions in relation to developments in physical cosmology and other sciences. In this respect, it assumes a more modest apologetic role in showing the consistency of faith claims with the findings of other disciplines (see Apologetics). Natural theology, then, is the activity of relating religion, science, history, morality, and sometimes the arts into a general world view.

Throughout its long history, natural theology has undergone three broad stages of development, away from the mythological stage in which God was conceived as another being in the world, to the stage of metaphysical theism in which God was conceived as a transcendent being who is personal, bodiless, and inaccessible to sense experience, to the idea of God as ultimate reality conceived in dynamic, creative, and active ways.

Often conceived as a branch of Christian theology, ancient Greek predecessors to natural theology can be found in the writings of Plato (*ca* 430–*ca* 345 BC) concerning rational arguments for the existence of divine reason at work in the world, and in the reflections of Aristotle (384–322 BC) on the 'final cause' or unmoved mover, who functions as the end or purpose of the process of nature. Utilizing and revising Aristotelian categories (see Aristotelianism), T. Aquinas, according to one classical interpretation of his work, produced the most important medieval milestone in the history of reconciling Christian faith with natural reason in his *Summa theologiae*, in the course of which he offered the 'Five Ways' as an initial framework for reflecting on the reality of God (*ST* 1.2.3). While defending versions of the cosmological and the teleological arguments for the existence of God, Aquinas maintained that the ontological argument made famous by Anselm of Canterbury failed, as it is not legitimate to move from the thought of something to its existence in reality. After Aquinas, the teleological argument, cosmological argument, and ontological arguments for the existence of God continued to exercise fascination, with the teleological (or 'design') argument receiving the most attention. The ontological argument underwent significant revisions in the twentieth century by C. Hartshorne (1897–2000) and A. Plantinga (b. 1932) with the aid of modal logic. More recent readings of Aquinas have tended to see his project less in terms of a semi-independent natural theology, and more as one of accommodating philosophical insights within a thoroughly Christian theological vision.

In the seventeenth century, popular works such as J. Ray's (1627–1705) *The Wisdom of God Manifested in the Works of the Creation* sought to celebrate God's handiwork in the creation as an aspect of the pursuit of modern science. Theologically inspired arguments reached their apogee a century later in W. Paley's (1743–1805) *Natural Theology; or, Evidences of the Existence and Attributes of the Deity, Collected from the Appearances of Nature* (1802). Included among those appearances were such examples as the hinges on bivalve shells and the plumes that facilitate wind dispersal of certain seeds. But the heart of Paley's argument was constructed around the analogy of a watchmaker. Imagine, Paley suggested, that you are walking across a heath and suddenly encounter a watch lying on the ground. After close inspection of the watch, you would be compelled to conclude that such an intricate device could not have been fashioned otherwise in order for it to work. It is only reasonable to assume 'that the watch must have had a maker: that there must have existed, at some time and at some place or other, an artificer or artificers who formed it for the purpose which we find it actually to answer, who comprehended its construction and designed its use' (*Works* 388). In the case of living organisms, the evidence for design is even greater, 'in a degree which exceeds all computation' (*Works* 390–1). Paley concluded, 'The marks of design are too strong to be gotten over. Design must have had a designer. That designer must have been a person. That person is God' (*Works* 468).

Though Paley's work was enormously popular, serious problems with the kind of argument he presented had been enumerated by D. Hume (1711–76) years before his book appeared. Hume's posthumously published *Dialogues Concerning Natural Religion* (1779) presented a devastating attack on natural theology's attempt to move inferentially and analogically from evidence in nature and human experience to the justification of religious orthodoxy. The *Dialogues* marshalled at least ten objections that struck at the heart of natural theology: (1) The leap from part to whole is too vast to be bridged by any inference based on causal analogy. (2) To select intelligence as the causal key to the cosmos is extremely provincial. (3) Human beings are much too ignorant about all the vastly different conditions that must have obtained when the world was being formed to claim confidently that intelligence alone produced it. (4) All causal analogy is inapplicable in an utterly unique instance such as the making of this universe: the causal sequences we know are all *within* nature and thus provide no basis for affirming a causal relation between God and *the whole of* nature (if it is a whole). (5) Nature is full of ambiguous evidence, and too much dissimilarity obtains between the world and direct manifestations of intelligence. (6) Inferring a divine intelligent cause is useless when we might, with equal justice, postulate some 'inherent faculty' in matter that makes it orderly. (7) The empirical argument is too indiscriminate and gives no basis for inferring an infinite mind, a perfect one, or a unified one. (8) A plausible case can be made for alternatives to purposive intelligence, thus casting doubt on the reasonableness of the theistic hypothesis. Finally,

Hume's major criticisms highlighted: (9) the vagueness and remoteness of the causal analogy and (10) the problems for theodicy posed by the idea of a designer God (viz., that, given human experience of evil, God is either all good but not all powerful, or all powerful but not all good). Natural theology, Hume seemed to conclude, was idle speculation, and if Christian teachings were to be believed at all, they must be believed on blind faith.

The import of Hume's attack was not immediately felt in the English-speaking world. Between the seventeenth and the nineteenth century, through the efforts of writers like Paley, natural theology flourished together with early modern science, both appealing to the wonders of nature. The relation between theology and 'natural philosophy', as science was called, was porous and shifting, with no clear boundaries. A frequent metaphor was that of the 'two books': the book of God's work (nature) and the book of God's word (SCRIPTURE). No conflict or segregation should occur between the two books, argued (for example) I. Newton (1643–1727), against the RATIONALISM of R. Descartes (1596–1650), for only an intelligent being could have calculated the correct tangent of all the planets' velocity, thus assuring their stable orbit.

It was C. Darwin's (1809–82) account of EVOLUTION by random and incremental processes of natural selection that provided the single most important new challenge to natural theology. If the variations on which natural selection worked were random rather than under divine supervision, the human race could not be viewed as the intended product of a divinely planned progression. Nor could the products of the human mind – natural theology among them – be considered reliable in generating knowledge of the divine. Furthermore, the explanatory power of any orthodox conception of the divine as an antecedent knowing, caring, and creating reality that answered the question of origins (whether of the cosmos as a whole or of life on earth) was diminished in so far as it was either another name for natural selection or else gave rise to the regression question, 'and what created *God*?' Nevertheless, Darwinism inspired many works that attempted to develop models of theistic evolution. One of the most important of these was that of the Anglican theologian A. Moore (1848–90) who wrote 'The Christian Doctrine of God' in the tremendously popular anthology *Lux Mundi* (1889). According to Moore:

> Science has pushed the deist's God further and further away, and at the moment when it seemed as if he would be thrust out altogether Darwinism appeared, and, under the guise of a foe, did the work of a friend. It has conferred upon philosophy and religion an inestimable benefit, by showing us that we must choose between two alternatives. Either God is everywhere present in nature, or He is nowhere (*Lux* 73).

By the middle of the twentieth century, N. Smart (1927–2001) could declare natural theology to be 'the Sick Man of Europe', buffeted as it was by the prevailing winds of logical positivism and neo-Kantianism. K. BARTH famously maintained the opposition of German liberalism to natural theology by offering a theological argument against its very possibility. Since the decisive self-revelation of the triune God is in Jesus Christ, it is not for us to establish a knowledge of God elsewhere. Any such notion would be a human construction and thus idolatrous. In the context of the German Church struggle, this resulted in his famous essay *Nein!* (1934), directed primarily against the views of E. Brunner (1889–1966). However, as the tide turned against foundationalism in philosophy, natural theology enjoyed something of resurgence in the last quarter of the twentieth century. This was accompanied by a willingness on the part of Reformed thinkers such as H. Berkhof (1914–95) to revise Barth's wholesale prohibition on natural theology. More recently, biblical scholars have also identified traces of natural theology in Scripture, particularly in its Wisdom literature and the preaching of the APOSTLES in Acts.

Abandoning demonstrative arguments, many natural theologians have taken a not-yet-proven-irrational defence of theism. The emergence of REFORMED EPISTEMOLOGY led to a shift away from the burden of providing sufficient reasons for religious faith in favour of the more modest expectation of showing, as Plantinga stated, that such faith can be 'entirely right, rational, reasonable, and proper to believe in God without any evidence or argument at all' ('Reason', 17). Natural theology was here no longer a necessary task to warrant belief in the existence of God, although it might remain as an ancillary responsibility to counter attempts at disproving or invalidating key claims of faith.

Fuelled also by a growing interest in science-and-religion studies, the topics central to natural theology have come to look new and intriguing in the context of recent scientific cosmology. Current questions centre on such topics as, for example, the coherence of the divine attributes of omniscience and omnipresence in light of theoretical physics and cosmology, or top-down divine causality in relation to quantum mechanics. Attention to cosmic fine-tuning and ANTHROPIC considerations has revived interest in the design argument, while debates about the initial singularity of the Big Bang has rekindled discussion of the *kalam* cosmological argument originally developed by Islamic thinkers. Within analytic philosophy of religion, R. Swinburne (b. 1934) has attemped a much-discussed series of probabilistic arguments for the existence of God which cumulatively render religious belief rational. Also at the forefront of current attention are epistemological questions about the canons of rationality and the conditions of plausibility. At stake in any way of doing natural theology in the twenty-first century is a host of underlying philosophical questions, still largely unresolved, concerning the relation between experience and interpretation, truth and reference, realism and anti-realism, naturalism and supernaturalism. Increased sensitivity to the historicity not only of scriptural texts but also of philosophical assumptions about 'nature', 'reason', and 'revelation' now influence the literature.

W. Wildman (b. 1961) has identified three major forms of natural theology that hold claim to some continuing vitality in different quarters of the field and according to differing criteria of evaluation. These three types, reflecting three different understandings of God, are: personal theisms, ground-of-being theologies, and PROCESS THEOLOGIES. Wildman outlines a new comparative natural theology that would not assert entailment relations from nature directly to a metaphysical account of ultimate reality. Instead, it would compare numerous compelling accounts of ultimacy in as many different aspects as are relevant. Assembling the raw materials, the natural theologian would then make inference-to-the-best-explanation arguments in favour of particular theories of ultimacy, making clear which are preferred, or not, according to the criteria reviewed. Measured against a complex grid of criteria and comparisons, Wildman himself rates ground-of-being theologies as scientifically and philosophically more coherent, as well as religiously more satisfying than the other options. Be that as it may, differentiating these three as classificatory types of natural theology allows a case to be made for the comparative strengths and weaknesses of each and encourages cross-cultural attention to a wide range of evidence and argument in religious texts. Within this new paradigm the natural theologian is called upon to serve no longer as apologist but as fruitful gadfly.

J. Barr, *Biblical Faith and Natural Theology* (Oxford University Press, 1993).

T. E. Long, ed. *Prospects for Natural Theology* (Catholic University of America Press, 1992).

D. Ospovat, *The Development of Darwin's Theory: Natural History, Natural Theology, and Natural Selection, 1838–1850* (Cambridge University Press, 1982).

A. Plantinga and N. Wolterstorff, eds., *Faith and Rationality: Reason and Belief in God* (University of Notre Dame Press, 1983).

J. F. Sennet and D. Groothuis, eds., *In Defense of Natural Theology: A Post-Humean Assessment* (InterVarsity Press, 2005).

W. Wildman, *'Comparative Natural Theology', American Journal of Theology and Philosophy* 27:2–3 (May/September 2006), 173–90.

NANCY FRANKENBERRY

NEGATIVE THEOLOGY: see APOPHATIC THEOLOGY.

NEO-CHALCEDONIANISM 'Neo-Chalcedonianism' is a name given in the twentieth century to attempts by various sixth and seventh-century Byzantine theologians to interpret the CHRISTOLOGY of the Council of CHALCEDON in a way that might be acceptable to its opponents – specifically, to those who thought the council's two-nature formula a betrayal of the authentic one-nature Christological tradition that they associated with CYRIL OF ALEXANDRIA. The non-Chalcedonians (see MIAPHYSITISM) tended to see Cyril's acceptance of a 'union of two natures' formula in the Formula of Reunion of 433 as a dangerous or even misleading compromise with his opponents (see NESTORIANISM), and saw his true position as represented by his insistence elsewhere on 'one incarnate nature of God the Word'. The neo-Chalcedonians, equally loyal to Cyril, insisted that both formulae could and should be held together, provided that each was interpreted correctly. Both non- and neo-Chalcedonians also tended to insist upon Cyril's twelfth anathema, against those who deny that 'the Word of God suffered in the flesh' (the so-called THEOPASCHITE formula).

Some neo-Chalcedonians argued that, while it might indeed be proper to distinguish two natures in the one, composite Christ formed by the HYPOSTATIC UNION (such that Christ could be said not only to have been formed *from* two natures but to exist *in* two natures), this can only be a distinction 'in thought' – a useful but purely conceptual abstraction from the actual inseparable union in which the two natures now exist in the incarnate one. They saw 'one-nature' formulae as a useful (or necessary) indication of this inseparability. Those sometimes now dubbed 'extreme neo-Chalcedonians' insisted that ORTHODOXY is *only* properly secured if both two-nature and one-nature formulae are used. 'Moderate' neo-Chalcedonians, on the other hand, while allowing that one-nature formulae can be given an acceptable interpretation and a useful function within a predominantly Chalcedonian framework, did not insist upon their use.

The name 'neo-Chalcedonianism' can suggest, somewhat inaccurately, that a Cyrillian interpretation of Chalcedon was an innovation by these Byzantine theologians. A significant number of participants at Chalcedon seem to have understood its formulae in a Cyrillian way from the very start, however, and the innovations of the neo-Chalcedonians thus lie more in the technicalities of their explanations than in their broad Cyrillian direction. The debates between them and the non-Chalcedonians were certainly in part arguments about the controversial substance of Christology, but they were also in part debates about the proper conceptual elucidation of the texts of the Cyrilline tradition, and some have therefore seen in these debates the emergence of a form of theological SCHOLASTICISM.

Already by the end of the fifth century, a collection of excerpts from Cyril – the *Florilegium Cyrillianum* –

had been compiled to illustrate the agreement between his theology and Chalcedon. It did not yet, however, indicate *how* one-nature and two-nature formulae are to be held together, nor whether the twelfth anathema could be given a Chalcedonian reading. In the early sixth century, Nephalius of Alexandria (*fl. ca* 510) appears to have written an apology for Chalcedon arguing that, though orthodox, it was guilty of a certain terminological crudity; he preferred to speak of 'two united natures' in Christ, seeing that as equivalent to talk of one nature formed from two. Further, more robust apologies for Chalcedon in Cyrillian terms were produced by John of Scythopolis (d. 550), who seems to have been the first to defend the compatibility of Chalcedon with Cyril's twelfth anathema, Ephrem of Amid (d. 546), John Philoponus ('the Grammarian', *ca* 490–*ca* 570), Anastasius of Antioch (d. 598), and Eulogius of Alexandria (d. 608). One of the most influential was Leontius of Jerusalem (*fl.* 535), who developed a strong focus on the hypostatic union in order to do justice to the unity upon which he took Cyril's one-nature formula to be insisting.

Some of the impetus behind neo-Chalcedonianism was generated by Emperor Justinian I (r. 527–65), who saw an irenic theological solution to the Church's post-Chalcedonian splits as necessary to imperial unity and peace. He took a very direct hand in theological debates, producing in 551 a neo-Chalcedonian 'Edict on the True Faith', before in 553 calling the second Council of Constantinople to further a neo-Chalcedonian agenda.

Neo-Chalcedonian theology continued to flourish into the seventh century, perhaps most significantly in the work of MAXIMUS THE CONFESSOR, whose strict insistence on Christ's two natures (and, in response to MONOTHELITISM, two wills) nevertheless went with an approval of Cyril's one-nature formula, and even at times an insistence that acceptance of that formula was necessary for the preservation of orthodoxy.

See also ORIENTAL ORTHODOX CHURCHES; SYRIAC CHRISTIAN THEOLOGY.

MIKE HIGTON

NEO-DARWINISM: see EVOLUTION.

NEO-ORTHODOXY The term was applied (perhaps chiefly by enemies of the movement) to a significant minority of European, North American, and British Protestant thinkers active between about 1914 and 1965 – a minority whose passion, erudition, and timeliness soon guaranteed that they would set the tone for serious theology, not only during their own lifetimes but for decades beyond, and not only among Protestants but for ecumenical Christianity as a whole. As an appropriate designation of the emphases of theologians as diverse as K. BARTH, P. TILLICH, E. Brunner (1889–1996), R. NIEBUHR, D. BONHOEFFER, R. Bultmann, G. Aulén (1879–1978), S. de Dietrich (1891–1981), W. Visser t'Hooft (1900–85), and others, the term 'neo-orthodoxy' was never satisfactory and is still disputed. Although all or most of these thinkers drew upon various Protestant and other doctrinal traditions of the past, none of them intended his or her work as a deliberate attempt to preserve this or that reputed ORTHODOXY. If they were *neo*-orthodox in any meaningful way, it was only in the sense that they used classical Protestant and other (e.g., Augustinian) expressions of the faith to critique the contemporary dominance of 'liberal' and 'modernist' theologies which, they felt, were irrelevant in the face of the great question marks being written over the whole modern project by the events and crises of their times (see LIBERAL THEOLOGY; MODERNISM). However greatly they may have differed in their positive or constructive theological proposals, they all shared a lively sense of the bankruptcy of nineteenth-century liberalism, with its reliance upon the ideology of historical progress and its naive trust in essential human goodness and perfectibility. Such optimism, reflecting the 'brave new world' of RATIONALISM and technological innovation, was simply incapable of addressing the dismal failure of modernity as it was made palpable by the global economic catastrophes of the 1920s and the devastations of two world wars, to say nothing of the nihilism, loss of confidence, and moral chaos that was engendered by and resulted from these events.

The first *Christian* expressions of this bold rejection of the present and return to the past for insight and wisdom occurred in Europe. The debunking of modernity on the part of Christians who were themselves schooled in modern liberal assumptions (as all these thinkers were) can be dated to the appearance of Barth's early works, especially his commentary on PAUL'S Epistle to the Romans. Ignoring the academic niceties of historical and biblical scholarship, Barth made a direct and prophetic appeal to SCRIPTURE. He described the 'strange, new world of the Bible' in such existentially gripping terms that (as his older contemporary, K. Adam (1876–1966), put it) his work 'fell like a bomb in the playground of the theologians' ('Krisis', 271).

In North America, which was spared the devastations of Europe for a few years longer, theological liberalism continued to dominate well into the 1940s and 1950s. When Bonhoeffer made his first appearance in the United States in 1930, his fellow students at Union Theological Seminary in New York City were astonished at his references to such 'antiquated theologians' as M. LUTHER and J. CALVIN! But in the city of Detroit R. Niebuhr, whose parishoners were pawns of fluctuations in automobile assembly lines, was beginning to experience the same 'shaking of the foundations' as those Barth had felt in his European context. And in 1934, following the events in Germany that brought A. Hitler (1889–1945) to power, it was Niebuhr, chiefly, who arranged for Tillich, the first non-Jewish intellectual to be dismissed from his university post in Germany, to come to Union Seminary and teach.

Tillich's 'neo-orthodoxy', if the term can be applied to him at all, was certainly different from that of either Barth or Niebuhr, though it was in some ways quite compatible with the approaches of Brunner in Switzerland and of H. R. Niebuhr (1894–1962) in the USA. Yet, while Tillich, a Lutheran, was often critical of what he saw as Barth's FIDEISM, the two had more in common than is often thought. Barth's appeal to Scripture was never literalistic, and in many ways he arguably *exemplifies* the correlation of GOSPEL and cultural context that Tillich championed. The Christian, as Barth famously declared, must have the Bible in one hand and the newspaper in the other.

In fact, despite their significant differences, all those loosely associated with the term 'neo-orthodox' manifest certain common assumptions, among them: (1) a new respect for the Bible, in *both* testaments, as well as TRADITION; (2) a sense of the unavoidable dialectical tension between divine REVELATION and human reason; (3) recognition of the historical conditioning of all religious thought and life; (4) the insistence that theology exists to serve the Church, which in turn exists to serve God's beloved world; (5) the realization that responsible theology from now on must be a corporate, *ecumenical* undertaking; (6) a quest for comprehensiveness – not necessarily in the form of expansive works of 'systematic' theology of the sort produced by Tillich, Barth, and Brunner, but at least as an ongoing attempt at intellectual wholeness and the integration of theological and ethical aspects of Christian witness (as found in the work of Bonhoeffer and the Niebuhrs).

The influence of this group of creative theologians was unfortunately, if understandably, interrupted – though never curtailed – by the religious and moral preoccupations of succeeding generations. Since the 1960s the most visible concerns of Christian thinkers and activists have centred in specific struggles ('culture wars'), causes (racial, gender, environmental), and identities. In the present need for a theological and ethical self-understanding comprehensive enough to address today's global realities (including substantive dialogue with other faiths), the works of this earlier generation of theologians may provide additional and valuable resources for insight and direction.

See also DIALECTICAL THEOLOGY.

G. Baum, *Twentieth Century Theology: An Overview* (Orbis, 1999).

D. J. Hall, *Remembered Voices: Reclaiming the Legacy of 'Neo-Orthodoxy'*, revised edn (Fortress Press, 2008).

W. Pauck, *From Luther to Tillich: The Reformers and their Heirs* (Harper & Row, 1984).

DOUGLAS JOHN HALL

NEOPLATONISM: see PLATONISM.

NESTORIANISM The term 'Nestorian' is used pejoratively to refer to the theology of those Christians who reject the decisions of the Council of EPHESUS, where Nestorius (*ca* 385–*ca* 450) was deposed from the PATRIARCHATE of Constantinople and the two-nature ('dyophysite') CHRISTOLOGY associated with him condemned. Proponents of this kind of strongly dyophysite Christology were already well established beyond the eastern boundaries of the Roman Empire prior to Ephesus and gradually spread through Persia and the Indian subcontinent to reach Mongolia and China by the seventh century. Though persecution led to their gradual disappearance from East Asia in the medieval period, significant communities of the 'Church of the East' remain in Iraq, Iran, and India.

Within the Roman Empire the Nestorian controversy developed as a dispute over the DOCTRINE of Christ's person. Though all parties accepted the full divinity of the Son as defined at the Councils of NICAEA and CONSTANTINOPLE, they disagreed over the character of the INCARNATION. Drawing on the work of theologians like Diodore of Tarsus (d. *ca* 390) and Theodore of Mopsuestia (*ca* 350–428), the dyophysite party (citing biblical texts like John 2:19) spoke of the divine Son 'indwelling' the human being Jesus of Nazareth and argued that a clear distinction between these two subjects was crucial to affirming the incarnate Christ as both fully divine and fully human. They therefore rejected the characterization of the Virgin Mary as *Theotokos* ('Mother of God'), arguing that she was the mother of the human being Jesus only – and that to predicate birth (or any other such characteristic) of God amounted to an idolatrous confusion of creature and Creator. The opposing party at Ephesus, led by CYRIL OF ALEXANDRIA, countered that this undermined the unity of Christ by implying that Jesus, as a mere human being, could not be worshipped as Lord.

The Nestorians denied that they divided Christ, but they conceived of his unity in different terms from their opponents. Instead of the HYPOSTATIC UNION (i.e., two natures in one HYPOSTASIS) promulgated at the Council of CHALCEDON, they developed a doctrine of 'parsopic union': a duality of natures *and* hypostases united in one person (*parsōpā* in Syriac). This formula was required because for the Nestorians hypostasis is the manifestation of a nature, such that it is impossible for a nature to be present without its own corresponding hypostasis. Thus, to say with the Chalcedonians that Christ had only one (divine) hypostasis is necessarily to make him less than fully human. This emphasis on Christ's humanity is rooted in a particular soteriological vision. In contrast to Cyril's emphasis on God's saving human beings by assuming – and thereby healing – human nature, for the Church of the East God saves by indwelling Jesus and living a life of obedience that passes through death to glory – a trail others are able to follow because the One who blazed it was also a particular human being.

See also Syriac Christian Theology.

S. Brock, 'The Christology of the Church of the East' in *Fire from Heaven: Studies in Syriac Theology and Liturgy* (Ashgate, 2006), 159–79.

S. Wessel, *Cyril of Alexandria and the Nestorian Controversy: The Making of a Saint and a Heretic* (Oxford University Press, 2004).

Ian A. McFarland

New Age Informed by heterodox interpretations of Christian premillennialism, the term 'New Age' was used in the mid-twentieth century (especially from the 1930s) to signify an imminent 'new age' of the spirit which would succeed the 'old age' of formal religions. The signs of transition from old to new dispensation were variously detected in the military and economic crises of the interwar and Cold War periods and, later, in prophecies of ecological disaster under global capitalism. Religion in the 'new age' would take the form of a new and ecumenical spirituality, expressed within and across religious traditions, and drawing on a perennial understanding of religious truth articulated outside the formal conventions of Christian systematic theology. Thus, the typical New Age disposition is lay, popular, and syncretistic, incorporating multiple traditions of belief and practice.

The specific discourse on a coming 'new age' took shape among Theosophists, Spiritualists, heterodox Christians and other religious 'seekers' in the early to mid-twentieth century. This broadly middle-class constituency was boosted from the late 1960s onwards by 'baby-boomer' members of the counter-culture in North America, Australia, South Africa, and northern Europe, who sometimes used the cognate term 'Age of Aquarius', which linked the new dispensation to astrological ideas. Although often pigeonholed as 'the New Age movement', the milieu of ideas and practices which was evident by the 1970s differed sociologically from prominent 'new religious movements' of the period such as the Unification Church and the International Society for Krishna Consciousness by dint of its lack of clear boundaries and centralized organization. 'New Age' religiosity typically drew on beliefs and practices concerning healing, meditation, divination, and body exercises, pursued in small groups, networks, and retreat centres, with no overarching authority and flexible tradition. Models of God and Christ were often present, but typically as depersonalized, abstract ideas; notions of powerful hidden energies and forces were drawn from the Victorian and Edwardian occult revival; and Hindu and Buddhist ideas and practices such as karma, reincarnation, yoga, and meditation were incorporated in de-traditionalized forms. New Age ideas and practices diffused into the wider culture in the 1980s and 1990s where, under psychological and humanistic influences, they acquired the name 'holistic' or 'mind–body–spirit' and spread into community centres, private healthcare provision, and mass-market publishing. In this period New Age also began to display signs of commodification which attracted criticism from both secular and religious positions.

The defining character of New Age religiosity remains a moot point. On the one hand it has been argued that it represents a secularization of Renaissance esoteric thought as this trickled down into modernity; on the other, that it expresses a modern Romantic subjectivity based on mystical introspection and contemplation of nature. In both cases the popular pursuit of vitalistic and holistic experiences is arguably a response to what M. Weber (1864–1920) called the 'iron cage' of rationalized modernity and its 'disenchantment of the world'. Other accounts have stressed the popular, grass-roots nature of the phenomenon, arguing that it is an expression of popular religion whose persistence in modernity has been obscured by a historiography based on an overly systematized model of religion. In the near future 'New Age' and 'holistic' may be displaced by new popular rubrics, but the underlying phenomenon is likely to persist and even grow among receptive social groups where the local culture is moderately secularized but religiously pluralized.

P. Heelas and L. Woodhead, *The Spiritual Revolution: Why Religion Is Giving Way to Spirituality* (Blackwell, 2005).

D. Kemp and J. R. Lewis, eds., *Handbook of New Age* (Brill, 2007).

Steven Sutcliffe

New Testament: see Scripture.

Newman, John Henry Perhaps the greatest religious thinker of modern England, John Henry Newman (1801–90) contributed to theological epistemology, hymnody, the theory of education, and (in *An Essay on the Development of Christian Doctrine* of 1845) provided an approach to the historical development of religious teaching that remains a landmark in the field. Newman rose to prominence as a leading thinker through his guiding role in the Oxford Movement, a mid-century effort to recover an authentic spiritual basis for the Church of England. By the mid-1840s, however, Newman's role as a religious leader within the established Church underwent a startling change. In an era when Catholics were still subject to grave public impediments, especially in politics and education, Newman's agonizing conversion to the Catholic Church in 1845 stunned Victorian Britain. For the rest of his life, Newman found himself attempting to explain the meaning and significance of his developing religious views to his contemporaries. After many years of ambivalent regard on the part of the Roman authorities, Newman was elevated as a cardinal in 1879. In many ways, Newman's life-journey enacted in a very public way much of the drama and confusion in which religious belief has found itself caught up since the beginning of modernity.

Newman's eight volumes of *Parochial and Plain Sermons* from his Anglican years comprise a coherent spiritual theology imbued with the patristic vision of holiness, often expressed in passages of striking beauty, redolent with the Christian PLATONISM of his favourite Alexandrian thinkers (especially ORIGEN and ATHANASIUS). Preached during the same period (between 1826 and 1843), the *Oxford University Sermons* were regarded by Newman as his best work, taken as a whole. Their remarkable sweep portrays a deeply perceptive mind making its way into the nettlesome central questions of the relationship between faith and reason in post-ENLIGHTENMENT thought. Newman deepened this analysis in what is often regarded as his most brilliant work, *An Essay in Aid of a Grammar of Assent* (1870). In the first part, Newman shows that it is not nonsense to believe what you cannot yet understand; in the second part he shows that one can rationally believe what one cannot prove. Thus Newman works against a positivist understanding of religious beliefs, seeing them as forming a believer for fuller encounters with truth.

Newman further explored the role of Christian theology in forming a mind free from narrowness in *The Idea of a University: Defined and Illustrated* (1853; enlarged in 1873). These often pointed and humorous lectures continue to set the agenda in any discussion of what counts for a truly liberal education. In his *Apologia pro Vita Sua* (1864) Newman defended the authenticity of his faith against a very public attack on his integrity. Though an account of one man's religious beliefs, it is also a classic study of the influences, questions, and aspirations that shape human experience and the human capacity to believe in God.

A. Dulles, *Newman* (Continuum, 2003).

I. Ker, *John Henry Newman: A Biography* (Oxford University Press, 1988).

MARK A. MCINTOSH

NICAEA, COUNCIL OF Reckoned as the first ecumenical COUNCIL, the (first) Council of Nicaea was summoned by Emperor Constantine I (*ca* 275–337) in 325. It met primarily in order to settle a dispute over the nature of the Son of God that had arisen in Egypt between Arius (*ca* 250–336) and Bishop Alexander of Alexandria (d. 326), but which had soon involved a number of important ecclesiastical figures throughout the Eastern Empire (see ARIAN CONTROVERSY). The council was originally to meet in Ancyra, the see of Marcellus (d. *ca* 375), a controversial bishop strongly opposed to Arius and the traditions of which he was a part; but Constantine summoned the bishops to Nicaea, a city close to the imperial residence at Nicomedia and easier to reach from the western half of the empire. The majority of those present were eastern bishops, with very few western representatives. The number in attendance is traditionally reckoned at 318 (the number of Abraham's servants in Gen. 14:14), but the true number was somewhere between 250 and 300.

The council was preceded by another, which met in Antioch in the spring of 325. Here Eusebius of Caesarea (*ca* 260–*ca* 340), one of Arius' most famous supporters, was put under preliminary condemnation. This context helps to show how much the council at Nicaea was an event organized in advance. At the same time, it is inappropriate to speak of a shared theological programme on the part of Nicaea's organizers beyond a clear opposition to Arius.

Constantine himself spoke at the opening of the council and was present during the key discussions. Unfortunately, we do not possess a detailed account of the council's proceedings. It seems that Eusebius of Nicomedia (d. 341), another of Arius' supporters, offered a statement of faith that was rejected. Eusebius of Caesarea offered the baptismal creed of Caesarea as his own statement, and while the council did not adopt this as its creed, Eusebius was accepted as orthodox. The final creed adopted by the council seems to have been a version of a baptismal creed from Syria or Palestine. In order to exclude Arius, the creed was modified to state that the Son was born 'from the substance of the Father' and was *HOMOOUSIOS* ('of the same substance') with the Father. The council also legislated on a number of matters of ecclesiastical order, including the date of Easter, the Melitian SCHISM (which had divided the Egyptian Church), and a number of other regulations concerning the relationships between local Churches.

The purpose of the creed adopted at Nicaea, beyond the immediate purpose of creating a standard to which Arius could not subscribe, was not at all clear: much thought about the function of a creed would happen before it assumed the status of a universal standard of belief. The council fathers doubtless assumed that they would continue to use their own local CREEDS, and it is a measure of this gulf between the prominence Nicaea would later assume in Christian theology and its perceived significance at the time that the NICENE CREED now recited in churches the world over is not the creed approved at Nicaea, but a modified version from the Council of CONSTANTINOPLE half a century later. Indeed, although the sheer size of the council and Constantine's role made it stand out, it was to be many years before the idea of an 'ecumenical council' had anything like a fixed place in Christian understanding.

R. P. C. Hanson, *The Search for the Christian Doctrine of God* (T&T Clark, 1988).

LEWIS AYRES

NICENE CREED The formula conventionally known as the Nicene (or Niceno-Constantinopolitan) Creed seems in fact to have been composed at the first Council of CONSTANTINOPLE (381), though the earliest official record of the text dates only from the Council of CHALCEDON (451). Though it shares certain textual features with the creed promulgated at the Council of NICAEA (325), it appears to have been an independent composition, probably based on a local baptismal creed from Palestine. It has served as the baptismal creed of the ORTHODOX Churches since the sixth century, and also established itself as the Eucharistic creed of the whole church, first in the East, and by the eleventh century in Rome. Like the APOSTLES' CREED, it was retained by both Lutheran and Reformed Churches after the REFORMATION.

The Nicene Creed preserves in liturgically more polished form the main Christological dogmas found in the creed of 325, including the confession that the Son was 'begotten not made' and 'of the same substance (*HOMOOUSIOS*) with the Father'. Its major difference from the earlier creed comes in the third article where, in response to attacks on the divinity of the Holy Spirit, the laconic 'And [I believe in] in the HOLY SPIRIT' of Nicaea was supplemented by a series of clauses designed to secure the Spirit's equality with the other two Persons of the TRINITY. One of these clauses, 'who proceeds from the Father', was later supplemented in the western Church by the addition of the phrase 'and the Son' (*FILIOQUE*), thereby occasioning what remains the chief doctrinal dispute separating the Orthodox and Catholic communions.

See also CREEDS.

J. N. D. Kelly, *Early Christian Creeds*, 3rd edn (Continuum, 2006).

IAN A. MCFARLAND

NIEBUHR, REINHOLD Reinhold Niebuhr (1892–1971) was an American theologian and political thinker, known for an interpretation of Christian social ethics that he called 'Christian realism'. He began his career as a pastor in Detroit (1915) and later joined the faculty of Union Theological Seminary in New York (1928), where he remained until retirement.

Niebuhr developed his theology during a time of general disillusionment with Protestant liberalism that followed World War I. In contrast to K. BARTH's renewed emphasis on obedience to the Word of God, however, Niebuhr's critique of LIBERAL THEOLOGY focused on the social context of Christian life and action. He argued that the teachings of Jesus and the words of SCRIPTURE provide little direct guidance for Christian social ethics, which must be concerned with a rough justice between competing interests, rather than a community of mutual love. Niebuhr's early works, *Moral Man and Immoral Society* (1932) and *An Interpretation of Christian Ethics* (1935), argued that change can only be brought about by power, and those who have power are inevitably guided chiefly by their own interests. Appeals on behalf of the poor and disenfranchised will have no effect on the powerful unless those who are victimized themselves acquire some form of power. Niebuhr's realistic politics influenced M. L. KING's philosophy of NONVIOLENCE on this point.

Niebuhr's most important work, *The Nature and Destiny of Man* (1941, 1943), argues that the biblical view of human nature, balanced between the image of God and the sinful creature, offers the most adequate account of what is possible for human life and human societies. Classical and modern alternatives tempt human pride with promises of unlimited power or, less frequently, relieve human beings of the anxiety that accompanies their finitude by allowing them to slip unresistingly into the forces and processes of nature. The biblical view, by contrast, allows human beings to face the realities of history without thinking either that they can end evil in the world or that they are only tragic victims of it. Those who see life in biblical terms are thus enabled to seek responsible choices between real human possibilities.

During World War II and the Cold War that followed, Niebuhr became increasingly convinced that democracy needs the guidance of this balanced, biblical understanding of human nature. In the words of an aphorism he coined for *The Children of Light and the Children of Darkness* (1944), 'Man's capacity for justice makes democracy possible; but man's inclination to injustice makes democracy necessary' (xiii). Niebuhr is perhaps best known among political thinkers for his exploration of historical limits on human projects and ironic reversals of overstated human expectations. In later years, he wrote little on theological topics, but his political philosophy is drawn from the interpretation of Christian tradition that he sets out most completely in *The Nature and Destiny of Man.*

See also NEO-ORTHODOXY.

R. W. Fox, *Reinhold Niebuhr: A Biography* (Cornell University Press, 1996).

L. Gilkey, *On Niebuhr: A Theological Study* (University of Chicago Press, 2001).

ROBIN W. LOVIN

NIETZSCHE, FRIEDRICH Among philosophers, Nietzsche's influence on twentieth and twenty-first century thought has probably been second to none. Born into a Lutheran parsonage in 1844, he developed into a brilliant classical philologist and was appointed to a professorship in the University of Basel in 1869. On account of ill health, he was pensioned off within ten years and thereafter led a roving existence in western Europe. In January 1889, he suffered a mental collapse from which he never recovered before his death in 1900.

There is agreement neither on the timing nor on the causes of Nietzsche's break with Christianity and adoption of an atheistic outlook; in fact, even the title 'atheist' has proved contentious. Historical criticism of SCRIPTURE and questions about the epistemic status of FAITH went into the mix. In his teen years Nietzsche was powerfully influenced by his exposure to the Greek ideal of an autonomous, strong humanity, something that collided with, and he deemed superior to, a Christian outlook. For a time, he intensely admired both A. Schopenhauer (1788–1860) and R. Wagner (1813–83) and saw in the latter's project for cultural renewal in Germany the glittering prospect of a kind of Greek Renaissance. But he became disillusioned and turned his literary guns against Christianity at the same time. Some of his objections were in what we might describe as a characteristically French ENLIGHTENMENT mould: Christianity was intellectually ridiculous, as both scientific and philosophical reason demonstrated. Above all, it demeaned humanity by virtue of its DOCTRINE of SIN. As he progressed in his outspoken opposition to Christianity, Nietzsche spoke of the 'death of God', an event of culturally momentous consequences whose significance contemporaries were failing to see even when they had turned intellectually in an atheistic direction. The death of God meant the death of objective moral order, but the survival of Christian morality in post-theistic European civilization was the supreme sickness of that civilization. A naturalistic re-evaluation of all values was called for, but Nietzsche did not live to offer it as he had hoped.

Nietzsche foresaw the coming of the *Übermensch*, sometimes (and rather unfortunately) translated the 'Superman', the strong and autonomous creator of values who will overcome all obstacles to forging a new type of humanity. His will be a morality for the strong, which will not succumb to the lure of weak compassion as trumpeted in the virtues of the rabble. Nietzsche's occasionally lyrical expression of this is accompanied by the conviction that the biological organism should be understood in terms of the maximization of the will to power rather than, as C. Darwin (1809–82) thought, in terms of preservation. It is not easy to say confidently to what extent this is a strictly biological and metaphysically realistic commitment and to what extent it is a perspectival stance that eschews metaphysical realism. At the heart of Nietzsche's mature thought lies another doctrine whose status is hotly contested: the eternal recurrence of all things. The question is (roughly) whether this is a quasi-scientific cosmological theory or a metaphor for uncompromising self-affirmation. Either way, existentially it means that we must redeem our past by owning it: 'I willed it thus'. This is dramatically set forth in *Thus Spoke Zarathustra* (1883–5).

In Nietzsche scholarship, there has for some time been a strong tendency to dismiss as false the familiar allegation that Nietzsche paved the way for Nazi anti-Semitism (see HOLOCAUST). However, there is no consensus on this or, indeed, on a great deal in Nietzsche's thought. Whatever we decide and whatever its force, a distinction has to be drawn between fostering anti-Semitism and advocating the 'immoralism' of the strong. Nietzsche's intellectual connections with postmodernity and poststructuralist views of language have also been explored since the late twentieth century. The connections may be significant, yet the main thread of Nietzsche's anti-Christian authorship – and his authorship overall might be defined as 'anti-Christian' – owes more to the direct attack on THEOLOGICAL ANTHROPOLOGY and its associated nauseating, repulsive view of God, than to a particular conceptual approach to language. He makes an important and revealing declaration in Section 132 of *The Gay Science* (1882): 'What is now decisive against Christianity is our taste, no longer our reasons'.

The intellectual quality and substantive merits of Nietzsche's work are subject to very widely differing estimations. Undoubtedly, he was a forceful writer. His insistence that the collapse of belief in God logically entails the collapse of Christian morality, and his accompanying insistence that there are no moral facts are intellectually and culturally momentous. From a logical point of view, Nietzsche was not rigorous, but attempts have been made to lay out his insights in a systematic philosophical form. He favoured the aphorism and the punchy paragraph. This was not a matter of sheer literary taste; insight, Nietzsche believed, came partly through psychological observation, and psychological observation was best conveyed in the form favoured by French *moralistes* like F. de La Rochefoucauld (1613–80). But he could also adopt the mode of more sustained argument, as in *On the Genealogy of Morality* (1887).

Nietzsche's principal work, *Thus Spoke Zarathustra*, is a kind of visionary and prophetic anti-Christian scripture. K. Jaspers (1883–1969) rightly remarked that 'in the end one cannot help but ask how a man who is by no means representative can still become as overwhelmingly significant as though he spoke for humanity itself' (*Nietzsche* 16). The passion of Nietzsche's attack on Christianity and his unflinching naturalism make him congenial in our time. Naturalism may be judged philosophically untenable, and Nietzsche's criticism of Christianity intellectually shallow, but he saw clearly what was at stake in Christianity and Christian morality and K. BARTH was right to conclude that Nietzsche 'rejected ... not a caricature of the Christian conception of humanity, but in the form of a caricature the conception itself' (*CD* III/2, 231)

R. J. Hollingdale, *Nietzsche: The Man and His Philosophy* (Cambridge University Press, 1999).

R. Safranski, *Nietzsche: A Philosophical Biography* (Norton, 2002).

H. Staten, *Nietzsche's Voice* (Cornell University Press, 1990).

STEPHEN N. WILLIAMS

Niles, D. T. Daniel Thambyrajah Niles (1908–70) was a Ceylonese Methodist minister who helped initiate the articulation of theology in South Asia and shaped the ecumenical movement in the first part of the twentieth century. The character of his theology and his scholarship, like that of his beloved J. Wesley, were shaped by his sermons and ministry.

Neo-orthodoxy lies at the heart of his theological commitments. This movement responding to the disillusionment with the optimism of the nineteenth century, called into question the way history was understood. It entailed a move from belief in an inner authority that helped one to know God to an emphasis on God as wholly other. Correspondingly, neo-orthodox thinkers read history from an apocalyptic point of view, in which God was both the sole visionary and key actor, revealing God's self in Jesus Christ, and thereby connecting to a broken and finite humanity. This kind of dialectical or paradoxical theology, juxtaposing the transcendent God with finite reality, created a framework for Niles to hold on to a unified, eschatological vision while paying attention to local expressions of Christian faith (see Dialectical Theology). Thus he was deeply ecumenical in his vision, participating in the creation of ecumenical bodies like the World Council of Churches and the East Asia Christian Conference, while at the same time serving as a theologian in the Methodist Church in Ceylon, searching to understand the Christian message in his own context.

Despite his Christocentrism, Niles broke with the neo-orthodox trend to reduce history to every era's eschatological encounter with the Christ event. Instead, his writings reflect the conviction that the epistemological key to the ongoing historical activity of the transcendent God is Jesus Christ. Understanding Christ as the epistemological key to, rather than exhaustive content of, God's saving work in history allowed Niles to emphasize God's transcendent freedom to do as God wills not only among Christians in different cultural contexts but also in non-Christian faiths. Indeed, Niles goes further to say Christians can only see ultimate reality if they use the light of Christ to read God at work in the local context. These ideas are developed in books like *Sir, We See Jesus* (1938), *Buddhism and the Claims of Christ* (1946), and *Who Is This Jesus?* (1968).

S. W. Ariarajah, *We Live by His Gifts: D. T. Niles – Preacher, Teacher, and Ecumenist* (Ecumenical Institute for Study and Dialogue, 2008).

Damayanthi Niles

Nominalism Although in the high Middle Ages 'nominalism' technically denoted a school of method in teaching logic, it became controversial when that logical analysis was applied to philosophical and theological problems. Despite a great deal of variation among individual thinkers, it is possible to outline a number of features which provide a general profile of nominalism. The most famous of these relate to the philosophical point that a 'universal' (e.g., 'whiteness') is a name and not a reality, and the associated idea that to speak of relation, quantity and the other Aristotelian categories as 'universals' soon leads to contradiction and is best avoided. Within theology nominalists stressed that created reality is a function of God's ordained power (*potentia ordinata*), and thus freely chosen by God in preference to other worlds that God might have created by virtue of God's absolute power (*potentia absoluta*). This emphasis on divine freedom also influenced nominalist theological anthropology, which stressed human beings' capacity to dispose themselves for the gift of salvation.

With respect to the issue of universals, nominalism represents a denial of the position that the most abstract (e.g., a general concept like 'whiteness' or 'humanity') is the most real ('realism'). On the contrary, for nominalists like William of Ockham (*ca* 1285–*ca* 1350), the mind is that which makes sense of the world and unifies it. With this principle in mind, Ockham maintained, 'No thing outside the soul is universal' (*CSent.* 1.2.7). This point of view can be seen as tending towards a subjectivism or perspectivism, but it also allows for an attention to particularity, in as much as for Ockham there are (for example) as many 'whitenesses' as there are white things, and each whiteness is distinct from each white thing. The key for Ockham is to recognize that any likeness between species lies only *in* them and not (as a 'realist' understanding of universals would have it) *between* them; yet similarity for Ockham is a real relation (*Ord.* 1.2.4–8).

The distinction between the *potentia absoluta* and the *potentia ordinata* of God is not intended to promote the idea of divine arbitrariness, but rather to offer reassurance that God has committed to be merciful in the covenant, and that this deliberate determination on God's part is more reliable than any idea of an intrinsically merciful nature. It could mean (contrary to the views of J. Duns Scotus) that the place of miracles, understood as God's occasional working according to his absolute power, was minimalized, since though nature is created and its laws could therefore be suspended by God, God's covenant faithfulness means that they will not. At the same time, the nominalist perspective notes that God deals with creation in a truly historical and contingent way, so that God's will in its faithfulness can adapt and transform creation over time.

Nominalist theologians like G. Biel (*ca* 1425–95) identified the image of God in humanity with free will, understood as the correlate of God's own free will. Using this freedom, Biel argued, sinners could dispose themselves for grace in the negative sense that they have the capacity to block meritorious acts being elicited by God, but not in the sense that they could do such acts on their own or choose to have the grace necessary to do them. Though also found in the writings of T. AQUINAS and others, the claim, rejected so emphatically by M. LUTHER, that 'God does not deny grace to those who do what is in them' was especially associated with the nominalist R. Holcot (*ca* 1290–1349), who thought REVELATION would come to all who lived according to NATURAL LAW and that the supernatural articles of faith go beyond but not against reason.

W. Courtenay, *Ockham and Ockhamism* (Brill, 2008).

H. Oberman, *The Harvest of Medieval Theology* (Harvard University Press, 1963).

P. V. Spade, *'Ockham's Nominalist Metaphysics: Some Main Themes'* in *Cambridge Companion to Ockham*, ed. P. V. Spade (Cambridge University Press, 1999), 100–17.

MARK W. ELLIOTT

NONVIOLENCE In many ways a specifically theological understanding of nonviolence must be developed on behalf of the many people who face the violence of underemployment, POVERTY, and war. Unfortunately, in these contexts RELIGION is very often abused for nationalistic purposes, exacerbating confrontation and warfare. It was the wisdom of one of the most famous practitioners of nonviolence in the modern era, M. K. Gandhi (1869–1948), to teach that religion and, more concretely, specific religiously motivated practices, should play a significant role in putting an end to wars instead of creating them. Though himself a Hindu, Gandhi was deeply influenced by the Christian theological writings of L. Tolstoy (1828–1910) and frequently referred to Jesus and especially to the SERMON ON THE MOUNT (especially passages like Matt. 5:39, 44) as a crucial source for his teaching on nonviolence.

A current example of the use of Christianity in furtherance of nonviolent social change can be seen through the major change in South Africa, the place in which Gandhi initiated his method of nonviolent action. One could argue that there would be no peace in South Africa without the decisive role played by religious leaders like D. Tutu (b. 1931), who has acted as a vehicle of nonviolent social transformation both before and since the end of apartheid. Other Christians whose understanding of nonviolence has been strongly influenced by Gandhi include D. BONHOEFFER in Nazi Germany and M. L. KING, Jr, in the USA.

The main ingredients of nonviolence for major architects of the nonviolence movement are: a common perception of an extreme injustice and a conviction that civil disobedience could offer a remedy. This kind of direct action or 'empowerment' meant, from the moment it was conceived, that a community's overcoming fear and recovery of self-respect could come through collective nonviolence. Gandhi's nonviolent method was initially described as 'passive resistance', but Gandhi rejected that term because it did not convey the active power of nonviolence. He then coined the term *satyagraha*, defined as the 'force of truth and LOVE'. From the outset, therefore, Gandhi wanted to emphasize the special power of *satyagraha* by distinguishing it from passive resistance or what he called *duragraha*, 'the force of bias'. *Duragraha* is the counterfeit of *satyagraha* because it implies a wrong use of power, coming from a selfish obstinacy. The passive resister or *duragrahi* may avoid physical violence yet still harbour enmity and anger within, using nonviolence as a tactic but lacking commitment to its core values of understanding, openness, and respect for the adversary. Writing from a distinctively Christian perspective, King affirmed the importance of this distinction when he also rejected 'passive resistance'. The nonviolence of *satyagraha*, King wrote, 'avoids not only external physical violence but also violence of spirit. The nonviolent resister not only refuses to shoot his opponent but he also refuses to hate him' (*Stride* 103).

Working out of specifically Christian traditions that long antedated Gandhi, a minority of communities, including the descendants of the radicals of the Reformation era (especially the Mennonites) and Quakers, have seen in Jesus' teaching in the Sermon on the Mount and elsewhere a basis for rejecting all Christian participation in war (pacifism). Contemporary advocates of nonviolence influenced by these more marginalized Christian traditions include the Mennonite J. H. Yoder (1927–97) and the Methodist S. Hauerwas (b. 1940).

See also MENNONITE THEOLOGY; QUAKER THEOLOGY.

D. Tutu, *No Future without Forgiveness* (Doubleday, 2000).

J. H. Yoder, *The Original Revolution: Essays on Christian Pacifism*, revised edn (Herald Press, 2003).

MICHAEL BATTLE

NORDIC THEOLOGY The Nordic context comprises the modern nations of Denmark, Finland, Iceland, Norway, and Sweden. Within these countries LUTHERAN THEOLOGY has predominated since the REFORMATION and has been taught at State faculties in Uppsala (established 1477), Copenhagen (1479), Turku (1640), Lund (1666), Helsinki (1828), Oslo (1813), and Reykjavik (1911). A Lutheran ORTHODOXY (later mediated by PIETISM and the ENLIGHTENMENT) reigned in these faculties well into the nineteenth century, when democratic institutions emerged, and cultural conflicts arose between the establishment, revivalist movements, and anti-Church groups. Despite secularization and immigration, however, the Evangelical–Lutheran Churches still constitute majority Churches in Nordic countries, with 74 to 82 per cent of the population as contributing members.

In a Nordic context, academic theology is generally supposed to play a mediating role between the living Christian TRADITION and contemporary culture (i.e., philosophy, arts, science). Theology is thus expected to have relevance for both believers and sceptics. This model of a 'loose coupling' between theology and Church, however, is no longer unquestioned. Conservatives want to have a stronger hold on theology, while critics see the faculties of theology as unfairly privileging the Christian tradition.

In the twentieth century, Swedish theology has produced several theological programmes in defence of theology's academic standing. In Lund A. Nygren (1890–1978) and G. Aulén (1879–1977) developed a programme for 'motif research', using a typological approach to the history of theology. Defining unconditional GRACE as the quintessential motif of Christian DOCTRINE, they argued for the purity of Pauline and Lutheran theology, seeing medieval theology as polluted by human *eros* and a mistaken notion of the human co-operation with God in salvation. Nygren's *Eros and Agape* (1930–6) and Aulén's *Christus Victor* (1931) became international bestsellers, though their views have hardly withstood historical criticism. Nygren's successor in Lund, G. Wingren (1910–2000), developed a more continental style of kerygmatic theology (see KERYGMA), counterbalanced by a CREATION theology based on IRENAEUS, M. LUTHER, and N. F. S. Grundtvig (1783–1872). Later, A. Jeffner (b. 1934) of Uppsala, in *Kriterien christlicher Glaubenslehre* (1976), criticized his colleagues in Lund, as well as German SYSTEMATIC THEOLOGY, for doing theology without rational criteria. In Uppsala, doctrinal studies were replaced by 'comparative studies of faiths and ideologies' (*Tros-och livsåskådningsvetenskap*). This programme continues to define major strands of Swedish systematic theology, some in empirical orientation, some in a more philosophical vein. Before leaving Sweden in 2006, W. Jeanrond (b. 1955) reinvigorated hermeneutical theology, and a younger generation now seeks to regain a space for constructive theology in alliances with FEMINIST THEOLOGY, Church-based theology, or postmodern philosophy. The establishment of many new schools of theology, in Göteborg and elsewhere, has led to a rapid pluralization of Swedish theology.

Danish and Norwegian theology has traditionally been more continental in orientation, though mediated by two outstanding figures of Golden Age Denmark: S. KIERKEGAARD and Grundtvig (who, like Kierkegaard – though in a very different idiom – was a persistent critic of both academic theology and the established Church). R. BULTMANN's existentialist approach has found resonance among Kierkegaardians in the movement known as *Tidehverv* ('Tides', dating from 1926), as well as among Grundtvigians drawing on Grundtvig's principle, 'First human, then Christian' (i.e., understanding precedes FAITH). The newly established theological faculty in Aarhus (1943) produced important theological work. In his widely read dogmatics, *Creation and Redemption* (1953), R. Prenter (1907–90) combined Luther and Grundtvig in a critical appropriation of K. BARTH. K. E. Løgstrup's (1905–81) *The Ethical Demand* (1956) became a cultural classic – still in print in several languages – seeing 'basic trust' as the ontological ground of ethics. Løgstrup's four-volume *Metaphysics* (1978–84) criticized Kantian theology for its ANTHROPOCENTRISM, and Kierkegaard for his 'pilgrim-mythic' interpretation of Christianity. The 'Scandinavian creation theology' of Løgstrup, Wingren, and Prenter thus formulated an alternative to both Barth and Kierkegaard, while using a phenomenological approach to theology that they argued was 'closer to experience' than secular world views (see PHENOMENOLOGY). Løgstrup also inspired the emerging ECOTHEOLOGY, science–religion dialogues, and ethical discussions. Still today there are rivalries between Grundtvigians and Kierkegaardians, both having Luther as a common point of reference, while using either F. SCHLEIERMACHER or P. TILLICH and W. Pannenberg (b. 1928) as mediating figures.

In Norway, too, the hermeneutical paradigm has reigned, expressed in excellent exegetical and historical scholarship. At the same time, Norwegian theology is still marked by tensions between a biblicist Pietism and LIBERAL THEOLOGY. In 1908 the 'Community Faculty' (*Menighetsfakultet*, today called the Norwegian School of Theology) was established in opposition to the more liberal faculty of the University of Oslo. O. Hallesby (1879–1961) was the overarching figure; and his 1953 radio address affirming the DAMNATION of all the unconverted inaugurated what became known as the 'HELL Debate'. In Norwegian theology ethical and political questions have taken centre stage in continuous public debates on women pastors, on DIVORCE, and on homosexuality. Today, however, even the *Menighetsfakultet* allows philosophical arguments in constructive theological work, while at the Oslo faculty the Grundtvig–Løgstrup tradition continues to be strong. Hermeneutical studies are here often combined with empirical investigations of what ordinary people actually think and do.

Finland has been influenced by both Pietism and Biblicism. The Helsinki faculty has consistently focused on the 'big' questions of Christian thought, gaining international recognition in NT scholarship, medieval semantics, and Reformation studies. S. Teinonen (1924–95) introduced ecumenical theology to Finland (see ECUMENISM), and, backed up by an educated leadership of the Church, ecumenical endeavours have been a persistent feature of Finnish theology. T. Mannermaa (b. 1937) established the so-called Finnish School of Luther Research, focusing on the thesis that Luther taught 'ontological presence' of Christ in believers, akin to Orthodox as well as Catholic traditions. Mannermaa's emphasis on Luther's views on *theosis* has influenced several ecumenical dialogues, including the *Joint Declaration of Justification* (1999). Also at Helsinki J. Knuutila (b. 1952) and colleagues are currently developing an analytical philosophy in contact with historical semantics, psychology, and cognitive sciences. The smaller Swedish-speaking faculty in Turku (re-established 1924) has created a theology in tandem with first the Lundensian, then the Uppsala tradition.

Icelandic theology has traditionally been closely connected to Denmark, but since Iceland's independence in 1944 domestic resources (especially rich in SPIRITUALITY and hymns) have been emphasized, in addition to an increasing orientation towards North American theology. This tendency of moving from the national towards the international scene may, on the whole, characterize the most recent decades of Nordic theology.

N. Hope, *German and Scandinavian Protestantism*, 1700–1918 (Oxford University Press, 1995).

J. Kristiansen and S. Rise, eds., *Moderne teologi: Tradisjon og nytænkning hos det 20. århundredets teologer* (Høyskoleforlaget, 2009).

NIELS HENRIK GREGERSEN

NOUVELLE THÉOLOGIE Foundations for the collection of ideas termed *nouvelle théologie* were laid at Ore Place, the Jesuit seminary in exile overlooking Hastings on the south coast of England. This existed from 1906 to 1926, combining the previously separate seminaries of the Lyons and Paris provinces and thus establishing an intense cross-provincial collegiality. Key scholars there included systematician L. de Grandmaison (1868–1927), NT scholars F. Prat (1857–1938) and J. Huby (1878–1948), and evolutionary theologian P. TEILHARD DE CHARDIN. Later, fresh impetus was given by the *Sources chrétiennes* series, founded in 1940 by H. DE LUBAC and J. Daniélou (1905–74), which made possible the *ressourcement* of theology by providing patristic texts in their original languages, accompanied by a parallel translation.

The movement's political and cultural origins must also be considered. In France the ban on Christian education completed in 1904 that had forced the Jesuits and other religious communities into exile made responding to secularism and its concrete effects a pressing concern. Members of religious orders enjoyed no exemption from the military draft, so were conscripted into the French army as soldiers or auxiliary personnel when war broke out. This experience irreversibly transformed the social and intellectual horizons of a whole generation of theologians, and conditioned them for spiritual resistance to Nazism. The Jesuit martyr Y. de Montcheuil (1899–1944) was notable for translating the philosophy of action developed by the Catholic lay philosopher M. Blondel (1861–1949) into the contemporary political context, and in his writings exhorting lay Christians, as the Church, to resist Nazi occupation can be seen important intellectual antecedents of the lay ECCLESIOLOGY of VATICAN COUNCIL II, as well as of LIBERATION THEOLOGY.

Theoretically, many of the tendencies referred to as *nouvelle théologie* originated in Blondel's philosophy of action and in the 'act of faith' DOCTRINE expounded by the Jesuit P. Rousselot (1878–1915). Blondel argued that divine activity was implicated in every true human action. Rousselot saw an interior act of faith involving the whole person as an essential corollary of outward Christian observance. These insights were developed by H. de Lubac in his seminal *Surnaturel*. In this work, de Lubac used the 'new theology' label pejoratively to refer to the separation of philosophy from theology that occurred around the sixteenth century, founded on the concept of a pure nature that sought only natural ends. Instead, he proposed an approach to theology that emphasized humankind's spiritual capacity and understood creation, and not only redemption, as an act of grace.

Key to the application of the *nouvelle théologie* in the Catholic Church were the Dominicans of the *studium* of the Saulchoir in Paris, especially Y. Congar (1904–95). They formed a more cohesive group than the Jesuits, having been presented as a 'school' in a 1937 manifesto by their regent, M.-D. Chenu (1895–1990). Apart from the theology of T. AQUINAS, the order's most celebrated son, their concerns included the preaching of the GOSPEL, mission (see MISSIOLOGY), ECUMENISM, and the worker-priest movement. In these ecclesiological endeavours they gained intellectual inspiration from the Catholic TÜBINGEN SCHOOL, which had reached its peak in Germany in the 1840s.

Like many theological tendencies, the *nouvelle théologie* was defined and given coherence primarily by critics. Characteristic criticisms are listed in *Humani generis*, the 1950 encyclical of Pope Pius XII (r. 1939–58), having been previously expounded by R. Garrigou-Lagrange (1877–1964) in a polemical 1946 article in *Angelicum*. They centre around the movement's refusal to read SCRIPTURE and patristic sources through the lenses of Catholic dogma and neo-Thomist philosophy (see THOMISM). Features identified in the encyclical include: (1) privileging the spiritual sense of Scripture over its literal sense; (2) denying that human reason can prove God's existence unaided by an act of FAITH; (3) accepting evolutionary theory and questioning the received concept of original SIN (including the denial that the world had a beginning or that all humans were descended from Adam); (4) destroying the gratuity of the supernatural order by arguing that God cannot create humans without predisposing them to the BEATIFIC VISION; (5) interpreting Christ's presence in the EUCHARIST symbolically rather than by the dogma of TRANSUBSTANTIATION; and (6) embracing a range of modern philosophical theories.

All these points require response. The *nouvelle théologie* in fact sought to establish the mutuality of the literal and spiritual senses of Scripture, defying the low CHRISTOLOGY of modernists like A. LOISY (see MODERNISM).

Likewise, the 'act of faith' doctrine implied that personal faith and reason were complementary, in contrast with the SCHOLASTICISM of *Humani generis* that separated them and thus presented a curious mirror image of the RATIONALISM of the ENLIGHTENMENT. The theory of EVOLUTION had raised profound questions about the relation of theology and scriptural exegesis to NATURAL SCIENCE, and many French-speaking theologians sought to synthesize these different sources of knowledge, encouraged by a strong Jesuit scientific community and a historic national predilection for Lamarckian evolutionary theory. The theory of the *surnaturel* corrected a picture of the world as existing independently of divine activity and with no intrinsic need of divine preservation. Most theologians in no way denied the real presence of Christ's body in the Eucharist, believing that the status of the Church as the body of Christ was dependent on this substantial Eucharistic presence and in no way abolished it. Modern philosophy was frequently engaged in order to unmask its deficiencies or to promote theological positions.

By seeking to defend theology against new methods and interpretation, neo-Thomist theologians had exiled it from the modern world and allowed secularism to take root in its place. The various figures and concepts associated with the *nouvelle théologie* unsettled this compromise by proposing a more ambitious mode of theology engaging modern society and culture.

H. Boersma, *Nouvelle Théologie and Sacramental Ontology: A Return to Mystery* (Oxford University Press, 2009).

D. Grumett, *De Lubac: A Guide for the Perplexed* (T&T Clark, 2007).

F. Kerr, *Twentieth Century Catholic Theologians: From Neoscholasticism to Nuptial Mystery* (Blackwell, 2006).

A. Nichols, *Catholic Thought Since the Enlightenment: A Survey* (Gracewing, 1998).

DAVID GRUMETT

NUPTIAL THEOLOGY The world's major religious traditions all have mystical dimensions in which the relationship between God and the human is suffused with erotic imagery. In Christianity, particularly in some strands of medieval and modern Catholicism, this takes the form of a nuptial theology in which the love between Christ and the Church is analogous to the love between husband and wife (cf. Eph. 5:22–33). In CATHOLIC THEOLOGY Mary as well as the Church is depicted as the bride of Christ, and also sometimes as spouse of the HOLY SPIRIT or of God the Father (see TRINITY).

Christian mystics used the language of sexual desire and married love to express the SOUL'S longing for Christ. For male mystics like Bernard of Clairvaux (1090–1153) and John of the Cross (1542–91), this involved the feminization of the soul, so that the mystic's voice becomes the bride addressing 'her' beloved, the male Christ. Debate continues as to how far such language constitutes a repressed form of homoeroticism. In the writings of female mystics, the language of the feminized soul tends to be more direct and explicitly erotic than in male writings, perhaps for the obvious reason that a woman can speak as herself, rather than projecting herself into the sexual other. For both sexes the eroticization of spirituality often went hand in hand with sometimes severe ascetic practices aimed at controlling the physical desires of the body (see ASCETICISM), and in male mystical writings this sometimes takes highly misogynistic forms.

Nuptial theology and its forms of mystical expression have their roots in the OT, where God is repeatedly depicted as the spouse of ISRAEL – a relationship patterned around wifely infidelity and harlotry on the part of Israel, and husbandly chastisement, anger, compassion, delight, forgiveness, and faithful LOVE on the part of God (e.g., Jer. 3; Hos.; Isa. 54). In Christianity, the story of CREATION and the FALL in Genesis 1–3 has shaped this nuptial imagery, with the marriage between Adam and Eve being projected onto that between Christ and the Church and/or Christ and Mary. The *Song of Songs* was also highly influential in informing Christian MYSTICAL THEOLOGY and MARIOLOGY. The fact that this book is included in the Christian canon has long been an enigma to biblical interpreters, with an enduring tendency to spiritualize a text which many today would recognize as an overtly erotic love poem celebrating human sexual desire.

The REFORMATION introduced a more personal and some might say individualistic understanding of the relationship between the believer and God, so that the idea of the Church as bride of Christ mediating salvation to the organic BODY of believers through her sacramental life was replaced by a more Bible-centred and less sacramental understanding of FAITH. While strands of the nuptial tradition persisted in the devotions of individuals and in some smaller Christian sects, it has not been a significant aspect of Protestant theology and practice. In the Catholic Church, the gendered, symbolic language of nuptial ecclesiology and Mariology was briefly eclipsed after the reforms of VATICAN COUNCIL II, but it has experienced a resurgence since the 1980s, particularly owing to the influence of the theologian H. von BALTHASAR on Pope John Paul II (r. 1978–2005) and on a number of modern theologians. John Paul II's nuptial theology of the body has attracted widespread interest.

Nuptial theology has arguably always served implicitly – and often explicitly – to reinforce patriarchal hierarchies in the Church and society, with husbandly authority and wifely submission providing a model for all human relationships (see PATRIARCHY). As the feminized soul submits to the masculine God, so the wife must submit to the husband and women must submit to male authority figures. The recent resurgence of Catholic nuptial theology may be a reaction to the influence of feminism and the challenge this poses to concepts of priesthood, hierarchical authority, and sacramentality (see FEMINIST THEOLOGY). During the twentieth century the Catholic Church dropped the language of wifely submission in favour of the language of complementarity in its theology of marriage, but the concept of the complementary characteristics of each sex still tends to be informed by what many would argue are anachronistic models of essentialized feminine obedience, passivity, and receptivity on the one hand, and masculine authority, activity, and initiative on the other.

For this reason, many liberal and feminist Catholics reject such nuptial imagery, although paradoxically this coincides with a growing interest in mysticism with its pervasive language of erotic love. Perhaps this will provide a stimulus to refigure the symbolic significance of MARRIAGE and human SEXUALITY. The emergence of more egalitarian, inclusive, and mutually supportive concepts of marriage might invite an understanding of God and the human wedded together in a relationship of harmonious rather than hierarchical difference – not God as the husband over and against the submissive and troublesome wife, but God as the other within and beyond the beloved. This would invite greater attentiveness to Christ's rejection of all hierarchical relationships of mastery and domination, and his invitation to his followers to be his friends, brothers, sisters and mothers (Matt. 12:48–50; Mark 3:33–4; Luke 8:21). Such concepts of married love as otherness in difference, mutual respect, and mutual service might usher in a new mystical sensibility through the reawakening of a sacramental imagination capable of weaving together God, the human, and the rest of creation. To imagine God and the human in a fertile love relationship based on enduring faithfulness and commitment, together sustaining and tending creation, nurturing the vulnerable and bringing all things to maturity and fulfilment in Christ, might offer a way of understanding the nuptial relationship which unites God, humanity, and nature in a fertile and faithful union, such as we sometimes glimpse in faithful human sexual love and in the dedication of parenthood.

T. Beattie, *New Catholic Feminism: Theology and Theory* (Routledge, 2006).

F. Kerr, *Twentieth Century Catholic Theologians: From Neoscholasticism to Nuptial Mystery* (Blackwell, 2006).

E. F. Rogers, Jr, ed., *Theology and Sexuality: Classic and Contemporary Readings* (Blackwell, 2001).

A. Cardinal Scola, *The Nuptial Mystery* (Eerdmans, 2005).

TINA BEATTIE

O

Oblation Derived from a Latin word for 'offering', 'oblation' has several meanings. In Catholic CANON LAW it is used for anything given over to the use of the Church. In the more narrowly liturgical context of the MASS, oblation refers to the Eucharistic elements of bread and wine, whether as brought in unconsecrated form to the altar during the offertory (the lesser oblation) or in their presentation after consecration (the greater oblation). Protestants generally restrict the use of oblation to the offertory, on the grounds that to designate the consecrated elements (in distinction from the unconsecrated bread and wine, as well as the monetary and other gifts brought forward in furtherance of the Church's ministry) as an oblation implies that in the celebration of the EUCHARIST the Church offers something to God rather than thankfully receiving what God offers it.

In the monastic context oblation refers to the medieval practice of dedicating children to religious life (cf. 1 Sam. 1:11, 22–8) by trusting them to the care of a monastery. Such children (known as oblates) were raised in the community until they were judged sufficiently mature to decide whether they wished to commit their lives to it by taking monastic vows. The reasons for dedicating children were varied, and often desperation (among the poor) and convenience or political calculation (among the rich) trumped religious motives. Nevertheless, oblation remains significant as a distinctly Christian form of ADOPTION, in which collective childrearing filled out the cenobitic model of a community organized around structures other than heterosexual MARRIAGE and the biological family.

See also MONASTICISM.

IAN A. MCFARLAND

Occasionalism Occasionalism is a metaphysical theory of causation, which regards God as the true and proper cause of all change and impact. Worldly causes are not in themselves effective, but are only 'occasions' for God's action. Nevertheless, God does not interfere at random, but follows a divine ECONOMY of regularity.

T. AQUINAS treated this theory (which had a considerable previous history in Arabic–Islamic theology) as contrary to his own view of the contingent but real efficiency of creaturely secondary causes acting under God as primary cause. Occasionalism was most fully elaborated in the wake of CARTESIANISM. Its leading theorist was the French Oratorian priest N. Malebranche (1638–1715). He set out this theory in his early writing *Recherche de la verité* (1762) and applied it then to many other subjects. A mature version is found in his *Entretiens sur la métaphysique et la religion* (1688).

Occasionalism was not, as claimed by B. Fontenelle (1657–1757) and G. Leibniz (1646–1716) and repeated until today, merely a convenient solution to the Cartesian problem of dualism: the question of how the two substances, spirit and matter, interact in human life. On the contrary, Malebranche applied his theory to mechanical as well as cognitive processes in an attempt to combine Cartesian science with the theocentrism of Augustinian metaphysics. He was particularly interested in countering any tendency to grant nature any causal autonomy at God's expense. He saw this as a particular danger among the 'Libertines': free-thinking popular writers who tried to install a quasi-mythical 'Nature' as source of all truth, goodness, and beauty – even of all religion. Malebranche's occasionalism was successful in so far as it complied with scientific procedure: disregarding all speculation on the essence of things, the occasionalist considers an event to have been explained if it can be described as an instance ('occasion') of a general, mathematically formulated natural law. After Malebranche's death, however, his system collapsed and was even invoked in defence of atheistic MATERIALISM. Today occasionalism has no prominent defenders, though it has been associated with the ENLIGHTENMENT-era theology of J. EDWARDS.

Most modern research on occasionalism is focused on accurate historical reconstruction of the Cartesian era. Malebranche's system is examined for its inconsistencies in order to discover how it developed into materialistic naturalism in the eighteenth century. Frequently, however, the theological inspiration of Malebranche's occasionalism goes unrecognized. At bottom, occasionalism is a kind of rational mysticism, according to which in his daily life the individual is in touch with God, who is the proper cause of all his actions. Humans have the means of being purified, illuminated, and united with God. As they assimilate themselves more and more to the divine order, they are enabled to overcome the powerlessness and error with which they are afflicted because of original SIN. Malebranche sees every thinking person in a dialogue with God, or, more specifically, with Christ, whose humanity plays a central role in his occasionalist system. This dialogue can be described as GRACE, and Christ serves as the occasional cause for its concrete realization.

N. Malebranche, *Dialogues on Metaphysics and Religion* (Cambridge University Press, 1997 [1688]).

D. Perler and U. Rudolph, *Occasionalismus: Theorien der Kausalität im arabisch-islamischen und im europäischen Denken* (Vanderhoeck & Ruprecht, 2000).

FRANZ JOSEPH BAUR

OFFERTORY: see MASS, CANON OF.

OLD TESTAMENT: see SCRIPTURE.

ONTOLOGICAL ARGUMENT The ontological argument attempts to demonstrate the impossibility of God's non-existence. There are different expressions of the argument, of which the simplest is a conceptual version proposed by R. Descartes (1596–1650): just as the concept of a bachelor implies that every bachelor is male, the concept of God implies that God exists. The existence of God, unlike the existence of any other being, is claimed to be soundly deduced from the concept of God.

ANSELM OF CANTERBURY is the originator of the ontological argument. His version, presented in his *Proslogion* (1077/8), can be summarized as follows:

(1) God is that than which none greater can be conceived.
(2) God exists as an idea in the mind.
(3) That which exists as an idea in the mind and in reality is greater than a being that exists only as an idea in the mind.
(4) Thus, if God exists only as an idea in the mind, then we can imagine something that is greater than God.
(5) But we cannot conceive something that is greater than God (i.e., something greater than that than which nothing greater can be conceived).
(6) Therefore, God exists.

Anselm's contemporary, Gaunilo, famously countered that this argument could be adapted to deduce the existence of a perfect island. To see the strategy, substitute for 'God' in the above argument 'piland', defined as 'an island none greater than which can be imagined'. But the criticism was unpersuasive because an island is not the kind of thing that admits of the kind of absolute perfection ascribed by Anselm to God.

I. KANT argued that premise (3) falsely presupposes existence is a property. Though Kant's reasoning is unclear, he seems correct. Existence seems to be a precondition for the instantiation of any properties and *not* itself a property (in, say, the way that being red is a property of an apple). A non-existent thing has no properties.

Other critics argue that, even if it were a property, existence is not a property that makes something better for having it. As N. Malcolm (1911–90) expressed the point, 'My future child will be a better man if he is honest than if he is not; but who would understand the saying that he will be a better man if he exists than if he does not?' ('Anselm', 43). Nevertheless, a number of modern philosophers and theologians, including K. BARTH and C. Hartshorne (1897–2000), have found the argument persuasive.

A. Plantinga (b. 1932) gives an influential modal version of the argument. Plantinga defines a being as *maximally great* in a world W if and only if it is omnipotent, omniscient, and morally perfect in every possible world and argues that the coherence of this definition implies such a being, i.e., God, exists in every possible world:

(1) The concept of a maximally great being is self-consistent.
(2) If (1), there is at least one logically possible world in which a maximally great being exists.
(3) If a maximally great being exists in one logically possible world, it exists in every logically possible world.
(4) Therefore, a maximally great being (i.e., God) exists in every logically possible world.

Critics have challenged the claim that the concept of a maximally great being is self-consistent, but have not produced a conclusive refutation of this admittedly obscure premise. In consequence, the ontological argument remains debated today in philosophy of RELIGION.

KENNETH EINAR HIMMA

OPEN THEISM Open theism is a theological vision within Christian theology in which God is believed to be 'open' to the world, that is, affected by and responsive to the creatures that God made and particularly to human beings. Open theists take God to be not so much an 'unmoved mover' as a 'most moved mover', able to be affected by historical change. They also believe that God is 'open' to the future, which they view as indeterminate in some respects, waiting to be determined by God and human beings in other respects. The complete future consists of things that are now settled and of things that are not yet settled. This means that human agents can by their actions make a difference as to how things will work out historically.

Open theism as a model arose first among evangelical philosophers such as W. Hasker (b. 1935) and D. Basinger (b. 1947) in North America, from whence it spread to biblical scholars and to theologians. It is an expression of free-will theism, varieties of which have always existed. It has roots in the Wesleyan/Arminian tradition (see ARMINIANISM; METHODIST THEOLOGY).

According to traditional theism, a perfect being such as God would have to possess the attribute of unchangeability, because any change in God would have to be a change for the better or a change for worse, neither of which would be compatible with traditional notions of perfection. According to the logic here, God has to be immutable, timeless, and impassible in order to rule out any change and, correspondingly, cannot be affected by creation in any way.

Open theism, for its part, rejects this way of thinking about God's perfections. It understands God as temporally everlasting, not timeless, and as the God who experiences the succession of events. God is everlasting. God has always existed and always will exist. Therefore, God's experience varies from time to time as God observes changes in the world and responds to creatures. Open theists believe that God, far from being impassible, is profoundly affected by what happens to creatures. God sympathizes and suffers with them, sharing in their joys and sorrows.

Unlike proponents of PROCESS THEOLOGY, open theists believe that God has the power to control the world unilaterally but has chosen not to do so. God chooses instead to bestow on his human creatures libertarian freedom. The idea of divine self-restraint in God is fundamental and human beings have the possibility of making genuine choices for or against the divine will. The gift of freedom makes possible a response of love and/or the possibility of turning away from God.

Accepting libertarian freedom, open theists deny MIDDLE KNOWLEDGE and believe that God manages the world without enjoying the degree of control over and the foreknowledge of contingent events that was traditionally ascribed to God. This requires, according to open theists, more wisdom and intelligence on God's part, but open theists trust that God is resourceful when it comes to carrying out his creation project.

Open theism has enjoyed a warm response from theologians like J. Moltmann (b. 1926) and J. Polkinghorne (b. 1930) and some appreciation from J. Cobb (b. 1925) and D. Griffin (b. 1939). The strongest opposition to it comes from more traditional interpreters of REFORMED THEOLOGY, whose views remain influential among conservative evangelicals.

C. Pinnock, *Most Moved Mover: A Theology of God's Openness* (Baker Academic, 2001).

C. Pinnock *et al.*, *The Openness of God: A Biblical Challenge to the Traditional Understanding of God* (InterVarsity Press, 1994).

CLARK PINNOCK

ORDERS 'Order' (Latin *ordo*) is an established corporation with a hierarchy, and 'orders' refers, correspondingly, to the offices into which people are ordained (i.e., legally incorporated) into an *ordo*. Those in 'Holy Orders' take office in the Church hierarchy, with the adjective 'holy' meaning, 'set apart for some purpose'. Being set apart for MINISTRY in the Church may be understood wholly functionally (i.e., in terms of the roles ordained persons perform) or also ontologically (i.e., in terms of what they become in themselves). Ontological understandings of orders vary and can include incorporation into Christ's priestly office (see THREEFOLD OFFICE) in a way that extends Christ's priestly ministry through time, as well as the belief that ordination, like BAPTISM, irreversibly imprints the SOUL (see Trent, *Ordin.*, Chapter 4). Ontological accounts most readily accompany teaching that ordination is a sacrament: an outward sign, instituted by Christ, of the conferring of GRACE necessary to the discharge of the office.

Those in orders serve the apostolic continuity of the Church. Whether through dogma, liturgical order, or structures, they are seen to stand in a line of succession going back to the twelve and the other APOSTLES whom Jesus called and sent (see APOSTOLIC SUCCESSION). Succession in ministry is focused in the act of ordination when the whole Church, through particular ministers, participates in ordaining those selected for the ministry of Word and Sacrament.

Three orders of bishop, presbyter, and deacon emerged probably in the first century and are evidenced unequivocally in the Ignatian epistles of the second century. The threefold ministry is retained today, with variations, by Catholic, Orthodox, Anglican, Eastern Catholic, Oriental Orthodox, Assyrian, Old Catholic, Independent Catholic, and some Lutheran Churches. These Churches regard the gift of orders as a sacrament, though Anglicans and Lutherans debate internally as to the extent.

Protestant Churches do not all recognize a separate order of bishops, for in the NT Church, overseers (*episkopoi*, or 'bishops') initially seem to have been identical with presbyters (*presbyteroi*, or 'elders'; see Acts 20:17–18; Phil. 1:1; Tit. 1:5, 7). The title of 'bishop' came to be reserved to presidents of presbyterate councils by the second century. The ministry of bishops arose out of the need for *episcopē*, which itself emerged as the number of local congregations multiplied. *Episcopē* includes oversight and visitation, and is the work of maintaining communion between congregations, safeguarding and handing on apostolic truth, and giving mutual support and leadership in witnessing to the GOSPEL. Non-episcopal Churches exercise *episcopē* through assemblies or eldership teams. Episcopal Churches exercise it through individual bishops and synods. Bishops delegate to presbyters/priests the authority to administer most sacraments, including, in the Catholic Church, CONFIRMATION, and in exceptional circumstances ordination. Ordinarily bishops reserve the authority to ordain because of their particular role in maintaining the unity and continuity of the Church (see EPISCOPACY).

The word 'priest' is a contraction of 'presbyter' (elder), but has also taken on connotations of offering sacrifice. 'Priest' is employed by Churches that regard *presbyteroi* as mediating by the HOLY SPIRIT Christ's unique priesthood (John 20:21–3). In this context, the order of 'priests' is understood to realize the PRIESTHOOD OF ALL BELIEVERS by enabling the Church to enter into the self-offering of Christ. 'Presbyter' is used by those Churches of the REFORMATION that reject agential notions of PRIESTHOOD as rivalling the unique and sufficient priesthood of Christ (Heb. 7:26; 1 Tim. 2:5), and which reserve language of priesthood for the body of all believers. The King James Version and some subsequent English translations of the NT regularly use 'priest' only in relation to the sacerdotal terms *hierys* and *hierateuma* (Latin, *sacerdos* and *sacerdotium*), which in the NT are applied to the Christian BODY as a whole, and not to individual ministers (1 Pet. 2:5, 9; Rev. 5:10). The Latin term *sacerdotes* was applied to Christian ministers by the end of the second century, initially to bishops, and, by the time of Cyprian of Carthage (d. 258), to presbyters (*Ep.* 61), because authority to consecrate in the EUCHARIST was delegated to them.

The DIACONATE is a distinctive order embodying the ministry of service to the whole body of Christ. It is traditionally seen as instituted in the ordination of the Seven in Acts 6:1–6 for service to the poor and distribution of alms. Presbyterians have two classes of deacon performing these two roles, as delineated in Calvin's *Institutes* (4.3.9). The Greek term *diakonos* ('servant') is used not in Acts 6, but is in Philippians 1:1 and 1 Timothy 3:8 for ministers who serve under presbyter-bishops. Within threefold ordained ministries, deacons serve pastorally and liturgically. Liturgical roles include preparing the altar for the Eucharist, and also leading the people in confession and the sharing of the peace. The Orthodox Churches have a larger permanent diaconate than in Catholic and Anglican Churches, but in all of these communions the majority of those ordained deacon are subsequently ordained priests. In some Lutheran Churches assistant parochial ministers are called deacons even though they are in full Lutheran orders.

Women are ordained in many Protestant, Lutheran, and Anglican Churches. They are not ordained in Orthodox or Catholic Churches. Debates over the propriety of women's ordination centre on the maleness of Christ and the Twelve, MARY MAGDALENE's role as first witness to the RESURRECTION, female leaders of NT Churches, and the Pauline language of 'headship' (1 Cor. 11:2–15). Sacramental issues arise over the unity and irreversibility of orders. Where ordination is understood as a sacrament, it is agreed that there is a single Sacrament of Orders. On this basis some argue that orders have been divided, altering the relationship between bishops and priests, in those Provinces of the Anglican Communion that ordain women as deacons and priests but have not agreed to ordain women as bishops. If orders cannot be reversed, this has particular relevance for communions unresolved about the ordination of women. Within Anglicanism, should the decision to ordain women be reversed? The reversal would not be of any ordination, but of synodical decisions. Women already in orders would continue to work out their ministry in recognition that they were duly and canonically ordained.

Full unity between Christian communions is achieved where Churches fully recognize one another's orders, as with the Lutheran and Anglican Churches of the Porvoo Agreement (1993). Partial recognition of orders is achieved elsewhere by western Churches, which generally uphold AUGUSTINE's position that even in HERESY or SCHISM a bishop can validly ordain, just as he can validly baptize or preside at the Eucharist. Therefore the Catholic Church does not re-ordain bishops and priests from the Orthodox Church, and Anglicans do not re-ordain Catholic priests. However, the Catholic Church does not recognize orders conferred within the Anglican Church. This is not, as is sometimes supposed, due to an alleged break in the historic succession of episcopal ordinations, for any break in succession was restored with Archbishop W. Laud (1573–1645), but due to supposed inadequacies in Anglican understandings of the priestly power to consecrate and offer Eucharistic sacrifice. By means of 'economy' Orthodox Churches often in practice recognize the orders of those ordained in the West. However, in principle the East retains the dominant view of the early (i.e., pre-Augustinian) Church that orders could not be given outside the Church. The Orthodox position highlights the significance of orders to the *esse* (essence or very being) of the Church, for, where orders are not recognized, the authenticity of a congregation as a Christian Church is denied.

See also POLITY; SACRAMENTOLOGY.

P. F. Bradshaw, *Ordination Rites of the Ancient Churches of East and West* (Pueblo, 1990).
A. Green, *A Theology of Women's Priesthood* (SPCK, 2009).
E. Schillebeeckx, *The Church with a Human Face: A New and Expanded Theology of Ministry* (SCM, 1985).
E. Schweizer, *Church Order in the New Testament* (SCM, 1961).

HARRIET A. HARRIS

ORDINATION: see ORDERS.

ORDO SALUTIS *Ordo salutis* (Latin for 'order of salvation') is the phrase used to describe the logical ordering of the elements in individual salvation. It became a commonplace in both REFORMED and LUTHERAN THEOLOGY by the seventeenth century.

The Bible itself offers a number of passages typically used in support of an *ordo salutis* concept, such as Romans 8:30 and Ephesians 1:3–10. In these passages, the structure of salvation is laid out on the basis of PREDESTINATION, followed by the various benefits brought in its wake. With the shift at the REFORMATION towards concerns with predestination, with JUSTIFICATION, with the need to maintain the importance of good works, and with personal ASSURANCE, these *ordo salutis* passages became theologically and pastorally significant.

Under polemical pressure from the Catholics (who pointed to the incipient ANTINOMIANISM of the Protestant position on justification) and to defend the importance of good works in the context of justification by GRACE through FAITH, early Reformers, most notably M. BUCER, accented the importance of predestination as the foundation of salvation, and the means whereby the act of faith and subsequent good works were held together in an unbreakable chain. For Bucer predestination was to a twofold justification: before God by imputation; before the world by impartation. J. CALVIN modified this structure to stress union with Christ as that to which the elect are predestined, with justification and SANCTIFICATION as its twofold benefit, albeit with justification having strict logical priority.

With its emphasis upon the eternal decree and its execution in time, Reformed theology continued to place a central emphasis upon the *ordo salutis* as the logical unfolding of the decree throughout the sixteenth century. Typically it was from ELECTION to calling to union with Christ to justification to sanctification to glorification. This idea was also developed with a strong pastoral tone, as evidenced in the work of T. Beza (1519–1605), and, more elaborately, in that of W. Perkins (1558–1602). The typical Protestant emphasis upon assurance, combined with an equal concern for the unknowability of God's eternal decree, fuelled the rise of pastoral literature which, in a manner qualified and subordinate to assurance based upon Christological considerations, allowed for a certain amount of inference back from sanctification to election (see PRACTICAL SYLLOGISM). This is most graphically demonstrated in Perkins' *A Golden Chaine* (1591), which contained an elaborate chart (based upon a Bezan original) showing how the various elements of the *ordo* connect the believer to election and to the work of Christ. Contrary to some arguments, the golden chain of salvation was not presented to demonstrate the logical deduction of salvation from the sovereignty of God but rather to show how each stage in the *ordo* is only comprehensible in the light of that which has gone before it and upon which it rests.

Lutheranism in the sixteenth century had not typically focused on a precise definition of predestination in the manner of the Reformed; yet, under the impact of intra-Lutheran doctrinal debates, seventeenth-century Lutheran systems did produce a carefully defined *ordo salutis* which typically took the following form: election to calling to justification to union with Christ to sanctification to glorification. In this ordering, Lutheranism made more explicit the logical priority of justification to sanctification than is the case in certain Reformed articulations, such as those of R. Baxter (1615–91).

Modern biblical scholarship, particularly in the field of Pauline studies, has raised significant questions about whether the emphasis upon the *ordo salutis* has not eclipsed the more biblical emphasis upon the *historia salutis* and displaced the story of ISRAEL and of Christ with an unhealthy emphasis upon the individual, thus fuelling a certain introspection and a distorted understanding of the Bible's teaching. Certainly, the earlier literature does not seem always to have captured the biblical emphasis on the corporate aspects of salvation; but the concerns of the *ordo salutis* are undoubtedly present within the biblical texts.

See also SOTERIOLOGY.

L. Berkhof, *Systematic Theology* (Banner of Truth Trust, 1958).

J. Murray, *Redemption Accomplished and Applied* (Eerdmans, 1955).

CARL R. TRUEMAN

ORIENTAL ORTHODOX CHURCHES The Oriental Orthodox Churches, sometimes called non-Chalcedonian or pre-Chalcedonian, are the Orthodox Churches that adhere to the first three COUNCILS of the Church (NICAEA, CONSTANTINOPLE, and EPHESUS), but historically refused to accept the Council of CHALCEDON, in lasting opposition to the dyophysitism implied in the phrase 'in two natures'. Similarly, the Oriental Orthodox Churches have opposed the *Tome* of Pope Leo I (r. 440–61), and especially the phrase 'each form does the acts which belong to it, in communion with the other'. Often falsely accused of monophysitism, the Oriental Orthodox recoil from this description, associated as it is with the denial of full INCARNATION in APOLLINARIANISM and EUTYCHIANISM. Maintaining their support for the classic formula of CYRIL OF ALEXANDRIA that in the incarnation, there is 'one nature of God the Word incarnate', they prefer the designation 'miaphysite'.

Geographically, the Oriental Orthodox were to the South and the East of the Byzantine Empire. They include the Syrian Orthodox Church (sometimes called the Jacobite Church, after the missionary James Baradaeus (d. 578)), the Coptic Church in Egypt, and the Ethiopian Orthodox Tawehedo Church ('Tawehedo' is a Ge'ez word meaning 'undivided', a reference to their miaphysite Christology). Also included among the Oriental Orthodox are the Armenians (though they were not actually present at Chalcedon, being out of touch with Byzantium) and the (Indian) Malankara Orthodox Church. The Apostolic Catholic Assyrian Church of the East (the 'Nestorian Church') was historically dyophysite and is not included among the Oriental Orthodox. The Oriental Orthodox, though in communion with each other, are independent hierarchically. Collectively, they provide an important non-Slavic, non-Greek voice. The Ethiopian Orthodox, with some 40 million members, is the largest Orthodox Church after the Russian.

The middle of the twentieth century saw far-reaching efforts to achieve understanding and bring about reconciliation between Chalcedonian and non-Chalcedonian Orthodox Christians. There were four unofficial theological consultations (Aarhus, 1964; Bristol, 1967; Geneva, 1970; and Addis Ababa, 1971), followed by the establishment of a Joint Commission of the Theological Dialogue between the Orthodox Church and the Oriental Orthodox Churches (Chambésy, 1985; Anba Bishoy, 1989; Chambésy, 1990 and 1993). A First Agreed Statement was produced at Anba Bishoy monastery, Egypt, in June 1989. This acknowledged the Nicene tradition as a common inheritance for all Orthodox Christians. It found common ground in the formulae of Cyril of Alexandria, that in Jesus Christ there is 'one nature (HYPOSTASIS) incarnate of God the Word', and that the Virgin Mary is *Theotokos*.

The very precisely worded statement affirmed that the *Logos*, eternally consubstantial with the Father and the Holy Spirit, in these last days, 'became incarnate' of the HOLY SPIRIT and the Virgin Mary *Theotokos*, and is thus truly God and truly human at the same time. The Churches clarified that when they spoke of the 'one composite [*synthetos*] hypostasis' of Christ, they do not affirm that in him a divine hypostasis and a human hypostasis came together. They are affirming that the one eternal hypostasis of the Word assumed human nature, *in that act* uniting it with his divine nature, to form an inseparably and unconfusedly united divine–human being, the natures of which are distinguishable only in abstract contemplation (*theoria*). The hypostasis of the *Logos* before the incarnation is not composite. The same hypostasis of the incarnate *Logos* is not composite either. The unique theandric person (*prosopon*) of Jesus Christ is the one eternal hypostasis who has assumed human nature, and that hypostasis is called 'composite' on account of the natures which are united to form one composite unity with all the properties and functions of the uncreated divine nature, inseparably and unconfusedly united with the created human nature, with all its properties and functions, including natural will. The two Church families also agreed in condemning the Nestorian and Eutychian heresies, and in retaining the four Chalcedonian adverbs, describing the union as being without confusion, without change, without separation, without division.

A Second Agreed Statement was reached in 1990 at Chambésy. This re-affirmed that both Church families rejected the heresies of Eutyches and Nestorius. Both affirmed that the hypostasis of the *Logos* became composite (*sunthetos*) by uniting to his divine uncreated nature created human nature, which he made his own, along with its natural will and energy. Both families agreed that *the one who acts* is always the one hypostasis of the Word incarnate. Both families agreed in rejecting interpretations of the Councils not in accord with the intention (*horos*) of the ecumenical Council of Ephesus and the Letter of Cyril of Alexandria to John of Antioch of 433.

In consequence both families agreed that all the ANATHEMAS and condemnations of the past which had hitherto divided them should be lifted. They agreed not to rebaptize each other's members, to resolve conflicts over mixed marriages, to have joint discussion on a common Orthodox response to the issues of ABORTION, of other Christian communities, and of the ordination of women to the priesthood.

These remarkable statements, drawing upon the terminological subtleties of both sides, were one of the ecumenical successes of the twentieth century. Actual progress has been slower, with some of the Chalcedonian Orthodox (especially those of Russia and Serbia) being hesitant. There is a question about the possibility and manner of lifting anathemas that were imposed by ecumenical councils, but deeper understanding is being forged.

In 1984 Pope John Paul II (r. 1978–2005) and Patriarch Zakka I Iwas of Antioch and All the East (r. 1980–) together confessed the NICENE CREED and acknowledged that the confusions and SCHISMS that had occurred between their Churches in the later centuries in no way affected the substance of their FAITH, since these arose only because of differences in terminology and culture. The dialogue continues.

P. Gregorios, W. H. Lazareth, and N. A. Nissiotis, eds., *Does Chalcedon Divide or Unite? Towards Convergence in Orthodox Christology* (WCC, 1981).

'Joint Commission for Theological Dialogue between the Orthodox Church and Oriental Orthodox Churches', *Sobornost* (*Eastern Churches Review*) 12:1 (1990), 78–80.

IAIN R. TORRANCE

ORIGEN OF ALEXANDRIA Although his name meant 'Child of Horus', Origen (*ca* 185–255) was the son of a Christian martyr, Leonides, and of a mother who was either Christian or Jewish, for she taught him the Psalms at an early age. Origen was the first Christian intellectual to have a truly international reputation as a philosopher and was, at one stage of his career, summoned to address the imperial entourage of J. Mammaea (*ca* 180–235). Her bursary to him assisted in a lifelong task he had set himself: to found a Christian academy at Caesarea Maritima in Roman Palestine, and to furnish it with a respectable library. His efforts were successful in his own lifetime and were sustained over several generations after him by learned bishops of Caesarea who followed his tradition.

The legend, based on a much later account of his life by Eusebius of Caesarea (*ca* 265–*ca* 340), that in his zeal for chastity he had himself castrated is almost certainly not true. His own writings must always be preferred for sorting the often conflicting accounts of Origen's history, and in his *Commentary on Matthew* (19.12) he declares that anyone who takes that evangelical saying about self-eunuchizing literally would be foolish indeed. His own references to the condition of eunuchs (which some scholars have looked to as confirmation of the legend) are all drawn from the medical writer Galen and show no personal experience. Eusebius' report is more plausibly explained as an attempt to account for Origen's rejection by his Alexandrian bishop (and the pope) on canonical grounds that monks of his own day would have sympathized with, rather than on the unpalatable fact that many thought he was heterodox even in his lifetime.

Origen was a religious philosopher who looked to divine REVELATION as the highest level of illumination. Thus, despite appearances of being highly speculative metaphysically, he follows a scriptural–exegetical method in all his theology. In his approach to the sacred text, he obeyed the scholarly traditions of contemporary Alexandrian literary analysis and set out for the Church rules of interpretation that would be massively influential for later ages. His theory of exegesis is dominated by the notion that SCRIPTURE was a single reality reflecting a single mind – that of the divine *LOGOS*. Its apparent multiplicities were, therefore, but the masking of the eternal revelation under the illusory appearances of historical relativity. A particular passage, therefore, always had several layers of meaning; usually this was witnessed in three layers: a historical or literal import, a moral meaning, and a mystical (spiritual or noetic) meaning. Take the story of the conquest of Canaan: the literal meaning was a historical account of a war; the moral meaning is a 'higher' sense and connotes the individual Christian's call to rise to a godly life by conquering vice; the third level is the still higher, mystical (eschatological) significance of entering the 'Promised Land', understood as referring to the SOUL's communion with God in the kingdom which is to come. This 'highest' allegorical (or spiritual) interpretation was his preferred method. Texts which had an 'impossible' meaning (morally questionable behaviour on the part of God or the OT patriarchs, for example) he saw as being like special 'page-markers' left in Scripture by God to make intelligent souls stop and realize that a deeper mystery lay buried like a treasure in the field. For Origen, those who stayed only with the literal meaning of the text were unenlightened souls who had not realized that Jesus gave some of his teaching in the valleys and some on mountain tops. Only to the disciples who could ascend the mountains did Jesus reveal himself transfigured.

From the time of his father's death during his teenage years, Origen turned to scholarship as a living, moving from the profession of grammarian to his own preferred self-definition as philosopher-rhetorician. He proved an active apologist who dealt intelligently and spaciously with the Gnostic movements that were still active in his time (see GNOSTICISM). He also wrote a learned response to the caustic attack on Christianity's rational coherence that the Greek philosopher Celsus had composed a generation earlier. His answer, known commonly as *Against Celsus*, is a brilliantly sustained defence of Christianity as a philosophical as well as a religious system, and calls for intellectuals to rise to the foreground of the Church. Here Origen plays with ideas of religious PLURALISM that have only recently come back into circulation. He also left a massive corpus of biblical commentaries which influenced almost all the great patristic writers of the classic era, even though Origen was himself (several times) condemned posthumously.

Origen's work as a theologian attempting to correlate biblical understandings with philosophical, cosmological, and metaphysical agendas, served as a stimulus to generations after him. He wrote what must be accounted as one of the first treatises of Christian systematic theology, *On First Principles* (*Peri Archōn* in Greek, or *De Principiis* in Latin), and his massive critical edition of the OT, the *Hexapla*, was the scholarly wonder of the age. His great *Commentary on the Song of Songs* has been regarded as the foundation of Christian MYSTICAL THEOLOGY, while his *Commentary on John* is a magnificent account that founded the Christian tradition of regarding the fourth Gospel as the 'first-fruits of the first fruits' of all Scripture. At the end of his life he was arrested and tortured during the Decian persecution. That he survived for two years afterwards meant that he did not win the accolade of MARTYRDOM, and thus his works were frequently subjected to waves of imperial, monastic, and ecclesiastical censure. That so much has survived into the present is a testimony to the manner in which he has been so deeply loved by Christian intellectuals of all ages.

See also ORIGENISM.

H. Crouzel, *Origen* (T&T Clark, 1989).

C. Kannengiesser and W. L. Petersen, eds., *Origen of Alexandria: His World and His Legacy* (University of Notre Dame Press, 1988).

J. A. McGuckin, *The Westminster Handbook to Origen* (John Knox Press, 2003).

J. W. Trigg, *Origen: The Bible and Philosophy in the Third Century Church* (John Knox Press, 1983).

JOHN A. MCGUCKIN

ORIGENISM 'Origenism' refers to a mixture of DOCTRINES, some of which go back to ORIGEN OF ALEXANDRIA and his follower, Evagrius Ponticus (345–99), but others of which arguably derive from exaggeration or misunderstanding of their teachings. Origenist ideas were especially popular among Christian ascetics and, in various forms, have deeply influenced the SPIRITUALITY and religious practice of the Christian East and West down to the present day.

Debates over Origenism arose initially in the early fourth century (*ca* 397–404) and included the following 'Origenist' doctrines: (1) the Son and the HOLY SPIRIT are both creatures; (2) before the creation of humankind, SOULS lived in the heavens among the rational creatures; (3) the waters above the heaven signify celestial, and the lower waters demonic, powers (cf. Gen. 1:6–7); (4) souls received bodies of different quality, according to their previous merits or faults; (5) the paradise story of Genesis 2–3 is to be interpreted allegorically (see ALLEGORY); (6) paradise was a spiritual state, in which human beings did not have bodily members; (7) when Adam was expelled from paradise, he lost the image and likeness in which God made him; (8) the 'garments of skin' in Genesis 3:21 refer to the human BODY;

(9) human flesh will not be resurrected; (10) ANGELS, demons, and humans can be transformed into one another depending upon their merits or wickedness; (11) innumerable worlds have existed in the past and will exist in the future; (12) Christ had often suffered and will also suffer for demons; (13) in the final restoration the DEVIL and demons will also be saved and will reign together with SAINTS (see UNIVERSALISM).

Whereas the focus of the fourth-century controversy was the primordial and final state of rational creatures, during the sixth-century debate (*ca* 514–53) Christological and soteriological questions took centre stage. Within the framework of speculations about the ontology of created intellects that owe more to Evagrius than to Origen, two important 'Origenist' groups formed, the so-called *Isochristoi*, and the *Prōtoktistoi* (or *Tetraditai*). The former proclaimed that in the final restoration (*apokatastasis*) created intellects will be so perfectly unified with each other as to be 'equals to Christ' (*isochristoi*), and that, by virtue of participating in God's power, this intellectual unity will be able to create new worlds. The latter seem to have emphasized the role that the 'first-born' (*prōtoktistos*), created mind of Christ, perfectly united with the divine *LOGOS*, played in the CREATION of the universe. They concluded that this Christ-intellect was a fourth hypostasis (*tetraditēs*) of the TRINITY and thus an operating principle both in creation and in subsequent divine ECONOMY.

Fifteen Origenist (or, more accurately, Evagrian) theses were anathematized by a pre-session of the second Council of Constantinople in 553, but it is disputed whether or not the ANATHEMAS were officially adopted by the council fathers. Origen, however, was condemned by name in the Council's official acts.

E. Clark, *The Origenist Controversy: The Cultural Construction of an Early Christian Debate* (Princeton University Press, 1992).

B. E. Daley, 'What did "Origenism" Mean in the Sixth Century?' in *Origeniana sexta*, ed. G. Dorival and A. Le Boulluec (Peeters, 1995), 627–38.

GYÖRGY HEIDL

ORIGINAL SIN: see SIN.

ORTHODOX THEOLOGY 'Orthodox theology' refers to the intellectual tradition of the Eastern Orthodox Christian Churches, which primarily, though not exclusively, includes those Christian communities with historical ties to the Byzantine tradition. There are at least two basic theological trajectories in the Byzantine tradition: the first concerns the well-known controversies around the person of Christ that occasioned the convening of the seven ecumenical councils (see CHALCEDON; CHRISTOLOGY; EPHESUS; NICAEA). The dogmatic proclamations of these Councils reflect non-negotiable axioms of Orthodox theology from the Byzantine tradition to the present, of which the most foundational is the affirmation of divine–human communion in the person of Jesus Christ. Some of the key figures of the Byzantine period who contributed to the theological controversies on the person of Christ and whose works are authoritative for Orthodox theology are ATHANASIUS OF ALEXANDRIA, Basil of Caesarea, Gregory of Nazianzus, Gregory of Nyssa (see CAPPADOCIAN FATHERS), CYRIL OF ALEXANDRIA, and MAXIMUS THE CONFESSOR.

The second trajectory in the Byzantine theological tradition is APOPHATIC theology, which is normally associated with DIONYSIUS THE AREOPAGITE, but which is also discernible in Gregory of Nyssa, and, in a much less developed form, in post- and ante-Nicene patristic thinkers, such as ORIGEN. Though often defined as understanding God in terms of what God is not, such a definition is simplistic and misleading, and does not capture the richness of the apophatic theological tradition in Eastern Christianity. Apophaticism, otherwise known as 'negative theology', is a form of Christian theology which simultaneously attempts to express the transcendence and immanence of God. In terms of the transcendence of God, apophaticism affirms the inadequacy of reason or language as definitive forms of knowledge of God; in terms of the immanence of God, apophaticism defines knowledge of God in terms of mystical union. It is because God is excessive to reason or language that knowledge of God is understood in terms of mystical experience. In Dionysian apophaticism, the God–world relation is best understood in terms of an *exitus/reditus* model. God's outpouring of Godself in creation (*exitus*) is the basis for cataphatic statements about God; the return of all in union with God (*reditus*) requires *apophasis*, or the negation of all positive statements about God. Union with God is the result of a double negation, since God is beyond the opposition of positive and negative statements. Debate exists over the Christological foundation of apophaticism, but within the Byzantine tradition, the apophatic affirmation of knowledge of God in terms of mystical union is logically derivative from the affirmation of divine–human communion in the person of Christ. The intersection of these two trajectories is evident in such apophatic, mystical thinkers as Symeon the New Theologian (949–1022), but especially in G. PALAMAS, who is the last of the authoritative and well-known patristic thinkers (see APOPHATIC THEOLOGY).

Palamas' thought emerges in reaction to an attack on HESYCHASM, a form of spirituality whose goal is union with God through the practice of the recitation of the Jesus Prayer ('Lord Jesus Christ, Son of God, have mercy on me, a sinner'). Palamas is especially known for his conceptualization of divine–human communion in terms of the categories of essence and energies, in which God is unknowable and transcendent in God's essence, but knowable and immanent in God's energies. The essence/energies distinction is discernible in earlier patristic writings, but receives its most developed form in Palamas. There is no tradition of 'systematic' or 'dogmatic' theology in the Byzantine tradition, though JOHN OF DAMASCUS' *Exposition of the Orthodox Faith* is an attempt at a systematization of theological themes, whose influence is evident in T. AQUINAS' *Summa theologiae*, but not on any later Byzantine texts. Byzantine theology was primarily developed in response to a variety of challenges to the foundational principle of divine–human communion in Christ, and to debates over the implications of this principle for the spiritual life.

After the fall of Constantinople to the Ottomans in 1453, it is not an overstatement to claim that theology in the Christian East went through a dark age where the intellectual tradition was sacrificed for the sake of survival. The Ottomans never reached as far as Russia, but at the end of the fifteenth century the Russians were just beginning to dust off the remnants of Mongol occupation. As a result of this experience of colonial oppression across Orthodox Christian territories, there was little sophisticated Orthodox theological engagement with the religious and intellectual movements occurring in Latin Christianity, such as the REFORMATION and the ENLIGHTENMENT. The first sign of revival of an intellectual tradition in the Christian East occurs in nineteenth-century Russia. This revival, however, is often seen by some Orthodox as another form of colonization, this time by the intellectual, cultural, political, and religious influences of western Europe introduced through the reforms of Tsars Peter I (r. 1682–1725) and Catherine II (r. 1762–96). A sign of this intellectual revival was the construction of new theological academies; however, at the most respected of these (e.g., Kiev), classes were taught in Latin.

The Ottoman occupation of formerly Byzantine Orthodox territories lasted until the beginning of the twentieth century. In the attempt to revive an Orthodox intellectual tradition, these formerly occupied territories immediately erected theological academies that were, like their Russian counterparts, based on western European models. Much of this revival of an Orthodox theological tradition was a postcolonial attempt to retrieve an Orthodox identity in the wake of centuries-long occupation; but, paradoxically, it relied on western European Christian models of theology and theological education. Inevitably, there was a reaction to this paradox in the form of a return to the intellectual and patristic resources of the Byzantine tradition. A negative consequence of this reaction, however, was the construction of the category of the 'West' and a diametrical opposition between this 'West' and the 'East'. Such an opposition is clearly evident, among other places, in twentieth-century treatments of AUGUSTINE by Orthodox theologians. In spite of the fact that one cannot locate a negative comment about Augustine in the Byzantine tradition, and that his work was even positively appropriated by Gregory Palamas, for many Orthodox theologians (particularly the Greek theologians of the 1960s), Augustine was responsible both for the theological heresies of the West, such as the *FILIOQUE* and PREDESTINATION, and for the solipsistic individualism of modern Western philosophy. The emphasis given to certain theological categories in twentieth-century Orthodox theology, such as the Palamite essence/energies distinction and Trinitarian understandings of personhood, are motivated as much by a postcolonial attempt at reclaiming an authentic Eastern Christian identity through a diametrical opposition of the 'West' and the 'East' as by genuine theological differences. This opposition and its effect on theological thinking are also evident in post-Communist Orthodox countries, especially in debates on the compatibility of liberal democracy and Orthodoxy.

The Ottoman and Communist occupations notwithstanding, the most notable of Orthodox theologians in the late nineteenth and twentieth centuries evince a remarkable continuity with the Byzantine tradition in their consensus on the foundational principle of Orthodox theology – divine–human communion (see DEIFICATION). This consensus is evident in the three major trajectories of contemporary Orthodox theology: Russian sophiology, the neo-patristic synthesis, and the relational ontology of J. Zizioulas (b. 1931). All three trajectories developed, in part, in reaction against the appropriation of Western, manual-style theology in Russia and the formerly Ottoman-occupied Orthodox counties.

V. Solovyov (1853–1900) is considered the father of Russian sophiology, which receives its most sophisticated development in the theology of S. BULGAKOV. Bulgakov's starting point is the Chalcedonian affirmation of the divine–human communion in the person of Christ. The conciliar tradition also achieves dogmatic clarity on the truth of God's being as TRINITY – Father, Son, and Holy Spirit. The patristic tradition, however, according to Bulgakov, failed to produce theological explanations on how God's being as Trinity is such that God is simultaneously immanent and transcendent to the world. Such an explanation requires a deduction of the Trinity based on the understanding of the Absolute as person. Inherent to the notion of person is self-positing, and the self-positing of the Absolute as person is the self-revelation of the Father to the Son. Such a self-positing of the Absolute is not conditioned by a 'not-I', as it is with human personhood, but by the hypostasis of the Son, the content of the self-revelation of the Father who is simultaneously 'I' and 'You'. The completion of the self-revelation is the Holy Spirit, who is the love that unites the Father and the Son. This self-revelation of the Father in the Son and the HOLY SPIRIT is what Bulgakov identifies as 'Sophia'. As the fullness of God's revelation it is all that God is in God's Trinitarian being, and though Bulgakov rejects that it is a fourth thing in the Trinity, neither is it simply HYPOSTASIS or *ousia*. Sophia is rather the ontological link between God and the world – what allows for the realism of divine–human communion. As the fullness of God's Trinitarian being, Sophia is God's relation to the world from all eternity. This does not mean that Bulgakov affirms an eternal creation, but simply that God cannot be conceived as not relating to the world from all eternity. Bulgakov, thus, identifies Sophia with 'divine-humanity' (*bogochelovechestvo*), a central concept in Russian sophiology. Divine-humanity is the ground and goal of creation, and is manifested in its fullness in the INCARNATION. As the image of the divine Sophia, CREATION is the repetition of God's self-revelation in time and space; it is, thus, the creaturely Sophia in the process of becoming united with its prototype – the divine Sophia.

Although presently experiencing a revival due to the translation of his work in English, Bulgakov's work was not influential after his death, due to the inaccessibility of his work and to critique by G. Florovsky (1893–1979) and V. Lossky (1903–58) that his theology betrayed more modern western philosophical than patristic influences. Both Lossky and Florovsky were Russian exiles who settled in Paris and are considered responsible for initiating the neo-patristic school in twentieth-century theology. The neo-patristic movement, like the Catholic *ressourcement*, called for a return to the fathers. Central to Lossky's theology was Dionysian apophaticism and the Palamite essence/energies distinction, which he opposed to neo-Scholastic understandings of knowledge of God and created grace. For Lossky, theology is necessarily apophatic, since God exceeds the limits of creation. Knowledge of God is, thus, mystical union, and the most adequate expression of the antinomy of God's transcendence and immanence is the antinomic distinction between God's unknowable essence and God's participable energies. Indicative of Lossky's influence is the ubiquitous presence of Dionysian apophaticism and Palamism throughout contemporary Orthodox theology, especially in such well-known Orthodox theologians as D. STĂNILOAE and C. Yannaras (b. 1935). Lossky's Trinitarian theology of personhood in terms of uniqueness and freedom was also influential on contemporary theologies of the Trinity in Eastern Orthodoxy, especially on the thought of the Greek theologians, such as Yannaras and Zizioulas.

Zizioulas' theology represents a break with the dominance of apophaticism and Palamism in contemporary Orthodox theology. Rather than Dionysius and Palamas, Zizioulas' patristic focus is the Cappadocian Fathers, whose Trinitarian theology he diametrically opposes to that of Augustine. According to Zizioulas, the Trinitarian theology of the Cappadocians represents an 'ontological revolution', where for the first time being is identified with person, particularity, relationality, and communion rather than with essence. Personhood, according to Zizioulas, is a relational reality constituted in particular relations of love and freedom. Zizioulas is also well known for interpreting through the lens of Trinitarian personhood the Eucharistic ecclesiology of N. Afanasiev (1893–1966), whose influence is evident on the *NOUVELLE THÉOLOGIE* of H. DE LUBAC.

A new generation of Orthodox theologians, such as J. Behr (b. 1966), is challenging the appropriation of the patristic texts in contemporary Orthodox theology (especially Zizioulas' Trinitarian ontology), raising the perennial issue in Orthodox theology of patristic interpretation. The work of D. B. Hart (b. 1965) also does not fit easily into the main currents of contemporary Orthodox theology, especially in his interpretation of divine–human communion in terms of beauty and use of Thomistic notions of ANALOGY.

See also RUSSIAN THEOLOGY.

J. Behr, *The Nicene Faith* (St Vladimir's Seminary Press, 2004).
S. Bulgakov, *On Divine Humanity*, 3 vols. (Eerdmans, 2002–8 [1933–45]).
D. B. Hart, *The Beauty of the Infinite: The Aesthetics of Christian Truth* (Eerdmans, 2003).
V. Lossky, *The Mystical Theology of the Eastern Church* (St Vladimir's Seminary Press, 1976).
A. Papanikolaou, *Being with God: Trinity, Apophaticism, and Divine–Human Communion* (University of Notre Dame Press, 2006).
J. Zizioulas, *Being as Communion: Studies in Personhood and the Church* (St Vladimir's Seminary Press, 1985).

ARISTOTLE PAPANIKOLAOU

ORTHODOXY 'Orthodoxy' is the transliteration of the Greek *orthodoxia*, which can be translated either 'right opinion' or 'right praise'. The term is used in theology to refer to DOCTRINE judged to be consistent with the GOSPEL of Jesus Christ and thus 'correct' from a specifically Christian perspective. In as much as Christians have from the earliest times recognized that not all teaching is equally consistent with the gospel (see Gal. 1:6; 1 John 4:1), the idea that only certain teachings should be regarded as orthodox has been a significant characteristic of Christian belief. At the same time, both the content and the criteria of orthodoxy are matters on which Christians from different traditions disagree. Thus, while in principle 'orthodoxy' encompasses all teaching that gives appropriate expression to the Christian FAITH, its specification is an ongoing and contested process.

Formal designation of a particular doctrine as orthodox is typically occasioned by controversy within the Church: someone proposes a particular way of articulating Christian belief that others find inconsistent with the faith (and thus open to condemnation as HERESY). While the vast majority of Christians regard conformity with SCRIPTURE and the TRADITION of the Church as important criteria of orthodoxy, there is considerable disagreement over how such conformity is measured. In CATHOLIC THEOLOGY the formal teaching of the MAGISTERIUM is decisive. Orthodox Christians, by contrast, accept as binding only those decisions of an ecumenical council received by local Churches (see ORTHODOX THEOLOGY), while for LUTHERAN and REFORMED THEOLOGY great weight is placed on agreement with official confessional documents (e.g., the AUGSBURG CONFESSION, the HEIDELBERG CATECHISM).

See also ANATHEMA; SYSTEMATIC THEOLOGY.

IAN A. MCFARLAND

ORTHOPRAXIS Literally meaning 'right practice', the term 'orthopraxis' is usually used in deliberate and intentional contrast to 'ORTHODOXY' as 'right teaching'. The core idea of orthopraxis is already present in SCRIPTURE. The prophets insist on right practice as the measure of true religion (Hos. 6:6). In the NT 'works' are demanded as a consequence of faith (Jas. 2:14–26). Both the Gospels (e.g., SERMON ON THE MOUNT) and paranesis in the NT letters (e.g., Rom. 12) include instruction in the right practice of the Christian life. Church history is replete with reform movements predicated on right practice (e.g., Franciscans, Waldenses, Methodism). Whenever orthodoxy threatens to diminish into mere rhetoric, the impulse to orthopraxis emerges as counterpoint.

In terms of theological method, an emphasis on orthopraxis aims to narrow the gap between theology and ethics and to co-ordinate the relationship between theory and practice. Since the nineteenth century the incorporation of insights from the social sciences into theological method has given a distinctive shape and character to the meaning of orthopraxis. In particular, the fourth of K. Marx's (1818–83) 'Theses on Feuerbach' (1845) has sparked new life into the concept of orthopraxis: 'Heretofore philosophy has attempted to *understand* the world; it should have attempted to *change* the world.'

The emergence of various forms of LIBERATION THEOLOGY in the late twentieth century places renewed stress on the centrality of liberating praxis as the goal of theological endeavour. Orthopraxis has come to define the very method of liberation theology, which includes the following elements: (1) a living encounter with conditions of oppression, (2) an ethical imperative to change those conditions, (3) drawing upon the appropriate resources of the social sciences (e.g., sociology, economics) to analyze the causes of oppression, (4) drawing upon biblical material, Church history, and the theological tradition for the cause of liberation, and (5) engagement in liberation practices to overcome oppression.

Theologies insisting on orthopraxis as the measure of theology raise critical questions about the necessary involvement of the theologian in movements for liberation. In this way, liberation theologies have questioned the validity of 'academic' theology with the intellectual context of the university as its primary social location. In so far as theological reflection may play a secondary role in this method, critics of liberation theology have sometimes accused it of rationalizing positions already taken on other grounds, rather than allowing theology to maintain its own distinctive voice. In particular, the emphasis on orthopraxis has sometimes been suspected of subordinating theology to Marxism. The emergence of the discipline of PRACTICAL THEOLOGY in the academy aims to incorporate more serious attention to the linkage of theory and practice according to the values of orthopraxis. Similarly, the theme of 'practices' in theological discourse demonstrates how concern for orthopraxis has been incorporated into the life of the Church.

See also BLACK THEOLOGY; DALIT THEOLOGY; FEMINIST THEOLOGY; KOREAN THEOLOGY; LATIN AMERICAN THEOLOGY; LATINO/A THEOLOGY; MUJERISTA THEOLOGY.

C. L. Nessan, *Orthopraxis or Heresy: The North American Response to Latin American Liberation Theology* (Scholars Press, 1989).

M. Volf and D. Bass, eds., *Practicing Theology: Beliefs and Practices in Christian Life* (Eerdmans, 2001).

CRAIG L. NESSAN

OTTO, RUDOLF Rudolf Otto (1869–1937), a self-described 'pietistic Lutheran' in the tradition of F. SCHLEIERMACHER and N. von Zinzendorf (1700–60), was professor of SYSTEMATIC THEOLOGY at Göttingen, Breslau, and Marburg, where he succeeded W. Herrmann (1846–1922). Otto's principal work, *The Idea of the Holy* (1917), was one of the most widely read theological books of the twentieth century. In it Otto coined the term 'numinous' to refer to a category of value that distinguishes RELIGION as a field of human experience that is *sui generis* or of its own kind, and described the object of numinous experience as a mystery that elicits dread and fascination simultaneously. Because in this and subsequent works Otto drew on numerous examples from non-Christian religions, his ideas had a greater impact on the nascent discipline of comparative religious studies than within academic theology. As a result, Otto's theological intentions have sometimes been insufficiently appreciated.

Two pressing intellectual challenges confronted liberal Protestant theologians in Germany in the late nineteenth and early twentieth centuries: the relativization of religious truth claims resulting from research into the historical origins of Christianity and other religions, and the threat posed by the ascendancy of scientific materialism to the validity of the theistic world view. Like that of his contemporary E. TROELTSCH, Otto's approach to theology was profoundly shaped by these concerns, which the theory of the religious a priori presented in *The Idea of the Holy* addresses. Earlier efforts to address related issues include *Life and Ministry of Jesus According to the Historical–Critical Method* (1901) and *Naturalism and Religion* (1904). Otto's position in *The Philosophy of Religion Based on Kant and Fries* (1909) reflects his involvement in the revival of the philosophy of J. Fries (1773–1843) led by his Göttingen colleague, L. Nelson (1882–1927). Otto sought to develop on the basis of Fries' doctrine of *Ahndung* or aesthetico-religious premonition, and the ideas of the Friesian theologian, W. De Wette (1780–1849), a more secure epistemological foundation for a theological science of religion than the one provided by Schleiermacher in his *Speeches on Religion*, an annotated edition of which had been published by Otto in 1899.

After World War I, Otto's scholarship came to focus increasingly on the analysis of non-Christian textual traditions. Otto produced several translations of classical Sanskrit texts as well as major comparative studies of Christianity and the Hindu *bhakti* tradition, and of the mysticism of Meister Eckhart and the Vedantic philosopher Shankara (*ca* 780–*ca* 820). In addition to his scholarly activity, for a period of time Otto promoted the work of the *Religiöser Menschheitsbund*, which encouraged moral co-operation among the followers of different religions. He also undertook travels to the Middle East, India, China, and Japan, in some cases to gather artefacts for the *Religionskundliche Sammlung*, which he established in Marburg as a museum devoted to the history of religion. Otto's emphasis on religious experience and his interest in non-Christian religions were severely criticized by the followers of theologians such as E. Brunner (1889–1966) and K. Barth (see Neo-Orthodoxy). One of Otto's last works, *The Kingdom of God and the Son of Man* (1934), can be read as a response to the existentialist interpretation of the kerygma proposed by his younger Marburg rival, R. Bultmann.

P. C. Almond, *Rudolf Otto: An Introduction to His Philosophical Theology* (University of North Carolina Press, 1984).

T. A. Gooch, *The Numinous and Modernity: An Interpretation of Rudolf Otto's Philosophy of Religion* (Walter de Gruyter, 2000).

Todd Gooch

Oxford Movement The Oxford movement refers to a programme of renewal within the Church of England in the second quarter of the nineteenth century, spearheaded by Anglican clergymen at the University of Oxford, most prominent among whom were J. Keble (1792–1866), J. H. Newman, and E. Pusey (1800–82). The movement sought to recover and renew the 'Catholic' (i.e., strongly tradition-conscious, or 'High Church') character of Anglicanism over against more evangelical and liberal interpretations of the tradition. Although Pusey in particular (whose significance was such that by 1840 the movement was often referred to as 'Puseyism') remained a leader in what came to be called Anglo-Catholicism through the latter part of the century, the heyday of the Oxford movement is generally identified with the period extending from Keble's 1833 sermon, 'National Apostasy', to Newman's conversion to Catholicism in 1845.

Keble's sermon was triggered by the British Parliament's passage of the Irish Church Temporalities Bill, which (as part of a program of cost-saving) dissolved ten Anglican bishoprics in Ireland and was seen by many as an assault on the independence of the Church that amounted to Erastianism. In the aftermath of the sermon, Keble, Newman, and their colleague R. H. Froude (1803–36) determined to promote their case for ecclesiastical independence from governmental interference through a series of intentionally provocative tracts (thanks to which the movement would also come to be known as Tractarianism and its proponents as Tractarians). The first of these *Tracts for the Times* appeared in September 1833, and their publication continued through the release of Newman's Tract 90 in 1841, with its arresting (if theologically questionable) claim that the Church of England's Thirty-Nine Articles were not inconsistent with the teaching of the Catholic Church.

The Tractarians' defence of ecclesiastical independence from State interference led them to focus quickly on what they regarded as the true ground of the Church's authority. Already in Tract 1 an emphasis on the principle of apostolic succession (along with a correlative stress on an episcopal polity) emerged as a central tenet of the Oxford movement. Over against any notion that the authority of the Church was somehow dependent on the State, the Tractarians argued that the British subject's loyalty to the Church rested not on any fortuitous political arrangements but solely and squarely on its apostolic (and, therefore, divine) commission.

Associated with this fundamental principle of Tractarian ecclesiology was a profound reverence for the writings of the fathers of the Church's early centuries. This reverence for patristic theology was distinctive from earlier forms of Anglican 'High Church' theology by virtue of the Tractarians' explicit elevation of the fathers over the theology of the Reformation, which Newman in particular came to regard as having unleashed a spirit of doubt and disorder that undermined the proper exercise of authority in the Church. This suspicion of Protestantism led to charges that the Tractarians were promoting a return to Rome, in response to which Newman in 1834 wrote the '*via media*' tracts (numbers 38 and 41), arguing that the Church of England represented the orthodox middle way (Latin *via media*) that 'lies *between* the (so called) Reformers and the Romanists' (Tract 38). Although Newman himself did eventually convert to Catholicism, this interpretation of Anglicanism as a *via media* equally distinct from Protestant and Catholic piety has remained an influential interpretation of Anglican theology to the present day.

A further dimension of the theology of the Oxford movement, closely linked to its emphasis on the sanctity of the clerical office as guaranteed by apostolic succession, was an insistence on the regenerative power of baptism. Over against the stress evangelical theologians (whether inside or outside the Church of England) placed on the importance of a subjective experience of conversion as the index of spiritual regeneration, Keble, Newman, and their colleagues insisted on the objective efficacy of baptism as God's gift to the baptized. Corresponding to this emphasis on the objectivity of grace in the sacraments was a de-emphasizing of faith as a central focus of theological reflection. This perspective intended no disparagement of faith, but reflected rather the view that it was a gift of God rather than an intellectual achievement of the believer. As Newman put it: 'true faith ... is but the medium through which the soul sees Christ; and the soul as little really rests upon and contemplates it, as the eye can see the air' (*Lectures* 337).

The major criticisms of the Oxford movement reflect the terms of the Tractarians' opposition to evangelicals and liberals: that their passion for tradition undermines the authority of Scripture in matters of doctrine (see *sola Scriptura*), and that their high ecclesiology and sacramentalism promote a clergy-centred, insular, and elitist Church (as exemplified by their commendation of the need for 'reserve' in communicating religious knowledge in Tract 80 and elsewhere). Nevertheless, the reverence for antiquity and tradition associated with the Oxford movement has been deeply influential within Anglicanism, especially on patterns of liturgy and personal devotion (e.g., the 1928 edition of the Book of Common Prayer). Along the same lines, Tractarianism's emphasis on the importance of a catholicity rooted in the fathers anticipated many of the values of the liturgical and ecumenical movements in the twentieth century.

See also Ecumenism; Evangelical Theology; Liberal Theology; Liturgical Movement.

O. Chadwick, ed., *The Mind of the Oxford Movement* (A. & C. Black, 1960).

C. B. Faught, *The Oxford Movement: A Thematic History of the Tractarians and Their Times* (Pennsylvania State University Press, 2003).

M. R. O'Connell, *The Oxford Conspirators: A History of the Oxford Movement 1833–1845* (Macmillan, 1969).

Ian A. McFarland

PAINTING, THEOLOGY AND The juxtaposition of theology (literally, *talk* about God) and painting can be seen as a kind of mistake, since painting, by its very mode of expression, was rarely if ever intended to carry a specifically theological (i.e., propositional) message. Depiction of various kinds has roots in the prehistoric era and may be evidence of humankind's yearning for expression, creativity, and appreciation of beauty. Depiction is found in the catacombs at the beginning of Christianity, and it may be accepted that from the beginning Christians valued the concretization and illustration that forms of depiction offered.

P

Christianity is a faith which pays close attention to words and acknowledges Jesus Christ as the Word of God incarnate. Although this is to confess word become person (and, more specifically, a person in whom was revealed GRACE and truth), elements of Christianity have always struggled with an acknowledgement that human language cannot encompass God, and, correspondingly, with the question of how mystery, which makes space for the ineffable, may be preserved in human forms of expression. The apostle PAUL regularly made use of paradox as a mode of indicating the utterly unanticipated path of God's salvation. How may paradox and ambiguity, over the centuries, when expressed verbally, not suffer a flattening? Or, given that Christianity is both didactic and prophetic of its nature, how may that didactic note avoid forms of closure which tend in a literalist direction?

While it is misleading to view Christian visual art as utilitarian and therefore derived, the traditions of art inspired by Christianity have enabled a verbal tradition to express itself as powerfully in question (*Why*, God?), in the subjunctive (the mays and mights), and in the optative (desire), as in the indicative. Art is always a human artefact and therefore contextualized. It follows that Christian visual art is an important witness to contextualized forms of devotion, prophecy and yearning. Christian history shows the gradual development of 'orthodox' faith. At their best, such orthodoxies strive to listen to what transcends them and avoid the marginalization of minority perceptions. The tradition of Christian art similarly developed classic themes and accepted handling of them. Yet Christian visual art can be at its most powerful and fluent when it is subversive of its own archetypes and so avoids the kinds of closure common in orthodox verbal exposition. Thus, while the late antique and medieval confidence that a true likeness of Christ had been preserved (in the Mandylion, or 'Image of Edessa', and, later, the veil of Veronica) constrained imagination, profundity could be offered through innovation in composition, perspective, and colour (as in, e.g., the *Last Supper* (1495–8) of L. da Vinci(1452–1519)).

What are the classic themes and archetypes of Christian visual art? Early traditions of Church decoration both illustrated the Christian story (didactic) and imitated the vault of heaven (various mosaics or frescos in the apse). The former were not naturalistic in that they could place together SAINTS and witnesses who were not contemporaneous. The latter were less decorative than ways of bringing worshippers into the nearer presence of God and transcending the physical limitations of a building. Outstanding surviving examples include the mosaics in Ravenna at the church of Sant' Apollinare Nuovo and the depiction of the resurrection on the last day in the apse of the church at Chora, Istanbul.

The eastern tradition saw the development of the ICONOSTASIS, as well as of the ICONS that covered it. The western tradition developed the altarpiece. This was no more 'art' in a contemporary sense than the frescos in an apse. The aim of the altarpiece was to focus worship and to open a window to the transcendent. Examples are Raphael's (1483–1520) *The Sistine Madonna* (*ca* 1512–14) and G. Bellini's (*ca* 1430–1516) *San Giobbe Altarpiece* (before 1478). An altarpiece was almost always the gift of a patron. As such (and, again, differently from contemporary art), the interests of the patron were accommodated within the overall purpose. An example is Raphael's *Entombment of Christ* (1507), which was commissioned by a mother whose son had died in a family feud. Altarpieces, while not always overtly theological in inspiration, could indicate profound theological commitment. An example is the Isenheim Altarpiece (1512–16), which depicts a crucifixion of particular agony. As the altarpiece was in a hospital for those suffering an excruciating skin disease, it focused the devotion of people in pain. The Swiss theologian K. BARTH kept a reproduction of the Isenheim Altarpiece in his study.

Classic themes emerged in Christian visual art. One such theme is that of the Adoration of the Magi (Matt. 2:11). This theme lent itself to various purposes: a depiction of the paradox of a baby who is Lord of all; the leadership role of kings; the universality of the Church. As Christian history unfolded, different landscapes 'hosted' the adoration, depicting both the locality and the catholicity of Christian belief. Such classic themes could also be played subversively, as for example in the *Adoration* (1564) by P. Bruegel the Elder (*ca* 1525–69). Painted in a time of suppression and threat, the artist shows the ugliness of power. Under Franciscan influence, attention shifted slowly but importantly from adoration of the kings to wonder at the INCARNATION. An outstanding example is G. de La Tour's (1593–1652) *The New-Born Child* (*ca* 1648).

Christian visual art from the nineteenth and twentieth centuries has no classics and few archetypes. Yet a combination of technique and intent has enabled it to excel at the depiction of human emotion or moral claims which are less successfully expressed in words. Examples of technique might include the late works of J. M. W. Turner (1775–1851) which, in their evocative loss of form indicate the effectiveness of refusing closure, thereby enlisting the imagination of the viewer. The Pre-Raphaelites combined precision and intent, painting biblical, historical, and social scenes with detailed realism. Examples are W. H. Hunt's (1827–1910) *The Awakening Conscience* (1854) and *The Light of the World* (1851–3). Contemporary symbolism and expressionism is capable of unlocking powerful and unexpected resonances. An example is J. Bellany's (b. 1942) triptych *Allegory* (1964), which depicts three gutted haddocks displayed in the style of the crucifixion, as voiceless metaphors for the suffering of humanity. The painting has allusions both to the Isenheim altarpiece and to Rembrandt's flayed oxen and thus stands loosely in a complex but still living tradition.

N. MacGregor, *Seeing Salvation* (Yale University Press, 2000).
L. Bourdua, *The Franciscans and Art Patronage in Late Medieval Italy* (Cambridge University Press, 2004)

IAIN R. TORRANCE

PALAMAS, GREGORY Gregory Palamas (1296–1359) was a mystic and ecclesiastical statesman whose major contribution to Greek theology was his robust defence of HESYCHASM and its theological account of PRAYER. Born to a noble family in Constantinople, Palamas benefited from a good education before retiring to Mt ATHOS around 1316. About twenty years later, the 'hesychast controversy' erupted when Barlaam (*ca* 1290–1348), a Greek monk and theologian from Calabria, disputed the claim by hesychast monks to have seen with their eyes the uncreated light of God which had shone at the TRANSFIGURATION on Mt Tabor. In his *Triads in Defence of the Holy Hesychasts*, Palamas maintained that the monks were indeed seeing and encountering the ENERGIES of God by which they were transformed, even deified (see DEIFICATION). This teaching was endorsed by the abbots of the Athonite monasteries in the *Hagioritic Tome* (1340). During this phase of the debate, immoderate language led Palamas to make claims regarding the relationship of the divine energies to the divine essence which he later moderated (albeit without abandoning his central contention that the energies, although really and not merely notionally distinct from the essence of God, are nevertheless properly regarded as God). He was challenged on these claims by Gregory Akindynos (*ca* 1300–48), a mutual acquaintance of his and Barlaam's. Akindynos was briefly supported by Patriarch John XIV of Constantinople (r. 1334–47), though this tide was reversed by the political ascent of Palamas' favoured party, followed by a series of synods over the next several decades which endorsed Palamite theology as normative ORTHODOXY. Palamas was made archbishop of Thessalonica in 1347, in which role he wrote numerous additional works of theology. Palamas was canonized in 1368 by Patriarch Philotheos of Constantinople (r. 1363–76), a former disciple.

Notwithstanding the prominence of his works in the *PHILOKALIA*, it is unclear whether Palamas' theology exercised an ongoing influence in the centuries following his death. However, during the early twentieth century his works became central to a revival in modern ORTHODOX THEOLOGY. The research that formed the basis to the articulation of 'neo-Palamism' was conducted chiefly in France by, e.g., D. STĂNILOAE, C. Kern (1899–1960), and J. Meyendorff (1926–92), but it was also from France that the earliest contemporary rejections of Palamite theology were launched by M. Jugie (1878–1954). Few modern Orthodox theologians have dissented from the consensus that identifies Palamism as the most satisfying expression of Trinitarian theology. Among Catholic and Reformed scholars, responses to Palamas' theology are more varied. A. de Halleux (1929–94) and T. Cardinal Špidlík (b. 1919) consider it a spiritual synthesis rather than a SYSTEMATIC THEOLOGY. On the other hand, G. Podskalsky (b. 1937) and D. Wendebourg (b. 1952) have criticized the implications of the Palamite energies–essence distinction, while still others have compared Palamas to major western theologians with sometimes intriguing results.

J. Meyendorff, *A Study of St Gregory Palamas*, 2nd edn (St Vladimir's Seminary Press, 1998 [1974]).
R. E. Sinkewicz, 'Gregory Palamas' in *La Théologie byzantine et sa tradition*, vol. II (Brepols, 2002), 131–88.

AUGUSTINE CASIDAY

PANENTHEISM Panentheism is the view that all is contained within the divine, although God is also more than the world. In the first place, then, it is a way to conceive the God–world relation. Yet panentheism has implications for other classical theological *loci*, including the question of DIVINE ACTION, CHRISTOLOGY, the HOLY SPIRIT, THEOLOGICAL ANTHROPOLOGY, and ESCHATOLOGY. The term entered into modern Christian theology through the work of K. Krause (1781–1832), though F. Schelling (1775–1854) had already used the phrase 'Pan + en + theismus' in the *Freiheitsschrift* of 1809. Since then it has grown to be one of the major systematic understandings of the God–world relation in twentieth-century philosophical theology, including among its advocates C. Hartshorne (1897–2000), J. Macquarrie (1919–2007), J. Moltmann (b. 1926), J. Cobb (b. 1925), M. Suchocki (b. 1933), E. Johnson (b. 1941), S. McFague (b. 1933), G. Jantzen (1948–2006), A. Peacocke (1924–2006), and M. Borg (b. 1942).

The theologies of many modern theologians have been called panentheistic (e.g., F. SCHLEIERMACHER, P. TILLICH, K. RAHNER, and H. von BALTHASAR), whether or not the term actually occurs in their writings. Although the etymology of the word places emphasis on all things being 'in' God, panentheism actually stands for the whole group of positions that seek a closer relationship between God and world than more traditional understandings of divine transcendence provide, yet without falling into PANTHEISM or ATHEISM.

Contemporary panentheists often distinguish their theologies from what they call 'classical theism', 'classical philosophical theism', 'perfect-being theology'. They express concern about the way in which the notion of substance functions in the later patristic and medieval periods, especially what they see as the way in which some theologians construe God and individual things as substances. Such 'philosophies of substance', it is alleged, have more trouble allowing for two things to be present at the same place and make it correspondingly more difficult to conceive relations of deep ontological interdependence.

Panentheists hold that creation takes place, and remains, within the being of God. Thus, God does not first create a world of separately existing substances and then enter into this world to carry out the divine will. Such a view would be foreign to the biblical model of God, the God 'in whom we live and move and have our being' (Acts 19:28). Also, developments within modern science make it harder to conceive of divine agency within the world unless the world already exists within and is permeated by the divine Spirit.

It is helpful to distinguish between 'specific' and 'generic' senses of panentheism. Panentheism, broadly conceived, stands for any emphasis on the closeness of God and divine immanence within theology. Much of the Bible could be said to be panentheistic in this sense; one thinks of many of the psalms, the Wisdom literature, Ephesians 1:10, Colossians 1:16, and the phrase 'in Christ', which is repeated over ninety times in the NT. Those theologians and mystics across the entire Christian tradition who stress the immanence of God might also be generic panentheists in this sense. In particular, the Orthodox tradition might be taken to affirm an eschatological panentheism in its doctrine of *theosis*, the gradual DEIFICATION of the world.

Panentheism in the specific sense involves those theologians since 1800 who have used modern philosophical and theological sources to resist the isolated, transcendent God (*deus ex machina*) of modern theism and to recover a more balanced theology of divine transcendence and immanence. Influential schools of theology have drawn, for example, on the resources of German IDEALISM, Romanticism, British neo-Idealism, Boston PERSONALISM, and the many branches of process thought (see PROCESS THEOLOGY). Understood in this way, panentheism is a contribution to modern philosophical or 'constructive' theology, and not necessarily a competitor to classical doctrinal theology.

Panentheism implies a twofold 'in': all created objects are in God, and God is in all things. Some, including A. N. Whitehead (1861–1947) and Hartshorne, interpret the twofold 'in' as a full symmetry; in their dipolar panentheism all that pertains to the divine side applies equally to the creaturely side. Others (e.g., Moltmann and the present author) strongly emphasize the asymmetries between the divine and the human sides, often by relying on Trinitarian categories. Some make the correlations between God and world metaphysically necessary; others make it a result of the free divine choice to create.

In virtually all cases, the 'in' is neither (merely) spatial or logical, but rather dialectical and ontological. Often an argument is presupposed that was first developed by G. W. F. HEGEL: since God as infinite must be that which encompasses *all* things, finite beings cannot exist outside the infinite God. Finite things do not thereby become infinite or become God; the result is emphatically not pantheism. Instead, panentheists advocate a dialectical ('both–and') framework in which co-inherence or 'internal relations' are possible (cf. classical Trinitarian PERICHORESIS). The point of the dialectical framework is to allow persons to be so closely linked to God that one can speak of them as being 'within' God, yet without being identified with, or identical to, God.

Panentheism represents a powerful means for conceiving divine action. If the world lies outside God, God would break natural law by intervening in its processes. By contrast, panentheists understand the regularities of the natural world as themselves expressions of the regularities of God's nature, somewhat like the autonomic functioning of the human BODY. Special divine action then represents God's intentional actions – roughly analogous to individual conscious actions by human agents.

Many of the details of panentheistic theologies vary among thinkers. It is important not to confuse specific proposals with necessary conditions for panentheism. For example, panentheism in the Orthodox tradition denies change in God but emphasizes the absolutely unique status of humans as *imago Dei*. Process panentheism in the Whiteheadian tradition emphasizes the temporality of God and God's responsiveness to the world. Some panentheists draw sharper distinctions between the human and divine natures. M. Brierley (b. 1973) identifies seven themes frequently found in panentheism: the cosmos as God's body; language of 'in and through'; the cosmos as sacrament; language of inextricable intertwining; God's dependence on the cosmos; the intrinsic, positive value of the cosmos; passibility; and degree Christology – though he acknowledges that panentheists respond differently to these topics.

Finally, some scholars are now using panentheism as a means for fostering dialogue between Christianity and other traditions. One finds significant panentheistic elements in parts of Judaism (Kaballah, certain forms of Hasidism, and various strands in twentieth-century Jewish theology), Islam (especially Sufism), and Hinduism (especially in the 'Brahman with personal attributes' school of Ramanuja).

P. Clayton, *Adventures in the Spirit: God, World, Divine Action* (Fortress Press, 2008).

J. Cooper, *Panentheism – The Other God of the Philosophers: From Plato to the Present* (Baker Academic, 2006).

C. Hartshorne and W. Reese, eds., *Philosophers Speak of God* (Humanity Books, 2000 [1953]).

A. Peacocke and P. Clayton, eds., *In Whom We Live and Move and Have Our Being: Panentheistic Reflections on God's Presence in a Scientific World* (Eerdmans, 2004).

PHILIP CLAYTON

PANTHEISM Etymologically, 'pantheism' can be defined as 'All [is] God'. While this may seem a straightforward definition, its significance depends on what one means by 'all' and 'God', as well as the proffered account of exactly what their identity amounts to. The term 'pantheism' is thought to have been coined by J. Tolland (1670–1722) in his *Pantheisticon: or The Form of Celebrating the Socratic Society* (1720), though the idea reaches much further back to ancient Greece and India. A central tenet of pantheism is that there is no *absolute* distinction between God and the universe and thus also no distinction between transcendence and immanence, but while the two are co-terminal and co-substantive, pantheism should not be taken to mean that a simple inventory of all that there is (the universe) would constitute and exhaust what pantheists mean when they use the word 'God'. At the same time, there is considerable diversity with respect to the interpretation of pantheism, though all forms share some commitment to the notion that there exists a real, unifying principle at the base of the universe, that this principle serves as a metaphysical ground and epistemological 'explanation' for all that is, and that it is divine.

There is a long history of pantheism and its various forms in particular traditions. In modern times the concept has most often – and perhaps unfairly – been used as a pejorative in contrast to theism, particularly by some Christians for whom pantheism and ATHEISM are virtually synonymous. This is, of course, strictly false since pantheists do hold that God exists, although they differ from traditional theists on the nature of God, salvation, CREATION, and evil, among other questions. Pantheism also differs from polytheism (the view that there are many Gods), monotheism (the belief in one God), PANENTHEISM (the view that all is *in* God), and what M. Müller (1823–1900) termed 'henotheism' (where individuals worship one god as supreme while acknowledging the existence of many other gods).

In the classical Greek thought of Plato, Plotinus, and the Stoics (see PLATONISM), as well as in the Hindu Advaita Vedanta and in some schools of Samkhya, one encounters the view that there exists ultimately only one true substance or principle. This radical monism entails pantheism, but monism is not necessary to pantheism. Philosophical Daoism as well as the thought of F. Schelling (1775–1854), G. W. F. HEGEL, P. TILLICH, and W. Whitman (1819–92), among others, could be said to be pantheistic but certainly not monist, and it will be useful here to distinguish the two clearly. The identification of monism with pantheism might be due to a naive association of pantheism with B. Spinoza's (1632–77) substance monism as found in his *Ethics* (1675). However, even here the story is not simple: while Spinoza maintains that there exists only substance and its modes (*Eth.* 1.28), the modes themselves are not self-caused and neither is their existence contingent. Spinoza's pantheism is thus neither the view that God is corporeal nor the identification of God with the totality of the universe. Rather Spinoza – the arch pantheist – is closer to the Hindu Advaita view that what exists is *nirguna* ('qualityless' Brahman, the divine reality per se) and *saguna* ('qualitied' Brahman, the divine reality in its self-effected form). The two are eternally distinct yet can be said truly to be identical. So while pantheism is naively (and pejoratively) thought to mean that the material universe simply *is* God without qualification, it is very difficult to find anyone who truly claims this position.

D. Berman, *A History of Atheism in Britain: From Hobbes to Russell* (Croom Helm, 1988).

R. Mason, *The God of Spinoza: A Philosophical Study* (Cambridge University Press, 1997).

TINU RUPARELL

PAPACY Belief that Peter was both commissioned by Jesus to be the leader among the apostles (see Matt. 16:13–20) and martyred at Rome has been central to the development of the theology and praxis of the papacy. The political context in which the early Church grew, first under persecution by the Roman Empire, then with official imperial support, and eventually in the void created by the empire's decline, is scarcely less significant.

Peter was said to be the first bishop of Rome, and those who succeeded him in that role eventually asserted not only their 'Petrine' office but also secular power that after the fall of the western empire replaced and imitated in some ways the governing authority of

Caesar. The imperial title of 'pontiff' (literally, 'bridge builder') was added to more Christian nomenclature such as 'vicar of Christ', 'vicar of Peter', and 'Servant of the Servants of God'. The degree to which the bishop of Rome might exercise some kind of primacy in relation to other bishops, and the nature of the relationship between popes and secular rulers – especially Christian ones – became long-term disputed points.

By the year 800, the western Church was less and less exclusively Mediterranean and more and more European. On Christmas day of that year, Pope Leo III (r. 795–816) crowned Charlemagne (r. 800–14) emperor of a Christian empire that included much of what is today Germany and France. Popes that followed liked to think that such a coronation implied subjection of emperor to pope, and superiority of Church over State, but few emperors saw things that way. Throughout the ninth and tenth centuries popes were chosen sometimes by the emperor, sometimes by Roman aristocrats, and sometimes by the Roman clergy. While bishops often sought to marginalize papal power, popes also found ways to circumvent the power of bishops. In 910 the abbey of Cluny was founded in France, and it became the mother house of a wide network of monastic foundations (see MONASTICISM). Popes granted these monasteries exemption from the authority of local bishops; later religious orders would enjoy a similar exemption from episcopal interference, though such exemption also meant for them dependence on the papacy.

In the eleventh century, several developments helped to set the course of the papacy in Christianity's second millennium. In 1054 the eastern Churches repudiated papal affirmations of a Roman primacy over other sees. In 1059 Pope Nicholas II (r. 1059–61) promulgated a decree restricting participation in papal elections to cardinals. This restriction would eventually be strictly enforced, with the requirement of a conclave to help guarantee the freedom of the electors from political and other pressures. Also, the Gregorian reform of Pope Gregory VII (r. 1073–85) insisted on a celibate clergy (see CELIBACY), and on curbing the role of the State in the institution of bishops.

In the high Middle Ages, papal authority was exerted in some new ways. As CANON LAW developed, many popes were trained lawyers, and the role of legislator became central to the papacy. The law maker could also dispense from legal obligations, and this power of dispensation proved to be an excellent source of income. Medieval Church councils met in various places in western Europe, and the claim that the pope was the person having the authority to call a council became a part of papal apologetics. As many new universities were created in various parts of Europe, often with a papal charter or other authorization from Rome, supervision of education soon became another prerogative claimed by the bishop of Rome.

Late medieval and Renaissance popes faced a variety of challenges and opportunities. In 1300 the first Holy Year was celebrated in Rome, exalting the city (and especially the tomb of Peter) as a special place of pilgrimage. In 1302 Boniface VIII (r. 1294–1303) declared in his bull *Unam sanctam* that only those persons subject to the Roman pontiff could be saved. A few years later, the papacy moved to Avignon, and to domination by the kingdom of France, for most of the fourteenth century. More problematic for papal authority was the Great Schism (1378–1417), during which there were two and then three rival claimants to the chair of Peter. Resolution of this schism came through a council called by an emperor, and this instance of successful conciliar Church governance would not be forgotten by those seeking to restrict papal power (see CONCILIARISM).

The sale of indulgences was one of the ways popes in the late medieval and Renaissance periods financed their political and cultural enterprises, and M. LUTHER's critique of indulgences is usually considered to be the start of the REFORMATION. Luther soon expanded his attack on the papacy to a thoroughgoing rejection of papal authority over Christian DOCTRINE and practice. For Luther the pope was a heretic, indeed the ANTICHRIST, leading the people away from salvation through a false doctrine of works, righteousness, and church-made laws that made a mockery of the GOSPEL teaching of JUSTIFICATION by FAITH alone. SCRIPTURE alone, Luther asserted, should be the source of Christian teaching, not papal decrees (see *SOLA SCRIPTURA*).

The Society of Jesus was approved by Pope Paul III (r. 1534–49) in 1540. Because the Jesuits considered the pope the universal pastor – the one who would know where the needs were greatest for preachers, teachers, confessors, and spiritual directors – they made themselves available to be missioned by the pope anywhere in the world. When Pope Gregory XV (r. 1621–23) created the Congregation for the Propagation of the Faith, in 1622, he indeed acted as a kind of universal pastor, seeking to ensure a greater measure of papal supervision of evangelization beyond the limits of Catholic Europe. Gregory's efforts sought also to limit the power of Catholic monarchs over the Church in their realms, but in the following centuries it was the monarchs of Spain, Portugal, and France that did the most to limit papal authority.

The French Revolution seemed for a time to have destroyed the papacy. The Papal States were occupied repeatedly by French troops; Pope Pius VI (r. 1775–99) died in France, a prisoner of Napoleon. His successor, Pius VII (r. 1800–23), agreed to a concordat with Napoleon governing the Church in France. Though the emperor violated the agreement and eventually imprisoned him, Pius outlived Napoleon's empire, returned to Rome in 1814, and presided over an impressive restoration of not only the papacy's temporal authority in Italy, but of papal prestige and influence more widely. Many new dioceses were created, especially in the Americas, and the role of the pope in the selection of bishops for these new sees was often greater than it had been for European dioceses.

In the nineteenth century, the pope would claim immediate jurisdiction over the entire Catholic Church, as well as, in certain circumstances, the possibility of making infallible doctrinal definitions (see INFALLIBILITY). Ultramontanists advocated such papal centralization, while those who advocated a more restricted papal role were increasingly marginalized if not altogether repudiated (see ULTRAMONTANISM). The ultramontanist agenda was promoted during the reign of Pius IX (r. 1846–78) and during VATICAN COUNCIL I, even as Italian unification brought termination of the pope's role as a temporal ruler. The void created by such a loss was quickly filled with an ever more frequent exercise of the papal MAGISTERIUM. Pius had defined the doctrine of the IMMACULATE CONCEPTION in 1854. He also wrote ENCYCLICALS. This form of papal teaching, not only on doctrinal and spiritual matters, but also on questions of social justice, subsequently became a major part of what popes did, beginning in the reign of Leo XIII (r. 1878–1903).

In times of warfare, popes increasingly adopted a neutral stance, and the twentieth century repeatedly tested this policy. During World War I the neutrality of Benedict XV (r. 1914–22) irritated governments on both sides, and the neutrality of Pius XII (r. 1939–58) during World War II remains controversial. The Lateran Accords of 1929 had recognized the autonomy of Vatican City, but recovery of sovereignty over a tiny State did not elicit a change in the policy on neutrality. Critics continue to contend that Pius XII should have played a more public and prophetic role, in particular by exposing and denouncing the HOLOCAUST.

While many popes sought to defend the rights of the Church by means of concordats and other accords with particular States, Pope John XXIII (r. 1958–63) made defence of human rights a central part of his pontificate. Addressing a postcolonial world, he pleaded for aid for developing countries in the southern hemisphere, and for peace between East and West. He also convened VATICAN COUNCIL II, though the council did most of its work in the pontificate of Paul VI (r. 1963–78). Vatican II vigorously affirmed the place of the Church in the modern world, promoted human rights and human dignity, and denounced nuclear weapons. It also affirmed the collegial nature of Church authority and sought to help heal divisions between Catholics and other Christians, as well as promoting respect for persons of other religious traditions.

Modern technology had made possible a different style of papacy, as itinerant as it was Roman. Paul VI's 1965 address to the United Nations helped to establish a new model of papacy: prophetic, on PILGRIMAGE, and concerned to promote the good of all human beings in this world as well as their salvation in the next. Pope John Paul II (r. 1978–2005) developed this model further, with much more travel, and with many encyclicals in defence of human dignity. A Pole, John Paul brought an end to several centuries of Italian-only papacy. But he also sought to strengthen the role of papal authority in the Church. For him modern technology facilitated the pope's personal presence throughout the world, and it also made possible ever greater and more immediate supervision of local Churches. The universal and immediate jurisdiction of the pope legislated at Vatican I has been facilitated by jet aeroplanes and by faxes, e-mail, and the internet. But is such centralization good for the Church? Or should the bishop of Rome minimize the role of universal and omnipresent administrator and focus rather on that of prophet and servant? Election of a German as pope in 2005 helped to confirm the end of Italian domination of the papacy, but it has left open many other questions.

P. Granfield, *The Limits of the Papacy: Authority and Autonomy in the Church* (Crossroad, 1987).
J. W. O'Malley, *What Happened at Vatican II* (Harvard University Press, 2008).
K. Schatz, *Papal Primacy: From Its Origins to the Present* (Liturgical Press, 1996).
F. A. Sullivan, *Magisterium: Teaching Authority in the Church* (Paulist Press, 1983).
J. M. R. Tillard, *The Bishop of Rome* (SPCK, 1983).

THOMAS WORCESTER

PARABLE Derived from the classical Greek word for 'comparison' or 'analogy', 'parable' is the term used in the first three Gospels to characterize the typical form of Jesus' teaching (e.g., Matt. 13:3, 34). Generally in the form of a short story (e.g., 'The Parable of the Sower' in Matt. 13:18–23; 'The Parable of the Rich Man and Lazarus' in Luke 16:19–31) or brief comparison (e.g., the sequence of parables that begin with the words 'The kingdom of heaven is like...' in Matt. 13:44–50), parables are understood by the evangelists as a form of discourse used to reveal 'the secrets of the kingdom of heaven' to Jesus' followers, while remaining opaque to those outside the community of faith (see Matt. 13:10–15; Mark 4:10–13; Luke 8:10; cf. Isa. 6:9–10).

Christian understanding of how to interpret the parables has been subject to considerable variation over the course of the Church's history. Most ancient and medieval commentators were inclined (following the lead of Jesus in, e.g., Matt. 13:37–43) to interpret the parables as a form of ALLEGORY, in which each element stands for a particular truth of the FAITH. Thus, for ORIGEN (*HLuke* 34.3) the 'Parable of the Good Samaritan' in Luke 10:30–7 summarized the whole history of redemption, with Jerusalem standing for paradise, Jericho for the world, the robbers for demonic powers, and so on. In the late nineteenth century A. Jülicher (1857–1938) overturned this tradition by arguing that the parables were in fact intended to communicate a single, relatively simple message (LOVE of neighbour in the case of the Good Samaritan). Contemporary exegetes tend to reject both these alternatives, stressing instead the way Jesus' parables generate tensions that defy easy resolution in terms of clearly defined moral or doctrinal content.

IAN A. MCFARLAND

PARACLETE: see HOLY SPIRIT.

PARADISE: see HEAVEN.

PARISH In ecclesiastical usage, 'parish' (from the Greek *paroikia*, or 'district') typically refers to the territory associated with a particular congregation and its clergy (viz., the parish church and its priest). Originally synonymous with 'diocese', the parish system of Church administration emerged gradually in the early medieval period as a means of ecclesiastical provision for and oversight of widely dispersed populations under the care of a single bishop. In Catholic, Orthodox, Anglican, and some Lutheran traditions, the parish remains a geographic and administrative subdivision of an episcopal diocese; in the Presbyterian context of the Church of Scotland, it is a subdivision of the local presbytery. The term can also be used loosely to refer to the members of a particular Christian congregation, without any geographical reference.

The parochial system expresses the commitment of the wider Church to ministry both across the whole of a territory and to each individual community within it. Yet in the modern period the rapid and frequent movement of populations, as well as the proliferation of Christian denominations, has placed stress on the parish as the fundamental unit of ecclesiastical organization. Particularly in urban areas, it is rarely possible to identify coherent communities geographically – leading the Catholic Church from the mid-nineteenth century to establish non-geographic 'national' parishes to serve ethnic minority populations. In so far as the parochial system emerged to serve the liturgical needs of a stable and confessionally uniform Christian population, the demise of the socio-political ideal of CHRISTENDOM renders its continued viability open to question.

IAN A. MCFARLAND

PAROUSIA The transliteration of a Greek word that can mean either 'presence' or 'arrival', 'parousia' is used in Christian theology to refer to Christ's future return in glory (the 'second coming'). The term is drawn directly from the NT, where it is used to refer to the eschatological 'coming of the Son of Man' (Matt. 24:27, 37, 39; cf. Dan. 7:13), who is identified with Jesus (Matt. 24:3; cf. 1 Thess. 2:19; 3:13; Jas. 5:7–8; 2 Pet. 3:4; 1 John 2:28). In his letters PAUL clearly understands this return as signalling the final vindication of Christ's lordship and the realization of the Christian HOPE of RESURRECTION to eternal life in communion with Christ (1 Cor. 15:22–4; 1 Thess. 4:13–17). Considered in a specifically Christological context, the parousia is a corollary of the DOCTRINE of the ASCENSION: in the same way that Christ ascended from earth to heaven after his resurrection, so will he come from HEAVEN to earth to usher in the KINGDOM OF GOD (Acts 1:11).

Though belief in Christ's return is a widely accepted feature of Christian ESCHATOLOGY enshrined in both the APOSTLES' and NICENE CREEDS, the relationship between this event and the end of history is contested. Among Christians from IRENAEUS to the many present-day evangelicals who subscribe to some version of PREMILLENNIALISM, the parousia inaugurates a 1,000-year reign of Christ and the SAINTS on earth prior to the Last Judgement (see MILLENNIUM); by contrast, the majority of Christian Churches (including the Catholic, Orthodox, and the majority of 'mainline' Protestant traditions) identify the parousia with the Last Judgement and the end of earthly history.

See also AMILLENNIALISM, CHRISTOLOGY, POSTMILLENNIALISM.

IAN A. MCFARLAND

PASCAL, BLAISE The last great polymath of early modernity, Blaise Pascal's (1623–62) work in physics and mathematics remains unchallenged. His 'first conversion' dates from his 1646 encounter with the neo-Augustinian doctrines propagated by J. Du Vergier de Hauranne (1581–1643), abbot of St Cyran, disciple of C. Jansen (1595–1638), defender of the latter's *Augustinus*, and chaplain to the Cistercian sisters at Port-Royal-des-Champs. Pascal became an intimate and disciple of St Cyran's successors: Le Maître de Sacy (1613–84), A. Arnauld (1612–94), and the other solitaries in permanent retreat near Port-Royal. He entered into the Jansenists' quarrel with the Jesuits over moral theology in the *Provincial Letters* (1656–57), his masterpiece of irony and polemic. During the night of 23 November 1654, Pascal experienced an intense mystical encounter (the 'second conversion') recorded in the *Memorial* found sewn inside his doublet upon his death.

In 1656, Pascal's niece at Port-Royal was believed to be miraculously cured by a relic of the Sacred Thorn of the Passion, provoking Pascal's desire to write a defence of Christianity based upon miracles. He soon realized that his projected *Apology for the Christian Religion* – the 800 or so fragments we read as the *Pensées* (the numbered order dates only from the turn of the twentieth century) – required an innovative and broader approach to Christian APOLOGETICS. Pascal predicted that he needed ten years respite from his long-standing ill health to finish his great project. In fact, only six, four consumed by severe illness, remained.

Pascal progressed as far as organizing half of his notes into twenty-eight 'classified chapters'. The first half presents an essentially anthropological analysis of the fallen human state and includes celebrated analyses of vanity, diversion, and the inherent contradiction of human potential and despair. This strategy is used so as not to alienate sceptics, atheists, and wavering Christians by immediately plunging into theology. He then turns to traditional Christian apologetics, expressly ignoring rational proofs of God's existence and branding them as sterile because they fail to lead to a Christocentric vision. Traditional proofs, he believed, could only lead the unbeliever to DEISM, a theology as abhorrent as ATHEISM itself.

Two key chapters from among the unclassified fragments were to have preceded the first half of the *Apology*. The 'Letter to a seeking friend . . .' is a highly polished analysis of disbelief. Pascal's celebrated 'Wager', a seeming proof of God's existence, was in fact designed only as a lure to attract those intrigued by his theories of probability to a provisional Christian life.

Pascal's arguments drawn from SCRIPTURE (particularly his literal reading of the prophecies) have long been discredited by an evolving BIBLICAL CRITICISM. His strict exposition of a *DEUS ABSCONDITUS* has failed to alter that semi-PELAGIANISM inherent in much everyday Catholicism. Yet Pascal's exposition of both affords unique access to the mental universe of baroque Catholicism. And Pascal's diagnosis of the human condition and the dilemma of disbelief remain as acute and authentic as ever.

See also JANSENISM.

N. Hammond, ed., *The Cambridge Companion to Pascal* (Cambridge University Press, 2003).

D. Wetsel, *Pascal and Disbelief: Conversion and Catechesis in the "Pensées" of Pascal* (Catholic University of America Press, 1995).

DAVID WETSEL

PASSION: see CROSS AND CRUCIFIXION.

PASTORAL THEOLOGY 'Pastoral theology' refers to a critical reflection on the nature and caring activity of God and of human persons before God, within the personal, social, communal, and cultural contexts of the world. It is described as *pastoral* because of its focus on the care of persons and communities. It is *theological* because it reflects on the nature and activity of God, and of humanity in relation to God, as portrayed and understood through various practices and documents of FAITH. Pastoral theology is a constructive PRACTICAL THEOLOGY that seeks to make contributions to both the disciplines of pastoral care and theology. Thus, the American Society for Pastoral Theology defines pastoral theology as 'a constructive practical theological enterprise focused on the religious care of persons, families and communities', emphasizing its constructive and practical nature.

Pastoral theology includes interpretive, constructive, and expressive reflections on the caring activities of God and of human communities throughout history as well as in the contemporary world. Pastoral theologians engage 'God' and 'care' critically – raising questions and exploring concepts and practices for their fidelity to understandings of faith and their effectiveness in caring for human persons, families, and communities in their respective contexts. Pastoral theologians engage interpretively by examining the meanings – both manifest and unconscious – of statements and practices of faith as they impinge upon practices of care. Pastoral theology is constructive in that it seeks to assist in the refining and redefining of notions of God with the purpose of disclosing more adequate ways of being present with and caring for human persons. Pastoral theologians seek to express their work through performative practices of care that include creative, liturgical, and artistic activities such as counselling, worship, preaching, teaching, group work, and community development.

Pastoral theology, then, is essentially a theology of pastoral care, or a theological reflection upon practices and theories of care. The relationship between theology on the one hand, and pastoral care on the other, is largely conceived of in pastoral theology as *dialogical* in nature. Consequently, there is an expectation that theology will inform care and that care will also inform theology. The assumption is that both theory and practice are *loci* of learning and REVELATION. Pastoral theologians expect to encounter God and learn about God through the practices of care they engage in. As such, various practices are engaged in with the express purpose of discovering more about God and learning more about the self that engages in acts of care. One important such practice is that of the writing and presentation of detailed accounts of encounters with patients and clients (called *verbatims*) to and in supervised groups. These accounts and the presentation and discussion of them become significant means of theological learning. Supervisors of clinical pastoral education groups are pastoral theologians who assist groups to engage in pastoral theology at the coalface of practice in hospitals and other sites of human need and care.

Pastoral theology has a wide scope, including the study of the theological underpinnings, understandings, and implications of the offices, roles, and functions of persons in ministry within as well as outside the Church. Historically 'pastoral' theology was restricted to a study of the clerical office. However, as the discipline has developed, especially during the twentieth century, there has been a deeper recognition of the multifarious and communal nature of the caring ministry of the Church. As such pastoral theology has focused increasingly on exploring the theological aspects of the care of persons rather than exclusively upon caregivers and their office and functions.

Traced historically, paradigms of pastoral care have morphed through classical–clerical, clinical–pastoral, communal–contextual, and intercultural–postmodern phases. Elements of each of these distinguishable paradigms are still very much in evidence today in various parts of the world. *Classical–clerical* pastoral care emphasized the office, role, and functions of ordained clergy as ministers and purveyors of the 'cure of SOULS' (*cura animarum*). Ordained clergy were theologically trained to offer ministrations that transmitted the grace of God to persons in need of healing, guiding, sustaining or reconciling. Pastoral theology in the classical clerical age was essentially a theology of ministry with a focus on the role and action of the ordained.

Clinical–pastoral care is modelled upon medical practice, with pastoral caregivers occupying the role of trained clinicians. 'Pastoral care and counselling' here is conceived of as a mental-health discipline with a spiritual component. Psychotherapy is the reigning paradigm, and pastoral care is largely synonymous with counselling. Chaplains and pastoral counsellors acquire therapeutic skills to be utilized with patients or clients. Pastoral theology in the clinical–pastoral model consists of theological reflections upon clinical encounters, with explorations of how God's presence is discernible in the therapeutic experience.

Communal–contextual care raised questions about the individualist tone and personal therapeutic nature of the practices of pastoral care. Pastoral theologians recognized the communitarian nature of the care of persons and emphasized the place of communities of faith and faith perspectives in the practice of care. The important influence of LIBERATION THEOLOGY in the development of FEMINIST, BLACK, WOMANIST, and other forms of explicitly contextual theology provided tools for the development of pastoral theology in different contexts. Pastoral theology in a communal contextual frame employs the methodologies of liberation theologies in seeking social and communal justice, drawing attention (as feminist theologians in particular have urged) to the interconnectedness between personal distress and socio-political conditions. Theology is examined for its liberative contributions to the human quest for wholeness and healing.

Intercultural–postmodern pastoral care continues to identify gender, race, class, sexuality, and culture as significant elements in the practice and theorizing of care and seeks to incorporate socio-cultural analysis into the theory and delivery of pastoral care. Global cultures and differences in pastoral care in different world situations have, correspondingly, begun to play a more prominent role in pastoral care. Pastoral theologians are beginning to pay closer attention to the way faith and religious tradition play a role in shaping the kind of care on offer and indeed upon the way in which meaning is made of human exigencies. Inter-religious dialogue and activity have begun to play a role in pastoral care and pastoral theology. Intercultural pastoral theology emphasizes THEOLOGICAL ANTHROPOLOGY arising from international contexts, is respectful of diversity, celebrates difference, and seeks meaningful and honest dialogue across differences.

The pastoral theology that has accompanied developments in pastoral care, growing out of classical and contemporary theological traditions has, in terms of methodology, taken the following forms: deductive, correlational, interdisciplinary, inductive, contextual, and constructive methodologies. *Deductive* pastoral theology arises where theological, experiential or documentary material is premised as the source out of which practices of care are derived. *Correlational* theological methods, made explicit in the work of P. TILLICH and later revised by D. Tracy (b. 1939), lay the existential realities of human life alongside the symbols and teachings of Christian faith. Tillichian correlational approaches are unidirectional, with questions arising from existence and answers from the symbols of faith. Revised correlational methods are more dialogical, allowing for mutual questioning and answering.

Interdisciplinary pastoral theology draws on a variety of disciplines in arriving at theologically recommended practices. Pastoral care has traditionally drawn on psychology as its scientific disciplinary partner. Under this paradigm pastoral theology has tended to assume the characteristics of a religion-and-science discussion, with psychology being the science. More recently, sociology, cognitive science, and neuroscience have been occupying that position. In *inductive* approaches to pastoral theology, human experience is the main source out of which pastoral care practices are sought. *Contextual* approaches emphasize social location, cultural dynamics, and anthropological considerations in the derivation of theologically appropriate practices of care. *Constructive* approaches largely in tune with PROCESS THEOLOGY seek to advance theological notions that reflect creativity and development within the divine sphere.

Pastoral theology is practical theology with a very clear orientation towards praxis, thereby emphasizing the necessary interaction between theory and practice in all practical theology. The relationship between theory and practice in practical theology has been expressed in at least four ways, all of which are in evidence among contemporary pastoral theologians: theory–practice, practice–theory, theory–practice–theory, or practice–theory–practice. Although the starting and ending points (with their particular stresses on the relative priority of theory and practice) distinguish these approaches from each other, each nevertheless includes as of necessity both theory and practice in some measure of interaction.

Pastoral theology fulfils the 'core tasks' of all practical theological endeavours, which have been usefully articulated by R. Osmer (b. 1950) as (1) descriptive–empirical, (2) interpretive, (3) normative, and (4) pragmatic. The *descriptive–empirical* task entails gathering information that helps in the discernment of patterns and dynamics in particular episodes, situations, or contexts. Pastoral theologians seek to develop acute observational skills that enable them to record carefully what is going on. Listening is a core skill for the pastoral theologian, as is asking questions that elicit clearer expressions of what is being experienced. The usage of narrative therapy in pastoral care, for example, begins with the facilitation of the uninhibited articulation of one's story. Much of pastoral care, including pastoral counselling, begins with listening to and hearing descriptions of empirical experience. But so does congregational or communal care engage social descriptive means to 'hear the story of the community'. Other important tools employed in pastoral care and pastoral theology include personal genograms, which are pictorial depictions of family relations and personal characteristics going back two or three generations, and community genograms, which identify significant social and cultural patterns in the historical development of communities.

The *interpretive* task draws on hermeneutical theories from the arts and sciences to unearth deeper understandings and explanations of the observed patterns and dynamics. In this activity the aim is to go beyond the superficial into deeper underlying forces and influences upon what is experienced or perceived. Meaning-seeking here employs an array of different possible theories in an attempt to account for experience. This task deliberately explores non-theological disciplines in the belief that they may actually also reflect the God of all creation who seeks to be revealed and known. It thereby reflects the interdisciplinarity that is basic to pastoral theology.

The *normative* task is pursued in expressly theological language and forms of thought. Theological concepts are used to interpret particular episodes, situations, or contexts, constructing ethical norms to guide responses, and learning from 'good practice'. Pastoral theology qua theology engages critically in theological discourse with a deep sense of the value and importance of theological thinking in the quest for appropriate and effective means of care and healing. Theological interpretation, far from being an intrusive add-on to a therapeutic process, actually serves to offer fresh and needed perspectives for the task of providing adequate care. Theological concepts often critique social scientific ones in helpful ways when the two are engaged dialogically. Similarly the human sciences can and do offer useful questions and critiques to theological interpretations.

The *pragmatic* task seeks to develop strategies of action that will influence situations in desirable ways. The goals of pastoral theology include the provision of appropriate and effective care of humans in our existential realities. In this context, 'God is LOVE' (1 John 4:8) is both a theological and a pastoral statement. Pastoral theologians seek to find ways in which this theological statement may be 'enfleshed' in the lives of living human persons within the networks of relationships in which we are embedded, in ways that will be beneficial for all. As such pastoral theologians tend not to end with the aesthetically satisfactory theological statement. Rather they push forward to find a pragmatically appropriate response that will be in keeping with sound theology, appropriate ethics, and effective care of persons.

V. Fabella and R. S. Sugirtharajah, eds., *Dictionary of Third World Theologies* (Orbis, 2000).
E. Y. Lartey, *Pastoral Theology in an Intercultural World* (Pilgrim, 2006).
R. Osmer, *Practical Theology: An Introduction* (Eerdmans, 2008).
N. J. Ramsay, ed., *Pastoral Care and Counseling: Redefining the Paradigms* (Abingdon Press, 2004).
D. Willows and J. Swinton, eds., *Spiritual Dimensions of Pastoral Care: Practical Theology in a Multidisciplinary Context* (Jessica Kingsley Publishers, 2000).

EMMANUEL Y. LARTEY

PATRIARCHATE, ECUMENICAL The Orthodox bishop of the ancient city of Constantinople (modern-day Istanbul, Turkey) holds the title 'archbishop of Constantinople, New Rome, and ecumenical patriarch'. As bishop of the city that once was the capital of the Byzantine Empire, he presides over a synod of bishops who hold titles of sees located in modern-day Turkey and certain Greek Islands in the Eastern Mediterranean Sea. Until recently, only these bishops constituted the permanent synod, but in March 2004 the composition was altered so that bishops from dioceses throughout the world could be considered permanent members. The bishops of dioceses in Northern Greece commemorate him as their patriarch, although they do not form part of this synodal structure, and in fact are administered by the Orthodox Church of Greece.

The ecumenical patriarch has direct oversight over a number of monastic communities, most notably those on the island of Patmos and the monastic confederation on Mount ATHOS in Greece. He further maintains jurisdiction over territorial dioceses throughout the world, which are headed by archbishops or metropolitan-bishops, as well as ethnic dioceses of Albanian, Russian, Ukrainian, and Carpatho-Russian communities, which exist outside their countries of origin. Beginning on 1 September 1992, the ecumenical patriarch has regularly summoned all active hierarchs under his jurisdiction for meetings and consultation. The synod in Constantinople, together with the bishops from abroad, elects a new patriarch upon vacancy in office. By Turkish law, the patriarch must be a Turkish citizen. Upon election, the new patriarch is enthroned in the patriarchal cathedral.

The patriarch of Constantinople oversees scholarly institutions in Athens, Thessalonika, Chambésy, and Berkeley, among others, as well as various offices of representation, agencies, and missionary centres. His most important scholarly institution is the Holy Trinity Theological School on the island of Halki, modern Heybeliada, one of the Princes Islands near Istanbul in the Sea of Marmara. This school served as the primary place for educating clergy for service in the patriarchate and in the Orthodox Church. The Turkish government closed this school in 1971 in a law that prohibited private institutions of higher learning. Although it does not function as a school, the patriarchate hosts conferences there and works tirelessly for permission from the Turkish government to reopen it.

Among the other Orthodox Churches, the ecumenical patriarch is considered to be 'first among equals'. Broadly speaking, he exercises his unique ministry within the Orthodox Church by maintaining and facilitating the unity of the different autocephalous and autonomous Orthodox Churches. He fulfils this ministry by initiating and co-ordinating inter-Orthodox gatherings, at which he also presides over whether they are of a liturgical or consultative character. Likewise, he leads the Orthodox participation in inter-religious dialogues.

The canonical tradition and historical circumstances have shaped the position of the ecumenical patriarch within the Orthodox Church. At the end of the fourth century at the first Council of CONSTANTINOPLE, the bishop of Constantinople was given 'privileges of honour after the bishop of Rome', because, the council reasoned, it is the New Rome. This position in the hierarchy of the Church was confirmed and enlarged by subsequent Church councils. After the estrangement between the Eastern and Western Churches at the turn of the first millennium, Constantinople assumed the position of primacy within the Orthodox Church. During the Ottoman Empire, this position was greatly expanded as he also became the effective civil leader of all Orthodox Christians in the Ottoman Empire, responsible for a census, collecting taxes, adjudicating disputes, and representing Orthodox Christians to the government.

The title 'ecumenical patriarch' first appears in the sixth century, when it is used as a form of address for Menas of Constantinople (r. 536–52), although at this point he signed official documents as 'bishop of Constantinople–Rome'. By the end of the same century, Archbishop John IV ('the Faster', r. 585–95) had adopted this title for his correspondence, and by the mid-ninth century, under Patriarch Photius I (r. 858–67, 877–86), it was used regularly. Initially the title's meaning was ambiguous and part of the flowery language common to the high levels of society in late antiquity. It did indicate that the incumbent was at the highest rank in the ecclesiastical hierarchy, second only to Rome. With the expansion of the activity of the patriarch over the course of history, the meaning of the title has also expanded.

T. Fitzgerald, *The Ecumenical Patriarchate and Christian Unity* (Holy Cross Orthodox Press, 1997).

V. Laurent, 'Le titre de patriarche œcuménique et la signature patriarcale', *Revue des études byzantines* 6 (1948), 5–26.

Maximos, Metropolitan of Sardes, *The Oecumenical Patriarchate in the Orthodox Church: A Study in the History and Canons of the Church* (Patriarchal Institute for Patristic Studies, 1976).

L. Patsavos, *Primacy and Conciliarity: Studies in the Primacy of the See of Constantinople and the Synodal Structure of the Orthodox Church* (Holy Cross Orthodox Press, 1995).

ALEXANDER RENTEL

PATRIARCHY The term 'patriarchy' translates directly as 'rule of the father'. It is used to describe many different societies in which women have access to cultural and material capital primarily through men. In patriarchal cultures, the structures of society uphold and reinforce the power and authority of the male head of the household, granting the dominant male legal, economic, and political privilege. Patriarchy, in this general sense, characterizes many cultures around the world and throughout much of history, even as the degree of male domination and the specific ways in which it is perpetuated vary considerably.

Patriarchy is best understood as part of a larger systemic pattern in which particular groups are granted structural privilege and power over others based on culturally determined characteristics such as sex, race, or age. Such systems of domination reinforce one another, maintain hierarchies of power, and sustain the acceptance of inequality. Interlocking systems of domination create, and are created by, societies in which the privileges of the few are purchased at the cost of the oppression of the many. Patriarchy is, therefore, inextricably linked with other systemic forms of exclusion and inequality, including racism and classism.

The multiple traditions of Christianity have been formed, transmitted, and interpreted in various patriarchal cultures. Thus they are deeply complicit in sustaining patriarchy. This happens in both explicit and implicit ways. Many Churches overtly endorse patriarchy by excluding women from positions of power, such as ordained ministry, and asserting that women should submit to male heads of households. Other Christian communities indirectly support patriarchy by using exclusively masculine language and imagery for God. In these ways and many others, Christian traditions often portray patriarchal social structures as divinely ordained.

Many contemporary feminists find Christianity, especially given its focus on a male saviour, to be inherently and irredeemably patriarchal and thus harmful to women. However, others see patriarchy as pervasive within, but not definitive of, the traditions of Christianity. In this view, patriarchy is part of the sinful brokenness of humanity and is contrary to the liberating message of the GOSPEL. It denies the theological affirmation that all people are created in the image of God. Proponents of this view also argue that the words and actions of Jesus, as described in the NT, refute the legitimacy of patriarchy by honouring persons marginalized by society and proclaiming God's love for all people.

An analysis of patriarchy, particularly in its systemic nature and its relation to other structures of oppression, highlights the radicality of certain Christian affirmations and practices. Claims regarding God's concern for justice, the value of all persons in the eyes of God, and the importance of caring for the poor stand in stark contrast to oppression. When Christian communities embody these values, they profoundly challenge patriarchal societies. Christian life includes the vocation to live into new forms of social relation that do not rely on, or perpetuate, structures of domination such as patriarchy.

See also ANDROCENTRISM, FEMINIST THEOLOGY.

SHANNON CRAIGO-SNELL

PATRIPASSIANISM The term is a nickname, probably invented by TERTULLIAN, and used by him to refer to the position of Praxeas (*fl. ca* 200) and his followers. It is derived from the Latin *Pater passus est* ('the Father suffered'), as Tertullian accused Praxeas of teaching that the Father himself suffered on the CROSS. However, even on the basis of Tertullian's own description of Praxeas' teaching, this accusation seems unfair. Praxeas did reject what would later become the orthodox DOCTRINE of the TRINITY. Instead, he distinguished between the Son, that is, the flesh of the man Jesus, who suffered on the cross, and the Father, identified with the HOLY SPIRIT, God, or Christ (*Prax.* 27). The Father did not suffer himself, but suffered *with* the Son. Tertullian rejected this attempt to safeguard divine impassibility (the doctrine that God cannot suffer), arguing that because compassion is a form of passion Praxeas implied that the Father himself suffered.

Patripassianism is, formally speaking, a Trinitarian HERESY, because proponents refused to make strict distinctions between the Father and the Son, on the grounds that this would compromise the unity (*monarchia*) of God. For them, the Son was a mode of appearance (*modus*) of the Father. Hence, contemporary scholarship prefers the terms MODALISM or modalistic monarchianism for this position. Sometimes it is also called Sabellianism, after Sabellius (*fl. ca* 220), a patripassianist mentioned by Hippolytus of Rome (*ca* 170–*ca* 235). Contemporary dogmaticians are wrong when they see in patripassianism a forerunner of modern rejections of God's impassibility: in spite of their assertion of the unity of God, patripassians tried to avoid denying God's impassibility.

See also ABBA, CHRISTOLOGY.

MARCEL SAROT

PATRISTICS 'Patristics' is the term conventionally used for the study of the writings of the 'Church fathers' (Latin *patres*) – those early figures regarded as having contributed positively to the formation of Christian DOCTRINES and practices. The term usually covers the period from the late first and the early second centuries (beginning with those 'APOSTOLIC FATHERS' not included in today's biblical canon) to the fifth and sixth centuries.

The term 'patristics' has become a bone of contention. The notion of the 'fathers' implies that they have (or had) authority, but this immediately raises the question of whether the study of their writings should be a purely historical exercise, or whether it should be normative. If the latter, the questions 'whose authority?' and 'authoritative for whom?' need to be asked. There is now, for example, increasing study of early writers from non-Chalcedonian Churches with a rich theological tradition and a sophisticated literary output which is worthy of detailed study from both historical and theological perspectives (see ORIENTAL ORTHODOX CHURCHES). Additionally, since the nineteenth century patristics has increasingly included the study of writers strictly beyond the boundaries of the Church. This is partly through the need to understand ideas developed against 'heretics'; partly because attention turned to more marginal texts as patristics as an academic discipline expanded, and partly because scholars questioned whether one could apply a clear boundary to early 'Catholic' or 'orthodox' Christianity.

The term 'patristics' has also been challenged by feminist scholars, such as E. Clark (b. 1938), who argue that a focus on the 'Church fathers' (and a doctrinal/philosophical theology almost exclusively produced by men) has obscured women's contribution to the development of early Christianity. Their work, together with that of scholars like P. Brown (b. 1935), has highlighted the historical, social, and cultural context of the fathers' writings, and has subjected the texts to rigorous readings which emphasize their character as particular kinds of discourse written in specific contexts, often by men with extremely sophisticated rhetorical training. This 'linguistic turn' has drawn the study of the 'fathers' into the broader discipline of late antiquity.

Historically, patristics developed from the work of Renaissance and humanist scholars who revived interest in neglected early Christian texts. In the nineteenth century, developments in historical, classical, and philosophical scholarship (especially in Germany) had a huge impact; furthermore, text-critical techniques were applied to the fathers, and linguists opened up texts in, e.g., Syriac, Coptic, and Armenian. Occasionally, new texts were discovered – most dramatically, the Nag Hammadi collection of Gnostic codices (see GNOSTICISM). Gradually patristics developed the character of a formal academic discipline with translations, critical editions, journals, and international conferences. Theological interpretation of the fathers did not cease, however: the OXFORD MOVEMENT encouraged historical and theological readings of the fathers (at both scholarly and popular levels). Theological interpretation was also invigorated in the mid-twentieth century by the *ressourcement* movement in CATHOLIC THEOLOGY and by the number of Orthodox émigrés in western Europe and North America. Challenging and creative responses to the texts have also been stimulated by thinkers such as J. Derrida (1930–2004).

MORWENNA LUDLOW

PAUL The year of Paul's birth is unknown (Acts 7:58 notes that he was a 'young man' at the time of Stephen's martyrdom). Probably born as a Roman citizen in Tarsus and raised there, he was thereafter (following Acts 22:3) educated in Jerusalem under Rabban Gamaliel I (d. *ca* 50); this would suggest that Paul (at that time, Saul) belonged to the moderate Hillelite school, though some have argued that his zeal suggests attachment to the school of Shammai. Galatians 1, Philippians 3, and Acts all give accounts of Paul's conversion. Thereafter, the chronology of Paul's ministry is constructed on the basis of Acts, and of the passing references in the epistles, with the help of external evidence such as Claudius' (10 BC–AD 54) expulsion of the Jews from Rome in 49 and Gallio's (d. 65) tenure as proconsul of Achaea in 51–2 (cf. Acts 18:1–2 and 12–17).

His four principal journeys led him as far as Rome in the West, though they focused on what are now Turkey and Greece. It is uncertain whether he ever reached Spain as he had planned (Rom. 15:23–4, 28). He supported himself as a tent-maker as he preached the GOSPEL. A number of scholars consider Paul only to have written Romans, 1 and 2 Corinthians, Galatians, Philippians, 1 Thessalonians, and Philemon; however, a growing number are accepting a larger corpus as authentic, especially including Ephesians, Colossians, and 2 Thessalonians. According to tradition, Paul died in Rome during the Neronian persecution (*ca* 64).

There has been considerable debate about where the 'centre' of Paul's theology lies. JUSTIFICATION has attracted a number of supporters, but reconciliation, ESCHATOLOGY, and others have also been proposed; in fact, no single concept can be identified as that from which all others stem. Primary in Paul's theology is the gospel of Christ's death for SINS and his RESURRECTION according to the Scriptures (described as 'of first importance' in 1 Cor. 15:3). The sequence of thought in Romans 1–3 presents Christ's atoning work as saving sinners from God's wrath (cf. Rom. 8:1–4); the LAW was never intended to be the way to salvation (Gal. 2:21). Christ bore the sins and the divine curse on behalf of God's people and in their place, receiving the penalty of death (Rom. 8:3; Gal. 3:13; 2 Cor. 5:21). It is on the basis of this atoning work of Jesus that God pronounces the justifying verdict upon sinners, who are counted by divine declaration as fully obedient, and accepted by God (Rom. 4:5). This righteousness is received by FAITH in Christ. Christ's work, however, not only involves displacing sinners, dying in their place; he also represents them as the head of his BODY, the Church. In his resurrection, as the first-fruits of the saved, he inaugurates a new creation (1 Cor. 15). The resurrection to new life in the HOLY SPIRIT makes possible a new obedience, the shape of which is imitation of Christ: this is the purpose of God, who predestined his people to be conformed to the image of Christ (Rom. 8:29–30).

This leads to the other pole of Paul's thought, the GLORY of God. It is the goal of God's own purposes (Rom. 15:8–9; Eph. 1:4–5, 11–12), and is thus to be the goal of human action also (1 Cor. 10:31). When Christ returns he will condemn the wicked, but those in Christ will be glorified in him (2 Thess. 1:5–10). In the meantime, Paul advocates patient expectation, purity, and the proclamation of the gospel.

Paul's letters almost certainly began to be collected already in the first century (see 2 Pet. 3.16; Ignatius, *Eph.* 16.2), perhaps even by members of his team during his lifetime. In the second century the interpretation of Paul's letters is contested. They are used by the orthodox, with Paul serving as a pattern to follow for Ignatius of Antioch (*ca* 35–*ca* 110) and Polycarp (*ca* 70–*ca* 155), but his letters are also used by the Valentinian school and by MARCION. This latter's influence continues in the third century, as Paul is enthusiastically taken up by the Manichees (see MANICHAEISM).

It is with the former Manichee, AUGUSTINE, that Paul's influence reaches its high watermark in the early Church. There was already an extensive tradition of Pauline commentary by his time, but Augustine himself develops Pauline teaching extensively, particularly in the articulation of his SOTERIOLOGY. Paul continued to be claimed, however, not only by Augustine's Manichaean opponents, but also by Pelagius, who himself wrote commentaries on Paul's epistles (see PELAGIANISM). Augustine ensured Paul's centrality to the medieval theological tradition, not least in T. AQUINAS.

Concentration specifically on Paul's soteriological concerns came to prominence again at the REFORMATION, particularly in the theology of M. LUTHER. Again, however, interest in the interpretation of Paul was sparked not only by reforming zeal but also by humanist and traditionalist, anti-Lutheran impulses. J. CALVIN and the Reformed tradition further emphasized the Augustinian focus on GRACE and PREDESTINATION, although Paul also became central to METHODIST THEOLOGY.

In the twentieth century, the most influential expositors of Paul were K. BARTH and R. BULTMANN. Barth's *Epistle to the Romans* (2nd edn, 1921) complained of the anaemic nature of most scholarly literature on Paul, and stressed the disturbing fact that Romans was about Christ. Barth's stance towards Paul also left a considerable impress upon his later *Church Dogmatics* (1932–67). The first volume of Bultmann's *Theology of the New Testament* (1952) focuses on Paul's theology, from the anthropological standpoints of the human situation in the world under sin, and 'man under faith'. Bultmann also considered that Paul himself had already engaged in a kind of DEMYTHOLOGIZATION of his Jewish world view, a point which encouraged Bultmann in his own project. The twentieth century also saw scholarly treatments of Paul by Jews and philosophers, as well as avowedly secular approaches making use of (for example) postcolonial theory.

Probably the most important recent change in Pauline scholarship has been a renewed focus upon the Jewish roots of Paul's theology. In Bultmann's day, the HISTORY OF RELIGION SCHOOL had constructed a Hellenistic–Gnostic framework for Paul's thought. Shortly after World War II, reflection upon the HOLOCAUST provided impetus to a renewed interest in the rabbinic background to Paul, and this was further supplemented by the new discoveries of the Dead Sea Scrolls, which showed that Jewish parallels to the dualistic elements in Paul were just as clear as Gnostic analogues. Appreciation of the Jewish background of Paul has, however, led in a number of different directions. In some hands, it has meant viewing Paul as a figure who remained thoroughly rooted in his traditional religion. For others, Jewish literature brings more sharply into focus the APOCALYPTIC dimension of Paul's thought, in which Christ has come out of a clear blue sky to judge and rectify the cosmos. Furthermore, it continues to be disputed how much Paul is in disagreement with his Jewish contemporaries on the question of justification by faith.

Another important development has been a focus on Paul's CHRISTOLOGY. Recently NT scholars have argued that Paul's Christology cannot merely be reduced to a human messiahship, since a variety of passages in Paul assume a Christology of divine identity and reflect the worship of Jesus. By its reformulation of the *Shema*, 1 Corinthians 8:6 refers to Jesus' identity as 'Lord' in OT terms. It also testifies to Jesus Christ's pre-existence and agency in creation: 'one Lord, Jesus Christ, *through whom all things come*'. Again, the great majority of interpreters view Philippians 2:6–11 as attesting to the pre-existence of Christ, and a number of scholars see a statement of divine identity there ('being in the form of God'). The end of this passage also refers to eschatological worship, in which Jesus receives the same acclamation as 'Lord', which in the OT is ascribed uniquely to the one God (Isa. 45:22–3). Here we see an important contribution of attention to the wider Pauline corpus, in contrast to a more exclusive focus on Romans and Galatians, where the traditional Pauline soteriological concerns are to the fore. This research also helps to illustrate the breadth of early Christian commitment to the divinity of Jesus, which has often been more narrowly rooted in John's Gospel.

R. J. Bauckham, *God Crucified: Monotheism and Christology in the New Testament* (Paternoster Press, 1998).

S. J. Gathercole, *Where Is Boasting? Early Jewish Soteriology and Paul's Response in Romans 1–5* (Eerdmans, 2002).

J. L. Martyn, *Theological Issues in the Letters of Paul* (T&T Clark, 1997).

T. H. L. Parker, *Commentaries on the Epistle to the Romans 1532–1542* (T&T Clark, 1986).

A. Souter, *Earliest Latin Commentaries on the Epistles of Paul* (Oxford University Press, 1927).

SIMON GATHERCOLE

PEDOBAPTISM: see BAPTISM.

PELAGIANISM 'Pelagianism' refers to a collection of beliefs about FREE WILL, SIN, and GRACE named after Pelagius (*ca* 355–*ca* 420), an Irish ascetic who sought to promote greater moral rigour in reaction to what he saw as a growing laxity in Christianity exemplified by AUGUSTINE's prayer, 'Command what you will and grant what you command' (*Conf.* 10.29). Pelagius himself was only one of a number of figures with distaste for Augustine's theology, and leaders of Pelagianism as a theological movement included Caelestius (*fl.* 415) and Julian of Eclanum (*ca* 385–*ca* 455).

Pelagius' main work, on the letter of PAUL to the Romans, was written before 410. He followed ORIGEN's interpretation of Romans 5:12, according to which Adam transmitted to his posterity merely a tendency to sin. For Pelagius, as for Ambrosiaster (*fl.* 380) and Origen, genuine sin requires a deliberate act of the will. He therefore taught that sin has not corrupted our inherited nature (as in Augustine's doctrine of original sin), that it is only habitual through repetition, and that it can be undone through PENANCE and obedience. According to Pelagius, Christ has the power to forgive past sins and has provided an example of righteousness. BAPTISM inaugurates a new way of life after the forgiveness of past sins. Thus, infants were not baptized to wash away sin, but rather to introduce them to the sacramental life of the Church with which they would grow to co-operate, overcoming a lifetime's ingrained habits through a lifetime of penance.

Pelagius appears to have taught that Adam was created mortal (i.e., that he would have died even if he had not sinned), so that the consequences of the FALL were moral but not ontological. For this he was condemned in 418 by Pope Zosimus (r. 417–18). Because Julian, bishop of Eclanum, would not subscribe to this condemnation, he and twenty-two other Italian bishops were exiled. For Julian, the doctrine of congenital, inherited sin articulated by Augustine and endorsed by the pope implied an ontological dualism inconsistent with the DOCTRINE of CREATION. He argued that Augustine effectively demonized MARRIAGE in so far as he identified the *locus* of sin's transmission in the moment of conception. For Julian, the biblical teaching that human nature was created good meant that marital relations, as part of that nature, could not be the source of sin.

In contrast to Augustine's insistence that grace be understood as a gratuitous divine enabling of damaged human abilities, Pelagius and his associates saw the grace more in terms of God's manifold ways (through the law as well as Christ) of encouraging the proper exercise of human capacities that were in principle sound. Correspondingly, Pelagian theology trusts in the goodness of humanity's nature as providing individual human beings with the wherewithal to move to God through VIRTUE, by the free choice of the will. Pelagianism thereby promotes a Church of faith in action over against one of 'cheap grace' and easy forgiveness, though this same principle also suggests that the Church is embodied in its elite individual performers more than in the average group of believers.

Pelagianism (specifically, the teaching of Caelestius) was condemned at a council in Carthage in 418, and again at the ecumenical Council of EPHESUS in 431. Later in the fifth century, a second wave of resistance to Augustine's views on grace and free will emerged in monasteries in what is now southern France. The cornerstone of this position was that the Christian was able to refrain from sin and initiate the life of faith apart from any gift of grace separate from those given through humanity's created nature and the gift of the LAW. These teachings (much later dubbed 'semi-Pelagianism') were condemned at the second Council of Orange in 529.

T. de Bruyn, *Pelagius's Commentary on St Paul's Epistle to the Romans* (Oxford University Press, 1993).

B. R. Rees, *Pelagius: A Reluctant Heretic* (Boydell, 1988).

O. Wermelinger, *Rom und Pelagius* (A. Hiersemann, 1975).

MARK W. ELLIOTT

PENANCE Penance and repentance have been related terms in the history of Christian theology and practice. Rooted in the Bible they have also reflected the differences among Christian confessions, most especially with regard to the Protestant REFORMATION in the western Church and its consequences for the various Christian communions. The dispute often revolved around the translation of the Latin *poenitentia* as penance, penitence, or repentance, with the disagreement rooted not so much in philological questions as in the theological meaning with which the term is invested. Is it part of a penitential practice understood within a sacramental context (as Catholics contended), or should it be interpreted alongside the hearing of FAITH that constitutes the conversion by the GOSPEL (as Protestants preferred)? The complicated history of repentance/penance reflects both these views.

Repentance in the OT is associated with CONVERSION, change of heart and mind, regret or CONTRITION for SIN, and turning from evil to God. The verb 'to repent' is used of God as well as humans, the latter imitating the divine with respect to a change of purpose. Therefore humans repent of their actions in the same way that God changes his mind to destroy Jerusalem by plague (1 Chron. 21:15). Or Moses pleads that God will repent of the evil against Israel by turning back from his fierce wrath (Exod. 32:12). The change from one state to another for humans is most often associated with sorrow over sin and adherence to the will or LAW of God. This may be a matter of the simple admission of sin exemplified by Moses: 'I have sinned this time; the LORD is in the right, and I and my people are in the wrong' (Exod. 9:27).

Although repentance is never mentioned in Psalm 51, all its elements are expressed. The appeal for mercy (v. 1) and cleansing (v. 2), the admission of sin (v. 3), and the justification of God (v. 4) culminate in the broken and contrite heart of the sinner (v. 18). Such is the basis for both the priestly and prophetic enactments of the call to repentance and reparation. In the case of the former, the priestly sacrifice of the sin offering is matched by his confession of the sins of the people over the scapegoat, which is sent away into the desert (Lev. 16:21). The prophets call ISRAEL to return to the Lord, foreshadowing the days when God will write the law upon their hearts (Jer. 31:31–4). In terms of individual responsibility repentance culminates in the exhortation that each is responsible for the sins one has committed even if this was preceded by a righteous life (Ezek. 3:16–21).

The oldest NT Gospel opens with the preaching of JOHN THE BAPTIST (Mark 1:4), followed by that of Jesus (Mark 1:15). Both exhort Israel to repentance and signify it through the administration of the water ablution of BAPTISM. After the death and RESURRECTION of Jesus, Christian baptism (Acts 2:38) follows a similar pattern, but with a fulfilment that the former could only foreshadow. Whereas John's baptism for the forgiveness of sins anticipated the coming of the Holy Spirit, Christian baptism entailed the imparting of the gift of the HOLY SPIRIT by the additional rite of the laying on of hands (Acts 8:14–19; 19:5–6). Later Christian penitential practices certainly imitate the Baptist's call that deeds must give evidence of repentance (Luke 3:10–14), something the apostle PAUL recognized in the repentance of members of the Corinthian Church who were 'grieved into repenting' (2 Cor. 7:9). The prophetic oracles in Revelation likewise follow a similar pattern calling the Churches to 'repent of their doings' (Rev. 2:22).

In the subsequent history of Christianity a threefold pattern emerges. Repentance or penance may be considered as a VIRTUE, a sacrament, or the fruit of a proper hearing of the gospel (viz., evangelical repentance). Despite the differences among Christian communions, one can affirm a commonality shared by all Christians. As in the parable of the Prodigal Son, the essence of repentance is to change one's mind – 'But when he came to himself, he said: ... I will arise and go to my Father' (Luke 15:17) – and acknowledge one's sins – 'Father, I have sinned against heaven and before you' (Luke 15:18). Associated with repentance (Greek *metanoia*, or 'change of mind') is sorrow for sin or contrition and the new life of faith in turning to God. How divine GRACE comports with these human actions is the subject of confessional controversy. The development of the sacrament of penance had much to do with this.

In antiquity ritual penance was considered a 'second plank' for those who had gravely sinned after baptism. This 'Canonical Penance' was severe and public, administered by the bishop and bestowed only once during a lifetime. Around the sixth century it was succeeded by 'Tariffed Penance', a form of penance promoted by Celtic monks. Still somewhat rigorous (more so for monks and clerics than for the LAITY), it was private and repeatable, thus paving the way for the emergence (beginning in the twelfth century) of the sacrament of penance, in which absolution preceded the assigned penance rather than following its performance as in the previous periods. In all these periods one may distinguish between the personal virtue of penance and canonical or sacramental acts of penance required for reconciliation with God and the Church.

The virtue of penance constituted one of the four essential elements of the medieval and modern sacrament. Contrition for sin precedes the confession of sins, absolution administered by the priest (forgiving the guilt of sin), and the satisfaction required for the alleviation of the temporal punishments of sin (i.e., healing the effects of sin in the penitent's life). This form of 'private confession', interpreted as a sacrament, has continued in the Catholic Church (as well as in the Orthodox Churches) and was the subject of reform at the time of the Reformation. Modified forms continued intermittently in the Anglican communion and the Lutheran Churches although founded upon a distinctly evangelical theology of penance.

The main dispute between upholders of the sacrament of penance and an evangelical repentance has to do with whether penance and its fruits in a transformed life – including acts of reparation – are considered essential for a living faith (for Catholics) or the consequence of it (for Protestants). While the integral act of penance in which the SANCTIFICATION of the penitent is enacted in all four aspects of the Catholic sacrament is still disputed by Protestants, it is safe to say that all Christian communions accept the burden of 'evangelical repentance': namely, sorrow for sin (including the resolution not to continue sinning) presupposes the theological virtue of faith, which is itself a gift of grace.

See also MORTAL SIN; SACRAMENTOLOGY.

M. J. Boda and G. T. Smith, eds., *Repentance in Christian Theology* (Liturgical Press, 2006).

D. M. Coffey, *The Sacrament of Reconciliation* (Liturgical Press, 2001).

M. Hebblethwaite and K. Donovan, S. J., *The Theology of Penance* (Clergy Book Service, 1979).

Pope John Paul II, *On Reconciliation and Penance in the Mission of the Church Today* (St Paul, 1984).

RALPH DEL COLLE

PENTECOST Originally a harvest festival celebrated on the fiftieth day after Passover (cf. Deut. 16:9–10), *Pentēcostē* ('fiftieth' in Greek) was becoming by the time of the NT a celebration of the giving of the LAW at Sinai (so, e.g., in the *Book of Jubilees* and at Qumran). Luke, additionally and especially, associates Pentecost with that initial gift of the HOLY SPIRIT from the risen Lord (Acts 1:5, 8; 2:38–9; cf. Luke 3:16–17; 24:49). This gift brought about ISRAEL's promised salvation/restoration as God's servant-witness to all nations to the 'end [*sic*] of the earth' (Acts 1:8; cf. Isa. 49:6). John also clarifies a post-resurrection gift of the Spirit to the Church, though without any specific attachment to the 'day of Pentecost' (see John 20:22–3; cf. 7:39; 14:15–17).

Acts 2 portrays Pentecost as a portentous 'theophany' of something 'like' fire and roaring wind (2:2–3; cf. Philo, *Dec.* 33; *Spec.* 2.189), and with distinctively 'Sinai' overtones. The expected 'prophet like Moses', leader of Israel, has ascended on high (to God's right hand, not Sinai) to receive a foundational gift (the Spirit rather than the law), which he then gives to his assembled, expectant, praying people (Acts 2:1–4, 33; cf. Josephus' wording on Sinai in *Ant.* 3.77–8). And as the fiery noise/voice in Philo's account transmutes into divine speech intelligible to all hearers to the extremities of the world, so in Acts 2:5–13 the miraculous tongues/languages address people from every nation under heaven as a proleptic fulfilment of the mission to follow.

For Luke, Pentecost contains both unique and paradigmatic elements. It uniquely begins Israel's restoration around 'the Twelve' (mini-Pentecosts in Acts 8 and 10 do the same for the surprising inclusion of Samaritans and Gentiles). But *all* believers are to expect the Spirit as promised by Joel (2:28–32; cf Acts 2:17–21, 33, 38–9), which in Acts is God's very own Spirit, quintessentially experienced as the 'Spirit of prophecy', granting REVELATION, charismatic WISDOM, prophetic speech, inspired doxology, and works of power. Luke predominantly portrays the Spirit as the One who directs, empowers, and confirms mission.

In the late eighteenth century, debate arose as to whether the Pentecost gift was *constitutive* of the Church, and soteriologically necessary (a traditional position), or whether it was a *donum superadditum*. J. WESLEY argued baptism in the Spirit was granted to those *already* Christian as a further distinct grace of 'entire SANCTIFICATION' and empowering. The early twentieth-century Pentecostal movements took this up but tended to narrow Luke's view of the Spirit *exclusively* to 'empowering for mission'. A quasi-parallel debate erupted in the 1940s in the wider Church, as to whether the Pentecost gift of the Spirit was given in the rite of CONFIRMATION or in BAPTISM.

In so far as appeal is made to Luke's view of Pentecost, the debates appear to hinge on false antitheses. For Luke the KINGDOM OF GOD and Israel's restoration begins with Jesus' Spirit-anointed ministry (Luke 4:16–21; 16:16); but with the 'exodus' (Luke 9:51) of Jesus in the ASCENSION, it can only continue – and intensify – through the Spirit poured out *by* the risen Lord. In accordance with Isaiah 32:15, 44:3, and Joel 2:28–32, the Spirit of prophecy he gives affords the very charisms which are *essential* to bring the self-revealing, relational, transformative, and empowering presence of God and his Christ *to* the believers; in this way, Pentecost is soteriological. But through believers it is brought to the outsider, and so is missiological as well. So Luke regards the Pentecost gift as strongly (but not inevitably) *related* to water baptism (2:38–9), yet he sees the same gift as profoundly missiologically orientated. Yet Luke does not contract the Pentecost-Spirit to some all-in-one event: he anticipates multiple 'fillings' of the same Spirit for different occasional needs and ministries.

The question of whether the Easter gift of John 20:22 is 'the Johannine Pentecost' is very finely debated. Has he theologically collapsed chronology to make it so? Or does he think there is a further, and more decisive, gift of the Spirit-Paraclete to be given beyond Jesus' complete ascension to the Father (thus bringing his position closer to that of Luke's 'Pentecost')? In any case, it is clear that for John the gift of the Paraclete is (1) a version of the 'Spirit of prophecy'; (2) soteriologically necessary in the sense that only direct immanent–relational, wisdom-giving, revelation of the Father and Son can bring the believer to what John means by 'salvation'; and (3) the means through which the believer can be made to confront 'the world'. In that respect, his chronology is theologically secondary.

Luke depicts Jesus as saying he, *himself*, will send the Spirit ('the promise of my Father' in 24:49). In his quotation of Joel at Acts 2:17, Luke adds that '*God declares* ... "I will pour out my Spirit"' and through Peter's lips interprets this to mean that Jesus 'has [received and] poured out' the Pentecostal Spirit at 2:33. Given that the Spirit was regarded as God's very own inner life and external vitality, this claim – that the Spirit of God is now also the Spirit of Jesus (cf. Acts 16:6–7) – is a justification for the 'Christomonotheism' expressed in Acts 2:34–6. The same dynamic is found in John. The ascended Jesus *sends* the Spirit from the Father, now as the ongoing presence of the Father and the Son, who will replace, continue, and interpret Jesus' ministry to and through the disciples. Once again this is the 'Spirit of prophecy', and thus both soteriological and missiological in character. In theological terms, in both Luke and John, Jesus metaphorically steps between the Father and his Spirit and thus includes himself within the one divine identity.

J. D. G. Dunn, *Baptism in the Holy Spirit* (SCM, 1970).
Jesus and the Spirit (SCM, 1975).
R. P. Menzies, *Empowered for Witness: The Spirit in Luke–Acts* (Sheffield Academic Press, 1994).
M. Turner, *Power from on High: The Spirit in Israel's Restoration and Witness in Luke–Acts* (Sheffield Academic Press, 1996).
The Holy Spirit and Spiritual Gifts (Paternoster Press, 1999).

MAX TURNER

PENTECOSTAL THEOLOGY 'Pentecostal theology' refers here to the theologies of those diverse movements and Churches that have emerged since the beginning of the twentieth century, with an emphasis on a personal experience of the HOLY SPIRIT and the exercise of spiritual gifts, including healing, prophecy, and speaking in tongues (see GLOSSOLALIA). A distinction can be made between the theology of 'classical' Pentecostal denominations that followed the Azusa Street revival of 1906–9 in Los Angeles, that of independent Pentecostal Churches of Africa and Asia that arose from about 1914 onwards, that of the charismatic movement within the older Churches from the middle of the century, and that of the newer charismatic independent Churches that have emerged globally since about 1975; but these various movements have common theological themes that are outlined here. Most Pentecostal denominations (e.g., the Assemblies of God) have an institutional headquarters that prescribes official doctrines and from time to time may modify them, but Pentecostals as a whole seldom use historical creeds.

The various expressions of Pentecostalism have one common experience and distinctive theme: a personal encounter with the Spirit of God empowering for service, often called the 'BAPTISM in the Spirit'. Pentecostals often declare that 'signs and wonders' accompany this experience, evidence of 'God with us'. Although they do not always agree on the precise formulation of their

Spirit theology, the emphasis on divine encounter and the resulting transformation is always there. Most Pentecostals believe that this Spirit baptism is normally accompanied by speaking in tongues. Classical Pentecostals are usually taught to believe in the two distinct doctrines of 'consequence' or 'initial evidence' (that speaking in tongues is the consequence, or primary evidence of Spirit baptism), and 'subsequence' (that Spirit baptism is a definite and subsequent experience to conversion). The doctrine of 'consequence' was probably first formulated by C. Parham (1873–1929), who made a theological link between tongues speaking and Spirit baptism. This was emphasized in the Azusa Street revival and has been a characteristic of American Pentecostalism ever since. The doctrine of 'subsequence' had origins in the nineteenth-century holiness movement, whose adherents thought that J. WESLEY had taught a second 'work of grace' (called 'perfect love' or 'SANCTIFICATION') subsequent to conversion. Some Pentecostals came to associate this experience with Spirit baptism, and the resulting 'holiness Pentecostalism', which stresses a post-conversion experience of sanctification as well as the experience of Spirit baptism, was the earliest form of Pentecostalism, though it represents only a minority of Pentecostals today.

The doctrines of 'consequence' and 'subsequence' have been hotly debated within Pentecostal circles. Some charismatics, while acknowledging a distinct experience of Spirit baptism, deny that speaking in tongues is the necessary evidence of this experience. Others see Spirit baptism as an initiatory experience that is part of (or the final stage of) the conversion process and maintain that gifts of the Spirit (including tongues) are given to all believers. Still others (especially Catholic charismatics) see Spirit baptism in sacramental terms, as a release of the Spirit already given in baptism. This view seeks to be more accommodating to the theological positions of older Church traditions.

Pentecostals read the Bible to find something that can be experienced as relevant to felt needs. Most Pentecostals rely on an experiential understanding of SCRIPTURE and believe in spiritual illumination: the immediacy of the Holy Spirit, who makes the Bible 'alive' and therefore different from any other book. They assign multiple meanings to biblical texts, with preachers often identifying a 'deeper significance' that can only be perceived by the help of the Spirit. In much Pentecostal preaching, narrative, illustration, and testimony dominate the sermon content rather than theory. Despite a tendency to literalism, Pentecostalism cannot be equated with FUNDAMENTALISM, because preachers constantly interplay Scripture with contemporary life and present the text as a reflection of common experience. Because Pentecostals believe that the Bible has direct relevance to life experience, they take it as it is and look for points of contact with real-life situations. They focus on divine intervention in these daily-life situations by emphasizing miraculous and unusual happenings in personal and communal experience. This experiential interpretation of the Bible as it is prayed, sung, danced, prophesied and preached in the worship implies an understanding of the Bible from the underside of society, where ordinary people interpret the Bible from the perspective of their own experiences and struggles. The Bible is believed to contain answers for 'this-worldly' needs: a sourcebook of miraculous answers to human need as well as confirmation of the reality of 'supernatural' experience. The strength of Pentecostal hermeneutics lies in the serious role it gives both biblical text and human experience, as Pentecostals tell personal stories of healing, deliverance from evil powers, the restoration of broken marriages, success in business ventures, and other needs met through miraculous intervention of God through the Spirit.

The style of 'freedom in the Spirit' that characterizes Pentecostalism all over the world has undoubtedly contributed to the appeal of these movements and has influenced the wider Christian Church irrevocably. A spontaneous liturgy that is mainly oral and narrative carries an emphasis on a direct experience of God through the Spirit. It results in the possibility of ordinary people being lifted out of mundane daily chores into a new realm of ecstasy. This is aided by the emphases on speaking in tongues, accompanied by loud and emotional prayer, joyful singing, clapping, raising hands, and dancing in the presence of God. These practices made Pentecostal worship more easily assimilated into a variety of cultural contexts, especially where a sense of divine immediacy is taken for granted; moreover, these liturgies contrasted sharply with the rationalistic, written, clergy-centred liturgies that were the main feature of most competing forms of Christianity. Indeed, the involvement of women and the laity became one of the most characteristic features of Pentecostal worship, contrasting with the dominant role played by the male priest or minister in the older Churches.

Classical Pentecostal eschatology is also predominantly premillennial, and belief in the imminent return of Christ overshadowed and motivated all early missionary activities (see PREMILLENIALISM). This tended to make Pentecostals poor strategists and little prepared for the rigours of living in different continents and cultures. It was believed that the new Pentecostal movement was the 'Latter Rain': the outpouring of the Spirit in the 'Last Days' prophesied to precede the second coming of Christ. One consequence of this belief in the imminence of the end was that there was little time for matters of social concern, as it was more important to 'save souls'. At the same time, the this-worldly emphasis of Pentecostal preaching and worship tended to blur the distinction and tension in ESCHATOLOGY between the 'already' and the 'not yet'. Because the promise of the Spirit was not only the fulfilment of prophecy and the sign of the 'last days', but also the tangible evidence that the 'last days' had already come, the eschatological benefits of healing, deliverance, and prosperity were now available for the poor and the oppressed.

In the second half of the twentieth century, the 'Positive Confession' or 'Word of Faith' movement surfaced in independent Pentecostalism in the USA, stimulated by healing evangelists and the charismatic movement; it is now a prominent teaching of Pentecostal and charismatic Churches all over the world (see Prosperity Gospel). This is a form of 'realized eschatology', supported by selective Bible quotations, in which it is believed that every believer should be physically healthy and materially prosperous and successful. This teaching emphasizes the importance of the 'word of faith': a positive confession of one's faith in healing and prosperity, despite the circumstances or symptoms. Among its questionable features is the belief that human faith may become a condition for divine action and that the strength of faith can be measured by results. Material and financial prosperity and health are sometimes seen as evidence of spirituality, while the role of persecution and suffering in discipleship is often ignored. While the Bible is not entirely silent on the question of material need – including the ideas that Christ's salvation is holistic, makes provision for all human need, and involves the enjoyment of God *and* God's gifts – nowhere in the Bible is faith related to the satisfaction of those needs as an irreversible law of cause and effect.

Pentecostals believe that the preaching of the Word in evangelism should be accompanied by 'signs and wonders', and that divine healing in particular is an indispensable part of their evangelistic strategy. In many cultures, where the religious specialist or 'person of God' has power to heal the sick and ward off evil spirits and sorcery, Pentecostalism's offer of healing has been one of its major attractions. In these cultures, people see Pentecostalism as a powerful religion that meets human needs. The numerous healings reported by Pentecostal missionaries and evangelists confirmed that God's Word was true. God's power was evidently on their ministries, with the result that many people were persuaded to leave their old beliefs and become Christians. Early Pentecostals stressed that healing was part of the provision of Christ in his atonement, following a theme that had emerged in the holiness movement. Pentecostals believe that the power of performing miracles reported in the NT has been restored in the present day to draw unbelievers to Christ. Though the importance of healing in Christian ministry is often directly proportional to the unavailability of medical resources, for people who believe themselves to have been healed, the gospel remains a potent remedy for their frequent experiences of affliction. Pentecostals have in this way responded to what they experienced as a void left by rationalistic forms of Christianity that had unwittingly initiated what amounted to the destruction of ancient spiritual values. Unfortunately, this message of power has in some cases become an occasion for the exploitation of people who are at their weakest.

Deliverance from demons or exorcism has always been a prominent part of Pentecostal praxis and exhibits a wide variety of procedures. Most Pentecostals believe in a personal Devil (Satan) and his messengers (known as demons or evil spirits). The reality of this dark spirit world and the need for liberation from it is particularly pertinent where unseen forces of evil are believed to be prevalent. Exorcism, or, as it is better known in Pentecostalism, 'deliverance', is regarded as a continuation of the NT tradition and is a feature of the ministry of healing evangelists, as well as of those regarded as having a special gift of 'deliverance ministry'. There are, however, differences among Pentecostals about what constitutes 'demonization'. Some believe that every mishap and illness is the work of Satan or evil spirits, while others attribute only certain types of mental illness to Satan. Another commonly held practice related to exorcism is 'spiritual warfare', an intense prayer activity where it is believed (on the basis of Eph. 6:12 and similar texts) that believers actively engage and resist the 'spiritual forces of wickedness' that take control of individuals, communities, cities, and nations. The emphasis on healing and deliverance from evil remains the main attraction of Pentecostalism in the developing world.

In other areas of theology, Pentecostals follow other Christian traditions closely, although a branch known as 'Oneness Pentecostalism' teaches a type of Sabellian Unitarianism, in which the Trinity is denied and the deity of the Godhead merged into one (see Modalism). There are Arminian and Reformed Pentecostals, Pentecostal sacramentalists, and radical orthodox Pentecostals (see Arminianism; Radical Orthodoxy; Reformed Theology). Pentecostal theology is diffuse, and this outline can only draw attention to its most significant points of distinctiveness.

A. Anderson, *Introduction to Pentecostalism: Global Charismatic Christianity* (Cambridge University Press, 2004).

M. Cartledge, *Encountering the Spirit: The Charismatic Tradition* (Darton, Longman and Todd, 2006).

D. W. Faupel, *The Everlasting Gospel: The Significance of Eschatology in the Development of Pentecostal Thought* (Sheffield Academic Press, 1996).

W. J. Hollenweger, *Pentecostalism: Origins and Developments Worldwide* (Hendrickson Publishers, 1997).

H. I. Lederle, *Treasures Old and New: Interpretations of 'Spirit-Baptism' in the Charismatic Renewal Movement* (Hendrickson Publishers, 1988).

F. Macchia, *Baptized in the Spirit: A Global Pentecostal Theology* (Zondervan, 2005).

Allan Heaton Anderson

PERFECTIONISM 'Perfectionism' is striving after 'perfection', understood as a return to the original image of God (Gen. 1:26–7), or freedom from SIN, or an escape from the material world and mystical union with God, or participation in the divine nature by self-denial or ASCETICISM. Christian concepts of perfectionism grow out of several biblical commands and injunctions. These include Leviticus 19:2: 'Say to the congregation of the people of Israel, You shall be holy; for I the LORD your God am holy'. YHWH (see TETRAGRAMMATON) is the source of all holiness, righteousness, and justice. God's people are called to perfection by 'walking before' their God in a right relationship with Him rather than according to any objective or external standard. 'Be perfect, therefore, as your heavenly Father is perfect' (Matt. 5:48). James presents wisdom as God's gift enabling believers to attain perfection (1:5–8) and promises that perfection will be granted to those who suffer and endure trials or persecution (1:2–4).

All types of perfectionism grow out of a reaction against the contemporary religious/moral lethargy. Most perfectionist movements ultimately lead to a more or less separate religious community apart from the main body of Christian believers. This usually results in a second 'higher' standard of life, led by individuals who have received special esoteric knowledge (*gnosis*) or enlightenment that functions as the superior norm or higher morality. Typically, perfectionist spirituality is ranked in a hierarchical fashion, with those who are said to have attained perfection placed at the top (e.g., the medieval Albigenses).

H. K. LaRondelle (b. 1929) identifies different types of perfectionist impulse. These include APOCALYPTIC perfectionism (MONTANISM, JOACHIM OF FIORE), moralistic–ascetic perfectionism (PELAGIANISM), ecclesiological perfectionism (DONATISM), Neoplatonic–ascetic perfectionism (ORIGEN OF ALEXANDRIA), monastic–contemplative perfectionism, and ethico-philosophical perfectionism (Wesleyan Methodism). There are also other motivations for perfectionism, including the overwhelming desire for greater knowledge of God and of self. For example, T. AQUINAS argued that human reason, coupled with LOVE, leads to the highest perfection attainable in the mortal state.

Modern Christian perfectionism is centred in J. WESLEY and his descendants, the Methodist Churches and the holiness and Pentecostal movements. Wesley's contribution to these groups came from his urging that Christians seek a second work of grace involving 'entire SANCTIFICATION'. This would be attained the moment a Christian, having progressed in holiness, became completely devoid of self-interest, in line with Wesley's principle, 'Gain all you can, save all you can, and give all you can' ('Use').

The dark side of perfectionism can be seen throughout history in that perfectionists have clung to a method for obtaining the perfect life, often to the extent that the method itself is confused with perfection. Eventually, such perfectionism tended to become ossified into a mere method or code that impales adherents on its sharp demanding thrusts.

See also DEIFICATION; METHODIST THEOLOGY; PENTECOSTAL THEOLOGY.

S. M. Burgess, *Reaching Beyond: Chapters in the History of Perfectionism* (Hendrickson Publishers, 1986).

H. K. LaRondelle, *Perfection and Perfectionism* (Andrews University Press, 1971).

STANLEY M. BURGESS

PERICHORESIS 'Perichoresis' is the English transliteration of a Greek term referring to the co-inherence or mutual interpenetration (Latin *circumincessio*) of the Persons of the TRINITY. The scriptural starting point for the notion lies in the language of the Johannine Jesus: 'I am in the Father and the Father is in me' (John 14:11; cf. 10:30, 38; 17:21).

Christian thinkers of the fourth century wrote of the Father and the Son being in one another, and the HOLY SPIRIT in both, and of the Trinitarian persons 'containing' one another, but this set of claims was not in fact termed 'perichoresis' for several hundred years. The word itself, which comes from the prefix *peri* ('around') and the verb *chōreō* ('to go' or 'to contain') was first used in CHRISTOLOGY, to describe the relationship of the two natures in Christ (or more particularly the penetration of the human nature by the divine). It was transferred into a Trinitarian context by an anonymous eighth-century thinker known as the pseudo-Cyril, and then taken up by JOHN OF DAMASCUS (*EOF* 1.8, 14).

Recent Trinitarian thinkers, especially those drawn towards social analogies to the Trinity, have laid considerable emphasis on the concept of perichoresis. In many cases there is a tendency for the underlying metaphors to shift from the spatial to the psychological and emotional, so that perichoresis is imagined as a peculiarly intense LOVE, empathy, or interpersonal closeness. In others perichoresis is used in a way that it was not by the fathers: as a means of characterizing God's oneness which is *in contrast with* the affirmation of a single divine *ousia* or substance.

See also ABBA; HYPOSTASIS.

G. L. Prestige, *God in Patristic Thought* (SPCK, 1959).

KAREN KILBY

PERSEVERANCE An important concept for REFORMED THEOLOGY in particular, 'perseverance' refers to the belief that the SAINTS, by virtue of the irrevocable character of God's eternal decree of ELECTION (Rom. 11:29; Rev. 13:8), cannot fall away completely from FAITH. This perseverance of the saints was one of the central points of DOCTRINE defined at the Reformed Synod of DORT (I.11), where it was defended as a necessary consequence of God's UNCONDITIONAL ELECTION of a definite number of people to salvation (I.7, 9–10). The doctrine does not mean that the elect do not commit SIN, but because God has already claimed them as children by ADOPTION, their sin does not sever them from God's LOVE, which is sealed in them by the power of the HOLY SPIRIT and thus invariably turns them to REPENTANCE and renewed faith.

Objections to the doctrine centre on the pastoral worry that it leads to presumption by failing to take with sufficient seriousness human responsibility for life with God. Thus, for example, the Arminians condemned at Dort argued that, while God protects Christians from all external assaults on their faith, the integrity of created human agency implies that they can nevertheless apostatize by their own will (see ARMINIANISM). The Reformed countered that perseverance is not inimical to human agency, both because the salvation to which the elect have been called includes works of SANCTIFICATION, and, still more fundamentally, because the immutability that guarantees perseverance belongs to the divine rather than the human will, which is in no way deactivated and remains throughout life subject to variation and change.

IAN A. MCFARLAND

PERSON: see HYPOSTASIS.

PERSONALISM Personalism is a philosophical movement most prevalent in continental Europe. Nevertheless proponents of personalism, both historical and contemporary, can be found in the USA and the UK. Early personalism appears towards the end of the eighteenth century in the works of F. Jacobi (1743–1819), F. Schelling (1775–1854), and F. SCHLEIERMACHER. In opposition to German IDEALISM, PANTHEISM, and ATHEISM, early personalism asserts the moral freedom of humans as communities of persons and leans towards a Christian concept of God.

The term 'person' has varied meaning and usage in different forms of personalism; in addition, there are a number of philosophies and theologies that express central tenets of personalism without using that specific terminology. In essence, personalism is a form of HUMANISM that need not be secular. It maintains that human persons have intrinsic value, that they exist and develop as subjects and objects in relationships with other persons, and that they have FREE WILL and are self-determining. In some versions of personalism, these principles are co-ordinated with belief in the existence of the SOUL as an ontological feature of human personhood, and in a personal divinity.

Two prominent scholars of personalism come to the fore in the twentieth century: B. Bowne (1847–1910) and E. Mounier (1905–50). Methodist theologian Bowne, from Boston University, focused on the concept of the person as an antidote to philosophical MATERIALISM, in which the category of person (whether applied to human beings or to God) had little place. Instead, Bowne sought to interpret reality from the standpoint of a person with a soul in relationship with a personal God. Mounier, who trained in and taught philosophy in France, referred to personalism as the philosophical antithesis of western individualism, with its promotion of isolated and defensive selves. Reacting against liberal bourgeois capitalism, established Catholicism, and Marxist collectivism, he asserted that the fundamental nature of persons is reflected in communication with others rather than separation from them. According to Mounier the spiritual value of embodied persons is central, and he was correspondingly critical of institutional Christianity for its connection with bourgeois individualism and private spirituality. In response to what he saw as a spiritual crisis in 1930s France, he founded the journal *L'Esprit* as a forum for discussion on responsible spiritual living. Though he was concerned with social justice rather than divine justice, his emphasis on relationality and spirituality as constitutive of human personhood is compatible with Christian THEOLOGICAL ANTHROPOLOGY.

Although personalism has never received wide acclaim in analytical philosophy, it has continued to develop in diverse locations. The Jewish philosopher M. Buber (1878–1965) wrote what remains perhaps the most widely read work of dialogical personalism, *I and Thou* (1923). The principal exponent of a personalist theory in the UK was J. Macmurray (1891–1976), whose Gifford lectures, published as *The Form of the Personal* (1957–61), remain influential. Other notable personalists include J. Oman (1860–1939), M. Blondel (1861–1949), M. Scheler (1874–1928), J. Maritain (1882–1973), G. Marcel (1889–1973), M. L. KING, Jr, and Pope John Paul II (r. 1978–2005).

B. P. Bowne, *Personalism* (Houghton Mifflin, 1908).
E. Mounier, *Personalism* (Routledge, 1952).

ESTHER MCINTOSH

PHENOMENOLOGY Phenomenology is a philosophical movement founded by E. Husserl (1859–1938) which aspires to construct a 'rigorous science' rooted in an examination of consciousness. Its significance is inseparable from its context: Husserl and his collaborators wrote in the aftermath of World War I, during which Europe was transformed by crises in industrial capitalism and faced with the rise of totalitarianisms of the left and right. Husserl, a mathematician by training, was aware that the mathematization of nature accomplished by natural science unleashed the enormous intellectual and technological power of modernity. But this very success, by eclipsing other functions of rationality, contributed to the betrayal of the ENLIGHTENMENT's great optimism regarding the possibility of justice, freedom, and continually unfolding understanding of nature and society. Although there are powerful methodological reasons for the reduction of phenomena to mathematical expression, this mathematization of reality expels much of what is most distinctively human from rigorous investigation: ethics, aesthetics, RELIGION, politics, and social analysis. The enormous complexity of consciousness becomes invisible and society is left with fewer resources to defend itself against the propaganda and ideology practised by all forms of twentieth-century totalitarianism. Phenomenology and the waves of continental philosophy indebted to it are preoccupied with defending concretely existing beings against their erasure by any form of totality: political, epistemological, social, or ethical.

Husserl's phenomenological method begins when, inspired by the lectures of F. Brentano (1838–1917), he turned from mathematics to an examination of the structures of consciousness. This analysis was a continual beginning and each of his works maps the territory a little differently. In the *Cartesian Meditations* (1931), Husserl argued that Descartes erred in his radical doubt by moving too quickly from doubt to the reification of an 'I' over against the world. It would be more correct to say not 'I think therefore I am', but 'There is thinking'. Husserl argued that examination of consciousness does not produce a subject–object dichotomy. In contrast to modernism's mind/BODY dualism, he described consciousness as constituted by a subject (noema), an object (noematic), and a mode of awareness (noesis). Consciousness is not an independent subject accidentally related to an object of sense data. Rather, consciousness is always already embedded in a world constituted by meanings and intersubjective connections. This unity of consciousness with the world it inhabits breaks down the dualisms of subject and object, of realism and idealism, and of fact and value characteristic of much modern epistemology.

Husserl was committed to an approach that allowed phenomena to shape the ways in which they were investigated, rather than being forced into conformity with a predetermined theory: '*zu Sachen selbst*' (to the things themselves) was his motto. One aspect of this was the bracketing of the 'natural attitude'. This is a temporary suspension or bracketing of the habit of attributing reality to objects of consciousness, thereby allowing phenomena to come forth according to the distinctive way they are given to consciousness rather than in terms of a pre-existing assumption about what they can or cannot be. For example, rather than saying that Ulysses is not 'real' because he was not a historical figure, a phenomenologist would examine consciousness to discover what *kind* of awareness came forth in consciousness of Ulysses. In this way the distinctive awareness appropriate to literature or mythology would be permitted to emerge. Husserl argued that phenomenology, precisely by attending to the distinctive ways in which the objects of consciousness are manifest, was a rigorous science (*Wissenschaft*). Rather than subjecting phenomena to Procrustean theoretical determinations, rationality should be carefully disciplined to become attuned to the various ways in which concrete phenomena exist and interact.

Although Husserl's rigorous investigation of consciousness found few direct followers, his attention to 'the things themselves' continued in the work of a wide assortment of philosophers. J.-P. Sartre (1905–80) and M. Heidegger (1889–1976) took up the question of existence, and thus an existential phenomenology was born. E. Stein (1891–1942) and M. Scheler (1874–1928) provided accounts of the dynamics of sympathy and compassion. M. Merleau-Ponty (1908–61) applied the method to an exploration of embodiment, which I. M. Young (1949–2006) refined in her investigations of female embodiment. The FRANKFURT SCHOOL used their training to examine the intersection of social and political structures, while H. Arendt (1906–75) interrogated the structures and logic of totalitarianism and its assault on ethics. G. Marcel (1889–1973) and K. Jaspers (1883–1969) explored the structures of intersubjectivity with great subtlety and also displayed acumen and moral passion in their analysis of the disasters that befell Europe in the middle of the twentieth century; and H.-G. Gadamer (1900–2002) turned in the direction of HERMENEUTICS. E. Levinas (1906–95) criticized certain features of phenomenology, but his own exposure of the 'face' as the foundation of ethics and reason is based in this method.

Phenomenology also proved a powerful instrument in the hands of a number of twentieth-century theologians. Used in the context of a contemporary APOLOGETICS, it interpreted the subject matter of religion to be irreducible either to institutions of authority or to self-enclosed 'language games'. As AUGUSTINE deployed PLATONISM and T. AQUINAS radicalized theology through his dialogue with ARISTOTELIANISM, a number of theologians have employed techniques of phenomenology to articulate Christianity in the contemporary situation. As a way of providing nuanced and multi-dimensional analysis of the human condition, phenomenology gave theologians a way of defending the relevance of Christian DOCTRINE. SIN and redemption, for example, are not accidents of a particular community's discourse but insightful ways of interpreting and responding to subjective, intersubjective, and social distortions of the human condition. R. BULTMANN used existential philosophy to 'demythologize' SCRIPTURE and recover its existential power. P. TILLICH and K. RAHNER are among those who are indebted to phenomenology for THEOLOGICAL ANTHROPOLOGY and for their method of describing the theocentric quality of human spirit.

Before and after World War II, phenomenology's chief architects dedicated themselves to a model that integrated ethics with rationality, and which remained open to the plurality of ways reality is manifest. They tried to find a way to avoid the epistemological and political logic of totality, which flattens out the uniqueness of particularity and the vibrancy of plurality.

Phenomenology also provided a way to think beyond the dichotomy of individualism and collectivism to expose ways in which individuals are constituted by intersubjective and social relations but possess an inherent dignity irreducible to larger totalities. The synthetic habit of mind that underlies phenomenological analysis represents an attempt to heal a major lacuna in modern thought by integrating ethical reflection into rationality itself. Its attention to concrete existence restores the significance of particularity for philosophy and theology. Phenomenology thus represents a critique of modernism by insisting on ethics as the foundation of rationality rather than a merely subjective epiphenomenon.

These impulses towards synthesis and concreteness highlight plurality as the natural and desirable condition of existence and thought, leading the way towards the greater appreciation of the distinctive ways in which women, persons of colour, people of various ethnicities, and so on experience the world and perform religion. The discipline of phenomenological thinking invites its practitioners to minimize the impulse to dominate the objects of thought or subject them to the contortions of theory. In this way, it can be understood as a kind of spiritual practice in which room is made for the 'other', both epistemologically and ethically. These ethical, political, and interdisciplinary attitudes in continental philosophy prepared the way for postmodern analysis in the later decades of the twentieth century (see POSTMODERNISM).

E. Husserl, *The Crisis of European Sciences and Transcendental Phenomenology* (Northwestern University Press, 1970 [1954]).

The Essential Husserl: Basic Writings in Transcendental Phenomenology, ed. D. Welton (Indiana University Press, 1999).

D. Moran, *Introduction to Phenomenology* (Routledge, 2000).

R. Sokolowski, *Introduction to Phenomenology* (Cambridge University Press, 2000).

H. Spiegelberg, *The Phenomenological Movement: A Historical Introduction* (M. Nijhoff, 1960).

WENDY FARLEY

PHILOKALIA Meaning 'love of the beautiful', the *Philokalia* is a collection of spiritual writings from the Orthodox tradition, originally assembled in the eighteenth century at Mt ATHOS by Bishop M. Notaras of Corinth (1731–1805) and Nikodimos of the Holy Mountain (1749–1809), and published in Venice in 1782. Though the collection had little immediate impact in Greek circles, a Slavonic translation (the *Dobrotolyubiye*) published in Moscow in 1793 proved extraordinarily influential on nineteenth-century Russian spirituality, as did the Russian translation of 1877 made by Theophan the Recluse (1815–94), which abridged some of the original texts but added a great many more, resulting in a collection much longer than the original. In the twentieth century an even more greatly expanded version (running to twelve volumes) in Romanian was completed by D. STĂNILOAE.

The aim of the *Philokalia* was to provide guidance in the discipline of PRAYER to the end of union with God (see DEIFICATION). Its compilers were traditionalists, deeply committed to patristic theology and the monastic traditions of HESYCHASM in the face of increasing western influence on Greek culture, and the texts they selected were largely drawn from the writings of Orthodox monks who lived between the fourth and the fifteenth centuries. The full original title of the work, the *Philokalia of the Holy Neptic Fathers*, reflects these monastic commitments ('neptic' refers to the capacity for vigilance of the mind associated with eastern MONASTICISM in general and hesychasm in particular).

Philokalia is also the title of a collection of writings from ORIGEN compiled in the fourth century by Gregory of Nazianzus and Basil of Caesarea (see CAPPADOCIAN FATHERS), which includes important fragments of the third and fourth books of *On First Principles*.

IAN A. MCFARLAND

PHILOSOPHICAL THEOLOGY The phrase 'philosophical theology' first came into prominence as the designation of an academic discipline with F. SCHLEIERMACHER, who in his *Brief Outline of Theology as a Field of Study* (1830) divides theology into HISTORICAL THEOLOGY, philosophical theology, and PRACTICAL THEOLOGY. On his view, philosophical theology has the normative role of defining the essence of Christianity in relation to other religions (APOLOGETICS) on the one hand, and internal deviations in belief (polemics) on the other. As such, it is the root of theology, but it does not include dogmatics (the systematic definition of DOCTRINE), which belongs to historical theology. This lack of an explicitly dogmatic component in Schleiermacher's definition of philosophical theology explains how the discipline can sometimes become almost synonymous with 'natural theology', as in F. R. Tennant's (1866–1957) classic *Philosophical Theology* (1928). While Schleiermacher's view is still remembered, philosophical theology is nowadays conceived differently, namely as the discipline that applies philosophical methods and tools to theological questions.

Philosophical theology in its contemporary sense is a branch of the philosophy of religion, and became important only in the 1970s. During the major part of the twentieth century, the philosophical climate in the English-speaking world was unfavourable for the philosophy of religion, both because analytical philosophy was predominantly atheistic, and because the influence of logical positivism made it difficult to account for the meaning of religious language. The 1960s and 1970s saw both the decline of logical positivism and a resurgence of interest in religious epistemology, especially in arguments for the existence of God and the related question of the rationality of religious belief (see COSMOLOGICAL ARGUMENT; MORAL ARGUMENT; ONTOLOGICAL ARGUMENT; TELEOLOGICAL ARGUMENT). In the 1970s and 1980s, the scope of the philosophy of religion widened. Philosophers started to apply the methods of philosophical analysis developed earlier in the century to conceptual issues in the doctrine of God. This development was prompted by considerations within religious epistemology. It became increasingly clear that one is only able to enquire whether God exists when one has a meaningful and coherent concept of God. The kind of coherent concept of God that lends itself to philosophical analysis, however, was not provided by contemporary dogmatics. The academic study of dogmatics had increasingly moved away from the development and defence of traditional Christian belief in God, and moved towards a rearticulation of faith in terms of existentialism and other continental forms of philosophy. The views of God that were thus developed lacked the distinctiveness and clarity that analytical philosophers needed in order to be able to assess whether it is rational to believe that God exists. Consequently, philosophers of religion decided to develop such a concept of God themselves, drawing on both ancient and medieval theological traditions, as well as on the tools developed in twentieth-century analytic philosophy. The first ventures in this direction were a sign of the rising self-consciousness of philosophers of religion as a result of the renaissance of religious epistemology. 'Philosophical theology' was the name by which the project became known.

Initially, philosophical theology devoted itself to the doctrine of God and to the divine attributes. One of the first landmarks in contemporary philosophical theology was *The Coherence of Theism* (1977) by R. Swinburne (b. 1934). The title clearly indicates the subject of the emerging new discipline: the belief in the one God which Jews, Christians, and Muslims have in common. In the initial stage of philosophical theology, topics included the concept of God, the coherence of the doctrine of God, and the individual attributes of God: eternity and God's relationship to time; omnipresence and God's relationship to space; omnipotence, omniscience, and human free will; simplicity; impassibility; and love. Among the leading scholars were V. Brümmer (b. 1932), S. T. Davis (b. 1940), Paul Helm (b. 1940), A. Kenny (b. 1931), A. Plantinga (b. 1932), K. Ward (b. 1938), and N. Wolterstorff (b. 1932). Leading journals were *Religious Studies* and, from 1983 onwards, *Faith and Philosophy*. In the mid-1980s the scope of philosophical theology started to widen, and from then on important new work was also done, e.g., on the doctrine of the ATONEMENT, INCARNATION and CHRISTOLOGY, the doctrine of the TRINITY, SANCTIFICATION, REVELATION, and so on. From the very beginnings both the doctrine of God and the other issues under discussion were continually related to the problem of evil and the question of THEODICY, and thus it might be claimed that philosophical theology has had three main foci: God, evil, and humanity. Generally, philosophical theologians align themselves with Christian ORTHODOXY, but there are important exceptions: (1) several atheists and agnostics critically contributed to philosophical theology (e.g., A. Kenny); (2) C. Hartshorne (1897–2000) and other process theologians have exerted considerable influence within philosophical theology (see PROCESS THEOLOGY); (3) D. Z. Phillips (1934–2006) untiringly contributed to philosophical theology from a Wittgensteinian, non-realist angle, and thus became an important and cherished sparring partner for many of his colleagues; (4) Jewish philosophers like J. (Y.) Gellman (b. 1940) have made notable contributions to philosophical theology.

Thus, theological issues became in a novel way a focus of philosophical research. The received view of the distinction between theology and philosophy – that theology has revelation as its source, philosophy reason – was rejected. On the received view, philosophers might either criticize religion, as L. FEUERBACH, K. Marx (1818–83), F. NIETZSCHE, and S. Freud (1856–1939) have done, or think constructively about it, as proponents of natural theology have done. Natural theology, however, is characterized by a restriction on its premises. Sense experience and scientific knowledge are admissible, but religious experience and revelation are not, because these are less generally accepted and less 'objective'. From its premises, natural theology argues to the existence and, to a certain extent, the nature of God. Philosophical theology lifts this restriction and admits doctrinal propositions that are not demonstrable apart from revelation as premises. Its premises characteristically take the form of assumptions, as follows: 'Assuming – for the sake of analysis – that God is impassible in the sense asserted by Christian orthodoxy, what does this imply for our understanding of the nature of God and of God's attributes such as mercy and love? How is it possible for an impassible God to become incarnate and to suffer? What view of 'passion' is presupposed in the doctrine of divine impassibility?' In this way, the 'logic' or 'grammar' of faith is analyzed: doctrinal propositions are tested, their presuppositions uncovered, their implications developed, their coherence (or lack of coherence) with other such propositions analyzed, etc. While the philosophical theologians engaged in this type of project may *believe* their conclusions to be true, because they *believe* their premises, they characteristically do not *prove* their conclusions to be true, because they do not *prove* their premises. In principle, then, anyone can engage in philosophical theology, regardless of her religious convictions; in practice, most philosophical theologians are personally involved in the doctrinal positions they analyze.

One form of reasoning that is common to many philosophical theologians is that of perfect-being theology. Following ANSELM OF CANTERBURY's form of argument in his *Proslogion* (1077/8), they assume that God is a being none greater than which can be conceived and argue that this being must be whatever it is better to be than not to be. Thus, intuitions and arguments about goodness and perfection acquire a decisive place in philosophical theology. Critics, mostly from a Reformed background, perceive as danger that in perfect-being theology reason becomes a separate source for philosophical theology, instead of being employed to analyze positions drawn from SCRIPTURE and TRADITION.

Philosophical theologians must not only decide which type of argument is acceptable and which is not; they must also decide on the meaning of religious language. Though it is sometimes argued that religious language is only about religious experiences (J. Hick (b. 1922)), moral attitudes (R. Braithwaite (1900–90)), or linguistic rules (D. Z. Phillips), most philosophical theologians maintain that it is also about God as a reality which is external to the human subject. God talk is not merely normative or expressive but also constative: it aims to describe what is in fact the case. In this sense, it is reality-depicting (J. Soskice (b. 1951)). Philosophical theologians by and large agree in their rejection of anti-realism and espousal of realism, but they have various strategies to avoid naive realism (the position that God exists in the same way that tables and chairs exist) and to explain in what way religious language can be literal, analogical, and metaphorical (see REALISM AND ANTI-REALISM).

Though philosophical theology emerged only in the twentieth century, it builds on a long tradition, and philosophical theologians often have recourse to the Church fathers and to medieval theologians like Anselm and T. AQUINAS – to the extent that several major contemporary philosophical theologians, including N. Kretzmann (1928–98) and M. McCord Adams (b. 1943) are also renowned specialists in medieval philosophy. One of the continuing debates among philosophical theologians is between those who accept the attributes of God as they were developed against the background of the western metaphysical tradition, and those who argue that a concept of God that is immediately rooted in the Bible stands in tension with this tradition. The two views are hotly debated among North American evangelicals and Reformed theologians, with those who stress the tension between 'metaphysical' and 'biblical' positions labelling the former 'classical theism' and the latter 'OPEN THEISM'. Where classical theism defines God as timeless, simple, immutable, impassible, omniscient, and omnipotent, open theists prefer to characterize God as everlasting, true to Godself, and reliable; moreover, they deny that God is impassible, that God is omniscient with respect to the future, and that God uses divine power to determine infallibly the free acts of human beings. While classical theism remains the dominant position among Christian philosophical theologians, prominent open theists include D. Basinger (b. 1947), W. Hasker (b. 1935), C. Pinnock (b. 1937), R. Rice (b. 1944), and J. Sanders (b. 1956).

Philosophical theologians often apply theories and models from other fields, e.g., physics or psychology, to their field of study. For example, L. van den Brom (b. 1946) applies physical theories of multidimensionality to explain God's omnipresence. When philosophical theologians study topics other than the concept of God, they, similarly, often apply such theories to the classical puzzles of theology. Thus, T. Morris (b. 1952) has attempted to clarify the relation between the divine and human natures in Christ by means of the relation between the conscious and the unconscious in ordinary humans, and P. Geach (b. 1916) and P. van Inwagen (b. 1942) have attempted to explain the doctrine of the Trinity in terms of the philosophical theory of relative identity.

In the near future, the relationship between philosophical theology on the one hand and Christian SYSTEMATIC THEOLOGY and dogmatics on the other needs to be clarified and improved. Systematic theologians often ignore developments in contemporary philosophical theology. Though the influence of French existentialism within systematic theology has faded away, systematic theologians still tend to derive their philosophical input primarily from continental thought (drawing heavily on German IDEALISM, French DECONSTRUCTION, and PHENOMENOLOGY) without attending to the work of philosophical theologians. Philosophical theology, on the other hand, often operates in lamentable isolation from the various theological disciplines. Much research in philosophical theology is done by philosophers without a background in the biblical languages and biblical exegesis, the history of Christianity, Christian theology and Christian doctrine, the world religions, and practical theology. Under these circumstances a certain onesidedness is unavoidable, which is used as an excuse by theologians who do not engage with philosophical theology at all. This is unfortunate, since philosophers who engage in philosophical theology are often right in criticizing theologians for being philosophically naive and correspondingly open to philosophical critiques of religion, as well as for giving up convictions that well admit of rational defence. What is urgently needed is a generation of philosophical theologians trained both in philosophy and in theology and able to integrate elements of both in plausible syntheses.

See also ANALOGY; ATHEISM; ATTRIBUTES, DIVINE; FIDEISM; HERMENEUTICS; RELIGIOUS LANGUAGE; THEODICY.

D. Brown, *Continental Philosophy and Modern Theology* (Blackwell, 1987).

H. A. Harris and C. J. Insole, eds., *Faith and Philosophical Analysis* (Ashgate, 2005).

B. Hebblethwaite, *Philosophical Theology and Christian Doctrine* (Blackwell, 2005).
T. V. Morris, ed., *The Concept of God* (Oxford University Press, 1987).
R. Swinburne, *The Coherence of Theism*, revised edn (Oxford University Press, 1993).
G. van den Brink and M. Sarot, eds., *Understanding the Attributes of God* (Peter Lang, 1999).

Marcel Sarot

Pietism Pietism became the most important religious-renewal movement in Germany and neighbouring lands after the Reformation. It marks an emphasis on the practice of the Christian life as well as on themes of repentance, regeneration, sanctification, biblical devotion, and (to varying degrees) premillennialism. Pietists established new forms of religious association – e.g., the *collegia pietatis* or 'coventicles' – and were among the first among Protestants to organize concerted missionary efforts beyond western Europe.

Scholars generally trace the origins of Pietism in a broader sense to a crisis of piety within German Protestantism around 1600 and new forms of devotional literature. J. Arndt (1555–1621), for instance, stressed the congruence of Christian thought and practice as well as the need for daily repentance. His *True Christianity* (1605) became one of the bestselling devotional works in German Protestantism, reintroducing elements of medieval mysticism to Protestants in a Lutheran redaction (see Lutheran Theology). Though controversial, Arndt was revered by many figures in Lutheran orthodoxy, including J. Gerhard (1582–1637). In this broader sense of the term, Pietism runs parallel to cognate movements in Europe including Puritanism in England and the *nadere Reformatie* in the Netherlands; in Germany, however, it remained largely literary in character.

Pietism in the narrower sense emerged as a distinct movement in Reformed and Lutheran areas during the 1660s and 1670s with a new emphasis on reform through gathering the pious within conventicles. In the Reformed tradition, the movement is represented by the moderate T. Untereyck (1635–93) in the Lower Rhine, and the separatist J. de Labadie (1610–74) in the Netherlands (see Reformed Theology). The most influential figure, however, was the Lutheran theologian P. Spener (1635–1705) in Frankfurt am Main.

In 1670 Spener instituted the *collegia pietatis* in Frankfurt and in 1675 published the *Pia desideria*, which laid out his reform programme. In contrast to earlier ideas of reform within Lutheran orthodoxy, Spener advocated a lay encounter with the entire Bible, the exercise of the common priesthood, improvement of pastoral training, and regular conventicle meetings, based on his understanding of the early apostolic gatherings in 1 Corinthians 14. He set these within an optimistic eschatology of 'hopes for better times' and a call for a reduction in religious polemics among Protestants.

Spener saw himself as a confessional Lutheran throughout his life, recovering and extending the spirit of the Reformation. His proposals regarding devotional gatherings outside worship and the expectation of the imminent conversion of the Jews engendered some opposition. He went beyond orthodox Lutheranism in his emphasis on the common priesthood, his attenuated premillennial eschatology, and his understanding of regeneration as repeatable – a position that paved the way for later Pietist theologies of conversion.

Spener's Pietist movement remained modest and relatively uncontroversial until the late 1680s and early 1690s when a series of prominent conflicts divided Lutherans into Pietist and orthodox parties and thrust a new generation of leaders to prominence. A. H. Francke (1663–1727), a protégé of Spener, initiated Pietist gatherings in Leipzig that, to the alarm of the authorities, moved beyond academic circles to include a range of lay people. As the gatherings spread to cities across Germany, some became the site of ecstatic experiences and visions, and a series of prophets arose that inflamed tensions and caused divisions within the Pietist movement.

This 'second wave' of Pietism marked a turning point. Moderate Pietists sought to institutionalize the movement within the Lutheran Church. In Halle, Francke established schools and an orphanage, which along with printing and pharmaceutical enterprises expanded into one of the largest institutions of its kind in Europe. Francke moderated more radical aspects of Pietism, including millenarian hopes, lay claims to authority, and conventicles. He emphasized personal conversion and biblical piety and made a corps of regenerate clergy central to his reform goals. In 1706 with Danish support, Francke sent missionaries to India, often identified as the first major Protestant missionary endeavour.

Radical Pietist criticisms of the established Churches were far-reaching, and theologically they were far more heterodox than ecclesial Pietists, often advocating the authority of the inner word, an imminent 1,000-year reign of Christ, universalism, and prophecy. Some, such as J. E. Petersen (1644–1724) and her husband J. W. Petersen (1649–1727), advocated premillennialism and the universalist 'restoration of all things' (*apokatastasis pantōn*) but did not formally separate from the Lutheran Church. Others sought to return to the practices of the primitive Church and formed new communities. The Schwarzenau Brethren (known in America as Dunkers) instituted adult baptism as a communal practice within radical Pietism. Some radicals advocated celibacy and experimented with forms of monasticism, including the Ephrata cloister in Pennsylvania. Others, such as the Inspirationists, institutionalized the practice of prophecy within their communities.

Nonetheless, the lines between ecclesial and radical Pietism could often be fluid. G. Arnold (1666–1714), whose *Impartial History of the Church and Heresy* (1699/1700) marks a turning point in the writing of Church history, was a leading radical who later moderated his views and became a Lutheran minister.

Pietism declined in influence after 1740 in many areas, but it gained a strong foothold within the Württemberg territorial Church, which in 1743 explicitly endorsed lay conventicle meetings. Led by the biblical scholar and millennial thinker J. A. Bengel (1687–1752), a distinctive form of Pietism developed in Württemberg among the middle and lower classes that remained vibrant well into the twentieth century.

The Renewed Unity of the Brethren (Moravians) represents another late expression of Pietism that had enduring success. Beginning in the 1720s under the leadership of N. von Zinzendorf (1700–60), Moravians established a communitarian form of Pietism that combined elements of the Hussite *Unitas fratrum* with Spener's conventicles. Appropriating Luther's theology of the cross (see *THEOLOGIA CRUCIS*), Zinzendorf developed a piety focusing on the blood and wounds of Christ and a deeply personal 'encounter with the Saviour'. He sought to unite Christians in an ecumenical society that transcended confessional divisions. Moravians were extraordinarily dynamic as preachers and missionaries, and transmitted many Pietist ideas to Protestants beyond Germany, including J. WESLEY.

In the late eighteenth and nineteenth centuries the legacy of Pietism continued among mission societies, the emerging revival movement in Germany and Scandinavia, and neo-Pietist movements. Pietism profoundly influenced modern Protestantism through its practices of small groups, missionary activity, hymnody, biblical devotion, and revival. These reflect important shifts in ECCLESIOLOGY, eschatology, and SOTERIOLOGY, but it is important to recognize that Pietists remained theologically heterogeneous, ranging from confessional Church leaders who valued religious experience to heterodox spiritualists who rejected all organized religion. What binds them together historically is less theological consensus than desire for renewal and an opposition to worldly Christianity.

M. Brecht *et al.*, *Geschichte des Pietismus*, 4 vols. (Vandenhoeck & Ruprecht, 1993–2004).
H. Schneider, *German Radical Pietism* (Scarecrow Press, 2007).
F. E. Stoeffler, *The Rise of Evangelical Pietism* (Brill, 1965).
German Pietism during the Eighteenth Century (Brill, 1973).

JONATHAN STROM

PILGRIMAGE The practice of pilgrimage, understood as a departure from daily life on a journey in search of spiritual BLESSING, has never been obligatory for Christians (as it is for, e.g., Muslims), but it has long been a significant aspect of Christian life and devotion. Early Christians journeyed to the Holy Land to walk in the footsteps of Jesus. Irish monks wandered across continental Europe as well as around the remoter shores of the British Isles, exiling themselves from home comforts and becoming perpetual pilgrims as a form of costly witness to the Son of Man who has nowhere to lay his head (Matt. 8:20). With the development of the cult of SAINTS in the Middle Ages, Christian pilgrimage reached its zenith, with thousands travelling for many months across Europe to Rome, Santiago de Compostela, St Andrews, and other shrines associated with APOSTLES and martyrs (see MARTYRDOM). Although largely banished from Protestant countries following the REFORMATION, pilgrimage has continued to thrive among Catholic and Orthodox Christians. In Europe Marian shrines like Lourdes, Fatima, and Medugorje attract hundreds of thousands annually (see MARIOLOGY). The last twenty-five years or so have seen a significant revival of interest and participation in pilgrimage among Protestants and Catholics alike.

Pilgrimage has interested anthropologists, notably V. (1920–83) and E. Turner (b. 1921), who pioneered its modern academic study, as well as writers on spirituality and devotion, like T. MERTON, more than it has theologians. Still, in the work of J. Moltmann (b. 1926), the pilgrim motif found in the OT story of the Exodus and the journey to the Promised Land has inspired a theology of journeying where God is seen as always on the move ahead of his people. The Irish monks' attachment to perpetual pilgrimage, given theological expression in the sermons of the sixth-century Irish monk Columbanus, has been a major theme of those seeking to identify and analyze a distinctive CELTIC THEOLOGY.

Some of the most fruitful recent theological applications of the concept of pilgrimage have come from Norway where, in common with the rest of Scandinavia, there has been a marked revival of interest in both its physical and metaphorical aspects. A number of publications from the Lutheran Church of Norway's liturgical centre in Nidaros have sought to work out a practical pilgrimage theology emphasizing themes of journey towards the holy and an ecclesiology of provisionality and movement. More widely, in the context of ever lower levels of Church attendance in Europe, there is increasing interest in exploring why people are apparently happier to walk than to talk the FAITH and in discerning the marks of a pilgrim Church (see VATICAN COUNCIL II, *LG*, §§48–50). As more and more Christians express their faith in terms of an ongoing journey rather than a sudden conversion experience, a new pilgrim theology is emerging in which the road to Emmaus is a more meaningful metaphor than the road to Damascus.

C. Bartholomew and F. Hughes, eds., *Explorations in a Christian Theology of Pilgrimage* (Ashgate, 2004).
I. Bradley, *Pilgrimage – A Cultural and Spiritual Journey* (Lion Hudson, 2009).

IAN BRADLEY

PLATONISM 'Platonism' refers to the tradition of thought descended from the teaching and writing of the Greek philosopher Plato (*ca* 430–*ca* 345 BC). Historians of philosophy distinguish several periods in the long history of the development of Platonic ideas, including 'Middle Platonism', which is generally dated the first century BC to the late second century AD and 'Neoplatonism', which is associated particularly with the work of the philosopher Plotinus (*ca* 205–70) and his followers. Taken at the highest possible level of generality, the defining features of Platonic thought include a fairly sharp distinction between the changeable, material world and a changeless realm of eternal forms or ideas that instantiate the good and the true, and of which the material order is understood to be a necessarily imperfect reflection. Platonic thought in its many forms promotes practices that facilitate the turning of the SOUL (understood as ontologically connected to the realm of ideas) from captivation with the passable world of matter (including the BODY) to contemplation of and participation in the eternal realm of truth.

In the process of articulating an identity predicated on LOVE and harmony, early Christians frequently contrasted their beliefs in God to the discordant plurality of Greco-Roman religion and philosophy – but also frequently made an explicit exception for Platonism. Of course, the historical relationship between Christianity and Platonism has been fraught: some Christians have at times outspokenly opposed any hint of Platonic influence in Christian theology. Even so Christians have been quicker to acknowledge their engagements (for better or for worse) with Platonism than they have with other such philosophical schools as Stoicism or ARISTOTELIANISM. Several features of Christian interaction with Platonism can be identified down the centuries. Apologists found in Platonism a vehicle for presenting themselves to their contemporaries (see APOLOGETICS). Theologians were enabled by Platonism to articulate their convictions about non-physical reality. Mystics adapted Neoplatonic exercises of inner ascent to cultivate a profounder awareness of God. Controversialists argued from the example of Platonism about the possibility of natural (as distinct from revealed) theology.

By endorsing themes current from Platonism, Christian apologists like Justin Martyr (d. *ca* 165) were able to communicate their beliefs in an idiom familiar to cultured but potentially hostile audiences. The way forward was prepared by the Hellenistic Jewish philosopher Philo of Alexandria (*ca* 20 BC– AD 50). Like Philo, Christians found Platonic philosophy conducive to further theological reflection, which was often justified by appealing to Platonic belief in the Good as the underlying, unifying principle of reality. Indeed, 'Middle' Platonists were prepared to identify the source of reality – the 'primary mind' – more precisely as God (Alcinous, *Hand.* 10.4–6). Another aspect of Platonism that appealed to early Christians is the availability of Platonic terms for describing non-material reality. In the same passage, Alcinous derides as absurdity any attempt to conceive of deity in terms of form and matter. This claim, as well as the suggestive account in Plato's *Timaeus* of a creator god, made Platonism seem to Christians to break through problems they perceived in other ancient philosophies. Thus, in accounting for his philosophical evolution, Justin Martyr relates how, after allying himself to a Stoic, then an Aristotelian, then a Pythagorean, he had begun to despair of progress:

> In my helpless condition it occurred to me to have a meeting with the Platonists, for their fame was great. I thereupon spent as much of my time as possible with one who had lately settled in our city – a sagacious man, holding a high position among the Platonists – and I progressed, and made the greatest improvements daily. And the perception of immaterial things quite overpowered me, and the contemplation of ideas furnished my mind with wings, so that in a little while I supposed that I had become wise; and such was my stupidity, I expected forthwith to look upon God, for this is the end of Plato's philosophy (*Trypho* 2).

Justin was not alone. Other early theologians and apologists who similarly privileged Platonism include Minucius Felix (*fl.* early third century) and still later AUGUSTINE, whose spiritual journey was also facilitated by the Platonic conception of non-material reality. Platonism was emerging as the provider of a valid but limited natural theology (cf. Augustine, *City* 8.4–12), complementary to Jewish theology, that could feed into Christian theology: 'For what is Plato but Moses speaking Attic Greek?' (Clement of Alexandria, *Strom.* 1.22.342). As competence in Greek became less common in western Europe, the direct availability of Platonic texts decreased. The influence of Platonism was therefore mediated by a few key figures, such as Boethius (*ca* 480–*ca* 525), who integrated Platonic themes into his philosophical, pedagogical, and theological works.

The incorporation of pagan philosophy into Christianity was not universally welcomed. TERTULLIAN was typically strident: 'Away with all attempts to produce a mottled Christianity of Stoic, Platonic, and dialectic composition!' (*Prae.* 7). Tertullian's outspokenness was unusual, although arguments about philosophical influence in Christianity were not uncommon. In sixth-century debates, Plato's name is used to stigmatize Christian opponents (e.g., Cyril of Scythopolis, *Cyr.* 13). Significantly, those debates were conducted in monasteries during a period when MONASTICISM was being reimagined as profoundly counter-cultural and even anti-intellectual. In this context, Plato had become a cipher for the corrupting influence of Hellenistic philosophy: the beliefs associated with his name were caricatures at best. Not all monastic reactions to Platonism were so immoderate. Anastasius of Sinai (*fl. ca* 650) relates a cautionary tale about a learned Christian whose habit was to curse Plato daily until Plato appeared to him in a vision, saying, 'You are merely harming yourself . . . when Christ descended into Hell, no one believed in him sooner than I did' (*Quest.* 3). No one made more of the potential than DIONYSIUS THE AREOPAGITE, the pen-name of a Christian theologian and mystic whose writings incorporated elements from the Neoplatonic philosophers of Athens, as well as from theological writings of the CAPPADOCIAN FATHERS. Dionysius' potent synthesis was a major vehicle for Platonic thinking in Christian society.

In the seventh century Dionysius' cosmic theology was taken up by MAXIMUS THE CONFESSOR, in whose *Ambigua* there is articulated a vision of the universe, its fall, and its restoration that rests ultimately on a Platonic foundation, albeit one by this point mediated by generations of Christian reflection. Even so, Maximus' contemplative meditations on the Monad and the Dyad, on the reconciliation of opposites, and on inter-relation of beings can be profitably understood by reference to the logic of predication outlined in the Neoplatonic philosopher Porphyry's (*ca* 235–*ca* 305) *Eisagoge.* Dionysius' and Maximus' cosmological writings were major landmarks in medieval Greek theology. They also came to influence western Christianity, thanks above all to the translation of and commentary upon their works by J. Scotus Eriugena (*ca* 800–*ca* 870).

A renewed interest in Plato's writings for their own sake was characteristic of the fifteenth century. The Council of Ferrara–Florence (1438–9) brought prominent Greeks like G. Gemistos Plethon (*ca* 1355–1450) to the West. Plethon's learning was vast and his lectures on Plato were very well received, and while the union sought by the council was elusive, the encounter sowed the seeds of the Renaissance in Italy. Under the patronage of the Medici family, a 'Platonic Academy' configured itself in Florence. Conspicuous participants in the conversations of this 'academy' were G. Pico della Mirandola (1463–94) and M. Ficino (1433–99). Ficino was in many respects the Italian answer to Plethon. His interests were equally wide-ranging. Ficino translated Plato's works into Latin and on the basis of those studies prepared a treatise on the immortality of the SOUL. Looking back to Augustine's commendation of Plato, Ficino appealed to Platonic theology to show 'that in the divinity of the created mind, as in a mirror in the center of all things, we should first observe the works of the Creator, and then contemplate and worship the mind of the Creator' (*PT,* Proem 3). Ficino's lively interest in hermetic philosophy and astrology led to accusations of practising magic and his theological contributions were not generally accepted by the Church.

By contrast, Ficino's contemporary Cardinal Bessarion (1403–72) – no less noted a translator into Latin and an advocate of Platonism, especially against the imprecations of George of Trebizond – enjoyed a long career within the Church of Rome, where he took refuge after participating in the Council of Ferrara–Florence and consequently being rejected in the East. Bessarion, like Ficino, was a major contributor to the return to Greek sources that shaped early Christian HUMANISM.

Interest in Christian Platonism was widespread across Europe, as the example of the English churchman and reformer J. Colet (1467–1519) demonstrates. Colet corresponded with Ficino, translated Dionysius afresh into Latin, incorporated Neoplatonism into his writings, and was praised for his knowledge of Plato and Plotinus by D. Erasmus (1466/9–1536). The humanist recourse to antiquity characteristic of Colet and Erasmus was sometimes coupled with a high-handed disdain for the Middle Ages. By returning to Plato, some Christian theologians sought to create for themselves an alternative to the perceived excesses of medieval SCHOLASTICISM or otherwise to find a new theological voice. In the seventeenth century, B. Whichcote (1609–83) and others formed a group of Anglican theologians and churchmen who looked back to Plato as a means of steering a course around Reformed PURITANISM and the MATERIALISM of T. Hobbes (1588–1679); they were therefore called the Cambridge Platonists. W. R. Inge (1860–1954), a great admirer of the Cambridge Platonists and a scholar of Plotinus, advocated a mystical, non-coercive Christian FAITH that was informed by his profound study of Platonic spirituality and distaste for the Church of Rome. More recently still, and in a more ecumenical spirit, the Platonic tradition has fed into the writings of J. Milbank (b. 1952), C. Pickstock (b. 1970), and other proponents of RADICAL ORTHODOXY. Creative Christian recourse to Platonism shows no sign of abating.

S. Gersh, *From Iamblichus to Eriugena: An Investigation of the Prehistory and Evolution of the Pseudo-Dionysian Tradition* (Brill, 1978).

J. J. E. Gracia and T. B. Noone, eds., *Companion to Philosophy in the Middle Ages* (Blackwell, 2005).

W. R. Inge, *The Platonic Tradition in English Religious Thought* (Longmans, Green and Co., 1926).

E. von Ivanka, *Plato Christianus: Ubernahme und Umgestaltung des Platonismus durch die Väter,* 2nd edn (Johannes Verlag, 1990).

C. Pickstock, *After Writing: On the Liturgical Consummation of Philosophy* (Blackwell, 1998).

AUGUSTINE CASIDAY

PLURALISM, RELIGIOUS From the outset Christians were confronted with religious pluralism. Three interesting attitudes to this reality are discernible within the first few centuries that continue to shape most contemporary Christians. First, there was a clear emphasis on the necessity of faith in Christ for salvation, echoing John 14:6: 'I am the way, and the truth, and the life; no one comes to the Father except through me'. This faith had an ecclesial dimension, including the necessity for BAPTISM into Christ's BODY, so that membership of the Church (always assuming active FAITH and LOVE) was also required for salvation. This first emphasis meant that Christianity was a vigorous missionary religion with an explicit desire to convert all peoples. 1 Timothy 2:4 holds that God 'desires everyone to be saved and to come to the knowledge of the truth'. This missionary drive excluded no religion, although large-scale Jewish rejection of the GOSPEL was always an embarrassment in the early days and led to a strong anti-Jewish polemic.

Second, some early Christian intellectuals had learnt greatly from Greek philosophy and could not help wonder at the wisdom they had found there: truths that were consonant with REVELATION, moral exhortation of a high order, and, indeed, philosophical frameworks that allowed for the sophisticated explication of Christian revelation and for its defence against philosophical attacks. They developed three crucial theories to explain pagan wisdom: the *prisca theologia* ('ancient theology'), the *preparatio evangelica* ('preparation for the gospel'), and the *semina verbi* ('seeds of the Word'). The first held that all pagan wisdom was actually an unacknowledged borrowing from the OT – a theory of plagiarism held by some divines until the seventeenth century. The latter two theories, by contrast, argued that God provided knowledge in nature and in cultures that led people to the truth of the gospel, such that it was possible to know God and find truth, goodness, and beauty outside the Christian revelation. This position is more characteristic of most Catholic, Orthodox, and Protestant Christians. Some Reformed theologians have tended to emphasize the damage of original SIN to qualify these two ideas, or even use them to emphasize why non-Christians who have never heard the gospel might be damned: they have known truth, yet rejected it.

Third, the early Christians were faced with the question of the righteous of ISRAEL: were they lost because they were born before the time of Christ? This was unthinkable. The SAINTS of Israel had valid faith in God, for they partook of the very covenant which is the root upon which the Church is grafted (Rom. 11:11–24). Ideas of the justice of God (in tandem with passages like Acts 2:7, Rom. 10:6–7, Eph. 4:8–9; 1 Pet. 3:18–20) led to the notion that these righteous awaited the coming of Christ, who as the creed has it, 'descended into HELL', where he preached salvation to those who deserved it so that they might be saved. This scenario led to the idea of the *limbus partum* ('LIMBO of the fathers') as a kind of holding tank for the righteous who died before Christ. Clement of Alexandria (*ca* 150–*ca* 215) and others included righteous pagans in the *limbus partum*, which suggested the possibility of salvation for all persons, not just Israelites. AUGUSTINE likewise insisted on an invisible Church from the time of Abel composed of the righteous.

Together, these three attitudes run throughout Christian history, leading to three widely adopted theologoumena: the necessity of Christ and his Church for salvation; the justice of God towards the righteous before the coming of Christ; the possibility of goodness, truth, and beauty being present in pagan traditions but never in a manner equal to Christianity in kind or degree. In evaluating this background, however, it is important to recognize that it was assumed by most theologians that after the time of Christ everyone knew the gospel. Therefore, if a person was not a Christian, that implied that they had explicitly rejected the truth of God. This meant that Judaism (from the start) and Islam (from the seventh century) were both seen as heretical and/or schismatic movements. An anti-Islamic polemic arose, which was fuelled greatly by European Christianity's territorial struggles with Islam. At the same time, there were also important instances of dialogue between Christianity and Islam, including mutual hospitality and respect (in medieval Spain, for example).

It is thus possible to see how all the central dogmatic topics bear upon the question of Christian relations to other faiths: CREATION, sin, CHRISTOLOGY, the TRINITY, ECCLESIOLOGY, SALVATION HISTORY, and ESCHATOLOGY. Further sub-areas in theology are also related to this question: MISSIOLOGY, INCULTURATION, and APOLOGETICS, to name the three most important. With the onset of the European 'age of discovery' in the fifteenth century, there was a growing recognition that countless people had never heard of the gospel through no fault of their own – with the possibility that they were analogous to the righteous pagans in *limbus partum*. In this context, it was no longer feasible to rely on T. AQUINAS' speculation that, were there to be a young boy bought up by wolves (and who thus had never heard the gospel), God's justice would require that an angel would visit him, or that he would have interior revelation. The evidence was that ANGELS had not visited non-Christian peoples en masse, and that if God had granted interior revelation, the many religions had not understood it aright. The sixteenth-century Dominicans of Salamanca F. de Vitoria (*ca* 1480–1546) and D. de Soto (1494–1560) laid the seeds for later Catholic theology on this topic in two ways. De Vitoria was outraged by the behaviour of the Christian *conquistadores* and argued that, unless the gospel was presented properly, without violence, threat, or coercion both before and after its preaching, the hearers were under no obligation to accept it and must not become enslaved. De Soto argued that implicit faith in Christ would suffice for those who had never heard the gospel but who followed the natural law evident in creation and through the use of reason. This meant that the necessity of the Church for salvation was contextualized, while nevertheless still viewed as binding. This remains the official Catholic position.

An alternative solution to this new problem arose from the emerging Reformed traditions. J. Calvin, drawing on Augustine, argued for predestination and, correspondingly, rejected medieval Catholic arguments for the possibility of salvation for pagans on the basis of God's justice as undermining the necessity of faith in Christ for salvation. According to Calvin, because God had predestined those who did not know the gospel to damnation, there was no question to be answered about how they might be saved or how God's justice might be compromised.

With the emergence of European empires during this period, Catholic and (later) Protestant missionaries travelled the world. This period is complex. Some of the *conquistadores* exemplified an imperial brutality and economic hunger that is often associated with missionaries. But there are also stories of deep sacrifice and careful transformation of cultures and lives so that people enjoyed better health, education, and civic developments catalyzed by their new faith. Sometimes, these were the incentives to convert. Some missionaries, like the Jesuits F. Xavier (1506–52) and R. de Nobili (1577–1656) found much to admire from the non-Christian cultures they encountered and saw clear evidence of the operation of natural law and grace, amidst superstition and error. The Orthodox Churches did not develop a theology regarding these matters until the modern period.

It is only in the modern period that an entirely new teaching called 'pluralism' emerges. It goes radically beyond the previous three 'classical' Christian attitudes towards non-Christian religions identified at the outset. With growing knowledge of other religions and a strong historical approach to truth, the nineteenth century saw the slow emergence of a Christian theological view that held all the great religions to be both salvific and equally marred with human error and superstition. Given the dark aspects of missionary history, the shame of empire, the Holocaust, and the wars of religion that ravaged Europe in the early modern period, the emergence of pluralism is not altogether surprising. Its seeds go back to the deists and rationalists of the seventeenth and eighteenth centuries, to I. Kant, a key figure of the German Enlightenment. His philosophical position soon became deeply theologized. Kant argued that God could not be just or wise to entrust his message to the contingencies of history, for this could never be a universal communication of the truths thereby revealed. Further, the arguments for the existence of God were also defective. How can one find God? Kant's answer was through the universal sense of obligation in ethics: the categorical imperative presupposed God. Christ's Sermon on the Mount was exemplary of this universal ethical requirement. Variants of all these arguments are found in the work of contemporary pluralists like J. Hick (b. 1922), P. Knitter (b. 1939), R. Haight (b. 1936), and P. Schmidt-Leukel (b. 1954). G. W. F. Hegel's dialectical philosophy has also undergirded this approach, which maintains that truth (which is always in the future) can be found only in dialogue and dialectics between religions. Pluralism's impact on key doctrines is significant and has heralded a profound theological revisionism, but its dependence on models of truth derived from the Enlightenment raises questions for many regarding its grounding in specifically Christian theological principles.

In light of these concerns, other theologians push towards pluralism, but stop short in serious ways. Catholics like K. Rahner and J. Dupuis (1923–2004) argue that, while non-Christian religions are (respectively) 'provisionally' or 'substitutionally' salvific, the cause of salvation is always the grace of Christ and the triune God. In the wake of the publication of the encyclical *Redemptoris missio* (1990) by Pope John Paul II (r. 1978–2005), there is also considerable debate among Catholic theologians about the extent to which the Holy Spirit may be found within the world religions. There has also been debate – especially in developing countries – about the way in which liberative movements in history, which include world religions, build the kingdom of God.

A further development has been the attempt to view non-Christian religions in their own terms, as proposing different ends and means, which should be respected, so that these religions are not simply viewed as varyingly deficient forms of Christianity. The discipline of comparative theology has emerged with writers like D. Burrell (b. 1933), F. Clooney (b. 1950), K. Ward (b. 1938), and J. Fredericks (b. 1951). Here the focus is on learning and patient conversation. Questions of personal salvation in particular and the salvific efficacy of religions in general are not central. Further, some, like Fredericks, argue that a generalized theology of religions is a bogus discipline, and that what matters is the specific engagements that happen when Christianity meets a particular religion. Each encounter will generate its own unique agenda to be addressed (including problems that require solution), as Christians theologize on the particular.

Feminist theology has also made its contribution by asking whether the fixation on the salvation of others is not part of the necrophilia latent within Christian theology (G. Jantzen (1948–2006)), whether theology has failed to recognize its material contexts and interdisciplinarity (J. Hill Fletcher (b. 1969)), and whether all religions are to be interrogated regarding their stultifying patriarchy, so that no single one stands on a perch judging others (R. Ruether (b. 1936)). There has also been a spirited and powerful defence of the exclusive Christological emphasis, with A. Plantinga (b. 1932) and other Reformed theologians offering a robust defence of 'exclusivist' positions, according to which salvation requires explicit faith in Jesus. Finally, since 9/11 Islam has become increasingly important in this debate for theologians in the West.

Much of the modern debate is affected by the extent to which modernity has shaped theology. It is of course impossible to simply resort to pre-modern thinking, but the pervasive influence of pluralism is indicative of this methodological issue. There is room for both a theology of religions (which attends to general dogmatic questions and determines the parameters within which enquiry can continue) and a theology with and for specific religions (see Buddhism and Christianity; Hinduism and Christianity; Islam and Christianity; Judaism and Christianity). In this latter area, there is also a profound requirement for historians of religions and phenomenologists to work with theologians in an interdisciplinary fashion. Through these investigations Christians will also learn how to most effectively present the gospel of Jesus Christ who is good news to Jews and Gentiles, religious and non-religious people.

G. D'Costa, *The Meeting of Religions and the Trinity* (T&T Clark, 2000).

J. A. DiNoia, *The Diversity of Religions. A Christian Perspective* (Catholic University of America Press, 1992).

J. Dupuis, *Towards a Christian Theology of Religious Pluralism* (Orbis, 1997).

J. Hick, *An Interpretation of Religion* (Macmillan, 1988).

D. Strange, *The Possibility of Salvation among the Unevangelised: An Analysis of Inclusivism in Recent Evangelical Theology* (Paternoster Press, 2002).

F. Sullivan, *Salvation Outside the Church? Tracing the History of the Catholic Response* (Paulist Press, 1992).

Gavin D'Costa

Pneumatology: see Holy Spirit.

Political Theology In the most general terms, political theology is theology which relates to the social, economic, and political orders, sometimes endorsing and justifying, sometimes challenging them, and sometimes shaping them. Although political theology as a recognized branch or class of theological study dates only from the early twentieth century, the concerns and approaches characteristic of political theology have been around for a very long time.

The ancient Greek city-states, for example, each had their civic gods, and patriotism and piety were indistinguishable from one another. The city was watched over by its gods, who shared in its joys and sorrows. The cult was a celebration and affirmation of the life of the city. One who came, like Socrates, asking questions, was quickly dismissed as seditious and impious. The pious person, the good person, and the loyal citizen were all one.

As the Roman Empire grew, there came the development of a highly formal imperial cult which served the turn of a civil religion, eliciting and affirming loyalty to the divine emperor. This made few demands and was held to be compatible with most other more local expressions of religion. Those of a more rationalist cast of mind, who despised popular superstition, developed a philosophical monotheism which drew parallels between the one god in heaven and the one emperor on earth, and provided a kind of rationalist theology for the imperial cult.

Judaism, as found in the Roman Empire, did not fit easily into the accepted pattern of a religion. In the Diaspora it differed from the profusion of religions and cults in its universalistic claims. The God of Israel, though most clearly recognized in Israel, is the universal Lord of all, whether this is acknowledged or not. The OT thus has a pervasive political theology around the conviction that Yahweh is the one God who is to be honoured and obeyed. In the NT the central concern is the proclamation of the kingdom of God, in which Jesus is Lord, and the exposition of which explores central themes of politics: justice, peace, charity, and so forth.

From the conversion of Constantine I (*ca* 275–337), Christianity became the official religion of the Roman Empire, and theological reflection on politics developed within three major 'schools', all of which are still active today. For Tertullian the Church was a kind of counterculture, and Christians were called to separate themselves from the *massa perditionis* of secular society, which was rushing towards its doom. 'There is nothing more alien to us than politics', he pronounced (*Apol.* 38:3). Christians are aliens in this world, for their real citizenship is in heaven. They live by their own standards, maintaining an absolutist ethic with a tendency towards pacifism and a millenarian expectation (see Premillennialism). The modern theologies of J. Yoder (1927–97) and S. Hauerwas (b. 1940) belong to this tradition.

At the other extreme, we find the political theology of Eusebius of Caesarea (*ca* 265–340), who sought to provide a political theology in the classical mode, suitable for the new relationship between the Christian Church and the Christian empire following the conversion of Constantine. Eusebius' theology is more monotheistic than Trinitarian: the one God in heaven is reflected in the one emperor on earth, and Eusebius sees the earthly rule of the emperor as a kind of participation in the kingly omnipotence of God himself. This type of political theology is rarely championed in modern times, but it lurks behind a number of authoritarian regimes.

Between the positions of Tertullian and Eusebius there stands the towering figure of Augustine of Hippo. In the immediate aftermath of the collapse of the

Roman Empire, Augustine thought in terms of two cities, the earthly and the heavenly. The earthly city is partial and incomplete, aiming at a provisional and always relative peace and justice, arising out of the balancing of claims and interests. The city of God, in contrast, transcends the earthly city and its values and objectives. It is a community united by 'a common love of the same things' (*City* 19.24). The highest love, which is the love of God, is the love which sustains the city of God, where true justice, true peace, and true and loving relationships are to be found. Augustine's political theology sparks between the two poles of the earthly city and the city of God. He holds back resolutely from deifying any temporal order or earthly ruler – even the Church – as he strives to discern the signs of the times as clues to God's purposes and working in the present age.

The first thinker in modern times to speak of political theology as such was a conservative and nationalistic German Catholic philosopher, C. Schmitt (1888–1985), whose *Politische Theologie* (1922) argued that political ideas and theories were derived from the tradition of monotheistic theology. Schmitt joined the Nazi Party, and was attacked by E. Peterson (1890–1960) in *Der Monotheismus als politisches Problem* (1935).

In the aftermath of World War II, there emerged two further types of political theology: theologies of HOPE and LIBERATION THEOLOGY. Both arose from dialogues with Marxism. A dissident Marxist, E. Bloch (1885–1977), published his monumental *The Principle of Hope* in 1959, and this work had tremendous impact among younger theologians, most notably J. Moltmann (b. 1926), whose books *Theology of Hope* (1964) and *The Experiment Hope* (1974) had considerable influence. Meanwhile a new political theology which was rooted in engagement with the realities of the social and economic problems of Latin America, and drew substantially on Marxist insights, flourished as liberation theology, which generated a large amount of challenging theological work, from L. Boff (b. 1938), J. Míguez Bonino (b. 1924), E. Cardenal (b. 1925), A. Fierro (b. 1936), and many others. Numerous theologians who would not label themselves political theologians engage productively and seriously with parts of the agenda of political theology – issues of justice, poverty, war and peace, equality, violence, and the like.

See also PUBLIC THEOLOGY.

H. de Vries and L. Sullivan, eds., *Political Theologies: Public Religions in a Post-Secular World* (Fordham, 2006).

D. B. Forrester, *Theology and Politics* (Blackwell, 1988).

A. Kee, ed., *Reader in Political Theology* (Westminster Press, 1974).

P. Scott and W. Cavanaugh, eds., *The Blackwell Companion to Political Theology* (Blackwell, 2004).

DUNCAN B. FORRESTER

POLITY Polity refers to the formal organization and governance of the Church, both within and across individual congregations. SCRIPTURE refers to a number of leadership positions in early Christian communities, including APOSTLES, prophets, teachers, and administrators (1 Cor. 12:28), evangelists and pastors (Eph. 4:11), bishops and deacons (Phil. 1:1; cf. 1 Tim. 3:1–2, 8–13), and elders (1 Tim. 5:17; Jas. 5:14). The precise roles of these persons in their communities are hard to reconstruct, and the divisions between them may not have been clear-cut (e.g., Tit. 1:5–7 suggests that 'bishop' and 'elder' refer to the same office). In the subsequent history of the Church, the terms 'bishop', 'elder', and 'deacon' in particular have played prominent roles in defining different forms of Christian polity.

In episcopal polities governance is centred in the office of bishop (*episkopos* in Greek), who has oversight (the literal meaning of *episkopos*) of all the congregations in a particular geographical area. The idea of the 'monarchical episcopate' (e.g., one bishop for a particular region) became the dominant form of Church government in the second century and remains that of the majority of Christians (including Anglicans, Catholics, Methodists, Orthodox, and some Lutherans). The bishop represents the unity of the Church gathered by and under a single Lord (see, e.g., Ignatius, *Trall.* 2:1; cf. Eph. 4:5–6), and this symbolism leads many Churches committed to the EPISCOPACY to assign one bishop in particular some sort of primacy in the wider Church. In some cases (e.g., the pope, or bishop of Rome, among Catholics), this primacy has well-defined juridical force; in others (e.g., the archbishop of Canterbury for Anglicans), it is largely symbolic.

Presbyterian polities are a defining feature of Churches in the Reformed tradition and take the office of elder (*presbyteros* in Greek) as the basis for Church organization. Each individual congregation is governed by a Church session, or council of elders. Members of congregational sessions, in turn, are appointed to the presbytery, which represents all the Churches in a local area. Presbyteries may gather in larger aggregations known as synods, and, at a national level, representatives of synods gather periodically as a general assembly. Theologically, presbyterian organization is seen as reflecting apostolic practice (see, e.g., Acts 14:23; 20:17; 21:18; 1 Pet. 5:1–4).

Finally, congregational polities, characteristic of Congregational, Baptist, and other free-Church traditions (e.g., Mennonites), affirm the juridical and doctrinal independence of individual congregations. Governance is agreed by members in a formal agreement (or COVENANT) covering matters of DOCTRINE and Church order. Generally, provision is made for an ordained minister and a congregational council (sometimes called a board of deacons) as the local Church officers. The congregational model is rooted in the belief that the local assembly of Christians in itself realizes the fullness of the Church (Matt. 18:20), and that such assemblies are the only visible realization of the universal Church prior to the eschaton.

See also Anglican Theology; Apostolic Succession; Baptist Theology; Mennonite Theology; Methodist Theology; Papacy; Patriarchate, Ecumenical; Reformed Theology.

E. L. Long, *Patterns of Polity: Varieties of Church Governance* (Pilgrim, 2001).

Ian A. McFarland

Pope: see Papacy.

Post-Christian Theology Simply put, post-Christian theology refers to any theology undertaken by those who no longer identify themselves as Christian. That is, because of the prefix 'post', post-Christian theologians acknowledge that their theology is always in part a response to Christianity – both past and present. Their central focus is a critique concerning the possibility and limits of Christian theology in response to a post-Enlightenment and post-Christendom world. This makes post-Christian theology strongly dialectical. Post-Christianity was initially a Protestant move that, arising out of H. Heine's (1797–1856) proclamation of God's death, found its anti-Christian nihilistic expression in F. Nietzsche. Conversely, in the first half of the twentieth century, influenced by G. W. F. Hegel, S. Kierkegaard, F. Schleiermacher, and biblical criticism, a neo-orthodox response focused on the possibilities of Christian expression in a post-Christian society (see Neo-Orthodoxy).

From the 1950s, following the translation of D. Bonhoeffer's prison letters into English, the central issue became the challenge of the expression of Christian belief in a modern, secular world 'after God'. Challenged in its belief in modern progress by R. Rubenstein's (b. 1924) *After Auschwitz* (1966), from the 1970s post-Christian theology expanded into a response to nihilism, secularism, technology, and the destruction of human life experienced by modern humanity in the twentieth century. In its rejection of a modernist hope in progress and technology, there was often an attempt to recover the apocalyptic roots of Christianity. More recently, it critiques the post-secular turn and the rise of conservative Christianity.

Two groups are often mislabelled post-Christian. The first are unorthodox reformers existing within yet challenging Christianity, including, e.g., L. Geering (b. 1918), D. Cupitt (b. 1934), and J. S. Spong (b. 1931); their concern is primarily in fostering theology's engagement with Enlightenment modernity. A second group are those represented by M. Kaufman's (b. 1929) description of a 'post-Christian theism', in which both theism and theology continue after a rejection of Christianity, often with a focus on the category of spirit. By an explicit rejection of Christianity what is offered is an alternative theism, not one in critical dialectic. This could be better described as either anti- or non-Christian theism. Another important strand is post-Christian feminist thought as typified by M. Daly (b. 1928) and D. Hampson (b. 1944). They critique and reject Christian patriarchy by positioning 'God' over and against 'Christian myth'. For such feminist thinkers, Christianity is rejected as inherently patriarchal and dangerous while 'post-Christianity' acts as liberation.

There is a tendency within such post-Christianity (especially via process theology) to become panentheistic or pantheistic (see Panentheism; Pantheism). P. Teilhard de Chardin is an important (if often unacknowledged) influence in such theologies.

Post-Christian theology proper emerged from the rejection of classical Christology expressed in the death of God theology that arose in America in the 1960s, primarily in the work of T. Altizer (b. 1927), W. Hamilton (b. 1924), and P. van Buren (1924–98). They were never a unified group, and in evaluating their work distinctions must be made between theologies that reject Christianity *in toto*, those that reject classical Christology and turn to a rethought historical Jesus, and those which reject the historical Jesus as unrecoverable and turn to either a totally kenotic immanent Son or Word or a new age of the Spirit. Much of this radical theology became forms of mythopoetic *gnosis* influenced by W. Blake (1757–1827) and M. Eliade (1907–86).

While death of God theology was a short-lived phenomenon, a continuing and different type of post-Christian theology arose out of the work of G. Vahanian (b. 1927): theology within a secular framework and society, often in conversation with continental and postmodern philosophy. While J. Caputo (b. 1940) is associated with one school that expressed an American secular theology highly influenced by J. Derrida (1930–2004), M. C. Taylor (b. 1945) leads a distinctively American engagement of post-Christian theology and cultural analysis that is increasingly focused on a response to technology. In recent decades a different form of post-Christian theology has emerged, primarily from a continental European perspective. This post-Christian European secular theology, influenced by the neo-Marxist critical theory of the Frankfurt School, engages with Christianity as a political, literary, and cultural text. Symbolized in the 1960s by E. Bloch (1885–1977), in more recent years it has been expressed by neo-Marxist thinkers such as G. Agamben (b. 1942), A. Badiou (b. 1937), and S. Zizek (b. 1949), who recover theology as the critique of religion.

G. Vattimo (b. 1936) provides a link between the neo-Marxist and the secular theologians. Offering a 'weak theology' expressed as a form of hermeneutics, Vattimo reformulates theology as a philosophy of response within a secular, late modernity against the expressions of more traditional, institutional 'strong' theology and piety. Central therefore to this post-Christian theology is the question of how to think and talk theologically in a secular, pluralist world. Rejecting confessional and dogmatic thought, while still using Christian language, terms, and texts as cultural, theological, and philosophical resources within a secular society, its focus is philosophy but not piety.

T. J. J. Altizer and W. Hamilton, *Radical Theology and the Death of God* (Bobbs-Merrill, 1966).

G. Vattimo, *After Christianity* (Columbia University Press, 2002).

Mike Grimshaw

Postcolonial Theology: see Colonialism and Postcolonialism.

Postliberal Theology It is helpful to distinguish three differing usages of the adjective 'postliberal' among English-speaking theologians. In America from the 1940s to the early 1960s the term found limited currency as a description of the new 'Christian realist' or 'neo-orthodox' trend in theology which, sparked by European developments in the 1920s, had fostered a return to classic and Reformation themes of sin, redemption, and revelation. These moves were usually accompanied by sharp criticisms of that form of liberal theology which, codified along lines established by A. Ritschl (1822–89) but with inspiration running back to F. Schleiermacher, had reigned among Protestant theologians in the late nineteenth and early twentieth centuries. By the later 1960s the term had clearly lost resonance in the rapidly changing intellectual situation and dropped out of sight.

Any memory of this earlier usage was eclipsed upon the publication of G. Lindbeck's (b. 1923) *The Nature of Doctrine: Religion and Theology in a Postliberal Age* (1984). The somewhat grandiose connotations of the book's subtitle are not at all characteristic of Lindbeck's careful delimitation of how he intends to employ the term. The technical use of the word is clearly 'methodological' in orientation; that is, it characterizes the presuppositions and procedures of theology more than its conclusions. It is intended to signify the incorporation into the practice of theology of a particular set of assumptions about the relation between experience and language, derived specifically from the anthropological and sociological modes of studying religion. The result is that a 'postliberal' theology in Lindbeck's sense derives its framework of interpretive concepts from a religion's explicit scriptural and dogmatic traditions in order to articulate the implicit, quasi-grammatical scheme that both constitutes the religion as a distinct 'symbol system' and regulates its testimony and practices. A 'postliberal' theology will accordingly refuse the basic 'liberal' move, in which those same traditions are understood as an always inadequate 'expression' of the Church's ineffable 'faith', where the latter is understood as the proper criterion for criticizing and reconstructing religious claims.

Though the wide currency of the term 'postliberalism' at present can be traced back to the discussions started by Lindbeck's book, it is arguable that it has come to be used in yet a third way. It no longer has the precision and methodological focus found in Lindbeck and his immediate interpreters; indeed it is often used without any explicit reference to Lindbeck and the 'Yale' tradition that was his context. There is also a corresponding decline in clarity concerning just what 'liberalism' consists in, for, whereas Lindbeck's conception derived its cogency from a particular way of defining its opponent, postliberalism in current usage is characterized more by a broad, at times even implicit, sensibility than by a focused methodological position. It tends to signal a confidence in theological formulations drawing directly on scriptural and creedal language, a questioning of typically modern strategies of biblical exegesis and of doctrinal analysis, and a suspicion that conceptualities and criteria not native to the Christian tradition are incommensurable with sound theological judgement.

See also Frei, Hans; Narrative Theology.

P. DeHart, *The Trial of the Witnesses: The Rise and Decline of Postliberal Theology* (Blackwell, 2006).

D. Kamitsuka, *Theology and Contemporary Culture: Liberation, Postliberal and Revisionary Perspectives* (Cambridge University Press, 1999).

Paul J. DeHart

Postmillennialism The term 'postmillennialism' refers to one of several approaches to Christian eschatology that are defined by the way in which they relate the expected return of Christ to the Millennium described in Revelation 20:1–6. Whereas advocates of premillennialism hold that Christ's parousia inaugurates – and thus comes *before* – the 1,000 years of Revelation 20, postmillennialists affirm that Christ will return only *after* the Millennium. Postmillennialists thus view Christ's return as signalling the end rather than a renewal of earthly history, a belief (along with a reluctance to interpret the Millennium as referring literally to 1,000 years) shared by proponents of amillennialism; but postmillennialists differ from amillennialists in understanding the millennial period as a time of the Church's steady and triumphant growth.

Postmillennial ideas find sophisticated elaboration in Reformed thought, especially in the Princeton Theology of C. Hodge and B. B. Warfield (1851–1921). In contrast to premillennialists, postmillennialists tend to de-emphasize the significance of Revelation 20 as the key to the end times; indeed, Warfield did not even view the chapter as having an eschatological reference.

The postmillennial emphasis on the Church's inexorable growth, is, correspondingly, more dependent on the depiction of Christ as one who conquers spiritually – with the sword that comes 'from his mouth' (Rev. 19:15, 21; cf. 6:2) – and on Jesus' promise that the 'GOSPEL of the kingdom will be preached throughout the whole world, as a testimony to all nations; and then the end will come' (Matt. 24:14; cf. Mark 13:10; Rom. 11:25–6). And while some postmillennialists believe that this inexorable progress of the gospel will ultimately be achieved by means of Christian political supremacy (see DOMINION THEOLOGY), the majority hold that it will be the product of cumulative effect of missionary activity rather than any sort of legal mandate. Indeed, one of the distinguishing marks of postmillennial thought over against premillennialism is the conviction that SCRIPTURE envisions no basic change in God's means of advancing the kingdom between PENTECOST and the Last Judgement.

One of the strengths of postmillennial eschatology is its stress on the ability of God to achieve God's aims in history through the operation of the HOLY SPIRIT in the Church. Its single-minded emphasis on the Church's missionary responsibility to preach the gospel throughout the world (Matt. 28:19; Mark 16:15) is thus supplemented by a level of optimism regarding the future of the Church that is not typical of either pre- or amillennial perspectives. Yet critics see in this notion of the gospel's steady, forward progress a potential weakness, since the connection posited between the growth of the KINGDOM OF GOD and the work of the Church can promote the kind of Christian triumphalism that merged all too easily with the very worldly project of western COLONIALISM in the past and is no less prone to exploitation by the neo-colonial dynamics of globalization in the present.

C. Hodge, *Systematic Theology* (Scribner, 1871–3), IV.iii, §§4–5.

B. B. Warfield, 'The Millennium and the Apocalypse' in *Biblical Doctrines* (Oxford University Press, 1929), 643–64.

IAN A. MCFARLAND

POSTMODERNISM 'Postmodernism' is a term loosely used to describe the critique of modernity across disciplines ranging from architecture to philosophy. Postmodernism criticizes some of the fundamental convictions of modern philosophers such as I. KANT and R. Descartes (1596–1650), particularly their 'foundationalism'. Foundationalism held out the promise that scholars and scientists – freed from religious and political biases – could know the world as it 'really' was. According to Descartes, for instance, knowledge properly acquired was constructed from the ground up, on the basis of 'certain' foundations. The most basic beliefs were supposed to satisfy the criteria of being self-evident and irrefutable. In Kant and others, this account of knowledge gave birth to the notion of a universal, neutral, autonomous reason as guarantor of universal truth. This foundationalist account of objective knowledge is one of the primary targets of postmodern critique (though, contrariwise, critics of postmodernism often charge that its anti-foundationalism leads to relativism).

According to philosophers such as M. Heidegger (1889–1976), H.-G. Gadamer (1900–2002), and J. Derrida (1935–2004), there is no knowledge which is not always already prejudiced. This is because our very perception of the world is conditioned by our 'horizons', and these horizons are relative to our particular socio-cultural histories. As such, there can be no universal, neutral, 'objective' knowledge, but rather interpretations of the world generated from within particular commitments. M. Foucault (1926–84) intensified this critique by arguing that knowledge is in fact conditioned by *power* – that our 'prejudices' stem from interests of power and domination. Most famously, J.-F. Lyotard (1924–98) has defined postmodernism as 'incredulity toward metanarratives'. By 'metanarratives', he does not mean simply 'large-scale' stories, but rather accounts of the world that seek to ground themselves by appeal to a universal, autonomous reason (as in Kant, G. W. F. HEGEL, or positivism). For Lyotard, all accounts of the world – even scientific ones – ultimately appeal to a founding 'narrative', analogous to a religious story or 'myth'. As such, all knowledge is rooted in the particularity of faith stories.

While postmodernism is often construed in negative and almost amoral terms (and admittedly, some of its more Nietzschean strains suggest this), at its core is a very positive concern about justice. In figures such as Derrida, E. Levinas (1906–95), Lyotard, R. Rorty (1931–2007), and Foucault we find a trenchant critique of the way in which social and institutional structures marginalize and dominate the powerless and oppressed. In Levinas this is directly informed by the biblical concern for 'the widow, the orphan, and the stranger'. Levinas has thus introduced deeply Hebraic conceptions of ethics into contemporary postmodern discourse, exerting a signal influence on Derrida. According to Levinas, and in contrast to the 'rights talk' of modernity, I am not first and foremost an individual with 'rights', but rather I find myself always already obligated to the face of the Other. The 'Other', for Levinas, is the other human being who at the same time 'incarnates' the Otherness or 'alterity' of God. In the postmodern concern for alterity, in contrast to the hegemonic 'sameness' of modernity, Christian theologians have found an important biblical basis for cultural critique and engagement.

J. K. A. Smith, *Who's Afraid of Postmodernism?* (Baker Academic, 2006).

K. Vanhoozer, ed., *The Cambridge Companion to Postmodern Theology* (Cambridge University Press, 2003).

JAMES K. A. SMITH

POVERTY Christian theology recognizes three types of poverty: *physical* poverty, or the lack of basic necessities for life; *spiritual* poverty, or the acknowledgement of one's sinful condition before God, manifested by humility of heart; and *voluntary/religious* poverty, or a vow to renounce personal possessions and serve God through a life of simplicity. Religious poverty seeks to enter into a stylized form of physical poverty in order to fully realize spiritual poverty.

Though the OT portrays nothing desirable about poverty, it reveals God as defender of the poor. Wealth is considered a blessing, and Israel is to treat the poor with sympathy, justice, and generosity. The LAW requires landowners to leave the corners of their fields unharvested and not to re-harvest vineyards or olive trees so the poor may glean them (Lev. 23:22). In the sabbatical year all debts are released and Jewish slaves freed (Deut. 15:1, 12; cf. Lev. 25:39–41). In the year of jubilee any sold land must be returned to its original family (Lev. 25:13–17). In this way the law mitigates the creation of a perpetual underclass.

The NT strikes a more wary tone about wealth and proclaims the poor and hungry blessed (e.g., Luke 6:20–1). Jesus' life of simplicity brings theological significance to poverty; he teaches that anything given to the poor is given to him (Matt. 25:40). James warns the Church to treat the poor with respect because God has chosen them to be rich in faith and heirs of the kingdom (Jas. 2:5).

Patristic writings have three recurring themes regarding the poor: a persistent call to *generous almsgiving* (with a promise of divine reward), a rejection of *radical* ASCETICISM, and a recognition that poverty and wealth present *spiritual opportunities and temptations*. There remains diversity on the topic, however. Clement of Alexandria (*ca* 150–*ca* 215) identified 'the poor' as both spiritually and physically poor believers. John Chrysostom (*ca* 345–407), exiled for preaching against the empress' luxury and licence, taught that need, not virtue, qualified one to receive alms. Cyprian (d. 258) warned the rich that by not sharing their wealth with the poor they were neglecting those with whom Christ identifies.

By the Middle Ages the Church's theological interpretation of poverty became intertwined with its understanding of salvation. A symbiotic relationship arose between the rich and the poor as part of the Church's penitential system. The poor embodied Christ and were favoured in God's sight; the rich needed them as objects of charity for their own sanctification. This became the 'social contract' of the Middle Ages, that is, the duty of the poor to remain poor so that the salvation of the rich might be secured. Poverty became not a problem to be solved but an opportunity for the rich to obtain merit.

The poor's spiritually favoured position gave rise to the practice of voluntary poverty by clergy. In feudal society poverty was primarily understood as humility and became a key concept for social reform. Knights left their violent lives to live in the humble brotherhood of monastic poverty. Poverty understood primarily as humility allowed the Benedictines to accumulate vast amounts of wealth while considering themselves 'the poor of God' (see MONASTICISM).

The period from the eleventh to the fourteenth century saw theological shifts as the Church grew in wealth and spiritual lethargy. In spite of Bernard of Clairvaux's (1090–1153) reforms, monasteries fell into spiritual decline. Poverty of spirit alone was no longer adequate. Francis of Assisi called for *usus pauper* or complete physical sacrifice, including three levels of poverty: a poverty of *outer things* (one garment, one walking stick, shoes only when necessary and – because Judas carried one – no money bag), a poverty in *relationships* (i.e., an attitude of humility), and a poverty *towards God* in recognition of our beggarliness as sinners. Francis also insisted his followers practise manual labour, like the poor, as they preached itinerantly. Furthermore his *Testament* forbade followers to own fixed property or hold offices invested with power.

Francis' theology of poverty clashed with the PAPACY's. After Francis' death Pope Gregory IX (r. 1227–41) declared Francis' interpretation of *usus pauper* non-binding, arguing instead that Franciscans had *usus rerum*, or a 'use' of things without real 'possession' of them. Divisions ensued, and two groups of Franciscans emerged. *Spirituals* argued that while external poverty may not guarantee spiritual poverty, its absence proved a lack of spiritual poverty. *Conventuals* maintained that the Church could hold material goods without detriment to spiritual perfection. The dispute culminated in the *usus pauper* controversy and a series of papal bulls declaring that spiritual perfection belongs to the realm of spiritual poverty only and has nothing to do with renouncing property. Francis' theology of *usus pauper* was effectively declared null and void.

Religious poverty had the unfortunate consequence of begetting myriads of able-bodied beggars. The REFORMATION challenged at its foundation this theology of poverty that permitted clergy to usurp the poor's alms and spiritual position. M. LUTHER's corrective of *sola fide* weakened not only the Church's idealization of poverty but also its theological legitimization. If salvation is a free gift by God's grace alone, then poverty – voluntary or involuntary – serves no one. Giving alms or taking a vow of poverty has no meritorious value.

For Luther, poverty was not a virtue to be idealized but the blasphemous result of a greedy Church, and he sought not to sanctify poverty but to abolish it. He restored the connection between worship and giving to neighbour by supplying the needs of the poor through a common chest. Nevertheless, Luther's early writings emptied the biblical language of poverty of its socio-economic meaning, spiritualizing it to mean those who desire God's Word. This understanding of poverty was an effective tool for the doctrinal reform of the Church, but it created disastrous consequences for his social ethics, as demonstrated in his response to the peasants' war. Though afterwards Luther's theological interpretation of poverty shifted to include socio-economic connotations, the critical time in history to influence German society had passed. J. CALVIN benefited from Luther's success and failures, and more fully integrated his theology of poverty into his CHRISTOLOGY, ECCLESIOLOGY, and understanding of the Christian life.

Catholic LIBERATION THEOLOGIES in Latin American have championed the place of the poor in theological discourse. Using Marxist class analysis, these theologians maintain the 'epistemological privilege of the poor' in their unique ability to understand the gospel's critique of unjust economic and political structures. G. Gutiérrez (b. 1928) contends communion with God occurs only when one identifies and sides with the cause of the poor, through whom God is revealed. Popes John Paul II (r. 1978–2005) and Benedict XVI (r. 2005–) have condemned certain elements of liberation theology, though they have also adopted the liberationist language of the 'option for the poor'.

See also PREFERENTIAL OPTION FOR THE POOR.

J. L. González, *Faith and Wealth: A History of Early Christian Ideas on the Origin, Significance, and Use of Money* (Harper & Row, 1990).

G. Gutiérrez, *A Theology of Liberation* (Orbis, 1973 [1971]).

C. Lindberg, *Beyond Charity: Reformation Initiatives for the Poor* (Fortress Press, 1993).

BONNIE PATTISON

PRACTICAL SYLLOGISM Within REFORMED THEOLOGY, 'practical syllogism' (Latin *syllogismus practicus*) refers to the principle that a person can come to know her ELECTION by a process of self-examination that focuses specifically on her good works. As such, the practical syllogism is closely bound up with the DOCTRINE of the believer's ASSURANCE of salvation. While most Reformed theologians denied that such assurance was an essential component of saving FAITH, they did believe that it was possible for believers to work 'to make their calling and election sure' (WC 18.3; cf. 3.8 and 2 Pet. 1:10). The practical syllogism provided a logical framework for carrying out this task, working from the principle that saving (or justifying) faith naturally leads to good works, according to the following line of reasoning: 'Whoever believes shall be saved; my good works give evidence that I believe; therefore, I shall be saved'.

The primary criticism of the practical syllogism is that it leads persons to look to themselves rather than to Christ as the ground of their assurance. While formally distinct from any form of JUSTIFICATION by works (since, as the major premise shows, its proponents held that human beings are justified by faith alone through grace), the syllogism's psychological effect was arguably to generate the same sort of tormented CONSCIENCE that led M. LUTHER to reject the late medieval Catholic penitential system. In both cases, an attempt to reassure doubting believers of their status before God easily produced just the opposite result: augmenting doubt by turning the believer's focus from the GOSPEL of God's unmerited gift of GRACE to the question of her own objective goodness.

IAN A. MCFARLAND

PRACTICAL THEOLOGY Practical theology is a vigorous, if somewhat contested, discipline in which a multiplicity of approaches and definitions abound. While its roots are in the historic and perennial activities of Christian nurture, reflection on the nature of the Church, and its proclamation and service to the wider world, in its contemporary manifestations it is characterized by its interactions with a range of non-theological disciplines, such as the modern psychologies, social and cultural theory, anthropology, and philosophy. The past thirty years have witnessed something of a reorientation of its core identity, and in particular the repudiation of itself as an 'applied' discipline concerned with the activities of the ordained ministry, towards a self-understanding as a primary theological discipline focusing on critical reflection on faithful practice in a variety of settings. This is about a move, essentially, from a model of 'applied theology' to one of 'theology of practice' in which contemporary experience is placed in a dialectical relationship with the sources and norms of tradition in order to generate the 'practical wisdom' by which the life of the Church can be directed.

Practical theology historically has occupied much common ground with PASTORAL THEOLOGY, although opinions differ as to whether they should be regarded as interchangeable terms or discrete disciplines. The tendency in North America and continental Europe has favoured pastoral theology as a specialist subdiscipline concerned with questions of pastoral care and counselling – the study of activities associated with 'shepherding' of the flock – while practical theology has embraced other aspects of the Church's ministry, such as preaching, Christian education, and congregational studies. In Germany and the Netherlands, the tradition of 'empirical theology' utilizes a range of qualitative and quantitative research methods as a means of generating data for the Church's ministry, usually in education, youth work, and ministerial formation. The British tradition has tended to elide the two terms to denote any issue affecting the practice of human care, interpersonal relations, rites of passage, mission, and ECCLESIOLOGY, through to theological perspectives on public issues. The recent turn to method, however, especially in the Anglo-American tradition, locates practical theology much more firmly as a broader meta-discipline which reflects on the nature of theological understanding in the light of Christian praxis in the world, while retaining a more specific understanding of pastoral theology as theologically informed responses to the human life-cycle.

Accounts of the historical development of practical theology insist upon the irreducibly practical nature of theology from the earliest years of the Christian Church. Following E. Charry's (b. 1947) evocation of the origins of Christian doctrine as essentially orientated towards the practice of discipleship and the cultivation of Christian virtue, E. Graham (b. 1959), H. Walton (b. 1957), and F. Ward (b. 1959) have suggested that all theological discourse emerged as the means of articulating the norms, narratives, and visions by which the various tasks of Christian formation, the building up of the BODY of Christ, and the communication of the FAITH were to be guided. Similarly, G. Heitink (b. 1938) has argued that theology emerged out of the processes by which the earliest Christian communities grappled with the nature of its life together and sought to give theological underpinning to the core activities of *KERYGMA* (proclamation), *didache* (instruction), and *paraklesis* (pastoral care).

As the Church consolidated its orders of apostolic ministries and sought to bring the regulation of individual and community care by clergy under the aegis of Church authority, literature emerged which focused on the work and duties of the pastor. The *Book of Pastoral Rule* (*ca* 590) of Pope Gregory I ('the Great', r. 590–604) was one of the most influential texts of late antiquity, and stressed the personal and spiritual qualities of the pastor and the importance of sensitive discernment of human personality in the cure of souls. The medieval period saw the emergence of 'MORAL THEOLOGY', in which the practice of pastoral care was linked to the administration of the sacraments, a tradition that endures in much Catholic pastoral theology to this day. In the Protestant tradition, exemplified by divines such as G. Herbert (1593–1633), R. HOOKER, and J. EDWARDS, the emphasis lay on the pastor as moral exemplar and shepherd of his flock.

A definitive phase in the history of practical theology came with the establishment of the academic study of theology under the German university system in the eighteenth century. In many respects, the intention of the architects of this system, chief among whom was F. SCHLEIERMACHER, was to affirm the public significance of the Protestant Church by placing the training of its ministers alongside that of other professions such as law and medicine. Also, for Schleiermacher, the 'scientific' pursuit of academic excellence in theology must, for the future leaders of the Church, be accompanied by a concern for its practical relevance, framed for him in terms of the tasks of management and governance of the Church. Schleiermacher's system proposed a threefold categorization of theology, in which PHILOSOPHICAL THEOLOGY constituted the 'roots' of the discipline, the historical field of Church history, exegesis, and dogmatics was the 'body' or 'trunk', and the practical, as the field of Church administration and ministry, the 'crown' or branches (*Outline*, §§24–31). Later critics have commented, however, that the legacy of such an institutionalization of theological study has been a deductive epistemology in which practice is derivative of doctrines formulated elsewhere, rather than the fertile ground in which the seeds of new philosophical and theological insights would be sown.

The stage was thus set for a subdivision of practical theology into areas such as HOMILETICS (preaching), liturgics (worship), CATECHESIS (Christian education), jurisprudence (administration), and poimenics (pastoral and spiritual care). Its relegation in the hierarchy of theological sciences was further institutionalized by the predominance of SYSTEMATIC THEOLOGY, biblical studies, and Church history within theological seminaries, with the study of 'pastoralia' frequently consigned to the early years of ordination, often on an apprenticeship model of acquiring 'hints and help' from more senior pastors.

In the twentieth century many of the constituent subdisciplines assimilated insights from secular disciplines, such as communication, sociology, or modern psychologies and psychotherapies. Such adoption tended to remain at an operational or pragmatic level, with little conscious attention to the implicit values inherent in such a process beyond its utility in enhancing ministerial technique. By the last quarter of the twentieth century, however, the predominance of 'applied theology' was giving way to an altogether more inductive and dialogical relationship between the practice of ministry and the resources of theological understanding.

One contributory element to this was a discomfort on the part of writers like T. Oden (b. 1931) at the privileged position of what were regarded as secular humanist sources at the expense of the classic sources of pastoral practice. While Oden's views were controversial, his intervention was a catalyst to the stimulation of debate about the very theological identity of Christian practice and the sources and norms by which it would be guided. Thus, D. Browning (b. 1934) put forward a vision of practical theology which concentrated less on the content of the curriculum than on constructing a methodological model which repudiated the 'theory–practice' emphasis of the deductive tradition in favour of a movement towards 'practice–theory–practice'. Under the influence of H.-G. Gadamer's (1900–2002) notion of the fusion of interpretative horizons in hermeneutics, and P. TILLICH's model of correlation in theological understanding, Browning offered a sophisticated reworking of the liberal correlational model in which practical theological discernment is drawn from the interaction between the human sciences and the normative texts of SCRIPTURE and TRADITION.

Other factors were also contributing to the reorientation of practical theology. Under the influence of VATICAN COUNCIL II and other movements to mobilize and educate the LAITY, ministry was no longer solely equated exclusively with the 'clerical paradigm', but understood as the province of the whole people of God, to be exercised in Church and world. Latin American LIBERATION THEOLOGY exerted a major influence by characterizing theology as the 'work of the people'; the basic ecclesial communities of Latin America, informed by the pedagogy of P. Freire (1921–97) and nurtured by the reforms of progressive Catholicism after Vatican II, provided an educational model to facilitate this process. Theology was conceived as an inductive process in which the sources and resources of the theological tradition were brought to bear on the practical dilemmas of everyday life. Inspired by Marxist reworkings of Aristotelian concepts of praxis, liberation theology recast theological discourse less as authenticated by the strictures of *ORTHODOXY* (right belief) and more as directed towards the necessities of *ORTHOPRAXIS* (faithful action).

In reaction to the ENLIGHTENMENT division of theory and practice (in Aristotelian terms, the privileging of *theoria*) and the relegation of practice to mere *technē*, E. Farley (b. 1929) argued for a recovery of the tradition of practical wisdom (*phronēsis*) in which theology was conceived as HABITUS, or a unity of reflection and action in which schooling in the disciplines of faith was indivisible from intellectual formation (*Theologia* 127). More recent contributions have argued that theology is fundamentally a 'performative' discipline, and that it is in the very practices of faith themselves that Christian communities embody and enact their truth claims. Theology is first practised and then reflected upon or systematized. Consequently, practical theology should be regarded as 'more "verb-like" than "noun-like"' (Veling, *Practical* 4).

Perhaps in reflection of its predominantly correlational tendencies, practical theology finds itself occupying the spaces between D. Tracy's (b. 1939) 'three publics' of academy, Church, and society. This triangulation will continue to shape its future priorities. Given its inductive–experiential bias, and the significance of 'the turn to the human' in its many forms during the twentieth century, practical theology will continue to engage productively with other branches of the humanities, such as cultural theory and the social sciences. Its flair for listening in to the cultural Zeitgeist can be seen in current interest in narrative, ethnography and qualitative research as means of generating new insights into the nature of its foundational (but often undertheorized) categories of experience and practice. Yet practical theology must also heed the warnings of its more neo-orthodox critics that any such theories of the person must also be rooted in traditional expressions of THEOLOGICAL ANTHROPOLOGY and DIVINE ACTION.

Practical theology also shows signs of moving into new approaches to culture and society, including consideration of how a study of theologically informed practice may be extended into examinations of the broader values and narratives that inform meaning and action in ostensibly 'secular' cultures and institutions. S. Pattison's (b. 1953) interest in the 'action-guiding worldviews and belief systems' that inform even the most secular of institutions and G. Lynch's (b. 1968) explorations of how forms of cultural practice offer frameworks for the expression of spiritual world views in the face of the decline of organized, creedal religion serve as means by which practical theology's perennial concern to interrogate the relationship between beliefs and actions might be carried into a post-secular, post-Christian context. Yet practical theology still suffers from a reputation as the 'Cinderella subject' of academic theology, and it remains to be seen whether Graham, Walton, and Ward's characterization of its task as the recontextualization of Christian doctrine will result in a greater recognition by systematic, philosophical, and biblical disciplines.

Essentially, however, practical theology focuses on the immediacy of the human condition from a fundamentally incarnational conviction that this is where 'talk about God' begins and ends: where words become flesh. Or, as T. Veling (b. 1959) puts it, practical theology roots itself in the real needs of the world 'on earth', in order to align it more closely to the vision of what will prevail 'in heaven' (*Practical* 17–18).

D. Browning, *A Fundamental Practical Theology: Descriptive and Strategic Proposals* (Fortress Press, 1991).

E. Graham, *Transforming Practice: Pastoral Theology in an Age of Uncertainty*, 2nd edn (Wipf and Stock, 2002).

E. Graham, H. Walton, and F. Ward, *Theological Reflection: Methods* (SCM, 2005).

S. Pattison, *The Challenge of Practical Theology: Selected Essays* (Jessica Kingsley Publishers, 2007).

J. Swinton and H. Mowat, *Practical Theology and Qualitative Research* (SCM, 2006).

T. Veling, *Practical Theology: 'On Earth as It Is in Heaven'* (Orbis, 2005).

ELAINE GRAHAM

PRAYER Prayer is a religious practice that Christians share with many other people. The human cry to the divine for help amid need and the human laud of the divine because of help received are found everywhere, formally organized in RELIGIONS, intimately experienced by human beings who have little religious formation, enacted in great public gatherings, and probably even inscribed in prehistoric petroglyphs of figures with hands upraised. Christians rightly assume that they engage in a widespread human undertaking when they pray.

But Christians also inherit a particular tradition of prayer. 'Pray in this way', says the Jesus of Matthew's Gospel (Matt. 6:9), criticizing both self-righteous display and 'empty phrases' and introducing one version of the characteristic and central Christian text called the LORD'S PRAYER. Furthermore, PAUL and the deutero-Pauline letters repeatedly combine prayer with thanksgiving (e.g., 1 Thess. 1:2; 5:17–18; Phil. 1:3–4; 4:6; Rom. 1:8–9; Col. 4:2) and assert that prayers and thanksgivings should be made for others, indeed for everyone (1 Tim. 2:1). In Christian use, then, prayer may mean thanksgiving and beseeching intertwined. It also may mean only the beseeching.

The Gospel tradition presents narratives of Jesus praying (e.g., Mark 1:35), including prayers he makes that remain significantly unanswered (Mark 14:32–42; 15:34). Finally, prayer is part of that 'everything' that Christians are to do 'in the name of the Lord Jesus, giving thanks to God the Father through him' (Col. 3:17). These NT texts bear witness to the early formation of a Christian TRADITION in prayer. That tradition has developed into a number of structures or patterns of Christian praying, structures that profoundly express particular central themes in Christian FAITH. Moreover, because of the way prayer expresses Christian faith in these structures, it can be seen as an important enacting of Christian theology and an important source for Christian theological reflection – or, at least, an important partner in a dialogue with theology about the meaning of Christian faith (see *LEX ORANDI LEX CREDENDI*; see also LITURGY).

Some of the structures of Christian prayer are exercised in the praying of a person alone. The Matthean Jesus says, 'Go into your room and shut the door' (6:6). The Markan Jesus finds a deserted place for prayer (1:35). Such patterns and practices of personal prayer may be common to a range of faith traditions and not distinctively Christian at all. Moreover, such prayer can become a matter of talking to oneself in wishful thinking or self-congratulation (cf. Luke 18:11) or with too many words (Matt. 6:7). But it can also be a profound address to the divine beyond the self. 'Help me!' or 'Thank you!' is spoken to the unknown darkness by people throughout the world. Indeed, these primal forms of plea and praise, however they are developed, indicate two deep and basic theological convictions, shared by many human beings: God can be addressed and God can help (cf. Heb. 11:6). They also introduce two serious theological problems. First, is God changed by prayer, or does petition have some other function (e.g., the cultivation of trust in God's will, as suggested by F. SCHLEIERMACHER in *CF*, §147)? And, second, what does it mean when God does not help? Where is God then? These problems continue to be discussed in any interaction of theology and prayer (see DIVINE ACTION).

Though such similarities with non-Christian practices of prayer are undeniable, much of Christian personal prayer has also been formed by encounter with the concrete patterns and characteristics of Christian communal prayer, as seen in, for example, personal use of the themes of thanksgiving, of prayer for the needs of others, and of prayer 'in the name of Jesus'. Christian patterns for personal or familial prayer at table, at sunrise, sunset, and going to rest, and at the seasons of the year have also been formed by communal practice and express the communal Christian conviction that God is the creator of all, that SIN and evil nonetheless haunt and possess the world, that God loves the world and redeems it in Jesus Christ, that the very rhythms of time can proclaim the DEATH and RESURRECTION of Christ, and that food and help should be shared. Even the idea of prayer 'without ceasing' (1 Thess. 5:17) may reflect the idea that the community has been formed to stand before God for the sake of the world in every circumstance of its members' lives.

Christians also have particular ways, drawn from the prayer of the community, of understanding the silence of God. Individuals can receive the communal tradition of praying or reading texts that also know that very silence (e.g., Pss. 42; 74; JOB), thereby learning to conjoin their personal experience with that of many other people and of the holy texts themselves. They can lament, along with the great biblical and communal tradition of lament. According to the central story of the community, they can know that 'prayer in Jesus' name' means prayer together with the One abandoned on the CROSS, God's own self experiencing the silence of God. They may also know of the prayer that responds to silence with silence, simply being before the triune God in contemplation, 'deep calling to deep'.

All this suggests that the primary locus of the specifically Christian tradition of prayer is communal or liturgical. The Lord's Prayer speaks in a plural voice – 'give us', 'forgive us', and 'deliver us', it prays. The Psalms, too, are sung by the community. Moreover, the 'supplications, prayers, intercessions, and thanksgivings . . . for everyone', urged in 1 Timothy 2:1, and so characteristic of Christianity, were probably originally intended as a practice of the gathered assembly. In any case, such prayers have become a major tradition of Christian worship in the 'Intercessions' or 'Prayers of the Faithful' of most Sunday liturgies. Furthermore, central moments of Christian liturgy are all marked by great prayers of both thanksgiving and beseeching, important communal enactments of the NT counsel. The prayer at the Eucharistic table (see MASS, CANON OF) is especially such a prayer. Prayers patterned after this model are said over the water of the font, at the lighting of the evening and paschal candles, at ordinations, and over the couple in a MARRIAGE blessing. Even the short prayers or 'collects' that traditionally mark the beginning of the western EUCHARIST – as well as the setting of its table and the end of its communion rite – are brief versions of thanksgiving conjoined with petition in a pattern called the 'collect form'. That prayer is primarily communal in Christianity implies an ECCLESIOLOGY.

This pattern of thanksgiving and beseeching arose not only from the example and the urging of the Pauline writings. In fact, Paul was himself receiving the great tradition of biblical prayer. The Psalms regularly interweave thanksgiving with prayer, praise with lament, and Christians have dealt with the Psalms as their principal 'school of prayer'. The pattern is also especially clear in the great prayer of Ezra in Nehemiah 9. Here the text begins with that recitation of the deeds of God that particularly marks biblical thanksgiving. Such open acknowledgement or praise is here interwoven with a confession of the failure and the need of the people. Then, at Nehemiah 9:32, the prayer turns. 'Now therefore, our God', the text runs as Ezra then proceeds to pray for God's action for the people now and in the future. This same structure was still alive in Jewish prayer at the time of Christian origins, being present in forms like the extended *berakoth* or *hodayoth* so important to Jewish liturgy and also found in the Qumran scrolls, forms that began 'Blessed are you' or 'We thank you', openly and praise-fully proclaiming the deeds of God and then going on to prayers and intercessions. These Jewish patterns had great effect on Christian practice. However, while the *berakah* had some ancient Christian use (cf. 2 Cor. 1:3–7 and Eph. 1:3–10), it was primarily the *hodayah* with its accent on thanksgiving that lived on in Christian liturgy.

This classic pattern of thanksgiving and beseeching brings to expression an important Christian conception of time and of ESCHATOLOGY. Together with Judaism, Christians believe that God has acted in the past and that God has promised to act in the future. Christian prayer, then, remembers God's actions in praise and begs for God's fidelity to the promises in hope. Then, characteristically, Christian prayer celebrates that Jesus Christ, the Risen One around whom the community gathers, is the summation of all of God's actions and is already the down payment on all of God's promises. Thanksgiving and bold – even confident – intercession are classic Christian traits of prayer 'in the name of Jesus', that is to say, in the presence and power of the Crucified-and-Risen One. When one understands that the HOLY SPIRIT gathers the community into Christ so that it may pray in his name before the God who acts and promises, one sees that Christian prayer expresses the faith in the TRINITY.

This same faith in the Trinity and this same sense of eschatology may be seen in the classic use of the Lord's Prayer. Christians trust that they are given this prayer by Jesus and pray it with him. They again and again use it as a summation of all of their prayers in his name, as a gift to those who are being baptized and as a table-prayer at the Eucharist. The prayer joins with all humanity in begging God for help at last, using the language of first-century Hellenistic–Jewish eschatology. Yet, as J. Jeremias (1900–79) has demonstrated, it also celebrates the gifts of the communal meal and of mutual forgiveness, understanding these as the Spirit-enlivened presence in the assembly of two matters that belong to the biblical conception of the end of time: the great final feast of the end of death (cf. Isa. 25:6–8) and the great final judgement of sin. According to current scholarship, it is most likely that these eschatological gifts, this bread and forgiveness, are the uniquely Christian matter of the prayer, not the supposed imitation of Jesus in the use of the address 'Father': the latter is more likely an ordinary Hellenistic way that anybody would pray. To be in this prayer is thus to be realistically among human needs, using the human practice of prayer. It is also to be with Jesus Christ, in the gifts of the Spirit, before the face of God, with past and future drawn into the present prayer. It is to be gathered into the very life of the triune God.

J. Jeremias, *The Prayers of Jesus* (Fortress Press, 1978).

G. Ramshaw, *God beyond Gender: Feminist–Christian God Language* (Fortress Press, 1995).

J. M. Robinson, 'The Historicality of Biblical Language' in *The Old Testament and Christian Faith*, ed. B. W. Anderson (Harper, 1963), 124–58.

D. Saliers, *The Soul in Paraphrase: Prayer and the Religious Affections* (Seabury Press, 1980).

K. Stevenson, *The Lord's Prayer: A Text in Tradition* (Fortress Press, 2004).

GORDON W. LATHROP

PREACHING: see HOMILETICS.

PREDESTINATION 'Predestination' refers to the eternal purpose of the triune God to save a particular number of human beings. Sometimes the term 'predestination' is used broadly to refer to God's foreordination of whatsoever will come to pass (Eph. 1:11, 22). More properly it refers to God's eternal purpose to save some human beings (as well as ANGELS) and not others. Predestination includes both God's foreknowledge of all that will come to pass and his will to save those whom he elects.

The biblical roots of the doctrine of predestination include the OT teaching of God's ELECTION of ISRAEL, the emphasis upon God's purposeful plan in redemption, and especially the teaching of PAUL in Romans 8:29–9:29 and Ephesians 1:3–14. In the biblical representation of God's works, what transpires in all of history occurs in accordance with the divine plan.

In the history of Christian theology, the doctrine of predestination is especially linked to the theology of AUGUSTINE in his dispute with Pelagius (see PELAGIANISM). Augustine taught that, as a consequence of original sin, all human beings belong to a *massa damnata*. The salvation of God's people depends upon God's sovereign choice to save some to whom he grants the gift of perseverance, and to leave others in their fallen estate.

Pelagius, whose view was condemned by a series of councils at Carthage from 416 to 419, taught that salvation depended upon human works performed in obedience to the commands of the GOSPEL. T. AQUINAS embraced the Augustinian view, though he modified Augustine's denial of FREE WILL by allowing a place for co-operation with the GRACE of God. At the time of the REFORMATION, M. LUTHER and especially J. CALVIN reaffirmed the Augustinian position that salvation depends ultimately upon the predestination of God. In the Churches in Calvin's tradition, a dispute arose between Calvin's followers and others who followed J. Arminius (1560–1609). Arminius sought to affirm divine predestination upon the basis of God's foreknowledge of all possible events, including the free choice of some to make proper use of his grace (see ARMINIANISM). In the twentieth century, K. BARTH reformulated the Augustinian/Reformed doctrine upon the basis of God's revelation in Christ, who is both the elected and reprobated man. Barth's reformulation of the doctrine derives the knowledge of election from the knowledge of Christ, and is often interpreted as a form of UNIVERSALISM.

The doctrine of predestination has provoked controversy in the history of theology, including debate over whether predestination is single (election only) or double (election and reprobation), and whether predestination is compatible with human freedom and responsibility. Despite its controversial nature, however, predestination expresses a fundamental conviction of Christian theology, namely, that the triune God, out of sheer and unmerited grace, is the exclusive Author of salvation, such that the story of salvation begins with God's free, eternal, and unchanging decision graciously to enter into fellowship with human beings.

See also INFRALAPSARIANISM AND SUPRALAPSARIANISM.

Augustine, *On the Predestination of the Saints* in *Nicene and Post-Nicene Fathers*, vol. V: *Saint Augustine: Anti-Pelagian Writings 1st series* (Eerdmans, 1887 [428]).

J. Calvin, *Concerning the Eternal Predestination of God* (James Clarke, 1961 [1552]).

CORNELIS P. VENEMA

PRE-EXISTENCE: see LOGOS.

PREFERENTIAL OPTION FOR THE POOR The phrase 'preferential option for the poor' arose in the specifically Catholic context of Latin American LIBERATION THEOLOGY, though it has also been appropriated – and criticized – by theologians writing out of other ecclesial and social locations. Closely associated with the work of theologian G. Gutiérrez (b. 1928), it was incorporated into the final document of the third General Conference of the Latin American Episcopal Council, held in the Mexican city of Puebla in 1979. Its immediate inspiration was Pope John XXIII's (r. 1958–63) affirmation that in the face of poverty the Church should show itself to be 'the Church of all, and especially the Church of the poor' ('Radio', §7.4). Among Catholics in particular, one way of framing the debate over the appropriateness of the preferential option for the poor centres on the question of whether it honours the pope's dual emphasis on the universality and particularity of the Church's mission.

Liberation theologians have generally argued that in the face of gross social and economic inequality, to be the Church of all means to be the Church of the poor, since failure to side with the poor invariably reinforces the structures that cause POVERTY and thereby belies the Church's commitment to the wellbeing of all people. Beyond this sociological point, however, they draw attention to SCRIPTURE's consistent condemnation of practices that promote and exploit poverty (e.g., Amos 2:6–7; 5:10–12) and, still more specifically, to Jesus' statements of solidarity with the poor (e.g., Matt. 25:40; cf. 11:4; Luke 4:18; 6:20–1) as decisive for Christian praxis: because Jesus identifies with the poor, his followers must commit themselves to the poor. In this context, to speak of an 'option' for the poor is to recognize that the Church must make a deliberate choice about the form of its MINISTRY when confronted with systemic poverty. To describe this option as 'preferential' is to affirm that it is relative rather than absolute: to opt for the poor is not to reject or ignore other groups, but to recognize that solidarity with the poor is God's means of realizing the blessings of the KINGDOM OF GOD for all people.

Though in his major ENCYCLICAL on Catholic social teaching Pope John Paul II (r. 1978–2005) clearly affirmed the Church's 'option or love of preference for the poor' (*Sollic.*, §42; cf. *Cent.*, §11), the Catholic MAGISTERIUM has been cautious in adopting the language of 'preferential option'. The Vatican has appeared more inclined to use the language of 'preferential love' as a means of affirming the Church's commitment to the poor while both avoiding any suggestion that this commitment is exclusive (John Paul II, *Eccl.*, §34) and distancing itself from explicitly Marxist principles of social analysis and revolutionary praxis (Benedict XVI, *Deus*, §§26–9).

G. Baum, 'Sociology and Salvation: Do We Need a Catholic Sociology?' *Theological Studies* 50 (1989), 718–743.

G. Gutiérrez, 'Option for the Poor', in *Systematic Theology: Perspectives from Liberation Theology* (Orbis, 1996), 22–37.

IAN A. MCFARLAND

PREMILLENNIALISM As a variety of Christian ESCHATOLOGY, premillennialism teaches that the second coming of Christ (see PAROUSIA) will occur before his establishment of a 1,000-year kingdom of peace and justice on the earth (see MILLENNIUM). Advocates point to a variety of biblical passages for support: those promising a future 'peaceable kingdom' (Isa. 2; 11; Jer. 31–3, Mic. 4) and various apocalyptic texts (Ezek. 36–9; Dan. 7–12; Zech. 1–6, the 'little apocalypse' in Mark 13, and Rev.). Premillennialism's most important text is Revelation 20:1–10, which describes the binding of Satan (see DEVIL) and two RESURRECTIONS separated by a 1,000-year reign of Christ.

Premillennialism in one form or another is found throughout the history of Christianity, though the term itself was not used until the nineteenth century. Earlier it was called 'chiliasm', from the Greek *chilia* ('thousand'). The core beliefs of premillennialism are as follows: as the present age draws to a close, a number of 'signs of the times' will be revealed, including 'wars and rumours of wars' (Mark 13:7), natural disasters and famines, religious APOSTASY, moral decay, the rise of the ANTICHRIST and the great tribulation, at the end of which Christ will return to bind Satan, defeat the antichrist at the Battle of Armageddon, resurrect the righteous dead, and establish his millennial kingdom in Jerusalem.

These beliefs began circulating in the second and third centuries, when the Church experienced occasional but intense persecution by the Roman Empire. Drawing on apocalyptic texts, Justin Martyr (d. *ca* 165) predicted the rise of the antichrist, the great tribulation, the return of Christ, two resurrections separated by 'a thousand years in Jerusalem', and the final judgement (*Trypho* 80–1, 110). IRENAEUS OF LYONS used texts from both testaments to come to similar conclusions (*AH* 5.25–36). TERTULLIAN connected such ideas with the 'new prophecy' of MONTANISM, which predicted the descent of the New Jerusalem in Asia Minor and the dawning of the Age of the HOLY SPIRIT (*Marc.* 3.25). Chiliasm is also found in *The Epistle of Barnabas* (15) and the *Divine Institutes* (14–27) of Hippolytus (*ca* 170–*ca* 235).

Such views were not universally held. ORIGEN OF ALEXANDRIA rejected chiliasm as a relic from Judaism and adopted an allegorical reading of Revelation (*Prin.* 2.11). When Christianity found favour in the empire in the fourth century, Eusebius of Caesarea (*ca* 260–*ca* 340) rejected chiliasm's condemnation of Rome and linked the Church's success to the empire's (*EH* 10). When Rome fell in the fifth century, AUGUSTINE divided the City of God and the City of Man and used an allegorical reading of Revelation to argue that, during the time between Christ's first and second comings, the SAINTS, living and dead, reigned with Christ in a spiritual millennium (*City* 20.7–20).

In the medieval period, it is difficult to find a systematic presentation of premillennialism, though many of its apocalyptic elements are detected in the rationale and expectations for the Crusades and in JOACHIM OF FIORE's alternative to Augustine in his thirteenth-century *Exposition of the Apocalypse*. The Taborites, the violent followers of J. Hus (*ca* 1370–1415) in the fifteenth century, used prophecy to fight both popes and emperors in anticipation of Christ's return.

Most leaders in the magisterial REFORMATION followed Augustine's eschatology, though they often used apocalyptic prophecy to label their enemies. Protestant radicals frequently adopted premillennialist themes. T. Muntzer (*ca* 1490–1525), M. LUTHER's former student and ally, used chiliasm to encourage the bloodshed of the peasants' revolt. M. Hoffman (*ca* 1495–1543) predicted Christ's return to Strasbourg in 1533; and in the mid-1530s the Anabaptists in charge of Münster declared the city the New Jerusalem, placed it under OT law, and prepared for the war leading up to the second coming. Virtually all the major Protestant confessions called chiliasm a HERESY.

Premillennialism experienced a revival among the English Puritans of the seventeenth century, thanks especially to J. Mede (1586–1639) of Cambridge, who predicted Christ's return in 1736, to be followed by his millennial kingdom. His views were adopted by the 'Fifth Monarchy Men', who unsuccessfully sought to establish a government of the saints in anticipation of Christ's return. Underpinning O. Cromwell's (1598–1658) Commonwealth were many prophetic views that looked forward to a new king and kingdom in the near future. After the Restoration, I. Newton (1643–1727) kept premillennialism alive in England, as did J. Bengel (1687–1752) in Germany.

Starting in the late eighteenth century, another premillennial revival occurred in England. At gatherings at Albury Park and Powerscourt Estate in the late 1820s and early 1830s, these new premillennialists affirmed a literal interpretation of biblical prophecy, the restoration of the Jews to the Holy Land, the apostasy of CHRISTENDOM, the decline of civilization, the imminent return of Christ, and the millennial kingdom. There were disagreements too, especially on how to understand the book of Revelation. *Historicists* believed the book contained prophecies covering the whole of the age of the Church, while *futurists* believed that it pointed to events just prior to the second coming. For some time historicists prevailed (e.g., the Millerites in the USA in the 1840s); but the futurists had strong leaders in E. Irving (1792–1834) and J. Darby (1800–82). Many Plymouth Brethren followed Darby's doctrinal system – DISPENSATIONALISM – which included the pretribulational RAPTURE, in which the Church escaped the antichrist's tribulation.

Dispensationalism had its greatest success in the USA, to which Darby travelled often after the American Civil War. Though initially rejected by postmillennialist-leaning evangelicals, dispensationalism eventually won a following, thanks to Bible and prophetic conferences, Bible institutes, and bestsellers like *The Scofield Reference Bible* (1909). By World War I, it was widely accepted in fundamentalist and Pentecostal circles (see FUNDAMENTALISM; PENTECOSTAL THEOLOGY). Its popularity continues, thanks to other bestsellers like *The Late Great Planet Earth* (1970) and the *Left Behind* series (1995–2004). Since the 1980s, many American premillennialists have used Bible prophecy to organize politically in support of the State of Israel and a strong military. Although most modern scholars prefer some form of 'realized eschatology', premillennialism retains a significant following among those who believe that the Bible contains a discernible and detailed blueprint for the future.

F. J. Baumgartner, *Longing for the End: A History of Millennialism in Western Civilization* (St Martin's Press, 1999).

S. Hunt, ed., *Christian Millennialism: From the Early Church to Waco* (Indiana University Press, 2001).

E. Weber, *Apocalypses: Prophecies, Cults, and Millennial Beliefs through the Ages* (Harvard University Press, 1999).

T. P. Weber, *On the Road to Armageddon: How Evangelicals Became Israel's Best Friend* (Baker Academic, 2004).

TIMOTHY P. WEBER

PRESBYTERIANISM: see POLITY.

PRIESTHOOD 'Priesthood' is a term that has had many meanings. In the history of religions it is normally applied to religious officials who take charge of the cult, offer sacrifices, and perform other sacred duties. In the Christian context it applies first of all to the priesthood of Jesus Christ, especially as described in Hebrews 4–10. Here Christ's priesthood is contrasted to the sacrificial priesthood of ISRAEL. Christ is the eternal high priest who offers himself once for all (Heb. 7:27, 10:14). Christ therefore remains the unique priest for Christians.

By analogy, however, the term 'priest' (Greek *hiereus*, Latin *sacerdos*) is applied to all Christians at least in the corporate sense in 1 Peter 2:4–10 and Revelation 1:6 (see Exod. 19:5–6). Besides Christ, the concept of priest is not applied to individual Christians in the NT. In the NT individual ministers are denominated by the secular titles *presbyteros* ('elder') and *episkopos* ('supervisor'). The terminology can be confusing because the English word 'priest' is derived etymologically from *presbyteros*, but its meaning is derived from sacerdotal vocabulary. By the end of the first century sacerdotal vocabulary begins to be used, at least obliquely, for Christian individuals (e.g., in *1 Clement* and the *Didache*). In the third century bishops and presbyters are clearly called priests in North Africa by Cyprian of Carthage (*Ep.* 63).

In the course of the western Middle Ages priesthood came to be defined more and more in terms of the presidency of the EUCHARIST and the power to absolve SINS in sacramental confession (see T. AQUINAS, *ST* 3.83.4). The result was uncertainty as to the distinction between priests (presbyters) and bishops, since both shared the same sacerdotal dignity. In his official capacity the priest acted 'in the person of Christ' (*in persona Christi*), and in the West (though not in the Orthodox Churches of the East) priests were required to be celibate.

The Protestant REFORMATION had varied responses to the traditional theology and practice of the priesthood. M. LUTHER (in both *The Babylonian Captivity of the Church* and *Letter to the Christian Nobility*) affirmed the PRIESTHOOD OF ALL BELIEVERS and denied that a special priesthood belonged to any class in the Church. Most of the Reformers agreed, although they retained the ministry of preaching the word, administering the sacraments, and pastoral care. The Anglican Reformation retained the language of episcopacy and priesthood but not the sacerdotal concept of the priesthood (at least at the outset). The Reformers also did away with the requirement that ordained ministers be celibate.

The Catholic Council of TRENT unequivocally reaffirmed traditional Catholic teaching on a distinct priesthood for ordained ministers (*Ordin.*). Modern Catholic theology of the priesthood was heavily influenced by the seventeenth-century French School, including Cardinal de Bérulle (1575–1629), J.-J. Olier (1608–57), and the Sulpicians. They emphasized the personal union between the ordained priest and Christ, especially in a life of self-sacrifice and in the celebration of the Eucharist. The priest thus came to be considered 'another Christ' (*alter Christus*).

With VATICAN COUNCIL II the Catholic Church recognized the episcopacy as a distinct order (*LG*, §21) and considerably broadened the understanding of the priesthood to encompass the threefold office of Christ: priest, prophet, and shepherd/king (*PO*; cf. THREEFOLD OFFICE). The Catholic Church has retained the discipline of CELIBACY for priests and has not seen itself able to ordain women to the priesthood. A number of other Christian Churches do ordain women to ministry. The WORLD COUNCIL OF CHURCHES produced a comprehensive ecumenical statement on ordained ministry and priesthood in *Baptism, Eucharist and Ministry* (1982).

JOHN F. BALDOVIN, S. J.

PRIESTHOOD OF ALL BELIEVERS Closely associated with the thought of M. LUTHER in particular and the REFORMATION more generally, the DOCTRINE of the PRIESTHOOD of all believers was not intended as a protest against the existence of a distinct class of persons within the Church (i.e., the clergy) with particular responsibility for preaching and celebrating the sacraments. In short, it does not mean that any baptized Christian is free to assume the responsibility for the public ministry of word and sacrament. On the contrary, the AUGSBURG CONFESSION clearly expresses the position articulated in all the major confessional documents of the Lutheran and Reformed traditions when it states that 'nobody should preach publicly in the church or administer the sacraments unless he has a regular call' (14). Nevertheless, the doctrine does represent a significant reinterpretation of ordained ministry, and, correspondingly, of the distinction between clergy and LAITY.

Although Luther himself never used the phrase 'priesthood of all believers', he did affirm that Christians 'are all consecrated priests' (*Nob.* 127; cf. 129) on the basis of his theology of BAPTISM, understood as the sacrament that establishes all baptized persons as equal before God. Drawing on the language of 1 Peter 2:9, in which the whole Church is described as 'a royal priesthood', Luther denied that the process of ordination constituted the clergy as a distinct 'spiritual' (viz., clerical) class or Christians ontologically distinct from and superior to the 'temporal' (viz., lay) order; instead, he insisted that 'all Christians are of the spiritual estate [*Stand*], and there is no difference among them except that of office' (*Nob.* 127). Indeed, Luther argued that it was precisely because Christians are all equal in status that offices like that of priest and bishop were established as a means of ensuring that the exercise of the authority common to all Christians is subject to the consent and oversight of the whole Church.

No less important to understanding Luther's position is an appreciation for the way in which his theology of priestly ministry is rooted in his CHRISTOLOGY. For Luther, Christ is the one and only true priest, who through his death has interceded with the Father on humanity's behalf once and for all. Thus, to regard all Christians as priests is not simply to comment on their *individual* status before God as secured by Christ but also to see this in the context of their *communal* location as persons commissioned to intercede on behalf of each other in Christ's name. In this context, Luther specifically identifies the power to declare the forgiveness of sins as common to all Christians, even though reasons of good order dictate that it is normally exercised by the clergy (*Pen.* 12, 21). In short, while the clergy have a special, public responsibility to preach the GOSPEL to the community as a whole, every Christian has a similar, personal responsibility to bear witness to the gospel to her brothers and sisters.

T. J. Wengert, *Priesthood, Pastors, Bishops: Public Ministry for the Reformation and Today* (Fortress Press, 2008).

IAN A. MCFARLAND

PRINCETON THEOLOGY The dominant theology of American Presbyterianism, Princeton theology was developed at Princeton Theological Seminary from its founding in 1812 until it was reorganized in 1929. Its foundations lay in the seminary charter's mandates to produce clergy who subscribe to the Westminster Confession (see WESTMINSTER STANDARDS), are highly educated in the ancient languages and the content of SCRIPTURE, knowledgeable in the history and controversies of the Church, committed to pastoral care using the distinctive features of Presbyterian POLITY, and faithful in corporate and private piety. By training over 6,000 students Princeton taught more pastors and missionaries than any other seminary up to 1912.

A. Alexander (1772–1851), Princeton's first professor and the most pastoral of the Princetonians, established themes that endured throughout its century-long history. He defended biblical authority, espoused a warm piety, advocated Scottish COMMONSENSE PHILOSOPHY and related biblical content to scientific findings. He taught Calvinism using Swiss theologian F. Turretin's (1623–87) *Institutio theologiae elencticae*. Converted during a revival, Alexander proved most amenable to American revivalism, though his successors faulted the Second Great Awakening for its defective theology and manipulative methods. Identifying with moderate Old School Presbyterians who opposed revising Calvinism, Alexander resisted extremist plans to expel the New School over doctrinal and polity differences, but he eventually voted to abrogate the ecumenical Plan of Union with Congregationalists, which resulted in the Old–New School SCHISM of 1837.

Alexander's protégé, C. HODGE, who joined the faculty in 1822, further developed Princeton's theology and world view for over fifty years. His three-volume *Systematic Theology* (1872–73) replaced Turretin in classroom instruction. He also founded the *Biblical Repertory and Princeton Review* (1825), one of the country's most respected religious journals which became the main organ for promulgating Princeton's Reformed perspective. Lengthy articles and reviews probed not only biblical, theological, and ecclesiastical matters, but explored a broad spectrum of intellectual topics and cultural interests: philosophical trends, the political state of the country, America's Civil War, abolitionism, and scientific views relating to human origins. The journal critiqued the theology and revivalist techniques of C. Finney (1792–1875), N. Taylor's (1786–1858) innovations to Calvinism, and the Mercersburg theology of J. Nevin (1803–86). Hodge's *Constitutional History of the Presbyterian Church in America* (1839) established the Old School position on the origins of Presbyterian polity and justified Princeton's acquiescence in the Church's 1837 division. *Conference Papers* (1879), a collection of talks Hodge delivered in Sunday-afternoon meetings on practical religion, displays his personal piety that set the spiritual tone of the seminary.

In the second half of the nineteenth century Princetonians addressed challenges posed by BIBLICAL CRITICISM and Darwinian EVOLUTION. From its inception Princeton endorsed the Westminster Confession's view of Scripture as the authoritative Word of God. Although all Princetonians held to a plenarily inspired and inerrant Bible as the historic teaching of the Church, in 1881 Hodge's son, A. Hodge (1823–86), wrote with B. Warfield (1851–1921) a definitive essay asserting that the original autographs were totally free from error (see Inerrancy). C. Hodge had concluded in *What Is Darwinism?* (1874) that Darwin's theory was atheistic because of its lack of teleology. The younger Hodge, however, conceded that not all theories of evolution were atheistic and that development of species occurred. Warfield further argued that evolution cannot explain creation, but it may illustrate divine providence. He also contended that antiquity of the human race was of no theological significance, but the unity of the human race was not negotiable.

Warfield never wrote a systematic theology, but his evidentialist apologetics and collected works on J. Calvin, Augustine, Christology, the Westminster divines, and perfectionism greatly enhanced Princeton's reputation. His trenchant reviews of European and American scholarship in *The Princeton Theological Review* demonstrated that theological innovation and liberal interpretations of the Bible resulted from imposing naturalistic world views on the text rather than careful exegesis of the text itself.

The last major figure of Old Princeton, J. Machen (1881–1937), professor of the NT, exhibited the same breadth of interest and command of literature as his predecessors. He defended orthodoxy in *The Origin of Paul's Religion* (1921) and *The Virgin Birth of Christ* (1930). His most effective work, *Christianity and Liberalism* (1923), written during the height of the fundamentalist–liberal controversy, demonstrated the disparity between historical Protestantism and modernism.

Presbyterians reorganized the seminary board in 1929 to permit a more inclusive theological perspective. Machen and several other conservatives resigned and founded Westminster Theological Seminary in Philadelphia to maintain Calvinist theology with modifications only in apologetic method. Princeton theology remains dominant today in confessionalist denominations and seminaries of the Reformed tradition and among scholars committed to historic evangelicalism.

See also Evangelical Theology; Reformed Theology.

W. A. Hoffecker, *Piety and the Princeton Theologians* (Baker Books, 1981).

M. A. Noll, *The Princeton Theology 1812–1921* (Baker Books, 1983).

J. C. Vander Stelt, *Philosophy and Scripture: A Study in Old Princeton and Westminster Theology* (Mack Publishing Company, 1978).

Andrew Hoffecker

PROCESS THEOLOGY Process theologies focus on the dynamic and relational nature of everything that exists, including God. In *Philosophers Speak of God* (1953), C. Hartshorne (1897–2000) and W. Reese (b. 1921) trace this process lineage throughout the centuries of western philosophical theology, including such figures as Heraclitus (*ca* 535–475 BC), Plotinus (204–70), Richard of St Victor (d. 1173), Nicholas of Cusa and Meister Eckhart in the fourteenth century, H. Bergson (1859–1941), S. Alexander (1859–1938), and A. N. Whitehead (1861–1947), the latter of whom is the primary catalyst for current process theologies.

Particularly characteristic of Whitehead is his grounding in mathematics and physics, from which he moves into dialogue with philosophies, and then into developing his own answer to the question, 'What must the nature of existence be, that it yields the data we discover through quantum physics?' His very complex answer focuses on the primacy of becoming, experience, and relationality. Everything that exists does so through its emergence from a particular past, in response to a call towards a particular future. This process is a creative synthesis; it is the emerging entity's own decisive integration of its actual past and its possible future into a present experience of subjective becoming. There is nothing underlying this, no concrete substance commanding the process. All is relation, becoming, experience.

And yet there is God, deeply influencing the process at every instance of becoming. God functions as that call to a particular future, that suggestion of ways in which this particular past might be integrated in this particular moment of experience. In a universe where all is relation, God cannot be outside of or untouched by relation. On the contrary, God must be that most relational of all forms of experience: that which relates not simply to a particular past, but to every past, integrating the vast universe of experience into the divine becoming at every moment. Through the completeness of this everlasting divine integration comes the fullness of God's knowledge of the world in every aspect of its becoming, and hence the aptness with which God feels a future for every new instance of becoming, influencing it towards its most optimum range of possibilities given its circumstances.

Every finite instance of becoming, then, is to be understood through three principles: the One, the Many, and Creativity. Its emergence is accounted for through its feelings of those occasions of experience that preceded it in its finite past (the Many), through its feelings of the influence of God towards its own possibilities for the immediate future (the One), and through its own creative response to both (Creativity). Thus it is both other-created and self-created.

These broad brushstrokes give an overview of process thought, but the above requires the further delineation of what Whitehead called the 'physical' and 'mental' poles of every becoming entity, including God. The physical pole refers simply to the capacity to feel that which is other. The way we use language suggests that there must first be a 'something' that then feels others, but a process perspective differs radically from this. Instead, to have come into existence at all is to have an effect, and this effect is like a birthing process forcing something new into existence – a successor entity. Multiply this by countless entities in some form of proximity, each of which is like an insistence on a successor occasion of experience. From this cacophony, the physical feelings of these effects emerge as the becoming of a new entity. This emergent feeling of otherness constitutes the physical pole of an entity.

The idea of the mental pole addresses the question of how these many physical feelings can be integrated into a unity of experience. Just as a physical pole has no necessary reference to what we call the physical dimensions of our existence, neither does the mental pole have a necessary reference to thought. The mental pole refers to the capacity to feel a possibility for unification given this particular complexity of feelings. Whitehead calls it a mental capacity because it feels that which does not exist, like an idea of what might be rather than what is. In this sense, the physical pole begins the process of emergence, and the mental pole provides the possibility of completing it by integrating the many feelings into a new experience of subjective unity.

This process of integration (called 'concrescence' by Whitehead) has several requirements. Instigated by the feeling of possibilities for unity in the midst of manyness, the emerging entity feels each of its discrete feelings in relation to all others (Whitehead calls this 'mutuality of subjective form') in a process of contrast and comparison. Judgements emerge (not yet necessarily in the form of thought), by which feelings might be negated, adapted, or adjusted. Finally, the process of unification is completed in what Whitehead called the 'satisfaction' of the entity. It has become itself through this whole process of integration. Having become, it now acts as a catalyst calling for the emergence of its own successors, and the process is repeated again and again and again, each time yielding new and unique occasions of experience.

The application of this process of becoming to God requires a reversal of the polar structure, and hence of the process of concrescence. Whitehead envisions God as the source of possibilities, so that the mental pole is primordial in God, existing as a dynamic togetherness of all possibilities whatsoever for any and every universe of becoming. God is the organizer of possibilities, everlastingly unifying them according to God's own pleasure, and always in a conjunction yielding infinite variations of the theme of adventure, zest, beauty, truth, and peace. Whereas in finite occasions of experience the mental pole follows the physical, in God the reverse is true: the mental grounds and gives rise to the physical. The physical, in turn, is God's feelings of the world in every moment of its completion. The world is felt within God's own nature, there to be integrated in the divine concrescence towards conformity with God's primordial nature. This integration has several facets: on the one hand, it can be developed in terms of the eschatological redemption of the world as it is judged and transformed within God's own becoming; on the other hand, how God integrates the just-completed world affects God's feelings of possibilities for the newly emergent world. God's provision of possibilities for the world follows from God's integration of the world within the divine concrescence.

As can be noted from the above, discussion of Whitehead's philosophical schematism quickly moves into a richness of theological possibilities. The adaptation of process thought to Christian theology began primarily at the University of Chicago Divinity School, first through the influence of H. Wieman's (1884–1975) creative interpretation of Whitehead, and then through Whitehead's own teaching assistant at Harvard, C. Hartshorne (1897–2000), who later joined the Chicago faculty. While Hartshorne developed his philosophical theology as a variation of the rationalistic side of Whitehead, others on the Chicago faculty focused on the empirical elements within Whitehead. But it was one of their students, J. B. Cobb, Jr. (b. 1925), who was to be the major force in applying the categories of process thought to Christian theology. *A Christian Natural Theology* (1965), *The Structure of Christian Existence* (1967), and *Christ in a Pluralistic Age* (1975) are among his major early theological works, later followed by collaborative exploration of the theological implications of process in areas as diverse as ecology, biology, physics, economics, politics, education, and inter-religious dialogue. With L. Ford (b. 1933), Cobb founded the journal *Process Studies* in 1970, and three years later established the Center for Process Studies at Claremont School of Theology. This centre, and Cobb's teaching at both Claremont School of Theology and Claremont Graduate School (now Claremont Graduate University), not only provided a stream of graduate students who would later teach and develop process theology at a variety of institutions, but also created a stream of influence affecting an increased emphasis on becoming, experience, and relationality within many other forms of contemporary Christian theology.

While theologies stemming explicitly from the process school differ in a variety of ways, they hold a number of themes in common. First, all assume that God creates through EVOLUTION. This follows naturally from the concept that God continuously calls the world into becoming. The world's responsiveness to God is a part of the evolving creative process. This leads to a second common theme, which is the location of the problem of evil (see THEODICY) within the evolutionary process. Some process theologians focus on the responsiveness of the world to God's call as the source of evil, because of the freedom entailed in that responsiveness. When an occasion deviates from the call of God, evil can be introduced into the world as SIN, which is analogous to a traditional Christian naming of sin as missing the mark of God's call. Other process theologians argue that a capacity for aggression is necessarily built into the evolutionary system in order to ensure the physical survival of complex and fragile forms of existence. When sustainability is reached God calls the organism to a spiritual form of existence, which requires a reversal of priorities. Rather than responding to others with aggression, spiritual existence entails responses in keeping with the reality of our interdependence. Long habits of self-interest interfere with the capacity for spirituality, and sin – or unnecessary evil – results.

Creative transformation as the mode through which God redeems the world is a third common theme. All process theologians stress the creative transformation that God enables within the world, and some also stress an eschatological transformation that yields a final redemption of the world beyond death (see ESCHATOLOGY). Both assume that God feels the world as it is and offers enabling possibilities for what the world might yet be. In so far as a finite entity acts on these possibilities, creative transformation occurs. Those who also argue for a final transformation in God base their argument on God's capacity to feel the entirety of each finite entity through God's physical pole, including the subjectivity of the entity. In this case, the finite world participates in its integration into the fullness of God, which is both its judgement and its redemption.

A fourth theme is INCARNATION. Far from being a problem in process thought, incarnation is God's way of working in the world. God inspires the world through God's offer of possibilities. In the maximum case of incarnation, or CHRISTOLOGY, process theologians argue that Jesus becomes Christ by responding fully to God's creative lure to manifest the divine nature in history, so that incarnation in this case is at the same time a full revelation of who God is for us. The teachings of Jesus reveal the LOVE of God, crucifixion reveals God's presence to us as co-sufferer in the midst of physical and spiritual pain; RESURRECTION reveals that God's presence is for the sake of our creative transformation, both in history and in God in so far as we are made partakers of the divine life. The full REVELATION of God's nature in Christ enables specific forms of creative transformation in the world through communal spiritual existence, which of course suggests a theology of the Church (see ECCLESIOLOGY).

Process theologies also uniformly suggest that religious PLURALISM is to be affirmed as the natural consequence of the fact that God works with the world contextually. Responsiveness to the call of God is cumulative and social, so that precisely how God calls depends upon previous answers to that call within the enormous complexity of the actual world. The more complicated the organism God calls, particularly at the personal and social levels of human development, the greater the range of diversity that will result.

Finally, process theologians within the Christian tradition speak of God as LOVE. A gracious God who offers and enables possibilities for creative transformation towards spiritual existence, who reveals the divine nature within the context of human history, who receives the world into the divine nature even when the world yields pain, sin, and tragedies, who suffers with the world for the sake of the world's own resurrection in history and beyond, is the ultimate form of love.

See also OPEN THEISM.

J. B. Cobb, Jr, *A Christian Natural Theology*, 2nd edn (John Knox Press, 2007).

D. Griffin, *God, Power, and Evil: A Process Theodicy* (Westminster Press, 1976).

C. Hartshorne, *The Divine Relativity: A Social Conception of God* (Yale University Press, 1974).

J. McDaniel and D. Bowman, eds., *Handbook of Process Theology* (Chalice Press, 2006).

M. Suchocki, *God Christ Church: A Practical Guide to Process Theology* (Crossroad, 1982).

MARJORIE HEWITT SUCHOCKI

PROCREATION Procreation has played a prominent role in the biblical and Christian theological traditions. In the OT humans were given the divine mandate to be fruitful and multiply in order to subdue the earth and assert their dominion over it (Gen. 1:28). Children were, therefore, received as a blessing, and infertility was seen as a curse. Moreover, offspring were the principal means of perpetuating the COVENANT community over time.

In the NT the divine mandate is qualified, thereby easing the obligation to procreate. PAUL, for example, was ambivalent about MARRIAGE and family, and recommended continence for believers (1 Cor. 7:25–8, 38). Many early converts refrained from sexual intercourse either because of their belief in the imminent return of Christ, or to reinforce the conviction that since *the* child had already been born there was no longer any urgent need to procreate. The Church, unlike ISRAEL, would not perpetuate itself through biological lineage but through BAPTISM.

In either case pagan Rome viewed such sexual renunciation with great suspicion. Procreation was a public duty rather than a private choice. The strength and fate of the empire depended upon children. Due to high infant mortality rates, it is estimated that every woman needed to give birth to five children to maintain a stable population. Consequently, Emperor Augustus (63 BC–14 AD) promulgated laws which fined free men if they did not marry by a certain age, and penalized them again if they had not produced a requisite number of legitimate children within a specified period of time. In this respect, the sexual renunciation of many Christians was not so much a result of moral taboo as it was a political statement – one that from

Rome's perspective was tantamount to sedition. In contrast to Rome, the hope of the Church was Christ and not its children.

The subsequent growth of the Church was accompanied by the tacit recognition that most of its members were married couples and parents. This acknowledgement can be seen in the NT's household codes (e.g., Col. 3:18–4:1) and other early Christian literature providing instruction on childrearing. It was still nonetheless assumed that continent singleness was a vastly superior way of life. Marriage and family were tolerated rather than affirmed because household responsibilities were an impediment to serving God with a single-hearted devotion. Christian spouses and parents were effectively portrayed as second-class believers.

It is with Augustine that a more constructive theological assessment of procreation is undertaken. In *The Good of Marriage* and *On Marriage and Concupiscence*, he characterizes marriage and parenthood as virtuous vocations that should be affirmed and supported by the Church. Raising children within a Christian household is a worthy pursuit that honours God. Consequently, offspring is one of the goods of marriage. Although Augustine continued to believe that singleness was superior to marriage and family, both are nonetheless Christian ways of life. Rather than denigrating marriage and family, he merely highlights their differences with singleness, using the analogy of a hill and a mountain: both are good, but the latter is greater than the former. Likewise, marriage and singleness are both good, but the latter is superior to the former. Subsequent generations of theologians would refine this Augustinian framework, eventually establishing more formally the sacramental status of marriage. In disavowing celibacy and monasticism, early Protestant theologians effectively re-established a public obligation to marry and procreate.

Procreation continues to generate a number of contemporary moral and political issues. With the widespread use of contraception, procreation has become largely a matter of private choice rather than a public obligation in most affluent societies. While most Protestant Churches view contraception as permissible, the Catholic Church rejects all forms of artificial birth control as contrary to the meaning and purpose of sexual intercourse. Still more controversially, various techniques are also being used increasingly to select the characteristics of offspring (e.g., sex) or the absence of deleterious or unwanted genetic indications. Some critics are troubled by this technological intervention into procreation, worrying that it represents a covert form of eugenics. In addition, some troubling demographic concerns are emerging. In many poorer nations overpopulation is often a problem resulting in widespread malnutrition, illness, and poverty. In contrast, declining birth rates in many affluent nations will create a number of serious economic issues when there are an insufficient number of productive workers to support a large population of unproductive pensioners.

See also Abortion; Bioethics; Sexuality; Virginity.

P. Brown, *The Body and Society: Men, Women and Sexual Renunciation in Early Christianity* (Faber and Faber, 1989).

B. Waters, *Reproductive Technology: Towards a Theology of Procreative Stewardship* (Darton, Longman and Todd, 2001).

Brent Waters

Prodromos: see John the Baptist.

Prophecy Prophecy is a prime feature of the OT and continues in modified form in the NT (see, e.g., Rom. 12:6; 1 Cor. 12:10; 1 Thess. 5:20; cf. Acts 21:9–10). Thereafter it is arguably a recurrent feature within Christian history down to the present day (see Pentecostal Theology), though problems of definition (What exactly counts as prophecy? How does Christian preaching relate to prophecy?) are acute.

Prophecy is essentially *speech on behalf of God* (though many prophets perform actions for God also). A classic depiction is found in Deuteronomy 5:27, where Israel makes the following request of Moses (which God immediately approves and implements in the succeeding verses): 'Go near, you yourself, and hear all that the Lord our God will say. Then tell us everything that the Lord our God tells you, and we will listen and do it'. Moses is to stand in proximity to God, a proximity that is implicitly moral and spiritual more than geographical, so that he has access to God's will. This access is with a view to conveying God's will to Israel, so that Israel can know how to live under God. Moses here is the paradigm of other prophets (Deut. 18:15–19). Such access to the will of God is sometimes spoken of as 'standing in the divine council' (Jer. 23:18, 22), for the prophet is privy to the divine will as a senior courtier or counsellor is privy to a king's/ruler's purposes (cf. Amos 3:7; 2 Kgs 4:27).

Intrinsic to speaking for God is the notion of being *sent*, a verb that is integral to prophetic commissionings (Exod. 3:13,15; Isa. 6:8; Jer. 1:7; Ezek. 2:3). This sending indicates that the speech is not self-generated, but constitutes a divine initiative that is humanly mediated. Hence a prophet characteristically speaks for God as a messenger speaks for his master, 'Thus says God/X' (compare Jacob's commissioning messengers for Esau in Gen. 32:3–4 with God's commissioning Moses for Pharaoh in Exod. 4:22–23). Although the OT primarily depicts the prophet speaking for God to Israel, some texts also depict the prophet as speaking for Israel to God in the form of intercessory prayer (e.g., 1 Sam. 12:19, 24, Jer. 27:18). The vocation to speak entails a vocation to care.

Prophecy is characteristically *response-seeking* speech, which depicts a possible future whose realization is contingent upon the response given in the present. (Compare 'I love you', where what happens next depends on the response given; or, the warning to a person carelessly stepping onto a busy road, 'You're going to be run over', where the words seek a response such that what is spoken of does *not* happen). This is formulated axiomatically in Jeremiah 18:7–10, where Jeremiah's commission is envisaged as leading to diverse outcomes: threatened disaster can be averted through turning/repentance (cf. Jer. 26:18–19; Jonah 3:4–10), and conversely promised good can be forfeited through complacency and corruption (as in Gen. 6:5–7; 1 Sam. 2:30; 15:11). A similar principle of response-related contingency for individuals is formulated in relation to Ezekiel's vocation to be a watchman/sentinel (Ezek. 33:1–16).

The NT also portrays individual 'prophets', though their precise role appears limited (see 1 Cor. 12:28; 14:1–40); but the prime continuity with the OT is in the figure of the APOSTLE (literally, 'one who is sent'), who is commissioned by God and the risen Jesus (e.g., John 20:21–2; Gal. 1:1) to bear witness to God's truth as now definitively known in Christ.

Modern scholarship has given much attention to issues related to the history of prophecy and the prophetic books: how does prophecy in Israel relate to comparable phenomena in the ancient Near East? How did prophecy develop within Israel? Why did prophecy become a written phenomenon from Amos onwards? How do the prophets relate to the LAW? How do the prophetic books relate to the prophetic figure they depict? Why did prophecy fade out after the exile?

Although theological issues regularly feature within such debates, some of the prime issues can be formulated on their own terms. First, it is important to avoid any competitive understanding of the divine and the human, as though the more one can locate and explain prophets within their historical context (sociologically, psychologically, etc.) the less one can ascribe what they say to God – though such a competitive understanding (tantamount to a 'god of the gaps' theology) regularly skews debate. God is not an 'explanation' analogous to that of the sciences, but is the sovereign reality who is recognized when people are open to moral and spiritual truth within prophetic speech.

Second, a prime critical issue concerns how to distinguish genuine claims to speak for God from those which are spurious; how does one differentiate between the divine in human mediation and the merely human which pretends to the divine? Although it may be supposed that one can only tell with hindsight, in terms of the realization or otherwise of what a prophet says (cf. Deut. 18:21–2), the prime critical criteria within the OT, not least within the extended treatment in Jeremiah 23:9–32, relate to (1) the conformity of the prophet's life to God's priorities (23:14, 15), and (2) the moral integrity of the challenge which the prophet speaks, such that it seeks to bring people to genuine engagement with God (usually through repentance, 23:21–2); for the divine is located in the moral and spiritual content of the prophetic person and message.

Third, the prophets operate with an understanding of divine action within history in relation to human integrity and corruption (as in Jeremiah's temple sermon in Jer. 7:1–15) that many find difficult today, when categories of politics, economics, sociology, and psychology tend to be the preferred categories for accounting for movements in history – even though the prophetic emphasis on justice still resonates. Not unrelated is an unease many have with the very idea that one could speak as confidently and categorically for God as the prophets do, given the complexities of life in the world and human potential for self-deception. However, a moral account complements rather than displaces other accounts, as the prophets along with other voices in the OT recognize that God's ways are frequently inscrutable (cf. Isa. 55:8), and much of what the prophets say represents a moral vision whose value only becomes apparent as and when it is appropriated within human living.

H. B. Huffmon, 'Prophecy' in *Anchor Bible Dictionary*, ed. D. N. Freedman vol. V (Doubleday, 1992), 477–502.

R. W. L. Moberly, *Prophecy and Discernment* (Cambridge University Press, 2006).

G. von Rad, *The Message of the Prophets* (SCM, 1968).

R. W. L. Moberly

Proskynēsis: see Dulia.

Prosperity Gospel Also known as 'prosperity doctrine' and (by critics) as 'name it and claim it' or 'health and wealth' theology, the prosperity gospel refers to Christian ministries whose hallmark is the belief that God intends prosperity (including material abundance, physical health, and financial success) for believers and, correspondingly, that such prosperity is rightly interpreted as a sign of divine favour and approval. For some this prosperity is interpreted as direct recompense for generosity in giving to the Church; by others it is understood as bestowed by God to enable such giving, whether as a reward for good works, a response to PRAYER, or even as a matter of PREDESTINATION. Though not limited to any particular Christian tradition, it is frequently associated with the Word of Faith (or Word-Faith) movement in Pentecostalism, which teaches that Christ died to bring material as well as spiritual benefits to believers (see Pentecostal Theology).

A key biblical text used by proponents of the prosperity gospel to support this position is 2 Corinthians 8:9 ('Jesus Christ … for your sakes became poor, so that … you might become rich'), though frequent reference is also made to OT texts in which material abundance is understood as a sign of God's COVENANT faithfulness (e.g., Deut. 8:18; cf. Gal. 3:9). Ministries associated with the prosperity gospel have been criticized on a number of fronts, including captivity to a shallow materialism inconsistent with the POVERTY of Jesus and the APOSTLES, failure to focus on SIN and the need for repentance, and promoting an individualism that undermines Christian social responsibility.

IAN A. MCFARLAND

PROTESTANTISM 'Protestantism' emerged during the sixteenth century as a broad term used to refer to a network of ecclesial movements in the western Church outside the body of the Catholic Church. From the outset, 'Protestantism' designated a series of movements rather than a single coherent entity. The use of the term is somewhat problematic for a number of reasons, not least that these reforming movements did not always see themselves as specific embodiments of a more general reality.

By the end of the 1520s, three broad strands can be discerned within the western European Church: the reforming movement which traced its origins back to M. LUTHER, initially based in north-eastern Germany, and which gradually came to be known as 'Lutheran'; the reforming movement initially associated with H. ZWINGLI and the city of Zurich, which later became consolidated under J. CALVIN and the city of Geneva and became widely described as 'Calvinist' (though it is today often referred to in scholarly literature as 'Reformed'); and more radical approaches to Christianity which emerged in the 1520s, and were often linked with a rejection of infant baptism and referred to as 'Anabaptist'. A distinct form of Protestantism, often referred to as 'Anglican', emerged in England, especially during the reign of Elizabeth I (r. 1558–1603). In the later part of the sixteenth century, Protestantism underwent considerable territorial expansion. Most significantly, it began to establish a presence in North America through emigration, initially from England, and subsequently from Germany and Scandinavia. The expansion continued during the eighteenth and nineteenth centuries, partly through colonial expansion of European powers such as Great Britain, and partly through the founding of mission societies.

Protestantism is characterized theologically by its emphasis upon the individual's right to interpret SCRIPTURE and its rejection of any notion of papal authority. The DOCTRINE of JUSTIFICATION by faith alone (*sola fide*) was a cornerstone of much early Protestant preaching and theological reflection. At the practical level, Protestantism was easily distinguished from Catholicism by its practice of offering EUCHARIST in both kinds, i.e., allowing the laity to receive both bread and wine in the Communion service. These ideas were expressed in Protestant 'Confessions of Faith', such as the Lutheran AUGSBURG CONFESSION (1530), the Calvinist Westminster Confession (1647; see WESTMINSTER STANDARDS), or the Anglican Thirty-Nine Articles (1566). Such confessions were seen as subordinate to both Scripture and the ecumenical CREEDS (both of which were held to possess universal authority) and tended to be viewed as local implementations or interpretations of the Christian FAITH.

Although sharing a common commitment to the authority of Scripture as a source of ethics and doctrine, Protestants found themselves disagreeing on its interpretation and application at many points. For this reason, the area of 'biblical hermeneutics' has played a much greater role in the shaping of the Protestant theological tradition than it did its Catholic or Orthodox counterparts. A multiplicity of approaches, synchronic and diachronic, to biblical interpretation has resulted in Protestantism showing a considerable degree of variation at any given time, as well as development over time. It is thus difficult to generalize about 'Protestant' attitudes or beliefs, as if these were permanently and clearly defined. Nevertheless, some general observations can be made.

Some strands of Protestantism have been persistently ambivalent about the place of the arts. The OT prohibition of images of the divine was taken very seriously within REFORMED THEOLOGY, which prohibited depictions of Jesus Christ or God in churches (see ICONS and ICONOCLASM). The Reformed tradition was also critical of the theatre and novels, in that both elevated works of fiction, intended to deceive, above factual and improving narratives. Substantially the same criticism would later be made of the cinema in the early twentieth century. Lutheranism and Anglicanism, in contrast, came to value the role of the visual arts and literature, both as an aid to piety and devotion, and for their own sakes. This legacy, combined with a weakening of Reformed hostility to the arts in the late twentieth century, has manifested itself in growing interest in the interface of Protestant theology and the visual arts on the one hand, and literature on the other (see FILM, THEOLOGY AND; PAINTING, THEOLOGY AND).

Discussion of the broader impact of Protestantism on western culture has been deeply marked by the 'Weber thesis', developed by the German sociologist M. Weber (1864–1920). This proposed that a new 'spirit of capitalism' emerged in the early modern period as a result of Protestant influence, especially within the Reformed tradition. Weber argued that Reformed piety in particular generated the psychological preconditions essential to the development of modern capitalism, partly on account of the way in which its doctrine of PREDESTINATION encouraged economic activism among believers, in the belief that material prosperity could be taken as a sign of divine blessing, and thus of ELECTION to salvation. Although this thesis has proved controversial, it continues to be influential.

A significant link can also be made between Protestantism (again, particularly in its Reformed manifestation) and the natural sciences from the later sxiteenth century. The reason for this intellectual synergy is not fully understood, but is widely believed to involve perceived parallels between the interpretation of the 'book of Scripture' and the 'book of nature'. Protestant writers increasingly came to see the interpretation of the 'two books' as interconnected, with both requiring direct attention to the 'data' unencumbered by traditional teaching. Serious tensions emerged in the later nineteenth century, when C. Darwin's (1809–82) theory of EVOLUTION appeared to call into question traditional Protestant interpretations of the Bible. This led to renewed engagement with the biblical CREATION narratives, leading some to adopt accommodationist understandings (see ACCOMMODATION), and others to propose a 'warfare' between science and religion. Theologically, this has manifested itself in growing interest in the relation of theology and the NATURAL SCIENCES, a trend especially evident in the writings of the Scottish theologian T. F. Torrance (1913–2007).

Although clearly showing roots in some important theological and spiritual trends of the late Middle Ages, Protestantism came into being through a series of ruptures with the medieval Catholic Church. With the passing of time and the softening of institutional memories, many began to wonder whether some form of *détente*, or even rapprochement, might be possible. This ecumenical interest took place at two levels: the fostering of better relationships, if not achieving visual unity, between Protestant denominations; and the attempts to bring about better relationships between Protestantism and Catholicism. Theologically, this has given rise to a serious engagement with Catholic and Orthodox theologians within Protestant theology since the 1960s. It is now welcomely routine for Protestant theologians to engage positively and appreciatively with writers such as K. RAHNER and H. U. VON BALTHASAR, just as Catholics have simultaneously taken K. BARTH with increasing seriousness.

Protestantism, like most other forms of Christianity, recognized the importance of education at every level. The founding of new schools, colleges, and universities in western Europe, and subsequently in North America, is a significant indication of the commitment to education. The commitment of Protestants to theological engagement was thus undergirded by a network of educational institutions which aimed at consolidating specific versions of Protestant theology and exploring their broader intellectual and cultural implications. In the twentieth century, however, the fundamentally religious basis of many of these colleges was called into question as a result of changes in society and academic culture. Many American colleges and universities with specifically Protestant foundations have seen these transmuted into more generalized Christian forms, or restated in essentially secular forms. Harvard University illustrates this trend well: its original motto of 1692, *Veritas Christo et Ecclesiae* ('Truth for Christ and the Church'), has been verbally and conceptually truncated to the single word *Veritas* ('Truth').

Finally, it must be noted that the twentieth century gave rise to some further significant developments within Protestantism. The growing economic and political significance of the USA led to American Protestantism playing an increasingly important role globally, particularly after World War II. Although there are now indications of multiple historical origins of Pentecostalism, it is traditionally held to have begun in the USA during the first decade of the twentieth century. The 'Azusa Street revival' was a harbinger of similar revivals elsewhere. Pentecostalism's emphasis upon a direct experience of God and an ensuing personal transformation proved to have a deep appeal to urban populations in Latin America, Asia, and Africa. In addition to giving a much higher profile to pneumatology in matters of theology, this has led to significant developments in some fields of biblical interpretation. More generally, there is some evidence of discomfort with the use of the word 'Protestant' in some circles on account of its possible sectarian overtones in Northern Ireland and western Scotland.

It must be concluded that Protestantism represents a theological work in progress. It remains unclear whether the movement's past allows us to predict its future.

See also ANGLICAN THEOLOGY; LUTHERAN THEOLOGY; PENTECOSTAL THEOLOGY; REFORMATION; REFORMED THEOLOGY.

J. C. Brauer, *Protestantism in America: A Narrative History* (Westminster Press, 1965).

P. Harrison, *The Bible, Protestantism, and the Rise of Natural Science* (Cambridge University Press, 1998).

M. E. Marty, *Protestantism* (Holt, Rinehart and Winston, 1972).

A. E. McGrath, *Christianity's Dangerous Idea: The Protestant Revolution* (HarperOne, 2007).

D. E. Miller, *Reinventing American Protestantism: Christianity in the New Millennium* (University of California Press, 1997).

ALISTER MCGRATH

PROVIDENCE The meaning of the concept of providence includes both senses of the Latin *providere*, from which it derives: foresight and providing. In SCRIPTURE God's providing for CREATION is celebrated at the end of the flood story (Gen. 8:22), where the regularity of the seasons is a sign of divine faithfulness, and in many of the psalms (e.g., Pss. 19, 104). Elsewhere, there is a sense of God struggling within nature and history to accomplish the divine rule and to overcome evil; this is powerfully attested, for example, in the closing stages of JOB. In the SERMON ON THE MOUNT, Jesus speaks of God's parental rule of nature and creaturely activity, a ruling that governs even the smallest detail

(Matt. 6:25–33). In light of the RESURRECTION as the sign of the coming kingdom, the early Church could proclaim the outworking of God's good purpose throughout the entire cosmos (Rom. 8:28; Rev. 1:17–18). Although the concept is not explicitly developed in Scripture itself, providence would later emerge as a unifying theme that integrated Christian convictions about creation, redemption, and ESCHATOLOGY. On a vertical axis, it is required to connect creation as the making of the world with its redemption in Christ and its final consummation. On a horizontal axis, its scope includes not only ISRAEL and the Church, but extends outwards to comprehend culture, history, the natural world, and the wider realms of the cosmos.

In the patristic period, theologians found resources in Stoic philosophy for articulating divine providence. Against those pagan philosophers who assigned greater scope to randomness and chance in the universe, the Stoics insisted upon the conformity of all events to the rational principles that informed the universe. For Christian theologians such as Theophilus of Antioch (d. *ca* 185) with their biblical convictions about divine rule, an alliance with Stoicism on this matter seemed compelling. One danger of this dependence, detected especially by modern theologians, was an impersonal determinism that threatened both the personal nature of God's rule and also the freedom granted to human creatures. While this determinism may have characterized doctrinal formulations more than scriptural interpretation in the early Church, the influence of Stoicism continued to be registered at later periods.

Within the classical western tradition, providence became a central theological doctrine. T. AQUINAS located it within the doctrine of God. As one of the divine perfections, providence belongs to God by virtue of divine omniscience and omnipotence. Nothing can happen that is not willed and known by God from all eternity. Since each thing owes its existence to God, its final end is bound to be directed by God. Aquinas here employs the model of God as artist. 'Since his knowledge is related to things like that of an artist to his works of art . . . it must be that all things are set under his ordering' (*ST* 1.22.2).

The presence of evil in the creation – a major challenge to the doctrine of providence – is also ruled by God, according to Aquinas. Though evils may conflict with the nature of some particular thing, these contribute to the overall end of nature. 'Were all evils to be denied entrance many good things would be lacking in the world: there would not be life for the lion were there no animals for its prey, and no patience of martyrs were there no persecution by tyrants' (1.22.2). The distinction between primary and secondary causality becomes crucial here in order to avoid the implication that God is the author of evil and SIN. The secondary causes which govern contingent entities are related to the primary cause of God's will, which is both their necessary and their sufficient condition; but it is the former that carry responsibility for the imperfections of the world. Elsewhere in Aquinas, the attention to human freedom, miracles, and prayer offer a more dramatic and less determinist account of the God–world relationship, in which divine initiative and creaturely response achieve a degree of mutuality. In the exercise of human agency, divine and creaturely causes belong to different orders, which are complementary and non-competitive. Likewise, in response to ancient anxieties about the efficacy and propriety of petitionary PRAYER, Aquinas argues that divine providence has ordered the world in such a way that the will of God is sometimes made effective through the agency of human prayer. Thus divine rule is compatible with human freedom, even to the extent of guaranteeing it.

J. CALVIN and the post-Reformation tradition located providence within the doctrine of creation. It is not essential to the divine being but is a necessary feature of God's relationship to the world. Calvin argues from the conviction that it is the teaching of Scripture that everything is ordained by God. Behind what appears uncertain and confused, there lies the steady and immutable will of God. The providence of God employs creaturely means for the fulfilment of the divine will. Like Aquinas, Calvin is careful to note that the attribution of all events to God's will does not entail that God is the cause of sin and evil. These are to be assigned to creaturely agencies which, although subordinate to the divine action, carry the sole responsibility for wrongdoing. The rays of the sun may cause the corpse to putrefy, yet the stink is to be attributed to the corpse and not to the sun (*Inst.* 1.17.5).

The comprehensive nature of God's ever-watchful rule informs Calvin's account and it promotes a particular type of piety. Attacking Epicurean notions of chance, he insists upon everything being ordained by God. All things come to pass by the divine dispensation. Tribulations are sent to chastise or steel us in the ways of discipleship. This elicits an attitude of trust that nothing can happen by fortune or chance. Everything is under the paternal care of God. There is a strong pastoral dimension to this DOCTRINE in the Reformed tradition. It provides a sense of assurance, guidance, and direction in the face of unexpected sickness, misfortune and political uncertainty. This is evident especially in the HEIDELBERG CATECHISM and in the ways in which the doctrine of providence governed expressions of personal and political identity. A related practical upshot of the Calvinist doctrine is the sense of confidence and trust that derives from the knowledge that the future is secured by God. This energizes the believer in serving God in the world. This lent support to the much-debated thesis of the German sociologist M. Weber (1864–1920) that the Protestant ethic fostered the spirit of capitalism in early modern Europe. In New England a strong sense of providentialism was found in the lives of Puritan immigrants and in theological expressions of the national identity, e.g., in John Cotton (1585–1652; see PURITANISM). Emerging from this Protestant tradition, the discourse of providence remains resonant within American political culture today and has many secular variants.

The Reformed and Lutheran ORTHODOXY of the seventeenth century further formalized the doctrine of providence by its commitment to a threefold pattern of *CONSERVATIO*, *CONCURSUS*, and *GUBERNATIO*. In preserving the world, God maintains its matter, laws, and creatures in order to accomplish the divine purpose. The preservation of the world is a mark of divine faithfulness and constancy. In co-operating with creatures, God enables them always to act in accordance with the divine will. (Reformed and Lutheran accounts had different emphases at this point, the former tending towards divine determinism rather than human freedom.) The distinction between primary and secondary causality was again vital in avoiding the implication that God was the author of sin, while also guaranteeing the consistency of divine rule with human freedom. In guiding and overruling all things to their appointed end, God ensures that all things fulfil the purpose for which they have been created. This scheme was intended to articulate the scriptural account of the divine relation to the world. In doing so, it avoided an 'extrinsicism' in which God becomes detached and remote from the world (as in DEISM) and also an 'intrinsicism' in which God was too closely identified and limited by the processes of the world (as in PANTHEISM).

Within this dogmatic tradition, a distinction between general and special providence was also frequently invoked. General providence comprised the laws and general order of the world, both natural and social, while special providence referred to the particular acts of divine rule in the lives of creatures, especially with respect to the Christian life. These included miracles, God's response to our prayers and the promptings of the HOLY SPIRIT.

While refusing to yield to synergist tendencies, K. BARTH's account of providence represents a significant revision to the classical tradition, especially its Reformed version. Complaining that this tradition was insufficiently related to the self-revealing acts of the TRINITY, Barth sought to offer a more Christocentric and scripturally adequate account that was less determinist and more tentative in how it read the providential works of God throughout nature and history (*CD* III/3). Providence is grounded in FAITH rather than speculative vision. We can see its outcomes only partially and with the eyes of faith. It is a doctrine that has creaturely freedom as one of its goals. For Barth, divine providence is evident not so much in secular history with its problematic claims for progress but in those events that are more closely linked to God's redeeming power in Jesus – the preservation of Holy Scripture, the maintenance of the Church, and the ongoing witness of the Jewish people. Only in their partial attestation of Jesus Christ can we perceive the rhythms of life, the order of the natural world, and political society as tokens of divine providence. As confirmation of God's rule through Christ amidst sin and evil, Barth suggests that providence might more authentically be affirmed on bad days of struggle and suffering than in better times of serene pleasure and contentment. It is grasped not by the speculative intellect, but only in faith, obedience, and prayer.

Elsewhere in modern theology, other attempts have been made at revisionist accounts of the classical doctrine, especially where it appears suggestive of an impersonal determinism that threatens human freedom and magnifies the problem of divine responsibility for evil. Some address these problems by making a strong distinction between divine permission and divine willing, affirming that divine foreknowledge of future events depends not upon God's preordained will but rather on divine foresight of creatures' genuinely free choices. These revisions were anticipated by (Catholic) Molinists (see MIDDLE KNOWLEDGE) and (Protestant) Arminians in the seventeenth century (see ARMINIANISM) and by Wesleyans in the eighteenth (see METHODIST THEOLOGY), and in important respects they recall features of the less determinist and monergistic doctrine of providence that can be found in the Orthodox tradition (e.g., in MAXIMUS THE CONFESSOR). In twentieth-century constructions, greater attention has been devoted to the personal nature of the divine rule, implying notions of co-operation and persuasion that are less developed in the classical tradition. This is a feature not only of PROCESS THEOLOGY, but also of varieties of PERSONALISM (e.g., J. Oman (1860–1939)), and more recently of OPEN THEISM and some Anglo-Saxon philosophies of religion with their abridgement of the doctrine of divine omniscience (e.g., J. Lucas (b. 1929) and R. Swinburne (b. 1934)). Here it is claimed that a genuinely free and open universe is one in which even God cannot entirely foreknow future outcomes. Divine providence thus takes the form of an improvising and ever-resourceful love. This approach has been further reinforced by readings of the OT, engagement with neo-Darwinian science with its stress on the openness and unpredictability of the evolutionary process, and also pastoral theologies that stress the importance of the language of complaint and lament in Scripture. The world is not the embodiment of a perfect divine blueprint – it is a dramatic work in progress in which everything is not yet in conformity with God's good will. While this has been criticized for allowing an element of risk and indeterminacy into the created order, exponents maintain that where it is held alongside creation out of nothing and a robust eschatology the risk is finally overruled by divine grace.

See also Divine Action; Free Will; Philosophical Theology; Theodicy.

K. Barth, *Church Dogmatics* (T&T Clark, 1961), III/3.
C. G. Berkouwer, *The Providence of God* (Eerdmans, 1952).
P. Helm, *The Providence of God* (InterVarsity Press, 1993).
J. Polkinghorne, *Science and Providence* (SPCK, 1989).
J. Sanders, *The God Who Risks: A Theology of Divine Providence*, 2nd ed (InterVarsity Press, 2007).
C. M. Wood, *The Question of Providence* (John Knox Press, 2008).

David A. S. Fergusson

Pseudo-Dionysius: see Dionysius the Areopagite.

Psychopannychism Also known as the doctrine of soul sleep, psychopannychism (from the Greek words for 'soul' and 'vigil') refers to the belief that the human soul subsists in an unconscious state between the time of bodily death and the final resurrection. While this belief does seem to be reflected in certain biblical texts (e.g., Ps. 6:5; Eccl. 9:5–6; Dan. 12:2; 1 Thess. 4:13–16), it seems inconsistent with others (see especially Luke 23:43; cf. Matt. 22:29–32; Luke 16:19–23; Acts 7:59). The term was coined by J. Calvin, who attacked the doctrine (as taught by some Anabaptists) in one of his earliest works, *Psychopannychia* (1534); the doctrine, however, was favoured by M. Luther.

Always a minority position among Christians, psychopannychism is inconsistent with the Catholic belief in the beatific vision and purgatory, and its implication that the soul is mortal was explicitly rejected at Lateran Council V (Session 8, 1513). Although the doctrine has most frequently been attacked for its incompatibility with belief in the immortality of the soul, this objection has been rendered problematic by the virtual consensus among contemporary scholars that no such belief is presupposed in the Bible. Yet, while psychopannychism does reflect biblical teaching that the life of the soul no less than that of the body derives from God alone (Job 34:14–15; cf. Eccl. 3:19–20), it can be challenged for its assumption that the dead remain time-bound (viz., that they have to wait for the resurrection), which runs counter to the biblical tendency to view death as the definitive end to a person's subjection to space and time (e.g., Phil. 1:21–5).

Ian A. McFarland

Public Theology The expression 'public theology' emerged among Christians in the North Atlantic (and, more specifically, North American) context in the last quarter of the twentieth century, though it has since been used in other contexts as well (see African Theology). Unlike liberation theology or feminist theology, public theology refers less to a theological programme than to a theological problem: how to bring theology to bear on issues of general concern (e.g., economic or military policy) within a pluralistic society. In other words, in the face of conventions that tend to limit theological discourse to the Church and (to a lesser extent) the academy, proponents of public theology seek to address matters of general (i.e., public) welfare from a perspective informed by the doctrines and symbols of Christianity, without presupposing that the public addressed shares a commitment to the Christian faith.

While the meaning of public theology has been an object of vigorous debate, the expression emerged as an attempt to identify a mode of public religious discourse that, in contrast to the kind of broadly shared but confessionally vague beliefs associated with civil religion, is rooted in a particular faith tradition. Because a 'public theology' in this sense does not presuppose the kind of consensus associated with civil religion, it is better positioned to adopt a more critical stance towards the attitudes and practices prevailing within the wider society. At the same time, public theology differs from political theology in being less focused on developing a Christian theology of politics than on influencing public policy across every dimension of the social world Christians share with non-Christians. Figures frequently named as exemplary practitioners of public theology include R. Niebuhr, M. L. King, Jr, and J. C. Murray (1904–67). On an ecclesial level, the statements *The Challenge of Peace* (1983) and *Economic Justice for All* (1986), produced by the National Conference of Catholic Bishops, are often cited as instances of public theology.

The practice of public theology faces numerous challenges. Chiefly, the goal of rooting one's contribution to public discourse in a particular faith tradition may conflict with the desire to give the contribution a form convincing to those outside that tradition, since (seemingly) the more widely the warrants for a particular position are acknowledged, the less they will bear the stamp of a particular faith community. With this tension in mind, some theologians have rejected the model of public theology on the grounds that it is inevitably temporizing: at once diluting Christian convictions and placing them at the service of non-Christian institutions or ideologies. Yet it is not clear that religious authenticity and public persuasiveness necessarily stand in such a zero-sum relationship. For example, within Catholic theology the category of natural law arguably provides a framework internal to the Christian tradition for dialogue with persons who do not locate themselves within that tradition. Alternatively, theologians who reject the idea of a priori common ground between revealed faith and human reason may still see in the unity of the world under God the basis for a deep and wide-ranging, if methodologically ad hoc, Christian engagement with a pluralistic culture.

R. F. Thiemann, *Constructing a Public Theology: The Church in a Pluralistic Culture* (John Knox Press, 1991).
B. Valentin, *Mapping Public Theology: Beyond Culture, Identity, and Difference* (Trinity Press, 2002).

IAN A. MCFARLAND

PURGATORY In CATHOLIC THEOLOGY 'purgatory' refers to a post-mortem state of temporary, disciplinary purification for those faithful who upon death have not made complete satisfaction for their SIN and thus are not yet ready to experience the BEATIFIC VISION. The fact that purgatory is a place of painful discipline distinguishes it from HEAVEN; the fact that its pains are temporary rather than eternal distinguishes it from HELL. Although not formally promulgated until 1215, the DOCTRINE of purgatory can be traced back to myths of purificatory fires in the afterlife prevalent in biblical and classical antiquity. Along with popular literature and folk beliefs in otherworldly tribulations, the doctrine of purgatory (and the practices related to it) constitutes a major source of western civilization's emphasis on individuality and self-discipline. The subject of purgatory has taken on a renewed currency in the light of the recent papal decision once again to allow indulgences to be acquired by the living on behalf of the dead.

Purgatory can be understood as a means of affirming the principle that grace always works with nature and never simply overrides it (*gratia non tollit sed perficit naturam*). Thus, while the guilt of previous sins is fully forgiven by GRACE through the sacraments of BAPTISM, PENANCE, and ANOINTING of the sick, the concrete damage to the SOUL caused by sin cannot simply be erased by fiat, but must undergo healing in accord with the basic characteristics of human nature, in the same way that in a physical illness the BODY may need considerable time to recover its full strength after the fever is broken. During one's lifetime this healing is accomplished through good works; purgatory is the place where such healing continues, as necessary, after death, as souls 'undergo purification, so as to achieve the holiness necessary to enter the joy of heaven' (*Cat.*, §1030). The classical biblical warrant for the doctrine is the practice of praying for the dead mentioned in 2 Maccabees 12:46.

The Orthodox Churches have tended to regard the Catholic doctrine of purgatory with suspicion, though they have been open to the idea that some souls experience a time of waiting after death before admission to GLORY. By contrast, the Protestant Reformers rejected the doctrine of purgatory absolutely, both as unscriptural (since they viewed 2 Maccabees as part of the APOCRYPHA) and as inconsistent with their guiding dogmatic principle of JUSTIFICATION by grace alone. They argued that, because Christ's death was the only satisfaction for sin, any talk of human satisfaction invariably implies that human beings somehow earned their salvation – and thereby undermines the soteriological sufficiency of Christ. As M. LUTHER put it, purgatory 'is contrary to the fundamental article that Christ alone, and not the work of man, can help souls' (*Smalc.* 2.2).

Alongside this specifically dogmatic perspective, however, purgatory has played an important role in the development of the idea of the individual in western culture. Individuality emerges in a society when the person maintains a strong sense of his or her own being and presence apart from inherited or acquired social statuses. Such a sense of presence is especially likely to emerge in encounters with the sacred (i.e., in moments of extraordinary opportunity and danger). Purgatory provided a MYTH and a set of practices by which the pilgrim or the Crusader, the monk or the ecstatic, could find protection from the most dangerous enemies to be met along the road or in the other world. For instance, in their fatal encounters with death, even the souls of princes and bishops might emerge naked and vulnerable, deprived of their worldly status; and yet, if they had turned this life into a time of purgatorial trial and discipline, these souls could nevertheless retain their integrity beyond death by virtue of their dedication to particular forms of penitential practice.

The doctrine of purgatory also allowed the Church to demonstrate its belief in its capacity to adjudge the mysteries of the soul and to assign the soul its proper place in the afterlife: a capacity long reflected in the Inquisition and in the history of monastic penitential disciplines. The very connection between penance and 'doing time' is a monastic contribution to western civilization. Like monastics, souls in purgatory also 'did time', until they were adjudged to be their own masters and thus fit for beatitude. In this life, souls who took on the purgatorial discipline of self-examination and repentance could spare themselves some of the tribulations of purgatory after death. The western preoccupation with time is reflected in the penitential discipline of praying with an intensity appropriate to purgatory itself – to the extent that if death occurred during such PRAYER, the penitent would be fit for beatitude.

Not only the modern penal system but the use of civil law to resolve conflict and redress grievances has affinities with the Church's use of its sacramental disciplines to make people whole. By the early sixteenth century, courts became a place where absolution and reconciliation could be sought without submitting to the authority and sacramental disciplines of the Church. And, as L. Huston (b. 1958) has noted, a secularization of purgatory also took place on the Shakespearean stage, where the living and the dead maintained their lively relationships with one another. In this way, attacks on the doctrine of purgatory came not only from Protestant theologians but from dramatists and lawyers who challenged the Church's procedures and authority. It was, after all, the lawyers who demanded that people be made whole through acts of civil restitution without the benefit of clergy.

In this way, modern visions of the State grew to provide a this-worldly, secular, purgatorial discipline. Thus, in J. Locke's (1632–1704) understanding of the role of the civil polity as a framework or school for souls, the secular authorities are like a viaticum: a source of comfort and reassurance to the citizen that undergird her attachment to the larger society. The executive branch administers punishment and thus risks being the object of the citizen's resentment, but without endangering the citizen's attachment to the polity. The modern republic, then, would be a form of purgatory, in which the polity prepares the soul for eternal life.

A. E. Bernstein, 'Esoteric Theology: William of Auvergne on the Fires of Hell and Purgatory', *Speculum* 57:3 (July 1982), 509–31.

L. Hutson, 'From Penitent to Suspect: Law, Purgatory, and Renaissance Drama', *The Huntington Library Quarterly* 65:3/4 (2002), 295–319.

J. Le Goff, *The Birth of Purgatory* (University of Chicago Press, 1984).

RICHARD FENN

PURITANISM 'Puritanism' is a term used to denote a movement, or movements, within the Anglican Church of the sixteenth and seventeenth centuries. The term was coined in the sixteenth century as a pejorative to refer to those Anglican Protestants who had over-scrupulous consciences in matters of theology and practice. Central figures in its development are often seen to include J. Knox (*ca* 1510–72), W. Perkins (1558–1602), R. Sibbes (1577–1635), R. Baxter (1615–91), and J. Owen (1616–83).

There is no real scholarly consensus on what exactly it is that constitutes the essence of Puritanism. In the 1960s Marxist scholars tended to identify it as the ideology of the rising mercantile class with England; more recent scholarship has focused on its theological dimensions. In this context, some scholars see its essence lying in a commitment to a further reformation of the Church of England along lines reflecting the approaches of Zurich and Geneva to polity and worship, where the emphasis tended to lie on simplicity of aesthetics. Thus, from the early 1550s aspects of the BOOK OF COMMON PRAYER and Anglican practice (such as kneeling at communion and the wearing of clerical vestments) were sources of contention, and to these were added, from the later sixteenth century, a strict SABBATARIANISM. These issues formed the focus of debate and served to distinguish Puritan from non-Puritan. Other scholars, however, see its primary focus as being an experiential piety which sees true Christian FAITH as evidenced by CONVERSION and other subjective, sometimes almost mystical, experiences.

The lack of scholarly consensus on the nature of Puritanism indicates its eclectic nature as a movement. Theologically, many Puritans drew heavily upon both late medieval anti-PELAGIANISM and contemporary streams of Reformed Orthodoxy. Nevertheless, this is not true of all those considered Puritans: J. Goodwin (1593–1665), for example, was an Arminian (see ARMINIANISM); and, indeed, there were many Reformed Orthodox members of the Church of England who were not Puritans, such as T. Barlow (1607–91), bishop of Lincoln and close friend of the Puritan J. Owen. This diversity is even more pronounced when considering ECCLESIOLOGY: Puritans held to a variety of positions on Church government, from moderate episcopalianism through to independency.

Central to later Puritan identity was the Westminster Assembly. This gathering, which was convened by Parliament in 1643, produced, among other things, two CATECHISMS, a confession, and a directory for public worship, each of which represented an attempt to change the face of Anglicanism in a more radically Reformed direction in terms of both its theology and, even more so, its government and liturgical practice (see WESTMINSTER STANDARDS).

In England, Puritanism enjoyed its heyday of influence under Parliament in the late 1640s and early 1650s. The execution of King Charles I (r. 1625–49), and then the policies of O. Cromwell (1598–1658) as Lord Protector, served to weaken and fragment the movement. Typically, it is regarded as dying out after the 1662 Act of Uniformity, which effectively removed Puritan dissent from within the Church of England and led to the birth of non-conformity. At the same time, scholars apply the term to North American religious movements as late as the 1700s, to refer to the religious heirs of the Pilgrim Fathers of the early seventeenth century.

P. Collinson, *The Elizabethan Puritan Movement* (Oxford University Press, 1990).

P. Lake, *Moderate Puritans and the Elizabethan Church* (Cambridge University Press, 2004).

CARL R. TRUEMAN

Quaker Theology Quakers' enduring suspicion of 'theology' can be traced back to G. Fox (1624–91), generally regarded as the founder of Quakerism, and his dissatisfaction with religious 'professors' – those who 'professed', and could mount an intellectual defence of, beliefs that were not reflected in their lives or actions. In contrast to such 'professors', Fox reported that he 'had received that opening from the Lord that to be bred at Oxford or Cambridge was not sufficient to fit a man to be a minister of Christ' (*Journal*, entry written in 1647). His own emphasis on knowledge of God that was experienced and lived out led to a relative de-emphasis within Quaker thought on arguments from Scripture, Christian tradition, or reason. While these sources remain important in Quaker thought, their use is conditioned by the need to speak from and to an individual's or a community's experience. Nonetheless, originating in a highly literate age in which religious controversy was central to public life, Quakers have from an early stage produced theology. The distinctive forms of Quaker practice – unprogrammed worship based on silence, 'quaking' and similar manifestations of emotional and religious fervour, the lack of traditional sacramental practice, women's preaching and ministry, actions and speech that challenged social hierarchy – provoked external challenges that in turn forced early Quakers to articulate what became 'Quaker theology'.

R. Barclay (1648–90), a Scottish Quaker trained in Catholic theology and philosophy, wrote his *Apology for the True Christian Divinity* (1678) as a systematic account of Quaker thought to defend Quakers against a range of accusations from other Christian groups, particularly in relation to their lack of traditional sacramental practice and their view of the Bible's status. Barclay's central discussion of the experience of the convicting and revealing light of Christ, given to the individual and recognized and confirmed by the worshipping community, formed an important basis for subsequent Quaker theology. Alongside his work must be set the vast number of shorter apologetic and controversial writings produced in the early years of Quakerism, several of which – for example, E. Bathurst's (*ca* 1655–85) *Truth's Vindication* (1679) – also provided systematic accounts of Quaker practice and its theological basis. Even today, it remains the case that much 'Quaker theology' arises from the desire to explain Quaker practice, for internal or external consumption. For example, Quaker participation in the ecumenical movement has led to the production of important texts on ministry, authority within the Church, membership, and forms of worship. Equally important, although more diffuse, are Quaker contributions to the literature on religious pacifism and on social responsibility.

'Testimony' is a crucial term in Quaker theology and self-definition. At its broadest, it refers to words or actions that bear witness to the activity of God and to the truth that God reveals. From early in Quaker history, it was used to refer to the ways in which Quakers as a community testified concerning the *un*truthfulness of certain claims, practices, or ways of life – for example, by refusing to swear oaths or to undertake military service. Quaker theology can usefully be understood as part of such wider traditions of testimony. Theology as testimony is explicitly not the 'theory' that gives rise to a community's 'practice'; rather, the writing of theology is one of a range of practices that together constitute the testimony given by the community.

It is not hard to see why the journal, a record of and reflection on an individual's experiences, has been a particularly significant theological genre for Quakers. The characteristic Quaker concern for speech rooted in lived experience gave the journal its authority for the reader and its importance for the writer. The journals of Fox and of J. Woolman (1720–72) have been among the most widely studied and cited. Woolman is of particular interest in the contemporary context because of his profound reflections on simplicity of life, justice in human relations (most famously, his opposition to slavery), and the stewardship of natural resources.

Quakerism since the eighteenth century has been increasingly diverse, both in theology and in practice. Wider theological movements and shifts – Quietism, evangelicalism and revivalism (see Evangelical theology), liberal theology – have had their impacts on Quaker thought and have in some cases given rise to lasting divisions. In the early twentieth century Quaker scholars and theologians made important contributions to the developing study of mysticism in religion – influenced to some extent by, but also departing significantly from, W. James' work on religious experience. R. Jones (1863–1948) is probably the best-known of these scholars. His characterization of Quakerism as mystical religion based on a potentially universal experience of God – together with the famous histories of Quakerism compiled by W. Braithwaite (1862–1922), which used Jones' work to construct a narrative of early Quaker experience – has had a decisive influence on liberal Quakerism from the early twentieth century to the present day. At the same time, evangelical Quakerism has flourished worldwide and has developed distinctive accounts of Quaker history and practice from within the frameworks of evangelical thought.

In recent years, Quaker theology has been supported by a range of academic institutions – by a journal (*Quaker Theology*), by Quaker study centres in the USA and the UK, and by conferences and ongoing seminars. These, together with the triennial gatherings of the Friends World Committee for Consultation (the body linking Quakers worldwide) and other world Quaker gatherings, provide forums for interaction between Quakers of different theological and liturgical traditions. Significant Quaker theological work has emerged from such interactions, which both highlights ongoing areas of disagreement – for example, the nature of biblical authority, and the centrality or otherwise of distinctively Christian expressions of faith – and reveals common ground, in reasserting the primacy of lived experience of the transforming presence of God.

R. Barclay, *Apology for the True Christian Divinity* (Standard Publications, 2006 [1675]).
G. Fox, *The Journal of George Fox*, ed. R. M. Jones (Friends United, 2006 [1694]).
J. Woolman, *The Journal and Major Essays of John Woolman*, ed. P. P. Moulton (Friends United, 1971 [1753–74]).

Rachel Muers

Queer Theology According to E. Sedgwick (1950–2009), 'Queer is a continuing moment, movement, motive – recurrent, eddying, *troublant* ... The immemorial current that *queer* represents is antiseparatist as it is antiassimilationist. Keenly, it is relational, and strange' (*Tend.* xii). In line with this perspective, Queer theory has three characteristics: the emphasis on the construction of sexuality, the element of plurality which needs to be present in any reflection, and the idea of ambivalence or the fluidity of sexual identities. But traditional forms of Christian theology have been organized around a givenness, a monotheism, and an exercise of the authority of the meta-narratives of heteronormativity. Therefore, Queer theory works as a new 'mediator science' in radical theologies. As G. Gutierrez (b. 1928) spoke of liberation theology as the irruption of the poor in theology, Queer theory has also facilitated the irruption of the marginalized in Christianity: people and institutional forms of organization at the margins of heteronormativity (gays, lesbians, transgenders), but also knowledge at the margin of heterosexuality, too.

Queer theology is an emerging discipline which takes as its starting point the radical, and as yet unexplored, nature of the doctrine of the incarnation. That the transcendent divine moved across into immanent flesh once and for all is the Queer ground that human beings inhabit – a ground which they are also required to traverse. Far from creating the same yesterday, today, and tomorrow (cf. Heb. 13:8), this incarnational dynamism is always propelling human beings forward into new curiosities and challenges, not shutting them off from the world, drawing them into more of themselves as they spiral in the human–divine dance. Christians who take this dynamism seriously are challenged to move beyond traditional metaphysics and the comfortable world that they can create. Queer theory with its postmodern roots asks for distrust of any master narrative, and there is no bigger one than metaphysics. Queer theology would like to take lives, including that of Jesus of Nazareth, in the raw and examine how we between us embody the transformative and spiralling reality of incarnation. Within Queer theology there are no boundaries: all stories tell us of the incarnation all human beings share and the redemptive space we strive for.

Queer theology is therefore a deep questioning or an exercise of multiple and diverse hermeneutical suspicions (see Hermeneutics). Theology has for some time now been reflecting on concerns for justice which have included using class, race, and gender as critical tools when thinking about God and human history. However, sexuality remains one of the most difficult and pervasive ideological areas of assumed understandings. Queering theology requires challenging the existing link between theology and sexual domestication, making courage a crucial tool in the theological kitbag. Theories of sexuality function as myths which organize a representation of history, and the coherence of certain social order and institutional life (including that of the Church) also depends on the mythical heteronormal matrix. In the context of this matrix, other sexual thinking appears as deviant. In theology the question is how the politics of heteronormal identities pre-empt the representation of God and reflection into the key themes of Christianity.

What has been lacking in much liberation theology is the relationship between profit and pleasure developed by R. Hennessy (b. 1950). Drawing on these insights, Queer theology does not see capitalist expansion as separate from more personal embodied issues, but understands the destruction of the environment and the politics of exclusion to lie in the relation between capitalism and sexuality, between western economic thinking and heterosexual thinking and ultimately to be rooted in the same heterosexual binary thinking that underpins traditional theological ethics and narrow Christian praxis. To regulate sexuality in the name of divinities means to regulate the order of affectionate exchanges but also other human exchanges such as the political and economic systems. For this reason Queer theology does not take its place at the centre of the theological discourses but at the margins. It strives for differentiation and plurality – a kind of biodiversity – in theology which, in the end, transforms and renews theological praxis.

Queer theology is a political and sexual queering of theology that goes beyond the gender paradigms of the early years of FEMINIST THEOLOGY, and also transcends the fixed assumptions of lesbian and gay theology. Queering theology (that is, questioning the (hetero) sexual underpinning of traditional theological reflections), exceeds the sphere of the private and also goes into the heart of the understanding of, e.g., the vision of exchange characteristic of the International Monetary Fund and the anthropology implicit in philosophies of globalization. As Hennessy has pointed out, heteronormativity presupposes a policy of division of labour by virtue of its commitment to gender hierarchies and the associated reification of sexual identities in capitalist societies (*Profit* 64). In this respect, Queer theology is a POLITICAL THEOLOGY.

As a genre, Queer theology partakes of irony, humour, and self-disclosure as does the Camp genre and Queer literature more generally. The self-disclosure style means also that Queer theology is an '*I*' theology. In this way, Queer theology is a form of autobiography because it implies an engagement and a disclosure of experiences which have been traditionally silenced in theology, including (for example) issues of sadomasochism, transvestism, or even the denunciation of heterosexuality as a construction which does not even apply to the real experiences of heterosexual people.

As a subversive force, Queer theology focuses on theological closets – what has not been said or has been hidden. More than anything else, Queer theology is an incarnated, body theology that deals with desire, but also with pleasure which has been ignored in theology for too long. Pleasure is, after all, the incarnation of desires. Like POSTMODERNISM, queer theology encourages theologians to de-mystify, undo, and subvert. Far from being unhelpful, this approach should be viewed as crucial to human wellbeing. Though it has drawn concern from both feminist and liberation theologians who have long felt that some postmodern theology lacks a critical political/moral edge, Queer theology in fact operates on those edges.

M. Althaus-Reid and L. Isherwood, *The Sexual Theologian: Essay on God, Sex and Politics* (T&T Clark, 2004).

R. Goss, *Queering Christ: Beyond Jesus Acted Up* (Pilgrim, 2002).

L. Isherwood, *The Power of Erotic Celibacy: Queering Heteropatriarchy* (T&T Clark, 2006).

G. Loughlin, *Queer Theology: Rethinking the Western Body* (Blackwell, 2007).

Lisa Isherwood

Quest of the Historical Jesus The composition of the four NT Gospels in the first century almost immediately prompted reflection on how to make sense of this fourfold witness to Jesus of Nazareth. Over against attempts to combine the four into a single harmony (the approach taken by Tatian (*ca* 110–*ca* 180) in his *Diatessaron*) or the decision to abandon the four NT Gospels and produce an alternative (e.g., the *Gospel of Thomas* or the *Gospel of Judas*), the strategy that became normative (given classical form in the theology of IRENAEUS) was to hold the four accounts together. With the advent of historical criticism in the modern period, however, the aim in describing Jesus was no longer to reflect upon the fourfold witness of the Gospels to the Son of God, but to seek a historical Jesus who was different from the Christ of the CREEDS, and who lay not so much in as *behind* the Gospel narratives. Thus the 'quest' began, to discover a previously unknown Jesus through the process of excavation.

The 'quest of the historical Jesus' is conventionally divided into three parts: (1) the nineteenth-century 'old quest', documented by A. Schweitzer (1875–1965); (2) the 'new quest', referring to the attempts by R. BULTMANN's students to retrieve something after the extreme minimalism of their teacher; and (3) the 'third quest', a rather uncertain category which can contain a number of otherwise divergent contemporary approaches.

In his classic *Quest of the Historical Jesus* (1906), Schweitzer made H. Reimarus (1694–1768) his starting point, though there had already been numerous attempts before Reimarus to produce an alternative Jesus using, but not relying upon, the Gospels (including the efforts of English deists, as well as a sceptical eighteenth-century Dutch school). Schweitzer's generally disapproving narrative is punctuated by reference to those he much admires, such as D. Strauss (1808–74), whose influence has been very deep both in his general anti-supernaturalism, and in his arguments that the words and deeds of the Gospels are often retrospective constructions from OT material. Schweitzer divided the key works into those liberal *Lives* which domesticate Jesus by modernizing him, and a minority that give due weight to Jesus' Jewish eschatological mindset and his will to turn the wheel of history, including the work of J. Weiss (1863–1914). Schweitzer claimed to have destroyed the possibility of a liberal Jesus, demonstrating instead that Jesus' mindset was one of 'thoroughgoing ESCHATOLOGY'.

Some have assumed that little happened between Schweitzer and World War II, but there are important episodes. Schweitzer included in the second edition of his *Quest* the debate over the existence of Jesus, prompted by a flurry of events and publications in 1909 and 1910. Also noteworthy are the attempts by theologians such as W. Grundmann (1906–76) in the 1930s to produce an Aryan Jesus. More central to scholarly discussion, however, has been the so-called 'new quest', initiated by the famous address by E. Käsemann (1906–98) in 1953, in which he stressed that, despite the historical character of Jesus having receded into the scholarly background, certain important features of his ministry and teaching were clearly identifiable. Central to this new quest were the criteria developed for the authenticity of Gospel materials: for example, the much-criticized criterion of dissimilarity required that sayings could be regarded as dominical if they were at variance both with the Jewish environment of the time and with the theology of the early Church.

In reaction to what was a fairly unproductive new quest, there emerged a so-called 'third quest', but which is really a multiplicity of quests. G. Vermes (b. 1924), for example, was one scholar who pushed for a Jesus understood firmly within his Jewish context; although the Jewish credentials of this Jesus might suggest that Vermes belongs in the third quest, his work feels more a part of the now old-fashioned approach of the new quest. Similarly, some locate the Jesus Seminar as part of the third quest (or as its nemesis), but its method again is reminiscent of older approaches. Most representative of the mainstream today are E. P. Sanders (b. 1937) and J. P. Meier (b. 1942). Their books are notable for stress on the Jewish context of Jesus, the identity of Jesus as an eschatological prophet, and reliance primarily on the synoptic Gospels for a historical understanding of Jesus, with some use of John, and little or no importance attached to apocryphal Gospels. Additionally, N. T. Wright (b. 1948) has exemplified a concern that the Church is not an unfortunate obstacle to Jesus research, but is rather a remarkable phenomenon which any view of the impact of the historical Jesus needs to explain. On the other hand, there remain members of the Jesus Seminar who pursue the line that each saying must be weighed individually, with the burden of proof set rather high irrespective of whether the source is a canonical or non-canonical Gospel.

There was some overlap (if not actual agreement) between K. BARTH and Bultmann on the lack of relevance of a historically reconstructed Jesus for Christian FAITH. More recently, however, some theologians such as W. Pannenberg (b. 1928) have placed a much higher value upon historical verifiability. M. Hengel (b. 1926) has argued for the importance of historical research on the grounds that the INCARNATION not only permits such historical investigation of Jesus but demands it. In contrast, L. Johnson (b. 1943) has emphasized the severe limits of historical reconstruction, especially as practised by the Jesus Seminar. Over against the tension between the historical Jesus and the Christ of faith characteristic of German thought in particular, British writers like C. H. Dodd (1884–1973) and D. Baillie (1887–1954) were much more inclined to see an identity. A similar confidence in the relationship between the two is seen among contemporary Catholic theologians such as Pope Benedict XVI (r. 2005–) and G. O'Collins (b. 1931).

J. Carleton Paget, 'Quests for the Historical Jesus' in *The Cambridge Companion to Jesus*, ed. M. N. A. Bockmuehl, (Cambridge University Press, 2001), 138–55.

J. D. G. Dunn and S. McKnight, eds., *The Historical Jesus in Recent Research* (Eisenbrauns, 2005).

S. Neill and N. T. Wright, *The Interpretation of the New Testament, 1861–1986* (Oxford University Press, 1988).

J. M. Robinson, *A New Quest of the Historical Jesus* (SCM, 1959).

SIMON GATHERCOLE

QUIETISM 'Quietism' describes a theology and practice of inner PRAYER that emphasizes a state of extreme passivity. The SOUL achieves a continuous union with God through contemplation, and in this union the self is annihilated as the individual will is absorbed into the divine will. This interior way leads to Christian perfection and LOVE. The main proponent of Quietism was the Spanish Catholic M. de Molinos (1628–96), who arrived in Rome in 1663 and achieved considerable influence as a spiritual director and as the author of *A Spiritual Guide* (1675). Molinos was arrested and condemned to life in prison in 1685, primarily on the grounds of his teaching and his confession to alleged immorality. Objections to Quietist teaching lay in its claim to a state of uninterrupted union with God, its failure to delineate individual responsibility while the soul is one with the divine will, its rejection of meditation, and its lack of emphasis on the practice of the virtues. Furthermore, Quietists maintained that there was 'an easy way' of contemplation, available to all, not requiring a special VOCATION. Such teachings put the Quietists at odds with much of Counter-Reformation Catholicism and particularly with Jesuit theology and practice.

Quietism spread among Catholics through small groups into France, where F. Malaval (1627–1719) was a proponent. French Quietists were well-versed in Rhinish and Spanish mysticism, and their form of contemplation was akin to but distinct from the prayer of quiet described by TERESA OF AVILA in which the will is overcome by the presence of God, resulting in joy and delight. They were also influenced by F. de Sales (1567–1622) with his emphasis on pure love resulting from spiritual practice. J. de La Mothe-Guyon (1648–1717), a lay teacher and author of *A Short and Easy Method of Prayer* (1685), claimed not to have known the teaching of Molinos directly but did have contact with Malaval. Well-read in the literature of the Church, Madame Guyon influenced for a time the circle of devout Catholics in the court of Louis XIV (r. 1643–1715) and also was a spiritual counsellor to F. Fénelon (1646–1715), bishop of Cambrai. Her teachings added nothing new to Quietist thought, but her lay status and criticism of meditative and intellectual approaches to God set her at odds with the religious and political establishment, leading eventually to her exile to Blois in 1703.

Fénelon defended Madame Guyon in an increasingly bitter and public debate with J.-B. Bossuet (1627–1704), bishop of Meaux, who condemned Quietism as 'new mysticism' and criticized the idea of continuous union with God as a logical impossibility. Fénelon's particular emphasis within Quietism was a theology of disinterested love, which he articulated as part of a continuous tradition within the Church in *The Maxims of the Saints* (1697). Exiled to his bishopric in 1697, Fénelon submitted to the censure of some of his writings in 1699 by Pope Innocent XII (r. 1691–1700).

The writings of Madame Guyon, as well as those of Molinos and of Fénelon, exercised considerable influence among German Pietists, Quakers, and other non-conformists. J. WESLEY, attracted to aspects of continental Catholic spirituality, rejected the 'stillness' of Moravian spirituality (which was rooted in Quietism) but was influenced by the doctrine of perfect or disinterested love which he incorporated into his theology of SANCTIFICATION. In North America T. Upham (1799–1872) reinterpreted Quietism in the context of nineteenth-century holiness REVIVALISM and its theology of sanctification. By this time, Quietism had become more generalized – 'a state of rest in God'.

See also PIETISM; QUAKER THEOLOGY.

J.-R. Argomathe, *Le Quiétisme* (Presses Universitaires de France, 1973).
P. Pourrat, *Christian Spirituality*, vol. IV (Newman, 1955).
P. A. Ward, *Experimental Theology in America: Madame Guyon, Fénelon, and Their Readers* (Baylor University Press, 2009).

PATRICIA A. WARD

R

Race Race is a category by which individuals, groups, and societies interpret diversity in the human family. As a way of making sense, race is founded in the interpretation of differences between human groups – most often differences in melanin content (colour), facial features, hair texture, and also culture. The primary function of race has been both to catalogue and, more significantly, to attribute meaning to these observed differences. The construction and continuing use of the category of race represents a particularly modern approach to a broader human tendency to construct regimes of knowledge that both ground and explain systems of socio-political hegemony by appeal to some putative substantial differences between peoples. While it has been a highly unstable category, race has been enduring in the modern period because of its presumed status as an objective description of reality. This use of race to legitimate systems of social power is a good point from which to explore the idea theologically. Such an exploration begins with some description of the interplay of religion and the social sciences during the formative period of modernity.

Race evolved as a sense-making tool during the period of western global hegemony – modernity – that also saw the rise of the modern physical and social sciences (see Natural Science). During this period Christianity (and religion more generally) was being challenged by the emerging scientific world view, yet during the eighteenth and much of the nineteenth century Christian assumptions about human history (including God's providential guidance of it) continued to frame the field of vision for these sciences. Consequently, many of the cultural categories – including race – that emerged in this period were formed by the dynamic relationship between religion, science, and western hegemony. This was nowhere more apparent than in the works of thinkers like J. Arthur, Comte de Gobineau (1816–82), who established the idea that race and culture were inextricably bound, and C. Linnaeus (1707–78), who contributed the idea that 'racial' characteristics were immutable. The works of these two men in creating a significant dimension of the commonsense modernity is an illustration of the interplay between religion, the sciences, and western hegemony because they illustrate the ways that their seemingly scientific conclusions were in fact religiously based.

A common yet frequently unnoticed feature of the modern scientific world view was the general acceptance by scientists like Gobineau and Linnaeus that the chronological framework within which human history unfolded, and thus the basis for its interpretation, was roughly 7,000 years – the timeframe established by the Bible. The effect of this biblical framing of human history was, first, to limit the scope of the history these scientists sought to describe, and, second, to structure this limited historical vision in a way that gave inordinate significance to the period of western ascendancy.

This historical frame further established two significant ideas that would largely define the cultural and social working of the idea of race: the cultural superiority of the West and God's providential direction of it. The importance of the first question is seen in the penchant of many biological and social scientists to approach their study of human history seeking explanations for why some societies developed so quickly and dominantly, while others seemingly did not. Race served as a heuristic device to make sense of human history and difference in light of the ascendancy of European military and economic interests, thereby providing a means for understanding how western dominance was consistent with scientifically verifiable dimensions of human difference.

The further identification of race as a product of God's providence was founded in the assumption that humanity existed in its current (i.e., racially diverse) form from its very beginnings. Thus, the differences in culture and relative military and economic power in the present were understood to be the consequence of inherent, divinely established differences among human subjects and not the result of variable, contingent adaptation over time. Again, western hegemony was explained by inherent racial differences. Together, these assumptions would predispose scientists to employ the category of race in ways that presumed the western (eventually conceived of as White) dominance of much of the world as being in the natural order of things.

Another dimension of the modern dynamism between science, religion, and hegemony was the tendency not only to subject the Bible to critical study, but also to read scientific common sense back into the text. Thus, when race became stabilized as a 'scientifically' verifiable category, the Bible came to be read as stories about *races* of people. The pre-eminent example of this practice is the racialized reading of the story of Noah's sons, in which the curse of Canaan (Gen. 9:25–7) was used to justify the institution of chattel slavery in the New World and the colonial exploitation in Africa. Theological categories like 'chosenness' and 'election' were also appropriated by this thinking in both sacred and secular contexts. This *racing* of the biblical narrative is the explicitly religious dimension of the dynamism between religion, science, and hegemony.

In the context of these many dimensions of the concept of race, it becomes important to ask how this intersection between the sciences, religion, and hegemony continues to serve as the basis for racial exploitation and oppression in the twenty-first century. The first step in answering this question is to recall that race is primarily an epistemological category (i.e., one that structures human knowing), born of religious and cultural ideas. If race is understood to be a social construction that affects the 'thinking' of certain persons and groups about others in ways that have very real material consequences, the way is opened to a genuinely theological analysis of the concept. Such an analysis might utilize PAUL's reference to the powers of this age. In Ephesians 6:12, Paul makes the claim that the struggle of humanity generally and the Church more specifically 'is not against enemies of blood and flesh, but against the rulers [powers], against the authorities [principalities], against the cosmic powers of this present darkness, against the spiritual forces of evil in the heavenly places'. While this text has been interpreted in numerous ways, a point upon which all commentators have agreed is that Paul is concerned here to identify forces beyond the mundane which exert power and influence on human affairs. Most often, these 'powers' work in ways that co-operate with iniquitous systems of temporal rule. The goal of these 'powers and principalities', according to Paul, is to be minimally a hindrance and maximally to replace the living God in the hearts of the faithful.

This schema that Paul offers of material and immaterial forces that strive to defeat God's good purposes in CREATION is particularly appropriate for a theological analysis of the workings of race, because of its recognition that the suprapersonal does impinge upon the material content of reality. Still more concretely, it exposes the truth that what may appear to be the 'natural order of things' may not be 'natural' at all, but rather the working of forces beyond immediate human comprehension and control. One does not have to share Paul's COSMOLOGY or world view to find these insights helpful, for they highlight the ways ideas impose themselves on the material reality of human existence (e.g., the racialization of human persons) and also that behind every material instantiation of reality there is an idea or interpretation which is the currency of that reality. This deployment of the Pauline schema also points to the fact that the legitimacy which accrues to systems of oppression and iniquity is fundamentally rooted in our acceptance of the regimes of knowledge in which they 'make sense'. This acceptance is the precondition of powers being able to determine the structure of material reality even though they may exist primarily in the ideational (or 'heavenly') realm.

In addition to speaking of race as a 'power', it is possible to take a further step and speak of race in relation to the idea of 'principalities'. To continue with the Pauline schema, principalities are those material structurings of human reality that work to impose the dominion of a power upon relations among persons and within the whole of creation. They might be thought of as the material accretions of the powers. Principalities manipulate the material character of existence in ways that further the powers which stand behind them. The ways in which economic life is ordered, intellectual life is pursued, social space is constructed, and social goods are distributed all reflect particular structurings of reality, which are expressions of 'powers' – the controlling systems of thought rooted in the founding idea. Perhaps the most notorious example of such a principality in recent American history is the social, political, economic, and cultural system of segregation, which characterized life throughout much of the twentieth century – and which was founded on the concept of race.

C. L. Brace, *Race is a Four Letter Word: The Genesis of the Concept* (Oxford University Press, 2005).

J. K. Carter, *Race: A Theological Account* (Oxford University Press, 2008).

S. Haynes, *Noah's Curse: The Biblical Justification of American Slavery* (Oxford University Press, 2007).

STEPHEN G. RAY, JR

RACOVIAN CATECHISM: see SOCINIANISM.

RADICAL ORTHODOXY Radical Orthodoxy is a theological programme which first arose in Cambridge in the 1990s and is particularly associated with the British theologians J. Milbank (b. 1952), C. Pickstock (b. 1970), and G. Ward (b. 1955). Under their general editorship an original series of fourteen books was published entitled 'Radical Orthodoxy'. This has been succeeded by further series under different titles. Radical Orthodoxy is broadly ecumenical and has provoked positive and negative critical engagement from a range of theological and philosophical perspectives.

Radical Orthodoxy seeks to recover the resources of the orthodox Christian tradition to meet the scientific, cultural, political, social and philosophical challenges of late modernity. It seeks to articulate the unique and properly radical nature of Christian theology, refusing accommodation with secular modes of thought which deny the reality of the transcendent. While many might see in this programme echoes of the NEO-ORTHODOXY associated with K. BARTH, Radical Orthodoxy has been suspicious of Barth's emphasis on the notion of God's *self*-revelation to the exclusion of philosophical modes of reason. While agreeing with Barth's rejection of NATURAL THEOLOGY, Radical Orthodoxy is nevertheless committed to a critical engagement with philosophy, for it sees theology as completing and surpassing philosophical reason in the direction of LITURGY and doxology. Theology and philosophy – and faith and reason – are intimately interwoven. Radical Orthodoxy therefore establishes connections more clearly with the *NOUVELLE THÉOLOGIE* of H. DE LUBAC and H. von BALTHASAR (particularly de Lubac's refusal of a dualism between nature and GRACE), as well as with the Anglican OXFORD MOVEMENT of the nineteenth century which sought to recover the resources of patristic theology.

One of the methods which Radical Orthodoxy appropriates from contemporary critical theory is 'genealogy'. This is deployed in response to the historical nature of theology and philosophy: concepts are not fixed across time and traditions, but have histories. Among the many concepts whose histories or 'genealogies' are traced (e.g., space, motion, the self, society, reason, REVELATION), an overarching narrative of the rise of the secular has become particularly associated with Radical Orthodoxy. This begins with the interweaving of Christian theology and philosophy (particularly Neoplatonism) in antiquity up to the high medieval period, with a positive emphasis on theurgy, divine simplicity, the so-called 'ontological difference' between God and creation, and the metaphysics of participation (see PLATONISM). CREATION is not autonomously self-standing but is, in itself, nothing. There is only one focus of being and truth, namely, God. However, this does not issue in PANTHEISM because creation arrives out of nothing as God's continual donation of participation in God's own substantiality. In other words, creation's existence is not its own; it exists by continual participation in the divine. That ability to participate in God is not 'proper' to creation, but is itself a gift of the divine. This gives rise to the title of the introduction to the first collection of articles, *Radical Orthodoxy*, 'Suspending the material': the material creation is 'suspended' over nothingness. Outside a relationship of participation in God, creation is nothing. Creation does not lie outside or alongside God but is 'enveloped' by the transcendent.

The implication of this doctrine of creation is that just as creation is not autonomous from God, so no discourse can be strictly autonomous from discourse about God. In their introduction to the volume *Radical Orthodoxy* (1999), Milbank, Pickstock, and Ward state: 'Participation, however, refuses any reserve of created territory, while allowing finite things their own integrity. Underpinning the present essays, therefore, is the idea that every discipline must be framed by a theological perspective; otherwise these disciplines will define a zone apart from God, grounded literally in nothing' (3). This leads to an understanding of the nature of theological discourse which Radical Orthodoxy sees articulated most clearly by T. AQUINAS: unlike other disciplines, theology, in being speech about God and all things in relation to God, has no delimited subject matter; in principle, theology encompasses all things. Other discourses do not have an autonomy from theological considerations. Nevertheless, they maintain their own integrity which reflects the integrity of creation gifted by God.

Radical Orthodoxy's broad genealogy sees the fracturing of this Christian theological vision beginning in the fourteenth century with the rise of belief in the univocity of being (i.e., that God's being, although infinite, is univocal with created being), NOMINALISM, and the view that knowledge is a mere representation of reality. These theological shifts herald the notion of a space and reality – the secular – which can be defined as strictly autonomous from God and the sacred. The secular is not understood as the residue of modernity's project of desacralization. Rather, the secular is the positive invention of a pseudo-theology of power which masquerades as the neutral sphere of indifferent and a-traditional reason. Radical Orthodoxy does not regard *post*modernity as the overcoming of modernity's attempt to establish the presence of an immanent and a-traditional foundation for knowledge. Rather, it is the realization of the absence of such secure knowledge which in turn issues in nihilism. Thus Radical Orthodoxy regards *late* modernity as a prime opportunity for Christian theology to assert an alternative vision.

Moving forward from this broad genealogy and emerging from an understanding of theology as a discourse which is not strictly bounded by a single subject matter, Radical Orthodoxy has sought to read theologically 'the signs of our times'. Its writers invest heavily in sites often thought to be occupied principally by secular modes of reason. Of particular note are Milbank's recent discussions of the nature of gift and Ward's concern with the politics and culture of belief in the context of late modernity.

Criticisms of Radical Orthodoxy have focused upon its understanding of the history of philosophy and theology. A particular source of controversy has been the reading of J. DUNS SCOTUS and the meaning and implications of his DOCTRINE of the univocity of being. Writers in the sphere of Radical Orthodoxy have been robust in defending their views and frequently point to the much broader trajectory of theological and philosophical scholarship within which Radical Orthodoxy finds its positive place.

It is possible that the term 'Radical Orthodoxy', because it first named a series of books which is now complete, may wane in use in coming years. However, the influence of this broad sensibility continues to gather pace in Europe and North America through further publications and research.

J. Milbank, *Theology and Social Theory: Beyond Secular Reason*, 2nd edn (Wiley-Blackwell, 2005).

J. Milbank, C. Pickstock, and G. Ward, eds., *Radical Orthodoxy: A New Theology* (Routledge, 1999).

S. Oliver and J. Milbank, eds., *The Radical Orthodoxy Reader* (Routledge, 2009).

J. K. A. Smith, *Introducing Radical Orthodoxy: Towards a Post-Secular Worldview* (Baker Academic, 2004).

SIMON OLIVER

RADICAL REFORMATION: see MENNONITE THEOLOGY.

RAHNER, KARL Karl Rahner was born in Freiburg im Breisgau, Germany, in 1904 and died in Innsbruck, Austria, in 1984. His work deeply influenced the Catholic Church and modern theology more widely. Rahner played a major role at VATICAN COUNCIL II as advisor to the German bishops and is one key architect of modern Catholicism.

Rahner was ordained a Jesuit priest in 1932. His doctoral work, which was turned down by his supervisor, was a groundbreaking attempt to read T. AQUINAS in engagement with modern philosophy, especially via I. KANT and M. Heidegger (1889–1976), breaking from the prevailing ahistorical neo-Scholasticism. This work, published as *Spirit in the World* (1939; 2nd edn 1957), helped promote Catholic engagement with modern philosophy as partner, rather than as opponent, as had been the dominant ethos during Rahner's education.

Rahner became a leading 'transcendental Thomist', seeking to navigate the apparent Kantian roadblock to natural theology. Following Aquinas, he argued that the path to God was through the senses. Every act of knowing always implied a transcendence beyond itself – a horizon that cannot itself be grasped but which is the very condition of our knowing. This infinite horizon, an unthematized mystery, keeps the question of God open, Rahner argued. REVELATION is the word spoken by this mystery, a thesis developed in his second major work, *Hearer of the Word* (1937). Rahner eventually came to distinguish transcendental revelation, the divine self-communication which is met in the depths of experience as the mysterious horizon draws near, from categorical revelation, occurring in history. Revelation in both senses reaches its peak in Jesus Christ.

H. von BALTHASAR criticized Rahner for building his theological edifice upon German IDEALISM rather than revelation. This criticism has been influential but is still debated. K. Kilby (b. 1964), for example, has argued against giving a greater weight to Rahner's early philosophical works than he himself did. Others, like Philip Endean (b. 1954), argue that it is in fact Ignatian spirituality rather than any philosophy which is the most important influence on Rahner's thought.

Rahner turned to the theology of the SYMBOL (how the intangible represents itself in the tangible, the uncreated in the created) to develop a theology of the INCARNATION, the TRINITY, the sacraments, and the Church. Historically, his writings were quite ad hoc, addressing a wide variety of issues: many were published as twenty-three volumes of essays, called the *Theological Investigations*. However, the overall concern of every essay was the making credible and intelligible central doctrines of the Catholic FAITH and showing how personally appropriating DOCTRINE led to DEIFICATION and participation in the life of God. That Rahner also wrote many classics of spirituality is consistent with the fact that for him all theology led to the mystery of God.

Rahner approached CHRISTOLOGY from different angles. He could work both 'from above' (i.e., from the Church's formal confession of faith) and 'from below' (i.e., from the humanity of the man Jesus). Working from below, he tried to show that our humanity, shared with Jesus, is a constant movement towards the mystery in every act of knowing and loving that constitutes our self-transcendence. Yet in Christ (and thus from above) we see this mystery grounded in Jesus' humanity, which is revealed as the speaking of God's Word in the second Person of the Trinity (from above). In this way, the locus of revelation is through nature itself, not abrogating nature, or reducible to nature, but in Thomist fashion, taking up and transforming nature. This line of Rahner's thought has been criticized for failing to register the deep rupture that sin caused and for minimizing the atoning act of the cross. B. Marshall (b. 1955) engages this Christological issue in his comparison of Rahner and K. BARTH.

With regard to the Trinity, Rahner developed the important thesis that the immanent Trinity (God in God's self) *is* the economic Trinity (God as revealed in history) and vice versa. This thesis safeguarded the reality of revelation from modern epistemological roadblocks, such as Kant's distinction between the noumenal and phenomenal. It also allowed Rahner to develop his theology of the symbol, because humanity itself could thereby be understood as the best 'medium' for God's revelation in a way that allowed the soteriological aspect of all doctrine to be highlighted. Nevertheless, Rahner's way of relating the immanent and economic trinities has been subject to the criticism that it fails to preserve the eternal mystery of God, who is always transcendent to the world.

From the doctrine of the incarnation and Trinity, Rahner developed a powerful ECCLESIOLOGY. Christ was the original symbol of God (the *Ursakrament*), and the Church's sacraments make present the reality of Christ. Rahner developed his sacramentology with a relentless Christological personalism in order to move away from the mechanical explanations of sacramental efficacy that had set in after the Council of TRENT. He also recognized the activity of God's transforming grace throughout creation, in acts of selfless love and hope, although this grace of necessity was always from Christ and found its fulfilment in Christ and his Church. This meant that the sacramental Church was the visible sign of salvation, but that grace and salvation was possible outside the visible Church (see ANONYMOUS CHRISTIANITY).

Rahner's theology built a bridge between the modern world and the Catholic Church. His view of grace in nature gave inspiration to LIBERATION and FEMINIST THEOLOGIES, and his massive output (more than 1,600 publications) transformed a generation of theologians around the Catholic world. Though towards the end of his life he wrote a comprehensive work of systematic theology, *Foundations of Christian Faith*

(1977), it is probably his published prayers that provide the best initial access to his work.

See also SUPERNATURAL EXISTENTIAL.

P. Endean, *Karl Rahner and Ignatian Spirituality* (Oxford University Press, 2004).
K. Kilby, *Rahner: Theology and Philosophy* (Routledge, 2004).
D. Marmion and M. Hines, eds., *The Cambridge Companion to Karl Rahner* (Cambridge University Press, 2005).
K. Rahner, *Encounters with Silence*, 2nd edn (St Augustine's Press, 1999 [1937]).

GAVIN D'COSTA

RAPTURE A central category in certain forms of Christian ESCHATOLOGY associated with Protestant PREMILLENNIALISM, the idea of the rapture is derived from PAUL's description of how at the time of Christ's PAROUSIA, all Christians, living and dead, 'will be caught up [*rapiemur* in the VULGATE] in the clouds ... to meet the Lord in the air' (1 Thess. 4:17) and, in line with the teaching on resurrection found in 1 Corinthians 15:44, given spiritual bodies. While premillennial eschatologies are characteristic of many early Christian writers, the rapture only became a prominent topic with the emergence of modern DISPENSATIONALISM in the first half of the nineteenth century. Likewise, though in earlier centuries 'rapture' could be used to describe Elijah's translation in 2 Kings 2:11, only in the twentieth century does it acquire the status of a technical theological term.

Within dispensationalist theology the rapture is closely associated with a period of persecution known as the tribulation. While there is consensus that the tribulation occurs immediately before the onset of the 1,000-year earthly reign of Christ and the SAINTS described in Revelation 20:4–6, there is disagreement over whether the rapture precedes or follows the tribulation. According to pre-tribulation theology, the rapture occurs beforehand: Christ removes the faithful from earth and then returns with them at the end of the tribulation period to inaugurate the MILLENNIUM. By contrast, in post-tribulation theology 1 Thessalonians 4:17 is interpreted in light of Matthew 24:29–31 (which, in the King James Version, speaks of Christ appearing 'after the tribulation of those days') to conclude that the rapture comes after the tribulation. Mid-tribulation and pre-wrath views locate the rapture at some point during the period of tribulation.

The debate between these various positions tends to be dominated by questions of exegesis, though participants also raise the more specifically theological question of whether it is more consistent with the vocation of the Church to be spared from or to share in the world's final trials prior to Christ's eschatological triumph. At the same time, Christians operating outside a dispensationalist framework (including Catholic, Orthodox, and most 'mainline' Protestant Churches) charge that the stress on the rapture characteristic of these theologies represents a distinctly modern development without adequate grounding in SCRIPTURE, where the imagery of the faithful being caught up in the air is limited to 1 Thessalonians 4:17 – and even there is marginal to Paul's primary point, which is simply to assure his correspondents that the faithful dead will not be excluded from participation in Christ's final victory.

IAN A. MCFARLAND

RATIONALISM Broadly considered, rationalism is confidence in the capacities of human reason in discerning the true nature of reality. However, the term has come to have slightly different meanings in philosophical and theological discourse.

In philosophy rationalism is a type of *epistemology*, or commitment regarding the way that persons come to knowledge. It is associated with a group of philosophers, including Plato (*ca* 430–*ca* 345 BC), R. Descartes (1596–1650), B. Spinoza (1632–77), G. Leibniz (1646–1716), and, in a modified sense, I. KANT, who share the conviction that rational discourse and investigation, as opposed to empirical or sensory means of investigation, provide the most trustworthy way to knowledge of reality. Plato argued that the senses tie us too strongly to the material world, a realm of impermanence where things constantly change and pass away (see PLATONISM). Instead, we should set our minds in pursuit of transcendent and timeless truths, such as the ultimate nature of Beauty or the Good, which can only be discerned and fully understood through rational discourse or logical demonstration similar to mathematical argument. Descartes embraced rationalism in the quest for an unquestionable foundation for knowledge, methodologically doubting everything he had come to believe (including the reality of the sensory world, the existence of God, and even the truth of mathematics) until he came to a bedrock conviction that he could not doubt (see CARTESIANISM).

In theology rationalism refers to modes of relating reason and FAITH that oppose FIDEISM, or the conviction that it is valid to make theological claims solely based upon faith and without recourse to the basic tenets of reason (often exemplified by the adage falsely attributed to TERTULLIAN, 'I believe because it is absurd'). Many theological rationalists tend to think of reason more broadly than philosophical rationalists, claiming that theological affirmations must stand up against both the tests of rationality (logical coherence) and empirical investigation (correspondence to sensory experience). Beyond these basic similarities, theological rationalists come in many stripes, differing largely based upon how each relates faith to reason.

Atheistic rationalists affirm that reason and faith are at odds, and that this creates a significant problem for religion. According to this view, religious faith is fundamentally irrational and no different from other ludicrous beliefs (e.g., that the earth is flat). Rationalists of this type typically believe that scientific methods provide the most reliable basis for ascertaining truth because science is more open to correction than religious faith. Such rationalists typically consider themselves agnostic when it comes to religious matters, though there are many – including 'new atheists' like R. Dawkins (b. 1941) and S. Harris (b. 1967) who believe that scientific rationalism necessarily leads to rejecting religion on intellectual and moral grounds.

Theistic rationalists affirm the possibility of integrating faith and reason, and they trace their roots to early Christian apologists like Justin Martyr (d. *ca* 165) and Clement of Alexandria (*ca* 150–*ca* 215), who sought to articulate Christian faith in terms conversant with the philosophies of their day. Such views, exemplified in different ways by ANSELM OF CANTERBURY and T. AQUINAS, affirm that the fundamentally rational nature of reality provides a context in which human reason and faith properly utilized can affirm and enhance each other. Anselm maintained that reason enhanced by the light of faith is a valid and important tool in properly ordering our theological affirmations. Aquinas argued that although there is a limit to what we may learn about God apart from faith and divine revelation, one may properly affirm God's existence and even certain aspects of God's character from the observable structures of the world. Both perspectives continue to be influential in contemporary theology.

Some theologians and philosophers (especially among Reformed thinkers), drawing upon the work of writers like S. KIERKEGAARD and L. Wittgenstein (1889–1951) and encouraged by developments within the philosophy of NATURAL SCIENCE, affirm what might be described as fideistic rationalism, or a form of fideism that seeks to take reason seriously as a tool of faith. According to these thinkers, all ultimate commitments, including those of science, are built upon a foundation that cannot be constructed on a purely rationalistic foundation. Christians have warrant to assume certain faith commitments as long as they lead to an effectively coherent world view and the inner logic of these commitments can stand up to the fundamental tests of rational coherence. Recent advocates of a position like this include A. Plantinga (b. 1932), N. Wolterstorff (b. 1932), and other proponents of REFORMED EPISTEMOLOGY.

A variation on this theme, largely influenced by American pragmatism, affirms the validity of faith as a starting point for Christian life and thought, but requires that faith stand the tests of both coherence *and* correspondence; it must be held provisionally and deliberately tested publicly in conversation with other communities of enquiry (e.g., other religions, the sciences, etc.) also making claims about reality. Proponents of this view include D. Tracy (b. 1939) and R. Neville (b. 1939).

R. Dawkins, *The God Delusion* (Houghton Mifflin, 2006).
A. Nelson, ed., *A Companion to Rationalism* (Blackwell, 2005).
R. C. Neville, *The Highroad around Modernism* (SUNY, 1992).

MARK H. MANN

REAL PRESENCE: see EUCHARIST.

REALISM AND ANTI-REALISM Realism and anti-realism are contrasting tendencies of thought or, more strongly, positions concerning whether the entities proposed by a particular domain of discourse (e.g., theology, mathematics, sense experience) exist independently of minds and perceptions, whether those entities may be known, and whether they may be spoken about truthfully. Concerning the disputed domain, realism affirms that reality is not invented, constructed, or projected by humans but discovered by them; that knowledge of it is a finding rather than a fashioning; and that there is an objective truth of things beyond interpretations and experiences.

The realism/anti-realism debate is at the centre of contemporary philosophy. In theology and philosophy of religion, realists typically hold that God exists independently of human beings (even though religion might be regarded as a human construct), that God may be known by them, and that God may be spoken about truthfully. Robust realist claims can be contested on several grounds. For example, it has been held that God exists but not independently of human minds, or that God exists independently of human minds but cannot be spoken about. Religious discourse has been regarded as making claims that are systematically false, as expressive rather than representational, or as true according to standards internal to the discourse rather than objectively.

Philosophical debate between the various versions of realism and anti-realism is complex and technical, and there is little consensus about how the positions ought to be spelt out in detail. As a result, both the usefulness of the distinction and the appropriateness of either position as it has been attributed to any particular thinker have been disputed. Although the distinction between medieval nominalists and realists concerned cognate matters (see NOMINALISM), the current theological debate has been shaped by contemporary thought in philosophy, science, ethics, literary theory, and cultural studies. Renewed theological discussion of such topics as divine aseity and the relationship between the immanent and the economic TRINITY promises to throw fresh light on the debate, as do increasing awareness of the influence of modernity on theology and the retrieval of classical conceptions of the nature and purpose of Christian DOCTRINE.

The word 'anti-realism' does not normally carry polemical overtones. In a philosophical context it is usually associated with the philosopher M. Dummett (b. 1925) who argues that the realism debate should be framed in terms of the question of whether there are truths for which we are in principle unable to provide evidence (in philosophical jargon, truths which are 'evidence transcendent'). Realists are regarded as having to affirm that there are since they typically argue for the view (known as 'metaphysical realism') that reality can be described as it really is, objectively, independently of any particular observer. This seems to mean that the realist is committed to holding, for example, that it is either true or false that it started raining at 8 a.m. on 25 October 4004 BC, even though no one is in a position to provide evidence. But as the example implies, establishing the truth of this – and other evidence-transcendent matters – is only possible for a being who knows what happens at any particular time: God. Dummett has frequently alluded to the theological implications of his philosophy and once stated that 'anti-realism is ultimately incoherent but ... realism is only tenable on a theistic basis' (*Truth* xxxix). D. MacKinnon (1913–94) kept the realism/anti-realism debate on the agenda of PHILOSOPHICAL THEOLOGY during the middle decades of the twentieth century. In his profound and taxing work on ontology (especially in relation to CHRISTOLOGY) and on realism and IDEALISM he emphasized the tendency of the latter to deny the reality of deeds done, and, in particular, of individual, tragic suffering, notably that of Jesus Christ.

There have been two principal impulses to the contemporary realism/anti-realism debate in theology and philosophy of religion. I. KANT held that the only means by which humans can come to have knowledge is through the senses; he also argued that the traditional arguments for God's existence fail. But rather than deny that God exists, he proposed that God is the necessary but unknowable foundation of morality (see MORAL ARGUMENT). Kant's influence is particularly evident in the work of a contemporary Christian anti-realist, D. Cupitt (b. 1934). Cupitt argues for an autonomous religion of salvation – purified of out-moded METAPHYSICS and ecclesiastically controlled heteronomy – according to which God is a projection of what he calls 'the religious requirement'. Although he denies the mind-independent existence of God, Cupitt also denies that he is an atheist. At its most radical, for example, in strands of poststructuralist thought, anti-realism can seem to affirm that reality is a human linguistic construction; in his later work Cupitt has held a similar position.

The influence of Kant is also found in G. Kaufman (b. 1925). He affirms the independent reality of an 'unknowable X' which we designate by the term 'God'; however, thought about this 'X' never succeeds in referring, for it is only ever a human imaginative construction. Theology will only serve its moral purpose when it acknowledges its constructive character and rids itself of its idolatrous tendency to reify concepts of the divine. From a different theological perspective, the assistance of Kant's thought in avoiding idolatry has also been explored by the philosopher M. Westphal (b. 1940). He argues that since only God knows things as they really are – God included – and since human beings are sinners who 'edit God to our convenience' ('Anti', 144), we should acknowledge our creaturely epistemic limitations and – here Westphal departs from Kant – wait on God's self-revelation. This leads us to the second principal impulse towards the current realism/anti-realism debate.

REVELATION assumed centre stage in theological method owing to the way in which theology opened itself to and internalized the epistemological challenges of modernity. In the twentieth century, the most significant of these came from the empiricist movement known as logical positivism. Its 'verification principle' stated that a meaningful sentence is one which can be empirically verified. Sentences which cannot be verified were held to be nonsense, hence metaphysics and discourse about God, ethics, and aesthetics were consigned to oblivion. Although logical positivism has been abandoned, verificationism has had a lasting impact in philosophy of religion and philosophical theology because of the way it focused attention on the character of religious language and the question of whether it can be taken to refer to an independently existing deity. The 'expressivist' account of ethical discourse is a descendant of verificationism. On this view, when we speak of an action as morally 'right' or 'wrong', we are not judging it in terms of an independently existing realm of moral values; rather we are expressing an attitude of approval or disapproval towards it. An attempt to extend expressivism into theology was made by R. Braithwaite (1900–90) who argued that 'the primary use of religious assertions is to announce allegiance to a set of moral principles' and that '[a] religious belief is an intention to act in a certain way' ('View', 82, 89).

The empiricism of which verificationism is an example aims 'to give a true account of what is observable' and therefore opposes interpretations of scientific theories which propose unobservable structures and processes to explain observable phenomena – that is, the scientific realist position. Two notable Catholic thinkers, the physicist P. Duhem (1861–1916) and the philosopher of science B. van Fraassen (b. 1941), have argued for versions of empiricism, and both have linked their philosophical and theological outlooks. The realism/anti-realism debate in the philosophy of science has been vigorously conducted and several defences of theological realism have been proposed on the basis of these arguments. I. Barbour (b. 1923) developed an approach to the statements of science and of religion which sought to overcome the empiricist challenge in both disciplines by showing parallels between the two. He also proposed a typology of statements in the two discourses: 'naive realism' interprets them as referring directly to, and therefore as literal descriptions of, reality; 'critical realism' takes them as referring indirectly, as providing only approximate descriptions of reality – though with a hope of ever-increasing accuracy as knowledge accumulates. More recently, J. Soskice (b. 1951) has deployed arguments for a realist interpretation of language about unobservable entities in science to mount a structurally similar argument for how language about God can succeed in referring and hence be 'reality depicting'. Her work has been widely influential in theological accounts of the realism/anti-realism debate.

For both theological and philosophical reasons, tendencies to assimilate theological to scientific discourse and to interpret the realism debate in terms drawn from the philosophy of science have not gone unchallenged. The philosophical influence of the later work of L. Wittgenstein (1889–1951) on philosophers of religion like D. Z. Phillips (1934–2006) and on theologians of the so-called Yale School – in particular G. Lindbeck (b. 1923) – has been important in questioning whether Christian discourse requires intellectual legitimation from philosophy or science. These thinkers have stressed that what it means for God to exist independently of human beings must be interpreted according to criteria internal to Christian discourse rather than by criteria borrowed from other disciplines. Likewise, what it is for a statement to be true must be assessed according to internal rather than external criteria. Critics of these views argue that they lead to relativist anti-realism, but neither Phillips nor Lindbeck would accept such an interpretation of their work or the framing of the debate it implies.

See also FIDEISM; IDEALISM; REFORMED EPISTEMOLOGY.

G. Kaufman, *In Face of Mystery* (Harvard University Press, 1993).
B. Marshall, *Trinity and Truth* (Cambridge University Press, 2000).
A. Moore, *Realism and Christian Faith* (Cambridge University Press, 2003).
J. M. Soskice, *Metaphor and Religious Language* (Oxford University Press, 1985).

ANDREW MOORE

RECAPITULATION 'Recapitulation' describes an understanding of the work of Christ characteristic above all of the thought of IRENAEUS OF LYONS. The Greek word *anakephalaiosis*, which it translates, means in everyday usage a summing up or drawing together (e.g., summarizing the contents of a book in a list of chapter titles). PAUL uses the cognate verb in Romans 13:9 (all God's COMMANDMENTS are 'summed up' in the command to LOVE), but the term really enters Christian theology from Ephesians 1:10, which speaks of 'summing up all things in Christ'. The idea was probably developed by Justin Martyr (d. *ca* 165); at least Irenaeus uses it in a phrase which seems to be part of a quotation from Justin (*AH* 4.6.2).

For Irenaeus, Christ 'comes through the whole dispensation and sums up all things in himself' (*AH* 3.16.6), including 'the long story of humankind, offering us salvation in concentrated form, so that what we had lost in Adam – that is, being in the image and likeness of God – we might recover in Christ Jesus' (3.18.1). That means retracing in some way the whole of human history and the whole of human experience. Thus, the seventy-two generations of Christ's genealogy in Luke correspond to and symbolize the seventy-two races and tongues inferred from Genesis (3.22.3). Similarly, Irenaeus takes John 8:57 to mean that Christ was about fifty at the time of his death – old in the reckoning of the ancient world – so that he 'passed through every age – becoming an infant for infants, sanctifying them; a child among children ... a youth among youths ... so also an old man among old men' (2.22.4). The seemingly obvious problem presented for this scheme by the fact that Christ was male is partially met by the symbolic correspondence which Irenaeus sees between Eve and Mary.

See also MARIOLOGY.

PAUL PARVIS

RECONCILIATION: see SOTERIOLOGY.

RECONSTRUCTIONISM, CHRISTIAN: see DOMINION THEOLOGY.

REDEMPTION: see SOTERIOLOGY.

REFORMATION While many movements in Christian history have been called 'Reformations', the simple term 'Reformation' almost invariably denotes the seismic change in western European Christianity in the sixteenth century. That process of change ended the medieval vision of a unitary transnational Church led by the Roman PAPACY. It divided European Churches and their colonial offshoots between the Catholic Church and the many, diverse strands of PROTESTANTISM. It inaugurated fundamental changes in the liturgies and polities of European Christianity, driven by theological principles and imperatives.

Despite putative 'forerunners' of the Reformation, the main story begins with the theological struggles and insights of M. LUTHER, Augustinian eremite and professor of theology at the University of Wittenberg in Electoral Saxony. Like many others of his time, Luther wrestled with the theological dilemma of how a righteous God could save sinners, given the demanding example set by Jesus in the NT. In Luther's case the quest became entangled with a dispute over the Church's authority to dispense 'indulgences'. These papal graces remitted the 'works of satisfaction' required of the living after sacramental confession; by implication they were also believed to diminish or end the pain suffered by the departed in purgatory. In 1517 Luther issued a set of Latin theses disputing the power of indulgences. These provoked a storm of controversy in a Germany already long used to questioning the spiritual and ethical credibility of the papacy, and their notoriety gave the papal curia little choice but to insist Luther recant his views. Unfortunately for Rome, the agents sent to enforce Luther's recantation lacked the theological skill to meet him in argument. After private meetings and public debates Luther became convinced that only arguments from Scripture and evident reason could lead him to withdraw his statements. Eventually, confronted with the young and devout emperor Charles V (r. 1519–56) and representatives of the Church hierarchy at Worms in April 1521, Luther steadfastly refused to shift his ground.

During and after the indulgence controversy Luther completed a new understanding of the doctrine of justification, rooted in Paul and Augustine, but with distinctive features. Luther drew a conceptual distinction (made much sharper by his theological followers) between the forgiveness of a sinner that removes the condemnation of God (justification, or 'deeming righteous') and the intrinsic process by which a person is made better (sanctification, or 'making righteous'). Whereas medieval theology typically fused the processes or made one depend on the other, Luther insisted that sinners were forgiven, for Christ's sake, with a gift of extrinsic or 'alien' righteousness apprehended through faith. Divine forgiveness covered sinners *despite* their underlying impurity and unworthiness. This extrinsic justification did not exhaust the process: sinners were also sanctified by the Holy Spirit, made better able to lead lives of charity and self-discipline. However, their intrinsic righteousness was never the formal reason for their acceptance by God.

This insight radically transformed the kind of 'works' appropriate to a Christian life and the ministries required to support them. Since Christianity ceased to be about moral and ritual self-purification, the disciplines of personal penitence, abstinence, asceticism, and monasticism lost their rationale. Since God's forgiveness was not mediated through a ritually separate priesthood in the sacraments, the role of the priest changed into that of preaching the grace of God verbally (in vernacular Scripture) and physically (through baptism and the Eucharist). Churches that drew their spiritual power from the gospel needed no structural link to a 'well of grace' at Rome. These insights would define the mission and vision of the mainstream Churches of the Protestant Reformation, though variously expressed by different writers who were often independent of Luther.

While bequeathing to the Reformation its core theological insights, Luther took personal stances destined to mark off those Churches derived from his personal leadership and example from other Protestants. Luther remained all his life a gradualist and minimalist regarding liturgical change: he postponed reform of the mass until he believed the people were ready to understand a new order and was not inclined to radical iconoclasm. Most significantly, Luther argued that the wording of Scripture demanded confession that Christ's body, not just his spiritual presence, was in the consecrated Eucharistic elements. His insistence on this point at Marburg in 1529 and subsequently helped to isolate his movement from those of other reformers (see Lutheran Theology).

From the early 1520s other religious thinkers reworked and reformulated the basic Reformation ideas on justification and the priority of Scripture over tradition and the Roman hierarchy in their own accents. H. Zwingli, a stipendiary preacher in Zurich, began concrete steps to change the religious life of his community from 1522, and the degree of his dependence on Luther has always been disputed. His sacramentology was marked by a sharp rejection of the principle that any physical rite or physical substance could achieve spiritual effects. Thus, while sacraments might convey a message about the intentions of human beings, they were signs and not what they signified. While this rationalist philosophizing, deeply influenced by humanism, earned Zwingli the interest of Renaissance intellectuals in the Swiss Confederation and southern Germany, it was met by angry disapproval on the part of Luther and his followers. Following his rejection of the material in theology and worship, Zwingli pursued a much more radical, thorough, and speedy reform of Churches and their apparatus than Luther: images were removed entirely from worship spaces, and liturgy was stripped down to its barest essentials. Followers of this simple style boasted that they had recovered the characteristic worship of the primitive Church.

Once the religious imagination was thus liberated, smaller groups emerged with agendas even bolder than those of Luther, Zwingli, and their respective followers. T. Müntzer (*ca* 1490–1525) believed that the time had come for a sweeping, and, if need be, violent transformation of society. Further south, reforming spirits in Zurich grew impatient of Zwingli's negotiating with the city council and envisaged a gathered community of the self-selected 'godly'. Early in 1525 followers of C. Grebel (*ca* 1500–26) and his associates began to form Churches defined by adult baptism of believers in the villages of Zurich canton. It is still disputed how far these first 'Anabaptist' brotherhoods helped to inspire the parallel movements that emerged across southern and central Germany in the middle to late 1520s. Meanwhile in spring 1525 nearly all of Germany was convulsed by diverse protest movements representing the rural peasantry and the artisans of small towns. These called for religious reforms as part of a loose package of economic and social change. Initially hesitant, the German princes, spurred on by a visibly panicked Luther, suppressed the movements ferociously. Although 1525 did not end the movements to establish reformed Churches in towns and principalities, it did bring the period of unrestrained and adventurous pamphleteering to a sudden halt. Lay men and women who had experimented with writing, publishing, and even preaching reformed ideas now retreated to more politically and socially conventional roles, with the significant exception of K. Zell (1497/8–1562) of Strasbourg.

The Reformation was far more than a theological or liturgical event. For its implementation and survival it depended on the ability and will of secular leaders to protect it. Luther in his *To the Christian Nobility* of 1520 supplied the theoretical justification for lay governments to take the management of religious affairs into their own hands without fear of sacrilege. As papacy and empire dithered over how to respond to the Luther affair, magistrates and princes, slowly at first then with greater conviction, took control of the religious establishments and foundations within their states. Leagues took shape between reformers and their opponents, informally first and then with greater coherence, as the political geography of Germany was redrawn. The eventual result was the Peace of Augsburg of 1555, which gave princes and some towns significant autonomy to choose Catholicism or Lutheranism.

Also during the middle decades of the sixteenth century, Rome sought to give a comprehensive response to the doctrinal and ecclesiological challenges of the Lutheran Reformation in particular at the Council of TRENT. Yet both the Peace of Augsburg and the Council of Trent failed to take into account important ongoing changes in the religious complexion of Europe. In the mid-1550s the French reformer J. CALVIN, a formerly local player in the reformed enterprise, rose to far greater fame, pushing the hitherto barely significant town of Geneva to international prominence. Calvin began his career as a classical scholar in Paris and became a self-taught theologian. Through his many writings (including especially the multiple editions of his *Institute of the Christian Religion*), Calvin brought unprecedented intellectual rigour, exegetical sophistication, rhetorical balance, and verbal economy to the ideas of the Reformation. He adopted the core Reformation message on justification, but discerned a more positive role for the LAW even for the elect (see THIRD USE OF THE LAW). He formulated a doctrine of real spiritual presence in the Eucharist that balanced the insights of Lutheran and Zwinglian theologians while avoiding the excesses of either. In liturgy Calvin inclined more to the Zurich model of stark simplicity, and this model rapidly came to be thought of as 'Calvinist' (see REFORMED THEOLOGY).

Although Calvin's authority in his adopted city of Geneva remained precarious almost to the end of his life, his charisma attracted settlers not only from France but from other regions of Europe, especially during the later 1540s and 1550s. From the 1560s the Genevan models of reformed doctrine, worship, and pastoral discipline found passionate adherents in France, the Low Countries, Scotland, Hungary, Poland, and even in the extreme north-west of the Italian peninsula. In England, which had followed a peculiar course dictated by its monarchs' personal preferences, the dominant reformed theology resembled Calvin's, though in Church politics the English reforming bishops of the 1560s often looked for advice to the Zurich Church led by Zwingli's successor, H. BULLINGER (see ANGLICAN THEOLOGY). Even in Germany, where Lutheranism was the only legally authorized form of Protestantism, educated princes, led by the Elector Palatine at Heidelberg, adopted Calvin's tastes in worship and doctrine. These ideas were usually mediated through (or disguised as) the 'Philippist' type of Lutheranism associated with Luther's colleague P. Melanchthon (1497–1560).

The end of the Reformation is usually associated with the onset of the 'confessional era' and the establishment of Lutheran and Reformed 'orthodoxies' in the late sixteenth century. Following often bitter debates within and between the major reformed traditions, formulae hammered out in precise detail the theological standards of the new 'confessional' Churches: the Second Helvetic Confession (1566), the Lutheran BOOK OF CONCORD, the decisions of the Reformed Synod of DORT and others. These formulae often provoked further conflict: in the century or so after 1580 Europe stumbled into a series of bitter wars greatly exacerbated, if not actually caused, by religious divisions and the international alliances linked to confessionalism. However, the fundamental and liberating insight of the Reformation, that people can be freed by unearned divine grace to lead lives of charity without morbid anxiety for the precise state of their souls, would endure beyond the conflicts that its first tumultuous discovery had generated.

See also BUCER; CRANMER.

P. Benedict, *Christ's Churches Purely Reformed: A Social History of Calvinism* (Yale University Press, 2002).

M. Brecht, *Martin Luther*, 3 vols. (Fortress Press, 1985–93).

E. Cameron, *The European Reformation*, 2nd edn (Oxford University Press, 2011).

D. MacCulloch, *The Reformation* (Viking Books, 2004).

A. Pettegree, ed., *The Reformation World* (Routledge, 2000).

EUAN CAMERON

REFORMED EPISTEMOLOGY Reformed epistemology, so called because of its association with REFORMED THEOLOGY, is a movement that has at its heart the view that belief in God can be rational even if it is not based on any arguments. The position, whose leading proponents include W. Alston (b. 1921), A. Plantinga (b. 1932), and N. Wolterstorff (b. 1932), came into its own with the publication of *Faith and Rationality* (1983). The most mature statement of it is Plantinga's *Warranted Christian Belief* (2000).

Reformed epistemology was proposed in response to a long-standing tradition in the philosophy of RELIGION that took for granted a view called 'evidentialism' held by both theists and non-theists alike. According to evidentialism, belief in God is rational only if it is based on good arguments. Reformed epistemologists reject this view. They point out that not all rational beliefs are based on arguments. Arguments have premises; and conclusions of arguments are rational only if their premises are. These premises might themselves be conclusions of other arguments the believer has in mind. But this cannot go on for ever. Nor can it go in a circle if the conclusions are to be rational. Thus, if any beliefs are to be rational, at least some premise beliefs must be rational without being based on any arguments. And once that is granted, the question arises: which beliefs can be rational without being based on arguments? In particular, can belief in God be like that? If so, then the evidentialist assumption is mistaken and, as Reformed epistemologists sometimes put it, belief in God can be *properly basic*. (For a belief to be *basic* is for it to not be inferred from other beliefs; for it to be *properly basic* is for it to be both rational and non-inferential.)

Reformed epistemology has been misunderstood in a number of ways. Its name has led some to think it supports PROTESTANTISM over Catholicism. Plantinga corrects this error by showing the roots of the position not only in J. CALVIN but also in T. AQUINAS and PAUL. Others assume that Reformed epistemology disapproves of arguments for God's existence; but its claim is only that good theistic arguments are not *necessary* for rational belief in God, not that there are none or that none should be developed. Some have also wrongly concluded that Reformed epistemology insists that proper belief in God is groundless. In fact, basic beliefs often have grounds. When you believe that you are in pain, you do not infer this from other beliefs or base it on any argument. Nevertheless, this belief has a ground, namely, your experience of pain. Likewise, Reformed epistemologists think that properly basic belief in God can have grounds such as religious experience, whether dramatic and mystical or more subtle and ordinary.

Reformed epistemology continues to be controversial among those (both theists and non-theists) who endorse evidentialism or think that the experiences Reformed epistemologists cite as grounds are not adequate for the rationality of theistic belief. Nevertheless, it has significantly altered the course of contemporary philosophy of religion. Evidentialism, with its emphasis on arguments for and against God's existence, is no longer an unquestioned assumption dominating the field.

A. Plantinga and N. Wolterstorff, eds. *Faith and Rationality: Reason and Belief in God* (University of Notre Dame Press, 1983).

A. Plantinga, *Warranted Christian Belief* (Oxford University Press, 2000).

MICHAEL BERGMANN

REFORMED THEOLOGY The term 'Reformed' commonly designates the branch of the sixteenth-century REFORMATION which began in 1519 with H. ZWINGLI in Zurich, as distinguished from the Lutheran, Anabaptist, and Anglican reformations (see ANGLICAN THEOLOGY; LUTHERAN THEOLOGY; MENNONITE THEOLOGY). In the course of the sixteenth century, Reformed influence and teaching spread eastwards and westwards in Europe – to France, the Netherlands, and Britain in the West, to Poland, Bohemia, and Hungary in the East. By contrast, Scandinavia became Lutheran and the German Empire divided for the most part between Catholicism and Lutheranism – though with significant Reformed patches, especially in western and north-western Germany. Reformed Churches subsequently spread throughout North America, as well as Africa, Asia, Oceania, and South America. They will soon be represented in the new World Communion of Reformed Churches, which with some 80 million members will be the largest family of Churches stemming from the Reformation.

From the beginning the Reformed shared most of the emphases of M. LUTHER, but disagreements about the nature of Christ's presence in the EUCHARIST led to the separation of the Lutheran and Reformed confessions. Unlike the Lutherans, the Reformed Churches returned to the biblical numbering of the TEN COMMANDMENTS, restoring and emphasizing the second commandment with its prohibition of images and image-worship. They also modified the pattern of worship services more radically than Luther: while he retained a form of the mass, they followed a style more reminiscent of the late medieval prone, which had become quite common in France and Germany: a short vernacular service said from the pulpit and inserted into the mass following the Gospel; it generally contained prayers, readings, the creed, sermon and exhortation, and the LORD'S PRAYER. Further points of difference, particularly in the Churches most influenced by J. CALVIN, were the Reformed emphasis on double PREDESTINATION and the outworking of Calvin's models of ecclesiastical offices, organization, and discipline. However, Reformed theology was by no means always confessionalist in the narrow sense; it has produced a considerable variety of types and emphases through the centuries and played a major role in the wider stream of Protestant and, more recently, ecumenical theology (see ECUMENISM; PROTESTANTISM).

In the sixteenth century major theologians in the Reformed arena were, in addition to Zwingli: his successor in Zurich, H. BULLINGER; M. BUCER, who worked in Strasbourg and Cambridge; Calvin and his successor T. Beza (1519–1605) in Geneva; the Polish nobleman J. Laski (1499–1560), who worked mainly in northwest Germany but for a time in London; the chief author of the HEIDELBERG CATECHISM, Z. Ursinus (1534–83); and in Scotland J. Knox (*ca* 1514–72) and A. Melville (1545–1622). Major Reformed thinkers in philosophy and political theory included P. de La Ramée (1515–72) in France, G. Buchanan (1506–82) and S. Rutherford (1600–61) in Scotland, and J. Althusius (1557–1638) in Germany. The high intellectual aspirations and demands of Reformed theology were reflected in the establishment of numerous new universities and academies across Europe, from Scotland to Transylvania.

Calvin has come to be regarded in retrospect as the most significant of all of those mentioned: his shaping of the Genevan Church, his preaching, letters, biblical commentaries, controversial and constructive theological writings – especially the *Institute of the Christian Religion* (ever and again wrongly rendered in English as a plural, *Institutes*) in the fourth and final edition of 1559 – continue even today to be more intensively studied than the work of his Reformed contemporaries. The equation of 'Reformed' and 'Calvinist' is, however, misleading.

The term 'Calvinist' is most commonly applied historically to the theology of Reformed Orthodoxy as it was systematized in the three generations following Calvin's death in 1564, first by Beza and then particularly in England and the Netherlands. Three influences were particularly significant: English PURITANISM, the Arminian controversy (see ARMINIANISM) together with its result, the decrees of the Synod of DORT, and the development of FEDERAL THEOLOGY.

For roughly a century from the time of Elizabeth I (r. 1558–1603) in England, the Church of England was a battlefield between what today would be called the 'High-Church' and 'Low-Church' parties, the latter mainly drawing their inspiration from Zurich and Geneva and seeking a more radical reformation in liturgy and Church government than either the queen or the High-Church party would countenance. R. HOOKER wrote his *Laws of Ecclesiastical Polity* to refute these Puritan demands and so became the classic advocate of what would come to be known as the Anglican *via media* (see ANGLICAN THEOLOGY). The conflicts continued through the first half of the seventeenth century and led to the establishing of Puritan exile settlements in New England. The victory of the Puritans in the English Civil War and the proclamation of the Commonwealth under O. Cromwell (1599–1658) brought a brief period of Puritan ascendancy, but this was followed in 1660 by the restoration of the monarchy and with it the Anglican ecclesiastical order, leading many (though not all) Puritans to separate from the Church of England. In Scotland the struggle finally went the other way and led to the establishment of Presbyterianism and the marginalizing of the episcopal elements in the Church of Scotland. Prominent English Puritan theologians included W. Perkins (1558–1602), W. Ames (1576–1633), J. Owen (1616–83), and R. Baxter (1615–91); on the literary side J. Milton (1608–74) and J. Bunyan (1628–88) were especially influential. The comprehensive 'official' statement of Puritan theology and (Presbyterian) ecclesiology is to be found in the documents of the Westminster Assembly (1643–8) but these only received ecclesiastical ratification in Scotland (see WESTMINSTER STANDARDS).

In the Netherlands, Beza's former student, J. Arminius (1560–1609), professor in Leyden, came under attack from his colleague F. Gomarus (1563–1641) for modifying Calvin's and Beza's teaching on double predestination – that God from all eternity had chosen to elect some to salvation and to condemn the others to judgement. Arminius believed that the elect are indeed chosen by God and the reprobate rejected, but only on the ground of the divine foreknowledge of who in fact would come to faith in the GOSPEL. This departed not only from Calvin's teaching but also from that of such earlier theologians as AUGUSTINE and T. AQUINAS – though with them the reprobation of the non-elect was less a positive divine decision than the collateral consequence of God's decision to save only some. Arminius' position was defended after his death in the *Remonstrance* of 1610, but finally condemned by the Synod of Dort. The Synod rejected five arguments of the Remonstrants and set against them what came to be called the 'Five Points' of Calvinism: TOTAL DEPRAVITY, UNCONDITIONAL ELECTION, LIMITED ATONEMENT, IRRESISTIBLE GRACE, and the PERSEVERANCE of the saints. These became the hallmark of classical confessional Calvinism, combining with an ever more complex federal theology.

The central concept of federal theology is that of 'COVENANT' (Latin *foedus*). The term had played a major role in Bullinger's arguments against the Anabaptists: the unity of the 'testament or covenant of God' established the parallel between circumcision and (infant) baptism. Federal theology was developed further in Heidelberg in the third quarter of the sixteenth century and spread throughout the Reformed world. A key distinction came to be made between the 'covenant of works' made by God with Adam and Eve in Paradise, which they broke, and the subsequent 'covenant of grace' which (already in the OT) replaced it: the covenants thus became the hermeneutical key to the interpretation of SCRIPTURE and the history of salvation (see SALVATION HISTORY). Later versions added a third 'covenant of redemption' between the Father and the

Son, anchoring the theme of the covenant within the doctrine of God. The most comprehensive exposition of Federal Theology is to be found in the work of the German Reformed theologian J. Cocceius (1603–69). The ramifications of the concept in practical Church politics are reflected in the Scottish 'National Covenant' of 1638, the 'Solemn League and Covenant' of 1643 and the history of the seventeenth-century Scottish Covenanters. Federal thought also had more general social, juridical, political, and philosophical ramifications (e.g., the notion of the 'social contract') and played a significant part in paving the way for the modern understanding of participatory democracy. It also gave rise to major theological conflicts, especially in eighteenth-century Scotland, because of the implied 'contractual' nature of God's relation to humankind and the 'conditionality' of the covenant of grace on repentance and faith.

In the later seventeenth and eighteenth centuries classical orthodox Calvinism lost much of its power in the face of the challenges raised by the ENLIGHTENMENT, but thinkers such as J. EDWARDS paved the way for a deepening dialogue with modern social, political, and scientific thought and the analysis of religious experience, themes which were to become more prominent in the nineteenth and twentieth centuries.

By 1800 there cannot be said to be any single uniform or dominant pattern of Reformed theology. F. SCHLEIERMACHER, 'the father of modern theology' in a more liberal and experience-oriented sense, was Reformed, as were the two friends E. Irving (1792–1834) and J. M. Campbell (1800–72), who were expelled from the ministry of the Church of Scotland – Irving for allegedly unorthodox CHRISTOLOGY and Campbell for his understanding of ASSURANCE – but are today recognized as significant figures in the history of theology. More traditional tendencies were reinforced in Germany by H. Heppe (1820–79), who made an influential compendium of orthodox Reformed dogmatics, in the Netherlands by A. KUYPER and at Princeton Seminary by C. HODGE and B. B. Warfield (1851–1931), and are still very much present in North America and elsewhere, especially in the Dutch Reformed tradition. A more liberal, ecumenical, and historically based approach to theology in North America was influentially represented by the Swiss-born Reformed theologian P. Schaff (1819–93); in general the century also brought a slow-spreading acceptance of the results of contemporary (mainly German) biblical criticism and LIBERAL THEOLOGY in the Anglo-Saxon countries, so that by 1900 there was also a recognizably more liberal (and larger) Reformed wing over against the conservative. In Britain and North America the nineteenth century also brought a new interest in liturgy, Church music, and architecture and a departure from what had come to be felt by many as the overly bleak, didactic, and verbalized tradition of Reformed worship. In addition, whereas earlier centuries had seen a good deal of splitting and dividing in the Reformed – especially the Presbyterian – family, serious efforts began in the latter part of the century to rediscover its common unity, leading to the foundation of the World Presbyterian Alliance (1875) and the International Congregational Council (1891). These united in 1970 to form the World Alliance of Reformed Churches, which in turn plans in the near future to unite with the numerically smaller Reformed Ecumenical Synod.

The twentieth century saw a new wave in the form of DIALECTICAL THEOLOGY, with two Swiss Reformed among its leaders, K. BARTH and E. Brunner (1889–1966). This theology sought to break radically with the approach opened up by Schleiermacher, to reject all forms of 'NATURAL THEOLOGY', and to ground theological thinking solely on the Word of God. Dialectical theology was not solely Reformed – several leading representatives were Lutheran and in general it can be said that most work in Protestant systematic theology today is not overtly or recognizably confessional in character – but Brunner and Barth came to exert considerable influence on Reformed theologians in Europe and America. In particular the development of Barth's theology from the early dialectical phase (stressing the absolute qualitative difference between God and the world) to his later emphasis in the *Church Dogmatics* on 'the humanity of God' and the centrality of the person of Christ in dogmatics found many followers. Among many prominent Reformed contemporaries were the brothers R. NIEBUHR and H. R. Niebuhr (1894–1962) in America, in Britain the brothers J. (1886–1960) and D. (1887–1954) Baillie, in the Netherlands K. Miskotte (1894–1976) and H. Berkhof (1914–95), in Germany O. Weber (1902–66) and W. Niesel (1903–88), and in Czechoslovakia J. Hromadka (1889–1969). More recent widely read Reformed theologians were T. F. Torrance (1913–2007), who wrote prolifically on historical, ecumenical, dogmatic, and scientific theology, and J. Moltmann (b. 1926), with early work on political theology and the theology of the cross and a later emphasis on ecology and CREATION.

See also PRINCETON THEOLOGY; SCOTTISH THEOLOGY.

ALASDAIR HERON

REGENERATION: see *ORDO SALUTIS*.

RELATIONS, DIVINE: see TRINITY.

RELICS: see SAINTS.

RELIGION Religion's referent can be endlessly illustrated, but its nature is notoriously hard to define. R. OTTO argued that a specific quality – a 'sense of the holy' – may be found in all its core instances, while M. Eliade (1907–86) highlighted the distinction between the sacred and the profane. Others have maintained that the luxuriant variety of rites, beliefs, and symbols that go under the label 'religion' can only be characterized by a kind of family resemblance or organized under a number of functional headings.

Co-ordinate with the question of what belongs in the category 'religion' is the question of what impels a need for the category at all. In the Indian subcontinent the parable of six blind men and an elephant was used to describe religious opinions: one person held the trunk of the elephant and believed it a snake, another touched a leg and believed it a tree, and so on. The perspectives of the blind men were likened to the beliefs of various schools of religious thought – the parable itself being told from the viewpoint of the sighted person among the blind, the holder of the single correct belief that stands above the others. From this perspective, 'religion' is a category used to group and characterize other peoples' firm but mistaken beliefs. Some Jain writers, however, are believed to have initiated the use of the parable to include their own view as one among many perspectives, and so to imply an idea of religion as a genus within which my own tradition falls as one (perhaps superior) species among others.

Within primordial traditions, neither of these ways of conceiving religion is necessarily appropriate, since the meaning such traditions conveyed was profoundly tied to local communities and contexts, in contrast to the more universal scope of the philosophies and religions (including, e.g., Buddhism and Christianity) that developed in the so-called 'axial age' (800–200 BC). When Socrates (470/69–399 BC) was charged by Athenian citizens with not believing in the gods of the city or early Christians were criticized as 'irreligious', this signalled an assumed seamless connection between the sacred and the communal characteristic of primordial traditions. A variety of rites corresponded to a variety of human communities. Rather than being distinguished as one sphere of human life separable from the political or the economic, primordial religion permeated all dimensions. Its obligations were inseparable from those of family, clan, city, and culture. Christianity stood out in its context by mixing these categories, bringing together in one faith people who otherwise belonged to various social–ethnic complexes which had their own 'sacred canopies'. Jewish monotheism had already instigated the view that others' gods were not real and rival, but empty. In Judaism, however, this belief was inextricably attached to the particular ethnicity and culture of Israel. Christianity's spread among the nations significantly altered the understanding of the nature of religion.

From NT times Christianity articulated its beliefs in connection with Judaism. When the two religious communities separated, Christians were compelled to recognize the truth of this tradition at least in its possession of revealed SCRIPTURE. The troubled relation with living Judaism represents Christian theology's original religion question. Christianity also articulated its beliefs in connection with a universal human condition known in part through general reason and experience (as in Greek philosophy), though the extent of such connections was subject to debate. In this context, T. AQUINAS defined religion as that which is owed to God by humans and outlined what portion of that obligation could be known and realized (as in moral practice) through the use of reason. K. BARTH defined religion somewhat similarly, as all human efforts to know and relate to God apart from dependence on God's self-revelation, but he saw it as an obstacle to authentic FAITH. If for Aquinas natural religion was an implicit foundation for GRACE, for Barth it was a distorting dimension present in all human spirituality, even the most explicitly Christian.

In the modern period, 'religion' became a particular object of study separated out by definition from other human spheres and constituted by a mix of methods from the social sciences and humanities. The materials treated (texts, rituals, or beliefs) remained the same as those that figured within the practice and teaching of faith traditions themselves. But interpretations drawn from history, social theory, or psychology replaced theological, commentarial, and devotional ones. This perspective on religion was largely the product of European history. On the one hand the REFORMATION and the religious wars that followed left a *de facto* reality of Christian pluralism. This diversity prompted reflection on 'natural religion' either as a shared Christian essence or a deist alternative to confessional Churches. ENLIGHTENMENT philosophy developed a general critique of religion, most notably in the work of D. Hume (1711–76). This critique addressed itself not to a single tradition but to putatively generic features of religion, such as miracles or supernatural beings.

On the other hand, the modern missionary movement and European COLONIALISM brought home concrete knowledge of non-biblical religious traditions. At the root of serious study of particular faiths and the discipline of religious studies itself stands the work of mission pioneers in translation and field knowledge. The mission movement also prompted a new energy in the Christian theology of religions, marked by missionary-scholar figures like J. N. Farquhar (1861–1929) and H. Kraemer (1888–1965). In biblical studies, the 'HISTORY OF RELIGION SCHOOL' in late nineteenth- and early twentieth-century Germany advanced the effort to understand SCRIPTURE in light of parallels to be found in Babylonian, Egyptian, and Hellenistic religious systems. For these scholars, expertise in these (largely dead) religions was necessary for adequate interpretation of Christian sources and hence of Christianity itself. Finally, increasing knowledge of cultural diversity gave rise to an anthropological perspective on religion whose impact is marked by *The Golden Bough* (1890) by J. Frazer (1854–1941). Frazer's exclusively literary exploration of the mythology of the world emphasized parallel versions of a shared fertility MYTH revolving around a dying and rising king, implying that Christianity was but a variation on a general theme. In all these ways, the category 'religion' itself bears a distinctly western pedigree.

In the face of these changes, the most decisive figure is F. SCHLEIERMACHER. No other thinker so dramatically changed the understanding of religion itself while working out a new theological programme on the basis of that understanding. For him the well of religion was piety, a subjective awareness of unconditional dependence on the divine. All features of theology could be reconceived in terms of the way in which they expressed and facilitated the reproduction of that disposition. Schleiermacher straightforwardly accepted that religion was rooted in one distinct sphere of human life among many, the realm of affect and experiential integration, the one that made the others whole. DOCTRINE, morality, and cult were its necessary vehicles but not its essence.

Among contemporary scholars, N. Smart (1927–2001) identified six dimensions of religions: doctrinal, experiential, social, moral, ritual, and mythological. Entire disciplines came to focus on each of these. Philosophy of religion treats the propositional aspect of religions, psychology of religion the experiential aspect, sociology of religion the social aspect, religious ethics the moral aspect, and literary and anthropological study the ritual and mythological aspects. Several of these fields produced aggressive reductive explanations of religion: psychological in S. Freud (1856–1939), economic in K. Marx (1818–83), and sociological in E. Durkheim (1858–1917).

While a writer like AUGUSTINE demonstrates that theology encompasses all of Smart's dimensions (since, for example, what we later regard as a doctrinal development was often enmeshed in concrete ritual, social and ethical concerns), theology tended to follow the lead of religious studies by self-differentiating into various sub-branches. Working against this trend, some scholars of religion, including most notably C. Geertz (1926–2006), developed a unified cultural–linguistic perspective that viewed religions more on the analogy of a language, a system of signification that constituted a life world. G. Lindbeck (b. 1923) developed a correlative view of theology as a regulative grammar, referring to its ultimate objects not in one-to-one correspondence between propositions and things but in the more comprehensive way that an entire linguistic system may be said to represent the world.

For much of the last century theology concerned itself primarily with secular critiques of religion, and only slowly awakened to the fact that the religions themselves remained its primary interlocutors. Once this took place, religious PLURALISM became a central theological topic, both in terms of the need for a theology of religions sophisticated enough to comport with the thick descriptions provided by religious studies and in terms of the pastoral issues raised by life in diverse societies, including issues of multiple religious practice and multiple religious belonging. VATICAN COUNCIL II's document *Nostra aetate*, treating Christianity's relation with other religions, was a key turning point in this process, as was the theology of K. RAHNER, who articulated a broadly inclusivist approach to religious diversity (see ANONYMOUS CHRISTIANITY). Inter-religious dialogue came to be seen as integral to the theological task, even while it was debated whether it was an aspect of, a complement to, or a replacement for existing understandings of Christian mission.

Religious pluralism had long figured in the debates of philosophical theology in that competing supernaturalist claims seemed to undercut the rational defence of any one. Such concerns led J. Hick (b. 1922) to become the pre-eminent advocate of a pluralist view of religions, in which each offers a culturally conditioned version of substantively the same human transformation from self-centredness towards focus on a transcendent reality. Other notable thinkers agreed in rejecting any exclusivist claims for one religion's truth or any inclusivist claims that the superior content of one tradition funded the saving power of others. W. C. Smith (1916–2000) did so as a religious historian who argued that the subjective experience of faith was the same in various traditions. And P. Knitter (b. 1939) did so on the ethical grounds that exclusivist beliefs led to discriminatory behaviour and that each religion had proven itself inadequate alone to heal the world's injustice. Much theological discussion has been driven by debate among various pluralist, inclusivist, and exclusivist views. Other approaches have arisen that question the assumptions of this typology, whether the assumption that religions must relate to only one religious end or the assumption that we are in a position to make the global assessments required to opt for one of the three options. Most notable is the fledgling discipline of comparative theology in which significant sources from another religious tradition are used as primary references in Christian theological reflection.

This turn towards direct engagement with the religions has coincided with the waning of severely reductive treatments of religion in psychology and sociology. What has grown in their place is biological, or evolutionary, theories. Cognitive science investigates the brain states that correspond to religious experience. Evolutionary theorists parse religious beliefs and practices in terms of their implicit effects on inclusive genetic fitness. Readings of religion in Freudian or Marxist terms tended to mark it as pathological or destined for extinction. Evolutionary ones are somewhat more equivocal. The 'new atheists' lean heavily on explanations of religion that see it as an evolutionary epiphenomenon (overextending human pattern-recognition into imaginary realms) or as an outmoded adaptation to conditions that no longer exist. But others argue that religion may be hard-wired in our neurology and too tightly integrated with positive cognitive abilities to be purged, regardless of its ultimate validity.

In summary, 'religion' is a moving target, whose meaning has often been reframed. It remains of inescapable importance for theology under at least three headings. First, religion can be taken to mean the living religions themselves, which are essential as dialogue partners with their own alternative readings of the human condition. Second, it can be taken to mean the field of religion, the cumulative scholarly work in religious studies in all the dimensions we have mentioned, which are relevant to virtually any topic the theologian touches. Finally, religion can be taken to mean the purely empirical descriptions of the phenomena of religious practice and experience arising as by-products of scientific disciplines, which provide a baseline for theology's communication with the wider public. In all these cases, religion offers theology light on its own subject that theology alone cannot provide.

K. Barth, *On Religion: The Revelation of God as the Sublimation of Religion* (T&T Clark, 2006 [1932]).

W. James, *The Varieties of Religious Experience: A Study in Human Nature* (Longmans, Green and Co., 1902).

P. Knitter, *Introducing Theologies of Religion* (Orbis, 2002).

F. Schleiermacher, *On Religion: Speeches to Its Cultured Despisers* (John Knox Press, 1994 [1799]).

N. Smart, *Dimensions of the Sacred: An Anatomy of the World's Beliefs* (University of California Press, 1999).

W. C. Smith, *The Meaning and End of Religion: A New Approach to the Religious Traditions of Mankind* (Macmillan, 1963).

S. MARK HEIM

RELIGIOUS LANGUAGE All religions must deal with the importance of language in relating to the divine or the supernatural. This is especially crucial, however, for a 'religion of the book' like Christianity that purports to have communicable REVELATION from God. Such revelation, as well as expressions of PRAYER and praise to God, are challenging because they are expressed in a particular, everyday language, such as the common (*koinē*) Greek in which the NT is written. Because the same language used to name creatures is being deployed to talk about the Creator, it is deeply strained to speak of God without IDOLATRY.

Three major options for addressing this problem have emerged through much of Christian history. One is the univocal approach, where language about God has basically the same literal meaning as when used in other contexts. This assures that words have cognitive meaning when used of God, but the danger is that God's mystery is limited. At the opposite end of the spectrum was a second option early in the Church, the *via negativa* or negative way, where all positive claims about God are denied as representing equivocal use of language, not for the sake of sceptical unbelief, but for the sake of the most intense mystical awareness of God possible (see APOPHATIC THEOLOGY). T. AQUINAS rejected both options in favour of an analogical way. In this manner, God's uniqueness is protected while also recognizing that the creation in some ways points back to its cause (see ANALOGY). J. DUNS SCOTUS affirmed the univocal way in the next generation, arguing that analogy was a false option and that only two choices are possible: words are either univocal or equivocal.

All of these approaches have been severely questioned. In the negative way, it is difficult to convey any sense of cognitive content. The univocal way seems to limit God too much. Even Aquinas' analogical way seemed to reduce analogy to the univocal approach in seeing God as the cause of all things: if 'cause' is not used univocally, then he is essentially making a circular argument, explaining analogy by an analogy.

The twentieth century became the century of the 'linguistic turn', in which almost every major philosophical movement became preoccupied with language, realizing that one could not consider thought or reason without taking seriously its expression in language. An initial example of this trend was quite critical of religious language. The logical positivists' 'verification principle' meant that words have cognitive meaning only in so far as they can be empirically verified, rendering most religious language not just false but also nonsense. The poststructuralist deconstruction of J. Derrida (1930–2004) also pushed towards a rejection of any kind of transcendent claim or meta-narrative, although, more recently, some have found in Derrida's thought room for a kind of negative theology that at least supports a 'hermeneutic of suspicion' that can clear the ground of ideology for a 'hermeneutic of testimony' (see Ricœur, *Essays* 119–54).

Further developments offered more positive perspectives for religious language. Philosophies of SYMBOL, metaphor, and story have pointed to what some see as the true point of Aquinas' category of analogy, namely, that figurative language does not have to be 'translated' into univocal language in order to be meaningful. This understanding of the original creative power of figurative language has rejuvenated the understanding of the biblical language that is dominated by narrative, poetry, and parables. One can thus never leave the Bible behind once its meaning has been clarified in univocal language, which has sometimes been a tendency in theology and preaching; rather, one must return to SCRIPTURE for insight over and over again in a hermeneutical spiral.

This does not remove a role for univocal explanation or propositions, but it makes them supplementary to figurative language rather than a replacement for it. In fact, the work of the later L. Wittgenstein (1889–1951) emphasized that even univocal language is more flexible than previously thought. As he put it, it has 'blurred edges', which allow for broader application (*PI*, §71). He also made the primary issue in assessing meaning-effective use, so a word has meaning if it has a use. The use, he pointed out, is usually particular to a community, so a word might mean something literally to one group but not another. Wittgenstein's emphasis on the 'language game' or the 'form of life' (*PI*, §§7, 19) as being essential to meaning led to warnings of the danger of 'Wittgensteinian FIDEISM', where no one who is not 'playing' the particular religious language game can criticize it. This kind of focus on the use of language bore fruit in J. L. Austin's *How to Do Things with Words* (1975). Austin pointed out the descriptive fallacy, which assumes that words usually just describe things. He noted that people do many things with words, such as covenanting, thanking, baptizing, exhorting, and commanding, which cannot be reduced to simple description.

Perhaps the richest development in the field of religious language has been various forms of NARRATIVE THEOLOGY. All of these assume that narratives cannot be simply reduced to literal language but have an integrity of their own, much like metaphor. In fact, they usually assume that literal and symbolic language have their meaning only in the context of a larger socio-cultural narrative ('our story') – a point made by figures like P. Ricœur (1913–2005) and A. MacIntyre (b. 1929). Others, such as J. McClendon (1924–2000), have emphasized the centrality of biographies ('my story', 'your story') for making sense of FAITH. The so-called Yale school of POSTLIBERAL THEOLOGY, particularly H. FREI and G. Lindbeck (b. 1923), can be seen as a type of narrative theology that emphasizes not so much the cultural story ('our story') but the biblical story ('*the* story'), such that Christians must allow the biblical world to serve as the framework for interpreting everyday reality.

These positive approaches to religious language have largely taken the place of the sceptical question of religious language that dominated the mid-twentieth century. The effect of this wide reflection on language and specifically religious language has offered much richer and nuanced resources that are still being plumbed for understanding Scripture and theology.

P. Ricœur, *Interpretation Theory: Discourse and the Surplus of Meaning* (Texas Christian University Press, 1976).

D. R. Stiver, *The Philosophy of Religious Language: Sign, Symbol, and Story* (Cambridge University Press, 1996).

N. Wolterstorff, *Divine Discourse: Philosophical Reflections on the Claim that God Speaks* (Cambridge University Press, 1995).

D. R. STIVER

REMONSTRANTS: see ARMINIANISM.

REPENTANCE According to the first Gospel, Jesus began his ministry by taking up JOHN THE BAPTIST's call to repent (Matt. 4:17). The idea of repentance originates in the OT, where it refers to a turning back (the literal meaning of the Hebrew *shub*) from a course of action or style of life. While there are references to God 'repenting' in the Bible (e.g., Exod. 32:14; Jer. 18:8), repentance is normally viewed as a human rather than a divine activity (see especially Num. 23:19; 1 Sam. 15:29). Specifically, it is seen as appropriate for one who has committed SIN, and it includes both sorrow for past deeds and a commitment to act righteously in the future that together evoke divine mercy (e.g., 1 Kgs 8:47–8; Jer. 34:15; Ezek. 18:30).

Jesus called for repentance in anticipation of God's eschatological judgement of the world. Though this expectation of an imminent end to history gradually waned in the Church, the idea that commitment to the GOSPEL demanded a radical reorientation of life remained a permanent feature of Christian belief. The importance of repentance in proclamation was safeguarded by its close association with BAPTISM (Acts 2:38; cf. Mark 1:4; Luke 3:3), while the emergence of rites of PENANCE made formal acts of repentance and FORGIVENESS an ongoing feature of Christian practice. In later REFORMED THEOLOGY repentance was given more technical definition as a change of mind (the literal meaning of the NT Greek *metanoia*) bestowed by the HOLY SPIRIT and entailing both the mortification of one's sinful nature and the quickening of FAITH.

See also *ORDO SALUTIS*.

IAN A. MCFARLAND

REPROBATION: see ELECTION.

***RESSOURCEMENT*:** see *NOUVELLE THÉOLOGIE*.

RESTORATIONISM The term 'restorationism' refers to a type of Christianity whose adherents seek to pattern contemporary practice exclusively on ancient norms, exemplified by the behaviour and teachings of the founder(s). Every Christian tradition is to some degree restorationist, in as much as they all appeal to the most ancient teachings and norms. But most Christian traditions mix that appeal with an appreciation for historical development. For example, Lutherans appeal to biblical norms, but also to the ways in which M. LUTHER appropriated those norms in the sixteenth century (see LUTHERAN THEOLOGY).

The unmistakable hallmark of restorationist Christianity is the complete and utter rejection of any historical mediation of ancient, founding norms. Authentic restorationist traditions, therefore, refuse to recognize any historical development. Instead, they appeal directly to founding events, teachings, and examples, ignoring the historical developments that inevitably mediate those teachings and events into the present.

Restorationist movements have appeared in all periods of Christian history. One finds, for example, the early stirrings of restorationist Christianity among early Christian thinkers who sought to combat GNOSTICISM, MARCION, and MONTANISM by appealing to the teachings of Jesus and the unbroken witness of the bishops.

In later centuries, reformers often employed restorationism as a way to combat the historical traditions they opposed. On this ground, both J. Hus (*ca* 1370–1415) and J. Wycliffe (*ca* 1325–84) argued against the DOCTRINE of TRANSUBSTANTIATION. At the time of the Reformation, H. ZWINGLI offered a strong perspective, since he measured every doctrine and practice by the standard of the biblical text. On that ground, for example, he banned from Christian worship both instrumental music and vocal singing since, according to one reading of the Greek text of the NT, PAUL admonished Christians to 'sing psalms and hymns and spiritual songs, making melody to God … *in your hearts*' (Col. 3:16). Originating in Zwingli's Zurich, the evangelical Anabaptists also embraced restorationist thinking, seeking to root their beliefs and behaviour squarely and exclusively in the teachings of Jesus.

The classic restorationist tradition in the USA – the Churches of Christ – emerged in the early nineteenth century under the leadership of A. Campbell (1788–1866) and B. Stone (1772–1844). Basing their faith and practice exclusively on the NT text, they sought to practice what the NT taught and rejected any practice the NT failed to authorize.

Largely because of their radical allegiance to the biblical text, and because that allegiance typically excludes a consideration of history and historical development, restorationists have often been blind to the very real ways in which history and culture have shaped and moulded their beliefs and practices in spite of their protests to the contrary.

R. T. Hughes and C. L. Allen, *Illusions of Innocence: Protestant Primitivism in America, 1630–1875* (University of Chicago Press, 1988).

F. H. Littell, *The Origins of Sectarian Protestantism* (Macmillan, 1952); reprinted as *The Anabaptist View of the Church* (Baptist Standard Bearer, 2001).

RICHARD T. HUGHES

RESURRECTION 'Resurrection' (Greek *anastasis*) denotes the return ('raising', 'standing up') to bodily life of a person or persons who had been bodily dead. It does not mean 'life after death', but a new life the other side of whatever immediate post-mortem existence there may be. However vividly such a post-mortem life may be imagined (as in, e.g., some ancient Egyptian world views), this is not the same as actual new bodily life.

Ancient paganism (with the possible exception of Zoroastrianism, though the evidence is hard to date) scoffed at the notion of resurrection. Homer (*fl.* 850 BC), Aeschylus (525/4–456/5 BC), Pliny the Elder (23–79) and many others insisted that resurrection was impossible. Plato (*ca* 430–*ca* 345 BC) and others declared that it was in any case undesirable, since the soul is better off without its bodily prison (see PLATONISM).

Ancient ISRAEL, celebrating the goodness of the present world, placed a much higher value on bodily life, and developed no detailed account of an afterlife. But, as Jewish thinkers reflected on present injustices, a fresh vision began to emerge, reaffirming the goodness of bodily existence by insisting that God the Creator would remake the world and people too. This belief, hinted at in Psalms (e.g., 16:10–11; 73:24) and prophets (Hos. 6:2; Isa. 26:19; Ezek. 37:1–14), came to full flowering when the particular injustices of persecution and martyrdom forced the question: how would God be faithful to his covenant with Israel, and to his whole CREATION? The answer 'resurrection' (e.g., 2 Macc. 8) was widely accepted among Jews in Jesus' day, and taught in particular by the populist Pharisees, for whom 'resurrection' was part of a vision of religious and political renewal, naturally opposed by the aristocratic Sadducees. At this period, too, many Jews (e.g., Philo of Alexandria (20 BC–AD 50)) had embraced the Greek vision of a continuing, disembodied, immortal SOUL.

This is sometimes confusing. To believe in resurrection means believing also in some kind of personal continuity between bodily death and new bodily life and thus a *temporary* disembodied immortality. At the same time, part of the point of resurrection, as is clearly seen in the letters of PAUL (e.g., 1 Cor. 15:52–4), is that it will constitute an *embodied* immortality (i.e., an incorruptible, non-dying body). It is therefore not possible to play off 'resurrection' against 'immortality'. The critical difference is, rather, between ultimate bodily life and ultimate non-bodily life.

Early Christians insisted that Jesus of Nazareth had, against all expectations, been raised already from the dead into this new bodily existence. This early Christian belief in resurrection modified existing Jewish belief in several respects. First, unlike the range of opinion in both Judaism and paganism, early Christianity knows virtually no spectrum of belief about the future: belief in resurrection is almost universal. Second, resurrection became a central doctrine, no longer peripheral as with the rabbis. Third, the meaning of 'resurrection' has been firmed up: a physicality now transformed, beyond the reach of corruption and death (cf. Rom. 6:9), something not always clear in, e.g., the Maccabean literature. In this way, Jesus' own resurrection, and that promised to his people, is distinguished from the 'raisings' of Jairus' daughter, the widow's son, and Lazarus (Mark 5:21–43; Luke 7:11–17; John 11:1–44), which, like their OT prototypes, were a return to normal, corruptible bodily life. Correspondingly, the 'spiritual body' (1 Cor. 15:42–9) is not a body 'made of spirit' but a (physical) body *animated by* God's HOLY SPIRIT as opposed to the present 'soul' (cf. Rom. 8:9–11). Fourth, 'the resurrection' has split into two moments, that of the Messiah Jesus in the past and that, still awaited, of his people (and, it seems, everyone else, including the wicked, according to John 5:28–9; Acts 24:15; Rev. 20:12–14; but cf. Rom. 8) in the future. Fifth, the word 'resurrection', while continuing to denote new, concrete, embodied life, has acquired fresh metaphorical resonances: whereas in Judaism it could function as a metaphor for 'return from exile' (Ezek. 37), for Paul and others it indicates the new life experienced by Christians in baptism and holiness (Rom. 6; Col. 3:1–4; 1 Pet. 1:3–4). Sixth, because in the Messiah the 'end' of history has been brought forward into the middle of ongoing space–time continuity, those who belong to him are called to engage in the work of transformation in the present. Seventh, no Jew supposed the Messiah would be raised from the dead, because no Jew imagined the Messiah dying as part of his VOCATION; but for Christians this was central. Eighth, the early Christians believed that evil had been judged and condemned in Jesus' crucifixion, so that his resurrection inaugurated the promised new world from which evil had been banished.

It is hard to see how these remarkable features of early Christianity, common right across the first two centuries, are explicable without some event very like that described in the closing chapters of the four canonical Gospels and the opening of Acts. It does not seem very plausible to dismiss these unique accounts as the ahistorical projection of 'early Christian faith', and one can argue that it is impossible to explain the dramatic rise of the Christian movement, following Jesus' shameful death, unless the claim to his having risen is well-founded.

Resurrection was central for patristic and medieval theologians like T. AQUINAS. However, later medieval concentration on PURGATORY, HEAVEN, and HELL as the immediate post-mortem destinations of individual souls (as portrayed, e.g., in Dante Alighieri's (*ca* 1265–1321) *Divine Comedy*) tended to displace attention from the hope of a bodily resurrection. Likewise, the ENLIGHTENMENT's renewed Platonism encouraged many Christians to substitute a disembodied heaven for ultimate resurrection. This cuts the nerve of the Christian vocation to implement God's victory in Jesus the Messiah, and to anticipate his promised renewal of all things, by working for renewal in the present world. The Orthodox Churches have retained the NT emphasis on resurrection as the transformation, rather than the abandonment, of the present world, though sometimes marginalizing the CROSS as God's necessary judgement on evil prior to that renewal. Recapturing the biblical vision of resurrection thus offers new possibilities both for mission and for ECUMENISM.

NICHOLAS THOMAS WRIGHT

REVELATION Divine revelation is constituted by disclosure of the nature and purposes of God. What is hidden is made known; what is veiled is uncovered. Revelation differs from INSPIRATION, in that the former refers to any act of divine self-disclosure in time and space, while the latter has to do more specifically with the claim that particular communicative events (e.g., the production of the biblical texts) are a matter of divine rather than human will. The frequent confusion of the two categories tends to be driven by epistemic motivations: the inspiration of Scripture has been a bedrock for theories of scriptural INERRANCY, so that attempts to conflate revelation with inspiration are closely connected with a desire to view the content of revelation in terms of fixed propositional content.

The most basic distinction within the DOCTRINE of revelation is between general and special revelation. In the former God is revealed in the natural world and in conscience; in the latter God is revealed in special actions in history (e.g., in the exodus of ISRAEL from Egypt, or in God's word to prophets). Special revelation, however, requires further extension in that there is 'extra-special' revelation in the INCARNATION of Jesus Christ, as well as person-relative revelation to individuals, say, with respect to their VOCATIONS.

The idea of general revelation differs radically from traditional forms of NATURAL THEOLOGY. The latter is a matter of various human inferences from the nature of the world or the concept of God *to* the existence of God; the former involves general and special acts undertaken *by* God. At the same time, divine revelation can constitute evidence of the existence of God, since a recipient of divine revelation *ipso facto* receives evidence that God exists, along with whatever may specifically be revealed about the nature and purposes of God. The evidence is tacit but no less genuine than other kinds of evidence. The distinction between divine revelation and religious experience is less secure. Some forms of divine revelation can take the form of religious experience. The existence and love of God can become manifest to a person directly or through the natural world; but revelation goes beyond this to include basic acts of God like speaking and incarnation.

Revelation is an epistemic concept and, as such, is readily associated with that family of general ideas constituted by intuition, reason, experience, and testimony. Thus it functions to provide warrant and justification for a host of claims about God. Following K. BARTH, many have thought that divine revelation rules out natural theology, arguing that natural theology leads to IDOLATRY in that it posits a god distinct from the God made known in Christ, that it negates divine GRACE by relying on human effort to reach the divine, and that it replaces JUSTIFICATION by FAITH with justification by our intellectual efforts and reasoning. If God is known solely, exclusively, and fully in Jesus

Christ, natural theology is theologically incoherent and spiritually otiose. Yet a contrasting tradition rejects both the initial premise of this line of argument and the conclusions drawn. In the cumulative case tradition of natural theology, revelation is seen as supplemented and complemented by the appeal to reason and experience, the charge of idolatry is resisted by attending to the contextual complexity involved in securing divine identity, and the commitment to grace and justification by faith is regarded as fully compatible with both old and revised forms of natural theology.

Special revelation in the Christian tradition does, however, have a privileged epistemic position. On the one hand, accompanied by the work of the Holy Spirit in the hearts of believers, it counteracts the noetic effects of sin, on account of which human agents readily and universally resist divine revelation, eschew divine assistance in the name of self-sufficiency, and readily misread the good purposes of God in creation and redemption. On the negative side, then, divine revelation corrects the working of human reasoning and the voice of conscience. More positively, divine revelation not only provides information above and beyond experience and inference (e.g., life after death), but also enriches formally and materially what is available in experience and reason. Thus special revelation functions as a threshold concept. Once one crosses over into the world of divine revelation, the whole of one's perspective is cast in a new light. This explains why the reception of divine revelation often involves radical conversion. It also explains why divine revelation evokes intense commitment and tenacity. Once accepted, divine revelation is construed as a form of knowledge that establishes a personal relationship; abandoning it without its initial credentials being undermined will therefore be seen as a form of apostasy and a betrayal of trust. Secular objections to this set of attitudes (on the grounds that the category of revelation simply masks an appeal to tradition, prejudice, and emotion) tend to miss the logic involved. Failing to enter into the new world of divine revelation, they cannot in the nature of the case see what has been revealed and the cognitive difference this makes to the believer.

Divine revelation relates in complex ways to the Church, as well as to Scripture and tradition. Western Christianity has explored the issues with extraordinary fecundity. There is general agreement that divine revelation is enshrined in Scripture; indeed, early reflection often reduced special revelation to divine speaking and, in turn, identified the latter with the canon of Scripture. Canon in this trajectory was seen as a norm or criterion of theological truth. Protestantism and Catholicism have long disputed the relation between Scripture and tradition, with each side evoking pertinent revisions across their divisions. Traditional Catholic theology saw tradition as imparting divine revelation on a par with Scripture; nowadays tradition is given a hermeneutical status as providing essential interpretation of special revelation expressed in a unique way in Scripture. Within this schema papal infallibility functions within the magisterium of the Church to settle disputed interpretations of Scripture related to crucial matters of faith and morals. Past polemics and genuine differences between Protestantism and Catholicism inhibit the recognition that both share an epistemic conception of Scripture that has grown organically but contestedly from their vision of special revelation. The deep irony is that the pope in his claim to infallibility is the ultimate form of Protestantism, as the papal office has developed over time into an epistemic mechanism for shoring up a complex and evolving doctrine of *sola Scriptura*.

An alternative vision inspired but not officially sanctioned by Orthodox theology sees revelation as enshrined more comprehensively in the canonical heritage of the Church as developed in a complex network of materials, persons, and practices. These operate as subtle, inter-related means of grace intended to foster holiness and the mind of Christ in both the Church and the individual believer. Scripture and tradition when retrieved to fit into the canonical heritage of the Church operate fundamentally soteriologically rather than epistemologically. They are not epistemic categories and become dysfunctional when treated in this manner. Epistemological issues do not disappear on this analysis; they require apt and thorough investigation in their own right.

Revelation, like inspiration, is a polymorphous activity. God is revealed in, with, and through the actions of God, so that revelation supervenes on other acts God performs. Just as one farms by harvesting crops, breeding cattle, checking the weather forecasts, and the like, so God reveals himself by creating and sustaining the world, speaking through conscience, making promises through chosen agents, becoming incarnate in Christ, and the like. Within this schema, special attention has long been given to revelation through the Word of God (see *Logos*). In the human situation, we would be impoverished if we did not have access to others' speech; even more so in the case of God, for God outside the incarnation does not have a body. Moreover, access to the speech of agents is often pivotal in discerning the purposes of their actions and may even have a role in the initial identification of particular events *as* actions. Thus, in so far as Jesus Christ is seen as the Word of God par excellence, all theology must pass through the test of compatibility with what he has revealed of God.

Because of such complexity, efforts to settle disputes about the site of special revelation cannot be resolved by a simple appeal to miracles. There can be special revelation without miracles; and miracles in themselves do not prove the presence of special revelation.

Arguments for miracles, moreover, often presuppose the presence of special revelation. Thus, because making sense of the Resurrection of Jesus requires reference to the special revelation given in his life and ministry, it is not the case that the resurrection by itself secures the reality of divine revelation. However, miracles can have weight in resolving disputes about the location of special revelation in that they highlight a teleological component in the interpretation of events. In this way, there is a measure of mutual coherence and reinforcement in play between special revelation and miracle.

The recognition of both revelation and miracle depends on a basic capacity to perceive divine agency at work in creation, in historical events, in the person of Jesus, and in our own lives. Some medieval theologians referred to this as *oculus contemplationis* ('contemplative eye'); others spoke of a *sensus divinitatis* ('sense of divinity'). The core idea is that God equips human agents with cognitive capacities akin to intuition and memory that operate under the appropriate circumstances and according to a divine design plan to give access to reality. This claim differs from appeal to the inner witness of the Holy Spirit as much as perception and discernment differ from testimony. These capacities are not infallible; nor are they static in nature, for they can be damaged, repaired, and enhanced in various ways through grace and the effects of divine revelation.

However much revelation is constituted by the manifestation of reality with regard to the divine, theologians have been quick to caution against a false confidence. The positive effects of divine revelation are identified under the heading of cataphatic theology, that is, what can be said positively and with assurance about God. However, this is balanced by apophatic theology, that is, by the insistence that all claims about God fall short of depicting the full reality of God. It is important to distinguish this caution from scepticism and doubt. The latter are grounded in worries about reaching warranted conclusions about God. By contrast, apophatic theology is driven by considerations within the world of divine revelation. On the one hand, our language about God draws on tools invented to deal with creaturely reality; on the other hand, the fullness of divine reality vastly overspills the content of divine revelation. Most importantly, apophatic theology is driven by an enduring and repeated sense that what is said cannot begin to do justice to what has been seen and heard in special revelation and experience of God. In this way, apophaticism is not just an abstract philosophical proposal, but a vision that is itself dependent on access to divine realities.

A further reason that supports the apophatic dimension of the reception of divine revelation is its necessary incompleteness. The full and final revelation of God lies in the future. 'But as it is written, eye hath not seen, nor ear heard, neither have entered into the heart of man, the things which God hath prepared for them that love him' (1 Cor. 2:9, King James Version). Hence we need to round off our initial demarcations within divine revelation by adding a distinction between revelation in this life and in the life to come. Necessarily the theologian focuses on the former; in the nature of the case we do not yet know what that full and final revelation of God will disclose.

W. J. Abraham, *Crossing the Threshold of Divine Revelation* (Eerdmans, 2007).

A. Dulles, *Models of Divine Revelation* (Doubleday, 1983).

R. King, *Obstacles to Divine Revelation: God and the Reorientation of Human Reason* (Continuum, 2008).

G. Mavrodes, *Revelation in Religious Belief* (Temple University Press, 1988).

S. Menssen and T. Sullivan, *The Agnostic Inquirer: Revelation from a Philosophical Standpoint* (Eerdmans, 2007).

B. Mitchell, *The Justification of Religious Belief* (Seabury Press, 1974).

William J. Abraham

Revivalism Revivalism refers to the desire for spiritual renewal in the Church, often including conversion, repentance, and commitment to holiness. The term 'revival' does not appear in the King James Version of the Bible, but prayers that God would 'revive' his people, or his work, appear in two critical passages: Psalms 85:6 and Habakuk 3:2. These verses have helped shape the expectation of periodic revival in the Church. Ordinarily, the concept of revival assumes a Church that was once thriving but has fallen into spiritual decline. A closely related and often interchangeable term for revival is 'awakening'. Revivalism has traditionally been a priority of conservative Protestants because of their focus on individual conversion, but themes of revivalism have appeared in many Christian denominations.

The term 'revival' was commonly used in early modern English parlance, but did not necessarily connote spiritual renewal. Nevertheless, by the mid-seventeenth century writers like J. Owen (1616–83) had begun to speak of 'a revival of the power [of religion] in the soules of men' in contrast to cold, formal practice (*Enquiry* 71). Puritan writers placed increasing emphasis on revival as a special event initiated by an outpouring of the Holy Spirit. Calls for moral reformation, especially in colonial New England, were slowly supplanted by calls for revival. In a 1674 election sermon in Massachusetts, S. Torrey (1632–1707) asserted that to restore a declining people, God would 'pour out [an] abundance of converting grace, and so revive and renew the work of Conversion' (*Exhort*. 10).

By the 1720s and 1730s, many pastors in colonial New England had become convinced that their Churches had fallen so far from their original zeal that only a new outpouring of the Holy Spirit could awaken them. Sermons like J. Webb's (1687–1750) *The Duty of a Degenerate People to Pray for the Reviving of God's Work* (1734) became standard fare.

The sense of spiritual crisis and prayers for revival set the stage for the coming of the First Great Awakening in America and the evangelical revival in Britain and continental Europe, led by new evangelical luminaries such as G. Whitefield (1714–70) and J. WESLEY. One of the distinguishing features of the new evangelical piety was an enhanced expectation of seasons of renewal. Although evangelicals often had to toil for years with no signs of revival, the quest for revivals became one of their chief passions.

Because many of the early evangelicals were Calvinists (see REFORMED THEOLOGY), they insisted that only God could create revivals. The most influential exponent of the Calvinist view of revival was J. EDWARDS of Northampton, Massachusetts. Edwards' widely read *Faithful Narrative of the Surprising Work of God* (1737) described the 1735 Northampton revival as 'surprising' because it was an unplanned work of God. God had done such an amazing work in the revival 'to show it to be his own peculiar and immediate work, and to secure the glory of it wholly to his almighty power and sovereign grace', Edwards wrote (*Faith.* 87).

As the evangelical movement grew in the early nineteenth century, an Arminian perspective on revival became more common (see ARMINIANISM). In this view, God was still responsible for revivals, but he had entrusted the means for them to the Church. Thus, many evangelical leaders like C. Finney (1792–1875) believed that Churches could choose to hold revivals. In his *Lectures on Revivals of Religion* (1835), Finney insisted that these occurrences were not miracles. Revivals, to Finney, were the 'purely philosophical result of the right use of the constituted means' (*Lect.* 12).

Finney was eager to use any method, such as the 'anxious seat' (a designated bench at the front of a church where sinners seeking repentance could pray), to promote conversions. Over the course of the nineteenth century, revivals tended to become professionally planned occasions more than popular outbursts of renewal.

Christians of various denominations often look to past revivals as shapers of their religious heritage. Many Pentecostals, for example, remember the Azusa Street revival of 1906 in Los Angeles as the first major outbreak of renewed charismatic gifts (see PENTECOSTAL THEOLOGY). Many Christians today continue to seek and promote revivals across the globe.

See also CHARISMATIC MOVEMENT.

T. S. Kidd, *The Great Awakening: The Roots of Evangelical Christianity in Colonial America* (Yale University Press, 2007).

W. R. Ward, *The Protestant Evangelical Awakening* (Cambridge University Press, 1992).

THOMAS S. KIDD

ROMAN CATHOLICISM: see CATHOLIC THEOLOGY.

RULE OF FAITH The phrase 'rule of faith' (or 'rule of truth') was used by theologians beginning in the late second century to refer to a summary of Christian teaching inherited from the APOSTLES (cf. 2 Tim. 1:13). IRENAEUS tends to identify 'the rule of our faith' with a basic Trinitarian confession (*Dem.* 6; cf. *AH* 1.22.1). For TERTULLIAN the 'rule of faith' (*regula fidei*) is defined by belief in God the Creator and in Jesus Christ as God's incarnate Son and giver of the HOLY SPIRIT (*Prae.* 13). ORIGEN equates what he calls the 'ecclesiastical rule' with 'the expression of sound doctrine' (*HJer.* 5.14) and also conceives it in broadly Trinitarian terms (e.g., *Prin.* 1.4).

Though this rule of faith clearly approximated the later CREEDS with respect to content and catechetical function, it was not identified with a fixed formula. Though Tertullian insisted that the rule of faith is 'one everywhere' (*Virg.* 1), he himself offers several versions, changing not only phrasing but also the way in which major topics (e.g., CHRISTOLOGY) are developed. Notwithstanding such variation, the rule of faith was understood as witness to a stable, publicly available core of Christian teaching that both served as a précis of SCRIPTURE and constrained theological speculation by providing a hermeneutical framework for Scripture's interpretation (see, e.g., Irenaeus, *AH* 1.9.4; Tertullian, *Prae.* 12.5). It thus functioned as a working criterion of ORTHODOXY in the period before the formal definition of doctrines and creeds.

R. Hanson, *Tradition in the Early Church* (Westminster Press, 1962).

IAN A. MCFARLAND

RUSSIAN THEOLOGY The precise origins of Russian theology are a matter of debate. On the one hand, already during the ninth and tenth centuries theological ideas had entered into Kievan Rus, as reflected in theological fragments recorded in the most ancient part of the Russian collected chronicles, the *Tales of Bygone Years.* Fundamental Christian concepts (e.g., the Trinitarianism of the CAPPADOCIAN FATHERS, and the DOCTRINE of Christ's two natures defined at the Council of CHALCEDON) are reflected there, though elements of apocryphal stories and the influence of Arianism are also encountered (see ARIAN CONTROVERSY). On the other hand, the texts which are actually Russian in origin date only to the eleventh century and the period of Grand Duke Yaroslav the Wise (*ca* 975–1054).

Among the dominant theological genres of this time are homilies, epistles, and exhortations. For example, 'The Word on Law and Grace' of Metropolitan Illarion (d. *ca* 1055) contained commonly accepted instruction about the OT as the prefiguration of the GOSPEL. The first Russian ascetic literature also started to appear at that time (see ASCETICISM). Thus, one of the founders of the Kievo-Pechersk monastery, F. Pecherski (d. 1074), wrote 'The Word on Patience and Love', which introduces the theme of spiritual work into Russian theology, including the significance of good works and personal human effort towards salvation. Though Illarion also composed a short dogmatic work (*The Confession of Faith*), for the most part Russian theology during this period was not self-reliant and made heavy use of Greek and South-Slavic (especially patristic) sources. All these trends are developed most fully during the twelfth century in the works of Metropolitan K. Smolyatich (d. *ca* 1165) and K. Turovsky (*ca* 1130–82). While Smolyatich interpreted the biblical narratives and symbols allegorically, and used a predominantly rational approach for seeking the Christian truth (allowing, for example, the use of Plato (*ca* 430–*ca* 345 BC) and Aristotle (384–22 BC)), Turovsky continued the ascetical tradition by emphasizing the practical appropriation of Christian virtues and human spiritual transformation. In subsequent history the latter approach assumed prominence, especially under the combined influence of Byzantine HESYCHASM and the Dionysian corpus (see DIONYSIUS THE AREOPAGITE). Yet in the fourteenth and fifteenth centuries Russian adaptation of hesychasm had a predominantly mystical–contemplative character, reflected in the iconographic works of Theophan the Greek (1330–1408) and A. Rublev (*ca* 1365–1427/30).

The theological expression of this influence occurred in the works of N. Sorsky (*ca* 1433–1508) towards the end of the fifteenth century. He used the works of J. Climacus (*ca* 525–606), Isaac the Syrian (died *ca* 700), and other Orthodox ascetics to elaborate a theology of the origin and consequences of passions, and to outline the ways of resisting them in a manner similar to the prayer practices of the hesychasts. A different theological approach was that of I. Volotsky (1440–1515), who put the main emphasis not on inner ascetic practice that detaches human beings from the sinful world, but on the transformation of the earthly life by the elimination of all heretical teachings. In polemical exchanges with 'Judaizers' in Novgorod, Volotsky systematized and elaborated fundamental theological notions (e.g., the unity and TRINITY of God, the God-humanity of Christ, the necessity of INCARNATION) with meticulous references to biblical texts and commentaries.

On the whole, the sixteenth century saw the codification of the canon of Russian literature relating to spiritual formation. At the same time, the compatibility of Russian theological standards with those of ORTHODOX THEOLOGY in general was questioned. A vivid example is the work of Maximos the Greek (*ca* 1470–1556), who had studied in Italy and who travelled to Russia to correct the texts used in the liturgy (the so-called 'correction of books'). This question of textual modification became more urgent in the seventeenth century, giving rise both to Church reform and to an opposition movement known as the Old Believers. The essence of the Old Believers' theological position consisted in the necessity to preserve all preceding traditions (whether textual, iconographic, or liturgical) as materially incarnating the spiritual meaning of Christianity. These claims were, in turn, connected with assumptions about the national–religious uniqueness of Russia as the only country which has preserved Christian faith and practice unadulterated into the eschatological epoch.

Though the Old Believers developed some distinctive, strongly apocalyptic theological views, the influence of their theology was not extensive. The focus of theological development in Russia during the seventeenth and eighteenth centuries was the formation of a distinctly Russian theological system in the process of both appropriating and reacting against western (Catholic and Protestant) theology. This process was influenced by the Greek theologians as well as by the Ukrainian hierarchs whose sway increased during the late seventeenth and early eighteenth centuries. Despite several polemical confrontations, elements of Scholastic Catholic theology are noticeable in the thinking and structure of the writings of Kievan theologians (see SCHOLASTICISM): it was not accidental that both the so-called Latinizing theologians like S. Medvedev (1641–91) and their opponents like E. Slavinetsky (d. *ca* 1675) were graduates of the Kiev schools.

A similar heterogeneity of the cultural environment, which combined western influence in education, science, and literature with the traditional eastern piety, was reflected in the work of the most controversial and most influential hierarch of the epoch, F. Prokopovich (1677–1736). From 1711 to 1716 he compiled an outline of the academic course in theological science, the structure of which represented a considerable innovation: the teaching of SCRIPTURE is presented in the introduction, but the body of the course itself was divided by Prokopovich into two parts: dogmatic and moral. The dogmatic part included two sections: on God and God's essence, and God in relation to creation, a pattern that continued to characterize Russian dogmatics into the nineteenth century. More substantively, Prokopovich clearly formulated the so-called 'juridical' understanding of the ATONEMENT, according to which the sacrifice of Jesus Christ on the cross was necessary for the satisfaction of the divine righteousness. The foundation of this doctrine, which remained typical for Russian theology until the end of the nineteenth century, was an understanding of the fall as entailing a deformation of mind and will that makes impossible justification by human power alone. Instead, justification was achieved only by faith – a contention that provoked a forceful theological debate between Prokopovich and F. Lopatinsky (d. 1741). Prokopovich insisted on justification by faith, yet distinguished justification from salvation, for the attainment of which works were needed. By contrast, Lopatinsky held that neither salvation nor justification was possible without works; in addition, he argued that sins are not only forgiven but taken away through justification.

The other essential theological moment in the second part of the eighteenth century was the strengthening of the ascetic practices associated with the Russian tradition of spiritual eldership (*starchestvo*). This emphasis on personal spiritual experience and the rebirth of the Orthodox spiritual practice were strongly shaped by T. Zadonsky (1724–83) and P. Velichkovsky (1722–94), author of the enormously influential *The Pilgrim's Tale*. By developing a biblically oriented moral theology, Zadonsky emphasized the necessity of fierce inner struggle for salvation as an analogy of Christ's passion in the circumstances of the approaching Kingdom of God, thus stressing the eschatological aspect of Christian ethics.

The activity of Metropolitan Platon (1737–1812) represents the peculiar summary of both academic and moral theology in the eighteenth century. Though organizing the theological curriculum in terms of the theological virtues, Platon followed Prokopovich's teaching on atonement and the relation between justification and salvation, augmenting it with a doctrine of a natural knowledge of God that precedes revelation. In the area of moral theology, he renewed the theme of the diminution of the power of the passions and freedom from them as the goal of spiritually heroic action (*podvig*), to which he attributed not so much a mystical as a rational character.

To a certain extent, Platon and his school influenced Metropolitan Filaret (1782–1867), a renowned theologian, preacher, and biblical scholar, who produced a number of methodological instructions for the translation of the Bible into contemporary Russian. The special attention given to Scripture and its interpretation prompted numerous quarrels and accusations about Protestant ideas which were seen as having infiltrated Russian theology. During the decades from 1830 to 1850, this resulted in an increasing emphasis on the need to augment Scripture with tradition (especially the writings of the Church fathers) as a second, necessary, source of theology.

The second half of the nineteenth century was characterized by the reform of Russian theology as a whole, the objective of which was the transition from rationalistic systematization to historical analysis. Ascetic theology also continued to be an important force, represented by figures like I. Brianchaninov (1807–67), Theophan the Recluse (1815–94), and I. Kronshtadsky (1829–1909). Speaking against the secularization of Church life, they denounced the possibility of achieving spiritual perfection within a framework of non-confessional morality. At the same time, they deplored the lack of appreciation for the role of monasticism as the way of true Christian perfection. This group of theologians underlined the necessity of a balanced approach to the purification of the heart, through recovery of medieval Russian monastic practice which itself followed the patristic stress upon prayer and the spiritual life. Yet another characteristic feature of the nineteenth century is the so-called 'worldly' tradition of Russian theology, related to philosophy and literature, which first emerged among the Slavophiles, led by A. Khomyakov (1804–60). Using various concepts from German Idealism, they viewed Orthodoxy as transcending the one-sidedness of Catholic and Protestant thinking. Analyzing the dialectical interaction of society and personality, Khomyakov made ecclesiology based on the concept of catholicity (*sobornost*) the central theme of his theology (see Sobornicity).

To the end of the nineteenth century belongs the creative activity of V. Solovyov (1853–1900), among whose theologically important works are the *Lectures on God-Humanity* and *The Justification of the Good.* All attempt to reveal the moral foundations of Christian experience, and in particular the dialogue 'Three Conversations' with 'The Short Tale of the Anti-Christ' (1900) contain prophetic (and, in an Orthodox context, very untraditional) reflections about the eschatological unity of the Church before the end of history.

At the beginning of the twentieth century, the legacy of Russian 'worldly' theology helped initiate a 'Russian religious renaissance', by focusing attention on the problems of the human person, culture, and society. This is found in the sophiology of P. Florensky (1882–1937), in N. Berdyaev's (1874–1948) studies in theological anthropology, and in the Christian personalism of N. Lossky (1870–1965). Within academic theology the debate on the ontological nature and moral implications of atonement emerged as central: a number of theologians attempted to highlight the narrowness of the 'juridical' conception of atonement and the overall legalistic view of the relationship between the human person and God, and also to develop a new teaching on Christian personality. A further dogmatic discussion in this period was the debate over onomatodoxy (*imyaslavie*), or the doctrine that the name and essence of God are identical: though officially condemned, it continues to be discussed in Orthodox circles.

The tendencies of the end of the nineteenth century and the beginning of the twentieth continued in the theology of Russian emigration, wherein several major lineages are present: the conservative theology of the Russian Church abroad; the eschatologically intensive motifs of ascetic theology; the sophiology of the Paris school (associated especially with S. Bulgakov); and the neo-patristic renaissance, which posited the goal of returning to the Byzantine fathers as the pinnacle of Orthodox thought. This is represented by figures such as V. Lossky (1903–58) and G. Florovsky (1893–1979).

G. Florovsky, *The Collected Works of Georges Florovsky, vols. V–VI: Ways of Russian Theology* (Vaduz and Belmont, 1987).

P. Gnedich, *Dogmat iskupleniya v russkoi bogoslovskoi nauke* (Sretenskii monastyr, Moskovskaia dukhovnaia akademiia, 2007).

M. N. Gromov, *Ideinye techenia drevnerusskoi mysli* (Izd-vo Russkogo Khristianskogo gumanitarnogo in-ta, 2001).

J. D. Kornblatt and R. F. Gustafson, eds., *Russian Religious Thought* (University of Wisconsin Press, 1996).

P. Valliere, *Modern Russian Theology: Bukharev, Soloviev, Bulgakov: Orthodox Theology in a New Key* (Eerdmans, 2000).

O. V. NESMIYANOVA

Sabbatarianism 'Sabbatarianism' is a term used to refer to any conflation of Christian and Jewish practice with respect to the observance of a weekly day of rest. Historically, this takes two main forms: first, the belief that Christians should honour the Jewish sabbath (viz., Saturday) rather than Sunday as their weekly day of rest; second, a scrupulous observance of Sunday as a day of rest and worship to the exclusion of all other activity.

S

The former type of sabbatarianism was defended by some Transylvanian Socinians in the sixteenth century (see Socinianism) and some English and American Baptists from the seventeenth century; it is today most widely practised by the Seventh-Day Adventist Church (see Adventism). Its proponents look both to the Ten Commandments, which explicitly name Saturday as the day of rest (Exod. 20:8–11; Deut. 5:12–15), and to Jesus' own practice of sabbath observance (e.g., Luke 4:16). Their opponents point out that Christian observance of Sunday, as the day of Jesus' resurrection, has been the normative practice of Christians from the earliest times, with clear roots in the NT (e.g., the reference to 'the Lord's day' in Rev. 1:10; Paul's designation of 'the first day of the week' for making offerings in 1 Cor. 16:2).

Scrupulous observance of the Sunday sabbath is historically associated with English-speaking Reformed Christianity, with its stress on the formal replacement of Saturday by Sunday as the divinely instituted sabbath – with all of its attendant obligations (see, e.g., WC 20.7). Against both types of sabbatarianism, M. Luther argued that, because Christ put an end to the law, it is not incumbent upon Christians to observe any day out of necessity, but only as a practical matter of providing a mutually agreed occasion for bodily rest and public worship (*LC*, Third Commandment; cf. AC 28).

Ian A. McFarland

Sabellianism: see Modalism.

SACRAMENTOLOGY In his introduction to a collection of essays published in 2001, the Louvain theologian L. Boeve (b. 1966) noted that in recent years theologizing about the sacraments (the meaning of 'sacramentology') had become an important scholarly discussion. He observed that in Catholic circles, in the 1960s, there had been a special theological interest in eschatology and ecclesiology, which in the 1970s had shifted to Christology, and in the 1980s and 1990s, to the doctrine of God and the Trinity. In the years around the millennium the new interest was doing theology from a sacramentological or liturgical angle, and this had shifted to the centre of theology.

If there has been a shift of theological interest, there has also been a shift in terminology. Older textbooks discussed 'sacraments' and 'sacramental theology', and the latter was still very much in circulation into the 1990s. In postmodern discussions, the key word has become 'sacramentality', and with a wider connotation than the older traditional sacramental theology. According to R. Williams (b. 1950), 'Sacramentality is not a general principle that the world is full of "sacredness": it is the very specific conviction that the world is full of the life of a God whose nature is known in Christ and the Spirit' ('Foreword', xiii). In reference to Williams' words, A. Loades (b. 1938) has suggested that the term might be understood as the divine initiative to mediate divine redemptive presence to us through the natural world, which may include not just familiar Church rituals, but poetry, dance, gardening, engineering, design, buildings, and public places. In some ways this broader approach of postmodern theology towards sacramentology is a return to a pre-modern early classical or even Semitic understanding of divine disclosure in the world.

The Greek term *mysterion* carries both a wider sense of mystery as something hidden and awesome and a narrower sense of a ritual action or symbol. Its Latin rendering as *sacramentum*, first attested by Tertullian, was perhaps unfortunate, since the Latin term had the meaning of a military oath, and carried a much narrower connotation than *mysterion*. Hilary of Poitiers (*ca* 300–68) taught that people and events in the OT that prefigured the Christian mysteries (i.e., events of salvation) could be considered sacraments; and for Augustine *sacramentum* was a sign of a sacred thing. However, in his *Sentences* P. Lombard (*ca* 1100–60) taught that something is properly called a sacrament because it is a sign of God's grace, and is such an image of invisible grace that it both bears its likeness and exists as its cause. It was Lombard who seems to have definitively formulated for the West the belief that sacraments were seven (a divine number): baptism, Eucharist, penance, confirmation, orders, marriage, and extreme unction (see Anointing). Drawing on Aristotelian concepts, William of Auxerre (d. 1231) defined sacraments as having *materia* (matter) and *forma* (form, formula); in the case of the Eucharist, the matter consisted of bread and wine, and the form was the words of institution in the canon of the mass. As a result of this definition of sacraments, the rites became divorced from their ritual and liturgical setting and took on an independent, quasi-metaphysical existence. Furthermore, although all the sacraments conveyed the grace of divine disclosure and presence, the TRANSUBSTANTIATION of the elements in the Eucharist was regarded as the sacramental act in which this occurred with the greatest intensity.

The Council of TRENT reiterated and made official these doctrinal beliefs. The sixteenth-century Reformers preferred a Christological basis for sacraments to an Aristotelian one, but in so doing restricted the term 'sacrament' to ordinances instituted by Christ: baptism and Eucharist only. For M. LUTHER, sacraments were authenticated by God's promise, and he insisted on a substantial presence in the elements of the mass, though rejected transubstantiation as illogical ARISTOTELIANISM. The Reformed theologians differed among themselves as to whether or not sacraments conveyed grace, and whether or not they exhibited what they symbolized. J. CALVIN, for example, regarded sacraments as instruments that exhibited and conveyed grace, but H. BULLINGER regarded them as 'implements' only, and as not conveying grace. Not wishing to privilege the Eucharist over baptism in mediating God's grace, the Reformed termed Christ's presence in the elements as 'sacramental' or 'spiritual' – which they regarded as no less 'real' than substantial presence. In the case of H. ZWINGLI and the leaders of the Radical REFORMATION, however, the sacraments were pictorial reminders or mental triggers of grace already given, with Zwingli seizing upon the older Latin meaning of *sacramentum* as an oath or badge. The logic of Zwingli's approach is found in some liberal Protestant theologians of the early twentieth century, who held that sacraments were the invention of the early Church, borrowed from mystery religions, and had never been instituted by Christ. For such theologians, sacraments were an embarrassment, and it was a waste of time to devote energy to what were at best 'holy customs' of the Church.

An older western tradition, represented by Hugh of St Victor (1096–1141), allowed for a much wider range of symbols and rituals which could be deemed sacraments, such as making the sign of the CROSS, and the ashes of Ash Wednesday. In the Syrian tradition the term usually translated as 'sacrament' (*raza*/*rozo*, meaning 'secret') was used even more widely. In the writings of Ephrem the Syrian (*ca* 305–73), for example, God is hidden, but allows himself to be revealed in creation. Divine disclosure comes through nature, symbols, and metaphors, but above all in the INCARNATION: 'instead of the borrowed similitudes with which God's Majesty had previously clothed itself, [God] clothed himself with real limbs, as the First-born and was mingled with humanity' (*Her.* 32:9). For Ephrem, Christ is the ultimate *raza* or disclosure of God, but God can potentially disclose himself in anything and anywhere – a feature of his thought that resonates powerfully with a postmodern concern with sacramentality.

Recent rethinking of sacraments can be seen to originate in the theologies of K. BARTH and K. RAHNER. Barth, for example, in reference to Christ and his death, wrote, 'This is the one *mysterium*, the one sacrament, and the one existential fact before and beside and after which there is no room for any other of the same rank' (*CD* IV/1, 296). Both argued that Christ is the primordial sacrament, and Rahner regarded the Church, as the BODY of Christ, as a 'foundational sacrament'. Celebrated through the Church, the traditional rites identified by Catholics as sacraments were ecclesial disclosers of the divine presence and grace. In other words, they are sacraments by derivation, being the rites of the Church, which itself derives its sacramental nature from the one primordial sacrament, Jesus Christ. In some ways this had been anticipated in a very different way by LUTHER (who could also speak of Christ as the one true sacrament) and the Anabaptist D. Philips (1504–68).

Postmodern theologians have attempted to break company with what they term 'ontotheology', rejecting both Aristotelian and Neoplatonist METAPHYSICS which they regard as underlying all earlier sacramentology. The French theologian L.-M. Chauvet (b. 1941) has developed a symbolic theology from within sacramental practices. He follows M. Heidegger (1889–1976) in rejecting the notion of causality, and prefers the relation of mutual and reciprocal gift between lovers as a better analogy for grace and sacrament. He appeals to studies of language and ritual as the basis for understanding divine disclosure and presence. The paschal event proclaims God's love to humanity as shown in the self-effacement of the divinity on the cross. Through the Spirit's power, God continues to disclose the divine nature as the other in human bodiliness, where he continues to efface himself. Sacraments disclose the presence of this self-giving and self-effacing triune God in the ecclesial body, which lives for others, as well as in the bodies of the suffering and despised.

In contrast, another French theologian, J.-L. Marion (b. 1946), proposes a sacramental theology that relies on the idea of openness to the iconic, but centres on the Eucharist. Marion views Heidegger as being still trapped in the ideas of 'Being' and ontotheology and argues instead that, though God is nothing of anything that is created, the distance between divine and creaturely is bridged by the divine initiative of self-giving LOVE. God is in this way revealed in gift. Likewise, God is named not from Being, but from the cross, which is also gift. In discerning the divine, the idol must be rejected (see IDOLATRY), and the ICON accepted, and it is through the icon that gift/giving is recognized. Marion embraces transubstantiation, but offers a non-metaphysical interpretation of it: the bread and wine become the transparent iconic gifts through which the divine *agape* shows forth. The bread and wine are the gift of divinity, given in human time.

A further important contribution comes from K. Osborne, who is critical of the older theologies that speak of 'baptism' or 'Eucharist' as though these are metaphysical prototypes which exist somewhere in eternity. Drawing on J. Duns Scotus' term *haecceitas* ('thisness'), Osborne insists that there are only actual baptisms and actual celebrations of the Eucharist, and only a particular marriage or ordination. Any theology therefore has to begin with the actual rites and events as they occur in time. Thus the liturgical rites – words, gestures, ceremonial – as experienced in actual time are crucial for understanding how the divine is mediated in, through, and to the ecclesial body. This very welcome contribution invites serious consideration of the actual liturgical celebrations, and in turn invites those responsible for the rites to be mindful of what they are intended to disclose (see *Lex orandi lex credendi*).

As a result of this broader approach, recent explorations in sacramentality have included subjects such as pilgrimage to the sacred sites in the Holy Land, the sacramentality of the world and creation, and Anglo-Saxon iconography and sculpture, as well as music as sacrament. One of the pioneers of this broader approach is D. Brown (b. 1948), who, in a range of interdisciplinary studies, explores the divine disclosure in such things as the human body (dance), classical music, pop music, Blues, and opera. Brown's plea is that divine disclosure and divine presence cannot and should not be limited to those rites more traditionally termed sacraments, where human beings are engaged in doing something that carries a promise of divine presence. Here perhaps Brown acknowledges the inherent subjectivity in this broader approach, where God may or may not be present to a person in a particular piece of music or a dance. Luther, too, agreed that God might be present anywhere God chooses, but wherever else God might or might not be present, God has promised (literally, giving the divine Word) to be present in baptism and the Eucharist: 'where baptism, the sacrament of the altar and the forgiveness of sins are administered, there hold fast and conclude most certainly that there is the house of God and the gate of heaven' (*LGen.* 28:16). Understanding these rituals in the life of the Church remains at the heart of sacramentology.

L. Boeve and L. Leijssen, *Sacramental Presence in a Postmodern Context* (Peeters, 2001).

D. Brown, *God and Grace of Body: Sacrament in Ordinary* (Oxford University Press, 2007).

L.-M. Chauvet, *Symbol and Sacrament: A Sacramental Reinterpretation of Christian Existence* (Liturgical Press, 1995 [1987]).

J.-L. Marion, *God without Being: Hors-Texte* (University of Chicago Press, 1995 [1991]).

K. B. Osborne, *Christian Sacraments in a Postmodern World: A Theology for the Third Millennium* (Paulist Press, 2000).

G. Rowell and C. Hall, *The Gestures of God: Explorations in Sacramentality* (Continuum, 2004).

Bryan D. Spinks

Sacrifice Christianity has always tended to use the term 'sacrifice' with caution, largely owing to its association with non-Christian religious practice. For example, sacrifice pervaded ancient pagan religion, where it usually ritualized the relationship between people and their gods, especially at focal moments in the year or in the human life-cycle. Animal sacrifice was central to Jewish worship, where it was employed for a wide range of occasions, the most significant of which are perhaps the slaughter of the lamb at Passover (Exod. 12) and the sprinkling of blood on the Day of Atonement (Lev. 16). For all the attention given to sacrificial rites in temple worship, Jewish piety included a strand of doubt about their real meaning, which is articulated in two ways. One is the criticism often levelled at sacrificial practice by the prophets, who repeatedly call the people of Israel to live lives worthy of the worship they are supposed to offer (e.g., Mic. 6:8). Another is the exploration of the relationship between worship and reconciliation in the context of penitence, which is a common theme in the Psalms (e.g., Ps. 51:18–19). By the time of the NT these influences are often understood to have led to a 'spiritualized' understanding of sacrifice: while the term is still applied to the rituals of temple worship, it now also refers to a life of worship and obedience.

The NT is full of the aroma of sacrifice, but it is carefully reinterpreted. Jesus dies at the Passover season, with the Last Supper forming a rite that is clearly influenced by the Passover, yet is distinct from it: the new covenant mentioned at the sharing of the cup (Matt. 26:28) is not the same as the old. However much Jesus' death is seen as a ransom for many (Mark 10:45b), it represents a new understanding of sacrifice, not an adjunct to the old. Paul wrestles with the Jewish background to his theology when in a key passage he articulates the meaning of Christ's death in terms of justification (an image from the law court) and redemption (an image from the slave market), as well as the cultic image of sacrifice (Rom. 3:24–5). The person and work of Christ are most thoroughly worked out in relation to sacrifice in Hebrews, where Christ is seen as the great high priest, who offered himself once and therefore renders superfluous the annual rituals of the Day of Atonement or any other form of repetition (Heb. 9:28). Yet this stands in some contrast to the view that faithful discipleship involves offering 'spiritual sacrifices' (1 Pet. 2:5), as well as Paul's powerful and paradoxical image of Christians offering their lives as a 'living sacrifice' (Rom. 12:1).

From that basis of adaptation and reinterpretation, Christian theologies of sacrifice have hovered, both expanding and contracting down the centuries. Sacrifice has been applied to the Eucharist from the earliest times, reflecting its background (at least in the understanding of Paul and the synoptic Gospels) in Passover rituals. At first, this imagery was expressed in general terms only, but in the medieval West the idea of Eucharistic sacrifice acquired increasing intensity, leading to the reaction against sacrificial language during the REFORMATION in favour of a stress on Christ's death as the only sacrifice that can be countenanced. BAPTISM was often interpreted sacrificially in preaching, as new Christians offered themselves in the newly embraced faith. And at the end of the fourth century, John Chrysostom (347–407) even described preaching as a sacrifice (*HRom.* 29.1). The ecumenical consensus of recent years has used better knowledge of antiquity and the more general approach to the topic of sacrifice characteristic of ORTHODOX THEOLOGY to heal some of the divisions of the sixteenth century by using the NT notion of 'memorial' or *anamnēsis* (1 Cor. 11:24, 25) as a way around any notion of the Eucharist either as a repetition of Calvary, or as an exclusively inward activity of the mind.

Though Christian theology, following the example of the NT writers themselves, uses different images in relation to Christ's death, the sacrificial image keeps recurring. The patristic understanding of Christ as our representative is akin to the Jewish peace-offering (Lev. 3:3). In the medieval West, however, understanding shifts in the direction of Christ as our substitute, nearer the notion of the sin offering (Lev. 4:3). Reformation piety often took this over into an image of Christ appeasing an angry God. In reaction to what was viewed as a mechanistic understanding of sacrifice as appeasement in some post-Reformation Protestant thought, there was a tendency for some nineteenth-century Protestant theology to underplay sacrifice altogether (see KENOTIC THEOLOGY); but the tragic wars of the twentieth century put paid to any popular diminution of sacrifice as an essential part of the theological repertoire.

The idea of sacrifice has the effect of preventing the meaning of Christ's death, and the gathering around the Lord's table, from becoming too easy and routine. At the heart of the GOSPEL, after all, stands the CROSS, and it is probably for this reason that Paul could not get away from sacrifice when he reflected on the meaning of Christ's death. It also explains when the Word is preached, when new Christians are washed in baptism, and when bread and wine are offered to God for blessing in the Eucharist, sacrifice is still an indispensable tool in the ever-expanding Christian vocabulary. Perhaps the most basic sacrificial dimension of the Eucharist in particular can be seen in the elements of bread and wine themselves, the result of wheat that is ground and baked, and grapes that are crushed and fermented. Experience suggests that attempts to nail down a precise meaning of sacrifice in Christian faith and practice strain the concept to its breaking point, but Christian theology seems unable to live without it.

R. J. Daly, *The Origins of the Christian Doctrine of Sacrifice* (Fortress Press, 1978).

K. W. Stevenson, *Eucharist and Offering* (Pueblo, 1986).

S. W. Sykes, ed., *Sacrifice and Redemption: Durham Essays in Theology* (Cambridge University Press, 1991).

F. Young, *Sacrifice and the Death of Christ* (SPCK, 1975).

KENNETH W. STEVENSON

SAINTS Derived from the Latin *sanctus*, the term 'saints' literally means 'holy ones'. Those members of Christ's mystical BODY, the Church, who responded to the impulses of divine GRACE and bore faithful witness to Christ, either by a martyr's death or by a life of heroic virtue, are commonly known as saints. In such NT writings as Acts, the Pauline and Petrine epistles, Hebrews, and Revelation, the term is applied generally to members of the Christian Church, made holy by BAPTISM and striving to live, individually and communally, according to the teachings of Jesus Christ. Later, however, the word became restricted to members of the Church triumphant, namely, those who, by grace, overcame TEMPTATION on earth, and, having embraced the beatitudes (Matt. 5:1–11) in this life, now rejoice to see God face to face in heaven (see BEATIFIC VISION).

Recognized as excellent models of Christian witness, owing either to MARTYRDOM or to a life of personal ASCETICISM, and acknowledged likewise as adopted co-heirs with Jesus Christ of the KINGDOM OF GOD (cf. Rom. 8:17), the saints also came to be invoked as intercessors pleading to Christ for the living and for SOULS still awaiting purification before their admission to the state of eternal beatitude. This union of charity among the Church on earth (the Church militant), the souls in purgatory (the Church suffering), and the saints already in glory (the Church triumphant) is known as the communion of saints. Catholic and Orthodox practice involves both extolling the virtues practised by 'so great a cloud of witnesses' (Heb. 12:1) and invoking them directly in order to obtain the benefit of their intercession.

Martyrs furnished examples of constancy in professing the Christian FAITH even to the point of bloodshed. The NT account of the martyrdom of Stephen (Acts 7:54–60) highlights crucial similarities with the death of Jesus: heroic uprightness of life, zeal for the glory of God, self-oblation, steadfastness in suffering, PRAYER for persecutors, commendation of one's departing spirit to God. Just as Jesus conquered death by his RESURRECTION and glorification, so too the martyr, by overcoming the weakness of the flesh, wins the reward of heaven. The *Martyrdom of Polycarp*, recounting the martyrdom of the second-century bishop of Smyrna, constitutes the earliest extant eyewitness account of a martyrdom outside the NT and, as such, was included by Eusebius of Caesarea (*ca* 260–*ca* 340) in his *Ecclesiastical History* (4.15). The record of the North African martyrs Perpetua, Felicity, and their companions in 207 likewise ranks high in the catalogue of saints' passions owing to its detail of presentation and theological insight.

Martyrdom was not the only form of heroic witness to Christian faith and life. As early as the fourth century, ascetics, dynamic apologists, learned pastors, and renowned leaders of local Churches found similar acclaim as the Church observed the anniversary of the death of these confessors of the faith. Hence such non-martyrs as Gregory Thaumaturgos (*ca* 210–*ca* 270), Pope Sylvester I (r. 314–35), Nicholas of Myra (*ca* 270–*ca* 350), Anthony of Egypt (251–356), Martin of Tours (d. 397), Ambrose of Milan (*ca* 340–97), and AUGUSTINE OF HIPPO also enjoyed annual commemoration, the widespread circulation of their *vitae* or lives, and the placing of churches under their patronage. Nor was the role of the saints restricted to that of modelling the ideal Christian life and death. By the third century, ORIGEN already recognized the intercessory power of the saints and mentioned that Christians in his day were invoking the aid of their prayers (*Ora.* 14).

The veneration of saints has taken the form both of private devotion and of more public, liturgical cult (see DULIA). Christians gathered to celebrate the EUCHARIST and offer prayers at their tombs on their anniversaries. These sites (*loca sancta*), hallowed by the earthly remains of the saints, became the object of PILGRIMAGE at other times. Antiphons honouring specific saints were inserted into the Eucharistic liturgy as early as the fifth century. Similarly, in the office of vigils, readings from the *vitae* or lives of the saints, as well as antiphons drawn primarily from these lives, marked the saints' anniversaries or feasts. The West was slower to adopt this practice (eighth century) than the East (fifth century). Given the meticulous preparation, marked by intense prayer and fasting, as well as the quasi-sacramental role of saints' icons in the East, it is scarcely surprising that veneration of the images of the saints has marked eastern LITURGY and spirituality – though not without concerns over possible IDOLATRY that gave rise to an extended period of ICONOCLASM that was settled definitively only in 843, with the affirmation of the decrees of the earlier second Council of Nicaea (787). In spite of the restoration of icons, the controversies probably exercised a restraining influence on the variety of media used in the representation of saints in the East, where the depiction of saints through statuary and stained glass (which would flourish in the Latin West) failed to take hold. The West also developed a particularly strong cult of saints' relics that reached its zenith in the late Middle Ages and continues today despite efforts at discouragement and even suppression associated with the REFORMATION and the ENLIGHTENMENT.

The most famous collection of saints' lives, *The Golden Legend*, compiled around 1265 by the Dominican James of Voragine (1230–98), rivalled the Bible in popularity, as attested by more than 1,000 surviving manuscripts of the work, as well as hundreds of printed editions not only in Latin but also in the vernacular languages of Europe. Presenting the accounts of saints' lives and MIRACLES according to the occurrence of their feast days on the liturgical calendar, it remains even today an essential key for interpreting the iconographic and artistic representations of the saints. Although its hagiographic liberties, exaggerations, and indeed fabrications invite valid criticism, it is not entirely clear that a historical–critical method of editing the biographies of saints on the calendar, as undertaken by the Bollandists since 1643, offers the only legitimate approach to a genre that perforce entails unusual phenomena and elements of supernatural mysteries (e.g., miracles, healings, apparitions).

Under the guidance of M. LUTHER, the AUGSBURG CONFESSION recognized the example of the saints but rejected their intercessory role as inconsistent with the exclusive mediation of Jesus Christ. The *Apology of the Augsburg Confession* (1530) admitted that the saints do pray for the universal Church, but still forbade any invocation of the saints. In response to such criticisms, the Council of TRENT (*Invoc.*) insisted on the goodness of invoking the saints to obtain benefits from God through Christ, who remains the one Redeemer. For Trent the saints' intercession, far from competing with Christ's role as Mediator, actually underscores the power of the redemption won by Christ and the vitality of his paschal mystery as the source of the Church's life and mission, since it is to Christ that the saints, motivated by love for the universal Church, appeal for benefits from the Father. The intercession of the saints, then, depends altogether on the pleasure of Christ who has raised humanity to this state of glory. More recently, VATICAN COUNCIL II has sought common ground with Churches and ecclesial communions separated from Rome, striking out at abuses yet confirming the intercessory power of the saints and the worthiness of invoking them without denying the mediatorship of Christ.

The process of recognizing the heroic holiness of individual saints and including their names in the list or canon of other officially acknowledged saints has undergone much change over the centuries. At first recognized by popular acclaim, saints would enjoy a local cultus, which included annual commemoration on the calendar of a particular Church and the visitation of their tombs by the faithful. As their reputations for holiness spread, whether in virtue of their heroism or due to miracles attributed to their intercession, they might be included on the calendars of other Churches.

Over the course of the Middle Ages a pattern emerged: the local bishop would direct the compilation of a biography of a person who died with a reputation for holiness; he would have the body exhumed and transferred to lie beneath an altar in a church; finally the bishop would pronounce the deceased as a saint and assign him or her a day on the calendar (usually the day of death, although in some cases the date of ordination). By the late tenth century, in response to abuses and excesses, a more formal, centralized process of canonization had taken shape with the official insertion of St Ulrich of Augsburg (d. 973) among the saints by a synod of the Lateran under Pope John XV (r. 985–96). Gradually, papal intervention dominated the process, first as a model, then as the norm. In 1234 Gregory IX (r. 1227–41) rendered papal CANONIZATION the only legitimate form of declaring saints, with formal procedures instituted by Sixtus V (r. 1585–90) and Urban VIII (r. 1623–44). Today the Congregation for Causes of the Saints, established in 1969, supervises the steps to beatification and canonization.

The universal call to holiness, that is to abiding communion with the TRINITY, itself a union of LOVE among the three divine Persons, continues to draw people from every race, tongue, walk of life, and personal aptitude to co-operate with the movements of grace in their lives. The whole Church thereby experiences renewal and spiritual growth as the mystical body continues its pilgrimage through time to the new and eternal Jerusalem (cf. Heb. 12:22; Rev. 3:12; 21:2, 10) where God will be all in all (1 Cor. 15:28), and the saints will offer endless praise and thanksgiving in eternal bliss (Rev. 4:8). Meanwhile the Church's earthly liturgy extols the goodness of God manifest in the work of the saints. The Second Preface for Holy Men and Women, which precedes the Sanctus and the Eucharistic Prayer, neatly summarizes the role of the saints: 'You [God] renew the Church in every age by raising up men and women outstanding in holiness, living witnesses of your unchanging love. They inspire us by their heroic lives, and help us by their constant prayers to be the living sign of your saving power.'

See also DEIFICATION; SANCTIFICATION.

P. Brown, *The Cult of the Saints in Later Antiquity and the Middle Ages* (Oxford University Press, 1999).

V. L. Kennedy, *The Saints of the Canon of the Mass*, second revised edn (Pontificio Istituto de Archeologia Cristiana, 1963).

W. E. Post, *Saints, Signs, and Symbols*, second edn (Morehouse, 1974).

M. Walsh, *A New Dictionary of Saints: East and West* (Liturgical Press, 2007).

K. L. Woodward, *Making Saints: How the Catholic Church Determines Who Becomes a Saint, Who Doesn't, and Why* (Simon & Schuster, 1990).

NEIL J. ROY

SALVATION: see SOTERIOLOGY.

SALVATION HISTORY Used loosely, 'salvation history' refers to the whole of God's work of reconciling the world and is thus roughly parallel to the patristic idea of the divine ECONOMY of salvation. As a technical piece of theological vocabulary (*Heilsgeschichte* in German), however, the phrase emerged in the nineteenth century to refer to a particular understanding of SCRIPTURE as a record of divine saving actions stretching from creation to the end of history. As such, its focus is less on the ontology of the relationship between Creator and creature (the heart of patristic reflection on the divine economy) than on historical and hermeneutical issues relating to the accuracy of the biblical accounts and their ability to ground Christian belief.

The idea of salvation history arose partly as a means of affirming the unity of the biblical canon in response to the breakdown of TYPOLOGY as the preferred means of relating events across the two testaments. Its roots lie in the FEDERAL THEOLOGY of the seventeenth century, in which God's redeeming work was subdivided into a series of discrete yet contiguous temporal periods, culminating in the coming of Christ and the advent of the KINGDOM OF GOD. Yet there were problems associated with this way of affirming the Bible's unity. Earlier generations had read the Bible as a single story centred on the Gospels' depiction of Christ but typologically incorporating the whole of prior and subsequent history. Federal theologians attempted to relate the various episodes of the Bible more systematically, but their view of Scripture as describing the stages of salvation as a temporal sequence made it difficult to see how earlier events were genuinely informed – not simply superseded – by later ones.

Loosed from the doctrinal presuppositions of federalism and shaped by the combined influence of historical criticism and philosophical idealism, these ideas took new form in nineteenth-century Germany with the emergence of the *heilsgeschichtliche Schule*. Proponents like J. C. K. von Hofmann (1810–77) saw the Bible depicting a particular stream of events within the larger context of world history. This stream of 'salvation history' was defined by the progressive fulfilment of divine purposes over time, with ideas and concepts only implicit or inchoate in early periods clarified and completed by later events. Similar themes were echoed in the 'biblical-theology' movement of the mid-twentieth century (see BIBLICAL THEOLOGY), with its view of FAITH as the human response to the 'mighty acts of God' in history. In both cases there was appreciation of the need to appeal to the broadest possible historical context for understanding the theological import of particular events; but the apologetic desire to avoid conflict with 'secular' historical judgement in the interpretation of the biblical record led the locus of 'salvation history' to be displaced from the events themselves to the minds of those interpreting them. As a result, the attempt to base faith in history was subtly undermined and Scripture rendered more a witness to than a ground of belief.

See also NARRATIVE THEOLOGY.

H. W. Frei, *The Eclipse of Biblical Narrative: A Study in Eighteenth and Nineteenth Century Hermeneutics* (Yale University Press, 1974).

W. Pannenberg, 'Redemptive Event and History' in *Basic Questions in Theology* (Fortress Press, 1970 [1967]), 1.15–80.

IAN A. MCFARLAND

SANCTIFICATION Sanctification is one of the fundamental topics of Christian theology. It stands for a particular aspect of the DOCTRINE of salvation and has deep roots in the biblical traditions. In the NT the Letter of James has often been seen as the key document for the doctrine of sanctification, stating that 'faith by itself, if it has no works, is dead' (Jas. 2:17). The idea of sanctification, or holiness, is grounded in the holiness of God. Christians are sanctified as their whole lives – both faith and works – are transformed into the image of God. In the OT this is one of the central concerns of Leviticus, where God's holiness is inextricably related to the sanctification of the people: 'For I am the Lord your God; sanctify yourselves, therefore, and be holy, for I am holy' (Lev. 11:44).

Notions of sanctification in early Christian theology can be found especially in the eastern part of the Roman Empire. ATHANASIUS, for instance, employed the notion of DEIFICATION (*theosis*), in reference to 2 Peter 1:4: 'Thus he has given us, through these things, his precious and very great promises, so that through them you may escape from the corruption that is in the world because of lust, and may become participants of the divine nature.' According to Athanasius, Christ 'assumed humanity that we might become God' (*Inc.* 54); 'being God, he later became man, that ... he might deify us' (*Ar.* 1.38–9). While deification in this context does not imply an absolute ontological change – humanity does not become God – it implies a real sharing of humans in the divine nature.

Later important steps in the development of the Christian doctrine of sanctification include the developments in Europe at the time of the REFORMATION of the sixteenth century. Here, sanctification is also a key issue, but in a less visible way. M. LUTHER's emphasis on JUSTIFICATION by FAITH has often been understood as a rejection of an alleged Catholic doctrine of 'works righteousness', which supposedly holds that human beings can earn their salvation by performing good works. In this context the doctrine of justification is seen as rejecting a particular understanding of sanctification, according to which human beings can produce their own holiness. In reaction against this understanding of sanctification, later Lutheranism, starting with Luther's successor P. Melanchthon (1497–1560), tended to understand justification in formal terms as a divine pronouncement on unjust sinners who thus were considered just without any real change and without the transformative aspect that is a central concern of the doctrine of sanctification. Luther's own notion of justification, however, includes both a formal pronouncement of justice and a real moment of transformation in which the justified are reshaped in the image of God. Luther himself occasionally even uses the term 'sanctification'. In the *Large Catechism*, he relates the third article of the Apostles' Creed to the notion of sanctification and states: 'Thus, until the last day, the Holy Ghost abides with the holy congregation or Christendom, by means of which He fetches us to Christ and which He employs to teach and preach to us the Word, whereby He works and promotes sanctification, causing it daily to grow and become strong in the faith and its fruits which He produces.'

The notion of sanctification is more explicitly addressed in the Reformed tradition, especially in the work of J. CALVIN. For Calvin, sanctification, as the process of being made holy, is rooted in the holiness of God. 'From what foundation may righteousness better arise than from the Scriptural warning that we must be made holy because our God is holy [Lev. 19:2; 1 Pet. 1:15–16]' (*Inst.* 3.6.2). As with Luther, sanctification is not a human work but the work of God, yet Calvin puts more emphasis on the role of humanity: 'not because we come into communion with him by virtue of our holiness! Rather, we ought first to cleave unto him so that, infused with his holiness, we may follow whither he calls. But since it is especially characteristic of his glory that he have no fellowship with wickedness and uncleanness' (*Inst.* 3.6.2). To be sure, the role of humanity is both negative and positive, as sanctification implies both a rejection of the self and a determination to follow God's commandments: 'This is also evidence of great progress: that, almost forgetful of ourselves, surely subordinating our self-concern, we try faithfully to devote our zeal to God and his commandments' (*Inst.* 3.7.2). The sociologist M. Weber (1864–1930) would later find the 'spirit of capitalism' in this theology, where progress in sanctification could be measured in terms of economic success. Much, however, depends on how the holiness of God is defined, and other streams within the Christian tradition have understood it not in terms of economic success but in terms of a rejection of money and power.

Since the traditions of the Reformation were developed in opposition to Catholic doctrine, it should be noted that in its fifth and sixth sessions the Catholic Council of TRENT, responding to the challenges of the Protestant Reformation, explicitly rejects the notion of works righteousness, affirms the primacy of God's GRACE in salvation, and seeks to integrate sanctification and good works into the process of justification. Contemporary conversations on justification have clarified some of the older tensions and condemnations. The recent *Joint Declaration on the Doctrine of Justification* by the Lutheran World Federation and the Catholic Church, for instance, articulates a 'consensus on the basic truths of the doctrine of justification', noting that 'by grace alone, in faith in Christ's saving work and not because of any merit on our part, we are accepted by

God and receive the Holy Spirit, who renews our hearts while equipping and calling us to good works' (*JDDJ*, §15). While there is agreement that justification is based on God's work alone, sanctification is once again a fundamental concern common to both traditions: 'We confess together that good works – a Christian life lived in faith, hope and love – follow justification and are its fruits' (*JDDJ*, §37). This means that sanctification necessarily grows out of justification.

In Christian theology the doctrine of sanctification has often been considered in anthropological perspective, so that the main focus is on the personal achievement of holiness. This focus must be seen in the context of modernity, where a shift from theocentric to anthropocentric points of view takes place. J. WESLEY, considered by many to be the father of a robust doctrine of sanctification that influenced both the holiness movements and Pentecostalisms that are now reshaping the face of Christianity, is a theologian of modernity. His home, eighteenth-century England, was deeply immersed in the modernization of philosophy, labour, economics, and politics. Although not endorsing modernity unilaterally, Wesley shares in the modern concern for the affairs of this world rather than the next. He begins his road-map to the doctrine of salvation with a reference to Ephesians 2:8: 'Ye have been saved', replacing the definition of salvation as 'going to heaven, eternal happiness' ('Scripture', 1.1) with an understanding of salvation as that which takes place here and now. The focus of Wesley's doctrine of sanctification is, thus, not on earning a place in heaven or achieving immortality but on life here and now, understood as the fulfilment of 'the will of him that sent us' ('Circumcision', 2.10), or as the restoration of God's image in us (*CP*). While focusing on the modern concern for life in this world, however, Wesley's doctrine of sanctification moves away form the ANTHROPOCENTRISM of modernity. Sanctification is about God's transformative power and not about human capacity, which is why even perfection cannot be ruled out (although for Wesley perfection does not apply to natural human limitations such as lack of knowledge). The historical traditions of Christianity, especially the theocentric traditions of the early Orthodox Churches, contributed to Wesley's distinct emphasis on the work of God. Perhaps equally important, Wesley was for the most part not dealing with an upper-class audience (i.e., with people who felt in a position of control); rather, Wesley was dealing with people who belonged to the emerging working classes and others on the margins, like the sick and those in prison. This perspective lends itself to a more realistic view of human potential.

Sanctification in this sense becomes once again a holistic project that pushes beyond the rather narrow modern categories of religion. If sanctification is the work of God and refers to real moments of transformation, it encompasses quite naturally every dimension of human life, private as well as public, including economics and politics. The notion of sanctification that develops here is relational, tying together divinity and humanity with an emphasis on the transformative power of God. Wesley advises, 'Let nothing satisfy thee but the power of godliness, but a religion that is spirit and life; the dwelling in God and God in thee' ('Disc. 13', 3.9). LIBERATION THEOLOGIES in the twentieth century have taken up similar notions of God's transformative power. Other contemporary theologies, focusing more on the ecclesiological implications of sanctification, have reminded us of the crucial role of the Church, as the community of the sanctified that makes a real difference in this world. Anabaptist traditions especially, the so-called 'left wing' of the Reformation, continue to yield substantial influence here, as seen in the work of J. Yoder (1927–97).

Sanctification is, thus, a central concern for Christianity. Nevertheless, a closer look at the place of sanctification in Christian theology is required. A common distinction between justification and sanctification states that justification is what God does for us through Christ and sanctification is what God does in us through the Holy Spirit. According to this logic, justification is God's imputed grace whereby sinful human beings are declared just without actually being made just. Sanctification, on the other hand, is God's imparted grace, which transforms sinful human beings. This distinction overlooks more complex notions of justification which include a real sense of being made just, i.e., of lives being shaped by God's justice. Though such complexity can be found in Luther's teaching, Luther failed to comprehend some of the deeper implications of PAUL's notion of justification. Paul understood that God's justice provides an alternative and a radical challenge to the justice of the Roman Empire. In this context, God's justice becomes real in the alternative lordship of Jesus Christ, according to which the common people are treated with respect in an alternative way of life in which the last are the first and the first are the last. Without this particular understanding of justice and justification, sanctification loses its most essential qualities.

Sanctification, in sum, is based on the alternative justice of the kingdom of God, which implies new relationships both to the neighbour (a key theme for both Wesley and Calvin) and the world. This insight prevents several traditional mistakes in the understanding of sanctification. A common misunderstanding holds that sanctification implies accommodation to some political or ecclesial status quo, and that the sanctified person must submit to the established authorities. If sanctification is measured according to God's alternative justice, however, sanctification cannot be the glorification of predetermined projects. Another common misunderstanding is embodied in a free-floating understanding of sanctification that today often takes the form of the 'PROSPERITY GOSPEL', where sanctification means personal economic success. Here, the ethos of free-market capitalism replaces God's justice. A final example for a misunderstanding of sanctification is to define it in terms of classical theism, which cannot easily be reconciled in terms of the alternative justice of the kingdom of God. It is no accident that an otherwise religiously pluralistic Roman Empire rejected Christianity. Christians were considered to be atheists, since their God could not be brought in line with the gods of the status quo. Justification should, therefore, not be considered to be merely a prerequisite step to sanctification that is then left behind, but indicates the direction which sanctification takes.

Athanasius, *On the Incarnation* (St Vladimir's Seminary Press, 1978).

D. W. Dayton, *Theological Roots of Pentecostalism* (Francis Asbury, 1987).

T. Runyon, ed., *Sanctification and Liberation: Liberation Theologies in Light of the Wesleyan Tradition* (Abingdon Press, 1981).

E. Tamez, *The Amnesty of Grace: Justification by Faith from a Latin American Perspective* (Abingdon Press, 1993).

J. Wesley, 'Sermon 40: On Christian Perfection' and 'Sermon 92: On Zeal' in *The Works of John Wesley*, vol. III, Sermons III (Abingdon Press, 1986).

J. H. Yoder, *The Politics of Jesus: Vicit Agnus Noster* (Eerdmans, 1972).

JOERG RIEGER

SATAN: see DEVIL.

SATISFACTION THEORY: see ATONEMENT.

SCANDINAVIAN THEOLOGY: see NORDIC THEOLOGY.

SCHILLEBEECKX, EDWARD One of the leading Catholic theologians of the twentieth century, Edward Schillebeeckx has made original contributions to the areas of SACRAMENTOLOGY, FUNDAMENTAL THEOLOGY, MINISTRY, and CHRISTOLOGY in a career that has spanned six decades. Born on 12 November 1914 in Antwerp, Belgium, the Flemish theologian joined the Dominicans in 1934, was ordained a priest in 1941, and taught dogmatic theology at the University of Louvain from 1947 until his appointment as chair of dogmatics and the history of theology at the University of Nijmegen (now Radboud University) in the Netherlands (1958–83). Although not a *peritus* (official advisor), Schillebeeckx exercised a significant influence on VATICAN COUNCIL II through his lectures attended by large numbers of bishops. He founded the Dutch journal *Tijdscrift voor Theologie* and was a founding editor of the international journal *Concilium*. In 1982 Schillebeeckx became the first (and to date the only) theologian to be awarded the Erasmus prize for contributions to the development of European culture.

Schillebeeckx first came to international prominence with his groundbreaking work on sacramental theology, *Christ, the Sacrament of the Encounter with God* (1963), a distillation of his 1951 doctoral dissertation. Situating the specific sacraments of the Church in the broader context of the sacramental economy of salvation where the encounter with God is mediated by created and human realities, he argued that the primary sacrament of encounter with God is Jesus Christ. The Church likewise functions as a sacrament of Christ's saving presence in the world; its ritual symbolic actions are 'effective signs' of that mystery celebrated at decisive points in human life.

Early on, Schillebeeckx adopted the insight of his philosophical mentor D. DePetter (1905–71) that there is an implicit experiential element which goes beyond conceptual knowledge in all human knowing. Schillebeeckx's later writings on REVELATION as located in, but not identical with, human experience retain the insight that conceptual frameworks are necessary, but never adequate, expressions of an encounter with God that is mediated more fundamentally in practical activity on behalf of humankind and creation. Correlatively, Schillebeeckx emphasized the importance of situating theological insights and texts in their historical contexts and doing theology in dialogue with the social and political movements of the day.

Schillebeeckx's major contribution to contemporary theology remains his two-volume soteriological CHRISTOLOGY: *Jesus: An Experiment in Christology* (1979) and *Christ: The Experience of Jesus as Lord* (1980). Calling for a narrative–practical approach to Christology and drawing on years of study of biblical exegesis, Schillebeeckx constructed a theological reading of the story of Jesus as 'PARABLE of God' and 'paradigm of humanity' and proposed the main lines of a contemporary social–political theology of grace or salvation. The goal of both widely acclaimed volumes is to prompt hope and action on behalf of the kingdom of God in a secularized and suffering world.

M. C. Hilkert and R. J. Schreiter, eds., *The Praxis of the Reign of God: An Introduction to the Theology of Edward Schillebeeckx* (Fordham University Press, 2002).

P. Kennedy, *Schillebeeckx* (Liturgical Press, 1993).

MARY CATHERINE HILKERT

SCHISM Only in the fourth century was schism, or separation from the established Christian congregation in a particular place (and, more specifically, from communion with its bishop), formally distinguished from HERESY, or false teaching. Classically, while heresy is a SIN against the FAITH that defines Christians' shared commitment to the GOSPEL, schism is a sin against the LOVE that holds Christians together as a community (see Aquinas, *ST* 2/2.39.1.3). In line with this distinction, AUGUSTINE (*Fid.* 10; *QMatt.* 11.2) had maintained that schismatics may hold the same doctrine as the true Church, though Jerome (*Tit.* 3.10) argued that proponents of schism invariably create heresy as a means of justifying their separation.

Basil of Caesarea (see Cappadocian Fathers) attempted to give practical significance to the distinction between heresy and schism by arguing that, while the baptism performed by heretics was to be rejected (so that converted heretics had to be rebaptized), that of schismatics was to be admitted (*Ep.* 188.1). In contemporary ecclesiology this distinction plays a significant role in the relationship between the Catholic and Orthodox Churches. The Catholic magisterium regards the Orthodox as formally in a state of schism from Rome and explicitly affirms the validity of Orthodox sacraments (Vatican Council II, *UR* 15). The Orthodox have shown a greater tendency to view Catholics as heretics, as evidenced by a more established (though by no means universally accepted or observed) tradition of rebaptizing Catholic converts, as well as by a greater reluctance to allow Eucharistic fellowship between the two communions.

Ian A. McFarland

Schleiermacher, Friedrich Widely regarded as the father of modern theology, Friedrich Schleiermacher (1768–1834) was also the main early modern theorist of religion, hermeneutics, and the critical arts and the classic translator of Plato (*ca* 430–*ca* 345 BC). A co-founder of the University of Berlin, Schleiermacher was professor of both theology and philosophy there during the last twenty-five of his forty years as pastor. Although he deliberately separated his substantial philosophical work from theology's content and eschewed natural theology, he deemed the two fields to be ultimately compatible. Similarly, biblical exegesis (which comprised half of his teaching load) required no deviation from general scientific principles, only shifts of attention to the religious contexts embedded in the texts.

In Schleiermacher's first famous work, *On Religion* (1799), and elsewhere he depicts the essential nature of religion as (1) rooted in feeling, (2) existing in numerous developmental stages, from fetishism up to the 'feeling of absolute dependence' in monotheism and distinctively in Christianity, (3) communal, and (4) quite diverse. Religion will evolve beyond the Christianity we know but not beyond Christ.

Schleiermacher's *Soliloquies* (1800) include references to a series of insights gained over the previous sixteen years, which together explain his extraordinarily fecund production as a theologian after 1796. While then entering the small circle of early German Romantics in Berlin, he also served as chaplain at Charité Hospital there (1796–1802), the second of five pastorates. From early on, the major themes of his theology demonstrably arose from his intensive experience as pastor, preacher, and leader in the Church. This experience yielded a stream of sermon volumes, lectures, exegetical works, ecclesial essays, and larger works including *Christmas Eve* (1806), *Luke* (1817), *Election* (1819), *Christian Ethics* (1822–3), *The Triune God* (1823), and *Reformed but Ever Reforming* (1830), a sermonic critique of the Augsburg Confession.

For Schleiermacher, Christian faith experience is rooted in the feeling that one's self, like everything else, is 'absolutely dependent' on God. Evangelical (i.e., Reformed and Lutheran) theology is to be formed only in relation to God's redemptive activity in Jesus' unique person and work, particularly his self-proclamation by word and deed. It always concerns relationship to God within Christian community. The grace proclaimed by Jesus occurs universally, responsive to humanity's need for redemption from both original sin (transmitted socially from others, not biologically from Adam) and actual sin. 'Preparatory grace' operates everywhere, most evidently in the Church. Because God does what God wills, redemption occurs by God's single eternal decree. God's decree includes creation of human beings partially free, but only one final destiny exists for them: to be one with God eternally. There is, therefore, no devil, hell, or damnation.

His masterpiece, *Christian Faith* (1821; 2nd edn, 1830), is structured such that the general features of divine–human interaction presupposed in Christian experience are presented in Part I, in distinction from those features that directly present the Christian experience of the overcoming of sinfulness by grace, laid out in Part II. Schleiermacher's understanding of faith led him to reformulate a wide range of traditional doctrines including the following:

(1) The NT is the sole authoritative witness to Christ, redemption, and the reign of God. Over time, historical perspectives on this witness change, with potentially increasing insight. In this way, a thoroughly Christ-centred perspective, operating in tandem with an established but open canon of Scripture, relates everything to the redemption God accomplishes in the historical Jesus.

(2) God is Trinity as one God in three roles or manifestations, not as three Persons. God's activity is manifested only in and through the world. God's self-revelation can manifest no intra-Trinitarian (immanent) relations, though what God does in the world (economically) involves 'making the supernatural natural' by presenting the infinite in finite conditions. God wisely governs the world in love, the only divine attribute really knowable.

(3) Christ, the only real 'miracle', is alone necessary for redemption and faith. Redemption occurs by Christ's original and continuing life – including the way he *faced* death but not (in contrast to many traditional atonement theories) *because of* his

death – and operates in exactly the same way for the first disciples as for the Church ever since. As a man possessing perfect God-consciousness, Christ has only one nature (human). His sinlessness and total blessedness complete God's creation of humankind and are communicated to individuals through the Church's 'common spirit' – the HOLY SPIRIT. Christ is not pre-existent, fully manifests God's presence with human beings, and is at death taken up in God.

(4) Mature 'Christian religious immediate self-consciousness' is always rooted in feeling and is at its best contemplative, but results in a 'dry asceticism' if not also expressed in thinking and action. These three elements together constitute 'piety', manifested through the developing community-based processes of BAPTISM, CONVERSION, regeneration, and SANCTIFICATION.

(5) In the ever-embodied 'invisible Church' all regenerated persons are one in the divine Spirit by which Christ is continually communicated. Within the 'visible Church' diversity is to be honoured in love and separation overcome. ECCLESIOLOGY and pneumatology are coterminous.

(6) Christian life consists not in achieving moral duties or virtues but in people's being faithful within their communal and individual lives everywhere – by presentational, propagating, and purifying action in community of life with Christ. Formally, Christian ethics is indicative, not imperative. Similarly, Christian PRAYER is essentially thanksgiving, not petition.

(7) Thoughts regarding the end of history, the Church's consummation, and the afterlife do not reflect Christian consciousness. ESCHATOLOGY is therefore only prefigurative ('prophetic'), not *doctrina fidei*.

In *Brief Outline of Theology as a Field of Study* (1811; 2nd edn 1830), Schleiermacher divided theology into three interdependent parts: (1) PHILOSOPHICAL THEOLOGY he subdivided into APOLOGETICS, which displays the Church's comparative self-definition (not external proof or defence), and polemics, which corrects diseased elements within it. (2) HISTORICAL THEOLOGY included NT exegesis; institutional and doctrinal history of the Church; and dogmatics, itself subdivided into 'faith-doctrine' (dogmatic propositions), 'life-doctrine' (ethics), and 'statistics' (socio-cultural accounts of the Church worldwide). (3) PRACTICAL THEOLOGY covered Church governance and both clerical and lay ministry. All theology is to be both 'scientific' (because it is methodologically general, rigorous, cohesive, and open to change) and 'ecclesial'.

See also LIBERAL THEOLOGY; SYSTEMATIC THEOLOGY.

J. Mariña, ed., *The Cambridge Companion to Friedrich Schleiermacher* (Cambridge University Press, 2005).

T. N. Tice, *Schleiermacher* (Abingdon Press, 2006).

H. Peiter, *Schleiermacher's Christian Ethics* (Wipf and Stock, 2008).

H. Dierkes, T. N. Tice, and W. Virmond, eds., *Schleiermacher, Romanticism and the Critical Arts* (Edwin Mellen Press, 2008).

TERRENCE N. TICE

SCHOLASTICISM As the etymology of the term suggests, 'Scholasticism' refers to theology done in 'schools', that is, within a formal academic context. While sometimes used as a pejorative label for any theology viewed as overly preoccupied with fine conceptual distinctions (and thus applied to patristic writers like MAXIMUS THE CONFESSOR and JOHN OF DAMASCUS), the term more properly refers to a way of doing theology practised in European universities from the twelfth to the eighteenth century. Taken in this latter sense, Scholasticism is best defined *formally* as a set of techniques for the presentation of theological ideas rather than *materially* in terms of specific doctrinal content. These formal characteristics of Scholastic theology include an emphasis on technical precision in the definition of terms and logical order in the subdivision and organization of topics. Together, these characteristics reflect an underlying methodological concern for clarity and order in theological scholarship, connected with the pedagogical aim of training competent clergy.

Medieval Scholasticism emerged out of the effort to develop a clear and consistent presentation of Christian doctrine in light of the apparent conflicts found in the writings of the Church fathers, as identified by P. Abelard (1079–1142) in his book *Sic et Non*. As Scholasticism developed in the universities during the thirteenth and fourteenth centuries, theologians like T. AQUINAS and J. DUNS SCOTUS also sought to defend the intellectual credibility of Christian belief in light of the introduction into medieval Europe of the philosophical and scientific writings of Aristotle (384–322 BC), as well as of the great medieval Muslim commentators on his work. One notable feature of medieval Scholastic theology (found, e.g., in the *Summa Theologiae* of Aquinas) was the use of format of the 'disputed question' (*quaestio disputata*), in which theological problems were addressed through a systematic examination of evidence and arguments for and against a given position.

Although the idea of 'school theology' received a pejorative connotation in Protestant circles during the early decades of the REFORMATION, Scholasticism was the characteristic form of much theology among Protestants as well as Catholics from the late sixteenth century, especially as Lutheran and Reformed theologians sought to give dogmatic precision to the theological insights of the first generation of reformers. Though continuing to draw on medieval antecedents (especially Aquinas), early modern Scholasticism was also heavily influenced by Renaissance HUMANISM, and was, correspondingly, characterized by increased attention to ancient languages and the use of rhetorical (versus demonstrative) forms of argumentation in comparison with Scholastics of earlier centuries. By contrast, the neo-Scholasticism associated with the revival of Thomism in late nineteenth-century Catholic theology was conceived much more as a repristination of medieval practice, albeit with a recognition of the need to replace particular ideas (e.g., the principles of Aristotelian physics) that subsequent history had shown to be untenable with more modern concepts and categories.

Throughout its history, Scholasticism was as much concerned with the defence of orthodoxy over against what was viewed as heresy as with theology's academic credibility. Scholastic theological argument focused on the formal and conceptual adequacy of competing definitions and divisions of dogmatic material, a process that included the critical evaluation as well as appropriation of the opinions of earlier theologians. It was deliberately formulaic and impersonal in tone, and its attention to conceptual and logical distinctions clearly differentiated it from the presentation of Christian belief found in other types of theological writing (e.g., catechisms, biblical exegesis) written at the same time – though it is important to note that many 'Scholastic' theologians in both the medieval and early modern periods also produced writing in these alternative genres.

W. J. van Asselt and E. Dekker, eds., *Reformation and Scholasticism: An Ecumenical Enterprise* (Baker Academic, 2001).

J. Pieper, *Scholasticism: Personalities and Problems of Medieval Philosophy* (Pantheon Books, 1960).

Ian A. McFarland

Science: see Natural Science.

Scientific Creationism: see Creationism.

Scotism: see Duns Scotus, John.

Scottish Theology Christian theology has a long and varied history in the nation of Scotland. Though perhaps most renowned for its predilection towards an austere brand of Calvinism (see Reformed Theology), Scottish theology has in truth been a more diverse affair across the centuries.

The first Scottish theologians belong to the world of medieval Scholasticism and include Richard of St Victor (d. 1173), J. Duns Scotus, J. Ireland (*ca* 1440–96), J. Mair (*ca* 1467–1550), and G. Lokert (*ca* 1488–1547). That these men all lived and taught theology (among other places) in Paris indicates the strong connections that Scottish theology and the Scottish Church had with continental Europe throughout this period; but it also indicates the importance already attributed to theological education in pre-Reformation Scotland, in which the Church and the state had co-operated to found three universities by 1500. From a theological perspective, the work of Scotus is undoubtedly the most enduring: his advancement of realist epistemology and linguistic univocality contra T. Aquinas remains significant in the history of western thought.

The initial impulse of the Reformation in Scotland was Lutheran, with the first Protestant martyr in Scotland being P. Hamilton (*ca* 1504–28). However, the strand of the Reformation that ultimately succeeded was decidedly Reformed, culminating in the Scottish Reformation of 1560. The leader of this movement was J. Knox (*ca* 1515–72), who had previously studied under Mair in Paris and sojourned with J. Calvin in Geneva. In 1560 Knox and his colleagues drew up the Scots Confession, a document firmly rooted in the theology of Geneva, and with its ratification by Parliament the same year the Scottish Reformation was complete. Its aim was the spiritual renewal of the entire nation, to which end the co-operation of both ecclesial and secular powers was mandated.

From the political and religious turmoil in Great Britain in the seventeenth century, the Westminster Confession of Faith emerged as the new subordinate standard for the Church of Scotland (see Westminster Standards). Over the ensuing decades and even centuries, it had a profound influence on Scottish theology in particular and on the Scottish character in general. This staunchly Calvinist and anti-Catholic document laid particular emphasis on the legal idea of the covenant between God and humanity (see Federal Theology), and taught the doctrines of limited atonement and double predestination. The balance of the resonances and dissonances between this Confession and the earlier Scots Confession remains a matter of theological debate.

Any rather legalistic picture of the Scottish theology of this time needs, however, to be complemented by an understanding of other features of the Scottish theological context. First, theology in Scotland was not simply an intellectual pursuit, but also called forth extraordinary expressions of piety and devotion, as seen in the letters of S. Rutherford (1600–61). Second, Scottish theology was marked by profound ethical and social concerns. While this led on the one hand to a certain rigour in matters of Church discipline, it led on the other hand to one of the finest educational systems in Europe.

Furthermore, although the Westminster Confession enjoyed the status of touchstone for orthodoxy in Scotland, the doctrinal standards it endorsed came to be increasingly questioned from the early years of the eighteenth century. On the one hand, it faced pressures internal to the Church, as a succession of academic theologians and Church ministers underwent heresy trials up until the early twentieth century. Perhaps the three most renowned instances are: the 'Marrow controversy' (1718–23), in which the Church's contractual understanding of good works and Christian ASSURANCE was challenged; the case of E. Irving (1792–1834), who ascribed a fallen human nature to Jesus Christ; and the case of J. M. Campbell (1800–72), who contested the Church's teaching on the penal and limited nature of the ATONEMENT. Also worthy of mention is the case of biblical scholar W. R. Smith (1846–94), whose articles for the *Encylopaedia Brittanica* led him to be tried for heresy by the Free Church of Scotland. In addition, there were a series of SCHISMS in the Church relating to issues of polity and patronage, notably in 1690, 1733, and 1761, culminating in the Great Disruption of 1843.

This questioning of theological norms was symptomatic of the growing appreciation of human reason in the emergence of the Scottish ENLIGHTENMENT. This movement coincided with the emergence of a 'moderate' (as opposed to the 'evangelical') party in the Church, holding a rather broader and more tolerant view of theological matters. Indeed, a number of 'moderates' – such as T. Reid (1710–96) and H. Blair (1718–1800) – made prominent contributions to the Scottish Enlightenment in diverse fields of study (see COMMON-SENSE PHILOSOPHY). Meanwhile, external pressures arising from the need to respond to the emergence of DEISM, empiricism, RATIONALISM, and BIBLICAL CRITICISM also contributed to the broadening of the terrain of Scottish theology from its earlier circumscription by the tenets of Reformed ORTHODOXY. In the nineteenth century, apologetic responses to these challenges came from members of the 'evangelical' party such as T. Chalmers (1800–47), although confidence in the faculty of human reason waned as the years passed.

The second half of the nineteenth century saw a pronounced re-emergence of theological engagement with continental philosophy, notably in the shape of I. KANT and G. W. F. HEGEL. Figures such as J. Caird (1820–98) and A. Pringle-Pattison (1856–1931) contested the inheritance of German IDEALISM but were also at the forefront of mediating its ideas to the English-speaking world. Later scholars such as J. Macmurray (1891–1976), who advanced a personalist philosophy centred on freedom and LOVE, and D. MacKinnon (1913–94), who explored the relationship between idealism and realism from a theological perspective, represent a continuation of this interdisciplinary feature of Scottish theology (see PERSONALISM).

Over this same period, however, the dominant tendency in Scottish theology has been to work with a narrower focus on theology as a discipline founded on REVELATION, again with a particular eye for developments in continental theology. Figures such as P. T. Forsyth (1848–1921) and H. R. Mackintosh (1870–1936) reflected continental kenotic understandings of Jesus Christ (see KENOTIC THEOLOGY), while later figures such as D. Baillie (1887–1954) and J. Baillie (1886–1960) exhibited a certain continental liberalism in their theology (see LIBERAL THEOLOGY). The influence of R. BULTMANN and D. BONHOEFFER was noticeable on the work of theologians such as R. G. Smith (1913–68) and J. Macquarrie (1919–2007). Arguably the most famous Scottish theologian of the past century, T. F. Torrance (1913–2007), was particularly influenced by the theology of K. BARTH, which he brought into constructive dialogue with his own reappropriation of the patristic tradition.

N. M. de S. Cameron *et al.*, eds., *Dictionary of Scottish Church History & Theology* (T&T Clark, 1993).

J. Macleod, *Scottish Theology in Relation to Church History since the Reformation* (John Knox Press, 1943).

T. F. Torrance, *Scottish Theology: From John Knox to John McLeod Campbell* (T&T Clark, 1996).

PAUL T. NIMMO

SCRIPTURAL REASONING 'Scriptural reasoning' refers to an approach to the study of the sacred texts of Judaism, Christianity, and Islam first introduced in Charlottesville, Virginia, and Cambridge, England, in the 1990s by the Society for Scriptural Reasoning, whose founding members included D. Ford (b. 1948), D. Hardy (1930–2007), and P. Ochs (b. 1950). The approach is characterized by (1) the corporate study of SCRIPTURE (2) by scholars who are also practising adherents of the three religions (3) who meet regularly in small groups (4) over a substantial period of time (usually two or more years). Scriptural reasoning is thus an experiment in corporate, inter-religious, Scripture study, rather than a prescribed method of biblical analysis like, say, form, redaction, or rhetorical criticism (see BIBLICAL CRITICISM). Typically, a scriptural-reasoning study group proceeds by selecting a set of Qur'anic and biblical verses for common study, directing attention first to 'plain sense' grammatical and historical readings, then to issues of canonical setting and history of interpretation, and, finally, to theological assessment of the selected passages in light of each other. The process is then repeated with a new set of texts. Participants label the interpretive activity generated by this dialogue 'scriptural reasoning', and sometimes make it the object of theoretical analysis. Scriptural reasoning seeks to foster a model of academic scriptural theology that allows participants to maintain the normativity of their own traditions while engaging sibling traditions in a spirit of hospitality, trust, and egalitarianism. Participants are 'first' but not 'final' authorities with respect to the Scriptures of their own tradition. Hence scriptural reasoning is also a corporate exercise in letting go of exclusive ownership of sacred traditions.

See also ISLAM AND CHRISTIANITY; JUDAISM AND CHRISTIANITY.

R. KENDALL SOULEN

SCRIPTURE Like the related Greek and Latin terms *graphē* and *scriptura*, 'scripture' refers in the first instance to the act of writing or to the individual written record. The term is partially synonymous with 'inscription'. Where the reference is to the Bible, 'scripture' is often qualified by 'holy' to indicate the distinctive category of writing that is intended. The general, non-religious usage of the term survived into the nineteenth century, but 'scripture' or 'the scriptures' finally become virtually synonymous with 'the Bible'. If there is a distinction, it is that 'Bible' tends to refer to a single printed volume whereas 'Scripture' highlights the phenomenon of writing or textuality as such. A further significant term, 'canon', draws attention to the boundary that marks off those scriptures deemed to be 'holy' from all other books or scriptures.

From the sixteenth century onwards, Protestant theology developed what came to be called a 'doctrine of Scripture' whose individual topics might include Scripture's INSPIRATION, authority, sufficiency, clarity, infallibility, or unity. This relatively late development is of lasting theological value, but it tends to take for granted the phenomenon of Scripture as such – as though this were too obvious to be worthy of consideration. To affirm the inspiration or authority of Scripture, in opposition perhaps to those who seem to deny it such attributes, is often to overlook the prior question about Scripture itself. Of the various roles that Christian faith and practice assign to written texts, the one assigned to 'Holy Scripture' would seem to be the most fundamental. But how is that role to be described?

Christian faith originates within the creative ferment of Second Temple Judaism, where the concept of Scripture is inseparable from its communal function. That Scripture is read and heard in community is no less fundamental to its existence than its 'writtenness' – for writing is a technology of long-range communication and exists purely in order to be read and heard. As is noted at the so-called 'Council of Jerusalem', Moses (viz., the written text) is read each sabbath in synagogues in every city (Acts 15:21), and this social fact is the model for the new institutional structures created by Christian mission. There is no reason to suppose that written texts are the special concern of the non-Christian Jewish community, and that within the early Church they are superseded by the living apostolic witness, as the letter gives way to the Spirit. On the contrary, the written text itself becomes living address every time it is read and heard. In its written existence it is nothing other than the unlimited potential of such living address – like a musical score, which exists only with a view to live performance.

Equally fundamental is the preaching, teaching, or instruction that follows the reading of Scripture, indicating that what is written, read, and heard relates not only to communal worship on the sabbath or Sunday but also to everyday life during the rest of the week. Scripture exists in order to generate certain forms of praxis. As Justin Martyr (d. *ca* 165) notes, when passages from the Gospels or prophetic texts have been read, it is customary for the president to 'instruct and exhort to the imitation of these good things' (*1Apol.* 67). The reading and preaching of Scripture occurs here within a Eucharistic context; conversely, the EUCHARIST is constituted in part by the reading and preaching of Scripture. In and through preaching, the scriptural text comes to shape the everyday world, providing a hermeneutical framework within which encountered reality in its negative and positive aspects may be interpreted. The interpretation of Scripture is not an end in itself but enables Scripture to perform its own hermeneutical function, and it needs to be both read and preached if it is to do so.

As regards its origin, Scripture is held to be the work of individuals designated 'prophets' (for the OT) or 'apostles' (for the NT), that is, of persons divinely mandated to communicate God's address to the world. It is not just its pragmatic function but also its transcendent origin that constitutes the holiness of 'the Holy Scriptures'. Indeed, the pragmatic function is itself grounded in the transcendent origin. Those who hear as the holy writings are read, and who receive the corresponding instruction, are themselves the addressees of the divine communication embodied in these texts. They do not simply overhear an address intended primarily for the prophet's or the apostle's contemporaries, with only indirect and tenuous relevance for later generations. On that account, the calling of the prophet or apostle would be to speak a word of limited scope, fortuitously preserved and transmitted by the artifice of writing. Such a view (according to which writing deracinates speech from its living context) reflects the assumption that speech and writing are somehow antagonistic to one another, and that writing must be downgraded and even denigrated if the essence of speech is to be preserved. This deep-rooted assumption is already attested in Plato's (*ca* 430–*ca* 345 BC) *Phaedrus*, and continues to affect and impair the discussion of Holy Scripture to this day. In reality, prophetic and apostolic speech is not limited but universal in its scope, for in ISRAEL and in Jesus Christ God addresses not just individuals or select communities but the world. It is writing that realizes this universal scope, serving speech by indefinitely extending its communicative range through both time and space. As already noted, however, this writing exists in order to be converted back into speech as it is 'performed' in reading and preaching. Writing derives from prior speech and is oriented towards future speech, and as such it is a fit mode of communication for the God who has already spoken and who will speak again on the basis of what was said before. It is only when Scripture is abstracted from its proper communicative and communal context that it can seem to represent a sterile fixity rather than a living word.

It is already clear from this that the *content* of scripture is inseparable from its *form*. Its content is divine address with universal scope, directed to every new present on the basis of what was once said in a specific past; and the textuality or 'writtenness' that is Scripture's most basic formal feature corresponds closely to this content. Could a specific word attain universal scope, and without detriment to its particularity, in any other way than through the technology of writing? If the Holy Scriptures are 'the Word of God' (as sixteenth- and seventeenth-century Reformed confessions so emphatically claim), then they are such *on account of* their writtenness, not *in spite of* it. 'Writtenness' is a necessary though not a sufficient condition for Scripture to be Word of God.

Divine address or Word of God is still, however, a relatively abstract characterization of the content of Scripture. It draws attention to the ultimate origin of Scripture, and thus to the authority and significance of what is said there, but we learn little from it of what the scriptural word is actually about. *That* God speaks is one thing; *what* God says is another. A second formal feature becomes relevant at this point, and this is the *bipartite* nature of Scripture in its Christian form. For Christians, though not for Jews, there is an 'Old Testament' and there is a 'New Testament', and the co-existence and inter-relatedness of the two canonical collections make the Christian OT a fundamentally different entity from the Jewish *Tanakh* – the Law (*Torah*), the Prophets (*Nebi'im*), and the Writings (*Kethubim*). Where Christian readers read these texts alongside Jews, it is appropriate to regard them as a 'Hebrew Bible' shared by both communities. And yet, where Christian faith operates on its own terrain, the *Old/New* terminology is indispensable. It draws attention to the event in relation to which one collection of writings is 'old', preceding that event and presupposed in it, whereas another is 'new', following that event and generated by it. In strictly chronological terms, there is no justification for such absolutizing terminology. Recent scholarship has tended towards late, post-exilic datings for the OT texts, and the editorial processes that shape their final canonical forms may in some cases extend into the Christian era itself. Historically speaking, the production of scriptural texts occurs within a chronological continuum; Christians might reasonably have adopted an *extended* scriptural canon, comprising perhaps law, prophets, writings, and gospels, rather than a bipartite one. Christian Scripture is bipartite for theological more than historical reasons. Its two major components are what they are in relation to the event that both differentiates and unites them: the event which the Gospels narrate as the life, ministry, death, and RESURRECTION of Jesus, and which PAUL construes as the singular divine act of the world's reconciliation.

That event is the core content of Scripture, and it is attested already in Scripture's bipartite form. For Christian faith, Scripture is significant only in relation to this event. When, in all four Gospels, JOHN THE BAPTIST is introduced in scriptural language as the one who 'prepares the way of the Lord', he enacts the role of the Christian OT as a whole, which is itself nothing other than a preparing of the way of the Lord. When Jesus himself comes onto the scene, he enters not some neutral space but a context already shaped by Israel's Scriptures, with their testimony to the divine creation of the world and election of Israel: both open-ended events awaiting resolution. If, as Christians claim, Jesus is the Scriptures' 'fulfilment', he is no less dependent on them than they on him. He and they mutually interpret one another; neither party is self-interpreting, that is, possessed of a self-evident significance that cannot be otherwise and that needs no interpretative engagement. And the agents of that mutual interpretation, of Scripture by Jesus and of Jesus by Scripture, are the first Christians, from whose testimony the writings of the NT derive. The NT, then, is the textual space where the mutual interpretation of Jesus and Scripture is enacted, and where the world itself is transformed in light of this three-sided hermeneutical event.

Once again, the form and the content of Scripture here prove to be inseparable. And it is precisely the most obvious and easily overlooked formal features – writtenness, communal function, bipartite construction – that turn out to be the most significant.

There are, of course, other such formal features. Two that have recently attracted particular attention are the genres of the biblical texts and the canonical limit. In the first case, a particularly fruitful development has been the rediscovery of the narrative form of many of the biblical writings in its integral relation to their content. In the second case, discussion is dominated either by purely historical issues or by the assumption that a canonical limit is inherently oppressive, and that recovery of the texts and groups it marginalized is an ethical obligation. Here, too, attention to the form/content relationship might suggest a more constructive way forward.

See also BIBLICAL THEOLOGY; HERMENEUTICS; INERRANCY.

B. S. Childs, *Introduction to the Old Testament as Scripture* (SCM, 1979).

H. W. Frei, *The Eclipse of Biblical Narrative: A Study in Eighteenth and Nineteenth Century Hermeneutics* (Yale University Press, 1974).

D. H. Kelsey, *Proving Doctrine: The Uses of Scripture in Modern Theology* (Trinity, 1999 [1975]).

P. Ricœur, *Hermeneutics and the Human Sciences: Essays on Language, Action and Interpretation* (Cambridge University Press, 1981).

F. Watson, *Text and Truth: Redefining Biblical Theology* (T&T Clark, 1997).

J. Webster, *Holy Scripture: A Dogmatic Sketch* (Cambridge University Press, 2003).

FRANCIS WATSON

SECOND COMING: see PAROUSIA.

SECULAR HUMANISM: see HUMANISM.

SECULARIZATION Secularization refers to an epochal process through which every facet of western society (political, sociological, economic, and religious) transitioned from ecclesial to non-ecclesial authority. Described by sociologist M. Weber (1864–1920) as 'the disenchantment of the world', the results of this process are perhaps best encapsulated in C. Taylor's (b. 1931) question, 'Why was it virtually impossible not to believe in God in ... 1500 in our Western society, while in 2000 many of us find this not only easy, but even inescapable?' (*Sec.* 25). While one might locate the seeds of secularization even earlier, the 500-year period Taylor references marks the genesis, articulation, maturation, and defence of this wide-ranging phenomenon.

At its height in the nineteenth century, secularization spoke of a cultural optimism that ENLIGHTENMENT reason, NATURAL SCIENCE, liberal democracy, market capitalism, and religious TOLERANCE would finally replace sectarian religion's stranglehold on western civilization. Energized by advancements in every sector of society from architecture to social roles, secularization imagined a type of public space whereby citizens could freely exist in a commonwealth no longer policed by religion. Yet hidden beneath its iconoclastic mantra, *Sapere aude!* ('Dare to know!'), secularization spirited its own self-justifying traditions, practices, narratives, and discourses even as it denigrated religion for those prejudices. In this way, secularization is a process that must be continuously reproduced, enacted, and performed, so that the justification of secularization ensues as a self-legitimating narrative. Hence, in recent years, scholars from every discipline have begun to rethink the terms of secularism, to the point where J. Milbank (b. 1952) could make the unexpected claim, 'Once there was no "secular" ... The secular as a domain had to be instituted or *imagined*, both in theory and practice' (*Theol.* 9).

Even those who would otherwise celebrate the cultural demise of CHRISTENDOM may lament secularization's agendas and the moral realities that have materialized in its wake, and an increasing number of detractors have arisen to interrogate secularization and offer interventions on its processes. For example, in renaming secularization 'dechristendomization' T. Larsen (b. 1967) rejects the arrogance of secularization while affirming the theological benefits of its political aspirations. Other thinkers have identified the ways in which secularization, in its efforts to rid or at least discipline religion, has displaced traditional forms of life dependent on religion.

Secularization has elicited a number of responses ranging from reactionary religious FUNDAMENTALISM to a redefinition of secular goals and methods, and Christianity has situated itself within many of these various articulations. For some, Christianity can be easily fitted within the terms of secularism by culling certain objectionable facets of the latter, while for others religious faithfulness mandates protracted resistance against secularism's idolatries. For example, D. Martin (b. 1929) and S. Bruce (b. 1954) have observed how religious sectarianism historically rendered religious toleration and pluralism characteristic of secularization, in turn producing two divergent yet conjoined responses on the part of Christians: the accommodating stance of Protestant liberalism and the oppositional stance of fundamentalist sectarianism. Thus, the two options available to a religious community in a secularized world are adaptation and rejection. The sociological impact of these two options is the same: the growth of secular space that guards its boundaries against the intrusions of religion.

There can be little doubt that Christianity and Christian theology have had to contend with secularization and find new articulations within its age. The effort to find religious expressions has led to what P. Berger (b. 1929) terms 'movements of counter-secularization', characterized by novel religious forms and passions. Berger contends that religion continues to play a social and/or political role even when the practice of that religion has diminished significantly.

P. L. Berger, J. Sacks *et al.*, *The Desecularization of the World: Resurgent Religion and World Politics* (Eerdmans, 1999).

S. Bruce, *A House Divided: Protestantism, Schism, and Secularization* (Routledge, 1990).

A. C. MacIntyre, *Whose Justice? Which Rationality?* (University of Notre Dame Press, 1989).

JONATHAN TRAN AND DANA BENESH

SEGUNDO, JUAN LUIS Juan Luis Segundo (1925–95), Catholic and Jesuit, anticipated and then participated in the first wave of the LIBERATION THEOLOGY of Latin America during the last third of the twentieth century. Born in Montevideo, Uruguay, he studied theology in Europe, first in Louvain, Belgium, and then in Paris during the 1950s. He was awarded the *Doctorat ès Lettres* by the University of Paris in 1963.

Segundo began his extensive career as a theological writer in the early 1960s with works dedicated to the INCULTURATION of the message and practice of the Church into the problems of the people of Latin America. He never held a university position as a professor of theology but founded and taught at a centre for theological reflection in 1965. When it was suppressed by the right-wing Uruguayan government in 1975, he continued to write and to lecture abroad.

Segundo learnt the centrality of freedom from N. Berdyaev (1874–1948), the embeddedness of thought in history from K. Marx (1818–83), and an evolutionary perspective from P. TEILHARD DE CHARDIN. His best-known works are his five-volume synthesis of Christian FAITH, written in an accessible style, entitled in English

Theology for Artisans of a New Humanity (1973–4), and a five-volume CHRISTOLOGY, including a FUNDAMENTAL THEOLOGY, entitled *Jesus of Nazareth Yesterday and Today* (1984–8). They represent an activist spirituality of engagement in the 'kingdom' project of history.

In contrast to some of his liberationist colleagues, Segundo reflected the largely secular and developed environment of Montevideo and mainly addressed a middle-class audience: for him, professionals and managers represented the dynamic element in society. But his theology was thoroughly shaped by a PREFERENTIAL OPTION FOR THE POOR.

See also LATIN AMERICAN THEOLOGY.

F. Stefano, *The Absolute Value of Human Action in the Theology of Juan Luis Segundo* (University Press of America, 1992).

ROGER HAIGHT, S. J.

SEMI-PELAGIANISM: see PELAGIANISM.

SENSUS FIDELIUM The Latin phrase *sensus fidelium* means 'sense of the faithful' and refers to the principle in CATHOLIC THEOLOGY that the CHARISM of INFALLIBILITY, though associated especially with the Church's MAGISTERIUM, is shared by all the faithful. The Dogmatic Constitution on the Church of VATICAN COUNCIL II states: 'The entire body of the faithful, anointed as they are by the Holy One, cannot err in matters of belief' (*LG*, §12). At the same time, the Constitution is clear that this 'supernatural discernment in matters of faith' (*supernaturalis sensus fidei*) is a function of the universal agreement of clergy and LAITY and thus is always 'exercised under the guidance of the sacred teaching authority' of the magisterium (*LG*, §12; cf. *Cat.*, §889).

This insistence on the guiding role of the magisterium helps guard against identifying the sense of the faithful either with simple majority opinion or with the prevailing sensibilities of a particular historical period. Nevertheless, the belief that DOCTRINE can develop 'through the contemplation and study made by believers ... of the spiritual realities which they experience' (Vatican Council II, *DV*, §8) gives the category of the *sensus fidelium* significant practical importance in Catholic theology. For example, the logic (if not the language) of the *sensus fidelium* was instrumental in defining the dogma of the IMMACULATE CONCEPTION (Pius IX, *Ineffabilis*, §5), and proponents of LIBERATION THEOLOGY have used the concept to stress the mutual accountability of hierarchy and laity in matters of theological judgement.

IAN A. MCFARLAND

SEPTUAGINT The Septuagint (LXX) is the oldest and most influential Greek translation of the OT. The name (from the Latin for 'seventy') comes from the legend that the translation was undertaken by seventy-two Jewish scholars at the command of the Egyptian ruler Ptolemy II Philadelphus (r. 283–246 BC). Modern scholars concur that the LXX originated in Alexandria between the third and first centuries BC. Regarded by the Jewish exegete Philo of Alexandria (*ca* 20 BC–*ca* 50) as divinely inspired, the LXX gained wide acceptance among Hellenistic Jews and is the version of the OT most frequently cited in the NT. It was partly in reaction to its appropriation by Christians that the LXX was eventually abandoned by Jews in favour of the Hebrew Masoretic Text (MT).

The LXX is more extensive than the MT, including the books rejected by JEROME and later Protestants as APOCRYPHA. It is also based on a different Hebrew original, leading to significant differences in the texts of certain books (e.g., Esther is longer and Job shorter in the LXX than in the MT). Though the LXX was the standard OT text among early Christians, Jerome's decision to base his VULGATE translation on the MT diminished its influence in the western Churches. Yet it is regarded as canonical SCRIPTURE by Orthodox Christians. The Orthodox Council of Jerusalem (1672) confirmed the OT canon as coextensive with the LXX, on the grounds that the Church's reception of the apocrypha is no less ancient than – and correspondingly inseparable from – its reception of the Gospels.

IAN A. MCFARLAND

SERMON ON THE MOUNT The longest continuous discourse attributed to Jesus in any of the canonical Gospels, the Sermon on the Mount runs from Matthew 5:3 to 7:27. Within the context of Matthew, the Sermon portrays Jesus as a new Moses who, like his predecessor, goes up a mountain (Matt. 5:1; cf. Exod. 19:3) to expound God's LAW (Matt. 5:17; cf. Exod. 19:7). It begins with the nine beatitudes (5:3–12), which describe the characteristics of Jesus' disciples that render them 'blessed' (i.e., happy) in the KINGDOM OF GOD. These are followed by Jesus' interpretation of the Mosaic law (5:17–48), in which he contrasts established teaching ('You have heard that it was said') with his own understanding ('But I say to you'). The Sermon continues with a series of contrasts between true and false piety (6:1–18) that includes the LORD'S PRAYER (vv. 9–13), followed by teaching on material goods (6:19–34). It concludes with a combination of warnings and exhortations about the practice of discipleship (7:1–27).

The Sermon has proved influential among non-Christians like M. K. Gandhi (1869–1948) as well as within the Church, though its proper interpretation continues to be a matter of debate. A central point of contention is how commands like the prohibition of oath-taking (5:34–7) and non-retaliation (5:39) are to be understood. In CATHOLIC THEOLOGY such principles have been understood as evangelical counsels that are binding only on those with a particular (viz., religious) VOCATION, in distinction from evangelical precepts (e.g., the Ten COMMANDMENTS) that are binding on all

Christians. During the Reformation this view came under sharp criticism. Anabaptists insisted that the Sermon's commands were binding on all Christians, and, correspondingly, refused to bear arms or swear oaths (see Mennonite Theology). Lutheran and Reformed theologians also insisted that Jesus intended his words to apply to all Christians, but they argued that his purpose was not to encourage obedience; rather, it was to show the impossibility of perfect obedience, so that they would come to rely on Christ's righteousness rather than their own.

The modern period has seen the emergence of still other approaches. Drawing on renewed appreciation of the degree to which Jesus' thought was shaped by eschatological expectation, A. Schweitzer (1875–1965) argued that the Sermon was meant to be taken literally, but that it represented an 'interim ethic' that presupposed an imminent end to the world. By contrast, D. Bonhoeffer challenged his own Lutheran tradition by reading the Sermon as a permanent summons to Christians, who can share in Jesus' grace only if they follow his path. From another perspective, R. Niebuhr argued that the Sermon represents an ethical ideal that can motivate social reform even though it is unrealizable in practice. He has been opposed by a range of thinkers, including W. Wink (b. 1935), who sees in Jesus' teaching a practical programme of resistance to imperial power, and S. Hauerwas (b. 1940), who interprets the Sermon as a means of schooling Christians in how to live in ways that challenge the assumptions of secular society.

Ian A. McFarland

Session, Heavenly: see Ascension and Session.

Seven Deadly Sins According to Catholic moral theology, to commit any sin is to choose a good which is disproportionate or disordered because it does not harmonize according to reason with human nature's fundamental inclination to the good. What causes someone to sin is complex, but one important element is that emotion takes over and pushes reason towards a false goal that is perceived more by feeling and may not be a real and legitimate need. Generally all disordered emotions push persons to sin but especially anger, sadness, and the desire for pleasure. Reason and will can co-operate with these disordered desires, leading to voluntary sin. The so-called seven deadly (or, more properly, seven capital) sins are those personal evils that flow from these feelings, moods, emotions, or passions, when they are attached to a disordered object or goal.

For T. Aquinas, the seven capital vices or sins – vainglory, avarice, envy, anger, gluttony, lust, and acedia (sometimes called sloth) – are the lieutenants of the chief of these vices, namely pride. Each of these lieutenants, when active, gives birth to certain dispositions to other sins. While thinkers differ on the particular vices with which they correlate these offspring, Aquinas always follows the opinion of Pope Gregory the Great (r. 590–604).

In the mind of Aquinas, then, there are really eight capital vices, but pride inspires the rest by refusing to live according to the limits or determinations set by God, as reflected in the natural law. However, many sins are committed not because of pride but due to weakness and ignorance following a false or erroneous conscience. Likewise, the first movements of these vices are only sins in a loose sense, because they are not yet consented to and when repulsed become the building blocks of virtues. Pride, vainglory, avarice, lust, and gluttony arise from false and chosen desires. Anger, which can be part of the virtue of justice or even charity, is its own sin when excessive. Finally, envy and acedia result from sadness and depression.

The *Catechism of the Catholic Church* conflates pride and vainglory into one vice and calls it pride (§1866). Pride can be either a particular vice as the inordinate desire for one's own excellence or a general vice of aversion from God. In this latter form it is the chief of the capital vices. By contrast, vainglory, though similar to pride, is the excessive desire for honour and praise from others. It usually comes about as a result of feeling inadequate and the individual feels the need for affirmation for its own sake. Its offspring are disobedience, boastfulness, hypocrisy, contention, obstinacy, discord, and love of novelties, all of which attempt to show others one's apparent or even real excellence.

Avarice may come about as a result of either pride or vainglory, but at its root it is a desire for material things for their own sake, perhaps to show off, perhaps to simply feel one's own excellence or power. Its offspring are treachery, fraud, falsehood, perjury, restlessness, violence, and insensibility to mercy.

Envy is a sadness at the success or good achieved by another. Someone's good fortune or even virtue is seen by someone captivated by this vice as a personal threat. Its offspring are tale-bearing, detraction, joy at another's misfortune, and grief at another's prosperity. The *Catechism* adds to this notion that it is a refusal of charity (§2540), which would be a rejoicing in the goodness of someone else as a gift from God to the community.

Anger wishes to punish someone verbally or legally because of a perceived injustice, which may be an illusion based upon an overly inflated opinion of oneself on any level. If someone thinks they are very handsome and is then contradicted, feelings of anger emerge. On the other hand, when real injustice occurs, it is reasonable to have anger to get the energy necessary to combat it. Sometimes, it can be a sin *not* to be angry when it is called for. Nevertheless, sinful anger's offspring are quarrelling, swelling of the mind, contumely, clamour, indignation, and blasphemy. The *Catechism* simply says that it is a desire for revenge (§2302).

Gluttony is easy to understand in principle as an excess in eating and drinking. It should be said that it is often not so easy to judge about one's own intake of food and drink: for what seems to be an excess in one person may in fact be reasonable. Its five offspring are unseemly joy, scurrility, uncleanness, loquaciousness, and dullness of mind.

Lust is simply the desire for the pleasure of sex for its own sake, whether married or unmarried. In treating one's spouse as an object of pleasure by sheer intentionality, as if he or she were an object of use, or simply enjoying pornography, lust does not really love. The person does not give herself to another and so may not be open to love and life. The offspring of this vice are many: blindness of mind, thoughtlessness, inconstancy, rashness, self-love, hatred of God, love of this world, and abhorrence or despair of a future world.

Finally, acedia is a vice of sadness, distinct from clinical depression, whereby someone begins to have no sense of morality. According to the *Catechism* (§2094), joy in God disappears. What is truly good is seen or perceived as an evil to be avoided, and what is truly a moral evil is pursued as a good. There are six offspring flowing from this vice: malice, spite, faint-heartedness, despair, sluggishness in regards to the COMMANDMENTS, and wandering of the mind after unlawful things.

T. Aquinas, *Summa theologiae* 2/2.35–6, 118, 132, 148, 153, 158, 162.
De Malo 8–15.
B. Cole, O. P., *The Hidden Enemies of the Priesthood* (Alba House, 2007).

BASIL COLE, O. P.

SEXUALITY The term 'sexuality' is a recent import into Christian theology and its theological uses remain unsettled. For theologians working in English, it began to gain currency only after 1950, when the cultural prominence of both psychoanalysis and sexological research pushed the term and its topics into academic speech. The term is now widely used in English-speaking theology, but its popularity has not made it any clearer. Like many of the concepts that theologians have borrowed from new sciences, 'sexuality' brought with it a confused history.

In English, 'sexuality' was originally a biological term for one degree or another of sexual differentiation. It was applied to the elements, processes, or effects of sexual reproduction in plants and animals. When applied to human beings, the term referred generally to erotic tendencies or dispositions, though these were still conceived reproductively as between male and female. A decisive shift away from reproductive contexts came at the end of the nineteenth century, when the term was redeployed alongside a cluster of new diagnoses for variations of sexual desire or behaviour that were considered pathological. 'Sexuality' was redefined as if reasoning backwards from specific diagnostic categories. Granted the clinical existence of homosexuality and heterosexuality, for example, it seemed that beneath them or before them there must be sexuality itself – that is, the complement of sexual impulses that could be configured in relation to particular objects, acts, or aims. This meaning of the term can be seen just before 1950 in statistical studies of human sexual behaviour (such as the original 'Kinsey Report') and in English translations of S. Freud's (1856–1939) writings on human sexual development.

When 'sexuality' passed soon thereafter into Christian theology, it often carried sexological or psychoanalytic connotations, but it also continued to serve as a euphemistic generalization for the whole of human erotic life. What is theologically significant is that in both its clinical and its generalized meanings, the term named human sexual desire and behaviour in relation to the pursuit of pleasure rather than procreation. It thus presented in miniature an old puzzle for Christian thinking: what are the created status and present moral value of sexual pleasure itself? When theologians began to speak of sexuality, they often betrayed their difficulty in conceiving erotic pleasures apart from the procreative purposes that Christianity had so long invoked to justify them.

Even after Christian theologians imported the term and its confusions, they were still not its primary users. Its meanings continued to change with developments outside theology. One significant change linked sexuality to sexual orientation conceived as an identity. 'Orientation' is a loose directional metaphor that could refer to many aspects of sexual preference, but in current usage it is restricted to the anatomical sex of one's preferred partners. Sexual orientation is conceived as a persistent desire for partners of one's own sex, of the other sex, or of both sexes – and the conception of orientation almost inevitably reinforces the notion that there are only two sexes, with nothing in between them or beyond them. A persistent desire for same or other or both is taken to reveal the person's psycho-social identity as homosexual, heterosexual, or bisexual. In contemporary English, having a sexual orientation means having an identity that is also described as a sexuality within the grid of heterosexual, homosexual, or bisexual. In these contexts, the term has not progressed much beyond the turn of meaning it took at the end of the nineteenth century, except that the imagined grid is now more restrictive.

In other contexts, the meaning has been greatly expanded – and repeatedly undone. Since the 1970s, 'sexuality' has figured prominently in feminist debates, where it has been defined and redefined in relation to two other terms, 'sex' and 'gender'. Many feminist thinkers have been intent on separating the facts of human sexual difference from the cultural discriminations built upon them, precisely so that they could deny patriarchal claims that female anatomy entails societal subordination. In their arguments, sexuality often occupies a middle place between anatomy and culture. It floats uneasily between fixed sex and conventional gender as a configuration of sexual desire that seemed partly genetic or physiological, partly conventional or personal. In some recent forms of feminism, especially those in conversation with Queer theory, distinctions between natural and conventional or fixed and changeable have been dislocated. One tendency has been to stress that both gender and sexual identity are constituted by compelled performances. On these accounts, to be a woman or a homosexual is to be coerced into citing the declarations or behaviours that make one into a woman or a homosexual. Another tendency has questioned the fixity of anatomy through critiques of ideological bias in medico-scientific knowledge or from evidence of transsexual identification and bodily modification. Recent feminist writing has also stressed the impossibility of discussing sexuality in abstraction from race, class, and other social markers.

Such a complicated and ongoing history suggests how many risks there are in borrowing 'sexuality' for use in Christian theology. Despite the risks, theologians have come to rely on the term because it promises to do what inherited Christian vocabularies cannot. Most obviously, the category of 'sexuality' helps Christian ethicists, pastoral counsellors, and religious educators reformulate the Churches' sexual teaching in the face of rapid changes in both expert and popular views of numerous sexual topics. Beginning in the late 1920s, for example, scientific and economic predictions about overpopulation pushed a growing number of denominations to reconsider their prohibitions against contraceptive practices within Christian marriages. These debates raised fundamental questions about the morality of sexual intercourse apart from an intention to procreate. Because the category of sexuality encapsulated just this separation, it proved useful in elaborating Christian justifications for the goods of married sex beyond PROCREATION – though it hardly settled the debates.

More troublesome for Christian thinking was the growing cultural acceptance of psychological or psychoanalytic models for the development of human sexuality from infancy to adolescence. The new models presented sexuality as a primary human impulse towards pleasure that was only indirectly tied to reproduction. They implicitly or explicitly contradicted theologies that appealed to reproduction in order to excuse sexual pleasure in a fallen world. The contradiction appeared at many points, but perhaps most clearly with regard to masturbation. From the eighteenth century onwards many Christian theologians were vociferous proponents of medical and educational campaigns against adolescent masturbation. They made extraordinary claims about its evil effects from scriptural exegesis or ethical argument, and they collaborated in severe measures to prevent and punish it. As the new models of human sexual development spread, these campaigns appeared to be cruel deductions from bogus premises. Masturbation, far from being a morbid pathology or a damning sin, began to seem a natural stage of sexual development. Though some denominations still condemn masturbation, most have mitigated their judgement in pastoral practice and almost none would endorse the sorts of campaigns against masturbation that once featured Christian leaders. They have done this by relying on developmental narratives embedded in the category of sexuality.

Christian ethics and pastoral theology have also appropriated the category when addressing rapid changes in the social acceptance of homosexuality. Over the span of a few decades, some historically Christian countries have moved from counting any homosexual activity a serious crime to recognizing same-sex unions or marriages. These legal changes have been accompanied by a more uneven, though still striking, shift in public attitudes within and without the Churches. Christian ethicists now share no consensus on homosexuality, but some patterns of disagreement are visible over the last half-century. Citing accumulating discoveries about created sexuality, some Christian ethicists urge a reform of Christian judgements on a range of sexual cases, including homosexuality. They propose replacing many of the inherited judgements with norms that stress mature consent, absence of harm, equality of power, covenanted faithfulness, and responsibility to the community. Ethicists in this group tend to evaluate relations between members of the same sex using the general moral norms they would apply to married relationships. A second group of Christian ethicists responds to the changes around homosexuality by insisting that the ideal sexual relationship for Christians remains a lifelong marriage of man and woman ordered to procreation, but they then mitigate negative judgements on those who cannot attain the ideal because of physiological or psychological limitations. So they might encourage believers who are constitutionally incapable of a heterosexual marriage to form permanent homosexual unions. A third group reaffirms not only the inherited ideals, but specific prescriptions about permissible sexual acts. These ethicists typically judge that same-sex genital relations are serious sins. Sometimes they advance a critique of the cultural relativism that they detect in sexology or psychoanalysis, but more recently they have enlisted psychological theories to support their condemnations.

The strategy of the third group illustrates some unsettling consequences of importing the category of sexuality into Christian theology. The category has indeed enabled Christian ethicists, pastors, and educators to join contemporary conversations about human sex that are driven by sexological or psychological assumptions. If it had refused to speak about sexuality or to narrate developmental stages, Christian theology would have been excluded from important public conversations and would have fallen silent before striking social changes. But joining those conversations through the language of sexuality has introduced a double discontinuity into Christian speech. One side of it is a historical discontinuity between modern Christian formulations and earlier theological vocabularies for classifying human sexual acts and their origins in fallen desire. The other side is an explanatory discontinuity between Christian sexual ethics and the basic accounts of the human being as a creature called to share in divine life (see THEOLOGICAL ANTHROPOLOGY).

The heat of Church controversy can conceal the historical discontinuity, especially because some controversialists insist that they are only repeating the letter of SCRIPTURE or Church TRADITION. In fact, the great majority of contemporary Christian authors about sex, including the most 'conservative', rely on terms and categories that would have been unrecognizable to Christian ethicists of even the mid-nineteenth century. Terms like 'sexuality', 'heterosexuality', and 'homosexuality' cannot be convincingly translated back into the Greek of the NT or the various forms of Latin used in western Christian moral theology up until the early modern period. This is not a matter of words only, but of the concepts they carry. The models of human psycho-sexual development that Christian ethicists of all types now share cannot easily be aligned with the pictures of human agency that underwrite the inherited library of Christian sexual ethics. As so often, debates over homosexuality showcase this more general problem. Some ethicists who wish to uphold inherited condemnations of same-sex acts concede that an individual's upbringing might have made heterosexual relations impossible. They counsel lifelong celibacy. Others who sustain the condemnations argue that there is therapeutic hope for undoing childhood patterns and so for entering heterosexual marriage successfully. Both positions presume models of the psychological genesis of homosexuality that contradict traditional accounts for which same-sex desire is the consequence of IDOLATRY, an occult inheritance from the city of Sodom, a contagious pollution, or demonic trickery. To conceive homosexuality as the result of psychological modifications of sexuality during infancy or childhood marks a major break from traditional Christian explanations of the desire.

The break between applied ethics and theological accounts of the human creature that comes with appropriating sexuality as a category of Christian ethics is illustrated by the fact that any assertion of sexual pleasure as a basic human good or as an intrinsic element of healthy adulthood meets resistance in canonical Christian anthropologies. Some of the resistance comes over the importance of sexuality in human life. Many forms of Christianity exalt or bless celibacy, pointing not only to the unmarried example of Jesus, but to the expressed wish of PAUL (1 Cor. 7). More general resistance to claims for sexuality arises from Christian analyses of the deep disorders of sinful desire. The BODY or the flesh are ancient Christian emblems for the fallen human condition, and theologians have often cited lust as a clear example of how original sin disrupted original human nature. There was constant suspicion of excessive pleasures within marriage – even by Christian traditions that made marriage almost obligatory. More positively, the eschatological hopes of Christian communities have often pictured human fulfilment beyond sex, in an angelic heaven where the redeemed are 'neither married nor given in marriage' (Matt. 22:30). Thus, a new Christian ethics of sexuality requires a fundamental reworking of theological anthropology.

The troubling consequences for theology of appropriating the category of sexuality go one step further, to the very prominence of sexuality in many contemporary cultures. M. Foucault (1926–84) famously claimed that this obsession with sexuality was a by-product of a new regime for managing the life and death of sexed bodies, a regime he called 'bio-power'. Foucault also suggested, less famously but no less significantly for Christian theology, that sexuality had rushed in to fill the void left by the 'death of God' in late modern cultures. The collapse of the old FAITH and of the certainties based upon it gave way to a new faith and a new certainty – about the saving importance of sexuality rightly exercised. The most important task for Christian theology might be to assess how far the category of sexuality is in fact implicated in prevailing regimes of power and their creeds. Christian theology might then offer, as both ethics and anthropology, alternative languages for redeeming desire, not least out of its own library of mystical testimonies, Church rituals, and liturgical poetry.

M. De la Torre, *A Lily among the Thorns: Imagining a New Christian Sexuality* (Jossey-Bass, 2007).
K. B. Douglas, *Sexuality and the Black Church: A Womanist Perspective* (Orbis, 1999).
S. J. Grenz, *Sexual Ethics: A Biblical Perspective* (Word, 1990).
C. E. Gudorf, *Body, Sex, and Pleasure: Reconstructing Christian Sexual Ethics* (Pilgrim, 1994).
M. Jordan, *The Ethics of Sex* (Blackwell, 2002).
H. Thielicke, *The Ethics of Sex* (Harper & Row, 1964).

MARK D. JORDAN

SHEOL: see HELL.

SHOAH: see HOLOCAUST.

SIMUL JUSTUS ET PECCATOR The Latin phrase *simul justus et peccator* means 'righteous and a sinner at the same time' and refers to a defining feature of the DOCTRINE of JUSTIFICATION in LUTHERAN THEOLOGY in particular. The phrase refers to the belief that the Christian is, on the one hand, completely sinful (and thus worthy of DAMNATION) when considered in terms of her own merits, but, on the other hand, also entirely righteous before God (i.e., justified, and thus worthy of salvation), by virtue of the fact that her sin has been covered by the righteousness of Christ. In other words, while the Christian can claim no righteousness of her own, she is justified by virtue of the righteousness of Christ (in Latin, *justitia aliena*, or 'alien righteousness').

The principle of *simul justus et peccator* was defined by M. LUTHER over against Catholic theologies of justification, according to which the work of justification involved the gradual increase of the individual believer's own righteousness, through a combination of God's free gift of GRACE and a person's own meritorious works. From this perspective, the more righteous one becomes, the less one is a sinner. Luther objected to this zero-sum understanding of the relationship between SIN and righteousness on the grounds that it leads the Christian to look to herself rather than to Christ alone as the ground of her salvation. Catholic theologians respond that it is theologically unacceptable to suggest that God declares someone righteous unless that person is objectively righteous.

See also SOTERIOLOGY.

IAN A. MCFARLAND

SIN The term 'sin' refers to a disordered or disrupted relationship to God. In Christian theology sin is first and foremost a theological concept, that is, a form of opposition or alienation from God, and only secondarily a moral category that designates wrongful actions or deeds. Classically the DOCTRINE of sin (or hamartiology) belongs to the doctrine of CREATION. At the core of the doctrine is the claim that sin is not intrinsic to human beings, who were graciously created in all their finitude as good. Sin signifies a falling away or distortion of humankind's original perfection through disobedience to God's beneficent will. Since sin enters the world by human choice, it incurs objective guilt in human beings. An equally significant aspect of the Christian notion of sin is its overarching soteriological context (see SOTERIOLOGY). God ultimately acts in the world through Christ *not* to judge the sinner, but rather to vanquish sin and accomplish human beings' salvation.

While the OT does not contain the idea of an original sin per se, Genesis 2–3 set the stage for the subsequent development of the idea. According to Genesis 3:1–7, sin arises through Adam and Eve's disobedience to the will of God. When they disobey God's directive not to eat from the tree of the knowledge of good and evil, they incur God's wrath and reap harsh consequences for themselves and all generations to come. While DEATH is not the immediate punishment for their actions, the cascade of violent events in Genesis 3–12 demonstrates that the consequences of human disobedience are both radical and far-reaching: sin disrupts the relationships between husband and wife, within families, among tribes and nations, and indeed with the rest of the created order.

Among the NT writers, it was PAUL who took the decisive step towards formulating the doctrine of original sin. Particularly in Romans 3:22–6 Paul argues for humanity's solidarity in sin based on the universal salvific will of God manifest in Christ. If all are saved in Christ, Paul contends, then all must have fallen in Adam. According to Paul, it is the function of the LAW to convict humankind of its sin. While the law is in itself good, it alone cannot justify humankind for the law is powerless to prevent individuals from succumbing to the power of sin. Christ is the only answer to human sin, by taking it unto himself and destroying it through his death and his rising to new life. Through faith in Christ, human beings are released from the slavery of sin and reborn into new life.

AUGUSTINE's theology of sin and GRACE quickly became the cornerstone of the western doctrine of sin, though it was by no means the only account of sin circulating in the early Church and has never been embraced within ORTHODOX THEOLOGY. Drawing on Paul's connection between sin and desire, Augustine defined sin as a disorder in the desires or loves of humankind, in which the creature places his or her love of self, of others, or of objects in the world before the love of God. Sin is pride (Latin *superbia*): a form of self-exaltation in which human beings place their will above that of God's and, in so doing, assume God's place as ultimate judge. Despite Augustine's ambivalent attitudes towards the BODY (and especially towards SEXUALITY), he did not root sin ultimately in the flesh. The wayward will lies at the heart of sin, and it affects us *in toto*, clouding our minds, disordering the desires of our bodies, and fracturing human beings' relationship with God, with one another, and with themselves.

Building on Paul's Adam–Christ typology in Romans 5:12–21, Augustine also formulated what became the classical western doctrine of *original* sin: a term that signifies both the first historical sin of humankind and the bondage to sin that afflicts all of humankind thereafter. According to Augustine, Adam fell when he refused to obey God's command. Although his nature as a creature of God was not destroyed, his nature was so seriously wounded that it was no longer able to avoid and conquer sin. Human beings are therefore no longer capable of discerning and pursuing the good unequivocally, and sin becomes inescapable (*non posse non peccare*). According to Augustine, human beings transmit this fundamental distortion of the will (CONCUPISCENCE) to the next generation through natural procreation as well as social reproduction. Particularly in his later writings against PELAGIANISM, Augustine stressed human beings' complete reliance on the unmerited grace of God given in and through Christ for the forgiveness of their sins and the healing of their disordered desires.

In the Middle Ages T. AQUINAS reworked the basic features of Augustine's theology of sin. Though upholding the notion of a historical FALL, he did not view the Garden of Eden as a paradise, but rather as a world in which Adam and Eve experienced TEMPTATION, toil, and spiritual struggle. They were able to withstand temptation and sin because they were sustained by God's habitual grace in a state of original righteousness. In turning away from God, however, Adam and Eve lost the gift of habitual grace on which their perfection rested. Aquinas defined the essence of sin formally as the loss of this original righteousness, and materially as concupiscence (i.e., the inordinateness of desire that becomes habitual in human beings with the loss of habitual grace). Aquinas argued for the biological transmission of sin through procreation, so that all individuals inherit an already distorted nature.

In the later Middle Ages J. DUNS SCOTUS revised Aquinas' theology of sin. For Scotus, concupiscence is a natural power of the soul and therefore cannot be the essence of sin, or else human beings would have been created fallen. Along the same lines, he argued that sin did not damage the nature of human beings, only their will, causing individuals to misuse their freedom. It was partly in response to this late Scholastic insistence on the postlapsarian integrity of human nature that the Protestant Reformers radicalized the western doctrine of sin. For example, M. LUTHER argued that sin distorted human nature *in toto* so that no natural righteousness remained at all in humankind. For Luther, original sin represents an active propensity towards evil that manifests itself in rebellion, self-centredness, and self-exaltation. Human beings seek to be their own judges, thereby usurping the role of God. Through such misguided self-trust, we mistake God, ourselves, and the world for what they truly are. For Luther, however, this is not cause to despair, since the Church provides an inn or infirmary for those who are sick and are in need of being made well.

Modernity brought severe challenges to the western doctrine of sin. For one, the modern concept of freedom as self-determination undermined a key tenet of the doctrine of original sin, namely, that every human being shoulders responsibility and guilt for sins that one did not personally commit. Also, the rise of historical criticism, along with developments in modern science, threw into doubt the traditional belief in a historical fall event, before which creation was free of disease, labour, and mortality, and after which all these natural evils suddenly emerged. According to the natural historical record, no such pristine state ever existed. So, too, evolutionary biology belies the notion of MONOGENISM, the idea that all of humankind stems from a common pair of ancestors, Adam and Eve, from whom they inherit a fundamental defect in their constitution. Without such a natural unity of all humankind, a new basis had to be found upon which to claim the universality of sin.

The most recent challenge to the western doctrine of sin arises from diverse POLITICAL and LIBERATION THEOLOGIES. Representatives of these theologies criticize the Augustinian tradition as too individualistic and overly focused on the internal dynamics of the soul and focus attention instead on social or structural sin – those systems that diminish human flourishing through oppression, domination, and exploitation of others. Moreover, political and liberation theologians question the traditional insistence on humankind's solidarity in sin, on the grounds that it obscures the differences between the perpetrators and the victims of sin, and renders it difficult to assign specific moral responsibility for injustices and for their remedy. Finally, feminist liberation theologians argue that certain western concepts of sin are themselves complicit in oppressive social systems; notions of sin as pride or wilful disobedience can be used as a mechanism of social control, i.e., to quell resistance to oppressive circumstances – be it among women or other socially marginalized groups (see FEMINIST THEOLOGY).

Under the pressure of these diverse modern critiques, the western theology of sin has been reconstructed in the twentieth century in unprecedented ways. Most notably, sin has been reconceived as a dilemma of the human subject – a false relationship to one's self characterized by existential alienation or anxiety. In modern THEOLOGICAL ANTHROPOLOGIES (e.g., those of R. NIEBUHR, P. TILLICH, and K. RAHNER) selfhood is understood as a task to be achieved through the exercise of personal freedom. Here sin appears either as a misplaced trust in oneself as the sole master of one's destiny or else as a failure to become a self, that is, to exercise one's freedom altogether. Rather than treating the fall as a historical event, the fall signifies a mythic reality that is realized in each person's self-consciousness, as he or she experiences the ongoing tension between their capacity for self-transcendence and the contingency of human existence. While these accounts of sin capture well the dilemma of creaturely freedom, they risk equating finitude with fallenness and psychologizing sin in such a way as to dissipate an individual's objective guilt before God. In addition, feminist theologians have criticized the paradigm of sin as the self-arrogating will as androcentric: it misdiagnoses the nature of women's alienation which might be better described as hiding, triviality, or self-loss (see ANDROCENTRISM).

A second reconstruction of sin put forward by political and liberation theologians interprets sin within the broader scheme of the divine redemption of creation. Here sin is a corruption of right relations, a societal self-contradiction that manifests itself in unjust and oppressive relationships among genders, races, or classes of society. Sin is defined primarily in social terms, but individuals commit sin by participating in rather than resisting oppressive structures and social systems. While liberationist accounts of sin prophetically disclose and critique structures of oppression, they also strain human solidarity in sin; in so doing, they risk demonizing one portion of humankind while too easily exonerating others.

A third strategy for reconstructing sin locates the doctrine within Christology. K. Barth pioneered this path, by defining Jesus Christ as the ontological basis of human beings. According to Barth, human beings discover the true nature of sin by looking at the mirror of Jesus Christ, in whom sin is exposed, judged, and overcome. Here one discovers sin's essence as the fateful attempt to live for oneself rather than for God and for one another. For Barth, sin is an 'impossible possibility' in so far as it has been already vanquished in Christ. Nonetheless, sin is real, since humanity seeks again and again to negate its total dependence on God. Barth rejects the notion of inherited original sin, on the grounds that it undercuts personal responsibility and guilt for one's actions. Nonetheless, he affirms universal human solidarity in sin; we are all in Adam in so far as God's judgement against this first man falls equally upon all of us. While Barth's Christological approach highlights well the theological dimension of sin as opposition to God, his analysis can at the same time appear as too abstract and remote from actual human existence to capture the existential realism of sin.

In the wake of these diverse efforts to reconstruct the doctrine of sin, little consensus exists today in Christian theology about the future direction of the doctrine. Some theologians continue to defend humankind's universal bondage to sin, by focusing on the social reproduction of sin through cultural–linguistic structures that human beings inherit and perpetuate through their own agency. Others advocate jettisoning the traditional fall narrative altogether in favour of a process or tragic view of creation, in which vulnerability to sin and evil is built into the matrix of creation. Still others focus on exposing a host of actual sins, be they forms of political, economic, or ecological exploitation and violence. For those who seek to defend the doctrine of original sin today, the perennial task remains: how to maintain the realism of humankind's bondage to sin, while also retaining a sense of human agency and moral responsibility. Even more, the challenge remains to construe sin as a 'grace-dependent' concept, that is, one which leads not to despair but rather to greater hope and trust in the universal salvific will of God in Christ.

See also Free Will.

K. Barth, *Church Dogmatics* (T&T Clark, 1956–8), IV/1–2.

S. Jones, *Feminist Theory and Christian Theology: Cartographies of Grace* (Fortress Press, 2000).

D. H. Kelsey, 'Whatever Happened to the Doctrine of Sin?', *Theology Today* 50:2 (1993), 169–78.

A. McFadyen, *Bound to Sin: Abuse, Holocaust and the Christian Doctrine of Sin* (Cambridge University Press, 2000).

I. McFarland, 'The Fall and Sin' in *The Oxford Handbook of Systematic Theology*, ed. J. Webster, K. Tanner, and I. Torrance (Oxford University Press, 2007), 140–59.

R. Williams, 'Sin and Evil' in *Christian Theology: An Introduction to Its Traditions and Tasks*, ed. P. C. Hodgson and R. H. King, updated edn (Fortress Press, 1994), 168–95.

Joy Ann McDougall

Sobornicity 'Sobornicity' comes from the Russian noun *sobornost* (adjective *sobornyj*), which means 'co-operation' or 'togetherness'. The concept was introduced to ecclesiology by Russian poet and theologian A. Khomyakov (1804–60). In Khomyakov's view, *sobornyj* is the correct Slavic translation of the Greek word 'Catholic' in the Nicene Creed, and it connotes 'universal' not in the geographic, territorial sense, but as a perfect, organic fellowship of redeemed people united by faith and love. In Khomyakov's words, 'The unity of the church follows of necessity from the unity of God; for the church is not a multitude of people in their separated individualities, but the oneness of a divine grace indwelling in reasonable creatures who freely submit themselves thereto' (*Church* II.3). Khomyakov does not narrowly believe that sobornicity is experienced in the historical reality of the Orthodox Church, but rather as belonging to the image of the Church which is comprehensible to the mind.

Khomyakov's ecclesiology was influenced by the German Catholic theologian J. A. Möhler's *Unity in the Church* (1825). In turn, Möhler (1796–1838) himself responded to and was influenced by Protestant theologian F. Schleiermacher. Khomyakov's and Möhler's views have influenced today's ecclesiology of communion, an ecclesiology with a proven potential to foster the ecumenical dialogue not only among Catholics and Orthodox but with Protestants as well. *Sobornyj* also made its way into the Romanian Orthodox translations of the Nicene Creed (as *sobornicească*) to express the catholicity of the Church. Romanian Orthodox theologian D. Stăniloae took the theology of *sobornost* one step further when in 1971 he introduced the concept of 'open sobornicity' as a tool meant to foster ecumenism.

Reflecting the patristic tradition, Stăniloae believed that during Pentecost the Holy Spirit infuses a common way of thinking in those who come to believe, making them understand one another despite all the differences of expression which may exist among them. This common way of thinking symbolizes the unity in diversity that the Church should reflect, because those who have received the same understanding preserved their distinctive languages. In his concept of 'open sobornicity', Stăniloae combined three elements: (1) Khomyakov's *sobornost* as a communion of persons and a unity in diversity, (2) the Pauline idea (1 Cor. 12:19–20) that the variety of gifts in the Church complement one another in order to satisfy every spiritual need of the faithful and of the entire Church, and (3) spiritual intercommunion – a practice promoting common prayer, study, and action (but not Eucharistic hospitality) among the Orthodox and other Christians.

In 'open sobornicity' every theological system is welcomed as offering some valid theological insight and contributing to a better understanding of the whole revealed divine reality and of the whole human reality. New ways to express the divine reality appear as complementary rather than contradictory. Through openness to others, one's understanding is enriched, and a more symphonic, although not uniform, understanding of the divine reality is achieved. Nevertheless, the weaknesses of each system must be criticized, because no system is capable of comprehending the entire divine reality.

D. Stăniloae, 'The Holy Spirit and the Sobornicity of the Church' in *Theology and the Church* (St Vladimir's Seminary Press, 1980), 45–72.

L. Turcescu, 'Eucharistic Ecclesiology or Open Sobornicity?' in *Dumitru Stăniloae: Tradition and Modernity in Theology*, ed. L. Turcescu (Center for Romanian Studies, 2002), 83–103.

Lucian Turcescu

Social Gospel In the late nineteenth and early twentieth centuries, movements for Christian Socialism arose and thrived in England, Germany, Switzerland, and several other industrializing nations. The American version arose in the early 1880s; it generally favoured decentralized economic democracy instead of State socialism; and it came to be called the 'Social Gospel'. For thirty years this movement was usually called 'applied Christianity' or 'social Christianity'. It created key ecumenical organizations in the mid-1880s, swept into leading seminaries and several denominations in the 1890s, and became a dominant religious movement in the first decade of the twentieth century. From 1897 to 1900, a radical Christian community in Muscogee County, Georgia, called the Christian Commonwealth Colony published a magazine named 'The Social Gospel'. By 1910 this term was used to designate the movement for social Christianity as a whole, which was then at the height of its influence and expectation.

The Social Gospel was not novel for its promotion of social causes, as the USA was the site of numerous anti-war, anti-slavery, temperance, and other Christian reform movements before the Progressive Era. What made the Social Gospel novel was its theology of 'social salvation', which depended on the idea of social structure, which was itself a product of the distinct social consciousness of the Progressive Era.

Only with the Social Gospel movement did Churches in the USA begin to say they had a mission to transform the structures of society in the direction of social justice. If there was such a thing as social structure, salvation had to have a social dimension. Not coincidentally, the Social Gospel, social salvation, social ethics, socialism, sociology, social Darwinism, and the term 'social justice' all arose at the same time, along with trade unionism, urbanization, corporate capitalism, and the ecumenical movement (see Ecumenism). Theologically, the Social Gospel was based on the idea that personal salvation and social salvation were inextricably interlinked. In the Social Gospel, society became the subject of redemption; Christianity had a mission to transform society as a whole.

The Social Gospel was fed by the wellsprings of eighteenth-century Enlightenment humanism, the nineteenth-century Home Missions movement, and the post-Civil War activism of the evangelical and liberal anti-slavery movements. Most of its early leaders were products of the evangelical Home Missions movement, which sought to extend and deepen the Protestant character of the United States. A few were spiritual descendants of the anti-slavery abolitionists of the 1840s and 1850s. The Social Gospel took root as a response to the corruption of the Gilded Age and the rise of industrialization and urbanization, goaded by reformist writers such as E. Bellamy (1850–98), S. Colwell (1800–72), H. George (1839–97), and H. Lloyd (1847–1903). It took inspiration from the Christian Socialist movement in England and rode on the back of a rising sociological consciousness and literature.

Above all, the Social Gospel was a response to a burgeoning labour movement, which blasted the Churches for doing nothing for poor and working-class people. Christian leaders judged that it was pointless to defend Christianity if labour leaders were right about the indifference of modern Churches to the struggles of working people.

The Social Gospel and liberal-theology movements were not identical, as some theological conservatives supported the Social Gospel and some theological liberals did not. In the south of the United States the Social Gospel tended to be conservative theologically. But the two movements rose to prominence at the same time in the north, where they were usually deeply intertwined.

The founders of the Social Gospel were W. Gladden (1836–1918), a Columbus, Ohio, Congregational pastor; R. Ely (1854–1943), an Episcopalian and Johns Hopkins University political scientist who co-founded the American Economic Association in 1885; W. Bliss (1856–1926), a Boston Episcopal priest who founded the Society of Christian Socialists in 1889; F. Peabody (1847–1936), a Unitarian and Harvard University professor who founded the discipline of social ethics; and

J. Strong (1847–1916), a Congregational minister and home missionary who organized major Social Gospel conferences in 1887, 1889, and 1893 as director of the Inter-Denominational Congress and the Evangelical Alliance of the United States.

These founders believed that modern scholarship had rediscovered the social meaning of Christianity in the kingdom-centred religion of Jesus. They embraced the theory of EVOLUTION and BIBLICAL CRITICISM, emphasized the immanence of God and the 'Godlikeness' of Jesus, and upheld a moral-influence view of ATONEMENT. Most of them idealized Anglo-Saxon culture and were inclined to say that American imperialism was not really imperialism, because of its good (democratic) intentions. As early advocates of sociology, they believed in the disciplinary unity of social science and its ethical character, which gave rise to social ethics. On a popular level the Social Gospel received a huge boost from C. Sheldon's (1857–1946) novel, *In His Steps* (1897), which urged readers to ask themselves, 'What would Jesus do?' For thousands of readers, Sheldon's idealism captured the essence of the gospel and legitimized the Social Gospel movement.

The greatest Social Gospel theologian and movement advocate was W. Rauschenbusch (1861–1918). A Northern Baptist, he ministered to a poor immigrant congregation in the Hell's Kitchen district of New York City in the 1890s; joined the faculty of Rochester Seminary in 1897; published a manifesto for Christian Socialism, *Christianity and the Social Crisis* (1907), which galvanized the entire movement; wrote several books and spoke widely during the movement's heyday; and published its defining theological textbook, *A Theology for the Social Gospel* (1917), one year before his death. *Christianity and the Social Crisis* was the movement's signature work, notwithstanding that it was politically more radical than the movement's mainstream. Rauschenbusch described the teaching of Jesus as a message of radical social transformation, offered an analysis of why Christianity obscured the revolutionary content of the GOSPEL, and urged that it was not too late for the Church to adopt the way and spirit of Jesus. In a closing chapter, 'What to Do', he made a rhetorically powerful case for democratic socialism.

In 1918 the newly founded Federal Council of Churches, comprising thirty-two denominations, issued a 'Social Creed of the Churches' that reflected the spirit and expectations of an ascending Social Gospel movement. It called for a living wage in every industry, abolition of child labour, the elimination of poverty, and wealth redistribution. The high tide of the movement's optimism came in 1912, when three of the four candidates in the US presidential election vied for the votes of progressives and Rauschenbusch contended in *Christianizing the Social Order* that most of American society was already 'Christianized', a term he used interchangeably with 'democratized'. The holdout was America's unregenerate economic system, which he characterized as predatory and selfish. Politically, the Social Gospel was a vision, even in its milder forms, of an increasingly co-operative and peaceful society.

This faith in the progress and essential goodness of modern democratic culture flew in the face of the vicious racism of American society, where the oppression of African Americans intensified during the very period that northern Social Gospelers proclaimed that American society was being 'Christianized'. Many Social Gospel leaders said little or nothing about racial injustice in response; others settled for building up African American schools, colleges, and universities, principally through the programmes of the American Missionary Society. A Black Church tradition of the Social Gospel took root in the 1890s, led by anti-lynching activists I. Wells-Barnett (1862–1931) and R. Ransom (1861–1959). It was active in the Federal Council of Churches, but White Social Gospelers rarely treated Black Christian leaders as equal partners in the building of social Christianity. Although most Social Gospel leaders supported the movement for women's suffrage, they shuddered at seeing women pursue careers outside the home.

The Social Gospel movement strongly resisted American intervention in World War I – until the USA declared war in 1917, whereupon most Social Gospelers promptly retracted their opposition and baptized the war as a mission to 'make the world safe for democracy'. Afterwards many of them regretted their support for the war and vowed never to do it again. The Social Gospel lost its world-changing energy and ambitions during the war, but it remained a powerful force in American Protestantism in the 1920s and 1930s, principally as an anti-war movement. Most mainline Protestant denominations vowed in the 1930s never to endorse another war, a situation that caused former Social Gospeler R. NIEBUHR to attack the Social Gospel for its pacifist idealism. Leading Social Gospelers of the 1920s and 1930s included Methodist bishop F. McConnell (1871–1953), *Christian Century* editor C. Morrison (1874–1966), Federal Council of Churches official C. MacFarland (1866–1956), pacifist author K. Page (1890–1957), and theologians G. Harkness (1891–1974) and S. Mathews (1863–1941).

S. Curtis, *A Consuming Faith: The Social Gospel and Modern American Culture* (University of Missouri Press, 1991).

G. Dorrien, *The Making of American Liberal Theology*, 3 vols. (John Knox Press, 2001–6).

R. T. Handy, ed., *The Social Gospel in America, 1870–1939* (Oxford University Press, 1966).

C. H. Hopkins, *The Rise of the Social Gospel in American Protestantism, 1865–1915* (Yale University Press, 1940).

R. E. Luker, *The Social Gospel in Black and White: American Racial Reform, 1885–1912* (University of North Carolina Press, 1991).

GARY DORRIEN

SOCINIANISM Derived from the name of the Sienese theologians L. Sozini (1525–62) and his nephew, F. Sozzini (1539–1604), 'Socinianism' was a term used by opponents for an anti-Trinitarian branch of the REFORMATION that first took root in Poland (where the younger Sozzini lived from 1579 until his death) and later attracted followers in the Netherlands and England. L. Sozini (who, unlike his nephew, spelled his name with a single 'z') had converted to PROTESTANTISM in the 1540s and spent time in Wittenberg, Basel, and Geneva before finally settling in Zurich. After his death, his nephew used his personal papers as the basis for an *Explicatio* of the prologue to the Gospel of JOHN (1563). He subsequently developed his uncle's ideas further in the treatise *De Jesu Christo servatore* (1578), rejecting both the DOCTRINE of the TRINITY and the classical CHRISTOLOGY of CHALCEDON in favour of a form of ADOPTIONISM, according to which God the Father bestowed divine rank and universal lordship on Christ at the ASCENSION as a reward for his obedience.

The chief doctrinal standard of the Socinian movement was the Racovian Catechism, published in 1605 in the Polish city of Raków for the Minor Reformed Church (or Polish Brethren), an anti-Trinitarian group that had broken away from the main body of Polish Reformed Christians in 1563, and with which Sozzini later became affiliated. Sozzini himself compiled the first draft of the Catechism, which was completed by colleagues after his death. The Catechism bears clear marks of its Protestant roots in its insistence on the sufficiency of SCRIPTURE over against TRADITION. At the same time, it breaks decisively with the main line of the Protestant theology developed in both Lutheran and Reformed confessions by its rejection of the Trinitarian and Christological dogmas of the ancient ecumenical COUNCILS. Instead, it affirms a strictly Unitarian doctrine of God and, correspondingly, that Jesus of Nazareth had a human nature only and was not the incarnation of a pre-existent divine person. Christ's soteriological significance consists in his status as a divinely commissioned teacher and moral example, sent by God to show people the way to eternal life. The Lord's Supper (see EUCHARIST) is only a commemoration of Christ's death and not a means of GRACE. Similarly, BAPTISM merely signifies a believer's commitment to follow Christ and is thus not appropriately given to infants.

Though it characterizes both the Trinity and Chalcedonian Christology as repugnant to reason, the Racovian Catechism is no less insistent that they are contrary to the witness of Scripture. Its teaching therefore should not be confused with DEISM or other forms of religious RATIONALISM. On the contrary, the Catechism accepts the doctrine of Christ's VIRGIN BIRTH and RESURRECTION as well as the biblical accounts of Christ's MIRACLES, and cites them as confirmation of Christ's status as God's chosen means to communicate the divine will to humankind. This strong affirmation of the supernatural dimensions of Christ's life renders Socinianism distinct from (though a precursor of) contemporary UNITARIANISM, as well as from DEISM and later RATIONALISM.

IAN A. MCFARLAND

SOELLE, DOROTHEE Dorothee Soelle (1929–2003), a German Catholic theologian, earned her Habilitation in philosophy in 1971 and taught for twelve years at Union Theological Seminary in New York. She influenced theologians as prominent and diverse as J. Moltmann (b. 1926) and R. Williams (b. 1950), yet her largest readership is outside the academy. Her writings range over a wide field, from her first book, *Christ the Representative* (1967), an academic work on CHRISTOLOGY, to the reflections collected in books like *Against the Wind* (1999). The tension between the need to follow Christ through suffering and the need to resist unjust suffering runs through Soelle's works. In *Suffering* (1975), she explicitly refuses what she calls 'Christian masochism', insisting that accepting 'the way of Jesus means also to hold onto the paradox' of the unity of CROSS and RESURRECTION (166). Two decades later, *The Silent Cry* (2001) links the strength of SOUL cultivated by core practices in mystical (and, to a lesser degree, ascetic) forms of Christian life to the power to resist the forces of oppression in the struggle for liberation.

Whether in poetry or in theological argument, Soelle held fast to the vision of God's redemption; she was interested in experiences of God as well as in the political work for social justice. She did not establish a 'school,' but she did influence many who heard in her voice both the love of God and the justice of God. The legacy of her work is a vision of Christian practice that combines the themes of resistance and mysticism in a FEMINIST THEOLOGY of liberation.

See also LIBERATION THEOLOGY.

S.K. Pinnock, ed., *The Theology of Dorothee Soelle* (Trinity Press International, 2003).

D. Soelle, *Suffering* (Fortress Press, 1984).

MEDI VOLPE

SOLA FIDE: see JUSTIFICATION.

SOLA GRATIA: see JUSTIFICATION.

SOLA SCRIPTURA Since the REFORMATION, the phrase *sola Scriptura* ('[by] scripture alone') has been used by Protestants to denote their opposition to Catholic acceptance of SCRIPTURE and unwritten TRADITION as valid sources of authority for Christian Churches. In conflict with the PAPACY, M. LUTHER defended his views by telling Cardinal Cajetan (1468–1534) in 1518 that 'divine truth, that is Scripture, is also master over the pope and I do not await human judgment when I have learned the judgment of God' (*Proc.* 277). At Worms in 1521 he declared: 'Unless I am convinced by the testimony of the scriptures or by clear reason, ... I am bound by the Scriptures I have quoted and my conscience is captive to the word of God' (*Diet* 112). In neither case did Luther mean to exclude other authorities entirely. In debate he often appealed to early Christian theologians like AUGUSTINE, but Scripture remained the final authority.

Sola Scriptura was a flexible principle with implications that were utilized by other reformers. Introducing his sixty-seven propositions for debate in 1523, H. ZWINGLI declared that he had preached them on the basis of Scripture and that he would permit himself to be better instructed but only 'out of the aforementioned scriptures' (*Art.* 37). J. CALVIN condemned the notion that Scripture received its authority from the Church, writing that 'Scripture exhibits fully as clear evidence of its own truth as white and black things do of their color, or sweet and bitter things do of their taste' (*Inst.* 1.7.2). According to W. Tyndale (*ca* 1495–1536), every baptized Christian could perceive the true meaning of Scripture 'if our hearts were taught the appointment made between God and us in Christ's blood when we were baptized' (*Exp.* 141). More than their magisterial counterparts, radical reformers insisted on a strict application of *sola Scriptura* to Christian life.

In 1546 the Council of TRENT declared that both written Scripture and unwritten traditions contained the truth of the GOSPEL (*Scrip.*), and in 1564 Pius IV (r. 1559–65) required assent to the proposition that the correct interpretation of the Bible was determined by the Church (*Injunc.*). In response, Protestant confessions and theologians from the late sixteenth to the seveneenth century maintained that Scripture was the sole and sufficient norm of FAITH and life. Though the precise nature of the relationship between Scripture and tradition is debated in Catholic circles, VATICAN COUNCIL II seemed to reaffirm a long-standing difference between Catholic and Protestant Churches when in 1965 it declared both Scripture and unwritten tradition to be sources of divine REVELATION (*DV*, §9).

Nonetheless, modern Protestants disagree among themselves about the meaning of *sola Scriptura*. Many conservative Churches have insisted on a literal reading of biblical verses that export their meanings directly to individuals without taking context critically into account (see INERRANCY). Most mainline Protestants, however, acknowledge that canonical Scripture speaks with authority not primarily to individuals but to Christian communities and that believers in those communities, aided by the Holy Spirit and one another, discern its meaning for their life together. In the words of K. BARTH, 'if Holy Scripture alone is the divine teacher ... we will not want to find ourselves in this school of the church without fellow-pupils, without cooperation with them, without the readiness to be instructed by older and more experienced fellow-pupils: as fellow-pupils, but to be instructed' (*CD*, I/2, 606–7).

SCOTT H. HENDRIX

SOPHIOLOGY: see ORTHODOX THEOLOGY.

SOTERIOLOGY The term 'soteriology', from the Greek *sōtēria* (salvation) and the Latin *soter* (saviour), refers in Christian theology to issues having to do with salvation. According to the most commonly held teachings of the Christian Church, God creates the world good, it falls into SIN and evil, and is redeemed by God through COVENANT with ISRAEL and its descendants by what culminates with Jesus Christ (see CHRISTOLOGY). The prominence of the salvific issues posed by these claims in Christian faith and doctrine becomes evident from even a brief overview of some of their most basic (1) scriptural elements, (2) elements in the history of DOCTRINE, (3) disputes over them that have occurred in this history, and (4) present-day emphases regarding them.

Characteristic of the OT affirmations is the Psalmist's confession that it is God alone from whom salvation comes (Ps. 62:1–2). In addition to the divine 'work' of creation (Gen. 2:1–3), God is described as 'working salvation in the earth' (Ps. 74:12). In the Pentateuch the God who alone is said to have called the good creation into being, and in Genesis 3 is then depicted as calling 'Where are you?' when the first human beings fall into disobedience and hide themselves from the presence of the Lord God, is also said to bring deliverance from bondage in the exodus from slavery of the chosen people Israel. The later prophets proclaim an extension of this deliverance to other peoples as well: 'Did I not bring Israel up from the land of Egypt, and the Philistines from Caphtor and the Arameans from Kir?' (Amos 9:7b). God's saving work from the particularity of Abraham's descendants to the promised universality of God's blessing to 'all the families of the earth' (Gen. 12: 3) is prophesied as comparable to nothing less than a new CREATION (Isa. 65:17). While the saving significance of such testimony carries a connotation of an afterlife 'for ever' in some OT writings (though not in others), a consistent message is that both life and death, individually and corporately, are subject to the *hesed*, or steadfast LOVE, of God that 'endures for ever' (see, e.g., Ps. 106:1; 107:1).

God's making of an 'everlasting covenant' with God's people, as it is repeatedly recalled throughout the OT, does not exempt them from affliction, nor does it allow them to evade the wrathful judgement of God upon their own evil doing. Thus in the Hebraic traditions of the OT there are issues of salvation raised with respect both to the innocent *affliction* of evil suffered and to the culpable *infliction* of evil caused by sin. What is variously attested to be saved by God's PROVIDENCE and reconciliation in each instance is the ultimate victory of God's righteous judgement of loving kindness, as well as what it incorporates as new creation over all that is inimical and in deadly opposition to it.

In the NT the coming of Jesus upon the scene as 'the one born in the city of David a Saviour, who is the Messiah, the Lord' (Luke 2:11) is introduced in Luke's account of JOHN THE BAPTIST's preparing the way by recalling the prophesy of Isaiah 40:3–5 that 'all flesh shall see the salvation of God' (Luke 3:6). The good news of God's salvation becomes focused upon what happens with Jesus, a name so chosen, according to Matthew, because it signifies one who will 'save his people from their sins' (Matt. 1:21). Of this good news concerning Jesus Christ as 'Son of God', PAUL writes that it is this GOSPEL that is 'the power of God for salvation to everyone who has faith, to the Jew first and also to the Greek' (Rom. 1:16). Equally, the Gospel of JOHN attests that God's sending of the Son into the world as God's Word made flesh was in order 'that the world might be saved through him' (John 3:17). The letters attributed to Paul, especially, provide the terminology and patterns of reflection that later come to mark the traditional tenets of the Church's soteriological doctrine. 'GRACE', 'JUSTIFICATION', 'SANCTIFICATION', 'reconciliation', 'ATONEMENT', 'redemption', 'PREDESTINATION', 'righteousness', 'works', as well as the 'CROSS', 'sin', and 'salvation', are rubrics employed historically in addressing the saving work of God who in Christ 'was reconciling the world to himself, not counting their trespasses against them, and entrusting the message of reconciliation to us' (2 Cor. 5:19–20). The testimony of Ephesians 2:8–10, whether from Paul's own hand or from one close to him, becomes a touchstone of Church teaching, that salvation is the gift of God's grace through FAITH, not the result *of* our works, but *for* the good works for which God has created us in Christ.

In sum, the writings in the NT canon in distinctive ways share a prime soteriological witness. To be saved is to be where Jesus Christ is, embraced in the grace of God-with-us, crucified, risen, and glorious, from which nothing in life and death can separate us (Rom. 8:38–9). In this Jesus Christ 'was life' is the message of John 1:4. 'The free gift of God is eternal life in Christ Jesus' is Paul's testimony in Romans 6:23.

When we turn to elements in the subsequent history of Church soteriological doctrine we see the earliest ecumenical councils confronting two decisive questions regarding this proclaimed gift of life in Christ. The one leading up to the first ecumenical council at NICAEA is whether the life that faith confesses to know in Jesus really is God's own eternal life, or something less. Against the Arians and others who held that it was something less (see ARIAN CONTROVERSY), the decision of Nicaea was that this life is *HOMOOUSIOS tōi patri* ('of the same substance with the Father'). This is the Nicene decision defended by ATHANASIUS OF ALEXANDRIA in his influential work *On the Incarnation of the Word.* The second and ensuing question is whether this life that faith confesses to know in what happens with Jesus is really our own true human life, or something other. Against positions implying that it was something other, the Council of CHALCEDON affirmed that this life in what happens with Jesus is *homoousios hēmin* ('of the same reality as we are ourselves', except for sin) just as truly as it is *homoousios tōi patri.* Chalcedon confesses the so-called 'two natures' of Jesus Christ to be *concurring* happenings by characterizing them adverbially as the actual taking place together – 'without confusion, without change, without division, without separation' – of our own true human life together with God's own eternal life in what comes to pass with Jesus. As J. CALVIN expresses it, Christ becomes for us 'Immanuel, that is, God with us ... in such a way that his divinity and our human nature might by mutual connection grow together' (*Inst.* 2.12.1).

How what happens with Jesus Christ's living and dying and rising affects our own and others' living and dying and rising is a question that atonement theories historically have sought to address in meditating upon how the righteousness of a just God is rendered its due in such a way that unjust creatures are thereby reckoned righteous, or justified, by faith. Atonement accounts differ in their emphasis as to whether the focus is upon how a righteous God looks with grace upon the fallen creature in Christ, or how the fallen creature is enabled by grace to look to God, but what is at stake in either instance is the belief that there is no affliction or infliction of evil befalling creation that is out of bounds to what takes place with Jesus Christ. In the words of Gregory of Nazianzus (see CAPPADOCIAN FATHERS), 'that which is not assumed is not healed' (*Ep.* 101) or, expressed positively, by virtue of Christ's assuming our humanity all that afflicts our humanity has become subject to Christ's healing power. Church doctrines of salvation speak of those God reckons justified as also sanctified, or made whole and holy, in a life of continuing *metanoia*, of repentance and changed orientation. This sanctification is said to involve a daily dying and rising with Christ, a mortification and vivification enacted in the sacraments of BAPTISM and EUCHARIST and in the discipleship of taking up the cross by ministering to, in Jesus' reported words, 'the least of these, my brothers and sisters' (Matt. 25:40, 44).

What comes to the fore in the REFORMATION, most associated with M. LUTHER, are different perceptions about the most faithful ways to affirm the relation between the *ability to respond* to saving grace without works of our doing and the *responsibility* in grace for our doing of good works. This pivotal issue is posed by Paul's claims of a paradoxical synergy of divine and human working with respect to saving grace: 'Work out your own salvation with fear and trembling; for it is God who is at work (*energōn*) in you, enabling you both to will and to work for his good pleasure' (Phil. 2:12–13); 'But by the grace of God I am what I am, and his grace towards me has not been in vain. On the contrary, I worked harder than any of them – though it was not I, but the grace of God that is with [*syn*] me' (1 Cor. 15:10). Such testimony gives rise to debates over the role of human works in the economy of salvation.

At their core the primary doctrinal differences, as notably identified since the fifth century with disputes between Augustinianism and Pelagianism, revolve around the scope and role of divine and human agency in the operation of God's saving grace and the freedom of the will (see Free Will). These are disputes over the determinative role of God's freely predestining will in Christ and the limits versus the universality of God's saving grace. Divisions arise as to whether such grace is offered with the proviso that it is conditional upon our act of acceptance – as articulated by J. Arminius (1560–1609), favoured by J. Wesley, and preached by modern revivalists, '*if only*' we desire such help – or whether faith as the individually predestined gift of grace to those who are elect instead actually 'produces both the will to believe and the act of believing also', as the Synod of Dort countered. In the twentieth century K. Barth notably dissents from both an Arminian synergism of conditional grace and Calvinism's 'double decree' of an individualized election of some to salvation and others to rejection by affirming that in Jesus Christ's exclusively inclusive election and rejection 'the whole world' has 'objectively' been reconciled 'without its merit or co-operation', even though 'the hand of God has not touched all in such a way that they ... perceive [it]' (*CD* IV/I, 148).

Present-day soteriological emphases provide fresh evidence of continuing differences regarding the scope and role of divine and human agency by bringing to the forefront concerns for the social contextualization of salvation as liberation. These are epitomized by the refusal to divorce the slavery of sin from the sin of slavery, or to view Luther's labelling of the ability to respond to grace without works as 'passive righteousness' as other than the activation of our responsibility to engage in the work for justice. Particularly prominent in contemporary discussions are questions over the import of Christian claims to the exclusiveness and inclusiveness of the life in Christ. These are voiced from a broad range of theological perspectives that (to indicate only several of the most representative examples) primarily address issues of religious pluralism, of the wellbeing of women for whom the result of self-demeaning self-disparagement may be seen to characterize sin more truly than traditionally defined notions of prideful self-assertion, of sexual minorities and Queer studies, of the poor for whom the biblical God is recognized to exercise a preferential option, and of the broader than anthropocentric ecology of an environmentally threatened planet and what is required for its just habitation.

See also Ordo salutis.

Augustine, *On the Predestination of the Saints*, in *Basic Writings of Saint Augustine*, vol. I (Random House, 1948), 777–817.

H. U. von Balthasar, *Theo-Drama: Theological Dramatic Theory*, vol. IV: *The Action* (Ignatius Press, 1994).

M. Luther, *The Freedom of a Christian*, in *Martin Luther's Basic Theological Writings*, 2nd edn (Fortress Press, 2005), 386–411.

J. Moltmann, *The Way of Jesus Christ: Christology in Messianic Dimensions* (HarperCollins, 1990).

C. Morse, 'Salvation' in *Not Every Spirit: A Dogmatics of Christian Disbelief*, 2nd edn (T&T Clark, 2009), 225–55.

R. R. Ruether, *Sexism and God-Talk* (Beacon Press, 1983).

Christopher Morse

Soul For much of the Christian tradition, 'soul' has referred to the spiritual part of a human distinct from the physical, often understood as an ontologically separate entity constitutive of the human person. In his treatise on the soul, Tertullian wrote,

> 'The soul, then, we define to be sprung from the breath of God, immortal, possessing body, having form, simple in its substance, intelligent in its own nature, developing its power in various ways, free in its determinations, subject to the changes of accident, in its faculties mutable, rational, supreme, endued with an instinct of presentiment, evolved out of one [archetypal soul]' (*An.* 22).

Ancient controversy regarding the origins of the soul notwithstanding, Tertullian accurately represents the theological tendency to assert (following the teaching of Platonism) the soul's immortality and its superiority over the body, including the related view that the person is detachable from his or her body, which, then, requires discipline in order to function as the soul's instrument. Theologians ancient and contemporary have found in body–soul dualism either the necessary supposition or the corollary of a number of theological *loci*, including creation in the divine image (see Theological Anthropology), free will and moral responsibility, hope of life after death, and ethics.

Objections against traditional body–soul dualism have arisen especially on two fronts. The first is biblical studies, which is almost unanimous in its support of a monist anthropology. The second is neuroscience which, since its seventeenth-century beginnings, has demonstrated at every turn the close mutual interrelations of physical and psychological occurrences, documenting the neural correlates of the various attributes traditionally allocated to the soul. Biblical scholars have underscored the testimony of Genesis that the human person does not possess a 'soul' but *is* a soul, noting that the same is also true of animals, who are 'souls' or, better, 'living beings' (Hebrew *nepheš*; cf. Gen. 1:30; 2:7). More generally, they have argued that the OT shows a general lack of interest in human essences while presenting the human person in profoundly relational terms. The background on which the NT writers drew was heavily influenced by Israel's Scriptures, but also by Greco-Roman perspectives on body and soul. The latter were more varied than usually represented. Although belief in a form of body–soul duality was widespread in philosophical circles, for example, most philosophers regarded the soul as composed of 'stuff'. Moreover, among ancient medical writers, one finds a keen emphasis on the inseparability of the internal processes of the body ('psychology') and its external aspects ('physiology'), since any differentiation between inner and outer was fluid and permeable. Taken as a whole, the biblical witness affirms the human being as a bio-psycho-spiritual unity and provides no support for the later substance dualism of R. Descartes (1596–1650). Accordingly, the term 'soul' would refer to embodied human life and especially to embodied human capacities for personal relatedness vis-à-vis the cosmos, the human family, and God.

Nevertheless, how best to account philosophically for the data remains controversial, not least among those who seek a terminological specificity beyond the more general categories offered by Scripture and the theological tradition. Current options among Christian philosophers and theologians include those excluding a distinct metaphysical entity, such as a soul, to account for human capacities as distinctive. For example, according to *non-reductive physicalism* distinctive human capacities are explainable in part as brain functions, but their full explanation requires attention to human social relations, cultural factors, and God's action in our lives. In *emergent monism* what emerges in the case of humans from the one, material substance is a psychosomatic unity capable of mental and physical activity. Finally, *constitutional monism* holds that human persons are constituted by their bodies without being identical with the bodies that constitute them. Among those emphasizing a second, metaphysical entity, proponents of *emergent dualism* argue that the mind/soul is generated and sustained as a discrete substance by the biological organism, and its activities are subserved and enabled by the functioning of the organism, while *holistic dualism* teaches that the human person, though composed of discrete elements, is nonetheless to be identified with the whole that constitutes a functional unity.

J. B. Green, *Body, Soul, and Human Life: The Nature of Humanity in the Bible* (Baker Academic, 2008).

N. Murphy, *Bodies and Souls, or Spirited Bodies?* (Cambridge University Press, 2006).

J. P. Wright and P. Potter, eds., *Psyche and Soma: Physicians and Metaphysicians on the Mind–Body Problem from Antiquity to Enlightenment* (Oxford University Press, 2000).

Joel B. Green

South Asian Theology The scope of South Asian theology is quite complex and wide due to several reasons. The geographical area of South Asia includes India, Pakistan, Bangladesh, Sri Lanka, and Nepal. Each of these nations has a different history with regard to the arrival and growth of Christianity. Each of them, while having a common history of British colonialism, has had distinctive political developments after colonial times. Such historical variety has influenced the development of Christian theologies in these nations, and theologies are developed in either colonial or postcolonial modes. South Asia is also the home of three major religious traditions other than Christianity, namely Buddhism, Hinduism, and Islam, in addition to Jainism, Sikhism, Zoroastrianism, and several traditional or primal religions. This multiplicity introduces variety into South Asian theology depending on the religious tradition with which a Christian theologian engages in conversation. Moreover, there are several hundred languages spoken in South Asia, such as Hindi, Urdu, Tamil, Sinhalese, Nepali, Bengali, and so on, each with its own massive literary corpus. Due to the colonial past, the English language is widely used in the whole area and most professional theological thinking and writing has depended on and emerged in English. Yet linguistic variety leads to multiple types of theologies because language not only offers a medium for theology but also shapes it through the distinctive categories and thought forms available. More recently, there has been increasing appreciation of the complexity of Christian theology in light of the impact that the social location of the theologian (e.g., in terms of class and caste) has on theological activity in South Asia. Given this complexity and breadth, one can only highlight in broad strokes the major developments, current debates, and future directions of theology in South Asia.

Among the nations in South Asia, India was the earliest to come in contact with Christianity, with the earliest work of evangelization traditionally ascribed to the apostle Thomas. It is quite probable that Sri Lanka and Pakistan had Christian communities by the fifth century. Since these early communities were accommodated into the existing religious settings without any noteworthy theological interaction, one would not find specifically South Asian theology as such during the early centuries. Starting with the arrival of the Portuguese at the beginning of the sixteenth century, Catholicism was introduced in South Asia. Protestant traditions came alongside of the East India Company's commercial enterprise in India and through the work of mission societies in the West. These traditions were assisted in their expansion by British colonial power. Catholics and Protestants dealt with the Hindu, Muslim, and other religious traditions in India mostly in a condescending manner because of the prevailing assumption of the superiority of European culture on the one hand, and the kind of missionary theology that sustained an expansionist view of Christian mission on the other (see Missiology). Even though a theology of separation from local culture and religion was promoted in such encounters, the Christianity practised by the people was much more syncretistic, with liturgical and ritualistic practices of Christians in South Asia reflecting a theology of accommodation and adaptation from the very beginning. An intentional and conscious attempt at contextual theologizing began in the nineteenth century and has continued through the twentieth and twenty-first centuries.

Since theological traditions of the West have been seen as the benchmark of proper theology in many other parts of the world, theology in South Asia finds itself in a position of differentiating itself from and defining itself over against western theological tradition. Such an anti-western stance coincided with the growing nationalism in the nineteenth and twentieth centuries and the emergence of independent nations freed from colonial powers during the middle of the twentieth century. One can easily detect such a stance in the writings of Indian theologians such as B. Upadhyaya (1861–1907), M. M. Thomas, K. T. Paul (1876–1931), and P. D. Devanandan (1901–62), and Sri Lankan theologians including S. Kulandran (b. 1900) and D. T. Niles. There has been a serious engagement with theological method as such because it gives to South Asian theology its distinctive character. The discussion of sources, hermeneutics, and methods in relation to Hindu and Buddhist philosophical traditions has been pivotal for this enterprise.

South Asian theologians found themselves in a setting where other saviours and paths to salvation were already present in religious traditions other than Christianity. None of them had to deal with the question of God as such, even though the understanding of the Ultimate was very different in various Hindu, Buddhist, and Islamic traditions. It was the figure of Christ as the one and only saviour that became the chief bone of contention. This meant that most of the South Asian theologians worked on Christology more than any other discipline within the Christian theological enterprise. Christ is seen as *Cit* (Upadhyaya), *avatar* (V. Chakkarai (1880–1957)), and so on. Since Hindus and Buddhists focused more on the teachings of Christ (e.g., R. M. Roy (1772–1833), M. K. Gandhi (1869–1948), and others), Christian theologians constructed Christologies that intentionally went beyond Christ as teacher.

Due to the missionary history of South Asian Christianity, theological writings tend to have a more 'apologetic' character than an intra-ecclesial catechetical form (see Apologetics). Theology is used to answer the question of how one might make the Christian faith intelligible to people who do not belong to the Christian community. Behind this desire to 'answer' one can detect both concerns of self-understanding and attempts to communicate the gospel to outsiders. The apologetic slant is not limited to answering alone; it is employed in defending Christian faith in a setting where Christians are a small minority among an overwhelming majority of Hindus (India and Nepal), Muslims (Pakistan and Bangladesh), or Buddhists (Sri Lanka).

Although almost all Catholic theological writings in South Asia (with the exception of hymns) are by members of various religious orders, among Protestants South Asian theology has been throughout history dominated by the presence and productivity of lay theologians, both men and women, including M. M. Thomas and others. Perhaps Protestant laity found both a freedom and the creativity to think in South Asian terms, unlike the ministers and theologians who were already schooled in western theological traditions. This supposition becomes much more plausible when it is recognized that most of the initial creative theological attempts in South Asia are not found in discursive theological writings in English, but rather in the hymns and songs of South Asian Christians in the various vernacular languages.

Two major themes or concerns have guided South Asian theologies throughout its history. One is the concern for inculturation and the other is the commitment to liberation or humanization. Inculturation focuses primarily on the religio-cultural aspect of life in South Asia, taking into account the religious and cultural pluralism of South Asia. What does it mean to be an indigenous Church *of* South Asia and not simply be located *in* South Asia? One way to address this question is through serious engagement with ecumenism. In each of the national contexts within South Asia there have been attempts (most often successful) to unite Churches. Ecumenical Churches such as the Church of South India (1947), the Church of North India (1970), the Church of Pakistan (1970), the United Mission to Nepal, and the various National Councils of Churches in each of the nations of South Asia have generated ecumenical theological thinking and writing. Since Vatican Council II, Catholics, too, have been more open to ecumenical co-operation.

Inculturation involves allowing the gospel to take root in the South Asian soil and flourish as an indigenous growth rather than 'a potted plant'. The hymnwriters did their share of inculturation of the Christian faith in very creative ways. In that process they generated highly creative theological articulations. V. Sastriar (1774–1864), N. V. Tilak (1861–1919), and G. Joshua (1895–1971) of India, the authors of hymns in *Sevok*

Sangeet (*Songs of Servants*) of Bangladesh, and D. T. Niles and M. Devananda (*fl.* 2000) of Sri Lanka are some of those. Another move is to use local religious and philosophical categories in the construction of one's own theology. For example, theologians in India interacted with the Hindu philosophical traditions, while theologians in Sri Lanka focused more on the Buddhist tradition and those in Pakistan on Islamic religious thought respectively. One discovers indigenous theological reflection and articulation in the artistic discourse among Christians in South Asia. The paintings of J. Sahi (b. 1944) and others offer fresh theological insights into the place of Christ and Christian faith in the culture of South Asia.

The dominant theme other than inculturation is the issue of humanization or liberation. This is focused more on the socio-economic and political realities of South Asia. Theologies that address this issue zero in on the situation of POVERTY and oppression in South Asian communities. One is the issue of responsible citizenship and involvement in nation-building. The other is to engage in activities that lead to the release of the poor from the shackles of dehumanization and offer them salvation as humanization.

Two major movements – DALIT THEOLOGY and women's theologies – attempt to integrate these two themes of inculturation and liberation. Dalit theology is articulated by Dalits – the so-called 'untouchables' of Indian caste hierarchy – for their own liberation. The caste system of India is both a religio-cultural system and a socio-economic arrangement. Therefore, in articulating their theologies, Dalit theologians, such as A. Nirmal (1936–95), S. Clarke (b. 1956), and others challenge the place of Dalits within the Hindu religious system and seek to empower them to engage in liberative praxis through effecting economic and political changes. Dalit theologies articulate theological visions in order to assist both the Dalits and the non-Dalits in this process of humanization. In the same manner, theological articulations carried out by Christian women in South Asia also integrate the twin concerns of inculturation and liberation. They use local religious categories, stories, and myths, fresh biblical HERMENEUTICS, and intense socio-political analysis. These theologies have a decisively public character since Dalit liberation and women's emancipation are not simply intra-Christian concerns, but pan-national and multi-religious ones.

Today, South Asia is caught up in processes of globalization that introduce some amount of cultural homogenization in the wider society, bring in new forms of urban and rural poverty, and give Christianity a neo-colonial face. The dominance of the English language in South Asia is growing in such a way that theological articulations in South Asian vernaculars need extra empowerment. Globalization also creates a new cadre of the poor, whether in a residual way or as a direct result of globalization. Christian theologies in South Asia need to face this new challenge.

Due to the omnipresence of western media and the proliferation of Christian TV programmes in South Asia, Christianity now appears as an imported religion more than ever before. A further contribution to this perception of Christianity as a western import has been the influx from the 1950s onwards of Christian fundamentalist theologies – most often of the American kind – in the life of the Churches in India. Other theologians in South Asia have also had to contend with the rise of Christian FUNDAMENTALISM while articulating either a theology of inculturation or a theology of liberation. Moreover, the rise of Christian fundamentalism has led to or emerged along with Hindu, Islamic, and Buddhist fundamentalisms, presenting a major challenge to all the nations of South Asia. From a specifically theological perspective, the reality of fundamentalism has helped bring the issue of religious CONVERSION to the forefront in South Asia, especially in India, with the earlier evangelical theology that sustained the missionary work of the Churches coming under severe criticism by both Christians and others. In the face of these realities, Christian theologians are challenged to articulate their theology of mission in a creative fashion and in more dialogical modes.

See also BUDDHISM AND CHRISTIANITY; HINDUISM AND CHRISTIANITY; ISLAM AND CHRISTIANITY.

N. Abeyasingha, *The Radical Tradition: The Changing Shape of Theological Reflection in Sri Lanka* (Ecumenical Institute, 1985).

R. Boyd, *An Introduction to Indian Christian Theology* (ISPCK, 1989).

J. C. England *et al.*, eds., *Asian Christian Theologies: A Research Guide to Authors, Movements, Sources* (Orbis, 2002).

S. C. H. Kim, ed., *Christian Theology in Asia* (Cambridge University Press, 2008).

R. S. Sugirtharajah, ed., *Frontiers in Asian Christian Theology: Emerging Trends* (Orbis, 1994).

M. THOMAS THANGARAJ

SPIRIT: see HOLY SPIRIT.

SPIRITUALITY In its current usage, referring to the entire range of human encounters with transcendence, the term 'spirituality' is of quite recent origin. Earlier eras would have spoken, in chronological order, of CONTEMPLATION, of ascetical and MYSTICAL THEOLOGY, and of spiritual theology. 'Spirituality' is now generally used to refer both to the practices (and lived experiences) by which humans encounter a spiritual dimension of reality, and to the theory and study of this encounter. While the academic discipline that studies spirituality continues to develop its range of sub-specializations (see the fine essays in Sheldrake and Holder), this article will focus on the history of Christian spirituality in terms of its significance for theology.

The challenge of thinking perceptively about spirituality in the modern era remains our post-ENLIGHTENMENT frame of reference, in which language used in the TRADITION about the spiritual dimension of life tends almost inevitably to be interpreted as language about interior mental states or conditions of the human subject. We may try to remind ourselves repeatedly that pre-modern spirituality is usually ecclesial and cosmological in reference rather than individualistic in the modern sense. Yet it may also be clarifying to recall that the human 'I' spoken of by PAUL, Ignatius of Antioch (d. *ca* 110), or AUGUSTINE is always already a self-in-encounter, a self radically constituted and transformed by the HOLY SPIRIT and given a new, relational identity in the community of Christ's body (see Rom. 8:11, 15–16). From its origins in the paschal mystery of Christ, Christian spirituality lives from this passing over from death to life by means of being drawn into Jesus' relation to the Father through the power of the Spirit. Thus one way of understanding Christian spirituality is as a movement *from* the community's encounter with God in Christ *to* its members' participation in ongoing mystery of life in the Spirit. This movement takes place through the practices, teachings, and imaginative vision of reality that shape believers' lives. In interpreting Christian spiritual texts, it is therefore important not to read their language in straightforwardly experiential terms: the language of experience may be used because it is the only means by which a spiritual writer can convey something of the divine reality itself. For example language that, if read literally, seems to be a report about inner experiences of darkness or nothingness, is more often a critique of religious experience as a source of truth about either God or the self.

So the interaction of spirituality and theology is complex and often indirect: spiritual texts and practices contribute to the deepening encounter with God that permits the community to clarify and develop its understanding of the FAITH it believes, and, reciprocally, the resulting theological teaching helps to inform and open vistas for the spiritual lives of believers. One further aspect of the phenomenon of Christian spirituality is therefore its role as a sign to theology of God's call to continuing conversion. In a seminal paper, A. Louth (b. 1944) writes, 'Spirituality does not exactly answer the question, "Who is God?" but it preserves the orientation, the perspective, within which this question remains a question that is being asked rather than a question that is being evaded or elided' ('Theology', 4). Conversely, spirituality that has grown divorced from theology is in danger of becoming merely self-referential, even idolatrous.

A historical theology of Christian spirituality would begin with the fundamentally biblical and ecclesial focus of early Christian spiritual teachers. For ORIGEN, biblical exegesis is the paradigmatic spiritual practice by which the Word draws the Church into transforming encounter. In the years after the end of Roman persecutions, the spirituality of the martyrs was transmuted into a new form of radical imitation of Christ in various forms of MONASTICISM, but here also the spiritual meaning of SCRIPTURE was sought through personal appropriation within the worshipping life of the community. A landmark spiritual text such as *The Life of Moses* by Gregory of Nyssa (see CAPPADOCIAN FATHERS) portrayed the spiritual journey in terms of the ascent of Moses towards the divine presence. Nyssa's text, depicting a ceaseless stretching forward of the spiritual life into the infinity of divine life whose dazzling brightness can only be experienced as a divine darkness, set important themes for the development of Christian mystical thought. The major theoretician of desert spirituality, Evagrius Ponticus (345–99), highlighted the interactions of the monks with one another as the scene of spiritual testing, and as a school in which to learn humility and the ways of mercy and grace through the struggles of community life. Evagrius' account of the eight *logismoi* or dominating 'thoughts' played a central role in the development of theories of spiritual discernment, and passed into western theology through the influential writings of J. Cassian (*ca* 360–435). Evagrius brilliantly evoked the stunting and constricting power of the passions and demonic spirits that turned spiritual seekers towards self-obsession and illusion instead of openness to the reality of the neighbour and of God.

The development of medieval spirituality is dominated by two figures. AUGUSTINE shaped the Christian spiritual universe of the West in incomparable ways: in the *Confessions* (*ca* 397–*ca* 400), his Psalm commentaries (*ca* 390–*ca* 420), and *The Trinity* (*ca* 400–*ca* 420), the attractive grace and supernal beauty of God is refracted through the bishop's reflections on the humility of Christ, the life of Christ's body the Church, and the mysterious rhythms by which human existence is drawn towards the beatifying vision of divine WISDOM. Alongside the influence of Augustine must be placed the thought of DIONYSIUS THE AREOPAGITE, whose remarkable conversion of late antique Neoplatonism (see PLATONISM) to the GOSPEL of Christ, though still a matter of some scholarly debate, profoundly influenced both the Christian vision of creation as theophany (found later in J. Scotus Eriugena (*ca* 800–*ca* 875), Bonaventure (1221–74), and T. AQUINAS), and also the apophatic tradition in Christian theology and spirituality. In this tradition, the meaning of each feature of SCRIPTURE or the LITURGY or CREATION itself is held open towards a yet deeper and more powerful significance beyond all power of conceptualization. The monastic spirituality of communal life and the encounter with Christ in Scripture reached a western high point in the early medieval writings of Bernard of Clairvaux (1090–1153) and other Cistercian writers. The more speculative contemporary spiritual teaching of Richard of St Victor (d. 1173) and William of St Thierry (*ca* 1075–1148) begins the important shift towards the systematic analysis of the stages and characteristic features of the spiritual journey.

Later medieval spirituality is marked especially by the rise of passion mysticism, in which the Franciscan embrace of Christ's earthly poverty and humility is extended into a deep personal appropriation and reflection upon the sufferings and death of Christ. Often linked with the development of vernacular and more popular spiritual practices, passion spirituality found notable exponents and interpreters in such figures as Hadewijch (*fl. ca* 1250), Angela of Foligno (*ca* 1250–1309), and JULIAN OF NORWICH. The great spiritual leader CATHERINE OF SIENA included elements of this spirituality in her teaching, drawing it together with more metaphysical spirituality that reached its high point in MEISTER ECKHART and J. van Ruusbroec (1293–1381). While Eckhart is sometimes regarded as radicalizing Christian apophatic traditions (see APOPHATIC THEOLOGY) to the extent of passing even beyond the TRINITY, more considered scholarship has begun to revise this view, seeing that in many ways Eckhart remains true to his Dominican forebears Albert the Great (*ca* 1200–80) and Aquinas: in Eckhart the eternal Trinitarian processions become translucent to a metaphysics of the infinite divine act of existence, flowing at the ground of every creature. This flowing of infinite being is appropriately envisioned in yet more explicitly Trinitarian terms in Ruusbroec, for whom the unity of God is the serene oneness of the divine Persons, a unity that eternally flows forth in the infinitely fruitful joy of the divine processions of the Persons.

From the time of the REFORMATION into modernity, Christian spirituality has been shaped fairly strongly by a new emphasis on the individual and inner experience as well as a tendency to sequester religion in general, and spirituality in particular, into the category of private, personal preference. This has led not only to new emphasis on heightened or unusual spiritual states as somehow the normal focus of spirituality, but also to a marginalization of spiritual life away from the communal or institutional life. The paradigmatic figures TERESA OF AVILA and John of the Cross (1542–91), even as they warn against according much significance to inner experiences, are, at the same time, prodded by their contemporaries' concern to root out false spiritualities into providing ever more elaborate psychologies and categorizations of inner states and affects. The doctrinal interface of Christian spirituality fades in these circumstances, making it easier for developing academic theology to regard spirituality as mere piety or devotion without a significant theological dimension. Indeed some modern movements of piety have returned the favour, consciously deploring the mere 'abstractions' of Christian theology and preferring an apparently universal spiritual feeling that is seen as expressing the deep common truth *behind* the supposedly constraining doctrines of institutional religions.

Working against this dominant trend in modernity were the efforts of new apostolic religious orders such as the Society of Jesus, whose founder Ignatius of Loyola (1491–1556) strongly shaped the Christian theology of spiritual discernment through his teaching embodied in the *Spiritual Exercises* (1548). Loyola, like other moderns, was deeply aware of his own interiority, but he made it possible to set the individual's spiritual motions within the heart of Christ, reframing one's self-understanding and sense of calling in terms of one's desire to love Christ more deeply so as to follow him more closely in everything, for the greater GLORY of God. In not dissimilar ways, the great Puritan preacher J. Bunyan (1628–88) in classic texts such as *Pilgrim's Progress* (1678) was able to portray the individual Christian's journey in luminous allegory, interpreted at every step against the vast landscape of the gospel story and in the light of a strong theology of salvation. America's foremost theologian and spiritual leader J. EDWARDS likewise sought to test a mounting modern enthusiasm for intense religious experiences against the overruling grace and providence of God, and to check religious affections against the measurable fruits of a community's spiritual health and its practical results in living a godly life. Edwards may also be seen as extending the work of the Cambridge Platonists of the previous generation, such as R. Cudworth (1617–88) and H. More (1614–87), along with the remarkable Anglican divine T. Traherne (1636/7–74), in renewing a Christian spiritual vision of the creation as the radiant sign of God's goodness and glory.

The nineteenth and twentieth centuries brought some signs of a possible reintegration of Christian spirituality and theology – or at least a renewed dialogue. Particularly notable in this regard are the writings of the eminent Carmelite thinker E. Stein (1891–1942), who died at Auschwitz, and of the brilliant French intellectual S. WEIL, who also died during World War II. In both cases the extremity of the human condition seemed to afford these spiritual teachers an urgent awareness of the mysterious willingness of God in Christ to be present even within the most alienated states of human existence and human perishing. Both thinkers offer a vision of the radical generosity of Trinitarian life, and the richness of its self-giving, as the foundation of creation and salvation. They write in ways that invite recognition of one's true spiritual condition, but only within the overriding reality of God which alone endues human life with transcendent meaning.

H. U. von Balthasar, *Explorations in Theology*, vol. I: *The Word Made Flesh* (Ignatius Press, 1989).

A. Holder, ed., *The Blackwell Companion to Christian Spirituality* (Blackwell, 2005).

B. McGinn, *The Presence of God: A History of Western Christian Mysticism*, 4 vols. (Herder and Herder, 1994–2005).

P. Sheldrake, ed., *The New Westminster Dictionary of Christian Spirituality* (John Knox Press, 2005).

A. Stolz, *The Doctrine of Spiritual Perfection* (Herder and Herder, 2001).

Mark A. McIntosh

Stăniloae, Dumitru The Romanian Orthodox theologian Dumitru Stăniloae (1903–93) was a major twentieth-century authority on ecclesiology, patristics, and ecumenism. A professor at the Universities of Sibiu and Bucharest for over five decades starting in the late 1920s, Stăniloae was trained as a Church historian and theologian at the Universities of Cernăuţi, Athens, Munich, Berlin, and Paris. His doctoral dissertation on Patriarch Dositheos of Jerusalem (1641–1707) presents Romania as a meeting place between the Greek and Slavic worlds and a guardian of the Byzantine heritage, while emphasizing that country's special position within the world Christian landscape as the only predominantly Romance-language Orthodox country. While studying in the West, he was drawn to the dialogical theology of M. Buber (1878–1965) and the French personalists, but more importantly to the theology of G. Palamas, the main promoter of hesychasm. These were formative experiences for Stăniloae's later development of a deeply personalist theology that wove together in a creative and coherent whole modern personalism, patristic theology, and Orthodox spirituality (including especially hesychasm).

While translating the *Dogmatics* of the Greek theologian C. Androutsos (1867–1935) in 1930, Stăniloae realized that his former professor had a pronounced Scholastic approach to theology. This, along with the rediscovery of the Church fathers, led Stăniloae to be among the first to break with the Scholastic approach that dominated Orthodox theology during the first half of the twentieth century. He increasingly came to view theology as a personal experience, a living encounter with a living God, rather than as an abstract system or philosophical theory. His three-volume *Orthodox Dogmatic Theology* (1978) is pervaded by this new spirit.

After the establishment of the Communist regime in Romania in 1946, Stăniloae was imprisoned for five years due to his involvement with an unofficial spirituality group holding right-wing views and promoting the Jesus prayer. Despite numerous limitations imposed on him by the Communists both before and after his imprisonment, Stăniloae's scholarly output was prodigious: he authored some twenty books and over 200 articles published both in Romania and abroad; he also translated into Romanian many authors, ancient and modern, including the *Philokalia*. A valuable collection of Stăniloae's essays, entitled *Theology and the Church*, has been available in English since 1980. More recently, the translation of his *Orthodox Dogmatic Theology* into English under the title *The Experience of God* has paved the way for the western public's direct contact with his theology. Increasing numbers of Orthodox, Catholics, and Protestants have written doctoral dissertations on Stăniloae's theology at western universities.

Because of his erudition and profound insights, Stăniloae has beeen hailed by some as one of the most important representatives of Orthodox theology, and by others as occupying a position in twentieth-century Orthodoxy comparable to that of K. Barth in Protestantism and K. Rahner in Catholicism.

Lucian Turcescu

Status confessionis The Latin phrase *status confessionis* is used in contemporary theology for the judgement that the Church is confronted with a doctrine or practice that puts the integrity of its witness to the gospel at risk. In other words, to declare that the Church is *in statu confessionis* is to claim the need for a clear, public declaration that speaks directly to a contested matter of Christian faith. For example, in the 1930s D. Bonhoeffer argued that the German government's anti-Jewish legislation placed the Church *in statu confessionis*. More recently, the general council of the World Alliance of Reformed Churches (WARC) declared in 1982 that the apartheid policy of the government of South Africa constituted a *status confessionis*. As the WARC statement makes clear, in current usage this claim is closely tied with the judgement that the Church is confronted with heresy.

This modern use of the term diverges significantly from its Reformation-era roots in debates among Lutherans over the appropriate stance to be taken with respect to adiaphora (matters of Church practice regarded as permissible, though not obligatory). The question was whether it was licit to agree to conform on matters of adiaphora 'in time of persecution and in a situation of confession [*in casu confessionis*]', and in absence of broader agreement on substantive matters of doctrine (*FC, Ep.* 10). The answer given was negative, on the grounds that in a situation of persecution such concessions would suggest agreement on doctrinal questions still in dispute and thereby offend the weak in faith.

Bonhoeffer drew on this history in his own reflection on the need for clear confession in the face of the racial laws of the Third Reich, not least because many German Protestants regarded the Nazi anti-Jewish legislation precisely as an adiaphoron. Though influenced by Bonhoeffer, K. Barth decoupled *status confessionis* from the question of adiaphora, identifying it instead with any situation where the faith of the Church 'is confronted and questioned from within or without by the phenomena of unbelief, superstition and heresy' in such a way as to demand unequivocal 'protest' (*CD* III/4, 79).

While the theological power of the claim of *status confessionis* in the face of practices like apartheid is undeniable, its separation from the particular question of compromise in time of persecution raises important questions about its use. Because the declaration of *status confessionis* bars further discussion, it risks premature closure of conversation among Christians about how the Church should be the Church in the midst of history's contingencies. Thus, in the face of the temptation to view any issue of pressing moral concern (e.g., world hunger) as constituting a *status confessionis*, many have argued (following the example of the Council of Jerusalem in Acts 15) that compromise and negotiation should be viewed as the normal response to disagreement within the Church.

D. Smit, 'A *Status Confessionis* in South Africa', *Journal of Theology for Southern Africa* 47 (1984), 21–46.

E. TeSelle, 'How Do We Recognize a *Status Confessionis*?', *Theology Today* 45:1 (April 1988), 71–8.

IAN A. MCFARLAND

STEWARDSHIP: see CREATION.

STIGMATA The Greek word *stigmata* was used in antiquity for the brands put on slaves. In a Christian context stigmata are wounds corresponding to those Christ received in his crucifixion (viz., in both hands, both feet, the side, and sometimes marks on the head, shoulders, and back associated with the scourging and the crown of thorns). Though Paul writes of bearing 'the marks [*stigmata*] of Jesus branded on my body' (Gal. 6:17), most critics interpret him as speaking metaphorically of scars received as the result of persecution. The earliest clear case of the reception of stigmata is that of Francis of Assisi (1181/2–1226). Since Francis' time, hundreds of other cases have been reported, with varying symptoms (e.g., some involving pain but no visible wounds, others with flowing blood).

The cause of stigmata remains a matter of controversy. Many (especially Catholic) Christians have understood them as supernatural, bearing witness to the recipient's close identification with Christ's sufferings. Others have viewed them as a psychosomatic phenomenon. In some instances (most notoriously, the case of Magdalena de la Cruz (1487–1560)) the wounds have been self-inflicted. The fact that unambiguous reports of stigmata date only from the thirteenth century, when the crucifix became an object of popular devotion, suggests that their occurrence may be influenced by the conventions of Christian iconography.

IAN A. MCFARLAND

SUPERNATURAL EXISTENTIAL In the theology of K. RAHNER, the supernatural existential is the free and forgiving offer of God's self-communication to humanity. It is an ontological self-communication, by which God offers God's self as the innermost constitutive element of humanity. It is a vocation to BEATIFIC VISION, an ordination to a supernatural end of eternal communion with God. Given always and everywhere, it reflects the universal salvific will of God. An aspect of all experience, it makes personal knowledge and love of God possible without reducing God to an object of comprehension. The supernatural existential exists in each human being in the mode of antecedent offer, of acceptance, or of rejection. While human freedom is active in accepting God's offer, such acceptance is borne by God and is, itself, GRACE. In acceptance, the supernatural existential is the indwelling of the Holy Spirit. 'Existential' indicates that this is a characteristic of the entire person; 'supernatural' declares it is a further unexacted gift of grace beyond CREATION.

Human transcendence is the obediential potency for the supernatural existential. This means that human transcendence has the possibility of elevation into the supernatural existential, and this possibility remains significant even if it is unfulfilled. God is not obliged to grant humanity a supernatural end, yet the offer of beatific vision is a fitting elevation of humanity's spiritual nature. Thus Rahner emphasizes both God's freedom and the significance of grace for everyday life. Furthermore, the fact that the supernatural existential is the obediential potency for the HYPOSTATIC UNION of divine and human natures in Christ confirms that the INCARNATION is deeply connected to the grace of God present throughout history.

SHANNON CRAIGO-SNELL

SUPERNATURALISM 'Supernaturalism' refers to a movement in German Protestant theology that emerged in the early eighteenth century in reaction to criticism of the Bible's accuracy by exponents of DEISM and RATIONALISM. Supernaturalists argued that biblical accounts of MIRACLES and the fulfilment of PROPHECY were veridical reports of supernatural events rather than products of superstition or ACCOMMODATION. Though supernaturalism is associated with theological conservatism, proponents like S. Baumgarten (1706–57) displayed a distinctly modern spirit in arguing for the credibility of SCRIPTURE on secular grounds, invoking criteria like the trustworthiness of the authors and the verisimilitude of the narratives rather than relying on naked appeals to INSPIRATION. Though pockets of supernaturalism persisted into the nineteenth century at Tübingen and elsewhere, it had by then ceased to be a vital force in German academic theology.

Scholars like H. FREI have pointed out that the supernaturalists (like later fundamentalists) were in many ways closer to their rationalist opponents than to earlier generations of interpreters, since they read the Bible as a report of past revelation rather than as a source of revelation in the present. In other words, in so far as both sides identified Scripture's meaning with the history *behind* the biblical accounts rather than locating it *within* the text, they agreed that the Bible was to be assessed in terms of its historical reliability, however much their assessments may have differed. In pre-modern Christian HERMENEUTICS, by contrast, the Bible's authority was grounded in its immediate use by God as a means of communication rather than in its conformity to independently derived, external criteria of authenticity.

IAN A. MCFARLAND

SUPERSESSIONISM The concept of supersessionism (also known as replacement theology) remains a deeply controverted topic with respect both to Christian theological reflection on ISRAEL and to the broader relationship between JUDAISM AND CHRISTIANITY. It refers to the question of the extent – if any – to which the Christian Church may be said to have replaced or superseded the Jewish people as the object of God's COVENANT with ABRAHAM, and thus as the elect people of God. Throughout most of the Church's history, Christian theology has been explicitly supersessionist: the majority of Jews' rejection of Jesus as Messiah and the subsequent destruction of the Jerusalem temple by the Romans were taken to be signs of God's rejection of the Jewish people. Christian complicity in the HOLOCAUST, the founding of the modern state of Israel, and renewed Christian appreciation for the significance of PAUL's claim that 'the gifts and calling of God are irrevocable' (Rom. 11:29) have led to near universal repudiation of this earlier position.

Current Christian discussion tends to take the Jews' status as God's elect as a given and focus instead on the question of the relevance of Jesus for Jews. Some aver that the very claim that Jesus is the Jewish Messiah invariably leads to the triumphalism and anti-Semitism associated with traditional Christian forms of supersessionism and, correspondingly, limit Jesus' significance to Gentiles. Others (often referring to Paul's complex argument in Rom. 9–11) deny that confessing Jesus as Israel's Messiah commits Christians to the idea that the Church has displaced Israel as the object of God's covenant love, though conceding that it does complicate the mode by which God's loving purposes for Israel are fulfilled.

IAN A. MCFARLAND

SUPRALAPSARIANISM: see INFRALAPSARIANISM AND SUPRALAPSARIANISM.

SYMBOL 'Symbol' is used in two senses, one proper and one derived. The proper sense refers to the intrinsic symbol, in which an empirical medium makes a transcendent reality concretely present. The classic example is the Catholic DOCTRINE of TRANSUBSTANTIATION, which holds that the appearances of bread and wine (the empirical media) remain while their substance is converted into Christ's body and blood (the transcendent reality). The derived sense refers to a sign, in which the medium evokes, through reminiscence, an abstract concept that it does not actually embody. Examples include national flags and traffic signals. Christian theologians have appealed to both senses, even as they have interpreted the proper sense of the word differently.

The intrinsic symbol's origins can be traced to the pre-Socratics, Plato, and Aristotle (see ARISTOTELIANISM; PLATONISM), but it becomes theologically significant with the development in the patristic period of reflection on the human person as the image and likeness of God (see THEOLOGICAL ANTHROPOLOGY). Gregory of Nyssa's (see CAPPADOCIAN FATHERS) notion of the SOUL as a mirror reflecting divinity and AUGUSTINE's so-called psychological analogy between the soul's powers and the TRINITY represent touchstones for the theological appropriation of symbol.

Sacramental theology instances diverging views of symbol. Augustine and Isidore of Seville (*ca* 560–636) define sacraments as efficacious rituals causing what they signify. P. Lombard (*ca* 1100–60) specifies this causation as 'concomitant occasional'. This view holds that sacraments are causally efficacious in so far as they convey knowledge: pointing to the grace that God confers directly with them, but not in and through them. A distance thus obtains between the sacramental symbol and what it signifies. M. LUTHER and J. CALVIN are indebted to this view. What became the standard Catholic position, on the other hand, was developed by T. AQUINAS. Harnessing Aristotle's category of instrumental causality, he interpreted the sacraments as grace-laden rituals that bring humanity into direct contact with the divine. While the symbol retains its distinctiveness, the distance between it and what it signifies collapses.

K. RAHNER and P. TILLICH stand out among the symbol's most recent theological interpreters. Indebted to F. SCHLEIERMACHER, Tillich affirms the object of theology to be God's manifestation, not God as such. Known in religious experience, this manifestation is articulated by theology in symbols. Although these participate in the divine reality they signify, they are culturally determined. Because religious symbols evanesce and new ones emerge, a distance obtains between them and the divine. By contrast, Rahner, indebted to Aquinas, collapses this distance, so that the Trinity, INCARNATION, Church, and sacraments consist in a self-expression called the *Realsymbol*. Thus, Christ's humanity immediately mediates the Word, even as the Church, as a human organization, immediately mediates Christ through the HOLY SPIRIT.

Christian theology has variously interpreted aesthetic objects as divine symbols. In ORTHODOX THEOLOGY the icon is viewed as akin to the *Realsymbol*: an intrinsic vehicle of transcendence, it shatters any merely religiously anamnestic function (see ICONS AND ICONOGRAPHY). This function is preserved in CATHOLIC THEOLOGY, for which objects called sacramentals (e.g., crucifixes, rosaries) work like signs. In some Reformed traditions, by contrast, the aesthetic sign used religiously is considered a blasphemous image.

R. Haight, *Jesus: Symbol of God* (Orbis, 1999).
H. P. Joseph, *Logos-Symbol in the Christology of Karl Rahner* (Libreria Ateneo Salesiano, 1984).

STEPHEN FIELDS

SYNAXIS: see EUCHARIST.

SYNERGISM Derived from the Greek for 'working together', synergism (or synergy) refers to the co-operation between divine and human agency in conversion and, more broadly, to the nature and extent of human participation in the processes of JUSTIFICATION and SANCTIFICATION. The term is generally used to describe a model of divine–human relationship according to which the success of any of God's efforts to effect some change of disposition or behaviour in human beings is contingent upon some independent activity of the human will. It is thus opposed to monergism, according to which God is the sole efficient cause of human conversion.

Though M. LUTHER had denied that human beings possessed any FREE WILL that contributed to their own salvation, after his death Lutherans involved in the so-called 'synergistic controversy' debated whether humans had any inherent disposition towards God that might enable them to prepare for GRACE. The dispute was resolved in favour of monergism: though it was acknowledged that the HOLY SPIRIT effects conversion by renewing the will, the idea that human beings possess any capacity whatsoever to either turn or respond to God was firmly denied (*FC, SD* 2). In the wake of the Council of DORT, Reformed theologians rejected synergism even more firmly by emphasizing the irresistible character of the Spirit's work in conversion (see IRRESISTIBLE GRACE). Both traditions regard synergism as a form of PELAGIANISM that compromises the sufficiency of divine GRACE for human salvation. By contrast, figures like J. WESLEY and the overwhelming majority of Orthodox theologians defend divine–human co-operation as a necessary implication of Christian belief in human freedom.

IAN A. MCFARLAND

SYRIAC CHRISTIAN THEOLOGY Syriac Christian theology has been preserved in a substantial corpus of ecclesiastical literature written in or translated into Syriac and belonging to different Syriac-speaking Christian denominations. Syriac language developed as a dialect of Aramaic in Edessa from the second century and spread over a vast territory from the eastern Mediterranean coast through Mesopotamia and Central Asia as far as the Malabar Coast of India and China. Two major trends in theology are represented by the main denominations of Syriac Christianity, both of which reject the CHRISTOLOGY of the Council of CHALCEDON: the Assyrian Church of the East (the East Syrian tradition; see NESTORIANISM), and the Syriac Orthodox Churches (the West Syrian tradition; see ORIENTAL ORTHODOX CHURCHES).

Syriac theology, rooted in the bilingual Arameo-Greek milieu, developed under the influence of Greek philosophy. Another factor was its engagement in polemic with Judaism and with dualistic teachings which spread through Palestine, Syria, and Iran, especially those of MARCION, Bardaisan (154–222) and Mani (216–76). Bardaisan was the first who wrote his philosophical and theological works in Syriac, and thus is considered as a creator of Syriac literary language. Equally influential for the Syriac tradition was Tatian (d. *ca* 175), the author of the *Diatessaron.* His thoughts on the nature of salvation as the union of God's spirit and human SOUL (the abode of the spirit) found their reflection in the early Syriac apocrypha, the *Acts of Judas Thomas* and the *Odes of Solomon.*

The most outstanding early Syriac theologians, Aphrahat (d. *ca* 345) and Ephrem the Syrian (*ca* 305–73), worked out a special system of theology built up mainly on ascetical practice (see ASCETICISM) and spiritual meditation. Its language was not that of Greek philosophy, but a sequence of images and metaphors. The main common idea of all the early Syriac theology is absolute transcendence and incomprehensibility of God. There are only three ways for humans to get knowledge of God: through FAITH and LOVE, through the types of God in SCRIPTURE (see TYPOLOGY) and SYMBOLS of God in nature (viz., CREATION), and, finally, through the INCARNATION, which is the only moment when God fully reveals God's self to the world by 'putting on the body'.

As already indicated, further development of Syriac theology focused mainly on the Christological controversies that divided the Churches over the course of the fifth century, leading to splits within Syriac Christianity itself and the formation of the major independent Syriac-speaking Churches. The major complicating feature of Syriac Christology is disagreement over the interpretation of the key Christological terms: *itūtā* (Greek *ousia*, 'essence/substance'), *kyānā* (Greek *physis*, 'nature'), *qnōmā* (roughly corresponding to HYPOSTASIS), and *parsōpā* (Greek *prosôpon*, 'person') by the opposing Syriac traditions. However, the common point of the Syriac theology (in both its Chalcedonian and its various non-Chalcedonian forms) is the confession of the Holy TRINITY as the three hypostases (*qnōmē*): the Father, the Son, and the Holy Spirit, in one essence of God. All the three *qnōmē* are consubstantial (Greek *HOMOOUSIOS*) with each other and the Trinity is itself without beginning, without change, and without division. Thus, all denominations of Syriac

Christianity officially recognize the Councils of Nicaea and Constantinople. In addition, the Syriac Orthodox Churches also recognize the Council of Ephesus.

In the West Syrian Christology, systematized by Severus of Antioch (*ca* 465–538), *itūtā* is an abstract reality or a generic feature, while *qnōmā* is a reality endowed with individual properties. *Kyānā* has a dual meaning – first, as a general nature (synonymous to *itūtā*), second, and most important, as an individual expression of the general essence (synonymous to *qnōmā*). *Parsōpā* is understood as an individual reality and is apparently equivalent to *qnōmā*. Strongly committed to miaphysitism, West Syrian theology teaches that Jesus Christ was born out of the two perfect natures – the divine and the human, which united incomprehensibly in one person of Christ and became 'one incarnate nature [*had kyānāmbasrā*] of God the Word' and one composite hypostasis. In the incarnation God the Word united to God's self, as an act of God's single will and through God's single operation, the human flesh endowed with the rational soul, assumed from the Virgin Mary (who is thus recognized, in line with the canons of the Council of Ephesus, as the Mother of God). In this natural and hypostatic union there is neither mixture or confusion, nor division or separation.

In the strongly diaphysite East Syrian Christology, developed systematically by Babai the Great (*ca* 551–628), *kyānā* is the complete and abstract nature, a generic feature (equivalent to *itūtā*), and *qnōmā* is the concrete nature, an individual manifestation of *kyānā*. Thus the two *kyānē* of Christ respectively imply the two *qnōmē*. *Parsōpā* means a set of the individual characteristics of a subject, which make it unique; thus it cannot be identified with *qnōmā*. In line with these definitions, the main East Syrian Christological formula is 'two natures [*kyānin*] with two hypostases [*qnōmin*] united in one person [*parsōpā*] of the Son'. In the moment of the Annunciation, God the Word, the second *qnōmā* of the Trinity, united to God's self, by God's own will, the *qnōmā* of humanity. Thus the two perfect natures (*kyāne*) in Christ, the divine and the human, were ineffably and unchangeably joined in an inseparable 'prosopic union', which cannot be considered as mixture, mingling, or confusion.

Syriac-speaking Chalcedonian Orthodox Christians (historically known as Melkites) confessed the union of two natures (*kyānē*) in one hypostasis (*qnōmā*) and one person (*parsōpā*) without confusion. They translated Greek ecclesiastical literature into Syriac but did not produce their own theologians, and by the seventeenth century Arabic eventually replaced Syriac as their liturgical language.

The Eastern Catholic Churches, which continue to use Syriac in liturgy and often as a vernacular language, follow the doctrinal teaching of the Catholic Church. The theology of the Maronite Church is thought to have undergone the influence of monothelitism around the seventh century. The reformed Malankara Marthoma Syrian Church follows Anglican theology.

S. Brock, *Fire from Heaven: Studies in Syriac Theology and Liturgy* (Ashgate, 2006).

R. C. Chesnut, *Three Monophysite Christologies: Severus of Antioch, Philoxenus of Mabbug, and Jacob of Serugh* (Oxford University Press, 1976).

Mgr J. Lebon, 'La Christologie du monophysitisme syrien', in *Das Konzil von Chalkedon: Geschichte und Gegenwart*, vol. I: *Der Glaube von Chalkedon* (Echter-Verlag, 1951), 425–580.

R. Murray, *Symbols of Church and Kingdom: A Study in Early Syriac Tradition*, revised edn (T&T Clark, 2006).

Natalia Smelova

SYSTEMATIC THEOLOGY The phrase 'systematic theology' came into common use in eighteenth-century Europe to refer to analytical (as opposed to biblical or historical) reflection on Christian doctrine. J. Buddeus (1667–1729), one of the first to use it, defined the task of systematic theology as twofold: first, to give a comprehensive and logically ordered presentation of Christian belief, and, second, to explain, test, and prove it (*Isagoge*, 303–4). Its appropriateness has been questioned by some (most famously K. Barth, who preferred the term 'dogmatics'), on the grounds that calling a theology 'systematic' implies that the theologian has a degree of methodological control over her subject matter that is inconsistent with the Christian belief that God cannot be contained by human categories or concepts. More recently, similar concern that the metaphor of a theological 'system' fails to attend to the inherently open-ended and dialogical character of the discipline has led others (especially in North America) to describe their work as 'constructive theology'.

Although systematic theology can be undertaken with the aim of interpreting the Christian faith in terms of a single, overarching metaphysical framework (as in, e.g., the work of P. Tillich), it can also be conceived more modestly. The literal meaning of theology is 'God talk', and systematic theology can be understood as the task of showing how the various things Christian communities say about God either do or do not 'stand together' (the literal meaning of the Greek verb from which the word 'systematic' derives) in a coherent and credible way. This process of describing, analyzing, and assessing the relationships among various Christian beliefs is arguably the central task of systematic theology, as well as the primary interest of those who describe their work as dogmatic or constructive theology.

Already in the NT Paul attempts to explain how confession of Jesus as the definitive revelation of God's righteousness holds together with the belief in the divine origin of the Mosaic law (see, e.g., Rom.

3:19–31). Similarly, at the end of the second century Irenaeus of Lyons argued that prayer to the God Jesus called Father held together with worship of the God of Israel against opponents who denied that they could possibly be the same God. Most early works of Christian theology were occasioned by this sort of more or less explicit challenge to the coherence or plausibility of Christian teaching. More formal attempts to give a comprehensive exposition of Christian doctrine (especially for the purposes of educating clergy) emerged somewhat later. One early example, *Exposition of the Orthodox Faith*, written by John of Damascus in the eighth century, continues to play a prominent role in Orthodox theology. In western Europe the *Sentences* of P. Lombard (*ca* 1100–60) served as the main textbook of Catholic theology through the medieval period, after which it tended to be replaced by the *Summa theologiae* of T. Aquinas.

While Protestants deployed a variety of theological manuals from the period of the Reformation onwards, the *Commonplaces* (1521) of P. Melanchthon (1497–1560) and J. Calvin's *Institute of the Christian Religion* (1559) were especially influential in Lutheran and Reformed circles respectively (see Lutheran Theology; Reformed Theology). In the nineteenth century F. Schleiermacher's *Christian Faith* (2nd edn, 1830) introduced a style of systematic theology more critical of traditional doctrinal language than was characteristic of either Protestant or Catholic theology to that point (see Liberal Theology). In the latter half of the twentieth century, increasing recognition of the effects of the economic, political, and cultural contexts within which theology is done on the form and content of theological argument led many theologians to give more explicit attention in their writing to the particular social locations out of which their theologies arise and to which they are directed (see Liberation Theology).

An important aspect of the history of systematic theology as a discipline – one already implicit in Buddeus' definition – is its dual location in the Church and the university. On the one hand, systematic theology is a straightforwardly ecclesial practice designed to serve the Church by clarifying the content of its teaching (i.e., evaluating whether a particular doctrine is genuinely *Christian*). On the other hand, systematic theology has also been an academic discipline that includes the task of clarifying the relationship between Christian doctrine and other forms of human knowledge (i.e., evaluating whether a particular doctrine is *true*). Schleiermacher identified these two dimensions of theological reflection as the 'polemical' and the 'apologetical' respectively, specifying that the former had an inward orientation focused on purifying the Church's teaching from deviant developments, and the latter an outward orientation focused on exhibiting the truth of Christian beliefs to the world at large (*Outline*, §§39–41).

In a very rough fashion, the different perspectives that lead theologians to characterize their work as 'dogmatic', 'systematic', or 'constructive' can be seen to reflect differing sensibilities about the relative weight to be given to the two dimensions of theological reflection identified by Schleiermacher. Thus, proponents of dogmatic theology tend to be more concerned with the 'polemical' task of defining and defending orthodoxy over against heresy, while the language of systematic and constructive theology tends to signal greater emphasis on the 'apologetical' work of defending the credibility of Christian teaching in the face of challenges raised from outside the Church (see Apologetics). Such distinctions are relative, since all theologies struggle both to do justice to the distinctiveness of Christian belief (the fundamental concern of the polemical) and at the same time to present those beliefs in a way that is intelligible (the basic interest of the apologetical). Nevertheless, a particular theologian's perception of the needs of the Church at any particular time will generally lead to one of these dimensions of theological reflection being given particular attention over the other.

Because all social groups have some functioning protocols for distinguishing themselves from and relating themselves to other groups, the distinction between the polemical and the apologetical is in no way unique to Christianity. In order to understand the character of systematic theology as a specifically Christian discipline, therefore, it is necessary to move beyond such formal features of theological reflection to identify some of the material factors that structure the description and evaluation of Christian teaching by Christian theologians. While any such list itself amounts to a theological proposal and is, as such, open to debate, the following three beliefs have proved central to Christian theological reflection in both its polemical and its apologetical modes:

(1) The God of Israel, Creator of heaven and earth, is the one, true God.
(2) This God is not to be identified with any creature.
(3) The life of the human being Jesus of Nazareth is nothing less than God's own life.

These three beliefs stand in some tension with each other: while the second seems to follow from the first (since it stands to reason that the one who is the origin of the whole of the spatio-temporal order cannot be equated with anything in space and time), the third seems to contradict it (since a human life is inherently bound by space and time). These tensions are the root of some of the historically most contested Christian doctrines, including the Trinity and Christology. They are also suggestive of some of the other topics (e.g., creation, revelation) that have been more or less explicit objects of theological analysis from Christianity's inception down to the present day.

The Christian confession that the one true God is the God of Israel, and that this God has taken flesh in Jesus of Nazareth, means that God can be identified accurately only by talking about the very particular, historical realities 'Israel' and 'Jesus'. The polemical dimension of Christian theology is shaped by these historical particularities. To the extent that talk about God is understood to be distinctively Christian only in so far as it refers to Israel and Jesus, it follows that whatever qualities theologians ascribe to God – e.g., omnipotence, omniscience, omnipresence, wisdom, love, mercy, and so on (see Attributes, Divine) – need to be grounded in and interpreted in terms of the stories of Israel and of Jesus. These stories, as found in the OT and NT of the Christian Bible (see Scripture), therefore play a central role in systematic theology. Engagement with biblical texts is generally viewed as essential to the construction of a theological argument, on the grounds that they are an indispensable means of demonstrating that the object of theological discourse is none other than the God of Israel and (therefore) of Jesus Christ.

At the same time, because the God of Israel is believed by Christians to be the source of all that is not God, the apologetical dimension of theology cannot be reduced to a mere tactic designed to help Christianity survive in or prevail over the world. On the contrary, because confessing God as creator of all that is means that talk about God necessarily implicates the whole of reality, Aquinas could define theology as encompassing all things in so far as they are related to God (*ST* 1.1.7). Moreover, because the divine source of that reality is one, Christians have a vested interest in seeing to it that the doctrines they derive from the Bible are consistent with knowledge of the world acquired without reference to Scripture. Only so can the God of Jesus Christ plausibly be identified as the source and ground of all reality.

Yet, while the peculiar characteristics of Christianity demand that attention be given both to the distinctiveness and to the comprehensiveness of doctrines in order to show how they hold together as a coherent whole, these two demands are qualified by the proviso that no words are finally equal to the task of talking about God. Though the aim of theological reflection is to test the Church's talk to see whether it bears genuine witness to God (1 John 4:1), the utter transcendence of God as creator requires the theologian to recognize that all talk about God is inadequate to its object: God is always more and other than whatever we say about God (Isa. 55:8–9; 1 Tim. 6:16). In this respect, there is much to be said for the idea that the job of systematic theology is not to generate a series of propositions that describe God, but rather to discipline Christian God talk so as to give witness precisely to God's character as the one who cannot be described.

Viewed from this perspective, the point of systematic theology is less to provide an exhaustive categorization of what Christians believe than to provide a framework or set of protocols that Christians can use to keep their talk about God flexible enough so that it can bear witness to God as the one who is not to be confused with any creaturely reality (including, according to the definition of Chalcedon, the human nature of Jesus Christ himself). Conceived in this way, an important aim of systematic theology is to help Christians identify what needs to be rejected as inconsistent with their faith. This is not to say that works of systematic theology will in every or even in most cases take the form of anathemas that explicitly reject particular doctrines as un-Christian, but it is to suggest that the function even of positive theological proposals is less to define the characteristics of divinity than to mark the limits outside or in disregard of which human language fails to bear witness to the God of Jesus Christ.

These last considerations should make it clear that systematic theology is not a matter of ivory-tower, theoretical speculation about the nature of God and the world, but rather a 'second step' (Gutiérrez, *Theology* 9) – critical reflection on the life and witness of the Church as it is undertaken in a particular time and place. Systematic theology in its various dimensions thus has the task of examining that life and witness to see whether they are consistent with the Church's commission to proclaim the gospel of Jesus to the whole creation (Mark 16:15; cf. Matt. 28:19–20). It may, in this respect, be understood as the process by which Christians reflect whether that proclamation is true enough to its origins in the preaching of Jesus that it can be heard and received by those within and without the Church as good news.

H. Frei, *Types of Christian Theology* (Yale University Press, 1992).
N. Lash, *The Beginning and the End of 'Religion'* (Cambridge University Press, 1996).
W. Pannenberg, *Theology and the Philosophy of Science* (Westminster Press, 1976).
D. Ritschl, *The Logic of Theology* (SCM, 1986).
K. Tanner, *Theories of Culture: A New Agenda for Theology* (Fortress Press, 1997).
R. Williams, *On Christian Theology* (Blackwell, 2000).

Ian A. McFarland

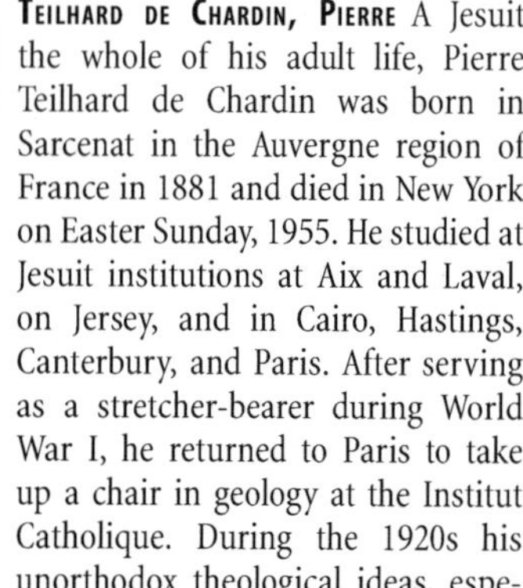

Taizé, Community of The Community of Taizé is an ecumenical monastic community located in southern Burgundy between the historic centres of western MONASTICISM: Cluny and Citeaux. It was founded in 1940 by Brother Roger (1915–2005). Deeply concerned with the division of Christians that he saw as a cause of tension and war in society, Brother Roger left the security of his native Switzerland (where he was a Reformed pastor) and settled, on his own, in the small village of Taizé. There he prayed three times a day and hid Jews fleeing Nazi-occupied France, bringing them safely to Switzerland. Forced to leave when the Gestapo invaded his house, he returned to Geneva where three other men joined him. The little community returned to Taizé in 1944 and quickly grew, attracting men from various Protestant denominations from throughout Europe. After VATICAN COUNCIL II it was also possible for Catholics to join the Community. Today, the Community of Taizé is constituted of brothers from all mainline denominations and from all continents.

Early on, the Community developed a musically rich LITURGY with the help of Father J. Gelineau, S. J. (1920–2008). Drawn by the beautiful liturgy and the novelty of a Protestant monastic community, the number of visitors steadily grew. The twelfth-century village church was soon too small and a larger church was built on the hill of Taizé – the Church of Reconciliation, which can hold up to 8,000 worshippers. With the cultural unrest of the 1960s, there was an explosion of young pilgrims to Taizé. This pilgrimage has continued unabated, and the Community annually hosts tens of thousands of visitors from all over the world.

The prayer of the Community is a simplified form of the classic liturgy of the hours (see DIVINE OFFICE). Comprising simple, repetitive chants (the 'songs of Taizé'), it introduces and carries the concerns, needs, and longings of the world.

The brothers who join the Community do not deny their faith of origin but remain part of the Churches in which they were nurtured. Together, they live and witness to the possibility of a reconciled Church. Many Church leaders, including patriarchs and popes, have praised the life of the Community as a PARABLE of communion. In 1986, Pope John Paul II (r. 1978–2005) visited Taizé and expressed his deep appreciation for the ecumenical witness of the Community.

Contrary to popular rumours, spun when Brother Roger received communion from the hands of the future Pope Benedict XVI (r. 2005–) at the funeral of John Paul II, Brother Roger never 'secretly' converted to Catholicism. Brother Roger was murdered in the Church of Reconciliation on 16 August 2005 during evening prayer, and Brother Alois, a German whom Brother Roger had designated as his successor in the late 1990s, became prior.

O. Clément, *Taizé: A Meaning to Life* (GIA, 1997).

M. Fidanzio, ed., *Brother Roger of Taizé – Essential Writings* (Orbis, 2006).

DIRK G. LANGE

Teilhard de Chardin, Pierre A Jesuit the whole of his adult life, Pierre Teilhard de Chardin was born in Sarcenat in the Auvergne region of France in 1881 and died in New York on Easter Sunday, 1955. He studied at Jesuit institutions at Aix and Laval, on Jersey, and in Cairo, Hastings, Canterbury, and Paris. After serving as a stretcher-bearer during World War I, he returned to Paris to take up a chair in geology at the Institut Catholique. During the 1920s his unorthodox theological ideas, especially about the FALL, came under increasing scrutiny from superiors. As a result, he was sent to China to spend more time on research into palaeontology, a discipline then transforming understanding of human origins.

His key theological works are *The Divine Milieu* (1957) and the collections *Writings in Time of War: 1916–1919* (1965) and *The Heart of Matter* (1976). In these, he unfolds a philosophical theology that in the twentieth century was unsurpassed in mystical and synthetic power. Human life is seen as a dialectic of action, in which humans co-operate with God's transforming activity, and passion, in which they experience diminishment and God's otherness. In a rich and dense COSMOLOGY, spirit provides the unifying principle of matter, and substance is preserved by a bond analogous with the presence of Christ in the EUCHARIST. Teilhard's theology is permeated with a striking vision of Christ revealing himself in the world by transforming human sensory perception of the world. Politically, Teilhard refutes both fascist and Marxist ideology and embraces a global social democracy.

He is best known for his theology of creative EVOLUTION, in which scholars of science and religion have shown much interest. This is developed in many essays and in his most famous work, *The Human Phenomenon* (1955). He accepts the classic Darwinian account of evolution, along with theories of emergence and complexity-consciousness, embedding these in a CHRISTOLOGY in which Christ is the alpha and omega of the created order. Humanity is becoming, he claims, the creative agent of its own future evolution through enhanced technological competence and its ability to manipulate matter and biological life. Key to this evolutionary theology is convergence, a theory in which there is currently renewed interest among palaeobiologists.

The Jesuit order banned Teilhard from publishing any theology during his lifetime, and he remained obedient to this injunction. His oeuvre was compiled and gradually published after his death to wide popular acclaim. Readers need to remember that he had no opportunity to respond to his public reception, or correct the many misinterpretations of his writings by both antagonists and enthusiasts. He therefore provides an easy target for unimaginative critics, but continues to inspire those theologians and Christians who possess a mystical sensibility, a passion for action, and a synthesizing vision.

D. Grumett, *Teilhard de Chardin: Theology, Humanity and Cosmos* (Peeters, 2005).

C. Raven, *Teilhard de Chardin: Scientist and Seer* (Harper & Row, 1962).

DAVID GRUMETT

TELEOLOGICAL ARGUMENT The teleological argument (from the Greek word *telos*, meaning 'goal' or 'end') is also known as the design argument. It involves reasoning from seemingly purposeful features of the natural world to the existence of God. In so far as it attempts to use reason and observation rather than REVELATION to draw conclusions about God, the teleological argument is a form of NATURAL THEOLOGY. In so far as it requires an observational premise, it is an a posteriori argument. Unlike the COSMOLOGICAL ARGUMENT, however, the observational premise of the teleological argument is not some general and incorrigible proposition such as 'there exists a contingent reality'. Rather, the versions of the teleological argument popular in any given era typically refer to specific discoveries of the best available science of that era. The most famous statement of the teleological argument is W. Paley's (1743–1805) *Natural Theology* (1802), in which he compares the exquisitely adapted structures of living creatures to artefacts like the watch and concludes that there quite probably exists a supernatural designer of living things. The force of Paley's argument diminished greatly when C. Darwin (1809–82) provided a fully naturalistic explanation of biological adaptation in *On the Origin of Species* (1859).

From that time the teleological argument lay mostly dormant for more than a century. New scientific discoveries in the latter half of the twentieth century, however, led to its revival. Physics and COSMOLOGY showed that the universe was 'fine-tuned' for life: if the basic parameters of the universe (e.g., its rate of expansion after the Big Bang) differed even slightly from their actual values, life of any sort could not have arisen anywhere in the universe. Consequently, some concluded the universe was designed rather than arose by chance. Furthermore, Big Bang cosmology, coupled with knowledge of the workings of life at the cellular level, opened the door for a new design argument from biology. The temporal and spatial finitude of the universe implied by the Big Bang meant that (contrary to earlier views) there were not unlimited opportunities for life to originate by chance. The alleged 'irreducible complexity' even of life's most basic structures (e.g., DNA) suggested to some that life is better explained as arising from design rather than by chance.

Some respond to the argument from fine-tuning by arguing that it ignores the possibility that our universe is but one in a much larger 'multiverse'. Its apparently fine-tuned features would then be explained in terms of the principle that observers should expect to find themselves in a part of the multiverse that meets whatever conditions are necessary for the existence of observers (see ANTHROPIC PRINCIPLE). Since in the multiverse it is highly likely that some universe is well suited for life, human observers should not be surprised to find themselves in just that sort of universe.

In response to the argument from irreducible complexity, it is said that Darwinian mechanisms are perfectly adequate for explaining even the most complex biological phenomena. And in response to all versions of the teleological argument, philosophers typically raise points made by D. Hume (1711–76) in *Dialogues Concerning Natural Religion* (1779). Even if there is evidence of design, they say, it cannot support the conclusion that the Christian God exists, but at best the conclusion that some limited designer(s) exist(s). Further, the evils and imperfections of the world block any inference to God. Lastly, if the teleological argument is to remain a form of natural theology, free of appeal to revelation, it requires defence of the further (and theologically treacherous) argument that God is likely to create a world like this one.

NEIL A. MANSON

TEMPTATION Biblical terms for 'temptation' (Hebrew *nissah*; Greek *peirasmos*) connote being tested. Christian theology has construed the 'test' of temptation ambivalently: sometimes as a moral danger to avoid, sometimes as a God-given trial to endure by GRACE (though cf. Jas. 1:13). This ambivalence is not surprising since, at its heart, temptation is a crisis of interpretation, a dilemma about the place of doubt in the life of FAITH. Christian discourse on temptation speaks to all manner of borderline dwelling places, from moral struggle to conform to a known right path, to confusion about the right direction, to entrapment in a state of distrust that afflicts the traumatized, depressed, or despairing and surrounds them with THEODICY questions. TEMPTATION's multifarious sources within theological discourse (e.g., sinful human nature, the demonic, God) amplify this hermeneutical struggle. Discourse on temptation snakes beneath the surface of other doctrinal discussions in sundry ways because, as a flashpoint for doubt, temptation marks the instability of movement between SIN and redemption. Temptation especially interrogates the doctrine of sin. As the test of faithfulness, temptation can be the path to sin, the effect of sin, or the sign of sin's redefining – whenever the Holy Spirit evokes a new vision of right relations.

Christian theologies tend to construe the more familiar face of temptation – the dynamics of moral and spiritual decay – through meditation upon the original story of deception among Eve, Adam, and a serpent in Genesis 2–3, often as informed by Paul's portrayal of the idolatrous root of human self-deception in Romans 1. Here temptation names the cluster of forces that invite our self-deception about what is good or evil – including the Devil, the flesh (understood as including embodied desires *and* spiritual passions), bad habits, the persuasive influence of 'the world', and an idolatrous 'will to power'. Typical theological treatments of temptation parse its psychological dynamics, origins, and types, and develop guides to overcoming it. Monastics like Ammonas (*fl. ca* 350) map ways to contend with the restless boredom (acedia) that tempts one away from prayerful warfare with sin. Augustine generated many fruitful trajectories for depicting the origin of temptation, which he frames in the context of original sin's effects in concupiscence: an inordinate desire for finite goods as ends in themselves, inherited from the old Adam and vying with the new Adam created in us by Christ's Spirit. Reflecting on motives for pranks, Augustine alludes to peer pressure and the gratuitousness of evil, committed for *no reason* (i.e., as a surd). Ultimately, perhaps, he locates temptation in the idolatrous desire to imitate God's sovereignty over moral norms by giddily defying them.

More sympathetic accounts of our vulnerability to temptation emerged in the twentieth century, but they form part of a longer tradition about another facet of temptation: doubt about what properly to name as sin. This is one way to construe recent reassessments of temptation shaped by post-Freudian psychology and shifts in attitudes about gender and sexuality. On the one hand, locating the origins of temptation in natural instincts and the unavoidable tensions accompanying our finitude fostered a more empathetic attitude to temptation as something less than insidious. On the other hand, feminist critiques illuminated the patriarchal dimensions of 'temptations' that demonize women by blaming them for men's sexual temptations (see Feminist Theology), while postmodern accounts of the saving goodness of eros have critiqued repressive, pathological dimensions of the discourse of temptation itself by celebrating passionate relationality and the transgressing of boundaries that establish normative – but oppressive – identities. These developments redefine what *constitutes* sin in ways that others might regard as *capitulating* to temptation, especially in so far as temptation presupposes our fallibility to an inveterate idolatry rooted in the structure of our finitude, our desire to secure and fulfil our mortal existence. Yet even where temptation entails rationalizing our decisions to commit known sin, temptation operates through our human capacities for introspection, doubting, and imagining multiple interpretive frameworks; sin's beginning – and redefining – starts with the serpent's question, 'Did God say ... ?' (Gen. 3:1). Indeed, the rhetoric of temptation can *itself* become a sinful weapon in struggles over competing interpretations of the Word and the Holy Spirit – especially concerning the configuration of the body of Christ itself. Faced with Gentile converts, what was the first Christian temptation: to break with God's Word in the Torah, or to resist the Spirit's nudging to extend and redefine Jesus' kingdom of God movement? Temptation-bearing questions appear in Christian debates ranging from definitions of heresy to the ordination of sexual minorities. Especially regarding contested interpretations of Scripture, when the rhetoric of temptation is wielded to demonize opponents, the greatest temptation is to stab the body of Christ itself.

Indeed, our relation to temptation falls into two types: temptation born of presumption (i.e., blind certainty of our rightness); and temptation born of despair (i.e., grave doubt about the goodness of ourselves, others, and/or God). As M. Luther affirmed, a *faithful* bearing of temptation to despair reads over the face of affliction by insisting upon the presence of God's redeeming Word. Faithfully met temptation endures the doubt in genuine uncertainty – including uncertainty about how to promote non-presumptively one's own convictions in a debate. But when a despairing form of temptation involves seemingly *divine* pressure to move in a direction that triggers moral queasiness (e.g., Peter feeling asked to eat unclean animals in Acts 10, or Abraham to sacrifice his son in Gen. 22), temptation draws us into the most perplexing questions of faith – into the hidden side of God, who might wear the mask of Satan for pedagogical *or* cryptic ends. For those seeking to know the Spirit's intentions, *and* for those whom God's Spirit abandons or oppresses, temptation stands at the spot of division – or conflation – between demonic and divine agency.

Christian response to all temptation entails participation in the life and grace of Christ, who is model, carrier, and healer of the tempted. Driven by God's Spirit to be tempted by Satan (Matt. 4:1–11 and pars.), Jesus identifies with all who face trial at God's behest; in faith, Christians participate in Christ's naming and rebuking demonic invitations to distort God's Word through selective interpretations that silence its wider fullness.

V. Burrus and C. Keller, *Toward a Theology of Eros: Transfiguring Passion at the Limits of Discipline* (Fordham University Press, 2006).

E. Farley, *Good and Evil: Interpreting a Human Condition* (Fortress Press, 1990).
W. E. Oates, *Temptation: A Biblical and Psychological Approach* (John Knox Press, 1991.
P. Ricœur, *The Symbolism of Evil* (Beacon Press, 1986).

AMY CARR

TERESA OF AVILA Teresa of Avila (1515–82) came from a well-to-do family of merchants. She entered the Carmelite monastery of the Incarnation in Avila (Spain) at the age of twenty. Twenty years later, she had a 'second CONVERSION' – an experience of tears before a statue of the wounded Christ, which she likened to AUGUSTINE's conversion in the *Confessions* – and this led her to plan a reform of the Carmelite Order, to return it to its early focus on contemplation. In 1562 she began her programme of reform with the founding of St Joseph's in Avila, which was followed by sixteen further foundations for nuns in the remaining twenty years of her life. She also set up a similar reform among the Carmelite friars, with John of the Cross (1542–91) as one of her first recruits. She wrote prolifically during this time, a dangerous activity for a woman in sixteenth-century Spain. She died in 1582, was canonized in 1622, and became a doctor of the Catholic Church in 1970. Her best-known works are her *Life* and *Way of Perfection* (both written before 1567), and the *Interior Castle* (1577).

Teresa has been studied in a variety of contexts in recent scholarship: as a mystic writing at the end of the great medieval flowering of mystical theology; as a religious reformer of the Catholic REFORMATION; as a feminine writer seeking authority against oppressive cultural and social forces; and as a theologian in her own right. It is now clear that Teresa was not the artless and theologically ignorant woman that she often said she was. While using homely images of watering the garden or spinning a cocoon, and mystical language of union, ecstasy, and so on, rather than scholastic language, she developed ideas of God's presence which contribute significantly to MYSTICAL THEOLOGY.

First, she reflects, especially in the *Interior Castle*, on the difficult process of integrating the relationship with God with human activity and development. She seeks to bring God's transcendence into the 'centre' of the person without removing its unlimited dynamism, thus giving the relationship between God's transcendence and immanence a creative theological–anthropological treatment. Second, Teresa's investigation of the 'interior' of the SOUL takes the theological and psychological journey into the soul, popular since Augustine, to new levels of detail, particularly in the examination of the state of mystical union. Union is mapped in a way which allows for the discernment of different kinds and stages of union, with unusual acuity. Third, Teresa's final position in the *Interior Castle*, that there is a union of contemplation and action, where prayer and virtuous work join together, though a common theme in late medieval mystical theology, is given a nicely constructed anthropological basis, showing how God-directed and world-directed activity can spring from a single 'interior root'. Finally, Teresa's reflections on the place of the TRINITY and Christ in union bring her practical concerns into conversation with questions of unity and difference in God, particularly concerning the humanity of Christ. She finds ways of distinguishing interior and exterior functions of the self in the life of prayer without dividing them – again bringing transcendence and immanence together in her anthropology – by setting them within Christological and Trinitarian patterns of distinction and unity.

E. Howells, *John of the Cross and Teresa of Avila: Mystical Knowing and Selfhood* (Crossroad, 2002).
R. Williams, *Teresa of Avila* (Geoffrey Chapman, 1991).

EDWARD HOWELLS

TERESA OF LISIEUX Marie-Françoise-Thérèse Martin was born on 2 January 1873 in Alençon and died on 30 September 1897 in Lisieux. She entered the Carmel of Lisieux in 1888 and is known in religious life as 'Teresa of the Child Jesus and of the Holy Face'. Canonized by Pius XI (r. 1922–39) in 1925 and proclaimed, with F. Xavier (1506–52), universal patron of the missions in 1927, she was declared the thirty-third doctor of the Church by John Paul II (r. 1978–2005) in 1997. Her feast is celebrated on 1 October in the ordinary Roman calendar.

One of the most popular Catholic SAINTS of modern times, Teresa is known for her teaching on spiritual childhood or 'the little way': Christians achieve holiness by performing well the small tasks of daily life with a childlike trust in God's mercy, an absolute confidence in God's will to save all who throw themselves upon God's goodness. For Teresa, the fundamental VOCATION of every human being is self-giving LOVE. Because a Christian's good deeds are only as valuable as the love that gives rise to them, great love makes even small deeds mighty. While such teaching is given consummate expression in her *Story of a Soul* (1898), the autobiography she was bidden to write by her superior, it is also found throughout her various if not voluminous writings, which include letters, conversations, prayers, poems, and plays. Devotion to St Teresa accompanied by the study of her writings has been widespread in all countries where the Catholic Church is present; her appeal has often extended beyond confessional and religious boundaries.

PETER A. KWASNIEWSKI

TERTULLIAN Septimius Tertullianus (Quintus Septimius Florens Tertullianus in medieval manuscripts) was a Christian author of the late second to early third century. His importance to Christian theology rests not only on the breadth of topics in thirty-one extant works and his rigorist attitudes (often expressed in a fiery style), but on his being the first Christian Latin-writing author whose works survived. Much of theology's Latin vocabulary is dependent on him.

The biographical details, mostly derived from Jerome and Eusebius of Caesarea (*ca* 260–*ca* 340), that he was the son of a centurion, was a presbyter of Carthage, was a lawyer or even a jurist working in Rome, and lapsed into Montanism and left (or was forced out of) the Church, are rejected convincingly by T. Barnes (b. 1942). What may be known comes from his own output: he converted to Christianity from paganism, he was a married man who admitted to adultery, he was highly educated with rhetorical training, and his literary base was probably Carthage itself. Though he was an adherent of Montanism, and this fact created tensions with those he viewed as less spiritual Christians, it should not be taken as indicating that he was schismatic.

As a writer Tertullian was a polemicist; he did not compose systematic and comprehensive theological treatises, but engaged in winning debates and refuting and correcting what he considered to be false beliefs. He used Scripture, non-Christian literature, historical and natural examples, and logic (even the natural logic of the untrained soul according to *De testimonio animae*) to win his case, making full use of classical rhetorical argumentation. In reading Tertullian's statements one must always place them in their rhetorical context by first determining the position held by his opponent, for inevitably he would argue against it, even if that involved contradicting something he had advanced elsewhere. For example, if an opponent believed a biblical passage should be read literally, Tertullian would argue for a figurative or allegorical reading, while in a different work with a different opponent he could argue for the opposite. So instances where Tertullian seems to contradict himself (and they are many) may reflect changes in his thinking over time, particularly as he becomes more uncompromising under the influence of Montanism (e.g., the rejection of further reconciliation after baptism – allowed in the early *De paenitentia* but rejected for serious sin in the later *De pudicitia* – or the legitimacy of second marriage after the death of a spouse – allowed in the earlier *Ad uxorem* but not in his later *De exhortation castitatis* and *De monogamia*); but they may also simply reflect his determination to win a debate using whatever arguments worked best at the time.

His most famous work is *Apologeticum*, in which he argued forensically that Christians were innocent of charges like incest, cannibalism, and murder, and were justified or misunderstood with regard to charges like atheism, sacrilege, and treason. To an ostensibly non-Christian readership he indicated Christian non-separatist support for state and society. In *Ad Scapulam*, a more hortatory work addressed to the local governor, Tertullian appealed for an end to persecution. *De pallio* argues that anyone with philosophical insight ought to be Christian. In a work for Christians, however, like *De spectaculis*, Tertullian argued that to participate in the spectacles of Roman entertainment and its associated religious underpinnings was to reject Christianity. In *De idololatria* he asserted that Christians must not contaminate themselves with the polluted world: sacred and secular were irreconcilable. Christian women need to be veiled to protect them from the snares of the world, as argued in *De cultu feminarum* and *De virginibus velandis*. In *Ad martyras* he offered martyrdom as the ultimate, desirable rejection of the world and in his commentary on the Lord's Prayer (*De oratione*) he desired the swift end of the present age. While at one time he expressed an understanding of those who avoided persecution (in *De patientia* and *Ad uxorem*), later (*De fuga in persecutione*) he found this intolerable. In *De corona militis* he rejected the possibility of Christians serving in the military.

In his longest work, *Adversus Marcionem*, Tertullian rejected the dualism of Marcion, who believed that the God revealed in the OT was a different, lesser God than the one revealed by Jesus in the Gospels. For Tertullian, Jesus revealed the OT creator, who was the same God who had announced the coming of the saviour. Tertullian also argued against the Gnostic Hermogenes, who believed that matter was eternal, which, for Tertullian, amounted to a belief in a second god (*Adversus Hermogenem*). Against the (possibly pseudonymous) Praxeas, who to defend the unity of God asserted that the Son was the Father in another guise (modalism or patripassianism), Tertullian advocated in *Adversus Praxean* that while there was a Trinity (*trinitas*) of Persons (*personarum*) there was only one God in one substance or being (*substantia*) – terminology that became standard in Latin theology. Even though Tertullian's Trinitarianism – according to which the Father was greater than the Son, who was greater than the Holy Spirit – does not correspond to later Nicene orthodoxy, neither was it some form of the emanationism taught by Valentinus (*Adversus Valentinianos*).

Tertullian taught that the human person is composed of body and soul, with each eternal soul being formed through conception (traducianism). Although he believed in the goodness of creation, he also believed in original sin (*De anima*) and the necessity of baptism for salvation (*De baptismo*). The importance of human flesh was seen in the fact that Christ was born with real flesh (*De carne Christi*) and that flesh will be resurrected (*De resurrectione mortuorum*). The Jews had been superseded in God's favour by the Christians (*Adversus Judaeos*), while heretics could not belong to the Church at all (*De praescriptione haereticorum*); and later – particularly under the influence of Montanism – he asserted that the Church consisted only of the pure, one sign of which was rigorous fasting (*De jejunio*).

T. D. Barnes, *Tertullian: A Historical and Literary Study*, revised edn (Oxford University Press, 1985).
G. D. Dunn, *Tertullian* (Routledge, 2004).
E. Osborn, *Tertullian: First Theologian of the West* (Cambridge University Press, 1997).

GEOFFREY D. DUNN

TETRAGRAMMATON The term 'tetragrammaton' (from the Greek for 'four-letter word') refers to the four Hebrew letters – generally transliterated YHWH – of the proper name of the God of Israel, as given to Moses in Exodus 3:15. The narrative of Exodus 3 suggests that the name is connected etymologically with the Hebrew word for 'to be' (*hayah*); nevertheless, its precise meaning and original pronunciation remain uncertain, though scholarly convention follows the conjecture of W. Gesenius (1786–1842) that the divine name was originally pronounced 'Yahweh'.

The Jewish sense of the sacredness of the divine name, combined with the explicit prohibition of its misuse in the Ten COMMANDMENTS (Exod. 20:7, Deut. 5:11; cf. Lev. 24:11–16) led to its dropping out of common speech, and even its liturgical use ceased after the destruction of the Jerusalem temple in AD 70. Instead, Jews adopted the custom of reading out the word 'adonai' ('My Lord') when encountering the tetragrammaton in the biblical text. This practice is reflected in the translation of the tetragrammaton by *kyrios* ('Lord') in the SEPTUAGINT, and has been followed in most Christian translations of the OT.

The custom of not pronouncing the divine name gives witness to shared Jewish and Christian conviction regarding God's transcendence: God is neither reducible to creaturely categories, nor subject to creatures' manipulation or control. At the same time, the putative links between the tetragrammaton and the Hebrew word for 'to be' have been interpreted as bearing witness to God's status as creator: the sole cause and ground of all creaturely being.

IAN A. MCFARLAND

THEODICY The problem of theodicy arises when faith in God's PROVIDENCE – God's goodness and power to care for us – is challenged by experiencing or witnessing evils beyond our control. G. Leibniz (1646–1716) coined the term 'theodicy' (from the Greek *theos*, 'god', and *dikē*, 'justice') in the 1690s to refer to the philosophical problem that arises for belief in God given the seeming incompatibility of four premises: (1) God exists; (2) God is good and just; (3) God is all-powerful; and (4) evil and suffering exist. Centuries before, Boethius (*ca* 480–*ca* 525) gave classic expression to this ancient problem: *Si Deus justus, unde malum?* ('If God is righteous, whence evil?'). Nonetheless, the term 'theodicy' need not be limited to the theoretical problem of justifying belief in God in the face of evil. A vast literature – ancient and modern – addresses the practical problem believers and unbelievers struggle with as they experience or witness evils that challenge either their sense of agency or what they have learnt about God from others (see Job 42:5).

We can classify theodicies based on their stance on the four premises mentioned above. One typology consists of theodicies that negate one of these four premises. One type denies the idea of *one God*, as in polytheistic beliefs in the involvement of gods in human fate and forms of Buddhism and Hinduism that understand gods and humans to be under the law of karma (moral retribution). A second denies *divine goodness and justice* (at least of a sort that humans can discern), as seen in references in ancient Near Eastern texts to the malicious behaviour of gods towards humans. A third type (often called 'dualism') denies *divine omnipotence* and includes both beliefs in a cosmic battle waged between a good deity and an evil antagonist and (albeit within a very different COSMOLOGY) PROCESS THEOLOGY. Finally, a fourth type (often called 'monism') denies the *existence of evil and suffering* and includes a Vedantic tradition, which defines suffering as *maya* (an illusion that does not affect the eternal soul), and PLATONISM, which defines evil as an absence of perfection and therefore as nothing in itself.

Another typology consists of theodicies found in SCRIPTURE and in most forms of Judaism and Christianity that draw on it. These theodicies affirm all four of the premises mentioned above. *Retribution theodicy*, central to the COVENANT theology of Israel, has sources in the Genesis story of CREATION and other biblical narratives, legal and prophetic literature, and eschatological, APOCALYPTIC, and WISDOM literature. It claims that evil and suffering result from God's wrath and justice on evildoers who disobey divine commands. *Educative theodicy*, found in much of the biblical tradition and in biblical writing that emerged during and after the historical crisis of the Babylonian exile, perceives suffering as something God uses to purify and educate believers, and to give them a more profound understanding of life. *Eschatological* or *recompense theodicy*, identified with eschatological and apocalyptic theology, comforts and exhorts righteous sufferers with the hope that God will ultimately vindicate their sufferings at the end of history. Stressing the *mystery of theodicy*, theodicies found in the lament psalms and the Wisdom tradition (especially JOB) focus on how humans cannot make God responsible for innocent suffering because finite human reason cannot fathom God's incomprehensible wisdom. Finally, *communion theodicy* spotlights how God is not only present with sufferers in a profound way, but also suffers for and with God's people. In particular, Isaiah 52:13–53:12 speaks of a mediator between God and the people whose vicarious sacrifice atones for the SINS and suffering of others. This text was influential not only for Christian interpretations of Jesus' death, but also (and especially when combined with eschatological and educative theodicies) for theologies that informed later Jewish and Christian theologies of MARTYRDOM.

Early Christians drew on these theodicies to interpret the 'scandal' of Jesus' death (1 Cor. 1:18–25) and their own experiences of suffering and evil. Presupposing God's wrath against sin and evil, they believed Jesus fulfilled eschatological and apocalyptic expectation. As Messiah, he not only became the sacrifice who vicariously atoned for the sins of all, but also even faced god-forsakenness himself. In addition, early Christians used educative motifs to interpret their own sufferings.

Church fathers like IRENAEUS and AUGUSTINE interpreted biblical theodicies in light of Middle Platonism. Countering Gnostic dualism, Irenaeus emphasized the unity of God and salvation history (see GNOSTICISM). Created in God's 'image', Adam and Eve were like children who had yet to mature into God's 'likeness'. Although their first 'trespass' interrupted their maturation, Jesus Christ, as the apex of salvation history, not only undoes the evils that resulted from their sin, but 'recapitulates' or 'sums up' all of creaturely existence. Participating in him, believers find that even the evils they experience are means by which they come to know God more fully.

Countering the dualism of MANICHAEISM, Augustine maintained that, as the supreme good, God is the most intensely real being; all that God creates receives its reality from God's goodness. Evil is merely a privation or perversion of something good and so lacks independent existence. It enters the created world because of the free choice of creatures, humans and angels. Their choice to sin is not a positive choice – again, evil has no real existence – but a turning away from the higher good, God, for a lower good. NATURAL EVILS, such as diseases, are divinely ordained consequences of a primeval fall. The choice to sin is itself an originating cause. Lacking any prior cause, its source lies in the mystery of human and angelic freedom. Nonetheless, because God seeks a relationship with free creatures, God's infinite creativity can use evil as a means to bring about even greater beauty and goodness in the universe.

The Reformers also drew on Augustine, but shifted attention to the divine creative righteousness that justifies sinners through GRACE. M. LUTHER'S *THEOLOGIA CRUCIS* counters human pretensions to goodness with Christ's suffering and death, which overcomes all sin, suffering, and death. Although J. CALVIN also emphasized God's electing providence as a comfort to sinners and sufferers, he was more emphatic than Luther in arguing for a double PREDESTINATION – the doctrine that God saves some and eternally damns others. Later Protestant ORTHODOXY argued that evil falls within God's universal rule of the world. Although God allows evil (without endorsing it), God nonetheless sets limits to it and will overcome it in the end.

Influenced by this approach, the Lutheran philosopher Leibniz developed his optimistic conception of this world as the 'best of all possible worlds', arguing that God's reasons for allowing evil are infinitely greater than our reasons; physical ills are simply a means for bringing about an even greater good. Voltaire (1694–1778) satirized this view and D. Hume (1711–76) countered it by arguing that the world's evils demonstrated that there was no intelligent God designing the universe. Undergirding these arguments was a shift in world view away from perceiving that the real world lies behind the appearances – and evils – we experience (as presupposed in Platonic metaphysics) to perceiving that the empirical world – with its evils – is the real world. Because of this shift, modern thinkers became preoccupied not with justifying God's goodness and power in the face of evil but with finding the intelligibility and meaning of life in a world of evil (e.g., I. KANT, G. W. F. HEGEL) or with examining the genesis of evil within human experience (e.g., F. NIETZSCHE and S. Freud (1856–1939)). After the HOLOCAUST, Hiroshima, and other mass murders (Rwanda, Bosnia, etc.), the philosophical problem of theodicy tends to be viewed with suspicion, on the grounds that attempts to justify God invariably diminish the suffering of the victims. Nevertheless, many thinkers, whether theist or not, continue to grapple with the problem of evil.

Contemporary Christian philosophers have sought to defend the intelligibility of belief in God in spite of evil in the face of criticisms based on logic (i.e., that a good and all-powerful God is incompatible with evil) and evidence, especially the evidence of 'gratuitous suffering' from which no good can possibly come. A. Plantinga (b. 1932) has argued for a 'free-will defence' – that God must create humans capable of moral evil in order to preserve free will. Process thinkers, starting with A. Whitehead (1861–1947) and C. Hartshorne (1897–2000) have argued that God is not omnipotent and thus there are evils (including gratuitous evils) which God cannot prevent, although God also enables humans to actualize their full potential in spite of evil. Drawing on Irenaeus and F. SCHLEIERMACHER, J. Hick (b. 1922) argues that humans come to maturity through the 'soul-making' that occurs as God guides their struggle with evil. M. McCord Adams (b. 1943) shifts attention to the devastation 'horrendous evils' bring to individual lives and argues, drawing on Trinitarian and Christological resources, that God's goodness defeats the 'depths of horrors' by participating in them – not only balancing them off but also endowing them with positive meaning.

Increasingly, Christian theologians have attended to theodicy not only as a theoretical problem, but also as a practical problem. This approach is characteristic both of systematic theologians like D. SOELLE and J. Moltmann (b. 1926) and practical theologians like S. Hauerwas (b. 1940) and J. Swinton (b. 1957). Human reason cannot resolve why God allows natural evil (e.g., earthquakes, floods), but we can attend to MORAL EVIL (the cruelty and injustice we inflict on each other) and the deleterious consequences of all evils. Foremost of all, theodicy must take the experience and witness of sufferers seriously, since God's providential ways always work towards the good of all. Further, as classic Christian teaching on SIN affirms, all people are responsible, albeit in varying ways, for how they contribute to and respond to the evils that befall others and themselves. Trinitarian and Christological belief affirms that God in Christ not only suffers with us in our struggle with evil – a participation that does not negate but is the most paradoxical expression of divine power and goodness – but also resists and defeats evil. Faced with God's mystery, evil may perplex us, but it cannot paralyze us. With FAITH in God's creative providence, we can learn and grow through our own suffering; moreover, funded by an eschatological hope in God's ultimate victory, human beings receive power to transform the consequences of evil in this world into good, especially for those who have the least power.

S. Davis, ed., *Encountering Evil*, 2nd edn (John Knox Press, 2001).
A. Laato and J. C. DeMoor, eds., *Theodicy in the World of the Bible* (Brill, 2003).
S. Niemann, *Evil in Modern Thought: An Alternative History of Philosophy* (Princeton University Press, 2002).
P. Ricœur, *The Symbolism of Evil* (Beacon Press, 1967).
K. Surin, *Theology and the Problem of Evil* (Blackwell, 1986).

LOIS MALCOLM

THEODORE THE STUDITE Though also a significant agent of monastic reform, Theodore the Studite (759–826) is best known as one of the leading defenders of icons during the second phase of the Byzantine iconoclastic controversy of the eighth and ninth centuries (see ICONOCLASM). Educated for a career in the imperial bureaucracy, Theodore became a monk under the influence of his maternal uncle and later abbot of the monastery of Studios in Constantinople. His career was marked by controversy with the imperial government, leading to three periods of exile: two (in 797 and from 809 to 811) for his opposition to the divorce and remarriage of Emperor Constantine VI (r. 780–97), and the third (from 815 to 821) for his defence of the icons.

In his three *Refutations of the Iconoclasts*, Theodore developed the Christological arguments pioneered by JOHN OF DAMASCUS and the second Council of Nicaea (787), according to which iconoclasm implies denial of Christ's humanity, since the capacity to be depicted is a constitutive feature of human beings as embodied entities. Against the iconoclasts' argument that an icon could only depict Christ's humanity and therefore was inconsistent with the Council of CHALCEDON's decree that Christ's divine and human natures were inseparable, Theodore countered that an icon did not depict human *nature* in the abstract, but rather an individual *person* whose attributes (eyes, hair, build, etc.) particularize that nature. In short, while Christ is able to be depicted because of his human nature (since that is the reason he has eyes, hair, and the like), what is depicted – and venerated – in the icon is the person present in that nature and not the nature itself.

R. Cholij, *Theodore the Stoudite: The Ordering of Holiness* (Oxford University Press, 2002).

IAN A. MCFARLAND

THEOLOGIA CRUCIS The Latin phrase *theologia crucis*, or 'theology of the CROSS', derives from M. LUTHER's *Heidelberg Disputation* of 1518. In that text Luther cites 1 Corinthians 1:21–5 and John 14:8–9 to contrast the 'theologian of the cross' with the 'theologian of glory'. He characterizes the former as the true Christian theologian, who presumes to see God only where God has made God's self visible, viz., in Christ and his cross. By contrast, the theologian of glory disregards God's own chosen form of revelation in Christ and imagines that it is possible to perceive God's invisible majesty (viz., the divine wisdom, power, and glory) in the created order without reference to the weakness and suffering of Christ's humanity.

Though Luther himself did not develop the 'theology of the cross' as an explicit theme in his later writings, his claim that 'true theology and recognition of God are in the crucified Christ' (*Heid.*, §20) has proved extraordinarily influential in modern Protestant theology as a critique of any form of NATURAL THEOLOGY that claims real knowledge of God apart from Christ. J. Moltmann (b. 1926) in particular has invoked the idea of a theology of the cross to argue that only a God capable of incorporating suffering and death into the divine life is credible in the wake of the unprecedented scale of human suffering (especially the HOLOCAUST) experienced in the twentieth century.

J. Moltmann, *The Crucified God: The Cross of Christ as the Foundation and Criticism of Christian Theology* (Fortress Press, 1993 [1972]).

IAN A. MCFARLAND

THEOLOGICAL ANTHROPOLOGY The phrase 'theological anthropology' refers to the Christian DOCTRINE of human being. Methodologically, it differs from social–scientific disciplines related to the study of humankind (e.g., cultural, physical, or social anthropology) in that it is specifically concerned with humanity's relationship to the triune God. Because human beings are understood to have been made by God like all other entities, theological anthropology is in the first instance a sub-topic of the doctrine of CREATION. At the same time, because the belief that the second Person of the Trinity has lived a specifically human life as the man Jesus of Nazareth is central to Christian faith, theological anthropology also stands in close relation to Christology.

The tension created by the affirmation of humanity's common origin with all other creatures on the one hand, and its special destiny as the one creature taken into the divine life through the incarnation on the other, has shaped the history of Christian reflection on human being. Something of this tension is visible already in the Old Testament. The first chapters of Genesis state that human beings were created on the same day (Gen. 1:24–7) and from the same material (Gen. 2:7, 19) as the other terrestrial animals, and that all are given the same food (Gen. 1:29–30); moreover, God's command for a weekly day of rest extends not only to human beings, but also to the animals that serve them (Deut. 5:12–14; cf. Deut. 25:4). At the same time, humanity is clearly set apart: animals are made with a view to human flourishing (Gen. 2:18–19), and human beings are given dominion over them (Gen. 1:28; cf. 9:2). Yet the witness of the Old Testament regarding humanity's place in the cosmos remains ambiguous: while Psalm 8 glories in humanity's distinctive place within the created order, the writer of Ecclesiastes sees no distinction between humanity and other animals (Eccl. 3:18–21; cf. Ps. 49:20).

As D. Kelsey (b. 1932) has argued, these differing perspectives on humanity can be seen as reflecting distinct anthropological plotlines within the biblical canon. According to one of these, human life is seen as securely positioned within the world of nature, within which it has its own particular contours, to be lived out in dependence on God's providential care (e.g., Job 10:5–12; 14:1–2; Ps. 39:4–7; 90:3–15; 103:13–18; Matt. 5:45; cf. Sir. 33:10–13). While from this perspective human suffering and mortality are a natural feature of finite (i.e., created) existence, a second plotline sees both as the unnatural consequence of human sin (Gen. 2:16–17; 3:16–19; Rom. 5:12–14; cf. Gen. 6:1–3), the effects of which can be overcome only by divine intervention (Rom. 5:6, 15–19; 1 Cor. 15:22; 2 Cor. 5:18–19). Taken together, these two plotlines bear witness to convictions affirming both humanity's being at home in the world and humanity's alienation from the basic form of its worldly existence as intended by God. Still a third anthropological plotline points to the hope of a destiny beyond the world that may be combined with either of the other two perspectives (Dan. 12:2–3; 1 Cor. 15:45–9; Rev. 21:1–5; 22:3–5).

Notwithstanding this pluralism of anthropological themes in Scripture, the presence of passages suggesting that even angels are in an inferior position before God when compared to human beings (1 Pet. 1:12) has resulted in a strong tendency for Christian theologians to construct anthropologies highlighting human distinctiveness from and superiority over other creatures, even if the effects of sin may obscure this fact in the present. At the same time, one approach especially prominent in Orthodox theology has been to interpret human distinctiveness precisely in terms of the close connection between humanity and the rest of creation. The fact that humans have, on the one hand, a material body like other animals and, on the other, a rational mind or soul like angels led Maximus the Confessor to argue that humanity is best understood as a microcosm: uniting both the material and spiritual dimensions of creation in such a way as to recapitulate the structure of the whole universe in miniature and so serve as the focal point through which God shapes and, ultimately, consummates the divine relationship to the whole of the created order (*Amb.* 41).

From the second century onwards, however, the majority of theologians in East and West focused on the biblical claim that human beings were created 'in the image of God' (Gen. 1:27) as the decisive clue to understanding how humankind is related both to the rest of creation and to God. Unfortunately, the Bible itself offers no definition of this enigmatic phrase, and theological consensus on its central importance has not translated into agreement regarding its meaning. Some, noting that God's intention to create human beings in the divine image is correlated with their being assigned dominion over the other animals (Gen. 1:26), have interpreted the phrase *functionally*: human beings bear God's image in that they rule over creation on God's behalf. In the modern period especially, others have argued that the parallelism between God's having created humankind 'in the image of God' and 'male and female' in Genesis 1:27 implies that the divine image should be understood *relationally*, as something found in those patterns of human mutuality typified by the loving union of man and woman in marriage. The most widely held position, however, has interpreted the divine image *noetically*, as referring to some mental capacity (e.g., reason, freedom, or self-consciousness) that elevates human beings above all other earthly creatures by virtue of the fact that they possess distinct spiritual capacities that reflect God's own transcendence of the material order.

Serious objections can be raised against each of these positions. Humanity's dominion over the other creatures is more naturally read as a consequence of creation in the divine image than as its content. And given that the biblical writers recognize that sexual dimorphism is not unique to humankind (Gen. 6:19), the juxtaposition of 'male and female' with 'the image of God' seems better explained as affirming that both men and women are created in God's image than as identifying the image with sexual difference. Finally, the various noetic approaches, for all their popularity, accord ill with the principle that no creaturely capacity, however powerful or distinctive, is ontologically more like God than any other, since the very fact that something is created renders it infinitely closer to other creatures than to the Creator. Nevertheless, all three approaches do attempt to make sense of the way in which humanity appears in the Bible as occupying a crucial place in the relationship between Creator and creation. For this reason, each provides a useful reference point for identifying key features of that broader relationship.

Although most traditional theological anthropologies have focused on humanity's noetic capacities as the decisive point of contact between the creaturely and the divine, the anthropological significance of the human body could never be ignored completely, given the central place belief in bodily RESURRECTION held for Christians from the earliest times (1 Cor. 15:12–19). IRENAEUS OF LYONS explicitly included the human body as part of the divine image (*AH* 5.6.1), and the idea of humanity as a microcosm exploits precisely human beings' embodiment as crucial to their place in the created order. Thus, if the kinship with the rest of the material order to which the body bears witness was sometimes a source of embarrassment for theologians, it explains Paul's view that humanity's longing for bodily redemption is shared by the whole of creation (Rom. 8:19–23) – as well as suggesting that modern science's claim of a common ancestry for all living things has more resonance with the biblical witness than its religious critics recognize.

A second feature of Christian belief regarding the character of human existence is also bound up with reflection on what unites humanity with other creatures. Though all creatures (precisely *as* creatures) are radically other than God, still the fact that they are from God means that they are bound to God as inescapably as they are bound to one another. In other words, to be *from* God is also in some way (which differs for every type of creature) to be *for* God, in the sense of having a purpose under God. Since God stands in no need of the creature, moreover, this purpose is none other than the continuous flourishing of creation itself as a theatre of God's glory. To be from God as a creature is therefore to have an integrity over against God as a distinct sort of being – a particular created 'nature' – the purpose of which is to be empowered by God (whether by natural or by supernatural means) to be just the nature it was created to be.

Needless to say, the claim that every creature exists to fulfil its nature raises all manner of questions about how any particular nature comes to be fulfilled. The debates in theological anthropology over the meaning of the divine image exemplify the difficulties associated with defining what is truly 'natural' for human beings. Nor have these disagreements been merely intellectual matters: the privileging of certain features (e.g., intelligence, especially as identified with particular cultural developments or predilections) has led to certain classes of people (especially males of European descent) being regarded as exemplifying human nature in a way that has led the humanity of others (e.g., men of colour and all women) to be judged deficient. Perhaps no feature of traditional theological anthropology has been more tenacious, notwithstanding strong biblical evidence against the idea of distinct classes of human beings (see, e.g., Acts 10:34; 15:8–9; Rom. 2:11; 3:22–3; Gal. 2:6).

Attention to the relationship between anthropology and Christology provides important resources for addressing these problems, which follow on every attempt to identify the fullness of human nature with the perfection of some particular characteristic identified with the image of God. For although the OT never defines what it means for humanity to have been created *in* God's image, the NT states that Jesus Christ *is* the image of God (2 Cor. 4:4; Col. 1:15; cf. Heb. 1:3), even though as regards his humanity he is in every respect like other people (Heb. 2:17; cf. Gal. 4:4). Combined with the promise that human destiny consists precisely in humanity's being transformed into Christ's image (Rom. 8:29; Col. 3:10), this affirmation suggests that human nature is best understood not as some set of qualities or attributes fixed at the beginning of time in abstraction from the actual course of human history, but rather as a dynamic reality that is generated in and through concrete human encounter with the person of Jesus.

This way of approaching the question of human being works against the temptation to reify any particular dimension of human existence as primary in a way that would justify establishing hierarchies according to which some people might be judged more fully human than others. Nor does it promote a homogenization of people that denies the significance of the differences among individuals in constituting a person's identity as a human being. On the contrary, if, for Paul, all are 'one in Christ Jesus' (Gal. 3:28), that in no way implies that all are the same. To the contrary, it is by virtue of their differences that they come to be 'in Christ' at all, for 'just as the body is one and has many members, and all the members of the body, though many, are one body, so it is with Christ' (1 Cor. 12:12; cf. Rom. 12:4–5). Because any person's humanity is a function of her distinctive place in Christ's 'body' (i.e., in the life that, according to Eph. 4:15–16; Col. 2:19, finds its unity, order, and source in Christ), it is impossible to speak of human nature in isolation from the totality of persons whose role in that body continues to emerge over time. Still more to the point, one's humanity is fundamentally not a matter of any property a person possesses intrinsically, but is rather established extrinsically, by Christ's having claimed that person as a member of his body.

H. U. von Balthasar, *A Theological Anthropology* (Sheed & Ward, 1967).

K. Barth, *Church Dogmatics* (T&T Clark, 1960), III/2.

M. Gonzalez, *Created in God's Image: An Introduction to Feminist Theological Anthropology* (Orbis, 2007).
D. Kelsey, *Eccentric Existence: A Theological Anthropology*, 2 vols. (John Knox Press, 2009).
I. A. McFarland, *Difference and Identity: A Theological Anthropology* (Pilgrim, 2001).
R. Niebuhr, *The Nature and Destiny of Man*, 2 vols. (Scribner, 1941, 1943).

IAN A. MCFARLAND

THEOPASCHITE CONTROVERSY Derived from the Greek words *theos* (God) and *paschein* (to suffer), theopaschitism is the position that the divine *LOGOS* (i.e., the second Person of the TRINITY) suffered on the CROSS. The *theos* in theopaschitism refers neither to God the Father nor to the Trinity as such, but to God the Son (or *Logos*), who took flesh in Jesus of Nazareth. Theopaschitism had been the subject of controversy long before the so-called theopaschite controversy proper started in the sixth century. Theopaschite language had been used from the beginnings of Christianity, but fell into disrepute when it was defended by Apollinaris of Laodicea (*ca* 310–*ca* 390), who was condemned for his denial of Christ's full humanity (see APOLLINARIANISM). It found a staunch defender in CYRIL OF ALEXANDRIA, who was vehemently opposed by Nestorius (*ca* 385–*ca* 450). Probably it was Nestorius, who also denied that Mary could truly be called *Theotokos* ('Mother of God') who coined the abusive term 'theopaschite'.

At the third ecumenical COUNCIL, held at EPHESUS, Nestorius was condemned and the use of the title *Theotokos* for Mary was approved, but no explicit decision on the legitimacy of theopaschite language was made. Many champions of theopaschitism were miaphysites (see MIAPHYSITISM). One of them, Peter the Fuller (d. 488), added the clause 'who was crucified for us' to the Trisagion in about 470 and enforced this revised form (which read, 'Holy God, Holy Strong One, Holy Immortal One, Who was crucified for us, have mercy upon us') in his diocese. This led to a revival of the debate on theopaschitism. The theopaschite controversy proper began in 519. In that year a group of Scythian monks led by John Maxentius (*fl.* 520) tried to get an authorization for the formula *Unus de trinitate passus est* ('One of the Trinity suffered') in Constantinople. These monks accepted the definition of the fourth ecumenical council at CHALCEDON that Jesus, though one HYPOSTASIS, had two natures, being truly God and truly a human being. They opposed, however, Nestorianizing interpretations of Chalcedon that so emphasized the distinction between Christ's two natures as to undermine his unity. By raising the suffering of God in Christ as a standard of ORTHODOXY, they attempted to ward off such interpretations. Initially, their formula met with resistance both in the Eastern and in the Western Churches, but after many difficulties, the fifth ecumenical council at Constantinople (553) approved it, thereby ending the theopaschite controversy.

It is important to recognize that, strictly speaking, the theopaschite formula is a *Christological* and not a *theological* formula. It does not assert that divinity as such (i.e., the triune Godhead) suffered. It affirms rather that the hypostasis of the *Logos* (i.e., the second Person of the Trinity), by virtue of the INCARNATION, suffered 'in the flesh' (i.e., *carne* or *secundum carnem*, or 'in the flesh'). In short, the formula asserts that the human nature of Jesus suffered, and that the second Person of the Trinity suffered by virtue of entering into a HYPOSTATIC UNION with that nature, but *not* that the divine nature of Jesus suffered. Accepting the theopaschite formula is a logical consequence of accepting the term *Theotokos*: if Mary was truly the Mother of God (i.e., the second Person of the Trinity), then God suffered.

See also MARIOLOGY; NESTORIANISM; PATRIPASSIANISM.

MARCEL SAROT

THEOSIS: see DEIFICATION.

THEOTOKOS: see EPHESUS, COUNCIL OF.

THIRD USE OF THE LAW In response to what he perceived as a Catholic tendency to see God's LAW as a means of JUSTIFICATION, M. LUTHER insisted that justification was accomplished exclusively by FAITH in the GOSPEL rather than by works of the law (cf. Rom. 3:28). Nevertheless, he also insisted (following Rom. 3:31) that the law, too, was given by God for the benefit of humankind. Later Protestant theologians sought to systematize this general principle by defining three divinely intended uses or functions of the law, the third of which proved a point of contention between Lutheran and Reformed branches of the REFORMATION.

The first use of the law (*usus civilis* or *politicus*) is to restrain evildoers. It refers to God's use of the law to guarantee the minimal conditions of human social life by providentially ensuring that certain basic moral precepts (e.g., prohibitions against theft and murder) are instilled in the human heart and enforced by governing authorities (cf. Rom. 13:1–4). This function of the law is not restricted to Christians but is common to all humankind.

The second use of the law (variously termed the *usus theologicus*, *spiritualis*, *paedagogicus*, or *elenchticus*) is specific to the ECONOMY of salvation and thus functions only among the faithful. Here God uses the law as a means of driving sinners to the gospel: by convicting them of their inability to fulfil the law's demands, which extend beyond external actions to include dispositions of the heart (cf., e.g., Matt. 5:21–2, 27–8), God leads them to rely solely on divine mercy for their salvation.

The third use of the law (*usus didacticus* or *normativus*) is also specific to the economy of salvation, but pertains to life after justification rather than the process through which people are justified. Here the law serves to give a definite pattern or rule of life for Christians.

The third use of the law was championed by Reformed theologians in particular, who stressed that according to its third use the law was in no sense a means of earning justification, but simply the God-given form in which to live out one's gratitude for having been justified (see, e.g., WC 19.6). Lutherans have argued that any preaching of the law as obligation invariably introduced the spectre of justification by works; they therefore hold that the law is to be preached among believers solely according to the second use, in order to convict them of sin (see *FC*, *Ep.* 6).

IAN A. MCFARLAND

THIRTY-NINE ARTICLES: see ANGLICAN THEOLOGY.

THOMAS, M. M. Madathiparampil Mammen Thomas (1916–96), popularly known as MM, is India's most renowned ecumenical leader. A self-educated lay theologian influenced by K. BARTH, R. NIEBUHR, N. Berdyaev (1874–1948), and H. Kraemer (1888–1965), MM was also a social analyst who began his career as a Gandhian, moved on to an appreciation of Marxism but redefined it in terms of a secular humanism. He was also a spiritual father to numerous subaltern movements, an advocate for dialogue and engagement with people of other faiths and ideologies, a prolific writer (in English and in his native tongue, Malayalam), editor of *Religion and Society* and *Guardian*, a Bible commentator, and a political resister who later became an elder statesman.

A member of the Marthoma Malankara Syrian Church, MM aspired to become an ordained minister of his Church but was rejected because of his Marxist leanings. His application to join the Communist party, too, was rejected because of his loyalty to the Christian GOSPEL. MM's lifelong quest was the integration of the gospel and social concerns, salvation and humanization, theology and ideology, and a search for the construction of 'Christian social *dharma*'. His pursuit took him to different places, as leader of the student movement in his Church, staff of the World Student Christian Federation in Geneva, director of the Christian Institute for the Study of Religion and Society in Bangalore, moderator of the Central Committee of the WORLD COUNCIL OF CHURCHES (WCC), chair of the Fifth General Assembly of the WCC in Nairobi, and, finally, governor of the State of Nagaland in Northeast India.

MM's evangelical piety and his early formation in the liturgical tradition of his Church served as a foundation of his Christocentric spirituality. Writing and theologizing in the context of postcolonial India and Asia, MM sought to discern God's work, the promise and judgement of Christ, in the midst of revolutionary economic, political, and social change, urging Christian participation in nation building. He was unwavering in his affirmation of 'the divine forgiveness through Christ as the source of renewal of humanity and the whole creation' (*Gospel* 1–2). This Christological commitment was articulated in terms of a spirituality of involvement in the struggles of people for justice and human dignity and interpreted salvation as humanization. Yet he was critical of the communalist pattern of the Church, with its insular mentality, and advocated the creation of Christ-centred secular fellowships outside the Church and within Hindu communities. In his works, *The Acknowledged Christ of the Indian Renaissance* (1969) and *The Secular Ideologies of India and Secular Meaning of Christ* (1976), and in his debates with L. Newbigin (1909–98) about CONVERSION and the necessity of belonging to a Christian community, MM challenged the traditional western MISSIOLOGY by arguing for the real – albeit partial – presence and activity of Christ outside the framework of the Church and the Christian community. He attempted to articulate a post-Kraemerian missiology that advocated a 'Christ-centred syncretism' in the midst of religious and cultural pluralism and spoke of *Risking Christ for Christ's Sake* (1987). MM's prophetic witness at crucial points where Christian faith and world's religions, cultures, and ideologies intersect made him a truly public theologian.

See also COLONIALISM AND POSTCOLONIALISM; HINDUISM AND CHRISTIANITY; SOUTH ASIAN THEOLOGY.

J. PAUL RAJASHEKAR

THOMISM While the writings of Thomas AQUINAS, the theologian after whom Thomism is named, were carefully preserved by his secretaries, he left no disciple who could expound and defend them effectively after his death in 1274. Long-standing suspicions of his interest in Aristotle (384–322 BC) led to the worry that some of Aquinas' ideas strayed outside the bounds of Christian ORTHODOXY. Thus, in 1279 the Franciscan W. de La Mare (d. *ca* 1290) excerpted 117 theses from Aquinas' work for 'correction', while in 1286 another Franciscan, J. Pecham (*ca* 1230–92), had one of Aquinas' best-known theories (that a human being has only one substantial form) declared heretical. However, by 1313 the Dominicans, incited by chauvinism, declared themselves 'obliged in a special way to follow' the teaching of their brother Thomas; and in 1323 Pope John XXII (r. 1316–34) declared Thomas a SAINT of the Church: a model in personal holiness but explicitly also in DOCTRINE.

Even with this approval, Thomism continued to develop adversarially. The first major interpretation of Aquinas was completed in 1432 by the French Dominican J. Cabrol or Capreolus (*ca* 1380–1444). Significantly entitled *Defensiones theologiae divi Thomae Aquinatis*, this massive work, widely read and influential, defends Aquinas against a host of adversaries, including J. DUNS SCOTUS and William of Ockham (both also Franciscans), defending both Aquinas' analogical sense of being over against Scotus' notion of univocity (see ANALOGY), and also his emphasis on God's wisdom over against Ockham's VOLUNTARISM.

Between 1507 and 1522 the Dominican T. de Vio (1465–1534), better known as Cajetan (from his birthplace, Gaeta), published a massive commentary on Thomas, which was regarded as definitive right into the twentieth century. By this time Thomism was regarded by some as the *via antiqua*, the 'old way', compared with the *via moderna*, the NOMINALISM allegedly followed by disciples of Ockham, which rejected the harmony between faith and reason, the doctrine that GRACE perfects nature, and suchlike optimistic ideas, with which Aquinas was indelibly associated.

Meanwhile, provoked by Spanish colonization of America, the Spanish Dominican F. de Vitoria (1483–1546) worked out a theory of natural human rights and a JUST-WAR doctrine, explicitly relying on Aquinas. He has been called the founder of international law. His pupils included M. Cano (1509–60), whose *De locis theologicis* expounded a conception of theology as a quasi-Aristotelian science and remained influential into the twentieth century (see ARISTOTELIANISM).

While few today would give unqualified endorsement to Cano's reading of Aquinas, there is no question that the thought both of Thomas and of those influenced by him are deeply influenced by engagement with Aristotle. For example, Thomas, rejecting what he understood as Platonic dualism (see PLATONISM), affirmed the Aristotelian understanding that the human SOUL is the form of the BODY. Its principal activity is intellectual; moreover, because the soul is non-bodily, immaterial, and incorruptible, thinking is not a physical or material activity, and intellection as such is not the work of any physical organ of the body. At the same time, Thomas' epistemology was anything but dismissive of the material world. On the contrary, attracted to Aristotle's brand of empiricism, Aquinas denied the existence of innate ideas, insisting instead that human beings do not think without turning to physical things as remembered, visualized, or otherwise perceived (*nisi convertendo ad phantasmatibus*). Even the soul has knowledge of itself only by way of reflecting on the activities in which we and others can see ourselves engaging. In short, human beings acquire knowledge over time and in space by means of discursive reasoning (unlike ANGELS, who have direct intuition).

Given this emphasis on the spatio-temporal character of human reasoning, it follows that the proper object of the human mind is the nature of material things and, correspondingly, that human beings therefore have no direct, intuitive knowledge of the existence of God, who is immaterial. On the contrary, knowledge of the existence of God is acquired only by way of reasoning from the existence of such features in the material world as change, contingency, causality, and so on. For this reason, however, it is not purely a matter of FAITH that God exists.

In created beings there is a real distinction between their essence or nature and their being or existence. In God, however, there is no distinction between essence and existence; rather, for Aquinas, God's essence is God's existence: God's nature is to be. The essence of God, metaphysically speaking, consists in the absolute fullness of pure existence (*ipsum esse per se subsistens*).

The natures of essences or created beings depend not on the sheer will of God, but on God's intellect. Accordingly, the NATURAL LAW, the basis of the moral life of rational creatures, depends on the mind of God. This means that certain actions are not bad simply because God forbids them (as if God might just as well have done otherwise); they are forbidden by God because they are against the inclinations towards the good which characterize a rational creature.

This understanding of the relationship between will and intellect in God is consistent with Aquinas' more general remarks on the topic, according to which the will moves the intellect in its actual operation; the intellect moves the will by presenting objects to it; and the beginning of all our acts is the apprehension and desire of good in general. Human beings desire happiness (*beatitudo*), not by a free deliberate choice but naturally and necessarily. The final happiness or everlasting bliss of the human creature consists in the vision of God (see BEATIFIC VISION).

While the expression 'physical premotion' is not found in Aquinas, Thomists regard it as recapitulating his doctrine that God works in every agent but in such a way that agents have their own proper activity (see CONCURSUS). As first cause of all change or movement, God's activity is always ontologically prior to that of the creature; moreover, God's working in the creature is not merely moral (i.e., persuasive) or occasional but real and permanent. Importantly, for Thomas this does not constitute an explanation of human freedom but simply its description: human beings remain free agents of their own moral life, while yet remaining radically dependent on God's all-embracing agency. Because their freedom is itself created and sustained by God, human beings are not in competition with God, so that there is no need to imagine some inevitable conflict between rational creatures as second causes of their moral life and God as primary cause of all that exists. In this way, God's work in us as first agent does not make our activity as secondary agents illusory or superfluous.

This position, however, gave rise to much controversy. The Spanish Jesuit L. de Molina (1535–1600) sought to reconcile the absolute sovereignty of God and the liberty of the human will by introducing the notion of MIDDLE KNOWLEDGE (*scientia media*): midway between God's knowledge of actually existent beings, past, present, and future, and God's knowledge of purely possible beings, this allowed for a knowledge of beings or states of being that certainly *would* exist if certain conditions were fulfilled. Surveying the endless possibilities, each with its own outcome, God chooses for creation – and actually creates – that which corresponds most perfectly to God's inscrutable designs. The Dominican D. Báñez (1528–1604) attacked this account on the grounds that it compromised the divine sovereignty by an anthropocentric focus on the interaction of God and creatures that amounted to PELAGIANISM. Báñez countered that God moves creatures to action, but only according to their natures – and so moves free creatures freely. This solution seemed to Molina and his followers to evade the issue and deprive human freedom of real self-determination. Worse still, it seemed to deny the existence of GRACE, in that without the physical premotion of God as first cause the human will remains radically incapable of salvific action. In effect, the Báñezian Thomist was, according to the Molinists, little better than 'Calvinist', denying any reality to the human response to divine grace (see J. CALVIN). This bitter dispute was referred to Rome in 1594: it was considered from 1598 to 1607 by the papal commission *Congregatio de auxiliis* and left unresolved, with Dominicans and Jesuits instructed to cease their mutual insults.

Notwithstanding this history of (specifically Dominican) defence of 'Thomist' ideas against Franciscan and Jesuit critique, it was only in the latter half of the nineteenth century that Thomism came into its own as the official theology of the Catholic Church, to be taught to all seminarians. For decades, culminating at VATICAN COUNCIL I, bishops, seminary professors, and suchlike had become increasingly alarmed by the effects on the teaching of Catholic doctrine of the philosophies of R. Descartes (1596–1650; see CARTESIANISM), I. KANT, and G. W. F. HEGEL. With the support of Pope Leo XIII (r. 1878–1903), whose ENCYCLICAL *Aeterni patris* (1879) urged the study of 'Thomistic philosophy' (not, it should be noted, theology), an initially quite small network of philosophers and theologians gradually established Aquinas' theology and especially what was taken to be his philosophy as the indispensable alternative to what they saw as the twin evils of idealist METAPHYSICS and rationalistic positivism (see IDEALISM; RATIONALISM). J. Kleutgen (1811–83), a German Jesuit who taught at Rome, was the key figure: in his defences of pre-modern theology and philosophy, he contended that a theology based upon post-Cartesian philosophy undermined Catholic doctrine, recommended a return to patristic theology and, more decisively, argued that the Aristotelian scientific method of Aquinas was the necessary basis for the theology the Church now required.

One prominent line in modern Thomism was thus defined in opposition to modern philosophy. Against the scepticism characteristic of post-Cartesian theories of knowledge, Thomists argued that there is no problem bridging the supposed gap between human consciousness and the outside world. On the contrary, human cognitive activity is nothing other than identifying the form of a thing in the mind with the form of the thing in the world, so that when some reality which is potentially intelligible becomes actually so, the mind is actually exercised. There is thus (*contra* idealists like Kant) no *tertium quid* between our minds and the world, such as sense data, impressions, or any other category that might open up the possibility that human knowledge is not of reality but rather of intermediaries of some kind. Once material objects have been perceived, moreover, the intellect can ascend to the knowledge of higher things, even of God. Thus, although knowledge begins by sense perception, the range of the intellect is far beyond that of the senses. In this way, Thomism gives to empiricism a degree of openness to transcendence.

Another motivation in Pope Leo XIII's decision to revive 'Thomist philosophy' was the reinvigoration – indeed, the inauguration – of the so-called social teaching of the Church. From his encyclical *Rerum novarum* (1891) on capital and labour, Leo XIII sought to open up a third way between the emerging spectre of communism and the visible brutalities of neo-liberal capitalism. These concerns were reiterated in *Studiorum ducem* (1923) by Pope Pius XI (r. 1922–39), emphasizing Aquinas' contributions, in morals, social theory, and law, in laying out principles of legal and social, commutative and distributive justice, and explaining the relations between justice and charity. He noted particularly 'those superb chapters in the second part of the *Summa theologiae* on paternal or domestic government, the lawful power of the State or the nation, natural and international law, peace and war, justice and property, laws and the obedience they command, the duty of helping individual citizens in their need and co-operating with all to secure the prosperity of the State, both in the natural and the supernatural order.' Pius hoped that the teachings of Aquinas, particularly his exposition of international law, would be taken into consideration in connection with the foundation of the League of Nations. As the 1930s unfolded, and in the aftermath of World War II, a widely read body of literature on these subjects developed, headed by explicitly Thomist thinkers like J. Maritain (1882–1973), but found among non-Catholics like the Anglican V. Demant (1893–1983).

See also GILSON, ÉTIENNE; LONERGAN, BERNARD; MARÉCHAL, JOSEPH; SCHOLASTICISM.

R. Cessario, *A Short History of Thomism* (Catholic University of America Press, 2005).
F. Kerr, *After Aquinas: Versions of Thomism* (Wiley-Blackwell, 2002).
N. Kretzmann and E. Stump, eds., *The Cambridge Companion to Aquinas* (Cambridge University Press, 1993).

G. A. McCool, *From Unity to Pluralism: Internal Evolution of Thomism* (Fordham University Press, 1989).
J. V. Schall, *Jacques Maritain: The Philosopher in Society* (Rowman & Littlefield, 1998).

FERGUS KERR

THREEFOLD OFFICE The concept of the threefold office (*munus triplex* in Latin) is a dimension of CHRISTOLOGY to the effect that Jesus of Nazareth, as the Messiah or Christ (literally, 'anointed one'), unites and sums up in himself the three roles (or 'offices') for which one was anointed in Jewish tradition, namely, those of prophet (cf. 1 Kgs 19:16b), priest (cf. Exod. 30:30), and king (cf. 2 Sam. 5:3). Generally, Jesus' anointing to these offices is identified with the descent of the HOLY SPIRIT on him at his BAPTISM (Matt. 3:13–17 and pars).

Eusebius of Caesarea (*ca* 275–*ca* 340) makes the earliest reference to Jesus' uniting in himself the three great OT offices (*EH* 1.3), and the idea is also alluded to by T. AQUINAS (*ST* 3.22.1.3). Nevertheless, it is in REFORMED THEOLOGY that the theme of the threefold office has been developed most systematically. Picking up M. BUCER's development of the idea, J. CALVIN gave a detailed account of the way in which Christ's saving work incorporates all three offices: he is prophet as the definitive teacher of sacred DOCTRINE (*Inst.* 2.15.1; cf. Heb. 1:1–2); he is king as the sole, eternal ruler of the Church (*Inst.* 2.15.3; cf. John 18:36); and he is priest as the one whose death made expiation for human sin, and who continues to intercede with God on our behalf (*Inst.* 2.15.6; cf. Heb. 9:22).

Most Reformed theologians of the sixteenth and seventeenth centuries employed the threefold office as a means of elaborating the full range of Christ's role as mediator between God and humankind. It was also used by Lutheran theologians, though some of them (especially prior to the mid-seventeenth century) were inclined to incorporate Christ's teaching ministry into his exercise of the priestly office. In the nineteenth century F. SCHLEIERMACHER retained the threefold schema as a means of giving appropriate expression to the comprehensive transformation of Jewish concepts into a specifically Christian form, according to which the individual's relationship to God is a function of her relationship to Jesus (*CF*, §§102–5). Still more recently, K. BARTH made the threefold office the organizing principle behind his exposition of the doctrine of reconciliation (*CD* IV/1–3).

Although the title 'Christ' was originally applied to Jesus because he was regarded as the promised heir of David (Matt. 1:1; 22:42 and pars; cf. *Inst.* 2.15.2), the letter to the Hebrews bears witness to early Christian interpretation of Jesus' career in priestly terms (cf. 1 John 2:1–2), and the Gospels report Jesus both referring to himself (Luke 13:33) and being referred to by others (Matt. 16:14 and pars) as a prophet. Although (as Schleiermacher points out) the NT applies many other titles to Jesus (e.g., Good Shepherd, Son of Man), the doctrine of the threefold office has the advantage of highlighting Christian belief that Jesus is the consummation of God's COVENANT with ISRAEL and the focal point of the divine ECONOMY: all the OT prophets, priests, and kings point to Jesus as the one in whom every dimension of God's desire for life with humankind is fully and irreversibly realized.

IAN A. MCFARLAND

THURMAN, HOWARD Howard Thurman (1899–1981) spoke and wrote on the ultimate worth of the self, community as the underlying nature and purpose of reality, and the experience of God as fundamental to religious knowledge, personal identity, and Christian discipleship. As an African American who experienced prejudice, discrimination, and segregation, Thurman identified race relations as a central spiritual and moral issue for theology and ecclesial witness. In 1944 in San Francisco, he co-founded The Church for the Fellowship of All Peoples, which was the USA's first interracial and intercultural Church in both membership and leadership. This Church was an inspiring example of racial reconciliation and the possibility for overcoming ecclesial practices of racial separation.

His books *Deep River* (1945) and *The Negro Spiritual Speaks of Life and Death* (1947) attested to the theological genius of Black slaves who bear testimony, under the most dehumanizing circumstances, to the nature and action of God. Thurman's *Jesus and the Disinherited* (1949) continued to develop the theme of God's liberating message coming directly to the disinherited. This book helped leaders of the American civil rights movement to interpret their goals and commitment to NONVIOLENCE as an expression of Jesus' love-ethic. It also influenced those who developed BLACK THEOLOGY. In addition to his university professorships and chapel deanships at Morehouse, Spelman, Howard, and Boston University, his thousands of speaking engagements influenced generations about the connection between mystical consciousness, social transformation, and inclusive community that celebrates both distinctive factors of identity and common factors of unity.

LUTHER E. SMITH, JR

TILLICH, PAUL After serving as a chaplain in the German Army during World War I, Paul Tillich (1886–1965) became known as a religious socialist and philosophical theologian during the fourteen turbulent years of the Weimar Republic. During this period he held posts at Phillips-Universität at Marburg (1924–5), Dresden Institute of Technology (1925–9), and Frankfurt am Main (1929–33). With the rise to power in 1933 of the Nazis, who banned and burnt his book, *The Socialist Decision* (1933), Tillich went underground and at the age of forty-seven emigrated to the USA, where he became one of the most influential Protestant systematic theologians of the twentieth century. In the USA he had appointments at Union Theological Seminary and Columbia University (1933–55), Harvard University (1955–63), and the University of Chicago (1962–5).

Tillich is perhaps best known for a theological 'method of correlation'. This method, as he writes in his three-volume *Systematic Theology* (1951–63), 'explains the contents of the Christian faith through existential questions and theological answers in mutual interdependence' (*STheol.* 1.60). The method 'correlates' interpretations of an existential situation with symbols from the Christian theological tradition. His own interpretation of the human situation was guided by M. Heidegger's (1889–1976) and S. KIERKEGAARD'S existentialist readings of being and existence. His interpretation of Christian tradition was shaped by the great symbols, God, Christ, and Spirit, which he interpreted as empowering 'New Being', through which existential estrangement was overcome through 'Spiritual Community'. The result was a creative re-reading of Christian existence that engaged many secular minds and invited inter-faith dialogue, even as his books and sermons were debated widely by Christians in Protestant, Catholic, and also Orthodox circles.

In spite of the significance of his *Systematic Theology,* the import of Tillich's pre-emigration writings is increasingly recognized. They show a perceptive and nuanced mind, exploring ultimate matters at one of the most dramatic sites of ruin and human creativity in twentieth-century European history: Weimar Germany, during which a society reeling from military defeat and the loss of its status as a colonial empire underwent a period of profound political, economic, and cultural transformation. After his own nervous breakdown following his traumatic war chaplaincy, Tillich had to rethink philosophy, theology, and culture, with powerful political spectres looming from every quarter, and personal morality and culture undergoing heightened levels of creative experimentation.

Published in these years was his *System of the Sciences according to Their Subjects and Methods* (1923), his bestselling *The Religious Situation* (1925), about the era's declining 'spirit of capitalist society', and *The Socialist Decision,* which fused a political ontology with 'religious socialism', in response to his times' tumultuous interplay of bourgeois society, conservative romanticisms, and proletarian revolution. These texts, along with many key articles Tillich wrote during this period, defined categories that would continue to mark Tillich's later theology, including power, *kairos,* the Protestant principle, theology of culture, and the demonic.

These early writings by Tillich seem to be occasioning a resurgence of Tillich's influence, particularly as many twenty-first-century political thinkers return to the conjunction of politics and ontology, and occasionally also to theology. That was the conjunction that Tillich probed in his formative, and arguably most creative, period. Even the decisive steps towards his later *Systematic Theology,* found in outline in his earlier *Dogmatik* (1925–7), were taken during this period. To this day, his extensive later works are most fruitfully read, their import best grasped, in light of the writings of the Weimar period.

MARK LEWIS TAYLOR

TOLERANCE Etymologically derived from the Latin verb *tolerare,* 'to put up with', tolerance has come to carry a variety of meanings in the milieu of late modernity, which is part of its allure. Within Christian history tolerance has often, but not always, marked the boundary between Christianity and the non-Christian world. The writings of early Christian thinkers such as Justin Martyr (d. *ca* 165) or Clement of Alexandria (*ca* 150–*ca* 215) invoke a kind of tolerance for philosophy and other religions because in the least they may possess a measure of the truth that Christianity has in full. Typifying the intellectual richness of the medieval period, T. AQUINAS would advance this mode of tolerance in his reception of Muslim and Jewish works, reflecting the much broader cultural tolerance of the pre-modern period. The ENLIGHTENMENT would prove to make tolerance both a problematic and, within that problematic, a VIRTUE.

The philosopher most strongly associated with the doctrine of toleration in this context is J. Locke (1632–1704). In his 'Letter Concerning Toleration' Locke proposed a remedy for the disastrous 'wars of religion' by championing the newly emerging nation-state as the benefactor of persons and property, elevating the power and promise of the secular State over against sectarian religions. In Locke's view the commonwealth was 'a society of men constituted only for the procuring, preserving, and advancing their own civil interests' (viz., life, liberty, health, property), whereas the Church was 'a voluntary society of men, joining themselves together of their own accord, in order to the public worshipping of God, in such a manner as they judge acceptable to him, and effectual to the salvation of their souls'. Within this framework toleration was to be the chief mark of the true religion and of any Church that sought a place in society.

Following that lineage, tolerance is used today to refer to 'putting up with' another's religion (or lack thereof), with the West in particular associated with a culture of 'religious toleration', which has come to denote at least two trajectories. One of these indicates a cultural abdication whereby nothing is taken seriously enough to warrant offence or protest. Difference is simply relegated to the realm of personal choice: one 'puts up with' another's difference because differences are seen as ineffectual and thus able to be 'tolerated'. Accordingly, literary theorist F. Jameson (b. 1934) has interpreted the postmodern suspicion of meta-narratives in terms of 'the cultural logic of capitalism', in which anything and everything demands acceptance as an articulation of freedom, and difference, though valued in principle, is not so much engaged as left alone. One can find precursors to contemporary expressions of this version of tolerance in cultural anthropologists like F. Boas (1858–1942), who articulated a nascent tolerance for difference based on cultural plurality. Embedded within this version of tolerance, however, is a set of commitments that entail proselytizing for it (e.g., arguing that people should be left alone, that 'freedom of choice' should go unquestioned) while at the same time rejecting other forms of proselytizing (e.g. religious) as inherently intolerant.

A second, thicker, and perhaps richer trajectory within which to develop the idea of tolerance would proffer not only acceptance of but also active engagement with the other. This approach would preserve the place of tolerance at the heart of liberal democracy as the political allowance for difference. For example, in his ethics, T. Englehardt (b. 1941) has made a robust affirmation of the moral significance of diversity as a way to challenge accounts of difference as discardable and illusory. Engelhardt goes on to offer a *res publica* that would allow for the proliferation of difference without the collateral reality of antagonistic violence. In this way, tolerance follows as the acknowledgement of difference as well as constructive patterns of mutual flourishing that are more substantive than a benign 'putting up with'. This goes beyond tolerance as 'the cultural logic of capitalism', because it situates agency in terms of an intersubjectivity that advances beyond modernity's understanding of the autonomous, sovereign, freely choosing self. Examples of this tolerance can be found in radical democratic theory, including authors such as R. Coles (b. 1959) and J. Stout (b. 1950), as well as emerging movements enabling diverse religious traditions to share common practices of SCRIPTURAL REASONING.

A. J. Conyers, *The Long Truce: How Toleration Made the World Safe for Power and Profit* (Baylor University Press, 2009).

J. B. Elshtain and P. Griffiths, 'Proselytizing for Tolerance', *First Things* 127 (November 2002), 30–6.

H. T. Engelhardt, *The Foundations of Bioethics*, 2nd edn (Oxford University Press, 1996).

JONATHAN TRAN AND DANA BENESH

TONGUES: see GLOSSOLALIA.

TORAH: see LAW.

TOTAL DEPRAVITY The DOCTRINE of total depravity (or total inability) was one of several theological positions (along with UNCONDITIONAL ELECTION, LIMITED ATONEMENT, IRRESISTIBLE GRACE, and PERSEVERANCE) defined as orthodox in the canons of the Reformed Synod of DORT (3/4.3). Unlike these other doctrines, however, it was not a point of disagreement with ARMINIANISM, whose proponents had affirmed it in the Five Articles of Remonstrance that were debated at the Synod. The doctrine affirms that as a result of original SIN human beings exist in a state of APOSTASY from God, such that apart from the GRACE of the HOLY SPIRIT, they are utterly unable to will or do anything either to turn to God or to transform their own sinfulness.

Objections to the doctrine (as found, e.g., in official Catholic teaching) are generally based in the claim that FREE WILL is a constitutive feature of human nature. To affirm that original sin renders human beings utterly incapable of any movement towards God thus implies that the FALL did not simply damage human nature but actually destroyed it, or, worse, that it made sin fallen humanity's essence in a way incompatible with Christian belief in the inalienable goodness of created natures. Defenders of total depravity counter that the doctrine teaches a profound perversion, not the destruction of the will, which remains free in so far as it sins willingly rather than by compulsion. They also maintain that affirming any human capacity to turn towards God undermines the principle that human beings are saved by grace alone.

IAN A. MCFARLAND

TRADITION The word 'tradition' derives from the Latin verbal root *tradere*, 'to hand down' or 'to bequeath', and in its Christian use refers to a body of authoritative beliefs, teachings, or practices that, in the faith of believers, conveys the gospel message of Jesus Christ. The earliest Christian appropriation of the idea occurs in 1 Corinthians, where PAUL, writing only two decades after the death of Jesus, instructs a nascent community of believers: 'For I handed on [*paredoka*] to you as of first importance what I in return had received: that Christ died for our sins in accordance with the scriptures, and that he was buried, and that he was raised on the third day in accordance with the scriptures, and that he appeared to Cephas, then to the twelve' (1 Cor. 15:3–5). This testimony is especially rich in elaborating the different aspects of tradition that Christians eventually distinguished. Tradition, for Paul, is a DOCTRINE that possesses a particular objective content about the saving death and RESURRECTION of Jesus, a content expressed in what seems to be a primitive Christian CREED. That content, though, is also a process, a 'traditioning', that unfolds in acts of believing, confessing, enacting, and receiving the faith from person to person and from generation to generation. By the same token, this faith was 'handed on' to Paul verbally, in the religion's earliest years before the appearance of Christian writing. Yet Paul justifies this early oral tradition by appeal to a sacred literary tradition of Jewish Scriptures that were embraced as God's word by the Jews whom we call the first Christians, a literary tradition that later Christians would judge Paul to have continued as his writings were included in the NT.

The human activity of speaking is far more common than that of writing, and so, through the ages, oral tradition has flourished as a practice in the daily lives of Christians much more than literary tradition. Writing, however, has proved to be far more consequential than speaking for the Christian understanding of tradition in several ways. First, along with Paul, a few first-century Christians committed to writing what was 'handed on' to them concerning the gospel of Jesus, expressing their faith in a variety of genres – letters, narratives of the saviour's life, history, and apocalypse (see, e.g., Luke 1:1–3). Through the use of these texts that reflected judgements about their truthfulness, Christians gradually ascribed divine authorship to some of these writings, and by the turn of the third century had settled on the belief that only these writings, and no new ones, could be regarded as divine REVELATION. This claim closed the canon of the NT, a sacred collection of writings that, they believed, fulfilled the story of God's revelation to Israel in what they now regarded as the OT.

This canon of sacred Scripture defined an orthodox content of what Christians believed they had received from previous generations and which they were obliged to 'hand on' to the next. Yet the unity and certainty sought by means of canonical closure proved elusive. Christians disagreed with each other – often vehemently – about the truthful way to interpret SCRIPTURE. In the fourth and fifth centuries, these disagreements centred on the nature and person of Christ, with Christians debating whether or not the saviour was fully divine and fully human. These disputes were adjudicated by bishops who met in Church COUNCILS to debate the issues and cast votes that defined a majority position. As time passed, the creedal teachings of these early councils – NICAEA, CONSTANTINOPLE, EPHESUS, and CHALCEDON – gained authority as the orthodox faith, a circumstance that stirred the belief that the HOLY SPIRIT was at work at these councils, divinely inspiring their results. The conciliar CREEDS functioned as an authoritative supplement to the Bible, as a lens for its truthful reading within the bounds of the Church. Although Christians regarded such things as liturgical practices, the veneration of the MARTYRS, and ecclesial structures as their tradition, the conciliar creeds achieved a special status in the deposit of faith for a host of reasons – their literary conciseness, their continuing role in securing ORTHODOXY in a relatively new religion struggling for identity, and, especially in the case of the NICENE CREED, for their liturgical value as communal statements of faith.

This conception of tradition as a literary supplement to the biblical canon appeared in late medieval Christianity in the authority that theologians accorded to earlier Christian writers whose work they judged to be thoroughly orthodox. For late medievals like P. Lombard (*ca* 1100–60) and T. AQUINAS, ancient patristic authors like AUGUSTINE, JOHN OF DAMASCUS, and the writer they knew as DIONYSIUS THE AREOPAGITE were unquestionable authorities before whom they had to justify their own theological opinion. Moreover, the theological culture of late medieval Catholicism assumed that all of these writings – the Bible, conciliar teachings, the orthodox fathers, and eventually papal decretals – voiced an ultimately harmonious and unified rendition of the gospel message, a *Scriptura sacra* whose uniform content, in the well-known phrase of the monk Vincent of Lérins (d. *ca* 450), was believed 'everywhere, always, and by all' (*Comm.* 4.3). Modern historical scholarship, of course, would show this assumption to be anything but true. But the medieval belief that God was finally the author of this single deposit of faith meant that even original theological contributions achieved authority only as they were judged to be in complete agreement with, and to offer not the slightest novelty to, this literary tradition.

The familiar distinction between 'Scripture' and 'tradition' did not exist in medieval Catholicism, but appeared in REFORMATION polemics. M. LUTHER's insistence that the biblical pages exhausted the scope of divine revelation became a basic belief of the Protestant Churches. That belief, expressed in Luther's watchword *sola Scriptura*, led the Reformers to portray extra-scriptural beliefs, practices, and authorities as a Catholic tradition of corruption, which the recovery of the authentic gospel could only reject. In turn, this charge against the mainstays of Catholic authority led Roman theologians to respond by writing the first theological treatises devoted to the topic '*De Traditione*', the first of which was the *De ecclesiasticis scripturis et dogmatibus* (1533) of J. Driedo (d. 1535). The Council of TRENT's teaching on Scripture and tradition reified the distinction that the Protestant polemic had hostilely begun. According to Trent, the 'truth and rule [of the gospel] are contained in written books and in unwritten traditions which were received by the apostles from the mouth of Christ himself, or else have come down to us, handed on as it were from the apostles themselves at the inspiration of the holy Spirit'. Moreover, the conciliar teaching 'accepts and venerates' traditions concerned with faith and morals 'with a like feeling of piety and reverence' it accords to the OT and NT (Session 4 (1546), DS 1,501).

This Catholic understanding of a single divine revelation communicated in Scripture and tradition was further reified in the nineteenth century with the emergence of a theology of the MAGISTERIUM. The practice of the shared teaching authority of the pope and bishops, especially in the growing frequency of papal encyclicals and in the definition of the dogma of papal INFALLIBILITY (1870), encouraged the belief that the orthodox tradition was explicitly clarified and safeguarded by the recurring exercise of magisterial teaching, even to the point that the clarity of magisterial teaching seemed to gain preference in Catholic sensibilities to the relative ambiguity of the biblical text. The *Dogmatic Constitution on Divine Revelation* (1965) of VATICAN COUNCIL II corrected this Tridentine imbalance by insisting on the mutual co-inherence of Scripture and tradition, while yet continuing to insist against the Protestant position that 'the church's certainty about all that is revealed is not drawn from the holy scripture alone', but from tradition too (*DV*, §2.9).

The nineteenth century also witnessed the birth of a modern theology of tradition as theologians, both Protestant and Catholic, faced the challenge posed by the new sense of historicity to the Christian belief in the timeless truth of divine revelation. The Reformed theologian F. SCHLEIERMACHER was the first to fashion a theory of doctrinal development in his early work on theological method, *Brief Outline of Theology as a Field of Study* (2nd edn, 1830). In Schleiermacher's account, valid Christian doctrine is always being reshaped in the experience of a believing community by the ongoing, temporal encounter between the orthodox past and what Schleiermacher called the 'heterodox', but truthful, present. Christian truth thus manifested itself fully in its developing historicity, a conceptualization that countered the ENLIGHTENMENT claim that time provided evidence for the corruption of the Church, the historical contradictions in the biblical story, and the capriciousness of orthodox settlements. Schleiermacher's Romantic sensibilities were embraced in their own way by Catholic theologians at the University of Tübingen, especially J. Drey (1777–1853) and J. Möhler (1796–1838), who, like Schleiermacher, found apologetic advantage in the notion of developing doctrine (see TÜBINGEN SCHOOL (CATHOLIC)).

Certainly, the best known and most influential theology of tradition of the nineteenth century was J. H. NEWMAN'S *Essay on the Development of Doctrine*. Written just as Newman was contemplating conversion from the Anglican to the Roman Catholic Church, the *Essay* offers a noetic metaphor for the movement of tradition that has since been claimed by liberals and conservatives alike. Newman portrayed doctrinal development as a process, informed and guided by the Holy Spirit, through which the community of faith clarifies its initially cloudy ideas concerning divine revelation and expresses its slowly achieved intelligibility with doctrinal precision. He was convinced by his own historical studies of ancient Church controversies that tradition is a providential sphere in which the Church gradually comes to an increasing awareness of God's saving truth. For Newman, this process is inexorably continuous – so much so that historical perspective enables later generations to see the incipience of a mature doctrine in the faith of early believers. Indeed, Newman regarded the continuity of tradition as so stable and consistent that, when it had truly unfolded, it could be measured by several criteria or, as he called them, 'notes' or 'tests', such as the developed doctrine's 'power of assimilation', 'logical sequence', or 'chronic vigour'.

That doctrine develops is an unquestioned axiom of modern theology, whether as a statement of historical fact or as a starting point for a theology of tradition, the latter especially for post-conciliar Catholics (both liberal and conservative), who continue to debate the authentic meaning of Vatican II. In spite of the Reformation polemic towards tradition, the history of authoritative readings of Scripture has functioned in Protestant Churches as a traditioning principle, and has even been claimed as such by the Lutheran theologian G. Ebeling (1912–2001). The most recent theologies of tradition have tended to question the classical assumption that tradition represents a universal truth and the modern, Romantic assumption that an unbroken continuity abides amidst the development of history. LIBERATION THEOLOGIES have called attention to the ways that claims for the universality of tradition bespeak the interests of empowered majorities, and attempt to reconstruct a more adequate account of tradition by drawing on the experience of traditionally excluded groups. Postmodern theologies have criticized the Romantic assumption that some essential content of faith capable of interpretive recovery certainly abides within a tradition's ever-changing cultural forms, thus problematizing the traditional category of continuity itself and the notion of development as progress. Much in the manner of the liberationist critique, postmodern theologies aim to expand the range of the authentically traditional. One approach along these lines regards Christian communities as contested spaces, shaped not thickly by continuous agreement but thinly by materials – texts, rituals, and histories – in which their members are invested and about which they are willing to argue continuously in order to approximate Christian faithfulness. Another approach, more typically Catholic, acknowledges the historical ruptures in the doctrinal record as cause for doubting the permanence of every traditional claim and as spaces within which new claims for authentic tradition might reconfigure previous understandings of traditional continuity.

See also CATHOLIC THEOLOGY; PAPACY; VATICAN COUNCIL I.

L. Boeve, *Interrupting Tradition: An Essay on Christian Faith in a Postmodern Context* (Peeters, 2003).
K. Tanner, *Theories of Culture: A New Agenda for Theology* (Fortress Press, 1997).
G. H. Tavard, *Holy Writ or Holy Church: The Crisis of the Protestant Reformation* (Harper, 1959).
J. E. Thiel, *Senses of Tradition: Continuity and Development in Catholic Faith* (Oxford University Press, 2000).
S. Wiedenhofer, 'Traditionsbrüche – Traditionsabbruch? Zur Identität des Glaubens' in *Traditionsabbruch – Ende des Christentums?*, ed. M. von Brück and J. Werbick (Echter-Verlag, 1994), 55–76.

JOHN E. THIEL

Traditional Religions and Christianity Traditional religions conventionally are regarded as preceding in time the spread of so-called missionary religions. As such and with varying results, they have been severely affected by colonialism, leading to their disappearance in some places and in others to their adapting to or adopting parts of the invading religions. J. Platvoet (b. 1935) calls traditional religions 'community' religions since they are 'particular to a single society' and thus are 'practised by all the members of the society and no one outside it'. He argues that before 250 BC this type of religion was the only kind in existence and 'most religions since then belong to this category'. Christianity, as a global religion, has been contrasted sharply in scholarly literature with traditional religions, which are often described as localized, kinship-orientated, and organized according to systems of lineage, with a primary focus on ancestors.

Christian missions actively began to seek converts among adherents to traditional religions during the nineteenth century at a time when small-scale, kinship-based societies were regarded widely among Europeans as occupying the lowest position on a model of cultural evolution, with western, Christian civilization at the apex. By trying to win traditionalists to Christian faith, missionaries, unlike many anthropologists of the mid-nineteenth century, affirmed that people living in a 'primitive' environment were fully human and capable of being lifted out of what often was depicted as their depraved living conditions. Overt attempts to correct widespread bias against traditional religions can be traced to Christian scholars of religion writing during the early to middle part of the twentieth century, who maintained that a rudimentary belief in God can be found among indigenous peoples around the world. This view was voiced most explicitly by missionary academics working in Africa, specifically E. Smith (1876–1957) and G. Parrinder (1910–2005), each of whom drew a line of continuity between the basic beliefs of African indigenous peoples and fully developed monotheism. Later, African scholars writing from within the Christian tradition, such as Parrinder's student E. Idowu (1913–93) and the Kenyan theologian J. Mbiti (b. 1931), used the idea of the universal belief in God to maintain that African religions deserve to be treated with respect and studied as religions in their own right alongside the other religious traditions around the world.

Parrinder made a fundamental contribution to the development of the study of traditional religions when in 1964, as professor of comparative religion at King's College London, he published *The World's Living Religions*, which (as he explained in the foreword) aimed at providing 'a short and impartial account of the major religions of the modern world' (*World* 7). Alongside chapters on 'Islam and the Arab World', 'Hinduism', 'Jains, Sikhs and Parsis', 'Buddhism in Southeast Asia', 'China's Three Ways', 'Japanese Shinto and Buddhism', 'Judaism', and 'Christianity', he inserted a chapter entitled 'Africans, Australians, and American Indians' in which he considered 'non-scriptural faiths' under one classification. He wrote, 'There is such great variety of tribes in many parts of the world, that one who wished to study a particular tribe must look for a specialist book on the subject', but 'there is enough similarity for comparative works to have been written, and these can now be referred to fairly easily' (125). Parrinder identified the subjects of such studies as peoples living in 'tiny groups' in North America, those still inhabiting the Central and South American forests, groups living in the Pacific Islands 'who still retain elements of their ancient faith', the aborigines of Australia who number 'some 50,000', the hill and jungle tribes of India, Southeast Asia, China, and Siberia 'that have for long resisted the encroachments of Hinduism and Buddhism', and, of course, the 'many tribes' of Africa 'which have their own religious practices, despite the inroads made in modern times by Islam and Christianity' (124). By including such a chapter in a book on the world's religions, Parrinder created a category for the study of peoples 'who do not follow one of the great historical religions, but have religious beliefs and practices that derive from ancient ideas and traditions' (124).

Parrinder's approach, the idea for which he first developed in the 1950s in Nigeria as a reaction against earlier descriptions of African traditional religions as primitive and 'fetishistic', could be regarded as apologetic in the sense that he wanted to foster respect for traditional religions among western and Christian audiences. His limitation of traditional religions to 'tribal' societies has now become outdated, particularly in light of the forces of globalization. Some scholars, such as A. Walls (b. 1928), a leading historian of Christianity, have argued that the encounter between localized religions and global religions favours conversion to one of the world religions. Walls contends that today traditional religions are being forced to change in response to western political, economic, educational, cultural, and religious institutions. These have created a 'disturbance of focus', which small-scale societies experience as threats to conventional values of worth, obligation, patterns of permission, and prohibition. Traditional world views are thus forced to expand beyond purely local concerns in order to account for the reality that they now form 'a part of a total world of events' ('Primal', 259). In this way, Christianity, with its universalist outlook, can provide traditionalists with a world view that enlarges or magnifies their original localized perspectives and thus enables them to engage positively with powerful international threats to their habitual way of life.

Traditional religions have not only been transformed under the impact of Christian missions, but they have also influenced the ways that Christianity is understood and practised, particularly in Africa, which since the beginning of the twentieth century has witnessed the exponential growth of African Independent Churches, otherwise referred to as African Initiated or Indigenous Churches (AIC). In his important study of Independent Churches in southern Africa, the missiologist M. Daneel (b. 1936) observed that AICs constitute 'a sort of "spiritual" or "prophetic revolution" in Africa' that 'involves an estimated 7000 groups with millions of followers' (*Quest* 25). Daneel contends that AICs demonstrate how Africans have reinterpreted their own traditional religions in Christian terms in order to reflect their own 'existential situation and world-view' (*Quest* 26). More recently, Pentecostal-type Churches have come to play an important role in African Christianity, but arguably both AICs and Pentecostal African Churches incorporate aspects of traditional practices, such as the emphasis on spirit possession, but in these cases by the Holy Spirit, and the banishment of evil forces, such as witches, interpreted in Christian terms as instruments of the DEVIL (see PENTECOSTAL THEOLOGY).

Despite the apparent detrimental effects of globalizing forces on local world views to which Walls refers and the indigenization of traditional religions as evidenced in AICs, a recent revival of cultural practices associated with traditional religions has been occurring in locations as far-reaching as Australia, under the leadership of the Rainbow Spirit Elders, through Alaska, where old men are instructing the young in the spiritual significance of traditional fishing equipment, to Siberia, which has witnessed an upsurge of interest in traditional shamanism. These events have led G. Harvey (b. 1959), a leading specialist on the study of indigenous religions, to argue that traditional cultural beliefs 'continue to provide resources for people surviving and thriving in the new globalized world' ('Understanding', 101). Harvey notes that indigenous people increasingly preserve their old patterns of life in diaspora communities, but in ways that respond dynamically to new circumstances foisted on them by modern economic, political, and communication systems. For this reason, today it may be better to replace the term 'traditional' with 'indigenous', which refers to those who are from a place, but due to the process of globalization, do not necessarily reside in that place. In contemporary times traditional religions can no longer be described as being bound inflexibly by 'tradition' but as having adapted to the wider world, often by adopting into their ancient religious practices new beliefs and ritual activities that have resulted from interacting with Christianity or other transcultural religions.

See also INCULTURATION; MISSIOLOGY; PLURALISM, RELIGIOUS.

M. L. Daneel, *Quest for Belonging: Introduction to a Study of African Independent Churches* (Mambo Press, 1987).

G. Harvey, 'Understanding Indigenous Religions' in *The New Lion Handbook of the World's Religions*, ed. C. H. Partridge (Lion Hudson, 2005), 100–4.

G. Parrinder, *The World's Living Religions* (Pan Books, 1964).

J. G. Platvoet, 'African Traditional Religions in the Religious History of Humankind' in *African Traditional Religions in Religious Education: A Resource Book with Special Reference to Zimbabwe*, ed. G. ter Haar, A. Moyo, and S. J. Nondo (Utrecht University, 1993), 11–28.

A. F. Walls, 'Primal Religious Traditions in Today's World' in *Religion in Today's World*, ed. F. Whaling (T&T Clark, 1987), 250–78.

JAMES L. COX

TRADUCIANISM Christian anthropology has typically viewed human beings as a composite of BODY and SOUL, but there is disagreement in the tradition over the origin of the soul and the mode by which it comes to be joined to the body. Traducianism (from the Latin term for 'transfer' or 'derive') is one of three prominent theories of the soul's origin, alongside pre-existence (advocated by ORIGEN) and CREATIONISM (the dominant position in both eastern and western Christianity). Most famously advocated by TERTULLIAN, traducianism has been a significant minority position in the tradition, entertained by Gregory of Nyssa (*Making* 17; see CAPPADOCIAN FATHERS), AUGUSTINE (*Ep.* 166), and M. LUTHER (*Prom.*), and subsequently favoured by a majority of Lutheran theologians. It teaches that the soul, like the body, is derived from the parents through genetic transmission. In contrast to creationists, therefore, traducianists affirm that the only human soul created directly by God was Adam's.

While Tertullian's traducianism was motivated largely by his desire to resist doctrines of pre-existence associated with PLATONISM and GNOSTICISM (*An.* 4, 18, 23), the chief source of its appeal among later theologians has been its usefulness in explaining the transmission of original SIN. Biblical support for the doctrine is claimed on the basis of passages like Hebrews 7:9–10 (which suggests a latent personal presence of descendants in the ancestor) and Genesis 2:2 (which suggests that there was no new CREATION after the sixth day). While traducianism does an excellent job of affirming the unity of the human race, it is criticized by its opponents as promoting a materialistic understanding of the soul.

IAN A. MCFARLAND

TRANSCENDENTALS, THE The roots of the medieval Scholastic doctrine of the transcendentals are to be found in Plato and especially in Aristotle (see ARISTOTELIANISM; PLATONISM). For *ens*, *unum*, *verum*, and *bonum* ('being', 'the one', 'the true', and 'the good') and sometimes *pulchrum* ('the beautiful') are held to transcend (i.e., 'go beyond') all of Aristotle's categories, which list the kinds of things there are. They 'transcend' because they are the fundamental properties of anything whatsoever and, as such, are held co-extensive with being itself. At the same time, the transcendentals do not have identical meaning. While extensionally equivalent, they are conceptually distinct.

The metaphysical importance of the doctrine of the transcendentals may be illustrated by the case of *bonum*. God is by definition good and every creature, in so far as it is, is good also. This means that evil has to be analyzed as *privatio boni*, not just as lack, but as abuse or deprivation of some actual or intended good.

The later Scholastic theologian, J. DUNS SCOTUS, is supposed to have held the transcendentals to be univocal in meaning, whether one is talking about God or creatures. Mainstream SCHOLASTICISM, represented by T. AQUINAS, held the transcendentals to be analogical. Scotus may be right about *unum* and *verum* (since these terms lack descriptive content), but Thomas is on surer ground where *ens*, *bonum*, and *pulchrum* are concerned. Given Thomas' understanding of the basic relationship between Creator and creature (often called the 'ANALOGY of being'), the ways in which both God and creatures are good and beautiful can only be analogical, too.

The informational content yielded by these basic analogies is minimal. For example, to call God 'good' is to affirm God's supreme value and desirability, but this says little or nothing about God's nature. As developed in revealed theology, the DOCTRINE of analogy goes far beyond the transcendentals in spelling out God's goodness in terms of steadfast LOVE. Love, taken as a revealed truth of God's nature, is not a transcendental. The same is true of many other analogical terms predicated of God in Christian theology, such as mind, wisdom, purpose, and agency. Justification for analogical predication in the case of these terms is held to stem from the revealed truth that humankind is made in the image of God (as most fully revealed in Jesus) rather than in a metaphysical concept like the transcendentals.

Another example of the limitations of the doctrine of the transcendentals may be seen in talk of God's unity. Essential though this is to every monotheistic religion, it does not rule out the development and articulation, whether on the basis of rational reflection or of revelation, of the doctrine of the TRINITY, in which the one God is recognized to be internally differentiated and inter-related in a way that justifies JOHN's assertion that God is love (1 John 4:8). Here, too, revealed theology takes Christian teaching beyond the doctrine of the transcendentals.

E. Coreth, *Metaphysics* (Seabury Press, 1973), Chapter 5.

N. Kretzmann, 'Trinity and Transcendentals' in *Trinity, Incarnation and Atonement*, ed. R. J. Feenstra and C. Plantinga, Jr (University of Notre Dame Press, 1989), 79–109.

BRIAN L. HEBBLETHWAITE

TRANSFIGURATION The transfiguration (*metamorphōsis* in Greek) of Christ, or his appearing in glory to Peter, James, and John, is an event described in Mark 9:2–10, Matthew 17:1–9, and Luke 9:28–36. It is also referred to in 2 Peter 1:16–19, and perhaps implied in John 1:14. Apocryphal sources that describe it include the *Apocalypse of Peter* and the *Acts of John*.

According to the Gospel narratives, either six (according to Matthew and Mark) or eight (according to Luke) days after the question posed by Jesus, 'Who do people say I am?' and the discussion that ensued, Jesus took Peter, James, and John, and led them to an unspecified 'high mountain'. ORIGEN identified this as Tabor, based on the verse, 'Tabor and Hermon shall rejoice in your name' (Ps. 89:12). This identification was adopted by virtually all subsequent writers, to such an extent that the expression 'Taboric light' refers unequivocally to the light of the transfiguration. On the mountain the garments of Jesus became a resplendent white, and his face shone brighter than the sun. Moses and Elijah appeared and were seen talking with Jesus, and Peter asked whether the disciples should make three tents for them. A bright cloud then overshadowed the mountain, while the voice of the Father was heard saying, 'This is my Son, the Beloved; with him I am well pleased; listen to him!' The disciples fell to the ground and were raised by Jesus after his transfiguration was over. On leaving the mountain, he instructed them to keep what they saw to themselves until after his RESURRECTION.

Although theophanies, or the self-revelation of a divinity to mortals, are attested in pre-Christian literature (e.g., Zeus' appearance to Semele in Greek myth), in the transfiguration of Jesus the divine nature is understood to be fully present in human form, even though it was experienced by the three APOSTLES only according to the degree that their human nature allowed. In other words, the transfiguration respects the transcendence of God's nature, but still constitutes a complete REVELATION of divinity in Christ, following the partial revelations of God to Moses (Exod. 33:18–23) and Elijah (2 Kgs 19:11–18) in the OT. Nevertheless, the reference to the three tents and several other elements of the narrative have been seen as evidence that the Gospel writers understood the transfiguration against the background of a specifically messianic understanding of the Feast of the Tabernacles (*Sukkot*), such that the event confirms Jesus' status as the Messiah. Likewise, the theme of the revelation of the Godhead in light has been read in the context of the Jewish concept of *kabod* (glory).

The first fathers who commented on the significance of the transfiguration – Origen, TERTULLIAN, and

IRENAEUS OF LYONS – connected it with the theological struggles of their time and saw it in the context of the unity of the OT and the NT. The presence of Elijah and Moses was seen by them as symbolic of the LAW and the prophets, which were fulfilled in and replaced by Christ. Other themes were increasingly explored by subsequent fathers, for whom elements of the biblical narrative such as the six/eight days, the ascent to Tabor, Peter's question, the voice of the Father, the symbolism of Moses, Elijah, and the three apostles, the white garments of Christ, and especially the light allowed them to explore the transfiguration in various ways, but with special emphasis on its status as a revelation of an eschatological nature. The most celebrated aspect of transfiguration theology, however, is connected with GREGORY PALAMAS, who saw the light of the transfiguration as a manifestation of the uncreated divine ENERGIES.

Although it is known that the transfiguration was celebrated from at least the fourth century in several parts of the East, it seems that there was no consistent, universal date for its feast. The current date of 6 August was introduced in the West by Pope Calixtus III (r. 1455–8) in 1456, but it is mentioned in much earlier eastern sources, such as the *Nomocanon* of Photios the Great (*ca* 810–93), which was compiled between the seventh and the twelfth centuries. The August date echoes the connection between the transfiguration and the passion, as it falls exactly forty days before the Feast of the Exaltation of the Cross, although there is evidence to suggest that the transfiguration was celebrated at other times in some parts of the East.

A. Andreopoulos, *Metamorphosis: The Transfiguration in Byzantine Theology and Iconography* (St Vladimir's Seminary Press, 2005).
D. A. Lee, *Transfiguration* (Continuum, 2004).
J. A. McGuckin, *The Transfiguration of Christ in Scripture and Tradition* (Edwin Mellen, 1986).

ANDREAS ANDREOPOULOS

TRANSUBSTANTIATION The DOCTRINE of transubstantiation is official Catholic teaching on the character of the consecrated elements in the EUCHARIST. The term first appears in a formal document of the MAGISTERIUM in 1215 at Lateran Council IV (Canon 1) and was formally defined at the Council of TRENT as the belief that 'by the consecration of the bread and wine there takes place a change [*conversionem*] of the whole substance of the bread into the substance of the body of Christ our Lord and of the whole substance of the wine into the substance of his blood' (*Euch.* 4; cf. *Cat.*, §1,376). This definition draws on Aristotelian metaphysical terminology, according to which a transformation of *substance* (or underlying essence) does not affect the *accidents* (or sensible properties) of the consecrated elements, which continue to manifest all the characteristics (e.g., appearance, taste, texture, etc.) of bread and wine.

The import of the doctrine remains unchanged since Lateran IV: the assurance that the same flesh and blood through which Christ entered into communion with humankind in the INCARNATION remains in the sacrament the medium of Christians' communion with Christ. The Reformed tradition objects that this (and other) claims that Christ's human nature is present in the consecrated elements is inconsistent with the creedal affirmation that the risen Christ's human body is in heaven at God's right hand. Lutherans accept Christ's presence in the consecrated elements, but regard transubstantiation as a needlessly complicated interpretation of this belief that lacks a clear grounding in SCRIPTURE or reason.

See also ARISTOTELIANISM; ASCENSION; UBIQUITY.

IAN A. MCFARLAND

TRAUMA, THEOLOGY OF Trauma is a life-threatening, life-altering experience of terror and helplessness which overwhelms normal resources, conventional understandings, coping abilities, and restraints. Trauma is an exceptional type of crisis, beyond normal developmental crises. Trauma can be simple or complex, a single event or a chronic, developmentally disruptive situation. In all cases, trauma has considerable effects on its victims, causing emotional, neurological, and biochemical damage. Where trauma occurs in the life-cycle is also significant, being most profound before the development of language. Trauma can cause such symptoms as flashbacks, hyperarousal, nightmares, mood swings, psychic numbing, and symbolic avoidance. Gender can play a significant role, such as when males cannot admit being victimized, or when females cannot recognize actual trauma because of stereotypical expectations. Trauma can also have vicarious effects on rescuers and caregivers. Many of these symptoms are grouped under the category 'post-traumatic stress disorder'.

But there are also less visible effects that directly impinge on SPIRITUALITY. Trauma survivors often find compromised their abilities to trust, find life-meaning, and marshal the emotional resources to deal with fear of chaos and DEATH. Religious beliefs can be shaken and one's self-understanding threatened. Individuals often feel guilty, debased, unworthy, and abandoned by God and others. Trauma can also be a group experience, distinctive to an ethnic, cultural, or racial community. Whole subcultures can pass down a collective memory of terror which colours group behaviour, beliefs, and religious experience. Increasing contemporary awareness of trauma includes renewed focus on the Bible's PREFERENTIAL OPTION FOR THE POOR, as well as work of various LIBERATION THEOLOGIES. While we have uncovered previously cloaked areas of trauma and denial, there has also been increased political repression and violence. Religious communities can exacerbate trauma through class, gender, race, and other biases, scapegoating, and minimizing local pain in favour of distant tragedies. They can promote healing by learning to recognize trauma, work co-operatively, and manage 'compassion fatigue'.

Caregivers need to take trauma seriously, not over-spiritualize it, yet offer a theology which helps restore faith. Constructive work must be done on such themes as SIN, evil, PROVIDENCE, FORGIVENESS, ATONEMENT, suffering, and GRACE. Theological suggestions include: differentiate sin from victimization, and find a term, such as 'anguish', for trauma and its spiritual damage; rethink our understanding of Jesus as God's victim, and atonement theories that attribute violence to God; explore where theology has justified terror and scapegoating, taking anti-Judaism as a tragic archetype; revitalize a theology of lament that eschews 'cheap' or premature forgiveness and reconciliation, and acknowledges that not all suffering is caused by personal sin; take human responsibility seriously so victimization does not turn into perpetration; reconsider whether God's power is coercive or influential, whether God is 'impassible', and how prayer works; contemplate whether our treatment of the earthly realm has promoted an inchoate form of trauma. Finally, theologians need to take seriously the subtle power of good, relentless divine grace, and the intention of God for abundant life now as well as in the future.

J. J. Means and M. A. Nelson, *Trauma and Evil: Healing the Wounded Soul* (Fortress Press, 2000).

L. Mercadante, 'Anguish: Unraveling Sin and Victimization', *Anglican Theological Review* 82:2 (spring 2000), 283–302.

LINDA MERCADANTE

TRENT, COUNCIL OF The COUNCIL known in English by this name met in the southernmost prince-bishopric of the Holy Roman Empire, a city at the very north of the Italian peninsula known as Trient or Trento. Its start had been repeatedly delayed, chiefly for political reasons, and these also contributed to prolonged interruptions, so that the Council effectively met in the years 1545–7, 1551–2, and 1562–3. Nevertheless, these meetings were finally recognized as a single council, producing a single set of decrees. The decrees alternated between two categories, doctrinal and disciplinary, although the latter were not lacking theological implications. This broadly reflected the stated reasons for papal summons of the Council, in the context of Protestant challenges during the first half of the sixteenth century: the ideal of Christian unity against the external danger of militant Islam, doctrinal clarification in the face of heretical deviation within CHRISTENDOM, and rectification of deficiencies in the life of the Church. The decrees of the Council were reviewed in Rome but published unaltered soon after the Council's end. Criticism of the content and limitations of the decrees swiftly followed, not only among those outside communion with Rome.

Only in 1551–2 were Protestant representatives present at Trent. They were non-voting members, the majority of whom were bishops. That many (indeed, for much of the Council's existence, a majority) of the latter were from the Italian peninsula did not in fact ensure outcomes desired at Rome, quite apart from the belated influence of Spanish and French participants. Professional theologians from the religious orders, especially Dominicans and eventually, and controversially, some Jesuits, advised the Council, and formal provisions ensured their knowledge of Protestant theology.

The Council enshrined the Latin VULGATE of the Bible for official purposes and asserted hierarchical control of access to SCRIPTURE, but did not outlaw all potential vernacular translations. Conventionally, the Council has been regarded as having crossed a theological Rubicon in 1547, in the decree on JUSTIFICATION, allegedly obstructing reunion with Lutherans or other Protestants. But already in 1546 the Council cited as the basis of Christian doctrine both Scripture and the Church's TRADITIONS (persistently misquoted as the singular 'tradition' in modern accounts). All further doctrinal decisions at the Council were thus reached on a basis not accepted by Protestants, quite apart from dispute over the identity of the canonical books of Scripture. To be sure, consideration of justification involved restatement of the DOCTRINE of original SIN, and hence the necessity of infant BAPTISM in normal circumstances, two issues where the essence of the Council's teaching ran in parallel to that of the magisterial Protestants. Nevertheless, the Council's definition of justification as the product of both FAITH and works entailed the firm rejection of the Protestant principle of justification by faith alone.

Against Protestant reduction of the sacraments to two, the Council reaffirmed the traditional western list of seven (see SACRAMENTOLOGY), with baptism and PENANCE receiving extensive and detailed analysis. Sacramental confession to a priest was reaffirmed as a regular adult obligation. By contrast, CONFIRMATION and unction (essentially clarified as extreme unction; see ANOINTING) were defined with a brevity which reflected a lack of theological consensus. For similar reasons, when the implications of original sin were considered, imposition of the doctrine of Mary's IMMACULATE CONCEPTION as a binding dogma was avoided. In considering the EUCHARIST the Council proclaimed the doctrine of Christ's real presence in the consecrated elements, retaining as the 'most apt' explanation of this the technical terminology of 'TRANSUBSTANTIATION', and so rejecting the alternative Lutheran and Reformed positions. This was logically related to the reassertion of the priestly and episcopal hierarchy of the Church in the decrees on the sacrament of ORDER.

The doctrinal decrees of the Council, more generally, were based on neither an intransigent anti-Protestantism nor an uncritical SCHOLASTICISM. The decrees on matrimony (see MARRIAGE) extended beyond vindication of ecclesiastical authority over the sacrament to establish a new discipline on the espoused (e.g., with respect to protocols for contracting marriage). The partners themselves administered the sacrament to each other, in what was taken as axiomatically an inviolable union of two Catholic Christians, one of each gender, both being freely consenting and of adequate age. While matrimony was classified as virtuous, chastity was exalted as a higher virtue, with defence of the binding vows of chastity taken by members of religious orders (see CELIBACY; MONASTICISM). It was also reaffirmed that the Church had authority to demand the discipline of celibacy for secular priests of the Western Rite.

The need for a better prepared clergy was recognized, owing especially to the new obligations of vernacular preaching imposed on bishops and parish priests, in addition to the priestly role in confession. Entirely new training was to be made available, by a seminary in each diocese, with scriptural study explicitly mentioned. A special set of decrees on the religious orders accepted the variety of their identity and regulated, especially for female religious, their institutions. After repeated discussions the Council left the PAPACY to decide whether under any conditions those other than the celebrant of the mass might receive communion in two kinds.

Despite internal and external resistance, pressures both within and without brought the Council to a speedy conclusion at the end of 1563, with PURGATORY, the invocation of the SAINTS, and the grant (ideally nonvenal) of indulgences given only summary revalidation. Visual art and music in the service of the Church were defended, but not subjected to any detailed regulation. Such rapid closure also left some ambiguity as to relations between the episcopate and the papacy. The Council explicitly devolved to the latter the interpretation as well as confirmation of the conciliar decrees, and also completion of the unfinished Index of Prohibited Books and official Catechism, both worked on by conciliar commissions. But even within Catholicism itself, professional theological controversy was not in fact ended: bitter internal dispute over the means of GRACE continued in the remaining decades of the sixteenth century in the Netherlands, Spain, and Italy. This was the prelude to the larger and more prolonged disputes, starting in the Netherlands and France in the mid-seventeenth century, associated with JANSENISM.

See also CATHOLIC THEOLOGY.

A. Dupront, 'Du Concile de Trente: réflexions', *Revue historique* (1951), 262–80.

A. Duval, *Des sacrements au Concile de Trente* (Cerf, 1985).

D. Fenlon, *Heresy and Obedience in Tridentine Italy: Cardinal Pole and the Counter-Reformation* (Cambridge University Press, 1972).

H. Jedin, *Crisis and Closure of the Council of Trent* (Sheed & Ward, 1967).

A. D. WRIGHT

TRIBULATION: see RAPTURE.

TRINITY The doctrine of the Trinity, which affirms that God is three Persons (traditionally designated, the Father, the Son, and the HOLY SPIRIT) in one substance, has been a touchstone of Christian ORTHODOXY since the late fourth century. In recent decades it has become the focus of an intense renewal of theological interest.

The technical language of the DOCTRINE of the Trinity is not biblical, and while the NT contains a number of threefold formulae for God (arguably 1 Cor. 6:11 and 12:4–6; Gal. 3:11–14; Heb. 10:29; 1 Pet 1:21 and most crucially Matt. 28:19) and some seemingly deliberate threefold patterning, the question of how God can be both three and one was not for the NT authors a locus of overt theological struggle or extended reflection. If it is not directly 'in' the NT, however, the doctrine did nevertheless arise from a problem bequeathed by the NT to the early Church, namely how to make sense of the fact that Christians find themselves both worshipping Christ as divine and continuing in the fundamental conviction that there is only one God.

While a variety of second- and third-century theologians wrestled with the issue of how to understand Son and Spirit in relation to the Father (including for example Justin Martyr (d. *ca* 165), IRENAEUS, TERTULLIAN – who introduced terms such as *trinitas* and *persona* into Latin theology – and ORIGEN), the long and bitter controversy which led eventually to the establishing of the doctrine of the Trinity was triggered by the preaching of Arius, a priest in Alexandria, in the early fourth century. Arius maintained that the Son, though divine, was not coeternal with the Father, and that he did not fully see or know the Father. Though Arius was excommunicated, the views he espoused found a sympathetic hearing among many bishops. The Council of NICAEA was called by Emperor Constantine I (*ca* 275–337) in the hope of ending the controversy. Here Arius was condemned, and the Son declared to be 'of the same substance' (*HOMOOUSIOS*) with the Father. The controversy, however, continued unabated after Nicaea; the Nicene bishops had been pressured by the emperor into accepting *homoousios*, but there was a good deal of uncertainty and suspicion surrounding the term, not only because it was unbiblical, but also because it seemed to many suggestive of MODALISM (see ARIAN CONTROVERSY).

ATHANASIUS, the bishop of Alexandria, became in the decades which followed a vigorous, theologically able, and highly combative defender of the Council and of *homoousios*. In so doing, he was driven primarily by soteriological considerations: only if the Son were consubstantial with the Father, he argued, could he be trusted as saviour, since otherwise there would be a limit to the Son's power that would vitiate his ability to guarantee salvation to those believing in him (*Ar.* 1.59–61; 2.8–10). Still, it was not until the cause was taken up in the following generation by the so-called CAPPADOCIAN FATHERS, Gregory of Nazianzus, Gregory of Nyssa, and Basil of Caesarea, that Nicene theology was framed with sufficient terminological clarity to allow the matter to be settled. The Cappadocians assuaged the anxieties of the more moderate of the opponents of Nicaea in part through the introduction of the Greek term HYPOSTASIS (conventionally translated into English as 'person') into their theology: in brief, they taught that, although Father and Son were *homoousios*, they were not simply identical in that they were distinct hypostases.

While controversy in relation to the Son's status was long and painful, debates surrounding the full divinity of the Holy Spirit were much briefer. Both Athanasius and Gregory of Nyssa had written in defence of the Spirit's divinity, but it is particularly Basil of Caesarea who is remembered for applying the kinds of arguments that had been developed with regard to the Son to the defence of the divinity of the Spirit, and in 381 his position was vindicated by the Council of CONSTANTINOPLE's expansion of the creed of Nicaea to include a more fully developed third article on the Spirit (see NICENE CREED). At the Council of Constantinople, then, the doctrine of the Trinity was finally established in its definitive formulation: God is one substance (*ousia*) and three Persons (*hypostases*).

To say that the doctrine was established, however, is not necessarily to say that its meaning was clear. A common Trinitarian language had been agreed, a language that clearly indicated a rejection of both modalism and any kind of subordination of the Son or Spirit to the Father (see ADOPTIONISM). Certain theological principles also became established, including the idea that the substantial unity of the triune God meant that the actions of the three hypostases in the world were always co-ordinated and never separate (expressed in the Latin phrase *opera Trinitatis ad extra sunt indivisa*). But it is interesting to note that the words *hypostasis* and *ousia*, before they were appropriated for Trinitarian purposes, were more or less synonymous philosophical terms (both would have been translated into English as 'substance'). Some twentieth- and twenty-first-century theologians (e.g., J. Zizioulas (b. 1931)) have suggested that in the distinct way they deployed the term *hypostasis* in a Trinitarian context the Cappadocians were responsible for a major breakthrough in ontology, but it is quite possible that AUGUSTINE, writing a generation after the Cappadocians, was closer to the truth in suggesting that we say three hypostases or persons not because of any particular adequacy of the words but 'in order to have a name to answer the question "Three what?"' (*Trin.* 7.4).

Attention to the history of its development is a vital element in understanding the doctrine of the Trinity. From it one sees that the doctrine does not arise out of abstract reflection about the one and the many or oneness and threeness, but out of struggle over CHRISTOLOGY and the proper interpretation of SCRIPTURE. Inevitably perhaps the doctrine gives rise to reflections on oneness and threeness and how they are compatible, and inevitably perhaps provokes a search for analogies, ranging from triangles, three-leaf clovers, and musical chords to the mind's activity of remembering, knowing, and loving itself, or to the love and unity of a small family or group of friends. Augustine, writing in the first generation after the Council of Constantinople, already spilt a good deal of ink and ingenuity in searching for VESTIGIA TRINITATIS, traces of the Trinity which one should expect to find in a world that has been created by the Trinity, and which should therefore help the pious mind ascend to some sort of understanding of God. But such efforts, absorbing though they may be – and in Augustine's case the search itself has a multi-layered and highly contemplative character – are not, if the origins of the doctrine are taken as significant, what lie at its very heart. Properly Trinitarian theology is not theology that has settled on just the right image, whether homely or metaphysically sophisticated, of three-in-oneness, but theology which properly combines Christology and pneumatology with an affirmation of FAITH in one God.

In recent years Trinitarian theology has been largely shaped by a double reaction; a reaction on the one hand against the ENLIGHTENMENT and LIBERAL THEOLOGY; and, on the other, against a situation where, in textbook theology and the faith of pious Christians, the Trinity had come to seem a sterile and religiously marginal intellectual difficulty.

The Enlightenment represented a profound shift in the fundamental patterning of thought about God, and in the context of this shift the doctrine of the Trinity more or less fell away – it was an irrelevance, an example of obscurantist superstition, a doctrine which gave rise to fanatical debates over an iota (the Greek letter distinguishing *homoiousios*, or 'of similar substance', from *homoousios*) and SCHISM over a single word (see *FILIOQUE*). Liberals in the nineteenth century, though not so wholeheartedly hostile to the doctrine, were nevertheless enough the inheritors of the Enlightenment to register in most cases a certain discomfort with it. F. SCHLEIERMACHER is usually taken as emblematic of this trend: he dealt with the Trinity only in a kind of appendix to his great systematic work, *Christian Faith* (2nd edn, 1830), and in fairly critical terms. Specifically, Schleiermacher argued that the doctrine, in so far as it involves assertions about eternal distinctions in God, is not an 'utterance concerning religious consciousness' (*CF*, §170.2) and so is secondary and in some sense extraneous to the proper business of theology.

One of the initiators of the twentieth-century revival of reflection on the Trinity was K. BARTH, who offered a several-hundred-page exploration of the doctrine in the first-part-volume of his *Church Dogmatics* (1932), making the deliberately provocative proposal that the Trinity must be the starting point of, rather than an appendix to, Christian theology. The content of Barth's work on the Trinity has not been especially influential in shaping what has followed, but the insistence on giving the doctrine renewed prominence has very much been taken up. An essay of K. RAHNER was also significant in drawing attention to the need for a rediscovery and rethinking of the doctrine. It had become so peripheral to most Christian thought, Rahner suggested, that if it was suddenly decided that the doctrine had been a mistake 'the major part of religious literature could well remain virtually unchanged' (*Trinity* 10–11). Partly to combat this sense of the doctrine as an abstraction lacking any living connection to the centre of Christian faith, Rahner proposed as a fundamental axiom that 'The "economic" Trinity is the "immanent" Trinity and the "immanent" Trinity is the "economic" Trinity' (*Trinity* 22). 'Economic Trinity' is a term referring to the Trinity as encountered in God's dealing with us, in the ECONOMY of salvation. In contrast, the 'immanent Trinity' is the Trinity in itself, as it is and would have been even apart from the world; it is a term attesting to the belief that God is not only Trinity in relation to us but really *is* three-in-one. Properly relating economic and immanent Trinity without either falling into modalism or seeming to set up two parallel trinities is a problem which has vexed recent theology, as can be seen by the reception of Rahner's axiom: quite a number of theologians have taken it up in some way, but often with rather different interpretations of what it means.

Social theories of the Trinity have been enormously influential in recent decades. Thinkers such as J. Moltmann (b. 1926), C. Gunton (1941–2003), and many others propose that the best model of the Trinity is not, as in Augustine, three faculties or activities of a single mind, but rather a small family or community so bound together in love and empathy as to be one. On such understandings the patristic notion of PERICHORESIS is the key which explains how the three Persons can nevertheless be one God, and the doctrine acquires an easily identifiable relevance through its implications for thought about the nature of family, society, politics, and in general the relation of persons to communities. Further, such 'social' theories of the Trinity tend to be closely bound up with the communion ecclesiologies which have been influential in recent decades in both Catholic and Orthodox contexts (see ECCLESIOLOGY).

Though the doctrine of the Trinity has been the focus of a great deal of theological activity in the twentieth and twenty-first centuries, there has not necessarily been an equal degree of clarity. All sides are at one in affirming that it is crucially important for Christian theology to be properly Trinitarian, but cannot seem to agree on what this means. Thus one can find thinkers such as Barth and Rahner suggesting that a social theory of the Trinity would amount to TRITHEISM, and social Trinitarians such as Moltmann insisting that Rahner and Barth are in fact modalists. Furthermore, while most recent theologians have been keen to return to the pre-modern tradition (especially theologians of the patristic period), there is a burgeoning literature on the misuse by systematic theologians of the patristic sources. This literature focuses specifically on objections to the contemporary appropriation of the Cappadocians and to the tendency to posit a fundamental divide between eastern and western (viz., Augustinian) understandings of the Trinity. Contemporary Christian theologians thus find themselves in the somewhat awkward position of being sure that the God they speak of must be understood not in abstract Enlightenment terms but in a distinctively Trinitarian way, but less sure about what this actually might mean.

See also ABBA; APPROPRIATION; *LOGOS*; SOTERIOLOGY.

E. Jüngel, *God As the Mystery of the World: On the Foundation of the Theology of the Crucified One in the Dispute between Theism and Atheism* (T&T Clark, 1999 [1977]).

W. Kasper, *The God of Jesus Christ* (Crossroad, 1991).

N. Lash, *Believing Three Ways in One God: A Reading of the Apostles' Creed* (University of Notre Dame Press, 1993).

J. Moltmann, *The Trinity and the Kingdom: The Doctrine of God* (Fortress Press, 1993 [1980]).

W. C. Placher, *The Triune God: An Essay in Postliberal Theology* (John Knox Press, 2007).

W. G. Rusch, ed., *The Trinitarian Controversy* (Fortress Press, 1980).

KAREN KILBY

TRITHEISM Tritheism, or belief in three Gods, is a position which at no point has been explicitly advocated within the Christian tradition (i.e., no theologian calls him- or herself a tritheist). But some interpreters of the DOCTRINE of the TRINITY have at times been judged to fall into this HERESY. A group of sixth-century miaphysites (see MIAPHYSITISM), of whom J. Philoponus (*ca* 490–*ca* 570) was the best known, are one case in point. Philoponus appears to have maintained that the divine HYPOSTASES must in reality be three substances, and that the one *ousia* of which the tradition speaks can only be a universal existing in the mind. He was condemned posthumously at the Third Council of Constantinople in 680–1. Roscelin of Compiègne (*ca* 1050–*ca* 1125) was condemned in the eleventh century for maintaining that the divine Persons were three individual beings, like three ANGELS.

Though such cases of a tritheism which has been formally recognized and rejected have been relatively marginal and rare, the worry about tritheism has played and continues to play a fairly significant role in Christian theology. The CAPPADOCIAN FATHERS, credited with the final triumph of what has become orthodox

Trinitarian theology in the fourth century, were themselves accused by some of their contemporaries of tritheism because of a tendency to account for the oneness of God in generic terms. In contemporary theology the proclivity of some theologians, including H. U. von Balthasar and many advocates of a 'social' model of the Trinity, to envisage three centres of consciousness and three 'I's in God raises similar questions.

Karen Kilby

Troeltsch, Ernst Ernst Troeltsch (1865–1923) was one of the leading representatives of German liberal theology in the early years of the twentieth century. He studied at Göttingen under A. Ritschl (1822–89), forming close friendships with a group of biblical scholars known as the 'History of Religion School'. He was appointed professor of systematic theology at Heidelberg in 1895, where he produced a number of influential writings epitomized by *The Absoluteness of Christianity* (1901), which drew out the theological and philosophical implications of the historical method, and which earned him the title 'systematic theologian' of the History of Religion School. He regarded historicism as one of the most important characteristics of the modern period, which differentiated it from the earlier 'ecclesiastical-unified period of European culture', in which he controversially included the Reformation.

Through his historical researches Troeltsch became increasingly interested in the different social forms of Christianity and formed a close working relationship with the sociologist M. Weber (1864–1920). Troeltsch's studies in social history resulted in the massive book *The Social Teaching of the Christian Churches* (1912), where he outlined the various ways in which the Christian ethos had been 'compromised' in particular historical settings. This led him to develop his threefold typology of Church, sect, and mysticism, which was taken up by later sociologists of religion. *The Social Teaching* was intended to provide a basis for a constructive theology, which would have blended the three types of religious organization, but which was never produced.

Having 'outgrown' the theological faculty, Troeltsch moved to the philosophical faculty at Berlin in 1915, concentrating his efforts on the philosophical analysis of history, and at the same time trying to understand the religious dimension of World War I. In the early Weimar Republic he played an active role in liberal politics. His historical researches resulted in *Der Historismus und seine Probleme* (1922), which was to have been supplemented by a 'material philosophy of history', which would have offered practical solutions to the ethical dilemmas of modernity. Although his sudden death meant that this remained unwritten, his work in this area was published posthumously in *Christian Thought* (1923). These lectures present an ethics of compromise based upon the relativity of all cultural constructs. Troeltsch aimed to use the resources of the past, drawn from the 'melting pot of historicism', to create a cultural synthesis ('Europeanism') for the present.

Troeltsch's reputation has suffered from his association with what was pejoratively called 'Culture Protestantism'; his move to philosophy was seen by K. Barth as marking the bankruptcy of liberal theology. However, Troeltsch was often deeply critical of his own culture and sought to introduce a thoroughgoing critical method into all aspects of thought, including theology. This was partly based on I. Kant's philosophy and showed a similar distrust of supernatural method and over-reliance on religious experience.

M. Chapman, *Ernst Troeltsch and Liberal Theology: Religion and Cultural Synthesis in Wilhelmine Germany* (Oxford University Press, 2001).

H.-G. Drescher, *Ernst Troeltsch: His Life and Work* (SCM, 1992).

Mark D. Chapman

Tübingen School (Catholic) In 1817 the Catholic theology faculty of the Ellwangen seminary moved to the University of Tübingen, long recognized as a centre for Lutheran theology. The first generation of Catholic scholars, most notably apologetic and dogmatic theologian J. S. Drey (1777–1853), moral and pastoral theologian J. B. Hirscher (1788–1865), and J. A. Möhler (1796–1838), who taught patristics, Church history, and canon law, inaugurated what the twentieth-century writers K. Adam (1876–1966) and J. Geiselmann (1890–1970) called a multi-generational, Catholic Tübingen 'School'. R. Reinhart (1928–2007) later demonstrated that there was no 'school' demarcated by a unified theological method or consistency in substantive theological positions. Nevertheless, there was a loosely held research agenda that sought to defend the truth of the Catholic faith by steering a course between critical assessments of Christianity characteristic of the Enlightenment and rationalism on the one hand, and defences of Catholic identity associated with fideism and ultramontanism on the other.

In 1812 Drey published an essay calling for a 'Revision of the Present State of Theology' and in 1819 he defended the public presence of Catholic theology in a modern university setting by contributing to the emerging genre of theological encyclopedia, engaging the views of F. Schleiermacher and F. Schelling (1775–1854). Drey concentrated on Jesus' teaching on the kingdom of God as the central idea of Christianity from which all others can be deduced. This idea proved pivotal in his apologetic theology and he constructed his dogmatic theology as a drama of the kingdom of God in four acts. Hirscher likewise constructed his moral theology, following his senior colleague Drey, in terms of the realization of the reign of God in creation and history, in the human subject and society.

Möhler never gave much attention to the idea of the kingdom of God. Instead he concentrated on the agency of the Holy Spirit in the nascent life of the individual and the Church. Subsequently he shifted to a resolutely Christocentric approach which marked his defence of the doctrines of the Catholic Church in *Symbolik* (1832), a book-length analysis of confessional differences with Protestant positions on theological anthropology, on faith and good works, and on Church and sacraments that was widely criticized, notably by F. C. Baur (1792–1860). Möhler's description of the Church as an ongoing incarnation proved very influential among his colleagues and students at Tübingen and with wider circles of theologians, including Roman-school theologians who were the architects of neo-Scholastic theology.

Drey in 1819 described Catholic Christianity as 'a living tradition', a motif which came to define Catholic Tübingen theology. Although the differences among Tübingen theologians on the nature of tradition are as important as the similarities, the sacramental, hierarchical, and organic understanding of the Church, its divine origins and goal, and the key role of theology in the Church were convictions shared by many Tübingen theologians. Likewise Drey and Möhler affirmed the importance of episcopal and papal authority, while rejecting contemporary forms of conciliarism and ultramontanism. However, Drey and Hirscher defended a role for theological criticism and public opinion in the Church, and the importance of local and provincial synods for addressing current pastoral issues. Möhler, by contrast, fashioned a distinctively confessional approach to theology and developed an antagonistic attitude towards reform-minded and modern attempts to call into question traditions such as mandatory priestly celibacyand the exercise of authority by the local and the regional Church and the papal office (see Papacy).

Bradford Hinze

Tübingen School (Protestant) The Protestant Tübingen School refers to a group of nineteenth-century historians, theologians, and biblical scholars in the University of Tübingen who were inspired and led by F. C. Baur (1792–1860). The school applied a rational 'objective criticism', a historical method shorn of all supernaturalist assumptions, to the study of the texts and broad context of early Christianity. Baur's approach was also informed by a dialectical conception of the historical process in which the earliest form of the emergent Christian community, a Semitic 'thesis' associated with the apostle Peter, was challenged by the radicalized 'antithesis', in the form of a Gentile-accepting representation of Jesus Christ. The resolution of this tension appeared in the 'synthesis' represented by early Catholicism.

This 'school' did not emerge in a vacuum but within a distinctive historical and social context. Theology has been taught in the University of Tübingen since its foundation in 1477. In the course of the implementation of the Reformation in Tübingen in the years after 1535, the close connection between academic and Church theology was newly consolidated in the faculty of theology and in the Tübingen Stift, the Protestant seminary that still supplies ministers for the Lutheran State Church of Baden-Württemberg. Candidates for the Stift were selected on the basis of ability and prepared in four special schools. Frequently an intense Schwabian Pietism informed both their familial and their academic background. Candidates were taught early the sacred languages of Latin, Greek, and Hebrew, and thus they commenced their studies in the Stift exceptionally well equipped to experience the intellectual tensions, first of the early modern period, and then of the German Enlightenment and Romanticism.

A 'first' Protestant Tübingen School is associated with J. Bengel (1687–1742) and G. Storr (1746–1805), conservative, supernaturalist biblical theologians and exegetes who represented an orthodox Christian theology anchored in evangelical Pietism (see Supernaturalism). In 1826 the Tübingen theological faculty underwent drastic reform that almost completely eliminated the influence of Pietism and traditional interpretation of the NT. Baur was appointed to a chair in theology and proceeded to publish a series of works that interrogated the assumptions of the theology in which he had been educated in the Stift. Building upon his early *Symbolik und Mythologie des Altertums oder die Naturreligion des Altertums* (1824–5), Baur produced studies of Manichaeism, Christian Gnosticism, the Corinthian Church, the (so-called) Pastoral Epistles, and the proto-Pauline Epistles and Acts, besides the Christian doctrines of reconciliation, the Trinity and the incarnation, and the later history of Christian theology. Baur's pupils did not for the most part attain established professorial positions and the overt influence of the 'School' declined from the late 1840s. Nonetheless, the extraordinary and contentious achievement of the Protestant Tübingen School set much of a critical agenda that endures to the present day.

H. Harris, *The Tübingen School: A Historical and Theological Investigation of the School of F.C. Baur* (Oxford University Press, 1975).

P. C. Hodgson, *The Formation of Historical Theology: A Study of F. C. Baur* (Harper & Row, 1966).

Richard H. Roberts

Two Kingdoms The category of two kingdoms (*zwei Reiche*) was introduced by M. Luther in his 1523 treatise, *Temporal Authority* (*Von weltlicher Oberkeit*), as a means of describing the Christian's responsibility to civil government. Both the temporal and the spiritual realm were ruled by God, and Luther referred to them as two regimes or governments (*zwei Regimente*) in order to avoid confusion between them and a third realm of sin and evil, in which the Devil held sway. It appears that K. Barth was the first theologian to refer to a doctrine of two kingdoms (*Zwei-Reiche-Lehre*), but neither Luther nor later Lutherans regarded it as a doctrine to be believed or a pattern that had to be followed (Braaten, 'Two', 498). The BOOK OF CONCORD made only occasional mention of two realms, but it did insist upon the integrity of each (Melanchthon, *Apol.* 16).

Forerunners of two kingdoms can be found in the two cities of AUGUSTINE and in the two powers or swords claimed by the medieval PAPACY, but Luther based his notion of two realms on SCRIPTURE. In *Temporal Authority* he wrestled with the issue of how Christians could live by the SERMON ON THE MOUNT and still obey the admonitions in Romans 13:1–7. As a solution he proposed that Christians lived in two realms, a spiritual kingdom, where Christ and the GOSPEL reigned, and a worldly or temporal kingdom, in which civil government and its LAWS were instituted by God to keep evil in check. Strictly speaking, the true home of believers was the spiritual kingdom, in which faith in Christ led to FORGIVENESS of SIN and salvation; but the temporal realm, though corrupted by sin, was also God's good CREATION, and Christians could and should serve in government, engage in business, and establish and nurture families – all with a good conscience as long as they did not set human judgement above divine authority (Acts 5:29). There were no perfect Christians, and forgiveness was always available in the kingdom of Christ; with that assurance, believers were encouraged to put their faith into action daily on behalf of others.

Luther's model required believers to affirm the integrity of both kingdoms and, unlike the medieval Church, to distinguish properly between them. Twentieth-century applications of two realms, however, have led to distortions and disagreements. By treating Luther's distinction between two kingdoms as a sharp separation and ignoring his rebukes of unjust princes, some German theologians in the 1930s argued that resistance to the Nazi dictatorship was not permitted to Christians because it did not involve their FAITH. In the BARMEN DECLARATION this view was resoundingly rejected by Lutheran and Reformed theologians, but in his influential book *Christ and Culture* (1951) H. R. Niebuhr (1894–1962) called two kingdoms a paradoxical way of relating Christ to culture that was vulnerable to passivity in the face of evil. Although that stigma is still alive, a proper distinction between the spiritual and temporal kingdoms helps to resist the persistent human tendency to mix religious zeal with political extremism.

SCOTT H. HENDRIX

TYPOLOGY 'These things happened to them to serve as an example [*tupikōs*], and they were written down to instruct us, on whom the ends of the ages have come' (1 Cor. 10:11). Etymologically a *tupos* was an impression made when a seal was struck. For Christians it was one of a series of words used to describe the way an event in the OT foreshadowed one in the NT, or the way a biblical happening presaged one in believers' lives. Typology (also known as figural reading) is thus an extension of ancient Christians' vision of the patterns in the Bible they came to call prophecy, as evidenced in PAUL's words to the Corinthians. If the 'ends of the ages' have indeed come, and the same God was at work before the crux of history, will we not see his fingerprints before Christ as well as after?

The word has carried a range of meanings. For example, Ignatius of Antioch (d. *ca* 110) could describe a bishop as a *tupon* of the Father. In mid-twentieth century Christianity it became a terminological way to distinguish a preferred non-literal interpretation of SCRIPTURE from one (usually called an 'ALLEGORY') that was not. Theologians sought to carve out space for what they called typological correspondence between, e.g., Isaiah's suffering servant and Christ's passion, or the Exodus and believers' experience of BAPTISM or the Civil Rights Movement in the USA. These readings are of actual, historical events that closely resemble one another while remaining distinct, with the emphasis placed on the literality of an act of interpretation rather than on a claim to historical verifiability of a past event. As ancient fourth-century Antiochene theologians argued against their third-century Alexandrian opponents, typological reading leaves intact the *historia*, or plain narrative meaning, of the biblical text. This plain meaning should not be obliterated as the exegete races off to whatever strikes her fancy – for example, finding spiritual states of the soul in the place names of the Israelite camps. In the words of Theodore of Mopsuestia (*ca* 350–428), allegorizers 'claim that Adam is not Adam, paradise is not paradise, the serpent not the serpent. I should like to tell them this: if they make history serve their own ends, they will have no history left' (*CGal.* 4:22–31).

In short, typology is usually contrasted with an assumed act of over-reading in which the allegorist leaps off from the text to eternal truths, leaving behind biblical, Hebraic, historical reality. To various degrees the Reformers and modern historical critics have seen their own reaction against allegory foreshadowed in Antiochene exegetes. But more recent scholarship has suggested that the line between typology and allegory is not so clear. Is a reading of the Song of Songs as a description of the LOVE of God for ISRAEL an allegory? Or is God's relationship with Israel not less 'historical' than anything else in Scripture?

D. Dawson, *Christian Figural Reading and the Fashioning of Identity* (University of California Press, 2002).
S. Fowl, *Engaging Scripture* (Blackwell, 1998).

JASON BYASSEE

Ubiquity The doctrine of the ubiquity (or omnipresence) of the human nature of Jesus is a feature of Lutheran theology that derives from M. Luther's teaching that Christ is present in the consecrated elements of the Eucharist in both his divine and human natures. Luther argued that restricting the real presence to the divine nature violated the Christology of Chalcedon, according to which both natures are united in Jesus' person without division or separation. In short, Luther maintained that to have Christ in his divinity only was not to have Christ at all, since the Christ is always the Word made flesh (John 1:14). In order to account for Christ's simultaneous presence in both natures in heaven (see Ascension and Session) and at an indefinite number of geographically separate celebrations of the Eucharist on earth, however, his human nature had to share the omnipresence characteristic of the divine nature (see Attributes, Divine).

Though Luther sometimes referred to medieval Scholastic distinctions between various modes of presence to justify his claims, he preferred to defend his position by appeal to biblical texts rather than through metaphysical speculation. Later Lutheran theologians grounded the omnipresence of Christ's human nature in the Christological doctrine of the communication of attributes (*communicatio idiomatum*). The Lutheran interpretation of this principle moved beyond the classical teaching that the properties of either nature could be predicated of Christ's person (so that, e.g., one could rightly ascribe hunger to the divine Son or omnipotence to Jesus of Nazareth), to argue for a real transfer of properties from the divine to the human nature (so that one could ascribe the divine attribute of omnipresence directly to Christ's humanity). This claim was justified on the grounds that in the incarnation the divine Son so assumed human nature that this nature has everything the Son has; therefore, the assumed human nature necessarily also acquires the attributes of the divine nature, since divinity is an essential characteristic of the Son as the second Person of the Trinity.

The principle of Christ's presence in the Eucharist in his human nature was affirmed in the Lutheran Book of Concord (*FC, Ep.* 8) and proved a major source of disagreement between Lutheran and Reformed theology. The Reformed argued that the Lutheran interpretation of the communication of attributes so blurred the distinction between the two natures that it effectively nullified Christ's humanity. In response to this charge, Lutherans insisted that one of the effects of the personal union of the natures in the incarnation was to bring new properties to Christ's human nature without thereby cancelling it out, in the same way that the application of heat can bring new properties (e.g., an orange glow, extreme malleability) to an iron bar without the bar ceasing to be fully and genuinely iron.

E. W. Gritsch and R. W. Jenson, *Lutheranism: The Theological Movement and Its Confessional Writings* (Fortress Press, 1976).

H. Schmid, *Doctrinal Theology of the Evangelical Lutheran Church* (Augsburg Publishing Press, 1961 [1899]).

Ian A. McFarland

U

Ultradispensationalism 'Ultradispensationalism' is a term used (generally by critics) to refer to a minority position within dispensationalism. All dispensationalist theologies draw a sharp distinction between Israel and the Church as distinct modes (or dispensations) of God's way of relating to humankind and, correspondingly, stress the importance of identifying the point of transition from one to the other. According to the majority ('Acts 2') dispensationalist position, the period of the Church begins with the pouring out of the Holy Spirit at Pentecost in Acts 2:4. Ultradispensationalists date the onset of the dispensation of the Church later, usually at Acts 28:26–8, interpreted as the inauguration of an exclusively Gentile Pauline mission. Those who date the onset of the Church at a position between Acts 2 and 28 are sometimes distinguished as hyperdispensationalists.

The debate between dispensationalists and ultradispensationalists turns on different understandings of the Church's defining characteristics. Defenders of Acts 2 dispensationalism focus on God's act in constituting the Church through the sending of the Holy Spirit, without reference to the Church's ethnic make-up. By contrast, ultradispensationalists stress the Church's character as a community marked by the inclusion of Gentiles and therefore argue that its foundation must come later than Acts' early chapters, which describe an apostolic mission to Jews only. Since they tend to see the defining characteristic of the Church as baptism in the Spirit, they generally reject baptism by water (as well as the celebration of the Eucharist) as a ritual holdover from the now superseded dispensation of Israel.

Ian A. McFarland

Ultramontanism Derived from the Latin for 'beyond the mountains', ultramontanism emerged in early modern Catholic theology, when European Catholics disputed the extent of the pope's authority in the countries north of (i.e., 'beyond') the Alps. The term 'ultramontane' was used pejoratively in seventeenth-century France for those who promoted the supremacy of the papacy over local Church traditions and more broadly in German-speaking areas in the following century for those who challenged secular rulers' authority in ecclesiastical affairs. Later usage is shaped by both these streams, so that in subsequent Catholic thought ultramontanism comes to refer to the position that in matters of Church POLITY papal authority trumps both the external claims of civil power and the internal claims of local bishops and even ecumenical COUNCILS.

The decrees of VATICAN COUNCIL I included the declaration that the pope has 'full and supreme power of jurisdiction over the whole church not only in matters of faith and morals, but also in ... the discipline and government of the church dispersed throughout the whole world' (Session 4, Chapter 3; cf. *Cat.*, §882). In reaction, some northern European Catholics broke with Rome, arguing that the Council's implicit affirmation of ultramontanism constituted a break with TRADITION. But the majority accepted the Council's reasoning that because the pope (as bishop of Rome) is the successor of Peter, who (following traditional Catholic exegesis of Matt. 16:16–19 and John 21:15–17) was appointed by Jesus to be the head of the Church on earth, the primacy of the pope derives from and represents that of Christ over the Church.

See also CONCILIARISM; INFALLIBILITY.

IAN A. MCFARLAND

UNCONDITIONAL ELECTION One of the central doctrines of classical REFORMED THEOLOGY defined at the Synod of DORT, unconditional ELECTION was conceived by its proponents as a necessary implication of the DOCTRINE of JUSTIFICATION. All the Reformed agreed that salvation was the consequence of God's eternal election of particular individuals, in line with biblical passages like Ephesians 1:4–6. In an effort to preserve some role for human freedom in the process of salvation, the Arminian party maintained that this election was based on God's foreknowledge of FAITH in the elect (see ARMINIANISM). Over against this position, the Canons of Dort (1.9–10) reason that, if human salvation is entirely a matter of GRACE, then it cannot be conditional on any quality or disposition in the person elected, but must be understood as grounded exclusively in God's own good pleasure.

The chief objections to unconditional election are, first, that it undermines FREE WILL, thereby making human beings completely passive objects of divine action; and, second, that it renders divine election arbitrary. The first charge is generally answered by arguing that in bringing the elect to GLORY God works through rather than against their wills. The most arresting response to the second charge is that of K. BARTH, who proposed a wholesale rethinking of the doctrine in which the immediate object of divine election is not some arbitrary set of individuals, but Jesus Christ, in whom God elects all human beings for God's self in order to nullify all human rejection of God (*CD* II/2, 94, 306).

See also IRRESISTIBLE GRACE.

IAN A. MCFARLAND

UNCTION, EXTREME: see ANOINTING.

UNIATE CHURCHES: see EASTERN CATHOLIC CHURCHES.

UNITARIANISM Unitarianism (Unitarian Universalism in the USA) is a liberal, non-creedal religious tradition that emphasizes free religious enquiry and embraces theological diversity. Unitarians are found in over forty countries, predominantly the USA and Romania (Transylvania), with significant numbers in Canada, Hungary, India, and the UK.

Unitarianism's roots lie in the radical REFORMATION and the ENLIGHTENMENT.

A specifically Unitarian theology emerged in the sixteenth century, primarily in eastern Europe, as the result of challenges to the doctrine of the TRINITY (see SOCINIANISM). Organized Unitarian movements appeared in England and the USA during the late eighteenth and early nineteenth centuries. In opposition to the Reformed DOCTRINES of original SIN and divine ELECTION, early Unitarians emphasized the human potential for goodness and divine love. Most affirmed some form of universal salvation, reflecting their theological affinity with UNIVERSALISM. Boston minister W. E. Channing (1780–1842) was the spiritual and intellectual leader of early nineteenth-century Unitarianism. His sermons and essays provided a firm theological grounding for Unitarianism and influenced liberal Christianity's approach to such matters as education, social reform, and peace.

Contemporary Unitarianism shares with other forms of LIBERAL THEOLOGY a modern emphasis on critical reason, the priority of ethics over doctrine, and the rejection of external authority in favour of autonomous judgement in matters of faith. It also shares with other descendants of the radical Reformation a strong commitment to liberty of conscience, separation of Church and State, and freedom of dissent, while avoiding the tendency towards withdrawal that characterizes many such groups. By maintaining a posture of critical engagement with modern culture, Unitarians remain responsive to current social circumstances and open to learning from the sciences and other areas of human knowledge. The most influential twentieth-century Unitarian theologian was J. L. Adams (1901–94), who made major contributions to the theology of liberal social ethics, the theory of voluntary associations, and the doctrine of the free Church.

Unitarianism today is marked by an enormous diversity of theological positions, ranging from Christian theism to non-theistic religious humanism, and in much of the world it is best understood as post-Christian (see POST-CHRISTIAN THEOLOGY). Nevertheless, the following theological principles are widely shared among Unitarians:

- *The fundamental unity and interdependence of all existence.* Reality is continuously recreated in a dynamic, open-ended evolutionary process.

- *Fundamental human freedom grounded in the inherent worth and dignity of all persons.* Within the constraints of biological, historical, and cultural circumstance, human beings are free moral agents who make choices for which they are accountable. This freedom is expressed in our human striving for a meaningful and fulfilling life and for liberation from all forms of oppression.
- *Principled theological openness.* Religious truth is not given just once for all time; no belief system or historical moment has any unique status. Religious meaning is constructed rather than given and may come through many sources.
- *Commitment to social justice.* Just communities reflect equal concern for all, respect for basic human rights and liberties, non-coercive institutions, consensual relationships, shared power, and inclusiveness. Human beings have a religious obligation to create institutions and social structures that reflect these values and enable all persons to live with dignity and respect.
- *The Church as a free covenanted fellowship.* The free Church emphasizes local autonomy in Church governance, non-hierarchical forms of ecclesial organization, and shared authority in decision-making; it does not require uniformity in belief.

P. Rasor, *Faith Without Certainty: Liberal Theology in the 21st Century* (Skinner House, 2005).
D. Robinson, *The Unitarians and the Universalists* (Greenwood Press, 1985).

PAUL RASOR

UNIVERSALISM Universalism in its classical sense means universal restoration (Greek *apokatastasis pantōn*). A universalist movement began in America in the eighteenth century that is often associated with UNITARIANISM. The movement propagated universal salvation, and its members consisted of Anglicans, New England Congregationalists, and various German immigrant groups, particularly those of Baptist, pietistic, and mystical persuasions (Dunkers, Schwenkfelders, etc.).

Consciousness of religious pluralism has produced a modern variety of universalism. According to J. Hick (b. 1922) there are many paths to God, since all religions are culturally conditioned responses to the ultimate mystery. Another view associated with P. Knitter (b. 1939) regards Christ as neither universally normative nor final and even suggests a plurality of ultimate ends. A more conservative stance defended by W. Visser't Hooft (1900–85), among others, upholds a universal salvation centred exclusively in Jesus Christ.

The origin of universalism is obscure. The classical term *apokatastasis* in its non-Christian usage means restitution of an earlier stage, such as restoration of health or return of the stars (planets) to their original positions. In GNOSTICISM and Neoplatonism (see PLATONISM) it expresses the return of the SOUL from its material captivity to the realm of light. Parseeism professes a dualism between good and evil, but all people have the chance of eventual purification. The evil god Ahriman and his demons will be destroyed, hell itself will be purified, and salvation will be bestowed on all.

Plato (*ca* 430–*ca* 345 BC) surmised that through cycles of reincarnation the soul will eventually be united with the divine. Those theologians most heavily influenced by Neoplatonic thought, therefore, concluded universal salvific significance from Christ's descent to the dead. Clement of Alexandria (*ca* 150–*ca* 215) declared: 'Out of all human beings who have been invited, the term "called" is applied only to those who have shown their willingness to respond' (*Strom.* 1.18). ORIGEN reasoned that 'to this beginning [of all creation] the end and consummation of all things must be recalled' (*Prin.* 3.6.7). This return to the beginning will be immaterial, since bodies are implicitly associated with corruption. Not even the DEVIL will be excluded from final spiritual unity with God. The Synod of Constantinople (543) condemned Origen's ideas, on the grounds that they extend future restitution to impious people and demons. Origen's condemnation was summarily repeated at the Fifth Ecumenical Council at Constantinople (553). Nevertheless, many minds in the early Church were inclined to universalism. Gregory of Nyssa (see CAPPADOCIAN FATHERS) claimed that punishment for the individual is restricted to the way one lived one's life. 'Those who have parted with evil will be united with [God]; and so, as the Apostle says, God will "be in all"' (*Soul*). While asserting that Christ 'will be all in all' (cf. Eph. 1:23 and Col. 3:11), Gregory advocated a cyclic understanding, a return to prelapsarian perfection. Unlike Origen, Gregory claimed that evil will be completely annihilated.

The NT mentions 'universal restoration' (*apokatastasis*) in Acts 3:21 only. It is unclear whether Luke refers here to the fulfilment of God's word through the prophets or cosmic restoration. Ephesians 1:10 employs the expression 'gather up all things'. The actual Greek is *anakephalaiōsis pantōn*, 'RECAPITULATION of everything', a phrase later used by IRENAEUS in his SOTERIOLOGY. Through the INCARNATION Christ 'recapitulated in himself the long line of human beings, and furnished us, in a brief, comprehensive manner, with salvation; so that what we had lost in Adam ... we might recover in Jesus Christ' (*AH* 3.18.1). Similarly in Ephesians 1:10 the apostle emphasizes that the Son restores cosmic harmony, bringing the fragmented, alienated elements of the universe together. Again, universalism is not clearly enunciated. The argument that the epistles, being earlier than the Gospels, allow for universalism, while the latter emphasize a twofold outcome, must not be allowed to obscure the fact that Jesus himself apparently used twofold illustrations.

The *Catechism of the Catholic Church* teaches that though 'God predestines no one to go to hell' (§1,037), there is 'the existence of hell and its eternity' (§1,035). At the same time it declares, 'The Church prays that no one should be lost . . . if it is true that no one can save himself, it is also true that God "desires all men to be saved" (1 Tim. 2:4), and that for him "all things are possible" (Matt. 9:26)' (§1,058). F. SCHLEIERMACHER saw traces in Scripture of that view 'that through the power of redemption there will one day be a universal restoration of all souls' (*CF*, §163, appendix). P. TILLICH similarly argues that the condemnation of one person would impair the heavenly bliss of others. He opts for 'essentialization' as a creative synthesis of a being's essential nature with the relationships of its temporal existence. Such a notion does not imply actual personal existence as one's eternal goal. Tillich finds the term *apokatastasis* problematic; K. BARTH rejects it outright, but then he allows it in through the back door by means of the ultimate triumph of GRACE. For Barth, Christ alone is rejected in our place, and we are elected. Since every person is predestined towards grace, the only question that remains is how long one can resist this divine election. K. RAHNER also tends towards universalism: 'The existence of the possibility that freedom will end in eternal loss stands alongside the doctrine that the world and the history of the world as a whole will *in fact* enter into eternal life with God' (*Found.* 444). Does the fear of a twofold outcome serve simply as an ethical stimulus, while God's all-encompassing benevolence will ultimately prevail? The NT cannot be adduced to support this approach; at least in its Gospels, it is KERYGMA, a proclamation addressed to the listeners which necessitates a response, ostensibly with eternal consequences. Yet neither is the kerygma a theory about other people, and we should not make their final destiny a question of dogma. HOPE for others should remain a pastoral issue, an aspect of Christian concern and LOVE.

See also DESCENT INTO HELL; ESCHATOLOGY; HELL; PLURALISM, RELIGIOUS.

G. C. Berkouwer, *The Triumph of Grace in the Theology of Karl Barth* (Eerdmans, 1956).

M. T. Marshall, *No Salvation Outside the Church? A Critical Inquiry* (Mellen, 1993).

J. F. Sanders, *No Other Name: An Investigation into the Destiny of the Unevangelized* (Eerdmans, 1992).

HANS SCHWARZ

USURY Usury is a SIN connected to lending or the extension of credit. This topic is theologically illuminating in three ways. First, Church prohibitions on usury represent a determined effort to extend the moral implications of Christianity to economic life. Second, the DOCTRINE drew on a metaphorical use of nature. Third, in its evolution, brought about by changing circumstances and mature theological reflection, what was once intrinsically evil became a sin dependent on degree and situation.

In the OT usury in lending to a fellow Hebrew is condemned (Lev. 25:36–7; cf. Deut. 23:19), for a blameless person 'does not put out his money at usury' (Ps. 15:5, VULGATE). In the NT Jesus says, 'But love your enemies, do good, and lend, expecting nothing in return' (Luke 6:35). These few verses coalesced with a metaphor widespread in the ancient Mediterranean world: as formulated by Aristotle (384–322 BC), lending money gave birth to offspring, and 'reproduction' of this kind was illicit because against nature (*Pol.* 1.10, 1,258b; cf. *Eth.* 5, 1,122a).

Buttressed by these biblical and philosophical texts, the Church fathers taught that usury was sinful. Usually, they focused on the harm done the debtor, but the rigorist JEROME saw sin in taking anything beyond the principal lent. Yet Roman law under Christian emperors was not altered to reflect this patristic consensus.

Probably because usury is most keenly felt in agricultural communities, the patristic ban only entered secular law under Charlemagne (r. 800–14) by way of the legal collection known as the *Hadriana*. Systematic consideration in CANON LAW followed in Gratian (*fl.* twelfth century), who wrote, 'Behold, it is evident, whatever is demanded beyond the principal is usury' (*Decr.*, Causa 14). By 1234, the *Decretals* of Gregory IX (r. 1227–41) contained a series of papal pronouncements on usury: it was found in mortgages and in sales on credit; it consisted in intention alone; and it could not be permitted in order to raise money for a good cause. On the other hand, it was not present in partnership (*societas*) where the loss of capital was risked, nor in annuities (*census*) where a right to income was purchased; also, it could be justified as interest when the lender incurred loss by lending.

Lawyers drew delicate and disputed lines. Expansion of commerce in the sixteenth century changed the economic environment. Both Catholic and Protestant reformers (e.g., Cardinal Cajetan (1468–1534) and J. CALVIN) rethought the old analyses. By 1600, most lending at interest could be accommodated, but battles continued until 1830, when Pius VIII (r. 1829–30) advised confessors that those who lent at a profit should not be disturbed.

Today an echo of the old prohibition can be found in laws against excessive interest and in concern expressed that the rich nations lessen the debt burdens of developing countries (e.g., John Paul II, *Tertio millenio adveniente*, 1994). Throughout, the ideas of justice and charity remain the animating principles of theological reflection.

J. T. Noonan, *The Scholastic Analysis of Usury* (Harvard University Press, 1957).

A Church That Can and Cannot Change (University of Notre Dame Press, 2005).

JOHN T. NOONAN

V

Vatican Council I Called by Pope Pius IX (r. 1846–78) on 8 December 1869 by the bull *Aeterni patris*, Vatican I was the first Catholic council since Trent, and is counted by Catholics as the twentieth ecumenical council. It was the first attended by a significant number of bishops from outside Europe. Its agenda was initially broad, with extensive preparatory work producing fifty-one *schemas* (draft documents) for the council fathers to consider. However, the Franco-Prussian war of 1870 forced the proceedings to conclude – without officially closing – after only four sessions, the first of which was merely preparatory. In fact, only two schemas were considered, and, apart from the opening proclamation, only three documents produced.

In their deliberations, the council fathers tended to adhere to one of two perspectives. The majority were ultramontane, supporting the Roman Curia's assertion of the absolute authority of the pope and the Church's rejection of modernity in all its forms (see Ultramontanism). The minority, which included J. H. Newman and many German-speaking bishops, were more liberal. The first document, a profession of faith, stressed conformity and obedience to the Church's teachings as necessary for salvation. The third session produced the dogmatic constitution on the Catholic faith, *Dei filius*, promulgated on 24 April 1870 as a papal bull. Here the council set out their understanding of the relation between faith and reason in response to the Enlightenment's questioning of the possibility of knowledge of God and the rationality of faith. The document draws on the by then traditional Catholic distinction between two levels of reality, nature and supernature, each with its own order of knowledge. God's existence can be known with certainty by natural reason without faith. Faith is an additional gift beyond our natural abilities. It is entirely consistent with reason, and reason should be used to explore faith's full meaning. Yet, since faith is a supernatural knowledge given by revelation alone, it cannot be based upon reason, nor can one reason independently to its knowledge. In this way, the council denied both religious rationalism and fideism (the latter attributed to Protestantism). The document continued the conciliar tradition of listing relevant erroneous propositions and anathematizing all who held them (see Anathema).

The final document, *Pastor aeternus*, a dogmatic constitution on the Church of Christ, caused a major controversy with its definition of the doctrine of the infallibility of papal teaching when pronounced *ex cathedra*. The document builds towards this, beginning with a strong emphasis upon the bishop of Rome's plenitude of power, and asserting the full primacy of his authority and jurisdiction over the whole Church not only with regard to faith and morals, but in discipline and governance too. The document displays animus towards those who question the Church's teachings, and incorporates anathemas directly within the document at the end of each chapter. The emphasis upon the Roman Church as the sole institution ordained by God to preserve and teach the faith with authority, together with its focus upon the Church's hierarchical structure, led to a one-sided ecclesiology not corrected until Vatican Council II.

See also Catholic Theology; Papacy.

Nicholas M. Healy

Vatican Council II Vatican Council II, regarded by the Catholic Church as the twenty-first ecumenical council, took place in Rome from 1962 to 1965. Called by Pope John XXIII (r. 1958–63), it brought together over 2000 bishops from all parts of the world, and produced a wide-ranging corpus of documents of major importance for the renewal of the Church in its mission today. The drafting and re-drafting of texts was marked by strong collaboration between the bishops and a remarkable group of theologians (*periti*). Pope Paul VI (r. 1963–78) succeeded Pope John in 1963 and guided the Council through some tumultuous phases to its conclusion.

When it was suspended in 1870, Vatican Council I left much unfinished business. Most notably, while the primacy and infallibility of the pope had been defined, the complementary role and responsibility of the bishops had not. The early twentieth century saw the rise of various movements that were to bear fruit in Vatican II's reflection on this and other issues. Outstanding were the biblical, liturgical, patristic, and ecumenical movements, the first three of which promoted a 'return to the sources' (*ressourcement*) that became a hallmark of Vatican II's methodology and doctrine. The 'updating' (*aggiornamento*) desired by Pope John was largely achieved by *ressourcement*, by putting the Church into vital contact with the wellsprings of its life, primarily with Christ himself as encountered in Scripture, the liturgy, the wisdom of the fathers, but also in and through the world of today, which is why Pope John wanted to open windows to the world, not only to give but also to receive. He prayed that the Council would be 'a new Pentecost'.

In his opening address, *Gaudet Mater Ecclesia* (11 October 1962), Pope John proclaimed: 'Christ is ever resplendent as the centre of history and of life.' He mapped a path for renewal within continuity: 'The substance of the ancient doctrine of the deposit of faith is one thing, and the way in which it is presented is another'; it was the latter that needed fresh consideration from a 'pastoral' point of view. He spoke of 'the paramount dignity of the human person', and affirmed that the Catholic Church considered it her duty to work for Christian unity. The teaching of Vatican II duly developed along pastoral lines, though with significant dogmatic advances, and was strongly personalist and Christocentric (see PERSONALISM). The Council also marked the entry of the Catholic Church into the ecumenical movement.

Initially, seventy-two draft texts were prepared, without any overall coherence. In December 1962, Cardinal Suenens (1904–96) proposed grouping all of them under two headings: the Church *ad intra* and the Church *ad extra*. The idea was enthusiastically embraced, and an orderly scheme of texts began to take shape thereafter.

Of the sixteen documents finally produced, four are called 'constitutions' and are of prime importance: *Sacrosanctum concilium* (*SC*, 1963) on the liturgy, *Lumen gentium* (*LG*, 1964) on the Church, *Dei verbum* (*DV*, 1965) on REVELATION, and *Gaudium et spes* (*GS*, 1965) on the Church in the modern world. Other texts deal with the office of bishops, the ministry of priests, the religious life, the apostolate of the LAITY, and missionary activity; particularly notable are *Unitatis redintegratio* (*UR*, 1964) on ECUMENISM, *Dignitatis humanae* (*DH*, 1965) on religious freedom, and *Nostra aetate* (*NA*, 1964) on non-Christian religions. *SC* taught that liturgy is actually the prayer of Christ himself to his Father, in which the Church participates as his BODY. All the faithful should actively participate, and the Council gave norms for the 'renewal' of the liturgy to enable this. Far-reaching reform of rites, especially the MASS, and language, extending to almost universal use of the vernacular, has been the most visible, though not trouble-free, result of the Council in the lives of the faithful.

LG directed that the Church be understood primarily as mystery and sacrament, and famously described it as the pilgrim people of God in which all the baptized have varied gifts and responsibilities. It also taught that bishops have the fullness of the sacrament of ORDERS (being 'high priests', not just governors), and that the college of bishops succeeds to the college of the APOSTLES, and together with the pope, its head, has 'supreme and full authority over the universal Church' – the doctrine of episcopal COLLEGIALITY (§22). *DV* taught that Christ himself is the fullness of God's revelation, and greatly promoted the place and study of Scripture in the life of the Catholic Church. This has been another area of notable results in the post-conciliar period. *GS* strongly advocated solidarity between the Church and the world: the Church believes that it is 'led by the Spirit of the Lord who fills the whole world' (§11). Hence the faithful should be attentive to 'the signs of the times' (§4) and discern what may be of God in them. Its central thesis was that only Christ can answer the questions and fulfil the desires that arise in every human heart. In a phrase much quoted by Pope John Paul II (r. 1978–2005), Christ 'reveals man to himself' (§22).

The Council saw the ecumenical movement as one of the 'signs of the times' and in *UR* it gave clear principles for Catholic participation in it. Another of the signs was the desire for religious freedom, and the Council made this doctrine its own in *DH*. Believing that this contradicted previous teaching, Archbishop M. Lefebvre (1905–91) and his followers, who also opposed the liturgical reforms, eventually went into SCHISM. Wishing particularly to reach out to the Jews, the Council deplored anti-Semitism and said that the Catholic Church rejects nothing of what is 'true and holy' in other religions (*NA*, 2). Since Vatican II, dialogue, both ecumenical and inter-religious, has been a major feature of Catholic life.

See also CATHOLIC THEOLOGY.

G. Alberigo and J. Komonchak, eds., *History of Vatican II*, 5 vols. (Orbis, 1995–2006).

A. Flannery, ed., *Vatican Council II: The Conciliar and Post Conciliar Documents*, vol. 1 revised edn (Costello, 1996).

H. Vorgrimler, ed., *Commentary on the Documents of Vatican II*, 5 vols. (Burns & Oates, 1967–9).

PAUL MCPARTLAN

VENERATION: see DULIA.

VENIAL SIN SIN is a breach in one's relationship with God. It is an offence against God and against truth and reason in the created order. The human being sins by an act of will and in doing so turns away from God's LOVE. This distorts the image of God in humanity and results in alienation from neighbour and oneself. According to Catholic tradition there are different types of sin with regard to their gravity and their effects vis-à-vis the state of GRACE of the one who sins. They differ according to the matter of the sin, the knowledge of the sinner, and the nature of her consent. Traditionally, Catholic theology identifies two types of sin in this regard: mortal and venial.

Venial sins concern less serious matters than MORTAL SIN. They may entail matters as grave as in mortal sin, but without sufficient knowledge and with less than free and deliberate consent. Venial sins do not destroy a person's state of grace. However, they still cause harm and wound the person who sins. Specifically, although the theological virtues – FAITH, HOPE, and charity (see LOVE) – persist in the SOUL, they are hindered by venial sin. Charity especially is weakened, and the culmination of many venial sins without repentance can endanger the soul and lead to mortal sin. Although the person who commits venial sin is still in COVENANT with God and possesses sanctifying grace, moral progress is hindered, and such sins merit temporal punishment (i.e., the damage the sin causes in one's life and character).

RALPH DEL COLLE

Vestigia Trinitatis The use of ANALOGIES drawn from the created world has been a feature of Christian accounts of God since the second century. The idea of *vestigia Trinitatis* (Latin for 'traces of the Trinity') is based in the presumption that the CREATION must in some way bear the imprint of its creator, so that if God is triune, there are genuine analogues to the TRINITY to be found in the world. Often, however, the phrase is more loosely used simply to refer to any proposed images or models of the Trinity.

Early theologians often reached for analogies of flowing water (the source, the stream, and the lake) and of light (the sun, the ray, and the radiance) to speak of the relationships of the persons of the Trinity. Basil of Caesarea (see CAPPADOCIAN FATHERS) introduced an image of a rainbow (*Ep.* 38), and AUGUSTINE, with whom the search for *vestigia* is above all associated, suggests that it is particularly to the human being, made in the image of God, that one should look (*Trin.* 9–11). Parallels to the Trinity have been drawn to an enormous variety of threesomes, including the three dimensions; weight, measure, and number; the first, third, and fifth of a musical chord; epic, lyric, and dramatic poetry; and so on. In recent decades social models of the Trinity, according to which the Trinity is imagined as an ideal community, have been influential.

The history of theology suggests both that the appeal to analogues of the Trinity within creation is hard to escape, and that God's transcendence of all created reality makes it important to avoid attributing too great an importance to any one of them.

KAREN KILBY

***Via negativa*:** see APOPHATIC THEOLOGY.

Virgin Birth The DOCTRINE of the virgin birth affirms that Mary was a virgin when she conceived Jesus (who thus lacks a biological father). In CATHOLIC THEOLOGY it also entails the claim that Mary retained her VIRGINITY (viz., the integrity of her hymen) in the parturition of Jesus. The idea of the virginal conception is derived from the infancy narratives of Matthew (1:18–25; cf. Isa. 7:14) and Luke (1:30–7); the teaching that Mary's virginity was preserved after Jesus' birth is an element of TRADITION not directly addressed in SCRIPTURE.

Scepticism regarding biblical miracles in general and Jesus' divinity in particular has caused the doctrine of the virgin birth to become a point of deep theological cleavage since the ENLIGHTENMENT. Many theologians, noting the highly stylized character of the birth narratives in Matthew and Luke (as well as the difficulty of harmonizing the two accounts), have argued for a symbolic interpretation of the virgin birth. In reaction to this approach, subscription to the literal truth of the doctrine has become a defining tenet of Christian FUNDAMENTALISM.

In the face of these debates (which are closely tied to disputes over biblical INERRANCY), it is important to note that though Matthew clearly interprets the virgin birth as a sign of Jesus' messianic status (since it fulfils the prophecy of Isa. 7:14), the doctrine is not directly relevant to the claim that Jesus is divine. As Pope Benedict XVI has argued, because the INCARNATION is a matter of ontology rather than biology, it does not depend on whether or not Jesus had a human father (*Intro.* 208). At the same time, this conclusion does not render the question of the virgin birth theologically irrelevant. As S. Truth (*ca* 1797–1883) noted in her address 'Ar'n't I a Woman?' (1851), the doctrine teaches that Christ came 'From God and a woman. Man had nothing to do with Him.' In a religious tradition strongly marked by ANDROCENTRISM, this claim that the incarnation completely bypassed male power and agency arguably gives the doctrine peculiar significance.

See also MARIOLOGY.

IAN A. MCFARLAND

Virginity In specifically theological as in colloquial discourse, virginity refers to the state of a person who has never engaged in sexual intercourse. As such, it is to be distinguished from CELIBACY, which refers to deliberate abstinence from intercourse by someone who may or may not have had intercourse previously. Virginity's significance for Christian faith remains a matter of contention across different confessional traditions. Though the OT places a strong emphasis on the virginity of women before marriage (Deut. 22:13–19), the permanent state of virginity had no positive significance in Judaism. On the contrary, God's command that humans should 'be fruitful and multiply' (Gen. 1:28), combined with the promise of innumerable progeny to ABRAHAM (Gen. 13:16; 15:5), led to a uniformly positive assessment of sex within the context of patriarchal marriage (see, e.g., Pss. 127:3–5; 128:3–4; Prov. 5:18–19; Eccl. 9:9). Nevertheless, in Christianity virginity came to be viewed favourably by virtue of its association with three chief characters in the NT: Mary, PAUL, and Jesus himself.

That Mary was a virgin when she conceived Jesus is explicitly affirmed in Matthew 1:18–23 and Luke 1:26–35, and according to TRADITION she retained her virginity throughout her life (see MARIOLOGY; VIRGIN BIRTH). In later theology her virginity was frequently interpreted as a necessary condition of Jesus' being born without original SIN and, especially in Catholic and Orthodox thought, was often closely correlated with affirmation of her own sinlessness. Though the NT nowhere calls either Jesus or Paul virgins, both have been regarded as such, since neither was married, and Judaism did not endorse sexual intercourse outside of marriage. Jesus commends virginity in relatively obscure terms: in response to his disciples' observation that it is better not to marry if divorce is forbidden, he notes that 'not everyone can accept this teaching, but only those to whom it is given', namely, those 'who have made themselves eunuchs for the kingdom of heaven' (Matt. 19:10–12). Paul is much more explicit in advocating perpetual virginity on the grounds that the married person's concern for his or her spouse distracts from single-minded service to Christ (1 Cor. 7:32–5). Together, Paul and Jesus' references to the significance of renunciation of marriage for the sake of the KINGDOM OF GOD remain central to contemporary Catholic teaching on virginity (*Cat.*, §922, 1,618–19). More controversially, Paul's judgement that 'he who marries his fiancée does well; and he who refrains from marriage will do better' (1 Cor. 7:38) was foundational for JEROME's contention that virginity is superior to marriage (*Jov.* 7).

The claim that virginity constitutes a mark of superior virtue was sharply contested by Protestants from the period of the REFORMATION onwards. While fully endorsing traditional beliefs regarding virginity prior to marriage and acknowledging perpetual virginity as a legitimate (though rare) calling, the Reformers viewed consigning large numbers of boys and girls to lives of virginity through monastic OBLATION as contrary to God's intention for the majority of human beings and correspondingly unnatural. Protestant suspicion of perpetual virginity, in turn, has come in for criticism as insufficiently sensitive to the way in which marriage can be an instrument of social control that limits the kind of freedom for the gospel that Paul was anxious to preserve.

IAN A. MCFARLAND

VIRTUE The last few decades have witnessed a lively renaissance of VIRTUE ETHICS, first in philosophical quarters, with subsequent attempts to (re)adopt it in Christian moral theology and various practical fields of ethics. The theological adoption has not been uncontroversial, and the discussion has largely moved between poles that can be seen as represented by two figures of the theological tradition: calls for a Christian adoption of classical virtue theory (predominantely, though not exclusively, by Catholic authors) have typically sought some grounding in the theology of T. AQUINAS (see *ST* 1/2.49–89); and a Christian (often Protestant) critique of such attempts has articulated itself along the lines of AUGUSTINE's attack on the virtues (*City* 5; 19) and its heirs in the REFORMATION era.

As a closer reading of the two perspectives reveals, they do not constitute polar opposites: Aquinas' interest in the Aristotelian concept of virtue entails no less its modification than its adoption (see ARISTOTELIANISM), and Augustine's criticism of existing virtues in the societies of the Roman Empire does not appear to rule out genuine virtue.

In any case, several features of the concept of virtue would seem attractive to a theological framework. First, it focuses on the 'goodness' of the moral agent as a whole person – as opposed to the 'rightness' or 'wrongness' of individual acts or principles behind these acts. This focus, which includes directing attention to the emotional aspects of character formation, seems congenial with Jesus' emphasis in the SERMON ON THE MOUNT on inward disposition of the act (Matt. 5:22, 28), as well as the idea in the OT that God 'looks on the heart' (1 Sam. 16:7). Second (and connected with this) the language of virtue connotes an emphasis on the permanence of disposition (Greek *hexis* or Latin *HABITUS*) to act in a certain way. A virtuous person is not someone who does individual virtuous acts as by chance (actualism), but who can be reliably expected to act in such a way. This emphasis on disposition resonates with Jesus' summons to be willing to forgive 'seventy times seven' times (Matt. 18:22).

A further advantage of the concept of virtue appears to be its pluriformity. There are always a number of virtues needed to circumscribe virtuous life, which counterbalance any one-sidedness found in monolinear concepts that claim to sufficiently describe the moral life by reference to just one major concept, as, for example, in J. Fletcher's (1905–91) 'agapeism'. Connected with this is a further practical advantage: the adaptability of virtue theories to the landscape of a growing number of specific 'genitive' ethics: virtue in general and individual virtues in particular seem comfortably applicable to old and new strands of moral discourse such as sexual ethics, business ethics, and bioethics.

The overarching point of attraction of virtue for Christian moral reasoning would seem to be in that it helps to make plausible and describable the DOCTRINE OF SANCTIFICATION – a doctrine which many think has paled down, in Protestant traditions in particular, to a mere afterthought to the doctrine of JUSTIFICATION. There are, however, several difficulties and obstacles which are associated with the adoptability of virtue theory to a theological framework. First among these is the acquisition of virtue through virtue. The so-called 'Meno problem' (named after the eponymous Platonic dialogue) describes the practical circularity by which becoming virtuous already presupposes a degree of virtuousness, for instance when it comes to recognizing which moral exemplars are worth emulating. Aristotle's solution to this problem in pointing to social convention – the standards of virtue embedded in the social consciousness of the polity – appears to be adjustable for theology: a Christian adoption of virtue ethics need not be embarrassed by acknowledging the particularity of its tradition and the conventionality of its standards as defined by the Church as a sort of polis. While a Christian framework can readily accept the givenness of the 'cloud of witnesses' (Heb. 12:1) or canon of SAINTS as moral exemplars, a more difficult issue arises with regard to accommodating the role of

Christ as more than a role model in virtue. As the Protestant Reformers in the sixteenth century in particular emphasized, before there can be an active 'imitation of Christ', there must be a passive justification through Christ. This insight was captured in M. LUTHER's formula of Christ as *sacramentum* before and over his role of *exemplum*.

Second, the model according to which virtue is actively acquired through performing virtuous acts has provoked theological caution with regard to its possible proximity to PELAGIANISM. High medieval accounts of *caritas* or LOVE as mother of all virtue provoked theological criticism by the Reformers, to the degree that these accounts emphasized the so-called 'initial love of God' as a natural human potential, the actualization of which, in turn, triggered the response of divine infusion of the supernatural virtues in the justificatory process. But even with a less ambiguous locating of virtue and its grounding in the order of sanctification as opposed to justification, the problem of the active versus passive/perceptive character remains virulent. The Christian equivalent to the classical virtue of courage (Greek *parrhêsia*, 'to speak with frankness and boldly'), for example, is portrayed in the NT not as engendered by a continuous practising of courageous acts, but as brought about through the HOLY SPIRIT (Acts 4:31).

A further difficulty that theological adoption of virtue faces is how to reinterpret the pluriformity of the concept: which individual specimens are to be counted in a list of Christian virtues? Is there a hierarchy of virtues, a singular 'mother virtue', and a unity of all virtues? It seems obvious that a specifically Christian adoption of virtue would eventually end up producing a different and distinctive list: among Christians mercy, for example, came to effectively replace the classical virtues of nobility and magnanimity, on the grounds that the condescending tendencies of the latter were unacceptable in a Christian context. A Christian theological framework would also work towards a redefining of uncontested virtues: courage, for example, would presumably no longer be understood according to the ideal of the brave soldier and his triumphant death on the battlefield, but according to the perseverance given to the martyrs; and for the case of the cardinal virtue of justice, acknowledging the FALL and the prerogative of God's judgement would eventually lead to a privileging of corrective justice over its distributive and commutative variants.

S. Hauerwas and C. Pinches, *Christians Among the Virtues: Theological Conversations with Ancient and Modern Ethics* (University of Notre Dame Press, 1997).

J. A. Herdt, *Putting on Virtue: The Legacy of the Splendid Vices* (University of Chicago Press, 2008).

A. MacIntyre, *After Virtue: A Study in Moral Theory*, 3rd edn (University of Notre Dame Press, 2007).

J. Pieper, *The Four Cardinal Virtues: Prudence, Justice, Fortitude, Temperance* (University of Notre Dame Press, 1990 [1954–9]).

J. Porter, *The Recovery of Virtue* (John Knox Press, 1990).

BERND WANNENWETSCH

VIRTUE ETHICS Virtue ethics is a mode of moral reasoning based in the cultivation of particular VIRTUES, understood as multivalent dispositions rather than as rigidly defined duties. Although its earliest expression is found in Aristotle's *Nicomachean Ethics*, it emerged in contemporary Christian theology as a reaction to I. KANT's deontological ethics. In *Groundwork to Metaphysics of Morals* (1785), Kant appropriated the western metaphysical tradition to produce a moral framework that relied on a notion of transcendence characteristic of Christianity without requiring adherence to orthodox Christian DOCTRINE. Configuring this framework as a 'tribunal of reason', Kant sought to establish the grounds of morality that might manage society without appealing to the moral doctrines of a particular religious tradition like Christianity. Through what he called the 'categorical imperative', Kant formulated a calculus that allowed the individual to negotiate various moral quandaries unencumbered by any prior moral obligations, religious or otherwise. Rather than locating ethical reasoning within communities of moral discourse, Kant utilized reason's ability to take account of a universal perspective (that is, a perspective above all other perspectives) to make appeal to objective duty the key to achieving moral consensus in a world of ineluctable moral diversity.

In the latter half of the twentieth century, theological ethicists began to rethink Kant's approach. At issue was Kant's stipulation that tradition plays no role in moral reasoning: that one 'think for oneself' and leave behind 'self-incurred tutelage'. Virtue ethicists found problematic this methodology (which they found counter-intuitive) and sought to restate tradition as a mode of moral discourse that relied on the very moral commitments Kant sought to displace. Hence, Christian virtue ethics advances T. AQUINAS' appropriation of an Aristotelian account of the virtues. Specifically, virtue ethics emphasizes the development of virtue through habituation of character. Communally derived moral intuitions mature as individuals regularly participate in constitutive practices. Morality ensues as a second nature rather than deliberate decision-making. In contrast to Kantian ethics, virtue ethics locates moral agency within a particular ordering of goods oriented towards an ultimate end (or *telos*) and relates the moral life to what Aristotle called *eudemonia*, or happiness. In this way, virtue ethics accords with ancient teleological ethics but should be distinguished from modern teleological ethics such as utilitarianism.

According to virtue ethics, within each community stands a table of virtues, and communal life can be largely understood as the processes by which one attains, enacts, and perfects those virtues. Though communities may vary in their understanding of the virtues, they are consistent in their reliance on shared life, practices, stories, texts, languages, descriptions, ordering of desires, and so on as necessary habituation to the life of virtue.

As examples, in Catholic moral theology the magisterial tradition emphasizes CASUISTRY and liturgical formation, while J. H. Yoder (1927–97), in the Anabaptist tradition, relies on 'body politics' as conditions necessary for moral excellence. Strongly influenced by Yoder, S. Hauerwas (b. 1940) has helped to bring the principles of virtue ethics into popular consciousness. The contention of virtue ethics is not that Kantian ethics relies on moral reasoning in a way that virtue ethics relies on TRADITION; rather, virtue ethicists argue that tradition is its own unique – and indispensible – mode of moral reasoning. In recent years, virtue ethics has been coupled with developments in the philosophy of language, particularly by L. Wittgenstein (1889–1951) and J. L. Austin (1911–60), as well as by thinkers like G. E. M. Anscombe (1919–2001) and P. Foot (b. 1920), for whom moral formation speaks of linguistic habits whereby individuals learn to speak about and see the world.

S. Hauerwas, *Character and the Christian Life: A Study in Theological Ethics* (University of Notre Dame Press, 1989).

J. J. Kotva, *The Christian Case for Virtue Ethics* (Georgetown University Press, 1996).

JONATHAN TRAN

VISION OF GOD: see BEATIFIC VISION.

VOCATION The theological concept of vocation (from the Latin *vocatio*, meaning 'invitation' or 'summons') derives from an idea central to the biblical narrative: the 'call' of God. In SCRIPTURE the divine call is a surprisingly wide-ranging idea, denoting an act of God in which people are drawn into relationship with God, either as objects of salvation, or as the means by which the saving purpose of God is furthered. As an abstract noun, 'vocation' can thus be taken in the biblical witness to refer to a complex of ideas, from the election of the COVENANT people (Isa. 41:8–9), to the address of the Lord to a prophet (1 Sam. 3:4–10), to the mission of Jesus (Mark 2:17), the summoning of the APOSTLES (Mark 1:20; 1 Cor. 1:1), the call to FAITH and obedience through the apostolic preaching (1 Cor. 1:2, 24), the inclusion of the Gentiles in the covenant people (Rom. 8:24–5), and even the heavenly, eschatological hope of the Church (1 Pet. 5:10).

A narrowing to a more limited semantic range is characteristic of the theology of vocation in the subsequent theological tradition. The patristic and medieval periods, which treated the Church and its sacraments as the appointed channels of GRACE, deemed those who served at the altar to be 'called' by way of an extension of the biblical usage, while the rise and rapid development of the monastic movement from the fourth century likewise transformed Christian understanding of vocation generally. In early Christianity, the ideal Christian life was frequently construed as that of the martyr, who imitated Christ in his passion by way of literal suffering or death. The metaphorical ('white') MARTYRDOM of the monk developed initially in a world in which this 'red' martyrdom had been made redundant, and modelled for the patristic and medieval periods a spiritual ideal attainable only by way of withdrawal from ordinary society. In the second and third centuries, a milkmaid or a cobbler might well have become a martyr; by the fourth century, however, the ideal of total self-giving was effectively no longer accessible to such Christians. Moreover, both classical civilization and the medieval world that was its heir privileged the contemplative life over the practical. Even the manual work required by the rules of the monastic orders was carried out as a discipline in the service of contemplation, rather than as an end in itself. Those engaged in labour for its own sake not only belonged to a separate order of society, but were understood to experience a separate and inferior spiritual life within the Church, while those summoned out of it to a life of Christian perfection were deemed to have a vocation.

There can be no doubt that a fundamental shift in the Christian understanding of calling is effected at the REFORMATION. The point at issue, however, can readily be misunderstood. Modern attitudes to the shift are largely shaped by the seminal study of M. Weber (1864–1920), who in *The Protestant Ethic and the Spirit of Capitalism* (1904–5) maintained that the rise of capitalism turned upon the Protestant and especially Reformed interpretation of calling, according to which worldly life was vested with full religious significance. M. LUTHER had argued in *To the Christian Nobility of the German Nation* (1520) that there is no true distinction between the 'spiritual' and 'secular' estates, and that the division drawn between the two amounted merely to the sinful, self-privileging claim of the clerical class. The core of Luther's theological riposte is that the distinction is alien to the very substance of GOSPEL, in which there is only a single status of Christians before God: that of being 'in Christ' by virtue of baptism and faith. REFORMED THEOLOGY, though developing along a separate theological trajectory, generally assumed these Lutheran insights, but added to them, in Weber's estimation, a distinctive and problematic emphasis on double PREDESTINATION, entailing that another distinction came to the fore: that between the elect and the reprobate. Weber's claim is that for the Reformed the proof of ELECTION was seen in one's bearing the fruit of faith in a worldly ASCETICISM. Combined with a rigorist ethic, Reformed Christianity thus constituted fertile soil for the development of a culture in which hard work, thrift, and economic success became measures of spiritual standing.

Against Weber, it should be noted that Luther, for instance, never equates calling flatly with occupation; his point, rather, is that the calling to love God and neighbour can be pursued in (or, indeed, despite) any social role. For their part, Reformed theologians throughout the modern period have known that a 'calling' is 'the work of God's Spirit, whereby, convincing us of our SIN and misery, enlightening our minds in the knowledge of Christ, and renewing our wills, he doth persuade and enable us to embrace Jesus Christ' (WSC 31). They knew, moreover, that there is scant support in Scripture (with the unlikely exception of 1 Cor. 7:17–24) for an understanding of calling that is not of a piece with the 'heavenly call' of God to faith and service (Phil. 3:13–14). Weber's thesis, by contrast, was attuned to an age in which the demand of reason was that RELIGION be constrained within the limits of this-worldly moralism.

More recent, and notable, trends in the theology of vocation include K. BARTH's massive Christological development of the theme in *Church Dogmatics* IV/3, in which the Christian is called by God to bear witness to the saving act of God in Christ, but in which also this witness is itself part of the reconciling work of Christ – and thus strictly not our doing. Barth's theology, though largely neglected at this point, makes an important point by seeking to return to the core of the gospel as the proper framework for a theology of Christian calling. Its best-known application has been in the *Missio Dei* movement in MISSIOLOGY and ECCLESIOLOGY, but its claim reaches well beyond this limited area to questions of CHRISTOLOGY, SOTERIOLOGY, and pneumatology.

A starkly different strand of thought can be identified in much contemporary liberal PROTESTANTISM, where vocation is shorthand for the realization of individual religious sensibility, typically as channelled into the occupational choice of lay or ordained ministry. What can be observed here again is a narrowing of focus, a forgetfulness of the broad salvation-historical outlook within which the concept of calling is located in the Bible, and, very often, a jarring tendency to speak of vocation primarily in the context of clerical selection and training. By contrast, the calling of the whole people of God to faith fundamentally, and so also to service, is profoundly present in the ecclesiological teaching of VATICAN COUNCIL II, which at this point represents a healthier theological alternative.

G. D. Badcock, *The Way of Life* (Eerdmans, 1998).

L. Hardy, *The Fabric of this World* (Eerdmans, 1990).

D. J. Schuurman, *Vocation: Discerning Our Callings in Life* (Eerdmans, 2004).

M. Volf, *Work in the Spirit* (Oxford University Press, 1991).

GARY D. BADCOCK

VOLUNTARISM 'Voluntarism' is a name given to a number of views that emphasize the priority or nobility of the will (*voluntas*) over the intellect in various contexts, but especially in the genesis of human action and in God's creative, legislative, and redemptive work.

A voluntarist with respect to human action holds that it is the will, rather than the intellect, that is the ultimate explanation for human choices. An intellectualist, by contrast, holds that the character of human acts is ultimately to be explained by the intellect's judgement concerning what is to be done. Accordingly, an intellectualist will insist that all wrongdoing is traceable to some intellectual mistake or misjudgement, whereas a voluntarist allows that one can will to sin even if one's intellectual judgement about what ought to be done is perfectly correct. In this way the voluntarist ascribes to the will a certain independence from the intellect and its judgements and regards human freedom and responsibility as rooted in the will, rather than in the human capacity for rational deliberation. This strand of voluntarism is discernible at least as far back as AUGUSTINE and is given clear expression in ANSELM's dialogues *De libertate arbitrii* and *De casu diaboli* (*ca* 1080–6), but it is most closely associated with Franciscan theologians such as J. DUNS SCOTUS, who wrote after the bishop of Paris had stigmatized various intellectualist doctrines in the Condemnation of 1277 on the grounds that they implied an objectionable form of determinism.

Voluntarism with respect to divine action emphasizes the supreme and unlimited sovereignty of the divine will in creating, establishing the moral law, and effecting human redemption. A voluntarist with respect to the moral law, for example, will argue that there are no limits, other than purely logical ones such as the law of non-contradiction, on God's power to establish whatever moral law God pleases. In this vein Scotus argued that it is entirely within God's power either to prohibit or not to prohibit murder or lying (*Ord.* 3.37), and William of Ockham (*ca* 1287–1347) went so far as to claim that God could command hatred of God, in which case hatred of God would be morally obligatory (*Rep.* 2.15 and 4.16; though the interpretation of these passages is the object of considerable controversy). Similarly, voluntarism with respect to human redemption emphasizes that God's decrees concerning who will be saved are entirely a matter of God's will and do not rest on any judgement on God's part that particular people ought to be saved (on account of foreseen merits, for example). To look for reasons that account for or justify God's decrees is, by the voluntarist's lights, simply to deny the sovereignty of the divine will.

B. Kent, *Virtues of the Will: The Transformation of Ethics in the Late Thirteenth Century* (Catholic University of America Press, 1995).

T. V. Morris, ed., *Divine and Human Action: Essays in the Metaphysics of Theism* (Cornell University Press, 1988).

THOMAS WILLIAMS

VOWS: see MONASTICISM.

VULGATE The Vulgate (from the Latin *versio vulgata*, or 'disseminated version') is the Latin translation of the Bible undertaken by JEROME in the late fourth century to improve the earlier Old Latin version. While Jerome initially focused on the Gospels and the Greek text of the Psalms, he eventually decided to translate the whole of the OT from the original Hebrew (though his translation of the Hebrew Psalter was unable to displace his earlier translation of the Greek). The gradual corruption of the text during the medieval period led to the publication in 1592 of the critically revised Clementine Vulgate, which remained the official version of the Catholic Church until 1979, when it was replaced by a further revision, the *Nova Vulgata*.

Though the Catholic Church has never disparaged critical study of Hebrew and Greek, the Council of TRENT (*Lib.*) decreed that the Vulgate, its authority vindicated 'by the lengthened usage of so many years', was to be 'held as authentic' for both liturgical and theological use. In other words, in so far as the Vulgate had served the Church faithfully as sacred SCRIPTURE, it could not be regarded as fundamentally in error. It is certainly the most influential translation of the Bible in the western Church. Not only did all medieval European theologians depend on it, but even M. LUTHER and J. CALVIN – though rejecting Catholic insistence on its authority – were educated in the Vulgate and freely cited it in their writings. Its influence on the translators of the English King James Version was also considerable.

IAN A. MCFARLAND

WAR: see JUST WAR.

WEIL, SIMONE Simone Weil (1909–43), born into a free-thinking Jewish family in Paris, was one of the first women graduates of the École Normale Supérieure. Throughout her life she was attentive to society's marginalized. Her writing addressed a variety of topics, including Greek philosophy, K. Marx (1818–83), Christianity, the Bhagavad Gita, literature, science, mathematics, politics, and ethics. Like Marx, she sought to reconnect theory and praxis by developing a philosophy of work. This commitment shows in her activities: teaching, working for a year in a factory, supporting French labour organizations and the unemployed, attempting to fight in the Spanish Civil War and working with the French Resistance in London, where she died in 1943.

Locating herself on the border of all things Christian and non-Christian, Weil simultaneously criticized and embraced the religion. Her critique was levelled at institutionalized Christianity, the church, and its collusion with any form of *empire* (whether fourth-century Rome or twentieth-century France), that produced a theology that excluded any *others* – whether religions, beliefs, cultures, or ideas. Weil embraced a unique version of Christianity, emphasizing inclusion, contemplation, renunciation, and truth. She saw Christ as revelatory, but not unique: INCARNATION occurs before and after Jesus, from the beginning of CREATION when 'the Word was with God' (John 1:1). The import of Christ is his decreative, or renunciatory, stance. He gives up his life in order to (1) attend to the least among us, (2) criticize institutional power, and (3) reveal the supernatural use of suffering. Thus, the CROSS AND CRUCIFIXION are more important than RESURRECTION.

S. Weil, *Waiting for God* (Perennial classics, 2001).

INESE RADZINS

WESLEY, JOHN John Wesley (1703–91), founder with his brother Charles (1707–88) of the Methodist movement, was born in an Anglican rectory in Epworth, England. Both of his grandfathers were Puritan ministers who lost their clerical positions in the Church of England after the Restoration of the monarchy in 1660 (see PURITANISM). Both his parents were nurtured in nonconformist households. Although they both conformed to the Church of England before their marriage and raised their children as devout Anglicans, they never lost the strain of Puritan moral rigorism and spiritual seriousness that they had imbibed from their parents.

Wesley earned his BA from Christ Church, Oxford, in 1724 and soon after experienced what is sometimes referred to as his 'Oxford Conversion' – a lasting resolution to be more devout and more disciplined in daily life. He was ordained a deacon of the Church of England in 1725, and only a few months later, in 1726, was elected fellow of Lincoln College, Oxford. The same year his younger brother Charles entered Christ Church, and in 1727 John completed his MA and was ordained a priest. Within a short time the Wesley brothers became the nucleus of a group of students that gradually transformed itself into a religious society as the members began replicating what they understood to have been the practices of 'primitive Christianity', earning the group disparaging names such as 'the Holy Club' and 'the Methodists'.

In 1735, both John and Charles (who was ordained for the purpose) accepted appointment as missionaries in the newly established American colony of Georgia. The most important result of what proved to be in general a disastrous experience was their exposure to continental PIETISM, especially through their acquaintance with the Moravians. Soon after returning to London in early 1738, John had a profound religious experience during a Moravian society meeting in Aldersgate Street when he felt his heart 'strangely warmed'. Although he soon came to have increasingly serious doubts about the 'QUIETISM' and 'ANTINOMIANISM' of the English Moravians and broke his connection with them in 1740, the influence of Pietism on his life and theology is unmistakable.

In 1739, at the urging of G. Whitefield (1714–70), Wesley became involved in an evangelistic religious revival around Bristol, then enlisted brother Charles. Their preaching ministry led to the emergence of religious societies, first in Bristol, then in London. This marked the beginning of the Methodist movement, which Wesley would lead for the next fifty-three years, though his personal life suffered as a consequence. In 1751 he married M. Vazeille (1710–81), a sailor's widow, but the marriage was a failure; she grew resentful of his ceaseless travels and jealous of his extensive correspondence with female Methodists, and they soon separated.

Methodism, which Wesley always insisted was a reform movement within the Church of England, spread to America in the 1760s. The American Revolution brought on a sacramental crisis for American Methodists because of the effective disappearance of the Church of England. After failing to secure ordination of some of his lay preachers for service in America from Anglican bishops in England, Wesley took matters into his own hands. Asserting that presbyters (i.e., priests like himself) had the same power to ordain as bishops, Wesley ordained two of his

W

preachers as deacons and then as elders, and then 'set apart' T. Coke (1747–1814) to be 'general superintendent' of Methodists in America along with F. Asbury (1745–1816). Coke was instructed to inform Asbury and the American preachers of these decisions, to ordain Asbury, and to form the American Methodists into a new Church. For this purpose Wesley edited the Book of Common Prayer to create the Sunday Service of the Methodists in America, and abridged the Anglican Articles of Religion from thirty-nine down to twenty-four.

The ordinations of 1784 created a lasting strain in the relationship between John and Charles: Charles insisted that his brother's actions meant the separation of the Methodists from the Church of England, but John refused to acknowledge this. When Charles died in 1788 he was buried in the graveyard of his parish church in London, but when John died three years later, at the age of eighty-seven, he was buried in the cemetery behind the Methodist City Road Chapel. His final words encapsulated his life and work: 'The best of all is, God is with us.'

See also Methodist Theology.

R. P. Heitzenrater, *John Wesley and the People Called Methodists* (Abingdon Press, 1991).

H. D. Rack, *Reasonable Enthusiast: John Wesley and the Rise of Methodism*, 3rd edn (Epworth, 2002).

Rex D. Matthews

Wesleyan Quadrilateral The so-called Wesleyan quadrilateral refers to the inter-relation of a fourfold set of sources and norms for Christian doctrine that is associated specifically with Methodist theology. As most commonly expressed, the quadrilateral states that the 'living core' of Christian faith is 'revealed in Scripture, illumined by tradition, vivified in personal experience, and confirmed by reason' (*BOD* 2008, 104). Another version describes Christian teaching and preaching as properly 'grounded in Scripture, informed by Christian tradition, enlivened in experience, and tested by reason' (*BOD* 2008, 101). These formulations, while not found verbatim in the writings of J. Wesley, are characterized by proponents as authentically Wesleyan because they point to a dynamic fourfold pattern of authority in Wesley's theological method. In that sense, they represent Wesley's addition of personal religious experience to the classical Anglican triad of Scripture, tradition, and reason (see Anglican Theology).

The quadrilateral first appeared in print when the report of a Theological Study Commission chaired by A. Outler (1908–89) was adopted by the 1972 General Conference of the United Methodist Church for inclusion in the *Book of Discipline*. The term 'quadrilateral' does not occur in the *Discipline* – it was borrowed from the Chicago–Lambeth Quadrilateral of 1888 and applied to the United Methodist formulation by Outler elsewhere – but it stuck, and soon became ubiquitous. Some critics of the quadrilateral assert that it is frequently misunderstood as an *equilateral* and so compromises the theological primacy of Scripture. Others claim that it confuses *objective* elements (Scripture and tradition) with *subjective* elements (experience and reason) and fails properly to distinguish between *sources* and *norms* for theology. Nonetheless, the quadrilateral, though variously interpreted, has been widely embraced among United Methodists as a useful and productive tool for theological reflection.

W. S. Gunter *et al.*, *Wesley and the Quadrilateral: Renewing the Conversation* (Abingdon Press, 1997).

Rex D. Matthews

Westminster Standards The Westminster Standards are the documents produced by the Westminster Assembly (1643–48), which was constituted by the English Parliament as an advisory body on the reform of the Church in the British Isles. The Standards include the Westminster Confession, the Westminster Shorter Catechism, the Westminster Larger Catechism, the Directory for Public Worship of God, and the Form of Presbyterial Church Government. Though their adoption by the English Parliament was nullified after the restoration of the monarchy in 1660, they remain (with some modification) the confessional documents of the Church of Scotland. They have also been immensely influential among English-speaking Reformed Christians around the world, especially those committed to Presbyterian polity. Together, the Westminster Standards constitute one of the most complete and co-ordinated statements of Reformed doctrine and Church order, and they are also significant for being one of the last great sets of confessional documents of the Reformation era.

Doctrinally, the Westminster Standards reflect the central principles of Reformed orthodoxy as defined at the Synod of Dort. At the same time, they go beyond Dort in their promotion of federal theology (WC 7; WSC 12–16, 20; WLC 20–2, 30). Though widely admired for their precision and clarity of expression, they have also been criticized even within Reformed circles on the grounds that their treatment of God, though formally orthodox, undermines the doctrine of the Trinity by decoupling the doctrine of God's eternal election from God's redeeming will as revealed in time in Jesus Christ. Their treatment of the relationship between Church and State (especially WC 30–1) was also viewed by many as overly Erastian (see Erastianism) and was frequently modified by churches otherwise loyal to the theology of Westminster Assembly.

Ian A. McFarland

Will: see Free Will.

Wisdom Wisdom (*sophia* in Greek) is an ancient theme undergoing a contemporary renaissance. As postmodernity challenges the West's modern scientism, wisdom may offer an alternative epistemology that is more holistic and less narrowly obsessed with self-evident starting points. Wisdom involves both the communication of tradition and reflective enquiry about its ongoing viability. In SCRIPTURE wisdom is the tree of life to which human beings cling so that by embracing God they may know how to live well (Prov. 3). For Augustine, whereas knowledge (*scientia*) relates to temporal things and human action, wisdom (*sapientia*) involves eternal verities – indeed, contemplation of the very divine life (*Trin.*, 12–13). The temporal and the eternal remain distinct but address us together in the incarnate *LOGOS*, who is at once divine and human. This offers the possibility that apparent tensions between creation and redemption, divine and human action, biblical command and common sense, and so forth might be resolved dynamically in reciprocal movement rather than statically in favour of one side or the other.

The biblical books categorized as Wisdom literature (viz., Proverbs, Ecclesiastes, Job) embody this possibility. On the one hand, Israel's particular COVENANT relationship with God centres on instruction (*torah* in Hebrew). Proverbs and other texts ground wisdom in fear of the Lord, which (in harmony with Deuteronomy) one pursues by loving divine LAW. On the other hand, wisdom texts also reflect study of the created order, contemplation of perennial human mysteries, and appropriation of knowledge from other cultures. At the same time, wisdom vocabulary is not uniformly positive; it can, for example, be associated with instrumental skill, which can be used for the sake of boastful human autonomy from God (e.g., Jer. 9:23–4).

Obeying God requires character formed communally, developing judgement to recognize how divine instruction pertains to particulars. The alternative is folly, which disrupts not only social but also cosmic harmony (*shalom* in Hebrew). Such harmony is a general expectation of the biblical writers due to the God-given order of creation, but the fact of human SIN means that it is not guaranteed. In the New Testament, the Old Testament's critique of prideful folly points to our need for Jesus Christ as God's Word, who both embodies wisdom on our behalf and enables us to attain it by the HOLY SPIRIT (see, e.g., 1 Cor. 1:18–2:16). Unlike Greek wisdom, Christian *sophia* is open to all in Christ rather than restricted to a heroic few contemplating eternal verities.

Drawing on ancient Christian identification of divine Wisdom (as depicted in, e.g., Prov. 8:22–31) with the Word who became flesh, contemporary feminist theologians have appropriated wisdom in the attempt to develop less stereotypically androcentric and hierarchical doctrines of God and Christ. While clearly present in the New Testament, the shape of Wisdom CHRISTOLOGY remains controversial, as Jewish encounters with the Greco-Roman world engendered a range of thematic connections to Jesus, and the extent to which contemporary theological moves reflect authentic Jesus traditions or biblical themes is contested.

In any case, wisdom, as knowledge is applied to a particular situation by means of judgement (*phronēsis*), remains vital for theological method. In line with its use by pre-modern theologians, it can serve as a unifying theme for both theological interpretation of Scripture and theological education by engaging the full range of moods and interests that characterize human reflective enquiry. Furthermore, the biblical theme of wisdom opens up possibilities for enriching Christian self-understanding through engagement both with Christianity's Jewish roots and with other faith traditions.

D. Ford, *Christian Wisdom: Desiring God and Learning in Love* (Cambridge University Press, 2007).
D. Treier, *Virtue and the Voice of God: Toward Theology as Wisdom* (Eerdmans, 2006).

DANIEL J. TREIER

WOMANIST THEOLOGY The term 'womanist' connotes a perspective or approach to theology, ethics, biblical studies, and religious studies which privileges the differentiated – that is, religious, personal, historical, cultural, social (i.e., political, economic, technological), psychological, and biological – experience of African-American women in enquiry and research, reflection and judgement.

In an essay in the 1970 groundbreaking collection *The Black Woman: An Anthology*, F. Beale (b. 1940) not only contested the notion that feminism was the province of White women, but pinpointed Black women's 'double jeopardy' through racial and gender oppression as well as the failure of White feminists to address racism and imperialism. Nearly a decade later (and while still doctoral students), K. Cannon (b. 1950), J. Grant (b. 1948), and D. Williams (b. 1934) extended Beale's analysis to include the marginalization of African-American women's perspectives and experiences within academic religious discourse, Black (male) and (White) feminist theologies, and the Black Church. Methodologically, these scholars argued that differentiation of experience was necessary for intellectually sound, pastorally adequate, and ethically responsible theological reflection. In order to distinguish their effort from that of African-American male and White female theologians, they named it womanist.

'Womanist' was initially coined by novelist A. Walker (b. 1944) and derived from the African-American cultural epithet, 'womanish' in her book *In Search of Our Mothers' Gardens* (1983). Walker denoted a womanist as a Black feminist or feminist of colour and thereby affirmed earlier attempts by thinkers and activists such as M. Stewart (1803–79), A. J. Cooper (1858/9–1964), and I. B. Wells-Barnett (1862–1931). Walker's definition explicitly encouraged Black women to embrace and to love their embodied selves in the midst of cognitive, religious, aesthetic, and social contexts that too frequently proved to be hostile to their intellectual and cultural creativity, spirituality, moral agency, emotionality, and SEXUALITY. Black women religious scholars turned this definition into a kind of manifesto through which to deepen awareness of ideology and practice of sexism within the Black community and to expose uncritical complicity in deformed societal and ecclesiastical structures.

Womanist theologians, ethicists, and exegetes do not constitute a school. Rather, perhaps because of the specificity of their point of departure, these scholars share a fundamental, practical, intellectual commitment to advocate for the survival and wholeness of an entire people, and therefore refuse to set Black women over against Black men. At the same time, debates have emerged among Black women religious scholars about the meaning and appropriation of the term 'womanist'. By explicitly including feminists of colour and recognizing the illimitable character of spirituality, Walker made space for the criticism raised by D. M. Majeed (b. 1954) of the unintentionally overweening Christian orientation of some womanists and the (corresponding unintentional) tendency to negate non-Christian womanists and traditions.

M. Coleman's (b. 1974) lead article for a Roundtable Discussion in the *Journal of Feminist Studies in Religion* (2006) provides a useful benchmark in charting new developments in womanist scholarship. Coleman queries both the content and the appropriation and imposition of the term 'womanist'; seven scholars respond, some self-identifying as womanist and some not. Coleman challenges womanists to focus on the theological, spiritual, and religious experiences of Black lesbians (and gays), to address social problems, and to contest homophobia. These issues resonate with the earlier work of second-generation womanist scholars, including K. Baker-Fletcher (b. 1959), K. B. Douglas (b. 1957), C. Gilkes (b. 1947), C. Kirk-Duggan (b. 1951), M. Riggs (b. 1958), E. Townes (b. 1955), and R. Weems (b. 1954).

Notwithstanding these links with the work of earlier scholars, Coleman's critiques of indiscriminate use of the term 'womanist', of Christocentrism, and of over-identification with the Black Church signal third-generation (or, as they refer to themselves, third-wave) concerns. Coleman argues that the success of first- and second-generation scholars ironically has made womanist identity *de rigueur.* Despite academic training and specialization, all Black women scholars now face being 'branded' as womanist. Such easy imposition dilutes and commodifies the meaning of womanist. Not all third-wave scholars have abandoned academic study of Christianity, but their cohort has enlarged and enriched womanist thought by engaging Islam, indigenous African, and Caribbean religions. These scholars, including S. Floyd-Thomas (b. 1969), R. St Clair (b. 1970), and N. L. Westfield (b. 1962) deploy interdisciplinary methods to interrogate suffering, praxis, and the Black BODY and sexuality.

Womanist thought has proved remarkably generative in confronting the biased ways in which Black women have been and are perceived not only in White, but in Black religious, cultural, social, and interpersonal contexts. Analysis of the interlocking and mutually conditioning forces of sexism, acquisitive MATERIALISM, homophobia, and anti-Black racism characterize the core of womanist thought. But its future lies in Black women's critical capacity for wonder, intellectual rigour, interdisciplinary openness, self-critique, and self-love.

K. G. Cannon, *Katie's Canon: Womanism and the Soul of the Black Community* (Continuum, 1995).

S. M. Floyd-Thomas, ed., *Deeper Shades of Purple: Womanism in Religion and Society* (New York University Press, 2006).

C. Gilkes, *'If it wasn't for the women – ': Black Women's Experience and Womanist Culture in Church and Community* (Orbis, 2001).

S. Mitchem, *Introducing Womanist Theology* (Orbis, 2002).

M. Shawn Copeland

Word: see *Logos.*

Words of Institution: see Mass, Canon of.

World Council of Churches The World Council of Churches (WCC) is the most significant worldwide ecumenical organization, comprising 349 member Churches representing nearly 560 million Christians from 110 countries. Its predecessor movements, 'Life and Work' and 'Faith and Order', were the major forces behind the incorporation of the WCC in Amsterdam in 1948 (see Ecumenism). The organization is a place of multilateral ecumenical work, where partner Churches of varying backgrounds and size meet together in the pursuit both of unity and of common work and witness. Originally conceived with the aim of providing a conciliar structure for member Churches, it has gradually become more of a forum for meetings and deliberations for ecclesial communities and movements of widely differing origins. Since 1948 the General Assembly of the WCC has met every six to eight years, with the first such meeting in the twenty-first century (the ninth overall) held at Porto Allegre, Brazil, in 2006. Between meetings of the General Assembly, an elected central committee manages the WCC from the Council's Geneva headquarters.

Alongside its work on achieving doctrinal consensus among Churches (especially through the work of its Faith and Order Commission, in which the Catholic Church, though not a member of the WCC, also takes part), the WCC participates in a broad network of social witness and assistance directed primarily to

Churches in developing countries. Its chief priorities are the pursuit of justice and peace, assistance to refugees, struggles against discrimination, education, and development at the international level as well as on the level of individual countries. Recognized as a non-governmental organization, the WCC can play a significant role in global affairs (as suggested by, e.g., its contribution to the end of the apartheid regime in South Africa).

M. van Elderen, *Introducing the World Council of Churches* (WCC, 1990).

ANDRÉ BIRMELÉ

Zwingli, Huldrych Huldrych Zwingli was born on 1 January, 1484 in Wildhaus (Switzerland). After he completed the Latin School in Weesen, Basel, and Bern, he studied in Vienna and enrolled at the University of Basel in 1502, receiving a Bachelors degree in 1504 and Masters in 1506. That same year he was ordained a priest, and was called as pastor to Glarus, where he dedicated himself to intensive study and fostered contact with Swiss humanists like J. Vadian (1484–1551) and H. Glarean (1488–1563). In 1516 Zwingli moved to Einsiedeln and continued his studies, focusing especially on the letters of Paul and the Gospel of John. At the end of 1518, he was called as pastor to Zurich, and in the following years Zwingli matured to a reformer whose sermons found a large audience and were the cornerstone for social change in Zurich.

Z

In 1522, when respected citizens publicly broke Lenten norms, conflict ensued with the bishop of Constance. Zwingli justified breaking the fast in *Concerning Freedom and Choice of Food*, which was a comparison between the Reformed principle of Scripture and the Catholic principle of tradition. That same year he demanded that the bishop of Constance remove the rule of clerical celibacy and that sermons be preached according to Scripture in his *Supplicatio ad Hugonem episcopum Constantiensem*, while in his *Apologeticus archeteles* he rebuked the bishop's authority altogether.

His preaching and actions met with some resistance in Zurich itself, prompting the city council to convene a hearing in January, 1523. To prepare for this disputation, Zwingli compiled his *67 Theses or Conclusions*, which were later published with his commentary as *Interpretation and Justification of the Theses and Articles*. The disputation brought official recognition to Zwingli's teachings and obliged pastors to preach according to Scripture. A second disputation took place that October concerning images and the mass and served to catalyze the reconfiguration of the Church and polity in the Reformed sense: eliminating the mass, removing images from the Churches, closing monasteries, and creating charity organizations and a law court outside the bishop's jurisdiction, along with a school of theology. Out of respect for the 'weaker ones in faith', these changes were not implemented overnight, leading to a break with some of Zwingli's more radical followers, including K. Grebel (*ca* 1495–1526) and F. Manz (*ca* 1495–1527), who broke with him and established Anabaptist communities.

Zwingli's main texts of systematic theology, *Commentary on True and False Religion* and *Divine and Human Righteousness*, were written between 1523 and 1525. The latter text was fundamental because it developed the relationship between the Church and political spheres that became a defining feature of the Zwinglian Reformation. The years after 1525 were marked by Zwingli's struggle against the use of Swiss as mercenaries, his effort to help the Reformation break through into the wider Swiss Confederation, and his attempts to give his form of Reformation international recognition. Zwingli actively participated in catalyzing the Reformation through the systematic construction of political alliances. At the same time, his intense battle with M. Luther over the presence of Christ in the Eucharist remained unresolved at the Marburg Colloquy of 1529 and had weighty consequences for confessional divisions within Protestantism.

Zurich's aggressive policies against the anti-Reformation factions of the Swiss Confederation were supported by Zwingli and led to the second Battle of Kappel, where Zwingli was killed on 11 October 1531. Zwingli's violent death was a heavy blow to the Swiss Reformation, but despite several modifications Zwingli's legacy in Zurich was preserved by his successor, H. Bullinger.

G. W. Locher, *Die Zwinglische Reformation im Rahmen der europäischen Kirchengeschichte* (Vandenhoeck & Ruprecht, 1979).

W. P. Stephens, *The Theology of Huldrych Zwingli* (Oxford University Press, 1986).

Christian Moser

References

1Clem — *1 Clement* (*ca* 100)
AC — Augsburg Confession (1530)
Adam, K.
  'Krisis' — 'Die Theologie der Krisis', *Hochland* XXIII (1925/6).
Alcinous
  Hand. — *Handbook of Platonism* (second century)
Anastasius of Sinai
  Quest. — *Questions and Responses* (seventh century)
AP — *Apophthegmata Patrum* (fifth century)
Aquinas, T.
  CRom. — *Commentary on Romans* (1272–3)
  CTrin. — *Commentary on the 'De Trinitate' of Boethius* (*ca* 1260)
  Pot. — *Quaestiones disputatae de potentia Dei* (1259–68)
  ScG — *Summa contra Gentiles* (1261–3)
  ST — *Summa theologiae* (1265–72)
  Ver. — *Quaestiones disputatae de veritate* (1256–9)
Aristotle
  Eth. — *Ethics* (fourth century BC)
  Meta. — *Metaphysics* (fourth century BC)
  Nico. — *Nicomachean Ethics* (fourth century BC)
  Pol. — *Politics* (fourth century BC)
  Rh. — *Rhetoric* (fourth century BC)
  Top. — *Topics* (fourth century BC)
Athanasius of Alexandria
  Ant. — *Vita Antonii* (*ca* 360)
  Ar. — *Orations against the Arians* (*ca* 340–*ca* 345)
  Gent. — *Contra Gentes* (*ca* 320–*ca* 340)
  Inc. — *De Incarnatione* (*ca* 320–*ca* 340)
Athenagoras
  Dep. — *Deprecatio pro Christanis* (late second century)
Augustine of Hippo
  Bapt. — *De baptismo* (*ca* 400)
  City — *The City of God* (*ca* 413–*ca* 427)
  Conf. — *Confessions* (*ca* 397–*ca* 400)
  Cred. — *De utilitate credendi* (*ca* 390)
  Ench. — *Enchiridion ad Laurentium* (421–3)
  Ep. — *Epistles* (386–429)
  Faust. — *Contra Faustum Manichaeum* (*ca* 400)
  Fid. — *De fide et symbolo* (*ca* 393)
  Gen. lit. — *De Genesi ad litteram* (*ca* 401–*ca* 415)
  Lib. — *De libero arbitrio* (*ca* 395)
  Nupt. — *De nuptiis et concupiscentia* (*ca* 420)
  Pet. — *Contra litteras Petiliani* (401–5)
  QMatt. — *Quaestiones in Matthaeum* (*ca* 400)
  Serm. — *Sermons* (*ca* 393–430)
  Sol. — *Soliloquies* (386/7)
  Trin. — *The Trinity* (*ca* 400–*ca* 420; ET: E. Hill, O. P. [New City Press, 1991])
Balthasar, H. U. von
  Epilogue — *Epilogue* (Ignatius Press, 1987)
Barn. — *Epistle of Barnabas* (*ca* 100)
Barth, K.
  CD — *Church Dogmatics*, 13 vols. (1932–67; authorized ET: ed. G. W. Bromiley and T. F. Torrance [T&T Clark, 1956–77])
Basil of Caesarea
  Ep. — *Epistles* (*ca* 357–*ca* 379)
  Spirit — *On the Holy Spirit* (*ca* 375)
BEM — *Baptism, Eucharist and Ministry* (Faith and Order Paper no. 111, 1982)
Benedict XVI [Ratzinger, J.]
  Deus — *Deus caritas est* (2005)
  Intro. — *Introduction to Christianity* (Seabury Press, 1968)
BOD 2008 — *The Book of Discipline of the United Methodist Church*, 2008
Braaten, C. E.
  'Two' — 'The Doctrine of Two Kingdoms Re-examined', *Currents in Theology and Mission* 15:6 (1988), 497–504

Braithwaite, R.
'View' 'An Empiricist's View of the Nature of Religious Belief', in *The Philosophy of Religion* ed. B. Mitchell (Oxford University Press, 1971), 72–91

Brakhage, S.
Essential *Essential Brakhage*, ed. B. R. McPherson (McPherson & Company 2001)

Brueggemann, W.
Theology *Theology of the Old Testament: Testimony, Dispute, Advocacy* (Fortress Press, 1997)

Buddeus, J. F.
Isagoge *Isagoge historico-theologica ad theologiam singualsque eius partes* (1727)

Bulgakov, S.
Burning *The Burning Bush: On the Orthodox Veneration of the Mother of God* (1927; ET: T. A. Smith [Eerdmans, 2008])
Lamb *The Lamb of God* (1933; ET: B. Jakim [Eerdmans, 2008])

Busch, E.
Barth *Karl Barth* (SCM, 1975)

Calvin, J.
CGen. *Commentary on Genesis* (1563)
Inst. *Institutes of the Christian Religion* (1559; ET: F. L. Battles [Westminster Press, 1960])
Predest. *Concerning the Eternal Predestination of God* (1552; ET: J. K. S. Reid [James Clarke, 1961])

Cat. *Catechism of the Catholic Church* (2nd edn, 1997 [1994])

Chaves, M.
Ordaining *Ordaining Women: Culture and Conflict in Religious Organizations* (Harvard University Press, 1997)

Chrysostom, J.
HRom. *Homilies on Romans* (*ca* 390)

Clement of Alexandria
Strom. *Stromata* (*ca* 200)

Costas, O. E.
Church *The Church and Its Mission: A Shattering Critique from the Third World* (Tyndale House Publishers, 1974)

Crites, S.
'Narrative' 'The Narrative Quality of Experience', *Journal of the American Academy of Religion* (1971), 291–311

CRS *Congressional Record, Senate*

Cyprian of Carthage
Ep. *Epistles* (*ca* 250–8)
Jealousy *On Jealousy and Envy* (*ca* 255)
Prayer *On the Lord's Prayer* (*ca* 250)

Cyril of Alexandria
CIsa. *Commentary on Isaiah* (*ca* 415–*ca* 425)
Ep. *Epistles* (early fifth century)

Cyril of Jerusalem
CO *Catechetical Orations* (*ca* 350)

Cyril of Scythopolis
Cyr. *Life of Cyriacus* (sixth century)

Daneel, M.
Quest *Quest for Belonging: Introduction to a Study of African Independent Churches* (Mambo Press, 1987)

de Beauvoir, S.
Second *The Second Sex* (1949; ET: Howard Parshley [Penguin, 1973])

de Lubac, H.
Cath. *Catholicisme* (Cerf, 1938)
Corp. *Corpus Mysticum: The Eucharist and the Church in the Middle Ages* (1944; ET: G. Simmonds with R. Price and C. Stephens [SCM, 2006])

Decret, F.
Mani *Mani et la tradition manichéenne* (Seuil, 1974)

Denck, H.
Schriften *Hans Denck Schriften* (early sixteenth century [1956])

Derrida, J.
Gram. *Of Grammatology* (1967; ET: G. C. Spivak [Johns Hopkins University Press, 1974])
Lim. *Limited Inc.* (Northwestern University Press, 1988)

Did. *Didache* (early second century)

Dionysius the Areopagite
Divine Names *Dionysius the Areopagite: The Mystical Theology and The Divine Names*, trans. C. E. Rolt (Dover Publications, 2004)
Hier. *Ecclesiastical Hierarchy* (sixth century)

DS H. Denzinger and A. Schönmetzer, eds.,

Enchiridion symbolorum, definitionum et declarationum de rebus fidei et morum (Herder, 1965)

Dummett, M.
- *Truth* — *Truth and Other Enigmas* (Harvard University Press, 1978)

Duns Scotus, J.
- *Ord.* — *Ordinatio* (*ca* 1300)

Edwards, J.
- *Faith.* — *A Faithful Narrative of the Surprising Work of God* (1737) in J. E. Smith *et al.*, *A Jonathan Edwards Reader* (Yale University Press, 1995)

Endo, S.
- *Jesus* — *A Life of Jesus* (Paulist Press, 1973)

Ephrem the Syrian
- *Her.* — *Hymns against Heresies* (*ca* 360–70)

Eusebius of Caesarea
- *Con.* — *Oration in Praise of the Emperor Constantine* (335)
- *EH* — *Ecclesiastical History* (*ca* 325)

Farley, E.
- *Theologia* — *Theologia: Fragmentation and Unity in Theological Education* (Fortress Press, 1983)

FC, Ep. — *Formula of Concord, Epitome* (1577)

FC, SD — *Formula of Concord, Solid Declaration* (1577)

Ficino, M.
- *PT* — *Platonic Theology* (1469–74; ET: M. Allen and J. Warden [Harvard University Press, 2001–4])

Finney, C.
- *Lect.* — *Lectures on Revivals of Religion* (2nd edn, Leavitt, Lord & Co., 1835)

Florensky, P.
- *Pillar* — *The Pillar and Ground of the Truth* (1914; ET: B. Jakim [Princeton University Press, 1997])

Foucault, M.
- *Care* — *The History of Sexuality*, vol. III: *The Care of the Self* (1984; ET: R. Hurley [Random House, 1986])

Fox, G.
- *Journal* — *Journal of George Fox* (1694)

Francis de Sales
- *Love* — *Treatise on the Love of God* (1616)

Galilei, G.
- *Opere* — *Le Opere di Galileo Galilei* (early seventeenth century [1966])

Gilson, É.
- *Intro.* — *Introduction au système de S. Thomas d'Aquin* (A. Vix & Cie, 1919)

Gratian
- *Decr.* — *Decretum* (twelfth century)

Gregory of Nazianzus
- *Ep.* — *Epistles* (*ca* 357–*ca* 385)
- *Or.* — *Theological Orations* (380)

Gregory of Nyssa
- *Making* — *On the Making of Humankind* (*ca* 380)
- *Or.* — *Catechetical Oration* (*ca* 385)
- *Soul* — *On the Soul and the Resurrection* (*ca.* 380)

Gregory the Great
- *Ep.* — *Epistles* (590–604)
- *HGos.* — *Homilies on the Gospels* (*ca* 590)

Gutiérrez, G.
- 'Theol.' — 'The Theology of Liberation: Perspectives and Tasks' in *Toward a New Heaven and a New Earth*, ed. F. F. Segovia (Orbis, 2003), 287–99
- *Theology* — *A Theology of Liberation: History, Politics, and Salvation* (1971; ET: M. J. O'Connell [Orbis, 1973])

Harnack, A. von
- *Christ.* — *What Is Christianity?* (1900; ET: T. B. Saunders [Harper & Row, 1957])

Harpham, G. G.
- *Ascetic* — *The Ascetic Imperative in Culture and Criticism* (University of Chicago Press, 1987)

Hennessy, R.
- *Profit* — *Profit and Pleasure: Sexual Identities in Late Capitalism* (Routledge, 2000)

Hiebert, P. G.
- *Transforming* — *Transforming Worldviews: An Anthropological Understanding of How People Change* (Baker Academic, 2008)

Hildegard of Bingen
- *Ep.* *Epistolarium* (1147–79)
- *Sciv.* *Scivias* (1141–51)

Hippolytus of Rome
- *Trad.* *Traditio apostolica* (*ca* 215)

Hooker, R.
- *Lawes* *Lawes of Ecclesiastical Polity* (1593)

Ignatius of Antioch
- *Eph.* *Ephesians* (*ca* 110)
- *Rom.* *Romans* (*ca* 110)
- *Trall.* *Trallians* (*ca* 110)

Irenaeus of Lyons
- *AH* *Against Heresies* (*ca* 180)
- *Dem.* *Demonstration of the Apostolic Preaching* (*ca* 180; ET: J. A. Robinson [SPCK, 1920])

Isaac the Syrian
- *Asc.* *Ascetical Homilies* (seventh century)

Jaspers, K.
- *Nietzsche* *Nietzsche: An Introduction to the Understanding of His Philosophical Activity* (University of Arizona Press, 1965)

JDDJ *Joint Declaration on the Doctrine of Justification* (1999)

Jenson, R. W.
- 'Spirit' 'You Wonder Where the Spirit Went', *Pro Ecclesia* 2 (1993), 296–304

Jerome
- *Jov.* *Adversus Jovinianum* (*ca* 392–3)
- *Tit.* *In Epistula ad Titum* (*ca* 387–8)

John XXIII
- *Ad Petri* *Ad Petri Cathedram* (1959)
- 'Address' 'Address on the Occasion of the Solemn Opening of the Most Holy Council' (1962)
- 'Radio' 'Radio Message to All the Christian Faithful One Month Before the Opening of the Second Vatican Ecumenical Council' (1962)

John of Damascus
- *EOF* *Exposition of the Orthodox Faith* (*ca* 745)
- *Jac.* *In Tractatum contra Jacobitas* (*ca* 740)
- *Three* *Three Treatises Against Those Who Attack the Holy Icons* (*ca* 726–*ca* 745)

John Paul II
- *Cent.* *Centesimus annus* (1991)
- *Eccl.* *Ecclesia in Asia* (1999)
- *Fid.* *Fides et ratio* (1998)
- *Red.* *Redemptoris missio* (1990)
- *Sollic.* *Sollicitudo rei socialis* (1987)

Josephus
- *Ant.* *The Jewish Antiquities* (*ca* 95)

Julian of Norwich
- *Show.* *Showings* (late fourteenth century)

Jüngel, E.
- *God* *God as the Mystery of the World: On the Foundation of the Theology of the Crucified One in the Dispute between Theism and Atheism* (T&T Clark, 1977)
- *Mög.* 'Die Möglichkeit theologischer Anthropologie auf dem Grunde der Analogie: Eine Untersuchung zum Analogieverständnis Karl Barths', *Evangelische Theologie* 22 (1962), 535–57

Justin Martyr
- *1Apol.* *First Apology* (mid-second century)
- *Trypho* *Dialogue with Trypho the Jew* (mid-second century)

Kähler, M.
- *Hist.* *The So-called Historical Jesus and the Historic, Biblical Christ* (1892; ET: C. E. Braaten [Fortress Press, 1964])

Khomyakov, A. S.
- *Church* *The Church is One* (SPCK, 1948)

King, M. L., Jr
- *Stride* *Stride Toward Freedom* (Ballantine Books, 1958)

LaRondelle, H. K.
- *Perf.* *Perfection and Perfectionism: A Dogmatic-Ethical Study of Biblical Perfection and Phenomenal Perfectionism* (Andrews University Press, 1971)

Leo I
- *Ep.* *Epistles* (442–60)

Lewis, C. S.
- *MC* *Mere Christianity* (Bles, 1952)

Lossky, V.
- *Mys.* *The Mystical Theology of the Eastern Church* (1944; ET: [James Clarke, 1957])

Louth, A.
'Theology' 'Theology and Spirituality', a paper read by A. Louth to the Origen Society on 30 October 1974, published by SLG Press in 1976

Luther, M.
Anti. *Against the Antinomians* (1539; ET: M. H. Bertram, in *Luther's Works* [*LW*], vol. XLVII [Fortress Press, 1971])
Bond. *On the Bondage of the Will* (1525; ET: P. S. Watson, in *LW*, vol. XXX [Fortress Press, 1972])
Diet *Luther at the Diet of Worms* (1521; ET: R. A. Hornsby, in *LW*, vol. XXXII [Fortress Press, 1958])
Freedom The Freedom of a Christian (1520; ET: W. A. Lambert, in *LW*, Vol. XXXI [Fortress Press, 1957])
Gal. *Lectures on Galatians* (1535; ET: J. Pelikan, in *LW*, vol. XXXVI [Concordia, 1963])
Heid. *Heidelberg Disputation* (1518; ET: H. J. Grimm, in *LW*, vol. XXXI [Fortress Press, 1957])
LC *Large Catechism* (1529)
LGen. *Lectures on Genesis* (1535–45; ET: G. V. Schick and P. D. Pahl, in *LW*, vols. I–VIII [Concordia, 1958–66])
Magn. *Magnificat* (1521; ET: A. T. W. Steinhauser, in *LW*, vol. XXI [Concordia, 1956])
Nob. *To the Christian Nobility of the German Nation* (1520; ET: C. M. Jacobs, in *LW*, vol. XLIV [Fortress Press, 1966])
Pen. *The Sacrament of Penance* (1519; ET: E. T. Bachmann, in *LW*, vol. XXXV [Fortress Press, 1960])
'Preface' Preface to Georg Rhau's *Symphoniae iucundae* (1538; ET: U. S. Leopold, in *LW*, vol. LIII [Fortress Press, 1965])
Proc. *Proceedings at Augsburg* (1518; ET: H. J. Grimm, in *LW*, vol. XXXI [Fortress Press, 1957])
Prom. *Die Promotionsdisputation von Petrus Hegemon* (1541)
Smalc. *Smalcald Articles* (1537)
Supp. *Confession Concerning Christ's Supper* (1528; ET: R. H. Fischer, in *LW*, vol. XXXVII [Fortress Press, 1961])

Malcolm, N.
'Anselm' 'Anselm's Ontological Arguments', *Philosophical Review* 69 (1960), 41–60

Maximus the Confessor
Amb. *Ambigua* (*ca* 630–*ca* 635)

Mechthild of Magdeburg
Flowing *The Flowing Light of the Godhead* (late thirteenth century; ET: F. J. Tobin [Paulist Press, 1998])

Meeks, Wayne
Origins *The Origins of Christian Morality: The First Two Centuries* (Yale University Press, 1993)

Meiderlin, P.
Paraenesis *Paraenesis votiva pro pace ecclesiae* (1626)

Melanchthon, P.
Apol. *The Apology [or Defence] of the Augsburg Confession* (1531; ET: *The Book of Concord: The Confessions of the Evangelical Lutheran Church*, ed. R. Kolb and T. Wengert [Fortress Press, 2000], 107–294)

Milbank, J.
Theol. *Theology and Social Theory: Beyond Secular Reason* (Blackwell, 1993)

Moltmann, J.
Hope *Theology of Hope* (1964; ET: [SCM 1967])

Lux *Lux mundi: A Series of Studies in the Religion of the Incarnation*, ed. C. Gore (Cambridge University Press, 1889)

Newman, J. H.
Lectures *Lectures on the Doctrine of Justification* (2nd edn, J. G. F. & J. Rivington, 1840)

Nicholas of Cusa
Vis. *De Visione Dei* (1453)

Niebuhr, R.
Irony *The Irony of American History* (Scribner, 1952)

Norris, R. A.
'Trinity' 'Trinity' in *The Holy Spirit: Classic and Contemporary Readings*, ed. E. F. Rogers, Jr (Wiley-Blackwell 2009), 19–43

Origen of Alexandria
Cels. *Contra Celsum* (*ca* 250)

CMatt. *Commentary on Matthew* (*ca* 245)
CSong *Commentary on the Song of Songs* (*ca* 245)
HJer. *Homilies on Jeremiah* (*ca* 235–40)
HLuke *Homilies on Luke* (*ca* 230–40)
Ora. *De Oratione* (*ca* 233–4)
Prin. *De principiis* (*ca* 225)

Owen, J.
Enquiry *An Enquiry into the Original, Nature, Institution, Power, Order and Communion of Evangelical Churches* (1681)

Paley, W.
Works *The Works of William Paley* (T. Nelson and P. Brown, 1831)

Parrinder, G.
World *The World's Living Religions* (Pan Books, 1964)

PG *Patrologiae Cursus Completus, Series Graeca*, ed. J. P. Migne (Imprimerie Catholique, 1857–66)

Philo of Alexandria
Dec. *Decalogue* (early first century)
Spec. *De specialis legibus* (early first century)

Pieris, A.
Love *Love Meets Wisdom: A Christian Experience of Buddhism* (Orbis, 1988)

Pius IV
Injunc. *Injunctum nobis* (1564)

Pius IX
Ineffabilis *Ineffabilis Deus* (1854)

Pius XII
Humani *Humani generis* (1950)

Plantinga, A.
'Reason' 'Reason and Belief in God' in *Faith and Rationality: Reason and Belief in God*, ed. A. Plantinga and N. Wolterstorff (University of Notre Dame Press, 1983), 16–93

Plato
Tim. *Timaeus* (*ca* 360 BC)

Prenter, R.
'Liturgie' 'Liturgie et dogme', *Revue d'histoire et de philosophie religieuses* 38 (1958), 115–28

Prosper of Aquitaine
Cap. *Capitula Coelestini* (aka *Indiculus de gratia Dei*, *ca* 430)

Puech, H. C.
Man. *Le Manichéisme* (Civilisations du Sud, 1949)

Rahner, K.
Found. *Foundations of the Christian Faith: An Introduction to the Idea of Christianity* (Crossroad, 1976)
Trinity *The Trinity* (1967; ET: J. Donceel [Crossroad, 1997])

Rauschenbusch, W.
Theol. *A Theology for the Social Gospel* (Macmillan, 1917)

Richard, J.
'Analyse' 'Analyse et symbolisme chez saint Thomas d'Aquin', *Laval théologique et philosophique* (1974), 379–406

Ricœur, P.
Essays *Essays on Biblical Interpretation* (Fortress Press, 1980)

Rousseau, J.-J.
Social *The Social Contract, or Principles of Political Right* (1762)

Rupert of Deutz
DO *De divinis officiis* (1112)

Schleiermacher, F.
CF *Christian Faith* (2nd edn, 1830; ET: H. R. Macintosh and J. S. Stewart [T&T Clark, 1928])
Outline *Brief Outline of Theology as a Field of Study* (1830; ET: W. Farrer [T&T Clark, 1850])
Speeches *On Religion: Speeches to Its Cultured Despisers* (1799; ET: R. Crouter [Cambridge University Press, 1988])

Schmid, H.
Doctrinal *Doctrinal Theology of the Evangelical Lutheran Church* (Lutheran Publication Society, 1875)

Sedgwick, E.
Tend. *Tendencies* (Duke University Press, 1993)

Shaftesbury, third earl of
Charac. *Characteristicks of Men, Manners, Opinions, Times* (1711)

Simons, M.
Writings *The Complete Writings of Menno Simons* (sixteenth century; ET: J. C. Wenger [Herald Press, 1956])

Snyder, C. A.
Footsteps *Following in the Footsteps of Christ: The Anabaptist Tradition* (Orbis, 2004)

Spener, P. J.
Pia — *Pia desideria* (1675; ET: T. G. Tappert [Fortress Press, 1964])

Spinoza, B.
Eth. — *Ethics* (1675)

Spitz, L.
RRGH — *The Religious Renaissance of the German Humanists* (Harvard University Press, 1963)

Tanner, K.
Economy — *Economy of Grace* (Fortress Press, 2005)

Taylor, C.
Sec. — *A Secular Age* (Harvard University Press, 2007)

Teresa of Avila
Life — *The Life of Teresa of Jesus: The Autobiography of St. Teresa of Avila* (*ca* 1565; ET: E. A. Peers [Doubleday, 1960])

Tertullian
An. — *De anima* (*ca* 205)
Apol. — *Apologeticum* (*ca* 197)
Carn. — *De carne Christi* (*ca* 210)
Jejun. — *De jejunio adversus Psychicos* (*ca* 210)
Marc. — *Adversus Marcionem* (*ca* 207–8)
Pat. — *De patientia* (*ca* 200)
Perp. — *Passion of St. Perpetua, St. Felicitas, and their Companions* (*ca* 205)
Prae. — *De praescriptione haereticorum* (*ca* 200; ET: P. Holmes and S. Thelwall, in *Ante-Nicene Fathers*, vol. III [T&T Clark, n.d.])
Prax. — *Adversus Praxean* (*ca* 215)
Resur. — *De resurrectione mortuorum* (*ca* 206–7)
Scap. — *Ad Scapulam* (*ca* 212)
Scorp. — *Scorpiace* (*ca* 211–12)
Virg. — *De virginibus velandis* (*ca* 209)

Theodore of Mopsuestia
CGal. — *Commentary on Galatians* (late fourth–early fifth century)

Theophilus of Antioch
Aut. — *To Autolycus* (*ca* 175)

Theophylact
Luc. — *Ennaratio in Evangelium Lucae* (*ca* 1100)

Thomas, M. M.
Gospel — *The Gospel of Forgiveness and Koinonia* (ISPCK & CSS, 1994)

Tillich, P.
STheol. — *Systematic Theology* (University of Chicago Press, 1951–63)

Torrey, S.
Exhort. — *An Exhortation unto Reformation* (1674)

Trent, Council of
Euch. — *De sanctissimo Eucharistiae Sacramento* (1551; ET: J. Waterworth [Dolman, 1848]))
Invoc. — *De Invocatione et reliquiis sanctorum et sacris imaginibus* (1563)
Lib. — *De editione et usu Sacrorum Librorum* (1546; ET: J. Waterworth [Dolman, 1848])
Ordin. — *Vera et catholica de Sacramento Ordinis doctrina* (1563)
Poen. — *De Sacramento Poenitentiae* (1551)
Sacr. — *De Sacramentis in genere* (1547)
Scrip. — *De Canonicis Scripturis* (1546)

Turretin, F.
IET — *Institutes of Elenctic Theology* (1679–85)

Tyndale, W.
Exp. — *Expositions and Notes on Sundry Portions of the Holy Scriptures* (1536 [1849])

Valantasis, R.
'Theory' — 'A Theory of the Social Function of Asceticism,' in *Asceticism*, ed. V. L. Wimbush and R. Valantasis (Oxford University Press, 1995), 544–52

Vatican Council II
DV — *Dei verbum* (1965)
GS — *Gaudium et spes* (1965)
LG — *Lumen gentium* (1964)
NA — *Nostra aetate* (1964)
PO — *Presbyterorum ordinis* (1965)
UR — *Unitas redintegratio* (1964)

Veling, T.
Practical — *Practical Theology: 'On Earth as It Is in Heaven'* (Orbis, 2005)

Vincent of Lérins
Comm. — *Commonitorium* (434)

Walls, A.
Cross — *The Cross-Cultural Process in Christian History* (Orbis, 2002)

WC — Westminster Confession (1647)

Wesley, J.
CP — *A Plain Account of Christian Perfection* (1777)

'Circumcision' — 'The Circumcision of the Heart' (1733)

'Scripture' — 'The Scripture Way of Salvation: A Sermon on Eph. 2:8' (1765)

'Disc. 13' — 'Upon our Lord's Sermon on the Mount: Discourse 13' (1750)

'Use' — 'The Use of Money: Sermon 50' (1760)

Works — *The Works of John Wesley* (eighteenth century [1984–])

Westphal, M.

'Anti' — 'Theological Anti-Realism' in *Realism and Religion: Philosophical and Theological Perspectives*, ed. A. Moore and M. Scott (Ashgate, 2007), 131–46

William of Ockham

Ord. — *Ordinatio* (*ca* 1320)

CSent. — *Commentary on the* Sentences (1317–18)

Rep. — *Reportata* (*ca* 1320–5)

Williams, R.

'Foreword' — 'Foreword' in *The Gestures of God: Explorations in Sacramentality*, ed. G. Rowell and C. Hall (Continuum, 2004), xiii–xiv

Wittgenstein, L.

PI — *Philosophical Investigations* (Blackwell, 1953)

WLC — Westminster Larger Catechism (1647)

WSC — Westminster Shorter Catechism (1647)

Zahn-Harnack, A. von

Harnack — *Adolf von Harnack* (H. Bott, 1936)

Zizioulas, J.

Communion — *Communion and Otherness* (T&T Clark, 2006)

Zwingli, H.

Art. — *Sixty-Seven Articles* (1523)

Printed in the United States
By Bookmasters